AN ANALYTIC DICTIONARY OF ENGLISH ETYMOLOGY

An Introduction

AN ANALYTIC DICTIONARY OF ENGLISH ETYMOLOGY

An Introduction

ANATOLY LIBERMAN

WITH THE ASSISTANCE OF J. LAWRENCE MITCHELL

University of Minnesota Press
Minneapolis
London

Published by the University of Minnesota Press
111 Third Avenue South, Suite 290
Minneapolis, MN 55401-2520
http://www.upress.umn.edu

Library of Congress Cataloging-in-Publication Data

Liberman, Anatoly.
An analytic dictionary of English etymology : an introduction / Anatoly Liberman ; with the assistance of J. Lawrence Mitchell.
p. cm.
Includes bibliographical references and index.
ISBN-13: 978-0-8166-5272-3 (alk. paper)
ISBN-10: 0-8166-5272-4 (alk. paper)
1. English language—Etymology—Dictionaries. I. Mitchell, J. Lawrence. II. Title.
PE1580.L53 2008
422.03—dc22

2007047224

Printed in the United States of America on acid-free paper

15 14 13 12 11 10 09 08 10 9 8 7 6 5 4 3 2 1

To the lasting memory of David R. Fesler

CONTENTS

ABBREVIATIONS OF LINGUISTIC TERMS AND NAMES OF LANGUAGES

For abbreviations of titles and proper names see the bibliography.

adj	adjective
adv	adverb
AF	Anglo-French
AFr	Anglo-Frisian
Amer	American
AS	Anglo-Saxon
Av	Avestan
AV	Authorized Version
Bav	Bavarian
Br	Breton
Bulg	Bulgarian
Celt	Celtic
Corn	Cornish
Dan	Danish
dial	dialect
dimin	diminutive
Du	Dutch
E	English
ed(s)	edition(s), editor(s), edited
EFr	East Frisian
esp	especially
f	feminine
F	French
Far	Faroese
fasc	fascicle
Finn	Finnish
Fl	Flemish
Fr	Frisian
G	German
Gael	Gaelic
gen	genitive
Gk	Classical Greek
Gmc	Germanic
Go	Gothic
Gr	Greek
Hebr	Hebrew
HG	High German
Hitt	Hittite
Icel	Icelandic
IE	Indo-European
Ir	Irish
IrE	Irish English
Ital	Italian
Kent	Kentish
L	Latin
Lanc	Lancashire
Latv	Latvian
LG	Low German
Lith	Lithuanian
loc cit	loco citato ("in the place cited")
LS	Low Saxon
m	masculine
MDu	Middle Dutch
ME	Middle English
MF	Middle French
MHG	Middle High German
MI	Middle Irish
ML	Medieval Latin
MLG	Middle Low German
ModAmerE	Modern American English
ModDu	Modern Dutch
ModE	Modern English

ModF	Modern French
ModG	Modern German
ModI	Modern Icelandic
ModIr	Modern Irish
ModIt	Modern Italian
ModSp	Modern Spanish
ModSw	Modern Swedish
MSw	Middle Swedish
n	neuter
N	Norwegian
n. d.	no date
Northumbr	Northumbrian
n. p.	no indication of publisher
OD	Old Danish
OE	Old English
OF	Old French
OFr	Old Frisian
OHG	Old High German
OI	Old Icelandic
OIr	Old Irish
OLG	Old Low German
OPr	Old Prussian
ORuss	Old Russian
OS	Old Saxon
OScand	Old Scandinavian
OSl	Old Slavic
Oss	Ossetic
OSp	Old Spanish
OSw	Old Swedish
Pers	Persian
PIE	Proto-Indo-European
pl	plural
Pol	Polish
Port	Portuguese
pp	past participle
Prov	Provençal
reg	regional
repr	reprint, reprinted
rev	reviewed, revised
Rom	Romance
Rum	Rumanian
Russ	Russian
sb	noun
Sc	Scots
Scand	Scandinavian
sec(s)	section(s)
Sem	Semitic
Skt	Sanskrit
Slav	Slavic
Sp	Spanish
Sw	Swedish
SwiG	Swiss German
trans	transitive
Ukr	Ukrainian
v	verb
Ved	Vedic
VL	Vulgar Latin
Wel	Welsh
Westph	Westphalian
WFl	West Flemish
WFr	West Frisian
WGmc	West Germanic

Introduction

THE PURPOSE AND CONTENT OF A NEW DICTIONARY OF ENGLISH ETYMOLOGY

> The dominant sense of the word *dictionary* for English-speaking people is a book which presents in alphabetic order the words of our language, with information as to their spelling, pronunciation, meaning and (as something more or less unintelligible and pointless) their etymology.
>
> —James R. Hulbert, *Dictionaries: English and American*, 1968

The Readership of Etymological Dictionaries

Disparaging statements like the one given in the epigraph above are many and at best mildly amusing. Richard Grant White wrote the following in his book *Words and their Uses Past and Present: A Study of the English Language* (Boston and New York: Houghton Mifflin Company, 1899 [this is a revised and corrected edition], pp. 342–43):

> With one exception, Etymology is the least valuable element in the making of a dictionary, as it is of interest only to those who wish to study the history of language. It helps no man in his use of the word *bishop* to know that it comes from two Greek words, *epi*, meaning upon, and *scopos*, meaning a looker, still less to be told into what forms those words have passed in Spanish, Arabic, and Persian. Yet it is in their etymologies that our dictionaries have shown most improvement during the last twenty-five years; they having profited in this respect by the recent great advancement in the etymological department of philology. The etymologies of words in our recently published dictionaries, although, as I have said before, they are of no great value for the purposes for which dictionaries are consulted, are little nests (sometimes slightly mare-ish) of curious and agreeable information, and afford a very pleasant and instructive pastime to those who have the opportunity and the inclination to look into them. But they are not worth, in a dictionary, all the labor that is spent on them, or all the room they occupy. The noteworthy spectacle has lately been shown of the casting over of the whole etymological freight of a well-known dictionary, and the taking on board of another. For the etymological part of the last edition of "Webster's American Dictionary," so called, Dr. Mahn, of Berlin, is responsible. When it was truly called Webster's Dictionary, it was in this respect discreditable to scholarship in this country, and even indicative of mental supineness in a people upon whom such a book could be imposed as having authority. And now that it is relieved of this blemish, it is, in this respect, neither Webster's Dictionary nor "American," but Mahn's and German.

Whether etymologies in our "thick" dictionaries are worth the labor that is spent on them and whether it was prudent to invite a German specialist in Romance linguistics to rewrite the etymologies in the most famous American dictionary of English are clearly a matter of opinion. But one notes with satisfaction that, despite the avowed uselessness, an undertaking like the present one will appeal to those who wish to study the history of the language and even afford them a very pleasant and instructive pastime. The main questions are: Where do we find such people? Is the readership of serious essays on the origin of words limited to professional philologists? These are not idle questions, for while the publisher brings out books to sell them, the author hopes to be noticed and appreciated. So who reads etymological dictionaries? A tolerably good market seems to exist for them. *The Oxford Dictionary of English Etymology* (ODEE), a volume of xiv + 1025 pages, was published in 1966 and reprinted again in 1966 and then in 1967, 1969, 1974, 1976, 1978, 1979, 1982 (twice), 1983, and 1985—a remarkable commercial success. Kluge's etymological dictionary of German has been around for more than a century, and its twenty-fourth edition, by Elmar Seebold, appeared in 2003. Of great importance are multivolume etymological dictionaries of French, Spanish, Italian, Russian, Tibetan, Sanskrit, and Hittite, to mention just a few.

The authors of etymological dictionaries often write forewords to the effect that their works will be accessible to a broad audience. However, ODEE, Kluge, and most other books of this type are thrillers only for the initiated. A few examples will suffice. ODEE explains that *bay* in the phrase *at bay* is traceable to Old French *bai* or is an aphetic derivative of Middle English *abay*, with *at abay* "being apprehended as *at a bay*." This is a simple etymology, but it presupposes a user who knows the periodization of English and French, is aware of the interplay between the two languages in the Middle Ages, and will not be discouraged by the term *aphetic derivative*.

In the entry *bone*, we read that Old English *bān* has cognates in Old Frisian, Old Saxon, Middle Dutch, Low German, Old High German, and Old Norse, that the Common Germanic (except Gothic) form was **bainam*, "of which no further cogn[ate]s are recognized." Here it is taken for granted that the reader is familiar with the entire spectrum of older Germanic languages and the meaning of asterisked forms and has been taught to look for cognates of English words outside Germanic. ODEE passes by the problem of *bone* being possibly related to Latin *femur* or representing the stump of Indo- European **(o)zdboiness*. Henry Cecil Wyld, the editor of *The Universal Dictionary of the English Language* and the author of detailed etymologies written expressly for that work, mentions the putative Latin cognate of *bone* but states that the tempting equation of *bone* with *femur* must be rejected. Who can be tempted by such an equation? Only Indo- European scholars versed in the niceties of media aspirata. The entry *thigh* in ODEE lists Germanic and several Indo-European cognates. It contains the following passage: "OE. *þēh* is repr[esented] immed[iately] by mod[ern] north[ern] *thee; thigh* descends from ME. *þīh* (xii), with *ę̄* raised to *ī* . . ." The editors missed *ę̄* in the list of phonetic symbols, but even if it had been included, the remark on the history of *thigh* is addressed to those with previous exposure to English historical phonetics.

Seebold, who was under pressure to bring out "Everyman's" etymological dictionary of German, says that *Mus* 'mousse, applesauce, fruit or vegetable purée' is a vriddhi formation on the same root as the *s*-stem word **mati-/ez* 'food.' How many Germans with a fondness for mousse have heard about the terms of Sanskrit grammar and consonantal stems? To be sure, the dictionary opens with a brief explanation of special terms, but is even a motivated user of the dictionary ready to look up special terms in the introduction every time they occur? Ásgeir Blöndal Magnússon, the author of the latest etymological dictionary of Modern Icelandic (xli + 1231 pages), was convinced that all Icelanders with a fondness for their mother tongue would benefit by his work. Did he really believe that his entry on *eiga* 'have, possess,' with its references to Old Indian, Avestan, and Tokharian B and discussion of short and long diphthongs and palatal velars in Indo-European, would appeal to the so-called educated lay reader?

Language historians cannot speak about etymologies without referring to the zero grade, *s-mobile*, prothetic consonants, aphetic forms, and so forth, but some modern so-called "lay" readers find it hard to distinguish even infinitives from participles, the genitive from the accusative, and nouns from adjectives. One needs little training to absorb the message of the entry *awning* in ODEE: "XVII. Of unkn[own] origin," but most of what is written in etymological dictionaries makes sense only to people familiar with historical linguistics. However, the commercial success of ventures like ODEE shows that despite high prices and changes in our educational system, enough individuals and libraries uphold the tradition and buy serious reference books on the history of language. At present, the market is flooded with popular but selective English etymological dictionaries and other compilations for a broad public. Yet the basic product has always been and should remain a dictionary whose author has evaluated all that is known about the origin and later fortunes of words. Such a dictionary is written for prepared readers. Concise versions and editions for schools shine with a reflected light.

The barrier existing today between scholarly etymological dictionaries and the public was erected in the last decades of the nineteenth century. The audience of Minsheu, Skinner, Junius, and Richardson could follow both their reasonable arguments and their fantasies. The situation changed with the discovery of regular sound correspondences and the efflorescence of Indo-European studies. Etymological dictionaries lost their status as pseudoscholarly adventure books and became supplements to manuals of historical linguistics. Country squires were slow to notice the change and kept on writing letters to *Notes and Queries,* which dutifully published them. Walter W. Skeat scolded such correspondents for their attempts to guess word origins instead of researching them. Some of his opponents refused to listen even in 1910, the year Skeat died. Nor were publishers in a hurry to recognize the emergence of a new branch of scholarship. Some still treat etymology largely as a divertissement; hence many of our woes.

The Information an Etymological Dictionary Is Expected to Provide

The structure of modern etymological dictionaries depends on the state of the art and the state of the market. The first etymological dictionary of English was written in 1617. If every edition of Mueller, Wedgwood, Skeat, Weekley, and so on is counted as a new dictionary, their sum total (from 1617 on) will exceed twenty-five. Their usefulness is partly open to doubt, for curiosity about the origin of English words can be satisfied by less sophisticated works. Thomas Blount (1656) started the tradition of giving etymologies in explanatory dictionaries, and his tradition has continued into the present. Although the focus of Webster, OED, *The Century Dictionary,* and others is on meaning and usage, they contain authoritative statements on etymology. As we have seen, Richard G. White was no friend of the tradition that Blount initiated.

Nonspecialists interested in the history of English words prefer simple conclusions to a string of mutually exclusive hypotheses. They will normally skip the cognates in Avestan and the remark on the raising of closed *ē* in Middle English. But specialists need informed surveys of the material that has accumulated over the years, and this is where English etymological dictionaries are at their most vulnerable. Indo-European linguistics, all its achievements notwithstanding, is unable to solve some of the riddles it confronts. Often none of the existing etymologies of an obscure word carries enough conviction. In other cases, modern scholarship has accepted certain hypotheses, which does not mean that the ones that have been rejected are wrong.

Unfortunately, the latest brand of English etymological lexicography adheres to the all-or-none principle. The following note on the activity of the Philological Society appeared in *The Athenaeum* (No. 4296, 1910, p. 254):

> A letter from Sir J.A.H. Murray was also read, stating that guesses at the derivation of words were deliberately kept out of the 'N. E. D.,' and that the entry after a word "etymology uncertain" or "of obscure origin" ought to be understood to mean that a careful discussion of all suggested derivations had been held, and since none of them was satisfactory, they had all been left alone. The editors should have credit for the exclusion of plausibilities and absurdities.

Since OED is not an etymological dictionary, Murray chose the most reasonable approach to presenting his data. The problem is that "plausibilities and absurdities" are sometimes hard to distinguish from correct solutions. The etymologies in OED are detailed and carefully thought out. The same is true of Wyld's dictionary, and Webster aspires to be a model of reliability and solid judgment. But it may be useful to listen to Weekley's verdict. Unlike the impatient and irascible Skeat, Weekley was restrained and civil in his published works. Yet this is what he said to the self-same Philological Society twenty-eight years after Murray (*TPS* 1939, p.138: a summary of the paper read on October 22, 1938) :

> An examination of the Shorter Oxford English Dictionary, the new Webster, and Professor Wyld's Universal Dictionary in their relation to recent work on etymology and the settlement of unsatisfactory derivations showed that they often repeated old absurdities, did not attach enough importance to the original meanings of words or made wrong assumptions about them, and neglected the guidance of semantic parallels.

Note the echo word *absurdities*.

One can understand the editors of "thick" dictionaries: etymology is only one of their concerns, and they have little space for discussion. But discussion should be the prime goal of an etymological dictionary—something that has not been generally recognized in the English-speaking world, though statements like the following are numerous:

> What would have been greatly useful for students and laymen alike would have been a sort of casebook selection with full commentary showing why the scholar chose and juxtaposed forms as he did, to what degree the etymologist seems to have illuminated the relations, what sort of further evidence we could most wish for in a given case, etc. etc. In short, it would be instructive for outsiders to see just how a sensitive and learned etymologist makes decisions and advances to further knowledge. . . . Many laymen have the notion that we progress simply by "finding new words" or by discovering startling distant cousins in far-off Tibet. The intelligent layman who I would like to think might read our most readable books ought to be fascinated by the implications unfolded when one spells out simply but pre-

> cisely how our understanding has improved in the case of words like *full* or *bridge*, or how dialect research has contributed to our grasp of *ain't*, *oxen*, or *gnat*. The findings, if readably reported, could be much more exciting and unforeseen than an exact account of the genesis of *OK* or *sputnik*. (From Erik P. Hamp's review of Alan S. C. Ross's *Etymology; With Special Reference to English*. Fair Lawn, NJ: Essential Books, an imprint of Oxford University Press, Inc., 1958. *Word* 17, 1961, pp. 96–97.)

For echoes of the same sentiments see André Martinet, "Pourquoi des dictionnaires étymologiques?" (*La Linguistique* 3, 1966, pp. 123–31) and J. Picoche, "Problèmes des dictionnaires étymologiques" (*Cahiers de lexicologie* 16/1, 1970, pp. 53–62).

Onions (ODEE), even more so than Skeat and Weekley, tended to avoid confrontation. For example, Michel Bréal compared *bone* and *femur*, while Herbert Petersson offered the form **(o)zdboiness*. The search by these outstanding scholars for non- Germanic cognates of **bainam* arose as part of the effort to find cognates for several seemingly isolated Indo-European words meaning 'bone.' Meillet's idea that Russian *kost'* 'bone' (allegedly, *k-ost'*) is related to Latin *ost-* owes its existence to a similar impulse. Bréal and Petersson may have been wrong, but reference to their hypotheses would not only have enriched the entry in ODEE: it should have constituted its main part. Since Onions preferred to sift the data behind the scenes and suppressed what seemed doubtful to him, his reader comes away with a set of unquestionable cognates and a morsel of distilled truth. When Onions failed to find a persuasive solution, he followed Murray's example and said: "Of unknown origin." Since the authors of the latest English etymological dictionaries seldom disclose their sources, the scope of their reading remains a secret. Articles and notes on the origin of words are hard to find. Titles like "Etymological Miscellany," "Etymologies," "Etymologisches," and "Wortdeutungen" give almost no clue to the content of the works. It is also a wellknown fact that etymologies are offered in writings on religion, history, literature, botany, and so forth, and words mentioned in such texts can seldom be recovered through bibliographies.

Etymology is a vague concept, as shown by the polite warfare between those who look on it as the science of reconstruction and those who allow it to subsume "the history of words." If the etymology of a word like *uncouth* is supposed to deal with its modern pronunciation (one would expect it to rhyme with *south* rather than *sooth*), the bibliographical search broadens considerably. The same uncertainty plagues the choice of comparative data. For instance, unraveling the history of the word *eel* naturally entails the study of its cognates, but what authors even of multivolume etymological dic tionaries have enough leisure to familiarize themselves with the literature on one fish name in eight Germanic languages and then go on to Latin *anguilla* and its kin? ODEE gives three cognates of *eel*, reconstructs the protoform **ǣlaz*, and concludes that the word in question is of unknown origin. If an etymological dictionary can go no further, why bother to write it? The situation with *eel* is typical. At one time, *colt* was believed to have several cognates outside Germanic, and this belief found its reflection in the dictionary by Walde-Pokorny. From ODEE we learn that *colt* is "of obscure origin," though three Swedish dialectal words are similar to it in sound and meaning. Onions seems to have treated *colt* as an isolated form. However, those who turn to his dictionary are interested not only in the editor's opinions: they expect to be introduced to the science of English etymology rather than be shielded from heresy.

Our current English etymological dictionaries are among the most insubstantial in

Indo-European linguistics. There is no comparison between them and their Dutch, German, French, Spanish, Russian, and Lithuanian counterparts, let alone the etymological dictionaries of Hittite, Classical Greek, Latin, Gothic, and Old Icelandic. An encyclopedic dictionary of English etymology like Vasmer's (Russian) or at the very least like Jan de Vries's (Old Icelandic, Dutch) is long overdue. Such a dictionary should summarize and assess what has been said about the origin of English words and cite the literature pertaining to the subject. Its authors need not conceal their views and pose as dispassionate chroniclers of past achievements. On the contrary, they should burn up the chaff, weigh the merits of various hypotheses, and draw conclusions, however guarded, from the material at their disposal. Their readers will then be able to pick up where the authors leave off.

The Body of an Etymological Dictionary

The first task confronting a dictionary maker is the selection of words for inclusion. Both publishers and the public have been taught to appreciate bulk. At first sight, the more words a dictionary contains, the greater its value. However, here, too, much depends on the state of the art (and of the market). Webster and *The Century Dictionary* attempted to collect every word that occurred in printed sources. Dialect dictionaries spread their net equally wide. Against this background, other lexicographers can be less ambitious but more practical. As early as 1858, *The Saturday Review* (Vol. 6, August 21, p. 183) carried an article entitled "Dictionary-Making." It contained the following passage:

> Surplusage is the first and great fault of dictionaries. Their compilers are goaded on by the same mania for collecting words which sometimes lays hold of the collectors of books and papers, and they defeat their own object in the same suicidal manner. Perhaps it never occurs to them that the labour of finding a paper or a word is in direct proportion to the number among which it has to be hunted out. Perhaps they look on a dictionary as a work of art, which such considerations of mere convenience would degrade. But if a dictionary is to be convenient, it must be compact; and if it is to be compact, all superfluous matter must be ruthlessly retrenched. It must be weeded of every word for which there is no real likelihood that any considerable number of students will inquire. Far, however, from practising this wholesome self-denial, it is rather a point of honor with lexicographers to reprint all that their predecessors have printed, and something more besides. Languages change, words grow, and words decay; but a word that has once found its way into the lexicographers' museum remains forever embalmed to meet the wondering gaze of distant generations who will be puzzled to pronounce it. The monstrous compounds in which South, Taylor, and the Caroline school loved to advertise their Latinity—the quaint distortions to which the Elizabethan poets resorted to meet the exigencies of their easy verse—are preserved with as religious a care as a saint's tooth or a medieval coin.

And almost half a century later, an anonymous reviewer of the first (1893) edition of Funk's *A Standard Dictionary of the English Language* (*The Nation*, vol. 58, March 8, 1894, p. 180) said the following:

> Great prominence is given in the advertisements to claims for this dictionary of an enormous number of words ("*Johnson*, 45,000; *Stormonth*, 50,000; *Worcester*, 105,000; *Webster* (International), 125,000; *Century*, 225,000; *Standard*, nearly 300,000"), although the strenuous effort of the good lexicographer is to *keep down* his vocabulary. In an ordinary dictionary of reference, 25,000 words comprise all that anybody ever looks out. The rest is obstructive rubbish.

Unfortunately, "the obstructive rubbish" is indispensable, for who looks up *bread, water,* or *boy* in a dictionary of one's native language? *Unrebarbative* and *ptosis* are a different matter. And yet the idea that swelling is no virtue in a dictionary deserves every respect. It is fully applicable to etymological dictionaries where *bread, water,* and *boy* are among the most important items, whereas rarities attract few people's attention.

The editors of etymological dictionaries do not explain how they select their vocabulary. The most frequent words are always included. The same holds for some obsolete and dialectal words with established cognates, for etymologists are perpetually on the lookout for fossils. Skeat wrote a middle-sized dictionary, but he did not miss *nesh* 'tender, soft,' because it goes back to Old English *hnesce* and is related to Gothic *hnasqus*. ODEE contains at least 10,000 words more than Skeat. It is instructive to study what has been added. To form an idea of the increment, we can look at the vocables beginning with *ga-*. These are the words absent from Skeat but featured in ODEE, with glosses added, to distinguish homonyms:

> gabbro (min.), gabelle, gad (*in* 'by gad'), gadget, Gadhelic, gadoid, gadroon, gadzooks, gaekwar (= gaikwar, guicower), Gael, gaff (sl.) 'secret', gaffe (sl.), gag (sl.) 'impose upon', gaga (sl.), gage (*reference word* = greengage), galacto-, galanty, galatea, galbanum, gale 'periodical payment of rent, freeminer's royalty' (Anglo-Ir.), galeeny, Galen, galena, galilee, galimatias, galliambic, gallimaufry, gallinazo, gallium, gallivant, galliwasp, gally, galoot (sl.), galumph, gamba, gambado 'large boot or gaiter attached to a saddle,' gambeson, gambier, gambrel (dial.), gammon 'lashing of the bowsprit,' gambroon, gamete (biol.), gamin, gamma 'third letter of the Greek alphabet,' gamma 'gamut,' gammadion, gammy (sl.), gamp (colloq.), gangue, ganoid, gantry (=gauntry), Ganymede, garage, garboard, garçon, gardenia, gare-fowl (= gairfowl), Gargantuan, garget, garial (*reference word* = gavial), garibaldi, garnet (naut.) 'kind of tackling for hoisting,' garron, garth, gas 'gasolene,' gasket (naut.), gasolene (gasoline), gasometer, gasteropod, gatling, gauche, Gaucho, gaudy 'rejoicing; annual college feast,' Gaulish, gault (geol.), gazebo.

The list does look a bit "obstructive." The following are technical terms: gabbro, gadoid, gadroon, galacto-, galena, galliambic, gallium, gambier, gamete, gammadion, gammon, gangue, ganoid, garboard, garnet, gasket, and gault. One can add the names of exotic plants and animals and ethnic terms: gaekwark, galbanum, galeeny, gallinazo, galliwasp, gardenia, garefowl, garron, gasteropod, Gaucho. Six words (gaff, gaffe, gag, gaga, galoot, and gammy) are marked 'slang.' Gammy and gambrel are dialectal (gammy is also slang), gale is Anglo- Irish, gadzooks is archaic, gambeson is dated, gamp is colloquial; gally (and garth?) hardly belong to literary usage. Gambroon, gamp, garibaldi, and gatling are "words from names," and so are Galen 'doctor' and Ganymede 'cupbearer,' and the adjective Gargantuan.

Although Onions added so many words to Skeat, his list could have been made still longer. Where are *gaberlunzie, gabionade, gablock, Gabrielite, gade, gadwall, Gaillardia, gain* 'straight,' *gain* 'groove,' *Galago, galbe, galiongee,* and others of the same type? Each group (technical terms, plant and animal names, archaic words, dialectal words, words used in describing objects and customs of the past, and so forth) is open-ended. The consequence of expansion is triviality. Consider the following entries: *gaekwar* native ruler of Baroda, India. XIX. Marathi *gāekwar,* lit. cowherd; *gamma* third letter of the Gr. alphabet . . . XIV . . .; the moth Plusius gamma, having gamma-like markings; (math.) of certain functions XIX. (Is this an etymology?); *galoot* (sl.) raw soldier or marine; U. S. (uncouth) fellow. XIX. of unkn. origin; *Gaucho* mixed European and Indian race of the S. American pampas. XIX. Sp., of native origin; *gault* (geol.) applied to beds of clay and marl. XVI. Local (E. Anglian) word of unkn. origin, taken up by geologists.

When it comes to borrowings, we learn the following: *gamin* street Arab. XIX. (Thackeray). F. prob. of dial. origin; *garçon* waiter. XIX. F., obl. case of OF. (mod. dial.) *gars* lad, of disputed origin. Together, *gamin* and *garçon* take up four and a half lines of almost useless text; *girl*, ten pages later, is given six and a half lines, though it is one of the most controversial words in English etymology. "Equal representation" is the death of an etymological dictionary. Someone who does not know that *galliwasp* is a small West Indian lizard (another word of unascertained origin) or that *gambier* is an astringent extract from the plant Uncaria gambir (from Malay *gambir*) should look them up in an encyclopedia or any other reference book.

Work on the present dictionary began with the understanding that as few words as possible would be selected, but each of them would be accorded maximum attention. Three large groups can be isolated in the vocabulary of Modern English. The first includes words of Germanic origin, regardless of the details of their history, such as *father* (a Germanic word with broad Indo-European connections), *bride* (a Common Germanic word without certain cognates outside Germanic), *play* (a West Germanic word), *grove* (a word going back to Old English but lacking unambiguous cognates), *window* (a Middle English word borrowed from Scandinavian), *keel* 'vessel' (a Middle English borrowing from Middle Low German or Middle Dutch), and *boy* (a Middle English word of unclear antecedents). Perhaps words like *wait* (a Germanic word borrowed by Old French and many centuries later reborrowed by Middle English in French guise) can also be subsumed under "Germanic."

The second group includes words of unknown (doubtful, questionable, uncertain, disputed) etymology. They may turn out to be native or borrowed (see *gault*, above). The combined evidence of several dictionaries, including OED, yielded about 1,200 "Germanic" and 1,800 "disputed" words if we subtract those marked *slang, dialectal, obsolete,* and *archaic,* technical terms, and "words from names." The third group includes borrowings from the non-Germanic, mainly Romance, languages. The borders between the groups are not sharp. For example, most sources treat *boy* as Germanic, while Onions follows Dobson (who reinvented Holthausen's etymology) and derives it from Old French; *ivy* is a West Germanic word, but dictionaries are not sure whether Latin *ibex* is its cognate; *colt* is either an isolated English word with unclarified connections to Scandinavian or a word firmly rooted in Indo-European. Yet an approximate classification is possible. About 3,000 words borrowed from non-Germanic languages also deserve detailed etymological analysis.

It seemed reasonable to start with English words of "unknown etymology." As shown in the previous section, the label *unknown* should not be taken literally. Most of such words have been at the center of attention for a long time, but unanimity about their origin is lacking. However, disagreement and ignorance are different things. Words of "unknown etymology" are stepchildren of English linguistics. Students of Indo-European and Germanic ignore them or make do with reference to the substrate. Students of English are equally unenthusiastic about this material: where Skeat, Murray, Bradley, and Weekley chose not to venture, the others usually fear to tread. Someone must finally descend from the asterisked heights of Indo-European and Proto-Germanic and subject those English words to an unbiased and unhurried treatment.

To give an idea of how English vocabulary can be stratified according to the principles outlined above, we may again turn to Onions and look at the words beginning with *ba-* (pp. 67–81). Among them, some are Germanic (with or without Gothic), with cognates in Indo-European:

> bairn (dial.?), bake, bale 'evil,' ballock (?), ban 'curse, denounce,' bane, bare, bark (of a dog), barley (cereal), barm 'yeast,' barm (dial.) 'bosom,' barrow 'mound,' bath (and bathe).

Barm and *bath* (*bathe*) could perhaps have been assigned to the small group of Germanic words (without Gothic) lacking Indo-European cognates, such as:

> back, bane, barn, barrow 'boar,' barrow (*as in* wheelbarrow), base (fish), bast.

The following words were borrowed from other Germanic languages:

> baas, babiana, backbite, bait, balefire, balk, ball (*as in* football), ballast, balm (cricket), band (for binding), bank 'slope,' bark (on trees), bask, batten 'grow fat.'

Four of the following six words came to English from Dutch. The immediate source of two words is German. None of them is native in those languages, so that it is probably better not to treat them as Germanic:

> bale 'bundle' (French), bamboo (Malay), bandoleer (French), barouche (Italian), basement (Italian), and basset-horn (both from French).

Two or three *ba-* words—*ban* 'proclamation,' (?)*band* 'company,' and *baste* 'sew loosely'–-are of the *wait* type: from French, ultimately from Germanic. It is unclear how to classify "words from names," some of them borrowed:

> badminton, bakelite, balbriggan, Banksian, bantam, barb 'Barbary horse and pigeon,' barège, Barker's mill ("the alleged inventor, a Dr. Barker ... has not been identified"), barsack, bass 'ale,' batiste, bawbee, possibly bant (*bant* is not a name but a backformation from *Banting*), bay-salt.

About twenty-five words of those listed above will end up in the Germanic fascicles. The number of isolated words and words of uncertain etymology is surprisingly high:

> babe (*and* baby), backgammon, bad, badger, baffle, baffy, bag, bail (in cricket), bald, balderdash, bally, ballyhoo, bamboozle, bandy (in tennis), bandy 'toss,' bandy 'curved inwards,' banter, bantling, barley 'call for a truce' (dial.), barnacle 'bit for a horse,' barrister, base (game), bass (fish name; possibly here), bass 'fibre,' baste 'pour fat,' bat 'club,' bat (animal name), battel (= batell), bavin, bawd.

The imitative words—*baa, babble, bah, bang, bash, bawl*—and the disguised compound *bandog* should probably be assigned to the foregoing group above, where the sum total is close to thirty.

In every dictionary of Modern English, most words are of French/Latin origin. The lists above yielded about sixty words gleaned from pp. 67–81 of ODEE, whereas the number of words borrowed into English from French and Latin (nearly all of them are from French) occurring within the same space is about 110. Approximately fifty of them are post-fifteenth century; they are given below with asterisks. The entire ODEE contains about 1,400 "Germanic," about 1,800 "questionable," and about 3,000 pre-16th century "French" words. (For comparison: among the 10,000 most frequent English words, "the native English element" comprises slightly over 35 percent, and "words of Latin origin" comprise almost 46 percent. See Edward Y. Lindsay, *An Etymological Study of the Ten Thousand Words in Thorndike's Teacher's Word Book.* Indiana University Studies, vol. XII, No. 65, 1925, p. 6.) Such words will constitute the bulk of the prospective dictionary.

Let us examine two more lists: 1) words from French and Latin, and 2) words from other languages (all of them are from the *ba-* section).

Borrowings from French and Latin

baboon, *babouche, *baccalaureate, *baccara(t), *bacchanal, bachelor, *bacillus, bacon, *bacterium, badge, *badinage, *bagatelle, *baignoire, bail 'security,' bailey, bailie (Scottish), bailiff, *bain-marie, *baize, balance, balas, baldric, bale 'lade out,' baleen, *ball 'assembly for dancing,' ballad, ballade, *ballet, *ballista, balm, balsam, *baluster, *banal, *bandage, *bandeau, *banderole, banish, *bank 'tier of oars' (*bank* 'bench' was borrowed in the thirteenth century), banner, banneret (a historical term), banquet, baptize, bar 'rod; barre˘r,' barb 'beard-like appendage,' *barbaresque, barbaric, *barbed, barber, *barberry, *barbette, barbican, bard 'horse armor,' bargain, barge, barnacle 'wild goose,' *barnacle (on the bottom of a ship), baron, *baroque (= barrok), *barque (= bark) 'boat,' *barquentine, *barrack 'soldiers, quarters,' *barrage, barrator, barrel, barren, *barricade, barrier, barring 'excepting,' barny (in heraldry), (? *bartizan, a word revived by Walter Scott), *basalt, *basan (= bazan), *bascule, base 'bottom,' base 'of low quality,' basil, *basilar, *basilica, *basilisk, basin, basinet, basis, basket, *bas-relief, bass 'deepsounding,' *basset, bassinette, bastard, bastille, *bastion, (*)bat 'pack-saddle' (first known only in compounds), bate 'beat the wings,' bate 'reduce,' *bateau, (*batman 'army officer's servant'; *only* bat *is from French*), *baton, *battalion, batter 'beat,' batter 'paste,' *battery, battle, battlement, *battology, *battue, bauble, baudekin, bauson (dial.), *bauxite (= beauxite), bay 'tree,' bay (in the sea), bay (*as in* bay-window), bay (*as in* at bay), bay 'reddish-brown,' bay 'bark,' *bayadère, (? bayard), *bayonet.

Borrowings from Languages Other than French and Latin

babiroussa, baboo (= babu), badmash (= budmash), bael (= bel), bagnio, bahadur, baksheesh, balalaika, balcony, baldac(c)hino, balibuntal (partly belonging to "words from names"), ballerina, bambino, ban 'governor in Hungary,' banana, bandanna, bandicoot, bandit, bandore, bangle, banian (= banyan), banjo, bankrupt, bannock, banshee, banxring, banzai, baobab, barbeque, bard 'minstrel,' barilla, baritone, barometz, barrack 'banter,' barytone, bashaw, bashi-bazouk, basistan, basso, bassoon, bastinado, bat 'colloquial speech of a foreign country,' batata, bath 'Hebrew liquid measure,' bathos, batik, batman 'Oriental weight,' batrachian, batta 'discount,' batta 'allowance,' bawn, bayou, bazaar (*cf. also socalled individual coinages:* barium, barometer, baryta, barytes, bathybius).

Every word needs a "biography," but some biographies are uninspiring. A specialized etymological dictionary gains little by filling its pages with curt statements that *baritone* is from Italian, ultimately from Greek, and that *bacterium* is from Latin, ultimately also from Greek. It has been argued above that *galliwasp* (the name of a small West Indian lizard) should be featured in encyclopedias and "thick" dictionaries rather than in books like ODEE. *Bari-*

tone and *bacterium* are relatively common words, but they clutter ODEE in equal measure. The sophisticated reader, used to consulting ODEE, undoubtedly consults other dictionaries, each of which offers the same information on *bacterium* and *baritone.* An etymological dictionary of English can probably dispense with words about which it has or chooses so little to say.

In the list "Borrowings from Languages Other than French and Latin," only *banana, bankrupt,* and perhaps *bannock* deserved a mention. The asterisked words in the list of borrowings from French and Latin are trivial from the perspective of an etymologist of English. Consider the entry *ballet:* ". . . XVII (*balette, ballat*).—F. *ballet*—It. *balletto*, dim. of *ballo* BALL[2]." or *basilica:* ". . . XVI.—L.—Gr. *basilikē,* sb. use of fem. of *basilikós* royal, f. *basileús* king." Most asterisked words (*babouche, baccara(t),* and so on) should have been included only if Onions had decided to treat their history in Greek, Latin, and Italian in depth. Among the "Germanic" and "questionable" words, obstructive rubbish is equally common, but there is less of it.

Dialectal words and slang pose special problems. Both explanatory and etymological dictionaries feature some "nonstandard" vocabulary, but on a relatively small scale. Even OED left out hundreds of so-called provincialisms; their absence is not due to oversight. A special etymological dictionary of dialectal vocabulary needs a good deal of preparatory work. Dialectal words of Scandinavian and Low German/Dutch origin have been studied in considerable detail, but the remainder—"words of unknown etymology"—is huge. Before all the recorded words of English dialects have been stratified according to the most elementary rubrics (words going back to Old English, borrowings from Scandinavian, borrowings from Low German/Dutch, Romance words, words of unknown origin, and so forth), it is pointless to include *bairn, barm, bauson,* and *nesh* in etymological dictionaries only because their history happens to be known. Some such words—for example, *oss(e)*—have been the object of protracted controversies and have "attained celebrity," yet they have to be left for the future.

Slang is an elusive concept. Although informal by definition, short-lived, and local, it often acquires a certain degree of respectability, stays in the language, and overcomes territorial barriers. However unscientific such a procedure may be, it is probably best to decide which slang words should go into an etymological dictionary by using one's intuition. Here are six "low" synonyms of *steal: purloin, cop, filch, mooch, pilfer,* and *swipe.* None of them is metaphoric in the sense in which the verbs *bone, cabbage, hook, lift, nick,* and *pinch* are. Probably even the most conservative lexicographers will not object to the presence of *purloin, filch, mooch,* and *pilfer* in an etymological dictionary, while the other two will be acceptable only to some. In the prospective dictionary, slang will occupy a modest place.

The Uses of the Prospective Dictionary of English Etymology

One of the functions of the prospective dictionary (represented below by fiftyfive samples) is to make the literature on English etymology available. Information on the origin of words that surfaced in Middle English and later is especially hard to collect. But this dictionary has not been conceived as a showcase of old and recent opinions. The user of Weekley, Partridge, Onions, Klein, and Barnhart learns little about researchers' and amateurs' doubts and almost nothing about their tortuous way to the truth. Dictionaries formulate their conclusions in such a way that few would suspect any depth behind the statements in their pages (compare what has been said about the treatment of *bone* in ODEE). Etymology, as it appears in English dictionaries, is the only philological science enjoying complete anonymity. Who suggested that *soot* is related to *sit?* Who detected *cock's egg* in *Cockney?* Who guessed that *surround* has nothing to do with *round?* Are these discoveries final? Indo-European linguistics is full of laws: Verner's Law, Sievers's Law, and dozens of others. It is sad that the most brilliant English etymologies are nameless waifs.

The format of the entry in Walde-Hofmann, Feist, Vasmer, and Jan de Vries reveals the extent of the authors' knowledge of their subject. In dealing with English etymological dictionaries, one has to take everything on trust. Onions could have done without *balalaika,* but he included it in ODEE and inadvertently revealed the danger of dogmatic entries. According to ODEE, *balalaika* is "Russ[ian], of Tatar origin." In a nondogmatic work, a reference would have supported his statement, but since ODEE almost never gives references, it begins to seem that no proof is needed: the Tatar origin of *balalaika* is apparently a fact. But it is not. Whoever wrote Slavic etymologies for ODEE could have looked up *balalaika* in several dictionaries of Slavic and found that the word is probably native. Why did ODEE prefer the less reliable etymology? Onions's Slavic consultants had a strong predilection for Tatar: they derived even *Kremlin,* an undoubtedly Russian word, from that language. If at the end of the entry on *balalaika* the source of information had been cited (as is done, for instance, under *Samoed*), the procedure could have been subjected to criticism, but in a dogmatic dictionary an insufficient familiarity with the material is hidden. An etymological dictionary is not a repository of aphorisms, and it should be written according to the rules valid for all linguistic works; that is, with a scholarly apparatus that allows the reader to see what is original and what is common knowledge in each entry, what authority stands behind the main formulations, and what the authors (editors, compilers) have read.

A still more important issue is the gap between English etymology as a science and as a body of information presented in dictionaries. One can assume with some confidence that Skeat, Murray, and Bradley tried to keep abreast of the times and followed the major publications on the history of English vocabulary. Since 1884–1928, the years in which OED was being published, thousands of articles and books on the origin of English words and their cognates have appeared. Most people take it for granted that the editors of our latest dictionaries are aware of those works; but if it were so, it would be hard to explain why ODEE, Partridge, Klein, and the rest show such disregard of post-1928 contributions. Most of the ongoing etymological research leaves no trace in English etymological dictionaries. Are the new ideas so bad that they do not even deserve refutation? In his review of Alistair Campbell's *Enlarged Addenda and Corrigenda* to Bosworth-Toller, R. I. Page wrote: "The difficulty . . . is that the reader does not know if Campbell's omissions are reasoned and intended, or accidental" (*Medium Ævum* vol. 44, 1975, p. 67). This is exactly where the shoe pinches the most. Etymology as a branch of linguistics is different from phonetics and grammar in that its practitioners do not meet at special conferences, few manuals summarize the latest contributions to the subject, and it is taught (when at all) only as a component of other courses. An article on the origin of an English word can make an impact on scholarship only if it is mentioned in an etymological dictionary.

Several circumstances disrupted the practice of coordinating dictionary work with achievements in English linguistics. The main one is the excellence of OED and Skeat[4].

Most etymologies in these dictionaries are so solid, even when incomplete and outdated, that recycling them guarantees a measure of success to any lexicographic enterprise. Second, English philology chose not to follow the example of Walde, Feist, Van Wijk, Vasmer, Jan de Vries, and others (more excellent models can be found in Romance linguistics) and did not develop an encyclopedic or analytic etymological dictionary. In a dogmatic dictionary, controversial ideas have no chance of being noticed. Finally, owing to the progress in comparative linguistics, most hypotheses advanced before roughly 1860–1880 appear obsolete; and old dictionaries, as well as old articles and books, have lost their appeal in the eyes of those who learned etymology from Brugmann, Noreen, and their contemporaries and pupils. Not only Skinner, Wachter, Junius, and Ihre, but also Mueller, who had the ill luck to publish the second edition of his dictionary shortly before Skeat, and Wedgwood, with his cavalier attitude toward phonetic correspondences, have been shelved once and for all. On one hand, English etymology abandoned its remote past as a laughable superstition. On the other, it became too self-sufficient to bother with recent contributions.

Everyone will probably applaud the effort made in this dictionary to discuss the post-1928 works that have not been given due credit. But to what extent are pre-Skeat and especially pre-Grimm books worthy of attention? The answer depends on the word under consideration. Many etymologies yield to a combination of Neogrammarian algebra, imagination, and serendipity. Recourse to phonetic correspondences makes certain hypotheses untenable by definition, but when a tempting etymology collapses under the weight of phonetic evidence, linguists have numerous ways to save the situation: the substrate, borrowing, hybrid forms (*Mischformen*), residual forms (*Restformen*), migratory words (*Kulturwörter* or *Wanderwörter*), sound symbolism, onomatopoeic and expressive formations, baby language, anagrams, individual coinages, taboo, and the multifarious forms of language play. Assimilation, dissimilation, metanalysis, metathesis, redistribution of morphemes, back formation, allegro forms, fear of homonymy, "corruption" (that is, folk etymology or mistakes in transmission), and analogy, for some reason usually called false, though being false is its only *raison d'être,* also prove useful. Contemporary knowledge of language families is another great asset. We no longer derive English from Hebrew, Greek, Latin, or German. But if an English word bears a close resemblance to a word in Hebrew, the two may be related. With the growth of Nostratic linguistics, modified versions of broad and even "global" etymologies, once favored and later ridiculed as fantasy, are again in vogue. Consequently, even reference to Hebrew words in old dictionaries can sometimes be put to use.

When etymology tries to solve the riddle of the origin of language, it fails. In Indo-European, one can seldom go beyond the roots posited by Brugmann, Walde, and Pokorny (with or without laryngeals): the circumstances in which allegedly primitive sound strings like **bhlag-, *ster,* and **wegh-* (in so far as they are not obviously onomatopoeic) came by their meanings is hidden. Older authors, even such learned men as Junius and Ihre, were at their weakest when correct solutions required the use of socalled sound laws, for they sought phonetic similarity, while we rely on correspondences. But thousands of etymologies are more or less inspired guesswork. *Strumpet* resembles English *strumpot* (whatever that means), French *tromper* 'cheat,' Latin *stuprum* 'disgrace,' and German *Strumpf* 'stocking' or 'trouser leg.' The more obscure the word, the more clues have to be examined. In such cases, the conjectures of old scholars have not necessarily lost their value.

An instructive example is the legacy of Wedgwood, the greatest authority on English etymology before Skeat. He took a keen interest in the distant roots of language (an interest he shared with Charles Darwin, his brother-in-law). His papers could at one time be found in every volume of the *Transactions of the Philological Society*. After the appearance of Skeat's dictionary (1882), he published a sizable book of objections to it, and although there was no love lost between the two scholars, Skeat accepted some of his rival's suggestions. Later, Skeat and OED upstaged Wedgwood; but in the sixties of the nineteenth century, George March, a leading specialist in the history of English, was so impressed with Wedgwood's dictionary that he envisaged an American edition of it with his additions and corrections (only the first volume appeared). Even Mayhew, who never missed a chance to denigrate his colleagues and who was aware of Wedgwood's faults, admired his ability to detect semantic connections. Regrettably, Wedgwood's works have fallen into oblivion.

In the prospective dictionary, more than one fourth of the words are of "obscure origin." In trying to unravel their past, old works with an etymological component have been occasionally found to be of use. References to forgotten and half-forgotten publications will benefit readers in several ways. Critical surveys will allow them to trace the path from the ancient rambles among words or word gossip (as this genre was called) to the terse formulations of ODEE. All modern solutions will be put into perspective. Even a hundred years ago, the most distinguished scholars in the field used to begin their articles with disclaimers such as: "My etymology is so simple that it must have occurred to someone else." Their fears were not always groundless. Our contemporaries find it difficult to master the scholarly literature that seemed vast as far back as 1880 (which is the reason they rarely try to do so) and need a detailed overview of books, articles, and notes in the style of Feist and Vasmer. Since such overviews exist for all the major Indo-European languages, English need not remain the only exception. Despite the emphasis on *survey* and *overview* above, the idea is not to publish an annotated bibliography disguised as an etymological dictionary. The surveys will examine early etymologies from chance juxtapositions to relatively convincing hypotheses. It will be hard to avoid some reference to uninformed opinions. Even those who will agree that we can learn something from Minsheu, Junius, and Skinner (and who welcomed the reprints of their dictionaries) may wonder why the fantasies of John B. Ker, Charles Mackay, Karl Faulmann, Frederick Ebener, M. M. Makovskii, Isaac E. Mozeson, and a few other researchers of the same type have not been ignored. The answer is simple. The history of linguistics is as erratic as all human history, and it is useful to be aware of this fact, the more so because our age produces "absurdities" with the enthusiasm and self-assurance even exceeding those of the past epochs.

The main situations we encounter are two: 1) A word has been given some attention in dictionaries and in special publications, but no one has discovered its etymology. Here the case will be presented and suggestions added, wherever possible. 2) The etymology of a word has been discovered, but English dictionaries keep repeating: "Origin unknown." For instance, the etymology of *cub* is no longer a puzzle, but articles on it and mentions of it in Scandinavian, German, and Dutch dictionaries escaped the attention of English lexicographers (the most probable explanation), or Onions and others found the existing hypotheses unconvincing and preferred not to rank them according to their worth. In such cases, everyone will be given a fair hearing and the best solution defended. This dictionary will close with a summary, a subject index, a word index, and a name index, so that lexicographers, etymologists, historians of ideas, specialists in the external history of English (including material culture), and students of any Indo- European language and of any aspect of the history of English will be able to retrace most of what they need.

Truly original etymological dictionaries of major Indo-European languages (that is, dictionaries in which every or almost every word receives a novel explanation) are no longer possible. Even such imaginative scholars as Ernst Zupitza and Francis A. Wood, quite naturally, found inspiration in the work of their predecessors; the same is true of de Saussure and Meillet. This is what Skeat said about his achievement in the last year of his life: "I have received so much assistance from so many kind friends that I fail to remember whence my ideas have come. May I say, once for all, that I claim to be no better than a compiler; and though some of the contributions have come from my own stores, I cannot always say which they are" (*Modern Language Review* vol. 6, 1911, p. 210; published posthumously).

On Methodology

By way of conclusion, it may be useful to formulate a few general principles on which the prospective dictionary is based. They are a mixture of a lexicographer's common sense and philology.

1. *Many Birds, One Stone.* An etymologist's first task is to find the cognates of any given word in the target language. By and large, the same etymology will be valid for the entire group. Once we agree that *fit* 'attack of illness; sudden onset,' *fiddle, fickle,* and so on belong together, the search for the origin of every member of the group resolves itself into documenting the attested forms. Dictionaries arrange words alphabetically and thereby destroy the ties they are supposed to restore. Even a dictionary devoted to the etymology of one language will gain if it partly follows the example of Fick, Walde, and others, whose format is "nests." In the entry FUCK, below, about twenty words with the presumable semantic core 'move back and forth' are etymologized. Some of them, like *fiddle*, deserve special treatment, but the rest can be dismissed summarily. The same holds for *miche, meech, mich, mouch, mooch,* and, possibly, *mug* 'waylay and rob; (ugly) face,' *hugger-mugger,* and *curmudgeon* (see MOOCH). See also GAWK and TOAD. Cross-references in etymological dictionaries invariably miss some of the words belonging to a large cluster, and since each headword has to be relatively self-sufficient, the same data are recycled over and over again, instead of relegating them to an index. It seems more profitable to write six pages on *mooch* and its kin than a half-dozen short entries that the reader will have to combine, in order to obtain a full picture. An average user has neither the time nor the expertise to do such work. The format advocated here enjoyed some popularity at the dawn of etymological lexicography but was later abandoned.

2. *Scorched Earth.* This principle, which is a variant of the previous one, was formulated by Skeat in his Canon 10: "It is useless to offer an explanation of an English word which will not *also* explain all the cognate forms." Skeat was right, but in the world of words kinship is not always evident. Consider the never-ending debate over the validity of lists in Walde-Pokorny and Pokorny. Even within one language group (Germanic), secondary ablaut produces forms whose relationship to one another constitutes the main part of etymological inquiry. For example, to understand the origin of *lad*, it is necessary to explore the prehistory of many Scandinavian, English, Old Saxon, and German words having *a, o,*

u, and other vowels between *l* and *d* (*ð, t*). Until all of them reveal their past, the origin of *lad* will remain uncertain. The same holds for *cob, cub, keb,* and the rest (also in several languages) and for *miche,* G *meucheln,* E *mug,* L *muger,* and so forth. Compare 7, below.

Etymologists prefer to concentrate on the obvious rather than distant, questionable, and spurious cognates. On the other hand, they will catch at the thinnest straw to explain the origin of a hard word. The purpose of the present dictionary is not only to discover the truth to the extent that we can do it with the information available today but also to expose all the false tracks. The entry KEY might be adequate without discussion of OI *kǫgurbarn,* but the temptation to connect **kag-* and **kaig-* is great, and a special note emphasizes their incompatibility. It comes as a surprise that in the Middle Ages stunted growth was considered a mental disease rather than a physical deformity and that dwarves were associated with lunacy. Every piece of evidence that illustrates this idea has value. Herein lies the justification of a long note on *altvile* appended to the entry DWARF. Only exhaustive critical surveys of all forms actually and allegedly related to the word under consideration and a thorough analysis of the *Wörter und Sachen* aspect of the problem at hand (which complement an overview of the state of the art) can weaken the speculative basis of etymology as a science.

The method employed in this dictionary owes little to Jost Trier's procedures despite some superficial similarity between them. Trier's overriding categories (fence building, young trees, the needs of a community, and so forth), which he treated as motors of semantic change, often produce doubtful and even wrong results because a bird's-eye view of word history cannot replace a painstaking study of the contexts in which words occur. Trier was an inspired scholar and saw far, but, as they say, God is in the details. This is true of etymology as much as of any other branch of scholarship.

3. *The Centrifugal Principle.* Tracing word origins is a game of probabilities. A language historian often reaches a stage when all the facts have been presented and it becomes necessary to weigh several hypotheses and choose the most probable or, to use a less charitable formation, the least improbable one. All other conditions being equal, tracing a word to a native root should be preferred to declaring it a borrowing. In similar fashion, it is more attractive to refer to an ascertainable foreign source than to an unidentifiable substrate. The origin of numerous plant and animal names, as well as of the names of tools, is obscure. Some scholars believe that *clover* and *ivy,* both limited to West Germanic, are substrate words taken over from a non-Indo-European language. Both propositions, most likely, are wrong because a persuasive Germanic etymology exists for *clover* ('sticky') and especially for *ivy* ('bitter'). However, the discovery of a plausible English source for *clover* and *ivy* does not mean that our task has been accomplished. By choosing an attested native etymon and refusing to deal with a plant name of non-Germanic origin, we only pay tribute to the centrifugal principle: the closer to the center, the better. OE *āfor* 'bitter' looks like a perfect match for *īfig*. Yet the relative value of the results obtained is self-evident.

4. *Say 'no' to 'obscurum per obscurius.'* When a word is isolated in one language (like *heifer:* only English), several languages (like *ivy:* West Germanic), or a language group (like *dwarf:* Germanic), etymologists make great efforts to find related forms elsewhere; see what is said above about their propensity to catch at the thinnest straw. As a rule, they succeed in discovering some word whose phonetic shape and meaning match those of the word un-

der discussion. It is usually hard to decide whether the alleged connection is valid. But the following principle provides some help: a word of unknown etymology in one language should never be compared with an equally obscure word in another language.

Heifer (< OE *heahfore*) resembles vaguely a few animal names outside English, Russ. *koza* 'nanny-goat' being among them. However the pair *heifer / koza* need not delay us, for the origin of *koza* remains a matter of debate (it may be a borrowing from some Turkic language). When Hoops suggested that *ivy* is related to L *ibex*, he found many supporters: both the plant and the animal are indeed climbers, whereas from the phonetic point of view the correspondence is flawless. But nothing is known about the origin of *ibex* (a substrate Alpine word?), which means that Hoops's etymology is unacceptable by definition. *Dwarf* (< OE *dweorg*) has exact counterparts in Old Frisian, Middle Dutch, Old High German, and Old Icelandic, but attempts to find its non-Germanic cognates have failed. Among those proposed are Avestan *drva*, the name of some physical deformity, Skt *dhvarás-* 'crooked, dishonest,' an epithet accompanying the demon Druh, and Gk σέρ(ι)φος 'midge' (or some other insect). The origin and the exact meaning of those three words are uncertain. It follows that they should not have been proposed, let alone taken seriously, as putative cognates of *dwarf*. Inevitably, after a short life in dictionaries (some of our best), they, especially *drva* and σέρ(ι)φος, returned to their obscurity, and the search for the derivation of *dwarf* started from scratch.

5. *Stylistic Congruity.* The deterioration and the amelioration of meaning are well-known phenomena. Yet the etymon of the word whose origin we are investigating should ideally be searched among the words of the same style. Reconstruction, let it be repeated, is about probabilities. Incredible semantic leaps have occurred in the history of words, but only such changes can be posited that have the support of documented analogs. According to a recent hypothesis, *girl*, though it surfaced in the thirteenth century, goes back to OE *gierela* (*gerela, girela, gyrela*) 'dress, apparel, adornment; banner.' A metonymy of this type (from clothes to a person wearing them) is common, but ME *girle* seems to have been an informal word that meant both 'young male' and 'young female' and was used mainly in the plural, whereas OE *gierela* appears to have belonged to a relatively elevated register and did not designate children's clothes. Inasmuch as the stylistic gap between OE *gierela* and ME *girle* remains unbridged, the former should be rejected as the source of the latter. Considerations of style are among the most neglected in etymological studies, though Voßler and Spitzer never tired of emphasizing them.

6. *Language at Play.* Sound correspondences remain the foundation of etymological analysis, but all branches of historical linguistics have to reckon with the existence of ludic forms. The union of Neogrammarian linguistics and phonosemantics should be welcomed, but only in so far as phonosemantics knows its place. Facile references to ideophones do not produce lasting results. It may be that the sound complex *k* + vowel + *b* conveys or at one time conveyed the idea of roundness, but even if so, the history of *cub* and *cob* remains obscure. We have to explain why both words were attested so late, how they are related to similar words in other Germanic languages, to what extent the many meanings of *cob* (noun and verb) belong together, whether it is legitimate to reconstruct a phonosemantic explosion in the history of English six or seven centuries ago, or whether earlier forms have to be reconstructed. Yet neither the strictest application of Neogrammarian laws nor the

broadest recognition of the role of sound symbolism, expressive gemination, and so forth will turn etymology into a strict science. It will forever depend on a combination of intuition, guesswork, and all-encompassing knowledge.

7. *Entries versus Essays.* The length of the entries in this book is untraditional. Some are longer than average journal articles, and even the shortest do not resemble those in Skeat, Kluge, or Feist. The format chosen for the entries is a consequence of the principle of scorched Earth. A single example will suffice. *Lad*, mentioned at the beginning of No. 2 ("Scorched earth"), has been compared with E *lead* (v), OE *lēod, hlāfǣta, *hlæda,* and *Ladda,* G *ledig,* Go *(jugga-)lauþs,* Gr λαός, Welsh *llawd,* VL *litus,* Hebr. *yeled,* and its cognate Arabic (*wa*)-*lad*-. In addition, a thicket of look-alikes surrounds it: OE *loddere,* OI *lydda,* MHG *(sumer)lat(t)e,* N *ladd,* and E *lath,* to mention the most important ones. A convincing etymology of *lad* can be offered only after all of them have been investigated and either weeded out or left as probable cognates of the English noun. Along the way, Hamlet's name turns up, and it, too, requires some attention. Discussion of so many side issues needs space. The apodictic, telegraphic style common among etymologists ("wrong cognates are offered by . . .", "different treatment can be found in . . .", without elaboration) would do a disservice to English, with its tradition of dogmatic dictionaries. A diffuse essay is preferable to an entry in which hints take precedence over detailed examination. After all, people not interested in circling the battlefield can come to the point at once, skip the digressions, and read only the summary and the conclusion.

Kluge, too, wrote a dogmatic dictionary, but his successors began to include references to the scholarly literature, and every new edition witnessed an increase in the number of works cited. In English etymological lexicography, even the few references Skeat chose to give have disappeared. The entries below are long because they follow every lead and contain exhaustive surveys of opinion going back to 1599 (Kilianus) or 1617 (Minsheu). A bibliography comparable in size to the text of the samples may seem excessive to some, but the time has come to cleanse the Augean stable of English etymology (a labor that is not only necessary but also pleasant). Another extenuating circumstance is that if this project were conceived by a German scholar, the book would be called *kurzgefasstes Wörterbuch*. Brevity is a matter of definition.

Otto Jespersen says the following in his review of Wyld's *The Universal English Dictionary:* "One of the distinctive features of this Dictionary is the great space given to etymology, and on the whole this part of the work is admirable. The author has shown much discrimination in selecting all that is reliable in recent etymological investigations without bewildering the reader, as some etymological dictionaries do, with a great many fanciful proposals that have found their way to linguistic periodicals" (*English Studies* vol. 15, 1933, p. 44). In the same paragraph, Jespersen notes that Wyld's interest in history sometimes carried him away. For example, "[t]he word *crinite,* from the English point of view certainly one of the most unimportant words, receives nine lines of etymology to half a line of definition." However, having said that and having adduced another instance of the same type, he remarks: "But why grumble if a man who gives us so much excellent information seems here and there to give us a little too much?" May his disarmingly kind question serve as a reminder that "fanciful proposals," both old and new, constitute the main body of etymological literature.

8. *The Samples.* The words treated in this book represent all the letters of the English al-

phabet except Q, V, X and Z. Most have been in the language since the earliest period, a few surfaced in Middle English; *slang* does not antedate the eighteenth century, *Lilliputian* and *jeep* are "coinages," and *kitty-corner* (whatever its age) was first attested in recent memory. Nouns predominate among the samples, but there are also verbs, two adverbs (*ever* and *yet*), and a numeral (*eena*). One entry (*heifer*) deals with a disguised compound. *Fieldfare, henbane, horehound*, and *ragamuffin* are still decomposable, but their constituent elements are partly or wholly opaque. In *understand*, both parts are transparent; it is their sum (*under + stand* = 'comprehend') that baffles the modern speaker. The same holds for *slowworm. Kitty-corner* (a phrase) has been included for the sake of the incomprehensible *kitty*.

The present book, a showcase of the entire project, contains words of various origins. *Brain, clover,* and *ivy* are West Germanic. *Beacon* is also West Germanic, but OI *bákn*, even if it is a borrowing from Old English, requires special attention. *Dwarf* has cognates all over the Germanic speaking world. The entries on *clover, ivy, beacon*, and *dwarf* demonstrate the treatment of the less isolated words of English. *Man* has cognates in Indo-Iranian and Slavic. Words with broad Indo-European connections, such as kin terms and ancient numerals, have not been included. The same holds for unquestionable borrowings even from other Germanic languages, but the question of language contacts turns up in the history of many words with obscure history. See the entries on *flatter, fuck, gawk, girl, rabbit*, and *strumpet*. Research into the possible sources of the seemingly isolated words plays a role in the etymology of *cushat, drab, filch, skedaddle,* and *stubborn*. The ghost of the substrate haunts the investigation of *clover, ivy,* and *key; adz(e)* resembles old migratory words.

Some entries form small cycles. *Clover* and *ever* end in *-er; cub* and *cob* are similar in sound and meaning; *boy* and *girl, lad* and *lass* are traditionally discussed together pairwise (this is especially true of *lad* and *lass*). *Doxy, drab, strumpet,* and *traipse* are near synonyms. The emphasis on plant and animal names is not due to chance (they are notoriously obscure), the more so as *hemlock, henbane,* and *horehound* share reference to poison.

The common denominator of all fifty-five words is their etymological opaqueness. The solutions offered here are, of necessity, controversial. If the history of *bird, cockney, slang*, and the rest were less troublesome, their etymology would have been discovered and accepted long ago. Some solutions look like a *tour de force* (see especially *fag(g)ot* and *pimp*), others may arouse no serious objections (for example, *cushat, stubborn*). The goal of the dictionary is to do justice to four centuries of research, not to close the science of English etymology. Fifty-five is a good number when it comes to etymological cruces and enough to give an idea of the project in its entirety.

A Few Practical Considerations

Since this book introduces a project of great magnitude, a few comments on its practical aspects may not be out of place. Work on the dictionary began in 1987. At that time, Anatoly Liberman (AL) and J. Lawrence Mitchell (JLM) were colleagues at the University of Minnesota. In 1988 JLM moved to Texas, where he spent sixteen years as Head of the Department of English at Texas A&M University. AL is a professor of Germanic Philology in the Department of German, Scandinavian and Dutch at the University of Minnesota (Minneapolis). He is responsible for the research and writes the etymologies. JLM prepared part of the volume for publication.

Before the first entry could be written, it was necessary to collect the literature on English etymology. The available bibliographies have yielded numerous relevant titles, but most references to the history of English words can be discovered only by screening journals *de visu*. Close to a hundred people have looked through major philological journals and numerous popular and semipopular publications dealing with English linguistics and photocopied the articles, reviews, and notes that, in their opinion, were useful for future work. All the works have been marked for the English words they contain and entered into the computer. This search is endless, for it is impossible to examine the entire corpus of old literature, while new journals and books appear every month. However, sufficiently detailed entries can be written on the basis of the files kept at the University of Minnesota. Etymological dictionaries of German, Swedish, Norwegian, Icelandic, Dutch, and several other languages have been indexed for English words. The writing of each entry begins with the production of two summaries: 1) everything said about the word in about two hundred dictionaries, and 2) everything said about it in articles and books. More about collecting the material has been said in the introduction to *A Bibliography of English Etymology,* being published simultaneously with these samples.

The authors of etymological dictionaries find it difficult to eliminate errors. In retrospect, one wonders how Walde could occasionally give a Latin word a wrong length or how Onions could spell a Czech word with letters nonexistent in that language. Reviewers call such mistakes abhorrent, unconscionable, and unpardonable. Moral indignation elevates the critic, but the fact remains that no one is fully qualified to write an etymological dictionary of an Indo-European language, especially of English. If authors and editors are versed in Old and Middle English, they are probably less comfortable in Old High German and Old Icelandic. If they spent years studying Classical Greek and Latin, they must have missed a good deal in Old Frisian and Middle Dutch, and if they know all those things, they could not have had enough exposure to Old French and Old Irish.

The present book has been written to test the chosen approach to the new dictionary. The entries reflect accurately the format to be followed in the future, but their text may not remain unchanged in the body of the dictionary. New information will inevitably lead to revision. Also, the longer one works on a project, the more experienced one becomes. Every new entry reveals some missed opportunities in the composition of those already written, brings new associations, and suggests formerly unsuspected moves. An etymologist describing the origin of *zip* and someone who, years before, pondered the origin of *adz(e)* are, figuratively speaking, different people. A noticeable distance separates Skeat's ideas in 1910 and in 1882, and, as is well known, OED improved from letter to letter, though even the first fascicle was superb. It would be ideal to complete the dictionary, use the acquired wisdom for revising all the early entries, and only then publish the whole work. But in this case one would lose the much appreciated "feedback" and run the risk of leaving behind only a heap of rough drafts on one's dying day.

To ensure readability, abbreviations have been used sparingly in the book. There is no period after abbreviations (thus, *v* or *dial*, not *v.* or *dial.*). Names are always given in full (thus, *Wedgwood* or *Chantraine,* not *Wedg.* or *Chantr.*), except for the instances like Meyer-Lübke (ML) and joint authors, such as Sievers-Brunner (SB). The titles of most dictionaries have been abbreviated; thus Jan de Vries's *Altnordisches etymologisches Wörterbuch* and *Nederlands etymologisch woordenboek* are referred to as AEW and NEW. Some choices have been arbitrary. Abbreviations like OED (= *The Oxford English Dictionary*) appear without the definite article, without periods after the capitals, and nonitalicized: OED, not *OED, the OED,* or (*the*) *O.E.D.* In the bibliography, some traditional abbreviations have been retained, for it seems that, for instance, *PBB* is still more familiar to most than *BGDSL.*

If the reference is Mueller, Wedgwood, and so forth (this is done only for dictionaries), it means that all the editions of the respective works contain the same information on the matter in question. Skeat's great 1882 dictionary was reset only for the 4th edition. Therefore, Skeat^1 means Skeat$^{1-3}$. Citations in the text have the form as in: Tobler (1846:46), or if the name occurs in parentheses, then: (Tobler [1846:46]), without a space between the colon and the page number. Dictionaries are cited without dates: Wright, IEW, and so on, but when a dictionary-maker is cited as the author of an article or book, the reference has the usual form, for instance, Skeat (1887:468, 470). When an article is contained within the space of one page, the page number has been left out: Collyns (1857), rather than Collyns (1857:258). Page numbers are also omitted when reference is to the whole work, for instance, Gusmani (1972). If a dictionary is arranged alphabetically and the letters are Greek or follow in the same order as in English, neither the page number nor the reference of the type *s.v., q.v.* is given. The same holds for Scandinavian dictionaries in which *æ, ø,* and *å;* or *å, ä,* and *ö* follow *z* (so in Danish/ Norwegian and Swedish respectively). In Icelandic, the last letters are *þ, æ* and *ö,* but in AEW *þ* follows *t,* as is done in dictionaries of Old English. Only in dictionaries of Old English *æ* either follows *a* or occupies the place of *ae.* A sentence like: "So Skeat$^{1-3}$ . . ." means that the etymology just cited can be found in the first three editions of Skeat's dictionary, under the headword. In references to the dictionaries of Sanskrit, Classical Greek, Hebrew, and Slavic and to dictionaries like WP, page numbers are always given.

Palatalized *c* and *g* in Old English words are not distinguished from their velar counterparts by dots or any other sign. In transliteration of words recorded in Cyrillic characters, diacritics have been avoided wherever possible. A Gothic word with an asterisk after it means that, although the word in question has been attested, the form cited in the book does not occur in the extant corpus. This is a convenient old tradition. In recent works, asterisks always appear before Gothic words, and the user of a dictionary gets the impression that most words of that language have not been recorded.

As far as the reliability of the forms cited in the book is concerned, see the introduction to the index.

Acknowledgments

Work on this book consisted of two parts. Since the idea of the dictionary was to produce analytic rather than dogmatic entries, a huge bibliography of English etymology had to be amassed. This work was done at Minnesota; see the acknowledgments in the introduction to the bibliography. It should only be repeated that the turning point in the support for the project was a meeting with the late David R. Fesler. He and his wife Mrs. Elizabeth (BJ) Fesler set up a fund without which screening journals and books and, consequently, the writing of etymologies would not have been completed. From benefactors the Feslers soon became my good friends, and it is appropriate that the "showcase" volume of the dictionary be dedicated to David's memory.

Most entries in the book end with references like Liberman (1988a) and Liberman (2003). Some etymologies featured below were published in *General Linguistics*, whose then editor Ernst A. Ebbinghaus liked the idea of an analytic dictionary and started a special rubric "Studies in Etymology" in his journal. After his death, my articles apxli ii peared in various journals, miscellaneous collections, and *Festschriften*. None of them is reprinted here unchanged. Their style has been reworked drastically. Countless additions have been made, mistakes corrected, doubtful formulations altered or expunged, and a few solutions modified. This is especially true of the earliest samples, but even the latest ones are in many respects new. References to their initial versions are of historical interest only: all those contributions have been "canceled" by the present publication.

The idea of the dictionary gained the support of several eminent scholars. Hans Aarsleff, Ernst A. Ebbinghaus, W.P. Lehmann, Albert L. Lloyd, and Edgar C. Polomé read twenty-three etymologies (this was years ago), and their approval of the format and the content of those early enteries was of inestimable importance. Recently, W.P. Lehmann and Albert L. Lloyd kindly have read almost the entire book. Three more attentive readers of my articles have been Bernhard Diensberg, David L. Gold, and Ladislav Zgusta. David L. Gold has also read about two-thirds of the text, and innumerable improvements in its final shape are due to his advice.

The initial stage of the preparation of the dictionary for print fell to the lot of Professor J. Lawrence Mitchell. This volume owes more to his patience and the diligence of his assistants than words can tell. Changes and additions on an almost weekly basis, endless telephone conversations about the form and content of the entries, an extremely difficult text that I submitted to him in barely legible longhand, and a multilingual bibliography needed the dedication of a scholar and the devotion of an old friend. Initial indexing has also been done at Texas. It is our pleasure to recognize the work of the following assistants at Texas A&M University: Dragana Djordjevic, Seunggu Lew, Hui Hui Li, and Polixenia Tohaneanu in particular, and especially Nathan E.J. Carlson at University of Minnesota, who worked tirelessly at polishing the book for over three years.

The timing of this project was truly auspicious. In the eighties, personal computers appeared in our offices, and where would we have been without copying machines? Card catalogs, too, were replaced with powerful computers, and WorldCat came into being. Then e-mail took care of our correspondence, and the era of online publications and downloading set in. May this page of acknowledgments express not only our gratitude to all those who helped us finish the work but also our joy that we are living in an age when unheard-of technical improvements serve basic sciences.

THE ETYMOLOGIES AT A GLANCE

The following etymologies aim at making the conclusions reached in the present volume easily available to those who are more interested in the results of the investigation than in going over conflicting hypotheses. They are also addressed to the etymological editors of "thick" dictionaries. The summaries will allow them to decide whether they want to read further and modify their entries in accordance with the solutions proposed here. "For many words, a thorough etymology can easily run to twenty or thirty pages of analysis. Obviously, no regular dictionary could allocate that much space for etymology. Nevertheless, most regular dictionaries could profitably incorporate the results of such an analysis into their brief presentation and at least reduce the shallowness of their etymologies" (Louis G. Heller, "Lexicographic Etymology: Practice versus Theory." *American Speech* 40, 1965, p. 118).

Although the volume contains fifty-five entries, it discusses hundreds of words (see the index), some of them in sufficient detail to justify summaries. The most characteristic examples are COB, FUCK, MOOCH, NUDGE, and RAGAMUFFIN. Therefore, this supplement presents the etymologies of 68 Modern English and three Old English words (*fæðel*, *ludgeat*, and *myltestre*).

ADZ(E) (880)
OE *adesa* and *adusa*, ME *ad(e)se*. ModE *adze* has been monosyllabic only since the seventeenth century. The word has no established cognates, though it resembles the names of the adz and the hammer in many languages. OE *adusa* is probably **acusa* 'ax,' with /d/ substituted for /k/ under the influence of some continental form like MLG *desele* 'adz.' The names of tools are among the most common migratory words (*Wanderwörter* and *Kulturwörter*). *Adz* seems to be one of them.

BEACON (900)
OE *bēacen* goes back to **baukn-*. It has cognates in all the Old Germanic languages except Gothic. The earliest sign for ships was probably **bak-*, preserved as LG *bak* and MDu *baec*. **Bak-* must have been one of the words designating objects capable of inflating themselves and making noise. A similar word was **bauk-* (cf G *Bauch* 'belly'), which may have acquired *-n* and a specialized meaning under the influence of its synonym **taikn-* 'token.' **Bak-* and **baukn-* were sound symbolic synonyms, not cognates.

BIRD (800)
OE *bird* is less frequent than *bridd* 'nestling.' Middle English, in which *bird* referred to various young animals and even human beings, may have preserved the original meaning of this word. Despite its early attestation, *bridd* is not necessarily the oldest form of *bird*. It is usually assumed that *-ir-* from *-ri-* arose by metathesis, but here, too, the Middle English form may go back to an ancient period. Gemination in *bridd* is typical of hypocoristic names and should not be ascribed to West Germanic gemination: the protoform with **-j-* in the second syllable has been set up for the sole purpose of explaining *-dd*. *Bird* (from **bird-*, not from *bridd*) was probably derived from the root of *beran* 'give birth' with the help of the suffix *-d*. Modern researchers have rejected this etymology, but it seems to be the best we have.

BOY (1260)
In Old English, only the proper name *Boia* has been recorded. ME *boi* meant 'churl, servant' and (rarely) 'devil.' In texts, the meaning 'male child' does not antedate 1400. ModE *boy* looks like a semantic blend of an onomatopoeic word for an evil spirit (**boi*) and a baby word for 'brother' (**bo*). The former may have survived in the exclamation *ataboy!*, whereas the latter gave rise to OE *Boia*. The derogatory senses of ME *boy* must go back to **boi* 'evil spirit, devil.' *Boy* 'servant' and *-boy* in compounds like *bellboy* reflect medieval usage.

BRAIN (1000)
Brain (OE *brægen*) has no established cognates outside West Germanic; Gk βρέγμα 'top of the head,' which many dictionaries cite, is hardly related to it. More probably, its etymon is PIE **bhragno* 'something broken.' From this protoform Irish has *bran* 'chaff, bran.' According to the reconstruction offered here, the Celtic word was borrowed by Old French, and from there it made its way into English. Consequently, *brægen* should be glossed as 'refuse,' almost coinciding with the modern phrase *gray matter*.

BUOY (1466)
Buoy is a borrowing from Middle Dutch, in which it is more probably native than a loan of OF *boie* ~ *buie* 'chain.' It is one of the names of inflatable, noisy objects like G *Bö* 'squall' and ME *boi* 'devil.' *See* BEACON and BOY.

CATER-COUSIN (1547)
Cater-cousin, now remembered only because it occurs in *The Merchant of Venice*, originally seems to have meant 'distant relative.' The element *cater-*, most probably of Scandinavian origin, means 'diagonally, across, askew.' Perhaps because of its regular use with reinforcing adverbs like *scarce*, *cater-cousin* acquired the meaning 'friend,' nearly the opposite of 'distant relative': *scarce cater-cousins* 'distant relatives of the remotest type' was misunderstood as 'not friends.' Confusion with *cater* 'provide' may have contributed to such a drastic semantic change. *See also* KITTY-CORNER.

CHIDE (1000)
OE *cīdan* 'chide' is probably related to OHG **kîdal* 'wedge' (> ModG *Keil*). The development must have been from *'brandish sticks' to 'scold, reprove.' OE *gecīd* 'strife, altercation' presumably also first had the meaning *'brandishing sticks in a fight.'

CLOVER (1000)
OE *clāfre* (> ModE *clover*) and *clǣfre* (> ModE *claver*) probably trace back to WGmc **klaiwaz-* 'sticky pap' (*klaiw-* as in ModE *cleave* 'adhere'). The sticky juice of clover was the base of the most popular sort of honey. *Clāfre* and *clǣfre* have the element *-re*, occurring in several plant names. That element may have been extracted from **-tro*, a suffix common in the Germanic botanical nomenclature.

COB 'round object' (1420)
Although known from texts only since the fifteenth century, *cob* belongs to a sizable group of words in the languages of Eurasia having a similar sound shape and a similar meaning. *Cob* often alternates with *cop* (whose predominant meaning is 'head'), but it is neither a variant nor a derivative of *cop*. Two meanings seem to have merged in *cob*: 'round object' and 'animal' (the latter possibly from 'lump'). The first of them is prominent in *cub*, a word closely connected with *cob*. *See also* CUB.

COB 'mixture of earth and straw' (1602)
Possibly from *cob* 'muddle, mess; badly executed work,' of onomatopoeic origin.

COB 'take a liking to someone; like one another' (1893)
The verb *cob*, poorly attested in British dialects but known in Australian and New Zealand English, is a back formation from *cobber* 'friend,' an argotic word whose etymon is Yiddish *khaver* 'friend,' from Hebrew.

COCKNEY (1362)
Cockney 'cock's egg,' a rare and seemingly obsolete word in Middle English, was, in all likelihood, not the etymon of ME *cokeney* 'milksop, simpleton; effeminate man; Londoner,' which is rather a reshaping of OF *acoquiné* 'spoiled' (participle). However, this derivation poses some phonetic problems that have not been resolved. *Cockney* does not go back to *cock*, ME *coquīna* 'kitchen,' or F *coquin* 'rogue, beggar.' An association between *cockney* and *cockaigne* is also late.

CUB (1530)
Cub is one of the numerous monosyllabic, less often disyllabic, animal names having the structure *k* + vowel + *b* or *bb*. Some connection between this group and words for 'piece of wood' with the structure *k* + vowel + *p* (as in *chip* < OE *cipp*) is possible. Most of them, whether ending in *-b* or *-p*, seem to be of onomatopoeic or sound symbolic origin. They are hard to distinguish from migratory words for 'cup,' 'cap,' and 'head.' *See also* COB 'round object.'

CURMUDGEON (1577)
The oldest meaning of *curmudgeon* was probably 'cantankerous person,' not 'miser.' The word must have been borrowed from Gaelic: *-mudgeon* (= *muigean* 'disagreeable person') with the intensifying prefix *ker-*, spelled *cur-*, as in *curfuffle* and many other Lowland Scots words. It is also possible that *-mudgeon* meant 'scowl'; *curmudgeon* would then have started out as 'big scowl.' Ties between *-mudgeon* and *mooch* (one of whose variants is *modge*), *mug*

'face,' and *-mugger* in *hugger-mugger* will turn out to be the same in both cases. The similarity between *cur* 'dog,' F *coeur* 'heart' and *cur-* is accidental. *See also* HUGGER-MUGGER, MOOCH, and MUG.

CUSHAT (700)
OE *cusceote,* most probably, had *ū* in the first syllable and was a compound, *cū-sceote* 'cow-shot.' A connection with cows may be due to the fact that pigeons are lactating birds. If *cusceote* is a reshaping of Wel *ysguthan* 'wood pigeon,' that connection may have been instrumental in producing the Old English form under the influence of folk etymology. The second element *-sceote* 'shot' referred to the bird's precipitous flight.

DOXY (1530)
Doxy probably goes back to LG *dokke* 'doll,' with the deterioration of meaning from 'sweetheart' and 'wench' to 'whore.'

DRAB 'slut' (1515)
Drab appears to be an etymological doublet of *traipse;* hence the meanings 'gadabout' and 'slut.' *See also* TRAIPSE.

DWARF (700)
The oldest recorded forms are OE *dweorg,* OS (*gi*)*twerg,* OHG (*gi*)*twerc,* and OI *dvergr.* The word has no established cognates outside Germanic. G *zwerch-* 'diagonally,' Skt *dhvarás* 'crooked,' Avestan *drva* (the name of some physical deformity), and Gk σέρ(ι)φος 'midge' are not related to *dwarf.* The consonant *r* in *dweorg* and its cognates is, most likely, the product of rhotacism. Gmc **dwer-g-* < **dwez-g-* < **dwes-g-* had the same root as OE *dwǣs,* OHG *twās,* and MDu *dwaes* (> ModDu *dwaas*), all of them meaning 'foolish.' This reconstruction presupposes that a foolish or mad person was said to be possessed by an evil spirit. Initially dwarves must have belonged with other supernatural beings, such as the gods and the elves, that caused people harm and inflicted diseases. Their short size and association with mountains and rocks are thus not their original features.

EENA (1855)
Eena is a reshaping of *one.* The origin of the counting out rhyme *eena, meena, mina, mo* from Celtic sheep scoring numerals and the source of the rhyme in the New World remain debatable.

ELVER 'young eel' (1640)
Elver is a variant of *eelfare* 'young eel.' Its second element (*-ver* and *-fare*) is probably identical with *-fare* in *fieldfare* and *-fer* in *heifer* (< OE *heahfore*). The original meaning of **ælfore* or **ælfare* may have been *'occupant of a place favored by eels,' later *'. . . by young eels.' *See also* FIELDFARE and HEIFER.

EVER (1000)
Æfre emerged in texts at the end of the Old English period and may have been coined by clerics or religious poets around that time. Its probable etymon is *ā* 'always,' reinforced by the suffix *-re,* the same as in the comparative form of adjectives. The umlauted variant *ǣ,*

rather than *ā*, may have been chosen unxii der the influence of other comparatives or because of the confusion between OE *ā* and *ǣ* 'law, covenant.' The meaning of the coinage was 'more than always,' that is, 'in all eternity.' The often suggested origin of *ever* in old prepositional phrases is unlikely.

[OE FÆDEL 'play actor'] The word occurs once in a gloss. *Fæð-* is probably akin to the root of the English verbs *faddle* and *fiddle*. The actor must have been a kind of juggler who entertained the public with quick movements. A word with a similar root but with postvocalic *-g-* is Pol *figlarz* 'juggler' (Pol *figiel* means 'trick, prank'). *See also* FIDDLE.

FAG 'servant; male homosexual' (1775); **FAG(G)OT** (1300)
Faggot (or *fagot*) 'bundle of wood' is a borrowing into Middle English, whereas the earliest known uses of *fag* 'servant' do not antedate the last quarter of the eighteenth century. The meanings of *fag* go all the way from 'drudge; junior in a public school' and 'male homosexual' to 'dish made of inferior portions of a pig or sheep.' Perhaps *faggot* acquired its derogotary meanings under the influence of *pimp* 'boy who does menial jobs; procurer of prostitutes' and also 'bundle of wood.' *Fag* is a clipped form of *faggot*. *See also* PIMP.

FIDDLE (1205)
The verb *fiddle*, first recorded in 1530 with the meaning 'make aimless or frivolous movements,' and *fiddle* (1205), the name of a musical instrument, go back to the same etymon. Their root *fid-* is indistinguishable from those in the words *fitful* and *fidget*, that is, 'move back and forth.' Those words belong with *faddle* 'caress; play; trifle,' *fiddle-faddle*, *fiddlesticks*, and *fiddle-de-dee*. A fiddle is an instrument that requires the 'fiddling' of a bow. ML **vitula* is a borrowing from Germanic rather than the etymon of OE **fitele* and OHG *fidula*.

FIDGET (1754)
Fidget is an extension of the earlier verb *fidge*, two of whose synonyms are *fig* and *fitch*. Final /ʤ/ sometimes lends verbs an expressive character. The development from *fig* to *fidge* and later to *fitch* is probable. In contrast, a verb like OI *fíkja* 'desire eagerly' is an unlikely etymon of *fidge*: the meanings do not match, and the few examples of /kj/ > /ʧ/ are controversial (the voicing of final /ʧ/, as in *hodgepodge* < *hotch-potch*, is common: it is the derivation of /ʧ/ that remains unclear). See NUDGE for examples of the alternation /g/~/ʤ/ and WITCH for /ʧ/ < /kj/.

FIELDFARE (1100)
Despite its seeming etymological transparency, this bird name poses problems, because 'fieldfarer' is too vague and makes little sense. More likely, *-fare* in it is a reflex of an old suffix that once meant 'belonging or pertaining to,' later 'dweller, occupant.' The fieldfare is thus 'field bird.' A reflex of the same suffix is present in Du *ooievaar* and G *adebar* (both mean 'stork') and OE *sceolfor* 'cormorant.' *See also* ELVER and HEIFER.

FILCH (1561?)
Filch is, most probably, an adaptation of G argotic *filzen* 'comb through.' OE *gefylcan* 'marshal troops' (> *filch* 'beat, attack') is a different word.

FINAGLE (1926)
Finagle is probably an extended form (a form with an infix) of *figgle* (*finagle* = *fi-na-gle*), which, in turn, is a phonetic variant of *fiddle* 'fidget about.' *Figgle* is a frequentative form of *fig*, the likeliest etymon of *fidge* (see FIDGET). Another similar extended form is SKEDADDLE.

FIT 'song' (800) and many more meanings; **'array of soldiers'** (1400) and other meanings
All the words spelled *fit* in Modern English are related. The basic meaning of the sound complex /fit/ is 'move back and forth; move up and down; make sporadic movements,' as seen in *fitful* and in the phrase *by fits and starts*. The other meanings, for instance, 'division of a poem' and 'match, suit; be a good fit; interval' are derivative. Go *fitan* 'be in labor,' Du *vitten* 'find fault with, carp,' and Icel *fitla* 'fidget' are akin to E *fit*.

FLATTER (1386)
Flatter is one of many onomatopoeic verbs beginning with *fl-* and denoting unsteady or light, repeated movement. *Flutter* and *flit* are similar formations. The original meaning of *flatter* must have been 'flit about,' whence 'dance attendance, ingratiate oneself by saying pleasant things.' *Flatter* is not related to the adjective *flat*. It is not a borrowing of L *flatāre* 'make big' or of F *flatter*. The French verb may be a borrowing from Middle English, but its history is unclear.

FUCK (1503)
Germanic words of similar form (*f* + vowel + consonant) and meaning 'copulate' are numerous. One of them is G *ficken*. They often have additional senses, especially 'cheat,' but their basic meaning is 'move back and forth.' As onomatopoeic or sound symbolic formations, FIDDLE (v), FIT, and FIDGET belong with FUCK. Most probably, *fuck* is a borrowing from Low German and has no cognates outside Germanic.

GAWK (1785, v; 1867, sb)
Gawk and *gawky* belong with several English, Dutch, and German words designating fools, simpletons, and awkward persons and their actions. It belongs with E *geck,* from Dutch, and *geek,* presumably from Low German. The history of *gawk* is inseparable from the history of *gowk,* an English reflex of the Scandinavian bird name *gaukr* 'cuckoo.' However, *gawk* need not have been derived from *gowk.* It is possibly another independent onomatopoeic formation with the structure *g-k*. *Gawk* 'fool; stare stupidly' was not derived from the dialectal adjective *gawk* 'left (hand),' believed mistakenly to be a contraction of its synonym *gaulick* ~ *gallock.* The development must have gone in the opposite direction: from 'clumsy' to 'left.' Nor was *gawk* formed on the base of the Scandinavian verb *gá* 'stare,' with the addition of the suffix *-k*. F *gauche* 'clumsy' is most probably a borrowing from Germanic; its influence on *gawk* is unlikely.

GIRL (1290)
Girl does not go back to any Old English or Old Germanic form. It is part of a large group of Germanic words whose root begins with *g* or *k* and ends in *r*. The final consonant in *girl* is a diminutive suffix. The *g-r* words denote young animals, children, and all kinds of creatures considered immature, worthless, or past their prime. Various vowels may occur be-

tween *g/k* and final *r*. ME *girl* seems to have been borrowed with a diminutive suffix from Low German (LG *Gör(e)* also means 'girl'). MLG *kerle*, OHG *karl* (both meant 'man'), OI *kerl* 'old woman,' MHG *gurre* 'old jade,' and N dial *gorre* 'wether, little boy; lazy person; glutton' belong to the *girl* ~ *Göre* group. They are loosely related as similar onomatopoeic or sound symbolic formations.

HEATHER (1730)
Heather continues *hadder*, one of several similar-sounding words (for example, *hadyr* and *hathir)* that designated the plant *Erica* in Middle English. Its etymon is supposedly OI **haðr*, whose origin is unknown. Perhaps **hað-* meant 'hair': *heather* is sometimes associated with shagginess. The vowel in *heath* goes back to **ai*, which, according to the rules of Germanic ablaut, cannot alternate with **a* in **haðr*. Consequently, *heather* and *heath* are unrelated despite their similarity and the existence of the German word *Heidekraut* 'heather,' literally 'heath grass.'

HEIFER (900)
Most probably, *ea* and *o* in *heahfore*, the earliest recorded form of *heifer*, were short, which excludes a connection between *heifer* and OE *hēah* 'high.' Old English seems to have had the word **hægfore* 'heifer.' The first element (**hæg-*) presumably meant 'enclosure' (as do *haw* and *hedge*), whereas *-fore* was a suffix meaning 'dweller, occupant' (see ELVER and FIELDFARE). By regular phonetic changes, **hægfore* became **hæhfore* and *heahfore*. In some dialects, *heahfore* yielded [heif\(r)], in others [hef\(r)]. Standard English *heifer* reflects the spelling of the first group and the pronunciation of the second. E dial *hekfore* has the same structure as **hægfore* (*heck* means 'rail; fence; gate').

HEMLOCK (700)
The earliest known forms of *hemlock* are OE *hymblicæ* and *hemlick*. Besides LG *Hemer* and *Hemern* 'hellbore,' they have cognates in the Slavic and Baltic languages. The root *hem-* means 'poison.' The origin of *-lock* is less clear, but an association with *lock*, whether the verb or the noun, is late. A probable etymon of *hemlock* is **hem-l-ig*, perhaps a variant of *hem-l-ing*. Both *-ling* and *-ig* are well-attested suffixes in plant names, as seen in G *Schierling* 'hemlock' and OE *īfig* 'ivy.'

HENBANE (1265)
The first element of *henbane* is *hen-* 'death.' This plant was originally called *henbell*, with *-bell* possibly traceable to *belene*, the Old English name of henbane. When the meaning of *hen-* had been forgotten, *-bell* was replaced with *bane* 'murder, death.' From a historical point of view, *henbane* is a tautological compound 'death-death.'

HOBBLEDEHOY (1540)
The original form of *hobbledehoy* seems to have been **Robert le Roy*, one of the many names of the Devil. Later the popular form *Hob* replaced *Rob*. The same *hob-* appears in *hobgoblin*. **Hobert le Roy* changed further to **Hobert le Hoy*, and that piece of alliterative gibberish yielded *hobbert-de-hoy*, apparently because the names of demons often contained *-de-* (*-di-*) or *-te-* (*-ti-*), as in *Flibbertigibbet* and *Hobberdidance*. Folk etymology substituted *hobble-* for

the meaningless element *hobbert-*, and the resulting compound *hobbledehoy* was associated with an unwieldy person. See RAGAMUFFIN for a similar development from the Devil's name to a derogatory name of a young man.

HOREHOUND (1000)
Hore- in *horehound* (< OE *hāre hūne*) means 'white' (< 'hoary'). One of the meanings of Gmc **hūn*seems to have been 'black.' Possibly, OE *hūne* was at one time the name of *Ballota nigra*, and *hāre* was chosen to modify *hūne* when *hūne* began to designate *Marrubium vulgare*. Final *-d* appeared in *horehound* in Middle English, perhaps because horehound was confused with alyssum, a plant whose name suggested that it could cure hydrophobia. Words like *gund* 'poison,' now current only in a limited area, may also have influenced the development of *-houn* to *-hound*.

HUGGER-MUGGER (1529)
Hugger-mugger remains a word of unclear origin mainly because we do not know whether *-mugger* has been coined to rhyme with *hugger-* or is traceable to an ascertainable etymon (with *-hugger* added as a nonsense word for rhyme's sake) or whether each element of the compound has its own etymon, so that the two were combined later and perhaps influenced each other's phonetic shape. *Hugger-mugger* has numerous variants, with *-k-*, *-g-*, and *-d-*, and it cannot be decided which of them is original and in need of an explanation. *Hugger-* has so far defied attempts to etymologize it (its derivation from *huddle* is unlikely), whereas *-mugger* is probably related to *mooch* (? < **mȳcan*). See CURMUDGEON and MUG. Therefore, a search for the origin of *hugger-mugger* should probably begin with *-mugger* rather than *-hugger*. See MOOCH for the history of the root **mȳc-* and its variants.

IVY (800)
OE *īfig* has established cognates only in German (*Efeu*; OHG *ebah* and *ebahewi*) and Dutch (*eiloof*), though the name of the mythic river *Ifing*, known from Old Icelandic, may also be akin to it. In all probability, *īfig* is related to OE *āfor* and OHG *eibar* 'pungent; bitter; fierce.' *Ivy* got its name because it was a bitter, pungent plant. The suffix *-ig* usually occurred in collective nouns, so that *īfig* initially must have meant *'place overgrown with ivy.' *Ivy* is not related to L *ibex* (as though both the plant and the animal were climbers).

JEEP (1940)
The vehicle was called after Eugene the Jeep, a small wonder-working animal in E. C. Segar's cartoon rather than from the abbreviation G. P. ('General Purpose') Vehicle that marked the first jeeps.

KEY (1000)
The etymon of OE *cǣg* ~ *cǣge* ~ *cǣga* was **kaig-jo-*. Its reflexes in Modern English are the noun *key* and the northern dialectal adjective *key* 'twisted.' The original meaning of **kaig-jo-* was presumably *'pin with a twisted end.' Words with the root **kai-* followed by a consonant meaning 'crooked, bent; twisted' are common only in the North Germanic languages. It is therefore likely that **kaigjo-* reached English and Frisian (the only language with a cognate of *cǣg*: OFr *kāi*) from Scandinavia. The **kaig-* words interacted with synonyms having

the root *kag-*. Despite their phonetic and semantic proximity, *key* and the cognates of G *Kegel* 'pin' (its *e* goes back to **a*) and E dial *cag* 'stiff point,' from Scandinavian, are not related, because **ai* and **a* belong to different ablaut series.

KICK (1386)
Kick is a borrowing from Scandinavian, as seen in OI *kikna* 'give way at the knees.' A near synonym of *kikna* is OI *keikja* 'bend back'; it has the same root but in the full grade of ablaut. Related to *kikna* and *keikja* are many words whose root ends in other consonants. All of them are united by the meaning 'bend, twist.' The doubts OED has about the Scandinavian origin of *kick* are probably unfounded. *See also* KEY and KITTY-CORNER.

KITTY-CORNER (1890)
Kitty-corner and *catty-corner* have nothing to do with F *quatre* 'four' or with cats. Both forms are folk etymological reshapings of *cater-corner*. The element *cater-*, most probably of Danish origin, means 'diagonally, across, askew.' Dan *kejte* means 'left hand' and *keitet* means 'clumsy.' *See also* CATER-COUSIN and KEY.

LAD (1300)
Lad reached northern English dialects from Scandinavia. Its etymon is N *ladd* 'hose; woolen stocking.' Words for socks, stockings, and shoes seem to have been current as terms of abuse for and nicknames of fools. However, Scand *ladd* *'fool' is unknown. *Ladd* has come down to us only in the compounds *Oskeladd* (or *Askeladd*) 'Boots, male Cinderella,' N *tusseladd* 'nincompoop' and *Laddfáfnir* (a name from a mythological poem). The vowels *a* and *o* alternated in the root **loð-* ~ *lað-* 'woolen sock; shoe.' **Lað-* is a secondary form of unclear origin, whereas **loð-* is the zero grade of **leuð* (as in OE *lēodan* 'grow'), with *o* < **u*. OI *Amlóði*, probably from **Amloði*, the etymon of Hamlet's name, belongs with *Oskeladd* and *Laddfáfnir*. The development must have been from 'stocking,' 'foolish youth' to 'youngster of inferior status' and (with an ameliorated meaning) to 'young fellow.' The Old English name *Ladda* emerged in texts two centuries before ME *ladde*. The evidence of their kinship is wanting. Scand *-ladd* was borrowed around 1300 and became a weak noun in Middle English. No English compounds with *-ladda* have been attested.

LASS (1300) The most probable etymon of *lass* is some Scandinavian word like ODan *las* 'rag.' Slang words for 'rag' sometimes acquire the jocular meaning 'child' and especially 'girl.' Middle English also had *lasce*, a diminutive of *las*. ModE dial *lassikie* is either a form parallel to it or a continuation of the Middle English word. *Lass* is not related to *lad* (only folk etymology connected them), though both words are of Scandinavian origin and surfaced in Middle English texts at the same time.

LILLIPUTIAN (1726)
Swift left no explanation about the origin of his coinage. *Lill(e)-* is probably a variant of *little*, and *-put* may be E *put(t)* 'lout, blockhead.' Swift must have been aware of the vulgar association that *put-* arouses in speakers of the Romance languages and of Sw *putte* 'boy.' Since *Lilliput* is easy to pronounce and carries derogatory overtones in many languages, it has found acceptance far beyond England. Later, Swift coined *Laputa* on the analogy of *Lilliputian*.

[OE LUDGEAT 'postern']

Lud- is cognate with OS *lud* '?functioning genitals' (usually glossed as 'form; figure; bodily strength; sexual power'), Sc *lud* 'buttocks,' and Sc *luddock* 'loin; buttock.' It is related to Gmc **leud-* 'grow' (as in OE *lēodan*). The most general meaning of *lud-* was 'object fully shaped.' OE **lud-* apparently meant *'posterior,' whence *ludgeat* 'back door, postern.'

MAN (971)

Man is not a cognate of L *homo* (through an etymon beginning with **g_hm-*) and has no ties with L *mannus* 'hand' or the Proto-Indo-European root **men-*, which allegedly meant 'think' or 'be aroused,' or 'breathe.' Most probably, *man* 'human being' is a secularized divine name. The god Mannus was believed to be the progenitor of the human race. The steps of the development seem to be as follows: *'the circle of Mannus's worshipers' → 'member of that circle' (Go *gaman* means both 'fellowship' and 'partner') → 'slave, servant' (from 'votary'; both meanings have been attested) → 'human being of either sex' → 'male.' The name *Mannus* seems to be of onomatopoeic origin, unless it is a baby word.

MOOCH (1460)

Mooch and its doublet *miche* are verbs of Germanic origin (*miche* is memorable because of Hamlet's *miching malico* 'sneaking mischief'). OE **mȳcan* or **myccan* meant *'conceal' and had cognates in Old High German, Old Irish, and Latin. Those words referred to all kinds of underhand dealings and criminal activities. The etymon of **mȳcan* may have been onomatopoeic, from *muk-* 'silence,' or a reflex of a root meaning 'darkness.' Whatever the distant origin of *mooch*, the verb **mȳcan* and its cognates have been part of European slang for at least two millennia. Many similar-sounding Romance words, including F *muser* 'hide' (< OF *mucier*), are probably borrowings from Germanic. *See* CURMUDGEON, HUGGER-MUGGER, and MUG.

MUG 'face' (1709); **MUG 'waylay and rob'** (1846)

Mug (v) probably derived from *mug* 'face,' which seems to go back to a word like Sc *mudgeon* 'scowl, grimace.' *See* CURMUDGEON.

[OE MYLTESTRE 'prostitute']

Myltestre has been explained as an adaptation of L *meretrix* 'prostitute.' However, the resemblance between the two words is insignificant. Speakers of Old English must have analyzed *myltestre* into *mylte* + *stre* (perhaps under the influence of *meltan* 'burn up' and *mieltan* 'digest; purge; exhaust'), since one of the words for 'brothel' was OE *myltenhūs*. An Old English cognate of G *Strünze* 'slattern,' originally a derogatory term for a woman, may also have existed, and one can even go so far as to imagine that the compound **myltestrunta* yielded *mylterstre*, especially because Old English had other words for 'prostitute' ending in *-re*. *Myltestre* should be recognized as a word of unknown origin rather than a "corruption" of L *meretrix*.

NUDGE (1675)

Nudge is one of many words having the structure *n* + short vowel + consonant (stop) and designating quick, partly repetitive movements that, as a rule, do not require a strong effort, for instance, *nibble*, *nod*, *nag*, and *knock*. Some verbs of that type occur only in dialects. They usually have cognates in Low German and Scandinavian. Verbs with postvocalic /d/ sometimes coexist with synonyms ending in /ʤ/. In the seventeenth century, *nud* 'boss with the head' and *nuddle* 'push' were recorded. *Nudge* may be a variant of *nud*, because /ʤ/, both initial and final, lends verbs like *jab*, *jolt*, *dodge*, and *budge* an expressive character. However, *nudge* may have had an Old English etymon, either **hnygelan* (only the noun *hnygelan* 'clippings' has been attested) or **cnyccan* 'push,' related to *cnucian* 'knock.' Sc *gnidge* 'rub; squeeze' is probably a variant or a cognate of *nudge*. Attempts to find a Proto-Indo-European root (for example,* *gen-*) from which all the Germanic verbs like *nudge* have been derived presuppose great antiquity of the whole group, but its old age need not be taken for granted. Gk νύττω and νύσσω 'push' are probably sound symbolic formations of the same type as *nudge*, not akin to it.

OAT (700)
Contrary to what most English dictionaries say, *oat* is not an isolated word: it has cognates in Frisian and some Dutch dialects. Of the etymologies proposed for *oat* the one that relates OE *āte* to Icel *eitill* 'nodule in stone' and OHG *-eizi* in *araweizi* 'pea' is probably the best, though the origin of *araweizi* (a borrowing from some non-Indo-European language?) is obscure. *Oat* is not akin to *eat* or *goat* and hardly a substrate word in West Germanic.

PIMP (1607)
Although E *p* before vowels corresponds to G *pf*, G *Pimpf* 'little boy' is a probable cognate of *pimp*. Judging by such recorded meanings of *pimp* as 'helper in mines; servant in logging camps,' this word was originally applied to boys and servants. The root *pimp-* ~ *pamp-* ~ *pump-* means 'swell'; a *Pimpf* was someone unable to give a big *Pumpf* 'fart.' Dial *pimp* 'bundle of wood' (that is, 'something swollen; armful') has the same root as *Pimpf*. The development must have been from 'boy; young inexperienced person' to 'servant; *despised servant' and finally to 'procurer of sex.' See FAG(G)OT, which also means 'bundle of wood', and is a term of abuse in sexual matters. *Pimp* does not owe its existence to any Romance word.

RABBIT (1398)
Germanic makes wide use of the root *r-b* in naming animals (G *Robbe* 'seal,' Fl *rabbe* ~ *robbe* 'rabbit,' and the like). E *rabbit* is apparently one such word. ME *rabet(t)* 'small rabbit' was a word mainly associated with French cuisine. *Rabbit* is a Germanic noun with a French suffix. Walloon *robett* (from Flemish) need not have been its etymon. F *râble* 'back and loins of certain quadrupeds, especially used of the rabbit and the hare,' F *rabouillère* 'rabbit hole,' Sp *rabo* 'tail,' Sp *raposo* (m) ~ *raposa* (f) 'fox,' let alone G *Raupe* ~ Du *rups* 'caterpillar,' and Russ *ryba* 'fish,' all of which have been suggested as cognates of *rabbit*, have nothing to do with it. *See also* ROBIN.

RAGAMUFFIN (1344)
Ragamuffin appeared in texts as one of the names of the Devil, and 'devil' seems to be the meaning of both *rag-* and *-muffin*. *Rag-* occurs in ME *Ragman* 'devil,' and *-muffi-* is akin to *Muffy* (in *Old Muffy*), another name of the Devil from F *maufé* 'ugly.' Final *-n* may have been added to *-muffi-* under the influence of *tatterdemallion* and other similar names of evil

spirits. Intrusive *-a-* between *rag-* and *-muffin* is the same as in *Jack-a-dandy* and so forth. The Devil was often presented as ragged in medieval mysteries, which explains the development from 'Devil' to 'ragged street urchin,' but the original *Ragamoffin* (the earliest spelling of the word) was a tautological compound *'devil-a-devil.' See HOBBLEDEHOY, another word with an infix and of comparable meaning, SLOWWORM (a tautological compound), and SKEDADDLE for words with infixation.

ROBIN (1549)
Despite the consensus that the etymon of *robin* is the proper name *Robin*, *robin* may be one of many animal names having the structure *r* + vowel + *b*. The last syllable in it is a diminutive suffix, as in *Dobbin* 'horse.' *See also* RABBIT.

SKEDADDLE (1861)
Skedaddle is probably a verb with an infix. Almost all such extended forms have three syllables with stress on the second one and are usually of dialectal origin. For example, *fundawdle* 'caress' is possibly *fondle* with the infix *-daw-*. See also FINAGLE. Most likely, *skedaddle* is E dial *scaddle* or **sceddle* 'scare, frighten' with the infix *-da-*. It has no connection with any word of Greek, Irish, or Swedish, and it is not a blend.

SLANG (1756)
One of the meanings of the word *slang* is 'narrow piece of land running up between other and larger divisions of ground.' *Slang* must also have meant *'territory over which hawkers, strolling showmen, and other itenerants traveled.' Later it came to mean *'those who were on the slang' and finally *'hawkers' patter'; hence the modern meaning. The phrase **on the slang* is a gloss on some Scandinavian phrase like Sw **på slänget* (E *slanget* has been recorded). *Slang* 'piece of land' is a word of Scandinavian origin, but its meaning may have been influenced by southern E *slang* 'border.' *Slang* 'informal speech' does not go back to F *langue* 'language,' and it is not a derivative of N *slengja* 'throw.'

SLOWWORM (900)
The only secure cognates of E *slowworm* are Sw and ODan *ormslå* and N *ormslo*. The element *slow-* goes back to OE *slā-* and has nothing to do with *slow*, *sloe*, or *slay*. Its most probable etymon is **slanhō-* related to G *Schlange* 'snake' (*h* and *g* alternate by Verner's Law). Since *-worm* also meant 'snake,' the whole turns out to be a tautological compound 'snake-snake.' Cf RAGAMUFFIN (another tautological compound) and possibly HOBBLEDEHOY.

STRUMPET (1327)
The words relevant for understanding the origin of *strumpet* are MHG *Strumpf* 'stump,' ModG *Strunze* 'slattern,' and ModI *strympa* 'bucket; big woman.' Some words without a nasal (*m*, *n*) belong here too, for instance, G *Gestrüpp* 'shrubbery' and G *strüppig* 'tousled.' The root of *strumpet* meant either *'rough; sticking out like a stump' or *'big, unwieldy,' the latter mainly occurring in the names of vessels. Either could have been the basis of a word meaning 'unpolished or unwieldy woman; virago.' Most probably, English borrowed a Low German cognate of *strunze*, added a French suffix (*-et*) to it, and narrowed down the

meaning of the loanword from *'ugly woman; virago' to 'prostitute.' In Modern German, *Strumpf* means 'hose' or 'stocking' (< 'stump'). See LAD for a tie between long socks and terms of abuse. E dial *strumpet* 'fat, hearty child' shows that in some areas, *strumpet* could refer to any unwieldy human being, not necessarily a woman. *Strumpet* is not a reshaping of L *stuprum* 'dishonor' or OI *striapach* 'prostitute.'

STUBBORN (1386)

An association between *stubborn* and *stub* is due to folk etymology. The only unquestionable cognate of *stubborn* is ModI *tybbin* 'obstinate.' The ancient meaning of **tub-* was probably 'swell.' *Stubborn* has the same root as *tybbin* (with *s-mobile*), but, unlike the well-attested Icelandic suffix *-in*, E *-orn* is of unknown origin.

TOAD (1000)

Old English had *tādige*, *tadde*, and *tosca* ~ *tocsa*, all meaning 'toad.' In the Scandinavian languages, similar forms are Sw and N dial *tossa* and Dan *tudse*. Most probably, *a* in *tadde* is the product of shortening (*a* < **ā*), but *ā* in *tādige* is **a* lengthened, possibly because the name of the toad is often changed as a result of taboo. North Sea Germanic has numerous words whose root begins with *t* and ends in *d*. They designate small objects and small movements, as in *tidbit* and *toddle*. *Tādige* and *tadde* belong to that group. The toad seems to have been named **tad-* because it is small or because it has warts, or because it moves in short steps. The Scandinavian words have a similar history.

TRAIPSE 'walk in an untidy way' (1593); **'slattern'** (1676)

The verb *traipse* is a doublet of *trape*. Both resemble G *traben* 'tramp' and other similar verbs meaning 'tramp; wander; flee' in several European languages. They seem to have been part of soldiers' and vagabonds' slang between 1400 and 1700. In all likelihood, they originated as onomatopoeias and spread to neighboring languages from Low German. *Traipse* 'slattern' is then 'woman who traipses': either 'untidy woman' or 'gadabout.' *See also* DRAB and TROT.

TROT 'old woman' (1352)

The most probable cognates of *trot* are MHG *trut*(*e*) 'female monster' and G *Drude* 'sorceress, incubus.' If they are related to E *tread* and G *treten*, *trot* originally meant 'gadabout.' Women often get disparaging names from their manner of walking, and a trot may have been 'someone with an ungainly gait; woman who treads heavily.' If at any time *trot* had the meaning 'useless, worthless, immature creature,' it may also have been applied to children; hence *trot* 'toddler; young animal.' See GIRL for a comparable semantic shift, as well as TRAIPSE and DRAB for disparaging names of women derived from their manner of walking.

UNDERSTAND (888)

Understand is one of several West Germanic verbs having the same meaning and the structure prefix + *stand* (for example, G *verstehen*). OE *understandan* competed with the synonyms *undergietan*, *underniman*, *underþencan*, and *forstandan*. The prefix *under-* meant 'under' and 'between; among,' whereas *for-* meant 'in front of.' Those verbs conveyed the idea of standing among the objects or in front of a thing and getting to know their properties. *Understandan* may have arisen as a blend of *forstandan* and *undergietan*, but the details and the age of that coinage can no longer be reconstructed with certainty.

WITCH (890)
None of the proposed etymologies of *witch* is free from phonetic or semantic difficulties. It is not known what OE *wicca* (m) and *wicce* (f) meant: the reference may have been to a seer(ess), a demon, a person possessing mantic knowledge, a miracle worker, or an enchanter (enchantress), to mention the main possibilities. Old English seems to have had three related words, namely *wita* 'wise man,' *witiga* or *witega* (that is, *wit-ig-a*) 'wise man; prophet, soothsayer,' and **witja* *'divinator' or perhaps 'healer' ('witch doctor'). Although secure examples are few, OE *-tj-* occasionally changed to *c'c'* (palatalized), as happened in OE *fecc(e)an*, presumably from *fetian* 'fetch' (v). Likewise, **witja* 'he who knows' probably became *wicca*. A Slavic analog of *witch* < **witja* would be, for example, Russ *ved'ma*: ORuss *ve‡d* meant both 'knowledge' and 'enchantment.' Later phonetic processes effaced the difference between *wicca* and *wicce*, and *witch* began to be associated with women. The usual word for a male witch is now *wizard*. Its most common meaning is 'magician.'

YET (888)
The Old English forms were *giet(a)*, *gīt(a)*, *gȳt(a)*, and *gēta*. The protoform of the first three seems to have been **iu-ta*, in which **iu-* meant 'already' and *-ta* (< **-do*) was an intensifying enclitic with cognates in and outside Germanic. As in many other cases, the rising diphthong *íu* became falling, and *íuta* yielded **iúta*, later *gȳta*. The vowels in *gīet(a)* and *gīt(a)* are traceable to *ȳ*. Despite the similarity between *gȳta* and *gēta*, their etymons must have been different, because *ē* in *gēta* cannot be derived from *ȳ* (*īe*, *ī*). The protoform of *gēta* was, as it seems, **ē-ta* (a synonym of **iu-ta*), which later got initial /j/ under the influence of *gȳ ta*, *gīeta*, *gīta*. The existence of /j/ in the protoform is less likely. ModE *yit*, now obsolete or dialectal, goes back to *gīt*. The history of G *jetzt* 'now' (< **iú-ze* < **īu-zuo*) is similar to that of *yet*. Monosyllabic and disyllabic forms (*gȳt* ~ *gȳta* and so forth) coexisted in Old English, so that ModE *yet* is not the product of apocope. The shortening of the vowel in *yet* is due to the conditions of sentence stress: *gȳta* was sometimes stressed and sometimes unstressed in a sentence. Modern English generalized the short vowel of the unstressed form. The synonyms of West Saxon *gȳta* and its side forms were Anglian *gēna*, *gīena*, and *geona* (the latter with a short vowel), none of which continued into Middle English. Contrary to what is usually said, *gȳta* was not an isolated Old English word: besides MHG *iezuo*, there are OFr *ēta* and *ieta*, MLG *jetto* (and many other forms), and Du *ooit* 'ever' (*-t* in *ooit* is akin to *-t* in *yet*), but the Hebrew, Greek, Latin, and Welsh words cited in older dictionaries are not related to it.

AN ANALYTIC DICTIONARY OF ENGLISH ETYMOLOGY

An Introduction

ADZ(E) (880)

The earlier forms of adz(e) *are OE* adesa *and ME* ad(e)se; *in dialects, only* nadge (a nadge < an adge)*, and so forth with initial* m-/n- *have been recorded.* Addice *remained the standard form until the 17*[th] *century. OE* adesa *has no obvious cognates but resembles the names of the ax in many Germanic and Romance languages; some of them begin with* a- *(such as Go* aquisi *and L* ascia*), others with* d- *(OHG* dehsala*). It may be a blend of two words for 'ax':* *acusa *and some ancestor of MLG* dessele*. The names of tools were part of workmen's international vocabulary and often changed their form in the process of borrowing. The phonetic shape of* adesa *may have been influenced by several such words. Most likely, the protoform of* adz(e) *is* *acusa *'ax,' with* d *substituted for* k *under the influence of some continental form like MLG* dessele *'adz.' If this reconstruction is correct,* adusa *is a blend.*

The sections are devoted to 1) the form of the English word, 2) its origin, and 3) the history of words for 'ax' in other languages and the possibility that OE adesa *is akin to Hitt* ateš.

1. The OE forms of *adz(e)* are *adesa* (m) and *adese* (f) (recorded once). *Adesa < adosa < adusa* (Mercian) is due to the Old English rule of dissimilation of two back vowels in unstressed syllables; *eadesa* in the *Vespasian Psalter* has *ea* < **æ* by velar umlaut (SB [sec 50, note 1, and sec 142]; Luick [1964:sec 342, note 1; 347]; A. Campbell [1959:sec 385]). **The spelling *addice* indicates that OE *s* rendered a voiceless fricative. The cause of the preservation of voicelessness is not clear.** Owing to the position between two unstressed vowels? (so Luick [1964:846]). One would rather expect voicing under no stress. As the result of the special status of the formative elements, with *ad-* understood as the root and *-es* as a suffix? (so A. Campbell [1959:sec 445, note 1]). Both (1909:47) treats *s* in *adesa* as a suffix and lists this word among isolated formations, but *adesa* was rather *ades-a* than *ad-es-a*.

Addice remained the standard form until the 17th century, and Johnson considered *adz(e)* to be a reprehensible corruption of *addice*, a view in which Kenrick followed him. No firm rule of syncope in the penultimate syllable of trisyllabic words existed: *Thames* (< *Temese*) has been monosyllabic since Middle English, but *temse* 'sieve' could be spelled *temize* even in the 17th century. In domesticated borrowings like *lettuce* and *trellis*, postradical vowels have been preserved. Although *adsan* (pl) occurs in Old English, the final stage of syncope in *addice* happened unusually late. Only when *i* was lost, did *addice* acquire the pronunciation [ædz] and the modern spelling *adz(e)*. For a more detailed discussion of syncope and voicing in this word see Skeat (1887 = 1892:252) and HL (959 and 963).

Among other forms, OED lists *atch* from the 17th century, and in the 1580 example *nads* appears (*an adz > a nads*). None of Scott's regional forms (1892:182)—*edge, eatch, eitch, eetch*—appears in EDD; nor does EDD note the confusion of *adz(e)* and *edge*. *Atch* may have arisen after syncope, with /s/ > /tʃ/, as in *sketch* (HL, 810, where Sc *its* 'adz' is mentioned), but *atch* 'adz' is hard to distinguish from *hatch* 'hatchet' (a short-lived word; the earliest citation in OED goes back to 1704: *hatch sb*[4]; see also Fehr [1910:317]). The only form of *adz(e)* in EDD is *nadge*; *mads*, presumably from *the mads < them ads,* was recorded in Connecticut in 1893 (Scott 1893:108-9).

2. ***Adz(e)* has no established cognates.** Makovskii's attempt to compare *adesa* and OE *ǣdre* 'vein,' related to OHG *âdra* (> ModG *Ader*) and OI *æðr* (> ModI *æð*) from the common base meaning 'cut, bend (for ritualistic purposes),' is typical of his irresponsible etymologizing (1991:139). In a later work (Makovskii [1992b:73]), he throws in OE *ād* 'fire,' *ādl* 'disease,' and *æðele* 'noble, glorious' but does not mention *ǣdre* (*ǣdre* and *æðele* recur on page 76, under the rubric 'blood'). This reconstruction appears once again in Makovskii (2000a:137-38).

Equally fanciful are Tucker's comparisons. He lists E *adz(e)*, L *arcia* and *astus* 'dexterity, craft,' *astutus* 'sly, shrewd,' from **ad-stutus*, and Gr ἀθάρη ~ L *ador* 'spelt' (sb) (originally an Egyptian word) ([n.d.]:11), all of which share the feature 'sharpness.' EG connect *adz(e)* with E *eat* ~ L *edo*, G *ätsen* 'etch,' L *esca* 'food,' and so on; *adz(e)* emerges as 'any instrument that is sharp and makes cut.' Both Tucker and EG are notorious for their wild guesses.

Still another unsubstantiated comparison is between OE *adesa*, understood as **ad-es-*, and Lith *vedegà* 'adz(e), icepick.' Allegedly, **ad-es-* was formed like *ax* and might, by association with it, have lost **w* (RHD[2]). The Lithuanian word is akin to Skt *vádhar-* 'deadly weapon,' from a verb meaning 'strike,' and its cognates (see the relevant forms and the literature in LEW, *vedegà*). A blend of **akwiz* and a noun like *vedegà* has no foundation in reality, for no cognate of *vedegà* exists in Germanic and no borrowing resembling it has been recorded. A cognate would have had *t*. OE **akwiz*, if it ever existed, would have lost its *w* early (Luick [1964:sec 618, note 2]), while **adwis-* is opaque.

***Adesa* resembles OE *æx* (*eax*) 'ax'** (with which

it sometimes forms an alliterative pair; on the relations between these words see also Buck [1949:561/9.25]), **Gk ἀξίνη** (Bailey [1721], not in 1730; Skinner), **L *ascia* (a cognate of *æx*), and several old and modern words in the Romance languages, such as Ital *azza* 'battle ax' and Sp *azuela* 'adz(e),' with which it was compared in the early dictionaries.** Of the more recent authors, Baly (1897:48) derives several European words for ax and, hesitatingly, *adz(e)* from the same root. CEDEL calls *adz(e)* a borrowing from Old French, but *adesa* existed in Old English before the Norman Conquest, as Dietz (1967:356, 358) and C. J. E. Ball (1970:68) noted. KD writes: "? cf OF *aze*."

Skeat[1] "suspected" that *adesa* was a "corruption" of **acesa* or **acwesa* (he may have added **acusa*), while Heyne (1908:5-6, note 9) suggested a prehistorical borrowing of L *ascia*. In both reconstructions, the attested Old English form comes out too garbled. In the fourth edition of his dictionary, Skeat abandoned his hypothesis; see also Brasch (1910:57). **OED calls *adesa* a word of unknown origin, a decision in which practically all later dictionaries, including AeEW, followed it.** The only exceptions are Partridge (1958), who asserts that *adz(e)* is akin to *ax* and cites "the extremely relevant Go. *aqizi*," and Shipley (1984:3), who traces *ax* and *adze* to PIE **agu(e)si*.

Some other words resembling *adusa* and *adosa* are OHG *dehsala* 'ax' (ModG *Dechsel* and *Dachsbeil*), MLG *dessele*, *de(i)ssel*, (M)Du *dissel* (<**þehsalon* 'adz(e)': see KS, OED [*thixel*], and IEW, 1058). DW (*Dechsel*) lists *adesa* among the cognates of *dehsala*, and so does, without certainty, Mueller[1] (noncommittally in the second edition). Minsheu gives two nouns at *addis*: LG *diesse* and Wel *neddau* 'adz(e).' He may have derived *neddau* from *(a)n addis*, but *neddau* and *neddyf* go back to the root of *naddu* 'cut' (so already Richards), from the base **snadh* (Lewis [1923:15]; see also Stokes [1894], 315; LE, *snath*; WP II:694, and IEW, 973). The same holds for Br *eze*, *neze* and other Celtic forms (which Thomson derives from "German" *egg* 'edge'). The counterparts of *adz(e)*, with and without *a-*, sounded similarly in much of Western Europe. **OE *adusa* seems to be **acusa* 'ax,' with *d* substituted for *k* under the influence of some continental form like MLG *dessele* 'adz.' Thus the form in need of an etymology is *adusa*, not *adesa*.** A blend seems more probable than pre-OE **adehsa* (< pre-Gmc **o-tékson*), as in OHG *dehsala* (Wood [1931:sec 18.10]; Wood examined prothetic vowels in Indo-European, and his **adehsa* turned out to be *a-dehsa*). Bugge (1874:158-59) thought that even F *tille* 'roofer's or cooper's ax' goes back to OHG *dehsala*.

3. The names of tools were among the many migratory words in the Middle Ages, such as Russ *topor* 'ax' < ORuss *toporŭ*, Arm *t'ap'ar*, OE *taper-æx* 'small ax,' Finn *tappara*, Middle Persian *tab'ar*, Skt *paraśúḥ* 'ax,' and Gk πέλεκυς 'ax,' probably from some non-Indo-European language of Asia (KEWA II:213), though Uhlenbeck (KEWAS, 156) thought of an Indo-European root. According to Abaev (IESOI, *færæt*), PIE **parta*, from which he derived Oss *færæt* and Skt *parasúḥ*, was borrowed by some people in the form **tapar* and spread as *tabar*, *taper*, *tappara* over a large territory; see also Thieme (1953:586-87), Ogonovs'ka (1989), and Georgiev (1953) on words for 'ax.' The history of OE *adesa* may be similar to that of OE *taper-*. Vennemann (2000:246) suggests a Basque origin of *adz*, but as is the case with KEY, there is probably no need to go so far.

The pronunciation of such words was often changed. For instance, F *hache*, known since the 13th century, Ital *azza*, and their Romance cognates were borrowed from Gmc (Franconian) **happia* (OHG *happa*, *heppa*, *happia*, *hebba*; see *Hippe* 'pruning knife; death's scythe' in KM and KS); Frings (1943:178) sets up **happja* as the protoform. FEW (XVI:147) and all modern etymological dictionaries of the Romance languages take the change of *-pp-* to other stops for granted; see also *hatchet* and the verbs *hack*, *hash*, and *hatch* in Lund (1935:114/3) and in dictionaries of English and *Hacke* in dictionaries of German. However, Seebold (KS, *Hippe*) emphasizes the unpredictability of sound substitution in such cases. Similar processes also happened at the dawn of Indo-European (Buck [1949:561/9.25]). See Rooth's remarks (1960-62:49) on the exchange of the names of tools between Romania and Germania. If *adesa* is a blend, its history brings to mind a similar convergence in the name of a shaft: OHG *dîhsala* (ModG *Deichsel*) and Ved *īṣā* (Meringer [1892:43], M. Bloomfield [1895:430, note 1]), let alone such hybrid forms as G reg *Geiskel* 'shaft' (*Geischel* + *Deichsel*; B. Martin [1923:256]). To be sure, Br *eze*, Ital *azza*, and E *adz(e)* are unrelated, but they seem to have become, by accident, part of carpenters' and coopers' *lingua franca*.

Finally, there is Hitt URUDU*ateš*. It occurs several times, but its exact meaning has not been established. J. Friedrich (HW, 38) glosses it as 'dish; metal plate,' with a question mark. Having the second meaning in mind, E. Sturtevant (1942:secs 46a and 47) compared *ateš* (or *ates*) with OE *e(o)dor* 'fence, roof,' a word with solid cognates in Germanic (AeEW [*eodor*]; AEW [*jaðarr*]; WP I: 121; IEW, 290, *edh₂*). But in Kronasser (1962:328/2 and 341/4), *ateš* is glossed 'ax.' Puhvel (HED, 227) gives *ates(sa)* 'adze, axe, hatchet,' without explaining how he obtained the more specific meanings ('adze, hatchet'). According to Čop (1955a:406-07, the most detailed discussion; 1955b:31; 1957:140; 1964:43), *ateš* and OE *adesa* are related; he cites that fact as proof of ancient Hittite-Germanic connections. Although the voicelessness of *s* in OE *adesa* poses problems, no evidence supports Čop's conclusion that OE *adosa* was stressed on the penult (hence *s*, not *z*, by Verner's Law). Nor are the etymologically obscure Latin words *asser* 'stake,' *assis* (with its doublet *axis*) 'board,' and *assula* 'piece of kindling, splinter' of much help. Čop derived them from **adh* 'cut' ('cut' → 'a thing cut off'). Tischler (1977-[90]:369) does not reject Čop's etymology. However, as Puhvel (HED, 228) observes, "The compelling adduction of OE *adesa*... does not clinch an Indo-European etymology. At best Hitt. *t-* and OE *-d-* would point to a common **-dd-*.... The odd shape of Hitt. *ateš* (normal spelling *e*, rather than accommodation to normal *s*-stem neuters like *nepis*) may point to its noninherited lexical character." He briefly discusses the literature mentioned above (a similar survey can be found in Tischler) and dismisses as improbable H. Eichner's reconstruction of PIE **E_1sw-e-dhE_1ti* 'having a good fit' versus PIE *o-dhE_1-ēs-* in Hitt *ateš*, Gmc **aðus-on* (Eichner's personal communication to Mayrhofer: KEWA III:804). GI (1984:716 / 1995:620) set up **a/od^{h}tt-es-*, based on the Hittite–Germanic–Indic correspondences, and MA (37) call *ates* ~ *adz* "a common inheritance of a PIE word;" but the Hittite word is too obscure to justify E. Sturtevant's and Čop's conjectures, while Eichner's gloss 'having a good fit' for 'adz' lacks foundation. **A migratory word for 'adz' is a possibility, but if *adesa* is a blend, Hitt *ateš* and OE *eodor* are not related to it. They are probably not related even if *adesa* is not a blend.**

BEACON (900)

Beacon *has cognates in all the old West Germanic languages (OE* bēacen, *OFr* bāken, bēken, *OS* bôkan, *OHG* bouhhan, *etc). OI* bákn *was, most likely, borrowed from West Germanic. The original meanings of the English word are 'banner' and 'portent.' The meaning 'signal fire' was not attested until the end of the 14th century.* Beacon *has been etymologized as '(object) before one's eyes,' 'bright (object),' 'bent sign for averting evil,' 'stick, pole,' and as a Germanized variant of L* būcina *'signal horn'; attempts have also been made to connect* bēacen *with OE* bēam *'tree' and* bōc *'book.'*

It is usually believed that beacon *goes back to some Proto-Indo-European root, but* *bauk- *was one of numerous 'local' Germanic words designating objects capable of swelling (cf OE* būc *'stomach') and taking on a monstrous appearance. It could refer to a nonspecific huge and formless mass. Its various ancient meanings and its suffix* -n *seem to have been adopted from* *taikn- *(E* token*), which, in Old English, functioned as a synonym of* bēacen. *Another object of the same type was* *bak *(Du* baak, *LG* bak, bake *'buoy, beacon'). It, too, belonged with the words denoting inflatable objects, sometimes frightening (cf E* bug*), sometimes harmless (cf E* bag *and, possibly,* buck *and* back*), and it probably meant 'buoy' from the start. Judging by the recorded forms,* bak *has always been a synonym of MDu* boy ~ boey. *Its falling together with* *baukn- *would be easy to explain. However,* bak *is not a shortened variant of* beacon; *nor is* beacon *an extended form of* bak.

Closely related to *baukn- *is* buoy *(1466), a loan word in English. According to the prevailing opinion, Gmc* *bōken *'beacon' became* boie *in Old French, and returned as* boeye ~ boye *'buoy' to Dutch, from which it spread over most of Europe. Yet the Middle Dutch form is, more likely, native. Many objects capable of inflating themselves and producing frightening sounds had, in Germanic, the form* bo, boo, *and so forth. Sometimes the aural aspect predominated, as, arguably, was the case with* boi *'devil'; sometimes both may have been present, as in Du* bui *'squall.' The primitive buoy was probably an anchored bladder or something similar.*

The sections are devoted to 1) the meaning of OE bēacen *and its cognates, 2) the proposed etymologies of* beacon, *3) an assessment of the semantic history of* beacon *and the relations between* *baukn- *and* *bak-, *4)* beacon *and other words having a similar phonetic shape, 5) the Germanic origin of* beacon *and the interaction of* beacon *with* token, *and 6)* beacon *and* buoy. *Section 7 is the conclusion.*

1. Gmc **baukn-* has reflexes in all the old languages except Gothic: OE *bēac(e)n*, Old EFr *bāken*, Old WFr *bēken* (Van Haeringen [1921:274]), OHG *bouhhan*, OS *bôkan*, and several others. In Modern Low German, *beeken* means 'straw torch' (Carstens [1879a:16; 1879b:93-94]). The Old Icelandic form is *bákn*, and since it has *ā*, as opposed to Gmc **au*, it is believed to be a borrowing from Old Frisian: see Bugge (1888b:179); Wadstein (1918-22:7, 1925:147, 1932:85; 1936:16); Mossé (1933:65), Feitsma (1962:108-9), Hoekstra (2001:139), and various etymological dictionaries. But Modéer (1943:132) was right that the lending language may have been Low German, for **au* yielded *ā* also in some Low German dialects. Ejder (1961-62:95-96) came to a similar conclusion.

The recorded words have a variety of meanings. **In Old English, *(ge)bēacen* has been attested in the senses 'sign, phenomenon, portent, appari-**

tion; banner' and once 'audible signal.' It occurs three times in *Beowulf.* In line 2777 (Klaeber [1950]), it means 'banner'; in line 3160, it refers to Beowulf's monument erected after his death (see R. Page [1975:66] on *bēacen* 'monument'), and in line 570, it is part of the kenning *bēacen Godes* 'sun,' reminiscent of *heofonbēacen* 'sign in the sky' in *Exodus* (see other examples in Klaeber [1912:122]). In the Old Saxon *Heliand,* the alliterative phrase *bôkan endi bilidi* 'signs [= miraculous signs] and pictures,' a rather close counterpart of Gk σημεῖα καί τέρατα 'signs and wonders,' memorable from the gospels, turns up. The Old Saxon compound *heribôcan* 'sign of war' corresponds in form to OHG *heripouhhan.* Their antonym is OE *friðobēacen* 'sign of peace.' OE *sigebēacen* 'sign (emblem) of victory, trophy' and 'the cross of Christ' has also been recorded several times.

OE *bēacenfȳr* 'beacon fire, lighthouse' and especially *bēacenstān* 'stone on which to light a beacon fire' (both in glosses) testify to the existence of *bēacen* in its modern sense (see Hill and Sharp [1997] on Anglo-Saxon beacon system, esp pp. 157-58). That **baukn-* often referred to miraculous things also follows from its Middle High German reflex *bouhnen* 'important event' (among other meanings), from a late-13th-century Low German gloss *boken* 'misterium, omen,' and from the Middle Dutch gloss *bokene* 'phantasma, spectrum' (Rooth 1960-62:50). The ease with which OHG *boununga, bauhnung(a)* 'significatio' (from *bouhnen* 'significare, innuere'), and OE *gebēacnung* 'categoria,' both of them derivatives of **baukn-,* passed into religious and philosophical language points in the same direction. Modern English has *beckon* (< OE *bēcnan*). The word *beck* in *at one's beck and call* is its truncated form.

Of special interest is OI *bákn.* As a loanword, it may have preserved the meaning it had in the lending West Germanic language, especially because it was of such rare occurrence. CV gloss *bákn* as a foreign word and refer to the compound *sigrbákn,* but the context is unrevealing ("the thing with which the king made signs in front of his horse is called *sigrbákn* in other countries"). Fritzner (ODGNS) explains: "A sign with which one hopes to ensure victory." In the absence of other relevant texts, more can hardly be said.

Bákn occurs only twice in Old Icelandic, both times in a verse—a situation, in principle, uncharacteristic of a foreign word. It is used (contemptuously or in wonderment) about a stallion's phallus worshipped by a benighted heathen couple (*Vǫlsa þáttr*) and about a troll woman (*Hjálmþérs saga*), that is, about a most unusual thing and an extraordinary figure. ModI *bákn* means 'huge and formless mass'; see Modéer (1943:143, note 3) for more details. **Any viable etymology of **baukn-* has to explain why this word so regularly refers to miraculous and supernatural phenomena and creatures (apparitions and trolls).** Modéer, in the note cited above, says that **baukn-* developed the secondary meaning 'monstrum, portentum, miraculum,' but no evidence suggests that this meaning is secondary.

2. The origin of **baukn-* has been explained in many different ways: 1) **Bugge (1888b:180) treated **baukn-* as **b-aukn* and traced it to **ba-augənán* 'an object before one's eyes.'** A. Noreen (1894:126, 165) and the authors of several etymological dictionaries supported him (FT, SEO, and, in a modified form, EWA). A similar but less sophisticated idea occurred to Skinner, who analyzed *bēacen* into OE *be-* (a prefix) and *[a]cennan* 'produce, show.' 2) **Möller** (1879:439-41), who noted that **baukn-,* like Go *bandwjan** 'make signs,' combines the meanings of 'shine' and 'speak,' **derived the Germanic word from the root **bhā-* 'shine.'** His etymology appears in numerous dictionaries because WP II:123 and IEW, 105, endorsed it. Skt *vi-bhāèvaḥ* 'shining, brilliant,' Gk φαέθων 'shining,' and other words are said to have the same root. Some modern researchers look on this derivation as fact: Loewenthal (1916:296/46), Austin (1958:206/5), Wood (1904:5/38; the same in 1923:334/21), and Ramat (1963a:53). Dietz (1967:359) prefers it for want of a better one. A related hypothesis connects the *beacon* group with Gk πιφαύσκειν 'make signs' (Skeat[1]; no longer in Skeat[4]). Hirt, in WHirt, gives this hypothesis as the most probable one, but Götze (EWDS[11]) calls it into question.

3) From **baukn-* 'shining object' a direct path leads to *bandwjan** (as indicated by Möller) and to Go *boka* 'book, letter,' OE *bōc,* and their cognates, to the extent those words are believed to be related to the name of the beech. **The first to connect **baukn-* and Old Icelandic *bók* was Ettmüller** (1851:299), but he failed to discern a semantic tie between them. H. Kuhn (1938:59-60 = 1969-78/III:473-74) thought of two words: *bók* 'book' and *bók* 'sign.' He cited an OS gloss *bôkon* 'knit' and OI *gullbóka* 'knit in gold' (once in the *Elder Edda*). From the phonetic point of view **au* and *ō* are viable partners, as one can see in OHG *goumo* (*ou* < **au*) 'palate' ~ OI *gómr* and OE *hrēam* 'fame, glory' (*ēa* < **au*) ~ OS *hrôm.* Later, H. Kuhn (1952:264 = 1969-78/II:104-05 and in the notes to the reprint of the 1938 article) distanced himself from his old

idea, but AEW mentions it (*bók* 2) and Szemerényi (1989:371) cites it with sympathy, if not with approval. Polomé (1985:7-8) characterized Kuhn's etymology as improbable.

4) Since Gmc **baum-* (OE *bēam,* OS *bôm,* OHG *boum* 'tree') are supposed in some obscure way to be connected with Go *bagms* and OI *baðmr,* **Uhlenbeck** (1905:263-64) **suggested that *bagms* is a blend of **baumaz* and **bagnaz,* with the root **bag-* or **bak-*.** Voyles (1968:743) reconstructed one root for **baum-* and *bagm-,* and Markey (1976:XIV) added **baukn-* to them. In his opinion, "[b]oth the semantic and formal relationships obtaining between Gmc **bagm-* and **baukna-* ... are clear." He proposed a derivation of Go *bagms* from **bhogh-m-* and of Gmc **baum-* from **bhough-m-*. "Both etyma (OE *bēam* and *bēacen*) derive from variants (*bhogh-* ~ *bhough-* ~ *bhoug-*) of the same root with nasal enlargements."

5) Hamp (1984:10; 1985; 1986b:345-6; 1988a:45) had his own protoforms to offer. At first, he did not object to Markey's idea but preferred PIE **bhorĝhmós* becoming Gmc **bargmaz,* with the subsequent development to *bagms, baðmr,* and **baumaz.* He reconstructed the earliest meaning of **baukn-* as 'signal fire' and set up PIE **bhor(ə)ĝ-no-* 'what shines' (related to Go *bairhts** 'bright') > **barkna-n* (Hamp [1985]) and thus ended up with two similar roots: Gmc **bargmaz* 'tree' and Gmc **barknan* 'beacon' (the same in the 1986b note). In Hamp (1984:10), he says that the vocalism of *bēacen* was early conflated with that of *bēam* < **bagmaz* and operates with the roots **bagma-* and **bakna-*. Later (Hamp [1986b and 1988b]) he withdrew his support of Markey's etymology. Hamp (and here he stands alone) is ready to accept OI *bákn* as a native Scandinavian word. Since all those reconstructions are mere linguistic algebra, their value is hard to assess. The original meaning of **baukn-* cannot be ascertained in a passing remark, as Hamp would like to do it, but in any case, **early 'beacons' (signs, special signs for sailors, apparitions, monsters, banners, and funeral mounds) were not trees. Nor were they exclusively signal fires, which makes all etymologies of **baukn-* based on the concepts of sheen and brightness suspect.**

6) According to **Senn** (1933:508), **baukn-* does not fall into *b* + *aukn.* He **asserts that **baukn-* is related to Latv *bauze* 'stick, cudgel' and *buõze* 'stick, cudgel, wedge, steelyard' and Lith *búožė* 'stick, cudgel.'** He does not elaborate on the connection 'sign' ~ 'stick.' E. Fraenkel (LEW, *baũžas,* and so on) makes no mention of Senn's etymology, and neither does anyone else.

7) Ettmüller (1851:299), who compared *bēacen* and *bōc,* also cited OHG *bûh* 'stomach' (ModG *Bauch*). He traced both words to the hypothetical verb **bēocan* or **būcan* 'prominere' ('protrude, project'). His reconstruction attracted no attention. Instead of **būcan,* the verb *būgan* 'bend, bow' emerged as the etymon of **baukn-*. Ten Doornkaat Koolman (1879-84, *bâke*) developed this etymology at great length. Presumably, people waved their hands or made movements with the head, to show the way to the ship. He listed *būk* (corresponding to OHG *bûh*) and the verb *bukken* along with *būgan* but did not explain how *g* and *k* are related. In addition, he supported Grimm's etymology (see the end of no. 8, below), so that the result came out confusing. Modéer (1943:145, note 4) dismissed Ten Doornkaat Koolman's idea as unworthy of discussion, and no one seems to have shown any interest in it except Goedel (1902, *Bak*), who copied Ten Doornkaat Koolman's text without referring to his source, until Güntert resuscitated or reinvented it, at which time it acquired some notoriety. **Güntert** (1928:134/22) **thought that **baukn-* could be derived from the root of Skt *bhogá-* 'coil, ring,' OI *baugr* ~ OE *bēag* 'ring,' OE *būc* ~ G *Bauch* (< OHG *bûh* 'body') ~ OI *búkr* 'body, trunk.' Beacons, he explained, were bent signs with the power to avert magic.** Since no evidence points to the existence of such signs, his etymology has become the favorite target of ridicule: it is called in some works amusing nonsense, a typical sample of "chairborne" philology, and the like.

8) **Modéer** (1943) offered a new etymology of **baukn-*; of related interest is also Modéer (1937:90-92). In the 1943 article, he analyzed all the extant meanings of the relevant words in Scandinavian and West Germanic and examined the reflexes of **baukn-* and their *n*-less counterparts, namely Du *baak* (known since the Middle Dutch period: *baec-*), LG *bak* and *bake,* Sw *båk,* Dan *båke,* N *båk(e)* (see these words in Hellquist [1929-30:805-6]). **He noted that OE *bēacen* could refer to an audible signal and took Gmc **baukn-* for a Germanized form of L *būcina* 'signal horn,'** which has come down to us as E *bassoon,* G *Posaune,* Sw *basun,* and so forth. Modéer submitted his paper as part of his application materials for a professorship at Lund. Three readers offered their comments, as Modéer recounts at the end of the article. Erik Noreen called the proposed etymology extremely hypothetical (and Modéer agreed), while Hjalmar Lindroth had no objections. Bengt Hesselman characterized it as bold, but still he preferred it to "some

fantastic etymologies of foreign scholars (Bugge, Kluge, and others)." DEO[3,4] (*båke*) and KM (*Bake*) considers the derivation of **baukn-* from *bucīna* probable. CEDEL gives it as the only one, but KS do not mention it, and J. de Vries (AEW [*bákn*] and NEW [*baak*]) calls it precarious. Polomé (1985:7-8) and EWA concur with this verdict; ÁBM (*bákn*) is noncommittal. Critics have only one counterargument: they point out that Gmc **au* could not render L *ū*. According to Okasha (1976:200), Modéer's reconstruction remains an attractive hypothesis, and J. de Vries's words are "perhaps a little too scathing." Page also found some value in Modéer's etymology (Okasha [1976:200, note 1]).

In a different form, the idea that **baukn-* originally designated an audible signal was offered long before Modéer. The Grimms (DW, *Bak*) related **baukn* to German *Pauke* 'kettledrum.' No progress has been made in the search for the origin of *Pauke* since the Grimms' times; even its connection with G *pochen* 'knock, thump' (another obscure word) is doubtful. Kauffmann (1887:510, 522) found the Grimms' etymology to be right. For more details he refers to Möller (1879:439-41), but von Friesen (1897:7, 13) criticized (deservedly as it seems) his comparison **baukn-* ~ Swabian *baokə* (pl) 'kettledrum.' Johansson (1900:360-61 and note on p. 361), whose work will be discussed below, explained the origin of many *b-k* words, including L *bucīna,* and doubted that Old English *bēacen* belonged with them (Weigand, however, derived *Pauke* directly from *bucīna*); he argued for the *bēacen* ~ *būgan* link. Thus *bucīna* turned up twice in the discussions of **baukn-*. *Pauke,* owing to the Grimms' reputation, occupied a more prominent place in the proposed etymologies of **baukn-,* but Modéer passed it by.

9) A few remarks to the effect that **baukn-* is related to some Hebrew word (בחן, that is, *b-h-n* 'try, prove; examine, as metals'; suggested by Parkhurst [1792:67] and rejected by Whiter III:333, who preferred derivation from *pick* because beacons "stick out"—III:286), that it was borrowed from Welsh or some other Celtic language (*beachd* 'watching, observation': Mackay [1877]), or that *beacon* is possibly akin to E reg *beck* (corresponding to G *Bach* 'stream, rivulet': Cameron [1892:220-21]) need not occupy us here. They are pure fancies.

10) The most authoritative dictionaries of English (OED, CD, Weekley, and Skeat) offer no etymology of *beacon.* An exception is UED. **Wyld's reconstruction escaped the notice of Germanic scholars and deserves to be quoted in full.** "O.E. *bēac(e)n,* 'sign, token,' also 'banner,' M. E. *beekne.* The certain cognates in other Gmc. languages are O. Fris. *bēken,* O.S. *bōkan,* O.H.G. *pouhhan.* Beyond this the etymol[ogy] seems not to have been carried, so far. We have here a Gmc. base **bauk-,* for wh[ich] we may confidently reconstruct an Aryan predecessor **bhoug-,* wh[ich] w[oul]d have also the grades **bheug-, *bhŭg-*. Such a base appears in Gk. *phéugō,* 'flee,' *phúza* (fr[om] **phug-ja*), 'headlong flight, rout'; Lat. *fugīre* [sic; apparently, *fugere* is meant] 'flee,' *fuga,* 'flight'. With these the etymologists connect Lith. *búgti,* 'terrify,' *baugùs,* 'frightful' &c. (See the prob[ably] related Gmc. base **biug-, *bŭg* &c. at BIGHT, BOW (I & II), where the development of meaning has gone on quite different lines.) The base **bheug-* then seems to have the sense of running away fr[om] something wh[ich] frightens one. It is now suggested that the base in Gmc. came to mean 'fear of something dangerous, danger, sign of danger, warning,' then, 'a sign or token' generally. Cf. also *beckon.*"

3. Some of the foregoing hypotheses are more probable than the others, but few of them pay sufficient attention to the semantic history of **baukn-*. For instance, how did the meanings 'specter, marvel; banner' develop from 'signal of a war trumpet?' What unites trees and sticks (cudgels) with 'signal fire'? If brightness is what gave the object in question its name **baukn-,* when and in what circumstances did the meanings 'specter, marvel; banner' emerge? Only Wyld was fully interested in this aspect of the problem.

No one says anything on the relationship between *bēacen, bāken, bēken, bôkan,* and *bouhhan* and their *n*-less partners. Stray remarks on *båk-* being a shortened form of *båk-en* have no value even for Scandinavian, as Modéer (1943:132) has shown, while deriving *baken* from an oblique case of *bake* (Collinder [1932:210]) can hardly be substantiated (besides this, it is **baukn-,* not *bāken* that has to be explained). Yet even Modéer made do with deriving **baukn-* and neglected the history of *bak* ~ *båk.* Although the *n*-less forms are poorer in content than the Old Germanic words ending in *-n* (they mean only 'beacon, beacon fire'), some link between the two sets must exist, and the opposition OE *bēacen* ~ OFr *bōken* versus MDu *baec* ~ LG *bak(e)* and so forth has to be explained. **If we assume that **bak-* is in some way related to **baukn-* (a regular connection cannot be postulated, for *ă* and *au* do not alternate by ablaut), Bugge's etymology, which depends crucially on the presence of *n,* and the etymologies based on the idea of **baukn-* as the past participle of some verb lose much of their appeal.** Caution is also invited in dealing with Proto-Germanic or Proto-Indo-European nasal enlargements: despite its late attestation, **bak-* may be the original form, whereas the *n*-forms need not be old.

4. It was noticed early on that short English and German words beginning with *b-* and *p-* convey the idea of swelling. J. Whitaker (1771-75:249-62) and Whiter III:191-205 offer a detailed discussion of such words. Since neither of them was aware of sound correspondences, they included numerous examples that should have been left out, but the observations they made were right. Johansson (1900:354-63) did not read authors like Whitaker and Whiter, but armed with the best achievements of comparative philology, he came to conclusions close to those of his distant predecessors. Gysseling (1987:52) reached similar results.

The list below is longer than Johansson's, though it is limited to English; the groups are *b-g, b-k, b-d, b-t, b-b, p-g, p-k, p-d,* and *p-t, p-p*. (*b–g*): *bag, big, bug* 'insect' and 'object of dread,' *bogey, boggle,* and so forth; cf E reg *bog* 'boastful' and *bug* 'big' (the last, most probably, of Scandinavian origin); (*b–k*): *?back, buck* (if the animal is 'a big beast'); in SEO, Hellquist (at *troll* 'troll,' sb) mentions Sw *troll-, trullpacka* and *troll-, trullbacka* 'witch'; in his opinion, the words with *b-* are older, as evidenced by Sw *rattbacka* and Dan *aftenbakke* 'bat'; this is probably right, but *-backa* need not be an alteration of *-blacka* 'flutter,' for rather *rattblacka* (the older form had one *t* in both Swedish and Danish) looks like a folk etymological alteration of *rattbacka*, with *-backa* being one of the words discussed here, that is, 'frightening creature' (Hellquist repeats an old opinion, which OED, *bat, sb*[1], calls into question, but ODEE, *bat*[2], endorses; the Middle English for *bat* was *backe*, apparently, from Scandinavian, for Old English had *hrēremūs;* the change from *back-* to *bat* has not been explained); Kluge's idea (KL, *bat*) that *backe* and so forth may be connected with *bacon* because in German dialects *Speckmaus*, literally 'flitchmouse,' occurs is fanciful; (*b-d*): *bud, body;* (*b-t*): *butt(ock), bottle, but* 'flatfish' and *-bot* in *turbot, button;* (*b-b*): *bob* 'bunch, knot,' *bobbin, bubble;* (*p-g*): *pig, pug* (cf LG *Pogge* 'frog'); (*p-k*): *pack, pock* 'pustule, pockmark' (cf G *Pocke*), *pocket, poke* 'sack,' *Puck, pucker, ?spook;* (*p-d*): *pad* 'small cushion, paw, etc' (compare the meaning of *padding* and G *Pfote* 'paw'), *pad* ~ *paddock* 'frog' (cf LG *Pogge,* above), *pod* (historically a variant of *cod*), *podge* ~ *pudge* 'short, fat person' (and the adjectives *pudsey, pudgy, podgy*), *poodle* (another dog is *pug,* above), *pud* 'hand of a child, paw of an animal'; (*p-t*) *?pate, pot, pout;* (*p-p*): *pap* 'nipple, teat.'

Some of those words (like *big*) have been the object of sustained etymological investigation; others (like *pate*) have attracted minimal attention. Most of them are of unclear origin, and a few may not belong here (this is especially true of words like *butt*: see Dahlberg [1955: 29-39] and the remarks on G *Butzemann* at BOY). *Bottle* and several others traveled back and forth between Germanic and Romance. In this case, details are less important than the principle. We have to admit the existence of a considerable number of vaguely synonymous words beginning with *b* or *p* followed by a vowel and a stop (*b, p, d, t, g, k;* however, *b* and *p* are rare).

Compare the following Russian words, some of which are near homonyms of the English ones: *byk* 'buck,' *bok* 'side' (related to E *back?*), *bukashka* 'little insect' (stress on the second syllable), *buka* 'bogey,' *biaka* 'bad, dirty thing,' *pug-* 'dread, fright,' *pugovitsa* 'button' (stress on the first syllable), *puzo* 'belly,' *puzyr'* 'bubble' (stress on the second syllable). They are not related to their English counterparts in the same way Russ *slab* 'weak' is sometimes believed to be related to E *sleep,* for the consonants in the two lists violate sound correspondences. For example, the Dutch for *pig* is *big* (*p : b*), the English for Russ *buka* is *bogey* (*k : g*), and so on. Yet the authors of Germanic etymological dictionaries regularly admit Slavic words through the back door, and their Slavic colleagues occasionally do the same with the German and Dutch words.

The English words given above have short (or so-called checked) vowels in the root. They are matched by *bū-* words with historically long vowels. Here we see nouns and verbs designating inflated objects that suddenly burst and the sounds they produce. **'Being swollen' and 'being noisy' are often inseparable.** Consider Russ *bukhnut'* 'make a loud sound' and 'swell'; *bukhnut'* 'swell' (usually with a prefix) has a synonym (practically, a doublet) *pukhnut'*. Similarly, E *puff* means 'emit steam' (cf *puff-puff* imitating the corresponding sound) and 'swell out' (cf *puffed up*). German has *pusten, pfusten* 'puff, blow' and *fauchen, pfauchen* 'hiss' (mainly said about cats; MHG *pfûchen*). *Bausch* 'paper ball, pleat on a curtain, bustle on a dress, puff on a sleeve' is not common, but the idiom *in Bausch und Bogen* 'completely' has universal currency, as do the *p-* words *pauschal,* said about an across-the-board estimated amount, and *Pausbacken* 'chubby cheeks,' *Backe* 'puffed up cheek,' along with L *bucca* (the same). E *back* and Russ *bok* form part of the first list. It follows that both parts of the compound *Pausbacken* have approximately the same origin (a tautological compound: see SLOWWORM. *Bauch* 'stomach, belly' (see sect 6 on Ettmüller and Güntert's etymology), is another *bū*-word. Seebold, who discusses the *Bausch* group in detail (KS), adds G *Bö* 'squall, gust' to it.

5. **MDu *baec*- [ModDu *baak*, LG *bak*, *bak(e)*] seem to belong with other *b-k* words, while **baukn-* belongs with OE *būk* and its cognates.** The earliest 'bak' must have been a float, a buoy (a similar case is ModI *dufl* 'buoy, beacon'; *dufla* 'splash about'). If 'growth' can be equated with 'swelling (out),' Go *bagms* will fit the *b-g* group, though *-m-* remains problematic. Gmc **bau-m-* easily aligns itself with *Bau-ch, Bau-sch,* for not only stops but also resonants can be attached to *bū* ~ *bau-,* as in G *Beule* 'bump, boil' (OHG *bûla, bŭla, būlla, bŭlla* 'bladder, *etc*'—note the wealth of forms typical of onomatopoeic and sound symbolic formations—OS *bûlia,* OE *bȳl, bȳle,* OFr *bēl, beil,* and Go *ufbauljan** 'puff up,' OI *bóla* 'boil,' alongside ModI *beyla* 'lump' and the unexplained Eddic name *Beyla*). It unnecessary to set up one etymon for *bagms* and *Baum. Bagms* may be a blend (**bag-az* with a suffix from **baum-az*; cf. Uhlenbeck, above).

Bogey, boggle, and the rest emphasize the frightening aspect of the objects designated by *b-g* words, so that a meaning like 'apparition' was not too remote even from *bac* 'buoy,' especially if ancient buoys were visible at night. But *beacon* is not a synonym of *buoy* (although the similarity of their function must have led to some influence in one or more directions), for beacons were signal fires on a coast, wooden towers, branches tied to poles, and so forth. **Baukn-* is particularly difficult because of its *-n*. **Neither *bak* nor **baukn-* should be mechanically projected to Proto-Indo-European. Both are members of the *big-bag-būk-pig* litter, and their age is indeterminate. Setting up ancient participles and an *n*-enlargement is a futile procedure. If Bugge's etymology is rejected, the origin of *-n* remains a puzzle. Most probably, it appeared in **baukn-* under the influence of **taikn-*, in which *-n* is a genuine suffix.**

Gmc **taikn-* had strong religious (magical) connotations. Finn *taika* (from Germanic) means 'divination, portent' (on this word see especially Collinder [1932:204-15]). OI *...krossa ok ǫll heilǫg tákn* 'crosses (acc pl) and all holy signs' (*Njáls saga,* quoted in CV under *tákn*) is reminiscent of OS *bôkan endi bilidi* and of the English biblical phrase *tokens and wonders* (see OED, *token, sb*[4]). *Tācen* and *bēacen* have almost completely overlapping glosses in dictionaries of Old English. *Bēacen:* "beacon," sign, token, phenomenon, portent, apparition; standard, banner; audible signal. *Tācen* "token," symbol, sign, signal, mark, indication, suggestion; portent, marvel, wonder, miracle; evidence, proof; standard, banner (Clark Hall). *Exodus* has both *friðobēacen* and *friðotācn* for 'sign of peace.' *Bēacen* and *tācen* often occurred together, as in *Beowulf* 140-41 (*...þā him gebēacnod wæs... sweotolan tācne...* 'when it was indicated to him by a manifest sign') and in *The Blickling Homilies* (*ealle þā tācno & þā forebēacno...,* quoted in OED, *token, sb*[5]), and see the examples in Klaeber (1912:122). Even the phonetic variation in the second syllables *bēacen* ~ *bēacn, tācen* ~ *tācn* is the same in both pairs. The fact of interaction between **baukn-* and **taikn-* is commonplace in etymological studies (WP II:123).

Three or four words meaning 'sign; omen' must at first have referred to different phenomena. For example, according to Üçok (1938:38-40), Go *bandwa** was restricted to concrete signs for demonstrating a meaning, and Go *fauratani** meant 'supernatural sign,' whereas *taikn* referred to any sign and was thus a general word (cited approvingly in Feist-Lehmann, **bandwa*). However, *taikn* also meant 'sign' and 'portent, miracle,' as did Gk σημεῖον (which that Gothic noun renders) and τέρας. Gothic did not have **baukn*; it would probably have turned up if it had existed. Its presumed nonexistence is indirect proof that **WGmc **baukn-* emerged late, crossed the path of **taikn-* (an old word), and partly usurped its functions.** Go *fauratani** must be another local innovation.

6. The etymology of *beacon* < **bauk-n-* will be incomplete without a few remarks on *buoy,* which is in turn connected with BOY. Diez's theory (1466, *boja*) reproduced in ODEE, traces MDu *bo(e)ye* (ModDu *boei*) to OF *boie* ~ *buie* 'chain, fetter,' a word that is mentioned elsewhere in Germanic etymologies: see Feist[3] at *baidjan** 'compel.' As Modéer (1943:141) pointed out, floating buoys are never *chained,* and being *anchored* could hardly be looked on as their most conspicuous feature. The main difficulty consists in the fact that the origin of the French word is unknown.

Diez's derivation of *boie* from Late L *boia* 'fetter' poses phonetic problems, regardless of whether *o* in *boia* is short or long. (See Vidos [1957:96, note 2], on the vowel length.) A. Tobler's attempt (1896:862) to rescue Diez's etymology met with little success. Nigra's conjecture (1903) that *bouée* goes back to L *bō(v)a* 'snake,' reg Ital *boa* 'rope or floating log used as a signal,' because the chain of a buoy reflects the light and resembles a water snake, also found few supporters (see only Pianigiani [*boia*]). Most other authors of the modern dictionaries of the Romance languages (for example, Battisti-Alessio, Devoto [*boia*], Corominas [*boya*]) and NEW trace the French word to MHG *bouchen* (the same, much earlier, Schuchardt [1901:346-47, 1903:611]) or Old Franconian *bôkan* (ML, 1005). In French, **bokan* allegedly changed to *boi* (as it did in F *jouer* 'play' from L *jocāri*) and returned to Middle Dutch as *bo(e)ye.* Considering the late appearance of the French word (the end of the 15th century), this reconstruction looks strained.

Vidos (1957:95-105, esp 103-04) suggested that the etymon of the French word is MDu *bo(e)ye* (*boie, boey, boei*), which owes its origin to OF *buie* 'chain,' from *boia.* His article deals with so-called organic etymology. This is how Szemerényi (1962:179) summarizes Vidos's views: "[I]f a member of a technical, especially nautical vocabulary, is of unknown origin, it is likely to derive from the same source as other words of the same field, especially if the first attestation is roughly of the same date as the others; if the word denotes an integral part of the object, the probability is even greater. The usefulness of the principle is demonstrated by Prof. Vidos on French *bouée* 'buoy,' which has at long last been traced to its Dutch source." In this case, the "organic" element is the progression *anchor—chain—buoy,* with *buoy* getting its name from an object that constitutes its inalienable part. FEW (XV:83, **baukn*) tentatively sides with Vidos. Modéer, whose investigation predates Vidos's by many years, subscribed to the **bokan* theory. Hardly anyone remembers that Bilderdijk I:120 saw a reflex of *bode* in Du *boei,* for beacons are signals ('messengers') of storms, or that Van den Helm (1861:207-08) traced Du *boie* to Ital *tempo boio* 'dark weather.'

Both Schuchardt's etymology (in its original form or modified by Meyer-Lübke [see also EWFS, *bouée*] and Vidos's radical revision of it presuppose that the word for 'buoy' wandered from a Germanic language to Old French and returned to Middle Dutch, to designate the same object in a new way. The question arises why Dutch speakers needed to borrow the Old French word. **It is more natural to suppose that MDu *bo(e)ye* was a native word and spread from its center to other languages.** French also had *beekenes* (pl) (Cameron [1892], Ott [1892]).

Boi and *boy* (see BOY) are creatures that frighten people with the sounds they make (*bo, boo,* and the like). But, as already pointed out, the same 'devils' could inflate themselves and inspire awe by being both loud and big, whence Du *bui* 'squall' (another word recorded late). Low German borrowed this word as *Bö* and *Böje,* High German as *Bö,* Swedish as *by,* but Danish as *byge; byge* resembles forms like E *bogey* more than Du *bui.* With MDu *bo(e)ye* as native, the following triad presents itself: MDu *bo(e)ye* 'buoy,' ME *boi* 'devil' (an almost extinct meaning), and late MDu *bui* 'squall.' If we allow 'inflation, swelling out' and 'noise' to be related concepts in describing demons, natural phenomena, and all kinds of objects, those three words will form a close-knit group. *Puck* and *boy* were probably evil spirits that struck fear in people by puffing themselves up and occasionally roaring, moaning, howling, and whistling. *Bui* was their inhuman incarnation, whereas man-made *buoys* were big and inflated.

7. Germanic had numerous words beginning with *b* and *p* and alternating vowels. All of them were vaguely synonymous, and their meanings were unpredictable: 'something big,' 'something loud (and frightening).' They could end in a consonant, as a rule in *g, k, d,* and *t,* but a resonant, most often *l,* was allowed too. Bugs and bogeys swelled out and made a lot of noise. Other words designated harmless objects. One such object was a float called *bak.* Since it showed the way to ships, it acquired the meaning 'sign.' Another sign was called **baukn-*. Perhaps it had some magical senses from the start, but, more probably, it acquired a set of elevated meanings and the suffix *-n* under the influence of the ancestor of modern *token* ~ *tecken* ~ *Zeichen.* ModI *bákn* still refers, nonspecifically, to a huge formless mass. The words discussed here are not restricted to Germanic: they occur, sometimes in identical form, in Sanskrit, Classical Greek, Romance, Slavic, and Celtic. They are products of primitive creation, and this circumstance makes tracing the routes of borrowings particularly difficult (Liberman [2001a:213-26]).

BIRD (800)

The most frequent Old English form of bird *is* bridd. *Since this noun has been assigned to the Germanic* ja-*stem* (*brid-ja-z, *bred-ja-z), -dd *appears to be due to West Germanic gemination.* Bird *surfaced late and is usually explained as a metathesized form of* brid(d). Brid(d) *supplanted OE* fugol *(ModE* fowl*) as the common name of a flying feathered animal. The oldest recorded meaning of* bird *was 'nestling,' but in late Middle English it occurred with reference to all kinds of young animals and human beings, from bees to devils.* Bird *has been compared with the verbs* breed ~ brood *and* bear *'give birth,' the adjective* broad, *and with several other words in and outside Germanic. Some etymologists believe in the derivation of* bird *from* brēdan *'breed,' but the difficulty of connecting OE* ē, *from umlauted* ō (brēdan < *brōdjan), *with OE* i *from* e *(or with old* i*) in* bridd *has not been solved, and most modern dictionaries call* bird *a word of unknown origin. The stumbling block in the* bird ~ beran *etymology is that the earliest recorded form is* bridd, *not* bird. *However, that etymology can be rescued if two assumptions are made: that in spite of the discrepancy in dates* bird, *not* brid(d), *is the original form and that the original meaning of* bird *was 'the young of any animal' (as recorded in Middle English), not 'nestling.' Then* bird, *from* *berd-jo-z, *would acquire the meaning 'born creature' and join such nouns as* *barn- *(OE* bearn*) 'child' ('bairn'), OE* gebyrd *'offspring,' OE* byre *'son,' Sc* birky (= bir-k-y) *'fellow,' and several others, with cognates elsewhere in Germanic, especially in German.*

The sections are devoted to 1) the attested forms of bird, *2) the attested meanings of* bird, *3) the proposed derivation of* bird *from* breed, *4) the proposed derivation of* bird *from* bear *(v), 5) other hypotheses on the origin of* bird, *and 6) the vindication of the etymology of* bird *from* bear. *Section 7 is the conclusion.*

1. The Old English forms of *bird* are *brid* and *bridd*. According to the microfiche concordance of the Toronto *Dictionary of Old English,* it occurs eleven times in the singular and fifty-four times in the plural, practically always with *dd*. *Bird* (pl *birdas*) has been recorded in Northumbrian glosses. ***Bridd*, assigned in grammars to the *ja*-stem, supposedly has a double consonant because of West Germanic gemination. *Birdas* is believed to be a metathesized form of *bridas*** (SB [sec 179.1]; A. Campbell [1959:sec 459.2]). The only analogue of such metathesis is *ðirda* (*þirda*) < *ðridda* (*þridda*) 'third.' In Middle English, both words underwent a second metathesis. Luick (1964:secs 432, note 1; 714.1 and note; 756.1) points out that in late Middle English, *dirt* and *thirty* were sometimes spelled *drit* and *thritty*, whereas the reverse process *ri* > *ir* in *þirde* and *bird* occurred in Old English. *Bird* has no prehistoric antecedents, so that when Kaluza (1906-07:I, secs 65a and 85a) calls *i* and *d* in *bridd* reflexes of Proto-Germanic (*Urgermanisch*), he has in mind a reconstructed rather than an attested form (**bridja*). He cites the same two Northumbrian words (*þirda* and *brid*) as examples of metathesis (sec 99a). OED gives the form **bridjo-z*, and it turns up in Hamp (1981:40, 1989:197-98): Pre-Germanic **b̄red-ja* > Gmc **b̄riddja* > OE *bridd*. The earliest occurrence of *brid* is in a gloss: *pullus, brid*. *Briddas* goes back to the year 1000.

2. **The forms **bridja-* and **bridjo-z* may never have existed.** *Brid(d)* ~ *bird* supplanted *fugol* (ModE *fowl*), the common Germanic name of a feathered animal, just as ME *pigge* (< **picga* 'pig') and OE *docga* 'dog' supplanted *swīn* and *hund*. Such newcomers are usually 'homey' words, borrowed from baby language or slang. They often contain expressive geminates and need not be native. Thus E *puppy* seems to be of French origin; *whelp* is English but without cognates outside Germanic, and *hjuppi* ~ *héppi* 'whelp' is only Icelandic. Typically, such words refer to more animals than one. For instance, *stag* is a male deer in Standard English, but in northern dialects it means 'horse'; OI *steggi* means 'drake,' but in Modern Icelandic, *steggur* is a male seabird and a male cat (ODEE cites OI *stagi* and *stagg* at *stag,* neither of which has been attested). Projecting *stag* and the like to Common Germanic and Proto-Indo-European is a risky, uncontrollable procedure.

Another fact to be considered is the early meaning of *bird*. **At the end of the 14th century, the words *bridd* and *byrd* begin to occur with reference to all kinds of young animals, such as adders, bees, fish, serpents, foxes, and wolves, as well as human beings and even fiends.** The unexpected meanings of *brydd* were the subject of an exchange between Maxwell (1891a), who cited an instance of *bird* 'wolf cub' without consulting OED, and his respondents (Murray [1891], Mayhew [1891a], and W. Logeman [1891]; see also Maxwell [1891b]). More recently, Lockwood (1981b:185) emphasized the importance of the Middle English meaning of *bird*. Although those examples fall into the period 1388-1591, slangy usage that would allow whelps, cubs, and young devils to be called 'bird' is hard to imagine. (Compare the transparent metaphor *jailbird*, based on the idea of a caged creature, or *gallows bird*.) It is more likely that the meaning 'the young of any animal' is ancient, even though the extant evidence is late. OE *brid* ~ *bird* was not a synonym of *fugol* 'bird, *avis*,' for *brid(d)* designated 'the young of the feathered tribes; a young bird; a chicken, eaglet, *etc*; a nestling.' OED adds: "The only sense in OE. found in literature down to 1600; still retained in north. dial. as 'a hen and her birds'." Older dictionaries were fond of quoting *1Henry IV*, V: 1, 60: "...you used us so / As that ungentle gull the cuckoo's bird / Useth the sparrow" (SG, *bird*, cites two more similar examples in Shakespeare).

3. Several etymologies of *bird* have been suggested and rejected. **Minsheu considered Dutch ("Belgian") *broeden* 'brood, sit on eggs' (his gloss is 'sit upon') to be the etymon of *bird*.** Skinner's correction "rather from OE *bredan* 'keep warm'" is reasonable, for why should an English word go back to Dutch rather than to an attested Old English form? But it does not change anything in principle, for OE *brēdan* 'produce or cherish a

brood,' that is, 'breed' is a cognate of G *brüten* (OHG *bruotan*) and MDu *brueden.* Junius cited *brydan,* but, apparently, he meant *brēdan.* Likewise, N. Bailey (1721 and 1730), Wedgwood, Ettmüller (1851:320), and Webster (1864 and 1880) traced *bird* to *brood.* That etymology then appears in Skeat[1], but in the *Errata et Addenda,* while defending himself against Stratmann's criticism, Skeat hedges and says that he "merely suggested a connection." *Connection* is a meaningless word in this context. Skeat must have realized the weakness of his defense because he added: "I still hold that the Teut[onic] base is BRU, whence also A[nglo]-S[axon] *brew, broth, bread, brood, breed,* etc. See Fick III: 217. If this be not the right form of the base, what is?" In CED between 1882 and 1900, he says that *bird* is "perhaps allied to *brood,*" and in Skeat[4] he admits that *bird* was understood as a thing bred. But a derivative of *brēdan* could be neither **bridjoz* nor **bredjoz.* The last edition of CED contains no etymology at all: Skeat only repeats Murray's verdict ("of unknown origin").

Brēdan* (< **brōdjan*) has vowels incompatible with *i* in *brid(d). One can perhaps reconstruct OE *ē* alternating with **ĕ* lowered to *i* before **j,* but no way leads from *ō* to *e.* Mayhew (1891a), a scholar much given to bullying his opponents, declared that "[t]o connect *brid* with *brōd* and *brēdan* is high treason against those severe laws which govern the relations of vowels to one another in the several 'Ablaut' series."

Yet the relatedness of *bird* to *breed ~ brood* seems so obvious that Minsheu's etymology lives on. Weekley noted that the connection between *bird* and *breed ~ brood* is doubtful (he does not say "out of the question"). Wyld (UED) suggested that it would be possible to overcome the phonetic difficulties if we assumed that *ō* in **brōdjan* goes back to PIE **oi;* then *i* in *brid* would be the zero grade of this diphthong. Unlike his predecessors, he considered *i* in *brid* to be old rather than a reflex of *e* lowered before *j* because of West Germanic breaking.

Finally, Hamp (1981:40) reconstructed the vowels in Gmc **brēð- ~ *brōð-* 'brood' as the lengthening grades of *ĕ, ŏ.* "As a back-formation from these **breð-ja-z* 'one of a brood' is perfectly intelligible as a neo-normal grade. Under the rules of Indo-European ablaut, in a thematic stem (and a derived *-io*-stem) derived from a noun (here **brōðō*) we expect **e* vocalism; cf *wild* beside *Wald...*" Theoretically, such a back formation is possible, but secure analogues are wanting. The alternation *ō ~ ĕ* is sometimes set up (Noreen [1894:54]) on the strength of pairs like OE *brōc* 'brook' and *brecan* 'break,' but all such etymologies are problematic. Hamp does not cite any examples illustrating the alleged pattern (long grade in a collective noun ~ normal grade in a word designating a member of the group), and it is unclear what G *wild ~ Wald* have to do with *ō ~ ĕ.* However, Markey (1987:277) supported Hamp. Both Wyld and Hamp believed that *brid(d)* is an ancient word with a prehistory reaching far back into Early Germanic and, like all supporters of Minsheu's idea, ignored the later meanings of *brid.* *Breed* must originally have meant 'hatch,' and *brood* refers only to young birds. **Deriving *brid* from *brēdan* leaves the problem of Middle English semantics (*brid* 'young bear,' and so forth) unsolved,** a circumstance even such an experienced etymologist as Trubachev (1980:9-10) disregarded.

4. **Another group of researchers derive *bird* from Gmc **beran* 'bear, give birth';** so Thomson, E. Adams (1858:101), the pre-1864 editions of Webster (from *bear* or the Welsh verb *bridaw* 'break forth'), and Leo (1877). Mueller, who cited Wedgwood and Ettmüller (*brid* from *breed*), preferred to trace *bird* to *beran.* By contrast, Scott connected *bird* and *beran* in the first edition of CD but switched to *breed ~ brood* in the second. **From the semantic point of view the *bird ~ beran* etymology is irreproachable.** The original meaning of *bird* would come out as 'a born creature,' which fits both the Middle English meanings and the meaning 'nestling.' OE *gebyrd* meant 'birth; descent, parentage, race' and 'offspring' (f, *i*-stem), while 'child' is one of the meanings of OHG *giburt* and MHG *geburt.* OE *gebyrd,* OHG *giburt,* and Go *gabaurþs*,* as well as OE *byrðen* and OHG *burdin* 'burden,' have the zero grade of the alternating vowel, whereas *bird,* if related to *beran,* would have *i* < **e,* the normal grade. A parallel in the normal grade would be Go *barn* 'child,' with cognates in all the Germanic languages (from an ancient past participle: *barn* = 'born creature'). Later dictionaries do not favor this etymology, but Specht (1944:148) cited it with some confidence. **The main problem with deriving *bird* from *beran* is that the original form of the Old English noun seems to have been *brid,* not *bird.*** For this reason, Mayhew (1891c:450) called the idea of tracing *bird* to *beran* impossible. It must have been Mayhew's criticism that made Scott revert to the *bird ~ breed* etymology.

5. **Other, more or less fanciful, attempts to explain the origin of *bird* will be mentioned here for completeness' sake.** Somner (1659:325) derived *bird* from Gk πτερόν 'feather, wing'—not a

bad idea, considering that πτερόν is a gloss for *feather* and its cognates. Tooke (1798-1805 I:348) may have been the first to connect *bird* and *broad*. In his opinion, *bird* was the past participle of OE *brǣdan* 'make broad, extend, spread, stretch out' (he usually derived nouns from participles), and he derived *board* from that word. Richardson gave no references, but his etymology of *bird* must be from Tooke: "So called from the increased breadth when the wings are expanded." EG also cited G *breiten* 'spread,' along with E *breed* and *brood,* and added Sc *birky* 'lively young fellow,' 'old boy' (from Jamieson), about which see below. W. Barnes (1862:28) gave *bird* under one of his imaginary roots *br*ng*: a bird is "what rises or is borne up"; *breed* and *brood* are cited there too. Mackay (1877), true to his program (all words are from Gaelic), declared *bird* to be a derivative or "corruption" of Gaelic *brid eun* 'little bird,' from *brid* (obsolete) 'little.' Rather early in his career (for the first and last time), Holthausen (1909:147) compared *bird* and L *fritinnire* 'chirp.' He offered no other conjectures on the etymology of *bird* but advised Götze to dissociate *bird* from *brood* (Holthausen [1935:167]). Garcia de Diego (1968:186, 187) considered the onomatopoeic origin of *bird* possible. If the original meaning of *bird* is 'any young animal,' Holthausen's and Garcia de Diego's proposals can be ruled out. The comparison *brid* ~ *broad* needs no further refutation.

The most recent and utterly fanciful etymologies of *bird* have been Makovskii's ([1977:60], repeated verbatim in Makovskii [1980:64]): 1) In the seventies, he was developing the theory that many common English words arose as the result of mistakes made by medieval glossators. L *pullus,* he observed, was most often glossed as *bird, brid,* but *pullus* allegedly also meant 'board, plank.' The Old English for 'board' was *bred.* The glossator may have looked at *pullus : bred* and decided that *bred* refers to a flying animal. Hence *brid* 'bird' (in sum: since *pullus* means 'bird' and supposedly 'board,' OE *bred* came to mean 'bird'). This and many similar hypotheses met with Shchur's approval (1982:153). 2) In his later publications, Makovskii (1989a:137, 1993:137) defended the *bird* ~ *breed* ~ *brood* etymology. 3) According to his other guess (Makovskii [1998:166]), *bird* is related to *breath,* for birds were believed to be the receptacles of souls. He made no mention of the fact that *breath* and *breed* are usually traced to the same Proto-Indo-European root. 4) In Makovskii (1999b:80), *bird* is compared with Latv *burts* 'letter' because ancient writing was allegedly connected with 'the birds' script,' a sacral language of the inhabitants of heaven. 5) Makovskii (1999a:61-62) is a variation on the themes of PIE **bher-* 'move fast,' gestures of prohibition, the World Egg, and breeding.

6. The result of several centuries of speculation is that *bird* joined the list of words of unknown origin, as stated in ODEE, AeEW, and elsewhere. However, **the connection *bird* ~ *beran* can perhaps be rescued.** The argument that OE *bird* is a secondary formation, a metathesized variant of *brid(d),* is not absolutely watertight. We only know that *brid(d)* antedates *bird* in Old English texts. Metathesis in words like *irnan* < **rinnan* 'run' and *birnan* < **brinnan* 'burn' occurred early; compare *gærs* 'grass,' *forst* 'frost,' *fersc* 'fresh,' and so forth (SB, sec 179). *Birdas* ~ *briddas, ðirdda* ~ *ðridda* do not form a class of their own ('before *d*') despite what is always asserted, because two words hardly constitute a distributional group. In West Germanic roots of the *TRET* ~ *TERT* type, the date of metathesis is hard to ascertain. The interaction of *burd* 'maiden' and *bride* in Middle and Early Modern English is reminiscent of an older confusion. **Both the most ancient form and the most ancient meaning of *bird* appear to have emerged in texts relatively late.**

Bird 'young animal' looks like a variant of the noun *(-)byrd,* with *d* in *bridd, briddas,* and so on lengthened, as usually happens in hypocoristic forms, though the masculine gender of *brid(d)* and the delabialization of *y* are irregular (see SB, sec 31, note 2 on OE *i* < *y*); however, OE *byrd* had the variant *bird.*

Many words were formed from the root of the verb *beran.* Beside OE *(ge)byr-d* and *bear-n* (*ea* < **a* by Old English breaking), OE *byre* 'child, son, descendant, youth' existed. Krogmann's idea (1938c:191) that OHG and OS *-boro* and OE *-bora* mean 'born' rather than 'bearer' is convincing (for instance, OE *wǣgbora* 'wave-born,' not 'waveborne'; the editors of *Beowulf* neither accept nor deny this interpretation, but OHG *eliboro* 'foreigner' originally meant 'born elsewhere'). *Byre* had no suffix. Jamieson and, unenthusiastically, OED compared Sc *birky* 'child, fellow; self-assertive man' with OI *berkja* 'boast, bluster.' Two words seem to have merged here. *Birky* 'crusty, independent, self-assertive man' may perhaps have developed its meaning under the influence of *berkja,* but *birky* 'child, fellow' is *byr(e)* followed by the diminutive suffix *-k,* as in ModI *Jónki, Sveinki,* and the like. *Birky* thus means 'sonny.' Against the background of *(ge)byrd, bearn* (< **barn*), *byre,* and *birk,* the word *bird,* that is, *bir-d* looks natural;

cf OHG *berd** 'growth, descendant' (only in *Tatian*; OE *beorðor*) (Kluge [1926:sec 141]; EWA: the references in the entry give no information about what can be found in Kluge).

7. Definitive conclusions cannot be expected in such a case. ***Bird* as 'born one, (some)one born; young creature' is possible.** In choosing the most common word for 'bird,' languages typically deviate from or oust the 'protoform': cf Sp *pájaro* and Ital *uccello* alongside L *ave* and *avis*. With regard to ModE *bird*, the only alternative to a confession of ignorance ("origin unknown" = "will never be discovered") is an etymology based on several assumptions. **To obtain a satisfactory etymology of *bird*, we have to agree that neither the original form nor the original meaning of this word was preserved in the oldest texts**. Whether such a solution requires a price in excess of its value is clearly a matter of opinion (Liberman [2003:376-81]).

BOY (1260)

The original meanings of ME boi *were 'churl, servant' and 'devil' (rare). This is why* boi *was often used as a derogatory word. The meaning 'male child' does not occur before 1400. Apparently, ModE* boy *is a blend of an onomatopoeic word for an evil spirit (*boi) and a baby word for 'little brother' (*bo). The latter may be extant in the proper name* Boia *(OE). Both words have numerous counterparts in and outside English and Germanic. They are not related to* boy *but belong to the same onomatopoeic and sound symbolic sphere. Hence the similarity between* boy *and words for 'child' in the languages of the world. A French etymon has been suggested for* boy; *however, the adduced evidence is either incorrect or inconclusive.*

The sections are devoted to 1) the proposed etymologies of boy, *2) the relations between* boy *and the proper name* Boi(a), *3)* boy *and words for '(little) brother,' 4)* boy *and words for 'frightening object; ghost; devil'; E* boy *and G* Bube, *5)* boy *in its Eurasian context; E* at(t)aboy *and* oh, boy; boy *as the result of a merger of two meanings ('brother' and 'devil'), and 6) the possibility that* boy *is a word of French origin.*

1. The etymology of *boy* has been the object of much speculation. In the literature on this word, the best-known work is Dobson (1940), but it seems that we are closer to the truth thanks to Dietz (1981a:361-405) and Roelandts (1984). More tangential but also important are Laistner (1888) and Mandel (1975). Three partly overlapping theories on the origin of *boy* have been offered.

1) ***Boy* is a baby word**. All over the world, we find similar words beginning with *b* and *p* and meaning 'child'; *boy* is allegedly one of them. Consider the list of look-alikes from W (1828; Greek words are given there without accents): "BOY, n. Pers. *bach*, a boy; W. *baçgen*, from *baç*, little; Arm. *buguel*, a child, *bugale*, boyish; Sw. *poike*, a young boy; Dan. *pog*, Fr[ench] *page*. See *Beagle* and *Pug*. *Boy* is a contracted word, and probably the L. *puer* for *puger*, for we see by *puella*, that *r* is not radical. So the Gk παις probably is contracted, for the derivative verb, παιζω, forms παιξω, παιχθεις. The radical letters probably are Bg or Pg."

A few of the words cited by Webster occur in the earliest etymological dictionaries of English, for example, in Minsheu and Skinner, and most of them can be found in books published two centuries later. Kilianus compared Du *boef* 'knave, rogue' and *boy*. Junius derived *boy* directly from the vocative of Gk παίς 'boy, servant' (παί = *boy*), while Skinner thought of βαιός 'small, insignificant.' The idea that G *Bube* comes from L *pūpus* enjoyed such popularity (see Pott [1833:193] and Wackernagel [1874b:287], first published in 1861) that as late as 1892 Franck (EWNT, *boef*) had to refute it. A list nearly a page long (examples, like those in Webster, from five continents) appears in Gottlund (1853:61), and a list from the Paleo-Siberian languages in Daa (1856:270). See also Thomsen (1869:273 = 1920:92). In the revised 1864 edition of Webster's dictionary, the original list is corrected and rearranged but, in principle, remains the same: "BOY, n. Prov. Ger. *bua*, *bue*, M. H. Ger. *buobe*, N. H. Ger. *bube*, M. D. *boeve*, N. D. *boef*. Cf. Lat. *pupus*, boy, child, and L. Ger. *pook*, Dan. *pog*, Sw. *pojke*, a young boy, Arm. *bugel*, *bugul*, child, boy, girl, Ir. & Gael. *beag*, little, W. *back*, id., Per. *batch*, child, boy, servant; A-S. & Dan. *pige*, Sw. *piga*, Icel. *pika*, a little girl." Although trimmed, the first part of the 1864 list can be found in numerous modern dictionaries. Sometimes *Bube*, *boef*, and so on are cited as cognates of *boy*, sometimes we are expected to "compare" these forms with the English word. The entry in Klein's CEDEL is characteristic: "BOY, n—ME. *boi*, rel. to the OE. PN. *Bōfa*, OFris, *boy*, 'a young gentleman', MDu. *boeve*, Du. *boef*, 'knave, villain', the OHG. PN. *Buobo*, MHG. *buobe*, G. *Bube*, 'boy', and in vowel gradational relationship to E. *babe*, *baby* (qq.v)."

Kluge related *babe* and *baby* to G *Bube* by ablaut. In EWDS[1-3], he called *boy* a borrowing from Dutch (*boy* < *boef*), but in the fourth edition he said more cautiously that it reminds one of *boef*. Götze (11th ed) listed *boy* "alongside" *Buobo*. Only Mitzka (16th ed) expunged reference to ablaut. E. Klein (CEDEL) may have reasoned that if *babe* is allied by ablaut to *Bube* and if *Bube* is a cognate of *boy*, the vowels in *boy* and *Bube* must be related. C. Ball

(1970:69) was surprised to find no mention of Dobson in E. Klein's dictionary. But Klein apparently did not read Dobson, for otherwise he would have known how inadequate the gloss 'young gentleman' given in OED for Ten Doornkaat Koolman's EFr (that is, LG) *Junge, Knabe* is (Dobson [1943:71], with reference to William Craigie).

In Fick[3] (214-15), E *boy* and G *Bube* are said to be related to G *beben* 'tremble, shake'; supposedly, *Bube* originally meant 'coward.' This bizarre etymology has never been repeated. It is the opinion of many that *Bube* is a reduplication of *boy* or of some form like *boy*. Thus Markey (1980:178): "MHG *buobe,* probably a reduplicated hypocoristic, cf *mama...* while *boy* is... employed as both an appellative and a personal name. Its further etymology is... obscure." However, he soon changed his opinion and related *buobe* to *boy* "by virtue of what appears to be an important and typically Ingwaeonic samprasārana," that is, by the rule of vocalization: *b* > *f*/*v* > *y* > zero (Markey [1983:104-5]).

According to another etymology of *boy*, the names of the young "are inseparably involved with the terms, denoting the lumpy, swelling out form, when considered either as in a little, small state, or as of larger dimensions, by whatever process it may have arisen, that their union has been effected" (Whiter [1825:171]). Likewise, Wedgwood[1] (an abridged version of the same appears in the later editions) believed that G *Bube* (which he compared with SwiG *bub* ~ *bue* and Swabian *buah,* "showing the passage of the pronunciation to E. *boy*"), is related to "Lat. *pupus,* a boy, *pupa,* a girl, a doll, which last is probably the earlier meaning. The origin seems the root *bob, bub, pop, pup,* in the sense of something protuberant, stumpy, thick and short, a small lump." He cited Russ *pup* 'navel,' Bavarian *Butzen* 'bud,' and so forth. Hilmer (1918:52) gives the same examples.

Whiter, Webster, and Wedgwood promoted the idea that words for 'boy, child' depend on the notion of universal baby talk. Richardson, at *boy,* says: "...the natural voice of children, asking for drink". Later, etymologists eliminated most of the spurious cognates. Even the connection *boy* ~ *Bube* ~ *boef* needs proof despite references to reduplication and samprasārana, but it is undeniable that in numerous languages, a similar sound complex is used to denote a male child. From the most ancient languages, Hurrian *purame* 'slave; servant' and Urartian *b*/*pura* 'slave' can be added (Ivanov [1999b:161]). The baby talk theory depends on the phenomenon that bilabial sounds appear early in language acquisition and for that reason complexes like *mama, baba, papa* are used widely for naming children and those who look after them. Yet each word—*boy, Bube, puer, pojke,* and the rest—has its own history that must be traced in detail.

2) ***Boy* is allegedly the same word as the Old English proper name *Boi(a),* which has a cognate in East Frisian, so that *boy* turns out to be of Low German origin.** This theory, forcibly put forward in Skeat[1] (less so in Skeat[4]), was expected to explain why the common name *boy* emerged so late (its first occurrence goes back to 1260; see Dobson [1940:126]) and offer a persuasive etymology of the Low German word. The family name *Boy(e)* is still common in North Frisian (Århammar [2001:349]; Timmermann [2001:386, 393]). A modified version of this theory sets up OE **boia.* It faces the same questions.

3) *Boy* is traced to an Anglo-French word with a Romance etymon, namely Late L *boia* 'fetter.' If this is so, the entire corpus of facts connected with baby talk and OE *Boia* has to be explained away.

4) Makovskii (1999a:70; 2000a:141) compares E *boy* with PIE **bhā-* 'burn,' for male firstborns were often sacrificed and burned on sacrificial pyres, and with OE *bōian* 'speak' and *ă-boian* 'keep silent' (this form does not appear in dictionaries, while *bōian* means 'boast' not 'speak') and comes to the result that *boy* (an aphetic form of **āboi?*) mirrors L *infans* 'unable to speak' (< *in* + the past participle of *fārī* 'to speak'). These etymologies need not be discussed here.

2. **The central issue in the etymology of *boy* is the relationship between ME *boi* and OE *Boi(a).*** *Boi(a)* violates Old English phonotactics, for Old English did not have the diphthong *oi* (the three examples in Dietz [1981] are also from Middle English), and in a native form one expects umlauted *o* before *i* (Dobson [1940:148]); the same holds for Old Frisian. But although *oi* looks like a foreign body in any ancient Germanic language, it was not unpronounceable in Old English, as seen from the weak verbs of the second class *bōian** (= *bōgan*) 'boast,' *gōian** 'lament, groan,' and *scōian** (= *scōgan*) 'put on a shoe' (SB, sec 415a; see the preserved forms in A. Campbell [1959:sec 761.7] and discussion in Dietz [1981a:392-93]). *Goian** has a reliable etymology (Jordan [1906:27-29]), *scōian** was derived from *scō(h)** 'shoe,' and *bōian* is, most likely, onomatopoeic: see sec 5, below. All of them had *ō* in Old English, with the syllable and morpheme boundary between *ō* and *i*. This seems to be the reason *Boia* is also supposed to have had *ō* (Kluge [1901b:944, 1050]; AeEW; HL, 376). How-

ever, J. Zupitza preferred to reconstruct a short diphthong in *Boia* (reported in O. Ritter [1910:473]), and Ritter agreed with him. If *oi* were short and monophonemic, the absence of umlaut would probably need no explanation. But the fact remains that *oi,* mono- or biphonemic, does not occur in any native Old English word, and the same is true of Middle English (Jordan[3] [1968:sec 131, note]). However, expressive words sometimes have marginal phonemes, a circumstance usually disregarded in dealing with the early history of *boy.*

The existence of *oi* is less obvious even in Middle Dutch than is sometimes believed. See the discussion of the element *Boid-* in place names (Mansion [1928:93]), the nickname *Boidin* (Tavernier-Vereecken [1968:198]), and *Boeye* (Haeserijn [1954:133]). (Similar difficulties occur in modern languages. E *ruin, Bruin,* and *Ewen* can be pronounced with [ui]. *Fuel* and *gruel* have the variants [fjuil] and [gruil]. Yet no phonological description of English recognizes the diphthong /ui/.)

NS (130-31) gave some attention to the distribution of the proper name *Boi(a);* Dobson (1940:148-49), Tengvik (1938:238-39), von Feilitzen and Blunt (1971:189-91), and Dietz (1981a:279-82, 361-405) investigated it in detail. Many men were at one time called *Boi* (a strong form) or *Boia* (a weak form). Whether all of them were immigrants from northern Franconia, as Dobson believed, or whether some of them were native-born but had a (partly?) domesticated foreign name cannot be decided. **Nor can the existence of the common Old English noun **boi(a),* with whatever meaning, be taken for granted. However, its reality will become more probable if we assume that **Boi(a)* was at one time a nickname.** The vast and varied vocabulary of Old Icelandic shows that numerous nicknames have not come down to us in any other capacity: they must have been too vulgar, conversational, or evanescent for occurring even in the sagas, and from Old English we have no texts resembling the saga literature of medieval Iceland. The meaning of a large number of Icelandic nicknames remains unclear today. The same holds for some names of mythological and legendary beings. Sublime or low, they were once semantically transparent and widespread. Yet they existed at the edges of Old Scandinavian vocabulary and disappeared the way much of modern slang does. Dietz (1981a) confines his discussion of nicknames to a few remarks on pp. 378 and 390.

Conflicting views are held on the origin of the English family name *Boys.* Some language historians think that it comes from F *bois* 'wood' and compare *De Bosco, Dubosc, De Bois, Bois, Boice,* and the like, so that *Boys* acquires the status of an etymological doublet of *Wood* (Charnock [1868]; Lower [1875]; Bardsley [1884:154]; Ewen [1931:204, 306], though on p. 204 *Boys* appears among Dutchmen in Essex; McKinley [1990:80]), while Reaney (1976) explains *Boys,* and the rest as *boy's.* Matthews (1966) seems to imply that all family names like *Boys* and *Bois* go back to *boy.* H. Harrison glosses *Boy(e)s* as 'dweller at a wood' and thus supports the French derivation of that name. The name *Boycott* was first recorded in 1256 (Reaney [1976]) and means 'woodhouse'.

The oldest place name containing the element *Boi* is *Boiwici.* It is dated to 785 (Dobson [1940:149]; von Feilitzen and Blunt [1971:190]; Dietz [1981a:375, 376, 378]), which means that either the name or the word *boi* had some currency in England before 1066. The early Middle English charter mentioning *Boiwic* is a fake (King Offa did not deliver such a charter), but regardless of the false ascription, it is based on reliable facts.

3. **Kluge EWDS[6] traced G *Bube,* Du *boef,* and E *boy* to some ancient word for 'brother.'** His idea became known to English etymologists from KL: "BOY ME. *boie* OE **bóïa,* perh. dimin. of a lost OE **bǫ́* 'brother' = Flem. *boe* 'brother': childish abbreviation of E *brother,* as G *bube.* OHG *buobo* is a reduplication of **bô* 'brother'?" Reference to *boy* later disappeared from the entry *Bube* in EWDS, but the idea that *Bube* and *boef* go back to a word for 'brother' has stayed. E. Zupitza (1900:237) and Vercoullie (1920:790-91) supported it; see a summary of Vercoullie's talk on pp. 779-80 of the same volume; p. 780 on *boy.* Later it made its way into IEW (164). Only J. de Vries (AEW, *Bófi;* NEW, *boef*) calls it "improbable" and "highly improbable," but his opinion is unfounded, as Roelandts (1984) made clear (first indicated in Roelandts [1966:271, 279]; cited in von Feilitzen and Blunt [1971:190-91]). Roelandts (1984) listed numerous Germanic names beginning with *Boi-* ~ *Boy-* and compared them with Dutch and Frisian words for 'little brother' and by implication, 'fellow.' He showed that ***Boio, Poio, Boiadus, Boiga, Boigea, Boga, Boye,* and even Scandinavian *Bo* may once have meant 'little brother'** rather than 'dweller' (from OE *būan,* OI *búa* 'live') or 'crooked' (from OE *būgan,* OI *bjúgr* 'bent'). (See the most important comparative material on such names in Schönfeld's dictionary [*Boio*] and in Much [1895:31-35].) Forms like *Boio* have probably always been slangy. See the etymological part of the entry *bully* in OED:

here again we find attempts to connect the designation of an adult man and a brother. *Boy* and *Boi(a)* can be the same word with the ancient meaning '(little) brother,' **but the problem is that *boy* 'little brother' has not been recorded in English texts or living speech and that even the meaning 'male child' is not original in it.**

4. Dobson (1940:126-47) distinguished the following meanings of *boy* in Middle English: 1) 'servant' or applied to persons engaged in some clearly indicated service of a humble sort, 2) applied without any specifically contemptuous intention to persons of the lower orders of society, often in clear or implied contrast to gentlefolk, 3) used more vaguely as a term of contempt or abuse, 4) various transitional uses, 5) the modern sense of 'male child.' **He concluded that the ordinary Middle English meaning of *boy* was 'churl,'** which should gloss all the examples under headings 1-3, except those for which 'servant' is required. *Boy* "never means 'male child' before 1400. The transitional and modern meanings are not substantiated until the 15th century" (p. 145). ODEE accepts Dobson's chronology of meanings (which is different from that in OED) without comment (see W. P. Lehmann [1966-67:625] on Onions's dogmatic style, with regard to *boy*). Makovskii (1977:69) gave the late Old English gloss *boi : diaconus,* but this is a mistake. He must have miscopied O. Ritter's reference (1910:472) to Iago (1903). The relevant place reads *boia diaconus* and means that one of the witnesses was a "diaconus" called *Boia.* **Mandel (1975) cited several cases of *boy* 'devil' in Chaucer.** His findings are correct, but they passed unnoticed. **The meaning ('devil'), which goes beyond "contempt or abuse," has parallels in continental West Germanic and in Scandinavian languages.** Here Du *boef* and G *Bube,* even though they are not cognates of *boy,* should again be mentioned.

Du *boef* means only 'scoundrel; criminal'; MDu *boeve* also meant 'servant.' Norn *bofi* is used in curses, in which it can be understood as 'devil' (EONSS). The recorded history of G *Bube* (see E. Müller [1968]) almost mirrors that of E *boy.* Like *boy, Bube,* a Southern German word, first appears as a personal name (OHG *Buobo*). In its Latinized form (*Bobo*) it was recorded as early as the 7th century: Zimmermann (1961:520-21); MHG *buobe* means 'young fellow' and 'libertine, gambler.' The meaning 'male child' does not appear until the 16th century. *Bub* is extant as a gross insult in some German dialects, and just as E *boy* 'servant, hired man' has survived in non-British usage (see the history of Indian *boy* in Vermeer [1971]) and in the compounds *bellboy, cowboy,* and *potboy,* the low status of *Bube* is obvious in the card name *Bube* 'jack, knave' and in the compounds *Lausbube, Spitzbube* 'villain, rogue,' and *Bubenstück, Bubenstreich* (= *Büberei*) 'knavish, villainous act.'

With the extinction of chivalry, knights' servants degenerated into urban riffraff (gamblers, beggars, thieves, pimps) or day laborers. The distance from a *cnafa* (the Old English for 'boy, youth; servant') to a knave has always been short, and the story of *ribald* shows how many turns one can expect on this road: from 'prostitute' (OHG *hrîba*) to 'retainer of low class' (OF *ribaut* ~ ME *ribald*) and further to 'rascal'; E. Müller suggests that *Bube* 'boy' is an innovation with its roots in casual every day speech but admits that *buobe* always meant 'male child.' If so, 'boy; servant' later developed into 'scoundrel.' We are faced with the same puzzling situation as in English: a derogatory meaning ('scoundrel; devil') coexists and seems to have coexisted for centuries with an affectionate one ('boy').

The striking parallelism in the recorded history of *boy* and *Bube* poses several questions. From 'little brother' one can perhaps get to 'a person of low status,' 'servant,' and 'knave' (in *varlet* from *valet* we have part of the same semantic development), but hardly to 'criminal' and especially to 'devil.' Nor is the path from 'devil' to 'little brother' probable. At most, one can expect the development 'devil' > 'imp' > 'little rascal; romp, scamp,' as in G *Nickel.* It is also odd that the meanings 'ruffian' and 'male child' did not get into each other's way, for even if the second meaning emerged later, the time interval was not long (in English, about a century and a half). **Two different sets of words seem to have coexisted in (West) Germanic: one denoted little boys and the other devils and rogues.**

5. **All over Eurasia, the combination of *b* with a back vowel is used to frighten people, especially children. For many words designating a male child one can find homonyms or near homonyms designating devils, ghosts, and the like.** Open syllables and the *bug-* ~ *bog-* group predominate in this sphere. In English, we have *bo* and *boo,* as in *say bo* (or *boh, boo*) *to a goose* (in Scotland, *to your blanket,* and several other variants; DOST) and in the verb *boo* 'hoot.' *Bo* was first recorded in 1430. Although the earliest version of "Little Bo-peep" goes back to 1810, a game (or an amusement) called *bo-peep* was known as early as 1364. *Bo-peep,* a counterpart of *peek-a-boo,* is the

simplest variant of hide-and-(go)-seek: a nurse would conceal the head of the infant and then remove the covering quickly, crying: "Bo-peep!" (AMG, 96, note 87).

Phonetically close to E *boo* is Du *bui* 'gust, squall,' the etymon of LG *Böj(e)* ~ *Büj(e)* and G *Bö*. Russ *boiat'sia* 'be afraid' (the root is *boi-*, stress falls on the syllable *-at-*) has cognates in Baltic and Indo-Iranian (ESSI II:163-64). The similarity between Du *bui* and Russ *bui-* 'violent, bold' was noticed long ago (Van Wijk [1909:30-31]). OE *bōian** 'boast' (see it in sec 2, above) is more probably a formation like *boo* than a cognate of L *fāri* 'speak' (suggested by Holthausen [1918b:238] and taken up by WP I:123-24). The heroic meaning of boasting was 'assert arrogantly one's superiority (before a battle).' Laistner (1888:153, 156) put together a list of *bo(o)-* words from the *Schweizerisches Idiotikon: bauwi, baui, boi, boy, böögk, bögk,* and *bök*. He also thought of E *boy* as traceable to *bo + g and of the name *Bēowulf* as containing this root (see also Kögel [1892:56] and [1893:272-73; however, Kögel believed that the root of Beowulf's name meant 'grain, cereals'] and Schönfeld [*Boio*] on *Bēow-*). Widdowson (1971) investigated the same material. German dialectal dictionaries contain many words like *boboks, boboz, Bögge, Bok,* and *Bokes(mann)* for 'scarecrow; object of dread; term of abuse.' Laistner was aware of the English words *bug* 'demon' and *bogle*. One can add *booman, boggard, buga-boo, boggle, bog(e)y, bog(e)yman, boodyman,* and so forth. Words with initial *p-* exist too; E *Puck*, mentioned at BEACON, and possibly *spook* are among them.

Almost the identical words have been recorded in Sanskrit, Greek, Latin, Slavic, and Celtic. It is not easy to decide whether each noun is a product of parallel formation or a borrowing, because the concept of borrowing becomes hazy when one deals with migratory words. G *Butz(emann)* 'bogeyman' is apparently native (see especially Webinger [1937a]), and so may be E *Puck*, but G *Popanz* 'bogeyman' seems to be a borrowing from some Slavic language. Russian has *buka* 'bogeyman' and its semantically depleted variant *biaka* 'bad or dirty thing.' Slavic etymological dictionaries tend to explain both as extended forms of *bu-* and *bia-* (though *-ka* has no lexical meaning) and never mention their counterparts elsewhere, for instance, E *Puck*, though Wedgwood already saw the connection. Russ *buka* was first recorded in the 18th century, but its occurrence as a nickname (*Mikhailo Buka*) goes back to 1377 (ESRI), a situation familiar from the history of *Boia, Bófi,* and *Buobo* versus *boy, boef,* and *Bube;* compare the history of RAGAMUFFIN.

For each of the aforementioned words a more or less plausible etymology has been offered. Princi Braccini (1984:149-57) follows FT (*Bus(s)emand*) and treats G *Butz(emann)* and many other *b-t* words as related to OHG *bôzan*, OE *bēatan*, OI *bauta* 'beat' (a solution accepted half-heartedly in KS), while Alexander Jóhannesson (IsEW) referred *Bófi* to onomatopoeic words like E *babble*, G *babblen*, and Gk βαβάζω, and in the demonic sphere, Berneker (36) offered the same etymology for Polish *zabobon* 'superstition' and its Slavic cognates. *Puck, spook, bug, bogey, boodyman, Butzemann, buka, biaka,* and the rest seem to be onomatopoeic baby words, and one etymology will probably be valid for all of them.

Both *bo-* series ('little brother' and 'evil spirit') are onomatopoeic or sound symbolic, and both originated in baby talk. The same is true of some extended forms like *Bube*. The two sets must have interacted for a long time. In some cultures, they stayed apart, in others they merged. **G *Bube* 'boy' and G *Bube* 'scoundrel'** (from which we have *Boofke*, a synonym for the 'ugly German': Stave [1965:134-36], Kaestner [1970:10]) **are, historically speaking, two different words even if the form of the one influenced that of the other and if at a certain stage *Bube* 'boy' was understood as a euphemism for *Bube* 'scoundrel, ?devil, ?imp.' The same is true of E *boy* and ME *boi* 'devil,' but in English, *boy* 'devil' did not continue into the postmedieval period, unless the exclamations *oh, boy!* and *at(t)aboy* are the last traces of the extinct word (see below).**

In any version of the history of *boy*, one has to account for either the amelioration of meaning (whether one starts with 'churl' or with 'devil') or an unbelievable zigzag (from 'little brother' to 'churl, devil' and back to 'boy'). **It is not improbable that 'object of dread, devil' gradually developed into 'scoundrel,' whereas its homonym 'little brother' acquired the meaning 'servant, person of low status.' At this stage, the two senses reached the points equidistant from 'churl,' though with opposite signs. 'Churl' and 'servant' coexisted for some time, then 'servant' won out and went a step higher to designate 'male child,' though words like *bellboy* and perhaps colonial *boy* have retained the meaning prevalent in the 14th and 15th centuries.**

As far as the exclamation *at(t)aboy* and *oh, boy!* are concerned, some facts from Early Modern Dutch seem to point to their original status as (mild?) curses. At the end of the 15th century, youngsters in the streets of Amsterdam used to throw stones at one another and shout: "Boye, boye, egellentier" (B. Van den Berg [1938]). *Egellentier* has been identified by all contributors to the discussion as *egel* 'hedgehog' (anonymous [1939: contains statements by Schönfeld and Th. H. d'Angremond] and Muller [1938-39:183-84]; *-tier* means 'animal'), but *boye* remained partly unexplained. We are dealing, it turns out, with two "generic" gangs. Apparently, one was called The Devils (or The Daredevils) and the other The Hedgehogs (bold, fierce, and prickly). The rock-throwing youths encouraged their comrades by shouting their gang's name. The examples from VV that Van den Berg quotes (*het heeft mi boy* 'I've had enough, I am sick and tired of it' and *hem boy maken* 'get angry') make sense if *boy* means 'devil.' Perhaps E *boy* 'devil' found its last resort in hunters' language in which it acquired the meaning 'hunted animal.' Can *at(t)aboy* go back to *à tout a boy!*, considering that *à tout,* a call to incite dogs, was well known? (See Russ *atu* in Vasmer I:96.) Other calls to the dogs are *hoicks a boy!* and *yoicks a Bewmont!* In any case, "the male-intimate affectionate sense" (Pinkerton [1982:40]) was hardly the original one in the imprecation *at(t)aboy* and *oh, boy.*

Dietz (1981a) endorses O. Ritter's hypothesis that E *boy* is a modern reflex of OE *Boi(a)* (the same in AeEW) and implies that the origin of *Boi(a)* is either beyond reconstruction or of no interest. He points out that *Boi(a)* was probably a native name, while the existence of **boia* cannot be proved. However, **without the common name *boia* the proper name (rather the nickname) *Boia* would hardly have arisen.** Whether OE **boia* meant 'brother,' 'devil,' or both will remain unknown. The two words may have been homonyms in the 8th century, as they were in the 14th, or **boia* may have meant 'brother' and **boi* may have been the word for an evil spirit. A popular name meaning 'buddy' is easier to imagine than a name meaning 'devil,' but consider such German surnames as *Teufel* and *Waldteufel* (with their phonetic variants).

Sw *pojke* 'boy' is probably related to E *boy* as E *boy* is related to *bogey.* It is far from obvious that *pojke* was borrowed from Finnish (*poika* 'boy, son'), as stated in SEO. Nor does Rocchi's 1989 article settle the argument (he believes that both OI *píka* 'girl' and Sw *pojke* reached Scandinavia from Finland). Thomsen (1869:40 = 1920:92) equated Sw *pojke,* Dan *pog,* and hesitatingly E *boy* with Finn *poika* but did not elaborate on their relations. Ahlqvist (1875:210) derived *-ka* in *poika* from Swedish, but *-ke* is also the most common diminutive suffix in Frisian and Low German. Consider Fr *boike, poaike,* and *poalke* (Brouwer [1964]) and the enigmatic *-ka* in Russ *buka* ~ *biaka.* Estonian *poeg,* Livian *puoga,* and their cognates, all meaning 'boy' (see especially Sauvageot 1930:28/34), testify to the stability of the velar in Finno-Ugric, thereby contradicting Ahlqvist's suggestion. SKES lists two pages of cognates but offers no etymology of *poika* and only notes that some Lapp words for 'boy' may have been borrowed from Scandinavian. On one hand, we are confronted by self-sufficient word clusters in every language group; on the other, *boi* ~ *poi-* 'male child' is a widespread Eurasian word. This is why it is so difficult to say anything definite about *-ke* in *pojke* and *-ka* in *poika.* The best work on the diminutive *-k* suffix is D. Hofmann (1961), but it contains no discussion of related forms or of *-k* outside Germanic.

6. **With such a solid Germanic background for E *boy,* strong arguments are needed to show that *boy* is an Anglo-French loanword.** An opinion to this effect exists, however. The first to suggest the Romance origin of *boy* was Holthausen (1900:365, 1903b:35). He remarked that words for 'child' often go back to the names of inanimate objects and offered the hypothesis that *boy* 'male child; servant' is the same word as ME *boie* 'executioner, hangman' and ModE *buoy.* Dobson (1940:150-51) suggested that every time an executioner is called *boi* in Middle English texts, reference is to a churl performing a hateful job (see also the end of the entry BEACON). However, the parallelism with the Romance words for 'hangman,' Walloon *boie,* OSp *boya,* and Ital *boja,* is astounding (more is said about devils, hangmen, and boys in connection with RAGAMUFFIN). The solution of this problem is of no consequence here. Of importance is only Holthausen's suggestion that L *boia* 'fetter; collar worn by slaves and criminals' is the same word as E *boy.* To reinforce his argument, Holthausen cites LG *kniəvəl* (cognate with G *Knebel*) 'handle' and 'ill-mannered person' and Sw *knävel* 'devil; hangman.' That 'hangman' and 'devil' complement each other in people's minds and that a lout can be called a piece of wood ('door handle') is understandable, but why should 'male child' come from 'fetter' and 'hangman'?

Dobson, who, judging by his references, was unaware of Holthausen's idea, discovered the same late Latin word (*boia*) and offered his own etymology of *boy.* His main argument was that ME *boy* had been recorded with the pronunciations [oi], [uoi], [we:], and [ui] and spelled *boige, boye, bwey, bway, bye, bey,* and *bai.* In his opinion, "[v]ariants comparable to these occur only in words adopted from French which in Anglo-Norman and standard Old French should normally have *ui*" (Dobson [1940:124]). He assumed a formation **un embuié* 'man in fetters,' from the verb *embiier* (whence 'slave, serf'), "which with Anglo-French aphesis of the *em-* would give the form **un buié*'" (pp. 124-25).

Dobson examined the distribution of the name *Boia* (his corpus was much smaller than Dietz's) and summarized his findings as follows: "If then we are to explain *boy* from *Boia,* we must assume that a foreign personal name came to be used as a common noun, or that a foreign common noun was introduced in addition to the personal name. Neither alternative is at all likely" (p. 149). Dobson's article was received with great enthusiasm. SOD[3] (with some hedging), OD, and ODEE repeat his etymology, and so does KD. But the entry in COD reflects the sorry plight in which etymologists working for great dictionaries find themselves. 5th ed: "...the origin of [ME *boi, boy*], subject of involved conjectures, remains unascertained"; 6th ed: reproduces Dobson's etymology; 8th and 9th eds: perhaps ultimately from L *boia* 'fetter.' Finally, in the 10th edition, *boy* is said to be a word of unknown etymology. The same state of uncertainty characterizes popular books on etymology. Ciardi (1980) copies from Dobson, while Pinkerton (1982:48-49) cites two possibilities—from OF *embuié* or from a word for 'brother.'

Critical voices were not wanting. William Craigie pointed out (in a letter to Dobson) that insufficient attention had been paid to the Frisian evidence (Dobson [1943:71]). Dobson devoted a special article (1943) to that problem and concluded that MDu *boye,* wherever it occurred, was a phonetic variant of *bode* 'messenger,' which could not be the etymon of ME *boi.* He followed VV (*bode*), but *boye* and *bode,* though close synonyms ('servant,' 'messenger'), seem to be different words. Leendertz (1918:270) observes that the regional form *booi,* the modern reflex of *boye,* is always pronounced with an open *o,* while *booien* = *boden* has closed *o.* However, Dobson's main argument concerned the development of OF *oi* in Anglo-French. In this area, his first critic was Bliss (1951-52:23-27). He had no quarrel with Dobson's results but found many mistakes in his exposition and offered improvements. "Dr. Dobson," says Bliss (1951-52:22, note 12), "asks me to say that he has long been conscious of errors in his article." A slightly revised version of Dobson's derivation of *boy* appears in Dobson (1957:817, sec 256, note 1).

Diensberg (1978 and 1981) subjected the reconstruction by Dobson and Bliss to devastating criticism. He showed that the phonetic base of their etymology is untenable and noted the obvious thing that *oi* of any origin could be expected to have the same development in Middle English. (See also Luick [1964:sec 544, note 3 and sec 803.3, note 1], who considered *w* in forms like *bwey* as intrusive after *b.*) In addition, Diensberg pointed out that OF *embuiier* 'fetter' (v) was all but unknown in Middle English: only OF *büie* ~ *boie* 'fetter' has been attested: a hapax legomenon in Barbour's *Bruce* (Diensberg [1978:346-47; 1981:80]). Yet he believes in the French origin of *boy,* which he traces to OF *boesse* ~ *baiesse* 'woman servant'; see also Diensberg [1985a:331]. Dietz (1981a:400-02) adds a few more phonetic arguments against Dobson's theory and calls into question the development 'chained' > 'man in fetters' > 'slave' > 'serf.' Nor is he supportive of Diensberg's bridge from 'female servant' to 'male servant.' Diensberg's latest conclusion (1994:213) is: "Recent and early attempts at providing a Dutch, Low German, or even a Frisian etymon for *boy*... failed to solve the problems connected with the Middle English phonological variants of *boy.*" Even if one accepts it, the French etymologies of *boy* do not become more attractive.

7. ***Boy* remains 'a word of uncertain etymology.' Yet unless some version of the French hypothesis again wins the day, it makes sense to recognize *boy* as an early semantic blend of **boi(a)* '(little) brother' and **bo* 'evil spirit' on Germanic soil.** The concept of ablaut is vacuous in dealing with such a word, so that *babe* and *baby* are better kept out of the present discussion. *Bube* and *boef* are not akin to *boy,* for *boy* has no cognates more or less by definition, but they belong to the same stock, and their development should be taken into account in the reconstruction of the English word (Liberman [2001a:201-13]).

A Note on the Eurasian Background of the Old English Name *Boi* ~ *Boia*

Many names sound like *Boi(a).* One of them is Ostrogothic *Boio.* Schönfeld shares the common opinion that *Boio* is a contracted form corresponding to OE *Bēawa* and OS *Bôio.* His reconstruction is acceptable but not necessary. A name like *Boio,* a baby word, could arise in many places independently and lack cognates in the sense in which *Zeus* or *father* have them. In citing *Bojo,* Schönfeld refers to Förstemann, but Förstemann (1900:324-25) lists

Boia, Baia, Beia, Beio, Peio, Beya, and so on, including some names that end in a velar (*Beic* and *Boiko*), exactly as they have been recorded: vowel length (*ô*) is the product of Schönfeld's view of the name's origin. OS *Bēowa* is not a perfect fit for **Bauja* because the expected form is OE **Bēawa*. Old English had *bēow* 'barley' and *bēaw* 'gadfly.' *Bēaw* is akin to LG *bau* and L *fūcus* 'drone' (WP II:164; AeEW). The etymology of *bēow* is less clear. AEW traces OI *bygg* 'barley' to **bewwu*. The history of the mythological name *Bēaw,* which, for some reason, alternates with *Bēo(w),* is lost (see the details in Klaeber [1950:xxiv-xxviii]). This name could have been understood as meaning 'barley,' whereupon it aligned itself with *Scēaf* 'sheaf' and thus formed the 'nature mythological' genealogy of the Danish kings that has been preserved in the opening section of *Beowulf. Bēowulf,* contrary to what is usually believed, is probably an expansion of *Bēow(a).*

The Celtic proper name *Boio* has also been recorded. In its Latinized form it is extant in the place name *Bavaria* (G *Bayern*). Schönfeld says that Celtic *Boio* is *undoubtedly* different from Gmc *Boio.* Here he refers to Holder, but this reference, like his previous one, is misleading. At the beginning of the entry, Holder (1896: 463-71) quotes his predecessors who think that *og* in L *Bogii* does not represent the diphthong [oi] and that *Boio* is related precisely to the Slavic and other words usually given in connection with Russ *boi-* in *boiat'sia* 'be afraid.' This opinion (which Holder seems to share), far from separating the Celtic and the Germanic names, connects them.

Words (roots) like E *boy, bug, Puck* ~ Russ *boi-, buka, pug-* and names like *Boia* ~ *Boiko* are spread over the same areas. Among Slavic proper names, ORuss *Boian* is of special interest, because its bearer is mentioned several times in the poem *The Lay of Igor's Host* as a singer who followed a different manner of composition from that adopted in the *Lay.* The prevalent trend in the discussion of *Boian* is that its meaning reflects the man's profession or character. If *Boian* was the singer's given name (*Bojan* is still current among the southern Slavic people), it cannot shed light on his later occupation or temperament, for the boy's parents had no way of knowing what would become of him. If, however, *Boian* is a nickname, it can mean 'singer' or 'narrator' (Russ *baiat'* means 'narrate'). At present, most students of *The Lay of Igor's Host* believe that the name *Boian* in it is of Eastern origin (see Miklosich's glossary, Korsch [1886:487-88], Melioranskii [1902:282-83], Menges [1951:16-18], and Baskakov [1985:143-46]), but disagreement remains over its place of origin and meaning: 'warlock,' 'rich man,' or 'singer.' Only Vasmer I:203 traces *Boian* to the noun *boi* 'battle,' but he adduces no proof that his conjecture is better than any other.

The history of proper names of the *Boi(o)* type is similar to that of the common names homonymous with them. Their original meaning was 'make a noise, frighten,' and a brave man could bear it with satisfaction. In different languages they evoked different associations: in some places with barley, in others with battles and impetuosity (which is what their etymology must have suggested in the first place, as seen in Russ *boi* 'battle' and *bui* 'hero') or performing skills, in still others with wealth (so in the Turkic languages) or with dwellers (farmers).

The last possibility offered itself to those who had the verb *búa* 'to live, dwell; cultivate land' (OI) and its cognates. Dictionaries explain the Scandinavian name *Bo* as 'dweller, inhabitant.' Dietz (1981a:384-85) interprets Ostrogothic *Boio* in a similar way, but Roelandts, as already stated, may be right that not only *Boio* but also *Bo* belongs with the words related to E *boy.* Nor should borrowing be excluded. *The Lay of Igor's Host* shows familiarity with skaldic poetry. Of the two singers, *Boian* is particularly reminiscent of a Scandinavian skald; see Sharypkin (1973; 1976). Consequently, the name *Boian* could be of Germanic origin. When one is confronted with such names, the direction of borrowing (from Scandinavian? from the East?) and the fact of borrowing cannot be demonstrated with desired persuasiveness.

BRAIN (1000)

Brain *has established cognates only in West Germanic. Despite the support of many authoritative dictionaries it is probably not connected with the Greek word for 'top of the head,' and there is no need to trace initial* br- *in it to* *mr-. *OE* brego *'ruler' and OI* bragr *'first, foremost' should also better be left out of the picture. The evidence of place names is inconclusive; in any case, OE* brægen *must have been a different word from* *brægen *'hill.' It is suggested below that OE* brægen *and Ir* bran *'chaff, bran' go back to the same etymon meaning 'refuse.' Apparently, those who coined the noun* brægen *associated brain with 'gray matter,' that is, slush. They gave no thought to its function in the organism or the role of the head as the seat of the brain.*

The sections are devoted to 1) the earliest and fanciful attempts to explain the origin of brain, *2) Graßmann and Johansson's hypotheses (which have been reproduced with minor modifications by all later dictionaries insofar as they venture any etymology of E* brain *and G* Brägen*), 3) the idea defended in this entry (*brain *and* bran*), and 4) other words for 'brain'* *that can be understood as 'refuse, waste, gray matter.'*

1. *Brain* (OE *brægen*), first recorded in 1000, has cognates in Frisian, Dutch, Low German, and Rhenish Franconian (see *brain, Brägen ~ Bregen*, and *brein* in etymological dictionaries of English, German, and Dutch and also Ten Doornkaat Koolman [1879-84: *Brägen*]; Stapelkamp [1950a], and Lerchner [1965:48]). The hypotheses on the origin of those words are not many. **Minsheu compared *brain* with Gk φρήν,** a noun used predominantly in the plural and having several meanings: 'diaphragm; chest; heart' and 'mind; thought.' *Brain* and φρήν sound alike, so that the gloss 'mind' in Greek dictionaries may have suggested to Minsheu a link between them. His idea irritated Junius (who called its author *vir minime indoctus*), yet as late as 1839, Kaltschmidt mentioned φρήν in the entry *Brägen*.

Helvigius was evidently the first to relate G *Brägen*, which he knew in the form *breeam* (= [brɛ:əm]?) **to Gk βρέγμα 'top of the head; fontanel.'** He wrote: "breeam / cerebrum, ab humiditate sortitum nomen. Βρέγω enim est humenectare, irrigare. Hinc βρέγμα synciput vocatur." His idea goes back to antiquity. The Greeks thought that βρέγμα and its doublet βρεγμός were akin to βρέγμα 'wet, moisten' because in infants the fontanel is wet or moist (the association is due to folk etymology: see Frisk and Chantraine). Skinner, possibly independent of Helvigius, also traced *brain* to βρέγμα. Many influential philologists, Junius, Wachter (*Bregen*), Diefenbach (1851:325), Webster, Kaltschmidt (*Brägen*), and Richardson among them, supported Skinner or shared his view.

However, a few other conjectures have been offered from time to time. **Schwenck** (*Bregen*) **pondered the derivation of G *Bregen* from G *Brei* 'mush, paste; porridge'** (not a bad idea, considering what the brain looks like), though he stressed the tentative character of his derivation. Kaltschmidt rejected the *Bregen ~ Brei* connection; however, Mueller found it worthy of note. **Richardson**, inspired by the Greek etymology of βρέγμα, **put forward the hypothesis that *brain* is a development of **be-rægn*, with *ber-* being pronounced *br-* and *-rægn* standing for OE *regn* 'rain.' MacKay,** who believed that most English words are traceable to Gaelic, **offered Gael *breith* 'judgment, wit, imagination, decision' as the etymon of *brain*** (only Stormonth copied his etymology). **May** (*Brägen*) **cited OI *brýnn*, which he mistranslated as 'forehead'** (*brýnn* is an adjective; the Icelandic for 'forehead' is *brún*) **and OI *brǫgðóttr* 'cunning'** (it would have been easier to refer to *bragð* 'deceit') **and wondered whether G *(sich) einprägen* 'impress' could be a variant of **(sich) einbrägen* from *Brägen*.** The last conjecture is ingenious but indefensible despite the obscurity that envelops the origin of *prägen*. **Mueller**, who gave *Brei* and βρέγμα as uncertain cognates of *brain*, **added G *Broden* 'foul-smelling vapor' to his short list of possibly related words** (*Broden* is akin to E *breath*). Those suggestions are now forgotten.

More recently, **Makovskii (1986:47-48 and 1999a) has offered a string of fantasies regarding the etymology of *brain*.** He begins by saying that in the anthropomorphic picture of the universe the brain is a symbol of the World Reason, which is related to the concept of a rising flame. He cites the roots **bhreg-* 'burn, shine' and **bhā-* 'to burn' and obtains OE *brægen* 'brain' from the sum **bha-* (< **bhū-* 'to be') + **arg-*, **areg-* 'burn, shine' (so in the 1999a work). In 1986, he gave **bhreu-* 'boil; ferment (v); violent, passionate' as the etymon of *brain*. Both entries contain E *brag, brochan* 'gruel, thin porridge,' *bragget* 'honey and ale fermented together,' and many other words from Sanskrit, Greek, and Lithuanian among others, as related to *brain*. According to Makovskii (1986), E *marrow* (< OE *mearg*) has the same root as *brain* (his sole supporter in this respect appears to be Jay Jasanoff; see Katz [1998: 211, note 77]). Partridge's hypothesis (1958) is at a comparable level: "IE r[oot] ?**breg(h)-*; r[oot] * *bherg(h)* would also account for G *(Ge)hirn*, OI *hiarni* [Patridge means OI *hjarni*], brain, for *hirn*, etc., may well be metathetic for **hrin-*."

2. **Major events in the investigation of *brain ~ Brägen ~ brein* were the appearance of Graßmann's and Johansson's works.** Graßmann (1863a:93, 118; 1863b:121; the main statement is on p. 93). Graßmann could not have been ignorant of the dictionaries everyone consulted in the middle of the 19th century, so that his comparison of OE *brægen* with Gk βρεγμός was not his discovery, but he added a semantic justification for bringing the two words together. In his opinion, the meaning of their root was 'enclose, cover,' as in Go *bairga-* (the first component of *bairgahei** 'mountainous region'). The alleged parallel Go *ƕairnei** 'skull' ~ OI *hjarni* 'brain' allowed him to conclude that the word *brægen* got its meaning from the name of the head or skull.

After the publication of Graßmann's article, references to Skinner disappeared, which is unfair, as the history of Webster's and Skeat's dictionaries makes especially clear. Webster (1828) cited βρέγμα among the cognates of *brain* (see above). His editors left the etymological part of the entry intact;

only in 1890 *perhaps* was added to it and in 1961 deleted. Continuity was restored, but the seemingly uninterrupted tradition consists of two periods: from Helvigius and Skinner to Graßmann and from Graßmann to the present. Although the Germanic/Greek connection has survived, the substance of the old etymology has changed, and, as will be shown later, more than once. Skeat[1-4] also mentioned βρέγμα and βρεγμός and created the impression that no progress had been made in the study of the word *brain* between 1882 and 1910.

In the year in which *perhaps* was added to the entry in Webster's dictionary, **Johansson** (1890:448) **reexamined the pair OE *brægen* ~ Gk βρεγμός and decided that the original sense of the root underlying them was not 'enclose, cover' but 'jut out, project.'** He interpreted βρεγμός as something protruding, sticking out and gave Gk κόρση 'cheek, temple,' Skt *śírṣan* 'head,' and (in a different grade of ablaut) Gk ἄρχω 'begin; go forward' as cognates. According to Johansson, another line leads from *brægen* to OE *brego* 'ruler.' He also mentioned OI *bragr* 'poetry' but left open the question of its origin.

Several of Johansson's predecessors believed that Greek and even Germanic *br-* could go back to **mr.* **Johansson** was of the same opinion and **reconstructed **m̥rghō-* as the etymon of βρεγμός and *brægen*** (but he did not combine *brægen* and *mearg* 'marrow'). Osthoff (1890:92) endorsed Johansson's reconstruction and devoted a long article to the putative reflexes of PIE **mr-*. Johansson-Osthoff's etymology of *brain* is a familiar part of many post-1890 dictionaries, including Fick[4], 279; WP II:314; and IEW, 750 (severely abridged in comparison with WP). See also E. Zupitza (1896:136 and 1900:242), Kluge (EWDS[5], *Brägen*, and 1913:80, sec 68, where *brægen* is given as the only example of the change *br* < *?mbr*), and Wood (1913-14:316/9). The only small addition to this etymology is Benveniste (1931), who cited Av *mrzu-* 'occipital bone, nape of the neck,' a form presumably related to *brain*.

Judging by the surveys in GI (1984:I, 813, note 1 = 1995:I, 712, note 24, continued on p. 713) and in a 1981 dissertation on the Germanic names of body parts (Egger 1981:35-36), no one has offered new ideas on the origin of *brain* since 1890. Wyld (UED) gives a lucid summary of the problem: "OE *brægen, bregen,* M. E. *brain,* O. Fris. & Du. *brein* ; cp. also O.E. *brego,* 'prince, king'; prob. cogn. w[ith] Gk. *brekhmós, brégma,* 'top of the head,' if this, as is suggested, stands for earlier **mreghmó,* Pr. Gmc. **mregn-,* of wh[ich] the full form w[oul]d. be **mereghn-*. It is further suggested that from a form of the same base w[ith] different gradation in both syllables **m̥rgh-,* the Gk. *arkhós,* 'leader, chief,' *árkhō,* 'I begin,' *arkhē,* 'beginning, cause' &c. are derived."

Watkins (AHD[1], 1530, *mregh-mo-*) reproduces Pokorny's etymology. A few dictionaries (CD and Weekley among them) list the Germanic cognates of *brain* and venture to go no further. The Oxford dictionaries, which follow OED, and the dictionaries derivative of Webster are satisfied with Skinner and ignore the *br-* ~ *mr-* relationship. Persson (1912:35) did not object to Osthoff's treatment of *brain,* traced OE *brego* and OI *bragr* 'first, foremost' to the root (or basis, as he called roots) **bheregh-* 'jut out, project' but admitted that they could "have been influenced" by that root, which is tantamount to saying that the association between *bragr, brego,* and *brægen* with **bheregh-* might be due to secondary processes. Polomé (1986b:185/21), in criticizing Johansson-Osthoff's etymology, pointed out that no examples testify to the change **mr-* or **mbr-* to **br-* in Early Germanic.

A side product of the *brægen* – βρέγμα etymology is the suggestion that OE *brægen* also meant 'hill,' even though that meaning is now preserved only in place names. Ekwall (1960: *Brāfield on the Green*) says that the first element of *Brāfield* is probably *brain* 'the crown of the head' and "in transferred use" 'hill.' A. Smith (1956, I:46) did without *probably*. Wakelin (1971 and especially 1979) pointed out that OE *brægen* had a rare doublet *bragen*. He also believed that *Bragenfeld, Braufeld, Brahefeld, Bramfeld,* and so on contained the element **bragen* 'hill.' His conclusion is unobjectionable, but it does not follow that **bragen-* 'hill' has anything to do with *bragen* 'brain.' Several Old and Middle English *br-g* words may have served as the etymon of *Bragen-*. For example, Ekwall gives *Bray* < OE *brēg* 'brow'; see also Sw *Bråviken* and *Bråvalla,* discussed by Adolf Noreen and cited in AEW, at *brá* 1. Holthausen (1942b:36/32) wrongly, as it appears, adduced OSw *Bragnhem* (> *Bragnam,* a modern Swedish place name) as proof that E *brain* does have a Scandinavian cognate after all. The only justification for ascribing the meaning 'hill, elevated place' to OE *brægen* ~ *bragen* is the almost universally accepted etymology of *brain,* but that etymology is hardly correct. ****Bragna-*, a word that must have existed before the Anglo-Saxon colonization of Britain, had no currency outside the northern German-Frisian area (whence its reflexes in Low German, Dutch, Frisian, and English), and its kinship with Gk βρέγμα ~ βρεγμός**

is unlikely.

3. Otkupshchikov (1961) devoted an article to the Irish word *bran* 'chaff, bran.' Its conclusions can perhaps be used for the clarification of the origin of *brain*. E *bran* is a borrowing, but its source has not been determined. Old French had *bran* 'bran,' whereas Modern French has *bran* 'excrement, muck, filth.' The earliest meaning of OF *bran* seems to have been approximately *'refuse, rejected matter' because in Modern French *bran* is usually called *bran de son* rather than simply *bran* (*son* also means 'bran,' a synonym of *bran* from a different part of the French-speaking area, so that *bran de son* is a tautological phrase, 'bran of bran'). *Bran de scie* means 'saw dust' (*scie* 'saw'). Otkupshchikov contends that *bran* 'bran' and *bran* 'excrement' are different words (their forms allegedly coincided in later French), but he may be mistaken.

A synonym of OF *bran* was *bren*, whence ModF *breneux* 'soiled with feces.' Old Spanish and Provençal also had *bren*. Sp *braña* 'summer pasture' developed its meaning from 'leaves or pieces of bark on the ground.' The Breton cognate of Irish, Welsh, and Gaelic *bran* is *brenn*. In Anglo-Latin, *brenn(i)um* and *brannum*, with the same alternation /e/ ~ /a/, have been recorded, and, as Wakelin showed, a rare Old English doublet of *brægen* was *bragen*. The Romance words and E *bran* may have been borrowed from Celtic, and this is what most dictionaries say, though von Wartburg (FEW) points out that the Celtic etymology of *bran* does not answer all questions. On the other hand, the source of E *bran* may have been Old French, and the Celtic words may have been borrowed from French or English. Otkupshchikov reasons that in Romance neither *bran* nor *bren* has even a tentative etymology, whereas the Celtic forms can be explained without any difficulty. He reconstructs PIE **bhrag-no-* '(something) broken,' with the specialized meaning *'flour together with bran; grain ground by a millstone,' later 'bran.' In his opinion, *bran* is a native Celtic word; the phonetic development of **bhragno-* to *bran* is parallel to that of **ueghno-* to Ir *fen* 'cart' and of at least two more words.

Otkupshchikov did not realize that the Germanic etymon of *brain* had been reconstructed as **bragna-*, a form identical with his PIE **bhragno-*. Apparently, despite von Wartburg's doubts, **Celtic **bragna-* existed. It was a "low" word for 'refuse,' perhaps 'rubbish.' Its expressive character must have made it popular among the Celts' Germanic and Romance neighbors. Those who borrowed **bragna-* had often seen heads split with a sword, with the brain, the refuse of the skull, as it were, oozing out. They had also seen the inside of animals' heads and got the same impression: an unpleasant looking gray mass, whose function in the organism did not bother them.**

4. **Glossing the etymon of *brain* as 'refuse' may seem unlikely, but a few other words for 'brain' confirm this reconstruction.** One of such words is G *Hirn* (< OHG *hirni* ~ *hirn*). On the strength of MDu *hersene* Seebold (EWDS[21-24]) gives the protoform of *Hirn* as **hersnja-* or **herznja-*. OHG *hirni* and OI *hjarni* (with *ja* < **e*) supposedly lost *z* between *r* and *n* (see also NEW: *hersenen*), but it is equally probable that *-z-*, or rather *-s-*, was a suffix *hirni* and *hjarni* never had. Mitzka (EWDS[20]) cites G *Hornisse* 'hornet,' alongside Du *horzel*, both allegedly going back to **hurzu-*, as another example of a spirant in *rzn* ~ *rsn* from **r(r)n*. Seebold expunged reference to *Hornisse* in the entry *Hirn*. He also has doubts that OI *hjarsi* ~ *hjassi* 'crown of the head' are related to *Hirn* and *hjarni*.

Only one point has not been contested, namely that *Hirn* acquired its meaning from a word meaning 'skull,' judging by its apparently unshakable cognates L *cerebrum* 'brain' and Gk κρανίον 'skull, cranium.' Despite the consensus, that etymology may be less secure than it seems. G *Harn* (< MHG < OHG *harn*) means 'urine,' but its original meaning was at one time *'bodily waste,' as suggested by MHG *hurmen* 'fertilize, spread manure over a field.' Its likely cognates (with *s-mobile*) are OI *skarn*, OE *scearn* 'dung, muck,' and L *ex-cer-mere* 'to separate' (akin to *ex-crē-mentum* 'excrement'). *Hirn* (with *i* < **e*) – *Harn* – *hurmen* form a perfect triad.

OI *hjarni* had a synonym *heili*. Its origin is unknown. The cognates proposed by older etymologists are unconvincing (AEW). Magnússon suggests its kinship with OI *hárr* 'gray' (< **haira-*; he traces *heili* to **hailar-* or **hailia-*) and glosses the protoform as 'gray matter.' The Germanic words for 'marrow' (OE *mearg*, OI *mergr*, and so on) have been shown to derive from the root **mozgo-*, whose Proto-Slavic reflex was **mozgu-* 'brain.' If Petersson's comparison of **mozgo-* with the cognates of E *mast* 'fruit of forest trees as food for pigs' is right (1915:125-6), the original meaning of **mozgo-* was *'fat.' Marrow looked like fat (gray substance) to those people. Some etymologists gloss Gmc **mergh-* as 'mass, lump, bunch' (Arnoldson 1915:6/2.03, with references). (However, Sverdrup [1916:41] perhaps went too far in believing that the existence of so many words related to *mearg* ~ *mergr* testifies to the early Indo-Europeans' proficiency in cooking meat.)

Baskett (1920:50, no. 39 A1) cites E reg *pash* 'brain,' a word defined as 'rotten or pulpy mass; mud and slush.' The idea of the brain as a mass is sometimes emphasized by the use of the corresponding words in the plural. In Russian, only the plural (*mozgi,* stress on the second syllable) denotes the dish brains, which is also the case in English. In German, the situation is different: the dish is *Hirn,* while the organ is more often *Gehirn,* a collective noun. Ten Doornkaat Koolman was wrong in connecting *Brägen* directly with *brechen,* but his idea that the brain was at one time understood as something broken into small pieces or something squeezed together testifies to his sound linguistic instinct. He also quoted the saying *Er hat keine Grütze im Kopfe* (literally 'He has no porridge in his head'), said about a stupid, brainless person. *Grütze* in this context is not unlike E reg *pash* and G *Brei,* which Schwenck offered as a cognate of *Brägen.*

Buck (1949:213/4.203) states: "Most of the words for 'brain' are cognate with words for 'head' or 'marrow'." Germanic words do not confirm the first part of his generalization. No common Indo-European name of the head and no common Germanic name of the brain existed. In the Scandinavian area, *hjarni* competed with *heili* ~ *heilir.* The usage in the mythological poems of the *Elder Edda* suggests that *heili* was the most ancient or most dignified word for the gray mass in the head. The primordial giant Ymir had a *heili* (the sky was made from it), not a *hjarni.* Perhaps the home of the etymon of *hjarni* should be sought to the south of the Scandinavian peninsula. Gmc **mazga-* probably also first meant 'brain.'

Learned coinages and local words must have existed at all times. One of them was OE *ex(e)* 'brain,' the origin of which is unknown (from **axe,* a variant of *asce* 'ashes' – 'ash-colored substance'?). When synonyms meet, they clash and narrow down their meaning, unless one of them disappears. Thus *heili* is lost in the continental Scandinavian languages (N and Dan *hjerne,* and Sw *hjärna* are reflexes of **hjarni*) but survives in Modern Icelandic, in which *hjarna-* occurs only in a few compounds; there is also *hjarni* 'skull.' In addition to *mergr,* Old Icelandic had *mœna* (> ModI *mæna*), related to *mœnir* 'ridge of the roof' and E *mane,* the original sense being evidently *'spine.' It is now a term used in describing vertebrates.

Fr *harsens* and Du *hersens* suggest that the prospective invaders of Britain also had a similar word. A late (1137) Old English hapax *hærn* 'brain' is hardly native, and E reg *harns,* as well as ME *hærnes, harnes,* and *hernes,* is from Scandinavian. **Early in their history, speakers of northern German and Frisian seem to have borrowed a "low" Celtic word that with time lost its slangy character. In Frisian and Dutch, it edged out the inherited name of the brain, whereas in Standard English it ousted the cognates of *harsens* ~ *hersens.* The doublets OE *brægen* ~ *bragen* may owe their origin not to some vagaries of Old English regional phonetics but to the existence of a similar pair in the lending language.** To sum up, *brægen* and *bragen* seem to have been taken over from the Celts with the meaning *'refuse, waste matter,' acquired the meaning 'brain,' competed with **harn-,* and eventually won out, but they never meant 'elevated place, hill' (Liberman [2004a]).

CHIDE (1000)

Chide (< OE cīdan) *has been compared with verbs of similar form and meaning in languages as remote as Sanskrit and Finnish, but it can hardly be related to any of them, and no reason exists to treat it as a migratory or onomatopoeic word. Although modern dictionaries characterize* chide *as isolated and etymologically opaque, OE* cīdan *'scold' and* gecīd *'strife' are probably related to OHG* *kîdal *'wedge' (MHG* kîdel, *ModG* Keil*). The early meaning of* *kîdal *must have been *'stick for splitting or cleaving.' If this suggestion is right,* gecīd *started from 'exchange of blows,' whereas* cīdan *probably meant 'brandish sticks,' with 'scold, reprove' being a later figurative use of the same.*

Section 1 discusses the existing derivations of chide, *and section 2 contains the proposed etymology.*

1. The verb *chide* is of unknown origin, though it has existed in written English since the year 1000 (it first occurs in Ælfric). OE *cīdan,* a weak verb of the first class, meant what it means today. The morphological variants—*chode* and *chidden* for *chided*—appeared later. **Old English had the noun *gecīd* 'strife, altercation; reproof,' and some dictionaries say that *cīdan* was derived from this noun** (see, for example, W[3] and AHD). **Even if *gecīd* is the etymon of *cīdan* rather than a back formation from it, the etymology of the root *cīd-* remains opaque.**

The oldest dictionaries offer many putative cognates and parallel formations of *chide:* G *schelten* 'scold,' Du *kijven* 'quarrel, wrangle' (Minsheu, he calls both words Belgian, that is, Flemish or Dutch; Skinner), Gk καίω 'burn, singe' (also Minsheu) and κυδάζω 'scold, vituperate' (Casaubon [1650:293]; still so Townsend [1824:81]), OI *kífa* 'strife, wrangle' and possibly L *cavēre* 'be on one's guard' and *cavillor* 'jeer, taunt' (Ihre, *kif;* he also mentions "Belgian" *kifwa*), Finn *kidata* and *kitistä* 'creak; shrink; press together' (Wedgwood: he misspelled the second verb), and Skt *hīḍ* 'be angry' (Leo [1877:286/39; he gives *hit* 'vociferavit'). The Finnish verbs are too remote from *chide* semantically to be of interest, and all the others have initial consonants that do not match OE *k*.

The complex *kid* or *kud* hardly renders the sound of creaking, shrieking, screaming, and so forth; yet both latest etymological dictionaries of Finnish (SKES and SSA) call *kidata,* as well as *kitistä* ~ *kitistää,* onomatopoeic. G *schelten* may be related to E *scold* and OI *skáld* 'poet' ('the author of vituperative verses'), but *l* belongs to the root in all three of them, so that the basis of comparison between *skeld-* ~ *skáld-* and *cīd* is absent. Initial *h-* in Skt *hīḍ* is incompatible with Gmc *k-*, and the origin of *hīḍ* is unknown (G *Geist* 'spirit,' E *ghost,* and so on are its possible cognates, KEWA III:60). Du *kijven* is related to G *kabbeln, kibbeln,* and *keifen* 'scold, wrangle' and to OE *cāf* 'quick, strenuous, bold' (a proper name *Cīfa* also existed). Sw reg *skvappa,* together with E reg *swabble* and E *squabble,* appear to belong to the *kabbeln—keifen* group. Their onomatopoeic or sound symbolic origin is not improbable, but, as *l* in *schelten* is part of the root, so is the labial in *kijven* and the rest.

Since positing the root *kī- 'wrangle, quarrel; scold' with the enlargements -*d* and -*b* (*f, p*) is an unappealing proposal, we can assume that none of the words listed above has anything to do with *chide*, even though the correspondence of sound and meaning between OE *cīdan* and Gk κυδάζω, to which ORuss *kuditi* 'scold' and Skt *kutsáyati* 'vituperates, scolds' should be added, is curious.

The onomatopoeic nature of OE *cīdan* cannot be ruled out. Compare G *kitzeln,* L *titillāre,* and Russ *shchekotat'* (stress on the final syllable), all meaning 'tickle.' Russ reg *shchekatit'* (stress on the second syllable) 'quarrel noisily and indecently' (Samuel Johnson's definition of *brawl*) sounds almost like *shchekotat'* 'tickle.' The sound shape of OE *citelian* 'tickle' is not particularly suggestive of the action it designates. For more words of the structure *k* + vowel + *d, t,* or *s* meaning 'battle, fight, press,' from Welsh to Chaldee, see the early editions of Webster's dictionary (1828; only Mahn expunged this array of words in the 1864 edition). An example of an onomatopoeic *kud* is Russ *kudakhtat'* 'cackle' (stress on the second syllable).

Wedgwood compared OE *cīdan* and SwiG *kiden* 'resound.' The Swiss verb appears in Stormonth and Mueller[1] as a tentative cognate of *cīdan,* but is was soon realized that Swi *kiden* is a reflex of **qvidan* (Go *qiþan*) 'speak' (Mueller[2]). Regel (1862:111) believed that at one time the verb *cīdan* had exact correspondences in most Germanic languages and treated Go *qiþan,* OE *cweðan,* and OI *kveða* as closely related to Gmc **cīdan.* Thomson cited "Gothic" (= Swedish) *kuida* [sic] and Saxon (?) *ciden* in his dictionary. Bosworth (1838) reproduced Regel's etymology at *cīdan,* but Toller (BT) deleted it. Pott (1859-76:IV, 838/1852) referred to Regel's article; however, he admitted that the problem had not been solved.

Skeat, in Skeat[1], hesitatingly compared *chide* with OE *cweðan,* and in the *Errata and Addenda* he cited, also with hesitation, Sw reg *ke(d)a* 'hurt, sadden' and Dan *kiede* (its modern spelling is *kede*) 'bore one,' which he found in Rietz and which Rietz compared with Skt *khid* 'hurt, sadden.' The Danish adjective *ked,* occurring in such phrases as *være ked (af noget)* 'feel irritated (by something),' *gøre nogen ked af noget* 'hurt, sadden,' goes back to OD *keed* and has close parallels in Swedish and Norwegian. According to DEO[4], -*d* in *ked* may be secondary, perhaps added under the influence of its synonym *led,* as in the tautological binomial *led og ked.* DEO[4] compares *ke(d)* and LG *keef,* N reg *keiv* 'crooked, twisted,' and so on. They lead either to **kib* 'split, turn aside' or to the root represented by OI *keikr* 'bent backward' and possibly by OI *keipr* 'rowlock, oarlock' and Dan *kejte* 'left hand.' See more on *kejte* and the rest at KEY and KITTY-CORNER. Although the adjectives and nouns united by the meanings 'bent, twisted, left-handed' form a rather cohesive group despite the variations in the postradical consonants, the words whose referents are 'strife, noisy quarrel; scold, wrangle; sadden' cannot be shown to belong to it. Rietz's Sanskrit verb (see *khidáti* 'he tears, presses' in KEWA I:309) is not related to OE *cīdan.*

Conjectures on the origin of *chide* gradually disappeared from dictionaries. Two more etymologies—by W. Barnes (1862:103, from the mythical root *k*ng* 'stop back anything') and Partridge (1958; *chide:* allegedly related to -*cīd-* in L *occīdere* 'slay')—may be dismissed out of hand. Dictionaries of Old and Modern English, including Holthausen's (AeEW, *cīdan*), agree in stating that *chide* is isolated and that nothing can be said about its history. Jellinghaus (1898a) listed 106 English words going back to Old English but having no cognates in Low German. *Chide* is one of them (p. 464). Attempts to find some traces of this verb in place names have failed. In Kent, in a village called Chiddingstone (formerly Chidingstone), near the church, a certain stone is popularly known as Chiding Stone. "The village tradition is that on it the priests used to chide the people, whence the name" (Lynn [1889]). But Ekwall's explanation (1960; probably from a personal name) destroys local etiological legend. In the later dictionaries of Germanic languages, *chide* turns up only once. Modern Icelandic has *kiða* (first recorded in the 17th century) 'rub, scratch, move with short steps'; the corresponding noun is *kið*. Exact parallels are wanting. Nynorsk *kjea* (< **kiða*) 'work negligently, bungle; wrangle' and OE *cīdan* are listed tentatively as its possible cognates and referred to the Germanic root **kī-* (< PIE * *ǵei-* 'split'; ÁBM). Ties between 'rub, move with short steps' and 'quarrel angrily' are hard to detect even if one takes *kiða* and *cīdan* for the full and zero grades of ablaut of the same root.

2. It is not surprising that all hypotheses on the etymology of OE *cīdan* revolve around the roots **kīd-* ~ **kīð-* or **kī-* followed by some other postradical consonant. However, stringing words with *kī-* is a formal procedure that can easily get out of control. For instance, Wortmann offers numerous words, supposedly related to G *keimen* 'germinate' (Go *keinan**, OS *kînan*, OHG *kînan* 'germinate'; OE *cīnan* 'gap, yawn, crack' is believed to have retained the original meaning of that verb). *Chide* is allegedly one of them (Wortmann [1964:57]). The semantic basic of *chide* would then be 'split of friendly relations.' This is a shaky bridge between **kī-* and *chide*, for *kīnan* and its derivatives consistently refer to the process of bursting forth, shoots, and branches, while *cīdan* with equal consistency denotes scolding and altercation rather than severance of friendship. The solution offered below is not different from some of those mentioned above, but it aims at reconstructing the semantic ties between the recorded meaning of *cīdan* and the postulated meaning of its ancient root.

One of the words traced to the base **kī-* is G *Keil* 'wedge.' Middle High German had *kîl* (< OHG *kîl*) and **kîdel* 'wedge, peg.' If *Keil* is connected with **kīnan*, its original meaning must have been 'tool for splitting or cleaving.' *Kîdel* apparently goes back to OHG **kîdal* (< **kî-ðla*), a doublet of **kī-þla* by Verner's Law. That etymology, offered by Sievers (1894:340), has never been contested and has found its way into works on Indo-European (Birgit Olsen [1988:15-16, sec 2.20]), though the relationship between *kîl* and **kîdal* is not clear. This question has been discussed in connection with the enigmatic change *þl* > *hl* in Germanic and especially with the history of G *Beil* (< *bîhal*) 'ax.' All of it is of little consequence for the etymology of *chide* if we disregard the suggestion that **kîdal* is a secondary formation or *kîl* with a syllable inserted, like 15th-century G *meder* for *mehr* 'more'; G *Speil* and *Speidel*, both also meaning 'wedge' and resembling *Keil* ~ *Keidel*, are words of obscure history (DW, *Keil*). MHG *kîdel* must be an ancient word. It survived in German dialects and has been preserved as a family name (*Keidel*), whatever the nature of the reference to 'wedge' may be (Gottschald and Brechenmacher give different explanations). E. Zupitza (1904:397) compared *kîl* (< **kīðl*) and Skt *kīlaḥ* 'wedge, peg,' but WP I:544 and IEW 355-56 rejected his idea of initial consonantal doublets (*k-* in Sanskrit and *k-* in Germanic).

The root *kīd-* probably meant 'stick,' and it seems to underlie both OE *gecīd* 'strife' and *cīdan* 'scold.' The original meaning of *gecīd* would then emerge as 'exchange of blows,' while *cīdan* could be glossed 'brandish sticks,' with 'scold, reprove' being a later figurative use of the same. E *haggle* from 'mangle with cuts' to 'wrangle in bargaining' and especially *rebuke* 'chide severely, reprimand' < AF *rebuker* = OF *rebuschier* provide a close semantic parallel. The verb *bushier* (OF *buchier, buskier*) meant 'beat, strike,' properly 'cut down wood,' for *busche* meant 'log' (ModF *bûche* 'log, cudgel'); see Skeat[4] and ODEE (*rebuke*). The development is obvious: from 'beat back' to 'reprove.' *Rebuff* and *upbraid* have come approximately the same way as *rebuke* and *chide*. One can also cite E *trounce*, assuming that it is related to *truncheon*, and Go *beitan** 'bite' versus *andbeitan** 'rebuke.' In the extensive recent discussion of F *chicane* and *chicaner* (the etymons of E *chicane* / *chicanery*), Littré's idea (he traced *chicane* to a Persian word for a club or bat used in polo – via Medieval Latin and Medieval Greek) has not been mentioned. It must have been given up as untenable, though Skeat, OED, and CD mention Littré's derivation as a distant possibility. Yet the reasoning in this case is instructive: from the game of mall, to a dispute in games, dispute in general, and to sharp practice in lawsuits, pettifogging, trickery, and all kinds of wrangling.

If the etymology proposed here is right, the verb *chide* owes nothing to onomatopoeia or sound symbolism. Nor is it related to any of the verbs in Sanskrit, Classical Greek, Welsh, Finnish, Dutch, and German, mentioned above. Even ModI *kiða* does not look like a cognate of *chide*. It would be tempting to connect *cīdan* and E *kid* 'tease,' but no recoverable tie seems to exist between them.

CLOVER (1000)

Clover *has cognates in all the West Germanic languages;*

the corresponding Scandinavian words are borrowings from Low German. The Old English forms were clāfre *and* clǣfre. *In Old English, several plant names had the suffix* -re. *The protoform need not have had* *i *or* *j *after* -r-, *for* ǣ *in* clǣfre *was probably not the result of umlaut. WGmc* *ā < *ai *and* *ǣ < *ā *(the latter corresponding to Go* $\bar{e}_1$*) could apparently alternate in the same root. However, the conditions under which that alternation occurred remain unclear. The etymology connecting* clover *with* cleave *'stick, adhere' seems to be right. Clover is sticky because its thick juice is one of the main sources of honey. Several European plant names with the root* pap *and its equivalents, as well as the meanings of E* honeysuck(le) *confirm that idea.*

The sections are devoted to 1) the arguments behind reconstructing *klaiwarjōn *and* *klaƀr(i)ōn, *2) the existing etymologies of E* clover *and G* Klee, *3) the origin of* ǣ *in OE* clǣfre *and the origin of the suffix* -re, *and 4) the semantic history of* clover *(clover as a sticky plant). Section 5 is the conclusion.*

1\. ***Clover* is a word with broad connections in West Germanic.** It is current in Frisian (*klaver*), Dutch (*klaver*), and German (the Standard form is *Klee* < MHG *klê* < OHG *klê* ~ *klêo*). In its Low German form (*klever*) it spread to Scandinavia and Russia: Dan *kløver* < *kleffuer*, N *kløver*, Sw *klöver* < *klever*, Russ *klever*. Yiddish also has *klever*. Alongside OHG *klê* (m), OE *clāfre* and *clǣfre* (n and f) occur. The protoform of *klê* must have been **klaiwa-*. Final *-a* was lost in Germanic, and *ai* became *ē* before *w* in German (as in *Schnee* 'snow' < **snaiwa-*) and *ā* in all positions in Old English; *-o* in OHG *klēo* is ancient *w* vocalized word finally.

The earliest Old English glossaries have *clābre* and *clāfre*, later West Saxon has *clǣfre* and *clǣfra*. Still later forms are *clouere* (13th century), *cleure* (15th century), *claver* (15th-17th centuries), and *clover* (16th century). *Clover* is rare before 1600 and did not prevail much before 1700. OED sets up **claƀre* ~ *clāfre* (weak feminine) as the oldest form in English. *Clover* continues ME *clāver*. *Claver* goes back to *clǣfre* with shortened *ǣ*. ODEE abridged and repeated the information given in OED but added that *claver* may represent OE *clǣfre*, with shortening of the stem vowel, or may be of Low Dutch origin.

The unfortunate term *Low Dutch* is old; in modern scholarship Llewellyn (1936) used it for Flemish, Dutch, Frisian, and Low German. Onions does not explain why he suggested the "Low Dutch" origin for ME *claver*; the vowel in the Dutch reflexes of *clāver(e)* is almost always long. His idea is original. See De Hoog (1909), Toll (1926), Llewellyn (1936), and Bense, none of whom mentions *clover*. Nor is reference to shortening (OED and Mayhew [1891d:452]), apparently before two consonants, sufficient in this case. OE *clǣfre* developed an epenthetic vowel (*clǣfre* > *clǣfere*, *clǣvere*), after which *ǣ* lost length in a trisyllabic word and the short-lived epenthesis was dropped: *clǣvere* became *clævre*, spelled *claver* (Luick [1964:secs 387.2 and 457.1]).

The presence of *ǣ* in OE *clǣfre* made etymologists reconstruct **i* in one of the postradical syllables, whence the asterisked forms **klaiwarjōn* and **klaiƀr(i)ōn* in most modern dictionaries: **i(j)* accounts for umlaut (ā* > *ǣ*), and the variation **ƀ* ~ **w* takes care of the difference between *w* in Old High German and *f*, that is, [v] in Low German and Old English.** Most etymologies of *clover* and its cognates are based on the assumption that this word is of Germanic origin and can be traced to some other Germanic word (see also Sauer [1992:386]). If *clover* goes back to an unknown substrate language (an idea acceptable to both J. de Vries [NEW, *claver*], Polomé [1986a:666, 1987:232], and Schrijver [1997:305]) the search becomes futile.

2\. The proposed derivations of *Klee* ~ *claver* ~ *clover* are as follows: 1) **Since L *trifolium* 'trefoil, clover' refers to the 'cloven' form of the leaf, the same must be true of *clover*, which appears to be related by this twist of logic to E *cleave* 'split,' Du *klieven*, G *klieben* (OE *cleofan*, OS *klioƀan*, OHG *chliuban*).** Such was the nearly unanimous opinion of early lexicographers, for example, Minsheu, Ihre (*klofwer*), Wachter (*Klee*), Todd (in Johnson-Todd), M. Höfer II:140-44, Kaltschmidt (*Klee*), Wedgwood, Leo (1877:360/26), Chambers, and May (*Klee*). Weigand's contemporaries disregarded his warning that *Klee* is not akin to *klieben*. Only Mueller took heed of it, and Schwenck observed that some form related to *klieben* 'cleave, split' rather than *klieben* must be a cognate of *Klee*. A connection between **klaiw-*, the base of the plant name, and **kleuƀ-*, the base of *cleave* 'split,' cannot be made out, because *ai* and *eu* belong to different ablaut series, and Schwenck's side form (*Nebenform*) has not been recorded. Skeat, in Skeat[1], did not reject that connection (he called it probable but not certain). However, in his CED, published in the same year, the corresponding phrase is "very doubtful." In Skeat[4], "very doubtful" is replaced with "impossible," and the idea is dismissed as being "inconsistent with phonology."

2\) **In the pre-1864 editions of Webster's dictionary, *clover* is associated with L *clāva* 'cudgel' and with Du *klaver*, which allegedly means 'club.'** **Klaver* 'club' must have been extracted

Clover

from Du *klaveren* 'clubs' (at cards) or from compounds beginning with *klaver-*. Although E *club* does not turn up among its cognates, *clover* is said to mean 'club-grass, club-wort' (which is wrong in respect of both *clover* and *clubmoss*). Prior gave an especially interesting comment along these lines. He preferred the form *claver* to *clover*: "It is evidently a noun in the plural number, probably a Frisian word, and means 'club,' from Latin *clava*, and refers to the clava trinodis of Hercules. It is in fact the *club* of our cards, French *trèfle*, which is so named from its resemblance in outline to a leaf with three leaflets." Du *klaveren*, a translation of F *trèfle* (< L *trifolium*), is of no help in elucidating the etymology of *clover* (EWNT[2]), but the history of the English name of the suit *clubs* is more complicated: "The suit of *clubs* upon the Spanish cards is not the trefoils as with us, but positively clubs, or cudgels, of which we retain the name, though we have lost the figures; the original name is *bastos*" (CD, quoting from Joseph Strutt's *Sports and Pastimes*).

3) The expression *in clover* evidently refers to cattle's delight in eating clover. Mackay (1877) arrived at the conclusion that the word *clover* was derived from this expression, glossed E *clover* as 'happiness,' and, following his preconceived idea that most English words are of Gaelic origin, suggested that its etymon is Gael *clumhor* ~ *clomhor* 'warm, sheltered, snug.' His etymology of *clover* stands out even among his other fanciful reconstructions.

4) **Kluge thought that, whatever the origin of *Klee* might be, OE *clǣfre* and all the related disyllabic forms were compound words, but he could not identify *-fre*.** In EWDS[1-3], he tentatively compared *-fre* with *-fre* in OE *heahfre* 'heifer,' possibly a syncopated variant of *heahfore*. (The origin of this *-fore* is still a matter of debate; see HEIFER.) Kluge also cited the German disguised compounds *Kiefer* 'pine tree' (< OHG *kienforaha*) and *Wimper* 'eyelash' (< OHG *wintbrâ(wa)*). In the fourth edition, he expunged reference to *heifer, Wimper*, and *Kiefer* but retained the idea that *clover* was a compound word (the same in EWDS[5-10]). His successors gave up that idea altogether, but it survived in OED, Vercoullie's dictionary of Dutch, and Weekley (1924).

Two attempts to etymologize *-fre* are known. **Pogatscher** (1898:97-98) **suggested that OE *clǣfre* consisted of **klaiwaz* and some word like Icel *smári* 'clover,' with or without *s-*.** By a series of phonetic changes **klaiw(s)mári* allegedly became *clāfre*. Since OE *clāfre* competed with *clǣfre*, Pogatscher reconstructed **klaiwaz* and **klaiwiz*, an *os/es*-noun. Although Pogatscher cited several words in which *ƀr* supposedly goes back to **mr*, his reconstruction found no support. The bulky form he proposed is not improbable, as N reg *kløversmære* shows (Nilsson [1984:201]). However, *kløversmære* is a late word, for *kløver*, as pointed out above, came to Scandinavia from Low German. More importantly, cognates of *smári* or its doublet **mári*, which Pogatscher compared with the obscure Greek plant names σμηρέα or μηρίς, have not been recorded in West Germanic; *smeer* 'clover' occurring in some English dialects is not a native word in them. Björkman (1901:227-28) summarized Pogatscher's etymology without comment, and etymological dictionaries never take it into consideration. The same holds for Walther's etymology (1893:135-36), who believed that the flower of clover resembles a berry and detected *-bere* in *clavere*. Foerste (1954:395) tactfully dismissed Walther's and Pogatscher's conjectures as indefensible.

5) **The etymology of *Klee* ~ *klaver* ~ *clover* that most modern dictionaries accept hesitatingly goes back to FT (*kløver*), who connected those words with *cleave* 'stick, adhere' (Du *kleven*, G *kleben*; OE *cleofian* and *clifian*, OS *kliƀon*, OHG *chlebên*), citing the sticky juice of the plant when it blooms as the reason.** WP I:620 and IEW, 364 (with a question mark), endorsed that hypothesis, though Kluge implicitly and Van Wijk (EWNT, *klaver*) explicitly rejected it. In German lexicography, reference to the sticky juice first appeared in Götze's rewording of Kluge's dictionary (EWDS[11]) and stayed there until Seebold (EWDS[22]) took it out. The usual objection to FT's etymology is that the juice of clover in bloom is not stickier than any other flower juice or sap. However, the feature chosen as the basis of the names of plants and animals need not be unique. For example, not only asters are radiated flowers resembling stars, and not only daisies are 'day's eyes.'

Yet the problem remains: What is so sticky about clover? The reasons for naming differ from plant to plant. Proto-Slavic **lipa* 'linden tree' was, most likely, called sticky (**lipati* 'stick, adhere') in consideration of its highly valued bast (ESSI [XV:114-16]). Foerste (1954:408-09) revived the idea developed by Ten Doornkaat Koolman (*klafer*) that clover is 'sticky' because it takes root and grows in almost any soil. The tenacity and ineradicability of clover hardly justify a name meaning 'clinger.' Clivers and cleavers are 'sticky' because they cling to the objects that come into contact with them, not because their roots are so sturdy. It is a curious fact that W. Barnes (1862:117), who worked with a set of imaginary bases, assigned *clover* to *cl*ng* 'cling.' He did not explain how he had arrived at his idea.

6) **According to Van Ginneken** (1941:363), **Gmc *klai-ja comes from a word meaning 'clay'** (cf Du *klei* and G *Klei*), because clover prefers sandy and loamy soils, that is, from the word *clay*. His etymology has never been discussed. **Baader** (1953:39-40) **traced the West Germanic name of *clover* to the "East European" root *gel- ~ *gloi- 'bright, shining.'** It is not sticky juice but intense color that is typical of clover, he said. Clover comes in several colors, but their intensity is about average, and the distance from **gel- ~ *gloi-* 'bright, happy, shining' to MHG *kleine* 'shining, dainty' hardly leads to *'white, reddish,' as Mitzka (KM, *Klee*) points out. Seebold (KS, *Klee*) mentions Baader's article without comment, and no one except Cohen (1972b:2/26) shared Baader's opinion.

7) **B. van den Berg** (1954:186-87) did not offer a new etymology of Du *klaver* but **suggested that its protoform was **klâwaz,* an *es/os*-stem, with **klâwira* as its plural.** The word for 'clover' often occurs in the plural (see Prior's etymology above), and Pogatscher assigned **klaiwaz* (not **klāwaz*) to the *es/os*-stem long before Van den Berg, who may have been unaware of this fact.

3. The traditional reconstruction of the protoform **klaib̄r(i)on* shies away from the question of why two forms—with and without *i*—existed. **Of interest is Foerste's observation** (1954:405-08; first, very briefly, as in 1955:3) **that *ǣ* in *clǣfre* does not have to be the umlaut of *ā*, for it can go back directly to Gmc *ǣ* (Go $\bar{e}_1$, WGmc *ā).** Instead of **klaib̄ron* and **klaib̄rion,* with *i* posited only to account for an allegedly umlauted vowel, he obtained the doublets *clāfra* (< **klaib̄ron*) and *clǣfre* (< **klāb̄ron*). Foerste cited several other word pairs in which old **ai* seems to have alternated with **ā;* Weijnen (1981:136) gave two more examples. None of those forms is fully convincing, and no reasons for the alternation have been offered. Yet Foerste's reconstruction has potential and can perhaps be accepted as a working hypothesis. Dutch and Low German dialects also have *klever* and *klaver*. Previous explanations of *a* were of two kinds: that it is of Frisian origin (an improbable hypothesis in light of OE *clāfre*) or that it is an Ingvaeonic feature. In addition to the works already mentioned, see Heeroma's discussion (1937:262-63, 265) of the "*â* map" in the linguistic atlas of Dutch (1949:30) and the bibliography in Brok's edition of Heukels (Heukels [1987:LXI]).

Foerste did not address the problem of monosyllabic forms (like G *Klee*) versus disyllabic ones (like Du *klaver* and E *clover*). According to Van den Berg (1954:191-92), **-wr-* became **-vr-* in *klaver,* and some examples in Dutch dialects bear out his statement. But *-fr-* in the Old English forms needs another explanation. For this reason, Foerste rejected Van den Berg's etymology (likewise, Lerchner [1965:143]).

The Germanic suffix **-ðro* was used in the naming of various trees. Such are OE *apuldre* (OHG *affoltra* or *apaldr*) 'apple tree,' *mapuldre* 'maple,' and many others. A reflex of **-ðro* shows up in G *Holunder* 'juniper' and possibly *Flieder* 'lilac.' Not only tree names have this suffix or a complex that came to be associated with it: it is also present in E *dodder* and *madder* (ME *doder;* OE *mædere*). The meaning of **-ðro* (perhaps 'bearer') was forgotten early, whence such creations of folk etymology as OE *æppeltre* (*æppeltrēow*), MLG *mapeldorn,* and so forth. After Sievers (1878:523-24) clarified the meaning and origin of **-ðro* in plant names, no one added anything new to his reconstruction. Only Wyld (UED, *heather*) pointed out that in Old English, the formative element of plant names *-re* had come into being, as in OE *ampre* 'dock, sorrel' and *clāfre* 'clover' (*ampre* is a reshaping of an adjective meaning 'bitter'; compare G *Ampfer* < OHG *ampfara ~ ampfaro*). His observation seems to be relevant also for Frisian, Low German, and Dutch, but it need not be assumed that *-re* is a continuation of **-ðro*. **The most natural etymology of OE *clāfre ~ clǣfre* would be **claiw- ~ *clǣw-* with the formative element *-re*. The suffixed forms **clāw- ~ clǣw- + -re (ra)* would also explain parallel forms with *-b-*: the group *wr-* was preserved in Old English intact (contrary to German and Dutch), but in the middle of the word it did not occur and was transformed into *-fr-* (pronounced [vr]) or *-br-*.**

4. An equally difficult part of the etymology of *clover* is the semantics of this plant name. **FT's idea that *clover* is akin to *cleave* 'adhere' can be accepted. Some property of clover made people associate it with a sticky, adhesive mass. A semantic parallel to *clover* is Icel *smári* 'clover.'** *Smári,* along with its doublet *smæra,* surfaced only at the end of the 17th century, but it must be old, for its cognates exist in Faroese and in the dialects of Swedish, Norwegian, and Danish (Nilsson [1984]; ÁBM, *smári, smæra*). The etymology of *smári* has been discussed sporadically and insufficiently. Jacob Grimm (1865:121) looked on it as a borrowing from Celtic: he cited Ir *seamar, seamrog* and Wel *samrog,* the etymon of E *shamrock,* Icel (he erroneously said "Old Icelandic") *smári,* and Dan (Jut-

land) *smære* (his spelling is *smäre*).

Bugge (1899:455-56/30) could not imagine that *smári* is a Celtic word and traced it to **smáirhon* (< **smarəkon-*). He reconstructed the Proto-Celtic form as **sembrako-* (< **semrako-*). **Smar-* and **semr-* emerged as different grades of ablaut of the same base. The Irish word appears in FT(N), but later Falk and Torp concluded that *seamar*, like OE *symmering-wyrt* 'violet' or 'anemone' (Förster [1917: 139/2] thought it was a variety of malva), is related to the Germanic word for 'summer' and expunged it from the German translation (FT(G), see *smære* in both editions). However, they never shared Bugge's view of the origin of *smári* and compared it with OE *smǣras* 'lips' (pl). They explained the name *smári* as 'leppeblomst,' that is, 'lip flower' (the same gloss in NEO, *smære),* allegedly because of some similarity between clover flowers and lips. FT's later etymology of Ir *seamar* 'clover' also seems to have been abandoned. WP II:624-25 and Pokorny (1949-50:135) derive *seamar* from PIE **stembros* 'stalk.'

FT's etymology of *smári* is even less credible than Walther's ("clover is like a berry"). Reference to L *laburnum* does not help, for laburnum is a tree whose bright yellow, pear-shaped flowers do not resemble clover. The origin of the Latin word is unknown, and its association with *labia* 'lip' is due to folk etymology. Charpentier (1912:140-41) supported enthusiastically the idea that *smári* is related to OE *gālsmǣre* 'jocose, frivolous,' a word mentioned in FT. He noted that the root **smei-* ~ **smi-* (as in E *smile*) meant both 'laugh' and 'bloom.' His observation is correct (see also Petersson [1916:290]), but the connection between laughter and flowers goes much deeper than he thought, for laughter was considered in many cultures to be a giver of life. The motif is too broad to be invoked in any etymology. See Propp (1984: no 9, esp p. 137 "Flowers That Bloom at Someone's Smile"; first published in 1939). Charpentier may have missed Benfey (1875), and Benfey was apparently unaware of the Icelandic word. In his discussion of the names of the plant hop (1875:213-16), Benfey mentions Gk σμῖλαξ 'convolvulus, dodder' (as well as 'yew tree') and considers the possibility of the protoform **smaila* or **smaira* in view of the Sanskrit plant name *smera-*. He notes that *smera* seems to be a derivation of **smi-* 'smile, laugh' and refers to the bright blossoms covering many climbing plants ('smiling' = 'in bloom'). "This would indeed be a very poetic designation," he says (pp. 215-16), but adds that some poetic names may be taken back to Proto-Indo-European. He would have been puzzled by Icel *smári,* another 'smiling' name of a plant not famous for its brightness and not a climber.

Both etymological dictionaries of Modern Icelandic (IEW, 909; ÁBM, *smári*) copied from FT, though a reasonable conjecture on the derivation of *smári* has been known for a long time. Holthausen (AeEW) pointed out that *gālsmǣre* should be kept away from *smǣras* and that the source of *ǣ* in OE *smǣre* 'lip' is WGmc **ǣ* (corresponding to Go $\bar{e}_1$) rather than the umlaut of *ā* from **ai,* as follows from the Anglian dative plural *smērum,* and cannot be related to *ā* in *smári* (see also Holthausen [1941:81] and Foerste's discussion of *clǣfru,* above; Knobloch [1959:41] disagrees with Holthausen without giving reasons for his disagreement). The cognate of *smári* is, according to Holthausen, OI *smjǫr* ~ *smør* 'butter.' E *cleave* 'adhere' is archaic, but in German, *kleben* and *schmieren* are not only synonymous but sometimes interchangeable. *Smør* and *schmieren* are closely related words.

Another semantic parallel to clover as a sticky flower is Russ *kashka,* the popular name of *klever* 'clover.' *Kasha* means 'porridge, hot cereal'; *kashka* 'pap' is its quasi-diminutive. According to the current explanations, *kashka* got its name either from its flowers collected into dense heads of short spikes resembling porridge (Dal' II:100) or from the fact that when it is ground in the hand, it feels like fine grain (Merkulova [1967:90]; ESRI II/8:105-06; ESSI IX:159-60 lists cognates but gives no etymology). Who grinds clover in the hand and why? With a word denoting pap (mash, pulp) we are not too far from *kleben* and *schmieren.*

The Russian word is in no way unusual. Among the popular names of German plants, we find *Pappel* and *Käsepappel;* G *pap-* is a cognate of E *pap* (Štech [1959:154-55]). Štech notes that all those plants, when squeezed or broken, excrete thick juice, which is, or was in the past, used for medicinal purposes. It is noteworthy how often various authors writing in German use the phrase *dicker Saft* 'thick juice.' FT and their followers refer to thick juice in their etymology of *kløver* and *Klee.* Štech says *dickflüssiger Saft,* and in WHirt *Latwerge* 'electuary' (= *dicker Heilsaft,* a medicinal powder mixed with honey or syrup) is defined as *durch Einkochen dicker Saft.*

Medieval pharmaceutical books regularly mention clover, but its role in healing ailments is not prominent. **The thick juice of clover is associated, even if vaguely, with honey.** The missing link between clover and stickiness (*Klee* and *kleben, klaver* and *kleven, clover* and *cleave* 'adhere') is the English word *honeysuckle* (its doublet is *honeysuck*), which until the end of the 17th century meant 'red clover, *Trefolium pratense.*' This meaning is still alive in dialects (EDD). Honey stalks mentioned in Shakespeare's *Titus Andronicus* (IV:4, 90) are stalks of clover. Not only the cattle appreciate the sweet taste of clover.

Although the cultivation of clover started in Europe in the 16th century (first in Brabant), neither bees nor beekeepers had to wait so long. In Kilian's 1599 Dutch dictionary, *klauern honigh* 'clover honey' is defined 'mel optimum & candidissimum, ex trifolio pratensi' ('good, very clear honey from purple clover'); the association between clover and honey was natural to him. Wherever clover grows, children chew it (as they chew honeysuckle and sometimes lilac) and enjoy the taste of this 'pap.' As recently as at the end of the 19th century, poor people in Iceland put clover into their milk and ate this 'cold cereal' (Nilsson 1984:202). **Clover is 'sticky,' because its thick juice is one of the main sources of honey.** Other examples illustrating the connection between the juice of a tree and the product made from it include Welsh *bedw* 'birch; birch grove,' called for the juice it excretes. *Bedw* is a rather secure cognate of E *cud*, OI *kváða* 'resin,' and G *Kitt* 'putty.' G *Weichsel* (OHG *wîhsila*) 'bird cherry' is akin to L *viscum* 'bird lime'; bird lime was made from these berries.

In popular botanical nomenclature, the same name is often applied to several different plants, and, conversely, one plant may have many names. The Old English glosses in which *clāfre* and *clǣfre* turn up are confusing because copyists could not know the exact meaning of *cirsium, crision, calta,* and other Latin words (BWA, I:35, II:23, III:52; Cockayne [1861, II:276]). That is why Skinner based his etymology of *clover* on the meaning 'violet,' arguing that clover and violets have a similar smell (the same, as always, in *Gazophylacium*), and the pre-1864 editions of Webster's dictionary emphasize that "[t]he Saxon word is rendered also marigold and violet." In the dialects of many Germanic languages, words like E *hare's foot,* Sw *röd-fikor, rö-tastar,* Icel *hrútafifl,* each denoting a different kind of clover, are widespread. So many compound words have *clǣfre* as their second element in Old English, including some exotic ones like *þunor-clǣfre* 'bugle,' that *clǣfre* became the name of almost any grass. Yet the main meaning of *clǣfre* ~ *clāfre* was probably the same as today, which did not prevent them from having synonyms. The word *clǣfre* is still discernible in numerous place names beginning with *Clare-, Clar-, Claver-,* and *Clover-*. *Clarendon* may be one of them (Ekwall [1960:113], A. H. Smith [1956, I:96]).

5. In sum, the history of *clover* and its West Germanic cognates looks as follows: 1) West Germanic had the form **klaiwaz,* most probably, an *a*-stem. Its direct continuation is High German *Klee* (< *klêo(w)*). 2) In English, Frisian, Dutch, and Low German, *-re,* a formative element of plant names, possibly extracted from < **-þro,* was added to **klaiw-,* and **klaiwre* yielded **klaifre* [-vre] and **klaibre.* The first variant won out. **Klaifre* developed into OE *clāfre* (> ModE *clover*). 3) In early West Germanic, **ai* sometimes alternated with **ǣ* (< **ā),* whence OE *clǣfre* (> ModE *claver*) and all continental forms with *-e-*. 4) Clover got its name from its sticky juice, its nectar, the base of the most popular sort of honey. The sound complex **klaiwaz* must have meant 'sticky pap.'

COB (1420?)

Cob, *in its various meanings, refers to animal names, the names of round and lumpy objects, and the head. It is often confused with* cop, *but, as a rule,* cop *means only 'head.' The history of* cop *is as obscure as the history of* G Kopf, L caput, *and their cognates. Late convergences and ancient ties are impossible to distinguish in this group. Possibly,* cob *'animal name' (related to* cub*) and* cob *'round ~ lumpy object' are historically distinct from* cob ~ cop *'head.' Of the animal names, only* cob *'male swan' can be understood as 'the head (swan).'* Cob *is not a borrowing from Scandinavian or Celtic in any of its meanings.* Cob *'basket' is perhaps related to* cubby(hole). Cob *'fight' (v) is of unknown origin; it is not necessarily a continuation of the rare Middle English verb* cob *'fight' (from French?).* Cob *'mixture of earth and straw' is so called from its having been made of heavy lumps of clay.* Cob *'harbor at Lyme Regis' may also have received its name from* cob *'roundish mass, lump' (< 'rounded skerry'?).*

The sections are devoted to 1) the range of meanings of cob *and the relations between* cob *and* cop, *2)* cob *as the name of various containers, 3)* cob *(v) 'fight,' 4) the treatment of* cob *by Makovskii and Abaev, 5)* cob *'mixture of earth and straw,' 6)* (Sea) Cob, *and 7) the family name* Cobb(e). *Section 8 is the conclusion.*

1. OED classifies the meanings of *cob* as follows: 1) containing the notion 'big' or 'stout,' 2) containing the notion 'rounded,' 'roundish mass,' or 'lump,' 3) with the notion 'head, top.' In addition, several compounds like *cob-house* 'house built by children out of corncobs, *etc*' and seven other nouns spelled *cob* or *cobb* are known. OED gives them as homonyms of *cob*. Du *kobbe*, apparently related to *cob*, is equally polysemous: Heeroma (1941-42:51).

For etymological purposes it is more advantageous to divide the meanings of *cob* into

1) those referring to animals, 2) those referring to round and lumpy objects, and 3) those referring to the head. Old dictionaries derived *cob* from *cop*, a word of regional origin with the principal signification 'head, top.' Wood (1920/97) also chose not to differentiate *cob* and *cop*. OED treats *cop* 'vessel' as a homonym of *cop* 'head.' About two dozen words in Germanic mean 'cap,' 'cup,' and 'cop' (that is, 'head') with synonyms in Romance and in non-Indo-European languages—not counting variants with final *-b* (as in *cob*) and initial *g-* (as in *goblet*). They may show no evidence of the First Consonant Shift (compare, for example, ML *cuppa* and E *cup*); sometimes only one stop is shifted (as in G *Kopf* 'head').

In all probability, they are migratory words that influenced one another's sound shape and semantics. H. Kuhn (1962) spoke of the Pre-Germanic substrate, and Reinisch (1873:201-02) cited similar-sounding words in African languages. Cowan's discussion (1974:247-49) is reminiscent of Kuhn's. G *Kopf* has been traced to sources as remote as Finno-Ugric and Mongolian. See a short survey in Augst (1970:167-172), Sapir (1937:73-75; Hebrew), and Ulenbrook (1967:536; Chinese).

English *cop* and *cob* must also have interacted. However, there is no compelling reason for calling **kobbi* ~ **kubbi* a sound symbolic variant of **kopi* ~ **kuppi*, as Lühr (1988:276) does. Similar solutions have been offered in the past. ODEE understands *flabby* as an expressive alternation of *flappy*, though it is unclear why *flabby* is more expressive than *flappy*. *Gaby* (reg) 'simpleton' may be related to Icel *gapi* 'reckless man' or E *gape*, and *-nap* in *kidnap* is believed to be the same word as *nab*. None of those etymologies is safe.

Attempts to unravel the history of *cobweb* (< ME *coppeweb(e)*) bring out the confusion of *cop* and *cob* with especial clarity. OED cites Westph *cobbenwebbe* (at *cobweb*) and *cobbe* 'spider,' also with *-bb-* (so Woeste [1930]) and Fl *koppe, kobbe* 'spider' (at *cob*[4]), with *-pp-/-bb-* (De Bo, *koppe*). Woeste (1871:356-7) identified *-cob* and *-cop* and glossed *attorcopa* as 'gift sucker' (as though from *keep* < **kopjan*). He referred to the belief that spiders suck poison from the air. This is a fanciful etymology.

Kaluza (1906-07, II:330, sec 402/f) mentions three English words with *b* < *p*: *cobweb* (< ME *coppewebbe*), *lobster* (< OE *loppestre*), and *pebble* (< OE *papol(stān)*). Jespersen (1909:sec 2.11) gives the same words. Luick (1964:1109, sec 799.1b) lists *cobweb* among such forms as *jobardy* (a 16th-century variant of *jeopardy*), but he admits that in *cobweb* the group *bw* may have developed from *pw*. Most of his examples are borrowed from Wyld (1920:312-13). See also Jordan (1974:sec 161) and Wakelin (1972:153). In HL (1017), *copweb* is said to have become *cobweb* by distant assimilation: *p–b* > *b–b* (cf Horn [1950:1691]).

The Old English for *spider* was *(ætter-)coppe*, probably 'poison head' (Dan *edderkop*, N *edderkopp*; only A. Noreen [1897:47] glosses the second element as 'lump'). The spider's other Old English names were *gange-wifre* 'weaver as it goes,' *hunta* 'hunter,' possibly *spīþra, (ætter)loppe*, and *lobbe* (E. Adams [1859], Cortelyou [1906:103-11]; Schlutter [1907:303]; Bradley [1916: no 5]; Stuart [1977]; Liberman [1992b:132-33 = 1994c:211]). *Lopp-* was related to *lobb-*, as *copp-* to *cobb-*, and all of them covered the same semantic territory: *lopp-* ~ *lobb-* 'flea'; 'spider'; heavy object. *Hor(e)cop* 'bastard' is probably **hor(e)cob*, that is, 'whore child.' OED (*horcop*) gives examples from 1430 to 1578, hesitatingly compares *-cop* with *cop* 'head, top' and admits that "the analytical sense is not clear."

Yet *cob* and *cop*, though close, are not identical. The main difficulty in deriving *cob* from *cop* is the fact, noted in OED, that *cob* has meanings irreducible to 'head,' while in *cop* the meaning 'head' predominates. Two words, possibly going back to the same etymon, seem to have merged in *cob*: one referring to animal names, with the original sense being 'round, lumpy object,' and the other referring to 'head.' Only the second one is a variant of *cop* (the first word is discussed in detail at CUB). Neither possessed expressive connotations and must have arisen along the lines suggested by Wyld and Luick, with certain dialects choosing the *-b* form and others the *-p* form. No animal name recorded at *cob* appears to have genetic ties with words outside Germanic.

2. In addition to being an animal name, *cob* can designate 'great man' (probably 'the head'). 'Testicle,' 'nut,' 'stone of the fruit,' 'piece of coal,' 'loaf of bread,' and 'coin' look like extensions of 'head' (= 'little head'). Since most of those meanings surfaced late, their history cannot be reconstructed with sufficient clarity. W. Barnes (1862:101) compared *cob* 'wicker basket' and *kib, kibble* 'basket used by miners'; OED suggests that *kibble* (*sb*[3]) was borrowed from German (G *Kübel* 'large container').

It seems safer to separate all the words designating containers (including coves, baskets, and sheds) from words for 'bunch, bundle, tuft, haystack, hair,' and the like. *Cob* 'tuft of hair, haystack, etc,' may be related to E *sheaf* (which is akin to G *Schober* 'haystack,' *Schaub* 'bunch of hay,' and *Schopf* 'forelock, tuft'), with *s-mobile,* while E *cove,* G

Schuppen 'shed,' and G *Schober* 'barn' belong to the 'container' group. None of them is related to E *cob* 'head,' though here, too, the semantic distance would be easy to bridge: 'hair' → 'hairy head' or 'head' → 'container' (cf E *cup* ~ G *Kopf,* E *hogshead,* LG *Bullenkop* 'measure of beer': see KM, *Oxhoft*). See also AEW (*kubbi*) and NEW (*kobbe*[1]). ***Cob* 'head; round object' hardly experienced a foreign influence.** Nearly all Scandinavian words sounding like *cob* are animal names (see them at CUB). Wedgwood and Skeat[1] (also Skeat [1887 = 1892:451]), among others, treated Wel *cob* 'top, tuft' as the etymon of E *cob,* but the meanings of the English noun are more varied than those of its Welsh counterpart, so that borrowing from English into Welsh seems incontestable.

3. OED labels *cob* (v; 1400) 'fight' (a single citation) as a possible onomatopoeia. ModI *kubba* (v) 'chop,' mentioned in Wedgwood[2] and CD as a cognate of *cob* 'fight,' belongs with the words discussed at CUB. E *cob* (v) 'strike,' especially 'strike as a punishment' (nautical use), was first attested in 1769, but *cobbing* is a word not confined to sailors' life (it was widespread among schoolboys; see the examples in OED and EDD and a note on *Cob Hall* 'prison' in Peacock [1889]). Davies (1855:228; 1880b:24/5, 48; 1885:14) derived *cob* (v) from Wel *cob* 'blow' ~ *cobio* 'thump' and treated F reg *cobir* 'fight' (in Roquefort, according to Davies) as a borrowing from Celtic. Whitaker (1771-75:298), likewise, argued for the Celtic origin of E *cob* (v), but he traced thousands of English words to Celtic. See a survey of early opinions on the Celtic etymon of this verb in W. Hudson (1950-51:291).

The French verb apparently continues OF *cobiri* ~ *cobbir*. Only two citations with *cobir* appear in Godefroy, who also cites *coffir* (from Ménage?). Sainte-Palaye gives *coffir* and *cotir* ~ *cottir* as variants, but *cotir* is a separate verb (Littré). TL mention only the noun *cobe* 'blow.' **ME *cobbe* may have been of French origin (MED), but insofar as the history of the English verb is undocumented between 1400 and 1769, it seems that ModE *cob* (v) does not continue ME *cobbe*.** (A similar difficulty occurs in the history of FAG and FILCH.) Since Wel *cobir* 'beat, strike, buffet, thump, peck (said about hens)' is first recorded for 1455-85 (GPC), it need not be considered the etymon of OF *cob(b)ir*. Wel *cobio* and ModE *cob* (v) are so close in meaning that one of them might be a borrowing. However, **the use of ModE *cob* in sailors' language makes it unlikely that this verb is from Welsh.** See the Celtic material in WP and in Falileyev and Isaac (1998: 203).

4. *Cob,* in its several meanings, has been an object of Makovskii's speculation for years. He referred to the alleged syncretism horse ~ mountain and derived *cob* 'horse' from PIE **keubh-, *koubh-, *kubh-* 'hill, peak' (1995:135), bypassing the problem of the initial consonant (*k-* in non-Germanic and *k-* in English). According to another hypothesis (Makovskii [1992b:51, 86, 115]), bird names and words for 'give birth' and 'genitalia' are often related. He thus combined *cob* 'sea mew,' 'testicle' and the verb *cob* 'like one another' (and further, Skt *gabhá-* 'vulva'). That verb was never current in English dialects; it appeared in only one of Wright's sources from Suffolk (EDD). A word of such low frequency and not recorded in Middle English is the most unlikely etymon of *cobber* 'friend,' once current in both Australia and New Zealand, though for want of a better etymology, both AND and DNZE derive it from *cob* 'be fond of one another.' It is a word of "opaque ancestry," as Görlach (1996:77) puts it. Yet Makovskii (1964:48) connects *cobber* and *cob* (v).

In Australia, *cobber* appeared in print in 1893 and in New Zealand, in 1897. It seems to be obsolescent in both countries (see Wilkes). According to Gold (1984:205), *cobber* is of Hebrew origin: Hebr חָבֵר (*chaver*) 'friend' > Yiddish *khaver* 'friend,' and further to English through the language of the German underworld. *Cob* 'be fond of one another' is then a back formation from *cobber*. The other *cobber* 'great lie, prodigious falsehood; thumber, whopper' (slang) is equally or even more obscure. Likewise, the meaning 'sea mew' is not central to the noun *cob*.

In his first attack on this word (1971:22), Makovskii compared E *cob* 'small stack of hay or grain; bunch or knot of hair; chignon' and SwiG *Chober* (SI III:110), but he glossed *Chober* as 'haystack,' when in fact *Chober* means 'container for hay kept behind a pigsty' and is therefore the same word as G *Kober* 'handbag, food basket, weir basket, fish trap' (see also G *Koben* 'pigsty, cage': KM, KS, DEW). Turning to *cob* 'beat,' Makovskii (1992b:52, 115) compared it with Gk κῑβωτός 'box arch,' L *cibus* 'food,' and L *cubō* 'lie' (v). Again we have a string of arbitrarily chosen words with initial *k-*. None of them is related to one another. See similar fantasies in Makovskii (2000a:140).

One of Makovskii's ideas is that some common words well represented in Germanic are due to scribal errors in old glosses (1980:53-123). Consider the following passage (translated, with forms as given in the original and minimal abbreviations): "Our data show that, in the Middle High

German period, glossators often confused the meaning of the Latin lemmata *pellex,* particularly in the form *pellice* 'concubina' and *pellicium, pellifex, pellicule* (< *pellis*). Thus, we read in Middle High German glosses: *pellicium* 'i. vestis de pellibus facta l. deceptio (Diefenbach, p. 421); *pellacia i fallacia l. pellis* 'deceptio' (ib.). The lemma *pellicula* is glossed in MHG as *hut,* among others, whereas G *hut* also corresponded to the lemma *tugurium* (Diefenbach, p. 601...). Finally, the lemma *tugurium* corresponded to G *cubisi, chubrisi, chupisi* (Schade, s.v.). Confusion of the above-mentioned Latin lemmata resulted in the acquisition by that German word of the meaning 'concubina' in late glosses, and this meaning entered both Modern German (*Kebse*) and the related languages: OE *cyfes* (along with *cebisse, cebisae, caebis*), OI *kefsir,* and so forth. As the result of the confusion of the Latin lemma *dolium* (= OE *cyf,* OHG *kuyp, koffe*) and *dolosus, dolos* (= OE *cyfes, caebis,* OHG *chebis*), their meanings were also confused. See Diefenbach, p. 187: *dulus. list, betregunge* and *ain zuber.* Of interest here is the modern argotic German word *Kübbe* (cf E reg *kip* 'a house of ill-fame'—EDD III:498) 'Hurenhaus,' *kobern* 'dem Dirnengewerbe nachgehen,' *sich kobern lassen* 'sich geschlechtlich preisgeben' (Wolf, p. 2806). Cf E reg *to cob* 'take a liking to anyone' (EDD I:675; and Lith *kẽkšė* 'Hure' and Pol *kochać* 'love,' Czech *kochati* 'love,' *kochati se* 'enjoy'; see BB 2:157 [= Bezzenberger 1878]; KZ 41:287 [= Ehrlich 1907]). Cf also German argotic *Kipper* 'Betrüger' and E reg *keb* 'a villain' (EDD, s.v.). Cf a similar semantic development of E *cullion* 'a base fellow' < *couillon* < L *coleus* 'testicles'; cf E *to cob* 'to deceive' (slang). Cf also German argotic *Kibitz* 'vulva' (S. Wolf [1956:2590]) and E reg *cob* 'a sowing-basket' (see SED IV:199). As Fraenkel [LEW] and Vasmer [I:698] have shown, the notion of 'concubina' is often connected with the names of animals and especially birds. One cannot help juxtaposing E *cob* 'seagull,' Late L *coppa* (R. Latham, p. 115) on one hand and E *cub* on the other..." (pp. 64-65).

The last statement recurs in Makovskii (1988a:103), where he says that words meaning 'give birth to, bring into the world' can acquire the meaning 'dog, cub; cattle.' Makovskii compared E *cur* and Russ *kuritsa* 'hen' versus Bulg *kuritsa* 'vulva,' E *cob* 'seagull,' *cub,* and (reg) *cobs* 'testicles,' and all of them with the verb *cob* 'take a liking to someone.' This is Makovskii's idea of what he calls linguistic genetics.

Nor does calling *cob* onomatopoeic (or rather sound symbolic) solve the problem. It is a fact that the complex *k-b* is used in many languages to designate round objects, a circumstance important to Abaev (IESOI [330-35, esp 331-32]), but one wonders whether Gk κύβος, L *cubus,* E *cup* (from Old English), and many other similar words in the languages of Asia and Africa are ideophones, that is, words without a past, words that arose as a result of primitive formation all over the world only because the combinations *k-b, k-p, g-b, g-p* (and *k-d*) evoke in the human mind the idea of plumpness. Russ *kub* 'cube,' unlike Russ *kub(ok)* 'goblet,' was borrowed from German, L *cubus* was taken over from Greek, and E *cup* came from Latin. They are not spontaneous formations. None of the English words spelled *cob* was recorded before 1420. Are we to assume that a series of phonosemantic eruptions in late Middle English and Early Modern English produced clones of Gk κύβος? If such an assumption has any merit, it has to be discussed in detail rather than being brought forward as an etymological master key (see the discussion in Voronin [1997:145] and Liberman [1999b:98-100]).

5. *Cob* 'mixture of earth and straw' (Southwestern England) is a word of debatable origin. According to anonymous (1857: 14), "[t]he etymology of *cob* has long puzzled the lexicographers," but the existing conjectures are few. OED (*cob sb*[2]) rejects Cope's idea (1883) that *cob* in this meaning derives from *cob* 'lump.' But Cope did not offer an etymology; he gave only a definition: "*Cob* 'a lump of clay, such as those with which walls, houses, &c are built." It was Wedgwood who tried to find a common origin for *cob* in all its meanings. He said: "*Cob* a blow, and thence as usual a lump or thick mass of anything" and beginning with the second edition, also "*cob* (for walls) from being laid on in lumps." He may have borrowed part of his explanation from Chapple (1785: 50, note), who suggested that *cob* was "possibly from the British [that is, Welsh] *Chwap* (Ictus) [that is, 'blow, thump'], à Gk Κοπτός, 'contusus' because the earth and straw ought to be well *beaten,* trod, or pounded together." A similar suggestion appears in Fraser (1853): "a cob-wall... is so called from its having been made of heavy lumps of clay, beaten one upon another." Boys (1857:65), who quotes Chapple, cites "the old French verb, *cobbir* (said to be borrowed from the nautical English), to bruise, bump, or break into pieces." Although OED hands down the verdict that identification of *cob* 'mixture of earth and straw' and *cob* 'lump' "is otherwise improbable," the meaning of *cob* 'muddle, mess, badly executed work' (EDD: *cob, sb*[2]) makes the old ideas about *cob* not wholly untenable. The derivation of *cob* from Spanish (Boys [1857]) or Arabic

(White [1858]) has no foundation in fact. See further discussion in Collyns (1857).

6. Equally hard is the *Cob* ~ *Cobb* ~ *Sea Cob*, the names of harbor or pier at Lyme Regis (Dorset). OED (under *cob sb*[7]) believes the *Cob* to be related to *cobblestone*. According to Ekwall (1960), *Cob* is identical with E *cob* 'roundish mass, lump' and seems to presuppose OE **cobb* or **cobbe*, which would be akin to Sw reg *kobbe* 'rounded skerry.' Other similar place names (for instance, *Cobhall, Cobham, Coventry*) are more likely traceable to OE *cofa* 'cave, den; small bay, creek' or to the proper name *Cofa*. Longman[2] derives *cob* 'mixture of earth and straw' tentatively from *cob* 'lump,' and refers all the other meanings of *cob* to the root of E *cot* ~ *cottage*. No further explanation appears at *cot*. The main part of this etymology is copied from W[3]. WP I:559 and IEW 394 compare L *guttur* 'throat,' which W[3] mentions too, with OI *koddi* 'pillow, testicle' and list the other, extended variants of the root **gēu-, *gəu-, *gū-*, namely, **gugā, *gupā*, and so forth. From the point of view of the history of English, *cob* and *cot* have nothing in common. Their relatedness hardly makes sense even at the level of Proto-Indo-European.

7. The origin of the last name *Cobb* ~ *Cobbe* is also disputable. Several homonymous names may have converged in the modern form. Lower's derivation of *Cobb* from *Cobb* of Lyme Regis (1875:I/71) did not meet with approval in his time (*Cobbe* occurs in Old English [Ewen (1931:88)]; all the Cobbs could hardly have been descendants of one small group of people in Dorset). E. C. Smith (1956) accepted that etymology as possible and offered the formulation: "Dweller near the roundish mass or lump." The blurred line between *cob* and *cop* is the cause of Bardsley's attempt to trace both *Cobb(e)* and *Copp* to *cob* 'head' (1884:124; the same in the earlier editions). The two most frequently offered etymologies of *Cobb(e)* are from *Jacob(s)* (Long [1883:95, 274; H. Harrison [1912]; Ewen [1931:271, 332, 334]; copied by E. C. Smith [1956; 1969:64]) or from OE *Cūðbeald* 'famous-bold' (so Matthews [1966:327]), though it is unclear whether *Cobb* can be viewed as an abbreviation of *Cobbald* ~ *Cobbold*, whose origin (< *Cūðbeald*) is not in doubt. According to RW, in the eastern counties of England, *Cobb* may go back to OI *Kobbi*.

8. Despite the vagueness of the general picture, certain conclusions can be drawn, even if cautiously. Two distinct words seem to have existed: *cob* 'head,' alternating with *cop* and probably belonging with *cup* and the other words of this group, and *cob* 'round lumpy object,' a variant of *cub* (*kab* ~ *kub* ~ *kib* ~ *keb*). The animal names discussed above, with the possible exception of *cob* 'male swan,' go back to the second word. *Cob* 'mixture of earth and straw,' *cob* at Lyme Regis, and *cob* 'round lumpy object' are not incompatible, but *cob* (v) 'fight' is a different (in all likelihood, native) word. *Cob* 'be fond of one another' is from Hebrew. None of those homonyms is the etymon of the family name *Cobb(e)*. See Liberman (1997:97-108) and CUB.

COCKNEY (1362)

Middle English seems to have had two words. One of them was cokeney (-ay)$_1$ *'cock('s) egg' (= 'defective egg'), that is,* cok-e-ney, *with intrusive* -e- *(like* -a- *in* cock-a-doodle-doo*) and* n *that arose by misdivision of* an ey > a ney. *It occured in some dialects and soon acquired the meaning 'the poorest meal.' The second was* cokeney *'milksop, pet child, simpleton, effeminate man, inhabitant of a town, Londoner.'* Cokeney$_2$ *may be an Anglicized variant of the aphetic Old French past participle* acoquiné *'spoiled,' whose root is probably* cock *(as in* cocker*), but this etymology is uncertain. No direct connection exists between* cockney *and L* coquīna *'kitchen.' An association with* Cockaigne *is late.*

The sections are devoted to 1) the earliest etymologies of cockney; cockney *and* Cockaigne, *2)* cockney *and L* coquīna *(and its derivatives), 3)* cockney *and* cock, *4)* cockney *and* cock's egg; *the controversy over this derivation, and 5) the putative etymology of* cockney.

1. The word *cockney* surfaced in two meanings almost simultaneously. Langland (1362) used it in an alliterative phrase whose interpretation remained unclear until **J. Murray (1890a) explained ME *cokeney* as 'cock's egg.'** In Chaucer (1386), *cokenay* means 'fool' or 'simpleton' and is pronounced without syncope, in three syllables. The post-Langland attestations of the meaning 'egg' are few and late (1568 and 1592), though a 1377 passage, cited in OED, may belong here too. *Cokeney (-ay)* 'egg' occurred only in descriptions of poor meals as part of set phrases (*be served a cockney, not have even a cockney*, and so on). By contrast, the meaning 'fool' has a long and uninterrupted history from 'milksop, pet child' to 'simpleton' and further to 'Londoner.'

Casaubon (1650:218, 308-9) **traced *cockney* to Gk οἰκογενής 'born and bred at home.'** His fanciful etymology, which even Casaubon's contemporaries rejected, turns up as late as 1868 (anonymous [1868b:137-38]). **Mackay** (1877; 1887:87-89), who believed that most English words have Gaelic roots, **explained *cockney* as a combination of Gael *caoch* 'empty' + *neoni* 'nobody' (= 'ignoramus').** Around the same time, two other equally improbable Celtic sources of *cockney* were offered: Wel *coeg* 'silly' and Corn *cok* 'folly' (Douce [1807, II:156], cf GAWK and see Skeat[1] in sec 2, below; the nonexistent Corn *cok* must have been contrived on the basis of *goc* 'foolish'). Thomson related *cockney* to "Gothic" *kauptona* 'emporium' and *gawken* 'jack sprout, coxcomb.' His *Gothic* usually means 'Swedish' and sometimes 'Old Icelandic'; here probably OI *kauptún* was meant. *Gawken* is a blend of some Scottish word and an Icelandic article (see GAWK and GOWK in OED). Thomson also mentioned several Romance forms, including *cockagney* (= *Cockaigne*). His reviewer (anonymous [1826: 111]) did not know enough to question the ghost forms but doubted their relevance (except for *cockagney*) in tracing the history of *cockney*.

The best-known old etymology of *cockney* goes back to Minsheu. According to his anecdote, a Londoner took his son for a ride in the country. The youngster had never seen animals before and when he heard a horse, he asked what it was that the horse had done and received the answer: "The horse doth neigh." Soon he heard a cock crow and asked: "Doth the cock neigh too?" Hence *cockney* ('cock-neigh'), a person "raw and unripe in countrymen's affairs." That story (recorded in OED and CD) was of course told tongue in cheek, for no Londoner could have grown up without seeing horses. More than two centuries later, J. Taylor (1818:36-37) explained the origin of *cockney* according to Minsheu, without mentioning any other hypotheses. He probably knew none.

Blount referred to Camden's derivation of *cockney* from the alleged ancient name of the Thames and added: "Others say the little brook which runs by Turnbole and Turnmillstreet, was anciently so called." (Camden says nothing similar in *Britannia...* or *Remaines...*, and the passage in Blount is absent in Förster [1941: 498], who discusses Camden's ideas in detail. An earlier search also failed to confirm Blount's reference: Curtis [1852].) A river name *Cockney* does not turn up in the books consulted, but the hydronyms *Cock Beck, Cocker, Coker,* and *Cocken* exist (Ekwall [1928; 1960], Förster [1941:158, 409, 425]). Only Phillips and Coles, whose dictionaries depend on Blount's, took that etymology seriously. Later (for example, in the 1696 edition), Phillips removed it but left the "absurd mis-expression" *cock neigh.*

Beginning with Hickes (1703-05: *Institutiones Grammaticæ Anglo-Saxonicæ & Moeso-Gothicæ,* p. 231, note 1), ***cockney* has been seen as the name of someone living in the land of Cockaigne** (Hickes writes *cokayne*), a fabulous country of abundance and, by inference, London. That was Bell's opinion (BPW, 230-31), and *Cockaigne* is still sometimes considered to be the etymon of *cockney,* though Skeat[1], in contradistinction to Mueller[1], denied the connection. And indeed, the meaning 'pet child, simpleton' hardly developed from 'inhabitant of the land of plenty' (Hickes explains: 'one fond of drinking and eating' → 'ignoramus' → 'one not versed in the affairs of country life'). Popular articles that set out to explain the "archeology" of *cockney* (like Carey [1822] and anonymous [1845]) usually end up describing the joys of E Cockaigne ~ F Cocagne ~ Ital Cocagna. *Cocknei* in *the King of Cocknei* does not mean 'London' (OED).

2. **Another cluster of hypotheses centers on Medieval L *coquīna* 'kitchen.'** The name *Cockaigne,* which is of Romance origin, probably means something like 'cookieland.' Since E *cook* and *kitchen* go back to *coquīna* and its derivatives, the two etymologies (from *Cockaigne* and from *coquīna*) share some ground. The intermediate stages were supposed to be: *coquīna* → *coquinātor* 'cook, scullion' → a general term of contempt → *cockney* (see, for instance, Tyrwhitt [1775:253-54, note on line 4206]). F *coquin* 'rogue, scoundrel' and *acoquiner* 'seduce; deprave' appeared to provide an additional link.

The first to suggest the French past participle *coquiné or acoquiné and coquin as the etymons of *cockney* was Thomas Henshaw, who was the editor of Skinner's posthumous dictionary in 1671. Henshaw took for granted that F *coquin* had at one time meant 'person fond of cookery' and that it was a cognate of L *coquīna.* His idea found wide acceptance. Webster adopted it (W [1828]), and even Ker (1837, II:131-32), who traced *cockney* to the nonexistent Dutch word *kokene-jong* (= *koksjongen*) 'scullion,' mentioned it in his book.

Skeat returned to Henshaw's etymology. In the 1882 edition of his dictionary, where he despaired of finding the origin of *cockney,* he listed ME *cokes* 'simpleton,' Wel *coegynnaidd* 'conceited, foppish' and Wel *coegennod* 'cocquette' (*-aidd* and *-od* are suffixes), as well as Corn *gocyneth* 'folly' and *gocy* 'foolish' (< *coc* 'empty vain'), but in the *Errata and Addenda* he disclaimed his Celtic hypothesis (because *coegynaidd* is stressed on the second syllable) and instead accepted Wedgwood's opinion. Wedgwood started from the verb *cocker* (*cockney* was thus supposed to signify 'a cockered child') and compared it with 16th-century Du *kokelen* ~ *keukelen* 'cocker' (Kilianus; see *kokelen* also in VV) and F *coqueliner* 'dandle, cocker, pamper' (Cotgrave). Skeat rejected that comparison, but

Wedgwood never gave it up. However, he did not contest Skeat's etymology (he could have done it in Wedgwood [1882]) and communicated his new idea, which is really Henshaw's, to Skeat. He now suggested that *cockney* was formed from OF *(*)coquiné* (< VL **coquinatus*) 'vagabond who hangs around the kitchen' or 'child brought up in the kitchen.' Skeat cited F *coquineau* 'scoundrel,' but the French word appeared in this reconstruction as a parallel to, not as the etymon of, *cockney*.

Skeat[2-3] reproduces the format of Skeat[1], though the third edition (1899) was published long after Skeat had abandoned his old etymology of *cockney* (see SKCW-5, 125, note on line 4208). He says, in Skeat (1885:576), that *cokeney* means 'cook's assistant, scullion, inferior cook' from VL *coquinatus* and explains: "It is easily seen how *coquinatus* might mean either (1) a person connected with the kitchen, as in M.E. *cokeney*, a scullion; (2) a child brought up in the kitchen, or pampered by servants, as in E. *cockney*, often used in this sense; and (3) a hanger-on to a kitchen, or pilfering rogue, whence F. *coquin*, as in Cotgrave." The same gloss 'cook's assistant, scullion, undercook, petted child, cockney' appears in Mayhew and Skeat (1888, *cokeney*).

In more recent scholarship, Holthausen traced *cockney* to Old French and thence to L **adcoquinātus* (EW). Weekley (1907-10:213-16; 1909:107) originally explained *cockney* and *coquin* as coming from *acoquiné* 'self-indulgent frequenter of the kitchen, unfit for manly doings, loafer,' hence 'milksop.' He considered the meaning 'child that sucketh long' secondary, whereas in *milksop* the process allegedly went in the opposite direction. He pointed out that in the eastern dialects of Old French, L *-atum* and *-atem* had usually become *ei(t)* rather than *é*. The loss of *a-* did not bother him. Thus ME *cockney* turned out to be OF *acoquiné* adopted with "the Burgundian pronunciation." Words like *country, valley,* and *attorney* were said to show the same development of the final vowel. But in his dictionary, 'frequenter of the kitchen' (that is, **adcoquinātus*) is absent. There he assumes an Old French form with *-ei* that was "made into" both OF *coquin* and ME *cokenei* and prefers to leave the etymology of *acoquiné* undiscussed. He also mentions Cotgrave's *coqueliner* 'dandle,' a verb known to Wedgwood (see above) and relevant only as the etymon of or a form similar to E *cocker*.

Klein (CEDEL) misunderstood and remodeled Weekley's entry. He referred to the northern (not eastern) French past participle *acoquine,* without a diacritic over *-e* (this is the form in Skeat's glossary to *Piers Plowman,* but is it not a misprint there?), derived the verb *acoquiner* 'make fond of' from *coquin,* and tentatively traced *coquin* to *coq* 'cock.' Since **coquiné* has not been attested, ME *cokenei* can be only a reflex of the aphetic form of the past participle. Weekley's etymology goes back to Henshaw and partly Cotgrave, who glossed *coquine* (f) 'a beggar-woman; also, a cockney, simperdecockit, nice thing' and thus posited a connection between *cockney* and *coquin(e)*.

3. **Some etymologists have tried to derive *cockney* not only from *cook* but also from *cock*.** In the few passages in which *cokenay (-ey)* seems to denote some kind of food, it was taken for 'a young or small cock, which had little flesh on its bones' and by transference 'weakly fellow' (WPP II: 580; WPW, 609). In DOPE, the first gloss of *cockney* is 'young cock,' but it is based on conjecture, not fact. The same holds for Skeat (1867:VIII, note 2; disclaimed in Skeat [1885:576]), Child (1860:295), and Mätzner (1878-85, I: *cokenei*).

Folk etymology connected *cockney* and *cock* long before philologists did that. *Cocknel(l)* (< VL *coconellus*), first recorded in 1570, meant 'cockney' and 'cockerel.' But if *cockney* is some sort of *cock*, what is *-nay (-ney)?* In early studies, only one suggested etymology tries to explain the final syllable (if we disregard the "cock neigh" anecdote). Cotgrave glossed *niais* (or *niez*) 'neastling, a young bird taken out of a neast; hence, a youngling, novice, cunnie, ninne, fop, noddie, cockney, etc.' OF *niais* denoted any bird of prey taken from the nest, as *faucon* [that is, *falcon*] *niais;* 'dunce, dummy' is a later meaning. That idea also found a few adherents. The reviewer of Nares (anonymous [1822b:616]) asserted that the second part of *cockney* is *niais*. J. Marshall (1890; published before J. Murray [1890a]) suggested that a slang phrase **coq niais* (or **coq niez*) had been applied to London apprentices in early time. We almost return to Minsheu, but instead of **cock neigh* obtain **coq niais,* with *i(j)* after *n-* left unaccounted for. Pegge (1803:22-29; 1814: XI, 21-28; 1844: V-VI, 16-26), Todd in Johnson-Todd, anonymous (1889b), and the works dealing with Shakespeare's use of *cockney* (see the end of this entry) give the most detailed surveys of the early etymologies of *cockney*.

4. Between 1882 and 1890, many dictionaries and books repeated Skeat's version of Wedgwood's etymology. CD[1] called the derivation of *cockney* from **coquiné* phonetically satisfactory but historically unsupported, a statement J. Murray (1890a) used for a violent attack on CD. K.M.E. Murray (1977:266-67) touches briefly on this epi-

sode, and Liberman (1996a) recounts it in detail. J. Murray destroyed the phonetic base of Wedgwood/Skeat's (and CD's) reconstruction by rejecting the postulated change of OF *-é* to ME *ay (ei).* Mayhew (1890) cited numerous words of the *attorney* type, allegedly with *-ey* < *é*, but J. Murray's rejoinder (1890b) leaves no doubt that Mayhew was wrong. Manuals of Middle English give no examples of a diphthong from OF *é(e).* See Jordan (1925:sec 25; the same in later editions), Weinstock (1968:34), and Luick (1964:442; only OF *fee* yielded ME *feie* 'fairy'). However, the reverse process—OF *-ée* corresponding to ME *ei (ay)*—seems to have occurred in F *haquenée* < ME *Hakenei* (AF *hakenei*) 'hackney' (from *Hackney* in Middlesex).

J. Murray also offered his own etymology of *cockney*. He interpreted *cokeney* as *coken-ey* 'cocks' (gen pl) egg.' *Cock's egg* and its German counterpart *Hahnenei* have some currency in Modern English and German dialects and folklore and mean all kinds of defective eggs, as in *cock's-egg* 'a small abortive egg' (Holloway), 'a small egg without a yoke; an abortive or wind egg' (EDD, *cock, sb*[1]). J. Murray concluded that 'defective egg' had yielded figurative uses: 'milksop, pet child; weakling, effeminate man; townsman; Londoner.' Even the attacked Americans hailed his discovery, though not without reservations (let it be remembered that the provocation for J. Murray's article [1890] was Scott's etymology of *cockney* in CD). In both countries, the origin of *cockney* aroused a good deal of public interest. The relevant literature is as follows. In England (in the order of appearance, after J. Murray [1890a]): Chance (1890a), Earle (1890), Mayhew (1890), J. Murray (1890b), Cook (1890), J. Murray (1890c and d), Wedgwood (1890a), F. Müller (1890), Chance (1890b), Wedgwood (1890b), Hales (1891). In the United States: anonymous (1890), Scott (1890; 1892:206-11, 220; 1894:107). Murray's gloss ('defective egg') explained the passage in Langland and in two similar later passages: the authors, it appeared, spoke not about 'diminutive cocks,' 'lean fowls,' 'lean or common meat,' 'chickens,' or 'scullions' but about small eggs. Perhaps only one example of the meaning 'small egg' needs a note. Florio cites *caccherelli* 'hens-cackling. Also eggs, as we say cockanegs.' Scott (1892:220) showed that Florio had misunderstood Boccaccio's 'hens' droppings' as 'hens' eggs.'

Murray's second conclusion, namely that *cokeney* 'defective egg' and *cokeney* 'spoiled child' are the same word is not persuasive. The meaning 'defective egg' was rare in Middle English and did not continue into later periods, whereas *cokeney* 'spoiled child, *etc*,' occurred often, so that its putative etymon could likewise be expected to have greater frequency. Since no one thought of a pun on 'defective egg' and 'spoiled child,' the two words hardly interacted. The semantic distance to be covered was not from 'bad egg' to 'bad child' but from 'bad egg' to 'beloved, overprotected child.' Murray's French example—*coco* 'egg; pet name for a child; contemptuous designation of a grownup man'—shows that the same word can designate an egg and a nestling, but who would call one's darling a cock's egg? A pet child did not have to be a weakling; the meaning 'weakling' developed from the idea of overindulgence and the child's ineptitude as the result of foolish upbringing (Chance [1890a]). Cooke (1988:116) noted that a word meaning 'small or misshapen egg' was applied to men thought to have small or misshapen testes and hence to any man who lacked virility. The sense 'milksop' or 'codling,' he says, was an obvious further development through 'effeminate fellow.' But he cites no examples of 'small egg' = 'small testis' and adduces no evidence that *cockeney* ever referred to male genitals. OED gives all seven passages in which *cokeney* 'bad egg' occurs in Middle English and Early Modern English.

Also, some morphological difficulties have to be taken into account. *Coken-* is an odd genitive plural of a strong native noun. Murray's other examples (*clerken-* and the like) are from Romance. *Coc* (or *cok*) may have been borrowed from French, but by the 14th century it had lost all traces of its foreignness (if it ever had any). *Cocks'* in the gloss 'cocks' egg' is equally odd. In G *Hahnenei* 'cock's egg' and *Gänsebraten* 'roast goose,' *hahnen-* and *gänse-* are old genitive singulars that were reinterpreted as plurals later and on which *Hühnerei* 'hen's (hens') egg' and so forth were modeled. Consider G *Mausefalle* 'mouse trap': the first element of that compound is obviously not a plural form, because the plural of *Maus* is *Mäuse.* In 14th-century English, such models of word formation did not exist (Chance [1890a], Scott [1892:209]).

Scott (1892:206) suggested the division *cokenay*, in which *nay* = *ay* 'egg.' He also noted that the genitive plural of *cok* (if weak, though the type of declension did not bother him), would have been *cokken-*, not *coken-* (Scott [1892:208]). Tyrwhitt (1778:IV, 239) guessed that Chaucer's *piggesnie* is *pigges-n-ie* 'pig's eye' (used at that time as a term of endearment), and Douce (1807:II, 154-55) thought that *cockney* was its vague synonym. He almost anticipated Murray, though *-ney* in *cockney* is *n-ey*, not *n-eye.* CD[2] explains *cockney* as "a form arising by misdivision of *an ay ~ an ey,* as *a nay ~ a ney.*" But by dismissing Murray's *cocken-ey,* Scott stayed with an unetymological middle vowel in *cok-e-ney* and could only refer to similar cases: *black-a-moor* = 'black Moor,' *pink-a-nye* 'small or narrow eye,' and *mold-e-warp* 'mole.' Another English compound obscurely connected with *-ei* 'egg' is *kidney,* but it provides no help in explaining *cockney.*

Murray's etymology that initially took English lexicographers by storm has lost much ground since 1890. As stated above, Holthausen did not recognize it, and Weekley agreed that *cokeney* may mean 'cock's egg' when it refers to something edible. The post-1890 dictionaries are divided between Murray's etymology and several alternative variants. Skeat[4] and all the Oxford dictionaries repeat the interpretation of OED. ODEE and SOD[3a] cite *cocker* as a possible influence on *cockney,* which is not a new idea: Junius already mentioned it at *cockney,* and Murray at *cocker.* All the editions of FW, UED, RHD[1-2], EB (through the fourteenth edition, 1971), and AHD[1] copy from OED. ED (in the volume that appeared in 1894) offers the old etymology (by Wedgwood-Skeat) and the new one (from OED) as equally probable. W[1] follows CD (that is, OED with Scott's correction), but W[2] prefers Weekley's explanation ("prob. fr. a reg form of OF *acoquiné* in sense of idle, pampered, luxurious, from *coquin* rogue, rascal, perh. < MLG *kāk* 'pillory'").

The origin of *coquin* is debatable, but its derivation from MLG *kāk,* offered in EWFS, is the least probable of all. W[3] returns to the cocks' egg theory, while Partridge (1958), CEDEL (in principle), and Barnhart copy from Weekley (Barnhart repeats the old hypothesis of the influence of *cockaigne* on *cockney*). NWD suggests tentatively that *coquin* interacted with *coken ey* 'cooked egg.' Since *cook* has always been a weak verb, the past participle *coken* is a ghost word. WNWD no longer reproduces that etymology. MED distinguishes between *cokenei* 1. 'a hen's egg, ?a bad egg' and 2. 'a pampered child; an effeminate youth, weakling.' It explains the first word as probably a facetious blend of *chicken ei* and *cok,* and the second as either a derisive use of the first or as adaptation of F *acoquiné* 'degraded.' Ernst (1894) referred to L *cokinus,* a 13th-century word that in England meant 'royal letter carrier of inferior rank,' and concluded that the *cokinus* (or cockney) "had something to do with the king's kitchen." Skeat (1894) disapproved of this attempt to return to an etymology he himself once embraced. Indeed, even though initially *cokini* "were simply a pair of hands from kitchen, used as casual messengers," (DMTP, *cokini*), this fact has no bearing on the origin of *cockney.* The equation *cokinus* = *cockney* is wrong. Someone who like Gerson (1983:1) will try "to learn quickly" the etymology of *cockney* from a dictionary will be lost among the conflicting hypotheses.

5. The conclusions that can be drawn from the foregoing are either negative or tentative. ME *cokeney* 'cock('s) egg' and 'milksop; simpleton' are probably different words. Both were first recorded toward the end of the 14th century. *Cokeney* (reg) 'egg' is the older of the two and should be explained as *cok-e-ney,* with intrusive *-e-* and *n-* added by misdivision of *an ey* as *a ney.* That etymology is nearly faultless. Intrusive *-e-* is not unusual in compounds. One can cite (in addition to Scott's examples) *chickabiddy* and refer to a certain rhythmic model. Thus, the incomprehensible Dutch phrase *ter kaap varen* 'go privateering' became the English compound *cap-a-barre* 'misappropriate government stores' (anonymous [1912]), and in words beginning with *cock-,* intrusive *-e-* is especially common: *cockagrice* 'a cock and a pig cooked together' (obsolete), *cock-a-leekie* 'soup made from a fowl boiled with leeks,' *cock-a-hoop* 'in a state of elation,' *cock-a-bondy* 'fly for angling' (reg), along with its near homonym *cock-a-bendy* 'instrument for twisting ropes,' *cock-a-rouse* 'person of distinction,' and *cock-a-doodle-doo. Cockalorum* 'whippersnapper' and some words borrowed from Dutch and French, for example, *cockatiel* 'a kind of parakeet,' *cockatoo* 'a kind of parrot,' the humorous word *cockamamie* 'ludicrous,' and *cockatrice* also have *-a-* after *cock.* Finally, many words have 'organic' *-e- ~ -a-* like *jack-a-napes* and *vis-à-vis;* see more at RAGAMUFFIN. If *cockenay* was stressed on the last syllable, it belonged with the jocular anapestic formations of the type known elsewhere in Germanic (Brøndum-Nielsen [1924]).

***Cokeney* (-ay) 'milksop, simpleton' should probably not be traced to *cokeney* 'cock('s) egg,' because their meanings are hard to reconcile and because *cokeney* was a rare word limited to dialects and even there just to a few set phrases.** Slang and obscenities are often borrowed, and $cokeney_2$ may indeed have come to Middle English from French, but its source is elusive. **Cock niais* has not been attested in Old French or in Anglo-French. *Coquin* 'rogue, rascal' is a strong term of abuse, and *coquin* 'beggar' cannot have developed into 'milksop, *etc.*' Nor is OF *acoquiné* 'spoiled,' though a good semantic and rhythmic match for ME *cokeney* 'spoiled child,' without problems as the etymon of *cockney*$_2$. The derivation from *acoquiné* presupposes a (highly frequent?) past participle changing into a slang noun in the borrowing language. Reference to an eastern variant of the Old French form with *-ei* is a bold attempt to save an otherwise shaky reconstruction. Native sources of *cokeney*$_2$ are absent: neither *cokeney*$_1$ nor *cocknell* is a viable possibility. **An association with *Cockaigne* is late.**

Since OF *coquin* and *acoquiner* probably have the root *coq* 'cock' (the basis of many humorous, depreciatory, and obscene words), *coquin, coquiner* ~ *acoquiné, cocker,* and *cockney* may in the end be related to one another and to *cockney* 'egg,' but even if so, we would still not know the mechanism by which *cokeney*$_2$ came into being. Those speakers of Middle English who did not use *cokeney*$_1$ must have noticed that *cokeney*$_2$ sounded like *cock('s) egg,* but, apparently, this fact did not bother them. In similar fashion, we use *cocktail* and *cockroach* without associating them with *cock, tail,* or *roach* (the name of a fish).

A Note on Shakespeare's Use of Cockney

Cockney occurs in Shakespeare twice: in *King Lear* II. 4, in the Fool's mocking speech (123ff; the numbering of the lines differs from edition to edition), and in *Twelfth Night,* also in the Fool's (Feste's) speech (IV. 1, 12ff). When Lear, stung by his daughters' ingratitude, exclaims: "O me! my heart, my rising heart! but, down!" the Fool retorts: "Cry to it, Nuncle, as the cockney did to the eels when she put 'em i'th'paste alive; she knapp'd'em o'th'coxcombs with a stick, and cried 'Down, wantons, down!' 'Twas her brother that, in pure kindness to his horse, buttered his hay."

The passage given above is partly responsible for the fact that *cockney* has sometimes been glossed 'cook' in several obscure passages (for instance, in Langland) and elsewhere. It has been suggested that the Fool alludes to some popular story, for 'numskulls attempting to cook animals alive' seems to have been a widespread motif in (late) medieval folklore. In Sebastian Brant's *Narrenschiff* [*The Ship of Fools*] (1494), an engraving shows two fools with clubs pushing a resistant pig into a kettle, and a proverbial line is quoted (Wuttke [(1994:10]). The proximity of the alliterating words (*cockney, knapped,* and *coxcombs*) suggests an old song or poem. The woman in the Fool's speech was too tender-hearted to kill the eels before putting them into a pie, and her brother, too, had the best intentions, but, like Lear, both made fatal mistakes.

Although those characters may have been Londoners ignorant of the ways of fish and horses, this is not the point, for the Fool's tale is part of the international folklore of stupid people. It is similar from China to Norway, and its protagonists can live anywhere. Mackay (1887) was right that the cockney and her brother are first and foremost fools, even if the woman also happens to be a cook. FH (998, note on line 227), in discussing the sentence from *The Tournament of Tottenham:* "Every v and v had a cokenay," insisted on the translation 'Every five had one cook' (instead of 'they had one poor egg to every five'), with reference to *King Lear,* in which *cockney* allegedly means 'cook.' The editors were here mistaken, and revisers did not repeat their gloss (see Sands [1966: 321, note on line 227]).

In *Twelfth Night,* Feste meets Sebastian whom he takes for Cesario, that is, for Viola and addresses him. Sebastian does not understand what Feste wants and finally says: "I prithee vent thy folly somewhere else, / Thou know'st not me." Feste, amused by Sebastian's phrase *Vent thy folly,* answers: "Vent my folly! He has heard that word of some great man, and now applies it to a fool. Vent my folly! I am afraid this great lubber, the world, will prove a cockney." Commentators know that Florio glossed *cocagna* as *lubberland* and they occasionally mention that circumstance in discussing *cockney* and the land of Cockaigne, another name for the legendary *lubberland* (H. Allen [1936:911 and note 18]), but they have missed the connection between the two in Feste's comment, in which *lubber* and *cockney* occur in the same short sentence. *Cockaigne* is not the etymon of *cockney,* but since with time, both came to designate London and sounded so much alike, they were seen as variants of the same name. Feste may have meant to say: "This great lubber [that is, Sebastian] will prove a cockney [that is, an idiot]"; *lubber* suggested *lubberland,* and he added *the world* in parenthesis. The sentence is obscure, but the aside can be understood as a blend of "My interlocutor is a fool" and "This land of fools is, after all, among us, cockneys, in our own land of Cockaigne." Many annotated editions of Shakespeare, glossaries, and special works on Shakespeare's plays tell the history of the word *cockney* in greater detail than it is told in dictionaries. See MSh 10 (116-17), W. Wright (1877:156-57), Furness (1880:148-49), ASh 17 (124; Henry N. Hudson's note), Muir (1952:84-85), Craig (n.d.:104); Furness (1901:250-52), Luce (1937: 134-35), LC (1975:116-17); Nares (*cockney*), Douce (1867:151-56), and also Herrtage (*cockney*).

CUB (1530)

Cub *is one of many Germanic words having the structure* k + vowel + b *and designating lumpy (round) objects and animals. It belongs with E* cob *'lump,' E* keb *'ewe that lost its lamb,' late MDu* kabbe *'young pig,' Sw reg* kib *'calf,' and so on, but is not related to any Celtic word for 'whelp' or 'dog.'*

The sections are devoted to 1) the existing etymologies of cub, *2)* cub, cob, *and other animal names having the* k-b *structure, 3) the putative Proto-Indo-European etymons of* cub, *and 4)* cub *among other obscure words of a similar phonetic shape.*

1. *Cub* was first recorded in the form *cubbe*, which remained in use for two centuries. *Cub* 'bring forth young' appeared only in Johnson. We do not know whether *cubbe* was ever pronounced in two syllables, for similar forms in related languages can be mono- and disyllabic: thus, OI *kið* and OHG *chizzi*, ME *kid* and *kide* 'kid.' The closest cognate of *cub* is LG *kübbelken* 'the weakest nestling' (Woeste [1876]). *Cub* ousted the native noun *whelp* from several spheres. Disregarding the ungrounded comparison of *cub* with F *cheau* 'bud on an onion sprout' (Thomson), the hypotheses about the etymology of *cub* are of three types.

1) **According to Minsheu (*cubbe*), the word *cub* derives from L *cubo* 'lie, repose'** because the *cub* "lies in his hole, and goeth not forth for prey as the *Reynard*, or old Fox doeth." He fortified his conjecture by citing Hebr *gor* 'young lion,' from *gor* 'dwell, abide,' and referred to the Hebrew text of Is. XI: 6 "the wolf also shall dwell with the lamb," in which he took *wolf* and *dwell* for derivatives of the root גר (*dl*). Minsheu's etymology, without the parallel from Hebrew, occurs as late as 1880 in Webster and is given with or without reference to its originator in Skinner, *Gazophylacium*, Bailey (1721; 1730), Lemon, Richardson, Oswald (1866:156; likewise in later editions), DDEL, and Webster (in the editions between 1864 and 1880). Mueller[2] and Mackay (1877) do not reject it outright. Mahn (in W [1864]) adds an alternative: *cub* < L *incubāre* 'brood, hatch' (found for the last time in W [1880]).

The derivation of *cub* from *cubo* is fanciful, for *cub* does not look like a coinage from a Latin root by an educated sportsman. *Cub* as the name of a young whale (1687) should also be taken into account in the assessment of this word's etymology.

2) **W (1828) says: "Allied perhaps to Ir. *caobh* 'a branch, a shoot,'** but the origin of the word is uncertain." Webster's Irish etymology stayed in dictionaries until 1864. ID (1850) reproduced it verbatim. Mackay (1877) suggested Gael *cu beag* 'puppy' (a free collocation, literally 'dog little') as the etymon of *cub*, and Skeat[1] cited Ir *cuib* 'whelp,' and Wel *cenau* 'whelp,' Gael *cuain* 'litter of whelps or pigs,' from **cú* 'dog,' Wel *ci* 'dog,' which are related to L *canis*, E *hound*, and so on. In Skeat (1887 [= 1892]:451), *cub* appears among words of Welsh origin. Stormonth, ED, and W[1] followed Skeat. While CD emphasizes that ModIr *cuib* 'cub, whelp, dog' is from English, W[1] compares *cub* and *cuib*, and OED mentions "a rare OIr. form *cuib*" but adds that no historical connection has been traced between *cuib* and E *cub*. Yet UED states: "[P]rob. fr. or cogn. w. Ir. *cuib* 'whelp'; cp. Gael. *cu* 'dog'." The Celtic hypothesis survived all the editions of FW and reemerged in Partridge (1958), Barnhart, and KD. The vowels in the two words (*u* and *ui*) are irreconcilable. In OIr *cuib*, even the consonants did not coincide with those of *cub*, for it was pronounced with a final fricative (LE, *cuib*). The same arguments militate against the idea that the Irish word was borrowed from English. The history of OIr *cuib* seems to be beyond reconstruction. The origin of Celt **cú* 'dog' is, by contrast, clear: see Fick[3] III:78 (*hunda*), WP I:466, IEW 633, and LE. Extracting *cub* from Wel *cu beag* (Mackay) is an untenable procedure. ***Cub* was not borrowed from Irish, and it is not related to the Celtic root **cú*,** for both begin with *k* (a Germanic cognate of **cú* would have had *h-*). Despite Drexel's statement to the contrary (1926:110), a similar form in a non-Indo-European family is of no interest for E *cub*.

3) **Wedgwood[1] (and only here) compared *cub* and OI *kobbi* 'young seal.'** His comparison recurs in R.G. Latham. Icelanders understand *kobbi* as a pet name of *kópr* with the same meaning. See CV and later dictionaries, including IsEW and ÁBM, though Jóhannesson (1932:6-7, 8, at *kobbi*; further discussion at *kjabbi* and *kubbi*) admits the possibility that *kobbi* is related to *kubbi*. According to AEW, *kobbi* is usually derived from *kubbi* 'block of wood' because of the animal's round head, which is also the etymon of E *cub* and *cob*. However, the picture is more complicated because a borrowed word for 'block' or even 'young seal' would hardly have acquired the meaning 'young fox' and 'young bear.'

In some form the idea that *cub* is related to E *cob* and to OI *kobbi* 'seal' ~ *kubbi* 'block of wood' appealed to Chambers, Johansson (1900:375), Skeat[4], Persson (1912:76 and 102-03), Weekley, EW, L. Bloomfield (1925: 100), WP I:395-96 (IEW, 561 does not mention *cub*), Schröer, CEDEL, W[2], and RHD. Mueller[1], Mackay (1877), Stormonth, Partridge (1958), and Barnhart mention that etymology as worthy of consideration. Weekley (following FT, *kobbe* and *kubbe*), SEO (*kobbe* and *kubb*), and others, reconstruct the original meaning of *cub* as 'lump, shapeless object.' Since borrowing does not explain the way from 'block' to 'whelp,' a Germanic root meaning 'lump' should rather be posited. OI *kobbi* is probably a word with this root and coined independently of *kópr*. *Kobbi*, which existed as a pet name of *Kolbeinn* and *Kolbrandr* (later also of *Jakob*), must have been connected with *kópr* through folk etymology or as a deliberate joke. In words of such phonetic structure, it is difficult to separate a common name from a hypocoristic proper name; consider, for example, E *cuddy* 'donkey,' allegedly from *Cuthbert*, and see Strandberg (1993). Swabian *kōb* 'old nag' can be an aphetic form of *Jakob*, unless it was borrowed from Slavic (Rosenfeld [1947:74-75]). Russ and Pol *kobyła* 'mare' (stress on the second syllable), its posited etymon, is also an etymological crux.

Germanic languages have a great number of monosyllabic roots like *kub* ~ *kob*, supposedly meaning 'lump, round object, soft object, *etc*.' They are found in all kinds of animal names, most of which were attested late. Such names tend to have expressive geminates, variable vocalism (secondary, or false ablaut), and alternations of the *bb* ~ *pp* (voiced ~ voiceless). See Björkman (1908; 1912:262-63, on *cub*) and Persson (1904:60, on Gmc *kubb-* ~ *kobb-* 'block of wood' and several animal names). Their referents are usually 'young ones.' *Kub* ~ *kob* words coexist with synonyms having the shape *mokk*, as in G reg *mocke* 'calf' and 'little pig' (Liberman [1988b:104-08]; some of the conclusions of that study should be modified), *lobb* ~ *lopp* and *rib* ~ *rabb* ~ *robb* (see further at RABBIT and ROBIN). NEO (at *hûn* 'bear cub' = OI *húnn* 'small piece of wood, young animal, boy, *etc*') mentions E *cub*, possibly as a case of analogous semantic development. *Cub* is one of many *mots populaires* (see the discussion of their phonetics and etymology in Seebold [1997]), and projecting it to Proto-Indo-European, where it was allegedly a borrowing (thus Beekes [1996:225, 227]), is not necessary.

2. The main problem for English is the relationship between *cub* and *cob*. E *cob* is the name of a male swan, several fishes, a short-legged, stout variety of horse, a gull, and a spider (but the latter is the same word as *ættor-cobbe*, probably 'poison head,' with the first element left out; see COB). *Cob* 'male swan' is especially hard to explain: it may be a shorter form of *cobswan* 'head swan' (as explained in Nares, at *cobloaf*, and in Toone), rather than containing the root *cob-* 'animal name.' *Cob* 'stout horse' is also obscure. No traces lead from it to L *caballus* 'pack horse,' the words derived from *caballus*, or E *hobby* (as Cockayne [1861:sec 305] suggested). *Cub* can also mean 'young whale,' 'young fox' ('bear, lion, tiger'), and 'small sea gull' ('gull' is a common occurrence in Scandinavian; the same in the Orkney dialect: EDD).

From the historical perspective, *cob* 'animal name' is indistinguishable from *cub*. Consider the following variants of *cub* ~ *cob* by false ablaut. Wedgwood[2-4] cites Du *kabbe, kebbe, kabbelen* 'little pig,' and *kabbelen* 'produce young.' *Kabbe* and *kabbelen* also appear in WNT. Kilianus gives *kabbe* and *kabbeken* 'porcellus'; *kibbe* 'pig' is widespread in Dutch dialects (NEW, *big*). Wedgwood's *kebbe* (which does not turn up in the dictionaries consulted) must be the same word as E *keb(b)* ~ *kebbe* 'ewe that has lost her lamb or whose lamb is stillborn,' known from written records since the end of the 15th century. DW compares G *kippe* ~ *kibbe* 'ewe' with Sc *keb*, E *kebber* ('refuse sheep taken out of the flock,' cited by Halliwell from a 1585 source), Dan *kippe* 'small calf,' Sw reg *kibb, kubbe*, and the like 'calf' (Rietz; Møller [1943-45:12-13] offers numerous such forms for 'calf' in Scandinavian dialects), and the Dutch words in Kilianus.

Almost identical words appear in earlier and later recordings. Among them are *kebbe* 'old useless cow or sheep' (similar to ME *kibber* 'block of wood tied to an animal to prevent it from straying,' *kible* 'block of wood,' *cubbel* = *kibber*) (MED) and *keb* 'sheep, any creature small of its kind; esp. an infant' (EDD). See more examples in von Friesen (1897:52-53), Kruppa-Kusch, and Wortmann (1964:38-42: the names of sheep in northern German dialects). Davies (1855:234) cites Lanc *kibble hound* 'beagle.'

Unless the are 'primitive creations' lacking tie with the rest of Germanic vocabulary, G *kibbe* ~ *kippe*, Sw reg *kibb*, and others lead from *kab-* ~ *kob-* / *keb-* ~ *kib-* to E *chip* 'small thin piece of wood' (< OE *cipp, cyp* 'beam'; OS *kip* 'post,' *kipa* 'stave'; OI *keppr* 'stick, staff,' and so on), within the framework of the syncretism 'child, little creature' / 'block of wood, stick' (see more at PIMP), and suggest their relationship with *chip* ~ *chap* ~ *chop*. Torp (1909) indicated that relationship in Fick[4] (III:43, *kîp*), and it turns up in AEW at *kjabbi* 'fat person,' but it escaped English etymological dictionaries. Nor do they mention the *kab* forms at *cub*. Likewise, although the proximity of *cub* and *cob* has become commonplace, OED and ODEE ignored it. OED calls English *keb* a word of uncertain etymology;

however, it is safely ensconced in a group of similar-sounding animal names all over the Germanic-speaking world.

3. Sound complexes designating small animals, useless animals, and whelps need not be ancient, and it is doubtful that the Germanic root *kab-* ~ *kob-* with all its variants has Indo-European cognates in the true sense of this term. Regardless of whether OI *keipr* 'rowlock' is akin to L *gibbus* 'hump' (Wood [1926:88/11.13]; Holthausen [1942a:272]; AEW), those words seem to be unrelated to *kab-* ~ *kob-*. Wortmann (1964) offered the most detailed discussion of the *kub-* ~ *kab-* ~ *keb-* ~ *kib-* group, but he mentioned too many words allegedly derived from the same hypothetical root with the help of various consonantal enlargements for their unity to deserve credence. He could not decide whether all of them go back to a root meaning 'split, sprout, put out shoots' (as in Go *keinan* and G *keimen*) or to a root with the basic meaning 'lumpy object,' and the difference is indeed far from obvious. See more on this root at CHIDE and KEY.

4. Some lexicographers do not side with any existing derivation of *cub*. Junius, Johnson (-Todd), Barclay, and ID² venture no hypotheses. The latest dictionaries almost unanimously call the etymology of *cub* uncertain or unknown (W³, Chambers [1983], ODEE, SOD, FW [1971], Hoad, and all editions of Longman). Klein's statement to the effect that *cub* is related to ML *cuppa* 'bowl, vessel, cup' is unfortunate (CEDEL). Some connection between *cob* and *cup* exists, but it is hard to disentangle the skein of twenty odd migratory words designating 'head,' 'cap,' and 'cup'; see also COB. (Liberman [1994a:11-14] and [1997:97-108]).

CUSHAT (700)

OE cusceote *is a compound, but neither the length of* u *nor the morphemic cut in it is immediately obvious. Hence several conflicting etymologies of the word. Most probably,* u *was long. The division* cūsc-eote *presupposes an incomprehensible element* -eote*; also,* cūsc- *'chaste' as the first component is an unexpected epithet for a bird, even for one whose fidelity to its mate has become proverbial.* Cū-sceote *yields approximately 'cow darter' (if* cū- *is 'cow'), and this is no less puzzling. Identification of* cu- *with ModE* coo *is suspect because* coo *surfaced in English late, and the resulting whole 'coo darter' or 'coo caller' (if* -sceote *is related to* shout *rather than* shoot*) would have no parallels. However, two possibilities to connect pigeons and cows exist. Birds regularly follow cattle and feed on insects flying over the herds and are therefore often jokingly called cow guards. More importantly, doves and pigeons are the only lactating birds in nature.* Cusceote *may have been an adaptation of the Celtic name of the wood pigeon. Then the connection between pigeons and cows led to the folk etymological reshaping of the word.* Cūsceote *was probably understood by the speakers of Anglo-Saxon as 'cow darter,' that is, 'cow-like darter' or 'swift-flying bird following cows (cattle).' The first interpretation is more specific and perhaps more preferable.*

Section 1 is devoted to the existing etymologies of cushat, *and section 2 treats the connection between pigeons and cows.*

1. *Cushat* 'wood pigeon' has been recorded in multiple forms: *cuscute, cuscote, cusceote* (in early 8th- and early 11th-century glosses), then after a long interval (1000-1483) *cowscott, cowschote, cowshut,* and so on. In Modern English, *cushat* is a North Country word, but Robert Burns and Walter Scott popularized it in their poetry. The length of *u* in OE *cusceote* is impossible to reconstruct with certainty, for the spelling may be due to folk etymology (Flasdieck [1958:389-90, sec 6.33]; see also a brief discussion of this vowel in Schlutter [1908b:433] and Skeat [1909]). **It is usually believed that *cū-* had a long vowel because *cŭsceote* is opaque**. But *cūsceote* makes little sense even if *cū-* is understood as OE *cū* 'cow.' Hence many attempts to separate reference to the cow from the bird name.

Todd in (Johnson-Todd) divided the Old English word into *cusc-* and *-ote* and identified *cusc-* with OE *cūsc* 'chaste' "because of the conjugal fidelity of the bird." His etymology recurs in Cockayne (1861:148/599) and Smythe Palmer (1883:79-80, *cow-shot;* Smythe Palmer corrects Bosworth's *cūs-sceote* to *cusc-eote*). Skeat (1886a), who missed Palmer's predecessors, pointed out that the division *cūsc-ote* involves an unknown suffix **-ote;* "moreover, *cúsc* is not clearly an Anglo-Saxon word, being probably a borrowing from Old Saxon at a later date than the occurrence of *cúscote.*" The element **-ote,* unless it is a variant of *-hād,* is indeed meaningless, and the suffix of an abstract noun would be inappropriate in such a word (Koch [1873:143]). Skeat was also right in his assessment of the Old English bookish word *cūsc* 'virtuous, chaste, modest.'

In German, in which OHG *kûski* has continued via MHG *kiusch(e)* into the present (*keusch*), it first meant 'proper in one's behavior, moral,' then 'showing restraint in eating,' and only later 'chaste, abstinent in sexual matters' (Frings and Müller [1951]). The etymon of the German word is believed to be L *conscius* 'sharing one's knowledge, conscious (of),' though at least one other hypothesis exists; see Kaspers (1945:151). Conjugal fidelity is not synonymous with chastity, and the concept of a chaste (restrained, moral) bird is incongruous.

The division *cu-sceote* presupposes the second component *sceot* 'quick.' Koch (1873:143) cited OE *sceota* 'trout' (='a quick fish') and OI *-skjóti* (which occurs only in the compounds *fararskjóti* and *reiðskjóti* 'means of transportation, horse, donkey') and concluded that *-sceote* referred to the cushat's ability to dart precipitously into the air. He identified *cu* with *cuc* (= *cwic*) 'living,' presumably used for reinforcing the meaning 'darter.' He did not comment on the absence of the form **cucsceote* or on the change of *cuc-* to *cū-*. Mueller included *cushat* only in the second edition of his dictionary and halfheartedly accepted Koch's etymology. The same etymology (*cushat* from **cuc-scote* 'quick-shooting, swift-flying') turns up as possible ("perhaps") in CD and FW. Pigeons as 'darters' are credible; compare OE *-sc(e)ote* and the Scandinavian regional words *skuda* (Bornholm) and *skuta* (Faroese, Swedish) 'wood pigeon' (Suolahti [1909:208]), and Ebbinghaus's tracing of OHG **attûba* to **atar-tuba* 'fast (flying) dove ~ pigeon' (1989:137), but the loss of *-c-* in **cucsceote* (dissimilation?) has not been explained.

Leo (1877:573) **offered an almost irrefutable derivation of *cushat*. He cited Wel *ysguthan* 'wood pigeon, ring dove,' from Wel *coed* 'forest,' and suggested that the form **cusguthan* or **cusguddan* had become OE *cusceote*.** Like the Welsh word, Corn *cudon* and Breton *kudon* mean 'wood pigeon, ringdove,' which, in all probability, excludes borrowing from English. Davies (1880a:16; independently of Leo?) came to the same conclusion. Skeat (1886a) admitted that *cū-sceote* could be "an English adaptation of a British name." If Leo guessed the origin of *cusceote*, in Old English we are dealing with folk etymology. It would still be interesting to find out what made early Anglo-Saxons connect pigeons and cows, though folk etymology defies logic. Leo's etymology has never been discussed except in a short note by Skeat, who preferred to think that *cusceote* was a native word. In his opinion, *cū-* has the same meaning as ModE *coo*, and he glossed the whole as 'coo-darter' (likewise in Skeat[4]), an unattractive compound.

OED expressed no enthusiasm for Skeat's etymology, but it gained the support of ID[2], Suolahti (1909:208; he cites G *Girr-Taube* as an analogue of *coo-darter*), Weekley (1924; he believed that *cushat* as 'darter' has a parallel in *dove* ~ *dive*, but those words are, most likely, unrelated), UED, and WNWD[1-2]. The verb *coo* was first recorded in 1670, and its age cannot be ascertained. It need not have existed a thousand years earlier. More often, and not only in Germanic, cooing is rendered by the sound strings *girr, kirr, garr, gurr, kurr, turr,* and the like. EDD cites *coo* in a poem and *coo-me-door* 'a term of endearment for a wood-pigeon.'

Among so-called natural sounds, one can find entire complexes like *cushat* imitating a bird's voice (for instance, Sw *kuish:* Hellquist [1915:150]; similarly, Hortling [1944:163] explains the Swedish bird name *kusk* as onomatopoeia), but OE *cusceote* is hardly an onomatopoeic word. Lockwood (1984) glossed *cusceote* as 'coo-shouter,' that is, as 'coo-caller.' *Shout* surfaced in English only in the 14th century. Its etymology is a matter of debate, and projecting this verb to the earliest Old English, along with *coo,* is a risky enterprise. Among other forms, Lockwood mentioned *queece,* a regional variant of *cushat* (a cross between some unknown word and **squeece* < *sceote* rather than from *cu-sceote?*) and see *quest* and *quist* in Terry (1881). Such variants of *cushat* beset us all the time. For example, *coscirila,* a 9th-century German gloss, copied from an OE gloss, is a (corrupted) form of *cusc-* with a diminutive suffix (Suolahti [1909:208]).

2. Regardless of whether *cusceote* is native or adapted from a Celtic word, its first element, if it is *cū* 'cow,' is not as incomprehensible as most sources call it, though even Kitson [1997:495] considered it as lacking an etymology. Pictet (1859, I:402-03; 495-60; II:58) devoted an illuminating chapter to pigeons in his book and noted that all over the Indo-European world words for 'pigeon' begin with the syllable *go-* ~ *ko-* ~ *gu-* ~ *ku-* (L *columba,* E *culver,* Russ *golub',* and so on). Birds, he went on to say, regularly follow cattle, feed on insects flying over the herds, and are often called ironically cow guards. (E *cowbird* shows that irony is not indispensable in such cases.) He cited G *Kuhstelze* (*Stelze* 'wagtail') and *Ziegenmelker.* The latter is called 'goatsucker' in English. Its etymon is L *caprimulgus,* a calque of Gk αἰγοθήλας (Suolahti [1909:XIV and 17]). Similar forms occur in Slavic (Russ *kozodoi* and its cognates). According to an ancient legend transmitted by Aristotle, goatsuckers visit goats at night and suck their udders. The bird's other German name is *Nachtschwalbe* (literally 'night swallow'), and its French name is *tette-chèvre* (literally 'teat goat'). (Likewise, butterflies have the ill fame of milk thieves: two 17th-century glosses on L *pāpilio* are G *Molcken/dieb, -stehler:* Bierwirth [1891:389].) **Pictet suggested that *cu-sceote* meant 'cow darter,' a bird flying toward a cow.** In Old English, *scēotan* 'shoot' often occurs in religious contexts with the sense 'injure.' One example is *ylfagescoten* 'elfshot,' that is, 'injured by

elves; sick' (see discussion in Ivanov [1999a:15, note 50] and at DWARF). *Cusceote* (if it was *cūsceote*) may have meant 'a quick bird following cattle (herds).' But if the same idea underlay the names *cūsceote* and αἰγοθήλας, the implied meaning could be 'cow injurer; milk thief.' Situations in which an animal is depicted as a sky dweller (Majut [1963] and Liberman [1988c]), that is, the opposite of the one discussed above ('from a bird to an animal'), have no relevancy here.

Another possibility of connecting pigeons and cows is more specific: doves are lactating birds. Lithuanian has two words for 'pigeon,' namely *balañdis* and *karvēlis;* they are roughly parallel to E *dove* and *pigeon.* Pictet did not miss Lith *karvēlis* and cited it among 'cow words' for 'pigeon.' Lith *karvė* (f) means 'cow,' and *karvēlis,* though it is a masculine, seems to mean 'little cow.' By a coincidence, *balañdis* means 'wild dove' and 'hornless cattle.'

J. Levin (1992:87-88) says the following about pigeons and cows: "The pigeon is the only bird that feeds milk to its young... The cock pigeon (in all species of genus *Columba*) is the only male vertebrate which normally produces... milk for his young... The hen pigeon is the only female that lactates. This characteristic sets pigeons and doves apart from all other feathered bipeds... Contrary to one's reasonable assumption, pigeon milk is not some regurgitated milky substance like milk. All pigeons and doves produce this creamy substance, with a make-up very similar to rabbit's milk, in their crops... Thus it is milk... that establishes a connection between *karvė* 'cow' and *balañdis* 'pigeon' that would support the metaphor, the parallelism, implied in the epithet *karvēlis* 'little cow.'" Since *karvēlis* also means 'a plant bearing blue flowers,' Karaliūnas (1993:110-11) seeks a color word behind *karvēlis* (*balañdis* has long since been explained as 'a white bird'; see LEW and the references there). But *karvė* 'cow' cannot be separated from its Indo-European kin: Slav *korova* 'cow,' L *cervus* 'deer,' Gmc **χerutaz* 'hart,' and so on. Nor is it desirable to divorce *karvēlis* from *karvė.*

Thus, pigeons could be considered 'cow injurers' that steal milk to feed their young. If *cūsceote* is a native word, some such idea probably gave rise to the name of cow-like darters. If, however, *cūsceote* is a Welsh word, a similar idea must have supported its folk etymological adaptation. Ekwall (1960, Shotley) suggests that *Shotley* goes back to **Scotta lēah* 'the *lea* of the Scots' or perhaps 'pigeon wood,' but OE **sc(e)ota* 'pigeon' does not seem to have existed.

It is no wonder that *cushat,* a word without cognates, poses almost insurmountable difficulties to etymologists. Hardly any name of the wild pigeon, from L *palumbēs* to Russ *viakhir',* reveals its inner form without complications. In addition to Pictet's survey, see also Edlinger (1886a, *Taube*).

DOXY (1530)

The most probable etymon of doxy *is LG* Dokke *'doll.' If this is right,* doxy *has experienced the not uncommon deterioration of meaning from 'wench, sweetheart' to 'whore.'*

Two etymologies of *doxy* 'whore' exist. 1. From LG *dokken* 'give quickly.' Partridge (1949a) traces *doxy* to *dock* 'copulate,' known, according to him, since 1536 and says: "A doxy is a woman one docks." This etymology goes back to Skinner and should be discarded. *Doxy* did not emerge in the meaning 'prostitute'; it existed for a long time as a term of endearment ('wench, sweetheart'). A neutral and even tender word for 'woman; the loved one' might yield 'prostitute.' Such is the history of *quean,* which, in the rare cases it is used in present-day English, means 'shameless jade, hussy' and in the north 'lass, woman' (< OE *cwene* 'woman'). Likewise, *whore* is related to L *cārus* 'dear' and OIr *cara* 'friend.' E *hussy* (< *huswif* 'housewife') and G *Dirne* 'whore,' originally 'maid(en),' have had a similar history. But the way up, from 'prostitute' to 'sweetheart,' is unimaginable. 2. **From LG **doketje,* a diminutive of *dokk,* or directly from *dokke,* both meaning 'doll.'** This etymology (which first appeared in W 1828) is better than Skinner's. Comparison of *doxy* with *duck* 'pet' (W[1]) lacks foundation. MLG *dôkmaget* 'whore,' literally 'maiden- [wearing a] kerchief' (*dôk* is a cognate HG *Tuch*—Schütte [1902]), resembles *doxy,* but no connection between it and *doxy* can be established.

Most modern dictionaries, insofar as they commit themselves to some hypothesis, derive *doxy* from a word for 'doll.' See a detailed explanation in CD, in all the editions of Webster, and in Partridge (1961). OED leaves the derivation of *doxy* open. It mentions only *dock,* one of whose meanings is 'the solid fleshy part of an animal's tail' (*dock sb*[2]), and relates it tentatively to Fr *dokke* 'bundle, bunch, ball (of twine, straw, etc),' LG *dokke* 'bundle (of straw, thread), skein of yarn, peg' (see Baader [1953 (1954):42/18 on the Low German word]), and G *Docke* 'bundle, skein; plug, peg.' Even in glossing *Docke,* OED avoids 'doll' and lists only 'bundle, skein, *etc.*' ODEE goes still further and dismisses *doxy* as a word of unknown origin. Under PIE **der* 'peel,' Shipley (1984:69) lists a string of ill-assorted words, including *drab* (sb, adj), *draff,* and *dross,* but offers no arguments to justify his choice. Wedgwood laid special emphasis on the fact that *doxy* at one time meant 'beggar's harlot.' He cited the pair *doxy – gixy* and sought a connection with F *guese* 'woman beggar.' His etymology (repeated only by R.G. Latham) is not superior to Brocket's *doxy* < F *doux-œil,* literally 'tender eye.'

Dolls were originally small bundles, objects swaddled and used as toys, and words designating bundles often serve as (pet) names for children and women. However devious the route of *baggage* 'pert, saucy woman' may be, the common association between soft packages and women ('bag and baggage') must have helped it stay in English. As analogues one can cite ModI *pjönkur* (pl of *pjanka*) 'bundle, baggage' versus Sw reg *panka* 'young pig; little girl' (ÁBM), as well as G reg *bönsel* (< *bünsel*) 'little boy' and *bunschel* 'bundle' (J. Müller [1911:182]). **The path from 'doll' to 'lassie, gal' and eventually to 'whore' is straightforward** (Liberman [1992a:80-81]).

DRAB 'slut' (1515)

Drab *seems to be etymologically related to* traipse. *If this suggestion has merit, it is easy to understand how the first word came to mean 'gadabout.'* Drab *is not a metaphorical use of E* drap *'kind of cloth' (which is from French). A connection between* drab *and OE* drabbe *'dregs' is equally unlikely. Similar-sounding Celtic words are probably borrowings from English.*

Dictionaries usually explain *drab* as a cognate of G *Treber* (earlier spelling *Träber*) and Du *drab* 'dregs, refuse, lees' (which is related to E *draff* 'yeast' and *drivel*). According to that etymology, a drab is a person from the dregs of society. But *drab* is not a bookish or churchy word, and in popular speech 'prostitute' refers to a woman's genitals, to her being common property, men's plaything, slovenly, dirty, or to her selling (exposing) herself, gadding about and idling, rather than to social stratification (Buck [1367-69:19.72]). Even when 'prostitute' is derivable from 'err,' 'err' means 'fornicate.'

In the vocabulary of English, *drab* is not 'woman who makes a false step,' 'fallen woman,' or 'erring sister.' It belongs with *broad, chippy, tart,* and the words featured in J. Stanley (1977:316-18); *draggle-tail* is especially close to it. ***Drab* seems to be a doublet of *traipse.*** Junius suggested the derivation of *drab* (which he spells *drabb*) from the old verb (?*) *drabben* 'cursitare, discurrere,' that is, 'run around,' but later researchers disregarded his etymology. His parallel Du *drille* 'featherbrained woman' ~ *drillen, trillen* 'loaf (v), *etc*' may be right. SwiG *leische* 'walk in a trailing way,' *leischa* 'whore,' and *läütsch* 'whore; bitch; idler' supply an additional semantic parallel (Singer [1924:231]). Junius's comparison sheds light on G *Trolle* ~ *Trulle* 'hussy' and E *trull* (Sc *troll*), which is related to *drille* by secondary ablaut; MHG *trollen* 'walk with short steps' is a counterpart of E *troll* (v) 'move about to and fro' and *stroll.* (MHG *trolle* meant 'hayseed,' originally 'ghost-like monster': KM, *trollen;* see further at TROT on the connection between monsters, walking lightly or heavily, and female gadabouts.)

Another possibility is to follow O. Ritter (1908:429), who connects *drab* 'slut' and *drab* 'kind of cloth,' apparently from F *drap,* another 16th-century word. Ritter cites F *torchon* 'rag' and 'slattern,' E *bit of calico (bit of muslin, bit of stuff)* 'prostitute,' *blowze* ~ *blouze* 'beggar's trull, slattern,' and LG *flicke* 'rag' ~ Sw *flicka* 'girl.' *Blowze* 'slattern' is hardly related to *blouse* 'shirtwaist,' but *torchon* provides a good parallel. See more about links between words for 'wench' and 'garment' (or 'cloth') at GIRL and LASS. Weekley preferrred Ritter's etymology of *drab* to all others. The most serious objection to it is that *drap,* unlike *calico* and *muslin,* was the name of coarse undyed cloth (as the meaning of E *drape* shows), of which women's skirts were seldom, if ever, made. Also, when sluts and trollops get their names from 'rag,' the association usually comes from some cloth draggling or hanging loosely and untidily.

OED is noncommittal with regard to the Celtic origin of *drab* (sb). Davies (1855:241), Hettema (1856:201; he cites MDu *dribbe,* sb 'cantankerous woman' and *dribben* 'tell falsehoods; slander' as parallels), and Skeat[1] derived *drab* from Celtic, but their idea was later abolished. O. Ritter and Skeat[4] trace Ir *drab* 'spot, stain,' Ir *drabog* 'dirty woman,' and Sc Gael *drabag* 'slut' to English (Liberman [1992a:91-92]).

DWARF (700)

OE dweorg *'dwarf' occurs in the earliest recorded English glosses. Its cognates turn up in all the old Germanic languages except Gothic and show no semantic variations. The differences in their phonetic makeup in Frisian, Dutch, German, and Icelandic are due to regular sound changes. Around the year 600, the West Germanic and Scandinavian root of this word must already have been* *dwerg-. *Numerous fanciful and several reasonable suggestions about the origin of* dwarf *circulate in the literature, but the more cautious etymologists accepted none of them. The origin of* *dwerg- *will become clear if we assume that* -r- *is the result of rhotacism* *and posit* *dwezg- *from* *dwes-g- *as the original form. The mythological dwarf, when he was called* *dwez-g-az *(if this noun was masculine and occurred in the singular) or when he was part of the collective whole* *dwez-g-ō- *(if only the neuter plural existed), shared the most prominent characteristics with other supernatural beings, such as the gods and the elves, and was thought of as neither small nor deformed. At that time, dwarves were not rock or earth dwellers. The root* *dwes- *is present in OE* gedwǣsnes *'dementia,' MHG* getwâs *'specter, ghost,' MDu* dwaes *'foolish,' and possibly in Gk* θεός *'god.' A foolish or mad person was said to be possessed by a god, an elf, a dwarf, a witch, and so forth. Judging by the extant Scandinavian myths, the dwarves emerged as the gods' servants; they were socially inferior, rather than short. Once* *dwez-g- *became* *dwerg-, *the word for 'dwarf' began to rhyme with* *berg- *'mountain,' and this is when dwarves came to be firmly associated with rocks. The outward appearance and habits of dwarves in medieval romances and later folklore provide no clue to the etymology of the word* dwarf.

The sections are devoted to 1) dwarves in myth and folklore, 2) the phonetic history of dwarf *and the short-lived etymologies offered for this word, 3) the names of* dwarf *outside Germanic and the four still current etymologies of the Germanic word, 4) the derivation of* dwarf *from* *dwe-s-g- *and the effect of the change* *dwezg- *to* *dwerg- *on the treatment of dwarves in folklore, 5) the loss by* dwerg- *of the ability to alternate with other words by ablaut and the consequences of this loss for the name of the female dwarf, and 6)* dwarf *and* quartz.

1. **To discover the etymology of the word *dwarf*, it is necessary to examine the place the most ancient dwarves occupied in Germanic beliefs.** Our resources are limited, because the myths of the Germanic nations outside Scandinavia are lost, and we do not know whether Southerners told tales reminiscent of those preserved in the lays of the *Elder Edda* and systematized by Snorri Sturluson.

According to Snorri, the dwarves came to life like maggots in the flesh of the primordial giant, but they received human understanding and the appearance of men from the gods despite the fact that they lived in the earth and in rocks. Some details in the wording of the *Elder Edda* are obscure, and even Snorri may not have understood them. It is unclear when the dwarves chose their habitat in rocks or why they developed into anthropomorphic creatures by order of the gods; however, once this happened, they came into their own. *Vǫlospá* ('The Seeress's Prophecy'), the opening lay of the *Elder Edda,* which devotes two lines to the creation of the dwarves, says that the most famous of them was Mótsognir and offers a catalog of dwarves' names. Later we are told that the foremost dwarf is called Dvalinn. All in all, in Old Icelandic literature (poetry and prose), over 200 such names occur.

Several dwarves supply the gods with their main treasures, including the mead of poetry; they occasionally render the same service to the heroes in the romantic sagas. In other tales, they appear as smiths. When Loki cut off the hair of Thor's (Þórr's) wife Sif, the sons of Ívaldi, called dark elves (who are indistinguishable from the dwarves), made her new hair from gold. They made Odin's (Óðinn's) spear and Frey's (Freyr's) ship. The dwarves Eitri and Brokkr forged a boar with bristles of gold, the ring Draupnir (the source of wealth that never gives out) and Thor's hammer. Four dwarves called North, South, East, and West (OI Norðri, Suðri, Austri, and Vestri) support the vault of heaven.

The dwarves are powerful and cunning, but they are almost never depicted as small. That circumstance has been noticed but not discussed in any detail or explained. See the following contradictory statements: *Gazophylacium* (*dwarf*: "Teutonic *Zwerch, Zwarg,* that is, one of short stature"), FT (*dwerg:* according to them, subterranean dwellers were visualized as short creatures), J. de Vries (1956a:254: dwarves are called the embodiment of the soul), Motz (1973-74:105; 1993:93: "[T]he modern observer may wonder why the important office of craftsman-priest was entrusted to a being of stunted size. The proportions of the creatures are not, however, mentioned in Germanic myth. While dwarfs were of religious significance, their appearance was of no importance. With the loss of function and the development into a figure of folk- and fairy-tale the picturesque aspect came to the fore, and as characters of modern stories size is their most important quality"), and Polomé (1997:449; a passing remark along the same lines). Only once do we hear that Regin, Sigurd's (Sigurðr's) foster father, was "a dwarf in stature" (Motz [1993:93, note 29]). In all likelihood, he ended up being a dwarf because he forged a wonderful sword. Such leaps of logic are typical of ancient ('primitive') thinking: since dwarves are smiths, smiths must be dwarves. In similar fashion, Regin's brother Fafnir lay on his gold and turned into a dragon: dragons guard treasure, so that a guardian of a hoard becomes a dragon. Even Vǫlundr, the Scandinavian counterpart of Wayland, not "a dwarf in stature," is called *álfa vísi* 'prince (lord) of the elves,' and by implication, of the dwarves, probably because he is a smith.

No conclusions regarding the dwarves' na-

ture can be drawn from their names, which have often been classified and analyzed. Many names are opaque, and few contain references to the dwarves' small size. Judging by ModI *nóri* 'something very small; small part of something; small lump; little boy; seal's cub; narrow creek,' the dwarf Nóri was tiny. Also *nabbi* means 'pimple, lump; blemish' in Modern Icelandic, which suggests that the eddic dwarf Nabbi was like Nóri, even though the common names *nóri* and *nabbi* were first recorded in the 17th century. Finally, Berlingr is an animated **berlingr* 'short stick' (attested as part of the compound *berlingsáss,* but *berling* occurs in Swedish and Norwegian dialects). Despite the preoccupation of the *Eddas* with the dwarves' names, the antiquity of most of them is in doubt, for the skalds mention only Dainn, Dvalinn, Falr, and Durnir (De Boor [1924:548]). Since the dwarves had descriptive names like Brown, and Shining, the same name could belong to a dwarf and another character or object, for example, to a fish, a hart, a ring, a rooster, a boar, a sword, Odin, and even a giant.

In myths, dwarves are never 'dwarved' by their surroundings. They were never "loathsome" (contrary to Arvidsson [2005:105]). Allvíss woos Thor's daughter; if she inherited her father's physique, she probably looked more like a giantess than an average woman. Both dwarves and giants lust for Freya (Freyja), who is reported to have slept with four dwarves in order to obtain a precious necklace. Dwarves occasionally get the better of giants (as in the myth of the mead of poetry). Loki was not tall, and yet Brokkr, one of two master smiths employed by the gods, sewed up Loki's mouth, without experiencing any inconvenience. All three eddic races (the gods, the dwarves, and the giants) were anthropomorphic. Their place in the universe, rather than their size, distinguished them: the gods ensured that the world would run its course, the giants fought to destroy order, and the dwarves were the gods' artisans, for without the tools (treasures) that the dwarves forged the gods would have been powerless and destitute. All the honor went to the elves, who were equal to the gods and who had a cult, but the memory of the elves as divinities was forgotten early. It is not unthinkable that some of the dwarves' names at one time belonged to the elves.

The *Edda*s give no account of the origin of the gods, but some conclusions can be drawn from the grammatical characteristics of the Icelandic noun *guð* (n). Aside from late references to the Christian god, it was used only in the plural. Go *galiuga-guð** and OHG *abgot* 'false god(s)' are likewise neuter (see an important discussion in De Tollenaere [1969:226-27]). Originally, the Scandinavians and, one can assume, all the speakers of the Germanic languages envisioned their gods as a collective whole. Although in the *Edda*s each god had a name and could be identified in the singular as an *Áss* or a *Vanr,* the plural forms—*Æsir* and *Vanir*—were in the absolute majority. Even today we sometimes use the plural when the idea of a whole is uppermost in our mind, for instance, *children* as in: "They have no children" (one child would suffice for stating that they have 'children'), germs (for what is a germ?), and so forth. Skeat preferred to list the form *bots* 'worms' in his dictionary, yet *bot*, singular, exists too (OED).

Despite the fact that OI *dvergr* is a masculine noun whose plural is *dvergar*, the dwarves must have started as a mass, a collective whole. The Old High German cognate of OE *dweorg* and OI *dvergr* was *(gi)twerc.* Its gender is impossible to determine from the extant texts, but in Middle High German *(ge)twerc* was nearly always neuter. Alongside *twerc,* the prefixed form *(ge)twerc* existed (see *Nib* 97/1, note); *ge-* occurs in nouns denoting groups of people or objects. The situation in Old and Middle High German is the most archaic, for the path from *guð* (n pl) to *guð* (m sg) and from *(ge)twerc* (n pl) to *twerc* (n m sg), that is, from an undifferentiated mass to an individual, is natural, whereas the reverse path is out of the question. Change of grammatical gender in such words was not uncommon (Brugmann [1907:318]). Note that OE *gāst* and *gǣst* 'ghost' must originally have belonged to the *s*-stem, which means that both words may at one time have been neuter (SB, sec 288, note 1; A. Campbell [1959:sec 636, end]; OED: *ghost*). Go *skohsl** 'demon' was neuter too, but no general rule obtains here, for MHG *orke* 'demonic creature' is masculine, and so is OE *orcnēas* (pl) 'evil spirits, monsters,' known from *Beowulf* 112. The gender of Gmc *orc-* was probably influenced by its etymon, L *orcus* 'god of death.'

Not only the fact that the gods and the dwarves were in the remote past members of 'hosts' rather than individual deities unites them. They seem to have been visualized and worshipped in a similar way. In Old Icelandic, two words spelled *áss* existed: one meant 'member of the Æsir family,' the other 'pole, beam' (as in *berlingsáss,* mentioned above). It is tempting to treat them as the descendants of the same etymon despite some doubts on this score. Columns and beams of all sorts have been objects of cults all over the world (Meringer [1904-05:159-66; 1907:296-306; 1908:269-70; Olrik [1910]; Weiser [1926:12]). See the discussion of the Gothic cognates of OI *áss₁* and *áss₂* in Feist[3-4] at *ans** 'beam' and *anses* '(demi)gods.' Of special interest is the ancient Venetian word *ahsu-*, which probably meant 'herma,' that is, a statue of Hermes mounted on a square stone post, and which can thus be related to both *áss₁* and *áss₂* (Sommer [1924:132]), Krahe [1929:325]). *Áss₁* and *áss₂* are now believed to be different words (Polomé [1953; 1957]), but it is remarkable, if it is a coincidence, that in medieval Iceland, *dvergar* meant 'dwarves' and 'short pillars that support the beams and rafters in a house.' See more on *dvergar* 'pillars' in Gunnell (2001:20-22; 2003:193).

The specialized meaning of *dvergar* is usually said to go back to the myth about four dwarves supporting the sky (ODGNS), but the development in the opposite direction is more probable: *dvergar* may have been understood as 'stalwarts,' as supports subservient to *æsir* 'beams,' and, once the world came into being, it was natural for Æsir to entrust four dwarves—North, South, East, and West—with propping up the new structure. The Old Icelandic for 'world' was *heimr* 'home,' so that "the big home" must have been modeled on human dwellings. The myth of four dwarves did not arise when the Scandinavians were cave dwellers. Likewise in Hittite, "[t]he typical *4 halhaltumari* are not merely the mundane corners of a house or hearth, they also denote the 'four corners of the universe,' that is, cardinal points in terms of movements of the sun and the winds" (Puhvel [1988:257]). *Æsir* and the *dvergar* as beams form a perfect correlation. An ornament called *dvergar*, one on each shoulder, mentioned in the *Elder Edda*, must have been a short support or a pin (Nerman [1954]).

We should approach the etymology of *dwarf* with the following considerations in mind: the eddic dwarves were the gods' most important servants, even culture heroes; they shared mythological space with the gods, elves, and giants, from all of whom they were in some cases indistinguishable; they did not emerge in people's fantasy as small creatures living in mountains and rocks; their names furnish no information about their origin; and the eddic dwarves may have had counterparts elsewhere in the Germanic speaking world.

2. The forms relevant for the etymology of *dwarf* are as follows: OE *dweorg*, OI *dvergr* (ModI *dvergur*, Far *dvørgur*, N *dverg*, Sw *dvärg*, Dan *dværg*), OFr *dwerch* and *dwirg*, OS *(gi)dwerg*, MLG and MDu *dwerch*, OHG and MHG *(gi)twerc*, *(ge)twerc* (G *Zwerg*). OED gives a detailed list of cognates in the Germanic languages and English dialects, but EDD barely mentions *dwarf* (only as part of plant names and such). Labialization in Faroese (*e* > *ø*) is late, and so is the irregular change of *tw-* to *zw-* in German. **The protoform immediately preceding the recorded forms must have been **dwerg-*.** The relation of OFr *dwerch* to *dwirg* will be discussed below.

The diphthong in OE *dweorg* is due to Old English breaking (*e* > *eo* before *rg*). The Middle English form was *dwerg(h)*. It is immaterial whether it goes back to *eo* smoothed (monophthongized) or to *e* that was not broken in the Anglian dialects. When ME *er* became *ar*, *dwerg* acquired the pronunciation *dwarg*, with *wa* later going over to *wo*. Detailed books on the history of English give an account of those changes; see, for example, Luick (1964:478, 697, 861). Hirt (1921:31) mistakenly referred the differences between *a* in *dwarf* and *e* in *Zwerg* to the differences in the influence of *i* in Germanic. In *Zwerg*, *e* is old (that is, not the result of umlaut), whereas in *dwarf*, *a* is not original.

The letter *g* in OE *dweorg* designated a fricative. That sound regularly became *f* in Middle English, with *gh* reflecting the oldest pronunciation of *-g*. It is due to chance that *dwarf* is not spelled *dwargh* or *dwergh* now. Koeppel (1904:34) notes that *-a-* in *dweorgas* was hardly "a guttural vowel" when fricative *g* yielded *w*, but by the time of the change *g* to *w* (whatever Koeppel's formulation means) *dweorg* had been monosyllabic for centuries. According to anonymous (1901a), Skeat cited reg *dwerk* and adduced it as proof that fricative *g* occasionally became *k*. The form *dwerk* is not listed in the sources consulted, and Skeat does not seem to have mentioned it in any of his published works. If *dwerk* exists, it is probably a variant of Scand *dverg*.

Most etymologists consider the word *dwarf* to be of unknown origin. J. de Vries (NEW, *dwerg*) suggested that it was a relic from a substrate language (was he thinking of a term of pre-Germanic religion?). His idea, although not repeated in AEW, found its way into Mackensen (*Zwerg*) as a remote possibility. Other modern dictionaries do not mention the substrate but have little to say about the history of *dwarf*. The hypotheses on the origin of this word are of two types. Some died without issue: no one supported them or the support was minimal. Others enjoyed considerable popularity for a long time. In this section, only the less fortunate conjectures will be mentioned.

Promising or fanciful, the etymologies of *dwarf* do not differ too much: all of them attempt to show that the original meaning of the word was 'short,' 'deformed,' or 'deviant,' none of which can be right.

Probably the oldest etymology of *dvergr* goes back to Guðmundur Andrésson, who referred this word to Gk θεός 'god' and ἔργον 'work.' Finn Magnusen (FML) found himself in agreement with Andrésson. Their etymology became widely known, because Jacob Grimm supported it (without references). He offered it in all four editions of his *Deutsche Mythologie* (1835:252; 1875:370). Since θεουργία meant 'divine work, miracle, magic, sorcery' (cf θεουργός 'one who does the work of God, priest') and has retained its meaning in modern use, as in E *theurgy* 'the working of some divine or supernatural agency in human affairs,' **Andrésson and others were justified in searching for links between the earliest sense of *dvergr* and the production of magical objects, but *dvergr* cannot be a relic of a disguised late Greek compound.** Those who referred to Grimm (they did not know his predecessors) added question marks. Mueller mentions him, but Ten Doornkaat Koolman (*dwarg, dwerg*), Kluge (EWDS: *Zwerg*), and Franck (EWNT: *dwerg*) make a point of distancing themselves from Grimm. Weigand combined Grimm's etymology with the *Zwerch* hypothesis (see below).

According to Skinner and Wachter, **Martinius** (apparently, not in Martinius [1701]) **compared *dwarf* and L *dīvergium,*** a word derived from Late L *dīvergere* 'turn aside,' because dwarves are deviant creatures. **Skinner refers to Martinius without comment and adds Belgian (that is, Flemish) *dweeis* 'obliqus.'** The closest one comes to *dweeis* is MDu *dwaes* 'foolish.' Wachter called Martinius's conjecture ingenious but doubted its validity. **Cleland** (1766:47), who set out to demonstrate the Celtic origin of most words, **looked on *dwarf* as the sum of the 'Celtic' privative prefix *de-* and OE *arf* 'inheritance.'** The expected result should have been 'disinherited' or 'dispossessed,' but Cleland says 'not grown.' Only Lemon took his etymology seriously. ***Dwarf* turns up in W. Barnes (1862:233) under one of his roots, namely *dw*ng* 'dwindle.'** Grouping together several mainly regional words beginning with *dw-* and having something to do with diminution and smallness was a good idea, but the root *dw*ng* does not exist. **Zollinger** (1952:89), ninety years later, in a book whose title is amusingly reminiscent of Barnes's, **compared PIE *dhu̯ergh, from IEW (279), and Egyptian *dnrg, dang, darg, da'g,*** all of which he glossed as 'dwarf.' Between 1862 and 1952, two more researchers dealt with this word. **According to Loewenthal** (1928:459), ***dvergr* should be understood as **dhu̯er-u̯okᵘos,* the second component being related to L *vox* 'voice.'** He glosses that compound as 'one saying fateful things,' though the dwarves are nowhere depicted as prophets. **Juret** (1942) **gave a thesaurus of his own roots. Under $ə_2t$ 'small, tiny,' we find, among others, E *dwarf* and *thin*** (p. 342).

3. 'Divergent,' 'dwindler,' 'sooth-sayer,' and 'producer of magical things for the gods' do not seem to be the original meanings of *dwarf.* Nor is the material outside Germanic of much help in approaching the Germanic word. 'Dwarf' does not appear in Buck, but some comparative material can be found in SN (708). Gk νάννος and νᾶννος, from which Latin has *nānus* (whence Ital *nano,* F *nain,* and Sp *enano*) and Hebrew has ננס (*nns*), is probably a baby word. Gk πυγμαῖος is from πυγμή 'fist,' a formation like G *Däumling,* E *Tom Thumb,* and OPr *parstuck* (Lith *pir̃štas* 'finger,' and so on). Russ *karlik,* with a diminutive suffix, and its cognates in Polish and Czech are slightly reshaped borrowings from German (OHG *karal,* MHG *karl,* G *Kerl* 'young man': Vasmer, *karla;* further references in ESRI [XI:72], *karlik*). See more on *Kerl* at GIRL. Lith *kaũkas* goes back to the root meaning 'elevation' (the *kaũkas* is visualized as a gland, pimple, knob; among the related words is Go *hauhs** 'high,' LEW). L *pumilio* is obscure. If it is from PIE **p(a)u-* 'small' (*pu-mi-l-ion*), *-m-* remains unexplained (WH); if it is from *pumi-l-ion* 'little hairy one' (as in D. Adams [1985:244, note 8]), the feature chosen for the nomination ('hairy') makes little sense. F *nabot* is equally opaque. From (O)I *Nabbi* (see it above)? A disguised compound from *nain* + *(pied)bot* 'clubfoot'? Both hypotheses look strained. Nothing is known about the history of *gnome,* first occurring in Paracelsus (KS, *Gnom*). Gmc **dwerg-* is neither a baby word nor 'manikin,' and unless it is a substrate word, it must have a recoverable root.

Over the years, four etymologies of *dwarf* (*dvergr, Zwerg*) have been recognized as holding out some promise.

1) ***Dwarf* is presumably a cognate of G *zwerch,* now extant in a few compounds like *Zwerchfell* 'diaphragm';** as an independent word it exists only in the form *quer* 'diagonally.' The originator of this etymology was Minsheu (*dwarf*), but it has the greatest appeal to German-speakers, for G *Zwerg* and *zwerch-* are near homonyms, and both *zwerg* and *zwirg* have been recorded as forms of *zwerch* (Much 1893:92), whereas in Low German,

dwerch combined the meanings of the two homonyms 'crippled, lopsided' and 'dwarf' (Lübben [1871:317]). In the other languages, the similarity between *dverg(r)* ~ *dwarf*, on one hand, and the cognates of *zwerch*, on the other, is not so great: compare Go *þwaírhs* 'quick-tempered,' OI *þverr* 'troublesome,' and OE *þweorh* 'hostile.' The semantic link between 'diagonally' and 'angry' is obvious; one can cite the English adverb *across* and the adjective *cross*. The only cognate of *þweorh* in Standard Modern English is *thwart* 'frustrate, challenge,' which is a borrowing from Scandinavian. Minsheu's etymology reemerged in Wachter (*Zwerg*), but neither bothered to explain the difference between *þw- and *dw-. Such an explanation could not be expected at that time.

Zwerg from *zwerch-* appears in Kaltschmidt (an early but serious dictionary), Terwen (*dwerg*; his only source is Kaltschmidt), Talbot (1847:37-38), Richardson, Chambers (1867), and Faulmann (from the nonexistent strong verb **zerben* 'turn oneself around'; with the explanation that deformed, hunchbacked people do not grow). Richardson, who borrowed his etymology from Wachter, noted that the word *dwarf* had perhaps originally been applied to certain imaginary creatures of thwart, cross, crooked, mischievous dispositions, and later to any thing stunted or perhaps deformed in its growth. Faulmann seems to be the latest proponent of the *zwerch* etymology (1893). As early as 1879, Ten Doornkaat Koolman rejected it as unconvincing. G *zwerch* and Go *þwairhs* can be related to L *torqueo* 'twist, bend.' L. Schmidt (1961:33-49), the author of a special work on *torqueo*, does not mention *Zwerg*.

The mythological dwarves, it should be repeated, were not deformed (crooked, hunchbacked, or stunted); only later folklore occasionally represented them as such (Siefert [1902:377]). Nor were they particularly mischievous or evil. Ethical norms are alien to myth, and the behavior of mythological characters is determined by expedience rather than morality. In the *Eddas*, dwarves do what they find useful at any given moment, and malice is not their most prominent feature. In recent time, J. de Vries (AEW, *dvergr*) partly revived Minsheu's idea. He cited a few words in which initial *þ-* and *d-* alternate and suggested that the most ancient meaning of the root was 'pin, peg, short stick.' A widespread syncretism 'child, little, creature' / 'block of wood' exists in the Germanic languages, so that a semantic link between 'shoot' and 'offshoot' is real (see CUB, KEY, and PIMP). Numerous words for 'child' go back to words meaning 'chip, chit, pin.' But two circumstances invalidate J. de Vries's hypothesis: 1) no recorded word containing the root *þver-* means 'branch, twig, pin, short stick,' and 2) mythological dwarves were not thought of as short. In his history of Germanic religion, J. de Vries (1956:253, 254) notes that the small size of all 'dwarf-like' creatures may be due to the conception of the soul being embodied in them. The eddic dwarves have nothing to do with the soul. W. Krause (1958:56) rejected J. de Vries's reconstruction, and it does not appear in any later etymological dictionary, seemingly, for a good reason.

Marginally related to the etymology discussed here is Te Winkel's conjecture that MDu *dwerch* is akin to OE *þweran*, which in poetry meant 'beat, forge,' for dwarves, as he says, were smiths, and Du *smeden* 'forge, weld' (a cognate of G *schmieden*) was a synonym of *þweran* (1875:111, see *dwerch* in the glossary). Here he erred slightly, for in the remote past, smiths were craftsmen, wrights, rather than workers in metal. Also, the meaning of OE *þweran* 'beat, forge' seems to have been derived from 'stir, churn' (hence 'soften, make malleable'). Te Winkel related MDu *dwerch* and OE *þweran* to Go *þwairhs* 'quick-tempered' (with the implication that 'irascible' = 'pugnacious'?) and OE *þyrs* 'giant, demon, wizard' (he could have added OI *þurs* 'giant'). Dwarves were, in his opinion, not unlike Cyclopes and later came to designate monsters, often but not necessarily small. He quotes Bilderdijk (*dwaarg*), who noted that in Dutch medieval romances *dwerg* was used interchangeably with *reus* 'giant,' both kinds of creatures being deformed but of enormous size (!) and presented as robbers, and finds ample evidence of huge dwarves in Jacob van Maerlant's *Roman van Torec*, which Te Winkel edited. However, initial *þ-* in *þyrs* ~ *þurs* (and OE *þweran*) cannot be reconciled with *d-* in *dwerg-*. It will be shown below that *r* of *dwerg-* and *þyrs* ~ *þurs* are equally irreconcilable. Nor is ablaut (*e-u*) to be expected in this case (sec 5, below). The origin of *þyrs* ~ *þurs* remains unclear (see AeEW, AEW, DEO[4]: *turs(e)*, and other Scandinavian etymological dictionaries).

2) **A. Kuhn (1852:201-02), in an article on evil creatures in Indo-European mythology, compared *dvergr* and Skt *dhvarás-* 'crooked, dishonest,' an epithet accompanying Druh, a demon; he traced them to the root *dvṛ.** Although his article appeared in volume 1 of the celebrated *Zeitschrift für vergleichende Sprachforschung* and Pictet (1859-63, II:637-38) referred to it, his proposal attracted little attention until it was incorporated into Fick[3] I:121

and III:155-56. *Dvergr* now joined Skt *dhvárati* 'fell, cause to fall,' L *fraus* 'detriment, harm, *etc*,' and many other words as a related form. In a kind of postscript, Fick compared Vedic *dhvarás-* 'evil fairy, demon of deceit' with Gmc **dverga-*. This remains the most often cited etymology of *dwarf*. No one subscribes to it wholeheartedly, but for want of a better solution dictionary makers mention it with various degrees of hedging. M. Schwartz's detailed analysis of the root **dhvar*[i] brought him to the conclusion that the Vedic word is not related to *dwarf* (1992:405-10, esp p. 410). Von Bradtke (1886:352, note 1) preferred *druh* to *dhvarás-* as a cognate of *dvergr*. Kuhn discussed both *druh* and *dhvarás-* before him and, as we have seen, made a different choice. If even Kuhn's comparison had to wait more than two decades before it found its way into a widely read manual (however, the users of Fick's compendium did not always know who offered the etymologies in it, for Fick gave no references), it could only be expected that Holmboe's idea, which was exactly the same (OI *dvergr*: Skt *dvṛ* 'bend, curve') and was also made public in 1852, passed without notice.

3) **Another attempt to link Gmc **dwerg-* to an Iranian word was Bartholomae's (1901:130-31, note 2). He connected *dvergr* and Avestan *drva*, the name of some (unidentifiable) physical deformity.** Bartholomae's etymology has found a number of supporters, the most confident of whom was Krogmann (1934-35). It is not obvious what unites *dvergr* and *drva* apart from the phonetic similarity between *d-v-r* and *d-r-v*. The dwarves of Scandinavian mythology were not deformed. Bartholomae and others may have been inspired by the circumstance that the dwarves and elves were believed to cause diseases and produce deformity in people.

This belief has left some traces in the Germanic languages, such as N *dvergskott* 'epizootic' = and 'dwarves' shot' (De Boor [1924:545]); the affected cattle are called *dvergslagen*. But in this respect dwarves do not differ from other spirits, fairies, and so on, as follows, for example, from G *Hexenschuß* and N *hekseskudd* ~ *hekseskott* 'lumbago,' OE *ylfa gesceot* 'disease attributed to evil spirits' (see *elfshot* in OED and *elf* in ODEE, Lessiak [1912:136-40], and Ivanov [1999a:4-5] for a broad discussion of diseases caused by elves and their kin). E *giddy*, from Late OE *gidig*, from **gydig* (the umlauted form of **guð-ig-az*) probably means 'possessed by a god.' Likewise, OE *ylfig* (*ielf, ylf, ylfe, ælf* 'elf') meant 'mad, deranged.' The Classical Greek noun ἐνθουσιασμός 'inspiration' derives from 'being possessed or inspired by a god,' so that *enthusiastic* is, as far as its inner form is concerned, close to *giddy*. The root of the word *ghost* meant 'terrify, afflict' (cf Go *usgaisjan** 'frighten').

Having a god in one might be beneficial or injurious to the person possessed. Although the dwarves, the gods, and the elves could cause insanity, it would be imprudent to look for the origin of the words *god, elf,* and *Hexe* (*hekse*) 'witch' among the names of demons, even if the first dwarf's name *Mótsognir* or *Móðsognir* means 'sucking strength' (Reichborn-Kjennerud [1931]). In Anglo-Saxon England, dwarves were said to cause convulsion (see BT II:*dweorg* and discussion in Ostheeren [1992:45]). Those names were too numerous and too varied.

Nothing is known about the Avestan word *drva* except that it occurs in a list of physical deformities (see Derolez [1945]). **Krogmann (1934-35) added Latv *drugt* 'collapse, diminish' to Avestan *drva* as a cognate of **dwerg-*.** Neither he nor those referring to *drugt* in their dictionaries realized that it is an obscure regional word, itself in need of an etymology. Von Grienberger (1900:59) tentavely connected it with Go *drauhsnos* 'fragments, crumbs,' but the form and the origin of the Gothic noun seem to be beyond reconstruction. The putative cognates of Latv *drugt* are OI *draugr* 'dry wood' (a homonym of *draugr* 'ghost' or the same word?), OE *drӯge* 'dry,' Go *driusan** 'fall,' and Lith *drugỹs* 'chill fever; butterfly' (see Russ *drozh'* 'shiver' in Vasmer I, 540-41); finally, Lith *druskà* 'salt' is sometimes drawn into this circle. It is anybody's guess whether *drugt* belongs with them. Berneker (231) mentions it, while Fraenkel (LEW, *drugỹs*) does not. Wood (1914a:69/7) combined E *dry* and Latv *drugt*, and Endzelīn in Mūhlenbachs (*drugt*) thought his idea to be reasonable, but Karulis did not include *drugt* in his dictionary. Endzelīn thought of a connection between *drugt and* E *dry* as possible. Etymologies based on the *obscurum per obscurius* principle seldom prove to be right. Two almost impenetrable words (*drva* and *drugt*) are hardly able to shed light on the seemingly isolated **dwerg-*, whose ties with those words are exactly what has to be established.

Since Skt *dhvárati* is believed to be a cognate of OHG *triogan* 'deceive' and since *dhvarás-* designates some demonic creature, **dwerg-* was assigned to the root **dreug-a-* 'deceive.' Seebold (1970:168-69) does not mention *Zwerg*; however, in KS he admits the possibility that *Zwerg* and (*be*)*trügen* are related. 'Dwarf' as 'deceiver' appears in FT(N) (the dwarves allegedly cause visual aberrations, or they are dangerous, harmful creatures). WP I:871-72 give *dhu̯ergh : drugh* 'dwarf-like, deformed' (likewise in IEW, 279); KEWA II:119 refers to IEW but translates the root *dhu̯er-, dhu̯erə* 'destroy by deception or cunning; injure.' It is the confusion of 'deformity' and 'deception' that makes the etymology of *dwarf* so vague. We constantly run into **dhrugh* 'harm, deceive' (as in Mogk [1918-19:597]—'schädigen, betrügen') or are told that harming results in deceiving (as in Detter's dictionary, *Zwerg*; edited out in Loewe's version).

Although no system can be detected in the practice of lexicographers' dealing with the origin of *dwarf*, in the dictionaries dependent on Fick[3] the gloss 'deformity' prevails (so, for example, in Zehetmayr), while Kluge (EWDS) and his followers prefer 'deception.' Those who treat dwarves as deceivers rely mainly on the Sanskrit cognate; those who look on dwarves as cripples cite the Avestan word. Practically, all of them leave the question open, list both etymologies as uncertain, and refuse to take sides. Certainty is rare (for instance, L. Bloomfield [1912:258/10] refers to Fick's solution as definitive). Equally rare are new attempts to explain the nature of dwarves from linguistic data. Thus, Scardigli and Gervasi (1978, *dwarf*) give **dhreugh-* 'deceive'? and suggest 'creatura misteriosa' as the original sense of *dwarf*; this is a rather mysterious gloss (do they mean 'belonging to so-called hidden people'?). Motz (1973-74:113-14) takes the ritual deformity of the mythological smith (Hephaistos and others) as her point of departure, and supports Bartholomae's etymology (Avestan *drva*, Gmc *dwerg-*). The statements in Motz (1983:117, 118) are more cautious. Vǫlundr, like Hephaistos, was indeed deformed, but none of the eddic dwarves is represented as a cripple.

4) One more hypothesis gained considerable currency at the end of the 19th and the beginning of the 20th century. **Holthausen (1886:554) suggested that *dvergr* is related to Gk σέρ(ι)φος 'midge.'** E. Zupitza (1896:99) supported Holthausen and later (1899:100, 103) added OIr *dergnat* 'flea' as a cognate of σέρφος. When A. Noreen (1894:224), Pedersen (1909:109, sec 65), and Vendryes (1912:286) gave this etymology their imprimatur, it became widely known. Skeat[1] borrowed his etymology from Fick[3], whereas Murray chose Holthausen's derivation, and it appeared as proven in OED, SOD[1-3], and ODEE. Only SOD[3a] makes no mention of it, presumably because Beeler (1970:322) expressed his surprise that a major English dictionary could offer an etymology classicists had never taken seriously.

Attempts to establish the origin of σέρ(ι)φος have failed. Venmans (1930:72) compared the Greek word with L *serpens* 'snake,' but Kretschmer (1933:181) and Specht (1944:266/6) rejected his etymology on phonetic grounds. Fernández (1959:98) tends to agree with Wood's idea (1919:250/101) that σέρφος belongs with συρφετός 'sweepings, refuse, litter,' and σύρμα 'sweepings, refuse, heap of straw,' σάρος 'broom, litter, refuse,' and σύρω 'drag along,' all of them allegedly from PIE **tu̯er-*. Frisk wonders whether σέρφος is an onomatopoeic word, but other compendia and dictionaries of Classical Greek (Prellwitz, Leo Meyer, Hofmann) venture no hypotheses. Frisk and Chantraine are of the opinion that σέρφος defies explanation. Only Boisacq compared σέρφος and Skt *dhvarāḥ* 'demon.' There is partial agreement on the fact that -φ- in σέρφος is a suffix (from **bh-*), which neither invalidates the comparison σέρ-φ-ος: **dwer-g-az* nor strengthens it. The main argument against Holthausen's etymology of *dwarf* ~ *Zwerg* ~ *dvergr* is, once again, the use of the *obscurum per obscurius* principle: the opaque Greek word σέρφος cannot reveal the origin of an equally opaque Germanic word. See Petersson (1921:18) for some arguments against the *dwarf*—σέρ(ι)φος connection.

This episode in the study of *dwarf* is typical in that it shows the lack of coordination among the various branches of Indo-European etymology as a science. Apparently, if *dwarf* is related to σέρφος, σέρφος is related to *dwarf* (*Zwerg, dvergr*). But despite the prestige of OED and the high esteem in which Holthausen was held, not a single etymological dictionary of Classical Greek considered *dvergr* as a possible cognate of σέρφος, and among Greek scholars only Boisacq comments on the implausibility of Holthausen's conjecture from the semantic point of view. Juret, who offered his own fanciful etymology of *dwarf*, made no mention of σέρφος. Apart from OED, Tamm (*dvärg*) accepted σέρφος as a cognate of the Germanic word, and SOAB followed him with some reservations (vol 7, containing *dvärg*, was published in 1925). Hellquist rejected Holthausen's etymology (SEO). The other national dictionaries of the Scandinavian languages and of Dutch offer the usual choice between Skt *dhvárati* and Avestan *drva*.

The latest admirer of the *dvergr*—σέρφος—*dergnat* etymology was Güntert (1919:235-37), who cited many instances of insects as spirits. However, nothing follows from his examples for *dvergr*. OIr *dergnat* is as obscure as σέρφος. Scandinavian folklore links dwarves and spiders, and the word *dvärg* means 'spider' in some Swedish dialects. A

Dwarf

dwarves' (or dwarf's) net (*dvärganet, dvärgsnet*) as the name of the spider's threads hanging in the air in autumn is current in many parts of Sweden. Rietz pointed out that the dwarves were likened to spiders because they were so skillful. Schwenck repeated Rietz's explanation in all the editions of his dictionary. The connection dwarf—spider has no value for etymology. The parallel *Loki* ~ Sw reg *loki* 'spider,' which SEO cites, is of no consequence, for, despite all efforts to prove the opposite, the Scandinavian god Loki has nothing to do with the spider (Liberman [1992b:132-33], repr in Liberman [1994c:219-20]), and the Welsh polysemous noun *cor* 'point; dwarf; spider' (Wilhelm Lehmann [1908:435-36]) does not make the triad *dwarf*—σέρφος—*dergnat* any more appealing. We can conclude that the dwarves did not get their name because they were associated with some insects or spiders and that σέρ(ι)φος and **dwerg-az* are not related. Obviously, a word like OI *dvergr* 'dog with a short tail' (May, *Zwerg*) does not clarify the original meaning of *dvergr* 'dwarf' either.

Some lexicographers have listed the cognates of *dwarf* but refrained from conjectures on its origin. Among them are Kilianus, Junius (who made the statement that since *dwarf* has no reliable etymons, it might be from Greek), Johnson, Todd in Johnson-Todd, Wedgwood, Mackay (1877), Stormonth, Skeat[4], Weekley, Partridge, Barnhart, and Webster. All the revisers of Webster's dictionary withstood the temptation of offering an etymology of *dwarf* until W[2] gave *dhvaras* (without a stress mark) as a tentative cognate and listed E *dream* as possibly related. In W[3], *dhvarati* (again without a diacritic) turns up. The changes from W[2] to W[3] show that in the absence of new ideas dictionaries substitute repackaging for research. This semblance of activity is typical. WNWD[1] gives the Indo-European base **dhwergh-* 'delude,' offers no cognates outside Germanic, and defines the etymon as 'deceptive (that is, magic-making) being, little devil'. Later editions add Skt *dhvárati* '(he) injures,' and **dhwer* acquires the gloss 'trick, injure.' When references to the scholarly literature are included, the choice is often unpredictable. IsEW lists many sources, among them Loewenthal (1928); NEW mentions IEW and Krogmann (1935), AEW adds Nerman (1954); DEO[3] cites Krogmann (1935), Derolez (1945), and Nerman (1954); KS makes do with Lecouteux (1981), whose article contains only one page (372-73) on matters etymological (Desportes's letter to the author and the conclusion that dwarves were deformed, evil creatures).

All that is known about the origin of *dwarf* can be summed up in two short statements: 1) *dwarf* has numerous Germanic cognates, and 2) two words, one Sanskrit and one Avestan, sound like **dwerg,* but their connection with **dwerg-* is unlikely. However, someone who would dare reexamine the etymology of *dwarf* will not start from scratch, for on a few occasions etymologists have been within reach of what seems to be the right solution.

4. Kluge (EWDS[1]) suggested that *Zwerg* may have developed from either **dwezgō* or **dwergō.* If he had pursued that line of reasoning, the etymology of *Zwerg* (*dvergr, dwarf*) would have been discovered then and there, but connecting the German word with a Sanskrit one looked attractive, and Kluge never returned to his idea that *r* in *Zwerg* is the product of rhotacism. However, **if we assume the protoroot **dwezg-*, everything will fall into place.** The sound *z* existed in early Germanic only as the result of the voicing of *s*, so that **dwezg-* must have been derived from **dwesg-* (cf Go *azgo** versus OI *aska* 'ashes'). In **dwesg-*, *s* was voiced between a vowel (*e*) and a voiced consonant (*g*). One has to reckon with the possibility that the protoform was **dwizg-* rather than **dwezg-* because, before *r* from *z*, *i* became *e* in all the Germanic languages except Gothic, which had no rhotacism (SB, sec 45, note 3; A. Campbell 1959:sec 123; BE, sec 31; Noreen 1970:sec 110.2, with references to Behaghel and Sievers; O. Ritter [1922:173-76]), but only **dwezg-* lends itself to etymological analysis. OFr *dwirg,* a doublet of *dwerch*, is due to the variation *e* ~ *i* before *r* (as in *werk* ~ *wirk* 'work,' *berd* ~ *bird* 'beard,' *herd* ~ *hird* 'hearth,' *werd* ~ *wird* 'word'; Steller [1928:sec 8, note 2]) and is irrelevant in reconstructing the Germanic protoform. Richthofen preferred *dwirg* as the Modern Frisian form, but later dictionaries (including WFT) give *dwerch. Dwerch* is the only form in AfWb.

Van Wijk was also close to discovering the origin of *dwarf,* but like Kluge, he missed his chance. In EWNT[2], he traced Du *bedaren* 'calm down; subside (of a storm, *etc*),' an obscure verb with cognates in Middle Low German and Frisian, to the root **daz-*, as in Du *bedeesd* 'timid' and MDu *daes* 'stupid' (ModDu *dwaas*; see Skinner, above). Thus he established a connection between *das-* and *dar-*, and only one step was needed to relate Du *dwerg* to *dwaas*. Van Haeringen (EWNT, Supplement) had doubts about Van Wijk's etymology of *bedaren*, but W. de Vries (1914:148) and Törnkvist (1969) accepted and developed it. In NEW (*bedaren*), the reference to EWNT is noncommittal. Van Wijk's combination is promising, and *bedaren* is probably one more instance of **d(w)ar-*, **dwer-* having *r* by rhotacism.

**Dwezg-*, from **dwes-g-*, is related by ablaut to OE *(ge)dwǣs* 'dull, foolish; clumsy impostor' (the same root in OE *gedwǣsmann* 'fool,' *dwǣsnes* 'folly, stupidity,' *gedwǣsnes* 'dementia') (DOE), MHG *twâs* 'fool,' MHG *getwâs* 'specter, ghost,' MDu *dwaes* 'foolish' (ModDu *dwaas;* see above) and *gedwas* (with a short vowel) 'stupidity, hallucination, ghost.' The meaning 'stupid' tends to develop from 'stunned,' 'pitiful,' 'unsociable,' 'blissfully unaware of the surrounding world,' 'too trustful' (such is, for instance, G *albern*), and 'too accommodating' (such is E *daft;* its etymological doublet is *deft*). In historical semantics, the line between 'stupid' and 'insane' is easy to cross, as seen in the origin of such words as *silly, foolish, mad, crazy, moron, imbecile,* and *idiot*: people called this are 'impaired,' 'unprotected,' 'benighted,' and 'possessed by a god or spirit' (see the discussion of *giddy* above). OE *dwǣs* and MHG *twâs* belong with the *giddy* group.

A *gedwǣsmann* and a *twâs* seem to have been people possessed by a **dwezgaz,* that is, by a dwarf. The ancient meaning of *dwǣs* and its cognates was forgotten early; compare the tautological Middle Dutch compound *alfsgedwas* 'phantom conjured up by elves' (Te Winkel [1875:101, glossary] and VV). Each kind of being possessed, whether by the gods, the elves, or the dwarves, must have been specific enough when the words for those states were coined, but today ancient distinctions can no longer be discerned. Modern *giddy* 'easily distracted; flighty; having a reeling sensation' (previously, 'mad, foolish') gives no clue to the difference between OE *gidig* and, for example, OE *ylfin,* usually glossed as 'raving mad.' This difference was hardly clear even twelve centuries ago, but at one time it must have been known; see discussion in Stuart (1976). All supernatural creatures were believed to act as incubi and succubi and to cause nightmare. The second part of the compound *nightmare* is related to the name of the Old Irish female demon Mor-rīgain (*-rīgain* 'queen'), a word with wide connections in Germanic and Slavic. The German for nightmare is *Alptraum; Alp ~ Alb* is 'elf.'

The dwarves, like the elves, may have exercised their power at night. Only Modern Dutch has retained the adjective *dwaas* 'foolish, stupid'; yet English has *dizzy,* a close synonym of *giddy.* OE *dysig,* like MDu *dwaes,* meant 'foolish, stupid, ignorant' (a meaning still current in certain modern English dialects) and had cognates in all the West Germanic languages except Yiddish. Ray cited *dizzy* 'mad with anger.' The same root (**dus-*), but with a long vowel, appears in MDu *dûselen* and ModDu *duizeln* 'be giddy or stupid.' The idea of sleep is present in OI *dús* 'lull, dead calm,' possibly in OI *dúsa* 'be quiet,' and ModI *dúsa* 'take one's time.' English may have borrowed the verb *doze* 'stupefy, muddle, perplex; sleep drowsily' from Scandinavian. However, the etymon of that word (some verb like Sw reg *dåsa*) may itself be of Low German origin. Middle Dutch had not only *dûselen* but also *dosich* 'sleepy.' The Modern German adjective *dösig* 'sleepy,' which emerged in the 19th century, is a borrowing from Low German, and so are Sw, N, and Dan *dösig ~ døsig* 'drowsy.' OI *dasast* 'become exhausted' (from which English has *daze* 'benumb the senses') and its cognates MDu *dasen* 'behave like a fool,' ModDu *dazen* 'talk nonsense, act stupidly,' and OI *dasi* 'lazybones' have never been discussed in connection with *doze, dizzy,* and the rest, though while browsing in etymological dictionaries (for instance, NEW and AEW), one eventually restores the ties severed by the practice of writing short entries on each word rather than essays on large families. It is unlikely that *dizzy* has the Indo-European root for 'breath' (so, following IEW, 269; MA, 82).

The root **dus-,* which we see in OE *dysig,* probably goes back to **dwus* (*w* was regularly lost in medial position before *u* in Old English [SB, 150; A. Campbell 1959:sec 470] and Old Norse [A. Noreen 1970:sec 235, 1a]), with **dwus* being the zero grade of **dwes.* A sound complex like **dwezg-* or **dwesk-* had no affiliation with any ablaut series in Germanic. Yet the strong verb **dweskan* or **dwezgan* 'stupefy; behave in an irrational way' is not unthinkable, for the weak Old English verb *gedwǣscan* 'extinguish fire; abolish; blot out enmity or sin; eliminate, perish' has been recorded. Karsten (1902:435-36) connected it with OE *dwīna* 'dwindle' (it appears erroneously). **Dweskan* would have belonged to the third class: **dweskan—*dwask—*dwuskun —*dwuskan(s),* so that **dwus-* fits the model. The same cannot be said about **dwes- ~ dwǣs,* for the alternation *e ~ ǣ* is irregular as long as we remain in the *e—a—u—u* series. Middle Dutch had the verb *dûselen,* apparently related to *dwaes* (*ū ~ ā*), which in turn is related to *gedwas* (*ā ~ ă*). The posited alternation OE *ĕ ~ ǣ* (= MHG and MDu *ĕ ~ ā*) in **dwes- ~ dwǣs* makes the picture even more complicated.

The alternations *ă ~ ā* and *ĕ ~ ā* both occur in Germanic, but they belong to different series, whereas the alternation *ū ~ ā* is irregular. Could it be that words denoting insanity, nonsense, and nightmare were often pronounced with emphatic lengthening and violated standard rules of derivation because they were subject to taboo? If so, we would witness a veritable triumph of iconicity: erratic forms designating erratic behavior. Boutkan (1999:19) briefly mentions words with "the deviant root-vocalism P[roto]Gmc. *ǣ—*a—*ō" and argues for their non-Indo-European substrate origin. It is puzzling why that type of "deviation" occurs with such regularity. Despite all the difficulties, it seems that *dizzy, daze, doze, dwǣs, dwǣscan; dûselen,* and *dūsa* culled from Modern English, Old English, Middle Dutch, and Old Icelandic belong together (see some of them in L. Bloomfield [1909-10:276/96]) and are related to **dwesk- ~ *dwezg-,* the root of the noun *dvergr ~ dweorg ~ twerc ~ twerch* 'dwarf.'

If OE *hæg-tes(se)* 'witch' goes back to **hage-tusjō, -*tusjō,* despite its initial *t,* may belong with the words discussed above, but the etymology of *-*tusjō-* is problematic (see more at WITCH). OE *hægtes(se)* is not given in WP or IEW. Nor does Mayrhofer (KEWA II:28-29) consider **-tusjō* as a cognate of *dásyuḥ* 'demon,' cited by Kauffmann (1894:155).

A parallel to **dweskan* is OHG *dwesben* 'destroy,' a weak verb occurring only in Otfrid, who also used *irdwesben* 'destroy, kill' and *firdwesben* 'destroy, kill; spoil' (Riecke [1997:207] quotes all five relevant passages). Riecke is probably right in interpreting <sb> as <sp>. He tries to save Petersson's etymology of *dwesben* (1906-07:367) and compares the Old High German verb with L *tesqua* 'desert, wasteland' (pp. 207-10), but it is more likely that **dwes-p-an* and **dwes-k-an* (a strong verb) had the root referring to the pernicious influence of dwarves. In Middle High German, *bedespen* and *verdespen,* both apparently meaning 'hide, bury,' have been recorded (Riecke, p. 210). Finally, Riecke (p. 209) cites G reg *dusper* 'dark, dusky,' which is related to *-despen* (as, for example, OE *derne* 'dark' is related to OE *darian* 'lie hid'), but *dusper* and *-despen* have nothing to do with the words containing the root **dwezg-.*

Since Kluge's form **dwezgō* faded from view, it is customary to reconstruct Gmc **dwergaz* and Go **dwairgs* (or **dverga* and **dvaírgs*) for *dwarf* (among the earlier authors see Schade). However, **the oldest Germanic form was either **dwezgaz* (if the word was masculine) or **dwezgam* (if it was neuter). If it occurred only in the neuter plural, the dwarves were called **dwezgō*.** The Goths must have had **dwisks* (if masculine; pl **dwizgos*), **dwisk* (if neuter), or **dwizga* (if only neuter plural). Three consonants in word final position did not contradict Gothic phonotactics: cf *asts* 'branch' from **azdaz.* Jessen (*dverg*), probably following not only Kluge but also Grimm, asked whether *dvergr* could go back to **dhwas-gh* and compared it with Gk θεός 'god.' Much later, Oehl (1921-22:768) listed *dvergr* as related to MHG *getwâs* 'specter, ghost' and Gk θεός and added Skt *dhvarás-* to them. Jessen's readership outside Scandinavia was limited, and Oehl buried his etymology in a long unindexed article on primitive word formation. He was right in bringing together *getwâs* and *dvergr,* but he offered no discussion, said nothing about either rhotacism or ablaut, and even if someone had paid attention to his etymology (as a matter of fact, no one did), it would not have made an impression on dictionary makers, because he did not have a clear idea of the development of the pronunciation and meaning of the word *dvergr.* In any case, by adding *dhvarás-,* which has old *r,* to *dvergr,* with *r* < **z,* he doomed his hypothesis, for *dvergr* cannot be related to both *getwâs* and *dhvarás-.*

Attempts to connect Germanic religious terms with Indo-Iranian ones have so far proved unconvincing. If *dhvarás-* turned out to be the only non-Germanic cognate of *dvergr,* it would be unique in that no other instance is known of a Germanic-Sanskrit correspondence without related forms in some language spoken between India and the territory occupied by ancient Germanic tribes; see Polomé's comments (1980) on Chemodanov (1962:105-07). In Gmc **dwezg-, -g-* is a suffix, whereas the root is **dheu̯es-* 'breathe' (IEW, 268-71). MHG *getwâs* and, more problematically, Gk θεός are both members of this family (the origin of **ϝεός* is still debatable, as it was a hundred years ago: L. Meyer [1902:413], WP I:867, IEW, 269; Frisk; M. Schwartz [1992:392] rejects the connection between the Greek word and **dhwes-*). If E *dull* and G *toll* 'mad' belong here too (which is not certain), we obtain one more word meaning 'insane,' remotely connected with the dwarves.

During the centuries the dwarves were called **dwezgōz* or **dwezgō*, they must have been thought of as having the same size as the gods and the elves. The turning point in the history of their names was the final stage of Germanic rhotacism. When **dwezg-* became **dweřg-* and **ř* merged with *r*, the word *dvergr* began to rhyme with *berg* 'mountain.' This is when the popular imagination resettled dwarves into rocks, and this is when OI *bergmál* 'echo' (literally 'mountains' talk') acquired the synonym *dvergmál* 'dwarves' talk.' Snorri knew myths, according to which the dwarves lived in the earth and in stones. One such myth (about a king lured into a rock by a dwarf), has been preserved in skaldic poetry (*Ynglinga Saga*, chapter 12). It contains an international folklore motif of the *open, Sesame* type. According to the eddic catalog of dwarves, eleven of them live in rocks (or boulders, or stones: *í steinom*). Before the final battle between the gods and the giants, dwarves are depicted as weeping in front of 'stone doors' (*fyr steindurom, Vǫlospá* 48:5-6). Yet the **dwezgōs* or **dwezgō* of the ancient Germanic religion must first have shared their habitat with the gods and the elves. The early Teutons venerated stones, but no evidence points to any original connection between stones and dwarves (see a broad discussion of dwarves, smiths, and stones in Motz [1983:87-140]).

As far as we can judge by inscriptions, Scandinavian rhotacism did not occur before the second half of the third century; neither did West Germanic rhotacism. The later rhyme *dverg- : berg-* presupposes the merger of *ř* and *r* dated tentatively to the 7th or 8th century (Makaev [1962:57]). It follows that the emergence of the dwarf, a rock dweller, did not happen before approximately the year 600. De Boor (1924) and J. de Vries (1956a:256) erred in their insistence that the dwarves had no roots in religion. The ancient **dwezgōs* (or **dwezgō*) were part of faith, whereas *dvergar*, their successors, were not. For this reason, the eddic episodes dealing with the dwarves (and those episodes may have been influenced by later folklore) do not compare too well with the fairy tales and local legends in which dwarves interact with people. When disparate stories are lumped together, as in Reichborn-Kjennerud (1934), the results carry little conviction.

The dwarves were created to serve the gods, and servants are socially inferior to their masters, so that the word **dwezgas* always had the potential for designating a small person. At first, the dwarves were diminutive in the sense in which a bellboy is a boy (see more on this matter at BOY), a waiter is a *garçon*, and a disciple is a *Jünger*. A chance fact emphasizes their status: *æsir*, when this noun designated part of a building, were huge crossbeams, and *dvergar* were ancillary supports. Finally, according to a popular belief, supernatural creatures were able to give people their own loathsome shape. Thus OI *trylla* (related to *troll* ~ *trǫll* 'troll') meant not only 'enchant' but also 'turn into a troll.' Perhaps dwarves were made responsible for stunted growth (which in the Middle Ages was looked on as a mental disease: see the supplement below) and gradually acquired the stature of their victims.

**Dwezga(z)* could not be the first word used in Germanic for an undersized person. While **dwezgō(z)* were supernatural beings akin to the gods and the elves, speakers must have had another name for a manikin, just as the Slavic speakers surely had another word for 'dwarf' before they borrowed *karl* from German. The extinct synonyms of Gmc **dwezga(z)* may be hidden among the numerous words for 'boy' in the Old Germanic languages. CD is ready to look for the original sense of *dwarf* in mythology but does not elaborate. In Old Icelandic, a *dvergr* was not a manikin, even if some dwarves were small.

Old English and Old High German glossators knew that the equivalent of *nanus, pumilio,* and *pygmæus* was *dweorg* ~ *twerc*. Medieval Europe enjoyed stories of the fabulous pygmies (Janni [1978; 1985]), and pygmies turn up in Isidore's *Etymologiæ* XI, 3, 26 and *Liber monstrorum de diversis generibus* 11, 7 (see, in addition to Janni [1978:49], Lutjens [1911:22, sec 31]). As late as 1887, notes like the following one could appear in a respectable journal: "A strange anthropological discovery is reported to have been made in the Eastern Pyrenees. In the valley of Ribas a race of dwarfs, called by the people 'Nanos,' is said to exist. They never attain more than four feet in height, and have high cheek bones and almond eyes of Mongolian type. They marry only amongst themselves, and are of a very low intellectual type" (anonymous [1887]). **The semantic change from **dwezgaz* 'supernatural being' to *dvergr* ~ *dweorg* ~ *twerc* 'manikin' seems to owe nothing to the transmission of classical folklore, let alone the distant memory of two races, giants and dwarves** (fantasies on this subject are popular; see De Montigny [1953]). **It is when rhotacism tied the dwarves to mountains and pushed their race underground that they became tiny in the human imagination.**

In English, sound symbolism may have accelerated dwarves' loss of stature. Words beginning with *dw-* frequently refer to diminution and diminutive objects. Modern dialects have *dwub* 'feeble person,' *dwable* 'flexible, shaky, feeble,' *dwine* 'waste away,' *dwinge* 'shirk, dwindle,' *dwingle* 'loiter,' and *dwizzen* 'shrink' (EDD). The origin of the recent American English slangism *dweeb* 'insignificant person' is unknown, but it looks like one of those given above (see especially *dwab*). Martin Schwartz has pointed out that *twerp*, a synonym of *dweeb,* resembles *dwarf* (personal communication). Whether *dweeb* and *twerp* (both recent) are in some obscure way related to *dwarf* or are products of so-called primitive creation (*Urschöpfung*) cannot be decided. The *dw-* group in *dweorg* made itself felt to such an extent that the Old English plant name *dweorgdoste* 'pennyroyal' even developed into *dweorgdwost(l)e* (Petersson [1914:136], and see Holthausen [1918a:253/29], who must have been unaware of Petersson's etymology of *-dwoste* from *-doste;* BWA I:49; Sauer [1992:401]: he also missed Petersson). Why the first part of that plant name is *dweorg-* 'dwarf' and whether *dweorgdwost(l)e* has cognates outside Germanic (see Hoops [1889:49] and KEWA II: 88-89, *dhattūraḥ*) is of no consequence in the present context. However, if the element *-dwost(l)e* is related to OE *dwǣs,* as Holthausen suggested, and if *dweorg-* goes back to **dwezg-,* both elements were at one time derived from the same root and we may be dealing with a tautological compound.

5. **All the dwarves mentioned in Scandinavian mythology are male, and in this respect their race was different from the races of the gods and the elves.** Female dwarves appeared only in later folktales. When need arose, German-speakers coined the noun *Zwergin.* **Old Icelandic *dyrgja* turned up first in *Þjalar-Jóns saga,* a 14th-century text (ODGNS, CV). It is not akin to *dvergr.*** Modern Icelandic has *dyrgja* 'fat, clumsy woman; hag' and *durgur* 'hulking, sullen man,' the latter recorded in the 19th century (ÁBM). Despite recent attestation, *durgur* gives the impression of being an old word rather than a neologism formed in retrospect as a missing partner of *dyrgja,* for the Old Icelandic nickname *dyrgill* (listed in both Jónsson [1907:300] and Kahle [1910:229]) must have meant 'moper,' 'fatty,' or something similar. Dictionaries give the amusingly literal gloss 'little dwarf, Zwergkin.'

The main question is whether *dyrgja* 'female dwarf' and *dyrgja* 'fat, clumsy woman' are related. A. Noreen (1970:145) set up the proportion *dvergr : dyrgja = verk* 'work, business' : *yrkja* 'perform work,' with *e* and *y* (< **u*) representing the normal and the zero grades of ablaut respectively. Yet a late word for a female dwarf would hardly have had such history. For purposes of comparison, we may take OI *gyðja* 'goddess,' arguably not an ancient but earlier word than *dyrgja* (*y* in *gyðja* is the umlaut of *u*), which has the same grade of ablaut as *guð*; a similar case is OE *ælf* and *ælfen.* Lindroth (1911-12:156 and note 5), despite several cautionary remarks, reconstructs **du̯ergiōn,* which, following the rule he formulated (*u̯e* occasionally becomes *y* after a consonant), allegedly yielded *dyrgin.* But if female dwarves did not exist, no one needed the Proto-Norse word **du̯ergion.* According to Motz (1973:107), the only female dwarf named in the sagas, also recorded late, is Herríðr. J. de Vries (AEW) endorsed Lindroth's reconstruction and added that the two meanings of *dyrgja* are not irreconcilable, because the same word designates supernatural beings, such as dwarves and trolls. But common names like *dvergr* 'dwarf' and *þurs* 'giant' substitute for one another only in later folklore, when they are subsumed under the concept 'monster.'

The original meaning of *dyrgja* was, in all probability, *'giantess, troll woman,' and folk etymology connected it with *dvergr.* The early history of *dyrgja* is unknown. IsEW (521) ties the word to *dorg* 'an angler's tackle' (*dorga* 'to fish'), an unappealing etymology, as de Vries (AEW) put it. *Dorga* is usually understood as a metathesized form of *draga* 'pull, draw.' Shetland *dwarg* 'rush; passing shower, *etc*' resembles OI *dvergr* but goes back to OI *dorg* (EONSS, *dwarg*); see also *dwarg* 'large, great,' recorded from Shetlands and Orkneys in EDD. Cannot *dyrgja* be cognate with OI *drjúgr* (*ju* < **eu*) 'solid, substantial' (OE *gedrēog* 'fitting, sober, serious,' Lith *drū́ktas, driúktas* 'thick,' and so on)?

The often-cited West Germanic parallel to *dyrgja,* allegedly reproducing the zero grade of ablaut of the root in *dverg,* is LG *dorf* 'dwarf' (Fick[3], FT, and others). Lindroth (loc cit) doubted the existence of *dorf.* As DW made clear (*Zwerg;* an outstanding etymological entry), *dorf* occurs only in BWb I: 231, which labels it as a swear word and classifies it with borrowings from English. **The idea that *Zwerg* and *dorf* are connected by ablaut is untenable.** Although DW 16 was published in 1954, Mitzka disregarded that information in KM[17-20], and only Seebold (KS) expunged reference to *dorf* at *Zwerg.* Almost certainly, no other word with medial *r* is related to *dvergr* by ablaut. Consequently, the dwarf name *Durinn* cannot be etymologized as 'the main dwarf' (Gutenbrunner's idea [1955:74]).

6. As a postscript to the story of *dwarf,* it can be worth mentioning that G *Quartz,* from which English has *quartz,* is called in Norwegian *dvergstein* 'dwarfstone' (De Boor [1924:540-41]). Although the origin of this word is debatable, the connection *Quartz* ~ *Zwerg* is not necessarily due to folk etymology, for both *kw-* and *zw-* can go back to *tw-* (cf G *quer,* above) (Liberman [2002a and c]).

A Note on MLG *altvile,* OI *Dvalinn* and *Dulinn,* and the Etymology of *Dwarf*

Additional support for an etymology connecting *dwarf* and insanity comes from MLG *altvile,* a hapax legomenon recorded only in the plural in the *Sachsenspiegel* (I:4), a 14th-century Civil Code. Among those who can inherit neither movable property nor a fief, mention is made of *dwerghe* 'dwarves' and *altvile.* Copies of the *Sachsenspiegel* containing the relevant sentence display a variety of forms *altfile, altveile, oltvile, oltuile, ultfyle, aldefil, alwile, antvile; altuvole, alczu vil,* and so forth (A. Höfer [1870a:4]). They show that scribes did not understand that word (which is amazing in light of Latendorf's [1880] communication: see below) and spelled it according to their folk etymological notions. The *Sachsenspiegel* was several times translated into Latin, but the Latin glosses for *altvile, dwerghe* ('dwarves'), and *Kropelkint* (n pl; 'those born with crippled bodies'), the names of the three categories of disenfranchised people, are often unclear (*nani, gnavi, neptunii, nepternii, homuncii, homunciones,* etc; A. Höfer [1870a:5, 6]; Latendorf [1877]), and it is sometimes hard to tell which Latin gloss corresponds to which German word. The phrase *filius fatuus gnavus aut contractus* seems to match *altvil* (sg) best of all. Pictures in the *Sachsenspiegel* are memorable. There, the *altvil* is represented as a small man, different from the *dwergh* but devoid of any specific features.

The idea that *altvile* in the *Sachsenspiegel* is a synonym of *dwerghe* is unconvincing, for the purpose of the statute must have been to target three, not two groups of people, whatever the original meaning of either word may have been. The form *altuvole* (corresponding to HG *alczu vil*) 'too many [organs?],' marks the beginning of the tradition, according to which *altvile* was understood as 'hermaphrodite.' 19th-century philologists, like their distant predecessors, realized that *altvile* is a compound but had trouble choosing between *al-tvile* and *alt-vile.* J. Grimm discussed that word three times (DW: *altwilisch* '?old, ancient,' with examples from Fischart; [1983:566], and [1848:947, note = 1868:657, note, continued on p 658], with reference to OHG *altâ* 'membrum') and offered conflicting interpretations of *al-* and *alt-,* but invariably came up with the result 'hermaphrodite'; the derivation of *altvil* from *altâ* + *vil* returned him to 'all zu viel.' OHG *wîdello* and OE *wīdl,* glossed as 'hermaphroditus,' which attracted Grimm's attention in *Deutsche Rechtsaltertümer* as possible counterparts of *-vile,* are words of unknown origin. WP I:225 give a few putative cognates of *wîdello* ~ *wīdl;* likewise Holthausen, AeEW. IEW does not reproduce any of them.

The German for 'hermaphrodite' is *Zwitter* (OHG *zwitarn,* from *zwie-* 'two'; *-tarn* is unclear: KS), and *-tv-* in *altvile,* assuming the division *al-tvile,* suggests the connection with some form of the numeral *two.* Both *al-tvile* and *alt-vile* have been made to yield the same meaning, though only LG *old, olde, ald,* and *alde* can correspond to HG *alt.* The most influential editors and translators of the *Sachsenspiegel,* as well as lexicographers, believed that it was dwarves, cripples, and hermaphrodites who could not inherit property in some parts of medieval Germany (see, for instance, von Sydow [1828:67-68], Homeyer [1830:560, glossary]; Lexer; Weiske [1840:156, glossary], Kosegarten [p. 286], Hildebrand [1876:125, glossary], and Rotermund [1895:20]). Hildebrand and Rotermund's example is instructive, for their works appeared long after the gloss 'hermaphrodite' had been discredited.

No reason would have justified singling out hermaphrodites along with people unable to defend themselves like dwarves and cripples or, for example, lepers (a provision added to that clause in some versions of the *Sachsenspiegel*). Hermaphrodites are born rarely, and the Germanic words that rendered L *hermaphroditus* in glosses—OHG *wîdello, wîbello, wîvello,* OE *bǣddel* (the putative etymon of ModE *bad*), and OE *scritta*—meant 'castrated man; effeminate person,' and 'devil,' but not 'a person with two sets of reproductive organs' (Leverkus; see his rough draft in Lübben [1871:320]), though OE *wǣpenwīfestre* (in a gloss; probably a nonce word, approximately like E *will-gill* or *willjill*), 'female creature with a penis' (see MAN for various interpretations of *wǣpen-*) reveals a clearer understanding of *hermaphroditus* (Kluge [1916a: 182/6]).

Germanic glossators, not versed in Ovid, did not seem to know exactly what *hermaphroditus* means and matched it with native words applicable to people with some deficiencies in the sexual sphere or even demons (the latter holds for OE *scritta*). Germanic mythology is poor in tales of hermaphrodites. Tacitus (*Germania* 2:1) mentions Tuisto, or Tuisco, the spouseless father of the good Mannus, but nothing is known about his appearance (see MAN). Only his name suggests 'two of something.' According to Snorri, Ymir, the primordial giant of the Scandinavian creation myth, fell into a sweat while he slept, whereupon a man and a woman grew under his arm; also, one of his legs got a son with the other. The name *Ymir,* even if it is related to several non-Germanic words for 'twin(s),' such as L *gemini*, provides no evidence that its bearer had the organs of a male and a female (Dörner [1993:6]), and Snorri does not intimate that Ymir was a hermaphrodite. Nor is the Indo-European etymology of *Ymir*, a typical paper construct, more convincing than the obvious one (*Ymir* 'making a lot of noise,' as Kure argues [2003]). Modern coinages, such as LG *helferling* (a term in pigeon breeding: Schütte [1912]), are usually transparent. The chance that MLG *altvile* meant 'hermaphrodites' is extremely small. Riccius (1750:66) noted that even if *altvile* had "two many" organs, it did not mean that the organs in question were genitalia (see also Mentz [1905:2])—an apt remark.

Four more interpretations of *altvile* exist. Woeste (1875) suggested that **altfil* might be *adlfil* 'leper,' with *-fil* as in Go *þrutsfill* 'leprosy.' Sachsse (1853:6-8), a law historian, indulged in fanciful operations with that word. However, one of his ideas that emerged from making sounds perform all kinds of tricks was not lost: he connected *altvile* and words for 'elf.' It may be that some old glosses (for example, *neptunii*) reflect a similar notion. As late as 1880, the word *altwil* 'elf' (a subterranean sprite substituting a changeling for an unbaptized baby) seems to have been current in the vicinity of Schwerin (Latendorf [1880]). The most consistent defender of *altvile* as 'elves' was Wilken (1872:449-50), who dismissed Sachsse's exercises in phonetics and believed *-t-* to be an excrescent sound; *alvile* from *altvile* can be understood as 'little elves.' He equated elflings with changelings and obtained a tautological binomial *dwerghe unde altvile* 'men of low stature.' That result invalidates his conclusion, at least with regard to the *Sachsenspiegel*. K. Haupt's aim (1870) was to support Sachsse's idea, but its subject is elves, not *altvile*, except in the introductory chapter (Haupt, too, reads *alvil*, not *altvil*). Mentz (1905 and 1908) believed in **alftwil*. Björkman (1899) offered a subtler defense of elves' relation to *altvile*. His starting point was the form **alfilus*, and he concluded that *altvile* were 'fools.' He also pointed to ME *alfin* ~ *alphin* 'bishop in chess; fool.'

A. Höfer's booklet (1870a), devoted to *altvile*, offers a survey of earlier scholarship and the most persuasive translation of *altvile*. Like several researchers before him, Höfer paired *altvil* and L *filius fatuus* 'stupid child' of the Latin version and concluded that the three categories of people not allowed to inherit property were dwarves, cripples, and imbeciles. But to justify his interpretation, he referred to the jocular Scots phrase *old file*, applied mainly to stupid women, with counterparts in Low German (pp. 25-40). Such a slang expression would be dramatically at variance with the surrounding text. The whole sounds like 'dwarves, persons with misshapen bodies, and old beans.' This is exactly what an anonymous reviewer said (anonymous 1870), only in German. A. Höfer's spirited rejoinder (1870b) did not make his etymology more attractive. (Judging by the text of the entry *altvil* in MW, the reviewer was Lübben.) The same holds for A. Höfer (1873). Smits (1870:152) asserted that he could see a file in the picture of the *altvil*. The triangular piece the *altvil* holds does not look like any identifiable object, but perhaps it points to three categories of the disinherited.

From an etymological point of view, the best interpretation of *altvile* is Leverkus-Lübben's (1871); see also Rochholz (1871:339-41), Koppmann (1876), and Lübben (1876). That interpretation is old; A. Höfer (1870a:5) knew but rejected it in favor of his own. ***Altvile* should be divided *al-tvile* and *-tvile* assigned to the root *dwal-*.** *Dwel-* would in some cases be its umlauted form, in others related to it by ablaut. The words containing the root *dwal-* ~ *dwel-* have seemingly incompatible meanings, namely 'tarry' and 'lead astray.' 'Have one's abode, spend time (on),' as in E *dwell* (both meanings were borrowed from Scandinavian), goes back to 'tarry'; 'be stupid' is the continuation of 'lead astray.' See details on this root in Siebs (1904:313), WP I:842-43, and IEW, 265-66, and Go *dwals** 'foolish,' Go *dulþs* 'festival,' G *toll* 'mad,' OE *dwellan* 'go; lead astray,' E *dwell* and *dull*, and OI *dvelja* 'tarry, delay' in etymological dictionaries.

Wyld (UED) follows WP and offers an outstanding analysis of *dwell* and its cognates. He arrives at the conclusion that the sense 'hinder, delay' "is the connecting link between that of 'wandering' and 'dwelling'; 'to wander, having lost one's way; to linger, delay, in doubt which way to go,' & finally, 'to remain where one is.'" On the strength of Gk θολός or θόλος 'sepia' (a dark fluid, ink) and θολερός 'muddy, troubled' (said about water, and so on), he glosses **dwal-* ~ *dwel* as 'go astray in the dark.' The sense 'obscure, dark, lacking clearness' could develop into both 'delay' and 'folly.'

Lübben (in Leverkus-Lübben [1871:324-29]) reconstructed an even more convincing original meaning with evidence only from Middle High German at his disposal. Some of his etymologies are wrong, but his examples show that the words clustered round **dwellan* (MHG *twellen*) once meant *'move in a circle.' A person moving in a circle gets nowhere (is delayed) and labors under the illusion of making progress (is led astray). *Altvile* were feeble-minded people, 'totally deranged' (*al-* is an intensifying prefix). In similar fashion, Till Eulenspiegel (Ulenspiegel) was Fool Eulenspiegel (he pretended to understand everything literally and behaved unconventionally), and William Tell was William (Wilhelm) the fool (he feigned madness). Cf Woeste's discussion of *til(l)* 'fool' (1875:209). Both *Till* and *Tell* were soubriquets (Pfannenschmid [1865:36-37], Lübben [1871:329-30], Rochholz [1871:340-41]). The numerous modern investigations of Till Eulenspiegel's name subject only *Eulenspiegel* and *Ulenspiegel* to serious scrutiny, while *Till* and *Dill* are disregarded. E *dally* and its cognates may have influenced the meaning of *Tell* and *Till* (Maak [1974, esp p. 379]). Conversely, attempts to connect *Tell* with the Scandinavian mythological names *Dellingr* and *Heimdall* can be dismissed as unsuccessful (the latest survey that puts this idea to rest is F. Neumann [1881]).

Two difficulties stand in the way of this otherwise well-argued etymology of *altvile*. It is based on the spelling *-w-*, rather than *-v-* (as in *dwell*), and *-d-* rather than *-t-* (one expects **aldwile*), because a Low German word is supposed to have unshifted *d*, as in E *dull* and *dwell*, not as in G *toll* or MHG *twellen*. Neither difficulty is insurmountable. In Middle High German, the alternation of the letters *v* and *f* followed rules that sometimes escape us today, regardless of whether they reflected phonetic reality or obeyed the scribes' whims. Since *w* also designated /v/ in that period, an occasional use of *v* for *w*, especially in a word with an obscure inner form, need not cause surprise; see *dvalitha* in Lübben (1871:324). It is hard to disagree with Woeste (1875:208) that the scribe who wrote *dwerge* would have written **altwile* if he pronounced [w] in it. However, *altvile* was an obscure word, and the scribe may have copied it in the form in which he saw it.

As regards *-t-* versus *-d-*, it is not known which form of the word *altvile* is 'correct.' Discussion centers on the verse from the *Sachsenspiegel*: "Uppe altvile unde uppe dwerghe / nirstirft weder lên noch erve, noch uppe kropelkint. / Swe denne de erven sint / unde ire nêsten mâge, / de solen se halden in irer plâge." ('On *altvile* and on dwarves /neither movable property nor a fief shall be devolved, nor on children born crippled./ Therefore, the [legitimate] heirs / and their [these people's] next of kin / are responsible for their care.') The pronunciation of *dwerghe* as [dwerwə] or [dvervə] follows from its rhyme with *erve*, but for the pronunciation of *altvile* we depend on the extant spelling, which, in the verse, is not more reliable than, for example, *aldefil*. Besides this, *dw-* and *tw-* were often confused in medieval German (Lübben [1871:323]).

M. Haupt (1848) pointed to *Markwart Altfil* occurring twice around 1180. Markwart's nickname is usually cited as proof of *t* being the original consonant in *altvile*, for the counterpart of LG *t* would have been HG *z*. But it proves the opposite. Since the High German word was recorded with *t*, the earliest Low German form must have had *d*. *Altfil* is indistinguishable from **Altvil*: after *t*, *v* had little chance of remaining voiced. M. Haupt divided *altfil* into *alt-* and *-fil*, glossed it as 'changeling' (because changelings look like children but are really old men and because folklore dwarves have gray beards), and took *alt-* for G *alt* 'old,' but he could offer no explanation for *-fil*. In all probability, the 12th-century character passed under the name Markwart the dolt. Björkman's arguments (1899) are different, but he arrived at the same conclusion. It is an almost incredible coincidence that E *dolt*, an etymological doublet of the now archaic *dold*, has the same alternation of consonants as in German. Other than that, *dol-t* looks like a viable cognate of **dwil* in another grade of ablaut. Although **aldwil* ~ **altwil* had some limited currency in the north and in the south, in most regions it seems to have gone out of use early, and only the phrase *altvile unde dwerghe* survived in some areas of Germany.

Even if the triad *altvile, dwerghe* [*unde*] *kropelkint* 'half-wits, dwarves, [and] cripples' has been unraveled, it is less compact than could be expected from a legal formula. Restrictions should have affected people of deficient physical and mental abilities. It was not necessary to make a special mention of dwarves. The binomial **dwile* [*unde*] *dwerg(e)* is based on alliteration. This fact presupposes a certain bond between the unit's members. The relation may go from closeness and near identity (as in *bed and board, safe and sound,* and *fret and fume*) to contrast (as in *through thick and thin*). Combining words to forge a quasi-idiom would be pointless. Children who did not grow were believed to be possessed by an evil spirit, and barbarous methods of exorcising it, like exposing the baby to great heat, were practiced in Europe. Derangement was ascribed to the same forces. **Medieval medicine treated stunted growth and mental retardation as caused by similar factors and in principle different from deformity.** Belief in changelings should also be reckoned with, but if any group among the *altvile, dwerghe,* and *kropelkint* in the *Sachsenspiegel* was looked on as consisting of changelings, it must have been the *dwerghe,* not the *altvile.*

***Dwerg-* is an ancient word. The legal language of medieval Germany needed a partner for it, to indicate another category of people possessed by spirits, and that is probably why **aldwil* came into existence.** Although this noun almost disappeared at the beginning of the second millennium, it does not mean that the coinage was inept, for attraction between the root *dwal-,* the basis of words meaning 'wander aimlessly, move without making progress; lead *or* go astray,' and dwarves can be traced to a remote epoch.

The name of the only prominent dwarf in Scandinavian mythology is *Dvalinn.* The other dwarves are his host, the sun is called his playmate (more likely, 'deceiver'), and some goddesses of fate are his daughters (see *Edda* I:326, index). However little onomastics may tell us about dwarves' nature, the similarity between *Dvalinn* and **dwile* (*altvile*) is significant.

AEW (*dvala,* end of the entry) repeats Magnusen's explanation in FML (without referring to the source) and cites N *dvalen* 'lazy, sleepy' in explaining the origin of *Dvalinn.* Mythological dwarves were neither lazy nor sleepy, but consider what has been said above about *dizzy* and *doze* and the root **dwesk-.* If we are allowed to cross the line separating a bearer of madness (a dwarf) and his victim, *Dvalinn* may be understood both as 'inflicting madness' and 'mad.' This gloss will also fit two other Dvalins recorded in the *Elder Edda*: Dvalin the hart ('precipitous?') and Dvalinn the warrior ('furious?'), the owner of the horse Móðinn 'courageous, spirited.' Frenzy characterized both. Another dwarf was Dulinn (see *LP*), whose name AEW etymologizes as 'hidden' (from OI *dylja* 'hide'). But dwarves became "hidden" only in later folklore, and *Dulinn* is even closer to OE *dol* 'foolish' (ModE *dull* is a borrowing from Scandinavian rather than a continuation of that Old English word) and G *toll* 'mad' than *Dvalinn* is. The senses involved here are 'drive crazy; lead astray, impede progress,' not 'lazy' or 'hide.' *Dvalinn* and *Dulinn* look like etymological doublets, with the root in the normal and the zero grade of ablaut respectively. **Whenever we meet dwarves, madness is close.** If **dwile* 'imbeciles' [and] *dwerg(e)* 'madmen, changelings' is an ancient formula, each of its parts may have referred to different types of mental aberration, but since *dvergr* and its cognates have not been recorded with the meaning 'madman,' such a hypothesis would need more proof.

The origin of the names *Dvalinn* and *Dulinn* attracted almost no attention, and few remember the exchange of opinions concerning *altvile* that seems to have ended in 1905. AHD devotes an entry to *altphil* 'bishop' (in chess) and identifies Markwart's soubriquet with it, but makes no connection between *altphil* and *altvile.* Dobozy (1999:210-11, note 28) contains minimal discussion. Only Janz (1989:68-75) examines the most important works on the subject and reproduces the illustration from the *Sachsenspiegel.* A. Höfer (1873:29) mentions "the impossible explanation by Messers de Vries and de Wal." Mentz, the author of an exhaustive survey of the *altvile* problem, tried to locate Vries and Wal's article (1905:6, note 7), but drew blank. In his book, A. Höfer promised to deal with their explanation later but must have thought better of his plan. The results obtained from the study of the medieval concepts of madness and the origin of *altvile, Til, Tell, Dvalinn,* and *Dulinn* are of some importance for understanding the nature of the mythological dwarf and, by implication, for the etymology of the word *dwarf.*

EENA (1855)

The ancient Celtic numeral that allegedly gave rise to eena *'one' is still current in England, especially in Yorkshire (along with similar words for 'two,' 'three,' 'four,' and 'five'), for counting sheep. According to some researchers, those pseudonumerals were brought to New England and used as tally marks in trading with the native population. They are now preserved only in children's games. Although counting out rhymes like* eena, meena, mina, mo *have been recorded in many languages, it is unlikely that all or most of them go back to a single source.*

OED dismisses *eena* as a nonsense word. AMG (250), calls the jingle "Eena, meena, mina, mo, Catch a nigger by the toe, / If he hollers, let him go, / Eena, meena, mina, mo" comparatively recent, without further comment.

An old exchange of opinions on "the ancient British numerals," known better among students of folklore than among etymologists, partly revealed the history of *eena* (the latest survey of this material [Barry 1969] appeared in *Folk Life;* see also Barry [1967] and Greene [1992:551-52], the latter is based on Barry's works). Here are the first five numerals used in scoring sheep in the Yorkshire Dales and transcribed by A. Ellis with the so-called Glossic signs he invented (1867): *yaan, taih'n, tedhuru, (m)edhuru, pi(m)p,* that is, [jain], ['taiən], ['teðərə], ['(m)eðərə], [pi(m)p] (Ellis [1870:117; 1871: XIX]).

I. Taylor's list of "ancient numerals which were formerly in use in the northwestern corner" of England (1877:338) is similar: *eina, peina, para, pattera, pith,* and so on. In his opinion, "these numerals are a relic of a language of the British kingdom of Strathclyde or Cumbria, which stretched northwards to Dumbarton, and whose southern boundary ran a few miles to the north of the place from whence these numerals have been obtained." He adds that according to a local tradition, "the numerals were brought to Craven by drovers from Scotland. This tradition in no way implies that the numerals are Gaelic, but may be sufficiently explained by the fact that a great part of the Cumbrian kingdom lay to the north of the modern Scottish border."

Ellis traced the Yorkshire numerals to Celtic, namely to "the Welsh branch, dreadfully disfigured in passing from mouth to mouth as mere nonsense." But Bradley (1877) wondered how Cymric numerals "could have become so familiarly known in Yorkshire" and believed "that they had descended traditionally from the time when a Cymric dialect was spoken in that district." He looked on them as ancient British rather than Welsh, and Taylor supported him. All the materials appeared in the same volume of *The Athenæum.* According to the editorial note (p. 43), *The Athenæum* received "a great many more communications on the subject" than the magazine could print. It printed only Westwood (1877), Ellwood (1877), Powell (1877), and Trumbull (1877). Later authors (like Beddoe and Rowe [1907:42]) repeated Bradley's conclusions. See the discussion in MacRitchie (1915) and more contemporary accounts in Potter (1949-50b) and Barry (1967). The numerals that Taylor, Ellis, and Bradley recorded are sometimes mere gibberish, with English words replacing the original forms (for example, *yahn* = [ja:n] 'one,' the local pronunciation of *one)* and rhyming words invented by informants.

A similar string of numerals was in use among the native population in North America, for example, *een, teen, tother, fither, pimp,* with the variant *eeny, teeny, tuthery, fethery, fip.* A list of Wawena numerals from Maine first appeared in Brunovicus (1868:180), with reference to a communication by R.K. Sewall, dated Winter 1867. Kohl (1869:91) suggested in passing that these numerals "bear a resemblance to the Icelandic" (which they do not). Trumbull (1871) corrected Kohl's mistake and pointed out that those scores were "to be regarded rather as *tally-marks* or *counters* than as true cardinal or ordinal numbers. They were used in counting by fives, tens or twenties. Traces of some such systems may be found in many school-boy rhymes for 'counting out'" (pp. 14-15). In his opinion, the numerals in question, were "brought to New England by English colonists and used by them in dealing with the Indians in counting fish, beaver skins, and other articles of traffic. When the memory of their origin was lost, the Anglo-Americans believed them to be Indian numerals, and the Indians, probably, believed them to be good English." Other variants of the rhyme in question abound (Newell [1883:194-203], Bolton [1888:103-08, numbers 568-646], A. Hall [1894], Abrahams and Rankin [1980: nos 119-411]); see also Witty (1927:44-45), Cassidy (1958:23-24), and Barry (1969). Gold (1990b) offers an especially detailed survey.

According to Potter (1949-50a), the second line of the rhyme goes back to a supposed French Canadian *cache ton poing derrière ton dos* 'hide your fist behind your back.' Misunderstood by Anglophone children, it allegedly turned, under the influence of their parents' conversations when the Fugitive Slave Law of 1850 was being debated, into *catch a nigger by the toe.* He does not exclude the role of an Indian or a half-breed intermediary and remarks that in the earliest variants (*eena, meena, mona, mite, basca, lora, hora, bite, hugga, bucca, bau; eggs, butter, cheese, bread, stick, stock, stone dead–O-U-T*) there is no mention of Negroes. According to OO [1951:156-57], the French Canadian hypothesis is interesting but hardly necessary. In fact, it is not interesting at all. As Gold indicates (1990b and personal communication), no native speaker of French would say *derrière TON dos,* and no evidence supports the rise of *eena, meena, mina, mo* among Canadian children. Even less credible is Potter's reconstruction of "an ancient magic rime-charm allegedly used in Druid times to choose the human victims to be ferried across the Menai Strait to the Isle of Mona to meet a horrible fate under the Golden Bough of the sacred mistletoe amid the holy oaks" (340). The most fanciful conjecture is Bickerton's (1982). He traces *eena, meena, mina, mo* to a phrase in São Tomense, "a creole language with a largely Portuguese vocabulary spoken on the island of São Tomé, off the West Coast of Africa, since the sixteenth century." Gold (1990b) provides decisive arguments against this conjecture.

Barry (1969:78-87) divides the hypotheses on the origin of the North Country numerals into two groups: survival from the Old Welsh language once spoken by the Britons and importation (from either Wales or Scotland) at a later date. Bradley (1877) supported the idea of survival, Ellis (1871:XIX) believed in importation. No conclusive proof in favor of either theory exists, and a definitive solution is impossible here.

Not only sheep are scored in the way described above, and not only in Yorkshire; see the examples in OED and in OO (1983:12-13). S. Levin (1995:422-23) discusses the opening line of the rhyme within the framework of his theory of displaced numerals. Gold (1990b) argues against the British origin of *eena, meena, mina, mo* in the New World, but he does not call into question *one* as the etymon of *eena*. If we do not follow Potter all the way to the Golden Bough, *meena* will appear as a variant of *eena*, while *mina* and *mo* seem to be nonsense words alliterating with *meeny* and leading up to the pair *mo* / *toe*. Nonsense words of this sort are to be expected in games: cf strips like *eensy-weensy* and *itty-bitty*. **It is not necessary to trace the counterparts of *eena* in various languages (and the entire line for that matter) to English, let alone Celtic.** Some similarities can be explained by the universal characteristics of children's language, but a few questions remain unanswered (Liberman [1994b:175-78]).

EVER (1000)

The etymon of OE ǣfre *(> ModE* ever*) has two morphemes, but whether the constituent elements are the root and a suffix or two roots within a compound, or whether a phrase preceded the emergence of this adverb remains a matter of debate. Of several etymologies of* ever *proposed in the 19th century, two are still occasionally cited because of the favorable treatment that OED gave them; both trace* ǣfre *to old prepositional phrases. However,* ǣfre*, contrary to the implicit assumption in all dictionaries, was probably coined late in ecclesiastical English by adding the suffix of the comparative degree to OE* āwa *'always,' a synonym of* ǣfre. *Words for 'ever, always,' especially the shorter ones, are regularly reinforced in the languages of the world. The vowel* ǣ, *rather than the expected* ā, *may have been chosen under the influence of other comparatives or because of the confusion between OE* ā *'always, ever' and* ǣ *'law, covenant.'*

The sections are devoted to 1) a survey of opinions on the origin of ever, *2) arguments for the derivation of* ǣfre *from* ǣw + re *(the suffix of the comparative degree), and 3) the later history of* ever.

1. **Most often, words for 'ever,' like words for 'always,' are compounds.** Such are L *semper* (from *sem-* 'one,' as in L *semel* 'one,' and *per* 'through'; approximately 'all the way through'), G *immer* (from OHG *io* 'ever' and *mêr* 'more'), Russ *vsegda* (an obscure formation but undoubtedly a compound; the same holds for its cognates in Slavic and Lithuanian: Vasmer I:362-63), Icel *alltaf* (= *allt* 'all,' n and *af-* 'of, *etc*') and *ætíð* (*æ* 'ever' and *tíð* 'time').

The earliest etymologists chanced on what seems to be the correct cognates of *ǣfre*: G *ewig* 'eternal,' Gk αἰών 'time, lifetime, generation, eternity, *etc*,' and L *aeternus* (Minsheu). Skinner compared *ever* and OE *ā* 'ever,' and Junius mentioned L *aevam* 'lifetime, generation' (with reference to Vossius). Wedgwood listed the same words and added several Finnish and Estonian look-alikes, which need not be related to *aevum* and the rest, but he was the first to refer to Go *aiws** 'time, eternity.' OI *ævi* 'lifetime, generation' turns up only in Chambers (1867). DDEL offers a string of the same cognates and traces them to the root **as* 'be.' Thomson detected the verb 'be' in *ver* but arranged the components in a different order: he represented OE *ǣfre* as the sum of OI *æ* 'always' and *vera* 'be' and noted the identity of *ever* and *aye*. W. Barnes (1862:323) compared *ever* with *every* and *ere*. *Every*, from OE *ǣfre ǣlc*, that is, 'ever each,' sheds no light on *ǣfre*, while *ēre* (< Gmc **airiz;* Go *airis*) is the comparative degree of **air* 'early' and is at best of typological interest for the history of *ever*, as will be seen below. In Gothic, the idea of perpetuity is expressed in the simplest way possible: *aiw* 'ever' is the accusative singular of the noun *aiws** 'time' (recorded only in negative clauses with *ni ... aiw* 'never'). **The etymology of *ǣfre* resolves itself into discovering the origin of *-fre*. A connection between *ǣ*- and some word designating time in Old English and elsewhere is secure, but whether that word is OE *ǣ* needs discussion.**

A reasonable, even if faulty, etymology of *ǣfre* appears in Ettmüller (1851:55). According to him, *ǣfre* is the dative of the noun *āw*, which is a cognate of Go *aiws*. He cites OE *hālor* 'salvation' (from *hāl* 'healthy, *etc*') and *pundur* 'weight.' It is unclear how those words bear on his argument (*hālor* contains a derivational suffix, and *pundur* is a borrowing from Latin), but since Go *aiw* is the accusative of *aiws**, the idea of interpreting *ǣfre* as a form of *ǣ(w)* is tempting. However, *-re* does not occur among the case endings in the declension of Old English nouns. The genitive and dative singular of OE *ǣ* is *ǣwe*, and texts display some vacillation between *ǣ* and *ǣw* (SB, sec 288, note 3); **ǣwre* as a case form of *ǣw* is unthinkable. Nevertheless, Mueller[1] reproduces Ettmüller's etymology without comment. Mueller[2] calls *ǣfre* an adverbial formation, a statement echoing Skeat[1]: "*-re* answers to the common A.S. [= Anglo-Saxon] ending of the dat. fem. sg. of adjectives and has an adverbial force." Skeat considered OE *ǣf-* to be related to OE *āwa* and Go *aiws* but did not explain how an ending of adjectives could be appended to a noun and give it adverbial force. In 1882, Skeat also brought out his CED, and there his statement is terse: "Related to A.S. *āwa*." Yet he clung to his original etymology for a long time. He called *-re* of *ǣfre* an adjectival ending, as in *gōd-re* (gen and dat sg of *gōd* 'good') in Skeat (1887 = 1892:274). CED says the same and refers to other Old English adverbs ending in the vowel *-e,* for instance, *ēce* 'ever.'

Cosijn (1879:267/2) **offered the first of the two durable etymologies of *ever*, though he explained *never* rather than *ever*. He derived it from some phrase like Go **ni aiw fairƕau* and pointed to Northumbr *nǣfra* "a *u*-stem."** **Bradley** (OED, *ever*) **cited OE *ā tō fēore*, which, he said, is equivalent to Go **aiw fairƕau* and OHG *nêo(i)naltre* 'never,' literally 'never in life.'** "This," he argued, "is supported by the agreement of the final *-a* of the Northumbr. *ǽfra* with the ending of the locative (dat.) of the *-u* declension, to which the sb. *feorh* life (:-**ferhwus*) originally belonged. The recorded forms of *feorh,* however, do not account for the umlaut; but cf the cognates OE. *fíras,* OS. *firihôs,* ON. *fírar* 'men'." Cosijn's discussion takes a line and a half (a footnote) in a long article written in Dutch and bearing the title 'De oudste Westsaksische chronicle' ('The Oldest West Saxon Chronicle'). If OED had not highlighted that footnote, no one would probably have known of it. In Horn's opinion (1921a:77/75), the etymon of *ever* was *aiw in fairƕau.*

Then came Hempl's (1889) **hypothesis. He reconstructed **ā-bifore* or **ā-buri* but preferred the latter**: "[f]inal *i* mutates *u* to *y* and this mutates the *á* to *ǽ* ... while the *e* < *y* ... being in unguarded position, is of course syncopated. According to this the original force of *ever* was 'in any case, at any time,'" as in G *jemals*. **Buri,* in Hempl's opinion, must have meant 'event, occasion' (cf OE *byre* 'time, opportunity,' perhaps 'occasion' and OHG *gaburi,* glossed as 'casus, eventus, occasio, tempus'). Hempl adds: "This also gives an explanation of the persistence of the writing *(n)æbre* (so always in the 'Cura Past[oralis]') when the labial fricative had come to be represented by *f,* and *b* was restricted to the representation of the labial stop. ... We should therefore recognize in the ultimate change of *ǽbre* > *ǽfre* ... a real change of *b* to *f* and not simply an alteration in the orthography." In looking for an instance of umlaut similar to that posited for **ā buri,* Hempl cited OE *ǣrende* 'message, mission, tidings.' Mayhew (1891c:sec 416) accepted that derivation of *ever* (*ǣfre* < *ǣ* + *byre*) but gave no reference, which caused Hempl's gentle rejoinder (1891) and Mayhew's unusually courteous apology (1891b). However, according to Mayhew (1891b), *ǣ* in *ǣrende* is a reflex of WG *ā* and is not due to umlaut. Hempl (1892b) disagreed. Bradley (OED) quoted both Cosijn and Hempl, without taking sides. Hence Hempl's comment (1892b): "I cannot understand how anyone can be contented to explain a mutation by saying that, though there is no *i* in the word involved (*feorh,* Goth. *faírhwus*), there is one in a word (*fíras*) that some have thought related to it."

Later dictionaries and manuals add nothing new to OED except for occasional mistakes. Skeat[4] and UED are not even sure that *ǣfre* is related to OE *ā*. Webster from 1828 onward, Weekley (1921), and Klein (CEDEL) believe that the relation exists. AeEW, EW[2,3], and Weekley (1924) say "? < *ā in fēore* 'ever in life'." Baly (1897:41) does without a question mark. RH[1] suggests kinship with Go *aiws**, but RH[2] makes no mention of it. Nicolai (1907:sec 92) follows Hempl. WNWD[1] gives *ā* + *byre* 'time, occasion' as the etymon of *ever,* while WNWD[3] inexplicably suggests *ā* + *feorr* 'far.' Kluge (KL) was positive that *ā* and *ǣ-* are cognates, but he only reproduced Bradley's text with abridgments. Barnhart states that some scholars derive *ever* from *ā in fēore,* whereas others trace it to *ā* + *-re,* "dat. fem. adj. suffix, often formative of adverbs." "Some scholars" are Skeat and Scott, the etymologist of CD. We thus have a set of shaky solutions, and dictionary makers, not knowing what to say, prefer to choose the safest variant rather than saying nothing. No one has refuted either Cosjin or Hempl, and the origin of *ever* is still believed to be unknown.

Two more deservedly forgotten conjectures on the origin of *ever* are Platt's and Pogatscher's. According to Platt (1892), who, without supplying a reference, says that he advanced his idea several years earlier, *ever* is "an adverb to the adjective *afor* with vowel modification." Probably he meant OE *afora* 'posterity, heir' rather than *afor*. The mechanism of the "modification" remains a mystery. Pogatscher (1898:97-98) endorsed Kluge's derivation of G *immer* from **ǣ-mre* (EWDS[4], *immer*) and traced *ǣfre* to this etymon, though Kluge gave up his unfortunate derivation in the next edition of EWDS and never returned to it.

2. Words for 'always, ever' are not necessarily disguised compounds; they may be phrases. Compare E *ever and ever* and the archaic binomial

ever and ay (*ay* is a Middle English borrowing from Old Norse; OI *ey* competed with *æ, ei,* and *øy*). G *immer,* already a compound (*io* 'ever' + *mêr* 'more'), swells to *immer wieder* 'ever again,' that is, 'again and again.' Horn, who shared Cosjin's views on the origin of *ǣfre* and noted that words for 'always, ever' are frequently replaced with new words (L *semper* with F *toujours,* and so forth) or reinforced, looked even on OE *ō*, the enigmatic doublet of OE *ā*, as *ā* pronounced with a high tone (HL, 747; Horn calls such emphatic forms *Hochtonformen*). Therefore, *ǣfre* may be a reinforced form of the adverb *āwa,* a variant of *ā* 'always,' with *-re* being the suffix of the comparative degree. The element *-re* may have been borrowed from words like *ǣdre* 'early' and *hlūtre* 'clearly,' but that is less likely. The forms of the comparative degree of both adjectives and adverbs that ended in *-ra* probably influenced *ǣfre.* Although the form *ǣfra* occurs only in Northumbrian, it is arguably the oldest. Some vacillation in the use of OE *-re* ~ *-ra* is not unthinkable: cf *clǣfre* and *clǣfra* 'clover' (see CLOVER).

The stumbling block of all etymologies of *ǣfre* is the origin of *ǣ-*. The vowel of OE *ǣ(w)* 'law,' an *i*-stem noun, owes its existence to umlaut. Go *aiws** was declined as an *a*-stem in the singular and an *i*-stem in the plural. OI *æ* 'ever' is usually traced to **aiwi.* But even if we disregard the semantic difficulty (OE *ǣ* ~ *ǣw* did not mean 'time'), ***ǣfre* cannot be the product of an adjectival or adverbial suffix grafted on a noun, for such hybrids do not exist.** That is why Ettmüller's and Skeat's etymologies of *ever* are untenable. Only *āwa* is a viable basis of *ǣfre,* and *ǣ* remains unexplained.

Foerste (1954:405-08) suggested that *ǣ* in *clǣfre* 'clover' and in a few other words in which umlaut is usually posited can be traced directly to Gmc **ǣ* (> Go *ē*, WGmc **ā*) that alternated with **ai;* see discusion at CLOVER. Such a shortcut would perhaps also be acceptable for *ǣfre* if *ǣfre* could be shown to go back to the remote past. But **it emerged only in Cynewulf, at the close of the Old English period, and its antiquity need not be taken for granted. *Ever* was then and remains to this day an elevated word, as opposed to *always,* and may be a coinage of clerics, in whose language reference to eternity would be common, or of religious poets.** Solemn phrases rendering L *in saeculum, in aeternum,* and *in perpetuum* were needed for prayers in native languages, and Go *in aiwins,* OHG *in then alten euuon* (Otfrid I:20, 25), and the like sprang up (Weisweiler [1924:457]). *Ever* belongs to the same style. Consequently, positing ancient West Germanic forms for it cannot be recommended, the more so because in the speech of officiating priests, phrases of such importance would not have shrunk to *ǣfre,* as happened, for instance, to G *nur* 'only' and Du *maar* 'but,' both of which were informal shortenings of *ni wâri* and *newâre.* A similar objection is applicable to Cosijn's and Hempl's etymons; *ǣfre* may not have had an asterisked prehistory. That OE *ǣfre* lacks cognates is commonplace (besides dictionaries, see Jellinghaus [1898a:463]).

If *ǣfre* was formed from *āwa* (with the ending *-a* syncopated) and contains the suffix *-re,* **āwre,* not *ǣwre* could be expected. Two factors probably affected the shape of the new word: 1) The noun *ǣ(w)* 'law' had the doublet *ā* and the variant *ǣ(w)* was more common. Some grounds for confusion existed in any derivative of this root. 2) Although the comparative degree did not need umlaut in Old English, some of the most frequent adjectives and adverbs, namely those with the suffix **-iza,* had mutated vowels: *i(e)ldra, yldra, eldra, ældra* (*eald, ald* 'old'), *grī(e)tra, grȳtra, gryttra* (*grēat* 'great'), *gingra* (*gung, geong* 'young'), *hī(e)r(r)a, hȳrra, hēgra* (*hēah, hēh* 'high'), *scyrtra* (*sceort* 'short'), occasionally *brǣdra* (*brād* 'broad') (SB, sec 307; A. Campbell [1959:sec 658]). **Against the background of *grȳtra, brǣdra,* and so forth, the neologism **ǣwra* would have sounded as natural as **āwra.* The suffixed forms *ǣ(w) + ra (re)* would also explain the variant with *-b-*: *ǣbre* 'ever' and *nǣbre* 'never' would develop like *clǣbre* 'clover.'** Both OED (*ever*) and Pogatscher (1898:97-98) emphasized the parallelism in the development of the *-br-* ~ *-fr-* group in the words *ever* and *clover.*

The suffix of the comparative degree, expressing increase and growth, is uniquely suited to serve as an element of semantic reinforcement, and it merges easily with adverbs and prepositions. The result is often the rise of new words. The history of *other, whether, after* (also Go *afar* 'after'), *over,* and their cognates in Germanic and elsewhere bears witness to this process. **Ǣwra* seems to have been coined (in the 10th century?) with the meaning 'more than always,' that is, 'for ever and ever,' 'in all eternity' and to be a lexicalized comparative degree of *āwa* 'always' with analogical umlaut. Proto-Indo-European had no word for 'eternity,' and the process of coining nouns and adverbs for this abstract concept did not stop in the prehistorical period. See Benveniste's numerous works on this subject (for instance, Benveniste [1937]) and *aiws* and *ajukduþs* in Feist[4] for more references. Assuming that such is the origin of *ever,* Skeat, it must be acknowledged, came closer to the truth than anyone else before or after him. It also follows that E *ever* does not belong with the words that became shorter on account of their frequency, as Mańczak (1987:90) suggested.

A connection between OE *ǣ* 'always' and *ǣ* 'law' is of tangential interest for reconstructing the origin of the adverb *ever*. Convinced by Weisweiler's arguments (1924), some researchers treat OHG *êwa* 'eternity' and 'law' as unrelated homonyms (see G *Ehe* 'marriage' and *ewig* 'eternal' in later etymological dictionaries and *a*- 2 'law' in OFED). But 'oath,' 'law,' 'covenant,' and 'institution sanctified by law' (inviolable things) are fitting measures of eternity within the limits of human experience. No compelling reason exists for seeking separate etymologies of OHG $\hat{e}wa_1$ and $\hat{e}wa_2$.

3. In Middle English, *ǣfre* became *evre*. Morsbach (1896:sec 61) and Luick (1964:sec 352, note 2) explain differently the loss of length in *ǣ*. Around the beginning of the 14th century, an epenthetic vowel (*e*) sprang up between *v* and *r* (Luick [1964:sec 449 and note 1]). In late Middle English, the forms *ĕr* and *ēr* were common (OED; Luick [1964:secs 454.1 and 745.2]). The semantic shift in *ever* is less obvious. In Old English, *ǣfre* usually meant 'at all times, always,' while the meaning 'at any time' can be detected primarily in negative constructions, as in Gothic (*ni ... aiws* 'never'). In the early modern period, *ever* acquired the force of an emphatic particle in *whatever, whoever, ever so much,* and the like (OED).

FAG 'servant; male homosexual, *etc*' (1775); **FAG(G)OT** (1300)

The original meaning of fag(g)ot *is 'bundle of firewood.' All the other meanings, 'drudge' and 'junior in a public school' among them, go back to the second half of the 18th century. The range of application is from 'ugly woman' to 'cheap meal' (all depreciatory).* Fag(g)ot *'bundle of firewood' may have come to designate 'menial servant' and 'male homosexual' under the influence of its near synonym* pimp *'bundle of firewood' and 'boy who does menial jobs,' 'procurer of prostitutes.'* Fag *is a clipping of* fag(g)ot. *Hence also* fag *(v),* fagged out, fag end, *and probably* fag *'end of a cigaret.'*

The sections are devoted to 1) the various meanings of fag *and 2) the origin of* fag.

1. The earliest known meaning of *fagot* is 'bundle of sticks, twigs, or small branches of trees bound together.' Later, 'bundle or bunch in general' and 'collection of things not forming any genuine unity' turned up. At the end of the 16th century, *fagot* 'old woman' appeared, and at the end of the 17th century, 'person temporarily hired to supply a deficiency at the muster or on the roll of a company or regiment.' Since 1882, *fagot* as a term of reproach, used about children, adults, and stray cows, has been recorded. In 1914 *fagot* '(male) homosexual' made its debut on a printed page in the United States.

ME *fagot* is a borrowing from French. According to Torp, the Romance word, which came to French from Italian, is of Germanic origin. However, VL **facus* and Gmc **fag* seem to be different words. Nynorsk *fagg* 'bundle, short fat man' corresponds to Icel *föggur* 'baggage' and Sw *faggorna,* the latter used only in such phrases as *ha döden i faggorna* 'have one foot in the grave,' literally 'have death in one's luggage.' Scand *fagg* is a possible etymon of E *fadge* (with [g] Anglicized to [ʤ]), but ME **fag* 'bundle' did not turn up. *Fadge* is a predominantly northern word. It means 'bundle of leather, sticks, wool, *etc*; bale of goods' (first recorded in 1588), 'large flat loaf; bannock' (1609), 'short, fat individual' (1765), and 'farthing' (1789).

It is unclear whether we are dealing with homonyms or different meanings of the same poorly attested noun and whether a connection can be assumed between *fadge* (sb) on one hand and *fadge* (v) 'fit, suit' (1573) and 'trudge' (1658) on the other; see more on *fadge* 'fit' at FUCK. *Fadge* 'farthing' is a typical name of a 'clumsy coin'; likewise, *cob* 'lump' meant 'old Spanish dollar' (Schwabe 1916-17, 106/6a and 8). If ME **fag* 'bundle' existed, it may have been viewed as a colloquial variant of F *fagot,* regardless of the origin of *fagot* in French. But since ME **fag* has not been found, its possible interaction with *fagot* and the derivation of *fadge* from it remain a matter of speculation.

Fadge and *fagot* did coexist in the north of England, but only *fagot,* though a borrowed word, became part of the standard language. See Skeat (1899-1902:665-66, *fadge* and *faggot*), NEO (*fagg*), SEO (*faggor*), ÁBM (*föggur*), Atkinson (*fadge;* he summarizes several earlier hypotheses and derives *fadge* from Welsh), and Holthausen (1932:67/15-17). OED (but not ODEE) cites OF *fais* 'bundle' (> ModF *faix* 'burden'); this trace leads nowhere. *Fag* 'drudge' surfaced in the seventeen-seventies, and its ties with the later meanings of *fagot* are obvious. Sheridan named a servant in *The Rivals* Fag (the play was first performed in January 1775). Names from recent colloquialisms were popular in 18th-century comedies; see also SLANG.

OED gives the following dates for the earliest occurrences of *fag* 'servant' and *fag* 'drudge, drudgery': 1775 'work hard,' 1780 'hard work,' 1785 'junior in a public school,' 1806 'be a fag,' 1824 'make a fag,' 1826 'weary one,' 1840 'fieldsman,'

1923 'homosexual.' We can assume that before the nineteen-twenties *fag* rarely (if at all) referred to sexual orientation. The fashion for *fag* 'servant, drudge' must have originated when it appeared in print. *Fag* 'servant' is an improbable continuation of **fag* 'bundle.'

The common belief that the starting point in the history of *fag* 'servant' is the verb *fag* 'decline,' which yielded 'wearied, fagged out,' 'drudgery,' and 'servant' has little to recommend it, for the 18th-century noun *fag* does not seem to have developed naturally from a word of comparable semantics; it has always belonged to specialized slang. The comparison between *fag* and *fatigue* (ODEE) is a product of etymological despair. (E. Edwards may have been the first to explain *fagged* 'weary' as a contraction of *fatigued.*) Two other conjectures concerning *fag* are even more fanciful: from F.A.G. (the Fifth Axiom of Geometry: Hotten; the anonymous reviser of the 1903 edition of Hotten's dictionary struck out this place but added reference to LG *fakk* 'wearied,' without identifying its source) and from Gael *faigh* 'get, obtain, acquire' (Mackay [1877]). School slang sometimes originates in the facetious use of Classical Greek and Latin words, for example, *fag* 'eatables' (Christ's Hospital; believed to be from Gk φᾰγεῖν 'eat') and *doul* 'fag' (sb and v) from Gk δοῦλος 'slave' (Shrewsbury and Durham; see both words in Farmer), but a classical etymon of E *fag* has not been found.

In all likelihood, *fag* emerged as a clipped form of *fagot,* whose pejorative meaning was known in the 1770's and brought to the New World. Lighter (*fag*[4]) says "short for *faggot*" but gives no proof. *Fag* must have been a low word from the start. A pun on *fag* 'young boy in service of a senior' and *fag end* or any other *fag* designating an object hanging loose is too obvious to miss in male company (cf *prick* as a term of abuse), but those must have been secondary developments. *Fag* 'drudge' and 'weary' are also late senses (a fag would, of course, be fagged out after all the fagging he had to do).

Some researchers believe that *fagged out,* applied to a rope with its 'whipping' gone, is an extension of *fag end* 'worthless remainder,' originally 'piece of rope whose end became untwisted' (a word current on shipboard) and that *fagged out* 'weary, tired' originated in sailors' slang (Wasson [1928-29:383]; see also Kuethe [1941:56]). But the earliest example of the nautical use of *fagged* in OED dates to 1841 and of *fagged out* to 1868. Therefore, it seems natural to view *fagged out* 'tired; untwisted' and *fag* 'work hard' as being coined at approximately the same time; also, *out* makes little sense when added to *fag* 'droop, decline.'

Fag end (said about a rope) is another 18th-century phrase (not attested before 1775), contemporaneous with *fag* 'work hard,' whereas *fag* 'something that hangs loose' was recorded in 1486, and *fag* 'flag, droop, decline' in 1530. If this *fag* is the etymon of *fagged out,* an interval of three centuries and a half between them in printed sources is hard to explain. (Similar queries arise in the history of COB (v) and FILCH.) *Fagged* in *fagged out* (said about a rope) bears some resemblance to *fake* 'one of the circles or windings of a cable or hawser, as it lies disposed in a coil.' The verb *fake* 'lay a rope in coils' was first recorded in 1400; the next example in OED is from 1860, and the noun *fake* surfaced in 1627. However, *fake* 'counterfeit' can be related to the FUCK group. See more on the interchange of postvocalic *k* and *g* in colloquial and slang words at MOOCH and NUDGE.

Servants, especially those bullied by their superiors, do not command respect. ***Fag* was an appellation meant to humiliate. That is another reason it could probably not have developed from such inoffensive words of low frequency as *fag* 'droop,' *fag* 'remnant,' or the polite, learned noun *fatigue.*** At Oxford and later at Harvard and Yale, paid servants were called *scouts.* The origin of this word is unknown, but it is usually believed to go back to *scout* 'spy.' *Scout* 'a term of the greatest contumely, applied to a woman; as equivalent to troll, or camp-troll' (Jamieson 1825, cited in OED) but used also in addressing men (clearly a borrowing from Scandinavian: both OI *skúti* and *skúta* refer to abuse [AEW]) is a likelier etymon; it would be a counterpart of *fag* (from 'fairy' to 'servant').

Oliver Twist was the thieves' fag. Could that circumstance have suggested the name *Fagin* to Dickens? In his youth, Dickens worked with a Bob Fagin and was on good terms with him. The often-repeated idea that he later bestowed that man's name on one of his most repulsive characters to take revenge on a Jew who had dared patronize him seems far-fetched. According to Paroissien (1986:XIII/228-48, nos 67-121), only Paroissien (1984) and Fleissner (1983) have tried to explain Fagin's name. (In his survey, he missed Davis's idea [1895] that *Fagin* is an anagram of Hebr *ganif* 'thief.')

Paroissien (1984) deals with the origin of the family name rather than with Dickens's reasons for choosing it. Fleisner's wanderings through associations between *Fagin,* "Old German" *Veigelein* 'violet' (the flower), and homosexuality or effeminacy are of little use, but he does quote (p 30) Robert W. Burchfield's improbable suggestion in *The New York Times Book Review* (November 26, 1972, p. 24): "*fag:* from Charles Dickens' character Fagin in *Oliver Twist,* 'a man who teaches boys to be dishonest.'" If *Fagin* is a pun on *fag,* homosexuality has nothing to do with it. Nor is it necessary to set up a special meaning for *fag,* because 'young boy in service of a senior' will do. Dickens denied accusations of anti-Semitism and noted that fences were or had often been Jews. Consciously or subconsciously, *fag* may have brought forth *Fagin,* and this automatically made "the old gentleman" Jewish. We will probably never discover the truth. The opposite way, from *Fagin* to *fag,* is impossible for chronological reasons. In slang, *Fagin* has been recorded with the meaning 'fence' (Eisiminger [1984:91]), but that usage testifies only to the popularity of Dickens's novel.

2. The most difficult question is how *fagot,* a foreign word for 'bundle,' could acquire the meanings 'old woman' and later 'bloke, brat' and 'stray cow,' thus becoming a vague synonym for 'scoundrel, rascal' and degenerating into a vulgar name for a homosexual. According to Hotten, *fagot* 'old woman' got its name because a bundle of firewood is like a shriveled old woman whose bones are like a bundle of sticks only fit to burn. Partridge [1949a] says that *fagot* could mean 'whore' as early as 1797 (not in Partridge [1961]); OED does not confirm his observation. Hotten's suggestion recurs in Edye (1886-87) and BL. Yet the semantic base of *fagot* is 'menial (hired) servant' or 'human trash,' rather than 'ugly, slovenly woman,' even though 'a term of contempt or reproach applied to women and children, a slattern, a worthless woman' (often pronounced *facket;* with an obsolete variant *fagoghe*) is the only gloss of its type in EDD. The word *fagot* progressed so far in its ability to refer to cheap objects and serve as a term of abuse that it came to designate even 'dish ... made of the fry, liver, or inferior portions of a pig or sheep' (EDD), and consider the following: "You stinking faggot, come here" said by a mother "in the lower parts of Plymouth" (Devonshire) to "the girl who is the object of the mother's wrath" (Hibyskwe [1885-86]). It is hard to tell whether *fag* 'sheep fly or tick' (OED, EDD) started as a generic derogatory term 'vermin.' In any case, *fag* also means 'loach' (EDD), whereas *loach* can mean 'simpleton.'

Perhaps *fagot* owes its later meanings to an interaction between *fagot* 'bundle of wood' and *pimp* 'pander' and (in southern counties) also 'bundle of wood' (see further at PIMP). Grose (1785) says that bundles of firewood (that is, fagots) are called *pimps* because they introduce the fire to the coals. The first English author to use *pimp* 'bundle' was Defoe (1742); see the quotations from Grose and Defoe in OED. Grose, who believed that *pimp* 'bundle' (a new word in his time) arose by association with *fagot,* was probably close to the truth, though the process must have gone in the opposite direction: *pimp* seems to be an old word in all its meanings, while *fagot* 'pander' is late.

The paths of *pimp* 'pander' and *fagot* 'firewood' cross in that pimps (panders) introduce lustful men to willing women as fagots (firewood) introduce the fire to flammable coals. One can also imagine that the existence of *fagot* 'slatternly woman or child' (almost a synonym for *whore* in popular usage) and *fagot* 'old, shriveled woman' ('match maker' by implication?) contributed to the semantic leap toward 'queer.' If today *pimp* 'pander' and *fagot* 'homosexual' are not synonyms, the reason may be that they developed differently from the meaning '(despised) party in sexual affairs': 'he who procures women' and 'he who acts like a woman.' BL suggested the influence of F *fagoté* 'dressed in ill-fitting, badly matched garments,' but no evidence points to the use of this participle among the lower classes in London. It is also most unlikely that *fagot* as a term of reproach has anything to do with the custom of making a recanter carry a faggot on his back for twelve months (G. P. [1885-86], Eisiminger [1984: 91]).

Fagots (wood) were common, and people treated them with rough familiarity as shown by the Dorset word *nickie* 'tiny faggot made to light fires' (anonymous [1935:179]). *Pimp* 'bundle of firewood' may have reached London by the forties of the 18th century and struck people as amusing because everyone in the capital knew the other meaning of *pimp.* **The emergence of *pimp* 'bundle of firewood' in London probably resulted in that *fagot* 'bundle of firewood' acquired the meaning 'despicable person' under the influence of its synonym.**

The fact that at present both *pimp* and *fagot* pertain to the gathering of wood and despised forms of sexual activities will be accounted for if we take into account the interaction of the two words in the middle of the 18th century. Consider also the parallelism between *pimp* 'boy who does menial jobs' and *fagot* 'person temporarily hired to supply a deficiency at the muster' (see more at PIMP). **Soon after *fagot* spread in its second meaning, *fag,* a clipped form of *fagot,* appeared as its double.** Sw (regional, colloquial) *fagott* 'fellow, guy' first turned up in Rietz and has been explained as an extension of *fagott* 'bassoon' (SEO). No connection seems to exist between the Swedish word and E *fagot*. Fort's derivation (1971:137) of *fagot* 'male homosexual' from Du *vangertje* 'tag' (a children's game) is of no interest.

FIELDFARE (1100)

Fieldfare was first recorded in the form feldefare. *ME* feldefare, *with nonsyncopated* -e-, *is probably from* *feldgefare, *feldgefore. *This bird name was early confused with OE* felofor *'brown one,' a kind of thrush (?), but also designating some large waterfowl (= L* porphyrio*). OE* scealfor *'diver, cormorant' and Du* ooievaar *'stork' (G* Adebar*) probably contain the same suffix as* fieldfare, *which may be identical with* -fora *and* -fara *in OE* innefora ~ innefara *'intestines' and also with* -fore *in OE* heahfore *'heifer' and* -ver *in ModE* elver *'young eel'; it presumably meant 'dweller (of).'* Fieldfare *is then 'field dweller,' the idea of 'fieldfarer' being the result of folk etymology. Reflexes of* feld(e)fore, feldgefore, *and* felofor *designate the same bird in modern dialects.*

The sections are devoted to 1) the earliest forms of fieldfare, *2) the existing etymologies of* fieldfare, *3) the protoform of* fieldfare *in Old English, 4)* -fare *in* fieldfare *in its relation to other animal names with supposedly the same suffix, 5) the proposed etymology of* fieldfare, *and 6) the place name* Fieldfare.

1. According to OED, *fieldfare* 'Old World thrush, *turdus pilaris*' (1100) was first recorded in the form *feldeware*. Although Förster (1917:113, note 4) pointed out that the word appears in the gloss as *feldefare*, MED believes in *w*. Even if the letter in the gloss is wyn, it should be dismissed as scribal error. See the discussion in Kitson (1997:487-88, esp 487). ***Feldefare* is a compound that violates the rule of West Germanic syncope: after a long syllable (*feld-*), medial *-e-* should have been lost.** Words like E *handiwork* and *landimere*, which L. Tobler (1868:46) tentatively compared with ME *feldefare*, had *-ge-* in Old English (*handgeweorc, landgemǣre*). He also mentioned reg *messigate* 'road to the church,' literally 'road to Mass' (see EDD), but 1100 is too early a date for the change *ge-* > *e-*. Chaucer pronounced ME *feldefare* in four syllables, and modern dialects have retained medial *-e-*. In one case it has even drawn stress to itself: EDD cites *vildéver*. Alongside *feldefare, fildefore,* and so on, modern dialects have *felfar, felfer, fellfaw,* and several other forms (EDD). They look like descendants of OE *felofor* (*felufor, fealefor, fealfor*; the Old High German glosses *felefor* and *felefer* were written by Old English scribes: Suolahti [1909:300] and Michiels [1912:69/28]), but *felofor* translates L *porphyrio*, the name of a pelican or some other big water fowl.

Dialects have many names for the fieldfare in the languages of Europe (M. Höfer [1815:2, 163], Newton [1893-96:249], and Lockwood [1981a:191-94]), and its English name appears in numerous variants in older texts. Therefore, etymologists cannot rely on one 'correct' form or a name that would bring out the bird's most conspicuous feature. I. Taylor (1873:106) says that the fieldfare is so called for its characteristic habit of moving across the fields, but this is a self-serving explanation, for the bird does not move in a particularly striking way.

In *Troilus and Criseyde* (III:861), Pandare says: "The harm is don and fare-wel feldefare." The meaning seems to be '...and the battle is lost' or '...and nobody cares' or '...and I am done with you.' This proverbial saying was first attested in Chaucer's poem. OED (*farewell* 2b) explains it as an allusion to the fieldfare's departure northward at the end of winter. The editors of the poem offer similar comments. "...fieldfares suddenly appear with the advent of cold weather and as suddenly depart. He, therefore, that would catch fieldfares...must not delay; for a warm day may come, and then, farewell, fieldfare!" (TC-B:145, note 2). "As fieldfares come here in the winter months, people are glad to see them go, as a sign of approaching summer. In the present case, the sense appears to be that, when an opportunity is missed, the harm is done; and people will cry, 'farewell fieldfare!' by way of derision." (SKCW-2:479, note to line 861); the same in TC-R:480-1, note to line 861. B. Whiting's quotation from Lydgate (1449) shows that the proverb goes back to a line in a song (1968:111, F130); consider the internal rhyme and alliteration *farewell* : *fieldfare* (Chaucer's line was not changed in a 17th-century modernization of the poem: TC-W:208/123). The choice of the bird name may have had nothing to do with the fieldfare's habits (all birds appear and disappear "suddenly"). H.C.K. (1858:511) traced *fieldfare* to *fealla-far* ~ *feala-for* 'something that is restless and always on the move' and accounted so for Chaucer's wording (allegedly, the fieldfare is particularly fickle because it "fares" a lot). Likewise, E. Edwards glosses OE *fe(a)la-for* 'something restless, and ever on the move.'

2. **Dictionaries usually state that *fieldfare* goes back to either *field* < *feld* + *fare* < *faran* and means 'field traveler'** (so all the editions of Webster's dictionary until W^2, Skeat, CD, EW, and many others) **or *fallow* < *fealu* + *fare* < *faran*, the meaning be-**

ing 'traverser over the fallow fields' (for example, Wedgwood; R. Latham, and EB). According to OED, the word is an obscure formation and apparently means 'field goer,' but the middle syllable is not accounted for, "and this, with the divergent spelling in the OE. gloss, suggests possibility of corruption from popular etymology." **Older scholars tended to identify OE *felofor* and ME *feldefare*** (Ettmüller [1851], 336; Stratmann[1-3]; Sweet [1897, *felofor*]; Brandl-Zippel, *feldfare*).

One often runs into the statement that OE *feldefare* is a reinterpretation of *felofor* (Mueller; Mätzner, both cautiously; Smythe Palmer [1883]; Sweet [1888:309/715]), but this view found no support in later research (anonymous [1897:610] and OED). **Pogatscher** (1903:181) noted that in Old English glosses L *scorellus* 'fieldfare' had often been translated *clodhamer* (*hamer* = *amer*: cf G *Ammer* 'bunting' and the pair G *Goldammer* ~ E *yellowhammer*, in which *-hammer* is the result of a folk etymology most appropriate for describing a woodpecker). He **reconstructed the string **felþu-amirōn* > **feldemre* (syncope, umlaut) > **feldeƀre*, **feldefre* (dissimilation of *mr* to *br*) > **feldefare* (folk etymology).** However, the history of OE *clodhamer* and ModE *yellow hammer* makes the development from *-amirōn* to *-efre* unlikely.

Some dictionaries say that *fieldfare* is a word of uncertain origin. For example, in Weekley's opinion (1921), the origin of *fieldfare* is doubtful, for *felofor* "may have changed its meaning, as bird names are often very vague." The stumbling block seems to be the relationship between *felde-* and *felo-*, but UED also calls into question the derivation of *-fare* from the verb *fare* 'go.' **MED, which took the nonexistent Old English spelling *feldeware* at face value, interpreted the word as 'field-dweller.'** Likewise W[2-3] and Longman; RHD[1] says that the change from *feldeware* to *feldefare* is due to *w* > *f* "by alliterative assimilation." W[3] no longer mentions that etymology, but RHD[2] does. Pogatscher (1900:222) suggested the alternation of OE *f* with *w* but did not find a single convincing example. Wedgwood, who traced *felde-* to *feolu-*, left *-fare* without comment. **Lockwood** (1981a:193; 1984; 1995b:373-4) **reconstructed Old English **fealu-fearh* 'grey piglet' (= 'fallow farrow'),** on the analogy of Wel *socen lwyd* 'fieldfare' and WFr *fjildbok* 'field billy-goat' ('fieldfare'); *socen*, allegedly an onomatopoeic word representing the bird's cry, can also mean 'pig.' Swainson, Swann, and Whitman add nothing new.

3. Despite the conflicting evidence, two points can be made with some certainty: 1) Although OE *felofor* and ME *feldefare* designate different birds, the two names interacted over the centuries: *fieldfare* goes back to *feldfare*, whereas *felfar* and its variants continue *felofor*. At some time, the true meaning of *felofor* must have been forgotten, and the word began to be used as the name of a 'wrong' bird. 2) The rule of West Germanic syncope makes the retention of medial *e* inexplicable. A. Campbell (1959:sec 367, note 3) called OE *mihtelēas* 'weak, powerless' and **feldefare* genitival compounds, but Lockwood observes that no other Old English compound beginning with *feld-* has *-e-*: even the word **feldware* 'dwellers in open country' deduced from place names lacks it. OE *felofor* could not have influenced **feldefare*, for then the form would presumably have been **feldofare* or **feldufare*.

The only solution seems to be positing OE **feldgefore*, a variant of **feldgefare* (see more on the alternation of OE *fore* ~ *fare* at HEIFER), which would be a product of folk etymology, for 'field traveler' and especially 'field companion' is a vapid phrase. Lockwood (1981a:192) notes that the concepts 'goer' and 'dweller' are alien to the popular ornithological nomenclature. The failure of the attempts to etymologize OHG *wargengil* 'butcher bird' as *warg-gengil*, from *warg* 'wolf' and *geng-il* 'goer' bears out the truth of that remark (Schlutter [1923:206]). The parallels that W. Grimm (1848:333) cites are unconvincing; see also Kralik (1914:131).

4. **Two bird names are relevant for discovering the origin of *fieldfare*. The first of them is OE *scealfor* (or *scealfra*) 'diver, cormorant';** see Kitson (1997:497-98) on its attestation. Kluge (1901a:199) derived *scealfor* from its synonym *scræf* (with cognates in West Germanic and Old Icelandic). Like many others, he cited a wrong form (it should have been *scræb*) and did not explain how *scealfor* got its second syllable. **Scræf*, with metathesis, supposedly yielded **scearf*; **scearf* may have become *scealf*, but where is *-or* from? Old English breaking rarely affected *æ* before metathesized *r*, except in the Anglian dialects. *Scealfor* seems to be a doublet of *scræb*, with the root vowel broken before *-lf*.

The second syllable of *scealfor* could not have meant 'traveler,' but Du *schollevaar*, with its variant *scholver* (the name of the same bird; MDu *scolfern*, *scolfaren*, *scolfaert*, MLG *scholver*, *schulver*, Fr *skolfer*; Suolahti [1909:395]), shows that *-for* is an integral part of *scealfor*. According to J. de Vries (NEW), *schollevaar* falls into *scholl(e)v-* and *-aar*, the latter on the analogy of *aer* 'eagle' (cf Du *dompelaar* 'cormorant' = *dompel-aar* from *dompelen* 'dive'; see that verb in KM at *Tümpel* 'pond'). More likely, *scholle-*

vaar is *scholl-(e)-vaar* and MLG *scalvaron* did not arise through dissimilation from **scarvaron*.

A second bird name important for understanding the origin of *fieldfare* is Du *ooievaar* 'stork,' which has numerous variants (Kosegarten, 101-02; Franck, VV, NEW, Gröger [1911:411], W. de Vries [1919:268-69], Blok-Stege [1995:29]). The Dutch word was so well known that one of its forms may even have made its way into Russian (Russ *aist* is a borrowing from Du or Low German; see Grot [1899]). The relations between Du *ooievaar* and G *Adebar* 'stork' have not been fully clarified. The first component of ModFr (1802) *earrebarre* (WFT) exhibits rhotacized *d*. The place name *Arbere* is, most probably, unrelated to *earrebare* (Naarding [1960]). J. Grimm (1844:638; the same in later editions; not yet in the 1835 edition) explained OHG *odebero* as 'luck bringer' (from OHG *ôt* 'wealth, luck' and *-bero* 'carrier'). The widespread attitude toward the stork as a sacred bird and the custom of telling children that babies are brought by storks (see the ditties in Kosegarten and in Linnig [1895:445]) supported Grimm's etymology. At the same time, J. Grimm (1966:147; first presented in 1845) reconstructed Gmc **uddjabaira* or **addjubaira* 'egg carrier.' (See a comment on this etymology in Lagarde [1877:94, end of No 1358].) Wackernagel (1874a:189, note 4; first published in 1860) compared *ade-* and L *uterus* 'womb.'

Grimm's etymology of *Adebar* ~ *ooievaar* dominated German and Dutch dictionaries for ninety years (the same in SEO, *stork*, Persson [1912:26], and Van Langenhove [1928:160-61]), though Suolahti (1909:369-71) showed that forms like Du reg *heilöver* and G *Heilebart*, all meaning 'luck bringer,' arose by folk etymology (see also Andresen [1889:119]). Gröger (1911:secs 70-71) pointed out that Old High German compound adjectives normally lost the connecting element when it followed a long-vocalic stem. If OHG *odebero* had had long *o* in the first syllable, medial *-e-* would have been syncopated. Holthausen (1924:116) came to a similar conclusion: in his opinion, LG *åderbår* testifies to *ŏ-* in this word. *Od-* with a short vowel cannot be understood as 'luck.'

Kluge tried to make Grimm's idea more palatable, but with little success. *Adebar* appears in EWDS[4] with the gloss 'Kindbringer,' that is, 'child bringer.' In EWDS[5-6], he took *ade-* (< *ode-*) to be a cognate of OI *jóð* 'child,' itself an obscure word; Persson (1912:26/3) tentatively followed that interpretation. EWDS[7-10] guardedly equated *-bero* with *-bero* in OHG *hornbero* 'hornet' and in proper names. In these editions, he also divided *odebero* into *od* and *obero* and traced *obero* to OHG *obassa* 'roof' ('luck bringer on the roof').

Numerous old conjectures, now forgotten, exist about the origin of *adebar*. Wachter (*Edebar*) already knew two "fanciful, almost ludicrous" (miras & tantam non ridiculas) derivations: *adebar* = *oudvater* 'old father' or *edel-bar* 'noble bird.' He explained *Edebar* (the form he preferred to *adebar*) as *edefar* 'traveling bird,' from *ede* 'bird' and G *fa(h)ren*, but did not specify the language in which he found *ede*. Apparently, he meant Wel *edn* 'bird.' The same etymology, with a reference to its originator, appears in Wiarda. Wachter's "ludicrous" list can be enlarged: 'bird traveling in flocks,' from L *avis* 'bird' (Terwen [1844]); 'bright-colored bird,' from OE *ād* 'fire' and MHG *var* 'color' or their cognates (Schwenck[1-2]); 'lamb-bringer,' from Du *oor* 'ewe' (Schwenck[4]; before Schwenck, Ten Kate compared *ooievaar* and L *ovis* 'sheep'), and finally, 'a bird believed to carry food in its entrails,' from G *Ader* 'vein' (Wasserzieher [1923:4-6]). (Wilken [1872:446] also noticed the similarity between *Adebar* and *Ader*—the stork allegedly had 'exposed veins'—but called it "too trivial.") The latest fantasy is Zollinger's (G *Adebar* and *Atem* 'breath' related to OI *jóð*; 1952:61, 81; 86, note 73). OI *jóð*, as we have seen, first turned up in connection with *adebar* in EWDS.[5-6]

Krogmann (1938a) disposed of the 'luck bringer' idea. He compared G *Adebar* with E *fieldfare* and identified *ade-* as a cognate of OE *waðum(a)* 'stream, lake' and G *-bar* as 'traveler' with *b* < *f* by Verner's Law. He offered a detailed analysis of the Germanic root for 'wet,' to which the Old English word is related (1936:35-38). However, Krogmann conceded that *-bar* had later been understood as 'carrier' and that *Adebar* might have been reinterpreted as 'luck bringer.' The post-1936 dictionaries follow Krogmann, and those who felt dissatisfied with his etymology, for instance, Karg-Gästerstadt (1941:211), Neuss (1973:131), Seebold (KS), and Hiersche, offered no counterarguments.

5. Thus, we have E *fieldfare*, OE *scealfor* (with cognates), and Du *ooievaar* (with cognates). OE *felofor*, mentioned above, also needs attention. Suolahti (1909:300-01) examined the variants *porfilio*, *polfir*, *folfir*, *philfor*, and *phelphur* and concluded that *felofor* was "a corruption" of L *porphyrio* under the influence of *scealfor*. AeEW derives *scealfor* directly from *porphyrio*.

A bird name ending in *-for* must have sounded natural to speakers of Old English. The history of that element is almost impenetrable. It first probably meant 'belonging or pertaining to,' and only by inference 'dweller' (a concept alien to the popular ornithological nomenclature, as pointed out above), but the original meaning seems to have been forgotten long before the emergence of Old English texts.

Perhaps the same suffix can be detected in OE *inneforan* ~ *innefaran* 'intestines, entrails.' If we assume that *-foran* is a variant of *-for(e)*, it can have its usual meaning in *innefora*, that is, 'in front of, in the presence of, before.' Gk ἔντερα 'bowels' consists of *en-* 'in' and *-ter* (a comparative suffix), the whole amounting to something like 'farther inside' (see WP I:217; IEW, 344, in both at *ēter*, and Brugmann [1897-1916:II/1, 324-26]). In Germanic, the designation of viscera had the prefix *in* followed by all kinds of unpredictable elements, as OE *innoð* and *innelfe* (*innifli, innylfe*), both with cognates in other Germanic languages; OI *ístr* ~ *ístra* 'fat of the paunch' (which AEW entatively derives from <**in-stra*, as in MDu *inster*; ÁBM suggests the etymon <**en(þ)s-tra*; see also *iðr* 'intestines'), and many others (Arnoldson [1915:150-59, especially 150-51], Baskett [1920:99-101, especially E1-2], Heinertz [1927:71-76], and AEW, *innyfli*). *Innyfli* consists of *inn-* and a suffix (the same suffix occurs in OI *dauðyfli* 'corpse': A. Sturtevant 1928:470-71). OE *innefora* has a similar structure and presumably means 'being inside.' See E. Sturtevant (1928:5) on the reverse process—the names of parts of the body becoming prepositions. AeEW (*-fora, -fara*) calls *innefora* a word of unknown origin. Later, Holthausen (1952:279, note 10) compared *-fora* and Gk πείρατα 'limit, boundary, rope, end of the rope,' with reference to L *viscēra* 'intestines' (< PIE **weis-* 'twist') and ModG *Geschlinge* (the same meaning; *schlingen* 'tie, wrap, plait'). But *innefora* belongs with the other *in(n)-* words: *intestines, entrails,* and so on. It is a counterpart of regional (or colloquial) *innards* 'viscera' (< *inwards*), known since the 13th century, and attempts to separate *-fora* in *innefora* from the adverb *fore* carry little conviction.

The existence of the suffix *-fore* finds additional confirmation in the history of HEIFER and especially of *elver* 'young eel' (1640), a variant of *eelfare* 'passage of young eels up a river' and 'brood of young eels.' In the earliest citation in OED (1533), *eelfare* means 'brood,' whereas the meaning 'passage of young eels' emerges only in 1836. The poor attestation of the word in texts (no data between 1533 and 1836) makes it advisable to reconstruct the history of *elver* on philological grounds rather than basing it on the chronology of the recorded examples.

Apparently, the change from *ēl- to ĕl-* occurred contemporaneously with the shortening of the stressed vowel in words like OE *ǣrende* (> ME *ĕrende*) 'errand' and OE *ǣmerge* (> ME *ĕmere* 'ember'), that is, in the 13th century at the latest (Luick [1964:secs 353 and 387]). The voicing of *-f-* in *elver* must be old, as ModE *wolves* and *culver* from OE *wulfas* and *culfer* show. OE **ǣlfore* ~ *ǣlfare* could not have had the sense 'young eel.' If, however, the suffix *-fore* ~ *-fare* designated inhabitants of restricted areas, it may occasionally have been used for designating areas and habitats as well. Perhaps **ǣlfore* meant 'territory favored by eels' (for spawning?) and, by implication, 'place favored by young eels,' whence 'brood of young eels.' The sense 'young eel' must have developed from the initial collective meaning of that noun. OE *heahfore* retained voiceless *f* when it became ME *heifer*, whereas **ǣlfore* or **ǣlfare* evidently split into **ēlver* and **ēlfare*. The latter, naturally, acquired the meaning 'passage of eels,' but it would not have yielded 'passage of young eels' if the connotation of the fish's age had not been present in the ancient form. When **ēlfare* went out of use, *elver* (<**ēlver*) retained the senses of both words.

6. This, then, is the picture in its entirety. **Old English had a bird name **feldfore* 'turdus pilaris,' which acquired a synonym **feldgefore*. Both meant approximately *'field bird.' Another bird, probably also a thrush, was called *felofor* 'brown one.' Although Old English scribes knew that L *porphyrio* designated some exotic waterfowl, with time the Latin word changed beyond recognition and merged with *felofor*. All three words continue into the present: *fieldfare* (< **feldfore*), *feldefore* and its variants (< **feldgefore*), and *felfar* and its variants (< *felofor*).** The modern forms with *feld-* (instead of *field-*, but not those with *fel-*) either never had lengthening before three consonants or underwent shortening in Middle English (HL, 705). Since by 1100, if not much earlier, the old meaning of the element *-fore* had been partly forgotten, compounds with it fell prey to folk etymology.

The same happened to the name of the stork in Dutch and German. Du *ooievaar* and G *Adebar* (*'swamp bird') share the second element with E *fieldfare*. Since in the beginning *vaar* ~ *-bar* ~ *-fare* ~ *-fore* had as little to do with traveling or traversing as with carrying, Krogmann's gloss of *Adebar* 'swamp goer' should be modified as 'swamp-er,' assuming that *ade-* is related to OE *waðum(a)*. OE *scealfor* and Du *scholver* ~ *schollevaar* have the same suffix. Whether *scealfor* goes back to *scræb* or has a verbal root (see Suolahti [1909:393-97] and AeEW),

-for in it was interpreted or even introduced as a suffix of a bird name.

7. I. Taylor (1873:119) mentions a mountain in Devon called *Fieldfare*. He explains it as a Scandinavian name (*Field* < *fjeld*), but in Dan *fjeld* 'mountain' the letter *d* never designated any sound (cf N *fjell*, Sw *fjäll*, OI *fjall*, *fell*). *Fieldfare* does not turn up in books on Devon toponymy (Liberman [1997:120-30]).

FILCH (1300? 1561?)

Filch *'steal' was, most likely, borrowed from thieves' cant. It is an adaptation of G* filzen *'comb through' (E* filch, sb, *means 'hook').* Filch *'beat; attack' is a different word, possibly from OE* gefylcian *'marshal troops,* etc.*'*

The date of the first occurrence of *filch* is unclear. OED doubts the connection between *filchid* (1300) and the modern verb (see *filch* and *bagle*). Both examples of *filch* (sb) in MED (ca 1300) and of *filch* (v; 14th century) presuppose the meaning 'attack,' not 'steal,' and are about dogs. The noun *ffylche* 'attack' was recorded in a poem of the first quarter of the 15th century. In 1561 *filch* 'steal' appeared and a year later *filchman* 'staff with a hook at one end used to steal articles from hedges, open windows, etc.' (Thieves using filchmans were popularly called anglers; *-man*, more often *-mans*, was a common suffix in thieves' language: H. Webster [1943:232].) The other relevant forms are *filching*, a verbal noun (1567); *filching*, a present participle (1570); *filcher* (1573); *filchingly* (1583); and *filch* = *filchman* (1622). See further examples in Partridge (1949a). OED marks *filch* 'hook' as obsolete, but Hotten[3] cites it as current. The meaning 'beat' (?< 'attack') was also preserved in later times (OED: *filch* v^3). OED transcribed *filch* with [ʧ] and [ʃ]. EDD has several words spelled *filsch*, possibly connected with *filch* 'rag' (for the [ʃ] ~ [ʧ] variation after resonants see Storm [1881:115, 126] and Luick [1964:1088, sec 788/2b]).

Numerous words appear in dictionaries as possible cognates of the verb *filch*: Gk φηλός 'deceitful' (Minsheu, Junius, Talbot), L *fallax* 'deceitful' (Minsheu), F *filou* 'thief, swindler' and *filouter* 'steal' (N. Bailey, Thomson, Mueller, Blackley [1869:202-03]), F *félon* 'traitor' (Holmboe, *veila*), Old Portuguese *filhar* 'seize,' perhaps allied to Ital *pigliare* 'seize' or F *piler* 'crush' (Marsh [1865:188]), OI *fela* 'hide' (Thomson, who calls Old Icelandic Gothic; he also has "Gothic" *filgia* and Sw(?) *filska*; cf Graham [1843:25]), OI *véla* 'defraud' (Holmboe), Go *filhan* 'steal' (Thomson's *fela* implies *filhan* and its cognates, including E reg *feal* 'hide'), G *filzig* 'greedy' (Skinner, *Gazophylacium*), Du *fielt* 'rascal' (Minsheu, who knew that the etymon of *fielt* is L *vīlis* 'base, mean'; he also cited Du *biel*, the same meaning), Gael *fealleaidh* 'knavish' (Mackay [1877]), SwiG *flöke* 'steal' (Wedgwood), Gael *peallaid* or *peallaij* 'skin of an animal, pelt' (Mackay [1877], Stormonth).

Filch can be akin to a word for 'pelt' only if it once meant 'rob an animal of its skin.' Analogous cases would be Go *wilwa* 'plunder' (if it is related to L *vellus* 'shorn wool,' and E *fleece* sb and v) and OE *hættian* 'scalp as punishment' from the root of *hæteru* (< **hætteru*) 'clothes.' Some of the comparisons, cited in the paragraph above, are ingenious. Blackley wrote a singularly uninformed book, but in addition to F *filouter* he offered a curious analogy: L *filum* (the etymon of F *fil* 'thread') is to *filch* as G *Strick* 'rope' to G *Strang* 'rope, cord' and 'rogue, scamp' (that is, 'gallowbird'). But thread was never used for hanging "rogues" and *filch* is not a noun. **Apparently, the sound complex *f-l* can designate some miscreant, vice, or misdeed in a dozen languages**. The (mainly regional) words cited in Wood (1913:19/159 and 64/48) also have the structure *f–l* but mean 'jerk; ruin by improper handling; fumble; flap, *etc*' and like various verbs from other languages for 'swing, shake' hardly have anything to do with *filch*. None of them except *fillip* (see it in the entry FUCK) has *i* in the root.

The Classical Greek and Latin forms are irrelevant, for, like *filch*, they begin with [f], but *filch* is not a bookish borrowing, and if the words cited above were cognates, the non-Germanic form would have had initial *p-*. The same holds for the Latin and Old Icelandic forms with *v-*. The origin of F *filou* (? < E *fellow*) is obscure. The word seems to be too late to have served as the etymon of *filch* (also *-ch* would remain unexplained) and is rather reminiscent of E *file* 'pickpocket,' with which W (1828) and Weekley compared it. *Filch* has a rhyming synonym *pilch*; Mueller[2] suggested that *filch* is its side form.

Skeat[1] considered *filch* to be related to Go *filhan* (see his reservations in the fourth edition) and derived it from OI *fela* 'hide' with a frequentative suffix, as in *tal-k, stal-k,* and *lur-k* versus *tell, steal,* and *lour* (*-k* as an intensifying suffix is also possible: cf *h(e)ar-k-(en)* and its cognates and see discussion at GAWK). To prove that the alternation *k* ~ *ch* existed, he cited *mil-k* ~ *mil-ch* (Skeat [1887 = 1892:468, 470]; Muller [1891:23] offers a list of such pairs). Hellquist (1891:142, note 1) and CD supported Skeat's etymology, and it appears in many dictionaries, including W[2]. But *filch* never meant 'hide.' Gothic etymological dictionaries take no cognizance of E *filch* in the entry *filhan.*

Holthausen (1904-05:295/9) **derived *filch* from OE **fylcan* and reconstructed Go **fulkjan,* related to Go *flokan** 'complain' and OE *flōcan* 'strike.'** His derivation presupposes that the verbs **ful-kjan* and *fl-ōkan* represent two variants of the zero grade, as do, for instance, Go *kun-i* 'race, generation' and its synonym kn-*ōþs*. *Flōcan* 'beat, strike' may be related to *filch* 'beat' and *filch* 'attack' but not to *filch* 'steal.' K. Malone (1955) traced ME *filch* to OE *(ge)fylcian* 'marshal (troops), draw (soldiers) up in battle,' later 'attack in a body, take as booty,' and his etymology appears in W^3. Recorded evidence does not fill the gaps between 'beat' or 'attack in a body' and 'pilfer.' The question arises why two centuries and a half separate the occurrences of a common verb. A similar difficulty confronts us in the history of COB 'beat' and FAG. In such cases, it is more reasonable not to postulate continuity. The unusual change from a literary style to low slang also requires an explanation.

If we dismiss the comparison of *filch* with the words given by Minsheu, Junius, Bailey, and others as fruitless and deny the connection between *filch* and Go *filhan* and OE **fylcan, (ge)fylcian,* two approaches can yield more or less satisfactory results. **Wedgwood cited N *pilka* (now, except in Nynorsk, spelled *pilke*) and Sc *pilk* 'to pick' and suggested that *filch* is a rhyming synonym of *pilch* (< *pilk*).** Mueller[2] found this etymology reasonable. OED does not associate *pilch* 'outer garment, *etc*,' first recorded in 1000 (E *pilch,* like G *Pelz* 'fur,' is from ML *pellicia* 'cloak'), and the verb *pilch* 'pick, pluck; pilfer, rob' (akin to LG *pül(e)ken, pölken,* N *pilke,* and a few Romance verbs given above), though *pilch* 'garment' ~ *pilch* 'rob' would be a pair like *fleece* (sb and v). *Pilch* (v) is a near doublet of *pluck* (see esp G *pflücken* in KM[20]), another verb of Romance origin, and seems to be in some way descended from L *pilāre* 'pull hair,' the etymon of E *peel* 'plunder' (obsolete), 'strip the outer layer,' a word etymologically distinct from *pelf, pilfer,* and *pillage.*

Despite the obvious similarity between the two verbs that Wedgwood and Mueller discussed, *filch* need not be a doublet of *pilch*. Ekwall (1903:21, note 4) **compared *filch* and Dan reg (Jutland) *filke* 'scrape, cut with a blunt knife,' and Oehl** (1933b:169) **tentatively supported him**. Like *pilk-* ~ *pilch,* presumably from *pil-k-* ~ *pil-ch,* Dan *filke* goes back to *fil-k-e* (ODS). Dan *file* (v) means 'scrape with a blunt knife; polish with a file; rub, scrub; pilfer'; the noun *fil* means 'file' (a tool). E *file* (< OE *fēol, fīl*), Du *vijl* (related to OS *fila*), G *Feile* (< OHG *fihala;* Dan *fil* and its Scandinavian cognates) are native Germanic words; see them and (O)I *þél* 'file' in etymological dictionaries. Although we obtain the proportion *pīl: pilk(e) ~ pilch = fīl: filk(e) ~ filch,* the connection between Dan *filke* 'scrape, scrub' and *pilke* 'pluck, peel; pick, peck; fish with a metal lure; jig' (so Feilberg, *filke*) is unlikely. *Filch* and *filke* are probably also distinct. **The English verb was recorded late, and **filk,* its putative base, has not been found. In addition, *filch* seems to have been coined as slang and has always meant only 'pilfer.' Therefore, *filch* 'hook' is the best starting point for tracing the origin of *filch* 'steal.'**

According to Jamieson (1808; 1867; 1879-82), *filchans* are 'rags patched or fastened together' ("hooked" in a bundle; see *filchmans,* above). The verb *filzen,* once current among German thieves, means 'comb through': Kluge (190lc:422 and 425). Early MHG *filzen* means 'search (a person),' a meaning still known. *Filz* is 'felt' (sb). Consequently, *filzen* comes from 'disentangle' (cf *verfilzt* 'tousled, *etc*') or 'sift through, filter'; 'filtering' needed sharp teeth (as on a comb) or 'hooks.' ***Filch* is probably an English adaptation of *filzen,* with [ʃ] and [tʃ] reproducing the German affricate [ts].** Hotten[3] derived *filch* from Romany *filichi* 'handkerchief' (implying that *filch* means 'steal handkerchiefs'?)—a dubious etymology, but since *filchans* 'rags' was part of international cant, the borrowing of the German verb into Early Modern English is likely. ME *filch* 'attack; beat' is a homonym of *filch* 'steal.' **E *filch* 'steal' seems to have appeared as a borrowing from German approximately when it was first recorded**. Its meaning may have been reinforced by *file* 'pickpocket' and *pilch.*

A Saxon last name *Filtsch,* limited to the Siebenbürgen area, is presumably of Slavic origin (from the root *velij-* 'big'). Its variants are *Filsch, Fielic, Fielke,* and *Fieltz.* See Keintzel-Schön (1976: index, and especially no 31 for 1933) and Gottschald (1954:584); not in Brechenmacher (1957). That name has no connection with the English verb (Liberman [1994b:169-73]).

FLATTER (1386)

Flatter is one of many Germanic words with the structure fl + vowel + t/d/ð, k/g *denoting unsteady or light, repeated movement, such as we find in* flutter *and* flicker. *The original meaning of* flatter *was 'flit about' (whence 'dance attendance'). The English verb is not derived from* flat *(adj), as though from 'smoothing,' L* flatāre *'make big' and thus 'inflate one's vanity,' or OF* flater *'flatter.' In this meaning, the Old French verb was more likely borrowed from Middle*

English and crossed the path of a similar verb meaning 'appease' and 'caress.' OI flaðra *'fawn on one' fits the phonetic scheme given above, but the relationship between* -t *and* -ð *remains unclear. Some* fl- *words have doublets beginning with* bl- *(for example, E* blatter *and* blather*); the origin of the interplay of* fl- *and* bl- *is also obscure.*

The sections are devoted to 1) flatter *and L* flatāre, flatter *and* flat, *and a few other proposed etymologies of* flatter, *2)* flatter *and G* flattern, *3) OI* flaðra, *and 4) the* bl- *words synonymous with* flatter.

1. **Early etymologists derived E and F *flatter* 'flatter' from L *flatāre* 'make big,'** which they understood as frequentative of *flāre* 'blow' (so Minsheu and Ménage), because flatterers 'inflate' another person's vanity and 'swell' their reputation in the eyes of those who listen to them or because they whisper ('blow') into the ears of their patrons. **Guyter (cited in Ménage) related F *flatter* to L *lactāre* 'dupe, entice,' < *flactāre.** According to Junius, **Ménage derived F *flatter* from *flagitāre* 'demand, importune'** (his source was not Ménage [1750]). Knobloch (1995:147) may not have known that he had such an early predecessor. **Storm** (1876:178-9) **suggested that **afflāre, *flatitāre,* and **afflaticāre* (> **flayer, *fléer*) meant 'flatter' and 'waft softly to make a fan move'** since OF *flavele* 'flattery' goes back to *flabellum* 'fan.' **Skinner derived E *flatter* from French, and F *flat(t)er* from L *blaterāre* 'blather.'** Junius also looked on the English verb as a borrowing from French but traced it to L *lactāre* < **flactāre*. **In addition, he believed that *flatter* could be derived from the English adjective *flat* because flatterers "smoothen down" those (with a flat hand, as it were) with whom they would curry favor.**

Junius's etymologies proved to be especially durable. The second of them turns up in Claiborne (1989:197) and in Shipley (1984:299), who compares *flatter* and L *plācāre* 'soothe,' both allegedly from PIE **pela*. A variation on 'smoothen down' is C. Smith's 'touch gently' (1865). Barbier (1932-35:112) cited what he believed to be a Romance parallel to *flatter* from *flat*. Kumada (1994:15), who argues for a sound symbolic origin of *flatter,* also assumes that the root of this verb is *flat*. See an incomplete survey of early French scholarship on this verb in NC, and of English, in Richardson and Mackay (1877). Woll (1986:2, 4) has shown how improbable the development from 'make flat' to 'fawn on, praise insincerely' is.

Bailey (1730), Barclay, and Johnson mark *flatter* as French. Todd, in Johnson-Todd, cites OI *fladra* [sic] and *flete* 'woman who flatters,' along with *fletsen*, "Teutonic" for 'flatter,' and *vleyden* (did he mean Du *vleien* 'flatter'?). R. Latham, despite his dependence on Johnson-Todd, ventures no discussion. Holmboe's etymology (he cites OI *flaðra*, F *flatter*, and Skt *laḍ* as cognates of *flatter*) rests on the idea of initial *f-mobile*. See *laḍ* at *lálati* (v) 'jests, plays' (v) in KEWAS, 259 and KEWA III:91. *Lálati*, which sounds like similar verbs in other languages, cannot be a cognate of *flatter*. Apart from phonetic difficulties, the meanings are irreconcilable. Lanman (1906:233) glosses *lálati* as 'sport, dally, play; behave in an artless and unconstrained manner.'

Gamillscheg (1921:633 and EWFS) **derived OF *flater* from Celtic **velno*** (cf Sc *feall* 'treason'), an etymology that ML rejected as phonetically indefensible. In Diez's opinion, OF *flatir* ~ *flater* are akin to OE/OD *flat(r)*, and OHG *flaz* 'flat.' The Old French noun *flat* meant 'stroke, blow' and the verb *flatir* meant 'dash down'; consequently, he interpreted the verb as 'stretch down' and referred to OI *fletja* 'make flat' (his string is 'dash down' > 'flatten' > 'caress' > 'flatter'). Brachet ignored Diez's etymology ("origin unknown"), ML (3356) and Brüch (1917:685) rejected it, but it appealed to von Wartburg (FEW).

2. **According to DW (*flattieren*), the etymon of all the verbs under consideration is G *flattern* because a flatterer flaps his wings as a dog wags its tail.** The Grimms' etymology goes back to Ihre. Scheler[1] follows Diez. Scheler[2] leans toward the Grimms' interpretation (likewise Mueller[2]), but in the third edition he again surveys the literature and hesitatingly returns to his initial idea. Tullberg (*flattera*) endorses the Grimms' derivation. Franck (*flatteren*) leaves the question open. Attempts have been made to explain OF *flater* as 'lick' (Cornu [1880:133]; Baist [1880] criticized Cornu's idea, but Gaston Paris supported it: see Cornu [1881:404, note 1, where Paris adds his comment], and Woll [1986:1-4], who distances himself from this etymology).

Contrary to the opinion of some eminent etymologists, E *flatter* cannot be a borrowing from French or Provençal. OED notes that F *flat-er* would have become *flat*, not *flatter*, in Middle English. CD and Skeat[4] found that argument convincing, but Kluge (in KL) continued to call *flatter* a borrowing from French (the fascicle of OED with *flatter* appeared in September 1896, and KL was published in 1899). MED shares the opinion of OED and compares the suffix in *flatter* with that in *flick-er-en* and *skim-er-en*.

Of decisive importance are the forms *ulateri* 'flattery' and *ulatour* 'flatterer' in the Middle English (Kentish) poem *Ayenbite of Inwit*. The voicing of initial fricatives in its text affects only native words (Wallenberg [1923:263, note 3]). This rule, which finds an analogy in Middle Dutch (Franck [1910:sec 81]), continued into later periods (Meech [1940-41:116]). Jensen (1908:38) and Dolle (1912:sec 139, 4.b) posited MDu *flatteren* as an intermediary between the Old French and the Old Kentish form, but the need for such an intermediary is not obvious, given that we are dealing with a sound change common to both areas.

Jordan (1925:sec 215) and Berndt (1960:180, note 2) support Wallenberg, but dictionaries are slow in accepting their conclusions, though ODEE is aware of the Kentish forms. Partridge (1958) and CEDEL copy from Diez and thus repeat Scheler[1,3]. Barnhart reproduces the etymology from MED. Weekley traces *flatter* to French, and so does W[3], which says, following Gaston Paris, that OF *flater* means 'lick, flatter.' RHD[1] dissociates E and F *flatter*, but RHD[2] states that E *flatter* was "reinforced" by the French verb.

Wedgwood modified slightly the Grimms' hypothesis and traced the meaning of the English verb to *'wag the tail' and that of F *flatter* to *'lick,' from which he derived 'stroke an animal' and 'flatter.' Skeat believed in the French origin of *flatter* and rejected Gmc *flat* as the etymon of OF *flater*. He noted OSw *fleckra* 'flatter' and Sw reg *fleka* 'caress' but did not know how to explain the alternation *t* ~ *k*. OED preferred to treat *flatter* as native, "an onomatopoeia expressive of light repeated movement"; it also cited the Swedish forms with *k* and mentioned OI *flaðra*. For the forms with *k*, *fleech* among them, see ODEE (*flatter*). A direct comparison of *flatter* with G *flehen* 'beseech,' still present in Skeat[1], cannot be sustained on phonetic grounds.

Although not a borrowing, *flatter*, probably a slang word when it came into use, superseded several other native words. The Old English verb meaning 'flatter' was *lyffettan, līcettan,* and *ōleccan* (TOE:04.06.02.06), though *līcettan* has more to do with hypocrisy than flattery (Thaning [1904:81], Brendal [?1908: nos 932 and 933]). The imperfectly known word *twaddung*, first discovered by Napier (anonymous [1904]), with its doublet *twædding*, which makes one think of E *twaddle* (AeEW), translates L *adūlātio*, thus 'flattery.'

If *flatter* is a cognate of G *flattern*, whose origin continues to puzzle German etymologists (DEW), its semantic development was 'flit, hover' > 'flit about' > 'dance attendance' > 'flatter.' It then follows that OF *flater* 'flatter' was borrowed from Middle English. The problem with this hypothesis is that in Anglo-French of the 12th to the 14th century, words of English origin are rare, while in continental dialects they hardly exist at all. Yet *flatter* may be one of them. Even Barbier, who was unwilling to recognize the presence of English words in early French, had to admit a few exceptions (Barbier [1938-43:308]). Old French had *flater* 'lick,' 'lie, deceive,' and 'dash down.' The etymon of each is contestable (Woll [1986] offers a detailed survey). The borrowing of a Middle English word may have "reinforced" the native meaning 'deceive.' The weakness of Woll's otherwise exemplary discussion is his disregard of the Germanic side of the problem.

Behr's suggestion (1935:78) that *flatter*, which she calls onomatopoeic, is a blend of *flacker* and *flutter* looks like a misunderstanding. Did she believe that E *flatter* means 'flutter'? The Dutch verb *flikflooien* 'flatter' is based on the same idea as *flatter* ('move around'); see the oldest conjectures on this word in Hoeufft (1835:293-94).

The derivation of OF *flater* 'flatter' (v) from Gmc **flat-* is improbable. OF *flater* 'flatter' and OF *flater* 'dash down' seem to be homonyms, and the latter may indeed go back to the Germanic adjective (so Woll [1986:11-12]). Judging by ModI *fletja* (v) 'roll (dough), cut (a fish), open and remove the backbone' and *fletja* (sb) 'roofing plank' (ÁBM), **flatjan* had predominantly specialized meanings. 'Dash down' (and thus 'make flat') may have been one of them (see FT, *flek*, the end of the entry, on the derivation of 'flatten' from 'strike'). OF **flatjan* probably arose before umlauting did and later merged with *flatir* ~ *flater* from Middle English.

3. OI *flaðra* occurs only once and seems to mean 'beat about the bush.' It has often been compared with E *flatter*. In Modern Icelandic, *flaðra* means 'fawn on one, jump around someone, cringe before one, flatter' (not 'wag the tail,' though *flaðra* is usually applied to dogs); see OED (*flether* and *flaither*). The etymology of *flaðra* is unknown (AEW, ÁBM). Like *flatter*, it has been traced to an adjective meaning 'flat,' that is, **flaðr* (although **flaðr* does not turn up in the texts, see its probable derivatives in NEO, 113 and 117). However, 'flatter' is usually a secondary meaning derived from 'inflate,' 'lick,' 'dupe,' and 'caress,' not 'make flat.' More importantly, *flaðra* means 'run around a master' (whence 'flatter') and has nothing to do with flatness.

Germanic possessed many verbs beginning with *fl-* and denoting unsteady or light repeated movement. Root vowels alternated in them by secondary ablaut. Equally variable were their root final consonants, so that E *flitter, flutter, flicker,* G *flattern,* OI *flaðra,* and so on are related through later associations, rather than genetically. All such verbs meant 'flap the wings,' 'run dog-like in circles,' 'flow lightly,' 'wave back and forth,' 'flash and die away by turns,' 'quiver, vibrate,' perhaps 'work nimbly with one's fingers' (for example, OI *fletta* and G *fleddern* mean 'rob a corpse'). **One of them was E *flatter* 'flit around' > 'behave like a sycophant.'** If *f-* in L *flagrāre* 'blaze, glow' is from **bh-,* the Latin verb cannot be related to OHG *flogarôn* (> ModG *flackern* 'flicker'), but the similarity between them is remarkable (Berneker [1898:364]). See also Wood (1899-1900:314/11) on *flicker* and *flutter.*

4. Many *fl-* words have doublets beginning with *bl-*. Skinner traced *flatter* to L *blaterāre* (see sec 1, above). The meanings of OI *flaðra* and *blaðra* overlap (ODGNS and CV, *blaðra*). Walde (1906:110) repeated CV without referring to their dictionary. Whether OI *blaðra* (sb) 'bubble' belongs here is uncertain. Of interest are E *blatter* and *blather,* which are not necessarily from Latin. *Blaðra* 'chatter' may have influenced *flaðra* ('talk idly and irresponsibly,' 'wag one's tongue' > 'talk insincerely' > 'flatter'). Likewise, E *blatter* may have affected the meaning of *flatter,* though *blatter* has at no time been frequent. Ir *blath* 'praise' and *blaith* 'plain, smooth,' which Webster (1828) mentioned at *flatter,* do not belong here, for the vowels are incompatible and Ir *bl-* is from *ml-* (Stokes [1897:51] and LE, *mláith*). Mackay's derivation of E *flatter* from Gael *blad* 'big, loud mouth,' *bladair* 'person with a big mouth; blatterer' (1877) is impossible on phonetic grounds (Liberman [1990 and 1991:227-28]). It may be noted that the variation *f-* ~ *b* is also known (E. Schröder [1909]).

FUCK (1503)

Many verbs in Germanic with the roots fik-, fak-, fuk-, fok-, *have a basic meaning 'move back and forth.' Their most common figurative meaning is 'cheat.' If Old English had such a verb, it seems to have been lost. ModE* fuck *is, most likely, a borrowing from Low German, rather than a direct continuation of a pre-15th-century native form.* Fuck *is part of a large group of loosely related verbs having the structure* f *+ vowel + stop. Intrusive* l *and* r *appear frequently between* f *and the vowel, so that* fit, fiddle, fidget, fib, fob, *as well as* flit, flip, flap, flop, flicker, frig, *and so on belong together, even though they cannot be called cognates in the strict sense of this term. Given such an indiscriminate mass of similar-sounding near synonyms, the task of discovering the Indo-European cognates of any of them holds out little promise.* L pungere *'prick, sting,'* L pugnere *'strike, fight,' and Gk* πυγή *'buttocks' are probably not related to* fuck. *The Germanic verb of copulation appears to have had some currency in the Romance-speaking countries; Ital* ficcare *looks like a borrowing from German.*

The sections are devoted to 1) the Germanic background of fuck, *2) words of similar sound and meaning, 3) the etymon of* fuck, *4) the English environment of* fuck, *5) the putative Indo-European cognates of* fuck, *and 6)* fuck *in English etymological lexicography and scholarship.*

1. **Numerous Germanic words have the root *fik- ~ fak- ~ fuk- ~ fok-*.** Here are some of them having *i.* G *ficken* (now relegated in this meaning to dialects) 'make short, quick movements; flog lightly.' The swish of the rod or cane is accompanied by the exclamation *fick, fick.* In dialects, *ficken* 'tap, rub, scratch, touch' has been recorded; OHG *ficchon* ~ MHG *vicken* 'rub' is evidently the same word. Early Modern Dutch and Dutch dialects have *fikken* and *fikkelen* with the same meaning (were the Dutch verbs imported from Frisian or Low German, for why is their *f-* not voiced?). Fl *fikken* 'tinker at something with a blunt knife', as well as Sw reg *ficka* 'hurry up' and *fikla* 'rummage about, work sloppily' (N reg *fikle*), belong here too. Compare G reg *Fickmülle* (a game in which stones are moved in different directions), *fickeln* 'play the violin' (*Fickelbogen* means 'bow for playing the violin'), *Fickel* 'penis,' and *Gefick* 'people running in different directions.' In Bavarian, *das ficht mich nicht an* 'it's not my concern' (from *anfechten*) coexists with *das fickt mich nicht an. Ficken* 'copulate' is widely known in dialects, but it is not the only meaning of this verb.

Noneuphemistic verbs denoting sexual intercourse, to the extent that they can be etymologized, usually mean 'thrust, strike, pierce, prick, rub.' See Buck 278:4.67 for a general overview, Goldberger (1932:103-18), and Holthausen (1955-56:97/16). The number of metaphorical expressions for 'copulate' is almost endless, as modern dictionaries of synonyms and annotated editions of Greek and Latin authors (Goldberger, loc cit and Herescu [1959-60]) show (this is equally true of dialects; see Gering [1920:302-03]), but in Germanic 'copulate' = 'thrust' is rare; however, see some examples in Barbier (1932-35:313) and Webinger (1937b:160).

'Move back and forth' as the semantic base of 'copulate' also occurs outside the *ficken* group. Such are OHG *rîban* 'rub; copulate' (ModG *reiben* 'rub'), MHG *baneken* (Ochs [1954:150-51]), G *ranzen* 'copulate' (said about animals), ultimately from MHG *ranken* 'move back and forth,' the now obsolete E *swive* (compare it with E *swivel,* G *schweben* 'float, hover, dangle,' and their cognates: OED), and the names of several Scandinavian gods, giants, and horses, seemingly meaning 'one rocking, moving back and forth' (AEW: *Vingnir, Vingskornir, Vingþórr,* and *vingull* 'a stallion's penis').

Words with *a:* G *fackeln* 'shilly-shally' (hardly from *Fackel* 'torch' because of its unsteady flame), *Faxen* in *Faxen machen* 'fool around,' *Faxen schneiden* 'pull faces,' and G reg *fäckli* 'flap of a garment, lap' and *fäck(t)en* 'wing.' OI *fǫkta* 'flee, retreat' (if *ǫ* is from *a*) may be part of this group. Magnússon (1953:15) compares *fǫkta* with ModI *fák* 'silly behavior,' *fákur* 'fool, simpleton,' and *fákur* ~ *fákhestur* 'steed' (from 'moving fast'), but the long vowel in the root makes the comparison difficult. He mentions E *fetch* 'apparition,' a word of obscure history (OED); the meaning 'coming and going' would be compatible with 'move back and forth.' The verb *fetch* has the same origin (sec 4, below). See the above-mentioned Modern Icelandic words in ÁBM. *Fick* and *fack* often go together. A Westphalian riddle about the broom contains the words *fick di fack;* cf G *fickfacken* 'run aimlessly back and forth; have a lot to do; scheme behind one's back, deceive, cheat; potter about; flog,' West Fl *fikfakken* 'spray with paint,' G *Fixefaxe* 'pranks, tomfoolery,' and G reg *facksen* 'write quickly and illegibly.' If the original meaning of G *fegen* was the same as today ('sweep') rather than 'cleanse, purge,' it may belong with *fickfacken* (Gerland [1869b:21-22, no 52]); its *e* probably goes back to *a.*

Words with *u, o*: G reg *fucken* 'move fast' and *fuck* 'great speed; advantage; quick movement; deception'; *fuckern,* and *fuckeln* 'cheat, especially in games; move quickly back and forth'; 'scratch'; *fucksen,* and *fuckseln* 'cheat in games, maltreat, torment, beat, steal.' Du reg *fokken* 'walk, run' (now obsolete); of the same type are G reg *focken* and MLG *vocken* 'tease, irritate; swindle,' Early ModDu and Du reg *vocken* 'quiver' (said about the flame), and the Early Modern German noun *Focker* ~ *Fucker* 'bellows' (ModDu *vocken* is the main verb for 'copulate': ErW), Sw reg *fokka* 'copulate' and *fokk* 'penis,' and Sw *slöfock* 'dullard, sluggard.' Dan reg *fok* 'the last sheaf' belongs here too on account of its connection with fertility rites (Bernard Olsen [1910:8-9]; Ellekilde [1937-38]; T. Andersen [1982:17 and 21, note 11]). This must have been the reason Mannhardt (1884:328) chose not to discuss its etymology. In all probability, G *Federfuchser* 'pettifogger; narrow-minded person' (that is, penpusher?) and *Pfennigfuchser* 'miser' have nothing to do with *Fuchs* 'fox'; neither does *fuchsen* 'annoy, vex' or *fuchs(teufels)wild* 'livid with rage, furious' (see also Bremmer [1992:66] on Du *vossen* 'study hard; copulate'; its connection with Du *vos* is due to folk etymology).

It will be seen that *fick(s)en, fack(s)en,* and *fuck(s)en,* as well as the verbs ending in *-eln* and *-ern,* are near synonyms. Their basic meaning is 'make quick movements; move back and forth' (hence 'copulate'). The most common figurative meanings of all those verbs are 'deceive, cheat; annoy, irritate; work with an imperfect tool.' See DW (*ficken*), Rietz (*fika(s), fokk, fokka*), FT (*fikle*), KS (*Faxe, Fuchs*[2] 'beginning student,' and *Federfuchser*), Gradl (1870:125-27), WF (117, *fikkelen-fikken*), Franck (1883:12-13), Laistner (1888:186), O. Weise (1902:243-44), L. Bloomfield (1909-10:266/54; an especially extensive list), Thomas (1909-10), Sperber (1912:413-14, 429-30, 436), Stoett (1917:65), W. de Vries (1924:135), Celander (1925), Stapelkamp (1957a:229), Müller-Graupa (1957:466-67), Carl (1957-58:357), and Rosenfeld (1955). Ochs (1921) can be consulted, but the article is confusing.

2. **The *fik-* ~ *fak-* ~ *fuk-* words have doublets with postvocalic *-t* or dental affricates** (Gradl [1870:125-30], Van Helten [1873:213-51], DW). Such are G reg *fitzen* 'flog, make stitches' (akin to OI *fitja upp* 'make the first stitches'), *pfitzen* 'run back and forth,' *fitschen* 'flutter about,' *fitscheln* 'play ducks and drakes; talk about nothing in particular,' *fätscheln* 'run back and forth,' *fatzen* 'cheat in games, *etc*,' *fätzen* 'wrangle, tease,' *pfutzen* ~ *futschen* 'run back and forth,' *pfutschen* 'gulp down,' *futsch* ~ *pfutsch* (interjections accompanying a quick movement), *fuschen* 'bungle one's work,' and Du *futselen* 'trifle with something.'

Another set of doublets begins with *fl-*. Here we find G *flicken* 'mend, darn' (= 'make stitches'); G reg *flicken* 'strike' and *jemanden flicken* 'strike up friendship with someone; copulate,' Du *flikken* 'patch (up)' and 'copulate.' Despite the prevailing opinion to the contrary (see NEW), Du *flikflooien* 'flatter' should not be separated from *flikken,* whatever the origin of *-flooien* may be (W. de Vries [1915:11-12]; for more, see FLATTER); Sw *flacka (omkring)* 'wander around,' and G reg *flotschen* 'flutter.' See Flom (1913), who surveys *fl-* words in Scandinavian, A. Kock (1895-98:1-3), and SEO (*flicka*). German *flattern* and English *flatter* also belong to that group. Some verbs with different vowels in the root have postvocalic *p:* OI *fipla* 'touch with the fingers,' LG *fipsen* 'make quick movements; copulate' and *fippen* 'go back and forth,' Du and G *foppen* 'cheat,' E *flip, flap, flop* (Du *flip* also means 'vagina' [ErW]).

Some of the German verbs listed above show

no effects of the Second Consonant Shift. For example, G *foppen, flicken,* and *flattern* have the same stops as do Du *foppen,* E *flicker,* and E *flatter.* Shifted forms exist, however: compare G *Fach* 'compartment, pigeon hole' versus OE *fæc* 'interval,' G *fuchtig,* a doublet of *fuchsig* 'very angry' (a synonym of *fuchsteufelswild*), G reg *Fuchtel* 'feather-brained woman,' and so on. G *Fächer* 'fan' may be an adaptation of a Latin word, but fanning presupposes movement back and forth. OE *fæc* is easy to understand in light of Du *vaak* 'often, frequently' (= 'at regular intervals, happening every now and then,' similar to 'move back and forth,' the meaning underlying the entire *f-k* group; Muller [1916]). If the basic meaning of G *Fach* is 'compartment,' then it refers to the same entity as OE *fæc,* but in space rather than in time. See the critique of Trier's ideas in Drosdowski (1950:61.6b and 63; Trier thought that OE *fæc* reflects the practice of making fences) and sec 4, below, on *fit.* When analyzing the Germanic root *fīst,* Rosenfeld (1958:357-420) mentioned dozens of words, whose pejorative connotations trace, in his opinion, to the meaning 'break wind,' but they much more likely belong with verbs of copulation. The words ending in *b, d, g* will be discussed below.

3. **Apparently, E *fuck* is one of the many words listed in sec 1 and 2,** as was clear to L. Bloomfield, **but it is hardly native, for English has never had a profusion of *fik- ~ fak- ~ fuk-* words.** In Old English, *fācen* 'deceit, sin, crime, blemish,' *fǣcne* 'deceitful, vile, worthless,' *ficol* 'cunning, tricky,' *gefic* 'deceit,' and *(be)fician* 'deceive, flatter' have been attested. If *fuck* ever occurred or still occurs with meanings other than 'copulate' (for example, *fuck the field* 'plant,' as a farmer informed J. Adams [1963:74]), they are derivative of the main one. The strong verb **fīcan* has not been recorded or reconstructed (for example, Seebold [1970] does not mention it), but ME *fike* 'move restlessly, bustle; act and speak deceitfully' may testify to its existence. Although current in the North, E reg *fike* does not seem to be a borrowing from Scandinavian, for OI *fíkjask* meant only 'strive eagerly,' while *fíkr* and *fíkinn* meant 'eager, desirous.' If, however, some such Old English verb existed, *fuck* is not its direct continuation. OE *befician* and **fīcan* may have meant *'copulate.'

In many languages, 'copulate' and 'deceive' are related concepts (so in E *screw*). The Czech cognate of Russ *ebat'* 'copulate' also means 'deceive' (the same meaning in Russ *naebyvat'*), while in Sorbian *jebać* 'deceive' has no sexual meaning (WONS). See Brugmann (1913:323-25; Slavic), ESSI VIII:188, Mackel (1905:269; LG *futän* 'bitch about, carp,' most probably going back to F *foutre* 'copulate'), Poetto (1984:198; English and Italian), Arditti (1987:215; Salonica Judezmo), Gold (1989:34, with references to his earlier works), and especially Foerste (1964a). Foerste cites nontrivial parallels for 'swing, jump, rub' (= 'move briskly back and forth') > 'deceive' and compares G *ficken* and OE *befician.* Sperber (1912) believed that the primary meaning of all such verbs was 'copulate.' *Screw* would be a counterexample, for it did not originate in the sexual sphere, but, in principle, his hypothesis is right: the development goes from 'have intercourse' to 'deceive' ('thrust forcibly, beat, nail down' > 'have intercourse' > 'be on top of it' > 'triumph' > 'look down upon' > 'deceive, mock, denigrate'; see also Goldberger [1932:110-18] and A. Keller [1871]). WONS admits both paths (from 'copulate' to 'deceive' and from 'deceive' to 'copulate'), but the evidence for the second path is lacking.

A third common meaning accompanying 'swing,' 'deceive,' and 'copulate,' is 'vex, annoy.' Such is LG *focken* 'tease.' Kück's derivation of that verb from MLG *vocke* 'toad' is fanciful (1905:15). Moving back and forth may appear as a physical representation, a visible image of inconstancy and hence of mockery and deceit. In societies in which steadfastness was a cardinal virtue, its opposite would easily develop into the most abhorrent vice (lack of loyalty). The history of E *fickle* shows the progress from 'treacherous' to 'inconstant,' though one would expect the reverse order. OE *fācen* means 'deceit, treachery, crime,' but the only recorded sense of *fācian* is 'try to obtain; reach' and of *fǣcan* 'wish to go.' The idea of movement underlies both (as well as OI *fíkjask* 'strive eagerly,' mentioned above); however, the evil connotations of *fācen* are absent in them. Thus we have no evidence that *fuck* is a native English verb. OI *fjúka* (*fauk, fuku, fokinn*) 'be tossed by the wind' has no cognates anywhere in Germanic and cannot support Lass's idea (1995) that *fuck* goes back to OE **fūcan.*

The earliest known example of *fuck* in English is dated to the second half of the 15th century (Revard [1977]). From 1503 onward, that verb has been continually in use (OED, DOST) and ousted *jape, sard,* and *swive* (see speculation on the longevity of *fuck* in Noguchi [1996]). Buck 278:4.67 cites the name *John le Fucker* (1278), for which he does not give the source. *Fucker* is probably a variant of *Fulcher,* along with *Fucher, Foker, Foucar,* as Sherman Kuhn suggested to Allen Walker Read

(Read [1976:4-5]). OED has no citations of *fucking* before 1568, but a reliable 1528 example is known in which the word apparently means 'copulating' (not an expletive: E. Wilson [1993]). Neither *fuck* nor its derivatives appear in Shakespeare. He knew the word, as follows from his pun on the *focative case,* but the vogue for it seems to have come later than roughly the years 1590-1610. The same is true of *Fucker, fuckster,* and puns on *fūcus.* See G. Williams (1994:562-65 and 1997:136), whose examples of *firk, fiddle, fig,* and others are equally valuable, and Webb (1989:42-43).

In the 16th century, *fuck(ing)* was applied mainly to lascivious monks and did not compete with the likes of *swive* in broader contexts. *Fuck(ing)* enjoyed special popularity in Scotland, though it points to Flanders and Germany rather than Scandinavia if we consider the late date of borrowing. Consequently, the word may have had too strong a northern coloring for Stratford-on-Avon. G. Williams (1994:562) seems to be right when he says that "Lowland Scots use of *fucksail* (foresail of a ship) for a woman's skirt suggests a more comfortable relationship with *fuck* than was found further south," but, as pointed out above, *fuck* might simply be a predominantly northern word. The bawdy allusion *fucus* = *fuck* was understood everywhere in England, however; see *fucus* in G. Williams (1994) and Henke (1979).

G *ficken* 'copulate' turned up in texts only in 1588 (WHirt), but the idea that a verb widespread in numerous (perhaps in all) dialects is old (so DW) must be correct. Unlike G *ficken,* E *fuck* has no support from modern **fick* and **fack.* It probably appeared in English when it surfaced in texts, that is, some time around 1450. The lending language was LG or Fl (hardly Scand). The borrowing must have occurred before E /u/ changed to /ʌ/. Early ModE *fuck(e)* is related to Du or Fl *vocken* as is E *buck* 'male of a deer' to its Dutch counterpart *bok.* However, it remains a puzzle why English speakers did not borrow the much more common *ficke(n)* and why the new word ousted the equally vulgar synonyms *jape, sard, swive,* and a host of others; T. Burton (1988:27-29) discusses some of them.

It is now taken for granted that Ital *ficcare,* OSp *ficar* (> ModSp *hincar*), Port *ficar,* and F *ficher* 'copulate' (cf also F *afficher* 'fasten, attach') have a Romance etymon, **ficticāre* or **figicāre* (< **fīccāre* < L *figere* 'attach'; F *ficher* replaced *foutre* only in the 17th century.) But perhaps the Romance words were borrowed from German. MHG *vicken* (*v* designated [f]) had the meanings 'rub' and 'fasten,' the second of which has also been derived from *figere.* Some contamination (G *ficken* X L *figere*) is not inconceivable, but if a sexual metaphor was at play, *ficken* 'fasten, attach' (= 'nail down') would accord well with *ficken* 'copulate.' Diez seems to have been the last scholar to wonder at the similarity between Sw *fikas* and Rom *ficcarsi* ('copulate'), both reflexive: see FEW 15/II:123 (*ficken*). Santangelo's few incoherent remarks on this subject (1953:68) are of no account. ML (3920) supported the oldest etymology (*ficcare* < **figicāre*; Del Rosal [?1537 - ?1613] already knew it: see Del Rosal [1992, *hincar*]), and modern dictionaries of the Romance languages repeat it (this is true of all the dictionaries consulted). Yet the Romance etymon of *ficcare* and its cognates remains a matter of speculation, and, if E *fuck* can be a borrowing from Low German, *ficcare* and the rest could also come from Germanic. The Italian verb first surfaced in Dante (DLLA, 1287). Bruckner (1899:13) supports Diez's derivation of Ital *fagno* 'rogue passing himself off as a dummy' from Go **faikns* (see OE *fǣcne,* above) but does not touch on *ficcare.* The words in question were unprintable for a long time, and this may be the reason they do not appear in Waltemath (1885), Mackel (1887), Goldschmidt (1887), Zaccaria (1901), Ulrix (1907), Bertoni (1914), Bonfante (1974), and others. Nor does Knobloch (1987:66) mention the connection of *ficcare* with the corresponding verbs in Germanic, whereas Luiselli (1992) deals with the periods too ancient for such a borrowing. According to Dietz (2000:80, note 7), *ficcare* and *ficken* are "definitely" unrelated (no other arguments given).

Russ *fukat'* and its Slavic cognates often mean 'make a noise' and are traditionally derived from the onomatopoeic complex **fu* (Vasmer IV:209), but note Russ *profukat'* 'waste (wealth),' Pol *fukać* 'berate,' and Slovenian *fukati* 'copulate.' Words from different etymons may have converged in Slavic. *Fick-* seems to have reached Czech at a period when speakers of Slavic languages still substituted *p* for foreign *f* (Janko [1926]). The Gmc verb enjoyed a truly international reputation (Spitzer [1915:213, note continued from p 212]). Verbs meaning 'copulate' are easily borrowed (Corominas [1942] gives one of many pertinent examples).

If the Italian verb is of German origin, *ficcare* from G *ficken* must have been reinforced by the obscene meaning of *fico* 'fig' (fruit and the gesture): ModIt *fica* means 'sexually appealing female'; a vulgar word (Goldberger [1930:64], Pisani [1979:314-16], and Scarpat [1969, esp 885-89]). Figs and fig leaves have had sexual connotations since at least biblical times. See Gold (1995a) on Ital *fica* and the several senses of *fig.* However vague the reconstruction advanced here may be, one can imagine a German profanity spreading north and south. More daring hypotheses turn up in the literature. For example, Stopa (1972:196) believes that "[t]he etymology of most obscene words in Slavonic languages (e.g. in the peasants' slang of Polish) leads to African." This is a baffling idea.

4. **Although English lacked the rich *fick-* ~ *fak-* ~ *fuk-* crop recorded elsewhere, it had many words of the type mentioned above; however, they ended in consonants other than *-k*.** The list opens with *fidge* (1575), transformed under unknown circumstances into *fidget* (1754; the noun *fidget* was first recorded in texts in 1674). OED notes that the meaning of *fidge* resembles closely that of *fike* and refers to G *ficken,* but adds, "...etymological connexion is hardly possible unless the form has undergone onomatopoeic modification." The obsolete verb *fig (about)* is another synonym of *fidge. Fadge* (obsolete and rare; OED gives citations between 1658 and 1876) meant, among other things, 'make one's way,' and it also occurred in the form *fodge.* One of the senses of *fudge* (1674) was 'thrust in awkwardly or irrelevantly,' while *fudgy* (1819!) means 'fretful.' All those meanings belong to the semantic field of G *ficken* and its variants. See a short discussion of *fudge* and *fidge* in Lockwood (1995a:70).

Some words have long vowels. *Feague* 'beat' (the end of the 16th century?) had a variant *feak* (1652). The second meaning of *feague* 'do for' (1688) resembles that of *fudge* (1674) and of *fake* (1812!). The similarity between G *ficken* and E *fidge* occurred to J. Grimm (DW), who wrote the proportion G *Brücke:* E *bridge* = G *ficken:* E *fidge,* but positing an old ancestor of *fidge* with a geminate is not a good idea, for the word surfaced late and its /ʤ/ may go back to /tʃ/, as in *Greenwich* and *hodgepodge.* Jamieson gives *fitch* 'move slowly from place to place, touch frequently,' and OED calls *fitch* (1637) an intermediate form between *fike* and *fidge* (an alternation like *seek* ~ *beseech*?). The simplest solution would be to recognize in *fidge* an expressive variant of *fig* (see NUDGE for similar occurrences). *Fitch* is *fidge* with a devoiced final affricate.

The regularity with which *fik-* alternates with *fit-* in German makes E *fit* a possible candidate for membership in the group discussed here. The verb *fit,* presumably from the adjective *fit,* emerged late, and their recorded history presents some difficulty, for both appeared in 1440 and are not attested again for more than a hundred years thereafter. Nor is it entirely clear whether *fit* 'canto, division of a poem' and *fit* 'paroxysm' are related to each other and to *fit* '(make) proper' (Jespersen [1962:167] doubted their kinship). None of those meanings can be easily deduced from 'move back and forth.' But consider *fitful* 'intermittent' and the phrase *by fits and starts.* Du *vitten* 'find fault, carp' corresponds to EFr and LG *fikje* ~ *fikke* (NEW), while OI *fitla* 'fidget' is almost the same word as Sw reg *fikla* 'rummage about' (N reg *fikle;* Bugge [1888b:120]), and Icel *fjatla* is a near synonym (the same in Far and Nynorsk: ÁBM). The much-discussed Du *fiets* 'bicycle' (1870!) can belong here too (its meaning will then be 'moving quickly'); see De Bont's survey (1973), especially pp. 53-54.

Go *fitan** 'be in labor, give birth to' is from an etymological point of view indistinguishable from E *fit* (W. de Vries [1923] and Feist[3]; see also Campanile [1969:22] on this word). *Fetch,* from OE *fecc(e)an,* is believed to be a late variant of *fetian.* Both may belong with *fit* rather than with OE *fæt* 'vat' (G *Faß*) and G *fassen* 'seize.' The primary meaning of *fetch* is 'go and bring back' (that is, 'go back and forth'). Go *fetjan** 'adorn' is of obscure origin, but in light of G *ficken* 'work with a needle' it poses no difficulties; see further OI *fat* 'vessel; clothes' in AEW and E *fetter* (OI *fetill*) in etymological dictionaries. If E *fit* 'canto, division of a poem' and 'swoon' belong to the *f-p/t/k* group, G *Fitze* 'bundle of yarn, skein' probably does too. Its cognate, in addition to OE *fitt* and OS *vittea* 'canto,' is OI *fit* 'the webbed foot of water birds.' The diminutives G *Fitzel* and *Fitz(el)chen* 'little bit' show that the original meaning of *fitze* was not 'web' or 'yarn' but rather 'a small piece, a product of division' which makes the kinship of *fit* and *Fitze,* with Gk πέζα 'foot; ankle; hem' unlikely. See *fit* in AEW and *Fitze* in KS.

Final *-d* often occurs among the postvocalic consonants in the words of the *f* + vowel + stop type that mean 'move in a certain way.' Consider E *fiddle (about)* 'make aimless or frivolous movements' (1530), *fiddle-faddle* 'trifling talk or action' (1577), *faddle* 'caress; play, trifle' (1755), less obviously, *fuddle* 'tipple, intoxicate' (1588; G reg *fuddeln* means 'swindle, work sloppily'), and the meaning of such words as *fiddlesticks* 'nonsense' and *fiddle-de-dee. Fiddle,* the instrument (OE *fiþele,* (M)Du *vedel,* OHG *fidula,* [G *Fiedel*], OI *fiðla*), must have had a related root (*fið-* 'pluck'). Compare the history of E *harp* (sb and v) and of G *Geige* 'fiddle'; assuming that the root of *Geige* means 'hesitate, doubt,' that is, 'change directions' (Hintner [1874:68]), *Geige* is an excellent match for *fiddle;* see KM and KS, which give conflicting explanations. Medieval Latin borrowed this word as **vitula.* If the borrowing had been from Latin, *t* would not have become *ð* in Germanic. (But the origin of **vitula* and *viola* remains debatable: H. Keller [1967:299].) The same root can perhaps be detected in OE *fæðel* 'play actor?' (once in a gloss). A word reminiscent of *fæðel* is Russ *figliar* 'clown, jester, buffoon,' from Polish. *Figli* means 'pranks,' and its root is probably *fig-* 'fig' (the obscene gesture). Both actors 'fidged' and 'fiddled' before the public. Spitzer (1915:213) seems to have guessed the origin of Pol *figli* correctly. Trier (1947:257) listed *fæðel* among the words he etymologized as 'belonging to the community'; his derivation can hardly be accepted.

Among the German, Dutch, and Scandinavian words of the *ficken* type, root final voiced stops (*b, d, g*) are rare (one example is G *vögeln,* a vulgar synonym of *ficken,* evidently not related to *Vogel* 'bird,' contrary to the popular view and Fokkema [1959]), but in English they occur regularly. In addition to *fig* (v), *feague,* and *fiddle ~ faddle ~ fuddle,* we find *fogger* (mainly in *pettifogger,* 1576), and *fib ~ fob ~ fab ~ fub. Fidge, fadge,* and *fudge,* with a voiced affricate, may perhaps also be cited here. Nothing is known about the history of *pettifogger;* its connection with the merchant name *Fugger* (OED) looks like a late pun. Rather, *fogger* was a hustler, running all over the place in search of petty clients. German dialects have *fuggern* 'trade; deceive,' and in British slang, *funny fugger* 'odd fish, rum card' has been recorded (George [1887:92]). Althaus (1963:69), like all his predecessors, derives *fuggern* and *Fugger* 'merchant, cheat' from the name of the Augsburg merchant *Fugger,* but it is more likely that *fuggern* is an old verb and that the first Fugger was called this because he was a *fugger* (cf *Smith, Cooper,* and the like).

Fob meant 'impostor' as early as 1353 (Langland). The verb *fob* 'cheat' (1593) is akin to Du and G *foppen.* G *Ficke* 'pocket' (now obsolete) has always been known to belong with *ficken:* either because a pocket is often opened and closed or because one constantly puts one's hand into it, or through an obscene association (*Ficke* 'vagina' and 'pocket'). Less convincing is the idea that *Ficke* got its name because pockets were attached to one's clothes (from MHG *ficken* 'attach'). E *fob* 'small pocket' was first recorded in 1653 and, like most European words for 'pocket,' is hard to etymologize (see OED), but the parallelism G *ficken—Ficke,* E *fob* (v)—*fob* (sb) is worthy of note. *Fib* (v) 'strike, deliver blows in quick succession' (1665) and 'lie, tell falsehoods' (1690) exemplifies a familiar semantic bundle. It may be that *fipple* 'play at the mouth of a wind instrument' and (reg) 'underlip' belong with *fib.* A direct connection between *fipple* and OI *flipr* (a nickname), and ModI *flipi* 'underlip of a horse' is doubtful.

In the study of *fik- ~ fak- ~ fuk-* words, a complicating factor is the presence of intrusive consonants between *f* and the vowel. As pointed out above, G *ficken* competes with *flicken.* In English, numerous *fl-* words designate unsteady movement. Among them are *flit* (1200), *flitter* (1563), *flicker* (1000), *flatter* (1386), *flip* (1616, it resembles *fillip,* 1543; cf G *Fips* 'fillip' and E *flippant,* 1622), *flap* (1362), *flop* (1622), and the verbs meaning 'beat, thrash, throw': *flack* (1393), *flick* (1447), *flog* (1676), perhaps even *flirt* ([sb], 1577; [v], 1583, originally 'tap, blow lightly, jerk'). Few of them antedate Chaucer, some are surprisingly late and rose to respectability from thieves' cant; see also D. Hofmann (1984).

Intrusive *r* is especially important for the history of English verbs referring to sexual intercourse. OE *frīcian* 'dance, move briskly' has been recorded once. OE *frek* 'brave' and E *frisk* may go back to the same Germanic etymon (Brüll [1913:129]; dictionaries are vague on this point). The verbs derived from the zero grade of *frīcian* (such as *frick* 'move briskly; and *frickle* 'fidget'; EDD) may have had sexual connotations, which would perhaps explain *Fricco,* the name given to the phallic figure of Freyr by Adam of Bremen. The attempts by Bugge (1904) and Jungner (1922:223) to relate *Fricco* to Πρίαπος failed (see, among others, Cahen [1923:147] and Loewenthal [1927:288]), but the idea was sound. Although Fricco is Freyr, the root of his name is identical with that of OI *Frigg* (Frigg was Óðinn's wife). Freyr had a female counterpart, Freyja. Freyja and Frigg are sometimes hard to distinguish, and *Frigg* is a phonetic variant of OHG *Frîja.* The etymology of *Freyr ~ Freyja* is disputable (see Go *frauja* and G *Frau* in etymological dictionaries), but insofar as *Fricco* is tied to *Frigg ~ Freyr,* it cannot be shown to be related to Πρίαπος or to **friðkan* 'amator' (Loewenthal [1927:288]), and its association with the verbs discussed above (if it existed) was a product of folk etmology.

E *fridge* 'move restlessly' appeared in 1550 and went out of use two centuries later. OED glosses *frig* (1550) 'move about restlessly, agitate the body limbs.' But it also meant 'masturbate' and 'copulate' and was interchangeable with *fuck* from the start (Pyles [1971:243]). *Firk* (*ferk*) 'carry, urge, move about briskly, play (a fiddle)' has the longest recorded history of them all: it surfaced in Old English and died out in the 18th century. OED and

AeEW treat it as a cognate of *fare*. Nares singles out 'strike' as its most usual sense but mentions its other, often unclear, licentious applications and says that some people connect it with L *ferio* 'strike, kill' (he gives no references). Yet its semantic kernel must be 'move about briskly, (dance, flaunt),' as in the 1595 citation, unless OE *fercian* and E *firk* ~ *ferk* are different verbs. *Firk,* a widespread synonym of *fuck,* is probably related to *freak* 'sudden change of fortune' (1563). *Fribble* 'stammer, falter; totter in walking; busy oneself to no purpose, fiddle' is even later (1627), and OED offers no etymology for it.

Like *ficken* ~ *facken* ~ *fucken,* the *fl-* ~ *fr-* words synonymous with them are said to be of unknown origin, but although each of them has its history traced in OED, research into their etymology will be of relatively little use. While it cannot be predicted when *l* or *r* will turn up, the result is clear: *f* + (short) vowel + stop alternate with *fl-* ~ *fr-* + (short) vowel + stop in verbs designating 'move back and forth; move briskly, unsteadily, restlessly' and their derived and figurative meanings: 'dance, dance attendance, speak insincerely; taunt, annoy, vex; copulate, masturbate.' Reference to an intrusive consonant may seem arbitrary. However, such consonants have always been recognized. EM call *c,* that is, [k] in L *fricāre* 'break up into small pieces' emphatic, as though *friāre* were traceable to *fricāre* 'rub.' Du *blutsen* 'beat' is a doublet of *botsen* (reg *butsen, boetsen*), E *fag* 'droop' is a doublet of *flag* (v), and inserted nasals are well-known from Indo-European reconstruction. See also Gonda (1943:419; examples from various languages), J. de Vries (1959; a collection of words with emphatic *r* in Germanic), Törnqvist (1970:23), and Falk's list of words with intrusive *j* in the Scandinavian languages (1896:212/46; N reg *fukla, fjukle, fikla, firla, fjarla* and Sw reg *fakkla, fikkla,* all meaning 'work sloppily').

These are the words of Modern English mentioned above; the ones no longer in use (except sometimes in dialects) have a dagger: *†faddle, †fadge, fake, †feague, †feak, fetch, fib, fickle, fiddle, †fidge, fidget, †fig* (v), *†fike, fillip, fipple, †firk, fit, †fitch, †flack, flap, flatter, †flick, flicker, flip, flirt, flit, flitter, flog, flop, flutter, fob, †fodge, (petti)fogger, fop, freak, fribble, frig, fuddle, fudge, fudgy.* It is tempting to add *fumble* to the list, even though its root ends in *-m* (*b* is excrescent). Not all forty of them are *fuck*'s next of kin, but they form one family. This was clear to Wedgwood (1852-53): see *flap* and *fickle* on pp 144 and 146; *fuck* is, of course, not discussed in the article. Unfortunately, Wedgwood allowed his ideas to carry him away and he made his list all-inclusive, but in retrospect it is his feeling for language as a living organism rather than his lack of critical judgment that impresses us today (a splendid car without brakes). If Hoptman's etymology of *finger* and *flunk* is correct (2000), that family is even larger.

Finding one's way among the cognates and homonyms of *fuck* is not always easy. The word *fuck* (adj and sb) occurs with the following meanings in only one German dialectal dictionary: 'immovable; ripe (about grapes), beginning to decay (about pears)' (German may have *Muckefuck* 'ersatz coffee' from *fuck* 'rotten,' with a possible pun on F *mocca faux*); 'hunger; bow in a girl's hair.' Close by we find *Fucke* 'willow pipe; weir basket; very short knitted undershirt'; *Fücksel* 'fir cone' (from *Fichte* 'fir tree'?); *fucken* (v) 'copulate; sell cattle (said only about Christian traders); jump, swing, whack, *etc*' (RhW II). The etymology of each of those words is problematic. The German last names *Fick, Fuck, Fix, Vix,* and *Figg* seem to have nothing to do with the verb in question (Gottschald [1954], Brechenmacher [1957]).

5. Vulgar verbs of copulation and breaking wind may have cognates in more than one language group and suggest a Proto-Indo-European origin. Skt *yábhati* 'copulates,' Gk οἴφω, and OSl **jĕbati* are apparently related (Polomé [1952:470]; Mayrhofer III:7, Frisk, Chantraine, WP I:198; IEW, 298; Arbeitman [1980:79], ESSI VIII:181; Bain [1991:72-74], with a superb bibliography). F. Müller (1897:9) and Möller (1911:109) believed in the existence of Semitic cognates of those words. Reference to taboo in the history of *jábhati* and its cognates is not necessary, for taboo need not be the cause of the aberrant vowel in Greek. Variation in a word of this type would be as natural in Greek as it is in Germanic. If **jebhati* was a low word, it would have been avoided in writing rather than tabooed. Its sounds would even have been 'scrambled' in play. A typical example is OI *serða* 'copulate, often, with the notion of Sodomitic practices' (CV, and see *serða* in ODGNS). Its principal parts are *sarð* and *sorðinn,* but *sorðinn* has the doublet *stroðinn,* from which the infinitive *streða* was formed, while *serða* has the quasi-synonym *sarða* 'polish.' The verb *streða* 'copulate' surfaced in the 17th century, *streða* 'work hard' in the 18th century; *sarða* is also an 18th-century word. *Stroðinn* has been explained as a metathesized by-form of *sorðinn,* with excrescent *t* between *s* and *r* (or a regular continuation of *serða;* see all the Icelandic words in ÁBM). That explanation carries no

more conviction than the taboo theory.

According to Hamp (1988b:181), we have no indication that PIE **i̯ebh-* was obscene, but the stylistic connotations of no word can be discovered without texts. The difference between so-called low and solemn words has always existed; the same does not necessarily hold for obscene. Verbs of copulation describe the physiological aspect of the sexual act, while ignoring its emotional side, and this (rather than reference to an activity of a certain type) tends to make them obscene. OE *(ge)brūcan, (ge)nēalæcan, licgan mid,* and others are not euphemisms for 'copulate,' as J. Coleman (1992) suggested, but expressions of love, physical union, and naturalness of sex in married life (Coleman admits the same at the end). Likewise, *husband, spouse, partner,* and *boy friend* are not euphemisms for *Fucker.*

The Indo-European background of *jábhati* suggests that *fuck,* too, can have connections outside Germanic. OE *fācen* and *ficol* appear in WP II:10-11 and IEW (795; **peiǵ-, *peiḱ-*); see also Ambrosini (1956:146). Holthausen (1955:204/51) compared Westph *fiuken* 'mate' (said about birds) with L *pungere* 'prick, sting' and *pūgio* 'dagger,' as well as with Lith *pìsti* 'copulate' and L *pinsere* 'grind.' *Pugnāre* 'fight, struggle' seems to be a better phonetic match for *fuck* than *pungere* (Holthausen derived *fiuken* from **fūkan*). Makovskii (2000a:144, note 12, continued on p. 145) cites PIE **(s)pien- ~ *poi-* 'pour, let one drink' as a cognate of *fuck,* but he has to change their meaning into 'pour semen,' 'drench with semen,' which makes the comparison useless.

The first to trace *fuck* and *pugnāre* to the same etymon was probably Loewenthal (1915:153). The same etymologoy occurred to Celander (1925:117), but long before them, Möller (1879:464-65) compared, mistakenly it seems, OE *fācen* and L *pugnāre* (he did not discuss *fuck,* but *fetch* is mentioned on p. 465). Read (1934:268) suggested that the original meaning of *fuck* had been 'knock' and cited E *knock up.* Bernard Bloch defended Read's idea in his lectures in the 1960's (Lass [1995:105, note 8]), whereas Lass (1995:104-05) related *fuck* to both *pungere* and *pugnāre* (p. 108). Whallon (1987:35) calls L *pugnāre* and *pungere* the most commonly mentioned cognates of *fuck.* See a semantic parallel in Fay's speculation on L *amāre* 'love' originally meaning 'pierce,' and, consequently, 'get a woman pregnant' (1906:20-23). He had the same association as Read: 'strike' = 'knock up' (Fay [1905:191/28]). However, *pugnāre,* unlike *prick* and *thrust,* is a durative verb: it meant 'fight, struggle, argue, quarrel, strive eagerly,' not 'strike, give a blow' and could hardly alternate with *futuere* outside the discourse on 'the battle of love.' *Pugnāre* and *ficken* belong to different styles. For a similar reason, WH found Gk φυτεύω 'plant' (v) incompatible with *futuere.*

Wachter compared *ficken* and *fregāre* 'rub' (which he correctly derived from L *fricāre*) and both of them with OE *fagung* 'scabies, lepra.' The word he meant is *fāgness* 'scab, ulcer, eruption,' that is, 'redness,' from OE *fāg* 'variegated, spotted.' It has nothing to do with the *fick- / fack-* verbs. Faulmann, the author of a wholly unreliable German etymological dictionary, was, however, right in comparing G *Fickfacker* 'unstable man, windbag, intriguer' and G *Ficke* 'pocket' with E *fickle,* but he made a fanciful guess that they are related to OHG *gifehan* 'be pleased with something.'

The most vexing problem in the search for the Indo-European etymon of *fuck* is the lack of one Germanic form to be etymologized. It will not do to say that *fuck* is a cognate of *pungere* or *pugnāre,* while *ficken* and *facken* represent other grades of ablaut. The Germanic material rather suggests that *ficken* is the main word, whereas *facken* and *fucken* (and *fokken*), along with *fl-* and *fr-* forms, are its modifications. Also, the well-documented meaning of all the Germanic *f*-words is 'move back and forth,' not 'prick' or 'fight.'

In Shipley's opinion, "the current term arose, by the natural looseness of uncultivated and coarse speech, and a simple semantic shift, from the word *firk*" (1977:24). He pooh-poohs possible objections and pronounces a harsh verdict on his immediate predecessors: "No connection can be traced to G *ficken* or Du *fokken.* 'Middle English type **fucken* not found' is the figment of a lexicographer's fancy. *Firk* is there" (p. 26). (Paros [1984:9-10] also prefers the derivation of *fuck* from *firk.*) However, Shipley (1984:42, 293) makes no mention of *firk* and assigns *fuck* to two roots at once: **bhreǵ- ~ *bhrei-* 'rub, prick, break' and *peig-* 'hostile'; neither connection can be justified.

By coincidence, L *futuere* is also an *f-* word. A convincing etymology of *futuere* has not been offered (ML, 3622). Perhaps Latin had echoic words like E *phut-phut-phut* (*phut* = *fut*) and *phit-phit-phit* (see them in OED: *phut,* 1888; OED cites Hindi and Urdu *phatnā* 'split, burst'; *phit,* 1894) or G *fick-fick, fickfack,* or *futsch ~ pfutsch* 'quick!' If such was the case, *futuere* did not have real cognates. Nor is there any evidence that *futuere* was borrowed from Germanic. It was an expressive word (EM) and has come down to us mainly from low comedy.

The same is true of *fuck:* "[A]ll the recorded examples of the verb and its derivatives are in contexts which are in some sense satiric or at least comic" (E. Wilson [1993:32, and see p. 35]).

The Common Germanic word for 'vagina' provides other false clues: OI *fuð-* (in compounds; ModI *fuð*), MHG *vut* (Modern German has *Fotze* and *Hundsfott* 'dog's vulva,' a swear word), and E reg *fud* (1785; ModAmerE slang *fatz* is from Yiddish: Gold [1985]). Whatever the origin of *fuð* ~ *fud* ~ *vut* (Van Helten [1908-09:195]), these words and Gk πῡγή 'buttocks' are unrelated to *fuck* (for a different opinion, not supported by any arguments, see Lass [1995:105, note 9]). A bewildering passage graces Partridge's book on Shakespeare (1947a; the same in the later editions): "*Fuck* is probably one of the sadistic group of words for the man's part in copulation (cf. *clap, cope, hit, strike, thump,* and the modern slang term, *bang*), for it seems to derive from Ger. *ficken,* 'to strike,' as Klüge [sic] maintains. Probably confirmatory rather than contradictory is Skt *ukshan* (a bull; lit. impregnator), which Bopp, in his *Comparative Grammar,* maintains to have originally been *fukshan* (where *shan* = the agential *-er*): with cognates in Gk *phutuein* and Ger. *Ochse.*"

Makaev (1970:236) believed that the etymology of *fuck* must begin with *ficken* and compared *fick* with Sw *spik* 'nail.' *Longman Dictionary of the English Language* lists a few Scandinavian forms, suggests the Scandinavian origin of *fuck,* and (probably following Read) gives L *pungere* as a possible cognate. WNWD mentions Sw reg *fokk* 'penis.' Bury (1883:79/9) traced πῡγή to φυχή and compared it with OHG *elinbogo* 'elbow' and E *bugger* ("a genuine word, though the prudish authors of English dictionaries do not usually include it"), and Makovskii (2002:75) cited Tocharian A *puk* 'believe, respect' as a cognate of *fuck.* No Tocharian sources consulted cite *puk* with such a meaning. Sheidlower (1999:XXV-XXXII) gives a detailed survey of recent conjectures on the origin of *fuck.* **The most reasonable conclusion from the foregoing survey will be that *fuck* has no Indo-European cognates. If so and if the many Germanic words given here are related, their putative Proto-Indo-European origin is illusory.** Du *vaak* and Gk πυκνός 'thick; frequent' (cited in Möller [1879:465], and Kluge [1884:182]), G *Fach,* Gk πήγνῡμι 'thrust,' and L *pugnāre, pungere,* and E *fuck* go their separate ways. Stone (1954) set out to show the influence of *suck* on *fuck.* His attempt will appeal only to other practitioners of psychoanalysis.

6. The word *fuck* has not always been unprintable. It appears in Florio (1611) as one of the glosses of Ital *fottere.* Minsheu (1617) included it in his dictionary and compared it with F *foutre,* Ital *fottere,* and L *futuere.* Skinner's posthumous editor Thomas Henshaw derived *fuck* from the same Romance etymon, assumed their kinship with Gk φυτεύω 'plant' (v), and added Fl ("Teutonic") *fuchten* from G *Futz* or Du *fotte,* or Dan *foder.* (Did he mean Dan *føde* 'breed' or *foder* 'fodder'?) According to Read (1934:269 and note 22), Henshaw took much of his material from Junius's treatment of the unrelated Gothic word *fodr* 'vagina.' But Go *fodr,* which occurs only in John XVIII:11, means 'sheath'; Gk θήκη 'casket; coffin, grave; sheath' did not mean 'vagina' either in recorded texts. The *Gazophylacium,* as always, copied from Skinner and glossed Dan *foder* as 'beget.' N. Bailey (1721) defined *fuck* as 'fæminam subagitare' and reproduced the entry from the *Gazophylacium* almost verbatim, but in his 1730 dictionary he wrote "a term used of a goat" and tentatively traced *fuck* to Dutch. *Fuck* also occurs in Ash.

Read consulted those dictionaries (except the *Gazophylacium*) years before they became available in modern reprints, and from him the story of the early attempts to etymologize *fuck* became known to other linguists. See a more recent version of this story in Rawson (1989:161). One often hears that *fuck* is an acronym: *fuck* = *f*or *u*nlawful *c*arnal *k*nowledge (Eisiminger [1979:582]) or *fuck* = *f*ornicate *u*nder *c*ommand of the *K*ing (allegedly, going back to the times of Black Death; G. Hughes [1988:25]). Sheidlower (1999:XXVI-XXVII) has more to say on such popular etymologies.

Then for over two hundred years the verb disappeared from English dictionaries. Anonymous (1865:181) states that Dwight (1859), in discussing the word *fauxbourg,* "adds to his list the most obscene word in our language"; no such list appears in the New York edition of Dwight's book. On two printed occurrences of *fuck* dated 1882 see Sheidlower (1999:XXXI-XXXII).

Lexicographers are expert in dodging obscenity laws. In the first edition of OED, *fuck* is conspicuous by its absence, but one finds *windfucker,* an obsolete name for the kestrel, or windhover (G. Hughes [1991:3, 161]). The single example from 1599 (*the kistrilles or windfuckers that filling themselues with winde, fly against winde evermore*) seems to suggest that *to fuck the wind* meant 'fly despite headwinds.' Du *fok* 'foresail' and *fokkemast* 'foremast' carry a similar idea. Swelling and thus being able to make headway looks like a perfect description of intercourse. Both E *fuck the wind* and Du *fok* might be metaphorical applications of *fuck(en)* ~ *fokken* 'copulate.'

Heeroma (1941-42:52) treats Du *fok* and *fokken* as related; however, he is probably wrong in reconstructing the original meaning of the root as *'rag.' OED gives no etymology of *windfucker* but compares it with northern reg *fuckwind* 'a species of hawk.' See *fuk, fuk-mast,* and *fuk-sail* in Sandahl (1958:38-41; their etymology is discussed on p. 41). For 1602-1616 OED cites several examples of *windfucker* as a term of opprobrium.

Fuck, printed *f*ck,* reemerges in Partridge (1961), where it is said to be related to both L *futuere* and G *ficken,* and in PED. In the United States, AHD seems to have been the first to break the ban. According to that dictionary, the Germanic verb in question originally meant 'strike, move quickly, penetrate,' with ME *fucken* (given without an asterisk) being akin to or perhaps borrowed from MDu *fokken* 'strike, copulate with.'

When the taboo on *fuck* was lifted in England, Burchfield felt such elation that he discussed this event in the introduction to Volume 1 of the *Supplement* to OED and two more times (Burchfield [1973:33, delivered in 1971; 1972]). See a short survey of censors' efforts to ban the word in Lebrun (1969-70) and McArthur (1996:54-58). The etymological note in the entry *fuck* in OED is disappointing. Its author reconstructs the form **fuk* and states that the word's ulterior etymology is unknown and that "synonymous G *ficken* cannot be shown to be related."

The etymology of *fuck* is obscure, but not hopelessly so. Most likely, this verb was borrowed into English in the second half of the 15th century from some Low German dialect. *Fuck(en) is one of many similar verbs known from Switzerland to Norway meaning 'move back and forth.' *Frig, fiddle, fidget,* obsolete *firk,* and possibly *fetch* belong to the same group, and so do numerous other verbs in Frisian, Dutch, German, and Scandinavian whose root begins with *f* and ends in a stop or an affricate. Vowels vary in them. None of those verbs, including *fuck,* has indubitable cognates outside Germanic. Judging by the entries *fuck* in G. Williams, HDAS, and Sheidlower, this view of the history of the English *f*-word is gaining ground (Liberman [1999a]).

A Note on Allen Walker Read's Correspondence about the *F*-Word

In 1971 Read sent letters to more than fifty people, asking them what they thought or knew about the origin of *fuck.* He was especially interested in the meaning of John le Fucker's name (mentioned in Buck) and in the reality of ME *fucken* (cited in AHD[1], *fuck*). Part of his correspondence, probably everything of importance, has been made public in Read (2002:277-300). No one offered a definitive etymology of *fuck,* but Read found confirmation of his belief that *Fucker* in *John le Fucker* has no relation to *fuck* and that ME *fucken* is a ghost word. Several of his most distinguished correspondents cited the Proto-Indo-European etymon of *fuck* (**peuk-* or *peug-*, or **pug-*). A. J. Aitken mentioned *fucksail* (p. 282). F. Cassidy remembered *windfucker* (though the form he gives—*fuckwind*—is wrong) (p. 285). Geart Droege mentioned E *fridge* and *fickle,* G *ficken* and *vögeln* (allegedly, a polite form), along with Fr *fojke* and *fokke,* which he considered to be the etymon of Du *fokken* 'breed or raise animals' (otherwise, initial *v*- could be expected) as belonging with the English verb. He offered an Proto-Indo-European etymon of the *fokken* group but called E *fick* (did he mean *fuck*?) "natively English" (p. 286). In Sherman Kuhn's opinion, *fuck* is "a borrowing from Dutch, not earlier than the sixteenth century" (p. 279).

GAWK (1785, 1837)

Gawk *and its derivatives were recorded in English late, and the date of their emergence in the language can no longer be determined. However, most of them must have been current as regional slang for several centuries. In addition to* gawk *'fool; simpleton; clumsy person' and 'stare stupidly,'* gawk *'left (hand)' exists in dialects. According to the hypotheses mentioned and partially defended in Skeat and OED,* gawk *'left' is either a contraction of its regional synonym* gaulick ~ gallock *(then from 'left-handed' to 'clumsy') or* gaw + k, *the root being a borrowing of the Scandinavian verb* gá *'stare.' Both hypotheses are probably wrong. The contraction* gaulick *or* gallock > gawk *has no parallels among many regional words with the suffix* -ock, *while the derivation of* gallock *from F reg* gôle *'benumbed' contradicts the usual way adjectives for 'left' acquire their meaning. The second etymology also runs into difficulties. The suffix* -k *is highly productive in the Scandinavian area, but* gawk *is unknown in the Scandinavian languages. In English,* -k *has never been productive, so that* gawk *as a native formation with this suffix is unlikely. Most early researchers traced* gawk *to* gowk *'cuckoo,' a borrowing of Scandinavian* gauk(r).

The Old Scandinavian diphthong au, *pronounced as* [æu] *or* [öy], *became* ou *in* gowk ~ gouk. *It may also have been reflected as* [au], *which, in English, would develop into a long vowel, as in the modern form* gawk. *It is not unthinkable that* gowk *and* gawk *are doublets, two variants of the same word. The cuckoo has been called a fool and a simpleton for millennia. But* gawk *may have arisen independently of* gowk. *It is one of many words having the root* g-k *or* g-g *and designating half-wits, clowns, and inept persons, such as E* geck *(from Dutch) and* geek *(presumably from Low German), G* Gaukel *'trickery,' and MHG* giege *'fool,' as well as sudden movements and swerving from the course (for instance, OI* geiga*), peeping (for instance, G* gucken*), foolish laughter (E* giggle *and its analogues in German and Dutch), and the like. All of them are onomatopoeic or sound symbolic formations and can be called related only in the loosest sense of this term.* Gaukr *and* cuckoo *are also onomatopoeias. Regardless of whether* gawk *is traceable to a bird name or is an independent creation of the* geck ~ geek *type, when it emerged in English, it began to interact with* gowk*; hence the multitude of meanings in* gawk *and* gawky*, including* gawky *'left.' F* gauche *'clumsy,' known since the 16th century, is not the etymon of* gawk*. It may be a borrowing of some Germanic word having the structure* *gok *and pronounced with an expressive geminate that later yielded* -ch(e).

The sections are devoted to 1) the meanings and attestation of gawk *and its derivatives, 2) the two current hypotheses on the origin of* gawk*, 3) the possibility that* gawk *continues the bird name* gauk(r)*, 4) other attempts to explain the origin of* gawk*, 5) German and Dutch words resembling* gawk*, especially G* Geck *and* Gaukel*, and 6) the conclusion that* gawk *may have been a reflex of a bird name or an independent formation.*

1. The relevant words, in the order in which they appear in OED, are as follows: *gawk* 'awkward person; fool; simpleton' (1837); *gawk* ~ *gauk* 'left,' competing in many northern English dialects with *gaulick-, gallick-, gaulish- (hand, handed)* (1703); *gawk* 'stare or gape stupidly' (first recorded in American dialects; 1785); *gawkish* 'awkward, clownish' (1876); *gawky* 'awkward and stupid; ungainly,' said about people (1785) and about things (1821); 'awkward, foolish person; lout; simpleton (1724); *gaw* 'gape, stare; look intently' (1200; the latest citation from a literary text dates back to 1566, but it appears in Jamieson's 1879-82 dictionary); *gowk* 'cuckoo' (1325) and 'fool; half-witted person' (1605; originally Scots and English northern regional); *gowk* 'stare stupidly' (rare; two citations in OED: 1513 and 1873), and *gawked* 'foolish' (1605; no citations after 1790).

Other dictionaries give the same or similar definitions of *gawk* and *gawky*. However, some note that *gawky* is applied to shy, tall, and overgrown individuals (for instance, *a gawky teenager*). Wyld (UED) uses this word in the definition of *hobbledehoy*. **The verb *gaw* is a borrowing of O-Scand *gá* 'heed, mark.' It surfaced in *Ormulum* and survived only in the north. The age of the other words is beyond recovery. They may have been current in dialects indefinitely long before making their way into print; in any case, it is unlikely that *gawk* (in either meaning) or *gawky* was coined only around 1703 or 1837.**

2. The main etymological problem consists in disentangling this knot of synonyms and (near) homonyms. OED offers suggestions on the origin of *gawk* and its kin. It notes that Johnson confused *gawk* 'fool' and *gowk* 'cuckoo,' with later lexicographers following him. By implication, this confusion should be avoided. According to OED, *gawk* 'fool' was perhaps derived from *gawk* 'left,' which is "of difficult etymology," possibly a contraction of some form like *gaulick*. *Gawk* 'stare' is said to be perhaps from the noun *gawk* or an iterative form of the verb *gaw*, with the suffix *-k*, as in *tal-k, wal-k, lur-k* (*stalk* and *hark*, the latter with its German cognate *horchen* of the same meaning, may be added to this list); cf FILCH. The second explanation (*gawk* < *gaw* + *k*) recurs in all the "Oxford" dictionaries. *Gawky*, which can be a noun or an adjective, is supposed to derive from the noun *gawk* or from the verb *gawk*. By contrast, the history of *gowk* 'cuckoo' is clear: here we have a borrowing of a Scandinavian bird name (OI *gaukr*, etc), which has multiple cognates: OE *gēac* (now extant only as reg *yeke*), OFr *gāk*, OS *gôk* ~ *gâk*, MDu *gooc*, MLG *gōk*, and OHG *gouh* (ModG *Gauch*). Most likely, **gauk-* is an onomatopoeia like *cuckoo*, the word that replaced *gaukr* and its congeners in several languages, including Standard English.

The two aforementioned hypotheses on the origin of *gawk*, even though they have been repeated in numerous dictionaries (with or without *perhaps*), carry little conviction. The verb *gawk* was hardly produced from *gaw* by means of adding the suffix *-k*. This verbal suffix, common in the Scandinavian languages (see Jóhannesson [1927:56-58], D. Hofmann [1961:112], and see the list in DEO[3-4]: *-ke*), is rare in English. The origin of *lurk, stalk,* and *walk* is obscure (their base is hard to isolate). *Talk* is certainly from *tal-*, as in *tale*, but it appeared in English texts only in the 13th century and may have been formed around that time on a Scandinavian model. If *gawk* had emerged as *gaw* + *k*, it could have been expected to have a history similar to that of *talk*, rather than being a borrowing from Scandinavian, because no similar verb has been recorded in any Scandinavian language and because among the verbs formed from verbs that Jóhannesson lists none occurs with the suffix *-k* following a vowel, if we disregard OI *þjáka* 'exhaust' from *þjá* 'enslave' (p. 58). Yet no native model has been found for *gawk* either.

The idea that *gawk* 'left' is a contraction of

***gaulick* is also implausible.** The phonetic development *gaulik* ~ *gallock* > *gawk* would be regular (cf *walk, talk, chalk*) only if the loss of the unstressed vowel could be taken for granted. Syncope in those words would be somewhat unusual, yet not improbable, but the presumed semantic development from 'fool(ish)' to 'left (hand)' would be without parallels. It is the word for the left hand (from 'bad; twisted, crooked; weak' or conversely, 'auspicious') that is always derivative. One can imagine the path from 'perverse; inept' to 'left hand' but not in the opposite direction. Therefore, it is better to separate *gaulick* ~ *gallock* from *gawk* despite the arguments that have been advanced for their identity and even despite the frequent occurrence of the spellings *golk* and *goilk* for *gowk* 'fool' in Lowland Scotch (Flom [1900:44]).

Skeat initially did not doubt that *gawk* is a variant of *gowk* (Skeat[1] and Skeat [1892:463, sec 424]) but later changed his mind (Skeat [1899-1902:278; reported in 1899: see Skeat [1901:114] and Skeat[4]). According to his later view, *gawk* is "a mere contraction from the fuller forms *gallock, gaulick,* and the like; where *-ick, -ock,* are mere suffixes. Hence the base is *gall-* or *gaul-*. This is evidently allied to the F. dial. *gôle,* 'benumbed,' especially applied to the hands." If *gôle* is the base of *gaulick* or *gallock,* the "mere suffix" must have been added to an adjectival root, but *-ock* forms diminutives only from other nouns. *Gawk* is not a word like *bullock* or *hillock.* Besides this, 'benumbed' would hardly have yielded 'left.' Whatever the origin of *gaulick, -ick* in it was mistaken for a suffix, because otherwise the form *gaulish,* also attested in North Country dialects, would not have arisen. However, this is a secondary development, and we need not be deceived by folk etymology.

3. **The question that will of necessity remain debatable is whether *gawk* and *gowk* should be kept apart.** At present, neither *gowk* nor *gawk* has the reconstructed vowel of OI *gaukr.* In the East Scandinavian languages, **au* was contracted: cf Sw *gök* and Dan *gøg* 'cuckoo.' In the Norwegian Bokmål, *au* has the approximate value of [æu]; in Modern Icelandic, of [öy]. Both pronunciations (especially the one with an ö-like nucleus) are old (for Icelandic see especially Böðvarsson [1951:163] and H. Benediktsson [1959:296]).

Some details in the adoption of **au* in Middle English remain unexplained. Sievers (1884:197) noted that even in Old English Scand *ǫu* was occasionally represented by the vowel *o*, and Stratmann (1883:441-2) cited several Middle English forms of the same type (ME *gōk* among them). Especially revealing are J. Zupitza's observations (1884). Skeat (1892:93 and 463) says that Scand *au* "was heard" as long *o* in *stoop* 'beaker' and *loose*. Grammars give several more examples and account for this correspondence by the absence of *ou* in Middle English except in word final position. The general assumption seems to be that this diphthong had the realization close to that in ModE *cow* and *town*. J. Zupitza (p. 155) suggested that at the time when words like ME *loos* (from *lauss*) appeared in English, it had three realizations in the speech of Scandinavian settlers: *au, ou,* and *ō*. This is a self-serving conjecture.

Although E /ou/, as in ModE *no* and *woke*, does not precede the Great Vowel Shift, it is unclear why English-speakers of the middle period could not replace the biphonemic Scandinavian diphthong by some combination of vowels. The phonetic history of *trust* and *fluster*, both from Scandinavian (Skeat [1892:463]), is obscure and provides no help in investigating the development of *au* in Middle English. See Björkman (1900:69), Luick (1964:388, sec 384.2), Jordan[3] (1968:sec 130.3), and Berndt (1960:76) for a brief discussion of this matter. The northern English form *gowk* that Wall (1898:104) and Luick mention (*gauk* ~ *gowk*) must have been borrowed either from Danish before the contraction of [au] or from Norwegian. Whichever language served as its source, [ou] is an imperfect rendering of a Scandinavian diphthong. The same holds for the original vowel of *gawk* if the word is of Scandinavian extraction, but this is precisely what we do not know. **Despite the admonition of OED, the idea that *gawk* and *gowk* are variants of the same etymon (doublets) is not totally groundless.**

If *gowk* and *gawk* go back to Scand *gauk-*, their later history can be envisioned in the following way. The Germanic word for 'cuckoo' (for instance, OHG *gouh*) has meant 'fool' for centuries. The folklore of the cuckoo is incredibly rich: a harbinger of spring, a bird prophesying people's age, the incarnation of the devil, a coward unable to brood and sustain its young, the slyest of all living creatures, and the stupidest of them all, to mention a few characteristics recorded in innumerable legends, songs, and proverbs. The cuckoo's name has been applied to every blameworthy creature and thing, from prostitutes to bad beer (Seelmann [1932-33:746-47]; Brand [1849:197-202: "Of the Word Cuckold"]).

The development may have been from 'someone doing a reprehensible, devilish thing' to 'outcast,' 'someone crazy; idiot; half-wit,' 'fool,' and 'simpleton.' (When *cuckoo* supplanted the reflexes of OE *gēac,* it inherited some of the old word's connotations, especially 'crazy.') Hence *gawk* (v) 'look stupidly,' as a sign of retardation ("To *gawk* is to 'stare about' like an awkward greenhorn. A *gawk* is properly a cuckoo and comes from the Old Norse." Greenough and Kittredge [1901:368]), and *gawky* 'stupid; clumsy, ungainly, hobbledehoyish; inept; left (hand).' The noun *gawky* looks as though it were an ironic diminutive of the *hubby* type. But this is not the only possible reconstruction. Cf Sec 6.

4. **The hypotheses on the origin of *gawk* and *gawky,* apart from those mentioned in OED, are not many.** The first to suggest that *gawk* is 'cuckoo' was Skinner, who cited G *Geck* 'fop, dandy' (pejorative) as its etymon and believed both to be onomatopoeic. Minsheu and N. Bailey do not list *gawk.* Junius, Johnson, Richardson, Mueller, Skeat[1], KL, and all the editions of Webster's dictionary through 1890 follow Skinner, though *Geck* as the etymon or a cognate of *gawk* is not included in their etymologies. AEW (*gaukr*) also mentions *gawk.*

W[1] and W[2], despite some hedging, copy from Skeat and use *gawk* 'left hand' as their starting point. W[3] derives the verb *gawk* from *gaw-* (which is said to have perhaps been influenced by E reg *gawk* 'left hand') and looks on *gawk* 'left-handed' as a possible source of *gawk* 'ungainly, clumsy, stupid fellow.' Despite Ogilvie's dependence on Webster's etymologies, he had two new suggestions (ID 1850; not repeated in ID 1882). In the entry *gawky,* he referred to F *gauche* 'left, awkward; warped, crooked' as a possible parallel and added that F *gauchir* 'shrink back or turn aside, use shifts, double, dodge' (those are the glosses in the dictionary) well express the actions of a jester or buffoon. Ogilvie also mentioned E *awk* as a form reminiscent of *gawk.* *Awk,* now associated only with the root of *awkward,* meant 'directed the other way or in the wrong direction, back-handed, from the left hand; untoward; froward [sic]; perverse, in nature or disposition; untoward to deal, awkward to use, clumsy' and is almost certainly of Scandinavian origin. It surfaced in texts in 1440 and seems to have died out by the end of the 17th century (no citations after 1674; the dates and definitions are from OED).

The similarity between *gawk* and *awk* is indeed striking, and the meaning 'ungainly, clumsy,' so prominent in *gawky,* may have arisen under the influence of *awk,* assuming that *gawk* was old enough to get partly confused with *awk.* Ogilvie's idea has been lost in later scholarship, except that E. Edwards (1881) wrote: "*Gawky*... from *awk,* the left hand [sic], *awkward,* with the prefix *g,*" and FW (1947) declared *gawk* 'left-handed' to be a blend of F *gauche* and ME *awk* 'back-handed.' This etymology is all the more surprising because in the treatment of *gawk(y)* the previous and later editions of FW do not deviate from OED. As noted, some interaction between the two words is not unthinkable, but 'clumsy' is probably too narrow a base for the multitude of meanings present in *gawk* and *gawky.* OED finds a connection between *gauche* and *gawk* improbable on phonetic grounds. (Skeat concurs with OED.) However, as will be shown in Sec 6, the question merits further investigation.

In Wedgwood[2-4], F *gauche* and *gauchir* are mentioned at *gawk* but, it seems, only as a semantic parallel (from 'warped' to 'left'), for next to *gauche,* unrelated and irrelevant OI *skjálgr* 'wry, oblique; squinted' is given. Wood (1899a:345-46/19) referred to *gawk* in his discussion of G *gucken* 'look; peep, peek.' "This word [*gucken*]," he says, "implies either stealth or foolish curiosity." Spitzer (1925:156) did not touch on *gawk* but suggested that *gucken* was a doublet of the verb *kucken* 'cuckoo.' In EW[1], only *gawk* (v), allegedly from *gaw* (OI *gá*), is given; the entry was removed from the second edition, but in EW[3] *gawk* 'cuckoo' [sic] and 'fool' are reinstated and traced to OD [sic] *gaukr.* Weekley (1921; 1924) makes do with the statement that the meanings of *gawk* "correspond with" *gauche* and is of the opinion that *gallock* may be the etymon of both *gawk* and *gauche.* Partridge (1958) cites *gawk* 'left-handed' and its regional synonym *cack-* ~ *keck-handed* (which has nothing to do with *gawk:* see KITTY-CORNER).

Some etymologies appear as though from nowhere. Such is the assertion in FW (1947) that *gawk* is a blend of *gauche* and *awk* (see above). Equally unexpected is the statement in RHD and ACD, affiliated with it, that *gawk* 'fool' and 'stare stupidly' apparently represent an Old English word meaning 'fool,' from *gagol* 'foolish' + *-oc (-ock),* used attributively in *gawk hand* ~ *gallock hand* 'left hand.' OE *ga(gol),* or *gāl* 'lust, luxury, wantonness, folly, levity; merry, light, wanton; proud, wicked' has cognates in several Germanic languages (G *geil,* etc) and is related to neither OI *gá* nor E *gawk;* cf the discussion of the suffix *-ock,* above. All the editions of WNWD say that *gawk,* from OI *gaukr* 'cuckoo,' is akin to G *Gauch,* with the etymological crux created by forms *gawk-hand, gallock-hand* 'left hand' being probably illusory (cf forms *golk, goilk* of *gawk*). This statement is hard to interpret.

Other than that, polemic does not go beyond cautious guesses and doubts as to their validity. For example, Mutschmann (1909:61, sec 168) derived Scots *gāke* 'gawky, silly' from Old English or Scand **gakk* and compared it with G *Geck,* but Björkman (1911:451) was not convinced. Hewett (1884:244) advised Kluge to list *gawk* among the cognates of G *Gauch* 'cuckoo,' and K. Malone (1956:349) gave similar advice to Alexander Jóhannesson (though without certainty) in connection with *gókr.* Jamieson objected to the identification of even *gowk* ~ *gouk* 'fool, simpleton' with the bird name. According to him, the congeners of *gowk* are G *Geck* and Icel *gikkr* 'fop; arrogant *or* intractable man' (he misspelled the Icelandic form and probably did not realize that *gikkr* is a borrowing from Middle Low German; so ÁMB). See the critical remarks on that score by Montgomerie-Fleming (1899:56), who pointed to the never-ending confusion of the two words: for instance, an English commentator of Burns misunderstood *gawky* 'foolish' as 'cuckooing.'

Thus, the choices open to a contemporary researcher who would like to pursue the origin of *gawk* and *gawky* are today nearly the same as at the end of the 19th century. The lines were drawn in OED and Skeat. Ties between those English words and *gowk* 'cuckoo' / *gawk* 'left-handed' have been accepted by some and denied by others.

5. ***Gawk* is less isolated than it seems, and its environment, however uncertain, may throw a sidelight on its origin.** Skinner was the first to compare *gawk* and G *Geck,* which leads to E *geck* and several other Dutch and English words. Skeat (1885-87:300-01 = 1901:115, first presented in 1885: see anonymous a, b) showed that E *geck* was borrowed from Dutch. In the last edition of his dictionary, he made a special point of the distinction between *geck* and three other words: *gowk, gawky,* and OE *gēac*. However, CD, which usually follows Skeat, shows greater reserve and only says that the connection between *geck* and *gowk* is doubtful.

E *geck* 'fool, simpleton, dupe' (1515) coexists with *geck* 'gesture of derision, expression of scorn or contempt' (Scots and northern regional, 1568; no citations after 1597, except in the phrases *get a geck* 'be deceived' and *give the geck* 'deceive,' but here, too, the only post-17th-century example is from Jamieson), and the verb *geck* 'scoff' (1583; the same provenance). OED cites Du *gek* and LG *geck* (sb) and *gecken* ~ *gekken,* related to G *gecken* 'croak.' The group turns out to be onomatopoeic, a fact made especially clear by the synonyms of *gecken*: *gecken, gacken, gicken, geckzen, kecken,* and *gäcken* ~ *käcken* (with long vowels: DW). *Geck* was originally a Low Saxon word. In 1385 *geck* turns up as the name of a court jester. The word has survived: *Gecken* ~ *Jecken* are the modern carnival 'fools' in the Lower Rhenish area. In its spread south, MHG *geck* encountered its synonyms *gagg, gaggel, gagger, gacks,* and the like (KS, *Geck*; *gacks* must be **gagg-s,* with the addition of the ending *-s,* on which see Bergerson [2004]). At present, there is a near consensus that in *geck* and other such words *ge-* and *ga-* render the inarticulate speech of the mentally retarded.

Knobloch seems to be only one to deny the onomatopoeic origin of *Geck* (Knobloch [1972:989-990 and 1995:148]; the latter is part of a list, with a brief reference to the earlier work), for he connected the rise and spread of this word with the cult of St. Jacob (G Jakob[us]). In so doing, he joined Wackernagel (1860:343-345 = 1874b:163-64), whose suggestions were not so far-reaching, however. Knobloch traced the names of many objects, including some of those called *jack* in English, to that cult and explained how 'fool' merged with 'blockhead' and simply 'wooden object.' His etymology runs into the same difficulty as the one that derives *gawk* from a bird name: each is separately convincing, but they ignore the larger picture.

W. Barnes (1862:71) derived hundreds of words from imaginary roots, and *Geck* ended up among the descendants of *g*ng*. This idea was of no value even when it was put forward, but his statement is not entirely devoid of interest in light of Knobloch's findings: "I hardly think that Jack, which is an element of many English words, is a form of the name John. It seems to carry some meaning of to go, to stir, or to act as a machine, or *ineundi,* as applied to the male of some animals." Thomson also wrote at *geck*: "See *gawk* and *jack*." He must have meant his *jack* 2 'mechanical instrument,' which he derived from *go,* but did not elaborate.

Thus we are advised not to confuse *gawk* with *gowk* (OED), *geck* with *gawk, geck* with *gowk* (Skeat), and *Geck* with various onomatopoeic words (Knobloch). If Knobloch is right, *geck* ~ *jeck* should be kept apart from *gagg, gacks,* and so forth, but this is an undesirable approach to the entire group.

Several proposals concerning the origin of *Geck* turn up in older literature. In Schwenck's opinion, *Geck* is allied to G *Gaukel* 'trickery' (< MHG *goukel* ~ *gougel*), *gaukeln* 'flit, flutter,' historically 'show tricks,' *Gaukler* 'medieval itinerant entertainer, juggler,' and *geigen* 'move back and forth' (now only regional; the meaning in the standard language is 'play the violin'). He reconstructed the initial meaning of the root as 'fluttering movement.' Kaltschmidt also listed most words, including MHG *giege* 'fool,' that were later compared with *Geck* and added *gähe* 'quick' (Standard German *jäh* ~ *jähe* 'sudden'), about whose origin nothing is known to this day. Lexer compared MHG *gek* and *gougel* ~ *goukel,* referred to Wackernagel's derivation of *gougel* from L *cauculus* 'magician's vessel (glass)', and concluded that two words had merged in the history of German: L *cauculator* 'magician' and some nomen agentis from *giugan* ~ *giukan* 'make a quick movement,' as in G *jucken* 'itch' (v).

Ten Doornkaat Koolman suggested that LG *gek* 'fool, simpleton' and *gek* 'revolving pole' (a sailors' term) are two meanings of the same word united by the idea of instability and cited MHG *giege* 'fool' and several Low German cognates of *Gauke*l and *gaukeln* as belonging with *gek.* He thought that both were like weathervanes. A similar idea occurred to Zabel (1922:11-12), who showed that 'mad' is often tantamount to 'turned; twisted.' According to Uhlenbeck (1901:297-98/22), *Geck* is related to OI *geiga* 'take a wrong direction,' OE *(for)gǣgan* 'transgress; trespass; pass by, omit,' and Go *-geigan* in **gageigan* 'desire.' (Feist doubted that the Gothic verb was akin to *geiga,* but Lehmann [Feist[4]] found their kinship probable.) Uhlenbeck's etymology is neither better nor worse than those of his predecessors.

At *gaukeln,* Mitzka (KM) mentions Austrian *gigerl* 'fop, dandy, masher, dude' (which Nutt [1900] compared with E *gawk*). He traces *Gigerl* to MHG *giege* 'fool,' allegedly related to Du *guig* 'grimace' (in *de guig aanstecken* 'poke fun' and other similar obsolete expressions), but denies it at *Gigerl* (see also KS: no connection). According to EWNT, *guig* is indeed allied to Du *gochelen* 'juggle, conjure' (a cognate of G *gaukeln*) and *giecheln* 'giggle.' E *giggle,* Du *giecheln,* G *kiechern,* Russ *khikhikat'* (stress on the second syllable) are among the most obvious onomatopoeias, like, for example, *gecko,* a Malay lizard, named so for its cry.

Faulmann derived all the words from strong verbs, sometimes attested, sometimes imaginary, but, as happens to most authors of erratic conceptions, he occasionally had rational ideas. He, too, thought that *Geck* and E *giggle* are related, while MHG *gehen* 'say, speak' (pronounced and sometimes spelled *jehan*), which he treated as their source, although not the etymon of *Geck,* may not be too distant from it, for it is usually compared with L *jocus* 'joke,' their reconstructed onomatopoeic root being **jek-* 'chat' (see *Beichte* 'confession,' from OHG *bijicht,* and *Urgicht* 'statement, declaration, confession' in German etymological dictionaries). Long before Indo-European scholars isolated the root of L *jocus,* E *joke* as a cognate of G *Gauch* and *Geck* occurred to Meidinger (1836:167).

Kluge (EWDS[1-7]) refused to see a connection between *Geck, gaukeln,* and MHG *giege.* In EWDS[4-6], he suggested combining G *Geck* and 'revolving pole' under one etymon. He did not refer to Doornmaat Koolman, whose dictionary he must have known well. Götze (EWDS[11], *Geck*) copied Uhlenbeck's etymology (OI *geiga,* etc). When Mitzka took over EWDS (beginning with the 17th edition), none of those words remained in the entry *Geck,* and *Geck* was treated as an onomatopoeia without ascertainable cognates. Both J. de Vries (NEW) and Seebold (KS) accepted Mitzka's treatment.

For completeness' sake a few more etymologies of *Geck* should be mentioned. Helvigius derived *Geck* from Gk εἰκαῖως 'vain, useless, futile; reckless, featherbrained' and Hebr חָקַק (*chak*) or חוֹק (*chok*) 'portray, carve,' and Wachter identified *Geck* with *Gauch* 'cuckoo.' He included three entries: *Gauch* 'cuckoo,' *Gauch* 'fool,' and *Gauch* 'juggler.' For the last of them he suggested the Welsh etymon *coey* 'empty, vain, good for nothing, insipid, foolish;' (cf COCKNEY). Wedgwood[1] reinvented Wachter's etymology; however, he removed it from the later editions. Jamieson misquoted Wachter but understood his idea correctly and found it unacceptable. Nares gave both occurrences of *geck* in Shakespeare (in *Twelfth Night* and *Cymbeline*) and remarked: "Capel says from *ghezzo,* Italian; but it is rather Teutonic, as Dr. Jamieson suggests." *Capel* must be a misspelling of E.W. Capell's name. This derivation could not be found in any of Capell's major works. In any case, *ghezzo* 'black' goes back to *Gyptius,* the aphetic form of *Ægyptius* 'Etyptian.' The development was from 'Africa' to 'black-colored' and 'fool' (cf E *blackamoor*).

Finally, there is E *geek* 'socially eccentric person' and 'someone engrossed in a single subject' (in combinations like *computer geek*). This meaning had such little currency even in the late sixties of the 20th century that AHD[1], published in 1969, does not mention it. For a long time only *geek* 'performer whose act consists of biting the head off a live chicken or snake' was known. "Cf *geek* n[oun]. A freak, usually a fake, who is one of the attractions in a pit-show. The word is reputed to have originated with a man named Wagner of Charleston, WV, whose hideous snake-eating act made him famous. Old timers remember his ballyhoo, part of which ran: 'Come and see Esau / Sittin' on a see-saw / Eatin' 'em raw'" (Maurer 1981:30).

The dependence of *geek* on LG *Geck* is undeniable despite the unexplained difference in vowels. OED (*geck, sb*) quotes an entry from an 1876 glossary of Whitby words (in the former North Riding of Yorkshire): "*Gawk, Geek, Gowk* or *Gowky* a fool; a person uncultivated; a dupe." The dictionaries that do not say "origin unknown" suggest that E *geek* is perhaps or probably a variant of LG *Geck*. The quotation from the Whitby glossary does not confirm this derivation, but it shows that *geck, geek, gawk,* and *gawky* were used interchangeably long ago.

6. Thus we have Gmc **gauk-* 'cuckoo' (G *Gauch,* E reg *gowk*, from Scandinavian, as well as the native form *yeke*) and from time immemorial 'simpleton'; G *Geck* and Du *gek* 'fool, jester,' both current for centuries (whence E *geck*); their southern German regional synonyms with the root *gagg-;* G *Geck* ~ Du *gek* 'revolving pole,' G *Gaukel* 'trickery,' also known since the Middle Ages; MHG *giege* 'fool,' Du *guig* 'grimace,' along with E *gawk* and *geek,* both recorded late. Several verbs may also be considered, though their affiliation with the previous loose group is doubtful: OI *geiga* 'take a wrong direction' (and its cognates in Old English and perhaps Gothic), Gmc **jukjan* 'itch,' MHG *gehen* 'speak' (< *'wag one's tongue'?), E *giggle* with its counterparts in German and Dutch, and perhaps even G *gucken* 'look' ~ *kucken*. The German adverb *gähe* ~ *jähe* may belong here too. Nor should *gauche,* though a French word, be disregarded.

All those words are probably onomatopoeic or sound symbolic; the two types tend to merge. For example, G *Geige* 'violin' is usually traced to *geigan* 'take a wrong direction,' but Seebold (KS) cites MHG *gîgen* and *gieksen* and explains *Geige* as a humorous name of an instrument making shrill music. If the history of *fiddle* provides a good parallel (see it at FUCK), the old hypothesis appears more persuasive, but the existence of *gieksen,* etc is a fact. See what is said about *gecken* and its synonyms, above. According to Skeat (1885-87:311), Du *gek* "is formed on a basis *GEK- that should be distinguished form GAUK-." In words like *Geck* and *Gauch,* clearly differentiated bases exist mainly on paper. While dealing with such formations, one is usually lost among countless pseudocognates; cf the forms discussed at FUCK and MOOCH. There is no need to derive *gawk* from *Geck* or *Geck* from *giege.* **These words are like mushrooms growing on the same stump: they are members of one rootless family.**

Onomatopoeic and expressive words do not obey sound laws. They travel easily across language borders, their age is usually indeterminable, and it is often hard to decide which of them are native and which are borrowed. Wackernagel and Lexer believed that G *Gaukler* goes back to L *cauculator*. (Du Cange cites *cauculatores* glossed as *cauclearii, coclearii, caucularii.* He does not give *cauculus* with the meaning ascribed to it by Wackernagel.) *Cauclearii* or *coclearii* were conjurers versed in weather magic. The Latin and the German word are almost homonyms, and so are OHG *gouggalâri* ~ MHG *goukalâri* and L *ioculārī,* another possible etymon of the German noun (see Mordek and Glatthaar [1993:39, note 29], where some references to the scholarly literature are given). Cf also the much-discussed history of E *jig* in its relation to OF *giguer* 'gambol, sport.' If, however, **jek-*, **jeg-*, **gek-*, **gak-*, **gag-*, **gok,* and so forth were the 'bases' on which slang words designating movement back and forth, sudden (quick) movement, and all kinds of prestidigitation were formed in Germanic and Romance, borrowing need not be posited every time such similarities turn up. Words like *gawk, geck,* and *geek* may emerge at any time, stay in the language for millennia, drop out, and be coined again. At the end of the 19th century, *gaga* 'mad, crazy' appeared in French and soon gained popularity in the English-speaking world.

Perhaps F *gauche* had a history similar to that of *gawk* and the rest. *Gauche* is believed to be a borrowing and reflect the Germanic root **walk-* (as in E *walk*). This etymology is hardly right. Weekley (1921, *gawk*) suggested that *gauche* is traceable to E *gaulick* 'left (hand)'; his hypothesis is even less plausible. If we assume that an old European slang word **gawk* was current in the 15th century (no earlier attestations of F *gauche* are known) and was borrowed by French with an emphatic pronunciation **gokk,* it would develop like **vacca* that yielded F *vache* 'cow.' *Gauche* would remain a Germanic word but of a humbler origin than has been supposed. However, the ground on which we stand here is so boggy that dogmatic exercises for students like: "Connect etymologically *gawky, gauche,* and *left-handed*" (so Hixson and Colodny 1939:117/11) should be avoided. Also to be avoided are equally misleading statements that "*[g]lawky* is the same word as the French *gauche,* and means left-handed, and therefore awkward" (Bett [1936:193]).

We have to return to the question whether E *gawk* may owe its origin to a bird name. Bird names not infrequently acquire the meaning 'fool' in various languages (cf E *goose, booby,* and *gull* among others), so that the path reconstructed tentatively in sec 3 is not improbable. Since such names are often onomatopoeic, it is no wonder that they can also be used to imitate inarticulate speech and refer to mental retardation. *Booby* is a typical example; *gowk* is another. **The history of *gawk* and its derivatives could have begun with *gauk-. However, it is possible that *gawk* was coined side by side with *gowk*. These would have been two variants of the same process.** *Gaga* 'crazy' need not have been derived directly from a verb for gaggling, but an association between them exists regardless of the details of the process. Be that as it may, once *gawk* and *gowk* appeared in English, they began to interact and produce new words, one of them probably being *gawk* 'left hand.' Little is gained by the fear of avoiding the confusion between *gawk, gowk,* and *geck.* Language "confused" them long ago.

The chances that *gawk* 'left hand' is a contraction of *gallok* or *gaulick* are low. In Wood's list of so-called *k*-formations (1913; ModE words: pp. 14-52), not only *gallack* and *gallock* (31/182) but also *ballack* ~ *ballock* 'left-handed, clumsy' (14/108) is given, so that it is unclear where to look for the original form. Wood lists a sizable number of nouns like *hullack* ~ *hullock* 'lazy, worthless person' (23/214), with *-ack* ~ *-ock* after *l;* none of them has a contracted variant. This suffix occurs with great regularity in words meaning 'trash; slovenly work,' 'mistreat'; 'gad about in an untidy way' (cf *flammock* and *flummox* 20/173, 174; the latter is known in modern slang with the meaning 'perplex'), 'fool; slattern; person with a dainty or fastidious appetite or manner,' and so forth. The presence of such a transparent suffix would probably have hindered contraction. Wood does not suggest any origin of *gallock.* It is unlikely that *gallok* was borrowed from regional French. This word should stay in etymological limbo, at least for the time being.

GIRL (1290)

Attempts to trace girl *to an Old English, Old Germanic, or Proto-Indo-European etymon have not yielded convincing results.* Girl *was probably borrowed into Middle English from Low German approximately when it surfaced in texts. The closest Low German form is* Gör(l) *'girl.' In* girl, l *is a diminutive suffix, and* gir-, *along with* gor(r)- *and* gur(r)-, *occurs in many Germanic words that designated children, (young) animals, and all kinds of creatures considered worthless.*

The sections are devoted to 1) the earliest attestation of girl, *2) words deriving (or believed to derive) from the* gor(r)- ~ gur(r)- *root, 3) the suggested Old English and Proto-Indo-European etymons of* girl, *4) the most recent suggestions about* girl, *and 5) suggestions about the origin of* girl *in old dictionaries.*

1. **In Middle English, *girle, gerle,* and *gurle* (*u* had the phonetic value of [y]) denoted a young person of either sex and was more often used in the plural ('children'),** a situation also known from the history of *wench.* A certain ambiguity in the meaning of *girl* seems to have continued into the present. In some British dialects, a common word for 'girl' is *child* ("Is it a boy or a child?"). The first literary example of this usage occurs in Shakespeare. Considering the earliest attested meaning of *girl,* the Old English gloss *gyrlgyden* to L *uesta,* that is, *Vesta,* cannot have meant 'virgin goddess' (so Sweet [1897] and Holthausen [1923:345/204]; corrected in AeEW, at *gierl-gyden*). Anonymous (1897:611) called into question this interpretation in a review of Sweet's dictionary. According to Meritt (1959:69), "It seems most likely that the glossator associated the lemma with *vestis,* as did *Isidore,* Etymologies 8, 11, 61, and that the first part of the gloss is equivalent to *gyrela,* 'garment'; note that at note 679 *stola* is glossed *gyrlan*" (the same in Schlutter [1908a:62-64]; it is less clear whether Ekwall [1903:27, note 1] approved of Sweet's idea). W[1] follows Sweet, and so do Hirt (1927:145, note 1), ACD (1947 and later editions), FW, and RHD[2]. WNWD[1] refers to OE **gyrelle* and *gyrela* "recorded as *gyrl.*" The words "recorded as *gyrl*" no longer appear in WNWD[2-3], but OE **gyrele* does. The etymologies proposed for *girl* vary according to whether the earliest attested Middle English forms are said to have had a lost antecedent in need of reconstruction or to have sprung up (or been borrowed) approximately when they were first recorded.

2. **Most likely *-l,* in *girl* is a diminutive suffix. The root of numerous regional words designating animals, people considered worthless, and children is *gur(r)-* or *gor(r)-*.** Some occur in Wedgwood; many more turn up in Rietz, NEO, EDD, and OED. Björkman (1912:260-61) gives a list compiled from various sources. It is partly reproduced below: 1) English regional: *gorr* 'seagull; red grouse; clownish fellow,' *gorr* 'unfledged bird,' *gurr* 'fish shanny; strong, thickset person; rough, knotty stick or tree.' *Gorrel* 'young pig; fat-paunched person' was borrowed from French, but

Anglo-French animal names like *gore, gorre,* and *gourre* 'pig, sow' are possibly of Germanic origin. Nothing is known about the history of E reg *gorlins* 'testicles of a ram.' *Gorr* 'unfledged bird' may not belong here at all, for it has a variant *gorb.* The same holds for *gorlin* 'unfledged bird, nestling; very young person,' a variant of *gorblin.* Nicklin (1904) cited E *grilse* 'young salmon,' whose first recorded use is dated 1413. Jamieson (1879-82) gives *grilse* and *girlss,* the latter being perhaps a misprint for *girlse,* and EDD adds *girling* and *gerling,* but it is doubtful whether *grilse* has the same root as *gorr* ~ *gurr* (see OED). 2) Northern Frisian: *gör* 'girl.' 3) Dutch regional: *gorre* 'horse, mare, especially old jade.' 4) German: MHG *gurre* 'old jade, bad horse' (so still in some modern dialects), MLG *gorre* ~ *gurre* 'mare,' SwiG *gurre* 'depreciatory term for a girl.' Duden 8 (p 373) gives SwiG *Gör* ~ *Göre* among synonyms for *Kind* 'child.' 5) Norwegian regional: *gurre* 'lamb,' *gorre* 'wether; little boy; lazy person; glutton.' 6) Swedish regional: *gorre, gurre* 'boy.' WNWD[1-2] suggests tentatively that OE *gyr(r)* 'pine tree' is a cognate of *girl,* but Holthausen (1918a:254/30; AeEW) explained *gyr(r)* as meaning 'prickly' (E *gorse* contains the same root). In Holthausen (1918a:254), Old English *gyr* and Modern English *girl* follow one another (nos 30 and 31). The etymological editor for the first edition of WNWD may have misread the two paragraphs as belonging together.

It is a commonplace of Germanic dialectology that some of the words listed above are akin to *girl.* See Outzen (1837 [completed before 1826], *gör*), Wedgwood (who was the first to note several cognates of *girl* in German), Mätzner (1860:241; English and Low German), W. Barnes (1862:91; his entry is confusing: "*gör* Fr. a girl, a grower," but *girl* is called a diminutive of *gör*), Koch (1882 [originally published in 1863]:363), Webster (beginning with 1864; especially in 1890 and later), Rietz (at *gårrä,* he gives Fr *gör* 'girl,' SwiG *Gorsch* 'child,' and Br *gour* 'man' in addition to the Scandinavian forms), MW (*gör*), Skeat (*Gürre,* "depreciatory term for a girl"; the same in Skeat [1887 = 1892:487, 489]: *girl* is said to be a borrowing from Low German), SwiG *Gürrli* 'mare' and *Gurreli* 'whore, *etc*' (SI II:409-10), WHirt (*Göre*) and Hirt (1921:21, 208), Holthausen (1900:366; he presents the relatedness of *girl* to MHG *gurre* 'old jade' as a new idea), EWDS (Kluge first mentioned *girl* at *Gör* in the seventh edition; since G *Gör* emerged in print only in 1593, he had doubts about its being a cognate of *girl,* yet he kept the reference in the later three editions; Götze removed it, but Mitzka [KM] restored it, and Seebold [KS] does not exclude the possibility that *Gör(e)* is related to *girl;* he offers no conjectures on the origin of MHG *gurre*: see *Gaul*), Björkman (1912:278), BZ, and CD. OED and ODEE mention the Low German form, but both are noncommittal on the etymology of *girl.* See Söhns (1888:7), Schumann (1904), and Sprenger (1905) for more information on LG *Göre;* Sprenger mentions E *girl.* Later dictionaries that say anything at all about the origin of *girl* (many of them only cite the Middle English word and call its origin unknown) usually mention LG *Gör(e)* and invite us to "compare" it with *girl.*

Among other *gor(r)-* ~ *gur(r)-* words, the name of the fictional Scandinavian sea king *Górr* is worthy of note. *Górr* appears in an Old Icelandic poem in immediate proximity with *Nórr,* and if it acquired *ō,* only to accommodate the rhyme, the original form **Gŏrr* may have meant 'urchin' and be identical with N reg *gorre.* (Sigfússon 1934-35:130; AEW does not find his etymology of *Górr* improbable, but ÁBM rejects it, and VEW does not mention it.) Then there are Du reg *garldegooi* 'trash, small fry,' *garlgoed* 'offal, trash,' *garlement* 'shivers, small fragments,' *gorrelen* 'pulverize, crash,' and *garl* 'piece' (in *aan garlen gooien* 'break to pieces'); the adjectives *gierelgooiig* 'thin' (said about soup) and *gierlegoi* 'thin' (said about coffee), *gorrel* 'thin' (said about cereal, porridge). *Gorlegooi* 'bad food' occurs in Middle Dutch (Van Lessen [1934]). Those words are apparently related to Du *goor* 'slimy, dingy.' See Du *goor,* OE *gor* 'dung,' OI *gør, gjǫr* 'dregs, sediment,' and OI *gor* 'half-digested food' in etymological dictionaries, WP I:685, and IEW, 494; Rooth (1962:62-65) also contains some relevant material.

If we stay with the most obvious cognates, we are left with a small nucleus of Swiss German and Scandinavian words resembling *gur-,* the root of ME *gurle,* in form and meaning and beginning with *gor(r)-* or *gur(r)-*. They designate young children and animals, people held in contempt, and all kinds of trash. (Cf the history of COB, CUB, and GAWK.)

Ties between *gor(r)-* ~ *gur(r)-* and *gaur-,* as in OI *gaurr* 'rough, uneducated man,' are more problematic. Torp (NEO) cites N reg *gaura* 'grow too fast, become lanky.' In Modern Icelandic, *gaur* means 'pole, post; rotten floating log; long thick bolt; thick (useless) needle; reproof, reproach; tall good-for-nothing; hayseed.' The only certain cognate of *gaur* is Far *geyrur* 'stalk of a large seaweed' (ÁBM). Jóhannesson (1942:221 and IsEW 360, 389) considered OI *gaurr* and Go *gaurs* 'sad, mournful' to be related (CV had the same suggestion), but doubted whether OI *gaurr* and ModI *gaur* could be called cognates. AEW posits the not uncommon development from 'pole, peg' to 'fellow, man,' but the kernel of most meanings of *gaurr* ~ *gaur* seems to be 'worthless (object).' The existence of ME *gaure(n), gawren, gowren,* and *gare* 'gape, stare; shout' (v) complicates the question. They are apparently from Scandinavian, though related to OE *gorian* ~ *gorettan* 'gaze, stare about.' That verb may be a cognate of N reg *gaura* 'pants with an opening behind worn by small children' and ModI *gaur* 'incomplete opening' (only in *standa upp á gaur* 'ajar,' first recorded in the 19th century: ÁBM), for both gaping and shouting imply a mouth wide open.

E reg *gowry* 'dull, stupid-looking' (Lidén [1937:]) goes back to ME *gaure(n),* which allowed Lidén to suggest that OI *gaurr* originally meant 'gaper' (discussed in Björkman [1900:188-89]). Holthausen (1901:379-80) supported Lidén's idea and gave up his previous etymology (*girl* from 'mare'), to which Braune also objected (see below). He now explained E *girl* and OI *gaurr* as representing different grades of ablaut of the same root. In Holthausen (1903b:38), *girl* appears as a cognate of *garish,* but the relatedness of *gaur-* and *garish* needs proof. If OI *gaurr* 'rough, uneducated man' is from 'gaper,' it cannot have anything to do with ModI *gaur.* Nor are then the *gorr-* ~ *gurr-* words related to *gaur:* however worthless, old jades, and so on, are not 'gapers.' But if, as seems likely, OI *gaurr* and ModI *gaur* are traceable to the same etymon, they should be separated from ME *gauren,* ModI *gaur* 'opening,' and N reg *gaura* (sb).

One can imagine a word with the meanings 'unwieldy, worthless object; thick needle, long thick bolt' applied to an able-bodied loafer and a yokel. *Gaurr* must have been a partial synonym, rather than a cognate, of *gorre.* ÁBM finds a genetic connection between *gaurr* and *gorre* improbable. The connection between OI *gaurr* 'rough, uneducated man' and Go *gaurs* 'sad' is even less probable. We can expect no clarity here, but it is advisable to keep apart *girl* and the *g-r* words with *au* in the root. WNWD[1] says that E reg *girls* 'primrose blossoms' and *girlopp* 'lout' (EDD) "substantiate strongly" OE *gyrl-* 'girl,' but *girls* appears to be a metaphor ('fresh and sweet'), while *girlopp* (known only in Devon) probably has the same root as the *gor(r)-* ~ *gur(r)-* words. That phrase and reference to *girlopp* disappeared from WNWD[2], though both E reg *girls* and LG *gore* remained. PIE **g̑her-* 'small' is cited as their possible etymon. It is also unclear how much importance (if any) should be attached to *girl* 'roebuck in its second year' (hunters' usage; recorded in 1486).

3. **Following Möller** (1880:542, note 1) **and A. Noreen** (1894:194), **Luick** (1897-98) **and Kluge** (KL) **reconstructed Gmc **gurwilōn* and OE **gyrele* (f), **gyrela* (m) 'girl.'** In Möller's opinion, Go **gaurwi* was like Go *mawi* 'child,' and Gmc **gaurwilo* like Go *mawilo* 'girl.' According to Luick, **gyrele* developed along the same lines as OE *byr(e)le* > ME *birle* 'cupbearer.' Both Luick ([1964:314] and Berndt [1960:34]) give *gyrl* along with *þyrl* 'hole,' *circe* 'church,' and other words that underwent syncope. On p. 837 of Luick's book, *gyrele* appears without an asterisk. The form **gyrela* ~ **gyrele* allowed Luick to explain why Middle English had the forms *gerle, gurle,* and *girle* (OE *y* allegedly yielded ME *i, e,* and *y,* spelled *u,* depending on the dialect). OED offers no etymology of *girl,* but ODEE agrees that the Middle English variants suggest an original *ü* (the same in Hoad). **Even if ME *i, e, u* go back to "an original *ü,*" it does not follow that OE **gyrela,* to say nothing of Gmc **gurwilōn,* ever existed.** Also, the diminutive suffix *-il* was absent from Old English (see ODEE, *-le*[1]). Consequently, whatever the etymon of ME *girle, gerle,* and *gurle,* it could not be an Old English form resembling Go *mawilo* 'girl' (from *mawi*) or *Attila* 'father' (from *atta*).

Girl rarely occurs outside the Standard: "the word now used by the poor is *wench*" (anonymous [1829:143]). In dialects, *lass, wench,* and *maid,* not *girl,* are the words for 'female child' (M. Keller [?1938:18-22], and Ellert [1946:39-40]). Despite Ekwall's statement (1903:27) that *girl* is "doubtless native," **the Middle English word was most probably borrowed from Low German**, though a few details remain unclear. Thus, *Gürrli* and *Gurreli* are Swiss German, not Low German words; the first means 'mare,' the second is only a term of abuse. LG *Gör(e)* 'girl' has no diminutive suffix, and its kinship with (MH)G *Gurre* 'old jade' cannot be taken for granted. Braune (1879:94) and DW deny a connection between *Gör* and *Gurre.* It was partly under Braune's influence that Holthausen (1901:379-80) modified his views on the origin of *girl* (see above). OED also preferred not to combine a 13th-century English word and a word first recorded in Low German in 1652. A 1593 occurrence of *Gör* is now known (see the relevant passage in WHirt and Kluge[7-10]). At the end of the 16th century, *gör* was current in Pomerania as a depreciatory or pejorative word for 'child,' and it still means 'saucy girl.' In 1697, *güre* 'mare' was recorded in Westphalia (KM, *Göre*).

With so many *gur(r)-* ~ *gor(r)-* words in existence, it does not seem too daring to suggest that G *Gurre* and *Gör(e)* are related. Pisani (1968:125) states, unfortunately without discussion, that *girl* is a borrowing from Low German, a diminutive of *Gör,* which he glosses 'ragazzo' [sic]. Whatever the origin of *Gör(e),* it will remain the most probable immediate etymon of E *girl.* In a late note, Skeat (1911-16:28) traced *girl* to Fr *gör.* He believed that both *boy* and *girl* came to English from Frisian. But *gör,* whose source also seems to have been Low German, has such limited currency in Frisian dialects that the chance of its being the etymon of the Middle English word is low. *Göre* may have been borrowed into late Old English or entered Middle English in the 13th century. Then the variants *i, e, u* reflect the uncertainty attending the pronunciation of a foreign word with the vowel *ö* rather than the split of "an original *ü.*" In any case, no word resembling **gyrle* turns up in the Old English material assembled by Bäck (1934).

G *Gören* (pl), like ME *girles,* means 'children,' but the singular is applied to a female. Middle English distinguished *gay girl* 'young female' from *knave girl* 'young male.' One and the same word often designates 'boy' and 'girl' (that is, 'child of a certain age'). Examples from Biblical Hebrew, Classical Greek, and modern languages abound (Gibbens [1955]). Later such words tend to narrow their sphere of application. Weekley (1921) suggested that the association between *girl* and females is due to the influence of *Gill.* His hypothesis is unverifiable. Perhaps LG *Gör(e)* and ME *girle* preserved their undifferentiated meaning because they were more commonly used in the plural. But the *gurr-* ~ *gorr-* words always refer to physically weak creatures, a circumstance that may have determined the ultimate choice of the referent. (However, Sw and N reg *gorre* means 'boy'!) In the later history of *girl,* only the pronunciations [gɛəl] and [gæ:l] and the affected variant with palatalized *g* have to be mentioned (Luick [1897-98:131; 1964:118, note 1; 1118, note 1], Horn [1935:49], and HL, 468-69, 1009).

Perhaps some connection exists between the *girl* group and F *garçon* 'boy.' The origin of the French word is obscure. See surveys of old conjectures in Roquefort I:148 and of more recent scholarship in FEW XVII:619-20, DCECH (*garçon*), Meier (1976:473-76; he derives *garçon* from *versus,* pp. 484-87), and Larson (1990). Kluge (1916b; 1921:684-85; 1922) traced *garçon* to southern Gmc **wrakjo* (OHG *reccheo,* OE *wrecca*—both mean 'exile, fugitive': ModG *Recke* 'warrior,' ModE *wretch*). Presumably, *garçon* entered French through VL **(g)w(a)raciō(n).* His etymology, which was first met with reserve, now appears in most dictionaries of the Romance languages (Ital *garzone* 'apprentice, errand boy'; in poetical use, 'youth'; Sp *garzón* 'boy, youth'; Port *garção* 'boy').

Kluge reproduced the relevant passage from his 1916 article in EWDS[9]. Only Seebold (KS) removed it. ODEE calls *garçon* a word of disputed origin (at *garçon*), but at *wretch* repeats Kluge's etymology. It is hard to understand how a word meaning 'exile' came to mean 'groom' (see a similar objection in Spitzer [1917:302]). Kluge rightly emphasized the inferior status of the people called *reccheo* and *garçon,* but an exile was the lowest of the low, whereas *garçon,* in *Chanson de Roland,* where it first occurred in Old French, is the name of a respectable occupation. Is it not possible that, whatever the ultimate origin of *garçon* < *gars* (*garçon* is an oblique case), its meaning and form were affected by some of the Gmc *gor(r)-* words? The influence of *garçon* on any Scandinavian name for 'boy' is unlikely, though Bugge (1888a:121) thought that Sw *gosse* 'boy' was a "nationalized" form of *garçon.* (Compare Anglo-Irish *gossoon* 'youth, boy,' ultimately from *garçon.*)

If the view of *girl* as a borrowing from Low German is justified and if LG *Gör* is one of the many recorded *gor(r)-* ~ *gur(r)-* nouns, attempts to reconstruct not only a Germanic but even a Proto-Indo-European etymon for *girl* should be abandoned. Möller (1880:542, note 1) related Gmc **gurwilōn* to L *virgo* 'virgin' and Gk παρθένος 'woman' and came up with PIE **ghᵘérghᵘ.* The approval of Prellwitz (1889:155) and A. Noreen (1894:194) lent glamour to Möller's reconstruction (though Prellwitz accepted **ghᵘérghᵘ* without recourse to Germanic). Pedersen (1893:257), Fay (1895:9, note 2), and Hirt (WHirt, *Göre*) supported it, though Hirt was aware of Brugmann's work on παρθένος (1906:173). Hirt (1921:21, 208) specifically praised the power of sound laws that brought to light the bond between παρθένος and *girl,* and later (Hirt 1927:145, note 1) called the Indo-European etymology of *girl* uncertain but revealing. However, OED and Björkman (1912:278, note 2) treated *girl* as unsuitable material for Indo-European reconstruction, and Pedersen (1930:61) disavowed his earlier views. In Pedersen (1949-50:5-6), he gave a different etymology of the Greek word. WH (*virgo*) mention *girl* but express no opinion on its origin.

Wood's idea to trace *girl* to PIE **gheu-* (and further to *ĝhouqʷ-* ~ *ĝhuōqʷ-* 'move rapidly') and

Tucker's derivation of *girl* from PIE **gher-* 'grow' will be discussed below. Bugge (in A. Noreen [1909:232, note on p. 66]) compared Sw and N reg *gorre* 'boy,' E *girl,* and LG *Gör(r)* with Ir *gerr* 'short,' Skt *hrasvá-* 'short, small' (and Skt *hrasati* 'diminish'). Torp (NEO, *gorre*) mentioned Bugge's idea without referring to the source. Jóhannesson (1942:221) and IsEW, 360, 389, traced Ir *gerr* ~ OIr *gair* and Skt *hrasvá-* to PIE **gher-*. Since Go *gaurs* often turns up in this context, two reconstructed Proto-Indo-European roots come into play: **gher-* 'small' and **ghou̯ros-* 'dreadful' (WP I:604-5, 636; IEW, 443, 453-54). When LG *Gör(e)* is said to be akin to G reg *gorig* 'small, miserable' (< OHG *gôrag*), we again end up with Go *gaurs* 'mournful,' Skt *ghorás* 'dreadful, awe-inspiring,' and their cognates.

4. Several etymologies of *girl* are more recent. The Middle English forms *gerle, girle,* and *gurle* resemble OE *gier(e)la, (ge)ger(e)la, (ge)girla,* and *(ge)gyr(e)la* (m) 'dress, apparel, adornment,' from **garwila,* that is, 'thing made ready (to wear).' OE *gearo* ~ *gearu* mean 'ready, prepared, equipped, finished' (Stroebe [1904:72]; AeEW, *gierela*); its feminine counterpart *gierelu* also existed. **It has been suggested that ME *girle* is the continuation of OE *girla* 'dress.'** See Rapp (1855:II/301); Mueller (he compares LG *Gör,* allegedly from G *Gehre* 'edge of a skirt; triangular piece' [akin to E *gore* 'triangular piece of cloth'; historically, 'triangular piece of land'], with *Gör* being understood as *Schoßkind* 'pampered child, child sitting in its mother's lap'; more guardedly in the second edition); Törnkvist (1959:15); MED ("? < OE **gyrela* < **gurw-,* akin to OE *gierela* <**garw* 'a garment'"; the volume with *girle* appeared in 1963); Robinson (1967; the main advocate of this etymology); Barnhart (prefers this etymology; tentatively considers *Gör* and so on to be either cognates or "simply accidental, vaguely similar forms"); Makovskii (1986:77; 1989b:80), and RHD[2].

Makovskii (1971:21) cites Sc and E reg (northern) *girl* 'neckcloth' (see EDD, *girl* v^1), but that noun, as well as *girl* or *gorl* (v) 'girdle; surround the roof of a stack with straw ropes...,' is a variant of *girdle* and has nothing to do with OE *gierela.* Makovskii (1992a:43) connects *girl* and the root **ker* 'produce sounds' with L *circulus* 'circle' (young women were allegedly associated with the circle, a symbol of infinity and chastity), but does not explain how all these etymologies can be combined. He further develops his fantasies in Makovskii (1999a:149-50). Now we are told that early Indo-Europeans buried their women according to the full military ritual, a fact that allegedly justifies the comparison between OE *girela* and L *gerere* 'fight,' because possibly *gerere arma* 'bear arms' is meant. The entry contains several wrong glosses, such as OE *gyrel* 'armor,' G *gären* 'move fast and chaotically,' and so forth. G *Groll* 'anger,' G *Gier* 'greed, lust,' the Sanskrit verb for 'to swallow,' and Oss *gyryn* 'give birth' appear as supporting evidence, with the conclusion that *girl* originated as 'someone swallowing the penis.'

The development from 'clothes' to 'a person wearing such clothes' (synecdoche) has often been recorded: compare E *skirt* 'woman,' *calico* 'woman' in colonial American English (Babcock [1950:138]), South African E *nylon* 'woman' (Gold [1992:107]), *gyp* 'college servant' (at Cambridge and Durham), believed to be from *gippo* (obsolete) 'tunic' (OED), and possibly G *Schranz(e)*: from 'torn clothes' to 'sycophant.' All such words are invariably slang. G. Neumann (1971:12), Markey (1983:103-4; 1987:282), and Terasawa (1993:338-41) supported Robinson, but Diensberg (1985a) and especially Moerdijk (1994) rejected his etymology.

The main arguments against it are as follows. Judging by the examples in BT, MacGillivray (1902:129 and sec 232), and Stroebe (1904:72-73), OE *gierela* at no time designated an article of children's clothing, as Robinson also admits. None of the numerous Old English words for 'boy' and 'girl' has its origin in a synecdoche. Robinson's etymology does not explain why ME *girle* mainly occurs in the plural. If OE *gierela* meant 'child,' it is surprising that this meaning found no reflections in written texts, considering how many informal Old English words for 'child' have come down to us. It is even more surprising that *girle* burst into bloom long after *gierela* was forgotten. Luick's Old English form **gyrele* would have been pronounced with initial [g] (umlauted vowels withstood diphthongization after velars), but OE *[ji(ə)rlə] would not have become [girl]. Robinson (1967:240) postulates northern influence on *girl,* though no evidence points to its being a northen word. In the 1992 postscript, Robinson (1993:180-81) subjects Diensberg to severe criticism, but the problems mentioned above remain unsolved. Bammesberger and Grzega (2001:1-4) have shown that in some Old English dialects *g-* could have remained velar in the reflexes of Gmc **garw-ilan,* but they did not refute the other arguments of Robinson's opponents. The main flaw of Robinson's etymology is that it disregards ties between E *girl* and similar words all over the Germanic-speaking world. Nor do Bammesberger and Grzega address that question; they only refer to "[a] particularly rich overview of past attempts at clarifying the etymology of *girl* in Liberman (1998)."

ME *girle* seems to be unrelated to OE *gierela.* Pedersen (1941-42) thought that E *wife* (< *wīf*) went back to a word meaning 'piece of clothing, kerchief,' but also without sufficient reason (Schmidt-Strunk [1989:253]). Robinson praises Berndt's hypothesis (1960:339-40), according to which ME *girle,* from **gyr(w)ela (-e),* was derived from OE *gyrwan* in the sense 'maturing, growing one.' However, OE *(ge)gyrwan* and its variants *(ge)gierwan* ~ *(ge)gerwan* meant 'prepare, cook; dress, adorn; direct,' not 'ripen' or 'grow.' Tucker (n.d.:9) anticipated Berndt: he traced *girl* to PIE **gher-* 'grow, be young, fresh, lively.' Another version of Tucker's idea is Nicklin's derivation of *girl, garth, yard, green,* and *grow* from the same stem (1904:246).

Schlutter (1908a:62-63, 1913a:153-54) **sought the etymology of *girl* in Gk χερ- (χεράς 'stream carrying stones and sand')** and referred to the Old English gloss *gerae* in *riui aggerum. congregatio aquarum i. gerae* 'the now smoothly flowing, now wild' river *Gera* and to G reg *Gören* 'canal' (Schleswig). Was he trying to suggest that *girl* should be interpreted as originally meaning 'brisk, impetuous'? (See Holthausen's puzzled query [1923:345/204].) If so, his predecessor was Wood (1902:52/88a), who posited the root **gheu-* 'move rapidly, whirl, turn,' as in Gk θήρ 'beast, animal,' L *ferus* 'wild; wild animal,' LG *Göre* 'boy, girl,' OE [sic] *gyrle* 'girl' (here Wood cites Lith *véikus* 'quick' and *vaĩkas* 'boy, girl'), and so on, including E *giddy.* Wood's derivation of *giddy* and *girl* is fanciful; see Klaeber's guarded criticism (1905:202) and discussion of *giddy* in DWARF.

By 1918 **Holthausen** must have felt disenchanted with his former etymologies of *girl* and **thought that *gyr-* in **gyrela* was a diminutive of OE *gor* 'dung, dirt, filth'** (ModE *gore* 'clotted blood,' distinct from *gore* 'triangular piece'; Holthausen [1918a:254]). He cited Westph *kyətəl* 'little heap of dirt' and 'boy' (akin to G *Kot* 'filth, excrement') and E *groom,* which he derived from OF *grom* (< L *grummus* = *grūmus* 'heap of earth, hillock'). In EW[2,3], Holthausen derived *girl* from OE *gor* without comment. He did not explain how OE *gor-,* when umlauted, produced three Middle English variants: *gerle* (the expected form), *girle,* and *gurle.* Nor did he come to terms with Björkman (1912), whom he had once supported with such enthusiasm. In a way, *girl* from *gor* is a perversion of Braune's idea: Braune (1879:94) explained LG *Gör* as being the same word as Du *geur* 'fragrance, odor, aroma' (allegedly, it all started with phrases like *sote göre* 'sweet smell' used as hypocoristic forms of address, but *geur* is probably a cognate of OE *gor* 'dung'; see NEW). According to still another interpretation, OE *gor* is a cognate of Go *gaurs* (Uhlenbeck [1905:289/132] and KEW[1] but removed from KEW[2]). Uhlenbeck's etymology again brings us to OI *gaurr* and the rest.

5. **Early etymologists had no clue to the origin of *girl.* They only assembled words for 'young female' that began with *g, k, h* and contained postvocalic *r, l* or explained it according to their views on women's nature.** See surveys in Johnson, Johnson-Todd, Richardson, Worcester, and Mackay (1877). Minsheu derived *girl* from L *garrula* 'garrulous' (f) (because young women are chatterboxes) or from *girella,* which he glossed as 'weathercock' (*Gazophylacium:* "from à Gyrando, thereby denoting their inconstancy"); see *girella* in OED. The first of his etymologies enjoyed such popularity that CD devoted a special statement to its refutation. Casaubon (1650:292) traced *girl* to Gk κόρη 'girl'. Not only Lemon and Cockayne (1861/282 and 1049) but even Wyld (UED) supported the *girl*—κόρη idea (Wyld says: "Possibly cognate with").

Skinner suggested OE *ceorl* 'man' as the etymon of *girl* or rather the imaginary feminine **ceorla* (though OI *kerla* 'woman' exists), and Hickes (1703-05:107) derived *girle* from OI *karlinna* 'woman.' Hickes's etymology proved equally long-lived. It turns up in Serenius (1757, *karl,* where he noted the similarity between *girl* and ModI *gervi* 'form' and *gervilegur* 'pretty'), Thomson, Webster (1864, among other possiblilities; 1874 and 1880), and in DDEL; reference to *karlinna* disappeared from Webster only in 1890. Van Kempe Valk (1880:168) cited OE *ceorl,* Du *kerel,* and E *girl* as self-evident cognates. Bernard compared *girl* and Pol *garzel* and *garlica* (? = *gardziel* 'throat' and *gardlica* 'turtle dove'). Junius mentioned Wel *herlodes* 'girl' (in fact, *herlod* means 'boy'), from which he seems to have derived E *girl* and *harlot* (*harlot* is from French, whereas Wel *herlod[es]* is most probably from English [Skeat[4]]; the origin of the French word is the subject of involved conjectures, to quote COD[5] on *boy*). Worcester adds Gael *cael* and *caileag* to this list; his modern supporter is Partridge (1958). (Was Worcester inspired by the pronunciation [gɛəl]?) Gael *caile* ~ *caileag,* Ir *caile,* and Br *plac'h* 'girl' are even more obscure than E *girl* (LE, *caile*). Comparison between those Celtic words, Gk παλλακή, and L *p(a)ellex* (both mean 'concubine'), favored at one time (MacBain, *caile;* Henry, *plac'h*), seems to be erroneous (WH, *paellex*).

W (1828) derived *girl* from "Low L. *gerula,* a young woman employed in tending children and carrying them about, from *gero,* to carry; a word probably received from the Romans while in England." This etymology stayed in Webster until 1860 and found its way into ID (1850), anonymous (1861:142), E. Edwards, Brewer, and Boag. According to Shipley (1945), Brewer derived *girl* from *girdle,* an object "worn by maids and loosed at the marriage," a derivation that does not turn up in any edition of Brewer's books consulted. Shipley found Brewer's idea "interesting" and surmised that *girl* is perhaps a "corruption" of *darling.* It will be seen that the line between so-called prescientific and modern guesswork is tenuous, the more so because some modern authors, like their distant predecessors, drop hints without going into details (for example, Hilmer [1914:35] asserts that most words for 'child,' including *girl,* are traceable to 'mass, piece, etc'). By contrast, some early philologists had enough common sense not to indulge in fruitless guessing (one of them was Tyrwhitt; see Tyrwhitt [1775:5, 85]).

Of old ideas, the one put forward by Skinner still has value. The group OE *ceorl* (ModE *churl*), MLG *kerle* (ModG *Kerl*), OI *karl,* and OHG *karl* (all of them mean 'man') reflects the same depreciatory attitude toward the persons involved that is noticeable in the *girl* group. A *ceorl* was a free man without rank; later *ceorl* acquired the meaning 'peasant, rustic, low base fellow, *etc.*' G *Kerl* has not degraded to the level of *churl,* but it is a familiar term: 'guy, bloke.' OI *kerling, kelli, kerla,* and *kella* 'old woman' are often synonymous with 'old hag.' The derivational model of *gir-l, kar-l,* and *ker-le* is the same. Seebold (KS) has justifiable doubts about the accepted etymology of G *Kerl* from PIE **ǵerə-* 'old,' whereas MLG *kerl(e)* and OHG *karl* need not be related by ablaut. More likely, they are variants of the same root, as are *gor(r) ~ gur(r).* Amosova (1956:183) rejects, on phonetic grounds, the idea that *girl* has anything to do with OE *ceorl.* To be sure, *gor(r)* and *ker- ~ kar-* are related (if at all) differently from L *ager* and Go *akrs* 'field,' but it seems that **Germanic had several near synonymous roots beginning with a velar stop and ending in *r*. They often appeared with the diminutive suffix *-l(e)*, and denoted young animals, children, and all kinds of creatures considered immature, worthless, or past their prime. In some situations, *gor(r)- ~ gur(r)-* and *ker- ~ kar-* functioned as doublets** (Liberman [1998]).

HEATHER (1730)

Heather *continues Northumbr* hadder, *which is most probably from OI* *haðr; -er *would be the same suffix as in* clover, madder, *and a few other plant names.* *Hað- *may have meant 'hair.' Its association with* heath *appears to be late.*

Heather emerged in the 14th century in the form *hathir* (later, *hadyr, haddyr, haddir, hedder, hadder, hather,* and *hether*). *Heather,* first recorded in the 18th century, is seemingly from *heath + er,* with vowel shortening in the stem syllable (Skeat[1] and the pre-OED works that discuss *heather*). **Usually *heather* appears at the end of the entry for *heath* as an obvious derivative.** Some researchers cite G *Heidekraut* 'heather' (literally 'heath grass') as proof that *heath* and *heather* are related in a natural way; G *Heide* (plant name) also existed (Wolff [1976]). Several etymologies of the word for 'heather' in the Indo-European languages (notably, of OI *lyng*) trace the name of this plant to the type of soil in which it grows. But *hathir* was originally confined to Scotland with the contiguous part of the English border, that is, to the regions in which *heath* was unknown, and an association between those words is late. One would expect *heather* to go back to **hedder, *hadder,* from **hædder* or **hæddre* (OED).

According to Skeat[4], who follows OED, *heath* and *heather* are etymologically unrelated, for Northumbr *hadder* points to some different origins. The other late dictionaries repeat OED with insignificant variations. UED adds that *heather* may have had the same formative suffix as in several other plant names. See discussion at CLOVER. In Ekwall's opinion (1908), *heath* and *heather* are cognates, with *heath* being native and *heather* going back to OI *heiðr.* To prove his idea, he reconstructed the change of Scand *ei* to *ā* in Middle English, the shortening of *ā* before *-r,* its narrowing to *e* in Scots (as in Sc *fether* 'father' and the like), and the reinterpretation of *r* as part of the root. Ekwall's examples of Scand *ei* > ME *ā* are less than fully convincing and no unambiguous evidence testifies to Scand **heiðr* 'heather,' but he was right that Scand *lyng* 'heather' had synonyms (see Moberg [1971] and Melefors [1984]).

Scand **haðr* 'heather,' unrelated to *heiðr,* probably existed. The old name of the Norwegian province *Hadaland* (now *Hadeland*) has been explained as containing the root *hǫð* 'battle' (akin to OE *heaðu-* and G *Hader* 'discontent') or **hað-* 'sea.' H. Kuhn (1941) supported the second etymology, but he did not mention *Hǫðr,* the legendary eponymous ancestor of the people of Hadaland, an important name in this context (see Much [1924:109]).

Both explanations seem to be wrong. OE *heaðo-līðende* (*Beowulf,* 1798 and 2955) probably means 'sea traveler,' but it does not follow that *Hadaland* should be understood as 'sea land.' It is also unlikely that a province called 'war land' existed. *Hadaland* rather meant 'heather land.' Knobloch (1980:198-99) related the root of such place names to OE *heaðor* 'restraint, confinement' (that is, 'wattle')—a rather contrived hypothesis. In late Old English, **haðr* and *hǣþ* must have been pronounced [hæðr] and [hæ:þ] respectively. **Folk etymology connected them and thereby saved **hæðr,* which spread south from its original home, while in Scandinavia it was ousted by *lyng.***

Many words with *a* and *ai* in the Germanic languages have the appearance of being related, but those vowels belong to different ablaut series. See more at KEY and OAT. H. Kuhn's etymologies (1954:144, 146, 151) are shaky. However, even if his approach to Gmc **a* were acceptable, coupling **haiþi-* ~ **haiði-* with **haðr* within the framework of his theory would presuppose that one of them is a term of agriculture or cattle-raising; yet heather is not a fodder crop.

****Haðr* may represent an *r*-less variant of the root **hazdaz* 'hair,'** as in OI *haddr* 'hair' (= 'long hair in need of combing,' hence 'woman's hair') and OE *-heord* 'hair' (in *bundenheord* 'with one's hair bound'); see also the history of E *hards* and *hurds* in etymological dictionaries. The West Germanic root **hezdon,* from which *-heord* was derived, did have an *r*-less variant: compare OE *hadswǣpe* 'bridesmaid,' literally 'one who brushes the bride's hair' (Pogatscher [1901:196-99; 1902:233-34], Roeder [1909:34-39]). *Hede* and *heide,* the Middle Low German forms for *hurds,* also lack [*r*]: cf Du *hede* and G *Hede.* If **haðr* goes back to an *r*-less variant of **hazdaz,* that is, if forms with and without *r* continued to be productive after rhotacism set in, **haðr* meant 'hairy.'

In some other Indo-European languages, the words for *heather* and *hair* also occasionally sound alike (O. Ritter [1922:52-53]). Their similarity is due to chance (IEW, 1139, 1155). An association of heather with shagginess in English dialects goes back to the confusion of the roots *hath-* and *hǣd-* 'hair.' EDD cites *hedder-faced* 'rough-faced, unshaven' and *hed(d)ery* 'rough, shaggy.' The noun *hathe* 'thick covering' occurs in the phrase *be in a hathe* 'be thickly covered with pustules of the small-pox or other eruptive disease; be matted closely together.' **Haðr* may have been an ancient *s*-stem, later interpreted as the plural, with the root of *hathir, haddyr, hadder, hedder,* and so forth meaning 'hair.' Plant names are often collective plurals. See CLOVER, IVY, and Bjorvand (1994:21-22), who suggested a similar origin for *lyng* 'heather' (the same in BjL, *lyng*). If *heather* once contained the element *-re,* in northern dialects this ancient suffix could be understood as a Scandinavian ending of the plural. The sense of the word would emerge as 'tract grown over with heather.' It is a mere curiosity that E *heather* and L *hedera* 'ivy' are near homonyms (Liberman [1988c:43-46]).

HEIFER (900)

In addition to the reflexes of OE heahfore, *ME* hayfore, *and many similar forms, modern dialects have* heckfore *and so forth. The explanation of* heahfore *as* hēahfōre *'high-farer, highstepper' makes little sense. The assumption that* -fore *is related to OE* fear(r) *'bull, ox' or Sc* ferry cow *'cow that is not with milk' does not clarify the meaning of the compound either. Most likely, OE* hĕahfŏre < *hægfore < *hæhfore *consisted of* *hæg *'enclosure' and the element* -fore *'dweller' = 'occupant of an enclosure.'* Heckfore *has the same structure (*hec *'rail; fence; gate'). A regular development* heahfore > heckfore *is possible, but the change* hf > kf *in it has few secure analogues. In some dialects,* heahfore *yielded* [heifə(r)], *in others* [hefə(r)]. *Standard English* heifer *reflects the spelling of the first group and the pronunciation of the second.*

The sections are devoted to 1) the hypotheses about the meaning of OE heah- *and* -fore, *with emphasis on vowel length and the connection between* -fore *and* faran, *2) the history of* -k- *in* heckfore *and of* heck- *'enclosure,' 3) similar animal names in English and other languages, and 4)* hĕahfŏre **'occupant of an enclosure.' Sec 5 is the conclusion.*

1. Old English had *heahfore, heahfru, heaf(a)re,* Northumbr *hehfore,* and a few other forms. *Heifer* has always meant 'young cow.' It is also a low colloquialism for 'woman' (see *Judges* XIV:18, Authorized Version: *if ye had not plowed with my heifer* 'if you had not used my wife's help'). An association between a heifer and a (young) woman is not limited to English. OIr *ainder* means 'young woman,' while Wel *anner* means 'heifer' (Schuchardt [1905:5-6]; Pedersen [1949-50:4], where Basque *and(e)re* ~ *anre* 'young woman' are discussed); see also the end of sec 4, below. According to Pokorny (1949-50:131-32), Irish and Welsh borrowed *ainder* ~ *anner* from Berber. Schrijver (2002) leans toward the Basque source of all those words.

See a few minor details of the phonetic history of OE *heahfore* in SB (sec 218, note 2: *heafre* < *heahfre*) and A. Campbell (1959:sec 392, *heafre, heahfore*). In modern dialects, *(h)ayfer, heckfore,* and many similar forms occur (EDD). Ben Jonson, in 1609, used *heicfar* 'woman' (OED). *Heahfore* apparently consists of two parts, so that ModE *heifer* is a disguised compound (Goetz [1971:10.26], Faiss [1978:131-34]; not listed in Bergsten [1911:9-24]). Despite the early loss of *-h-*, *-f-* remained voiceless in this word, and no forms have been attested with *-v-* at any period, unlike, for example, OE *clāfre* 'clover' and OE *frōfer* ~ *frōfor* (> ME *frover*) 'consolation.'

Words for 'young cow' are varied in Germanic. Their original meaning can be 'small creature,' 'barren,' that is, not yet impregnated, 'of one year old,' 'female,' and the like. Those who believe that *heahfore* had *ēa* (Skinner, Lemon, and many others) usually gloss it as 'highstepper, highgoer,' for they derive *-fore* from *faran* 'go' (as in OE *fara* 'traveler'), with *o* from *a* under secondary stress (more likely before *r*; see below).

The names of calves, lambs, and kids may perhaps contain the root of a verb meaning 'go, pass' when they refer to those animals' age. Such are possibly Oss *ræwæd* 'heifer' and its cognates in several Iranian languages (W. Miller [1907:332/69], IESOI, II:289-90). But Abaev's later etymology (1997:218/390): *ræwæd* < **fra-wata-*, in which *wata-* means 'year,' is more convincing. Similar formations would be OI *gymbr* 'ewe one year old' (ModI *gimbur*), with reflexes in all the Scandinavian languages (a cognate of L *hiems* 'winter': AEW, *gymbr;* ÁBM, *gimbr*; OED, *gimmel*; doubts about the origin of this word can now be dismissed), E reg *twinter* 'heifer' (that is, 'cow two winters old'), and others. Apart from the fact that OE *heahfore,* even if construed with a long diphthong, will not yield the meaning 'a creature of an advanced (high) age,' heifers are young, not old.

Garrison (1955:279) suggested that 'highstepper' referred to calves' long legs, but his interpretation *hēah* 'high' + *fore* 'in the front' is irreconcilable with the fact that Old English compounds never had the structure adjective + adverb of place. One could interpret **highstepper* as 'cow whose udder is (still) high above the ground,' but the likelihood of such an interpretation is not strong.

The element *-fore* has also been explained as a cognate of OE *fear(r)* 'bull, ox' (akin to G *Farre(n)* < *far(ro)* 'bullock') and of G *Färse* ~ Du *vaars* 'young cow' (OHG, MHG, OLG, MDu *verse*: EWDS[1-10] and KS, *Färse*; EWNT; Vercoullie, *vaarkoe* and *vaars* 'heifer'; not in EWDS[11-21] or NEW). The semantic tie between 'bull' and 'young cow' is less apparent than it seems: *'cow that goes to the bull for the first time'? Skeat (in the first edition of his dictionary and in Skeat [1887 = 1892]:424, 494, 496) defended the comparison of *-fore* with OE *fearr,* but in the fourth edition he disclaimed his views. See also R. Morris (1903:135), who treats OE *heahfore* like OE *hēahdēor* 'roebuck,' literally 'high (tall) animal' (UED says the same). E. Klein (1911) relates *-fore* to *faran* on p. 15 and to *fearr* on p. 41. Sweet (1888:354/1731), Mayhew (1891c:secs 708, 745, 801), BT, and Luick (1964:sec 516, note 5) do not discuss the etymology of *heahfore* but write *hēah-*.

***'Highstepper' as the name of a young cow would be a kenning, which alone makes this etymology of *heifer* improbable.** *Hēahdēor* 'stag, deer' is a usual bahuvrihi (Last [1925:21]). Among the Old English compounds beginning with *hēah-*, none has the semantic structure of a kenning. In *hēahseld* 'throne,' *hēahsetl* 'place of honor,' *hēahsynn* 'deadly sin,' and so on, *hēah-* either means 'high' or approaches the status of a reinforcing particle. Even a bookish bahuvrihi like *hēahrūn* 'pythoness' would be more transparent than *hēahfore* 'young cow,' a word of the peasants' vocabulary. The interpretation of Germanic nonpoetic compounds as elaborate metaphors and kennings is not justified (Binnig [1984]). For this reason, N.P. Willis's explanation (*heifer* = 'stepping superbly,' 'a young creature who has borne no burthens'; see Shulman [1948:41-42]) should be rejected.

Drake's idea (1907:221-22, no 518n, and 252, no 606n) that *-fore* in *heahfore* is related to *-fur* in OE *calfur,* plural of *cælf* 'calf,' does not merit discussion. Equally fanciful is Makovskii's attempt to interpret *heahfore* in light of an alleged mythological unity 'heaven' ~ 'cow' (1992b:154). He compared *heah-* with E reg *higgs* 'white cumuli' (EDD), and *-fore* with Russ *poroz* 'bull, boar,' a word of debatable etymology but probably related to OE *fear(r)* (Vasmer III:330-31).

IEW 818 derives *heah-* in *heahfore* from OE *hēah* 'high' and classifies *-fore* with cognates of ME *farrow* 'not in calf' (akin to Sc *ferry cow* 'cow that is not with calf and therefore continues to give milk through the winter' and Fl *vare koe* 'cow that gives no more milk': Jamieson [1879-82]). According to ODEE, *farrow* (adj), unrelated to *farrow* 'litter of pigs' (< OE *fearh;* PIE **porkos*), is of unknown origin, but Holthausen's hypothesis in AeEW is attractive: he compares *farrow* (adj) with Westph *fear* 'barren,' WFr *fear* 'barren,' and OE *fearr* 'ox' ('barren' and 'ox' share the feature 'nonproductive'; see the words of this root in Holthausen [1913:334] and in AeEW: *fearr* and *for*). **Although irreproachable phonetically, the etymology in IEW shares the main weakness of the previous one. Special names are bestowed on one-year-old animals precisely because they are not full-grown (see CD[1]).**

The proposed interpretation of *-fore* is tenable, but *heah-* in *heahfore* cannot mean 'high.'

Forby (1830), whose main concern was East Anglian *heifker,* wanted the word "to express a *half-cow;* a cow half-grown, not yet come to full size and maturity," a most reasonable hypothesis, considering the attempts to interpret *heah-* as *hēah-*. He cited the 1579 Norfolk form *heckfordes* or *heckforthes* 'heifers.' These, he thought, lost *d* or *th* (as in the place name *Thetfor'* < *Thetford*) and became *heifker* by metathesis, whereas *heckfer* allegedly emerged as the "mispronunciation" of *heifker*. Forby's reconstruction, however, is of little interest today, for it does not take into account OE *heahfore.* Rye (1895) deleted the entire note, but the forms ending in *-forde* ~ *-forthe,* to which OED adds *hecfurthe,* need an explanation; folk etymology must have been at work in them. East Anglian *heifker,* with its diphthong, looks like a blend, a cross between *[heifə(r)] and [hekfə(r)].

Kluge (EWDS[1-3], *Klee*) connected *-fore* in *heahfore* and *-fre* in OE *clāfre* 'clover' but later never returned to this idea; see CLOVER. Another daring guess about the element *-fore* is Shipley's. He traced *-fore* to PIE **per* 'pristine, primary' and cited *farrow* (he did not say which) as a cognate (1984:306, *per* VIc); Shipley's derivations are usually of this type.

The Latin glosses of OE *heahfore* were *altila* and *altilium* 'fatted calf' (from *alo* 'nourish'). Junius (*haifer*) thought that *heahfore* was a variant of *heahfodro*. His guess has little to recommend it despite Baly's support of it (1897:643, note 1). In Old English, *altile,* the Latin lemma for *heahfore,* occurred twice as *antile.* According to A. Brown (1972), *heahfore* is some glossator's attempt to render *altile* ~ *antile*: *heah* for *alt(us)* and *fore* for *ant(e)* (compare Garrison's etymology 'high-in-the-front'). He suggested that *heahfore* was never meant to be a real word. *Heahfru* is, in his opinion, a nominative back formation from the *-f(a)re* forms in oblique cases. If such were the origin of *heahfore,* it would be impossible to understand how this ghost word became known to the translators of Bede, gained currency in dialects, and stayed in the language of the peasants for twelve centuries. The glossator, more likely, wrote *antile* instead of *altile,* influenced by *-fore.*

W. S. Morris (1967:70-71) maintains that *heah-* was used to distinguish the genders of *fear(r)* (m) 'beast of burden, ox, bull' and *heafre* (f) 'young cow.' He believes the distinction to be due to an early misinterpretation of L *alitilia* 'nourished, fattened,' usually written *altilia,* as though it were a derivative of *altus* 'high,' which would correspond to OE *hēah-*. Such a misuse of *hēah-* would be unique, and Anglo-Saxon farmers did not know Latin. The rather frequent juxtaposition of OE *fear* and *heahfore* (> *heafre*) goes back to the predilection of Old English authors for paronomasia (see Frank [1972]).

2. **Wedgwood recognized a word for 'enclosure' in *heckfore.*** He cited Du *hokkeling* 'heifer' from *hok* 'pen' as a parallel case. His etymology reached the public (Paley [1882:462]), and it became customary to treat the *heah-* and *hek-* forms as parallel (so Mueller and CD). According to Kluge (KL), OE **hægre* is from **heah-* ~ **hæg-* 'enclosure.' He detected the same root in OE *heahfore* and in G reg *hagen* and *hegel* 'bull, ox' and compared *-fore* with OE *fearr*. Jordan (1903:179), who writes *hĕahfore,* and Weekley say the same. Theirs is a fruitful approach, though *Hagen* and *Hegel* are probably unrelated (DW; WP I:33-4; IEW, 522; KM: *Hecke*[1], *Hecke*[2], and *Hag*), and neither seems to be related to words for 'enclosure.' Smythe Palmer (1883, *heifer*) also compared *heck-* in E reg *heckfor* with *heck* 'enclosure' and ascribed the similarity to folk etymology. ID says that R. Morris derived the first part of *heifer* from a word for 'pen, stall,' but the form cited (*hea*) and the reference (oral communication? nothing similar occurs in any of his books) are dubious. EB, which gives the same strange form, prefers the meaning 'high-stepper.'

The relationship between *heah-* and *hek-* in the history of *heifer* remains a matter of dispute. Kluge (1901b:1003) proposed a rule whereby ME *hf* became *kf* (as allegedly in *heahfore* > *hekfere*), analogous to the change of Gmc *-s* to *-ks*. His idea found many supporters; see O. Ritter (1904:303; 1906a:149), Wyld (1899-1902:22; 1899:248-49), Luick (1964:718/4 and 770, note), Jordan (1968:sec 168, note 2), and HL (862, 1041-42). Kalb (1937:51), with reference to Horn (1901:94), cites several examples of *k* > *h* in Middle English, but the history of the word *hockamore* (a doublet of *hock* 'sort of wine'), first recorded in the 17th century, sheds no light on *heckfor,* because it is an Anglicised pronunciation of G *Hochheimer*. Skeat (1899-1902:446-47) disagreed with the formulation "*h* becomes *k* before a spirant" and pointed out that final *h* in *heah-* had either to disappear in Middle English or change. According to him, in some dialects, -[χ] yielded *-k* (as in *elk* < *eolh*), whereas in others the usual change of -[χ] to *-f* occurred, as in *rūh* > *rough.* When **hēahfore* became **hēaffore,* the vowel, he said, shortened and the word acquired its modern pronunciation. Since OE *hĕahfore* is a more likely form than *hēahfore*, Skeat's intermediate stage can be dispensed with.

The shortening of *ei* in *heifer* may be compared with that in *leisure* (when it rhymes with *pleasure*), *Leister*, and *nonpareil* (Kaluza [1906-07, II:298, sec 381/e]), but it is not necessary to explain [e] in *heifer* by the influence of *heckfer* (this is the suggestion in HL, 308, 727). The change from [χ] to *k* is extremely rare. If we disregard the animal names *elk*, from *eolh*, and reg *selk*, from *seolh* 'seal' (on which see Hamp [1994], among others), only reg *ekt* (< OE **hēht*) 'height' and possibly [hok] 'hough' (? < OE *hōhsinu*) remain. The evidence of place names is ambiguous. It is not necessary to trace *Haxtead* (Surrey), *Hickstead* (Sussex), and *Heckfeld* to OE *hēah-* or *Freek's* (Sussex) to OE *fyrhðe* 'woodland' (so Mawer [1937:127], but see *Haxtead* and *Heckfeld* in Ekwall [1960]). *Heahfore* was not a literary word, which explains its low frequency in OE texts. OE **hecfore*, not derived from *heahfore*, may have existed, though it has not been attested.

3. **Other animal names are useless in establishing the etymology of *heifer*.** The origin of Russ *koza* 'nanny goat' (stress on the second syllable) is obscure. Even if it is related to Go *hakuls** 'cloak' and OE *hǣcen* ~ *hēcen* 'goat' (Woeste [1857:431-32]; Feist[3-4], AEW, *hǫkull*; WP I:336; IEW, 517), nothing follows from this fact for *heifer*, despite Raucq's statement to the contrary (1939:49). The Russian word loses all relevancy if it is a cognate of Skt *ajáḥ* 'billy goat,' regardless of whether *k-* in *koza* is old or prothetic. But *koza* may be of Turkic origin (see the conflicting views on this word in Vasmer II:277-78; ESSI XII:19-20, and Chernykh I:408). Etymological links between *heifer* and OE *hæfer* 'goat' (related to OI *hafr*, L *caper*, Ir *gabhar*, and so on)—Skinner, Leo (1842:512), Smythe Palmer, Shipley (1945), and Gottlieb (1931:17)—based on the idea that both mean 'swift, bounding animal' (Pictet [1859-63, I:347, 368]: L *caper* and Skt *capala* 'swift') should be dismissed on phonetic grounds. The etymologies that relate *heifer* to some form of the root *hang* (for a heifer is covered *a tauro*: W. Barnes [1862:142]), E *havier* 'gelded fallow deer' (G. W. [1850]), OE *eofer* 'boar' (Paley [1882:462]), and OE *cælf* 'calf' (Drake 1907: 221-22/ 518n) lack all foundation.

Hebr פַּר (*par*) 'bull,' פָּרָה (*parah*) 'cow' and other related Semitic words (CEDHL, 522) can be compared with *heifer*, Gk πόρις 'heifer,' and the rest only if the second component of *heahfore* is a cognate of OE *fear(r)* and if this animal name is a migratory Eurasian word (see W [1828], Charnock [1889], P. Haupt [1889-90:114-5, note], Muss-Arnolt [1890:250], P. Haupt [1906:155, note 1], Cohen [1975] with reference to his earlier discussion; Möller [1911:112], at *[1]*k̑e-*, where *-fer* in OE *hehfor* [sic], mistranslated as *Bock*, is said to be related not only to L *caper*, OI *hafr*, and so on but also to OE *s-ceap* 'sheep'; L. Brunner does not mention *heifer* [1969]). The similarity between the Hebrew and the Germanic word attracted the attention of Luther, who regularly used *farre* where the Vulgate text had *vitulus*. Apparently, he searched for both a gloss and a look-alike (Ising [1960: 48]).

4. **In *hĕahfŏre*, the most likely Old English form of *heifer*, *hĕah-* is probably related to **hæg* 'enclosure,' as Wedgwood suggested.** The element *-fore* might be a weakened variant of *-fare* = *fear(r)* 'bullock' or of the Old English etymon of *farrow* 'not in calf,' because in West Germanic, *a* and *o* tended to alternate before and after *r*. Some examples include OFr *fora* ~ *fara* 'before,' OE *rador* ~ *rodor* 'heaven,' MHG *verwarren* ~ *verworren* 'confused,' and the Middle English doublets *scorn* ~ *scarn* 'scorn' (see more at RABBIT).

However, the fact that Old English lacked a cognate of MDu *verse* and that *farrow* surfaced only in the 15th century makes such an etymology vulnerable. **The second element of *heahfore* seems to be the same suffix as in OE *felofor* and a few other words (see FIELDFARE). *Heahfore* then meant 'occupant of an enclosure.'** This is admittedly a vague gloss. At present, bull calves are castrated about six months after they are born, at which point the calves are separated from their mothers but are kept together. If in older days the castration of young bulls occurred later, young cows may have been put into special enclosures, to protect them from the male animals. Or perhaps (a less likely hypothesis) *heahfore* was first applied to all calves and only with time acquired its more special meaning. A more definitive answer about the origin of *heifer* would be possible if we knew more about cattle breeding in the days of King Alfred.

Words designating 'place for sucking calves' abound: cf *cauf kit*, *cauf crib*, *kid crow*, and *kid crew* in the Cheshire dialect (Wilbraham [1821:22, 30]). Animal names from animals' 'houses' are common. Such are *stallion* from *stall*, Du *hokkeling* from *hok* (see above), and, according to Must (1957:63), OE *hengest*, but no one seems to have accepted his etymology. OE *hlōse* 'pigsty' provides a possible parallel, assuming that *hlōs* meant 'pig' or 'boar.' Note the numerous attempts to connect OI *kvíga* 'heifer' with *kví* 'enclosure for the cattle' or, conversely, to dissociate one from the other (Elmevik

[1971] and [1984:134-40], both with exhaustive references to earlier works).

Of interest is Skt *gṛṣṭíḥ* 'heifer.' Uhlenbeck calls this word unexplained (KEWAS, 82) and does not discuss it. Petersson (1916:240-44) relates it to the root **g^{u}erbh* ~ **g^{u}erebh* 'be bursting with life's force' (as in Skt *gárbhaḥ* 'womb, fruit of the womb,' Gk βρέφος 'fruit, child, *etc*,' and Russ *zherebenok* 'foal'). Liebert (1949:195) supported that etymology, and KEWA, I:344, finds it "not improbable." None of them mentioned Fay's conjecture (1913:31): *gṛṣṭíḥ* from **g(h)ṛd(h)-sthis* 'standing in a stall' (supposedly akin to Av *gərəda-* 'hole'). Fay's whole section "Names of Animals and their Stalls" (1913:31-32) is instructive. Assuming that the etymology of *heahfore* proposed here is persuasive, the 'enclosing' of heifers has nothing to do with building fences around or gathering together herds, as a supporter of Trier might conclude. See Go *wiþrus* 'herd (of pigs)' in Feist[3-4] and J. de Vries's variations on the theme of Trier's fence at *reini* 'horse' and *ráði* 'boar' in AEW.

The change *-fore* > *-fre* in *heahfore* may be due to syncope (though *-fre* occurs in other animal names: one of them is OE *culfre* 'culver, wood pigeon'), but *-fru* poses problems. Some changes caused by folk etymology are possible under the influence of a word meaning 'woman': cf the West Norwegian cow name *Hornfru* and the like (Stoltz [1935:52]; see also Edlinger [1886:99], Falk [1925b:136-7], and NEW, *kween*).

According to IEW, 537-38, *hek-* in ME *hekfer* may have meant 'horn.' However, in the name of a young cow, *hec-* and *hek-* (OE **hec* as in OE *fōdderhec* 'ruck for fodder, crib for hay') much more probably referred to 'fence, rail, gate.' **If OE **hecfore* existed, it must have been understood as a doublet of **hægfore* since both *hæg-* and *hec-* designated some sort of enclosure. When *-g* (the fricative [ɣ]) was devoiced, **hæhfore* (< **hægfore*) became *heahfore* by Old English breaking. The two forms (**hecfore* and *heahfore* < **hæhfore*) continued as variants of the same word into early Middle English.**

Although when calves are weaned and given hay, the change is sometimes reflected in their names (see G *Heurind, Heukalb* in Gabriel [1986:165]), *hay* 'dry grass' is unrelated to *heifer* (despite the suggestions to this effect by Minsheu and Skinner). The Old English for *hay* was *hieg, heg* and *hig*. A. Brown (1972:84, note 7) suggests that the modern spelling of *heifer* may be partly due to a folk etymological connection with *hay*. In that case, the idea of the change [ei] > [e] is wrong, but the pronunciation [hefə(r)] is not reminiscent of [hei]. Folk etymology would have affected the sound shape of the word rather than its spelling.

5. *Heifer* is so hard to explain that most old dictionaries limit their etymological rubrics to the reference: OE *heahfore*. Some authors label it as a word of unknown origin (Mätzner [1878-85:398], Skeat[4], OED, LEDEL). **The etymology offered here resolves itself into the following. OE **hægfore* consisted of **hæg-* 'enclosure' and the suffix *-fore*, the overall meaning being 'occupant of an enclosure.' By later phonetic processes, **hægfore* became **hæhfore* and the latter became *hĕahfore*. It may have had a doublet, OE **hecfore* (in which *hec-* meant 'rail, fence, gate' and *-fore* meant 'occupant,' as above). In some dialects, *heahfore* yielded [heifə(r)], in others, [hefə(r)]. Standard English *heifer* reflects the spelling of the first group and the pronunciation of the second. A change from *-hf-* to *-kf-* in the history of this word is unlikely** (Liberman [1988a and b]).

HEMLOCK (700)

The closest cognate of hemlock *is LG* Hemer(n) *'hellebore.' The root* hem-, *as follows from the Slavic and Baltic cognates of* Hemer(n), *means 'poison, sickness; injury.' The Old English name of this plant is extant in the variants* hymblicæ, hymlic, *and* hemlic. *Comparative data show that* b *in* hymblicæ *is not an intrusive consonant caused by the presence of* m. *Nor is it necessary to regard* hemlic *as a Kentish form. Rather we have three related roots:* hym- *and* hem-, *connected by ablaut, and* hymb-. *Those roots are in turn reminiscent of* han-, hen-, hun-, *designating 'death, poison; mutilation.' The suffix* -lic, *also attested in OE* cerlic *'charlock,' is probably akin to Gmc* -ling, *occurring in G* Schierling *'hemlock.' The original form of the Old English word may have been* *hem-l-ing *or* *hem-l-ig, *with* -ig *as in* īfig *'ivy.' The suffix* -lic *was rare and unproductive, whence folk etymological substitutions, one of which yielded ModE* hemlock.

The sections are devoted to 1) the existing etymologies of hemlock, *2) the origin of* hem-, *and 3) the history of* -lock.

1. OE *hymblicæ* first occurs in the *Epinal Glosses* (700), where it is paired with L *cicūta*, for which Old English glosses also offer *wōdewistle*, literally 'a whistle (that is, stalk) of madness.' *Wōd-* had the same root as the divine name *Wōdan*. Could *wōdewistle* originally mean Wodan's 'whistle'? Religious connotations have been detected in HENBANE as well. The form *hemlic* surfaced in the year 1000. This chronology gave rise to the idea that *e* in *hemlock* is of Kentish origin (the earliest example of *y* > *e* in Kent is dated 958; see Luick [1964:sec 183], SB [1965:sec 31, note 1], and esp A. Campbell

[1959:secs 289-90]). The etymology of *hemlock* revolves around the following questions: 1) What is the relation of *hym-* to *hem-?* 2) What is the etymological value of *b* in *hymblicæ?* 3) Since the word *hemlic* consists of two parts, what is *hem-* ~ *hymb-*, and what is *-lik?* 4) Insofar as *luc* in *hemeluc* dates to 1265, while *hem(e)lok* turned up for the first time in 1400, how did *-lic* change to *-lock*?

The etymologists of the pre-Skeat era (Minsheu, Skinner, Junius, Lemon, Todd in Johnson-Todd, Richardson, and Wedgwood) offer no hypotheses on the derivation of *hemlock.* Minsheu gives *Wüterich* as the German name of the plant. Craig's dictionary (1848-49) mentions *water hemlock,* which it misidentifies with *cowbane* (*cowbane* is *Cicuta virosa,* in contradistinction to *hemlock* '*Cicuta maculata*'). The roots of all species of *Cicuta* are a deadly poison.

The earliest guess on the origin of *hemlock* belongs to **Webster** (1828), who **suggested**, although without certainty, **that *hemlock* may have meant *hem-lock* 'border-plant, a plant growing in hedges.'** His etymology disappeared from Webster's dictionary only in 1890. Ettmüller (1851:453, 463) and Koch (1867:321) conjecture the same. Ettmüller offered the series **himan—*ham—*hēmun—*humen* 'heap up, raise up; cover, hide; hinder, hamper,' which he believed to have recognized in Go *himins* 'heaven.' He cited *hem* 'leather sock; stripped-off clothes' (the language of this word is not specified, but cf OE *hemming* 'boot' and OFr *hemminge* 'leather sack; boot'). With some hesitation he proposed to interpret *hemlock* as meaning 'border plant.' But such a gloss name would fit plantain rather than hemlock, which thrives not on the roadside but in waste places, on banks, and under walls.

Mueller said, in the first edition of his dictionary, that *hem-* is hardly the same element as *haem* ~ *hām* often occurring in plant names, and in the second edition he only amplified Ettmüller's gloss. Almost at the same time, Chambers's dictionary cited, with a question mark, *hæm* and *healm* 'stubble, from the straw-like appearance of the withered plant' as a possible cognate of *hem-*. Is this what Mueller meant by *haem* and *hām*? OE *he(a)lm* 'haulm' never appears without *l.* Stratmann (see Stratmann[3]) compared *hem-* in *hemlock* with ME *heme* (related to MHG *hem*) 'malign,' but, like his predecessors, added a question mark. He cited the phrase *heme and hine.* Although the Middle High German adjective has the meaning 'rebellious, evil,' the Middle English phrase contains a different word. Bradley, in his revision of Stratmann's dictionary, wrote *hēme and hine* and glossed *hēme* (with a long vowel) 'from ?*hām;* man, head of family' (so 'the head of a family and his domestics'). MED says 'household servants.'

Skeat[1] acknowledged that the meaning of ME *hem* was "not quite certain" but added that *hem-* in *hemlock* "still means something bad." Later he proposed a different etymology (Skeat [1907-10:340]). **He pointed to the similarity of *hymb-* in OE *hymblicæ* to Lith *kum̃pas* 'crooked.'** He would have offered what seems to be an acceptable solution if he had not stopped at the meaning of *kum̃pas,* which suggested to him "that *hymblicæ* meant precisely 'crooked-like'; from the remarkably angular growth of its jointed branches." Crookedness could not have been chosen as the most conspicuous feature of a plant like hemlock. (In the last edition of CED, that etymology has been omitted.)

The problem of *-b-* also remains. **Holthausen (AeEW) wondered whether *hymlice* was not related to OE *hymele* 'hop' (a plant name).** His shaky suggestion, repeated in W[3], WNWD[3], and Barnhart, should be abandoned. The only basis for Holthausen's etymology is the phonetic similarity between the two words. Despite several authoritative statements to the contrary, OE *hymele* (related to OI *humli*) is isolated in Germanic. Comparison with Nynorsk *hamla* and *humla* 'grope around' has little value. *Climb* and *grope* are not synonyms, and just as *hemlock* is not another angular plant, *hymele* is not another climber. *Hymele* seems to have reached Europe from the East (see a detailed discussion in ESSI VIII:141-45), whereas hemlock is a native plant, and its name is probably also native. Folk etymology may have connected *hymele* and *hymlic* (it would be strange if it did not: one plant kills, the other deprives people of the power of reasoning), but that late association has nothing to do with their origin.

2. **The guesses on the origin of *hemlock* are the result of a rare oversight, for the etymology of its closest kin LG *Hemern* (OHG *hemera,* MHG *hemer, hemere,* LG *Hemer* and *Hemern* 'hellebore' = G *Nieswurz* 'Helleborus L.' and 'Veratrum L.') was explained long ago. Its cognate in Proto-Slavic is **chemeru* ~ **chemera.*** Here are the meanings of some of the reflexes of **chemeru* in the modern Slavic languages (ESSI IV:52-53): 'misfortune,' 'poison,' 'devil,' 'bitterness,' 'chagrin, disgust, fury,' 'pus in a wound; gall.' They designate numerous diseases of human beings and animals and a certain poisonous plant, which often has a suffix: for example, *chemeritsa* and *chemerka;* see ESSI

IV:52-53 and Vasmer IV:331-32 (*chemer*), where Baltic cognates are cited. Apparently, we have the reflexes of Balto-Slavic and Germanic **kem-er,* with *kem-* meaning 'poison; sickness; injury.'

In Germanic, many words may be related to *hem-* in G *Hem-er* and E *hem-lock.* Although the derivation of some of them is debatable, a provisional list is worth giving. OHG *hamm* 'infirm' (only in Otfrid III, 4:8), OHG *hamal* 'wether, castrated ram' (ModG *Hammel,* from the adjective *hamal* 'mutilated;' the same element occurs in OI *hamalkyrni* 'some sort of grain,' possibly without bristles); MHG *hem* 'rebellious, evil,' mentioned above (ModG *hämisch*). The confusion of MHG *hemisch* and *heimisch* that troubles Seebold (KS: *hämish*) has an exact parallel in the examples cited by Siebs (1892:151; alongside *Fru Hinn*—about whom see HENBANE—*Freund Hein* 'devil' is known; he is Old Henry's German counterpart). The meaning of MHG *hamen* and *hemmen* (ModG *hemmen* 'hinder, hamper'), E *hem,* and OI *hemja* 'hold back, restrain' accords well with the idea of debilitating and castrating ('mutilate, cut off' and 'delimit, enclose, hinder'). E *ham* 'plot of pasture or meadow land' and *ham* 'hollow or bend of the knee,' later 'thigh of a hog used for food,' may belong here too. Both compound verbs with *ham-* (*hamstring* and *hamshackle*) refer to injury. Less clear is the origin of E *hamper* (v).

In the zero grade, we find E *humble-(bee)* and E reg *humble* 'hornless' (said about cows). However natural it may seem to explain *humble-bee, bumble-bee*'s twin, as a humming insect, such an explanation is almost certainly wrong, for the Proto-Indo-European root of *humble-* is **kem- ~ *kom.* ESSI IV:145-46 and X:169-71 supports the idea of the onomatopoeic origin of **kem- ~ *kom-,* but strong faith is needed to hear [kem] or [kom] in the sounds made by bees and mosquitoes. In the past, humble-bees were often confused with drones, and it was known that drones did not collect honey. A humble-bee is thus 'a defective bee,' belonging with a hornless cow and a castrated ram.

The protocow of Scandinavian mythology was called *Auðhumla.* The element *humla* corresponds to E *humble* 'hornless' and a few similar adjectives in Germanic dialects (OED; its cognates in Baltic and Slavic are less certain; see Sabaliauskas [1964:59-61], and ESSI VII:18-19, XI:174-75). A. Noreen (1918) glossed the name as 'rich hornless cow,' which makes little sense, even though according to Icelandic tradition, Búkolla, the hornless cow, was endowed with magical properties (see especially Uspenskij [2000:121-22]). In Icelandic, *-hum(b)l-* 'hornless' has not been recorded.

Three words were spelled *auðr* in Old Icelandic. Besides *auðr* 'riches' (and *auðr* 'fate'), *auðr* 'desolate; desert' occurred. The *Younger Edda* tells that when the frost surrounding the world thawed, it became a cow called *Auðhumla.* Her milk fed the primordial giant, and she licked the first man out of the salty ice blocks. She was probably 'the destroyer of the desert.' Ebbinghaus (1989b:4) discussed similar possibilities (*auð-* 'wasteland' and 'wealth') in deciphering the *cognomenta* of two Germanic matronae and glossed AVDRINEHAE ~ AVTHRINEHAE as 'matres of the waste land.' Kure (2003:315) developed a theory that the universe of the Scandinavian myth was created from "a scream" and understood *Auðhumla* as 'abundance of humming.' This is a fanciful etymology.

The above survey shows that *-b-* appears in the *ham- ~ hum-* words too regularly to be dismissed as a parasitic sound caused by the presence of *m-*, as in E *nimble* and *fumble.* We have E *hamble* versus OE *hamelian,* along with E *humble-bee,* and OHG *humbal* versus Du *hommel.* Even *Auðhumla* had the doublet *Auðhumbla.* Go *hamfs** 'maimed,' Lith *kum̃pas* 'crooked,' the Sanskrit glossary word *kumpaḥ* 'with maimed hands,' and Gk σκαμβός 'bow-legged' (IEW:918) make it clear that the labial consonant does not depend on the position between *m* and *l.* H. Schröder (1910:16-21) included a few more words (for example, E *hive*) in his entry on *hamble, humbal,* and others, but those already cited point unambiguously to **han- ~ *hen- ~ *hun-* and **hamb- ~ *humf-,* all of them referring to death, poison, and mutilation.

It seems as though *b* were caused by the presence of *m,* but in reality **n* probably changed to *m* before *b* or *f,* and the result was **han- ~ *hanf-,* and so on. We find that root in *hymblicæ* and *hymlic. Hemlic* may be a Kentish form, but more probably *hymlic* and *hemlic* were variants of the same word, whereas *hymblicæ* is an independent variant of that plant name.

3. The second part of *hemlock* is more obscure than the first. Mahn (in W [1864]), compared *hemlock* with *charlock,* another name of wild mustard. Old English had *cydilc, cedelc,* and *cyrlic* (again with the alternation *e ~ y*). In Modern English, *charlock* coexists with *kedlock* (OED also cites *cadlock,* first recorded in 1655) and reg *carlock, carlick, kerlock, kellock, kedlock,* and *kilk.* Its cognates are G *Kettich,* LG *ködich,* and Dan (reg) *kiddik* (H. Schröder [1909:588]). **In both *hemlock* and *charlock*, *-lock* appeared relatively late. It is *-lic* and *-lc* that need an explanation.**

In Partridge's opinion (1958), "the suffix *-lic* suggests that the Old English noun was originally an adjective: perhaps *hymlīce* is a contraction of **hymelelīc* '(a herb) like the hop vine of the bryony or the convolvulus,' OE *hymele* being applied indifferently to all three vine-like or climbing herbs. There may even be some obscure pun on the deadliness of the hemlock—and of the products of the hop." Partridge did not elaborate on the nature of the pun.

Mueller[1] believed that *-lic* was OE *lēac* 'leek,' as in *garlick,* for *lēac* sometimes referred to any garden herb. Even UED says that *-lock* may be a weakened form of OE *lēac* 'vegetable,' as in *lēac-tūn* 'kitchen garden,' though Skeat (1887 = 1892:424) realized that *-lice* can hardly be *-leek,* and **OED remarks (at *charlock*): "There appears no basis for the guess that the second syllable is *lēac,* 'leek'."**

In the first edition of his dictionary, Skeat explained *-ley* in *barley* as a reflex of *lēac,* but convinced by Murray's etymology of *barley* in OED (*-ley* is from *-līk,* as in the suffix *-ly;* the original meaning of the word was 'like barley'), he considered the possibility that *-lic* in *hemlic* was of the same origin. However, the whole point is that the English suffix *-lic* acquired a Scandinavian pronunciation [lij] and lost *-k,* while *-leek* and *garlic* show *k* where it has always been.

The German for 'hemlock' is *Schierling* (OHG *skerning* and *skeriling*), now, following A. Kuhn, usually explained as 'a plant growing on dung heaps,' from **skarna-* 'dung.' The correctness of that etymology is not at issue here, but *-ling* may shed light on *-lock.* The ancient Germanic suffix *-ling* is especially common in German. J. Grimm (1890:370) cited a long list of the names of mushrooms ending in *-ling.* This suffix is a contraction of **-l-inga* (< PIE *-*lo-ē-ko*). Apparently, *-ling* alternated with *-ig* in plant names, at least in English. For instance, *ivy* descended from *īfig* (Old High German had *ebah*: see IVY). It must have been easy to borrow L *radic-* and turn it into OE *rædic* 'radish,' for the word sounded like *ræd-ic.*

Hemlic* probably goes back to *hem-l-ic,* a variant of **hem-l-ing* or **hem-l-ig. For some reasons, *-l-ic* has been recorded only in *hem-l-ic* and *cyr-l-ic* (with its doublet *cyr-l-c*), but by the year 700 the suffix had become unproductive and dead; hence the recorded forms ending in *-luk* and *-lok.* An association with *lock* is due to folk etymology, as happened in *wedlock, killock* 'stone used as an anchor' (1630), and so forth. If Skeat's etymology of *fetlock,* from *fet-l-ock* (with a double suffix), is right, we have a case reminiscent of *hem-l-ic.* ***Hemlic* (*hymlic, hymblic*) is 'a destructive, poisonous plant.' The first syllable "means something bad," as Skeat put it, and the second is a suffix whose meaning was forgotten before the settlement of Britain by Germanic tribes, assuming that *hemlic* and *hym(b)lic* were in use alongside *hemera* from time immemorial** (Liberman [2001b:135-39]).

HENBANE (1265)

The first element of the plant name henbane *seems to go back to the root* *hen- *'death,' preserved in the names of places, people, and gods. Originally, henbane was called* henbell *'death bell.' Once the meaning* *hen- *'murder, death' had been forgotten, an association of* hen- *with the bird* hen *arose,* henbell *became opaque (no connection can be established between hens and bells), and the second element was replaced with* -bane. *The resulting compound is tautological from the historical point of view ('death-murder' or 'death-death'). The belief that henbane is particularly poisonous to domestic fowls is due to an attempt to rationalize the otherwise incomprehensible word.*

The sections are devoted to 1) the existing etymologies of henbane *and 2) the ancient meaning of* hen- *and the substitution of* -bane *for* -bell.

1. *Henbane,* the common name of the plant *Hyoscyamus niger,* has no recognizable cognates except ME *hendwale* (one 1450 citation in OED; *dwale* meant 'sleeping potion') and ModG *Hühnertod* (about which see below). F *hanebane* (a variant of *hennebanne*), which De Morgan (1869) cites as a related form, is a 14th-century borrowing from English. The extant Old English name of the plant is *belene,* a migratory word. OED says that OE *hennebelle* designates the same plant.

The earliest citations of *henne-belle,* that is, *henbell,* go back to the year 1000 and then disappear until they turn up again in the herbals of 1500 and 1597, never to come to life again. The gloss *simphoniaca* does not explain *-belle,* for the resemblance between a calyx and a bell is a trivial fact (compare *bluebell, bellflower,* and the like). But the flowers of henbane (assuming that we are speaking about the same plant) do not resemble bells, and the word *henne-belle* looks like a blend of OE **hennebana* and *belene,* in which folk etymology turned *belene* into *belle* 'bell.' See some suggestions on this point in Foerste (1964b:142). Smythe Palmer (1883) thought of an earlier form **henge-belle,* but his guess has no foundation. The sentence from the *Læcebōc* (in translation: "This plant which... some people call *henne-belle*"), dated 1000, suggests that the word had limited currency.

OED explains *henbell* as *hen* + *bell.* A similar etymology has been applied to *henbane* from *hen(n)eban(e): hen + bane.* CD asserts that "the herb acts as a deadly poison to man and most animals, and is especially destructive to domestic fowls (whence the name). Swine are said to eat it with impunity." **Seeing that the narcotic and poisonous properties of henbane have been known for a long time, it is surprising that hens were chosen as its particularly vulnerable victims,** the more so as henbane grows on waste ground and on rubbish about villages and old houses (EB[11] specifies: castles), where hens hardly ever stray, while ducks and geese are attracted by ponds rather than rubbish heaps, old castles, and wasteland. Skeat glossed *henbane* as 'fowl-poison' in all the editions of his dictionary. Wyld's 'hen's pest' (UED) is similar. The names of poisonous plants like E *dogbane, cowbane,* and even *wolf's bane* (a calque from Greek via Latin) or Russ *liutik* 'buttercup' (< *liut-* 'evil, terrible'), a possible calque of L *(Ranunculus) sceleratus,* make more sense than *henbane,* as does *chicken weed,* a counterpart of the notorious *sparrow grass* < *asparagus,* admittedly a noninformative name.

Skinner thought that *henbane* is a calque of Gk ὑοσκύαμος 'pig bean' ("swine are said to eat it with impunity") and traced *-bane* to *bean*. But he failed to explain the first part. His editor Thomas Henshaw retained *hen-beans,* because the flowers of this plant "are not unlike to a bean in its blossom," to quote the translation of Skinner's remarks in *Gazophylacium.* He gave the German parallel *Saubohne* 'henbane' (now no longer used in this meaning: KS), a calque of the Greek word, possibly suggested by F *jusquiame* or Ital *giusquiamo,* both continuing the Greek-Latin name, and offered the French and Latin glosses *la mort aux oyes, anserum venenum* ('goose-bane,' as it were). Those glosses amused **Lemon**, a lexicographer who always sought the Greek origins of English words. He **was content with deriving *hen-*, or rather *(h)en-*, from Gk ἰος 'poison'; the result appeared to be **hion-bean* or **ion-bean* 'baneful bean.'** Such is the short history of the question.

2. **In all likelihood, *henbane* does not mean 'fowl poison, hen's pest' even if this plant is deadly to domestic fowls.** MA (267) say, without references, that henbane was "employed by Danish chicken-thieves to stun their victims." Etymologists have overlooked an important contribution to the history of Germanic religion that is relevant to *henbane.* Siebs (1892) reconstructed a Germanic god of death whose Old High German name he gave as **Henno Wôtan* (= Mercury). Independent of Siebs, Gallée (1901) came to the conclusion that *hen (hin)- ~ han- ~ hun-* at one time meant 'death' (independent, because he missed Siebs's article and learned about it only after the appearance of his own work; hence the sequel: Gallée [1902]). Siebs returned to this subject many years later (1930).

The traces of *hen- ~ han- ~ hun-* show up in old proper names, in place names, in magic formulas like MHG *iâ henne* (it corresponds exactly to E *oh, boy!,* for *boy,* too, meant 'bogeyman' in addition to 'little brother, servant'; see BOY), swear words, mythological names like LG *Fru Hinne,* LG *hennekled* 'shroud' and LG *henbedde* 'deathbed.' In some varieties of Dutch, the plant *Solanum Dulcamara* is called *henneblômen* (*-blômen* 'flower'), and in others, *doodebezen* 'death berries.' *Haonblom, hunenbere,* and *hunschkraut* also occur. Both Siebs and Gallée derive *hen-* from the root **ken-,* as in Gk καίνω 'kill' (aorist 2: ἔκανον).

In a short article that only Siebs (1930) and Flasdieck (1937:279, and note 3) seem to have noticed, Sarrazin (1911) detected the root *hen-* 'death' in numerous words that ostensibly have no relation to hens. Among other things, he discussed Herne the hunter, whom Shakespeare mentioned in *The Merry Wives of Windsor* (IV:4). Siebs (1930:58-59) developed his idea in detail, but Flasdieck (1937:333-36) showed that *Herne* and *Henne* are incompatible from the phonetic point of view. He admitted (1937:278-80, 282) that the Germanic god *Henno* is a shadowy figure but accepted the existence of Henno Wodan.

Because of taboo, the names of chthonic deities are often changed beyond recognition, which makes isolating them in modern words difficult. For example, *hein-* (in *Heinrich*) may be a doublet of *hen-,* but this is not certain. G *Hain* is apparently a continuation of *Hagene* (Güntert [1919:117]), while attempts to discover the root *hein-* in G *Heimchen* 'cricket' and connect crickets with the souls of either unborn or departing souls fail to convince. See Menzel (1861), Much (1932:48), KM (rewritten in KS but still with reference to Much) and MOOCH, sec 2.

Sarrazin's list of English place names beginning with *Hen-* is of special interest. Many of them go back to OE *hēan-* 'high' (accusative) and *hinde* 'hind, doe,' but some defy an explanation. Neither Ekwall (1960) nor A. H. Smith (1956) was aware of the works by Sarrazin, Siebs, and Gallée. **Sarrazin suggested that *hen-* in *henbane* meant 'death.' This is a reasonable hypothesis.**

The oldest name of henbane evidently was *henbell,* whatever the origin of the second element *-belle* 'bell' may have been. Hens do not wear bells, and, as pointed out, the flowers of henbane are not bell-shaped. The meaning of *hen-* was forgotten, and *-bane* replaced *bell.* From the historical point of view, *henbane* is a tautology ('death-death,' 'death-murder,' or 'poison-death')—not a rare phenomenon in the development of disguised and even transparent compounds; see SLOWWORM for a detailed discussion of tautological compounds. G *Hühnertod* is also the result of folk or pseudolearned etymology (HDA). Siebs (1930:61) cited *Himmelloch* 'a hole in heaven' and *Hühnerloch* 'hens' hole' for *Hinnerloch* 'hell,' a more nonsensical word than *Hühnertod.* Förster (1917:130, note 4) cited G *Hühnerlochkraut.*

Henno was not the only name of Wodan ~ Wuotan used in the West Germanic popular flower lore. Another one may have been related to OI *Njótr:* see Bierbaumer's explanation of the Old English plant name *Fornētes folm* (1974). Some Dutch plant names beginning with *hemd-* and Danish plant names beginning with *hund-* may also contain the root **hen- ~ *hun-.* Perhaps *hen-* initially referred to the medicinal properties of *hennebelle,* a pain*killer* (for example, it alleviated tooth pain). See Alessio's comments on L *vāticina* 'henbane' and its religious connotations (1969:92-94). But the origin of the name *hennebelle* as a pharmaceutical term is, on the whole, unlikely.

**Ken-* had a double, namely, **kent-* 'pierce.' The root **kent-* seems to be present in G *Himbeere* < *hindberi ~ hintberi* 'raspberry,' related to OE *hindberie ~ hindberige*: Hermodsson (1990) (Liberman [2001b:132-35]).

A Note on *hebenon* in *Hamlet* I, 5:62

The Ghost tells Hamlet that Claudius poured "juice of cursèd hebenon" into his ears. Such a plant does not exist and guesses about the origin of Shakespeare's word have been numerous. Even in the 17th century no one seemed to know for sure what substance was meant, for alongside *Hebenon* of First Folio (1623), *Hebona* occurs in the Quartos (see the forms in J. Wilson [1934:380]). Furness (1877:101-02) lists the earlier conjectures: 1) *hebenon* is the metathesized form of *henebon* 'henbane,' 2) *hebenon* stands for *ebony,* regardless of whether the English or some Romance word occurred in the manuscript (Nares was among the supporters of this view), 3) perhaps *hemlock* was intended, 4) *hebenon* may have been a misspelling of *enoron,* one of the names, at that time, of *Solanum maniacum,* called also deadly nightshade. The equations *hebenon = henbane* or *ebony* can be supported by references to other authors of the Elizabethan epoch.

Since 1877 *hebenon* has been discussed in several publications. Nicholson (1880-82) advanced a series of arguments against the henbane theory and proposed to identify hebenon with yew (E *yew* < OE *īw ~ ēow;* G *Eibe* < OHG *îwa;* OI *ýr*). Among his followers were W. Harrison (1880-82) and Sigismund (1885). The latter, surprisingly, did not mention his predecessors, whose works he only summarized, and thus misled German students of Shakespeare. Even F. Schröder (1941:7) treated Sigismund as an authority on the meaning of *hebenon.* Nicholson and Harrison insisted on the impossibility of metathesis in Shakespeare. However, Furnivall's examples, sent to Harrison in a letter and quoted by him (p 320), show that syllables in *henebon* were occasionally transposed in the 17th century. More to the point are medical considerations. Shakespeare's contemporaries often mentioned the deleterious effect of the yew concoction, and the symptoms the Ghost described match those we find in doctors' works. OED offers an informative entry on *hebenon, hebon,* and *hebona* without taking sides, whereas CD says: "Thought to be a corruption of *henbane.*" SG has "(?) yew."

Although Nicholson and Harrison made a strong point for hebenon = yew, the case was not closed. Thiselton-Dyer (1916:506) found the equation *hebenon = henbane* the most plausible of all. Bradley (1920) shared his opinion. He, like most of his predecessors, refused to ascribe the coincidence between *juice of cursed hebenon* and Marlowe's *juice of Hebon* to chance (*Jew of Malta* III:4, 98; in some editions, 101). Since the English word *ebon* was often written with *h-,* Shakespeare (Bradley remarked) may have not distinguished between *hebenon* and *henbane.* Both Thiselton-Dyer and Bradley emphasized that, in the 16th century, henbane was believed to be deadly. Finally, according to Montgomery (1920), Shakespeare did not confuse henbane with (h)ebony, for "*hebenon* or *hebona* has its proper sense of *ebony.*" "Shakespeare, sharing a common view, regarded *lignum vitae* as a species of *ebony* and used the general term for the particular. Following a well-known tradition he then attributed to the 'juice of hebona' (that is, *guaiac*) the power of producing, in certain cases, a loathsome and leprous-like disease" (p. 306).

Many years later, the scale was again tipped in favor of henbane. R. Simpson (1947:582) pointed out that guaicum is the resin of a tree, while the Ghost mentions the juice. "The old alchemists would not be likely to use the term 'juice' loosely for two such distinctive products. Next it was a distilment and again the pharmacologists would distil henbane but not guiacum [sic]. In addition henbane in a fraction of a grain is a very potent poison. But the medicinal dose of guiacum [sic] is 5-15 grains." Simpson did not discuss the idea that hebenon could mean 'yew.'

The case is hopeless because it rests on two irreconcilable propositions: 1) Shakespeare must have had a definite plant in mind, and he was an expert in plants and poisons, 2) no plant was called *hebenon*. It is no wonder that Jenkins (1982:457) found it "probably a mistake to seek to equate *hebenon* with any familiar plant. No doubt Shakespeare drew on what he had heard or read of well-known poisons, but he surely relied (like Marlowe, to judge from his context) on a suggestion of the fabulous to intensify the horror."

Other editors are equally noncommittal. Only P. Edwards (1985:108) refers to Simpson. Most popular books, like Savage (1923:150), equate hebenon with yew. However, from the standpoint of medicine and pharmacology, *henbane* would be a better gloss for *hebenon*. Such is also Dent's opinion (1971:63-64). Of the works dealing specifically with Shakespeare's flora, only Grindon (1883:47, note) deserves mention, for, as he says, he had proposed the equation hebenon = yew twenty years before Nicholson and Harrison.

Hebenon was probably henbane, but it remains a mystery why Marlowe and Shakespeare did not say so in plain (Elizabethan) English.

HOBBLEDEHOY (1540)

Hobbledehoy *occurred in numerous variants. The first element has been compared to E* hobble, *E* hoyden, *OF* hubi *(the past participle of* hubir *'cause to thrive'), OF* hobe ~ *E* hobby, *F* hobel ~ hoberel ~ hob(e)ran *'country squire,' F* hober *'remove from place to place,' Sp* hombre *'today,' and some nonexistent Dutch words. Those etymologists seem to have been on the right track who understood* hob- *as a pet name for* Robert, *which was also one of the names of the Devil. The second element is less clear, but the whole may have started as* *Robert-le-Roy *and* *Rob-le-Roy. *When* Hob- *was substituted for* Rob-, Roy *followed suit, which resulted in the meaningless jingle* *hobert-le-hoy *and later* hobbledehoy *under the influence of folk etymology, as though the hobbledehoy had an awkward and clumsy gait ("hobbled"). In its present form,* hobbledehoy *has an 'infix'* -de-. *Both* -de- *and* -te- *often occur in the names of devils and sprites* (Flibber-ti-gibbet *and the like). These infixes have the same function as* -a- *in* ragamuffin, *so that* hobbledehoy *turns out to be an extended form. It can be glossed approximately as 'devil-a-devil'.*

The sections are devoted to 1) the attested forms of hobbledehoy *and the early attempts to explain the word's origin, 2)* Hob *as a pet name for* Robert *and the development of* *Robert-le-Roy *to* hobbledehoy, *3) a short summary of the proposed etymology and the further history of* -dehoy, *and 4) the role of* -de- ~ -te- *as infixes used in extended forms.*

1. The recorded variants of the noun *hobbledehoy* (1540) are unusually many. It was spelled with two hyphens or without any and as two or three separate words. The first element appeared in the forms *hob(b)le-*, *hob(b)a-*, as well as *hobbe-*, *hobby-*, *hobo-*, *hobbi-*, *hobbard-*, and *hab(b)er-* (OED; a similar array of forms appears in EDD). *Hobble-*, *hobbe-*, and *hobber(d)-* reflect different pronunciations rather than the instability of spelling; this is especially true of *hobble* and *hobber-*. The middle syllable could be *-de-*, *-di-*, *-dy-*, *-da-*, and *-ty-*.

According to OED, *hobbledehoy* is "[a] colloquial word of unsettled form and uncertain origin. One instance in *hobble-* occurs in 1540; otherwise *hober-*, *hobber-*, are the prevailing forms before 1700; these, with the forms *hobe-* ~ *hobby-*, suggest that the word is analogous in structure to *Hoberdidance*, *hobbididance*, and *hobidy-booby*, q.v.: cf. also HOBERD. Some of the variants are evidently due to the effort of popular etymology to put some sense into an odd and absurd-looking word. It is now perh[aps] most frequently associated with *hobble*, and taken to have ludicrous reference to an awkward and clumsy gait." A brief mention of the fact that Ray, Jamieson, Forby, and Skeat tried to explain *hobbledehoy* follows that summary. The derivation of *hobbledehoy* from F *hob(e)rau* 'hobby' (a kind of hawk) is then called into question, but OED offers no etymology of its own. *Hobbididance* is a fiend like *flibbertigibbet*; OED has two citations for it (1603 and 1605). *Hoberd* (one citation, 1450) is a term of reproach. *Hobidy-booby* (1720, also one citation) possibly means 'scarecrow.'

W (1864) cites E reg *hobbledygee* (without a reference, but the source is Halliwell) 'with a limping movement' and suggests that we compare it with *hobbledehoy*. The main question is whether the tie between *hobbledehoy* and *hobble* is original. Chance (1887:524) answered it in the affirmative. A lad from fourteen upward, he says, "is uncertain, physically and morally, whether he will turn out ill or well. And besides this he frequently has an awkward and shambling gait, to which the term may more especially have been applied." But OED is probably right in stating that *hobbledehoy* is only now most frequently associated with *hobble*. Before 1700, the prevailing forms were those with *hober-* and *hobber*. *Hobbledygee* and *hobble-de-poise* may allude to unsteady movement, but it does not follow that *hobbledehoy* belongs with them. The picture becomes even more blurred if *hubble-te-shives* (Halliwell), a synonym of *hubbleshow* or *hubbleshoo* 'commotion, hubbub' (1515; OED), is taken into account. It is not necessary to reduce all *hobble-* and *hubble-* words to a single etymon (and no one has tried to connect *hubble-te-shives* and *hobbledehoy*).

Most early conjectures on the origin of *hobbledehoy* mentioned but not summarized in OED are unrevealing. Ray (whom Skeat and Forby quote) derived *hobbledehoy* from Sp *hombre de hoy* 'man of today'— a meaningless gloss. Forby (1830:161-62) combined OF *hubi*, the past participle of *hubir* 'cause to thrive by wholesome diet,' and *hui* 'today' (as in F *aujour d'hui*) and obtained 'one well thriven [sic] now,' that is, 'well-grown lad.' "The change of vowels," he says, "is absolutely nothing. It may have been made after the word became ours, for the rhyme's sake ('hobi-de-hoy, / Neither man nor boy')." Wilbraham suggested to Forby that *Hobby* is *Robin*, and *hoy* is *hoyt*, or *hoyden* (see his comments on *Hobbity Hoy* in Wilbraham [1821:28]). According to his etymology, *hobbledehoy* is *Robin the hoyden*, or *hoyt*. Forby treated Wilbraham's suggestion as probable: "...by a metathesis in the last word, we come immediately to *hobbitehoy*." Jamieson thought that *hobbledehoy* is a French word and cited F *hobreau* (as it occurs in Cotgrave) 'country squire' ("*hobbledehoy* has been undoubtedly borrowed from the French *Hobereau;*" note the use of *undoubtedly*, so common in works on word origin).

Ker derived *hobbledehoy* from (what he called Dutch) *hoop beldt de hoy* 'it is by being formed into the heap (by heapings) that grass matures into hay,' implying, as he explains, that "with the various gradations of heapings and gradual increasings of size (well known to haymakers), grass in the last and largest of such forms, becomes hay, and is considered fit for its intended use." The result is that *hobbledehoy* is 'he whose increase of size portends a near approach to the maturity of manhood, neither man nor boy' (Ker 1837, I:84).

Skeat (1885-87:302-03 = 1901:731-32) traced *hobbledehoy* to F *hobel* (= *hoberel, hob(e)ran*), originally 'country squire,' which he misunderstood as 'villain,' and *de hoy* 'today,' that is, he partly repeated the etymologies of Ray and Forby. His translation of the compound from French was 'vile fellow of today.' Neither the gloss nor the contrived etymology has much appeal (see Chance's critique [1887:523]). *Hobel*, in Skeat's opinion, "is a diminutive of OFr. *hobe*, a hobby, and is allied to the E. *hobby*, a sparrow-hawk, a hawk of small size and inferior kind, whence it passed into a term of contempt." In the last edition of his concise dictionary, not a trace of that early etymology is left (*hobbledehoy* is said to be of unknown origin). Skeat called *hoy* an unmeaning suffix and mentioned Sc *hoy* 'shout' (noun and verb). But in the full edition, he again cited (for comparison) F *hober* 'remove from place to place' (Cotgrave's gloss) that he mentioned in his early article and added *hopptihopp* 'a giddy, flighty, eccentric man' (from Alsace) and *hupperling* 'boy who jumps about and cannot be still' (from Low German). **However, he ended his entry with reference to *hobby* 'pet name for *Robert*,' as did Wilbraham, and herein lies the most important clue to the origin of *hobbledehoy*.**

2. *Hob* 'sprite, elf' is short for *Rob*. This name also happens to be the first element of *hobgoblin*. Robin Godfellow (English) and Knecht Ruprecht (German) are medieval names of evil spirits (see ROBIN). It is reasonable to assume that the spelling *hoberdehoy* renders *hoberd-de-hoy* and that *hobbledehoy* is a folk etymological reshaping of that form. In 1557 Thomas Tusser published the book *Fiue Hundred Pointes of Good Husbandrie*. In one of its chapters, a human life is divided into twelve periods, each lasting seven years. The chapter begins so (see it in Tusser 1878:138, 60/3): "The first seuen years, bring vp a childe; / The next, to learning, for waxing too wilde; / The next, keepe under sir hobbard-de-hoy."

Tusser's verse has often been discussed in connection with *hobbledehoy* (Johnson-Todd, Halliwell, W.W.E.T. [1852], H.B.F. [1872], Skeat [1885-87:302-03]). Skeat understood *under* as an adverb (*keepe under / sir hobbard-de-hoy*, not *keep [the child] / under sir hobbard-de-hoy*). No other reading makes sense. The meaning then is: until the age of seven, bring up (take care of) your child; at the age between seven and fourteen, teach him, lest he get out of hand; at the age between fourteen and twenty-one, suppress Sir Hobbard de Hoy. Sir Hobbard de Hoy is the Devil, the call of sex. Tusser had a clear notion of when lust should be satisfied, when it is too late to start, and when it stops being attractive. Evidently, before a young man turns twenty-one, it should be kept in check. *Hobbard* is a side-form of *Robert*. (Perhaps a trace of the ancient devilry can be discerned in E reg *hobblety-hoy* 'large, unmanageable top': Brocket.)

The second half of the puzzle is *-dehoy*. *Hoy*, as Wilbraham pointed out, is reminiscent of *hoyden*, originally 'rude person of either sex.' Both Richardson and Ogilvie (ID, 1850) compared them. Skinner believed that *hoyden* was an Anglicized variant of MDu *heiden* 'heathen, gipsy.' OED accepted his etymology for want of a better one. But in the entry on *hoit* 'indulge in riotous and noisy mirth; move clumsily' (the word that is the basis of *hoity-toity* 'riotous behavior, romping'), it follows Brandreth (1885:vii), and *hoyden* turns up again. *Hoyden*, understood as *hoitin*, with intervocalic *d* from *t*, is more likely than *hoyden* identified with MDu *heiden*. The Celtic derivation of *hoyden* (see Johnson-Todd, with additions in Mackay [1877]) has been discredited, for the Welsh word is apparently a borrowing from English. *Hoyden* hardly has any connections with *hobbledehoy*.

Chance (1887:524) compared *hobbledygee* ~ *hobbledehoy* with carters' and waggoners' cry *gee-haw*. (Is Skeat's *hoy*, a shout used in Scotland, an attempt to improve on Chance's hypothesis?) According to him, the first word meant 'turning right' and the other, 'turning left.' He visualized balances as in *hobberdepoise*, with the needle wobbling about the middle point. Then, he says, these terms began to be applied to people, but he was at a loss to explain why a hobbledehoy should be someone inclining to the left.

The alliteration binding the elements of *hobbledehoy* is obvious. RHD states that *hobbledehoy* consists of *hoberd* (which seems to be correct) + *y* + *hoy* for *boy*, with *b* > *h* for alliteration. The part of the etymology about -*y* + *boy* (as in Forby) lacks foundation. **More persuasive is J. Hughes's conjecture (1954:606). He posits the initial form **Robert le Roy*, that is, King Robert. After *Robert* became *Hobar(d)*, *Roy* followed suit, and its *r* also changed to *h*.** The existence of King Robert is probable, and there must have been an element of humor in giving Robert Bruce an affectionate name King Hobbe. Hobard-de-Hoy is a sibling of three fiends mentioned in *King Lear*, namely Hobberdidance, Obidicut (also known as Haberdicut), and Flibbertigibbet. One of them danced, another may have been fond of cutting capers (Chance 1887:524, note), but *hobber* in their names, contrary to Chance's suggestion, did not refer to hopping.

3. The development of *hobbledehoy* can be reconstructed so: 1) One of the many names of an evil spirit, or the Devil, was **Robert le Roy*. 2) In popular speech, Robert was replaced with *Hob, Hobard, *Hobert*, and so on. 3) *Roy* adjusted to the new pronunciation and became *hoy*; the result was a piece of alliterative gibberish. 4) **Hobert le Hoy* degraded further into *Hobert-de-hoy*, for fiends' names typically had -*de*- in the middle. Although a desemanticized word in Tusser's days, it was still remembered as the Devil's name. 5) Evil sprites and all kinds of hobgoblins are occasionally represented as diminutive creatures, and conversely, children tend to be associated with devils of small stature. A classic example is the history of *imp*: from 'offshoot' in Old English to 'offspring, child' in Middle English, and to 'child of the Devil, little demon' in Early Modern English. 6) When *hobert-de-hoy* became the designation of an unwieldy adolescent, *hobert* turned into *hobble*, and the word acquired its present day form.

At a certain time, -*dehoy* may have begun to lead a semi-independent existence. Jamieson (1879-82) cited *ride cockerdehoy* 'sit on one, or on both the shoulders of another, in imitation of riding on horseback' and traced the component -*dehoy* to F *de haut* 'from on high.' Chance (1887:524-25) explained the Scots phrase as meaning originally 'sit on the left shoulder,' which is hardly credible. It probably means 'ride in the position of a cocker (that is, fighter, winner) and shout *hoy*.' Chance states that "...the *dehoy* [in *cockerdehoy*] ought to have the same meaning as *hobbledehoy*." His conclusion is not self-evident. The question remains open. Like **Hobard le Roy* that changed to *Hobard de hoy*, to provide the phrase with alliteration, *cockerdehoy* produced a doublet *cockerdecosie*.

4. The persuasiveness of what has been said above (**Hobert le Hoy* > *Hobert-de-hoy*) partly depends on whether a sufficient number of forms with unetymological -*de*- can be shown to have existed. The number is not great, but some humorous coinages are noteworthy, because they bring out the productivity of -*de*-. One of them is *simper-de-cocket* (OED gives citations from 1524 to 1707), a term of relativity mild abuse for a woman; the original meaning must have been 'simpering coquette.' Unlike *figgle-le-gee* 'finical, foppish' (Jamieson), in which -*le*- is a kind of reduplication -[l-li-]- of the same type as in *la-di-da* 'affectedly swell' or *fiddle-de-dee* 'nonsense,' the augment -*de*- in *simper-de-cocket* did not arise for phonetic reasons. The same holds for *gobbledegook* ~ *gobbledygook*.

In the study of such compounds, French models from *Cœur de Lion* to *dent-de-lion* (> *dandelion*) spring to mind, but -*de*- probably has more than one source, and in this respect it shares some common ground with -*a*- occurring in *ragamuffin*, that is, *rag-a-muffin* (see RAGAMUFFIN for a detailed discussion of this element). In *musterdevillers*, the name of woolen cloth well known between the 14th and the 16th century (the latest citation in OED is dated 1564), -*de*- is from French. But *dandiprat* 'small 16th-century coin' and 'worthless fellow' (no recorded examples before 1520) is obscure. Weekley (1921) wonders: "? Of the same family as *Jack Sprat*—'This Jack Prat will go boast / And say he hath cowed me'—*Misogonus*, ii, I, c. 1550." *Dandy*, itself of dubious origin, surfaced only in the 18th century. *Prat* could be a nickname (cf *prat* 'trick' and *prat* 'buttock'), or it could refer to *prate* and *prattle*. Neither component of *dandiprat* is of French origin, but the whole looks like *dan-di-prat*. Parasitic *-di-* occurs in several words denoting hubbub, ruckus, that is, noisy commotion and disturbance in the names of disreputable people and demons, in one of which it varies with *-te-*. The form *-te-* also speaks against the French origin of this augment.

Here are some of the *-de-* ~ *-te-* words: *haggerdecash* 'in a disorderly state, topsy-turvy' (Jamieson), *hubble-te-shives* 'confusion,' *flipper-de-flapper* 'noise and confusion'; *haydegines* or *heiedegynes* (see Whiter 1822-25, I:699-700 and its other forms in OED, *hay sb*[4], 2, explained there tentatively as *hay de Guy; hay* 'dance'); *slabberdegullion* 'lout' (a 17th-century word), *tatterdemalian* 'ragged person,' *grizzle-de-mundy* 'stupid person who is always grinning,' a synonym of *grinagog*; *Flibber-ti-gibbet* has been recorded in numerous variants, including *Flibberdigibbet*

The syllables *-de-* and *-te-* are common in Dutch, and some English words with those augments are probably of Low German / Dutch rather than Romance origin. In German we find *rumpel-de-pumpel* (Sprenger [1887]) and *holder-di(e)-polter* 'upside down.' Its Dutch cognate is *holder de bolder* 'helter-skelter,' whereas Low German has *hulter-(de-)fulter* and *hullerdebuller*, along with *hulterpulter*, the last one without an augment (NEW, *holderdebolder*); see more variants in Hauschild (1899-1900:8/3) and more Low German words of this type in Koppmann (1899-1900:42.k). The number and variety of such forms refute Partridge's statement (1949b and 1958) that *-de-* in *hobbledehoy* is "euphonic," "an intrusive, meaningless element introduced for ease of pronunciation."

H. Schröder (1906) regarded G *Schlaraffen-* in *Schlaraffenland* (the German counterpart of the English Land of Cockaign) as an extended form *schl(ar)aff(e)* from *schlaff* 'loose, lax.' Schröder's term is *Streckform*. See more about such forms at RAGAMUFFIN and SKEDADDLE. Kluge (1906:401) found a mistake in Schröder's quotation and hauled him over the coals for it. However regrettable his mistake might be, it did not invalidate Schröder's conclusion. The curious thing is that *Schlaraffen* developed from *slû-de-raffe* 'prosperous idler.' Consequently, one way or the other, *Schlaraffen* is an extended form (see esp KS).

French and Low German must have contributed in equal measure to the spread of *-de-* in English. Once this type of word formation came into being, hybrids like *hobble-de-poise* 'easily balanced' (half-Germanic, half-French), modeled on *avoirdupois*, and coinages like *gobbledygook* met with no resistance.

Chance (1887:524, note) remarks that E *-de-* "is not used as the French *de* is. It seems rather to mark some loose, often ill-definable relation between the two words which it connects, and may apparently be translated by *with regard to*, *as* or *like*, *in*, *about*, *on*, or *towards*." His formulation will not hold for *-a-*. However, *-a-* and *-de-* have sometimes been used interchangingly: cf *cater-a-fran* and *cater-de-flamp* (EDD; both mean 'askew'); OED cites *raggedemuffin*, 1612. (Liberman [2004b:100-04].)

HOREHOUND (1000)

Hore- in horehound *(also spelled* hoar-*) means 'hoary,' that is, 'white.' The Old English forms* hūne *and* hāre hūne *show that* -d *in* -hound *is late and invalidate attempts to find a connection between this plant name and dogs (hounds). Final* -d *may be excrescent (as in* sound*). It may also be due to the confusion between horehound and alyssum (a plant used to cure hydrophobia) and to the influence of* gund *'poison.' One of the several meanings of the Germanic root* *hūn- *seems to have been 'dark, black.' Possibly, OE* hūne *was at first the name of* Ballota nigra. *If so,* hāre *was chosen to modify* hūne *only when* hūne *came to designate* Marrubium vulgare.

The sections are devoted to 1) various attempts to relate horehound *to* hound, *2) the ancient meaning of the root* hūn- *and its possible congeners, 3) the proposed etymology of* horehound, *and 4)* horehound *among other plant names containing reference to poison.*

1. At present, etymologists agree that **the first part in OE *hāre hūne* 'Marrubium vulgare' means 'hoary' because the flowers of horehound are white or because its stem and leaves are covered with white, cottony pubescence (OED),** from *hār* 'grayish-white.' Skeat[1] concluded that Anglo-Saxons also knew black horehound, *Ballota nigra*, for otherwise the phrase *hwīte hāre hūne* would not have been coined. As usual in such cases, the same name has been applied to various plants (Pheifer [1974:103, note to line 657]).

The impenetrable part of *hāre hūne* is *-hūne*, whose reflex is ModE *-hound*. The form with *-d* after *n-* (*hoarhunde*) was recorded late (1486) and is of no value for etymological purposes. However, **an association between horehound and dogs is old,** because horehound was confused with alyssum, or gold dust (see the 1551 quotation in OED, *alyssum*), a plant whose name suggested that it could appease anger and even cure hydrophobia. Since Gk ἄλυσσον looks like the neuter of ἄλυσσος 'curing canine madness,' from the privative α- and λύσσα 'fury; passionate outburst; rabies' (according to a more convincing version, it was used to check hiccup: λύζω 'hiccup, *etc*'), the same healing properties were ascribed to horehound. "The species *alyssum*, a native of Spain and Italy, is called Galen's Madwort, because it was, at one time, a specific in cases of Hydrophobia" (Booth [1836:108]). Belief in horehound as a remedy for the bite of a mad dog was still remembered in the middle of the 19th century; both Richardson and Chambers mention it. This may explain why *hāre hūne* acquired *d* after *e* had been apocopated (but see the end of the entry). On the other hand, E *sound* 'auditory signal' and *bound* 'prepared to go' have excrescent *d* for no particular reason (Weekley [1921]: *horehound*). Barnhart's cautious reference to the Old English plant name *hundes tunge* as a possible source of *d* in *horehound* is an unsubstantiated guess.

Greppin (1997:72-73) points out that the medieval Arabic word for 'horehound' was *hašīsāt-al-kalāb* 'dog's plant.' He goes on to say that OE *hund* may have had two forms, namely *hund* and **hun* because *houne* sometimes occurs in Middle English without *d*. However, ME *houn(e)* cannot be projected to early English. The formant *d* in *hund* is Common Germanic (Go *hunds** and its cognates regularly have it), but postnasal *d* was often lost in both English and Frisian. Consider the recorded forms in Modern Frisian dialects (OFr *hund*, Standard Frisian *houn*): *hûnd, hônd* and *huhn, hûn, hunn', hün, hyn, hoen, hŷn', huwn(e), hôᵘn, hôn*, and so on (Siebs [1889:178]). Deriving them from two sources (*hund* and *hun*) is out of the question, whereas the change *nd* > *n* is a common occurrence, though it is more characteristic of the Scandinavian languages than of West Germanic. Gmc **χundaz* had a short vowel, and *ū* in English is due to the lengthening before *nd*. If **hun* had existed, it would either have retained its form in Middle English and become modern reg **hun* [hun] ~ [hʌn] or had lengthened *u* in **hune*. ME *ŭ*, when it lengthened before a single consonant (in so-called open syllables; cf IVY, sec 1) and preserved its length in later periods, yielded *ǭ*, so that the form Greppin cites would have been spelled **ho(o)ne*, not *houne*.

Maimonides could not offer a good explanation of the Arabic term (Greppin [1997:73]). The difficulty he faced is typical. Consider E *dogwood (dogberry, dogtree), dogrose, dog poison* (= *fool's parsley*), and many others. In some cases, 'prefixes' like *dog-* and *horse-* are added to designate inferior varieties of plants (Hoops [1920:40], Loewe [1938:52-53]). In English plant names, the name of an animal is typically the first element (*foxglove, harebell, cowslip*, and so forth), which makes the derivation of *-hound* from the noun *hound* improbable.

2. Dictionaries offer almost no suggestions on the origin of *horehound*. Thomson spells *hoarhund* and says: "Saxon *hun* signified wasting of strength, consumption for which this plant was esteemed a remedy." This is an interesting etymology, but Thomson did not indicate his source (in Somner [1659]), Junius, and Lye *hun* does not appear). **Skeat[1] compared *-hūn* and L *cun-īla*, Gk κονίλη 'a species of origanum,' and Skt *knūj-* 'stink'** (OE *cunelle* ~ *cunille* 'wild thyme,' OS *quenela*, OHG *quenela*, and MHG ~ ModG *Quendel* are from Latin). If the Greek word meant 'strong-scented,' little is left of the connection between wild thyme and horehound, for a strong smell is not characteristic of *Marrubium vulgare*. Besides this, the first vowel is short in Latin and Greek, and, to save Skeat's etymology, a prolonged grade in Germanic has to be set up (see below). W (1890) copied Skeat's etymology, but it did not reemerge in more recent editions, and Skeat expunged the reference to *cunīla* from the fourth edition of his dictionary ("origin unknown"). OE *hāre hūne* was a phrase rather than a compound, in which *hūne* may have been the primary word, with *hāre* added as a modifier. Conversely, *hāre hūne* originally may have been an indivisible group, with *hūne* abstracted from it. Alongside *hāre hūne, hārhune* has been recorded. Holthausen (AeEW) gives *hūne* as a separate entry and says only: "To *hūn* 'bear cub'?"

Gallée (1901:57) quoted from the Bern Low German glosses: "hun en crut elleborum." In Old High German glosses, this plant (*krut*) is called *hûnisch wurzû*. The English correspondence of *elleborum* is *hellebore* < ME *ellebre* < OF *elebre* < ML *eleborus* (L *elleborus* goes back to Gk ἐλλέβορος, rarely ἐλλέβορος), "[a] name given by the ancients to certain plants having poisonous and medicinal properties, and especially reputed as specifics for mental disease; identified with species of *Helleborus* and *Veratrum*..." (OED). Gallée observed that since vowel length is not marked in the Bern glosses, *hun* might stand for *hūn*, as in OE *hāre hūne*. He also cited OE *hun* 'impurity' and *hunel* 'foul, wanton.' *Hunel* is a ghost word. *Hune*, with its synonym *adle*, glossed L *tabo*. All the words are in the dative. *Tābum* means 'pus,' but OE *ādle* means 'disease, infirmity, sickness.' Consequently, *hune* may be 'poison' but may be 'disease' (or both). If *hune* is *hŭne* (the likeliest variant), it is one of the words discussed at HENBANE.

Since the pronunciation of a word for 'poison' might have been altered as the result of a taboo, *hūne* < *hŭn* is not inconceivable. If so, *hāre hūne* means 'white poison.' Poisonous plants and herbs known for their medicinal properties often share names, because every medicine is poison used with discretion. G *Wüterich* 'henbane' was supposed to cure madness; thus it did not cause but avert 'fury' (*Wut*). OE *ātorlāðe* was a plant used as an antidote to poison (*ātor* 'poison,' *lāð* 'injury'), and *lybcorn* was some medicinal seed (*lybb* 'poison,' *corn* 'seed'). Even if *hŭn-* and *hūn-* are in the end related, they seem to have been different words in early Old English, and *hāre hūne* need not have meant 'white poison.' Gallée approved of Skeat's comparison *-hūne* with *cunīla* and suggested that the root in question may have had two forms, with *ŭ* and with *ū*.

Siebs (1892:155 and 1930:55) explained LG *hunnebedde, hünebett,* and *heunenbett* as 'death bed' and E reg *hunbarrow* 'tumulus,' a word recorded in EDD and briefly discussed by Mayhew (1900), as 'burial mound.' By so doing, he evaded the problem of vowel length in *hŭn* ~ *hūn*. The *hūn-* element of Old Germanic proper names like *Folchūn* is usually compared with Celtic *kunos* 'high.' Hoops (1902:176-79) proposed that the initial meaning of *hūn-* was not 'great' but 'dark, black, brown,' as is probably the case in OI *húnaflói, Húna-vatn* 'dark water,' and the like. It is this adjective that he recognized in OE *hune* and *hāre hūne.* In his opinion, *hūne* referred to *Ballota nigra,* whereas *hāre hūne* was later applied to *Marrubium.* In Tyrolese, *Helleborus niger* is called *hainwurz,* and in Silesian *schwarzwurz* is the name of *Helleborus viridis.* Likewise, he explained OI *húnn* 'bear cub' as 'brown one.'

Helm (1903:83-85; 1905) supported Hoops's idea and pointed out that *hūn* may be related to Go *hauns* 'humble' (Go *haunjan* 'abase' and *hauneins** 'lowliness' have also been recorded), whose cognates are OE *hēan* 'lowly, despised,' OHG *hôni* 'despised,' and OHG *hôna* (ModG *Hohn*) 'scorn.' He reconstructed PIE **k̑ewo* 'big,' with the possibility of its denoting things very high ('great') or very low ('deep'), like L *altus* 'high; deep' and G *steigen* 'go up' or 'go down.' From 'low, deep' he deduced 'dark, black.' This sounds like an acceptable hypothesis. However, Helm did not touch on the possible ties between *hun-* 'death' and *hūn* 'low, deep, dark,' and before him Hoops (1902:176/3) observed that he would not discuss *hünebett, hünengrab,* and *hunbarrow,* which Siebs separated from MHG *hiune* (ModG *Hüne*) 'giant.' According to Siebs, those words had nothing to do with giants or Hunns and had always had a short vowel in the root.

Perhaps alongside the meaning 'death,' the complex *hŭn* developed the meaning 'earth, ground' by ablaut *u* : *ū* (De Vaan [2003:286]) **or with expressive lengthening. Then 'black, brown, dark' would be derivative of 'earth-colored,'** and *hiune* 'giant,' presumably an ancient word even though first recorded in Middle High German, could be understood as having originally referred to any frightening chthonic being, a sibling of those who have the appellations *jǫtunn, risi, þurs,* and *troll* ~ *trǫll* in Scandinavian mythology and folklore. The meaning 'abase' (from 'a-base') in Go *haunjan,* OE *hȳnan,* OS *hônian,* and OHG *hônen* fits **hūn* 'earth' perfectly; compare L *humilis* 'low, humble' from *humus* 'ground.'

The alternation *ū* ~ *au* is not a hindrance to such a reconstruction. Similar alternations occur in the second class of strong verbs (OE *scūfan* 'shove' ~ OHG *scioban,* with *io* < **au*) and in the normal grade (OE *hrēam* 'fame, glory,' with *ēa* < **au,* ~ OS *hrôm,* with *ea* < **au*). But it is equally possible that *hŭn* and *hūn* are not related. Gerland (1861) glossed **hūnaz* as 'swollen,' and Steinhauser (1976:510-15) followed him or came to the same conclusion. Those two reconstructed meanings do not necessarily contradict each other. 'Big' is easier to derive from 'swollen' than from 'dark' ('earth-colored' can then be bypassed), but we should not disregard the later recorded senses of the reflexes of **hūnaz*. 'Swollen' (applied to rivers), 'full of poison' (applied to the udder, as in one of Steinhauser's examples) could develop the connotation 'dark' and 'poisonous.' Consider also the discussion of Go *hauns* and its cognates, above. **Regardless of the most ancient meaning of *hūnaz, in *horehound* the reference seems to be to the flower's color.** 'Poisonous' is less likely.

3. In sum, the following tentative etymology of *horehound* can be offered. **Two roots existed in Germanic, both with non-Germanic cognates. One was **hen-* ~ **han-* ~ **hun-* 'death; poison.'** It often occurred in the names of poisonous plants (see HENBANE). **The other was **hūn-*.** Its etymology is less clear. **Words with **hūn-* meant 'black; low; big,' assuming that all of them belong together.** Perhaps we have a case of enantiosemy, as Helm thought. But perhaps **hūn-* is *hŭn-* by ablaut

or with expressive lengthening. If it is an emphatic form, its Indo-European cognates should be discounted. ***Hūn* may have meant 'earth,' whence 'black; low' and, in special circumstances, 'a creature of the earth, giant.'** One more unknown is the origin of the ethnic name *Hunn,* a word that may have influenced the meaning of MHG *hiune.*

Whatever the origin of *hūn* 'black' (from **hūn-* or from **hŭn-* lengthened), the Old English plant name *hūne* gets an explanation if we agree that in the beginning *hūne* meant *Ballota nigra.* When this word came to designate *Marrubium, hāre* was chosen to modify it. *Hwīte hāre hūne* is puzzling. Apparently, *hār* 'hoary, old' supplanted *hār* 'grey,' and the color term receded from active use. With time *hāre hūne* became a regular compound *hārhūne* (which may not have happened, as OE *hāre-wyrt* shows). After apocope, *-d* was appended to *hūn,* possibly because of the confusion of horehound and alyssum, the traditional remedy for canine madness.

4. When trying to unravel the remote origins of some poisonous plant names, we constantly run into near homonymous sound complexes with the meaning 'poison, injury' and should reckon with the possibility that the extant form is the result of folk etymology or a cross between a native and some migratory word. In addition to *hen-* ~ *han-* ~ *hun-,* as in *henbane, hem(b)* ~ *hym(b),* as in *hemlock,* and *hend-,* as in G *Himbeere,* have been recorded. **Hun-* 'poison, death' and **hend-* 'pierce' competed with *gund,* as in Go *gund* 'gangrene,' OE *gund* 'pus,' and OHG *gunt* ~ *gund* 'pus.' Their modern reflexes are N reg *gund* 'scurf' and E reg *gund* 'a disease of sheep that affects the skin' (EDD, only Dorset; Sigma [1890:125], and see A. Campbell's discussion [1969:306] of OE **healsgund* 'neck tumor').

The plant nightshade (bittersweet, belladona), that is, *Solanum nigrum* or *Solanum Dulcamara,* is called *hondemiegersholt* in the Dutch dialect of Drente and *hounebeishout* or *stinkhout* in Frisian, which reminds us of the "strong-scented" κονΐλη (Naarding [1954:94-95]). *Hand* 'hand' and *hond* or *houn* 'dog' are close by to suggest folk etymological solutions, but they should be disregarded. Du *hondsdraf* 'ground ivy' replaced *onderhave* and *onderhaaf,* and the earlier form was *gondrâve* (related to OHG *gundareba* > MHG *grunderebe* > ModG *Gundelrebe*). **Hun-* 'death' and *gund* 'poison' are the likeliest roots of those words.

Onderhave sounds amazingly like G *Andorn* 'horehound.' Of several etymologies of *Andorn* EWA prefers the one that is based on the comparison of the German word and Gk ἄνθος 'bloom, sheen,' but it appears that we are dealing with a plant name known in approximately the same form in Indo-European and Semitic (Möller [1911:10-11, *andh-*], WP I:67-68, *andhos;* IEW 40-41, *andh-;* none of them mentions *Andorn*). See also Loewe (1935:255-56), Pokorny (1949-50:131-32), Schwentner (1951:244), and Mayrhofer (1952b:48). Vasmer IV:404 notes that Russ *shandra* 'horehound' is almost the same word as Skt *candrás* 'shining' and refers to *Weisleuchte,* literally 'white lamp,' the popular German name of horehound. He is unable to reconstruct the circumstances in which *shandra* and its Polish cognate could have been borrowed from a language of India. Yet the fact remains that *shandra,* if we take away *sh-,* bears an uncanny resemblance to Du *onder(have)* and G *Andorn.* In case several such words were known to the speakers of Middle English, the change from *horehoun* to *horehound* may find an additional explanation (Liberman [2001b:139-43]).

IVY (800).

OE īfig *has established cognates only in German and Dutch. The origin of* ī *is debatable, but despite the prevailing opinion to the contrary,* īfig *probably does not go back to* if-hēg *(-*hēg *'hay') with compensatory lengthening after the loss of* -h-. *It is more likely that OE* īf-ig *and OHG* eb-ah *(both mean 'ivy') have different grades of ablaut in the root and in the suffix.*

In the languages of the world, the name of ivy is occasionally borrowed, and īfig ~ ebah *have been compared with many plant names in Germanic, Latin, and Greek. Although such comparisons have not yielded convincing results, the idea of a non-native, perhaps non-Indo-European origin of* *ib- *has not been abandoned. Only one of the proposed etymologies of* ivy *as an Indo-European word has survived until the present. According to it,* īfig *is related to L* ibex *and means 'climber.' But* ibex *appears to be an Alpine substrate word, and the Indo-European root* *ibh- *'climb' has not been recorded. All the skepticism notwithstanding,* ivy *can be a noun of Germanic origin, related to OE* āfor *and OHG* eibar *'pungent; bitter; fierce.' Likewise,* Ifing, *the name of a mythic river, occurring once in the* Elder Edda, *might mean 'violent (stream).' Yet a single obscure Scandinavian word is not sufficient for setting up a common Germanic root* *īƀ- *'bitter.' The resemblance between* Ifing *and other similar river names outside Scandinavia is probably accidental.*

The sections are devoted to 1) the phonetic structure of OE īfig, *2) the rejected etymologies of* ivy *and words for 'ivy' in various languages, 3) the one still current etymology of* ivy *and the etymology that holds out the greatest promise, and 4) the Scandinavian connection and the possibility of setting up a Germanic root* *īƀ.

1. The Old English forms of *ivy* are spelled *ifeg* and *ifig;* the form *īfegn* will be discussed at the end of sec 3. **It is now universally accepted that *ifig* goes back to *if-* followed by a word for 'hay.'** Standard reference books give **if-hieg* (Luick [1964:sec 250]; the same in BWA I:91), **iƀ-hēg* (SB, secs 121 and 218, note 1), **if-hīg* (Mayhew[1891c: sec 811]), and **if-hieg* (A. Campbell [1959:secs 240.2 and 468]). Kluge (1889:586) reconstructed **ifhīg*. Sievers (ASG[3], sec 217) and Holthausen (1894; 1903b:39) followed him and recognized the existence of pre-OE **ifhīg*. According to them, *-h-* was lost in **if-hi(e)g,* as a result of which radical *i* underwent compensatory lengthening. OHG *eba-hewi* 'ivy' provided the main support for OE **if-hieg*. The equation **if-hieg* = *eba-hewi* has long since become commonplace. See Charpentier (1918:39) and Trier (1963:2) among the best-known names.

The first vowel of OE *ifig* was long. Before a single consonant (or in so-called open syllables; cf HOREHOUND, end of sec 1), *ĭ* yielded *ę̄* not *ī*. Ten Brink (1884:25) believed that *ivy* constituted a rare exception to the rule and that *ifig* became *īvy*, but his idea has been rejected (see especially Morsbach [1888:182]). By the 13th century at the latest, *ifig* must have had *ī*, for otherwise the present-day form would have been **ivvy* (with the vowel of *give*) or **evy* (with the vowel of *eve*). Morsbach, in reconstructing *ī* in *ifig,* referred to Du *eiloof* 'ivy' (that is, *ei-loof; loof* means 'leave'). According to a more recent view, *ei-* in *eiloof* has no value for tracing the origin of *ivy* because *eiloof* is allegedly a 'bastardized' form, the product of interplay between MDu *iw-lôf, iff-lôf, i-loof,* and *eig-lôf* (Ceelen [1958:21-29]). That view is not necessarily correct (see the end of sec 3, below).

Despite the fact that *īfig* could not develop from *ĭfig,* that OHG *ebah* points to a short initial vowel, and that the second component of OHG *ebihewi* meant 'hay,' OE **if-hieg* probably did not exist. Björkman (1901:226) listed numerous forms of the Old High German name for 'ivy' and ascribed *eba-hewi* to folk etymology, which allegedly substituted *hewi* 'hay' for the ancient suffix *-ah.* By contrast, OE **if-hieg* is believed to be the original, primary etymon of *īf-ig*. Those reconstructions are at cross-purposes. *Īfig* matches *eb-ah,* though each word contains a root and a suffix in different grades of ablaut. Not inconceivably, OE *-ig* is from **-ag*. OE *bodig* 'body,' *manig* 'many,' and *hunig* 'honey' correspond to OHG *botah,* Go *manags**, and OHG *honag,* and neither *body* nor *honey* had umlaut (in *many* it occurred late). If *-ag* is the original form of the suffix, **if-hieg* is no longer needed even as a possibility, unless *ebah* derives from *ebihewi*—an improbable development. Another alternative is to set up OE **if-hieg* versus OHG *ebah,* which is also a bad solution because an independent word **if-* has not been recorded and no known component could attract *hieg* as the second element of **if-hieg.*

We are bound to admit that Old English had *īfig,* while German had *ebah,* but that in German, *ebah* competed with *eba-hewi,* perhaps not so much under the influence of folk etymology as for practical reasons: ivy leaves were, and in some places still are, regularly used as fodder in winter (see more on *-hewi* in sec 2). HDA called into question the connection between *ivy* and *hay,* but Trier (1963:2) clarified it and T. Klein (1977:364-66) explained it in overwhelming detail. See also ESSI III:59-61 on the same subject, but the conclusion drawn there is less convincing.

Works on Germanic word formation are silent on the meaning of OHG *-ah.* Only Seebold (KS, *Efeu*) mentions its collective force. Kluge (1926:sec 67) points out that in Old High German, the suffix **-ahja* was productive in the names of areas with a concentration of certain plants: for instance, *boum* meant 'tree' and *boumahi* meant 'place grown over with trees, woods.' A similar word is OHG *rîsahi* (> ModG *Reisig* 'brushwood') from *rîs* 'twig.' KrM (sec 146), Kubriakova (1963:106), and EWA (*ebah*) repeat the same information. At one time, *ebah* probably referred to areas covered with ivy. **The neuter gender of *ebah* and *īfig* bears out the conjecture that they were collective nouns.** OHG *ebah* may have had the meaning that *ivery* has in the modern Sussex dialect (Gepp included it in his books and discussed in Gepp [1922:107]). Change of gender in the history of German nouns is common. G *Efeu* is now masculine, even though *Heu* 'hay' is neuter. Sauer (1992:403) calls *īfig* a native simplex. *Īfig* and *ebah,* although not compounds, were bimorphemic.

The origin of the intervocalic consonant in *īfig* also poses problems. Old English *f* regularly corresponds to Old High German *b* (as in OE *giefan* versus OHG *geban* 'give'), but since intervocalic fricatives underwent voicing in Old English, the reflexes of PIE **bh* (to use the traditional value of this phoneme) and **p* merged: *lufu* 'love' (with *f* < **bh*), *belīfan* 'remain' (with *f* < **p* in a stressed syllable), and *seofon* 'seven' (with *f* < **p* preceding stress by Verner's Law) had [v] (Bahder [1903] offers the most detailed discussion of such words). Thus we can be certain that OE *īfig* was pronounced ['i:vij], but the exact origin of the fricative remains unclear. The zero grade of the root vowel in OHG *ibah suggests final stress, while ī in OE *īfig* makes initial stress the most natural option. **We may therefore reconstruct pre-OE **īfig* and pre-OHG **iƀáh,* though **ībhig* and **ibháh* would have yielded the same pronunciations.** However, setting up **bh* in such forms presupposes their great antiquity, and this is exactly what has to be demonstrated.

2. The proposed etymologies of *ivy* and its cognates are numerous. The word is West Germanic (N *eføy* is a borrowing from German). **Minsheu (*ivie*) derived *ivy* from Gk ἐπιζάινω 'invade'** but found no supporters. Many plant names resemble *īfig* ~ *ebah* and have been compared with them. Among them G *Eibe* (< OHG *īwa*) ~ E *yew* (< OE *īw* ~ *ēow*) are particularly prominent (so Skinner, *Gazophylacium,* and Meidinger [1836:32]). Skinner's reconstruction seems to be such: arrows were made of yew, and Gk ἰος 'arrow' is reminiscent of *yew* and *ivy*. According to him, **the first to compare *ivy* and *yew* was Casaubon.**

Junius (*ivie*) cited Gk ἶφι 'strongly, boldly,' because ivy kills the tree by twisting it hard. He probably did not realize that ἶφι goes back to *ινόφι, the archaic dative of ἴς 'sinew, strength.' Lemon found Junius's etymology acceptable: *ivy,* he said, is called "from its cleaving close to, adhering to, or affectionately embracing every thing it lays hold on." **Since ivy was dedicated to Bacchus, a tradition emerged that connected OHG *ebah* either with Bacchus's name directly or with 'ευαν, an exclamation in honor of Bacchus (Casaubon, Skinner, Junius, *Gazophylacium*).**

Charnock (1889) **derived *yew* from Go *aiw*,** which he glossed 'of age,' and suggested that *ivy* is akin to G *ewig* 'eternal,' for it is an evergreen plant. The same etymology could have been obtained without reference to *yew,* by comparing OE *īfig* with some cognate of G *ewig* (so Kaltschmidt, *Epheu*). Confusion between the derivatives of *Efeu* and *Eibe* and between both of them and *ewig* occurred not only in the minds of linguists but also in popular usage, as T. Klein showed (1977:363-67) and as follows from the existence of *ewig,* one of the regional names of ivy in German.

Next comes Gk ἄπιον 'pear,' the putative source of L *apium* 'parsley,' which yielded F *ache* 'parsley, celery' and which German borrowed as *Eppich* 'celery' and sometimes 'ivy' (*e* is the umlaut of **a*). Reference to *Eibe* and *Eppig* in the discussion of *ivy* and its cognates was usual, and Vercoullie devoted a whole entry to separating *ifte* from *ijf* 'yew' and *eppe* 'parsley.' **Schwenck connected *Efeu, Eppich,* and *Eibe* with L *abiēs* 'fir',** reasoning that their original meaning was 'green.' Both ἄπιον and *apium* turn up as possible cognates of *ivy* in Weigand (*Epheu*), Mueller[1], and Skeat[1].

Petersson (1908-09:161) **compared *Efeu* and ἰψός,** known only from Hesychios, and glossed ἰψός as 'ivy,' but, according to Frisk, the Greek word means cork oak. **Then there is ME *ive,* or *herbe ive,*** remembered mainly because it occurs in *Canterbury Tales* (not recorded in English texts after 1611: OED). Skeat first thought that *ive* meant 'ivy' (see the report in *The Athenæum* 1889/I:762-63), but, as he said later: "The etymology of the F. *ive* is unknown. There is no reason for connecting it with E. *ivy,* nor with E. *yew,* both of which Littré mentions, but does not seem to favour" (Skeat [1901:145]). His attempt to derive *ive* from OF *ive* (L *equa*) 'mare' (Skeat [see the report in *The Athenæum* 1900/I:630; Skeat [1901:145-46]) has no bearing on the etymology of *ivy.*

None of the conjectures summarized above brings to light the origin of *ivy,* and some do not merit discussion, but the similarity between OHG *ebah,* Gk ἄπιον and ἰψός, and L *apium* (the Indo-European word for 'apple' can also be added to this list) is obvious. Some old (pre-Indo-European?) migratory plant name beginning with *ap-* or *ip-* may have become known to speakers of Germanic and been associated with *Hedera Helix.* It need not have been the name of ivy, as the gulf between 'pear' in Greek and 'parsley' in Latin or between Arabic *rībās* 'sorrel' and E *ribes* 'currants' (OED) shows. Latv *efeja* and *eepjes* (Schachmatov [1912:196]) and N *eføy* make it clear that ivy may have a foreign name even in the countries where it grows in abundance. It also seems that *ebah* was not the main popular word for 'ivy' in medieval Germany. In late MHG, *ephöu,* that is, *ep-höu, ph* was taken for Greek *ph* and the pronunciation with [f] instead of [ph] set in. A spelling pronunciation would not have prevailed among illiterate peasants. It is hard to imagine E *uphill* becoming **ufill* or, conversely, *telephone* becoming **telep-hone* in a completely literate society.

Besides possibly being a substrate word, *ivy* may have changed because of a taboo. Although ivy, as far as we can judge, has never been prominent in medicine and was not used in Germanic religious rites (its use in ancient cults is known well; in addition to standard reference works, see F. Tobler [1912:137-51], and R. Palmer [1972]), it plays and played in the past a noticeable role in superstitions, especially in Germany (HDA).

The names of ivy are varied (Ceelen [1958] lists over thirty for Dutch alone), and their origin is sometimes obscure. The etymologically transparent ones are formations like Du *klimop,* literally 'climber up,' compounds like Sw *murgröna,* literally 'wallgreen,' or reflexes of a well-attested word: for example, the names of 'ivy' in the modern standard Romance languages go back to L *hedera.* Among the Classical Greek names of ivy (Olck [1905:2827-28]), none, including κισσός, which has often been discussed (see especially Güntert [1932:22-23]), has an established etymology. The same is true of L *hedera.* At one time, it was believed to be akin to L *prehendĕre* 'seize' (so in most older dictionaries, and see WP I:531-33 and 589; IEW, 438), but in WH that connection is dismissed. Stokes (1894:29) traced Welsh *eiddew* and its Celtic cognates to **<p>edenno, *<p>edjevo* and compared them with Gk πέδη 'fetter,' L *pedica* 'shackle, snare,' and so on. Even Brythonic *iliô* was squeezed into this protoform (Henry). In a footnote, Henry quotes Ernout's suggestion that *iliô* is a blend of **pedenno* and some other plant name, for example, *illy* 'sorb apple.' But Hamp (1974:90) reconstructed **ed-is- ~ *ed-ies* followed by the suffix of the superlative and glossed it as 'very eating, voracious.' Those conjectures do not inspire confidence. Russ *pliushch* alternates with *bliushch.* Their connection with *plevat'* 'to spit' and *blevat'* 'to vomit' is obvious, but whether those two verbs provide a reliable clue to the etymology of *pliuschch ~ bliuschch* is less clear (Vasmer I:179, ESSI II:138-39). Proto-Slavic **brŭščīľanŭ* remains a matter of dispute (ESSI III:59-61).

In Germanic, Du *hondsdraf* is no less opaque than *ivy* (see the end of the entry HOREHOUND). Late in the 16th century, it replaced the similar-sounding *onderhave ~ onderhaaf* (NEW). The second component (*-have ~ -haaf*) is reminiscent of the English plant name *hove,* which also occurs in E *alehoof* 'ground ivy,' another replacement, this time of *hayhove.* OED relates *hay-* in *hayhove* to *haw* and understands that compound as *hawhove,* but the history of OHG *ebihewi* shows that such a conclusion is not necessary.

The origin of OE *hōfe* 'ground ivy' is unknown (AeEW). No one seems to have compared *hōfe* with Du *-have ~ -haaf* since Jellinghaus (1898a:464) included it in his list. OED suggests that *alehoof* got its first element "in allusion to its alleged use in brewing instead of hops." However, *alehoof* looks so much like Du *eiloof,* pronounced and spelled in English, that the connection with *ale* and *hove* (< *hōfe*) may be due to folk etymology. Only Scott (CD, *alehoof*) noted the similarity but looked on the Dutch word as a borrowing from English. His guess can hardly be substantiated. De Hoog (1909), Toll (1926), Llewellyn (1936), and Bense do not discuss *alehoof.* A vague tie could perhaps be sensed between *hove, hop(s),* and the reflexes of OE *hēope* 'fruit of the (wild) rose' (> ME *heppe ~ heepe* > ModE *hip*) (see EWNT[2], *hop*). Is it possible that Old High German had a cognate of OE *hōfe,* a form like **huoba* or **huowa,* and that **ebahuowa* rather than *ebah* became *ebihewi? Veil,* another Dutch word for 'ivy,' is equally difficult: native? from Latin? (See Te Winkel [1893:54], Franck [1893:29-30], Grootaers [1954:93], and Ceelen [1958:22-23], besides EWNT and NEW.)

Those examples go a long way toward showing that the obscurity of *īfig ~ ebah* should be taken in stride and weaken references to taboo and the substrate. So many words for 'ivy' could probably not have been reshaped in the course of history or be borrowed from extinct non-Indo-European languages. In recent scholarship, Seebold (KS, *Efeu*) is ready to admit that Germanic borrowed the element *eb-* in *ebah* but offers no discussion.

Several relatively modern etymologies of *ivy* have been proposed in passing and attracted little or no attention. **According to Wedgwood[2-4], *ivy* is related to Wel *eiddew* and Gael *eidheann*.** In the first edition of his dictionary, Gael *eid* 'cloth' turns up (ivy allegedly clothes the objects on which it grows). Only E. Edwards repeated Wedgwood's derivation, but a similar idea occurred much later to K. **Malone** (1952:531), who **compared *if-* in OI *ifingr* 'headscarf'** (a hapax legomenon in Snorri's *Edda*) **and Go *iftuma** 'next, following'** ("a headcloth is something put upon the head"). **He detected the same element (*īf-*) in OE *īfig*, allegedly from **if-heg*:** "[H]ere again the plant is to be thought of as an object found upon something." Thomson offered a similar conjecture in 1826: *ivy* from G *uppa ~ ybba* (did he mean Sw *uppå* 'on'?) 'climb up,' as in Du *klimop.* Despite the mysterious words he cites, he clearly meant that *ivy* was akin to *up.*

The cognates of Go *iftuma** had caught the fancy of other researchers interested in the origin of *ebah ~ īfig.* Thus **Petersson** (1908-09) **traced OHG *ebah*, Gk ἰψός, and Go *ibuks** 'back' (adj) to the root **ibh-* 'bend.'** Feist[2-3] referred to Petersson without comment. First to connect *ebah* and *ibuks** (with a question mark) was Kluge. *Ibuks** does not appear as a cognate of *Efeu* in any edition of EWDS. That etymology was tried in KL (*ivy*), where no one seems to have noticed it. **Juret** (1942: 253), whose etymological dictionary is full of fanciful hypotheses, **listed Gk ὄφις 'snake,' ἴψ-, and *ivy* as belonging together (the root $ə_2p$ 'crawl; reptile'). FT compared *eføy* and Gk ἴφυον 'vegetable(s)'**—an excellent match, but neither the exact meaning nor the origin of the Greek word is known. **Makovskii** (1999a:182)**, true to his method of decomposing English words into two Indo-European roots, represented *ivy* as PIE **ei* 'to move' + **pag-* ~ **pak-* 'seize, get hold of' (because ivy clings to the pole on which it grows).** These etymologies are not better than those we find in the works by Casaubon, Skinner, and others.

3. There has been only one breakthough in the study of *ebah* ~ *īfig*. Hoops (1903:483-85) assumed that OE *īfegn* was a more ancient form than *īfig* and compared it with OE *holegn* 'holly,' both of which he assigned to the Indo-European *k*-stem (*īfe-g-n, hole-g-n*). He admitted that *īfegn* and the cognates of *holly* belonged to different declensions but referred to Skt *çalāka* (that is, *śalāka*) 'splinter,' which was, according to Stokes (1894:91), related to OIr *cuilenn* 'holly.' Neither Uhlenbeck (KEWAS, 305) nor Mayrhofer (KEWA III:314-15) mentions OE *holegn* among the cognates of *śalāka*. For *īfegn* Hoops could not cite even such doubtful related forms, but he followed Osthoff (1901:181-98, esp 181-87) and treated *-n* in both English plant names as an adjectival suffix (Osthoff cited G *Ahorn* 'maple' and L *acernus* 'made of maple' and looked on *Ahorn* as a substantivized adjective).

Whether or not those ideas are valid, Hoops must be given credit for taking notice of *īfegn*. O. Ritter (1936:87) had the same opinion as Hoops. However, Germanic shows no traces of the *k*-stem. Whatever the remote history of OE *holegn, -egn* must have been understood as a suffix in Old English and after *holegn* became *holen*. OE *sealh* 'willow, sallow' is akin to OHG *salaha*. Is *-h-* not a reduced variant of *-ah(a)*? And is *-eg-* in *holegn* not the same suffix by Verner's Law? Both ivy and holly are evergreens, so that rather than projecting *īfegn* to the *k*-stem, it may be more logical to suppose that *-egn* achieved the status of a suffix of plant names and that *īf-egn* was formed as a doublet of *if-ig*. See HEATHER for the emergence of such secondary suffixes.

Having discussed the morphemic structure of *īfegn*, Hoops suggested that a cognate of this word was L *ibex*. The ibex is a mountain goat. It is called *Steinbock* in German, and the German word sometimes occurs in the English zoological nomenclature. In Hoops's opinion, *h* in *ebah* < **eƀah-z* or **eƀah-az* (< **iƀ-ah-z*), or **īƀah-az* alternates with *g* in OE *īfegn* (< **īƀag-nā*) by Verner's Law, whereas **īƀahz* goes back to PIE **ībháks*, the etymon of L *ibex* (< **ibeks*). Both are 'climbers.'

Hoops's etymology made no impression on Skeat or Kluge, but Götze gave it as definite in EWDS[11] and TDW (*Efeu* in both). With or without reservations it appears in WHirt (*Efeu*), Hirt (1921:197), Mackensen, Hiersche (*Efeu* in both), EWA (*ebuh*), AHD, KM, KS (*Efeu*), SOD[3a], WNWD[1] (less definitely in the second edition), and many other dictionaries and compendia. The most circumspect authors say as does ODEE (*ivy*): "... of unkn[own] origin unless referable to the base of L. IBEX, with the sense 'climber' (cf. Fris., Du. *klimop* ivy, lit[erally] 'climb-up')." Some dictionaries have given up *ivy* ~ *Efeu* altogether. They only cite the cognates and state: "Origin unknown." See Skeat[4], EWDS[1-10] (the post-1903 editions are 7-10), Weekley, UED, and RHD.

It may be that a questionable etymology is better than no etymology at all, but **Hoops's comparison of *ebah* and *īfig* with *ibex*, however ingenious and persuasive at first sight, is almost certainly wrong.** Among the Indo-European roots as Brugmann and Walde have codified them, we find no **ibh-* 'climb.' Uhlenbeck (1909:170/13) pointed to this difficulty, discussed the Sanskrit, Greek, and Slavic words for 'copulate' derived from **i̯ebh-* (see them at FUCK, sec 5), and added Skt *íbha* 'elephant' and G *Eber* 'boar,' both of which he was ready to understand as 'mounters.' 'Mount' and 'climb' are not synonyms, however. Uhlenbeck did not reject Hoops's etymology, but his assent was lukewarm. He suggested (with a question mark) Gk αἰπύς 'steep' (adj) as a cognate of *ebah*. Van Wijk (EWNT[2], *klimop*) cited αἰπύς with two question marks.

Petersson (1908-09:161) accepted the equation *ebah* = *ibex* but approached it from a different angle. According to him, the root of both is **bheu̯gh-* 'bend.' The ibex, he argued, got its name on account of long backward-curving horns. In his reconstruction, the goat and the plant are 'twisters' rather than 'climbers.' He did not explain the origin of initial *i-*. All that is probably of no avail, for L *ibex* is now universally believed to be an Alpine substrate word like the etymon of *chamois* (EM). Polomé (1983:51-52) repeated Uhlenbeck's objections to Hoops and emphasized the non-Indo-European origin of *ibex*. In his opinion, Hoops's etymology of *ivy* is insupportable. Among the Latin etymological dictionaries, only WH mention *Efeu*, and the comment on Petersson's hypothesis is: "Wrong in all its parts." FT(G) reproduces the text from the Norwegian edition intact. In the bibliographical supplement (p 1453), Hoops's and Petersson's hypotheses are added without discussion. Even if we admitted for the sake of argument that *ibex* is an Indo-European animal name, it would be unsound to refer to it in the etymology of *ivy*. A word of obscure origin cannot shed light on another equally obscure word.

One more etymology of *ivy* exists. Loewenthal (1917:109/65) took Gmc **ibvan* ~ **ibvum* (as they appear in Torp [1909:28]), obtained PIE **ībhu̯om*, related it to **āibh* 'burn, be bitter,' and compared it with OHG *eibar* 'bitter, pungent; disgusting' and *ebah* 'ivy,' which he glossed as 'poisonous berry' because the berries of ivy have an unpleasant taste. Despite the artificial method of reconstruction typical of all Loewenthal's etymologies, the match *eibar* : *ebah* is flawless. In Old English, the corresponding pair is *īfig* : *āfor*. Another debatable *i* ~ *ā* pair is OE *ides* 'woman' and *ād* 'fire,' understood as 'hearth' on the analogy of L *aedēs* 'house, hearth' (AeEW). OE *idig* 'industrious' and OI *ið* ~ *íð* 'labor' probably have the same root. A good semantic analogue of *īfig* 'poisonous plant' would be OHG *gund-reba* 'ivy,' literally 'poison grass.'

However, we need not insist that *āfor* ~ *eibar* meant 'poisonous.' In both Old English and Old High German, this adjective occurs many times with exactly the same referents. In Old English: fierce (in poetry); harsh, severe (in medical recipes, of a remedy or its operation); bitter, acid, pungent (of taste); glossing L *rancidus*, apparently, in the sense 'bitter' (said about cries of remorse); in Latin texts: acerbus, rancidus (*with* amarus, foetidus) (DOE). According to Clark Hall: bitter, acid, sour, sharp; dire, fierce, severe, harsh, impetuous. In BT, vol 1: vehement, dire, hateful, rough, austere; atrox, odiosus, asterus, acerbus. None of the Latin glosses except *acerbus* appears in DOE, but Toller (vol 2) left them intact, though he struck off Bosworth's etymology (Go *aibrs* 'strong'). In Old High German: scharf, bitter; widerwärtig, abscheulich; heftig, leidenschaftlich; quälend, peinigend ('sharp, bitter; disgusting, loathsome; vehement or violent, passionate; torturous, distressful'); in glosses: acerbus, horridus, immanis, amarus (AHW).

Schade derived Ital *afro* 'sour, acid,' OF *afre* 'fright,' and F *affres* 'anguish' ~ *affreux* 'frightful, atrocious' from the root of OHG *eibar*, but his etymology is untenable. At best, the Romance words are traceable to Go *abrs* 'great,' for Go *aibr* 'offering' (not 'strong,' as in Bosworth!) is probably a scribal error for **tibr*. *Āfor* did not continue even into Middle English, but reflexes of *eibar* are extant in Modern German dialects and in archaic texts.

The answer to the etymological puzzle is then: *īfig* ~ *ebah* = 'bitter (unpleasant to the taste).' Another 'bitter' plant is OE *ampre*, OHG *ampfara* ~ *ampfaro* (see *amper* 'bitter, sour' in FT, NEW, WP I:179, and IEW, 777). **English had two words in the normal grade of ablaut (*īfig* and *āfor*), whereas in German the plant name was derived from the zero grade (*ebah*).** Du *eiloof* is harder to assess. If it is a blend, the original vowel was *i*. But if *eiloof* is a substitution for some old word with genuine *ei*, to which *loof* 'leaf' was added, then *ei* may be a cognate of *ei* in OHG *eibar*.

4. ***Ivy* has established cognates only in West Germanic, but perhaps one Old Icelandic word has the same root.** It is almost a homonym of *ifingr* that K. Malone suggested. **A myth in the *Elder Edda*** (*Vafþrúðnismál*, 15) **contains the name of a never-freezing river that separates the worlds inhabited by the gods and the giants. The name, *Ifing*, is a hapax legomenon, and we do not know the length of the first *i* in it.** Gering (1927:166) connected it with OI *ýr* 'yew.' H. Pipping (1928:25-26), M. Olsen (1964:15/6), F. Schröder (1941:8), and Holthausen (VEW) agreed with Gering, but J. de Vries's skepticism (AEW) is justified. What is a yew river, even though *Ífa* occurs in skaldic poetry, and why should a stream of cosmic importance be associated with yew trees? Although the yew tree played an important role in cult and legend (Läffler [1911:646-67], Bertoldi [1928], F. Schröder [1941:1-8]), this fact is irrelevant for understanding the origin of *Ifing*.

J. de Vries's suggestion is better. He cites OE *āfor* and OHG *eibar* and concludes that Ifing was a stormy, violent river. OE *āfor* 'fierce' (in poetry) and OHG *eibar* 'violent, vehement' fit his gloss *ungestüm* 'stormy, impetuous,' though he derives 'ungestüm' from G *Eifer* and Du *ijver* 'zeal, ardor, eagerness,' whose origin is obscure (see both words in German and Dutch etymological dictionaries and especially in EWA, *eibar*[1]). Regardless of their origin and of the vowel length in *Ifing*, the river between the two worlds seems, in all likelihood, to have been called fierce, violent, stormy. Machan (1988:77) finds 'yew river' and 'violent river' equally probable glosses of *Ifing*. The interpretation 'yew river,' that is, 'flowing past yew trees,' is too unimpressive in the context of the eddic lay to deserve credence despite F. Schröder's attempts to prove the opposite. J. de Vries, perhaps following FML, cites ModI *ýfing* 'ripples; incitement; strife' ('the state of agitation'). However, *ýfing* belongs with the words clustering around Go *ubils* 'evil' and its cognates and hardly has anything to do with *Ifing*.

Scandinavian cognates of *ivy* have been proposed more than once. Falk (1925a:242) suggested that the Old Icelandic names of the (tame?) falcon, *ifill, ifli,* and *ifjungr,* are related to both *ifingr* (this is the word in K. Malone) and *Ifing* (in which he leaves the first vowel short). In his opinion, all those words, as well as OI *ifrǫðull* 'sun' (poetic), contain the root **ibh-* 'wind' (v). The tame falcon, he thought, got its name from some band in the form of a ring, while the sun would be 'turning body.' Each of the Icelandic words Falk cited occurs only once, and, unlike *Ifing,* in the so-called *þulur* (lists of names), not in a consecutive text. His etymology recurred in IsEW, 80. Falk, who added OHG *ebah, ebihewi,* and OE *īfig, īfegn* as related to *ifill, Ifing,* and the rest, referred to Petersson (1908-09:161) but did not mention Hoops. Finally, J. de Vries (AEW) compared *āfor* ~ *eibar* and *Ífing*. Although he did not discuss *ebah* ~ *īfig* in his entry, the fragments of the picture are familiar from Loewenthal's combination *eibar* ~ *ebah*. Consequently, the isolation of *īfig* ~ *ebah* within West Germanic has not always been taken for granted.

If the etymology of *ivy* proposed above is correct, not all the words that Falk gathered belong together. The pair *īfig* ~ *ebah* / *āfor* ~ *eibar* excludes *ifingr* 'headscarf' and the Icelandic names of the falcon ('bitter' is too remote from any bird name). A connection between *ifill* ~ *ifli* ~ *ifjungr* and winding is so hard to establish that this loss does not seem to be too great either. OI *rǫðull,* a word of obscure origin, means 'sun' even without *if-* (as follows from OE *rodor* ~ *rador* 'ether, sky'), and *if-* does not occur as the first element in any other compound. See ÁBM for an appraisal of the origin of *ifrǫðull, Ífing, ifill,* and so on (only a survey; no new suggestions and no mention of *ivy*). When discussing a fanciful Pelasgian etymology of Gk κισσός, Hester (1964-65:357) asked: "Is the ivy a 'twisting plant'?" It is such only for the non-botanist, but climbing, winding, and twisting are close insofar as the properties of plants are concerned. However, other associations have been equally important in naming ivy.

No explanation of *Ifing, ifingr,* and *ifill* or of *īfig* and *āfor* can overcome the obstacle that their postulated roots do not occur elsewhere in Germanic, let alone the rest of Indo-European, and that the words under discussion are, except for *īfig* ~ *ebah,* rare, even exotic. A single Icelandic word (a hapax legomenon) resembling *īfig* is not sufficient for setting up a common Germanic rather than a West Germanic protoform, but its existence should not be disregarded.

WP I:6 and IEW 11 propose a Proto-Indo-European root of *āfor* and *eibar* and suggest a link to PIE **ai-* 'burn.' Yet the reality of PIE **ai-* is doubtful, for it has been attested only with enlargements. It is no more than the common part of numerous words with a loose semantic base (from 'ashes' to 'rage'). The West Germanic root **īf-*, that is, **īƀ-* 'bitter, sour; frightful,' recorded in all grades of ablaut (*ī* / *ei* / *i*) is more probable.

The Slavic river names *Ibar* (Serbo-Croatian), *Ibr* (Russian, Ukrainian), and a few others are even more obscure than *Ifing,* but it is instructive to observe the ever-recurring hypotheses on their origin: a substrate word? a derivative of PIE **iebh-* 'copulate'? a cognate of Basque *ibai* 'river' (cf *Iberia* and the name of the river *Ebro* in Spain)? See Vasmer III: 113, *Ibr* and ESSI VIII:205-06 for an incomplete and inconclusive discussion of the Slavic hydronyms.

Some Old Scandinavian mythological names go back to antiquity, others are late inventions of priests (compare the remarks on *Auðhumla* at HEMLOCK). *Ifing* is an old name (otherwise, it would probably have been more transparent), and that circumstance increases its value for reconstructing the origin of *ivy* and of the Germanic root **īƀ-* (Liberman 2002b).

JEEP (1940)

The first jeeps left the assembly line in 1940. Since they were marked G.P., it is usually believed that the coinage jeep, *widely known by September 1941, goes back to this abbreviation (which has been expanded in various ways) and that it was later associated with Eugene the Jeep. But most people who remembered the early days of the jeep connected its name only with the fabulous animal from E.C. Segar's cartoon, and apparently for a good reason.* Jeep *'inexperienced man, rookie' hardly affected the derivation, meaning, and spread of the new word.*

Several companies vied for the honor of having produced the first jeep, and conflicting versions exist of how this vehicle got its name. McCloskey (1943) recollects: "As far back as the early twenties the forerunner of the present jeep was being developed concurrently at the Infantry Tank School at Fort George G. Meade (Maryland) and at the Cavalry School, Fort Riley (Kansas). ...From the days of the early experiments at the Infantry and Cavalry schools it was variously referred to as a 'puddle jumper,' 'blitz buggy,' 'jeep,' and 'peep'—regardless of whether it was a 1/4-ton or a 1/2-ton truck.... In April 1940...I founded *Army Motors,* a magazine for the motor transport service.... I... had found that the mechanics and test drivers ... had settled on 'jeep' for the 1/2-ton truck because the first production models they had seen came marked 'GP' (General Production). I laid down an editorial ukase that the 1/4-ton truck was thereafter to be the 'jeep' and the 1/2-ton the 'peep'—and since our circulation ran into the hundreds of thousands the names stuck.... From all that I can discover, the marking 'GP' just happened to be put on the production jeeps merely to avoid confusing them with the various pilot models. It had probably been applied before, and if 'jeep' had not been one of the many names then current for the 1/4-ton and the 1/2-ton vehicles, there would have been no association of terms to produce the final 'jeep' designation for the 1/4-ton truck."

McCloskey's article appeared in response to H.L. Mencken's query (*ANQ* 3, 1943:119) in which he asked whether someone could supply the true etymology and history of *jeep.* "A great many folk etymologies are in circulation," he observed, "but they are extremely unconvincing." As will be seen, "a great many folk etymologies" have not turned up in printed sources. The editors of *ANQ* pointed out that, according to a letter in *Life* (November 3, 1944:5), *jeep* was the name, in a "Popeye" comic strip, of a "quasi-rodent" with "extraordinary powers." That information is given not in the letter but by the editors, who say that, "[u]sed by soldiers, it is their name of endearment and seal of approval on any particularly satisfactory piece of equipment. It has been applied to reconnaissance-command cars, light tanks, the 1/4-ton reconnaissance car and to anti-aircraft directors. Peep is a new word, carrying the same emotional charge, so far applied only to the 1/4-ton reconnaissance car."

With a single exception, all the other communications concern themselves with details. For example, according to Q.W. (1944), "Erle Palmer Halliburton, miner, manufacturer and oil financier, of Oklahoma and California, turned out, in 1937, a commercial vehicle—half truck and half tractor—*which he himself named the 'Jeep'* ... Mr. Halliburton proposed to convey an impression of the same remarkable omniscience with which Eugene the Jeep in 'The Thimble Theater' was endowed" (emphasis added).

Wells (1946:33-39), who reviewed some of the etymological material that had appeared in *ANQ,* quotes a letter from the G.&C. Merriam Company: "We have been interested in *jeep* as the name of the midget army vehicle and trace its origin to a pronunciation of the Army G.P. (General Purpose), a designation appearing on the first modeling, influenced by the word *jeep* appearing in the Segar comic strip. Before that in the earlier thirties the slang term *jeep* had been applied to an acrobatic dance, to a no-good worker, a wash-out, and the adjective *jeepy* meant, in the lingo of itenerants, foolish. Some believe that *jeep* had application among soldiers to anything insignificant, awkward, ill-shaped, or ridiculous prior to the use in the comic strip. This we have not investigated." B.W. (1946) reproduces the answer from the G.&C. Merriam Company and points out that if this suggestion was made on good grounds, the date of the word, apart from its use as a proper name, could be pushed back considerably.

Most likely, the fact that Halliburton called his tractor *Jeep* had no bearing on the naming of the famous car, though he was moved by the same impulse as those who dealt with the war vehicle. The earliest secure date of the wartime coinage is 1940: "...the original jeep was designed and manufactured by the Minneapolis-Moline Power Implement Company and *was given its name* from the 'Popeye' comic strip—during the Fourth Army Maneuvers at Camp Ripley, Minnesota, during the later part of August and first part of September, 1940.... A so-called 'big brother' of M-M's jeep—"Jeepers Creepers'—was described in the November 19, 1940 issue of the Minneapolis *Times Tribune*" (McFarlane [1943, emphasis added]). This event was remembered on August 12, 2002 in the rubric "Today in Minnesota History" (the Minneapolis *StarTribune,* Aug. 12, 2002, Variety, p. 1). According to G. Ritter (1943-44), "the first model of a 1/4-ton combat car was delivered by the American Bantam Car Company in September, 1940, and was called a Bantam, not a jeep." (Ritter discusses the names *Bantam* and *Willys* but offers no etymology of *jeep.*) His statement finds confirmation in all the literature devoted to the history of the jeep.

Another important statement is Ralph Martin's (1944:39): "The name first broke into newspaper print on February 22, 1941, when the jeep gave an exhibition of what it could do by climbing the steps of the nation's Capitol. Some reporter asked the driver what he called his vehicle, and the driver said, 'Why, I call it a jeep. Everybody does.'" Martin, who served overseas, was aware of both hypotheses concerning the origin of *jeep.* Mention of his feature in *The New York Times Magazine* appears in the bibliography in *American Speech* 19, 1944, p. 297. King (1962:77) cites the same article. According to his recollections, those "in uniform and on maneuvers during the summer and fall of 1941 referred to that car as a jeep."

Martin's date needs an adjustment. *Jeep* also turns up two days earlier (RHHDAS), but **the name "broke into print" in the St. Paul *Pioneer Press* on August 14, 1940.** Since neither Wells (1946:33), who correctly identifies the date, nor RHHDAS quotes this place (RHHDAS only refers to the files of Merriam-Webster, Inc., formerly G.&C. Merriam Co. and WCD[10] for the date 1940), it may be useful to reproduce it. On page 2, under two photos, a short unsigned note reads "'The Jeep' and the General See Action." Its opening sentences run as follows: "When the Germans crashed through Belgium and France, they used mechanical units like the one in the upper picture, a part of the United States Army equipment being utilized in the battle of Camp Ripley. Officially known as a prime mover, the soldiers call it a 'jeep.'"

The etymology of *jeep* has not been settled to this day. Letters to the editor written during the war (*TLS,* May 6, 1944:223; May 13, 1944:236; May 27, 1944:259; *NQ* 184, 1943:349; 185, 1943:28; 188, 1945:87) go back and forth between *G.P.* and Segar's *Jeep.* Rapkin (1945) contains the following addition: "...the designers of the car, the Willys Automobile Corporation of Toledo, Ohio, just recently were refused a copyright on the word 'Jeep'." An anonymous note in the German journal *Der Sprachdienst* (7, 1963:102) mentions Paul W. Spillner and Ward Cannel as researchers into the origin of *jeep,* but gives no references. Judging by Spillner (1963), he was the author of the note. The information the journal supplies is not new. A curious detail is added in anonymous (1963:165): many Germans think that *Jeep* is the name of the German who constructed the car! In the postwar years, the deeds of the omnipotent rodent were still remembered. Hardie Gramatky's book for children *Creeper's Jeep* (Eau Clare, Wisconsin: E. M. Hale Co, 1948) features a jeep that "did the plowing, milked the cows, and many other helpful things."

Dictionaries, if they say anything at all on this subject, state that *jeep* is "prob[ably] alter[ation] (influenced by Eugene the Jeep, a small fanciful wonder-working animal in the comic strip Thimble Theatre by Elzie C. Segar...) of g.p. (abbr[eviation] of *general purpose*" (W[3]; compare WNWD[1]: "< Eugene the Jeep, *later associated* with G.P. = General Purpose Car" [emphasis added]). The only unexpected explanation appears in WBD: "American English; reduction of "Jeepers Creepers!" (the exclamation of Major General George Lynch, Chief of Infantry, U.S. Army, upon the occasion of his first ride in the prototype model of the vehicle in 1939 at Fort Myer, Virginia; coined at the time by Mr. Charles H. Payne, his companion in, and designer of, the vehicle); perhaps later influenced by the initials G.P., for General Purpose, official designation of the vehicle."

Stewart (1992:63) called the origin of *jeep* obscure but added: "Most likely, it was a pejorative Army term for anything insignificant or not yet proven reliable, like a new recruit or a test vehicle." This also seems to have been Colby's opinion. Mencken[4] (p. 759) came to the conclusion that the history of the word is almost as obscure as the history of the car itself: "The fact that the code symbol of Ford on Army cars was *G.P.* has led to the surmise that the word *jeep* was born there and then, but there is no evidence for it. Nor is there any evidence that the word came from the same letters in the sense of *general purpose,* for the first *jeeps* were not called, officially, *general purpose cars,* but *half-ton four-by-four command-reconnaissance cars.*" In his opinion, it seems to be much more probable that the name was borrowed from the cartoon.

New documents that will elucidate the origin of *jeep* cannot be expected to turn up. **The facts at our disposal are as follows. *Jeep,* the combat car, got its name in August 1940 at the latest. By February 1941 "everybody" in the army, but, apparently, not among journalists, knew the word *jeep.* The first jeeps were marked *G.P.* McCloskey's decipherment of the abbreviation ('General Production'), if it is correct, was reinterpreted 'For General Purpose.'** Alexander (1944:279) mentions both possibilities, but his case is an exception. 'For General Purpose' has the variant 'For General Purposes.' It follows from Roscoe (1944) and Partridge (1947b:146) that the preferred variant in England was the plural.

The practice of giving etymologies in dictionaries without references makes it impossible to trace the editors' sources and evaluate their conclusions. What they say about the origin of *jeep* sometimes seems to be arbitrary. For example, in AHD[1], the explanation is: "Originally *G.P.,* 'general purpose'." AHD[2] has a longer entry: "[A]lter[ation] of G.P. (for General Purpose) Vehicle, a special use of Eugene the Jeep, name of fabulous animal in comic strip 'Popeye' by E. C. Segar." Finally, in AHD[3], *jeep* is etymologized so: "[P]robably pronunciation of the name of this vehicle in the manufacturer's parts numbering system: *G(overnment) + P,* designator for 80-inch wheel-base reconnaissance car." According to the universal conviction of war participants, *jeep* was named after Segar's Jeep (in England, *Thimble Theatre* was published in the

Daily Mirror, though it does not seem to have enjoyed the same popularity as in the United States: Olybrius [1943]). During the war, researchers shared this conviction (Fleece [1943:69]). However, the official point of view (assuming that it existed) favored the derivation from *G.P.* 'General Purposes.' Jeepers-Creepers was Jeep's 'big brother' (see McFarlane, above), but no confirmation of WBD's etymology has been found.

It is true that the first jeeps were not general purpose cars, and Bishop (1946:244), to whom Mencken refers, emphasizes that *G.P.* is not a normal Army abbreviation. Also, the development from the pronunciation *g–p* to *jeep* would be unusual. The idea that *jeep* was a pejorative army term for anything insignificant or not yet proven reliable runs contrary to the widely held opinion about *jeep* as a term of endearment for the wonder-working vehicle. The earliest examples of *jeep* 'foolish, inexperienced, or offensive individual; recruit or basic trainee' in RHHDAS do not antedate July 1938. No connection can be established between Eugene the Jeep and the slang word for 'recruit, rookie.'

With the emergence of the car, *jeep* 'recruit' did not drop out of the language, and the two coexisted through (most of?) the war; the latest example from that period in RHHDAS is dated 1943. *Jeep*, according to WFl, is "[f]rom the Army term 'GP' (general purpose) reinforced by the noise 'jeep' made by a mythical animal who could do almost anything, in E.C. Segar's comic strip, 'Popeye'." *Jeep* is glossed in their dictionary as 'new Army recruit, rookie; link trainer; naval escort carrier; slow, painstaking man' (not common), and 'complaint' (not common). *Jeepers,* and *jeepers creepers* (euphemisms for *Jesus!* and *Jesus Christ!*) were first recorded in 1928 (RHHDAS). *Jeep* (the car) had some short-lived progeny. *American Speech* 19 (1944:233) lists among trade name novelties *jeeps* 'a make of shoe in white or army russet with popular wedgie heel.'

The derivation of *jeep* from the cartoon character is acceptable. Both Segar's fabulous creature and the new car could "perform anything." The abbreviation *G.P.*, marking the first jeeps, was an unlikely source of the car's name. The suggestion that *jeep* owes something to *jeepers (creepers)* or that it is an extension of *jeep* 'recruit' does not carry conviction. The case of *jeep* is instructive: the word was coined in the full light of history, we have eyewitness reports (conflicting as such reports always are) of the car's production, and we still have doubts about the origin of its name.

KEY (1000)

The word key *has cognates only in Old Frisian:* kāie *and* kēie. *From an etymological point of view, it is probably the same word as English northern regional* key *'twisted.' The West Germanic protoform* *kaigjō- *must have designated a pin with a curved end. Judging by the recorded cognates, OE* cǣg(e) ~ cǣga *reached English and Frisian dialects from Scandinavia.*

The sections are devoted to 1) the protoform of key, *2) the earliest attempts at etymologizing* key, *3) E* key *and G* Kegel, *4)* key *and the Germanic root* *kī-, *5) the proposed etymology of* key, *6) the interaction of* *kāg- *and* *kăg- *words in Scandinavian, and 7) the homonyms of* key.

1. Dictionaries and manuals state that Old English had competing forms: *cǣg* (f *jō*-stem), *cǣge* (f weak), and *cǣga* (m weak), but they do not explain how the *jō*-stem and the length of the root vowel have been established. It may be useful to do so. OE *cǣge* was feminine; see phrases like *seo cæg* and *þære cægean* (BT, A.S.C. Ross [1937:67-68, 86], and DOE). In Old English, short-syllabic strong feminine nouns preserved their endings and could look like *caru* 'sorrow' (*ō*-stem), *beadu* 'battle' (*wō*-stem), or *duru* 'door' (*u*-stem). Short-syllabic *jō*-nouns like *brycg* 'bridge' had geminated root final consonants. OE *cæg* never ended in *-u* or had *-w* in oblique cases, and *g* in it was always short. Consequently, its vowel was long. That conclusion is borne out by the fact that the few Old English words ending in [j] and spelled with the letter ȝ, *ǣg* 'egg,' *cǣg*, and *clǣg* 'clay' among them, had long vowels or diphthongs in the root (SB, sec 175.2).

The vowel *ǣ* in *cǣg* could not be a reflex of Gmc *$\bar{e}_1$ because before *$\bar{e}_1$ initial *k* would have become an affricate, but before *ǣ* < **ā*, as before all umlauted vowels, *k* preserved its velar character (cf *chin* < *cinn* versus *kin* < *cynne*). It follows that *ǣ* in *cǣg* is the product of *i*-umlaut. The cause of the different treatment of velars before old and new front vowels, the chronology of umlaut in relation to the change *k* > *ḱ* (palatalized), and the syllabic structure of Old English words (discussed in detail in Hogg [1979] and Colman [1986]) are immaterial for the etymology of *key*.

Among phonetic details, the history of *-g* in *cǣg* deserves mention. That OE *cǣg* was [kæ:j] rather than [kæ:g] follows from the modern pronunciation [kei], the predecessor of [ki:], and from the fact that in Anglian dialects it did not become **cēg:* Anglian *ǣ* lost its open character before velars and remained unchanged before palatalized consonants (A. Campbell [1959:sec 233]). In the string *[kæ:g] > *[kæ:ǵ] > *[kæ:j] > *[ke:j] > [kei] > [ki:], only the last link is puzzling. The modern pronunciation of *key* is usually ascribed to Northern influence, though it is unclear why the Scottish norm should have prevailed in the South (Diensberg [1999:107]). Kaluza (1906-07:II, sec 356, note 1, and 385f) cites *weak, bleak* (from Scand *veikr* and *bleikr*), and *either* ~ *neither* (when they rhyme with *bequeather*) as also having [i:] from [ei], as well as *ley* 'pasture,' a doublet of *lea.*

Since *ǣ in cǣg* could not go back to **ē* and was the product of ī-umlaut, *cǣg* must have developed from **kāg* before *i* or *j*. The only regular source of OE *ā* is Gmc **ai*; consequently, an earlier form of **kāg* must have been **kaig*. The necessity to reconstruct *i* or *j* after the root leaves us with two choices: the *i*-stem or the *jō*-stem. However, strong long-syllabic feminine nouns of the *i*-declension (such as *bēn* 'plea') had the same form in the nominative and the accusative singular, while the accusative of *cǣg* was *cǣge*. Consequently, *cǣg* belonged to the *jō*-declension and had the protoform **kaig-jō-*. See SB (secs 257 and 276, note 5), Wright and Wright (1914:sec 275), A. Campbell (1959:secs 429, 439, 593), Kaluza (1906-07:I, secs 60, 89, 90a, 109), Luick (1964:sec 187, 238, 361.1, 373, 378b, 400, 408, 637.1, 709.3, 710), HL (287-88), and OED (the last mainly on the modern pronunciation of *key*).

2. **The earliest attempts to discover the origin of *key* did not go beyond the comparison between *key* and L *clāvis* 'key,' L *claudo* 'shut, close,' Gk κλείω 'shut,' and so on.** Ital *chiave* offered an especially tempting model: by "striking out" *l*, one obtained a form resembling *key* [kei]. Cockayne (1861:sec 822) and Lynn (1884) kept deriving *key* from *clāvis*. More cautious etymologists cited only the Old English form. Thus Junius, although he was the first to discover a cognate in Frisian (Old Frisian had *kāi* and *kēi*), could not think of any etymology of *key* (spelled *cey* in his dictionary). **Somner introduced the nonexistent infinitive *cæggian* (with a short vowel) 'obserare,' 'shut fast or lock.'** Tooke (1798-1805:375) declared *cǣg* to be the past participle of this ghost verb (he looked on most words as past participles) and listed a few other words he thought related to it: *cage, gage, wages, gag, keg,* and *quay.*

Wedgwood followed Tooke in that he tried to find the same etymology for *key* and its homonym *quay.* He correctly identified the Celtic ancestry of F *quai* and suggested the loss of *l* in Celtic, so that L *clāvis* again turned out to be the etymon of *key.* He referred to G *schließen* 'close' (with *l*) and E *shut* (without *l*), but as we now know, those verbs are not cognate. Many later dictionaries contain variations on Tooke's and Wedgwood's themes; see Johnson-Todd (OE *cæggian* 'shut up'), Richardson (*quay* and *cæggian* 'shut up, confine'), Mackay (1877; he repeats Wedgwood), Chambers (1868; he cites Welsh and Latin forms), and DDEW (L *clāvis*). Skeat[1] reconstructs the protoform **kagan,* denies its connection with *quay,* and says that the origin of *key* is unknown. Skeat[4] gives only the English and Frisian forms.

W (1828) cites Old English *cæg* but offers no etymology (that tradition continued into the present: throughout its history, no edition of Webster's dictionary has risked a hypothesis on the origin of *key*). The same holds for OED, all the "Oxford" dictionaries, and Weekley. The verb **cæggian* had an amazingly long life. It appears in Bosworth (1838) with reference to Somner and in BT, vol. 1. Only Toller entered *cæggian* and said: "delete." OED cited the Middle English forms but found it necessary to add: "An OE *cǽggian* is alleged by Somner."

When an etymology does not immediately suggest itself, one usually witnesses various attempts to guess the origin of a difficult word. Most conjectures turn out to be wrong, if not fanciful. But *key* provides relatively little food to an imaginative researcher. The Latin hypothesis (*key* < *clāvis*) died a quiet death because Skeat did not mention, let alone endorse, it. A Celtic connection, prompted by the Celtic origin of *quay,* has been explored and abandoned. The first to suggest that *key* is related to (or borrowed from) Welsh *cau* may have been Bosworth (1838), who gave the Welsh form with a misprint (as *can* 'shut, inclose'). Jellinghaus (1898a:464) cited the form correctly and followed it, in its putative capacity as a cognate of the Anglo-Frisian word, by a question mark. (Old) Welsh *cau* 'close, clasp; conclude; shut; hollow: enclosed' (from **kou̯os:* GPC) cannot be related to E *key* (from **kaigjō-*). A loan from Welsh is equally improbable. Neither Celtic nor English etymologists seem to have shown much interest in the Welsh hypothesis, and today it is forgotten.

Key surfaced in one of the oldest Scandinavian dictionaries with an etymological component. Serenius (1757) compared it with OI *kúga* 'tyrannize, force,' whose very Latin gloss ('cogo,' that is, 'force, compel; collect') looked like a cognate. He was not an original etymologist and was probably repeating the derivation of one of his predecessors. Those were rather numerous (Rogström [1998:179-201]), but *key* does not turn up in any of them. Nor does it appear in Ihre, in whose dictionary we find Sw *kag*, but not E *key.* If OI *kúga,* a verb of obscure origin, goes back to **kúfga* (AEW, ÁBM), it may be related to G *Kugel* 'bullet,' E *cog*, Sw *kugge* 'cog,' and perhaps E *cudgel*. The meaning 'compel' will not be part of it. Finally, W. Barnes (1862:96) listed *key* under one of his all-encompassing roots, namely *k*ng* 'stop back anything.'

One can see that **early etymologists, insofar as they did not derive *key* from Latin or Welsh, sought its origin in words designating some sort of restriction or confinement, and this is the reason their labors yielded nothing worth salvaging.** *Key* is not obviously related to any verb, and it contains no suffix of a *nomen agentis*. EWDS[11] says that English words for 'key' are of Romance origin. Holthausen (1934:35) was quick to point out the mistake, and it was expunged from later editions.

3. Students of English have given up the etymology of *key* as hopeless, but **the word often appeared in German and Dutch scholarly sources, in which it was compared with G *Kegel* 'skittle, ninepin.'** The first vowel of OHG *kegil* 'nail, pin' is the product of *i*-umlaut (*kegil* < **kagila*), and the cognates of **kag-* are well-known. *Kag* 'stalk, cabbage stump' is current in southern German dialects. Schmid mentioned it but could not think of a better comparison than Swabian *Kag* ~ L *cavus* 'hollow.' Some other words having the root **kag-* are Sw reg *kage* 'low bush' (compare E reg *cag* 'stump,' of Scandinavian origin), N *kage* 'low bush,' OI *Kagi* (a nickname), OE *ceacga* 'broom; furze' (mod reg *chag*), MDu *kegghe* 'wedge' (> ModDu *keg* ~ *kegge*), OI *kaggi* 'keg, cask' (the etymon of E *keg*), possibly MDu *kâke* ~ *kaek* and MLG *kāk* 'pillory,' OI *kakki* 'water jug,' and several words with the infix *n* (KM, AEW). Whatever the causes of the alternation *-gg-/-kk-* may be, the words with the voiced and the voiceless geminate seem to belong together (see especially Tamm, *kagge* 'keg').

Kegel does not have any reliable cognates outside Germanic. Several Greek words have been proposed as candidates and dismissed (Uhlenbeck [1901:299-300]). Bezzenberger and Fick (1881:237/27) compared *Kegel* and Lith *žaginỹs* 'pole, stake,' and Fick (1891:320) traced *Keģel* and L *baculum* 'stick' to the etymon **gagló-*. *Žaginỹs*, along with *žãgaras* 'dry branch,' and *žãgrė* 'plow, plowshare,' turns up in most modern etymological dictionaries featuring G *Kegel*. However, Fraenkel (LEW; *žaginỹs*: see *žãgas*) may have doubted the connection, for he compared *Kegel* only with Lith *gẽgnė* 'rafter.' Uhlenbeck (1896:101-02) added Russ *zhezl* 'rod, baton' to the Lithuanian words, but, according to Trubachev (1960:137-40), it should be kept apart from the Baltic group. Even more remote is Arm *cag* 'top, peak' (WP I:570; IEW, 354), though Holthausen (VEW) gives it in the entry *kǫggull* without discussion. **The *Kegel* group probably has no cognates outside Germanic.**

A single native English word related to *Kegel* is *chag* (reg). Schwenck[1-3] connected *Kegel* and *key* and cited OE **cægjan* [sic]. In Schwenck[4], *key* is absent. His dictionary enjoyed considerable popularity both among lay readers and in professional circles. Bezzenberger must have consulted it, but Bezzenberger and Fick (1881:237/27) do not refer to any predecessors (this is where OHG *kegil* and OE *cǣg* are for the first time compared with Lith *žaginỹs* 'stake, pole'). Holbrooke (1910:254) glossed OE *cǣg* as 'binder, bar, key' and listed it with OI *kaggi* and many other words having the root *[s]kag* ~ *[s]kaggi*.

Kluge apparently disapproved of Schwenck's etymology, yet it made its way into Dutch dictionaries, perhaps independently of Schwenck. Franck did not deny the possibility that Du *keg* ~ *kegge* are related to *key*. In EWNT[2], Van Wijk deleted Franck's *perhaps*, but in the supplement to the same edition, he declared the old etymology untenable, because, if OE *cǣg* were related to Du *keg*, its initial velar would, he said, have become an affricate. Here he was wrong, for an affricate, as has been shown in sec 1, above, did not arise before umlauted front vowels.

Vercoullie[1-3] compared Du *keg* and E *key*, but Indo-European dictionaries did not recognize his comparison. Torp (1909:33, *kag*) made no mention of *key*. WP I:569-70 cited OE *cǣg* and ModE *cag* under the root **gĕ̄g(h)-* ~ **gog(h)* 'branch; stake; bush,' yet on p. 570 this etymology of *key* is called into question. IEW (354) replaced "unlikely" with "unclear." **If *key* goes back to **kaigjō-*, it cannot be related to **kag*, for **ai* and **a* belong to different ablaut series.** The same problem arises in the etymology of HEATHER and OAT. Unless we agree that *ai* and **ā* may alternate in the same root (compare Foerste's rule about the alternation **ai* ~ **a*, discussed at CLOVER), *key* and *Kegel* must be separated as impossible partners. Van Haeringen made a brief statement to that effect (see his supplement: *keg*), and it is strange to find Vercoullie's etymology in Van Veen (*keg*).

Van Veen is not the only supporter of Schwenck's etymology. Markey (1979; 1983:98-100) offered a detailed investigation of the extant forms of the word for 'key' in Frisian dialects (Siebs [1889:202] and Löfstedt [1963-65:316] give a full array of the relevant forms; the Standard has *kaei*, plural *kaeijen*) and place names with the element *kōg* (< *kāg*; ModDu *kaag* and *koog* 'polder,' that is, a piece of low-lying land reclaimed from the sea or a river and protected by dikes). He concluded that *kōg* "was regarded as an opening, a central break in the water, the aperture for subsequent territorial expansion: it was a 'key' to the formation of new land, and Frisian *kōg* ~ *kāg* ~ *kēg* < *kaug(i)* is thus semantically related to Anglo-Frisian *key* < *kaigi-* as apophonic variants of a common root (**ǵogh*)" (1979:50). The Anglo-Frisian term for *key* is said to have "originally denoted the locus, the aperture receptive to the object employed to perform that act" (p. 41). The semantic base of Markey's reconstruction will be discussed below, but the main problem with his hypothesis is the reference to "apophonic variants of a common root."

Less clear-cut are Lerchner's examples (1965:129-30). The head word in his list is *kei* (m, f) 'cobblestone, boulder, oblong stone.' The etymology of this Dutch noun is debatable (NEW). If the original meaning was *'wedge-shaped stone,' then *kei* is a cognate of G *Kegel.* A connection between Du *kei* and *kiezel* 'gravel' (G *Kies* 'gravel,' *Kiesel* 'pebble,' and so on) is less probable. Lerchner borrowed his etymology from E. Zupitza (1896:194), though Zupitza's formulation is not clear. Makovskii (1968:133) mistranslated Lerchner's gloss and rejected his conclusion. He pointed to the difference in meaning between E *key* and Du *kei*, but the incompatibility of their etymons, whatever the origin of the Dutch word, is more important.

In a book full of far-reaching but shaky hypotheses, Zollinger (1952:46-47) noted that words for 'hook' have the root *kag-* all over the world. Examples in works of this type usually do not bear close scrutiny. Among words from Germanic, Slavic, Basque, Japanese, and other languages, Zollinger cites OE *kǣg* and E *key* (p. 46). He does not seem to be aware of the literature discussed above; nor can attention to details be expected from such compilations, and this makes them practically useless. Vennemann (1995:70), who noted the irregularities in the *hook* set, believes that *key,* like *hook,* is a substrate word and compares it with Basque (reg) *kakho* 'hook' and *gako* 'key' (Vennemann 2002:233-36). Unless it can be shown that we deal with a key of some special construction (otherwise the borrowing is hard to explain), his hypothesis has little appeal. Nor is the phonetic match (Basque [ak(h)] versus pre-OE *[āg]) close enough, at first sight.

Although one can surmise that *kāg-* and **kăg-* interacted and were occasionally confused in the oldest northern dialects, for etymological purposes the two roots should be kept apart. The Germanic words for 'hook' furnish a parallel to the *kăg-* / *kāg* relation, but here we have a case of regular ablaut. The words of the *hook* group also had varying root final consonants (see E *hook,* G *Haken,* E *hoop,* and E *hasp,* with their cognates, in etymological dictionaries).

4. **The next group of attempts to explain the origin of *key* centers round the root *kī-, attested in all the Old Germanic languages.** Go *keinan** 'sprout' has correspondences in Scandinavian and West Germanic, OE *cīnan* 'gape, yawn, crack' being one of them. The only Modern English reflex of **kī-* is probably *chine* 'crack,' which would have disappeared too if it had not been generalized from place names in Hampshire and the Isle of Wight in the meaning 'deep narrow ravine cut by a stream' (OED, ODEE). In some obscure way, *chink* must be related to *chine.* In German, words with the root **kī* have wide currency: *Kien* 'pine tree, pine branch used for kindling; torch' (< OHG *kien;* OE *cēn* occurs only as the name of a rune), *Keim* 'shoot, sprout' (< OHG *kîmo*), *keimen* 'germinate' (< OHG *kînan*), and *Keil* 'wedge' (< OHG *kîl*) (see *Keim, Keil,* and *Kien* in KM and KS, *keinan* in Feist[3-4], and *kiem* in NEW; see also WP I:544 and IEW, 355). OHG *kîl* had a Middle High German doublet *kîdel* related to OE *cīð* 'seed, sprout; mote'; see CHIDE. Thus we obtain the complexes *kī-l, kī-m, kī-n,* and *kī-ð.* The original verb has been assigned the meaning 'break open, burst open' (Seebold [1970:290-91] and KS, *Keim, Kien*), which takes care of sprouting, splitting, producing cracks and fissures, and so forth. The reconstructed form **kaigiō-* 'key' may belong to the *kī-* group, for unlike *a* in OHG **kagila, ī* is a legitimate apophonic partner of *ai.*

Wood (1902:52/92a; repeated in Wood 1920:340/135) was the first to connect OE *cǣg* and the words of the *kī-* group. He also mentioned G *Keil* and OI *keipr* 'oarlock, rowlock' as possibly derived from the root **ǵei̯o-* 'move suddenly, jerk, snatch.' *Keipr* is problematic (see below), but *Keil* has found its place in etymological dictionaries with Go *keinan* and the rest. Holthausen (1912:48), who may have missed Wood's etymology, advanced a similar hypothesis, but the cognates he lists do not cohere too well. He begins by connecting OE *cǣg* and OHG *kegil* and then adds MDu *keige* 'javelin, spear,' MHG *kîdel* ~ *kîl* 'wedge,' and OI *kill* 'inlet, canal.' He traces those words to **kaijō(n),* in ablaut relation with **kī-,* and argues that ancient keys were simply pins or pegs. However, he cites only OE *cīð* as a possible cognate of *cǣg(e)* in AeEW and gives no etymology of *key* in EW. The weakest part of Holthausen's reconstruction is that he lumped together words of the *Kegel* and the **kī-* groups.

Although OE *cǣg* and *cīnan* may belong together (though *cǣg* would then turn out to be the only word of the structure **kī-g-* ~ **kai-g-* among the cognates of Go **keinan* in any grade of ablaut), the semantic base of this etymology is not fully convincing. Nouns related to the verb **kīnan,* with its dominant meaning 'burst into bloom,' could hardly designate pieces of deadwood (like pins, pegs, and splinters), whereas resinous branches, shoots, and sprouts are unsuitable for barring doors.

In the first ten editions of EWDS (but not in KL), OE *cǣg* turns up as a possible cognate of *Keil.* Götze removed the English word from the entry, and it never appeared in Kluge's dictionary again.

5. **The English word denoting an instrument for moving the bolt of a lock is unusual in that it is opaque and has no cognates except in Frisian.** The isolated nature of *cǣg* ~ *kēi* has been recognized for a long time (Jellinghaus [1898a:464], E. Schwartz [1951:210]). Nor does *key* resemble its counterparts in the other Germanic languages, such as Du *sleutel,* G *Schlüssel,* and (O)I *lykill,* all of which are etymologically transparent (Kluge [1926:sec 90]). Words designating keys, latches, and bolts may be borrowed. Such are, for example, E *pin* (Förster [1902:324-27]), OE *clūstor* (< L *clūstrum;* SN II:324), E *latch, bar,* and *bolt,* and see other examples in Buck (1949:7.24), to which Russ *shchekolda* 'latch, bar, bolt'–stress on the second syllable–apparently, from LG *Steckholt* (Vasmer IV:500) can be added. They may have unexpected origins. Consider E reg *haggaday* 'latch,' an obscure word (Skeat [1895]), G *Riegel* (equally obscure), and G *Dietrich* 'skeleton key' (from a proper name, like E *jenny*). But *cǣg* < **kaigjō-*, if we disregard the Basque connection, seems to be a native word, and at one time it must have been coined from an easily identifiable root.

In most cases, words for 'key,' unless they mean 'lock-er' ~ 'clos-er' ~ 'shut-ter,' are derived from words for 'peg,' 'nail,' 'pin,' and 'hook.' The most primitive keys, when they were keys rather than bars, had bits. In many languages, the root of the word for 'key' means 'curvature.' See WP I:492-94, *qlēu,* and IEW, 604-05, *klēu-*; WH (*clāva, claudo*) also give the comparative material. A typical example is Russ *kliuch* 'key,' related to *kliuka* (stress on the second syllable) 'hooked staff, crook.' SN II:327 reproduce several pictures of old keys. The earliest extant locks used by speakers of the Germanic languages show the influence of Roman locksmiths (Falk [1918-19]), but the native Germanic words for 'key' go back to an older period (Heyne [1899:31]). Wattle doors of the type designated by Go *haurds* (its English cognate is *hurdle*) had openings in the front wall, not real doors; they did not need elaborate locks. Go *-lūkan* 'lock up' and its congeners originally meant 'bend, turn' (Feist[3-4]). Since G *schließen,* Du *sluiten* 'lock up, close,' and so on are related to L *clāvis,* they, too, must have meant 'put a bolt across the door.'

At all times, some keys have been made to lock the door, others only to unlock it (so that we should distinguish between 'closers' and 'openers'), and still others to perform both functions. Keys and locks of medieval Scandinavia have been especially well researched. If the answer to Old English Riddle 44 from the *Exeter Book* is 'penis' and 'key,' the key it describes has a modern form. Most of the oldest Norwegian, Danish, and Swedish devices for fastening the door do not antedate the epoch of the Vikings, but the shape of some of them is archaic (Berg at al [1966:48-61], Norberg [1967]). The long discussion on words for 'key' in Scandinavia has a bearing on both the linguistic and the material aspects of keys everywhere in the Germanic Middle Ages. See Brøndum-Nielsen (1931-32, 1933-34, 1971-73) and R. Pipping (1933-34); Brøndum-Nielsen (1931-32) contains numerous illustrations. Nor are relations between OI *lykill* and **nykill* irrelavant for understanding how keys got their names elsewhere. See Jirlow (1936), Andersson (1936), Hamp (1971-73) and Holm (1993:109-10). If **nykill* is not a phonetic variant of *lykill* (Byskov [1909]; DEO[3-4], *nøgle;* this point of view is much better argued than Andersson and Hamp's), then **nykill* should be understood as a bent stick. It will be suggested below that *cǣg,* too, was 'a curved pin,' as Holthausen proposed.

E *key* is both a noun and an adjective. Preserved now only in northern dialects and as follows from the occasional spellings *kay* and *keigh,* pronounced [kei], *key* (adj) goes back to Middle English. OED (*kay, key*) gives two citations, one dated 13??, the other 1611, but the material in EDD (*key*) is abundant, even though by Wright's time the adjective *key* was obsolescent in some areas (Audrey [1883-84]). *Key* (adj) has been traced to Scandinavian. OED refers to Sw reg *kaja* 'left hand' and *kajhandt* 'left-handed.' EDD cites Sw reg *kaja* (from Rietz) and also northern Frisian *kei* 'awkward; inarticulate, lacking fluency.' In English dialects, the most widely-known meaning of *key* is 'twisted,' as in *key-legged* 'knock-kneed, crooked' and *key-leg* 'crooked or bandy leg.' The verb *key* means 'twist, bend,' used especially with reference to the legs twisted by illness, and so forth.

'Left' must have originated as 'twisted' and 'bent,' like OI *vinstri* 'left' (< **wenistru*), with **wen-* most plausibly glossed by Huisman (1953:105) as 'bent downward' (see also AEW, *vinstri*). Despite Frisk's doubt (GrEW), Gk λαιός, L *laevus*, Proto-Slavic **lěvŭ*, and their cognates, including E *left*, originally seem to have meant 'bent down, twisted.' See etymological dictionaries and Beekes (1994:89). Malkiel (1979:esp 517 and 520) discusses words for 'left' and 'right' against a broad background and refers to a few important earlier works. OI *skeifr* 'oblique' and G *schief* 'crooked, lopsided, tilted' (from Low German) versus L *scaevus* 'left' provide a parallel to the Scandinavian word, which served as the source of E *key* 'left.'

Without *s-* we have not only Sw reg *kaja* 'left hand' but also (with root final *v*) Nynorsk *keiv(en)* 'clumsy, awkward; false, unfortunate,' *keivhendt* 'left-handed' and *keiva* 'the left hand of a left-handed person'; Dan reg *kei* 'left hand' goes back to **kêg* (NEO, *keiv*). Next come words with root final *t*, for example, Dan *kejtet* 'left-handed, awkward,' *kejthåndet* 'left-handed,' and *kejte* 'left hand' (cf Sc *katy-handed* 'left-handed') and words with root final *k:* OI *keikja* 'bend back,' from *keikr* 'bent backward.' A near synonym of *keikja* in the zero grade is OI *kikna* 'give way at the knees' (*kikna* must be the etymon of E *kick,* as Skeat suggested; OED and ODEE deny the connection and call *kick* a word of unknown origin). Alongside *kei-f, kei-g, kei-k,* and *kei-t, kei-p* has been recorded. The etymology of OI *keipr* 'oarlock, rowlock' (see sec 4, above) is debatable, but several scholars (Torp in NEO, *keip*, and see the references in AEW, *keipr*) treat *keipr* and *keikr* as related.

EDD lists several words with final *k* and *g* (from all over England) that resemble *keikja, keck-fisted, -handed, cack-handed,* and *cag-handed* (the last two sometimes end in *-fisted*) 'left-handed; clumsy, awkward.' From Warwickshire, EDD has *keggy* and *ceggy* 'left-handed.' *Keggle* and *kiggle* 'be unstable, stand insecurely' appear to be related to *cag-* and *keggy.* The northern forms *keck* and *kecker* may also belong here. A kecker is "the bar which connects the body of a cart with thills; a piece of wood or iron in front of a tumbril to enable the body of a cart to be raised to any angle. ...When the cart is kecked, the front is raised, and a peg is put into one of the holes in the kecker to keep it at the required angle" (EDD). The verb *keck* can mean 'twist to one side.' AHD[3] (*cack-handed*, chiefly British 'left-handed; awkward, chumsy') offers a plausible etymology: "Perhaps from Old Norse *keikr*, 'bent backwards'; akin to Danish *keite,* 'left-handed'," except that *kejte* means 'left hand,' while the derivation in Longman 1984 (*kack-handed,* the same definition, but in the opposite order 'awkward, clumsy; *derog[atory]* 'left-handed') is unacceptable: allegedly, from E reg *cack* 'excrement, muck,' from ME *cakken* 'defecate,' from L *cacāre.* SOD (DG, 241-42) offers a rich pallet of words for 'left-handed': *cack-handed, cat-handed, cuddy-handed, kaggy-handed, kay-reived, keck-handed, keggy-handed,* and *kittaghy* among others.

In all likelihood, both E reg *key* 'twisted' and the noun *key* (< **kaig-jō*) belong with the words given above. The same holds for OFr *kēie* and *kāie.* ***Key* was then 'a stick (pin, peg) with a twisted end.' It may have been a northern word from the start.** Many links connect it with Old Icelandic and modern Scandinavian dialects (however, according to ÁBM, ModI *kigi* 'the front part of a beam' is not related to OE *cǣg*), while leads to old and modern West Germanic are absent. *Scyttel(s)* and *forescyttels* testify to other Old English words for 'key.' They, too, designated a bar, for they represent the zero grade of *scēotan* and were thus 'shot' across the door like modern bolts. The phrase *īsen scytel* 'iron bolt' (OE) was synonymous with *īsen steng.* Bolts could also be used on wattle doors, as follows from OI *loka* and *hurðarloka.*

The disappearance of OE *scyttel(s)* is probably due to the fact that it was used too broadly: it also meant 'dart, missile, arrow.' In similar manner, *shuttle* 'weaving implement,' which emerged in texts in the 14th century, has been recorded with the meanings 'floodgate' and 'drawer.' Anything that can be shot or shut is potentially a 'scyttel' or a 'shuttle' (see *shuttle* in OED). On the other hand, neither Scand **lukila, *hnukila* (assuming that **hnukila* existed) nor OHG *sluzzil* ~ LG *slutil* had English cognates. E reg *slot(e)* ~ *sloat* 'lock' (akin to G *Schloss*) are borrowings from Middle Low German or Middle Dutch (OED). They are not related to *slot* 'groove.'

Frisian had *kāie* ~ *kēie* and *sletel.* Both may have been borrowed: the first from Scandinavian, the second from Dutch. Scandinavian dialects have not preserved a cognate of OE *cǣg* meaning 'key,' and this circumstance weakens the hypothesis of the northern provenance of *key,* but cases when a word survives as a borrowing but is lost in the lending language are not uncommon.

The Old English noun and its Old Frisian cognate must have had the same meaning. Markey's idea that in most Germanic languages the word for 'key' refers to a tool, whereas in Frisian it refers to an orifice, lacks foundation. We have no evidence that the object called **kaigjō-* needed an orifice. It was rather a bolt, a synonym of OE *grindel.* Furthermore, the key probably never derives its name from the hole into which it is inserted.

6. Proto-Old English **kaig-jō* gave way to **kāgji,* with **ai* smoothed (monophthongized) but **g* still a velar stop, though palatalized as, for instance, in ModI *elgi* 'elk,' *engi* 'meadow,' and *ergi* 'malice.' The root *kāg-*, which meant 'crooked, bent, twisted,' came into contact with a near homonym and partial synonym *kăg-*, not limited to the North. Consider OI *kaga* 'bend forward; peep, pry, gaze' and *kǫggull* 'joint in the finger or the toe' (usually in the plural: *kǫglur*). OI *kœgill* 'small barrel, any small vessel; ladle' can be understood as a diminutive of *kaggi* 'keg, small wine barrel,' another *kag*-word (it had a doublet *kaggr*): wooden vessels were made by weaving wattling or by interlacing pliant twigs (see these words in AEW and ÁBM). The geminate *-gg-* in *kaggi* and *kaggr* may be of expressive origin (Martinet [1937:116]). The cognates of *Kegel* do not necessarily have the connotation of curvature, but those mentioned above do. The English verb *kedge* 'change the position of a ship by winding in a hawser attached to a small anchor,' that is, 'warp a ship,' known from texts since the 15th century, may be related to OI *kaga*. In the 14th century, *cagge* denoted the action described by *kedge*. The final consonant of *kedge* could arise only in a native or an Anglicized word, but like OI *kaga,* it refers to bending or moving sideways. *Cadge,* a regional variant of *kedge,* is even closer to *kaga.*

The following picture emerges from the exposition offered here. A Scandinavian root **kaig-* 'crooked, curved, twisted, bent, oblique' alternated with **kaif-, *kaik-, *kait-,* and probably **kaip-*. It was the base of several verbs, adjectives, and nouns. One of those adjectives entered northern English and Frisian dialects; its reflex is E reg *key* 'left.' Some local designation of a device for fastening a door (a stick with its end turned down or bent), namely **kaigjō-*, reached the north of England and Frisian dialects before *i*-umlaut, the palatalization of *g* and the monophthongization of Proto-Old English **ai* to *ā*. English adopted it as a feminine *jō*-stem, but the word never acquired one standard form: in the feminine, it vacillated between the strong and the weak declension (*cǣg* and *cǣge*) and could also be a weak masculine noun (*cǣga*). After the monophthongization of **ai,* the word was pronounced **kāgji* or **kāgi* and interacted with synonyms having the root **kăg-*. The late occurrence of *cǣg(e)* and *cǣg(a)* in Old English texts (no recorded examples before the year 1000) does not necessarily mean that they had reached southern dialects only by the end of the 10th century.

7. *Key* 'low island,' in place names, is a different word, and OED explained its origin correctly (*key sb*³ and *cay*). The spelling of *Key* must have been affected by the English noun *key*. From an etymological point of view, it is the same word as *quay,* and it goes back to Sp *cayo* 'shoal, rock, barrier reef.' Later research (Friederici and DCECH, *cayo*) adds nothing new to this information. FEW II:46b states that the pronunciation of *Key* is the result of the confusion of the two homonyms in English, but the pronunciation of *quay* shows that it is not necessary to posit the influence of *key* on *Key.* The literature on Florida place names (books, dissertations, newspaper articles) contains discussion of the origin of particular names like *Key West* but not of the word *Key*. The only exception is McMullen Jr (1953).

The other words spelled *key,* for instance, *key* 'clef,' developed from the basic meaning of *key.* Only *key* 'pericarp of certain trees,' briefly mentioned above, looks problematic, but the explanation in OED appears adequate. See *key sb*³ IV.14: 'a dry fruit with a thin membranous wing, usually growing in bunches, as in the ash and sycamore' and the 1562 quotation: "They are called in Englishe ashe Keyes, because they hangh in bunches, after the manner of Keyes."

A Note on OI *kǫgurbarn* and G *mit Kind und Kegel*

In the history of the *k-g* words referring to curvature, OI *kǫgurbarn* 'infant' and G *Kegel* 'ninepin' are of special interest. The latter is also known from the phrase *mit Kind und Kegel* 'with the whole family' and is extant as the last names *Kegl, Kegelmann,* and *Kögel* (KS). OI *kǫgurbarn* (akin to Far *køgilsbarn,* Nynorsk *koggebarn:* AEW) carries a strong overtone of contempt. A despised child was most often born out of wedlock, and, as could be expected, MHG *kegel* meant 'bastard.' Seebold (KS, *Kegel*) is not sure whether *Kegel* and *kǫgurbarn* are related. They probably are, and OScand **kǫgurr* may have been a word of much stronger abuse than its Old Icelandic reflex.

AEW suggests the derivation of *kǫgur(barn)* from *kagi* ('low bush' in Modern Icelandic). In light of the widespread syncretism of branch, shoot, stump / child in Germanic, this suggestion makes sense (the same in Holthausen [1900]), but it leaves out of account the negative connotations of *kǫgurr* and *Kegel.* Couldn't these words contain reference to crookedness and hence illegitimacy, a conceptual ancestor of *bend sinister?* The idea of curvature is especially strong in the words with the infix *n:* OI *kengr* 'bend, hook' (E *kink* and *akimbo* reached English from Low German and Scandinavian respectively; both contain the same root as *kengr*), *kǫngurváfa* and *kǫngulvafa* 'spider' (spinner, like G *Spinne* 'spider'), *kǫngur* 'texture,' and *kǫngull* 'cluster of grapes or other berries,' reminiscent of E *key* 'pericarp of an ash.' Proto-Scand **kankur,* which yielded OI *kakki* (only in *vatnkakki* 'water basin') and *kǫkkr* 'ball' (ModI *kökkur* 'lump, clod'; Nynorsk *kokk* ~ *kakk* 'small wooden vessel'), belongs here too.

If OI *kǫgurr* 'quilt with a fringe, counterpane, bed cover, pall (over a coffin)' is a native word, it is not akin to *kǫgur,* as follows from Russ *kovër* 'rug, carpet,' earlier also 'thick cloth for carrying or perhaps burying a dead body.' We seem to be dealing with a migratory culture word, whose association with *kǫgurbarn* is due to folk etymology. See Fritzner (1883:28-29), Detter (1898:56), Sahlgren (1928:258-71), H. Andersen (1930), M. Olsen (1940), Elmevik (1974), IsEW (323-24), and AEW (*kǫgurr,* with references to earlier etymologies). Consider also Götze's fanciful etymology of *Kegel* in *Kind und Kegel* [1921:287] that can be found in all the editions of KM. None of those authors, except partly J. de Vries, is ready to dissociate *kǫgurr* from *kǫgurbarn.* On the Icelandic place name *Kǫgurr* see Jónsson (1916:78).

KITTY-CORNER (1890)

Kitty- *in* kitty-corner *(as in* the drug store is kitty-corner from the gas station*) is a jocular substitution for or a folk etymology of* cater-corner, *through a possible intermediate stage* catty-corner. *Numerous compounds have* cater- *as their first element. The verb* cater *'place diagonally' was first recorded in the middle of the 16th century. The compounds with* cater- *occur mainly in dialects, and their attestation does not predate the end of the 18th century; the only exception is* cater-cousin *(1547). Attempts to trace* cater- *to F* quatre *'four' and (for* cater-cousin*) to* cater *'supply food' did not yield satisfactory results.* Cater- *means 'across, askew, diagonally,' and its etymon was probably some Danish word like Dan* kejte *'left hand' or* kejtet *'clumsy.' Folk etymology connected* cater-corner *with* cat, *and* cater-cousin *with* cater *'supply food.' Some evidence points to a synonymous root of similar form, namely Gmc* kat-, *but it seems to have left no traces in English.*

The sections are devoted to 1) the dating of kitty-corner, *2) the Scandinavian origin of* cater-, *3) the etymology of* cater-cousin, *and 4) words with the root* kat- *and the possibility of projecting the roots of* cater- *and* kat- *words to Proto-Indo-European.*

1. According to DARE, *kitty-corner* was first recorded in 1890 and is a possibly folk etymological variant of *cater-cornered* 'placed diagonally.' OED has *cater-cornered* and its synonym *cater-ways* but no pre-1874 example of either. However, the verb *cater* 'cut (move, go) diagonally' turned up in 1577. Since *cater* 'place diagonally' was known in the 16th century, any compound with it may be equally old or older. **Although dictionaries agree in calling *cater-ways* an Americanism, it originated in British dialects** and is one of many similar compounds featured in EDD: *cater-cornelled, cater-flampered, cater-slant,* and seven more, all meaning approximately the same: 'askew, out of proportion, oblique, lopsided.' **On the other hand, *kitty-corner,* pronounced *kiddy-corner,* can be marked as an Americanism.**

2. **The best-known suggestion about the origin of *cater-* in *cater-ways* traces it to early ModE *cater* 'four'** (F *quatre*; see *cater sb*[2] and *quater* in OED). Not only amateurs like Terry (1883), Fishwick (1883), and G.L.G. (1883) but also the editors of OED found that etymology plausible. All later dictionaries repeated it. The idea of diagonal placement allegedly goes back to the shape of a square object (so Fishwick), but no one explained why a square came to be associated with a diagonal rather than a straight line. Numerals occasionally form the foundation of idioms. Such are E *be at sixes and sevens* 'be in confusion' (a folk etymological reshaping of a metaphor borrowed from dice: Whiting [1968:522, S359]) and G *fünf gerade sein lassen* 'turn a blind eye to an obvious transgression,' literally 'let five be straight,' but it is unimaginable that a specialized foreign numeral (its principal sphere of application was dice) should have become a fully domesticated adverb meaning 'across.' Equally puzzling would be the development from 'square' to 'out of square.'

The conjecture that *cater-* is related to G *quer* 'across' (H.E.W. [1883]; the author invites "cunning linguists" to find out what happened to the sounds) caused Skeat (1883) to write one of his fiery letters to the editor. Walsh (1939) begins his note so: "This word of interesting etymology (French *quatre coins*)..." His implication seems to be that *cater-cornered* is a calque of the French phrase. But, although some French phrase like *les quatre coins du monde (du pays, de la terre)* 'everywhere' and even *courir les quatre coins* 'run from place to place' (there is also a children's game *les quatre coins,* figuratively 'wild goose chase') have easily recognizable counterparts in English: *the four corners of the earth, within the four corners,* and *the four corners* 'crossroads,' this fact is not ground enough for explaining the origin of *cater-cornered,* especially because *cater-* is the first element of a whole series of compounds that have nothing to do with corners.

Most probably, *cater-* is a loan from an East Scandinavian language. Consider Dan *kejte* and Sw reg *kaitu* 'left hand' (see Rietz, *kaja*). *Kejte* goes back to Old Danish (ODS, OÆDS). 'Left,' as opposed to 'right,' often contains the idea 'bent, twisted,' as opposed to 'straight.' (See more on this subject at KEY.) T.T.W. (1872) elucidated the usage of *cater-* in Lancashire: "An angular stone or piece of wood is... said to be 'cater-cornered' when one of the angles is 'out of square' or too far distant from the rest. A person is also said to walk 'cater-cornered' when he moves with one side in advance of the other. This is specially applied to those who have suffered from paralysis" (the same, E.S.C. [1872]). Here the meaning 'bent, not straight' agrees with Dan *kejtet* 'clumsy, awkward.'

OIr *cittach* 'left handed; awkward' (> IrE *kithogue*) had the same source as the English *cater-* words (see the comment in O'Muirithe [1997:68]). It is a curious coincidence that not only *cater-* 'out of shape' but also *clumsy, awkward,* and possibly *gawky* are of Scandinavian origin (see GAWK). Were they first used to describe Scandinavian settlers? Final *-r* must have been added to disyllabic **cate* (< *kejte*) under the influence of some similar forms. Compare *caterpillar* from AF *katplöz* (it may have been pronounced **cat-a-pillar* for some time) and see what is said about *caterwaul* at RAGAMUFFIN. The verb *cater* 'bend' is probably a back formation from compounds beginning with *cater-*. Compounds with *cater-* as their first element must have been borrowed centuries before the time of their attestation.

3. **Additional light on *cater-cornered* and its kin comes from the history of *cater-cousin* (1547).** Today this word is remembered only because it occurs in *The Merchant of Venice* (II, 2, the line number differs from edition to edition: 125, 139 [OED], 143 [SG]): "His Maister and he ... are scarce cater-cosins," which is an ironic litotes for 'they are hardly friends' = 'they hate each other.' OED observes that the derivation and original literal meaning of *cater-cousin* are doubtful. In the 1547 citation, *cater-cousin* is explained as 'cousin-german,' that is, 'intimate friend but not cousin (relative) by blood.' This meaning appears to be late. T.T.W. (1872), in a note quoted above, states that in Lancashire, *cater-cousin* "is applied to those relationships which are extremely distant or very doubtful. When a person claims relationship to any of our local ancient families he is immediately twitted with being 'only a cater-cousin,' in intimation that his connection is both doubtful and distant." EDD refers to this note and gives two glosses of *cater-cousins*: 'intimate friends' and sometimes, though not generally, 'distant relations' (cf P.P. [1872]). DOPE glosses *cater-cousin* 1. 'intimate friend,' 2. 'parasite' (!), but without citations or references.

They are scarce cater-cousins may have had the sense 'they are distant relatives of the remotest type imaginable,' with *scarce* having its oldest meaning 'scanty, niggardly, *deficient in quality'. A connection between *cater-* in *caterways, cater-cornered,* and so on and *cater* in *cater-cousin* was forgotten, so much so that even the editors of OED, who saw these words on the same page, did not think of it. If *cater-cousin* was more often used with reinforcing adverbs like *scarce,* it was misinterpreted as 'friend,' the opposite of what it once meant. Also, *cater-* 'caterer' perhaps made people think of providers and helped to ameliorate the ancient term; see below. (Although the following is not an analogue, it may be of some use as an example of how a phrase can acquire the opposite meaning. Goldsmith still uses the idiom *there's no love lost between them* when he wants to say 'they love each other'—*She Stoops to Conquer* IV:1. And this makes perfect sense: their love is not lost! Now the idiom means only 'they hate each other,' with the implication that there was no love to lose.)

The author of the first etymology of *cater-cousin* was Skinner. He wrote (*quater-cosin*; the original is in Latin): "... we say about those who bear no secret ill will against each other that they are not cater or Quater cosins; in French ils ne sont pas de Quatre cousins. There are seven degrees of kinship, but only four principal ones. Thus, when we use this phrase, we refer not to close relatives, not to the ties of kinship." Skinner probably invented the "absurdly impossible" (OED) French idiom *quatre cousins.* Samuel Johnson mentioned "the ridiculousness of calling cousin or relation to so remote a degree." Lye (in Junius), copied Skinner's etymology, and reference to *quatre* remained in all the editions of Webster's until W^1. OE had the legal term *sibfæc* 'degree of affinity,' but *cater-cousin* has nothing to do with that usage.

Nares's definition of *cater-cousins* as 'friends so familiar that they eat together' must have reflected his identification of *cater-* with *cater* 'provide food.' Hales (1875:287 = 1884a:177) states emphatically that Skinner's French phrase does not exist and suggests a connection with *cater(er),* for cater-cousins are messfellows. He adds: "This explanation has been offered before; but it may still require confirmation." No confirmation has been found. Yet OED supported the messfellow idea, and *cater-cousin* emerged as a compound of allegedly the same type as *foster father, foster brother,* and *foster child.* But foster parents really foster (nourish) their foster children, while cater-cousins are not known to have provided for each other or boarded together. See a short survey of opinions on Shakespeare's word in Furness (1895:72). Skeat included *cater-cousin* only in the fourth edition of his dictionary and adopted the idea of OED. All the "Oxford" dictionaries, RHD, and AHD did the same. CD had Skinner's etymology, and, surprisingly, UED says: "Intimate friend; originally *quarter-cousin,* meaning distant or fourth cousin." This is almost exactly what one can find in Richardson: *cater cousin* 'quatre cousin.' ED also leaned toward *cater-* = *quatre. Quatre* as the etymon of *cater-* in *cater-cousin* is useless; *cater(er)* yields good sense, but its ties with *cater-cousin* are a product of folk etymology that may have played some role in its semantic history.

4. If *cater-* goes back to Dan *kejte* or some similar form, the search for its etymon can be considered almost closed. The only problem would be the absence of corresponding Scandinavian compounds. Conversely, in the history of *lad* compounds with *-ladd* have been found, whereas the simplex exists only in English. Most likely, *lad, lass, slang,* and *key* are also words of Scandinavian origin (see KEY, LAD, LASS, SLANG), but the most careful search yields only their non-immediate etymons. One is bound to admit that English speakers reshaped and restructured them.

From a historical point of view, *cater-corner* has nothing to do with *cat,* but folk etymology connected them, whence *catty-* and *kitty-corner.* An almost identical process happened elsewhere in Germanic. Kaspers (1938) examined the place names *Katwijk* (Holland), *Kattewegel* (Flanders), *Katthagen* (northern Germany), *Kattsund(sgatan)* (Sweden), and many others, including G *Katzwinkel* (*-winkel* 'corner'), with the elements *Kat(t)-, Katz-,* and *Kett-,* and came to the conclusion that all of them could not mean 'cat's village,' 'cat's hedge (haw, enclosure),' 'cat's bay,' and so forth. All those places are crooked, situated in a corner, and are in general associated with curvature. Northern G *Kattrepel* (Redslob [1913-14:32]) may belong here too. In Westphalia, the past participle *verkat* means 'wrong, perverse,' and Kaspers (1938:220, note 2) wonders whether the expression *für die Katz,* literally 'for the cat,' used about the work that turned out to be a waste of time, has the same origin. He does not deny the possibility that some place names he investigated contain allusions to cats, but many others must have meant 'crooked street (piece of land, *etc*).' If so, *Katzwinkel* and *Katzecke* are tautologies unless they really were the favorite haunts of alley cats or resembled such. Judging by the fanciful conjectures offered at one time about such German place names (Bause [1907]; see also Carstens's response [1908]), Kaspers was the first to offer a plausible etymology of *Katwijk* and others, but the discussion continued for a long time. See Gülzow (1938, 1943-49; 1950) on LG *Katschüße* 'narrow passage between two houses.'

Unlike E *catty-cornered,* Du *Katwijk* and the rest are neither folk etymologies of *keit-* words nor their cognates (*ei* and *a* belong to different series of ablaut). E *key* cannot be confidently referred to any Proto-Indo-European root, for the existence of PIE **gei-* 'bend, twist' (WP I:545-46; IEW, 354), whose putative reflexes are discussed at KEY, is doubtful. A list of the forms clustered around PIE **geu-,* a synonym of **gei-,* covers seven pages in WP I:555-62. In IEW, this material takes up only a page and a half (pp. 393-94; Pokorny also expunged the entire section on L *scaevus* 'left hand' from WP I:537). Kaspers's Proto-Indo-European root **ge-* 'crooked, bent,' from which he derived Gmc **kat,* is a typical product of root etymology. With vocalic enlargements he obtained **geu-* and **gei-,* while a dental enlargement in the *a*-grade yielded **gad-, *god-* and Gmc **kat-.* Amputating one consonant after another until a minimally short residuum like *ge-* is allowed to carry the meaning 'curve' is a procedure to be avoided. Germanic probably had at least three synonymous roots, **kāg-, *kăg-,* and **kat-,* meaning 'bend, curve.' Their ultimate origin is obscure, but nothing suggests an ancient element **kă̄* to which different consonants were appended in the manner of word-formative suffixes.

LAD (1300)

Several etymologies of lad *have been offered—from Hebr* yeled *'boy' to Go* (jugga)lauþs *'youth' and the past participle of OE* lǣdan *'lead'* (lad = *'one led'). But* lad, *as was also suggested long ago, appears to be a word of Scandinavian origin, though its etymon has not been found. The closest analogues of ME* ladde *are OI* lodd- *in the name* Loddfáfnir, *along with* -ladd *in N* Oskeladd *'male Cinderella' and* tusseladd *'nincompoop.' Numerous Scandinavian words were formed in the zero grade of the Germanic root* *leudh- *'grow.' Their radical vowel is either* u *or* o *from* *u. *They designate fully-shaped objects and attributes of luxuriant growth: 'furry, hairy; woolen; covered with thick grass.' The root* lud- *was stable, but the root* lod < loð- *alternated with* lad-.

One of the nouns belonging to this group is N ladd *'hose; woolen stocking (sock).' Its* a *is secondary; the original vowel was* o < *u. *Words for socks, stockings, and shoes seem to have been current as terms of abuse for and as nicknames of losers and fools.* Lad(d) 'youngster,' *with an ending of the weak declension (ME* ladde*), must have emerged in the north of England. The existence of many other similar words with the* l-ð, l-d, l-t *structure probably contributed to the rise of* lad *with its slightly patronizing meaning 'young fellow,' while OI* liði *'follower, retainer,' which is possibly a blend of Gmc* *galidja- *'follower' and ML* litus *'person belonging to a group between freedmen and serfs,' may have played a role in its acquiring the earliest recorded sense 'serving man, attendant.' The proper name* Ladda *(OE) surfaced in texts two centuries before ME* ladde *did, but the evidence of their kinship is wanting. The same holds for the few Middle English place names beginning with* Lad(d).

The sections are devoted to 1) the dead-end etymologies of lad, *2) Germanic words having the structure l + vowel + dental, and 3) the proposed Scandinavian-English origin of ME* lad; lad *and* liði ~ litus; lad *and* Ladda.

1. All the better-known etymologies of *lad* were offered long ago.

1) **Minsheu derived *lad* from Hebr יֶלֶד (*yeled* 'boy').** A similar idea occurred to Webster (W [1828]), who set up a 'class,' that is, a root **ld* 'procreate' and cited allegedly related forms from Hebrew, Arabic, Ethiopian, and several other languages. A. Hall (1904) reinvented this etymology and connected Go *liudan** 'grow,' as well as some words from Greek, Arabic, and Assyrian, with E *lad*. Cohen (1972a) cites a suggestion by one of his correspondents, "that lad (ladde) is a loan-word from Arabic, a product of the age of the Crusades and intense commerce and intercourse between Europe and the Near East." Cohen comments: "My friend Gilbert Davidowitz had already in 1965 pointed out to me the similarity between English *lad* and Arabic (wa-) lad-, Hebrew (ye-) led (boy). There is therefore an awareness among some people that *lad* may be connected with Semitic *-lad-*, but this awareness has not yet reached the writers of etymological dictionaries (even as a possibility to be rejected)." In fact, this awareness goes back to 1617 at the latest. **The history of *lad*, originally a regional word restricted to the north of England and alien to the other countries that took an active part in the crusades, speaks against the idea of its being a loan from Arabic.** Not unexpectedly, Mozeson favors the Hebrew etymology of *lad* (see Gold [1990a:117] and [1995b:373]: *lad* is mentioned as one of the words figuring in Mozeson's fantasies).

2) **Another possible connection, according to Minsheu, is between *lad* and the English verb *lead*.** Skinner supported this idea and compared *lad* and "Belgian" (= Flemish) *leyden (= leiden)*, because "lads are led by the hand or educated to manly virtues" (the English formulation is from *Gazophylacium*), though he did not object to deriving *lad* from OE *lȳt* 'little' as the etymon of *lad*. Junius also treated the verb *lead* as the etymon of *lad* (only he cited OE *lǣdan* rather than a Dutch form). Minsheu's etymology turns up in Johnson and Johnson-Todd. Richardson mentions it among others.

3) **For a long time, the most popular derivation of *lad* was from OE *lēod* 'man'.** According to Lemon, its originator was Casaubon (*lad* does not appear in the index to Casaubon [1650]). Lye, in his additions to Junius, gravitates toward that etymology. Reid and Robert Latham followed Lye. CD[1] had almost nothing to say about the origin of *lad* but made a special point of separating it from *lēod*.

4) **OED revived the suggestion that *lad* goes back to OE *lǣdan*.** Bradley (1894) published a note in which he says the following: "The word *ladde* coincides with the adjectival form of the past participle of the verb *to lead*. It seems not impossible that this may be the real origin of the word; a 'ladde,' in the older sense, being one of those *led* in the train of a lord or commander. We may compare the Italian *condotto*, explained by Tommaseo as 'soldato di banda, mercenario.' Holthausen (1896:266; the same in 1903a:323) supported Bradley. (In his 1903 review, Holthausen faults Kaluza for tracing *a* in *lad* to OE *a*; in Kaluza [1906-07], that place no longer appears.) Skeat[4] repeated Bradley's etymology but added *probably*.

Bradley's formulation in OED is slightly different from his earlier one: "ME. *ladde*, of obscure origin. Possibly a use of the definite form of the pa. pple. of *lead* v.; in ME *lad* is a regional variant of *led* pa. pple. The use might have originated in the application of the plural *ladde* elliptically to the followers of the lord. Actual evidence, however, is wanting. It is noteworthy that a 'Godric *Ladda*' attests a document written 1088-1123 (Earle *Land Charters* 270). If this cognomen be (as is possible) identical with ME *ladde*, its evidence is unfavourable to the derivation suggested above."

CD[2] ignored Bradley's hypothesis, but an anonymous reviewer (anonymous [1901b]) endorsed it and suggested kinship of *lad* with Gk λάτρις 'servant, slave; messenger; priest' and L *latro* 'mercenary; robber' from the Proto-Indo-European root **lat-* 'follow; serve,' related to Gmc **lith-* 'go,' whence the verb *lead.* It is unclear why Bradley no longer mentioned Ital *condotto*, the only semantic analogue he had of a substantivized past participle meaning 'servant.' Among the numerous Germanic words for 'follower, attendant,' none seems to have the derivational model reconstructed by Bradley for *lad.* One would expect some recorded examples to bear out his idea that the plural form *ladde* could be applied elliptically to the lord's retainers, but as is said in the entry, actual evidence is wanting. The origin of the cognomen *Ladda* is unknown (see sec 3, below). The existence of *Ladda* cannot be used as an argument either for or against Bradley's later suggestion.

5) **Wedgwood had a few innovative conjectures on the origin of *lad*.** He listed all kinds of words supposedly related to *lad*. **In the first edition of his dictionary, he equated *lad* and OHG *lâz* 'freedman'** (actually, *lâzze*; it is a Middle High German word), **a noun that made him think of E *lass*, and mentioned in passing Welsh *llawd* 'youth.' But in the fourth edition, he derived *lad* directly from *llawd* and Ir *lath* 'youth, companion,' while G *Leute* 'people' and Go *juggalauþs* 'youth' are said to be distinct from *lad*.** G *Leute* would have returned him to OE *lēod; -lauþs*, a suffix related to Go *liudan** 'grow,' is also akin to *lēod.* Skeat[1] agreed with Wedgwood but cited Go *-lauþs* as a cognate of *lad*, which he separated from G *Lasse* ~ MHG *lâzze* 'a vassal of a lord' (Skeat's gloss).

OED declared all those ideas untenable: "Quite inadmissible, both on the ground of phonology and meaning, is the current statement that the word is cognate with the last syllable of the Goth. *juggalauþs* young man; the ending *-lauþs* (stem *-lauda-* adj., *laudi-** sb.), which does not occur as an independent word, has in compounds the sense 'having (a certain) growth or size,' as in *hwelauþs* how great, *swalauþs** so great, *samalauþs** equally great. The Celtic derivations commonly alleged are also worthless: the Welsh *llawd* is a dictionary figment invented to explain the feminine *'lodes* (in Dictionaries *llodes*), which Prof. Rhys has shown to be shortened from *herlodes*, fem. of *herlawd*, a ME *herlot* 'harlot'; and the Irish *lath* does not exist in either the earlier or later sense of 'lad,' but means 'hero' or 'champion'."

6) Few of Thomson's etymologies have withstood the test of time. The same holds for his treatment of *lad*, but in this case some of his suggestions are not devoid of interest. Like Wedgwood after him, he was in the habit of stringing together various look-alikes if their meaning matched that of the head word. Thus at *lad* we find Go *laud-* and *lauþ-*, as well as OE *lēode* 'a rustic,' all of which "are apparently from *leod*, 'the people,' G and Sw *ledig* 'single, unmarried'" (he derived *ledig* from E *let* and its cognates: "Our Lads and Lasses are invariably understood to be young unmarried persons"), and VL *lati, lidi, lassi, lazzi,* and *latones*, who "were freed servants, not engaged either to a feudal lord or in marriage." Thomson mentions the unindentifiable "Gothic" nouns *lætingi* and *leisinghi*, but his statement that they correspond to Gk λύθεν (the epic third p pl aorist passive of λύω 'untie, set free') or λύτο (the second mediopassive of the same verb, third p. sing.), anticipates Bradley's idea; only Bradley wanted lads to be led ones, whereas Thomson thought of freed people. He may have known Lemon's derivation of *lad* from λαός 'people,' "quasi λαοδ, leod, lad; a common, vulgar boy." **Lemon compared *lad* and *lewd* and traced both to λύω, the same verb that attracted Thomson's attention**.

Mueller was unable to offer a convincing etymology of *lad*, but he **remarked that OE *lēod* could be the etymon of the English word only if VL *litus ~ lidus ~ ledus*, cited by Du Cange, served as intermediaries between them.** A *litus* (with numerous variants) was a person called a *colonus* in Rome, someone belonging to a group between those of freemen and serfs. Niermeyer's list (see *litus*) is even longer than Du Cange's: *litus, letus, lidus, ledus, liddus, lito* and *liddo*. These words turn up in numerous legal codes of medieval Germanic tribes.

Weekley (1921), who thought he had discovered a tie between *lad* and OI *liði* 'retainer,' **offered the following etymology of *lad*: "? Corrupt[ion] of ON. *lithi*... from *lith*, people, host.** I am led to make this unphonetic conjecture by the fact that the surname *Summerlad* is undoubtedly ON. *sumarlithi*, viking, summer adventurer, a common ON. personal name, found also (*Sumerled, Sumerleda, Sumerluda*, etc.) in E[ngland] before the Conquest. The corresponding *Winterlad* once existed, but is now app[arently] obs[olete]. *Ladda* also occurs, like *boy*...as a surname earlier than a common noun." (See the names listed by Weekley in Reaney.)

7) A few suggestions disappeared without a trace. **H.C.C. (1853) compared *lad* and *lady* and observed that the oldest form might begin with *hl-*.** He pointed out that the change OE *hlāfǣta* > *lad* would be parallel to *hlāford* > *lord* and *hlāfdige* > *lady*. *Hlāfǣta*, which is literally 'loaf eater,' meant 'dependant,' and, but for phonetic difficulties (*t* > *d*, *ǣ* > *ă*), a better etymology could not be imagined. **Townsend** (1824:340) **noted the similarity between *lad* and Russ *molodoi* 'young.' According to Glenvarloch** (1892), ***lad* goes back to the Sanskrit root LI 'helmet,'** with the basic meaning 'cover,' because a lad is "the nobleman's son who was allowed to remain *covered* in presence of royalty." This is a sad retreat by an amateur from former scholarly achievements.

Hellquist (1891:144) **wondered if Sw reg *larker* 'adolescent boy' (*halfvuxen pojke*) was allied to *lad*.** The answer is no, unless Sw *r* can be shown to go back to *d*. This type of rhotacism (*r* < *d*) is common in West Germanic dialects, and Mayhew (1894) suggested that the Australian English noun *larrikin* 'rowdy' is a phonetic variant of **laddikin* 'little lad.' The Swedish word occurs only in one area (so Rietz), and its connection with *larrikin* cannot be made out, but the coincidence is curious.

Tengvik (1938:257) **suggested that *lad* is "a hypocoristic form **Hlædda* < OE **hlæda*, a weakly inflected variant of OE *hlæd* 'load; heap, pile,' formed from a stem with the original meaning of 'to heap, accumulate.' ... Cf. discussion of OE *Mocca* (< Germ[anic] *mok(k)* 'to heap up, accumulate')..."** Since his reconstruction does not explain how the meaning 'heap' could change to 'serving man,' his proposal fell on deaf ears. Note, however, the reemergence of the idea that *l-* in *lad* goes back to *hl-*.

Makovskii offers a usual assortment of wild guesses: *lad* is a ghost word, the sum of *l* (the last letter of L *vel* 'or' in a gloss) and the Latin preposition *ad*, a combination some scribe misunderstood for an English noun (1977:62-63) (Shchur [1982:153] cited this suggestion approvingly); *lad* is a cognate of Go *-leiþan* 'go' and also of Russ *letat'* 'fly' (v), as well as of E reg *led* 'spare, extra,' so that *lad* turns out to mean 'heir' (1988b:141); *lad* and *lath* go back to the root **al-* 'burn': *lath* because it is hard, *lad* because it is shining (1988a:17); *lad* is related to Go *-leiþan*, Russ *lad'ia* 'boat' (because the souls of the departed were carried to the kingdom of the dead in boats) and L *lētum* 'death'; *lad* originally meant 'man, human being' (1993:132; the same in 1999a, *lad*), but Makovskii (1999a) mentions OI *eldr* (because male firstborns were sacrificed and thrown into the fire), along with OI *lindi* 'belt' (the victim was usually tied up), OE *hland* 'urine,' Sw *led* 'member' (because boys have penises), and G *Latte* 'lath' (because words for 'boy' and 'wood' are often connected). In a footnote, he added OE *lēodan* 'grow' and Indo-Aryan **laddika* 'boy, servant.'

8) A definitive conjecture on the origin of *lad* goes back to FT; see sec 3, below. **If we disregard implausible guesses and apparent nonsense, the results of the pre-FT research into the origin of *lad* are as follows. *Lad* resembles words for 'boy' in several languages of the East, but no connection between them can be made out; although *lad* bears some resemblance to at least one Irish word, it is not of Celtic origin; neither OE *lēod* nor *hlāfǣta* would have become *lad* for phonetic reasons; *lad*, from the past participle of OE *lǣdan* (because lads were instructed or led by their superiors), would be unique among the recorded names for servants in the Germanic languages; the Latinized Germanic words for 'freedman' known at one time over a large territory of Germania magna merit further consideration.**

2. **Here are the most important words that may be relevant for the etymology of *lad*.** All of them begin with *l-* and end in *d*, *t*, and *ð*, with vowels alternating in the root, and nearly all of them figure in someone's explanation of the origin of *lad*. See them in etymological dictionaries of Germanic languages, MW (*lod(d)er*), VV, WP II: 382, and IEW, 684-85.

1) Words with *-o-*, *-u-*, and *-ū-* between *l* and a dental: OE *loddere* 'beggar,' ME *lodder* 'wretched,' LG *lod(d)er*, *loderer* 'idler' and *luddern* 'to be idle,' G *verlottern* 'degrade, run to seed,' *lott(e)rig* 'slovenly,' *Lotterbett* 'old bed,' and *Lotterbube* 'wastrel' (the last two nouns are obsolete and can be used only humorously). The radical vowel *o* goes back to *u* and is part of the ablaut series **eu—*au—*u—*u*. In the normal grade, **eu* sometimes seems to have alternated with **ū*, which, when fronted to *ȳ* by umlaut, is occasionally represented by *ī*. Therefore, *loddere* and the rest are probably related not only to OE *lȳðre* 'bad, wicked, wretched' (E *lither*) but also to G *liederlich* 'dissolute, slovenly.' E *loiter*, most likely a borrowing from Dutch (Du *leuteren*), is now considered to be a doublet of *lôteren* (differently in EWNT[2]) despite its diphthong.

Several Icelandic words and their cognates in other Scandinavian languages and dialects belong here too: OI *lydda* 'rogue, wretch, scoundrel, nonentity, coward,' *lodda* 'whore' (and a term of abuse in general), *Lodd-* in the mythological name *Loddfáfnir*, and *loðrmenni* 'wretch, bungler.' OI *loða* 'cling fast, stick (to)' has the same root structure but a different meaning. OI *lúðra* 'stoop, cringe' may perhaps be compared with MDu *lôteren*.

Alongside the terms of abuse, similar words designating rags and articles of clothing exist, some in the normal, some in the zero grade: OHG *lûdara* ~ OS *lûđara* 'rag, diaper' and OE *loða* 'upper garment, mantle, cloak,' with cognates in several languages. Their best-known modern reflexes are G *Loden* 'loden,' that is, 'thick, heavily fulled fabric,' and Du *luier* 'napkin.' OI *loði* 'fur cloak, a cloak made of coarse wool' (LP) and perhaps 'fur' (Mohr [1939:158]) was a rare word; it occurred only in poetry and did not continue into Modern Icelandic. J. de Vries (AEW) relates OI *loði* 'fur coat' to OS *lûđara* 'rag,' and OI *loðinn* 'shaggy, thick' to Go *liudan** 'grow' and its cognates, so that *loðinn* would, in his view, mean *'overgrown' and be unrelated to *loði*. At *Loden*, KM and KS cite OI *loði* but not *loðinn*. Johansson (1890:346) preferred not to separate *loði* from *loðinn*, while AEW (*loðinn*) is ready to admit only their later interaction.

2) Words with *a* between *l* and a dental: E *lath* goes back to OE *lætt*; its *th* is at least as old as Middle English. The origin of the doublets OHG *latto* ~ *latta* 'lath,' with unshifted *-tt-*, and *lazza* is obscure. Old Saxon and Middle Dutch had *latta* and *latte*, respectively. The source of *tt* in OHG *latto* may be **þþ*, but reliable examples of WGmc **þþ* ~ **ðð* > *tt* are lacking. Reference to an expressive geminate in such a word would be vacuous, even though the lath is held to be the embodiment of thinness in both English and German (*thin as a lath, eine lange Latte*). Assuming that *lath* has cognates outside Germanic, the geminate may be the result of assimilation (Lühr [1988:252]: *tt* < *þχ*? or *tt* < *χþ*?), but the most ancient reconstructed meaning would still come out as *'rod, slat.' MHG *lade(n)* 'board' is apparently akin to *Latte*. ModG *Laden* 'shop, store' owes its meaning to *laden* 'board, counter'; *d* in it must be from *þ* (cf E *cloth* ~ G *Kleid*). West Germanic seems to have had the words **laþ-* and **lat-* 'thin narrow strip of wood.' The Yorkshire word *lad* means 'the upright bar of an old-fashioned spinning-wheel, which turns the wheel; a stay for timber work; a back stay for corves or wagons' (EDD, *lad sb*[3]). Regardless of whether the word is of English, Scandinavian, or 'mixed' origin (a blend of two synonyms), its similarity with E *lath* and G *Latte* is remarkable.

3) Words with *ŏ*, not derived from **u*, between *l* and a dental, and with *ŏ* going back to **au*. Here we find several words for 'sapling, seedling': Du *loot* (MDu *lote*), Fr *leat* (*ea* < **au*), and Fr *loat*. G *Lode*, not attested before the 15th century, is from Low German: its High German counterpart is *Lote*. Old Saxon had *lŏda* and *lada*. In MHG *sumerlat(t)e* 'sapling, one-year-old tree' (as opposed to OS *sumarloda*), *a*, according to KM and KS (*Latte*), should be ascribed to the influence of *Latte*. The etymology of the words with a long vowel is clear thanks to the existence of Go *liudan**, OHG *arliotan*, OS *liodan*, and OE *lēodan* 'grow.' If OI *loðinn* 'hairy, shaggy,' mentioned above, has been explained correctly, the unattested Old Icelandic strong verb **ljóða* must be reconstructed, of which *loðinn* is the past participle. OE *lēod*, OHG *liut* (ModG *Leute*), OI *lýðr* 'people,' and so forth, possibly including L *līberi* 'children,' have the same root as *loðinn*. In Gothic, the hapax legomenon *laudi** (dat sg) 'shape, form' and the suffix *-lauþs* (which Bradley discussed in his refutation of the idea that *lad* is a cognate of Go *juggalauþs* 'youth, young man') represent the *au* grade; in the zero grade, we find Go *ludja** 'face.'

Among the words having the structure *l* + vowel + *d*/*t*/*ð*, the following are especially close to *lad* phonetically: OS *-lada* 'seedling, sapling,' MHG *lade* 'board,' E reg *lad* 'stay for timber work,' and if words with *-o-* can be considered, then also OE *loddere* 'beggar,' ME *lodder* 'wretched,' OE *loða* 'cloak,' and OI *lodda* (a term of abuse). They do not form a unified group with regard to their origin (which is often unknown), but they sound so much alike that when their reflexes coexisted in one and the same language, their paths must sometimes have crossed. Various metaphors facilitated their confusion. The syncretism 'peg'/'child,' 'wood'/'child' guaranteed the interaction of *lath* and *lad*. E *lath* and G *Latte* mean 'strip of wood' and E *stripling* means "quasi 'one who is slender as a strip'" (ODEE). The distance between 'garment' and 'child' is also short. Here a good example is OIr *bratt* 'mantle' and E *brat*, from Irish (see also GIRL and LASS, sec 3). The proximity between 'lad' and 'seedling' and between 'lad' and 'one grown' needs no proof.

3. **The turning point in the search for the origin of *lad* was a remark by FT in the entry *ladd*.** The text in both editions is the same. It is given here in an English translation: "*Ladd* 'stocking put on over another piece of clothing, woolen sock,' in dialects also *lodde*, Sw reg *ladder* f pl 'old shoes,' *lädder* 'socks,' *lodde* 'Frisian shoe.' The forms with *o* seem to belong with *lodden* ['shaggy, hairy, covered

with grass'], cf Nynorsk *raggar* and *lugg* with the same meaning. The vowel *a* may owe its origin to the synonymous N reg *labbar* 'woolen socks,' but Sw reg *lädda* with old umlaut speaks against this conclusion; the forms with *a* are perhaps related especially closely to Celtic *lâtro-*, as in Welsh *llawdr* 'trousers,' Cornish *loder* 'shoe.' Nynorsk *ladda* 'shuffle, slouch along' are also related; cf *labbe* and *tøfle af* [the same meaning; N *tøffel* 'shoe, slipper']. Other words belonging here are *tusseladd,* and *Askeladd,* that is, 'someone who walks awkwardly, clumsily' (perhaps borrowed by English as *lad*)." Torp's entry is the same, but the references to Celtic are gone. Askeladd (actually, Oskeladd) 'ash-lad' is male Cinderella, the third son in fairy tales, a counterpart of Icel *kolbítr* (literally 'coal-biter'), Boots, as he is called in George W. Dasent's translation of Asbjørnsen and Moe's collection of folklore. ODEE (*lad*), too, uses *Boots* in glossing those words. *Tusseladd* means 'nincompoop.'

The idea that *lad* was borrowed from Norwegian found an enthusiastic supporter in Björkman (1903-05:503; 1912:272). The comment in ODEE is also favorable: "...the earliest evidence and even modern currency point to concentration in the east and west midlands and so perh[aps] to Scand[inavian] origin (cf. Norw. *aske/ladd* neglected child, Boots, *tusse/ladd* duffer, muff." Diensberg (1985a:330, note 7; 334) has a similiar opinion. However, FT's suggestion bypassed several difficulties: 1) *Ladd* has not been recorded in any Scandinavian language with the meaning *'(young) fellow.' 2) *Tusseladd* and *askeladd (oskeladd)* seem to be the only compounds with *-ladd,* and neither could be known well enough to produce the basis for a new English word. 3) Despite some parallels, it is unclear why someone wearing woolen socks or old shoes and walking awkwardly should be called 'fool,' the more so because E *lad* never meant 'fool, duffer, nincompoop.' 4) Finally, the earliest recorded English form is *ladde,* and Tengvik (1938:257) is right that *-e* was not a mere graphical character in it.

On the other hand, a connection between a disparaging word for 'young person' and 'shagginess' ~ 'hose, stocking, trousers' has been recorded elsewhere, namely among the words having the same root as E *strumpet.* Since the entry STRUMPET contains all the data, it will suffice to cite here only the main forms, with and without a nasal: E *strumpet* 'prostitute' and in one dialect 'fat hearty child,' G *struppig* 'disheveled,' G *Strumpf* 'hose, trouser leg, stocking,' originally 'stub, stump'; G *Strunze* 'slattern,' MHG *strunze* 'stump'; early ModI *strympa* (its present day variant is *strumpa*) 'dipper; tall hat; bucket; building with a cone-shaped roof; virago, big woman' are its cognates. The way from 'rag' to '(thing with an) uneven surface' and 'contemptible person' is also short: compare OI *rǫgg* 'tuft, shagginess (said about the fur on a cloak)' (CV), Sw *ragg* 'coarse hair; goat's hair' (see the other cognates in AEW), and Sw *Raggen* 'devil' (even if the association with *ragg* is secondary; SEO), as well as such a recent coinage as Sw *raggare* 'hippie' (see more on *Raggen* at RAGAMUFFIN); G *Lumpen* 'rag' and *Lump* 'scoundrel' (from a historical point of view *Lump* and *Lumpen* are variants of the same word). E *ragtag* (or *tagrag*) *and bobtail* 'rabble' (OED, *rag-tag*) are words of the same type.

OI **lodd* must have existed as an informal word meaning *'ragtag; worthless fellow.' For some reason, it has come down to us only in the compound *Loddfáfnir.* Lindquist (1956:150-52) suggested that the educational verses incorporated into *Hávamál* (strophes 112-37) and addressed to the otherwise unknown Loddfáfnir, were part of the initiation rite. The use of an address form consisting of an offensive slang word (**lodd*) and the name of a great mythological figure (Fáfnir was the dragon killed by Sigurd [Sigurðr]) would not be out of place in the rite of initiation (a youth of no consequence becomes a warrior and a [potential] husband).

The etymology of *lodd-* poses problems, but, contrary to Bechtel's hesitant suggestion (1877:215), its *-dd* does not go back to *zd.* It is rather a geminate typical of many expressive formations, including pet names, and its alternation with *ð* would be regular, for reinforced fricatives in Icelandic yield long stops, as in *Stebbi,* a pet name for *Stefán,* and OI *koddi* 'pillow, scrotum' versus ModI *koðri* 'scrotum' (numerous similar examples in the old language and in living speech). Grammatical, nonemphatic alternations are equally numerous. For instance, the past of *loða* is *loddi.* It follows that *lodd-* is probably related to the Icelandic *loð-* words. The absence of an independent noun **lodd* and the fact that in its disparaging sense it may be extant only in *Loddfáfnir* remain unexplained.

A connection between Du *lot* ~ G *Lode* and **leudh-* is certain. The same holds for Go *-lauþs* ~ *laudi** and a few words in the zero grade: Go *ludja**, OE *lud-* in *ludgæt*, and Sc *lud(dock).* Their meanings range from 'seedling' (*lot, Lode*) to '*Gestalt*' (*laudi**), 'object fully shaped' ('face,' 'posterior,' 'loin': *ludja**, *lud, luddock*), and 'shaped' (in the suffix *-lauþs*). The few recorded words for 'matted hair, thick fur,' and the like (for instance, OI *loðinn*) align themselves with the *lud-* words, for in both West Germanic and Old Norse, *u* changes to *o* according to regular sound laws.

OI *loða* 'cling, stick to' is more problematic. Things that adhere to the surface make it shaggy, hairy, and rough. This is especially obvious in plant names. Middle Dutch *lodwort 'Symphytum officinale'* (comfrey) has cognates in Low German. Stapelkamp (1946:57-60) related *lod-* to G *Lode* and explained the compound as 'fast-growing plant with a tall stalk.' But a similar plant name was OE *leloðre,* though the Latin part of the gloss is *Lapadium* ('silverweed'?) perhaps from **lē(a)-loðre* (*lēah* 'meadow, lea'), and both plants can owe their names to the hairs on their leaves (Wilhelm Lehmann [1906:298/6]). Despite some disagreement between Pheifer (1974:99, note 606) and Bierbaumer (BWA 3:160-65), they accept Lehmann's etymology. It is preferable not to separate OI *loði* ~ OE *loða* 'fur cloak' from OI *loðinn* 'shaggy.' Whether the Icelandic word is a borrowing from Old English, as Mohr (1939:158) suggested, or native (which is more likely) is immaterial for the present discussion. The verb *loða* should be added to the *loði* / *-loðre* group.

A particularly important word is OI *Amlóði* 'fool,' famous as the source of Shakespeare's *Hamlet.* If *ó* (the long vowel) in *Amlóði* is old, it cannot alternate with *ŏ.* But the original form was probably *Amloði* (E. Kock [1940:sec 3221] suggested the unlikely variant *Ámloðí*). Only Nordfelt (1927:62-69) doubted that *Amlóði* is a compound. See some even less credible suggestions in Gollancz (1898:XXXV, note). Saxo's Amlóði, the hero of a Danish chronicle, must have been called this because, to avenge his father's murder, he acted in an irrational manner. The modern reflexes of **amlóði* (such a common name was not recorded in Old Icelandic) are ModI *amlóði* 'wretch, bungler, fool' and Nynorsk *amlod* 'nincompoop.'

K. Malone (1923:52-58; 1927; 1928) summarized the extensive research into the proper name *Amlóði* and the homonymous common name and offered his own bold hypothesis. See also Detter (1892:6-7), Meißner (1927:382-88), and ÁBM. Both *aml-óði* and *am-lóði* lend themselves to an etymological analysis. If **Amloði* changed to *amlóði* under the influence of *óði* 'mad,' it perhaps meant **am-loði* 'ember lad.' This was Bergdal's idea (1929). K. Malone (1929) vehemently contested it, but a good deal of what Bergdal (1931) says in his rejoinder makes sense. **Am-loði* looks like an exact counterpart of *Askeladd (Oskeladd).* Jóhannesson (1940:2-5 and ISEW, 87) also assumed that *-lóði* is akin to Icel *lydda* and originally had a short vowel.

A question that has not been answered in a satisfactory manner concerns the relation between *-loð-* ~ *-lodd* and *-ladd.* Whitehall (1939:22), the author of the etymology of *lad* in MED and of the most authoritative article on this subject, traces *sumarlota* to the root **leudh-,* as in Go *liudan** 'grow' and its cognates, and remarks that "...OHG *-lota, -lata, -latta* ... is ultimately an ablaut derivative" of this root. The adverb *ultimately* has little value because Germanic *a* and *o* belong to different ablaut series and no evidence supports Whitehall's statement on the same page that all those words, "as we have seen," are related to **leudh-.* We have seen only this: "...he [Bradley] was unable to reconcile the *au* of Goth. *-lauþs* with the *a* of ME. *ladde* on simple phonological grounds. Yet a moment's thought on the peculiar social conditions of the Middle Ages should serve to reveal how easily a primary notion 'growing youth, one not yet of man's condition' would pass over into the notion 'one attendant upon or in service to another'" (ibidem). But that is semantics, not phonetics. Stapelkamp (1946:58), who also says that *-lode* and *-lade* are related by ablaut, cites several occurrences of LG *laide* but offers no explanation of the spelling. References to ablaut in this case should be abandoned.

West Germanic alternating forms like *sumerlatte* ~ *sumarlode* may have arisen as the result of the confusion of two roots (see KM, KS, *Latte*), but in the Scandinavian languages and dialects, *-ladd* is the only word of this structure with *a.* We must admit that in both West Germanic and Scandinavian, the root *lod(d)-* alternated with synonymous *ladd-.* No regular phonetic change connects them, and they are not related by ablaut. Perhaps initially they were regional variants, like ModE *strap* and *strop.*

4. If the premises set forth above are acceptable, the early history of *lad,* though still containing a few gaps, will no longer look obscure or uncertain. A biography with a blank here and there is not the same as an undocumented life. After all, we know more about Shakespeare than about Homer. **The Germanic root **leudh-* 'grow' has been attested in all grades of ablaut. In the zero grade, the words important for unraveling the origin of *lad* have *u* and *o* < *u*. The kinship of some of them is controversial, but they form a cohesive group, with the meanings referable to such concepts as 'well-shaped,' 'grown,' 'furry, hairy, shaggy,' not improbably 'cling, stick to, adhere.'** Words with old $\bar{o}$ occasionally have a

meaning suggestive of 'growth,' but they are not related to the derivatives of *leudh-. The root of *lath* and *Latte* is not related to them either, but *loð-*, for unascertained reasons, alternated with *lað-*, at least in the Scandinavian area, and the lack of stability may have resulted in some confusion of the two groups.

One of the words designating furry (woolen, hairy) objects was **loð- ~ *lað-* 'woolen sock; hose; stocking; shoe.' It acquired the figurative meaning *'worthless fellow,' but, again for unclear reasons, it has come down to us only in a few compound names and nicknames, and usually with an expressive geminate: OI *Loddfáfnir,* and **Amloði* (asterisked because the recorded form has *ó*) and N *Askeladd* (or *Oskeladd*) 'ashlad' and *tusseladd* (a word with folkloric overtones). OI *lydda* shows that other possibilities for coining worthless people's names from the zero grade of **leudh-* also existed. Since neither **ladd* nor **lodd* has been attested as a free form (*'wretch, nincompoop') in any Scandinavian language, it must be assumed that the semisuffix *-ladd,* as in *tusseladd,* gained special popularity in northern England and developed into a regular word for *'worthless person,' later 'person of low birth.' To become fully independent, it joined the weak declension (ladd* > ME *ladde*). This is the most probable origin of E *lad.* Consequently, *lad* is not a borrowing from Scandinavian, but rather a product of a northern English dialect heavily influenced by Scandinavian (Norwegian?) usage.**

The idea that *lad* is a "corruption" of *liði* does not deserve credence, but *liði* might influence the earliest feudal sense of ME *lad* 'serving man, attendant, varlet.' Although ML *litus* and its many variants were not in active use in Scandinavia, their undiscovered Germanic etymon, usually given as **laetus* (the original radical vowel in it may have been *ă* or *ā*), probably interacted with similar-sounding synonyms derived from other roots. "A G[erman]ic **liþu-, *leþu-,* though swamped by **lēta-,* has left some traces. OI *liðar...* may well represent a type P[roto] G[erman]ic *galidjan-* 'one who travels along' The compounds *sumar-liði, vetr-liði* are irrelevant]; yet a technical term **liþu-* may have been merged with it and may also have contributed to the formation of *lið* n. 'retinue' (**galidja-*)" (L. Bloomfield [1930:90-91]). See also Szemerényi (1962:186, with reference to Marco Scovazzi).

The Old English name *Ladda* (from Somerset) that Bradley (OED) found in Earle (1888:270), appears in a collection of documents dated 1088-1122. The context is not helpful: Godric Ladda is mentioned as a witness ("herto is gewitnesse godric ladda"). If *Ladda* is the precursor of ME *ladde,* the recorded history of *lad* will, as Weekley noted, mirror that of *boy*: first the (nick)name, then the common name. However, the actual order of events must have been the opposite. *Ladda,* identified with N *-ladd,* would not be a respectable cognomen for a witness, but official medieval nicknames were often derogatory (see more on nicknames at LILLIPUTIAN). O. Ritter (1910:472-74) dissociated himself from Bradley's etymology of *lad* 'one led' and emphasized a connection between *lad* and *Ladda.* Holthausen agreed with Ritter (1935-36:326) but later preferred to derive *Ladda* from *Landberht* or *Landfrið* (Holthausen [1951-52:9/107]). These ever-changing hypotheses found their reflection in his dictionary: three possibilities (< OE *Ladda?,* < N *ladd?,* < OE *lǣdda?*) (EW[1]), no etymology, only the Middle English form (EW[2]: < ME *ladde*), and from OE *Ladda* < *Landberht* (EW[3]). In extensive lists of Scandinavian cognomens, *Ladda* does not turn up (Lind [1905-15; 1920-21]; Jónsson [1907], Kahle [1903; 1910], Hellquist [1912]).

Ekwall (1960) traces *Lad-* in the place name *Ladhill* (Warwickshire) to *Hlod-,* whose etymology is unclear. A.H. Smith II:10 mentions *Ladgate* and *Ladhill* in Yorkshire. Barnhart leaves open the question of the origin of *Laddedale* (ca 1160). Not only Godric Ladda had such a name. One finds *Richard Ladde* (Northamptonshire, ca 1175), *Ywein Ladde* (1177), *Rog. Lade* (Hampshire, 1200), *Steph. Ladde* (Essex, 1205), *Ricardus Ladde* (1210), *Walter le Ladd* (Kent, 1242), and *Thom. le Lad* (Sussex, 1254). Dietz (1981a:398-99) does not doubt that those names can be identified with ME *ladde,* though the impression is that their bearers were people occupying a comparatively high place in the feudal hierarchy (note the emphasis on their real or assumed French heritage).

However, since *Oskeladd* is called *Boots* in English, we again have reference to footwear. Bergerson (2002) is probably right in comparing *Boots* with Afrikaans *botje* 'pal' and E *buddy* and arguing for the Dutch origin of all three nouns. *Boots* may have been a folk etymological interpretation of some word like *buddy,* and the idea that it is the name of a youngster cleaning gentlemen's boots could arise in retrospect. The late attestation of *Boots* (1798) makes all conjectures on this subject fruitless, but it is hard to imagine that Dasent would have chosen the name of a servant at a hotel for the Norwegian folklore hero. *Boots* satisfied

English readers of fairy tales, and OED mentions the phrase *lad of wax* 'shoemaker.' Consequently, the presence of Sw reg *ladder* 'old shoe' among the cognates of N *ladd* has a few marginal counterparts on English soil.

The root **leudh-* is not isolated in Germanic (see Feist, *liudan*), but since the vowel *a* in *lad* (assuming that the reconstruction offered above is correct) is unetymological, Latin and Greek words like *latro* 'robber; mercenary,' λάτρον 'remuneration,' and λάτρις 'servant' cannot be cognates of *lad*. By contrast, a study of words with initial *s-* (Icel *sladdi* 'slattern' and E *slattern*) may broaden our knowledge of the English word's field of application but will not add anything to what we have learned about the origin of either OE *Ladda* or ME *ladde*. The same is true of *slat*, almost a doublet of *lath* ~ *Latte*, for *lath* ~ *Latte* ~ *slat* and *lad* share nothing except the thinness of their referents in the real world.

A Note on Some Other Words with the Structure *l* + vowel + *d* (ð)

***Lad* emerged against the background of numerous *l* - *d* (ð) words with sexual connotations. We do not know whether they interacted with Scand *-ladd* and contributed to the pejorative sense of *lad* or to its becoming a free form. They are given below, to make the picture complete.** Some words with long vowels between *l* and a dental seem to have no bearing on the cognates of *lad*; see, for instance, *ljótr* 'ugly' in AEW. However, it is instructive that in this group *-t* and *-þ* also alternate, as they allegedly did in E *lath* ~ G *Latte*, and that paronyms turn up here too: OI *leiðr* 'loathsome' has approximately the same meaning as *ljótr*.

1) Words with ō, not derived from **ū*/**au*, between *l-* and a dental

ModI *lóða* (adj) 'in heat' surfaced only in the 16th century and is at present hard to distinguish from the noun *lóð* in the adverbial phrase *á lóðum*, also meaning 'in heat' (ÁBM, 5 *lóð*, 1 *lóða*). CV misleadingly included *lóða* and derived it from *loða* 'cling fast'—an excellent semantic match, but ŏ and ō are incompatible. Despite the late attestation, *lóða* must be an old word, for it has Celtic and less certainly Slavic cognates (Lidén [1937:91-92]; IEW, 680; WP II:428; ESSI XVII:19-20, *lětu*). From Scandinavian it reached Frisian (Löfstedt [1948:80-81]). OI *lóð* 'produce of the land' is akin to *láð* 'land' and cannot be traced to **leudh-*. G *Luder*, originally a hunting term ('bait'), now a term of abuse ('impertinent woman'), also had a long vowel in the past, judging by MHG *luoder* and MLG *lôder*. The Scandinavian divine name *Lóðurr* occurs only once in Old Icelandic. Nothing is known about the god Lóðurr, except that, while traveling with Óðinn and Hœnir, he met Askr and Embla, two trees destined to become the first human couple.

2) Some words of obscure origin having the structure *l* + vowel + dental

One such word is OI *litr*, recorded in the phrase *litom fœra*. In *Bergbúaþáttr*, *litr* means 'oar.' In the scurrilous eddic verse *Hárbarðzlióð* 50[3-4], the sense may be 'penis' (see all the proposed interpretations of *litom fœra* in von See et al [1997:243-45]). According to the Old Norse creation myth (*Vǫlospá* 18), the first human couple lacked, among other things, *lito góða*, and received it from the god Lóðurr (see above). His gift may have been good genitals rather than good complexion, as is usually believed. The origin of his name remains a matter of dispute. If it has the same root as *lóð(a)* '(in) heat,' *Lóðurr* may have been a god of sexual urge, and his gift of the genitals would be in character. A connection with *lóð* 'the produce of the land' would fit his appearance in the capacity as a fertility god. The length of the vowel in *Lóðurr* is uncertain (cf *Amloði*, above). **Lóðurr*, a hairy (= virile) god, would likewise be a proper deity to supply the first man and woman with the organs of reproduction.

Another obscure word is OS *lud* (*Heliand* 154). After having the prophesy about himself and Elisabeth, Zacharias says that to both of them is "lud geliđen, lîk gidrusnod" ('our *lud* is gone, our bodies are withered'). *Lud*, usually glossed as 'form, figure' or 'bodily strength,' is allegedly derived from the same root as Go *liudan** (see a survey in Grau [1908:205-06]). Sehrt gives the traditional gloss 'Gestalt (?),' but, according to Rauch (1975), 'sexual power' is meant. Rauch cited Sc *lud* 'buttocks,' a variant of *luddock*. The gloss in OED is: *luddock* 'the loin, or the buttock.' It appears that *lud-* words could designate anything that is fully shaped and recognizable as a *Gestalt*. The concrete manifestation of the *Gestalt* would be impossible to predict. In Gothic, it was the face. In Old Saxon, it was probably functioning genitals (a less abstract referent than sexual power). In some circumstances, it might even mean 'womb.' Whether the *Gestalt* was in front or behind did not matter, whence *luddock* both 'loin' and 'buttock' (for an initial approach to these words see Liberman [1995:265] and [1996b:80]). Herein lies the origin of the hitherto unexplained OE *ludgæt* 'postern, a door behind the house.' One can imagine *lud-* 'fetus' or even 'child.' Thus the Old English cognate of Go *kilþei** 'womb' and *inkilþo* 'pregnant' is *cild* 'child.' *Lud-* words occurred so rarely because except in Gothic they were probably considered not delicate enough for literary use; compare OI *lydda* 'nonentity' ('a prick'?).

Runic inscription 8 of Maeshowe, Orkney, reads: "Ingibjǫrg, hin fagra ekkja. Mǫrg kona hefir farit lút inn hér. Mikill ofláti. Erlingr." The transcription is from M. Barnes (1994:99), who translates: "Ingibjǫrg, the fair widow. Many a woman has gone stooping in here. A great show-off. Erlingr." The graffito is undoubtedly obscene, especially if *lut* or *lud* rather than *lút* is meant, for *fara lut* may be synonymous with *fœra litom* in *Hárbarðzlióð* 50 ('many a woman had a ride on a *lut* in here'). If the Old Swedish deity Lytir (less likely Lýtir) can be identified with Freyr in his function of a fertility god, his name makes one think of *Loðurr* (or *Lóðurr*), OS *lud,* and OI *lut* (that is, of a phallic idol) rather than of OI *lýta* 'deform, disgrace' (which would turn Lýtir into the devil), as Strömbäck (1928:292-93) believed, or of OI *hljóta* 'get by lot' (*Lýtir* 'soothsayer'), as Elmevik (1990:497-503) suggested.

LASS (1300)

Contrary to the belief that held out for several centuries, lad *and* lass *are unrelated, that is,* lass *is not a contracted form of* *ladess *or* *ladse. *However, both words surfaced in English simultaneously in the same northern texts, and both are of Scandinavian origin. The two seem to result from a similar jocular usage (slang) that encouraged the transfer of the names of (worthless) clothes to children. The etymon of* lad *means 'woolen stocking; hose; old shoe,' while* lass *is traceable to Dan* las *'rag' and its cognates in Swedish dialects and Old Norwegian.* Lass *never meant 'young unmarried woman' except by implication. Consequently, MSw* lösk kona *'free woman,' a phrase cited in OED and repeated in most later dictionaries, is neither a possible etymon nor an analogue of the English word.*

The sections are devoted to 1) the rejected etymologies of lass *(old and recent), 2) Bradley's etymology of* lass, *3) the metaphorical origin of* lass *('rag' → 'girl'), and 4) the interaction between the* las- *and* lask- *forms in and outside the Scandinavian area;* lass *and* windlass.

1. According to the oldest etymological dictionaries of English, the originator of the idea that *lass* goes back to **ladess* was George Hickes (Hickesius), but none gives an exact reference. From the point of view of the history of English *ladess* is a ghost word. Coined in 1768 by Horace Walpole, it has not taken root in the language (nor was it meant to). Skeat[1] tentatively derived *lad* from **ladess,* though the suffix *-ess* is said to be of Welsh rather than of French origin. *Lad* and *lass* were habitually regarded as borrowings from Celtic at that time (see, for example, Boase [1881:377].

O. Ritter (1910:478) **explained *lass*** as a substantivized comparative, that is, **as the continuation of OE (*sēo*) *lǣ̆sse* (f), literally 'the lesser one,'** and cited as analogues OE *þā ieldran* 'parents,' *se ieldra* 'father,' *se geongra* 'youth, disciple, vassal,' and a few others. It may be added that *Jünger* is still the only German word for 'disciple,' and E *elders* has retained a meaning not too different from G *Eltern* 'parents.'

Two arguments weaken Ritter's etymology. First, it is unclear who would call girls, and why only girls, 'the lesser one(s).' *Eltern* and *Jünger* presuppose a deferential attitude toward the parents and the teacher on the part of the followers and children. *Lass* belongs to a different style. Ritter cited G *die Kleine* (f) 'the little one' as a synonym for 'sweetheart.' However, *lass* is not a term of endearment typical of wooers' language. The parents might perhaps call their daughter 'the lesser one,' to distinguish her from the mother of the family when the division of property or inheritance rights were at stake (cf *John Smith Jr.*), but *lass* has never been a legal term. Second, it is preferable to have the etymology of *lass* that would take into account the word's northern provenance; *lass* understood as 'the lesser one' has no recorded counterparts in any Scandinavian language.

The other hypotheses (except Holthausen's: see below) are worth mentioning only for completeness' sake. The same people who thought they knew the origin of *lad* often had something to say about *lass.* H.C.C. (1853:257) traced *lass* to OE **hlāfestre,* the nonexistent feminine of OE *hlāfǣta* 'servant' on the analogy of *lad,* allegedly from *hlāfǣta* (see LAD for discussion). Makovskii (1977:63 and 1980:67) suggested that *lass* is the result of a misunderstood gloss: *puluis,* that is, *pulvis* 'dust, ashes,' was allegedly confused with *puella* 'maiden,' and the gloss *l.asce* 'or ashes' merged into *lasce,* whence the English word. He did not explain how *lasce* < *l.asce* became a common word and why it surfaced only in Middle English. (Shchur [1982:153] cited both of Makovskii's etymologies—of *lad* and of *lass*—approvingly.) Later he derived *lass* from the concept 'squeeze (milk)' and related it to L *lāc* 'milk' or to Skt *lạśah* 'resin' and *lasīkā* 'lymph, serum,' as well to Lith *lāšas* 'drop' (sb) ([1992a:52]; he did not mention a different opinion in KEWA III:94, 96). Finally, he said that *lass* was akin to words meaning 'battle' (*lass* 'warrior maiden'), such as L *līs* 'dispute, lawsuit' and Skt *las* 'move' (v), though Skt *las* 'appear,' he added, should not be ignored either (*lass* emerged as 'the producer of children'). As an afterthought, he mentioned OE *lǣs* 'field' and E reg *lash* 'comb,' because fights play themselves out on battlefields, while the comb is a metaphor for the woman's genitals (1999a:190-91).

2. Modern dictionaries call *lass* a word of obscure origin but often cite Bradley's etymology (1894) as tenable. This is how Bradley presented it in his article: "The feminine *lass* first occurs about the year 1300 in two Northern works, the 'Metrical Homilies' and the 'Cursor Mundi,' and in both passages is spelt *lasce*. This spelling suggests that the word is one of those in which Northern dialects represent a Scandinavian *sk* by *ss*, as in *ass* for ashes (Scandinavian *aska*), Sc *buss* for bush (Scandinavian *buskr*). Hence the etymology of the word may be sought in the Scandinavian **laskw*, the feminine of an adjective meaning unmarried; cf. Middle Swedish *lösk kona*, unmarried woman. ...The original sense of the adjective (which is etymologically akin to the verb *to let*) is 'free from ties, loose,' whence the meaning 'vagrant,' also found in Middle Swedish, and the Icelandic sense (*...löskr*) 'idle, weak.' The association of the words *lad* and *lass* is, if this explanation be correct, due to their accidental similarity in sound." OED and ODEE repeated Bradley's etymology in an abridged form. Although Thomson, as usual, cited several unidentifiable forms, he had an idea similar to Bradley's: *lass*, he suggested, means 'free, single,' with reference to a word that looks like OI *lǫsk*. ***Lass*, as Bradley pointed out, was first recorded in northern texts, and it is current mainly in northern and north midland dialects, so that its Scandinavian origin is likely.** However, **laskw*, the presumed etymon of *lass*, did not exist (Ekwall [1938:259]). Nor is it necessary to reconstruct the substitution of *ss* for *sk* in this word.

3. **The most probable etymon of *lass* is, as Björkman** (1912:272) **suggested, a word like Old Danish *las* 'rag,'** which has identical cognates in Swedish dialects and Old Norwegian. In a way, Björkman's predecessor was Holthausen (1903b:39), who compared *lass* and E *lash* and referred to his earlier etymology of Sw *flicka* 'girl' from Sw *flicka* ~ G *flicken* (v) 'mend, darn' (1900:366). But *lash* 'make fast with a cord' surfaced in English only in the 17th century and is probably a borrowing from Low German, like the analogous Scandinavian words discussed at the end of this entry, while the verbs G *flicken* ~ Sw *flicka* belong with *flip, flop*, and the like (see FUCK). The sought-for similarity at the semantic level is between *las* 'rag' ~ *lass* 'girl' and *flicka* 'patch, shred' ~ *flicka* 'girl.' Holthausen wanted to correlate his conclusion with Bradley's and suggested that *lass* was the development of the northern form *lash* (< **lask*).

In slang, words for 'rag' frequently acquire the jocular meaning 'child' and especially 'girl.' See some examples in Gebhardt [1911:1896]. Pauli (1919:225-26) cites various Romance examples and endorses Björkman's derivation of *lass* (see p. 225, note 5). Not only Sw *flicka* 'girl' but also E *brat*, from *brat* 'ragged garments,' has a similar origin (Sc *bratchart* may be an extension of *brat*, though the usual idea is that *brat* is a clipped form of *bratchart*); compare the history of *dud* (if it is from *dud* 'coarse cloak') and LAD, end of sec 2.

Sometimes the path from 'piece of cloth' to 'child' was from 'diapers' or from the similarity between a baby and a doll (dolls were made of rags), or from the practice of calling females after the clothes they wore (see the examples given at DRAB and GIRL, sec 4). In other cases, the transfer of the name followed more circuitous routes. OI *lébarn* 'infant, baby in arms' corresponds to E *bastard* (< OF *bastard*), held to be from *bastum* 'bat, packsaddle' (OED). With regards to *lébarn*, see N reg *ljo* 'padding for a pack saddle, consisting of a woolen blanket, a straw cushion and a skin'; *barn* means 'child' (AEW *lébarn*; Elmevik [1986:84]). Initially, the suffix *-ard* need not have had a depreciatory meaning.

Despite the guarded support by OED and Skeat of Mahn's idea that E *bantling* 'illegitimate child' is a "corruption" of G *Bänkling*, from *Bank* 'bench' ('a child begotten on or under a bench'), the old derivation from **band-ling* 'one wrapped in swaddling bands' may be correct, the *d* ~ *t* problem notwithstanding. Since *Bänkling*, which first occurs in Fischart (the same example in DW [*Bänkling*] and HDGF [*Bank*]), seems to have had minimal currency in Germany, its spread to England in this form would be hard to demonstrate.

Old designations of illegitimate children were not always coined as terms of abuse, and *bastard* was probably no closer to 'packsaddle son' (whatever it is supposed to mean) than *lébarn*. Likewise, OF *coitrart* (from *coite* 'quilt') and LG *Mantelkind* 'mantle child' that ODEE cites (*bastard*) do not sound offensive. In all those cases, '(piece of) cloth' served as the foundation of a word for 'child.'

Like LAD, ultimately from 'old or unseemly,

or worthless garment' ('hose; sock; shoe'), *lass* emerged from the metaphorical use of a word for 'rag.' Both are words of Scandinavian origin, but neither is, strictly speaking, a borrowing, for they do not mean 'youngster' and 'girl' in any Scandinavian language. Their recorded Middle English meanings developed in the northern dialects of England. If this reconstruction is acceptable, the only unanswered question will be whether ME *lass* and *lasce* are related. Bradley suggested that *lasce* was the original form, with *sc* later simplified to *ss*, but the interplay of *las-* and *lask-* is typical of the word for 'rag' far beyond the Scandinavian area.

4. Although ModG *Lasche* means, among other things, 'loop; tongue of a shoe; flap of a pocket,' MHG *lasche* and MLG *lassce* (with several variants) meant 'rag; patch; gusset' (KM, KS). The technical senses of the Middle Low German word contributed to its popularity in other countries. Dan *lask* is a doublet of *las* 'rag, patch' (the same in Nynorsk). In Swedish, *lask* 'metal plate' occurs, while in Icelandic, *laski* means 'crack in the wood, top of a glove, loop in knitting, splinter; section of an orange; slip of dry ground between two streams, *etc*' (ÁBM). Some of these senses must have developed on Scandinavian soil, others may have been taken over with the German word.

G **las* has not been recorded, whereas forms like *la(s)ka* 'rag, patch, shred' are known over a large territory: such are Gk λακίς 'rag,' L *lacer* 'torn,' Russ *loskut* 'shred,' Sp and Port *lasca* 'piece of leather, chip,' and many others. Gmc **laska* is possible, but its origin and the relationship between the Germanic and the Romance forms are unknown (in addition to etymological dictionaries, see Hubschmid [1953:84-85]). Meyer-Lübke rejected Gmc **laska* as the etymon of the Spanish and Portuguese word in all the editions of his dictionary (ML 4919), and it is strange that Holthausen (1929a:108 and GEW, **laska*) repeated Gröber's opinion to the contrary (1886:510) without comment. We seem to be dealing with a European word traceable to an ancient etymon, but borrowing and chance are the probable causes of the similarity that would otherwise be natural to ascribe to common heritage.

Gmc **laska* and Dan *las* may be unconnected despite the near identity of sound and meaning. *Las* 'rag' seems to be akin to Go *lasiws* 'weak,' but regardless of whether this etymology is correct, **ME *lasce* was, in all likelihood, a Middle English diminutive of *las*,** for *lask(e)* is known to have appeared in the Scandinavian languages only in the 18th century, and that is why it is believed to be a borrowing from Middle Low German. *Lasce* must have been a word like ME *polke* 'small pool,' ME *dalk* 'small valley (dale),' OFr *dönk* 'small dune' [sic], and OFr *tenk* 'small pail' (Kluge [1926:sec 61a]; KrM, 214). E reg *lassikie* (EDD) is a formation parallel with it or a continuation of ME *lasce*.

Windlass (1500) has nothing to do with *lass*; its etymon is OI *vindáss*. It may have been influenced by some word like ME *windle* 'winnowing fan,' but once *windlass* came into existence, it was felt to be *wind* + *lass*. Humorous and grim references to females in the names of tools and weapons are not rare. Consider *Scavenger's daughter* 'instrument of torture,' *Dutch wife* (in tropical countries) 'open framework used in bed as a rest for the limbs'; *maiden*, one of whose meanings is 'guillotine'; *gun*, held to be the first syllable of *Gunnhild(r)*, as well as *Big Bertha* and *Katyusha* (cannons). See *gun* in Weekley (1921) for many more examples of the same type.

LILLIPUTIAN (1726)

The word Lilliput(ian) *became known in 1726, when Jonathan Swift brought out the first (anonymous) edition of* Gulliver's Travels. *Like most of Swift's neologisms,* Lilliputian *has been the object of numerous attempts to explain its origin. English, French, and Latin words have been cited as its possible etymons. Some conjectures centered on codes and anagrams. Probably* lill(e)- *is a variant of* little *and* -put *is E* put(t) *'lout, blockhead.' However,* put- *is the root of a vulgar or colloquial word for 'boy, lad' in Latin, as well as in the modern Romance and Scandinavian languages.* Lilliputian *has a common European look—a circumstance that Swift could not fail to have noticed and that contributed to its worldwide popularity. Later he seems to have modeled* Laputa *(= the whore?) on* Lilliputian. *A definitive answer about the origin of a coinage can be given only by its originator, but Swift left no hints to the history of the words he invented.*

We can only try to guess at the origin of *Lilliput(ian)*, a word Swift coined. He did not elucidate the meaning of this name, but even if he had done so, his explanation might have been offered in jest, to confuse and mislead rather than enlighten. For example, Gulliver mentions two etymologies of *Laputa:* one by local sages and one that occurred to him. It is hard to tell whether both ridicule contemporary philologists or whether Gulliver's interpretation contains a clue to Swift's parody.

***Lilli-* is almost certainly a variant of *little*,** despite the fact that the second *i* is unetymological and may have been inserted for euphony's sake. The earliest conjectures on the origin of *Lilliputian* do not antedate the eighties of the 19th century.

Kleinpaul (1885:17-18) traced the German family name *Lütke* (the spelling *Lüdtke* also exists) to LG *lütje* (= HG *lützel*) 'little' rather than *Ludwig* and added in passing that Swedish and Danish *lille* 'little' seems to be the first part of *Lilliput.* **Chance** (1889) found Kleinpaul's hypothesis plausible and **suggested that *Lilliput* was a Scandinavian-Italian hybrid: *lille* + Ital *putto* 'boy.'** At the same time, **H. Morley** (1890:17-18), the most authoritative editor of Swift's works, **wrote the following: "The small representative of lordly man has a name of contempt familiar in Swift's time; he was a 'put.' But he was of the little—lilli—people, as Swift's 'little language' phrased it, of the land of Lilli-put.** 'Put' may have been from the Latin 'putus,' a little boy, allied to *puer.* But it was used in Romance languages—the *put* and *pute* of old French, the Spanish and Portuguese *puto* and *puta,* the Italian *putta*—in the sense of boy or girl stained by the vices of men. This made it once current in England as a word of scorn; and it has been suggested that the root was in the Latin *putidus,* stinking, disgusting. This use of the word was probably repeated in Laputa." Most of what has been said on *Lilliputian* since 1890 represents variations on Morley's hypothesis, and some researchers (for example, Kelling [1951:772]) see no need to modify it (but see below).

E *put(t)* 'blockhead' turned up in printed texts no later than in 1688 (OED). *Country put* means 'lout, bumpkin.' According to R. Smith (1954:186), "it may have come into English from Irish *pait, puite, pota* 'pot'; cf. *poteen* (Ir. *poitín,* 'illicitly distilled whisky, little pot'). Swift probably heard the word many times, since it appears in both Lhuyd and Begley." The etymology of *put(t),* be it from Latin (*put* = 'stinker') or Irish (*put* = 'pot') is of no consequence for the modern attempts to decipher the workings of Swift's mind. Important only is the fact that *Lilliput* may have been composed of two English words, whatever their ultimate origin.

Swift knew and disliked the phrase *country put,* defined as 'silly, shallow-pated fellow' in 1700, for he had a strong aversion to recent monosyllables (see, among others, J. Neumann [1943:200, note 50] and Söderlind [1968:75]). Söderlind remarks that Swift's dislike of the word *put* "does not preclude its occurrence as an element in the title of Gulliver's first story, but it detracts a little from the probability of that derivation." This is a *non sequitur.* Swift would have relished the idea of endowing the citizens of the great empire of Lilliput (and by implication, of Blefuscu) with the name he detested.

K. Crook (1998:171) **considered an association between *-put* and L *caput* 'head,' and Clark** (1953:606) **mentions and rejects the interpretation *Lilliput* = 'put little.'** Clark's own etymology (1953:606) seems fanciful. He says that, according to OED, "*put* was a dialectical form of the word *pretty,* or, rather ... a truncated familiar form of *putty,* which is one of several variants of *pretty.* ... Moreover, children commonly pronounce the adult *pretty* as *piti.* If Swift's usual interchange of *u* for *i* is effected, a form *puti* is obtained, a form consistent with a good dialectical English and the 'baby talk' of the element *lilli.* In other words, Swift has combined the two adjectives describing his fictional land according to the practice he followed with *Langro* and *Peplon. Little* (and) *pretty* (in the sense of delicate, nice, elegant, 'without grandeur') were combined as *Lilli-putti....* Finally, of course, *pretty* may be used adverbially, as *pretty little,* proper and common usage in Swift's time as in our own." Still another idea is Brückmann's (1974). She says that since "[e]verything is small among the Lilliputians, not least their conceptions, of every kind," Swift may have had L *puto* 'reckon, suppose, judge, think, imagine' in mind; the Lilliputians would then translate 'petty-minded.'

One finds the strongest defense of *Lilliput(ian)* as a nonce word of Scandinavian origin in Söderlind (1968). **His perspective is that of a Swede, "who cannot hear the word *Lilliput* without associating it with the perfectly natural and usual Swedish phrase *lille Putte,* where *lille* means "little" and *Putte* is a pet name for a little boy"** (p. 77). Söderlind goes on to show that Swift's knowledge of Swedish and interest in Sweden justify his hypothesis.

Baker (1956) **suggested that Swift had borrowed his word from Catullus 53:5.** In the episode related by Catullus, someone who heard Calvus's speech in court exclaimed: "Di magni, salaputium disertum!" ('Great gods! What an articulate [fellow]!'). Baker contends that *Lilliputian* rather than *Lilliput* needs an etymology and that *salaputium* may have provided the inspiration for Swift's word. The same idea occurred to Torpusman (1998:31).

Salaputium has not been recorded anywhere else in Latin literature; only the name *Salaputis* (in the ablative) occurs in an African inscription. The manuscripts have *salapantium* and even *salafantium* (*f* = *ph*), but Seneca, who quotes Catullus's phrase, says *salaputtium,* whence *salaputium* (with one *t*) in all modern editions. The origin of the Latin word (in whichever form) is unknown. The conjecture that *putus,* a vulgar form of *puer* 'boy,' and *salēre* 'mount' (in reference to copulating animals) contributed to this coinage may not be wide of the mark. Similarity between *salaputium* and *praeputium* 'foreskin' is also obvious. Except for Whatmough's derivation of *salaputium* from Celtic (1953:65), all the others are at least probable, though rarely attractive. See Thielmann (1887), Garrod (1914), L.A. Mackay (1933; mentions *solipugas* 'a species of ants'), Bickel (1953; glosses the word as 'penis'), and Pisani (1953:181-82). For a brief survey of earlier opinions see Kelly (1854:41, note 1) and Knobloch (1969:25, note 5). Etymological dictionaries and editions add nothing new. See the most detailed commentary in Riese (1884:100), Benois-Thomas (1890:497), G. Friedrich (1908:240), and Fordyce (1961:223-25).

The latest translators vie with one another in searching for particularly obscene words to render *salaputium,* but its meaning is presumably lost. The fact that it occurs in an inscription does not necessarily add to its respectability: the most opprobrious nicknames had wide currency and were used openly and even officially, strange as it may seem today. The bystander said something that according to the poem, made Catullus laugh (perhaps approximately: "This (little) fellow can ejaculate, he can!"), and the speaker may have used a regional word, which would have enhanced the comic effect. Seneca states that Calvus was short. It is then the small size of the orator and the high level of his performance that suggested the joke. If *salaputium* really made one think of coitus and genitalia, everybody would have understood the allusion.

Catullus was known in England long before Swift. The first author in Duckett's anthology (Duckett [1925:14]) is John Skelton (1460?-1529), and Swift's fondness of Catullus is a fact (McPeek [1939:53, 249; 287, note 42; 307, note 33; 376, end of note 204; 387, note 30]; Baker [1956:478]). Although H. Williams does not mention Catullus in his survey (1932:42-48), Swift owned the 1686 and the 1711 editions of Catullus's poems (LeFanu [1988:15], and see the catalog appended to Williams's book). However, Swift did not translate no 53 and his works contain no echoes of it. The early Italian editions of Catullus ([1554:58]; the same throughout the 16th century) call Catullus's poem "Ad rusticum" and include it in "Epigrammata" (after "Liber Quartus"). The word in question appears as *salapantium.* The extensive commentary in the 1554 edition discusses its obscurity, and the relevant passage from Seneca is quoted. Catullus (1686:27, "De quodam, & Calvo," already numbered 53) and Catullus (1702:49, the same title, no 54), substitute *salapantium* for *salaputium* but give no textual notes. This practice prevailed for a long time (see, for instance, Catullus [1715]). **Unless Swift knew and remembered that Seneca had once called Calvus short (*paruolus statura*), he would hardly have thought of *salaputium* when selecting the name for his little people.**

The Catullus connection, however unlikely, should not be disregarded, because the question it raises is of crucial importance to students of Swift's language games. Did Swift want his readers to guess the meaning of the words he coined? As a rule, literary riddles are asked to be solved. If that rule applies to Swift, the use of an obscure word from Catullus would have defied its purpose, but, considering how impenetrable some of Swift's coinages are, one cannot be sure that he did not indulge in verbal games only for his own (and occasionally Stella's) amusement.

Since the appearance of Pons (1936), **Rabelais's influence on *Gulliver's Travels* has been commonplace. Pons showed that the phrases in the Lilliputian language made sense when 'translated' into Rabelais's French** (which does not testify to Swift's interest in being deciphered!). He endorsed Morley's hypothesis (p. 224) and, like Morley, believed that *Lilliput* and *Laputa* belong together; see the same reasoning in Argent (1996:39, note 2). Despite a few attempts to understand *Laputa* as a near anagram of *Utopia, All-up-at,* and the like, the first association it arouses is with Sp *la puta* 'the whore,' and the clue could not have been offered as a red herring. That circumstance increases the probability that *Lilliputian* contains some scurrilous or at least impolite allusion.

The simplest way of reconstructing Swift's process of arriving at the name he sought for is this: He needed a word meaning 'contemptible little fellow' and came by *little put,* which he changed to **lillput* and added a connecting vowel (*lill-i-put*) on the model of other words of this rhythmic structure (see them at COCKNEY and RAGAMUFFIN). When the word was coined, he must have noticed how lucky his find was, for *put-* is also the root of a colloquial word for 'boy, lad' in the Romance languages. If his knowledge of Swedish was sufficient, he could congratulate himself on reaching out to Scandinavia as well. *Laputa* came as a reward for inventing *Lilliput.* The fact that Ireland was always uppermost in Swift's mind makes plausible V. Glendinning's suggestion about the debt of *Gulliver's Travels* to Irish folklore and the Irish language (1998:164), but *Lilliput(ian)* does not seem to owe anything to Irish. In light of the reconstruction proposed here, the Swedish hypothesis is beginning to look uninviting.

Henrion (1962:53-63), the author of a bilingual (English-French) book on Swift's alleged alphanumerical code, deciphered *Lilliput* as *Nowhere* and *Laputa* as *Saxony* (= England). If so, it remains unclear why Swift should have buried his secret so deep, why only the kingdom of the Lilliputians emerges as some kind of Thomas Moore's Utopia or Samuel Butler's Erehwon, and why *Lilliput* and *Laputa* despite their phonetic near identity should have yielded such dissimilar glosses.

Since Swift did not explain how he created his neologisms, of which *Lilliput* is the most successful (it entered many other European languages), our conjectures are doomed to remain guesswork, and the etymology of *Lilliput,* like that of any 'natural' word, resolves itself into choosing the least improbable variant. Dictionaries, which usually discuss the origin of coinages (*gas, theodolite,* and so forth), only state that *Lilliput* was Swift's invention.

MAN (971)

Man *has cognates in all the Germanic languages, and its most probable congeners are the divine names Gmc* Mannus ~ *Skt* Mánu *and some words for 'man' in Slavic. The relevant Germanic forms of the word for 'man' are nouns with the thematic vowels* -i- *(in two ethnic names) and* -a-, *as well as athematic (weak) nouns. If* Mannus ~ Mánu *belong here, the* u*-declension for this word should also be reconstructed. There have been attempts to combine* mann- *and Gmc* *guma ~ *L* homo, *but the artificial etymon* *ghmonon- *carries little conviction. Two other hypotheses (ignoring the fanciful ones) trace the word for 'man' to the root of L* manus *'hand' or to the Proto-Indo-European root* *men-, *glossed as *'think' or *'be excited, aroused', or *'breathe.' The probability of those reconstructs is low.*

Among the earliest meanings of man *and its cognates 'slave' and 'servant' are prominent. Occasionally such words refer to women; OI* man *could be neuter. Go* gaman *'partnership' and 'partner' (originally, as its suffix shows, a collective noun) provides the main clue to the origin of* man. *Evidently,* gaman *at one time meant *'partnership in the god Mannus,' that is, a group of his votaries (men and women alike). Hence the ancient sense 'servant.' Later, *'partnership in Mannus' yielded the meaning *'votary, worshipper of Mannus'; the Gothic word still designates both a group and an individual. The subsequent secularization of this word resulted in the attested sense 'human being.' Likewise, G* Mensch *(<* mennisco*) must have been coined with the meaning *'belonging to Mannus.' The god's name seems to have meant 'causing madness,' as is typical of ancient words for supernatural beings. Words for 'man' sound alike in various language families. It remains unclear whether we are dealing with a near universal baby word or with reflexes of a so-called Nostratic formation.*

The sections are devoted to 1) the morphological structure of the most ancient Germanic words for 'man,' 2) the attempts to etymologize man, *3) the suggested connection between* man *and* Mannus, *and 4) the origin of the name* Mannus.

1. The oldest recorded forms to be considered are Go *manna,* OI *maðr,* OE/OFr *mann* ~ *monn,* and OHG/OS *man.* In addition, there is *Mannus,* the mythic progenitor of the Teutons, whom Tacitus mentions in Chapter 2 of *Germania,* a proper name, apparently but not necessarily related to *manna* and the rest. The theme *(Stammvokal)* of the original noun is unclear, because there are unusually many variants. **Since the etymology of *manna* and its cognates partly depends on how we will reconstruct their declension, the question of their morphology has to be discussed before everything else.**

Gothic had *manna* (weak, *n*-stem) and two forms entering into compounds: *man-* (as in *manleika* 'likeness, image') and *mana-* (as in *mana-seþs* 'world, mankind,' *mana-maurþrja* 'murderer,' and *un-mana-riggws* 'wild, cruel'). *Manauli*,* possibly *man-auli,* rendering Gk σχῆμα 'likeness, shape,' and the indefinite pronoun *ni-manna-hun* 'no one' belong here too. In Old English, *mann* was an athematic noun, but compound names ending in *-mann* seem to have been declined as *a*-stems (A. Campbell [1959:secs 620–22[). In Old High German, *man,* also an athematic noun, had the geminate in all cases except the nominative (SB secs 238–39). OS *man,* athematic, had occasional forms from the *a*-declension (Holthausen [1921:sec 322]). The situation in Old Norse is the same as in West Germanic: although *maðr* (cf the attested runic form **man[n]R**) is athematic, as the first element of compounds it has a geminate and ends in *-a (manna-).* In two compounds, *man-* appears. CV (*maðr*) cite *Manheimar,* the name of a farm in western Iceland and make a special point of the local pronunciation: *man-,* not *mann-*. Both CV and Fritzner (ODGNS) give *mannvit* 'understanding'; however, Bugge, in a note appended to Fritzner's dictionary (vol 3, p. 1110), says that *manvit* is a better form, and A. Noreen (1970:sec 318, note 5) shares his opinion.

A. Kuhn (1853:463, 465, and esp 466–67) **compared the Germanic forms with Skt *Mánu* (the Old Indian counterpart of Germanic *Mannus*). He came to the conclusion that *nn* had developed from **nw*** and cited Go *kinnus** 'cheek' as one of several similar cases. Numerous researchers, including Delbrück (1870:406), Feist (1888:75, *manna*), and Pedersen (1893:253), accepted his reconstruction (it can also be found in DW), though it runs into both morphological and phonetic difficulties. The overwhelming evidence of Germanic forms points to athematic *mann,* and even in Gothic, in which the *u*-declension was productive, **mannus* did not occur. The thematic vowels of Gothic nouns were usually preserved in compounds (for example, *fotus* was a *u*-stem, and, predictably, *-u-* shows up in *fotu-baurd* 'footstool'). Only *kinnus** (cognate with γένυς) is a fairly certain example of the change **nw* > *nn* in Germanic, but Bammesberger (1999:3, note 6) tried to discredit even that single example.

Later, another etymology of the geminate was offered. Bezzenberger (1890) took Feist to task for repeating "the old but improbable explanation [of *mann*] from *manv,* though the parallelism *abne, abnam : manne, mannam* cannot escape anyone" (Go *aba* means 'man, husband,' and its forms in the genitive and dative plural differ from those of other weak masculine nouns, such as *hanane, hanam,* of *hana* 'rooster'). Wiedemann (1893:149) reconstructed the original paradigm (in the singular) so: **man-ē, *man-n-az, *man-n-i,* with the second *-n-* carried over into the nominative. It appears that the originator of this reconstruction was J. Schmidt, who, according to his statement (Schmidt [1893:253, note]), had taught "for years" that the earliest form of *mann* was **manan-* (weak). Thus **the first *-n-* was said to belong to the root, with the second being a thematic consonant.** The two allegedly came into contact after the syncope of **a,* but in **manns* (genitive singular), the geminate was simplified, as in *mins* 'less' (adverb): cf *minniza* 'lesser' (adjective). Since Schmidt expressed his opinion only in his lectures, one wonders how Feist could be aware of it.

In KrM 43-47, the ancient paradigm of *hana* has the following appearance: **hanēn* (or **hanōn*), **hanenes* (or *-os*), **haneni, *hanonm̥; *hanones, *hanonōm, *hanonmiz, *hananuns.* Asterisked paradigms change according to the changing views on unstressed vowels in Germanic (see for comparison J. Wright [1954:sec 207]; first published in 1910). Bammesberger (1999:4), with special reference to Boutkan, offers such a set of the protoforms of *manna: *manōn, *mannaz,* (the dative is not given), **mananu(n); *mannenez, *manno(n),* and (accusative plural) **mannunz.*

After 1893, references to Bezzenberger, Wiedemann, and Schmidt became an indispensable element of the works on *manna.* Uhlenbeck's change of mind is a case in point. In the first edition of his Gothic etymological dictionary (KEWGS), *manna* is traced to **monus, *monwes* (or **mn̥wés*). Streitberg (1897:255) made the same objection to him that Bezzenberger had made to Feist (see also Streitberg 1896:140, note 1), and in the second edition, Uhlenbeck gave the expected three references and modified his views. Brugmann (Brugmann and Delbrück 1906:303) followed suit (see Trutmann [1972:26, note 77] on the change of Brugmann's position). Feist held out longer. He repeated the statement from his 1888 work in Feist[1], but in Feist[2] no mention of **nw* remained. Kluge (as evidenced by Kluge [1913:16, sec 59]) never abandoned Kuhn's idea.

Among the recent philologists, Lühr (1982:133, note 2) is unswayed by Schmidt's reconstruction, though she mentions *-nn-* < **-nw-* in passing and offers no discussion. Lubotsky (1988:43) was mainly concerned with short *a* in the Sanskrit word (the regular vowel in this open syllable would have been long, according to Brugmann's Law) and notes that "this word probably had hysterodynamic inflection in P[roto]-I[ndo]-E[uropean], cf. Germ. **mann-* < **monu.*" Boutkan (OFED: *man*) finds this explanation probable; "alternatively, we can perhaps assume **monHa-*, both forms yielding regular gemination of the **-n-*." Since he reconstructs the laryngeal only to explain the geminate, his hypothesis has no value. The prevailing opinion on *manna* does not differ from Van Helten's: *manna* supposedly originated as a weak noun and changed to the athematic declension later (Van Helten 1905:225). Uhlenbeck concluded that since *mann-* does not go back to **manw-*, *manna* cannot be related to *Mannus.* Most researchers still associate the Germanic word for 'man' with *Mannus.* Connecting them has even become commonplace (see Bammesberger [1999:3], among others).

According to Ramat (1963b:25), the compounds *manamaurþrja* and *manaseþs* preserve the most ancient form of the root in question. OHG *manslaht* ~ OE *manslieht* 'murder,' he says, point in the same direction. He compared *andbeitan* *'scold' (v) ~ *andabeit* 'rebuke' — traditionally explained as **andbéitan* ~ **ándabeit* — *with bruþfaþs* 'bridegroom' ~ *hundafaþs* 'centurion' and reconstructed *hundáfaþs* (p. 28). Given his premises, the antiquity of **mana-* and **man-*, as opposed to **mann-*, is incontestable; yet he recognized the primacy of the weak declension and did not assign **man-* to the *a*-stem.

Mitzka's editions of EWDS state that three declensions can be discerned in the Germanic word for 'man': weak, athematic, and thematic (*-i-*, in the tribal names *Marcomanni* and *Alamanni*). However, if we do not follow Uhlenbeck all the way and do not give up *Mannus* as a cognate of *manna*, the admission is inevitable that at some time somewhere in Germania the *u*-stem played a role in the morphology of the word for 'man,' because, judging by Skt *Mánu-*, and the Iranian personal name *Manuš.čiθra* (H. Bailey [1959:113]), *Mannus* was a genuine Germanic rather than a Latinized form of the god's name. Christensen (1916) is especially important for Iranian.

Since Gothic compounds show that **man(n)-* was sometimes declined as an *a*-stem word, nothing can be said against positing at least four, rather than three, declensions of the word for 'man' (so Delbrück [1870:406]). By a coincidence (?), L *mānes*, too, had the by-form *mānis* (according to the *i*-declension). Beekes (1995:346) reproduced the ancient Scandinavian runic alphabet *(futhark)* and gave the name of the **M** rune as *mannaz*. Bammesberger (1996:314) contends that no facts justify such a form, but he does not discuss Gothic compounds. According to him (Bammesberger 1999:6), **M** could be called **mannz, *mannuz,* or **mannōn*. He both denies the role of the *u*-stem in the history of **man(n)-* and accepts Skt *Mánu-* as a cognate of Gmc **mannu-* (pp. 2-3); his position is contradictory. See a detailed discussion of the morphology of **man(n)-* in Wagner (1994). Feist (1888) suggested that in *manaseþs* and other compounds, *-a-* appeared on the analogy of the most productive declension. This is possible but unlikely. Gothic preserved relics of several morphological types, and all of them look genuine. **No reason exists for giving preference to any of the five declensions (*-n-*, *-a-*, *-i-*, *-u-*, and athematic) in reconstructing the history of the Germanic word for 'man.' This grammatical instability, the impossibility to set up a secure protoform (**manōn?*, **manas?*, **manis?*, **manus?*, **mans?*) cannot be disregarded in the search for the etymology of **man(n)-*.**

2. All the conjectures surveyed below aimed at finding an ancient meaning of **man(n)-* that would adequately describe some properties or habits of human beings. However, it is not immediately obvious what we are looking for. The ancient word for 'man' could have designated 'one possessing in high degree the distinctive qualities of manhood' (that is, 'vis') or 'being of the speaker's race and language, his like, of his kind or kin.' As Trumbull (1871:139 and esp 158) points out, *man* 'individual, *homo*' is untranslatable into any Native American lanugage, for distinction is always made between native and foreigner, chief and counselor, male and female, etc. 1) **Kluge traced *mann-* (with *nn* from **nw*) to the root of Gmc **guma* and L *homo* and came up with **ghmonon-*, "possibly a sideform of **ghemo*."** **Ghmonon* appeared in the fourth edition of EWDS and stayed there until Kluge's death. His reconstruction gained wide approval. Berneker (1898:361) cited Go *magaþs** 'maiden,' allegedly from **ĝhmoghī*, as a parallel case, for he believed that *magaþs** and Lith *žmogùs* went back to **ghmōghus*. Similar operations were performed on ἄνθρωπος 'man' and ἀνήρ 'male, man.' Here the most popular protoform was *m̥θρωπος, presumably related to OHG *muntar* 'awake, lively' and so on (Bezzenberger [1880:160]; see similar combinations in Sabler [1892:276] and J. Schmidt [1895:82] and discussion in Güntert [1915:6]).

Götze and others who reworked Kluge's dictionary expunged both *nn* from **nw* and **ghmonon-*, and it became customary to express one's disagreement with Berneker. However, **gmanōn-* as a Germanic development of **gumōn-*, which seemed realistic to Wyld (UED), reemerged in Seebold's editions of EWDS, along with Lith *žmónės* 'people.' The title of Berneker's article opens the short bibliography appended to the entry *Mann* in EWDS[22-24]. Berneker was aware of the fact that not a single example of the change *gm-* > *m* had been attested in Germanic but said that such a simplification was a natural process. His argument does not go far because no Germanic word ever began with *gm-*. Mańczak (1998) argued against the simplification of **gm-* with reference to his idea that words for 'man' usually become shorter; in his opinion, the uniform change **gm-* > *m-* in all the Germanic languages would be uncharacteristic from the point of view of his theory. Yet if the posited change occurred early, *man-* < **gman-* can be ascribed to Common Germanic. The phonetic handicap is not the only one. **By combining *Mann* with *guma* ~ *homo*, Kluge destroyed the connection between **man(n)*, *Mannus*, and *Mánu* — an undesirable situation** (see what was said above about Uhlenbeck). Hermodsson (1991:229) rejected Seebold's etymology on those grounds, without entering into the history of the question, but the entry in EWDS[23-24] is the same as in EWDS[22].

2) **Another etymology traces Gmc **mann-* to the root of L *manus* 'hand.'** Its author is Hempl (1901, esp pp. 426–28), who wrote: "The figurative use of *hand* for the whole *man* is very natural and appears in almost every language. It refers to the hand as the skillful member and generally designates a laborer or a skillful person" (p. 426). Brug-

mann (1905–06:423, note 1), once an advocate of Kluge's derivation of *mann* from **manw-*, found Hempl's hypothesis persuasive, and so did Niedermann (1911:35), who, however, offered a different semantic development ('hand' > *'a handful of people, team' > 'man' — from a group to an individual), but Uhlenbeck (1905:301/232) and WP II, 266 disagreed.

Uhlenbeck doubted that Gmc **mann-*, an athematic noun, could have been derived from the root of *manus*, and Walde offered the counterargument that at the dawn of civilization women did all the work (that consideration could at most have undermined Niedermann's, not Hempl's idea). Among the supporters of Hempl's etymology we find Paschall (1943:9, note 45), who devoted his study to the Proto-Indo-European root **nem-* 'to grasp, grab' but as an afterthought suggested that **nem-* may be related to **men-* and said at the end of his article: "Perhaps Goth. *manna* and Skt. *mánuš* 'man' belong together with Lat. *manus.* The presence of a Lat. *a* in the *e-o* series need no longer trouble anyone, and the connection in meaning should not seem difficult. Hempl's connection of these words…might have appealed more to Walde…if the latter had grown up on an American farm and had learned from actual experience how often *man* and *hand* are synonymous terms." Wüst (1956:43, note 1) quoted Paschall's statement approvingly, though his starting point was the hunt with its taboo terms.

Hempl's reconstruction disregards a serious difficulty of word formation. Germanic had a cognate of *manus,* namely *mund* (f) 'hand' (OE, OI; OHG *munt*), whereas **man-* 'hand' has not been attested. Go *manwus* 'ready' is isolated (there are also the adverb *manwuba,* the verb *manwjan* 'prepare,' and so on). Hempl glossed *manwus* as 'ready at hand; handy' (p. 428), but since related words in the same grade of ablaut are unknown, it is better not to explain *obscurum per obscurius,* the more so as the origin of *manus* is equally unclear. *Manwus* and *manus* have been compared more than once (see Feist[3]), and Kroes (1955), in a one-paragraph note, revived that comparison without new arguments or discussion. Lehmann (see Feist[4]) followed him, but, as it seems, on insufficient grounds.

The widespread existence of the synecdoche 'hand'/'man' needs no proof. Yet hardly any old word for 'man' is based on it. **Like Kluge, Hempl sacrificed a tie between **mann-* and *Mannus,* though the chance of their affinity is higher than that between **mann* and *manus.***

3) **Perhaps the oldest hypothesis traces the Germanic word for 'man' to the root **men-* 'think'** (so A. Kuhn [1853:466]). Since, outside Germanic, **e* alternates by ablaut with **a*, rather than **o* (compare the comment in *OED, man*), the supporters of this etymology posited **mon* 'man' that alternated with **man* or only later became **man.* ****Mann-* and *Mannus ~ Mánu* again turned out to be unrelated.** However, primitive man as 'thinker' did not appeal to anyone, except perhaps to Rudolf Steiner's followers (Beckh [1954:34-35]), not only because such a derivation has little, if any, typological support but also because in the remote past people endowed animals with the same mental capacities as human beings.

To save the situation, various detours have been proposed. One of them is to interpret the noun with the root *mon-* (in ablaut relation to *men-*) as 'geistig erregt' (approximately, 'mentally alert') or simply 'erregt' ('excited' or perhaps 'aroused'). The gloss 'aroused' would satisfy those who stress the link between thought and sex and cite *mentula* 'penis' as possibly belonging to the root *men-*. See an early discussion of *mentula* in Aufrecht (1885:220–21) and a more recent one in Katz (1998:211, note 79). 'Thinker' and 'one mentally alert' are close. With respect to excitement, Gk ἀνήρ 'male, man' ~ Proto-Slavic **nrovŭ* (Russ *nrav,* with cognates in other Slavic languages) 'habit; character' may furnish a parallel, assuming that they are related (Greppin [1983:284] takes their kinship for granted).

Since *men-* is the root of L *memini* 'remember' (Go *gamunds** 'memory, remembrance,' in the zero grade, is akin to it), of interest is Skalmowski's attempt (1998:105–06) to trace **martia,* the Iranian word for 'man,' as in Old Persian *martiya-,* not to the root **mar-* 'die' but to **smr̥-* (Skt *smárati* 'remember, recollect,' Av *mara* 'notice'). Skalmowski derived the Iranian word from a past participle 'remembered, called to mind' and (by implication) 'recognizable, familiar; one's own; a member of one's tribe.' However, the Germanic word for 'man' was so short (often athematic) that it hardly meant 'remembered' or 'aroused, alert' (cf also the unsuccessful attempts to connect the Gothic adjective *filu-deisei** 'cunning' with OI *dís* and OE *ides* 'woman;' see Feist).

FT explained that since **men-* 'think' is too abstract for providing the etymon of 'man,' it must have developed from a more concrete meaning, for example, 'breathe, blow.' Numerous laudatory references to their explanation cannot conceal the fact that the path from 'breathe' to 'think' remains unmapped. The cryptic note: "compare μαίνομαι" sheds no light on **mann-*. Gk μαίνομαι 'I am furious' and μανία 'madness' are akin to *mens, mentis* 'mind,' but neither has anything to do with breathing. Wüst (loc cit), too, looked for a concrete meaning of which 'think' would have been a derivative, but his reference to the hunt is obscure. Despite occasional disclaimers, the derivation of **mann-* from **men-* is the preferred one. In this respect, little has changed in the period between A. Kuhn (1853:466-67), Müllenhoff (1900:115) and Bammesberger (1990:201). See also Curtius (1873:101–02) and WP II, 264, but Pokorny (IEW, 700) isolated the root **manu* 'man,' which, he says, is perhaps related to **men-* 'think.' The same wording occurs in Meid (1992:497). **It will probably not be an exaggeration to state that the **mann-/*men-* etymology has survived not because it has merit but because, to quote OED, "no plausible alternative explanation has been suggested."**

4) **A few more conjectures on the origin of the Germanic word for 'man' exist.** Vaniček (1881:208) repeated Curtius's etymology but added L *manēre* 'stay, remain' as a cognate of G *Mann*. Loewenthal (1917:127–29/95) reconstructed the root **man- ~ *men-* 'catch, seize, grab' ('ergreifen'). From 'catch' he moved to 'grasp' (in the figurative sense 'understand') and etymologized **men(u̯)ós,* the alleged protoform of *man* (he obviously traced *-nn-* to **-nw-*) as 'der Ergreifer, der Umarmer' ('he who grasps; embraces'). He proposed a similar interpretation for Oscan *ner* 'man,' OI *fírar* 'men' (pl), and *vir* 'man': all of them turned out to be grabbers and graspers. No one seems to have taken his proposal seriously.

Tucker (1931, *homo*) says that *man* and *mann* are probably related to the root of L *mons* 'mountain' and *eminēre* 'stand out, excel.' Under *mons* his comment is: "ult[imately] this root does not differ from **men-* 'turn, bend' (*emineo* 'stand out, project')." Tucker easily crossed the line between etymology and fantacizing. Holbrooke's long list of allegedly related words (1910:79) does not inspire confidence either. His root is **ma-* 'grasp, measure, *etc.*' The coincidence with Loewenthal's 'grab, grasp' (suggested seven years later) is probably fortuitous. We are not told how 'man' is connected with grasping (Tucker) or turning, bending, and jutting out.

Jensen (1951) is another researcher who came up with **men-* 'project' (v) as the etymon of *man*. He found **men-* 'rise; project, jut out; tower (over)' among WP's five homonymous roots and proposed to etymologize 'man' as 'an erect being' (in opposition to animals), citing analogues in Paleo-Siberian languages. In a favorable comment on Jensen's article, Kähler (1952) gave examples from Austronesian languages in which the word for 'man' coincides with those for 'pole, stake, mast, trunk,' but they hardly confirm Jensen's derivation. The syncretism 'branch'/'child,' that is, 'offshoot'/offspring' is widely known, and Kähler's examples should probably be understood in its light: from 'tree trunk' to 'child' and 'man.' Seiler's doubts (1953:232, continued on p. 233) about Jensen's reconstruction seem to be justified.

Mezger (1946:239, note 41) understood **mann-* as 'small' and 'growing': "Is *manu-* 'small, little' connected with the word for 'human being'? Skt. *mánu-, manú-* 'human being,' with its difference of accent, may be explained as an original *u*-adjective with the accent on *u,* whereas *mánu-* would represent the substantive. The Germanic has consonantic *n*-inflection, *o*-stem (Goth. *manaseþs* etc.) beside the ancient *u*-stem, which, as Skt. *Manu-* 'god of law' illustrates, belongs in the realm of the cult. If there is a connection between Arm. *manr* 'small, little' and Skt. *manú,* etc., the noun *mánu* would have originally designated a growing human being in contrast to the grown-up person; the meaning small, little would be secondary. This explanation of *manu* agrees with the name of the god *Mánu-* 'the progenitor of mankind.' In general, a derivation of a word meaning 'human being' from a term meaning 'growing (engender)' is much more in conformity with that of other comparable expressions than a connection of *mann-* with **men* 'to think.'"

Of all the etymologies discussed above, Mezger's is the most plausible, but a nearly imperceptible substitution of concepts ruins it. For 'a human being' we need 'growing' or 'grown,' whereas the progenitor is 'grower.' Mezger says: "growing (engender)"; the two are not synonyms when we deal with an engenderer and an engendered (small but growing) creature. Besides this, putting too much credence in the idea that 'small' is a concept derivative of 'growing' cannot be recommended.

5) Makovskii has dealt with the Germanic word for 'man' in several articles, reviews, and books. Since he often repeats himself, reference will be made only to one review (Makovskii 1988:139–40) and four books of his (Makovskii 1988a:131; 1992:42; 1999a:207–08; 2000b:216–17). As usual, he offers a series of alleged cognates compatible only within the framework of his picture of an ancient pagan world (without any specifics: just primitive and pagan) and his laws of reconstruction that are based on uncontrollable semantic

transitions (allegedly happening in that primitive world), the broadest comparison of languages and dialects, and the thesis that most initial consonants are potential prefixes (like *s-mobile*) and can therefore be subtracted at will. Sound correspondences rarely play a role in his reasoning. Makovskii's ideas are reproduced here for completeness' sake. None of them merits discussion.

Proto-Indo-European **men-* 'compress' yields 'earth' (man as an earthly creature: cf OI *maðr* and OE *maða* 'worm, maggot') and 'liquid' (cf L *māno* 'flow, pour out' and *mānes* 'deified ghosts of the dead'). Sperm is one of such liquids (cf Go *mimz* 'flesh'). 'Compress' also yields 'soul' because souls were believed to reach the underworld by water. In addition, 'compress' (< *'bend') could develop the meaning *'fire,' whence **men* 'rise' (said originally about fire). Fire leaves spots, hence 'crime, harm' (cf OE *mān* 'crime') and *mōna* 'moon,' because the moon is a symbol of sickness and death. (The moon appears in Wüst, loc cit, too, though in a different and unclear context.) Fire is inseparable from burning. The role of fire is not restricted to leaving spots. Human beings are born by fire and are cremated after death. Therefore, OE *man* goes back to **marn* 'heat.' Likewise, L *homo* is related to Russ *kormit'* 'feed' and Russ reg *komet'* 'bend' (said about the flame). OE *hæl-eð* 'man, hero' is cognate with OE *ælan* [sic] 'burn' (*h* < **k* is a prefix). OE *ceorl* 'free man' is the sum of **ker* (< **er; k* is the same prefix) + **el-*, **al-;* both roots mean 'burn.' Gk ἄνθρωπος is the sum of **ater-* 'fire' and **peuor* 'fire,' whereas Russ *chelovek* 'man' is made up of **kel-* 'burn' + *uek-*, **og-*, **ag-* 'fire' (the same root occurs in OI *mǫgr* 'young man,' in which *m-* is a prefix). *Mano* 'in the morning' should be understood as 'the growing light of dawn.'

OI *maðr*, which has already been compared with words for worms and maggots, can also be compared with OE *māðum* 'treasure.' *Man* is obviously related to Gk μόνος 'alone, single' (literally 'put together, compressed' < *'bent'). According to another version, a single unit is a symbol of creativity, strength, courage, and superiority: cf L *mons* 'mountain' (printed with a typo; Tucker, also mentioned *mons* in connection with *men* but gave no explanation; Makovskii has a high opinion of Tucker's dictionary) and OI *mœna* 'jut out, project' (a conclusion probably arrived at without the influence of Loewenthal: Makovskii refers only to entire books and usually in an appended bibliography, not in the text). Further cognates: L *mundus* 'clean' (< *'purified by fire') and *manus* 'hand' (<*'bent'), OI *meiðr* 'tree' (printed with two typos), OE *wullmod* 'distaff,' *mōd* 'spirit; power, etc' (printed with a typo), and *mand* 'basket' (Kroes, too, mentioned E reg *maund*, which he, naturally, knew from Du *mand* 'basket'), and G *Minne* 'love.'

"According to pagan beliefs, the world is the scene of constant reincarnation, of constant transformations. Man appears as a creature perpetually 'changing masks': cf E *man* versus Russ *meniat'(sia)* 'change, alter' and Lith *mainýti* (the same meaning); Russ *chelo-vek* 'man' versus IE **kel-* 'move; turn (into)'. We witness not only a constant change of life and death but also the reincarnation of souls" (Makovskii [2000b:217]).

3. It is usually taken for granted that linguists have to explain the original meaning of the word **man(n)-*, while the etymology of *Mannus* will take care of itself because Mannus is simply 'man.' As a general rule, words for 'man' (= 'human being') arise to mark the opposition 'child of the earth; mortal' versus 'inhabitant of the heavens; immortal' (see, for example, Buck 1949:79-80/2.1), though in polytheistic religions the concept of an individual god emerges late, if at all: more often we find a collective plural, as in Old Icelandic (*guð* 'gods'). J. de Vries (1935-37:216) said: "Mannus is of course to be understood as protoman *(Urmensch)*."

However, no one needs a god or an eponymous ancestor called 'man.' Drees (1974) found credible traces of Mannus's cult, and personal names testify to its existence too. In *Hartmann* and the like, *-mann* means 'man,' but some of the old names beginning with *man-* must have been like Scandinavian names with the first element *Þor-* ~ *Þór-*. Schönfeld (1911:160) cites *Mannelebus*, Meyer-Lübke (1905:40, 86) and von Grienberger (1913:48) add a few others. In Searle's *Onomasticon* (1877:347–49) and in Förstemann's *Namenbuch* (1900:1088–1089), such names occupy several pages, though in the *Namenbuch* most end in *-mann*. If J. Grimm's conjecture (1835:XXVII) is right that Old Scandinavian *Ítermon* contains the same root, *Mannus* had worshippers not only among the western Germanic tribes. E. Martin (1907:77) doubted that *Manalaub, Maneleub, Manipert, Manedruda, Manifrid*, and *Managold* had any relation to 'man' and compared their first element with *menni* = *monīle* 'necklace,' but the connection with *Mannus* is more likely: cf OI *Þorvaldr*, *Þorveig*, *Freyfaxi*, and so forth.

Perhaps we will make progress in the search for the origin of *man* if we agree that all the ancient Germanic tribes venerated a god called Mannus, and that it is the etymology of the divine name that has to be explained because the

common name **man(n)-* is the derivative of *Mannus.* Gothic and Old Icelandic seem to have preserved an early stage in secularizing Mannus's name. Gothic had *gaman* (n) 'fellowship' and 'partner'; OI *man* (n or f) meant 'bondsman; girl, maid; concubine.' Feist[3] considers Go *gaman* to be a collective noun to *man-*, as in *manaseþs* and *manleika,* and J. de Vries (AEW) treats OI *man* as a cognate of the Gothic word (in Old Norse, prefixes were lost, so that Scandinavian **gaman* is probable). The original meaning of *gaman* must have been 'a group of Mannus's worshippers.' The word consisted of a collective prefix, the root of Mannus's name (which, as Ramat observed, did not have a geminate), and an ending *(*-an* or **-am),* lost before the time of the earliest texts. Trier's favorite *Mannring* was in this case *Mannus-ring.*

The way from a collective plural to an individual is usual in the history of such words. For example, OHG *wîb* (> ModG *Weib*) and OE *wīf (> wife)* were neuter nouns and at one time probably meant 'a woman and her family.' Old Gutnish *þiauþ* 'man' is neuter. The Old English cognate of OHG *liuti* 'people'(> ModG *Leute)* was *lēod,* but *lēod* also meant 'prince.' G *Stute* 'mare' corresponds to E *stud* whereas Rum *feméie* 'woman' meant 'family' (< *familia;* Niedermann [1911:35, note on *manus*]). L *mānes* 'deified ghosts of the dead' (m pl) later meant 'corpse.' OI *guð* 'gods' has been mentioned above, and see DWARF. Go *gaman* is especially interesting because it means both 'fellowship' and 'partner,' whereas OI *man* points to the inferior status of him or her who constituted the 'fellowhip' ('bondsman; concubine'), regardless of the sex.

MHG *man* had a wide spectrum of meanings ('human being; man; male, son; lover; fiancé; brave warrior, servant, vassal'), but in courtly poetry 'vassal' predominated (cf the English phrase *all the king's men*), and in chess any piece except the king and the queen could be called *man.* 'Son,' 'lover,' 'fiancé,' and 'warrior' are lexicalized contextual meanings, but 'human being' and 'servant' are not. The first of them allowed the pronouns *man, jemand* 'someone,' and *niemand* 'no one' to arise (*-d* is excrescent). The situation in Old English is similar. The meaning 'human being' is present in the compounds *wæpnedmann* 'male,' *wīfmann* 'woman,' and *gumman* 'person.' The pronoun *man* was used in the same sense as in German, and *man* 'vassal; serf' has also been recorded. The weak form *manna,* common in legal texts, meant 'any person' and 'slave,' but not 'vassal' (see a survey of Old English usage in dictionaries and in Stibbe [1935:32–33]). The Old Icelandic counterparts of OE *wæpnedmann* and *wīfmann* were *karlmaðr* and *kvennmaðr*.

Compounds like *mannsaldr* 'human age' show that *maðr* could mean both 'man' and 'woman' (any human being). Apparently, 'servant' is not a secondary feudal meaning of *man(n)-*; only 'vassal' and 'serf' are. Mannus's earthly votaries and worshippers were mortal human being and his servants; the two meanings are inseparable. All together — men and women — formed a *gaman.* **The development was from 'fellowhip in Mannus' to 'a fellow in Mannus' ('partner,' as in Gothic) and further to 'human being' and 'person of low status' (first in relation to the deity, then to the lord — 'slave,' 'concubine,' and so on).**

It follows that, unlike the cognates of Go *wair* and *guma* (both mean 'man'), which go back to Proto-Indo-European, ****man(n)-* emerged comparatively late.** (However, runic **man(n)R** is roughly contemporaneous with Tacitus's *Germania.*) **It was abstracted from the compound **gaman-*, and herein must lie the reason for the instability of its grammatical form.** The new coinage could be assigned to any declension fit for a masculine noun.

Attempts to find one and only one protoform were doomed to failure. *Mannus,* a *u*-stem word, existed, but the common name does not seem to have ever been declined like *fōtus,* and here Bammesberger is right. It naturally joined the *a*-declension, the most productive of them all (*wair* and *Karl* ~ *karl* ~ *ceorl* were also *a*-nouns); hence *manaseþs* and so on. In the plural, when used as the second element of tribal names, it, for unknown reasons, followed the *i*-declension, that is, behaved like Go *wegs* 'wave, billow' and *aiws* 'time, lifetime.' The bare form *man-*, devoid of the support of tradition, was a good candidate for the athematic declension, and perhaps under the influence of its synonym *guma,* it was sometimes declined weak.

The geminate in *manna* may have arisen as J. Schmidt and Ramat suggested, but *-n-* may have alternated with *-nn-* because a tie between the new word for 'man' and *Mannus* was as obvious to early speakers as its tie with **gaman-*. In *Mannus, -nn-* probably had the same origin geminates have in other divine names, that is, from the emphatic vocative: cf *-p-* in *Jūpiter* versus *-pp-* in *Juppiter* and *-nn-* in Beothian Μέννες (Leumann [1954:3]).

When parallel grammatical forms compete in a system, they tend to acquire distinctions in meaning and usage. This is what happended to E *brothers* and *brethren, proved* and *proven, struck* and *stricken, my* and *mine* and in three German plurals: *Männer, Mannen,* and *Mann* (each has its own sphere of application). As already pointed out, OE *manna* did not mean 'vassal, retainer.' Similar distinctions must have existed in Germanic between **mans, *manōn,* and **manas*, but the details are now beyond reconstruction.

Two scholars came close to discovering what appears to be the correct etymology of *man(n)-*. J. Grimm (1983:419-20) knew, as a matter of course, all the facts discussed above and concluded that the earliest Germanic word for *servus* had been *man,* but he hastened to add: "However, this does not allow us to trace the origin of the Teutons *(des deutschen volks),* whose progenitor was called *Mannus,* to an ignoble, subjugated tribe *(einem unedlen, unfreien stamme);* I believe that *mann,* in contradistinction to god, should be understood as a person created by and subservient to the Supreme Being *(als der erschaffne dem höchsten wesen dienstbare mensch [mannisco]).* Those two ancient words [that is, *Mannus* and *mann*] are no more demeaning than *homo* and ἄνθρωπος; rather, they are based on the concept of noble and natural dependence of all earthly creatures; likewise, the Latin and Greek words are sometimes used contemptuously with reference to worldly servitude" (the same in the later editions). Grimm realized that 'servant' was one of the original meanings of **mann-* and that this meaning is tied to Mannus's name.

Years later, Kluge (1901-02:43-44) developed a similar idea. He must have noted the incongruity of calling a god 'man' because he gave Mannus the gloss 'protoman (*Urmensch*).' Like Grimm (whose name does not turn up in his article), he emphasized the importance of the word *Mensch* 'human being' and suggested that *Mensch (< mennisco)* was not a substantivized form of an adjective 'pertaining to man' but a derivative of the root *man-* with a suffix meaning 'of a certain origin, descent.' He concluded that men were understood as Mannus's progeny (the same, in passing, already in Kluge [1897]). One can only wonder why he kept inventing complicated etymologies of *Mann* in his dictionary in disregard of his own insights.

Grimm and Kluge were right in that they approached *man* from *Mannus*. They were also right that *servus* 'slave' is one of the earliest meanings of the Germanic word for 'man' (Grimm) and that Go *mannisks** and its cognates should be understood as 'belonging to Mannus' rather than 'belonging to man' (Kluge). However, Kluge may have been mistaken in reconstructing the original meaning of *mannisks** as 'the progeny of Mannus'; more probably, it meant '(the circle of) Mannus's worshippers; members of the *gaman*.' Having explained *mannisks**, he failed to explain **man(n)-*, and his derivation of G *Mann* obscured his view. According to GI I:396, in the opposition gods : humans, **manu-*, as in Sanskrit and Germanic, represents the human element. But more likely, *manu-* emerged as the name of the Godhead. In Germanic, its circle of votaries was called *gaman-*. The movement from a group to an individual produced the concept of man, and this is how Go *manna* and its congeners originated (see also Eichner [1994:78-79]).

4. In the words of Scott, the author of etymologies for CD: "It is not likely that any orig[inal] significant term old enough to have become a general designation for 'man' before the Aryan dispersion would have retained its orig[inal] signification." In principle, he was right, but a few facts should be mentiond that seldom attract the attention of Germanic etymologists.

The sound complex *man-* designates 'man' not only in Germanic and not only in Indo-European. Güntert (1930:20) and Jensen (1936:163) cited Korean *myång* (or *myăng*). According to Jensen, the coincidence is more likely due to chance than to language contacts. Chinese *manu* also means 'man' (see the discussion in Ulving [1968:950]). In the Austronesian languages, the words for 'man' are *anaq muani, mone̱,* and *m̯wä̱än* (Dyen [1970:439/73]).

Illich-Svitych (1976:58–59/292) isolated the Nostratic root *mänʌ* 'man, male' common to the Hamito-Semitic, Indo-European, Uralic, Finno-Ugric, and Dravidian languages. In so doing, he partly followed Trombetti, to whom he referred. However, this root is absent in Bomhard-Kerns (1994). Andreev (1986:176/150; 1994:10–11) listed *M–N-* among his "Boreal" roots (*Boreal* is also Trombetti's term) and assigned the meanings 'man; think, thinking; ponder; remember, memory' to it. The meanings ('man' versus the rest) are too divergent to convince skeptics. The words he gives from a variety of languages are glossed as 'man; mind; memory; brain; say, talk over; remember; sly, cunning; tombstone with an inscription.' Since the etymology of man as 'thinker' or 'someone endowed with memory' is precisely what needs proof, it would be advisable to stay with *M–N-* 'think' (assuming for the sake of argument that such a Nostratic root is real) and leave 'man' alone. Ruhlen's list (1994:301-12), like Illich-Svitych's, is more to the point. It contains words meaning 'man, male, father, boy; a phallic deity; herdsman; warrior; woman; people, kin.' The similarity is noteworthy because the languages that yield the examples cover the whole globe and sound alike: *monō, mun, iman, manja, mancho, meno,* and so forth.

Oehl, who compiled lists of the same type long before the emergence of Nostratic linguistics, treated the complex *man* as a universal baby word (Oehl [1921–22:771; 1933a:43]). WH, 28 (the end of the entry *mānēs*) and 54 (the end of the entry *mātūrus*) do not deny the possibility that *ma-* is the root of some baby words. Feist[3] *(manna)* refers to Oehl (1933a) without comment.

At an early stage in the development of religious thinking, gods, spirits, and elves are distinguished mainly according to the harm they can cause. People with mental aberrations were said to be possessed by a god, shot by an elf, and the like. Bogeymen of all kinds inflate themselves, make a lot of noise, and frighten people. The names of such demons are sometimes similar all over Eurasia. See BOY and DWARF. Since such words are usually expressive and onomatopoeic, sound correspondences may be violated in them.

In Indo-European, the syllable *man* is often connected with the idea of evil spirits and madness. The Slavic material is especially rich. See the words collected under the roots **mamu, *manija,* and **manu* in ESSI 17, 190–91, 201–03. They mean 'enticement; deception; fury; an unclean spirit; apparition, ghost' and a few more like them. Greek has μανία 'mania,' and Latin has *moneo* 'warn; instruct, tell,' a cognate of G *mahnen (< manôn)* 'admonish.' Perhaps (as has been suggested) the original meaning of such words was 'beckon, make a sign; a demon making such signs.' *Mānes* 'deified ghosts of the dead' may belong here too. Dictionaries assign μανία and the rest to the root **men-* 'to think.' More likely, *man-* 'make a sign; ghost' is a separate root.

Both *Mánu* and *Mannus* probably arose in human consciousness as frightening, awe-inspiring creatures. Μάνης, the mythic progenitor of the Phrygeans and a common Phrygean name, may be their next of kin (Fick [1892:240]; Hermann [1918:228–29]) . Like so many other gods, with time they acquired benevolent features. Wodan (OI Óðinn), the furious one, turned into the creator of culture and founder of kingship. Þórr, the embodiment of thunder, spent his time maintaining law and order. The Slavic-Iranian **bog-* may have made it all the way from *bogey ~ buka* to a dispenser of riches. Mánu and Mannus became divine 'protomen.' Those who belonged to *Mánu* and *Mannus* were called *mānuṣa ~ mānava* and *mannisks* ~ mennisco,* respectively. All together, Mannus's people formed a **gaman-.*

The syllable *man* may, after all, be a baby word: first a bogeyman with whom to scare little children, then an evil spirit striking fear in the hearts of adults, then a (wrathful?) god, and finally, the progenitor of the human race. Such seems to have been the history of the Germanic word. The syllable *ma-* tends to combine with *n, r,* and semivowels to produce words meaning 'mirage, apparition,' and the like (Solmsen [1908; p. 581 on *ma-n*]). This is how a similar word may come into being in the absence of a deity. For example, Proto-Slavic **man-gi* or **man-gu* 'man' (Russ. *muzh,* and so on) is parallel to *mānuṣa- ~ mennisco,* but there is no Slavic *Mannus.* Hiersche (1984:89) says that the secular meaning of the Slavic word deprives it of any importance for reconstructing the ancient Indo-Iranian religious vocabulary. This is not necessarily true, for religious vocabulary is hard to separate from the vocabulary of belief and superstition.

MOOCH (1460)

The verb mooch *has numerous variants and doublets. Among the doublets,* miche *is especially important.* Mooch *and* miche *should be traced to the same etymon. Two main conjectures on the origin of* miche *and, by implication, of* mooch *exist: it is either a borrowing from French or a reflex of OE* *mȳcan, *a cognate of several words in Old High German and Old Irish. More probably,* mooch *and* miche *continue an Old Germanic verb whose root had cognates in Celtic and Latin, whereas the French and Italian words of the same type were taken over from Germanic. That verb possibly had a root with the initial meaning 'darkness; mist,' whence all kinds of underhand dealings and illegal actions. But its onomatopoeic origin is not unthinkable either. In English, the second component of* hugger-mugger, *as well as* -mudgeon *in* curmudgeon *and* mug *'(ugly) face' and* mug *(v), seems to be related to* mooch.

The sections are devoted to 1) the forms of mooch ~ miche *and their variants, 2) the Romance and the Germanic suggestions about the origin of* miche, *3) the probable Germanic origin of OF* muser *'hide' and the existence of several early European slang words for concealment and cheating, 4) the origin of* hugger-mugger, *5) the origin of* curmudgeon, *and 6) the origin of* mug, *noun and verb. Section 7 is the conclusion.*

1. The verb *mooch,* although known for a long time, appeared in etymological dictionaries late. OED gives its meanings as '?act the miser, pretend poverty,' 'play truant; *in later use* play truant in order to pick blackberries; *hence* pick (blackberries),' 'loaf, skulk, sneak, loiter; hang about, slouch along,' 'pilfer, steal,' and 'sponge, slink away and allow others to pay for your entertainment.' The last of those glosses was borrowed from BL. For

mooching as blackberry picking see EDD and Venables (1875). 'Loaf' and 'steal' appeared in print only in the middle of the 19th century. *Moocher* and *mooching* are equally late. The meaning 'sponge, etc' seems to have always been the prevalent one in American English, but no American dictionary before NCD recorded *mooch.* The citations for this verb in OED show a gap between 1460 and 1622. 'Pretend poverty' and 'obtain by cajolery or begging' are close, but the meaning 'play truant, loiter,' although it also refers to a socially unacceptable activity, bears no similarity to them.

The following forms (or variants) of *mooch* have been attested: *mowche, mouche, mootch, mooche, moach, moche, modge,* and *mouch. Modge,* with its voiced final consonant, is especially important for reconstructing the history of *mug, mugger,* and *-mudgeon.* OED gives the head word as *mooch, mouch,* with one pronunciation for both. However, *mouch* is rather a doublet of *mowch* [-au-], as follows from the name of Miss Mowcher, a heroic dwarf in *David Copperfield*. The now obsolete or regional verb *mouch* 'eat up, eat greedily' (1570) also exists. Yet Miss Mowcher was not a glutton; she feigned levity and merriment, while being a stealthy observer of human nature. *Mooch* has several variants, *mowch(e)* and *modge* among them, and a doublet *miche* (1225), which has its own variants, namely *mitch(e), mich,* and *meech. Micher* 'petty thief' and *miche* surfaced in the same year. The form *meech* does not antedate, as far as we know, the 19th century.

2. **Despite the wide range of vowels, *mooch* and *miche,* along with *mouch, meech,* and so forth, probably have the same etymon.** All etymological dictionaries of English discuss *miche* (or *mich;* Skeat), and Hamlet's *miching malicho* (III,2:148), understood as 'sneaking mischief,' made the verb *miche* famous among philologists. *Micher* in *1Henry IV* II, 4:455 means 'truant.'

The earliest guess about the origin of *miche* proved to be the most durable. **Minsheu derived *miche* from F *muser* (= *musser*) 'hide,'** and so did Skinner, whose starting point was *micher* 'miser,' for a miser won't spare one a crumb of bread (*mica panis*); he apparently connected E *miche,* F *musser,* and L *mica.* Whiter III:197 made fun of Skinner's etymology. Todd (in Johnson-Todd), Mahn (W [1864]), Wedgwood, and Skeat[1] followed Minsheu, though each of them, especially Mahn, added a few forms and a few details. Wedgwood's material is particularly interesting.

Between 1617 (Minsheu) and 1862 (Wedgwood), only two original etymologies of *miche* were offered. Whiter III:197 compared *micher* with *mud* (because, in his opinion, the most ancient meaning of all words was 'earth') and added *hugger-mugger* to a list of their cognates. *Hugger-mugger* will be discussed in sec 4. W (1828) and the later editions until 1864 connected *miche* and Sw *maka,* which they glossed as 'withdraw.' However, Sw *maka* means 'move (a little)'; like Dan *mage* 'manage, arrange' and late OI *maka* 'make,' it goes back to MLG *maken* 'make' and cannot be a cognate of *miche.*

Richardson supported Skinner (*miche* from F *muser*). His entry is a typical illustration of the state of the art when Wedgwood became active: "A *micher,* a covetous man, either from Lat. *miser,* or from the Fr. *miche; mica panis,* because he counts all the crumbs that fall from his table (Skinner). The later etymology is undoubtedly the true one. Mr. Tyrwhitt tells us that in the *Promptorium parvum* 'mychyn' stands as equivalent to 'pryvely stelyn *smale* thyngs' and Lambarde in his *Eirenarchia,* says that one justice may charge constables to arrest such, as shall be suspected to be *'draw-latches, miching* or *mightie theeves'* contrasting these different sorts of plunderers. The Fr. *Miche,* Lat. *mica,* is a small thing." Like other etymologists, Richardson was prone to using *undoubtedly* in stating controversial cases.

Wedgwood noted the similarity between *miche* and a set of verbs in German, namely SwiG *mauchen, mucheln,* and *mauscheln* 'enjoy delicacies in secret; steal.' He cited G *verschmauchen* 'smouch, or secretly purloin eatables; conceal,' SwiG *smussla* 'do anything furtively,' E *smouch* (v), and E *smuggle* as related. In Wedgwood[1], the list was even longer. There we find E *mucker* 'hoard up' and Ital *mucchio* 'heap.' The noun *mucchio* remained at *miche* in Wedgwood[2-4], but the verb *mucker* did not. However, he missed G *meucheln* 'assassinate (treacherously),' *meuchlings* 'treacherously,' and several old and newer compounds like *Meuchelmord* 'treacherous assassination' and failed to explain why an English word with such strong ties elsewhere in Germanic should be classified with borrowings from French.

Kluge (EWDS, without references) developed Wedgwood's etymology at *meucheln* but gave up the French connection and reconstructed OE **mȳcan* 'lie in hiding' (< Gmc **mûk-* 'waylay' < PIE **mûg-*). The form *mūg-* has been attested in Old Irish, and Zimmer (1879:210-11) linked OIr *rumúgsat* 'they have hidden,' *formúichdetu* 'concealment,' and a few others to such Old High German forms as *mûhhôn* 'waylay' and *mûheo* 'thief.'

In choosing the glosses 'lie in hiding, waylay,' Kluge projected the meaning of G *meucheln* to Germanic and Proto-Indo-European. He also thought that G *mucken* 'mutter' and *munkeln* 'speak secretly' are akin to G *meucheln* and E *mitch*, for both have connotations of indistinctness and secrecy. Reference to Zimmer appears for the first time in EWDS[6]; Götze (EWDS[11]) removed it, and it has never been reinstated. The most important works on the family of *meucheln* are Birlinger (1870:149 and 1872). Words with the root *mûch-* ~ *mauch-* invariably refer to underhand dealings. See also Weigand (*meucheln*) for examples and discussion.

The same root (*mûh-*) seems to occur in OHG *mûhheimo* 'cricket' (= 'hidden house spirit'; ModG *Heimchen* has lost the first component). This etymology of *mûhheimo* is old (see Schade and Schwenck). Kluge preferred to equate *mûh-* with Go *muka(modei)** 'gentleness, meekness' but supplied his derivation with a question mark. Götze deleted the question mark, and the explanation of *mûhheimo* as 'soft- (chirping) spirit' has prevailed. Seebold (KS) admits the possibility of a different semantic interpretation of *Heimchen* but does not elaborate. However, several Old High German animal names have the component *mûh-* (Birlinger [1872:317-18]), and in none of them would 'gentle' make sense. 'Hidden house spirit' is preferable to Schwabe's '[secret] gnawer' (1917:223); he related *heim-* to the root **sk̑(h)ēi* 'sever, separate, cut' (see L *scio* in WH), the association with 'house' being due to folk etymology. See also HENBANE, sec 2.

Kluge's **mycan* (with *y̆*) as the protoform of *miche* ~ *mi(t)ch* appears in W (1890), in which OE (properly, ME) **michen* is compared with OHG *mûhhen (= mûhhôn)*. But English etymologists did not come to terms with the origin of *mooch* ~ *miche*, for it remained unclear whether OF *musser* (or any of its multiple variants) played a role in the history of the English words. W[1] is noncommittal as to whether *miche* is ultimately of Romance or Germanic origin. Although W[2] traces this verb to OF *muchier* ~ *musser* 'conceal, lurk,' from Celtic, it mentions OE **mȳcan* as a possible etymon. W[3] does not list *mich(e)*, states that *micher* is akin to *meecher* from Old French, and derives *mooch* from F reg *muchier* 'hide, lurk.' Both the French and the German verbs appear in the entry *meucheln* in Walshe, a student's dictionary that was the main source of German etymologies in Partridge (1958; *mooch)*.

OED follows J. Payne (see his suggestion in anonymous [1872:310]) and considers only OF *muchier*), though Bradley, in MED(B), *müchen*, repeats Kluge. Skeat[4] (*mich*) no longer mentions OF *muc(i)er*, cites G *meuchlings*, and reconstructs OE **my̆ccan*, while CD (*miche*) remains true to Skeat's earlier etymology. UED gives *mooch* and *mouch* different pronunciations and derives them from OF *muchier* 'slink, skulk,' but *miching* (there is no entry *miche*) is said to be etymologically doubtful, possibly from OF *muchier* 'hide.' Wyld glossed the same verb differently in different entries (or rather he broke one gloss into two), and it comes as a surprise that the origin of *mooch* is certain, whereas that of *miching* is doubtful. Was Wyld not sure that *mooch* and *miche* are related? Or is the discrepancy the result of an editorial oversight? RHD and AHD (*mooch*) took their etymologies from OED.

Diensberg (1985b:172-73) contests Zettersten's derivation of *miche* from **mycan* (1965:231), but his real opponent is Kluge. In Diensberg's opinion, it is easier to explain the vocalic variations (*miche, mooch*, and so on) if we take the Old French verb as the etymon of *miche*. However, OE **mȳcan* could easily develop into ME **mēken, *mouken* (*ou* = [u:]), and **mīken*. The absence of the Old English verb in the extant monuments may be due to the fact that no appropriate context existed for it, especially if it referred only to furtive behavior rather than murder, as in Old High German, and lacked the stylistic dignity of OHG *mûhhôn*.

3. One can neither derive E *mooch* from OF *mucier* and simply "compare" it with OHG *mûhhôn* nor leave it in its Germanic nest in disregard of the French verb. The supposition of a root common to Celtic and Germanic goes back to Zimmer (1879:210-11; see above) and Stokes (1894:219). They are the authorities for such reconstructed roots as Celt **mūc-*, the putative etymon of several Romance words (Körting 6327), and Gaulish **mūkyāre* (ML 5723), which the latest English dictionaries copied, or **mūciare* (EWFS). Weekley (1921) traced *mooch* to Old French, whose root appears "in both Celt[ic] and Teut[onic]." Hirt (1921:108) included G *meuchel-* in his list of the Germanic-Celtic stock. E. Zupitza (1896:216) compared L *muger* 'a cheat at dice' with the Old Irish words, and according to Uhlenbeck (KEWAS, 228), Skt *mûhyati* 'is bewildered, mistaken' is a cognate of *muger*. Charpentier (1912:134), WH (*muger*), and KEWA (662) rejected his idea, so that it will be safer to do without the Sanskrit verb.

Regardless of whether OE **mȳcan* or **myccan* existed, we obtain an old word for cheating and concealment current in several Indo-European languages. The French verb may have been borrowed from Gaulish but may have been a loan from Germanic. If it originated in Germanic, nothing prevented its return home. For example, the second component of G *Duckmäuser* 'sleazy individual, creep' continues MHG *mûsen* 'behave secretively like a thief' (KM), which seems to be a reborrowing of a German verb from French, but E *mooch* need not be of Romance origin.

French etymologists do not agree on the origin of *mucier* despite the now prevalent reference to a Celtic root in etymological dictionaries. Diez (645) believed that OF *mucier* was connected in some way with MHG *mûzen* 'change, exchange' (not to be confused with MHG *mûsen*) and cited Ital *smucciare* 'slip away, escape' among its cognates. Meyer-Lübke initially followed W. Meyer (1888:256-57) and gravitated toward a Germanic etymon of *mucier* (so in the 1911 edition of his dictionary, at that time ML 5722), but Brüch's considerations on the phonetic shape and spread of this verb (1919:208) made him change his opinion in favor of Gaulish **mukȳare*. FW VI:193 gives a Gaulish form as the etymon of F *musser*; in BW *musser* is absent. Gamillscheg (1927:295) saw no reason to doubt the Gaulish origin of *musser* despite Sainéan's statement (1925-30, II:202, 284; III:170) that the etymology of that verb (which he preferred to treat as native) is unknown. Scheler compared *musser* with G *meuchlings*.

Scaliger's derivation of *musser* from the future infinitive of Gk μυέω 'initiate, teach,' which Ménage dismissed but NC accepted, has long since been abandoned (Scheler[1] seems to be the last to mention it). EWFS rejects the connection of Gk μυχός 'the innermost part of a house, the remotest part' with *musser*, but, according to Frisk, μυχός is akin to OI *smuga* 'narrow cleft, hole,' which in turn is related to OI *smjúga* and OE *smūgan* 'creep'; all of them resemble *mooch* and *musser*. Since μυέω is probably an onomatopoeic word like E *mum* and G *mucks*, genetic ties between it and other similar Indo-European and non-Indo-European verbs are hard to establish. However, no serious objections exist to deriving *musser* from Germanic rather than Gaulish.

According to Arcamone (1982; 1983:768-70), **the Italian regional verbs with and without *s*-, traceable to the etymon she gives as **mucciare*, are of Germanic (Langobardian) origin.** They have the following principal meanings: 'flee, escape,' 'steal,' 'command silence,' and 'strike gently.' Closely related are the verbs meaning 'cast a sidelong glance' (Arcamone [1983:770-73]). Those facts can be used as circumstantial evidence to support the hypothesis that OF *mucier* is of Germanic origin. Finally, we have F *mouchard* 'police informer, stoolie' (1589) and F *mouche* 'spy' going back to the 16th century (BW). Wedgwood's suggestion (1856:14) that *mouchard* belongs with *hugger-mugger* and *smuggle* looks plausible (see sec 4). Birlinger (1872:320) proposed the same origin for *mouchard*. Judging by Körting (6330 and 6398), ML, and BW, Romance linguists are unaware of that etymology. The idea that *mouchard* goes back to a proper name seems also to be given up. Wyld (UED, *mooch*) gave F *moucheur* 'plainclothes detective' as akin to *mooch* and *miching*, but he traced the English words to French (see above).

If L *muger* is related to OHG *mûhhôn* and OIr *rumúgstat*, we obtain a rare example of ancient common European slang that has existed for at least two millennia (*muger* already occurs in Festus). WP II:255 and WH (*muger*) share this opinion, though they do not use the term *slang*. The entry in WH is especially detailed and includes OHG *mûh-heimo* 'cricket' (among other German words), E *miche* < OE [sic] *mȳcan*, and ME *micher*. It follows FT (*smug* I) and draws E *smuggle* into this circle; see a comparable list in Gray (1930:193).

The many words with the root *(s)mug*- that qualify as cognates of *mooch* pose the problem of the final consonant, for OHG *mûhhôn* goes back to **mūk-*. In such cases, an ancient voiced ~ voiceless alternation is usually pressed into service, but it is better not to refer an attested alternation in a slang word to an asterisked etymon. **Apparently, a number of low class verbs (and even nouns, as *muger* shows) with the roots **mŭ̄g*- and **mŭ̄k*- circulated in Europe.** (However, Russ *muchit'* 'torment' [v] does not belong here.) For a similar situation, see NUDGE.

As already pointed out, Kluge's gloss 'waylay' for Gmc **mycan* is too specific. The verb's meaning must have been something like *'surreptitious act, underhand dealings, conceal(ment),' going all the way from 'invidious deed,' like assassination by a hired killer, to 'cheating at dice (cards)' and 'playing truant.' **Unless this group emerged as an onomatopoeic formation designating silence (keeping mum), the main sense of **mug*- and **muk*- may have been 'darkness'** or something similar (see Russ *mgla* 'darkness' and its cognates). Wachter, who compared G *meucheln* and Gk μύχιος 'deep, inner' and ὀμίχλη 'mist, impenetrable darkness,' was not too far from the truth, whereas Kaltschmidt's hypothesis that traced *meucheln* to a mythical root *μ-χ 'move' is fanciful. **Mūhen* 'move in a desultory way, wander about' may be related to the *mooch* group (see what is said above about OI *smuga*), but the evidence is weak. Stürmer (1929:339, note 5) reconstructed PIE **(s)mē-* 'crawl, creep across' (*darüberhinstreichen*), which led him to 'crawl (away)' (*sich verkriechen*) and to criminal activities, as in G *meucheln*, but root etymology is of little help in tracing the history of *mooch* and its kin.

4. **Several words mentioned in connection with *miche* ~ *mooch* seem to have been correctly identified as related to it. One of them is *-mugger* in *hugger-mugger* (1529).** Whiter III:197 noted the structural similarity of such reduplicating compounds with initial *h-* as *hugger-mugger, hocus-pocus* (1655), *hodge-podge* (1622), and *higgledy-piggledy* (1598) ~ *huddledy-puddledy* (his spelling is *hygledy-piggledy*). Smithers (1954:86) points out that in ideophones "one voiced stop is naturally substituted for another ... since all three have the same type of expressive quality." However, for etymological purposes it is not irrelevant whether the original form was *hudder-mudder* (1461) or *hugger-mugger* (see both in OED, which proposes different etymons for each of those two words). *Hucker-mucker* and *hucker-mocker* also existed.

Skinner thought that he could detect the roots of OE **hogan* 'observe' (the correct forms would be either *hogian* 'think; intend' or its synonyms *hycgan*) and of some word like *murk* (he cites a Danish form) in the English compound ('observation in the dark'; the same in N. Bailey [1721; 1730]). Johnson understood *hugger-mugger* as 'hug or embrace in the dark.' Stoddart (1845:120-21) gives a survey of the early attempts to explain the origin of *hugger-mugger* and calls Skinner's etymology "alike improbable and inappropriate." He has the following to say about Johnson's idea that *hugger-mugger* is corrupted perhaps from *hug er morcker*: "... in what language *hug er morcker* has this signification he [Johnson] does not mention, nor does any phrase correspondent to the English *hugger-mugger* appear to have ever become proverbial in any other language." "The Spanish," he goes on, "affords the nearest approach, to the separate parts of this expression; for *hogar* is a chimmey corner, and *mujer* is a woman; and if we could suppose *hugger mugger* to be taken from that language it might refer to the notion of a woman cowering in the chimmey corner; but as nothing can be more delusive than to be guided in etymology by mere similarity of sound, we may safely reject this derivation of the phrase in question."

Unfortunately, Stoddart does not say who proposed the Dutch etymon of *hugger-mugger*, which he discusses in detail. "The last etymology that we shall mention is from the Dutch title Hoog Moogende, (His Mightiness) given to the State General, and much ridiculed by some of our English writers, as in *Hudibras—But I have sent him for a token / To your Low-country Hogen-Mogen*. It has been supposed that *hugger-mugger*, corrupted from *Hogen-Mogen*, was meant in derision of the secret transactions of their mightiness; but it is probable that the former word was known in English before the latter." Radcliffe (1853) was aware of the *Hoog Moogende* etymology but did not refer to the source either. The publisher of *Notes and Queries* quoted a few lines from Stoddart's article in a postscript to Radcliffe's letter.

However ridiculous the derivation of *hugger-mugger* from *Hoog Moogende* may be, Ker's 'Dutch' etymology (1837:146) is even more fanciful: "*Heugh er maergher*; q. e. *a place where there is little hope*; a cheerless position; a situation of poor comfort; there where little expectation can be indulged in; a dismal cheerless abode. *Er*, there, the place or situation alluded to. *Heughe, hoghe*, hope, expectation, future prospect: joy, delight, pleasure: mind, shallow, poor. So that the phrase refers to the consequent state of mind of him who is confined against his will, not to secrecy. And Johnson's notion that the expression is *hugger-morcker* as *a hug in the dark*, is something below even a whim. *Heugh er maegher* sounds *hugger-mugger*."

Ker, who used to invent Dutch words and phrases and pass them off as the etymons of English words and who never missed a chance to attack Johnson, did, however, quote the relevant places from Samuel Butler's *Hudibras*. Yet *hugger-mugger* must have been known by the 1660's from *Hamlet*, if not as a pre-Shakespearean colloquialism, and Butler's use of the word could not be viewed as a novelty. *Hogen-Mogen* occurs in *Hudibras* twice. Bohn (1859: 318, note 3) explains verses 1439-1442 ("But I have sent him for a token / To your low-country Hogen-Mogen, / To whose infernal shores I hope / He'll hang like skippers in a rope"): "...the infernal Hogen-Mogen (from the Dutch *Hoog mogende*, high and mighty, or the devil"). Butler did not associate *hugger-mugger* with *Hogen-Mogen*, but couldn't Ker's idea that *hugger-mugger* goes back to Dutch and his quotation from *Hudibras* inspire someone to connect those links (*Hudibras, hugger-mugger*, and *Hoogen-Mogen*)? No serious student of Dutch loanwords in English mentions *hugger-mugger*.

The next passage from Stoddard has another 'epic' reference to the source of information: "Some persons supposed *hugger-mugger* to be derived from the old English word *hoker*; because Sir Thomas More, it is said, uses the word *hoker-moker*; but it is not very clear that he meant by it what we mean by *hugger-mugger*; and if he did, no great stress is to be laid on a casual variation of orthography in that age, when spelling had nothing like fixed rules. The word *hoker*, had no reference in point of meaning, to the idea conveyed by the word *hugger-mugger*; for it signified peevish, froward..." He concludes his argument so: "...upon the whole it seems most probable that *hugger* is a mere intensive form of *hug*, and that *mugger* is a reduplication of sound with a slight variation..." It remains unexplained what "a mere intensive form" means.

Richardson does not list the opinions of his predecessors and says only: "*Hugger-mugger*. This is the common way of writing this word from Udal [sic] to the present time. Sir Thomas More is said to have written it *hoker-moker*; others write *hucker-mucker*, and Ascham, *hudder-mother*. No probable etymology has yet been given... The reading of Ascham (though single) suggests the conjecture, that these words, however written, are formed from *hood* or *hud*, and *mud*; q. d. *hud-mud*, the diminutives *huddle-muddle*, *hudder-mudder*, *hugger-mugger*." He cites Jamieson's *hudge mudge* and *huggrie muggrie*. ODEE proposes the derivation of *hugger-mugger* from reg *mucker* (< ME *mokere*) and ME *hoder* 'huddle, wrap up' ("ult[imate] origin unkn[own]"). However, it is unlikely that the components of *hugger-mugger* are traceable to different sources and later influenced each other, though this is what OED suggests (the entry in ODEE is an abbreviated version of the entry in OED).

Most probably, *-mucker* is a variant of *-mugger*, and Wedgwood's comparison of *-mugger* with Sc *hudgemudge* 'a side talk in a low tone, a suppressed talking' (Jamieson) is unobjectionable. Both he and Kluge cited G *muck* in connection with G *meucheln* and E *hugger-mugger*, and Wedgwood's mention of F *musser* and Dan *i smug* 'secretly, privately' anticipated FT (*smug* I; *hugger-mugger* turns up in this entry too). Skeat (according to anonymous [1877b]) shared Wedgwood's opinion.

Guesses about the relatedness of *-mugger* and *smuggle* go back to a rather early day (L [1853:391]). Two etymologists invoked Sc *hugger-muggans* 'stockings with the feet worn away' in the discussion of *hugger-mugger* (anonymous [1822b:617] and Mayhew [1912:323-24]), but the origin of the Scots word is unknown. Since hugger-muggans are gaiters, a shoeless person walking in them makes no noise. That fact may have contributed to the form of *hugger-muggans*, but it sheds no light on the etymon of *hugger-mugger*. In all likelihood, *-mugger* is part of the *mugger—mooch—meucheln* family. The statement that "*mugger*, meaningless itself, merely repeats the idea of *hugger*" (Van Draat [1940:165]) should not be taken on trust. Krogmann (1952:29) cites several compounds of the *schurimuri* type (German) and believes that in all of them, including *hugger-mugger*, the second element reproduces the first, with *h-* substituting for any initial consonant. His generalization is too broad, and his opinion does not hold for *hugger-mugger*. In English, words like *hubble-bubble* and *pitter-patter*, in which the 'basic' element is the second, are numerous.

5. **The suggestion that *-mudgeon* in *curmudgeon* (1577) is related to *mooch* seems to be correct**. Numerous fanciful etymologies of *curmudgeon* exist: 1) From F *cœur méchant* 'evil heart' (proposed to Johnson by one of his correspondents). Todd told the story of John Ash's misunderstanding of this phrase and it has often been repeated. To some extent, Weekley (1915) supported Johnson. The 14th-century personal name *Boselinus Curmegen* that he unearthed would then mean 'a wicked man known as evil heart' (compare G *böse* 'wicked, evil; angry'). Groth (1922) must have been unaware of Weekley's discovery, for he offered the same facts. ODEE mentions *Boselinus Curmegen*, calls it remarkable, but offers no comments. Here is what Weekley says in his dictionary (1921): "... the spelling *curmegient* is found (1626), and ... *Curmegan*, occurring as a medieval nickname or surname (*Ramsey Cartulary*), is not impossibly F. *cœur méchant*." It follows that the name or nickname almost identical with *curmudgeon* turned up long before the common name (a usual situation: see BOY and LAD, though the case of *Ladda* ~ *lad* is unclear) and that folk etymology interpreted *curmudgeon* as a French phrase. Similarly, *bonfire* was taken for 'good fire.' The popular misconception does not make *curmudgeon* less opaque.

2) From the alleged OE **ceorlmodigan* 'churlish-minded' (Brewer [1873] and in his dictionary; Rule [1873]) or from 'chary-minded': OE *cearg* + *mōd* (Mitchell [1908:216]). 3) From ML *corimedis* ~ *curmedus* 'dependant who is liable to heriot' (see *curmedia* in Du Cange); Todd in Johnson-Todd added: "Some may perhaps think the word allied to a snarling cur." 4) From 'cur in the manger' (Richardson).

Whiter III:412-13 examined many words allegedly connected with mucus and mentioned L *muger* as a term of contempt. This was the first time (long before Zupitza) *muger* turned up in the discussion of the extended *mooch* family. Mackay (1877), whose Gaelic etymologies of English words are usually insupportable, suggested a derivation of *curmudgeon* that, by pure chance, as will be shown, is probably almost correct: from Gael *cearr* 'wrong, wrong-headed, perverse' and *muig* 'a scowl, a frown, a discontented expression of the face'; *muigean* 'a churlish, disagreeable person,' hence *cearr-muigean.*

Much has been made of *cornmudgeon* 'hoarder of corn' (1600). Wedgwood reconstructed *corn-merchant* as the original form of *curmudgeon* (the same in W [1864], Mueller, and Skeat[1]), but "Hollands's *corn-mudgin* is an alteration for the nonce by assim[ilation] to *corn* to render L. *frumentarius* corn-dealer" (ODEE). At present, *curmudgeon* is considered to be a word of unknown origin, though, according to OED, the idea that *cur-* in *curmudgeon* should be equated with *cur* 'dog' "is worthy of note" (no longer in ODEE), and Skeat[4] has 'grumbling cur' as a possible gloss of *curmudgeon.*

Partridge (1958) says that *curmudgeon* is perhaps akin to the echoic Sc *curmurring,* a low rumbling or murmuring (*cur-mur*), a source of grumbling; he gives as a possible parallel the Shetland and Orkney adjective *curmullyit* 'dark, ill-favored fellow' (EDD). A similar idea must have occurred to Todd, who after mentioning a snarling dog cited OE *murcnung* 'complaint.' OE *murc(nian)* 'complain,' G *murren* 'grumble,' and L *murmurāre* 'murmur' are onomatopoeic verbs. Sc *curmurring* is reminiscent of *curmudgeon,* and *curmullyit* is almost a doublet of E *cormullion* 'miser' (1596: OED has one citation).

The *cœur méchant* derivation suggested the French origin of E *-mudgeon.* Skeat[1] relates *-mudgeon* to *mooch,* which at that time he thought to be a borrowing from Old French. More recently, Spitzer (1942a) pointed to a possible French etymon of *curmudgeon* and cited OF *chamorge* 'glandered (horse)' (the glanders is a contagious disease in horses, marked by swellings beneath the jaws and discharge of mucous matter from the nostrils). Spitzer reconstructed "a simile suggested by the intermittent, dribbling, 'niggardly' discharge of excretions." Besides this, the glanders is attended with choking, and money "chokes" the miser (see F argot *râleur* 'one who gasps, rattles in his throat' > 'miser'). According to Spitzer, the development of *curmudgeon* from a general term of abuse to 'miser' is impossible. He explained *-on* as a French suffix "used in Romance to indicate a person afflicted with a certain malady or defect." The entire process looks as follows: **carmouge* 'glanders' > **carmougeon* 'glandered' > E *curmudgeon.* His reconstruction is ingenious but far-fetched.

One of the handicaps in the search for the etymon of *curmudgeon* is that only the origin of the meaning 'miser' has usually been sought. Both OED and ODEE quote Johnson's gloss: "avaricious churlish fellow," but the 'churlish' part is seldom taken into account. Among the British lexicographers, only Wyld (UED) gives a nontraditional definition: "a churlish, cross-grained, surly, ill-tempered, cantankerous fellow." Note that he uses five synonyms for 'contentious, querulous, grouchy' and not a single epithet for 'greedy.' Wyld's curmudgeon is disagreeable but not stingy. The same is true of *curmudgeon* in American English. Consider the following definitions. AHD[1]: "1. 'A cantankerous person.' 2. *Rare* a miser." RHD[2]: "A bad-tempered, difficult, cantankerous person." It took American lexicographers a long time to notice the difference between British and American usage with regard to *curmudgeon.* CD[2] still says: "An avaricious, churlish fellow; a miser; a niggard; a churl." W[1] and W[2] agree: "An avaricious, grasping fellow; a miser; niggard; churl," and only in W[3] the definitions are: "1. *Archaic*: a grasping, avaricious man: Miser. 2. a crusty, ill-tempered, or difficult and often elderly person." The meaning 'cantankerous person,' prevalent in American English may be at least as old as 'miser.'

Skeat[4] mentions Lowland Sc *murgeon* (see Jamieson and EDD) 'mock, grumble' and *mudgeon* 'grimace.' 'Grumble' and 'grimace' fit the idea of a peevish, disgruntled man well. Not improbably, *curmudgeon* was first applied to an unpleasant, unsociable person and by extension to someone who stays away from jovial company for fear of being robbed or asked to help the less fortunate. One of the meanings of the Italian regional verbs derived from the putative Langobardian cognate of *meucheln* is 'cast a sidelong glance.'

EDD gives E reg *motch* 'eat little, slowly, quietly and secretly; consume or waste imperceptibly' (*motch* is a doublet of *modge*). *Motching,* used attributively, means 'fond of dainties, with the idea of eating in secret,' and the verbal noun *motching* is defined as 'slow, quiet eating, with the idea of fondness for good living; imperceptible use, with the notion of thriftlessness.' A **motcher* would then be someone enjoying his riches in secret. One of the secretive actions designated by the **mug- ~ *muk-* verbs must have been *'look stealthily *or* askance'; hence the attested senses 'grimace, scowl, air of discontent' and the connotation 'churlish, cantankerous' in *curmudgeon.*

Spitzer erred in refusing to posit the development from a broad pejorative term to 'miser.' The reconstructed change in *curmudgeon* from 'churl, grumbler' to 'miser' would not be without analogues. Consider (obsolete) G *Kalmäuser,* first 'brooding recluse,' then 'skinflint.' (The origin of this word is unknown, and it is irrelevant in the present context. See some early conjectures in K. Krause [1888]; Lenz [1898:35] must have been the only one to compare *Kalmäuser* and *curmudgeon.*) Another example is Russ *skared* 'penny pincher,' which meant 'abominable' in Old Russian. Its Slavic cognates are now glossed 'excrement, dung' (Vasmer III:633-34).

Cur- in *curmudgeon* cannot be *cur* 'dog,' for nothing would explain the Romance word order **cur mudgin(g)* in an English phrase, and a late bahuvrihi **dogscowl* 'churl' is most unlikely. Wood (1910-11:191) equated *cur-* with *ca-* in *cahoots.* Since *cahoots* is a word of obscure origin, it would be more expedient to refer to E *kerfuffle* or *curfuffle* 'disorder, flurry' (sb and v, 1583). OED features *ker-* in the chiefly American echoic and onomatopoeic words of the *kerslash* type but does not suggest any etymology. However, in the entry *curfuffle* (v), OED says that "the first syllable is perh. Gaelic *car* twist, bend, turn about, used in combination in *car-fhocal* quibble, prevarication, *car-shúil* rolling eye, *car-tuaitheal* wrong turn: cf. the Lowland Sc. *curcuddoch, curdoo, curgloff, curjute, curmurring, curnoited,* in which the prefix seems to have the sense of L. *dis-.*" *Tuffle* (1536) is a synonym, nearly a doublet, of *curfuffle.*

The source of the American *ker-* verbs is probably Dutch, for in that language words with reinforcing *ka-* ~ *ker-* are common (see De Bont [1948:28], Dutch; Coetzee [1995], Afrikaans). Whatever the genetic relation between Du *ker-* and Gael *cur-,* since *-mudgeon* is of Gaelic origin, *cur-* in *curmudgeon* can hardly be from Dutch. This means that, for a change, Mackay guessed well. *Curmudgeon* is, most likely, 'extraordinary churl,' if *-mudgeon* = *muigean* 'disagreeable person,' with *cur-* added for emphasis.

6. **Sc *mud(e)geon* may likewise be the etymon or a cognate of *mug* 'face,'** as in *mug shot. Mudgeon* coexists with Sc *murgeon* 'face.' If *murgeon* goes back to F *morgue,* whose original meaning was 'grimace; grave and serious countenance,' and if *mudgeon* is related to the *mooch* group, their phonetic near identity is due to chance and they became interchangeable synonyms only after their paths crossed. But nothing supports the idea that *mug* is a "corruption" of F *morgue,* as suggested in anonymous (1859:578) and Smythe Palmer (1883). The origin of F *morgue* is unknown.

The tinkers of the south of Scotland were known as *muggers.* Their language, formerly referred to as *cant,* contains many Romani words (MacRitchie [1911:547-48]), so that *mug* was believed to be of Romanic origin. CD mentions that derivation, and so does Cohen in his comments on Gore (Gore [1993:6]), but a more convincing etymology of *mug* is needed.

An anonymous reviewer of Atkinson's dictionary (anonymous [1868a:836]) believed that *mug* 'face' is a humorous extension of *mug* 'drinking vessel' because grotesque faces were the chief adornment of ale pitchers. Whoever was the first to offer this etymology, which does not appear in any early dictionary consulted, it gained the cautious support of OED. Wedgwood related *mug* to *mock* < F *moquer* (compare Sp *mueca* 'wry face, grin, mocking grimace') and Gael *smuig* 'snout, face in ridicule' and added E *muzzle* to his list of cognates. OF *mocquer* 'mock' and *musel* 'snout' (ModF *museau*) are words of unknown origin, and it is unclear whether they belong to the *mooch* group, but E *mug* 'face' seems to be akin to Sc *mudgeon* and, consequently, to *mooch, miche, meucheln,* and the rest. The verb *mug* is almost an exact gloss of G *meucheln,* and their closeness need not be a coincidence.

Delatte (1935) points out that E *mug* 'face' "may be compared with similar words in Dutch dialects: *smikkel* and *smoel* (a possible contraction of **smogel*), which are also vulgar expressions for 'mouth.' There is no difficulty in finding a common base for these various forms: *(s)m...g,* or, with unvoiced guttural, *(s)m...k,* the addition of *s* being a common phenomenon." That is a reasonable comparison.

The German verb *mogeln* 'cheat' has been discussed in detail (Birnbaum [1935], Weißbrodt [1935], Birnbaum [1955], M. Fraenkel [1960:19; 1966:87], Wolf [1962:184], and see it in all the editions of EWDS, Wolf [1956], WDU-1963, and WDU-1970). Despite the guarded conclusions of most dictionary makers, Birnbaum's arguments against the Yiddish origin of *mogeln* are irrefutable. *Mogeln* is, more likely, related to *mooch* and its congeners. By the same token, E *smouch* 'pilfer' (1826), a doublet of *smooch* 'mooch,' is probably not a borrowing from Yiddish, regardless of the origin of *smouch* 'derogatory name for a Jew.' Russian borrowed the verb *mukhlevat'* 'cheat' (stress on the last syllable) from German (Vasmer III:19). Vasmer followed EWDS[11] and supported the Yiddish derivation of G *mogeln*. In Dutch studies, Weijnen (1998:157-58/26) shares the same misconception. *Smouch* 'kiss,' insofar as it goes back to the meaning 'mouth,' may be related to *mooch*.

7. As always, when proposing a common origin for a motley group of words of similar structure and meaning, one wonders where to stop. Verbs and nouns with the root **muk-* ~ **mug-* designated secret (and, consequently, sometimes illegal) actions for millennia. They may be traceable to onomatopoeia (**muk* 'keep mum'; this was Braune's suggestion [1897:220, note 4]) or to an ancient word for 'mist' (things done under the cover of darkness). They occurred in Latin, Old Irish, and Germanic. In Romance, they are either from Celtic or from Germanic, the latter being a more probable source. The English words *mooch, miche,* as well as *smouch* (v), *smuggle, hugger-mugger, (cur)mudgeon, mug* 'face' and *mug* (v), G *meucheln, mogeln, mucks,* and *-mäuser* in *Duckmäuser,* F *musser,* and L *muger,* are members of this group, each with its individual history. E *mock* and *muzzle,* both from French, may be related. Several verbs meaning 'crawl' should probably be kept apart from *mooch* and its more certain cognates. If such is the history of *mooch,* it provides a rare glimpse into the spread of ancient European slang.

NUDGE (1675)

Nudge was first recorded in 1675, even though its uninterrupted history starts only in 1838. Nud *'boss with the head' and* nuddle *'push, squeeze,' both regional, surfaced at the same time. The affricate in* nudge *suggests that despite this verb's late attestation and its seeming isolation in and outside English it was not borrowed from Scandinavian or Low German.* Nud *and* nudge *do not look like cognates, because in the history of English,* d *yields an affricate only before the yod. Regardless of a possible historical bond between* nudge *and* nud, *it is likely that* nudge *had been known in some dialects long before it entered the Standard. Word initial and word final /ʤ/ sometimes appear unexpectedly (for example,* smudge *and* jog *have doublets* smutch ~ smut *and* shog*) and seems to be endowed with sound symbolic value. The barrier between* nud *and* nudge *is perhaps not as impassable as it seems.*

The initial consonant of nudge *poses additional problems.* Nudge *may at one time have begun with* gn-, kn-, *or* hn- *and belonged with verbs like OE* cnocian, cnucian, gnagan, *and* hnappian *(ModE* knock, gnaw, *and* nap*). The* gn- ~ kn- ~ hn- *words form a loosely connected group whose underlying meaning is hard to reconstruct (it is usually given as 'compress'), but despite disagreement over details belief in such a meaning is widespread. The phonetic shape of such words is inconstant: all short (checked) vowels occur in them, and any stop and an occasional fricative may follow the vowel. Etymologists interested in the remote origin of the* gn- ~ kn- ~ hn- *group posit a root (PIE* *gen- *or* *ǵen-, *Gmc* *ken- *or* *knə-*) from which the recorded forms have allegedly been produced with the help of enlargements. The great antiquity and the ancient kinship of the* gn- ~ kn- ~ hn- *words, to which* sn- *should be added, is doubtful, but the existence of several subsets united by a common meaning is indubitable.* Nudge *belongs with the verbs designating light, sometimes repetitive, regular movements* (gnaw, nibble, nod, knock, *and the like).*

Two plausible etymologies of nudge *have been proposed. One connects* nudge *with OE* hnygelan *'clippings,' the other derives it from OE* cnucian *'knock.' A form like* *hnycgelan *or* *cnyccan *probably existed.* Nudge *may also have arisen as an expressive variant of* nud, *a form closely related to* nod, *but such coinages are sporadic, and their history cannot be traced with confidence.*

The sections are devoted to 1) the status of the final affricate in nudge *and in some other English words, 2) the semantics of the* gn- ~ kn- ~ hn- *group, and 3) the proposed etymologies of* nudge *and the borders of the* gn- ~ kn- ~ hn- *group, with emphasis laid on the words that may not belong to it.*

1. A colloquial English word, first recorded in 1675 and seemingly isolated in and outside English, looks like a borrowing. However, **the final /ʤ/ of *nudge* points to a high degree of domestication: a word taken over from Scandinavian or Low German in the 17th century would have had -/g/**. Although, as the first citation in OED shows, *nudge* was known in 1675, it had to wait for a century and a half until it found its way into respectable prose. OED gives no examples of the verb between 1675 and 1838, when Dickens, with his ear always attuned to street slang, used it in *Nicholas Nickleby*. Two years earlier, the noun *nudge* turned up.

***Nudge* surfaced almost simultaneously with *nud* 'boss with the head' (one citation in 1688; in 1887 it was recorded in a Cheshire glossary) and with the frequentative (iterative) verb *nuddle* 'push; beat; press; squeeze' (1650; now regional)**. For *nuddle* further records are also absent until the 19th century. **OED does not connect *nudge* with *nud* and *nuddle*,** because /d/ does not yield an affricate unless it is followed by /j/, as in *verdure, education,* and *did you;* the form **nudjan* has not been recorded. However, **in some way they must belong together**. *Nud* and *nuddle* never made it to the Standard, whereas *nudge* reached London and stayed there.

Final /ʤ/ has several sources in English. It occurs in many words of French origin, such as *lodge* and *rage*. In *Greenwich* and the like, /ʤ/ is the continuation of the voiceless affricate /tʃ/, but the variation /tʃ/ ~ /ʤ/ has been recorded not only in disyllables. One of the variants of *mooch* is *modge* (see MOOCH). *Hodgepodge* and *splodge* are doublets of *hotchpotch* (altered from *hotchpot*) and *splotch*. *Smudge* coexists with its synonym *smutch*. *Nudge* is related to *nud* as *smutch* is to *smut*, but, although *smut* has easily recognizable cognates (see *Schmutz* in KM and KS), -/t/ and -/tʃ/ share the fate of the pair -/d/ and -/ʤ/: no phonetic law governs their relationship.

In native words, /ʤ/ is the reflex of Old English /ǵǵ/ (palatalized), as in *bridge*. *Nudge* is hardly a borrowing from French (no similar words have been found in any Romance language), which leaves the possibility of /ʤ/ from /tʃ/, from OE /ćć/ or /ǵǵ/. All the words rhyming with *nudge*, except *judge* (from French), are of obscure etymology. *Budge* (1890) and *grudge* (1461) (< *grutch*; 1225) are believed to be borrowings from French (another doublet of *grudge* is *grouch*), but their ultimate origin is unknown. *Drudge* (1494) is perhaps related to ME *drugge* 'drag or pull heavily'; its /ʤ/ remains unexplained. *Dredge*, first recorded in 1471, seems to be akin to early Sc *dreg* and poses the same problem. *Fudge* (v, 1674) has a doublet *fadge* (1592), and *sludge* (1649) is almost indistinguishable from its synonyms *slutch* (1669) and *slush* (1641); their origin has not been clarified either. *Trudge* (1547), *tredge*, and *tridge* form an equally opaque set. It is tempting to relate *tredge* to *tread*, but /ʤ/ stands like a wall between them. *Squeege* surfaced in 1782 as a "strengthened form of *squeeze*" (1601; OED), a verb of questionable antecedents.

The verb *nidge* 'dress stone with a sharp-pointed hammer' deserves mention here. Its appearance in print does not antedate 1842, but a presumably native technical term of masonry could hardly be of such recent coinage. Nothing is known about its origin, and the existence of the equally impenetrable words *nidge* 'shake' (1802) and *nidget* 'triangular horseshoe used in Kent and Sussex' (1769) are of no immediate use in reconstructing its past. Wedgwood and Skeat compare *dodge* (1631) with Sc *dod(d)* 'jog' and *dodder* 'shake'. OED notes that their etymology fails to address the difference between the final consonants. *Stodge* 'fill quite full' (1674) may be, according to OED, a blend of *stuff* and *podge* 'short, fat person.' Blending in past epochs is usually impossible to trace.

The examples listed above show that *nudge* forms part of a group of (Early) Modern English words whose etymology would become clearer if their final /ʤ/ could be shown to derive from /d/. OED and ODEE often resort to the phrases *phonetically symbolic* (see OED: *stodge*) and *symbolically expressive formation* (ODEE: *slush*, *slutch*, and *sludge*). Such formations need not always obey so-called sound laws. Verbs like *budge, grudge, nudge, smudge, trudge, dodge,* and *stodge* are to a certain degree expressive, and a few of them may have started as slang. **Final /ʤ/, at first perhaps coincidentally, marked them as colloquial variants of stylistically neutral verbs.** The same might hold for nouns and adjectives: *smug* had a parallel form *smudge* (OED), like *sludge* with its doublet *slush*.

The symbolic value of final /ʤ/ is less obvious than that of initial *gl-* and *sl-*, for example, and a persuasive etymology cannot rest on it, but examples like *smug* ~ *smudge* show that /ʤ/ in *nudge* is not necessarily an impassable barrier between this verb and, for example, *nud*. Verbs denoting all kinds of movement, from a gentle push to a tight squeeze, often begin with /ʤ/ and, likewise, have no established etymology. References to sound symbolism prevail in discussion of their origin. See *jab* (and its synonym *job*), *jag* 'stab, prick' (reg), *jam, jaunt, jerk, jib* 'stop and refuse to go on,' *jink, jitter, jog* (a doublet of *shog*: Skeat), *jolt, jounce, jumble,* and *jump* in etymological dictionaries.

2. The original onset of the verb *nudge* is no less problematic than its coda. OED compares, though with some hesitation, *nudge* and N reg *nugga* ~ *nuggja* 'push, rub.' ODEE does the same, but at *niggard* it cites Sw *njugg* 'scarce; miserly' and its regional variants Sw reg *nugg* and Sw reg *nygg*, traceable to OI *hnøggr* 'stingy' (in the text, the Norwegian and the Icelandic forms are misspelled). N reg *nugga* 'push' and Sw reg *nugg* 'stingy' are almost homonyms, so that a bond emerges between *nudge* (despite its -/ʤ/) and *nigg-ard*. **Since *hnøggr* begins with *hn-*, *nudge*, too, may have *n-* from *hn-*.** English spelling retains initial *kn-* and *gn-* but disallows *hn-*. Therefore, if we did not know that *nap* 'short sleep' and *neck* go back to OE *hnappian* and *hnecca* respectively, we would not be able to reconstruct *hn-* in them. *Nudge* surfaced late, and its earlier form, in English or in the lending language (if it is a borrowing), is unknown. In light of the *nugga* ~ *nugg* ~ *hnøggr* connection, we may suppose that it began with *hn-*.

Boutkan and Kossman (1998:9) contend that until we have clarified the relationship between initial *kn- and *hn- in Early Germanic, nothing definite can be said about the origin of the words beginning with those groups. But the desired clarification should come as a reward for successful etymologizing rather than be a prerequisite for it. We face the coexistence of Du *klomp* and *(be)knibbelen* with E *lump* and *nibble*. Some such words (like E *lump*) have been recorded only in this form, others, like OI *kringr* and *hringr* (both nouns mean 'ring') are doublets. Projecting them to asterisked anti-quity is a self-defeating procedure.

Gallée (1885) compiled a long list of words that, in his opinion, avoided the First Consonant Shift. Sw *klippa* and Du *plat* mean the same as E *cliff* and *flat*, but *f* in them is believed to go back to **p*, while *p* in the first pair looks like a fossilized reflex of PIE **p*. Likewise, Dutch has *knijpen* 'pinch, squeeze' (with *k-*), as opposed to OI *hnippa* (with *h-*). E *nip* and *snip* are probably related to them, but the first has been known from texts only since the 14th and the second since the 16th century, respectively, and they may not be native.

Confronted with several hundred words (so-called *Restformen*) that allegedly proved immune to the First Consonant Shift, we must discover the causes of their invulnerability. Gallée did not go so far. Recourse to the substrate or dialect mixture is here ineffective. It may at best elucidate the history of one or two words but not of the entire group. OI *gn-* and *kn-* were later weakened to *hn-* (cf ModI *hnífur* 'knife' and *hneggja* 'neigh'), while in English *g* and *k* before *n* disappeared altogether. Perhaps at the periods known as Old English, Old High German, Middle Dutch, and so on, the change of *gn-*, *kn-* and *hn-* to *n* was underway, with both forms competing as stylistic variants. This trivial conjecture leaves the causes of the sound change open, but for etymology they are irrelevant.

The history of Germanic words like *gnaw*, *knock*, and *nap* shows that they form a loosely connected semantic group despite the wide range of postvocalic consonants (all stops and an occasional fricative) and the workings of secondary ablaut. Words with initial *gn-*, *kn-*, and *hn-* designate the following objects, actions, and properties. Nouns: peg, nail, summit, knot, knob, knuckle (and 'bone' in general), lump; point, hook; the nape of the head, fist; knife, clippings. Verbs: turn, bend, pinch, compress, push; gnaw, chew, rub; shake, tremble; crawl; (onomatopoeic) scratch, bang, sneeze, neigh. Adjectives: quick, sharp, smart; blunt, having short hair, bald, sparse. This is an abridged version of the list in J. de Vries (1956b:139) that also includes many animal names.

Similar lists have been compiled in the past. W. Barnes (1862:173-74) set up numerous roots and dealt with them as did his other contemporaries and later linguists. Most of the words he assigned to his roots have nothing to do with one another, but something in the *n-g* group makes different people arrive at similar conclusions. W. Barnes united *nog* 'slice,' *nog* 'ale,' *nugget*, *nag* 'sharp taste,' *snag*, *nudge*, *nick*, *nook*, and *notch* (among others), all of which, in his opinion, conveyed the idea of cutting and gripping.

Hilmer (1914:237-69) wrote a book about sound imitation, which he almost ruined by ascribing the onomatopoeic function to many words devoid of it, but his material should not be disregarded. He discussed the sound complexes *knap*, *knop*, *knup*, *knub*, *knep*, *knip*, *knat*, *knot*, *knut*, *knet*, *knack*, *knock*, *knuck*, and *knick*. He usually glossed the words from OED and dialectal dictionaries as 'strike, break, crack, nibble; protuberance, knot, lump.' Hilmer did not say that they are related; his goal was to point to their origin as so-called sound gestures.

H. Schröder's starting point (1910:21-26) was the concept 'short stick, peg,' and he cited several hundred German and Scandinavian words that have or once had that meaning. His list sometimes overlaps with Hilmer's, but his English examples are few (*knob*, *chump* 'log of wood,' *knop*, and *knave*). It will be seen that W. Barnes, H. Schröder, Braune, Hilmer, and J. de Vries, although they approached their examples from different directions, did not disagree over matters of principle.

Several attempts have been made to find a unifying meaning for all the *gn-* ~ *kn-* ~ *hn-* words. Van Helten (1873:32-37) reconstructed it as 'move(ment) back and forth.' That is how he explained *nap* in *take a nap* (= 'doze off and wake up') and some verbs of chewing like *nibble*. According to Torp (1909:48-51), the basic meaning underlying most of the *gn-* ~ *kn-* ~ *hn-* words is 'squeeze, compress.' Persson (1912:88-94), WP I:580-83, and IEW, 370-73, accepted this view. See also Nielsen (1964:196-99) and AHD[1] (1516: "*gen-* '[t]o compress into a ball.' Hypothetical Indo-European base of a range of Germanic words referring to compact, knobby bodies and projections, sharp blows, etc.").

Johansson (1889:340-43) explained the origin of several *gn-* ~ *kn-* ~ *hn-* words and derived their meaning from the participles designating 'shorn, scraped, cut' and from their active counterparts 'shearing, scraping, cutting.' However, it was Braune (1912:15-28) who undertook the most detailed analysis of the group in question. He started from the meaning 'something gnarled, bony, knotted.' His result did not differ from Torp's, but Braune rejected 'compress into a ball' as the unifying feature of the group and believed that verbs designating actions like *gnaw* and *nibble* and onomatopoeic words like *knock* imitiate by their consonants the sound one gets when dealing with bone. OI *knefi* ~ *hnefi* 'fist' (cf E reg *neif*, from Scandinavian) turned out to be a ball (made) of bone; hence the verbs of pushing. Braune did not mention *nudge*, but he cited E reg *nubble* and *knobble* (related to G *knuffen*) that combine the form of *nibble* and the meaning of *nudge*. Seebold (KS, *Knalle*) says that words beginning with *kn-* designate thick objects and that a connection with words for 'compress' is possible. See also *Knauf* and *Knochen* in KS and Zubatý (1898:173; Zubatý's article was inspired by Johansson [1889]).

To discover the etymology of *nudge*, it is not necessary to decide whether all the words constituting the *kn-* ~ *gn-* ~ *hn-* group belong together. Torp, Walde, and Pokorny did not only look for a semantic common denominator: they posited an ancient root (the same in Froehde [1886:299]). Thus, for Germanic Torp gave the root the form **knə-*, the reduction or the zero grade of PIE **gen-*. With the help of a series of enlargements **knə-* was supposed to produce the recorded forms. Since the reflexes of PIE **g* and **ǵ* merged in Germanic, PIE **ǵen-* is another possible source of *knock, knob, knot,* and so on. Güntert (1928:124-29) and Schüwer (1977) favored **ǵen-* over **gen-,* though they offered conflicting interpretations of the etymon: Güntert suggested the initial meaning 'bend, curvature,' whereas Schüwer followed Trier and believed that the original meaning of the **gen-* words must be sought in people's contacts with the underbrush (*Niederwald*).

The idea that the zero grade of an Indo-European root gave rise to several dozen heterogeneous verbs, nouns, and adjectives, some of which may have been coined late, is suspect. However, within the *gn-* ~ *kn-* ~ *hn-* group, several words belong together—a fact recognized long ago. See *Knochen, Knoten,* and *Knopf* in DW 5, which appeared in 1873. The author of the entries was Hildebrand, and Schüwer begins his survey with a quick look at them. FT (see especially *knude*) and other etymological dictionaries develop Hildebrand's idea. In the present context, rather than trying to define the alleged basic meaning of the entire *gn-* ~ *kn-* ~ *hn-* group, it would be more expedient to isolate the subset of which *nudge* is a probable member.

3. ***Nudge* belongs with the verbs designating quick, partly repetitive, regular movements that usually do not require a strong effort**. Among them are E *gnaw* (< OE *gnagan*), *nag, knock, nibble,* reg *knubble,* and *nod. Knuckle, nugget, noggin, knob, nub,* and *knot,* that is, all kinds of small objects (lumps) may have developed from similar original meanings. In regional words, final consonants vary even more than in the Standard. For example, *nug* can mean 'knot' and also 'nod; nudge' (verbs), while *nub* is a variant of *nudge* (EDD). Among many words for 'lump,' we find *nudgel*. Across language borders, the picture is similar: for example, the Middle Low German for *nod* is *nucken* (see it in Wood's list below).

Vowels change by secondary (false) ablaut in this group. In some dialects, the humorous word *noddle* 'head' occurs, in others, the corresponding forms are *naddle* and *nuddle* (EDD). Many words are expressive and refer to a push, a pull, a careless manner, and so forth, as do *nud* and *nug*. Some, like *niggle* 'work in a trifling way' (a cognate of *niggard*), have been known for several centuries (OED) and seem to have been borrowed from Scandinavian; others may have originated in English.

It follows that *nudge*, whether native or not, should, as already suggested, be traced to a verb beginning with *gn-* or *kn-* (*hn-* is, from the historical point of view, their weakened reflex). The problem of final consonants remains partly unsolved. If we refuse to treat *nub, nud, nug,* and the rest as reflexes of **knə-* with various enlargements, their relatedness to one another becomes questionable. (See BEACON, FUCK, MOOCH, and TOAD, which pose a similar problem.) Countless vaguely synonymous words in the modern languages have common parts (the stubs that remain after the 'subtraction' of postvocalic consonants), but the remainders need not be equated with ancient roots, the bearers of basic meanings. The kinship of *nug, nub,* and *nud* is probable, but its nature needs elucidation. *Nigg(ard), nudge,* and *nod* may be cognates despite the fact that no phonetic change connects -/d/ and -/g/ in Old and Middle English and that /d/ yielded /ʤ/ only before /j/. By the same token, *nibble* and *knock* are their cognates, a fact that will remain even if no use is made of Persson's enlargements.

Two good etymologies of *nudge* have been proposed. Wood (1907-08:272-74/30) listed OI *hnúka* 'sit cowering,' MHG *nucken* ~ *nücken* 'nod; stop suddenly, shy (said about horses); nod off, take a nap,' MLG *nucken* 'shake one's head in disagreement,' *nugen* 'bend,' ModI *hnykkja* 'pull violently; clinch, rivet,' and OE **hnygela* 'shred, clipping' (recorded as *hnygelan* and *hnigelan* 'clippings,' pl). He gave ModE *nudge* in his list without comments and did not reconstruct OE **hnycgelan*, whose modern continuation would have been *nudge*. (Wood returned to the *kn-* words several more times but did not mention *nudge* again.)

O. Ritter (1910:478-79) set up **knudge* as a side form of **knutch* < **hnucchen* < **cnyccan* 'push,' related to OE *cnocian* ~ *cnucian* 'knock.' He viewed Sc *gnidge* 'rub; squeeze' (verbs); 'squeeze; nudge' (nouns) as a variant of *nudge*. The vowel *y* in **cnyccan* would have developed as it did in *clutch* and the like (see a list of similar words at STUBBORN). The etymon of *nudge* can thus be reconstructed with a high degree of probability as OE **hnycgan* or **cnyccan*. This verb was colloquial (as it still is), perhaps even slang, and, like *niggle, nuddle*, and *knubble*, it had no currency outside a narrow regional area. But *nudge* may be an expressive variant of *nud*. The problem with such an etymology is not its implausibility; it is rather the absence of a regular pattern that makes the barrier between *nud* and *nudge* hard to overcome.

ODEE says the following about *nudge*: "[O]f unkn[own] origin; perh[aps] in much earlier use and rel[ated] ult[imately] to Norw. dial. *nugga, nygja* push, rub." OED is more optimistic and calls *nudge* a word of obscure origin; however, it does not suggest "much earlier use" (ODEE offers no arguments in support of its statement). ODEE replaced OED's "perh[aps] related" with "ult[imately] related." The phrase *ultimately related* is of little value here. All the words, brought together by Torp, Persson, Walde, Pokorny, and others may be "ultimately related," but each has its own history.

If MLG and MHG *nucken* is part of the aforementioned group, E *nick* 'notch' may be too. But ODEE echoes OED ("of unknown origin") and denies its ties with Du *nikken* and LG *nicken* 'nod.' OED, likewise, dismissed *nod* as a word of obscure origin and called its connection with MHG *notten* 'move about' doubtful. ODEE suggests a Low German etymon for *nod* and gives *notten* as the nearest corresponding form but offers no 'ultimate' etymology. Both dictionaries recognize *nugget* as a diminutive of reg *nug* 'lump,' whose origin is again unknown. *Nag* 'small riding horse' appears to be another word of unknown or obscure origin despite the reference to early MDu *negghe* 'dwarf horse.' Björkman's examples (1912:266) make it clear that the original meaning of the Norwegian, Dutch, and Low German nouns corresponding to *nag* is 'stump' and that all the animals called *neg, nag*, and *nagge* are small. *Nag* is akin to *niggle, niggard*, and so forth, all of which carry the idea of smallness. Thus *nag* and *niggle* are 'ultimately related' to *nugget, nudge, nod, nick*, and probably *noggin*. The same holds for numerous *sn-* words, from *snip* to *snug*. See Schrijnen (1904:93-98; a detailed list of *sn* - ~ *gn-* ~ *kn-* ~ *hn-* words), Siebs (1904:315; on *nip—snip—snipe*), Stapelkamp (1950b:100; on E *nib* and its cognates), and Frankis (1960:384; on *nick—snick* and *nip—snip—gnip—knip*).

The question about the volume of any multitude has two sides: what to include and what to leave out. Some English words, cited above, have a short recorded history and no known cognates. Others, like *nod*, have one cognate in Low German, so that the source of borrowing remains unclear (see Jellinghaus [1898b:31] on *nig* 'small piece' and *niggling*). Still others, like the noun *nag*, resemble many words in Low German and Scandinavian. Occasionally putative cognates in Lithuanian turn up (see, for example, LEW, *gniaužti* 'press, compress'), and, as usual, several promising look-alikes have been found in Hebrew, Sanskrit, and Greek (Lemon, *nudge*; Davies [1855:253, *nod*, and 261, *knock*]). Presumably, none of them began with *gn-* or *kn-*. Yet Frisk (νύσσω, νύττω 'push, strike, jostle') mentions G *nucken* as a possible cognate of the Greek verb. See also WP II:323, IEW, 767, and the etymology of E *nut* and L *nux* in old and new dictionaries. The entries in our reference works do not reflect the progress made since the days of Murray, Bradley, and Skeat in the study of each of those nouns and verbs, including *nod* (on which see Verdam [1897:165-70] and Krogmann [1933:382]).

In a search like the present one, we constantly run the risk of including extra words whose similarity with *nudge* is misleading, for we are facing forms merging with one another ("Wohl zusammengehörige Gruppe von Wörtern mit einer schwer abgrenzenden Verwandtschaft" [Probably a group of related words whose affinity is hard to determine], Seebold [KS, *Nock*] and see MOOCH, sec 7). For example, *notch* seems to be an ideal 'partner' of *nick* and *nudge*, and this impression may be correct, but both Skeat (1901: 198-99) and Weekley (1910:312-14) insist that *notch* is of French origin and that the synonyms F *oche* and E *nock* were associated in Anglo-French (AF *noche*). Likewise, *knife* is regularly mentioned with *nock, nick*, and the rest, and if at one time *knife* designated a stabbing tool or weapon, a kind of bayonet, its name will align itself effortlessly with the other *kn-* words (with respect to *-f,* see *neif* 'fist' above). Yet Vennemann (1997) believes that *knife* is a borrowing from Basque. No record of *niblick* exists before 1862. The comment in OED is "of unknown formation." Of the other dictionaries only RHD ventures a guess: from *nibble + ick,* a variant of *-ock.* Such a late word must presumably have been coined by a golfer or a sport journalist. *Nib* means 'point,' and a niblick is a golf club having a small round heavy ball. Another lump is called *knub.* A nib would be a small knub. Perhaps, someone made up the word *niblick* from the elements *nib* and *-lick,* as in *frolic* or *garlic,* with a facetious reference to the verb *lick,* quasi *nib-lick.* People often name a stick after the part that comes into contact with the object it strikes. Such is, for instance, *cudgel,* whose root is reminiscent of *cog* and G *Kugel* 'bullet' (KS, *Keule*). EDD cites *nudgel* not only for 'lump' but also for 'cudgel.' A bird's eye view of the entire *gn- ~ kn- ~ hn- ~ (sn-)* multitude cannot replace a meticulous analysis of every word.

The origin of *nudge* is certainly not unknown, even though the contours of the group to which it belongs are blurred. An Old English etymon of *nudge*—hnycgan* or its cognate **knyccan*—seems to have existed. When this verb emerged from its regional obscurity, it became part of the *budge—grudge—trudge* set, a circumstance that reinforced its expressive, slangy character.**

OAT (700)

Contrary to what is said in most English dictionaries, oat *(OE* āte*) is not an isolated word in Germanic. It has cognates in Frisian and in several Dutch dialects. In Old English,* āte *designated only wild oats* (avena fatua)*, but the extant occurrences are few, and our knowledge of the use of oats before the Conquest is limited. OE* āte *coexisted with* ǣte *and* ātih*. In some situations, all three words seem to have been synonymous. It remains a riddle why English lacked the common Germanic name of* oats *akin to G* Hafer*.*

In several languages, the word for 'oats' and 'goat' are strikingly similar; in German, Haber *means both. However, E* oat *and* goat *are not related. Some etymologists tried to relate OE* āte *and* etan *'eat.' Attempts in that direction are of no value, because OE* ā *and* e *belong to different ablaut series. A few other fanciful derivations of* oat *have not advanced the search for its history. It is now customary to call* oat *a word of unknown origin. Yet Skeat proposed a good etymology of* oat *and Binz improved it. Most German, Dutch, and Scandinavian scholars accepted it, but OED rejected it and later English philologists passed it by. According to Skeat and Binz, OE* āte *is related to Icel* eitill *'nodule, kernel, gland' and MHG* eiz *'swelling.' The original meaning of the root* *ait- *must have been 'grain.' Binz discovered the same root in OHG* araweizi *'pea' (ModG* Erbse*), literally 'pea grain.' Go* atisk *'grain field' looks like another good cognate of OE* āte*, but Gmc* *ai *and* *a *are as incompatible as OE* ā *and* e*.*

The sections are devoted to 1) the form and meaning of the Old English words for 'oats,' 2) oats and goats, 3) the improbable etymologies of oat *from Minsheu's days to the present, 4) the etymology by Skeat and Binz, and 5) the relationship between OE* āte *and Go* atisk*.*

1. ***Oat* occurs for the first time in the gloss '*lolium atae*,' and the meaning 'wild oat(s)' (*avena fatua*) is the usual one for *āte* in Old English,** though the recorded examples are few: most references occur in the parable of the enemy who sowed tares in a grain field; see BWA I:7 and III:5. **In Middle English, *otes* refers to the cultivated variety, that is, to *avena sativa*** (Bremmer [1993:24]). The plural forms (*ātan,* etc) predominate in Old and Middle English. Today, *oat* is familiar only from compounds and phrases like *oatcake, oatmeal,* and *oat grass;* otherwise, *oats* is used. OED compares *oats* with such plurals as *beans* and *potatoes* and infers "that primarily *oat* was not the plant or the produce in the mass, but denoted an individual grain; cf. *groat* with its collective pl. *groats.* This may point to oats being eaten originally in the grains, not like wheat and barley, in the form of meal or flour...but the scanty early evidence is not sufficient to show this." Since OE *āte* had the side form *ǣte,* it may have been declined as both an *-ōn* and a *-jōn* stem (like *hrūse* 'earth'), a circumstance passed over in the standard grammars of Old English.

According to OED, *āte,* an isolated word in Indo-European, is of obscure origin. ODEE, following its style sheet, substitutes *unknown* for *obscure* and says "peculiar to Eng[lish] and of unkn[own] origin." **Its verdict is all the more surprising as Bosworth (1838) cited Fr *oat* and Toller retained it.** It also appears in W (1864; 1890). Probably under the influence of OED, W^1 expunged Fr *oat,* and it did not return to $W^{2,3}$. CD, Partridge (1958), CEDEL, and RHD give no cognates of *oat,* while Weekley asserts that none are known. However, Bosworth's source of information was fully reliable (Bremmer [1993:25]; E. Stanley [1990, esp p. 436]) and should not have been ignored. **Several Dutch regional forms are also akin to E *oat*:** Fl *ate ~ ote* and Zeelandic *ôôte* (Bülbring [1900a:110, note], Vercoullie [1920], Heeroma [1942:86], Weijnen [1965:393], Bremmer [1993:24-28]; NEW, *oot*).

Besides *āte* and *ǣte,* Old English had *ātih* 'weeds' (continued in northern E reg *oatty* 'oats of very short stalks' and 'mixed with wild oat'), a collective noun of the type not uncommon in naming plants (-*ig* in OE *īfig* has the same origin; see IVY and O. Ritter [1922:60]). A parallel formation is Russ *ovës* 'oats' ~ *ovsiug* 'wild oats' (both words are stressed on the last syllable). The names of weeds and cultivated plants often sound alike (a typical example is Du *tarwe* 'wheat' and E *tare*) because several species of grain arise from weeds growing in sown fields or because they resemble one another.

It is not known when and from what area oats migrated to the Germanic-speaking world (Classen [1931:256]), where they must have been used both as fodder and for human consumption. However, the literary evidence on this subject, as already pointed out, is too scarce for drawing definite conclusions. Grube (1934:142) summarized the solution as follows: "The limited occurrence of O.E. *ate* indicates that oats were not very prominent among the grains as human food. This is further suggested by the glossing of *ate* with Latin *lolium* and *zizania*, 'weeds,' 'tares,' in several glosses.... *Zizania*, in Matthew 13, 38, which is translated *weod* by the Rushworth MS and *coccel* by the Corpus and Hatton MSS, is glossed *ata, sifeða, unwæstm* by the Lindisfarne MS. Essentially the same distinction is made in Matthew 13, 27, again in verse 30 of the same chapter. In the latter instance, the Lindisfarne version speaks of *wilde ata*, which would suggest that oats were cultivated, although the association of oats with tares would lead us to suppose that the grain was discredited as a food for humans. Use in the medical recipes is largely confined to poultices (e.g., Cockayne, III, 8). However, oatmeal, *ætena mela*, is mentioned in the *Leech Book* (Cockayne, II, 84), and a fragment containing some charms and recipes in a Twelfth century hand gives the following.... (Cockayne, III, 292). The direction is to eat these ingredients, including the groats of oats and the powdered oat-bran, *etriman dust*, with the substance of the oats, the pith. The passage presents several difficulties (one of them: what is 'oak drink'?), and is here presented merely as a record of the terms associated with 'oats.'"

2. **The oldest Germanic name of *oat* has been preserved in G *Hafer* (OHG *habaro*), Du *haver* (OS *haƀero*), and Dan, N, Sw *havre* (OI *hafri*, recorded a single time in poetry).** Its etymology is debatable, and the existing hypotheses are of little help in tracing the origin of *oat*. Only one circumstance is worthy of mention. G *Hafer* is a Low German variant of *Haber* and thus a homonym of *Haber* 'billy goat.' J. Grimm (1848: 66-67 = 1868:47) assumed that *Haber* 'oat(s)' was called this because it had been used as fodder for goats and sheep. He referred to several similar pairs, for example, Russ *ovës* ~ L *avēna* and Russ *ovtsa* 'sheep' ~ L *ovis*, and to Gk αἰγίλωψ 'wild oats,' but had doubts about coupling OE *āte* with some animal name.

Heyne, who wrote the entry *Haber* in DW and Schrader, in his notes to Hehn (Hehn [1894:539]), called into question Grimm's derivation of *ovës* ~ *avēna*. Opinions on G *Haber* are divided. FT (*havre*) and EWDS, including the latest editions, endorse Grimm's idea. Some etymologists remain noncommittal (see E. Zupitza and Lochner-Hüttenbach [1967:52]). If *Haber* 'billy goat' and *Haber* 'oats' have different cognates outside Germanic (see Uhlenbeck [1894:330/5] and Stalmaczczyk and Witczak [1991-92], among others), the two words may have nothing to do with each other. Solmsen (1904:6), Petersson (1918:19), WP I:24, EWNT², and J. de Vries (AEW, *hafri*; NEW, *haver*) follow Pedersen (1895:42-43) and look on the kinship between *Haber*$_1$ and *Haber*$_2$ as nearly or absolutely improbable. Russ *ovës* and *ovtsa* have been dissociated in the modern etymological dictionaries. The same holds for their cognates in the other Slavic languages. In αἰγίλωψ, the second component (-λωψ) is opaque (Frisk, Chantraine); this word also designated a variety of oak. Contrary to αἰγίλωψ, αἰγίλως seems to have meant only 'wild oats.'

E *oat* poses a problem of its own (as was clear to Grimm), because *g*- in *goat* cannot be explained away. However, Makovskii (1985:49) sees no difficulty here. In the eighties he developed so-called combinatorial etymology and made the following statement: "Contamination of OE *hæfer* 'billy goat' and *hæfer* 'oat' resulted in that OE *gāt* 'goat,' a synonym of *hæfer* 'goat,' acquired the fictitious meaning 'oat' (OE *āt* 'oat' < **gāt;* with regard to the elision of the initial consonant, cf Russ *koza* 'nanny goat' versus Lith *ožỹs*)." The origin of Russ *koza* is obscure (see more about it at HEIFER), and OE *hæfer* 'oats' did not exist (in the 14th century, *haver* 'oats' surfaced in northern English dialects, and it is still current in Scots, but this word is universally believed to be a borrowing from Scandinavian).

3. **An old etymology connected *oat* with OE *etan* 'eat,'** "because every where it is forage for horses and in some places of men" (Skinner, as translated by Richardson; similarly in *Gazophylacium*: "for it is forage for horses in all places; and in some, provision for men"). The first to derive *āte* from *etan* was Minsheu, who offered the same reason. Johnson's definition of oats (inspired by Robert Burton? [G. Thompson 1887]) 'a grain,

which in England is generally given to horses, but in Scotland supports the people' made Skinner's formulation offensive. Pictet (1859, I:259), J. Meyer (1880:15), Wedgwood, and Mueller (hesitatingly) supported Minsheu's etymology (without references).

Words for 'oats' and 'food' sound alike not only in English. We are facing an analogue of the *oat* ~ *goat* type, but here the most important evidence comes from Icelandic rather than German: OI *át* and *áta* mean 'eating' and 'food' respectively. However, the Old English cognate of *át* is predictably *ǣt*. OE *ǣte* 'oats' must have been a later form than *āte*, coined either to denote fodder or, more likely, as a *-jon* doublet of *āte*, because *ā* could not develop from *ǣ*, and the narrowing of meaning from 'food' to 'oats' is less likely than the broadening from 'cereal' to 'food' (cf E *barley* and its Slavic cognates meaning 'food'). Schrader (1901:321; the same in SN, 428) considered OE *āte* to be an isolated form and abandoned his old idea, offered tentatively in Hehn (1894:539), that *āte* is related to Gk εἶδαρ 'food.' Etymological dictionaries of Greek never mention *oat* under εἶδαρ. (In Schrader's works, OE *āte* appears as *āta*; SN corrected the mistake.) In Curtius (2329), *oat* does turn up but only in connection with the words for 'eat' (tentatively).

Contrary to other cereals, **oats have panicles that sway in the gentlest wind**. That circumstance gave rise to the comparison between G *Hafer* and Skt *kámpate* 'trembles' and *capaláḥ* 'moving, shaking unsteadily' (see *Hafer* in DW). Modern etymological dictionaries of German and Dutch do not discuss this comparison (see KEWA I:160, 374), but Wood (1919-20:568) reasoned in a similar way. He compared *Hafer* with OE *hæf* 'sea' and E *heave*: "The sea was naturally described as 'that which heaves, rises and falls,' and *haven* as a 'roadstead,' i.e., where ships ride at anchor." He interpreted OHG *habaro* as 'swelling, tuft.' The feature uniting them would thus be the swelling of the tuft and the swell of waves.

An idea close to the one in DW found an indirect reflection in Tucker (*aedes*), who explained *Hafer* "'oats,' from their shaking" and analyzed *āte* into OE **ĕ̄i+* **d*: "the primitive notion of this **ĕ̄i+* is that of expansive, restless, shaking, flickering or shivering." As a parallel to *oats* 'shivering grass' Tucker cited *totter bells* (*totter grass* is 'quaking grass,' according to CD and OED). Minsheu, though for different reasons, considered but gave up the parallel E *oats* ~ Gk ἄζω 'burn,' a cognate of L *aedes* 'temple' (originally 'hearth').

Attempts have been made to reconstruct a single etymon for G *Hafer* and L *avēna*. Kaltschmidt (*Hafer*) set up the root χ-π that absorbed the most various words, *avēna* and *Hafer* among them. A. Noreen (1894:149) considered the possibility of reconstructing **havēna* for L *avēna*—an ingenious but unacceptable protoform because it severs the ties between the Latin and the Balto-Slavic words. However, early English etymologists seem to have thought that *oats* rather than *Hafer* was related to Russ *ovës*, which would make it a cognate of *avēna*: see Minsheu, Hickes, and W (1828; expunged in 1864). It remains unclear what common features Minsheu and others detected in the two words, for even the vowels in them do not match. Equally incomprehensible is Partridge's statement (1958) that "one is tempted to compare [*oat* with] Lettish [= Latvian] *àuza* and O[ld] S[lavic] *ovisŭ*, which would bring us to L *auēna*." The nature of the inducement is even more obscure than the word under discussion.

After producing *āt-* from *gāt*, Makovskii had two more ideas: 1) He said that Go *hlaifs* 'bread' was a cognate of Hitt *harpai-* 'begin(ning),' and E *bread* a cognate of Sw *börja* 'begin.' Likewise, OE *āt-* is allegedly akin to Gmc **andjas* 'beginning-end' and OE *ent* 'giant' (Makovskii [1996:123 and continuation of footnote 9 on page 124). 2) Cereals have been objects of worship since antiquity (cf E reg *ait* 'custom, habit'); hence the affinity between E *oat* and all kinds of words meaning 'shield' and 'move.' He explains that when a grain falls into the ground, struggle begins (cf OI *at* 'struggle'): the grain first dies (cf OI *eyða* 'destroy, waste') and then comes alive (cf PIE **aid-* 'swell') (Makovsii [1999a, *oat*]). Evidently, E *oat*, E *end*, OE *ent*, OI *at* from *etja* 'incite, egg on,' OI *eyða*, and the rest are all related. W. Barnes (1862:320) traced *oat* to one of his inscrutable roots, this time *ng, and explained *oat* as 'sharp-eared plant.'

4. Since almost the only source of OE *ā* is Gmc **ai*, it is reasonable to try to derive OE *āt-* from **ait-*. Skeat[1] did exactly that and compared OE *āte* with Icel *eitill* 'nodule in stone,' a word (which also means 'nodule in wood') first recorded in the 17th century (ÁBM). *Eitill* has cognates in Faroese, Nynorsk, and in Swedish dialects; see *eitel* in FT and Torp. Other cognates include MHG *eiz* 'abscess,' presumably Russ *iadro* 'kernel' (stress on the last syllable; Vasmer IV:547-48 rejects that correspondence, and ESSI VI:65-66 does not even mention Germanic forms, but IEW, 774 repeats the information from WP I:166-67 and treats the Proto-Slavic form as a nasalized variant of PIE **oid-*), Gk οἶδος 'swelling' and the words, collected in WP and

IEW at *oid. OE *ättor* 'poison' is one of them. According to this theory, *oat* originally meant 'kernel, nodule' or simply 'grain.' One might expect a more concrete etymon, but OE *ātan* designated 'darnel, cockle, tares (lolium, zizania)' and may in prehistorical times have been applied to several kinds of weeds. If so, the name need not have been specific.

OED ignored Skeat's etymology, and later lexicographers classified *oat* with words of unknown origin. However, Skeat remained true to his idea. The entry in ODEE, which follows OED, contains no remarks on Skeat, whereas the criticism by Scott (CD) and Wyld (UED) misses the point. CD cites the suggestions that *oat* is related to *eitill* or to *eat* and concludes "... but why oats should be singled out, as 'that which has a rounded shape' or 'that which is eaten,' from other grains of which the same is equally or more true, is not clear." However, 'kernel' = 'grain' should be given precedence to 'that which has a rounded shape.'

UED lays special emphasis on οἶδος 'swelling,' which is "prob[ably] cogn[ate]" with OE *ättor* 'poison' ("a connexion has been suggested w[ith] O.H.G. *eitar*, 'poison' ...") and says: "This is not convincing because oats are among the last of the cereals to suggest the idea of swelling." 'Swelling' is a derivative of 'gland.' It is not necessary to detect the meaning of the reconstructed root in every attested form in all languages. Wyld must have been misled by the end of Skeat's early statement: "If this [proposed derivation of *oats*] be right, the original meaning of *oat* was grain, corn, kernel, with reference to the manner of its growth, the grains being of bullet-like form; and it is derived from √ID, to swell," not from √AD, to eat. *Growth* here means 'shape' rather than 'process of growing.' Skeat[4] replaced √OID with √EID.

Skeat's etymology is acceptable even on its own terms, but it received confirmation from German. Binz (1906:371) endorsed the comparison OE *āt-e* ~ Icel *eit-ill*, added Alemannic *aisse* 'abscess,' a reflex of MHG *eiz*, and suggested that OHG *araweiz* 'pea' (ModG *Erbse*) be divided *araw-eiz*, with *ar(a)w-* being akin to OE *earban* (an oblique case of *earfe* 'tare'; again 'tare'!) and L *ervum* 'wild pea,' and *eiz* meaning what Skeat reconstructed as the original sense of *āte*. He pointed out that understanding *oat* as 'kernel, nodule, *etc*' tallies with the pronouncement in OED: "...primarily *oat* was not the plant or the produce in the mass, but denoted an individual grain."

Kluge accepted this etymology. The entry *Erbse* in EWDS[7-10] (from 1910 to Kluge's death) contains Binz's explanation and a reference to his article. Götze (EWDS[11]) removed the reference but left the etymology unchanged, and it is still present in EWDS (with respect to the latest edition see Seebold [1967:127/10]). Hirt (1921:135) viewed *araweiz, ervum,* and two Greek words as belonging together but unrelated (consequently, as borrowed from an unknown source), and Duden 7 (*Erbse*) shares his opinion. Ipsen (1924:231) found the reconstructed Germanic forms **arawaita-* and **arawīta* incompatible with **aita-* because of the alternation *-ai-* ~ *-i-*. It matters little whether all those forms are true cognates or local variants of some migratory words. Such words always exist in several variants (see Debrunner [1918:445]). Skt *aravinda* (a plant name) is too obscure (see KEWAS 12, Porzig [1927:268-69], Van Windekens [1957], and KEWA I:48; III:632) to provide any help in solving the etymology of *oat*. WP I:166, with reference to Binz, and IEW, 774, without a reference, concur with Kluge.

In the Netherlands, Vercoullie (1920:936) had no objections to equating OE *āt-* and Icel *eit-*; neither did Van Wijk (EWNT[2], *erwt*), who followed Kluge's example. The same holds for Weijnen (1965:393). In Scandinavian dictionaries, *oats* appears with the disclaimer "some people compare..." So, for example, SEO (*ärt*). Torp (*eitel*) refers to *eiter* 'poison' but passes over E *oat*. BjL (*ert*) continue Torp's tradition. J. de Vries sided with Hirt. In AEW (*ertr*), he asserts that Binz was wrong, because *-eiz* in *araweiz* is a suffix, as in Go *aglaitei** 'licentiousness' (an idea going back to Bugge [1899:439] and Wiedemann [1904:46]), and that *ervum, Erbse,* and *ertr* reached Germanic speakers from some unknown language. In NEW (*erwt*), he did not mention Binz's etymology. Reference to *aglaitei** should have been left out. Feist points out that the origin and the type of formation of the Gothic word are obscure (likewise, Feist-Lehmann).

Even if *araweiz* is a borrowing from an unidentifiable language, it does not follow that the element *-eiz* is hopelessly obscure. L *ervum*, OE *earfe*, and OHG *araw-* probably go back to a non-Indo European substrate, but *-eiz* may be of Germanic origin. If a borrowed plant name could end in a native suffix, it could equally well be coupled with a transparent word (*-eiz*) that would have made its meaning more precise and its shape less foreign. The conclusion in EWA (310) that Binz's etymology is "totally ungrounded" is needlessly severe. ÁBM cites E *oats* at *eitill* as its unquestionable cognate, but at *erta* 'pea' he defers to J. de

Vries and wonders whether *-eiz* in OHG *araweiz* is not a suffix. IsEW, 982, expresses no such doubts.

Despite the fact that Binz's article contains the word *oats* in the title, English philologists overlooked it, and of course no one writing on E *oats* would think of consulting the entry *Erbse, erwt*, or *ertr*. (However, *oats* turns up in the indexes to WP and IEW and could be 'reclaimed.') Skeat died in 1910 and may not have seen the German article published in 1906. Even Weekley was ignorant of it, and Binz's irritation at being disregarded (1927:181-82) is easy to understand. Wood (1914b:500/4) cites many words cognate with *eitill*, including MHG *eiz*, but does not discuss G *Erbse*, whereas Wood (1919-20:568) once again presents OE *ātan* against the background of words for 'swelling' and glosses it as 'tuft, panicle' (see above).

Binz's etymology makes it clear that the impulse for calling *avena fatua āte* could come from OE *āttor* (OI *eitr*) 'poison.' The view of oats as a degenerate culture is old and stems from the confusion of *avena sativa* and *avena fatua* (this was Pliny's opinion; see the quotation and discussion in Hoops [1905:409]), but the meaning 'poison' in *āttor* must have developed from 'matter inside a swelling,' while *āt-* ~ *eit-* designated any nodule or gland. Binz touches on this subject too. **At present, Skeat and Binz's conjecture is probably the best**. Occasional references to the substrate origin of *oat*, as, for instance, in Claiborne (1989:179 "... more likely borrowed from some aboriginal people in northwestern Europe, where the grain probably originated") lack foundation. It would have been strange for the Anglo-Saxons to borrow an exotic (migratory?) word and apply it to a common weed.

5. Several words sounding like Old English *āte* refer to plants, parks, and so forth. The most conspicuous of them is Gothic *atisk* 'grain field,' with cognates in German and Dutch (ModDu *es*, in the old orthography *esch*, 'cultivated fields of a village'). Another one is OE *edisc* 'enclosed pasture,' whose *-d-* makes its kinship with OHG *ezzesc(a)* ~ MHG *ezzich* 'sown grain field' suspect. To complicate matters, *e* in OE *edisc* may be the product of umlaut and ModE *eddish* 'aftergrowth, stubble,' known from texts only since the 15th century, need not be the continuation of OE *edisc*. Then there is L *ador* 'spelt,' presumably akin to Gk ἀθήρ 'ear of grain.' For *atisk*, as for OE *āte*, affinity with the verb 'eat' has been proposed and rejected (see Feist[3,4]). See an exhaustive analysis of OHG *ezzesca* and its cognates in EWA (the head word there is *ezzisca*).

If OE *āte* were isolated or had only Frisian and Dutch cognates, it might be possible to suggest that its *ā* does not go back to **ai* but is the result of emphatic lengthening or some such process (see the suggestion on the origin of OE *ā* in *tāde* at TOAD), but the existence of MHG *eiz* and Icel *eitill* rules out this possibility. To relate Go *atisk* to OE *āte*, the familiar **ai* ~ **a* barrier has to be overcome (see HEATHER and KEY). H. Kuhn (1954) conjures up the ghost of an ancient fashion for *ă*, which allegedly set in when the Indo-Europeans were learning agriculture. 'Common sense' suggested to him that *oak* < **aik-* and *acorn* < **akarn-* are related (p. 147). Likewise, he refused to separate **aito(n)* 'oats' from *atisk* 'grain field' (pp. 144 and 147).

According to GI (1984:665 = 1995:I, 564, sec 4.2.2.1), Go *atisk* contains the most ancient Indo-European name of 'grain,' but they do not mention *āte* or refer to Kuhn in their compendium. 'Common sense' tells us that OI *hafri* and *hagri** (both mean 'oats'), Go *atisk* and OE *edisc*, as well as **aik-* and **akarn-* are related pairwise. In similar fashion, an association between oats and goats in one language after another, between *atisk* and **aito(-n)*, and between *heath* and *heather* cannot, as it seems, be fortuitous. Yet if we break the rules of the game, we cannot win it: the game will stop.

Given the present state of our knowledge, Gmc **ai* and *ă* are incompatible. Although a fashion for *a* may have existed, to connect **ait-* and **at-*, we need a 'law' rather than a feeling that it would be a good thing to do so or special dispensation. In the absence of such a law Go *atisk* and OE *āte* will remain unrelated in our books. Kuhn would have probably taken this conclusion in stride, for, as he says (p. 159), his goal was to stimulate research rather than convince.

PIMP (1607)

Despite its initial p-, pimp *seems to be a cognate of* G Pimpf *'little boy'* (Pimpf *for* *Pfimpf). Pimp *'helper in mines' and pimp 'servant in logging camps' have comparable meanings. The development was probably from *'despised weakling' to 'despised go-between' ~ 'procurer of sex.' The Germanic root* *pimp – *pamp – *pump *means 'swell.* G Pimpf *was someone unable to give a big* Pumpf *'fart'; E* pimp *must have had the same meaning.* Pimp *'bundle of firewood' is also 'small swollen object.' Since* pimp *'pander' is not the original meaning of this word, Middle French* pimper *'dress up smartly,' F* pimpant *'spruce,' and other similar Romance words provide no clue to its origin.*

The sections are devoted to 1) the relationship between E pimp *and G* Pimpf *and the proposed connection between* pimp *and some word for 'penis,' 2)* pimp *among other* pimp-*words, 3)* pimp *and a few other similar-sounding words out-*

side English, and 4) pimp *'procurer of sex' and 'bundle of wood.'*

1. **In addition to 'provider of prostitutes,' *pimp* means 'boy who does menial jobs at a logging camp, boy who carries water, washes dishes, or the like'** (R. Chapman). The *paper collar stiff's cigarette* was known among loggers as *pimp stick* (Stevens [1925:138], R. Adams), for lumberjacks despised those who smoked such cigarettes. A helper in northern Idaho mines was also called a pimp (Lehman [1922], Pethtel [1965:283]). OED treats *pimp* 'small bundle of chopped wood used for lighting fires' (1742; the word is still in use in Kent and Sussex; see Schur [1994:497-98]) as a homonym of *pimp* 'provider of prostitutes,' but the two words seem to have the same etymon.

A rather obvious cognate of *pimp* is G *Pimpf* 'little (inexperienced) boy.' Under the Nazis, *Pimpf* meant 'member of a patriotic youth organization, wolf cub.' Before the Nazi era, it was current mainly in Austria, and this must be the reason *pimp* and *Pimpf* have never been compared. *Pimpf* appeared in German dictionaries late: it does not occur in DW (vol 13, 1889), WH (1909-10), or Paul[1], and it was added to EWDS only by Mitzka. The authors of the most widely read works on English etymology published since roughly 1860 must have been unaware of this word. Mitzka's earliest citation is dated "before 1868" (KM). At that time, *Pimpf* was still a street word, and even Mueller (a native German) may not have heard it. *Pimpf,* once missed, remained in its isolation. German etymologists, for their part, overlooked *pimp* because they had no need to go outside German.

Unlike *pimp*, *Pimpf* poses no problem for an etymologist. It was originally a contemptuous designation for a youngster too weak to produce a big *Pumpf*, that is, a big fart. *Pimp* had similar connotations, going from 'ninny, raw novice' (Hibbard [1977]), *'weak boy; weakling; person considered worthless' to 'servant at the lowest level of the social hierarchy' and 'pander.' E *boy* 'servant,' F *garçon* 'waiter,' and Sp *muchacho* 'servant' developed in the same way (see BOY for more details).

Folk etymology seems to have connected *pimp* and *pimpernel,* which was understood as a flower lacking the power of resistance. E reg (Dorset) *pimpersheen* means 'one who is not good at enduring hardships' (anonymous [1935:178]). **Spitzer** (1951:216-17) **considered *pimp* to be a clipped form of *pimpernel,* but this is an unattractive hypothesis**. An association between *pimp* and some slang name for 'penis' may have suggested the meaning 'procurer of sex.' *Pimp* 'penis' has not been attested in Germanic (Arnoldson [1915:165-70], Baskett [1920:106-11]), but in northern German the vulgar verb *pimpern* means 'have sexual intercourse'; according to Duden, it can be a "side form" of LG *pümpern* 'grind with a pestle in a mortar.' *Pimmel* 'penis' is allegedly of similar origin (KS). *Pimmel* (? < **Pimpel*) is phonetically close to E *pintle* (< OE *pintel*), Du *pint*, and ModI *pintill* 'penis' (the latter could also mean 'pestle': ÁBM).

2. Indo-European and Germanic have many words formed from the root *pimp – pamp – pump* (a baby word, according to Oehl [1933a:44]), including the strong verb **pimpan* 'swell.' Those having *i* tend to designate small objects (such as *pimp* and *pimple*), those with *u* and *a* are more often tied to big things, for example, *pamper,* originally 'overfeed' (opposed to obsolete E *pimper* 'coddle, pamper') and G *pampig* 'arrogant.' Initial *p-* often alternates with *b-*.

If *pimp* is related to G *Pimpf,* it is unclear why the German form is not **Pfimpf.* Perhaps such a short word with the affricate *pf* in initial and final position was hard to pronounce. *Pfropf* 'cork' is a deliberate reshaping of a Low German noun according to the High German phonetic norm. *Pfropfen* (v) 'graft' is an equally deliberate attempt to render a Latin word in High German. *Pimpf* may also have originated in the north, later spread south, and retained traces of its Low German origin. But since its recorded 'home' is Austria, this hypothesis can hardly be entertained. A similar difficulty confronts us in the history of HG *foppen* 'tease,' with its unshifted *p*.

OED was close to guessing the origin of *pimp.* At *pimping* (adj) 'small, trifling, peddling, paltry, petty, mean; in poor health or condition, sickly' (first recorded in 1687), it says, "Of uncertain origin; dialectally *pimpy* is found in same sense. Cf *pimp sb²* [that is, 'bundle of firewood'] and Cornish dialect. *pimpey* 'weak watery cider'; also Du. *pimpel* 'weak little man,' G *pimpelig* 'effeminate, sickly, puling,' which imply a stem *pimp*." (*Pimpey* is not in Williams.) If the editors had not missed E *pimp* 'servant' and G *Pimpf,* they would have realized that *pimp* was originally 'weak little man,' rather than 'one who provides opportunities for sexual intercourse.' But even Spitzer missed them.

3. ***Pimp* resembles Middle French *pimper* 'dress up smartly' and F *pimpreneau ~ pimperneau* 'kind of eel; knave' (a slippery or shifty creature and individual). Skeat derived E *pimp* from some such word or from F *pimpant* 'smart, spruce; chic and attractive.'** Littré believed that the root of *pimpant* was a nasalized form of *pip-*. **Under Lit-**

tré's influence Skeat explained *pimp* as a 'piper who ensnares women.' Weekley regarded *pimp* as a shortened form of the Latinized word *pimpinio*. Spitzer (1951:216) **assumed the existence of OF *pimpre (= pimprenele) 'rascal,' later 'pander.' Skinner and Lemon derived *pimp* from Gr πέμπω 'I send'; προπομπός** 'accompanying person' gave them the necessary meaning 'provider.' Skinner compared *pimp* with Ital *pinco*, F *pinge*, and L *pēnis*. His etymology appears in all the editions of Johnson's dictionary and in Kenrick. Finally, Mackay (1877), who looked on most English words as rebuses with a key in Gaelic, presented *pimp* as Gael *pighe(pi')* 'bird' + *uimpe* 'around her' = 'decoy.' All those etymologies, whether fanciful or reasonable, assume the initial meaning to have been 'smart fellow, rascal, pander.' R. Chapman posited the influence of *imp* on *pimp*. Nothing supports this conjecture.

4. ***Pimp* 'bundle of wood' accords well with **pimp* 'swell.'** A similar case would be Ital (Piemont) *bafra* 'full belly,' *bafrè* 'swell,' F *bâfrer* 'gorge oneself with food,' and OF *baffe* 'bundle of sticks'; *baffe* is believed to be the etymon of E *bavin*, with the same meaning (Körting, 1152); see also García de Diego (156-59, *baf*). A distant etymology for a word whose recorded history begins in 1742 is risky, but both *pimp* 'boy' and *pimp* 'bundle of sticks' are probably old. If they go back to the root **pimp – *pamp – *pump* and remained in regional use for centuries, their coexistence may have been supported by the syncretism 'peg'/'child' and 'child'/'wood.' Compare E *chit* 'young of a beast, very young person' and 'potato shoot,' related to OE *cīþ* 'shoot, sprout, seed, mote in the eye'; G *Kind* 'child' and OS *kidlek* 'tax on bundles of wood.' OI *hrís* means 'brushwood' and 'branches cut off from a tree,' while *hrísi* means 'illegitimate child (boy).' Its feminine counterpart is *hrísa*. The traditional explanation that a *hrísi* is 'a child begotten in the woods' is "too ingenious," to quote a phrase Partridge used on a different occasion. Trier's explanation (1963:183-84) that *hrísi* is simply a side branch is more persuasive.

In such cases, the association may have been from 'offshoot' to 'offspring, child,' as in *imp, scion, stripling, slip* (of a girl), and many others, possibly including OE *hyse* 'boy,' all of which meant 'offshoot' (Ekwall [1928:205-06], Bäck [1934:176-79], Trier [1952:55, 60-61]), or it may have been from 'chip off an old block,' or from 'stub, stump' (something formless, 'swollen') to 'child.' Johansson (1900:373-78, 381-82) and Much (1909) cite Germanic words for 'boy,' 'girl,' and 'child' that can be etymologized as 'stump, piece of wood, *etc*.' See also H. Logeman (1906:279, note 2) and a more general discussion of 'men and trees' in Smythe Palmer (1876, chapter 7), Pauli (1919:284-85), Trier (1952; 1963), Ader (1958:32-33), and Weber (1993). Perhaps *Víðarr*, the name of Óðinn's son, belongs here too (if it is a cognate of OI *víðir* 'willow').

Fag(got) and the obscure English word *bung* provide other parallels. Besides *bung* 'stopper,' there are also *bung* 'nickname for the master's assistant who superintends the serving of the grog' (nautical), as well as *bung* 'bundle of hemp stalks' and (in pottery) 'pile of clay cases in which fine stoneware is baked.' OED seems to treat *bung* 'assistant' as a humorous extension of *bung* 'stopper.' This is not unthinkable. For instance, ModI *spons* (from Danish) 'bung' and 'child' is a word traceable to the same Latin etymon as are E *bung* and G *Stöpsel* 'bung' and 'child,' but OED suggests that *bung* 'pile' is "perhaps not the same word." In light of the history of *pimp* and *fag(g)ot*, *bung* 'assistant' (that is, 'servant') and *bung* 'pile' need not be separated (see FAGGOT). *Pimp* means 'small bundle of wood' and 'servant at a logging camp,' presumably because for a logger an association between the two would not be far-fetched. In searching for the origin of the syncretism 'child'/'bundle of wood,' we should turn to the experience of those in whose life the forest played a decisive role. Such people would naturally animate trees, brushwood, and stumps, and even bestow names on them: compare the Dorset word *nickie* 'a tiny faggot made to light fires' (anonymous [1935:179]), cited at FAGGOT. See more on the 'child'/'wood' syncretism at CUB (Liberman [1992a:71-80, 86-87]).

RABBIT (?1398)

Outside English, only Walloon robett *'rabbit' is in some way connected with* rabbit. *However, the English word need not be a borrowing from a Romance language. It is rather one of many Germanic animal names having the structure* r + vowel + b *(such as G* Robbe *'seal' and Icel* robbi *'sheep, ram') and a French suffix. This etymon is not traceable to E* rub, *OE* rēofan *'break,' or G* reiben *'rub.' Many similar-sounding words that have been compared with* rabbit *are not related. Among them are G* Raupe *'caterpillar,' Russ* ryba *'fish,' and several Eurasian names of the fox (Sp* raposa, *OI* refr, *and others). F* râble *'back and loin of the rabbit,' F* rabouillère *'rabbit hole,' and Sp* rabo *'tail' are not viable etymons of* rabbit. *The derivation of* rabbit *from the proper name* Robert *is also unlikely.*

The sections are devoted to 1) the earliest conjectures on the origin of rabbit, *2)* rabbit *and similar words, especially in French; Germanic animal names having the structure* r +

vowel + b, *3)* r-b *words outside Germanic, 4)* rabbit *and* Robert ~ Rabbet, *and 5)* (d)rabbit *and* Welsh rabbit.

1. According to OED, the earliest example of *rabbit* in Middle English goes back to 1398, but Skeat (1903-06:256) cites two examples that antedate the first quotation in OED by approximately a decade. Another English name of this rodent is *con(e)y*. Its traditional pronunciation ['kʌni] gave rise to an obscene pun, believed to be the reason *cony* was replaced with *rabbit* (see, for example, G. Hughes [1988:48]). The ousting of OF *connin* by *lapin* has been attributed to a similar cause. Since *cony* occurs in the *Authorised Version of the Bible*, the pronunciation [kouni] was introduced "for solemn reading."

The closest cognates of *rabbit* first appeared in Minsheu, who cited **Fl ('Belgian')** ***robbe, robbeken*** **'rabbit.'** Less successful was the early search for the distant origin of *rabbit*. Minsheu suggested **Hebr רבה (*rabah*) 'copulate'** as the word's etymon, on account of the animal's fecundity. Surprisingly, he missed Gk λαγώς 'hare' and λάγνος 'lascivious.' Had he known more languages, he might have noticed the pair Russ *zaiats* 'hare' (with cognates elsewhere in Slavic) and Lith *žáisti* 'play, jump; copulate.' Mitchell repeated or reinvented Minsheu's Hebrew etymology (1908:85). Skinner traced *rabbit* to **L** ***rapidus*** **'swift,'** while Junius derived it from the compound ***roughfet*** **'rough foot,'** as in the Greek compound δασύποὒς 'hare' (δασύς 'hairy, furry' + πούς 'foot'), and supported his idea with the alleged derivation of E *hare* from *hair* and of Wel *ceinach* 'hare' from *cedenog* 'hairy.' This etymology also enjoyed some prestige at the beginning of the 20th century (Lydekker [1907:248]).

Cleland (1766:39) decomposed *rabbit* into ***er*** **'earth' +** ***abit*** and glossed the whole as 'digging into the earth, to form its burrow.' Whiter II:1233, a scholar who believed that all words were derived from the concept of the earth, arrived at a similar result from a different direction: he connected *rabbit* ~ *robbe* ~ *robbeken* with the phrase ***rib land*** 'give it half plowing.' Likewise, Balliolensis (1853) looked for a tie between *rabbit* and **Ir** ***rap*** 'creature that digs and burrows in the ground.' Bingham (1862) referred to the West-country pronunciation of *rabbit* as ***herpet*** and cited Gk **ἑρπετόν** 'creeper.' Keightley (1862a and b) traced *rabbit* and **F** ***lapin*** **to Gk δασύποὒς** (he probably did not know Junius), citing alternations between *d*, *l*, and *r* (his etymology was subjected to scathing criticism by Chance [1862], who, it appears, also missed Junius), while A. Hall (1890) compared *rabbit* and ***rat***, and Hopkinson (1890:123) looked for the origin of *rabbit* in **E** ***rub*** **and G** ***reiben*** (rabbit = scraper, burrower). Carnoy derived *rabbit* from *rub* as a matter of course (1955:121). Drake (1907:64, note 67n), inspired by Biblical **Hebr אַרְנֶבֶת (*ar(e)nebet*) 'hare, rabbit,'** which he transliterated as *har(e)nebet*), treated both E *hare* and *rabbit* as possible cognates of this word. According to CEDHL (56), the root of אַרְנֶבֶת may be a verb meaning 'jump.' No evidence points to the fact that the Semitic name for 'hare' and 'rabbit' has spread to Western Europe. Skeat[4] mentioned **Nynorsk** ***rabbla*** **'snap'** as a possible cognate of *rabbit*. Makovskii (1992b:121) etymologized *rabbit* as 'moving fast' and compared it with **L** ***rabiēs*** **'madness' and** ***rōbustus*** **'oaken; firm, strong,'** allegedly going back to the root 'bend; cut.' Santangelo (1953:10-11) offered a few other equally contrived etymologies.

2. **The discovery of Walloon** ***robett*** **'rabbit' (Wedgwood) posed the question of the Romance origin of the English word. According to OED, the path was from Flemish to Walloon and from northern France to England. A few other Romance words resemble** ***rabbit.*** Chance (1862) cited F *râble* 'back and loins of certain quadrupeds ... especially used of the rabbit and the hare' and *rabouillère* 'rabbit hole.' He tentatively compared *râble* with L *rapidus* (see Skinner, above), E *rasp*, and G *raffen* 'pile, heap' (v), so that *rabbit* emerged as a swift 'scraping (scratching)' animal (see Balliolensis, above).

Smythe Palmer (1876) mentionsed Sp *rabo* 'tail,' *rabadilla* 'scut,' and *rabón*, which he glossed 'curtal' (that is, 'horse with its tail cut short or docked'), and cited as a parallel E *bunny* from Gael *bun* 'tail.' He overlooked a case that could have reinforced his etymology, namely the history of E *coward* cognate with OF *coart* (the name of the hare in *Roman de Renart*), allegedly from a word for 'tail' (L *cauda*). OED and ODEE reject the derivation of *bunny* from *bun*.

The main part of Smythe Palmer's etymology is also weak. The Iberian word for 'tail' could not have become the basis of a late Middle English (14th century) designation of a common rodent. Unlike L *cunīculus*, probably a word of Iberian origin (the Romans learned about rabbits from the Spaniards) that developed into Sp *conejo*, with cognates elsewhere in Romance, and was later borrowed into Germanic (E *coney* ~ *cony*, Du *conijn*, G *Kaninchen*), Sp *rabo* 'tail,' Sp, Port *raposa* 'fox,' and so on had no channels for spreading to English. Yet Skeat gives Sp *rabo* 'tail, hind quarters' and *rabear* 'wag the tail' with a question mark, along with MDu *robbe*, as the possibile etymons of *rabbit*.

The origin of Sp *rabo,* Sp *raposa,* and F *râble* is unknown, but F *râble* could have yielded E *rabbit* only if French had a corresponding well-known animal name. Despite the circumstantial evidence of F *rabot* 'carpenter's plane' (allegedly called this because it looks like a rabbit lying on the ground) and *rabouillère* 'rabbit burrow,' such a name does not seem to have existed. *Rabouillère* (1534), also used as the name for a hole in which shrimp are kept, has, according to most dictionaries, the prefix *ra-*, while F reg *rabotte* 'rabbit' is probably an extension of *rabot* 'plane.' If so, then the rabbit looks like the tool, not the tool like the rabbit. (Can it be that the root of F *rabot,* a word of disputed etymology, is a reshaping of LG *rûbank* 'big plane'? Russ *rubanok* 'plane' came from Low German and among the Romance names of tools F *hache* 'hatchet' is another word of Germanic origin, from Franconian **happia.*) Nor does F *lapereau* 'young rabbit' testify to the existence of **rabbereau* (suggested in EWFS and rejected by ML, 4905). Güntert (1932:19-20) thought a connection between *rabouillère* (his *rabbouilère* is probably a misprint) and *rabbit* possible. F reg *rabote* 'toad' (? < **rainebot,* see especially Sainéan [1907:127]) has no connection with the words under discussion despite Makovskii's assurance to the contrary (1992a:121).

No one doubts that Walloon *robett* is a borrowing from Flemish, but the problem is to show how this word reached England. Whatever the origin of central French *rabotte,* the etymon of E *rabbit,* if it is a Romance word, could have been only a northern French form. Gamillscheg (1926:247) recognized the difficulty of tracing E *rabbit,* with its *a* in the root, to *robette* and referred to the rule of vocalic dissimilation that allegedly produced *rabotte* from **robotte.* However, that rule applies only to central French. Judging by the examples in OED, the earliest meaning of ME *rabet(t)* was 'small rabbit,' a word mainly associated with French cuisine. The association makes the presence of a Romance diminutive suffix in *rabbit* natural, but it does not furnish sufficient proof that the entire noun is French.

The etymon of Walloon *robett* is not an isolated word in Flemish. (Most of the facts surveyed below were known to Gamillscheg, loc cit.) Germanic makes wide use of the root *r-b* in naming animals. Fr, MDu, Fl, and G *robbe* ~ *Robbe* mean 'seal, *phoca,*' but Kilianus knew only *robbe* 'rabbit'; the Low German for 'seal' is *rubbe* (one of the variants). De Bo (*robbe*) gives *rabbe* and *robbe* 'rabbit' and comments that when rabbits are called, people say: "Ribbe, ribbe!"; see also W. de Vries (1919:297-98) on this subject. In Groningen, *rōb* and *rībe* are words used in addressing little children (Van Lessen [1928: 93, note]). A considerable number of instances when the same word designates a child and an animal have been recorded. Perhaps the best-known example is OI *kind* (f) 'child' ~ ModI *kind* 'sheep.' The playful nature of the *r-b* words is especially obvious in Dutch. *Robbeknot* turns up as a name in Bredero (1585-1616) (Van Lessen [1928:93]), and Hexham gives *robbenknol* 'a little person with a great belly' (as Charnock [1889] noted). The first element of Du *robbedoes* 'romping child, hoyden, bumpkin' is more probably derived from *robbe* 'seal' than from *robben* 'romp.' *Does* poses its own problems (NEW), but its connection with the cognates of E *dizzy* (on which see DWARF) is probable (Van der Meulen [1917:5]). ModI *robbi* means 'sheep, ram' (see further at ROBIN).

Dutch and German etymologists have long treated Du and G *robbe* ~ *Robbe* and E *rabbit* as related (see Mueller, VV, Franck, Vercoullie, KL, and NEW, among others), but the best English dictionaries remain noncommittal and only list the Walloon and Flemish words (Skeat[4]) or say "etymology uncertain" (UED) or "etymology unknown" (Weekley). French forms appear and disappear in the entries for no apparent reason. W[1] does not cite them. W[2] derives *rabbit* from OF *rabot* 'carpenter's plane,' but in W[3] the reference to the Old French word is gone. EW mentions Walloon *robett* (< Fl *robbe*) in the first edition. The second edition adds OF *rabot* 'plane, *rabbit' to *robett,* and the third edition leaves only the Old French word. According to ODEE, late ME *rabet(te)* is perhaps an adaptation of an Old French form reproduced by F reg *rabotte, rabouillet* 'young rabbit,' and *rabouillère* 'rabbit burrow,' possibly of 'Low Dutch' origin. CEDEL finds the French and the Middle Dutch origin of *rabbit* equally possible. Derocquigny (1904:75), Plate (1934:29), and De Schutter (1996:53) present the hypothesis that *rabbit* reached England from France as fact.

Since the northern French etymon of *rabbit* has not been found and since even in central French dialects *rabotte* is not a common word, the idea that E *rabbit* goes back to French looks unattractive. It is more likely that a French suffix attached itself to the Middle English root *rab-*. According to OED and ODEE, *-et* became an English formative in the 16th century, but a few examples are earlier. Especially characteristic is *strumpet,* 1327 (see STRUMPET). **An Anglo-French hybrid (Gmc *rab-* + F *-et*) is probable. Given this reconstruction, E *rabbit* will appear as an Anglo-French**

formation similar to the Walloon word rather than a borrowing from an unidentifiable dialect of Old French. *Robin* bears out the existence of the Middle English root *rab-* ~ *rob-* (see ROBIN). If *rabbit* was coined in England, the problem of *a* ~ *o* in this word (from *robbet* to *rabbit*) loses its poignancy. The alternation *a* ~ *o* after *r* is not rare (Middle English for 'rat' was *ratte*, but *rotte* occurred once too; Low German had the alteration *rat* ~ *ratte* ~ *rot;* see also the Scandinavian examples, above, and at HEIFER, sec 4); therefore, it is not necessary to set up ME **robett* or compare *rabbit* and ME *rabbet* ~ *rabit* 'Arabian horse' (Skeat[4]) to account for *a* from *o*.

The root *r-b* is sometimes said to be akin to LG *rubben* 'rub' (the supposed etymon of E *rub*, ModI *rubla* 'rub,' Sw *rubba* 'move, shift,' Dan and N *rubbe* 'scrape, scratch'), EFr *rubben* 'rough,' and LG *rubbelig* ~ *rubberig* 'uneven, rugged' (FT, *rubbe*; Carnoy [1955:121, *kun-iko*]), as well as OE *rēofan* ~ OI *rjúfa* 'reave, break.' EWDS[11] asserts that G *Robbe* 'seal' is related to *Raupe* 'caterpillar,' both allegedly from **rūb* 'bristly' (so beginning with the eleventh edition, Kluge-Götze). NEW (*rups*) expresses doubts about the connection between *Robbe* ~ *Raupe* and points out that not all caterpillars are hairy. Van Lessen (1928:93) finds it incredible that a seal, an animal with especially smooth hair, should have been called bristly (the same is true of rabbits and sheep).

An older etymology of *Raupe* emphasized its similarity with Russ *ryba* 'fish' (nearly the same form in the other Slavic languages), definitely not a hairy or bristly creature, the end result of this etymology being the reconstruction of the protomeaning *'worm.' Wood (1920:238/98) gives *Raupe, Robbe,* and *ryba* under one heading. Du *rups* 'caterpillar,' with its variants *risp(e)* and *rips,* is even more obscure than G *Raupe* (see W. de Vries [1919:299-300] and NEW, among others). Boutkan and Kossmann (1998) offer the most detailed discussion of *Raupe* ~ *rups* (with the conclusion that it is a substrate word). De Vaan (2000) rejects their conclusion and traces both words to a verb meaning 'pick, pluck, strip' (Go *raupjan* and its cognates). Seebold (KS) retained Götze's etymology but noted that the word for 'bristles,' presumably represented by *Robbe* 'seal' and *robbe(ken)* 'rabbit,' had been postulated on the evidence of *Raupe* rather than attested.

Van Lessen (1928:93) tried to explain *rob* 'seal' from *robben* (v), a late doublet of *ravotten* 'romp,' but that verb cannot account for the existence of *r-b* words outside Dutch. Van Wijk (EWNT[2], *rob*) does not support the idea that *rob* is a 'romper,' yet NEW looks on it as worthy of consideration. Ties between G *Raupe*, Du *rups*, LG *rubben*, E *rub*, Du *rubbelig* and the root *r-b* do not go far enough to assign the meaning 'hairy,' let alone 'bristly,' to it. *Raupe* and possibly *rups* had a long vowel in the older periods and cannot be related to G *Robbe*, Russ *ryba*, or E *rabbit*. The root before us lacks a remote etymology, and all its semantic depth is on the surface. It does not, in principle, differ from G reg *boppi* 'fat dog,' N reg *tobba* 'mare' (Wood [1920/91 and 176], OFr *bobba-*, ME *babi* 'baby,' and a host of others of the same type.

3. The Germanic words having the structure *r-b* resemble many Eurasian names of the fox, such as Sp and Port *raposa*. Etymological dictionaries give them due attention (see also Huss [1935:204-07] and Reinisch's daring comparison of Skt *lopāśáḥ* with the root of *lynx* in Indo-European and African languages [1873:151]). Of apparently the same origin is Finn *repo*, with cognates in the other Finno-Ugric languages (see *refr* in AEW and Rédei [1986:46/18]). In Germanic, only Scandinavian has such a word: OI *refr* (Dan *ræv*, Sw *räv*, N *rev*); the expressive variants of ModI *refur* are *rebbi* and *rebbali* (ÁBM). Whether they go back to the color name 'red' (Much [1901-02:285], Frisk [1931:99]) cannot be decided. Brøndal (1929:10-11, 13, 27) looked for the etymon of this migratory word in some Sarmatian languages. However, when people begin to call animals *kobbi, robbei, tobbai, boppi* and call the flea and the spider *coppe* or *loppe*, or *noppe* (see EFr –LG?- *noppe* in Holthausen [1924: 115]; it is not in Ten Doornkaat Koolman), coincidences are bound to arise in languages that have never been in contact. Skt *lopāśáḥ*, Sp *raposa*, Finn *repo*, OI *refr*, and others may go back to different etymons and their similarity may be due to chance. If a migratory word that originated somewhere in ancient Iranian had reached Germanic, it would hardly have survived only in Scandinavian.

OIr *robb* 'body,' recorded in the forms *rop* and *rap*, has no accepted etymology (related to L *rupe* 'fat man; slab'? LE). In Modern Irish, *rap* is 'any creature that draws its food towards it' (O'Reilly's gloss). Only Balliolensis compared Ir *rap* and E *rabbit* (see *robb, rop* 'animal' and *robb* 'body' in CDIL). LE (*robb*) admits the possibility of an expressive formation. WP II:354-55 derives MI *robb* from **reub-*, as in E *rip*; IEW (869) gives that etymology with a question mark.

Essays on the origin of the rabbit's name in the Baltic and Romance languages (see especially Güntert [1932:12-13] and Hubschmid [1943]) show that the feature people choose for naming this animal is almost unpredictable. The 77 names invented for a hare in a 13th-century English poem (they are all terms of abuse: A. Ross [1932]) bear additional testimony to human resourcefulness in this area. Rabbits were well known in the British Isles by the year 1200, but the word *rabbit* surfaced two centuries later. Most likely, speakers of English coined many words for the new animal. They are all lost, while *rabbit* has survived. The sound complex *r-b* in the name of the rabbit has no parallels outside Germanic.

4. A popular etymology traces *rabbit* to the name *Robert.* This is how CD explains not only *rabbit* but also the entire Germanic group (G *Robbe* and the rest); it also compares *rabbit* and *robin*. Such a hypothesis fails even for *robin,* but it would be a minor miracle if speakers of Dutch, Flemish, English, German, and Icelandic chose the same proper name for deriving the name of the seal, the rabbit, and the sheep. The etymology from CD turns up in W², UED, Partridge (1958), CEDEL, and in books and articles for the general reader (for example, L. Smith [1926:214] and Espy [1978:199, 201]). Weekley, who derives *rabbit* from *Robert,* cites the last name *Rabbetts* and the custom of calling rabbits *Robert* in Devon. Neither fact makes his idea convincing. *Rabbetts* itself needs an etymology, and the tie between *rabbit* and *Robert* in Devon is secondary (compare the form of Russ *petukh* 'rooster,' stress on the second syllable, from *pet'* 'sing,' which induced that bird to be called *Petia,* diminutive of *Petr,* in Russian folklore). Weekley (1933:130) does not repeat his old derivation. The last name *Rabbett* (*Rabet, Rabbitt, Rabut*) may perhaps go back to *rabbit.* Someone called Mr. Rabbit, regardless of the spelling, would look less conspicuous than Mr. Heifer, Hound, Panther, and even Mr. Cattle, Kine, and Oxen (Lower [1875:I, 187]; H. Harrison).

The association of *Rabbet* with the animal name may be old (Ewen [1931:332]), but other possibilities also exist: from **radbod ~ *rædbod,* which H. Harrison glosses as 'swift messenger' (he means OE **rædboda*), from OE **rǣdbodo* 'counsel messenger' (RW, *rādbodo,* but *rādbodo* may have meant only 'travel messenger'), or from *Robert* (E. Smith [1969:289]; Cottle). Charnock's *rat-brecht* 'distinguished for counsel' (= *rǣd-breht?*) (1868) resembles **hrædboda ~ rǣdbodo*; however, it enabled him to explain *Rabbett, Radbod, Redpath, Ratpet,* and *Ratperth* in one fell swoop. E. Smith (1969:289) mentions *(Little) Rab,* a hypocoristic form of *raven* (OE *hræfn*). Some of those conjectures, with their recurring references to "Old German," are guesswork by people without sufficient schooling in the history of English. Weekley (1937) preferred not to discuss the etymology of the last name *Rabbett.*

5. The old vulgarism *(d)rabbit* 'darn it' (for example, *rabbit the child! drabbit the girl!*) was first traced to F *rabattre* 'beat down' (Addis [1868], F.C.H. [1868]; Skeat [1868] = Skeat [1896/39]). Its variant *rat it!, drat it* (Tew [1868]) may have been due to *rat* substituted for *rabbit,* but Skeat (loc cit) and J. C. M. (1868) derived *drat it* from *drot it* < **'od rot it* 'God rot it.' OED denies *(d)rabbit* an etymology of its own and explains it as a possible fanciful alternation of *drat*. Cohen's conjecture (1987:4) that *drat* became *drabbit* for euphemistic reasons or because of "the seaman's superstition that rabbits bring bad luck" needs further substantiation.

OED compares *Welsh rabbit* (1725) 'dish of toasted cheese' with *Scotch rabbit* (1743; the same meaning?) and *capon,* a name humorously applied to various fish, for instance, *capon = dried haddock.* Such names are not uncommon. Among them are *Irish lemons* or *Irish apricots* 'potatoes,' *Essex lion* 'calf' and locally 'veal dish' (Tylor [1874:505]; T. R. [1945]), *Arkansas chicken* 'salt pork,' *Cape Cod turkey* 'salt codfish' (J. Carr [1907:183]), *Kansas City fish* = Arkansas chicken (Babcock [1950:139]), *Gourock hens* or *Norfolk capons* 'red herrings,' and *Gravesend sweetmeats* 'shrimps.' B. Chapman (1947:258) says: "The Welsh were supposed to be so poverty-stricken they could not afford even rabbit meat but had to substitute cheese for it." This sounds like an ad hoc explanation.

The joke resolves itself into giving something cheap and unappetizing the name of an expensive dainty. However, *Welsh rabbit* does not duplicate the usual juxtaposition of two types of meat ~ fish ~ fowl (pork ~ chicken, fish ~ turkey ~ game ~ cheese). EB (*rabbit*) gives better parallels: *prarie oyster* 'the yolk of an egg with vinegar, pepper, &c added' and Scotch *woodcock* 'a savory of buttered eggs on anchovy toast.' It contends that "the alteration to Welsh rare-bit is due to a failure to see the joke as it is." Indeed, the allusion has never been clear. See a few more examples in anonymous (1889a:50). Consider Rees's (1987:219) lighthearted remark with regard to *Welsh rabbit*: "Well, Bombay duck is a fish and mock-turtle soup has nothing to do with turtle."

The use of the words *hare* and *rabbit* is not unusual in this kind of travesty. Pennsylvania Dutch *Paanhaas* (that is, 'panhare') means 'maize flour boiled in the metzel soup, afterward fried and seasoned like a hare' (Chamberlain [1889], with reference to Haldeman [1872:20]), and Ashkenazic Russ *fal'shivyi zaiats* (that is, 'false hare') is a dish of roast and egg. Popular books and some dictionaries explain *Welsh rabbit* (1785) as folk etymology of *Welsh rarebit*, but as OED states, no evidence points to the independent existence of *rarebit*. In Fowler's words (1965:651), *Welsh rabbit* is amusing and right, and *Welsh rarebit* stupid and wrong (Liberman [1997:108-17]).

RAGAMUFFIN (1344)

Ragamuffin *first appeared in texts as one of the medieval names of the Devil. It is a compound, and the origin of each of its parts is problematic. Etymologizing only* rag- *and dismissing* -amuffin *as a fanciful ending leaves this word without a reconstructed past. In all probability,* ragamuffin *has a connecting element* (rag-a-muffin) *and is thus an extended form like* cockney *from* cock-e-nei. *The most convincing hypothesis traces both* rag- *and* -muffin *to words for 'devil,' as in OF* Rogomant *(though in French it may have been a borrowing from Germanic), preserved in E* Ragman *and* Ragman's roll (> rigmarole), *and* Old Muffy, *from AF* maufé *'ugly; the Evil One.'* Ragamuffin *is then a semantic reduplication with an augment (*-a-*) in the middle, *'devil-a-devil.' An association with rags is late and due to folk etymology.*

The proposed derivation of ragamuffin *finds partial confirmation in the history of* hobbledehoy. *Both* ragamuffin *and* hobbledehoy *were first names of the Devil. The meaning of both has changed to 'ragged man' (often 'ragged urchin') and 'hobbling (awkward) youth' respectively, and both are extended forms, though with different augments.*

The sections are devoted to 1) rag- *'devil,' 2)* -muffin *as a reflex of one of the Devil's names, 3) the role of* -a- *in* ragamuffin *and in similar words, and 4) a brief comparison of* ragamuffin *and* hobbledehoy.

1. **It has been known for a long time that in Langland's *Piers Plowman,* 1393** (c, XXI:183, Skeat's edition, 1886, vol 1) **a devil called Ragamoffin is mentioned**. OED quotes the relevant passage. According to MED, the name *Isabella Ragamoffyn* occurred in 1344. For two centuries *ragamuffin* (with any spelling) did not appear in written documents. Its uninterrupted history goes back to 1581. OED says the following about its origin: "[P]rob[ably] from RAG *sb.*[1] (cf. RAGGED 1c), with fanciful ending." The second part of *ragabush* 'worthless person' (now chiefly regional) is also said to contain a fanciful ending added to *rag*. **The concept of the fanciful ending does not make sense when applied to sound strings like *-amuffin* and *-abush*.** Shipley (1945, *ragamuffin*) adds *-mudgeon* in *curmudgeon* (on which see MOOCH, sec 5) and *-scallion* in *rapscallion* to the list of such misbegotten creations. Whatever the origin of *ragamuffin,* its present day sense was influenced by *rag,* but it does not follow that the first ragamuffin was ragged or wore rags.

The entry *Ragman* 'devil' in OED contains a passing remark: "cf. RAGAMUFFIN, RAGGED, Sw[edish] *ragg-en* ['devil']." In the entry *ragged,* several examples make it clear that the Devil was often portrayed as having a ragged appearance. Sw *raggen* can be understood as 'the shaggy (hairy) one,' a tempting interpretation in light of the material from Middle English in OED, or as 'the evil one' (*rag* is also a metathesized form of Sw *arg* 'evil, wicked'). Hellquist preferred the second alternative, while OED took the first one for granted. Spitzer (1947:91) derived *rageman* (this is Langland's spelling) from French. The idea that *Ragemon (le bon)* and *Rogomant* were folk etymologized into *rageman* ~ *Rageman* carries more conviction than that *raggen* was borrowed from Swedish, because Sw *raggen* is a word unrecorded in the other Scandinavian languages. On *Rageman* see also *rigmarole* in English etymological dictionaries.

The French origin of *ragman* and *ragamuffin* was suggested (for the first time?) by anonymous (1822b:618), but neither Spitzer nor his predecessors succeeded in discovering the ultimate etymon of the French name, which may have been Germanic, especially if an old attempt to connect E *rag* and Ital *ragazzo* 'boy, youth' is not dismissed out of hand (then *ragazzo* would come out as 'little devil,' not 'person in rags': Liberman [2006:197-98]). Probably no other word of Italian has been discussed so often with such meager results.

The Germanic root **rag-* 'fury' is probable: compare Du reg *raggen* 'run around in a state of wild excitement' (*lopen en raggen* has the same meaning), alternating with Du reg *rakken* (Weijnen [1939-40]: detailed discussion without a definitive etymology). Sw *rag(g)la* 'wobble,' and ModI *ragla* 'wander about' may belong with the Dutch verb, but the chances are not so good, because the meanings—'move in violent agitation' and 'wander aimlessly, move unsteadily'—do not match. The nasalized forms (N *rangle,* and so forth), except for late MHG *ranzen* 'jump violently' (FT, *rangle* and *rage* III; ÁBM, *ragla*; KS, *Range* and *ranzen*), are synonymous with *ragla*.

If such a root existed, it need not have been identical with **arg-* 'copulate' (said about animals), though their derivatives were partly synonymous in various languages and though one could develop from the other by metathesis, as happened in Old Norse. (Can E *rag* 'scold' be of similar origin and can G *regen* 'stir' be related to this **ragen* rather than G *ragen* 'rise, tower, jut out'?) A pagan divinity called Rageman, someone like the Old English *Herla cyning* 'King Herla,' is not unthinkable (cf *Wōdan* from **wōð-* 'fury,' as in G *Wut*). The same name of the Devil seems to have been known in the Baltic languages: Lithuanian *rãgana* and Latvian *ragana* mean 'witch' (another much-discussed word; see, for example, Otkupshchikov [1977]).

2. Conjectures on the etymology of *-muffin* have been inconclusive: from Sp *mofar* 'mock' or Ital *muffo* 'musty' (W 1828 and in all the editions until 1864), from G reg *muffen* 'smell musty' (W 1864; the same until 1890), from Gael *maoidh* 'threaten' (Mackay [1877]; Mackay, who derived hundreds of words of European languages from Gaelic, combined Gael *ragair* 'thief, villain' with *maoidh,* so that *ragamuffin* turned out to be 'dangerous scoundrel'), and from E *muff* 'stupid, clumsy person' (thus UED, which only "compares" *-muffin* with *muff*).

John Ker traced numerous English words to nonexistent Dutch phrases, and his derivations are among the most ludicrous in the history of English etymology. He derived *ragamuffin* from *rag er moffin* 'poverty shews itself in that countenance.' "Literally, the *Westphalian* boor predominates in his person. *Mof* is the nickname of the Westphalian labourer.... The word *mof* is founded in the thema *mo-en,* in the import of, to cut, *to mow;* and the term means strictly, *a mower.... Moffin* is *the female* of this class.... And I have no doubts our term muffin is the ellipsis of *moffincoeck,* the pastry of the *muffin* who cries it, as that which she is employed to carry about to dispose of" (Ker 1837:I, 89). His gloss of *rag er moffin* 'may it show' goes back (as he says) to the Dutch or German verb *ragen* 'project' in the subjunctive and *er* 'there.' With Ker we are pushed to the edge of normalcy, but in a small way he was vindicated: the nickname *mof* turns up in Mueller[2] and UED (*ragamuffin*), and *rag-* may be akin to the verb *ragen,* though not the one he meant.

Richardson thought of *ragabash* and *raggabrash* as "a corruption of *ragged* (or perhaps *rakell* ['profligate']) rubbish," but "of *ragamuffin,*" he says, "the examples found have afforded no clue to the true origin." Mueller[2] cites G *muffen* 'smell musty, moldy' and E *muff* 'stupid fellow' (the same word as in Ker). He mentions *Ragamofin,* the name of a demon in some of the old mysteries, and of all English etymologists he seems to be the only one to suggest a tie between E *ragamuffin* and Ital *ragazzo* 'boy.' ID (1850) follows Webster but also offers a possible derivation from *rag* and obsolete *mof, muff* 'long sleeve.'

In Spitzer's opinion (1947:93), *ragamuffin* goes back to F "**Rogom-oufl[l]e* or **Ragam-oufl[l]e,* which must be a blend of *Ragemon* 'devil,' and such words as OF [sic] *ruffien* of the fourteenth century... or F *maroufle* ['scoundrel']; again, it could even be a coinage from the *ragemon* stem formed with the OF suffix *-oufl[le],* like *maroufle* itself.... The idea of 'ragged' appears in *ragamuffin* only as late as 1440, and is consequently quite secondary." Spitzer adds that *ragamuffin* still means a (ragged) street urchin and that perhaps 'street urchin' was the original meaning, whence an association with 'devil, demon, imp, heathen.'

W (1890) leaves *ragamuffin* without any etymology and mentions only the name of Langland's demon. For a long time dictionaries have followed this example. Only Wyld (UED) risked a tentative comparison of *-muffin* with *muff,* which he may have found independently of his predecessors or in Mueller[2] (for no one read Ker). Skeat did not include *ragamuffin* in his dictionary, but in his edition of *Piers Plowman* (1886:II, 257, note on line 283) he wrote: "Mr. Halliwell... remarks that *Ragamofin* is a name of a demon in some of the old mysteries. It has since passed into a sort of familiar slang term for any one poorly clad. The demons, it may be observed, took the comic parts in the old mysteries, and were therefore sometimes fitted with odd names." However, E. Stanley (1968:110) points out in his comment on Halliwell's statement that there is no existence for the use of *Ragamofin* in old medieval plays.

Against this background, the entry in AHD[3,4] is all the more surprising. It traces *-muffin* to MDu *moffel* ~ *muff* 'mitten' (is a bahuvrihi of the *Redcap* type meant: *Ragamuffin* = *ragmitten* or *ragged mitten?*). The entry has a supplementary word history in which we read that the discovery of the name *Isabella Ragamoffyn* disproves the current derivation of *ragamuffin* from a devil's name. But *ragamuffin* has always been understood as a vague continuation rather than a reflex of *ragamoffyn* in *Piers Plowman.* Apparently, the woman in question had the character that earned her the unusual soubriquet.

Some of the conjectures listed above can be ruled out by definition. **An English compound need not have an element straight from Spanish, Italian, German, Gaelic, or Middle Dutch**. One can look for English cognates of these words, but E *-muffin* has not been recorded (*muffin* 'cake' became known in the 18th century and has always meant what it means now). Spitzer's etymology is learned but too speculative. E *muff,* which Mueller and Wyld cite, first occurs in Dickens in 1837, and this must have been the time it gained currency in the streets of London. It has no ancestors, except *muff* 'deprecatory term of a German or Swiss, sometimes loosely applied to other foreigners,' which does not occur in extant texts after 1697. Du *muff* 'lout' (< *mof,* originally the same meaning as in E *muff*) and G *Muffel* were recorded much later than *ragamuffin*. Even if their history were less opaque, their late attestation and the absence of cognates in Middle English make a connection with *ragamuffin* improbable. However, *muff* may have been an import from the continent.

A seemingly correct etymology of *-muffin* can be deduced from the information in an article by Smythe Palmer. He read Prevost (1905) and noted the phrase *Auld Muffy* used by the older dalesmen for the Devil. As he observes: "The expression is now but seldom heard, and in a few years, probably it will be as extinct as the dodo." Muffy is AF *maufé* 'ugly, ill-featured,' "which was once synonymous with the Evil One," a creature "notoriously hideous and deformed"; cf *Satan le maufé* (Smythe Palmer [1910:545-46]; additional details on p. 546). E reg *muffy* 'hermaphrodite' is said to be an alteration of *morfrodite,* but if Old Muffy was known more widely in the past, the two words may have interacted. See the supplement to DWARF on hermaphrodites, and Prescott (1995) on *muffy*.

Both components of *ragamuffin* seem to mean 'devil'. Only the origin of final *-n* is not quite clear, but so many nouns ended in *-an, -en* (like *guardian, warden,* and formations of the *slabberdegullion* and *tatterdemal(l)ion* type) that **ragamauffi* could easily have become **ragamauffi(an)*. Note that the earliest spelling is *ragamoffyn* (with *o* for F *au?*) and that Shakespeare has *rag of Muffin* or *rag of Muffian* in *1Henry IV*, IV, iii:272.

3. Words with unetymological *-a-* are discussed in some detail at COCKNEY. In Middle and Modern English, intrusive *-a-* has more than one source. When the connecting schwa occurs in French words like *vis-à-vis* and *cap-à-pie,* it is a preposition. In the native vocabulary, *-a-* is a reduced form of *on* or *of,* as in *twice a day, cat-o'-nine-tails, man-o'-war, Tam o'Shanter*. But when a model establishes itself, new formations arise and neologisms begin to be cast in the same predictable mold. *Tam o'Shanter* was *Tam Shanter* in Burns's poems and acquired its *o'* on the analogy of *John o'Groats* and so forth. *Fustianapes* is an allegro form of *fustian of Naples*, but *jackanapes* developed from *Jac(k) Napes*, not **Jack on* or *of Naples*, and *Jack-a-dandy* never was **Jack of* or *on dandy*. *Will with the wisp* forfeited its *with the* (*o'* substituted for them), and in a similar way the older form of *lack-a-day*, the basis of *lackadaisical,* was *alack the day* (see these words in OED and ODEE).

The origin of many words with *-a-* will of necessity remain obscure, which does not mean that they should be given up as hopeless. ODEE states that *a* in *Blackamoor* (< *black More*) is unexplained. The comment in OED is longer: "Of the connecting *a* no satisfactory explanation has been offered. The suggestion that it was a retention of the final *-e* of ME *black-e* (obs[olete] in prose before 1400) is, in the present state of evidence, at variance with the phonetic history of the language, and the analogy of other *black-* compounds. Cf. *black-a-vised*." In the entry *black-a-vised* 'dark-complexioned' (first recorded in 1758, over two centuries later than *black-a-moor*), we read: "... perh[aps] originally *black-a-vis* or *black o' vis*; but this is uncertain." *Black-a-top* 'black-headed' (a single 1773 citation) is left without an etymology.

ODEE says that the first element of *caterwaul* is perhaps related to or borrowed from LG or Du *kater* 'male cat,' unless *-er-* "is merely an arbitrary connective syll[able]"; we recognize here a paraphrase of "some kind of suffix or connective merely" (OED). Neither Murray nor Onions realized that *cat-er-waul* (= *cat-a-waul?*) is not an isolated example. It is unprofitable to label insertions as merely arbitrary connective syllables or some kind of suffix. CD calls *-a-* in *black-a-moor* and *jack-a-dandy* a meaningless syllable. This is true enough but not particularly illuminating.

Cock-e-ney is the earliest certain recorded extended form with schwa, and the 14th century must have been approximately the time when such words arose. Unstressed *i* was also drawn into the process of coining extended *-a-* forms. *Cock-a-leekie* has a doublet *cockie-leekie*, though *ie* in *cockie* is not a suffix. A similar case is *piggyback* 'carry on one's shoulders,' from *pickaback*. According to Skeat, *huckaback* 'coarse durable linen' (earlier *hugaback* and *hag-a-bag*) is the English pronunciation of LG *huckebak* 'pick-a-back': at one time, it presumably designated a pedlar's ware, but the evidence is lacking, and OED says "origin unknown." If Skeat guessed well, *huckaback* is a close analogue of *pickaback* ~ *piggyback*. Kück's note on the Low German word (1905:14-15) supports Skeat's etymology.

Assuming that the reconstruction given here is correct and *ragamuffin* (1344) is a tautological extended form with the initial meaning *'devil-a-devil,' we will obtain a word of this type whose attestation slightly predates *cockney* < *cockeney*

(1362). It will emerge as a coinage not unlike *muck-a-muck* 'person of distinction.' Some confirmation of the proposed etymology comes from the history of *hobbledehoy*, arguably another extended form of similar structure and meaning. See HOBBLEDEHOY, SKEDADDLE (on extended forms) and SLOWWORM (on tautological compounds).

4. **Both *ragamuffin* and *hobbledehoy* seem to have been coined as the names of fiends (devils, sprites). Their original meanings are now forgotten, but the negative connotations they once possessed have survived.** *Ragamuffin* is a word that can be applied to a person of any age, though perhaps more often to a youngster (see Spitzer's remarks above), as in the title of James Greenwood's novel *The True History of a Little Ragamuffin*. The definition in AHD runs as follows: '[a] dirty or unkempt child.' RHD says: "1. a ragged, disreputable person; tatterdemalion. 2. a child in ragged, ill-fitting, dirty clothes." OED found it necessary to gloss ragamuffin "a ragged, dirty, disreputable man *or boy*" (italics added). King Rag(e)man, Auld Maufi, and King Robert were full-grown devils, but the loss of status resulted in their loss of stature. In *boy*, a baby word for 'brother' and a word for 'devil' have merged; its case is reminiscent of both *ragamuffin* and *hobbledehoy*. In Middle English, *boy* may have meant 'executioner,' and *ragman* 'hangman's assistant' has also been recorded. The proper name *Boy(e)* was current several centuries before the common name turned up in texts for the first time (see the details at BOY), and this is what happened to *ragamuffin* and presumably to *hobbledehoy*. *Rag-a-muffin* and *hobble-de-hoy* have not only had a similar semantic history; both are extended forms, though with different augments. (Liberman [2004b:97-100; 2006:191-200]).

ROBIN (1549)

The common name robin *is usually understood as* Robin *extended to a bird, but it is possibly an animal name with the structure* r + vowel + b + *diminutive suffix.*

The sections are devoted to 1) the alleged ties between robin *and* Robert *and the suffix -in, 2) robin as one of many words with the root* r-b, *notably in superstitions, and 3) the phrase* round robin.

1. Robin 'Robin redbreast, *Erithacus rubecula,*' originally a Scots word, has cognates in Dutch (*robijntje*) and Frisian (*robyntsje* and *robynderke* 'linnet'; WNT). Several other red birds and plants are also called robin in English. The older dictionaries, beginning with Skinner's, derived *robin* from L *rubecula*. This derivation cannot explain why a borrowing from Latin appeared in English so late and in such a changed form. E *redbreast* (1401) is a compound of the same type as G *Rotkelchen* (literally 'little red neck') and ModI *rauðbrystingur*. The recorded hybrids *robynet redbreast* and *Robyn redbreast* go back to 1425 and 1451. With time, the second part was shed, and *robin* became the regular name of the bird.

Richardson may have been the first to suggest a connection between *robin* and the proper name *Robin*, with reference to other animals called *Tom, Jack,* and so on. Wedgwood[1] explained *robin* as a familiar use of *Robin* on the analogy of *magpie* (< *Mag* + *pie*) and *parrot* (< *Pierrot*). Chambers, Skeat, and OED accepted Richardson's etymology, and most modern dictionaries, including Lockwood's (1984), repeat it. In later lexicography, only Charnock traced *robin* to L *rōbus* 'red.' Those who call into question the recognized etymology offer no improvement. When *wren, daw,* and *pie* developed the variants *Jenny wren* (1648), *jackdaw* (1543), and *magpie* (1605), they did not, except in idiosyncratic usage, become *jenny, jack,* and *mag*. The same is true of many other animal names of the *jackass* type; only *robin redbreast* allegedly did without the second element.

An older name of the robin redbreast was *ruddock* (< OE *rudduc*, 1100, a gloss on L *rubisca*). OE *salthaga* 'one good at hopping' may have designated the same bird. Palander (1905:126-27) suggested that *robin* is a folk etymological variant of OF *rubienne* 'robin redbreast' and referred to the popularity of the name *Robin* in England after the conquest (William's eldest son was called *Robin*). The difficulty with his suggestion is that E *robin* emerged only in the 16th century. A much earlier date could be expected if *robin* went back to an Old French word.

Although Greenough and Kittredge (1901:130) say that "[r]obin is of course a diminutive of Robert," this is only a guess (otherwise they would not have said *of course*). No evidence supports it: all we have are ingenious arguments explaining why this particular bird was named *robin* from *Robin* (S. Levin [1976]). Another guess, which H. Allen (1936:919) partly anticipated, may be worth a try. In the discussion of cub (see CUB), the sound strings *kab-, kob-, keb-,* and *kib-* were shown to have produced a variety of animal names. *Rob-* ~ *rab-* ~ *rib-* follow a similar pattern. The Dutch and Frisian forms (see them above) suggest that *robin* is one of such words. Like *ruddock* (that is, *rudd-ock*), *robin* has a diminutive suffix.

OED and ODEE mention the suffix *-en* (as in *kitten, chicken,* and ME *ticchen* 'kid') but not *-in*. Yet

-in is not identical with *-en*, and it turns up in some words, more often in dialects. The nuthatch is called *jobbin* because it is a jobbing bird (*job*, v, 'strike with a sharp bill'); *jobbin* is either a variant of *jobbing* or a formation like *robin* (OED cites only *nutjobber*, but see Swainson [1886:35, *nuthatch*] and Lockwood [1984, *nut jobber*]). *Hoggin* 'screened or sifted ground' (1861) may be the same word as *hogging* (OED), but it has the appearance of *hog* + *in*, even though the connection with *hog* is unclear.

The merger of *-in* with *-ing* in regional and colloquial use increased the number of words with *-in*. The history of *biffin* 'variety of apple' (< *beefing*) is typical. In Cheshire, *buggin* means 'louse' (see EDD and OED, at *bug*[2] 'insect,' end of the etymological introduction). *Dobbin* 'horse' (1596) is a diminutive of *Dob*. *Piggin* (1554) is a small pail; it seems to be a diminutive of *pig* 'pot, pitcher, *etc*.' *Pig* 'vessel' without a suffix matches *hogshead* 'large cask.' *Noggin* (1630) 'small drinking vessel' belongs with *piggin*. Unlike *bobbin* (1530), none of the words given above has been borrowed from French, but a bobbin 'reel, spool' is also a small object. In dialectal glossaries, one regularly runs into such words as *nedlins* ~ *netlins* 'small intestines of a pig' (anonymous [1935: 178] and Bagg [1935:208]; it is probably the same word as *nudlens* (< *noodle*) in Baskett [1920:100/113D1]). The diminutive suffix *-in* was at one time productive in dialects and competed with its near double *-en*. To the extent that the first recordings reflect the dates of words' appearance in language, *robin* (1549) falls roughly into the same period as *bobbin, piggin,* and *noggin* (1530-1630), but judging by *robinet* (1425), it must have existed long before the middle of the 16th century.

2. At a time when the sound strings *cob* and *cub* were used as the names of horses, whelps, fishes, and sea-gulls, and *rabb-* ~ *robb-* ousted the old names of the seal and the cony in Germany, England, and elsewhere, the 'generic' syllable *rob-* with a diminutive suffix could as easily have ousted *ruddock*. *Rabbit*, too, has a diminutive suffix (see more at RABBIT). *Robin ruddock* can be interpreted as a hybrid form that appeared before the change had been completed. Finally, if *robin* is from *Robin*, the question remains how Frisian and Dutch got the same bird name. One would have to posit a borrowing by all three languages from French (S. Levin [1976:130]), but what was so attractive in the French name? *Robin*, like *cob*, designates various fishes (the earliest citation in OED is dated 1618; see *robin* and *Round Robin*[6]). One of the north English words for 'earwig' is *forkin-robin*, that is, 'robin with a little fork.' E. Adams (1858:99) glosses *forkin-robin* from the dialect of the Isle of Wight as *straddle-bob*. He is right in doubting "whether this *bob* is the contraction of Robert," for *bob* is a usual second component in the names of insects and the like.

In Old French, sheep were often called *Robin* (Weekley [1933:130]). The Vikings may have brought this name to France from their historical homes, and its origin in the Scandinavian languages is not far to seek: ModI *robbi* means 'sheep, ram.' It was recorded only in the 19th century, but it is probably old. ÁBM compares it with Nynorsk *robbe* (m) 'bugaboo,' G *Robbe* 'seal,' and so forth. NEO offers only insignificant conjectures about Nynorsk *robbe* and mentions its synonym *bobbe*. Another ModI *robbi* means 'the male of the white partridge.' ÁBM thinks that it is a pet name for *rjúpkerri* or *rjúpkarri*, or *ropkarri* (the same meaning), but a tie between *robbi* and *rjúp-* ~ *rop-* may be an illusion, as is the case with OI *kobbi*, allegedly a pet name for *kópr* (see CUB) and with *robin* taken to be the same word as *Robin*. In medieval Scandinavia, where the personal name *Robin* had no currency (Lind 1905-15:857), the sound complex *rob(b)* was used as in the rest of the Germanic speaking world.

Nynorsk *robbe* 'bugaboo' explains E *Roblet* 'goblin leading persons astray in the dark' (obsolete and rare), which OED connects with *Robinet*, once used as the name of a goblin. Such a connection exists, but only via the meaning preserved by Nynorsk *robbe*, a word that may throw a sidelight on Robin Goodfellow. This character was especially well known in the 16th and 17th centuries, when the word *robin* also gained ground in English (*good* is a euphemism for *evil*), though Robin Goodfellow is hard to separate from the German Knecht Ruprecht, St. Nicholas's companion (*Ruprecht* < *Rupert* < *Ruodperht*, the Old High German etymon of F *Robert*; Güntert [1919:76, note, and 124]), and from *hobgoblin* (or *Hob Goblin* = *Rob Goblin*) and *hobbledehoy* (see more on *hob* ~ *rob* at HOBBLEDEHOY). *Robin* occupied a special place in folklore (Höfler [1934:48-49] and H. Allen [1936]). F *rabouin* 'devil' may belong here (Barbier [1932-35:117-18]).

3. The phrase *round robin* was first recorded in 1536 (Hooper [1897]). At that time, it was applied facetiously to a sacramental wafer and apparently meant 'piece of bread' or 'cookie,' which corresponds to *round robin* 'small pancake' (Devon). Chance (1897:131, and note) believed that *robin* here is a specific use of the name *Robin*, like *Jack* in *flapjack*, another provincial name of a pancake. E.

Marshall (1897) mentions 'robin rolls' sold in Oxford shops. Assuming that a baker named Robin was the originator of some such dainty, we could have let *round robin* join *charlotte* in our etymological dictionaries if the phrase *round robin* 'petition with signatures arranged in circle' were not to be accounted for. F. Adams (1896 and 1897; see the reference in F. Adams [1897:177, note]) gives a 1659 example of *round robin* in this sense. It appears that round robins had their origin in the navy. James included *round robin* in his dictionary (at *round*) with the following explanation: "[A] corruption of *Ruban rond*, which signifies a round ribbon." Todd (in Johnson-Todd) reprinted that explanation (only he substituted *riband* for *ribbon*); Smythe Palmer (1883) and other dictionaries copied his information. Webster had the same explanation until 1864; Mahn (in W [1864]) left *round robin* without any etymology. W (1880) restored the old etymology ("perh[aps] fr[om] Fr[ench] *rond + ruban*"), and there it stayed until it was again removed in 1961 (W^3).

Since F *ruban rond* should have become E *robin round*, some lexicographers (including Ogilvie: ID) produced the spurious source *rond ruban* or resorted to diplomatic formulations like Webster's (1880). The *ruban rond* ~ *rond ruban* theory can be dismissed because of the difficulties with the word order and because French dictionaries do not cite such an expression (F. Adams [1896:392]). If the phrase **ruband rond* had any currency among French officers at the end of the 18th century, it must have existed as an adaptation of E *round robin* refashioned after *ruban rouge, ruban bleu* (ribbons for orders), and the like. F. Adams (loc cit) attempted to connect *robin* in *round robin* and *roband* 'short length of rope yarn or cord for lashing sails to yards,' formerly called *robbin* or *robin* (see *ruband, roband, robbin, ribband,* and *ribbon* in OED). But **round roband* (that is, 'round ribbon') 'loop' is fiction. Despite the uncertainty (see Hooper [1897]), it is better not to separate *round robin* 'pancake' (or 'cookie') from *round robin* 'circular petition.' The technical senses 'hood' and so forth (Chance [1897]) reinforce the idea that **a round robin is simply a round object.** Not improbably, the local meaning of *round robin* 'pancake' was first applied to the document by natives of Devonshire, "that county having been well represented in the navy," as F. Adams (1896:392) put it (Liberman [1997:117-19]).

SKEDADDLE (1861)

Attempts have been made to trace skedaddle *to Greek, Irish, Welsh, Swedish, and Danish or to explain it as a blend of some kind, but the word is, most likely, an extended form of* skaddle *or* *skeddle *'scare, frighten.'*

The sections are devoted to 1) the proposed etymologies of skedaddle, *2)* skedaddle *and its putative etymons in an English dialect, and 3)* skedaddle *as a* Streckform *(an extended form).*

1. **The word *skedaddle* was first recorded in an American newspaper in the form *skidaddle*** (DAE) and soon became known all over the country. The noun *skedaddle* 'precipitous flight' is contemporary with the verb (Cohen [1979:5; 1985a:31]); compare *The Great Skedaddle* 'flight to the north and toward the mountains in Pennsylvania' (Brumbaugh [1965]). *Skedaddler* surfaced in 1866 (Thornton, and cf *Skedaddlers Ridge* in New Brunswick, noted as a Canadianism; see McDavid [1967:57]). E.B. (1877:514) noted that in England, *skedaddle* "had firmly established itself. ...among light and humorous writers it has made itself a pet. It is often met with in Blackwood." **The conjectures on the origin of *skedaddle* are of at least four types.**

1) ***Skedaddle* is either a cognate of Gk σκεδάννυμι 'disperse, rout (a crowd)' or a jocular distortion of the Greek verb**. That idea occurred more or less simultaneously to several people. Writing in 1880, Samelson noted: "When first I heard this American slang term, some eighteen years ago, I was at once reminded of the Homeric (and for that matter modern) skedazo, *that is,* disperse, scatter." Cohen's quotations with such statements (1979:16; 1985a:42) also go back to 1862. In the third edition of his dictionary (1864), Hotten expressed an opinion that *skedaddle* "is very fair Greek... and it was probably set afloat by some professor at Harvard." The Greek etymology was often reinvented (or repeated) in the seventies of the 19th century (Gardner [1871], F.J.J. [1876:338/3], anonymous [1877a:233 and 748], and Mackay [1877]). Some people who compared the English and the Classical Greek verbs preferred to trace them to the same etymon, rather than classifying *skedaddle* with borrowings. Among them was Skeat (1875:372), but he left *skedaddle* out of his dictionary (1882), apparently dissatisfied with the existing hypotheses.

Not everyone agreed to speak of *skedaddle* and σκεδάννυμι in one breath. Hotten's reviewers (anonymous [1864a:558; 1864b:545]) found the Greek derivation "more than doubtful" and "taxing our credulity." Later, Green (1906:27-28) held it up to ridicule. But it is still alive. Partridge (1958) did not exclude the possiblility of "some scholarly wit's blend of *sked* annunai + either '*paddle* away' or '*saddle* up and depart.'" From Partridge the Greek etymology of *skedaddle* may have found its way into Flexner (1976:92); see Cohen [1979:17, note 1; 1985a:43, note 1, cont on p. 44]. Cohen (1976:6-7; 1979:17, note 1) defended the Greek hypothesis (his remarks are reproduced in Cohen [1985a:44-47]) but later changed his mind (1985a:47) and cited the argument that had been known for more than a century: *skedaddle* "belongs to a rural setting... and such a setting does not seem conducive to Greek influence, either directly or from the schoolmaster via his students"; see also Sleeth (1981:5).

2) ***Skedaddle* goes back to some Celtic source**. Mackay (1888) attempted to represent *skedaddle* as the sum of two Gaelic words (his usual practice), but more often one finds mention of Wel *ysgudaw* 'run about' and "OIr" *sgedad-ol*, allegedly occurring in the New Testament quotation (Matt XXVI: 31, *Authorized Version*): "I will smite the shepherd, and the sheep of the flock shall be *scattered* abroad." The first edition of the New Testament in Irish (TNJC-1) appeared in 1602 (Quigley [1917:52]). In transliteration the relevant passage is: *búailfid mé an tao˙duire, agus SCABFUI˙D˙TEAR cáoirig an tréada* (the verbal form in question is given here in capitals). *Scabfuı̇ḋṫear* (the passive) does not resemble **sgedadol*, a form whose existence in the Irish Bible or anywhere in Irish is much in doubt. The same text appears in the 1681 edition (TNJC-2) and in the editions published in the 19th century; for instance, TNJC-3 has *scabfuidhtear*. *Scáin-*, the verbal root of ModIr *sgabaim* 'scatter, disperse' has no established etymology (LE).

Bartlett (1860) dates the earliest reference to Welsh 1877, and Cohen (1979:14-15; 1985a:39-40) dug up only one sympathetic response to **sgedadol* as the etymon of *skedaddle* (Clapin). However, Hamp (in a letter to Cohen: see Cohen et al [1979:20-22]; Cohen [1985a:41], and Sleeth's favorable comment [1981:7]) found some virtue in the Irish hypothesis. He mentions Sc Gael *sgad* 'loss, mischance,' Ir *sceinnim* 'flee,' and *scaoilim* 'scatter, shed, let loose.' He does not explain how any of those words could have been transformed into E *skedaddle* with stress on the second syllable. Attempts to trace *skedaddle* to other similar-sounding Irish words like *scea˙tra˙c* 'vomit, spawn' and also 'anything of scattered or untidy make,' *sceideal* 'excitement, anxiety' (the glosses are from Dinneen) are unprofitable.

3) **According to Mahn in W (1864), *skedaddle* "is said to be of Swedish and Danish origin, and to have been in common use for several years throughout the Northwest, in the vicinity of immigrants from these nations."** Cohen's remark (1979:10, note 1; 1985a:37, note 1) that OED incorrectly cites W (1864) is based on a misunderstanding: the entry in W (1864) appears where OED says it does. Mahn's derivation has little value, for he mentions no Swedish or Danish words. However, Scandinavian words vaguely reminiscent of *skedaddle* exist, as Keyworth (1880) notes: Dan *skynde* [sgønə] 'hurry, rush' (transitive and intransitive). Cohen (1979:10; 1985a:37) refers to ES's glib criticism of Mahn's idea (p. 290).

4) ***Skedaddle* has stress on the second syllable, which suggested to some researchers that the word is a blend**: *skid* + *daddle* 'walk unsteadily' (J.C.R. [1880]), *sket* 'quickly' + *daddle* (Barrère-Leland), or *skee(t)* 'squirt; spread, distribute, scatter; hasten, move quickly' + *daddle* (Wood [1910-11:176, note 44). SND tentatively derives *skedaddle* from *skiddle* 'spill' + *skail* 'scatter, disperse,' whereas Wescott (1977a:13) decomposed the verb into *s-* (as in *smash*) + *ke* (as in *boom* ~ *kaboom*) + palindromic *-dad-* (approximately as in *dodder*) + frequentative *-le* (see also Cohen [1979:4, 15; 1985a:30], who received further comments from the author). Green (1906:27-28) mentions someone's derivation of *skedaddle* from *sky* + *Daedalus*; see also Partridge's Greek-English blend (above). Cohen (1979:21-24; 1985a:48-52) now defends the etymology *skedaddle* = *skiddle* 'spill' + *jabble* 'spill' assimilated to **skidabble* > *skedaddle*. Some of the derivations listed above are not improbable, but, like most conjectures relying on blends, they are guesswork by definition.

In his comments on Bartlett[3], the reviewer mentions *skedaddle*, "of which the etymology is laboriously but fruitlessly discussed" by the author (anonymous 1878:171). W (1890) marks *skedaddle* as a word of unknown origin. OED labels it a fanciful formation. Giles W. Shurteleff was believed to have coined *skedaddle*, and Weekley shared the view that *skedaddle* belonged to the same type as its artificial synonyms *vamo(o)se* and *absquatulate*. Schele de Vere (1872:284-86), Bartlett (1860), Thornton (1912-39), and Mencken (1945:239: supplement to the 1936 ed) give surveys of early scholarship. See a sober assessment of various conjectures in Russell (1893:530). Green (1906:27-28) provided a sarcastic survey, and in recent years Cohen has explored the history of *skedaddle* in detail. Popularizers (see Brewer [1882], E. Edwards, and Hargrave) usually found it difficult to choose the best etymology and cited several as equally probable.

2. **The only reliable clue to the origin of *skedaddle* comes from the verb *skedaddle* 'spill milk.'** Mackay knew it from Dumfriesshire. His source may have been the often-cited letter to the *Times*, October 13, 1862, from Dumfriesshire (see its text in ES (291) and in Cohen (1979:8-9; 1985a:35-36). The writer of the letter says that one can skedaddle not only milk but also "coals, potatoes, or apples, and other substances falling from a cart in travelling from one place to another." Anonymous (1877a:234) says the same. Correspondents from the north of England, too, were familiar with this verb.

Of some interest is a letter in *Manchester City News* from R.D.S. Since it has never surfaced in linguistic literature, it is reproduced here in full (R.D.S. [1880a]): "I believe 'skedaddle' is taken from the word 'skeindaddle,' a term used in the north to express running over or spilling milk or water when carried in pails by the yoke or skein across the shoulders. In order to travel with the pails nearly full it was usual to put into each pail a thin slice of wood, called a daddle; and if any of the milk or water was spilled it was usual for the bearer to be scolded for allowing it to skeindaddle." In 1880b, R.D.S. added that as he had heard, "the word [*skeindaddle*] was much in use in both Glasgow and Edinburgh fifty years since, and also in North Yorkshire" and that his wife "frequently heard it when a young girl." A compound consisting of two nouns (*skein* 'yoke' + *daddle* 'slice of wood') could not have yielded a verb, especially one meaning 'spill.' *Skeindaddle* is a folk etymological variant of *skedaddle*, rather than its etymon, and it testifies to the widespread use of *skedaddle*, which is a late word in Scots (Cohen [1979:9, note 3; 1985a:36, note 2], with reference to A.J. Aitken).

Skedaddle 'spill' and *skedaddle* 'retreat hastily' may be parallel formations (Mencken [1945:239]). Green (1906:27-28) cites Lancashire and Northumbr *skedaddle* 'spill' and 'disperse,' and so does Wright (EDD). However, Wright's quotation from Northumberland ("The American war familiarized this term in 1862; but it has been commonly used on Tyneside long before;" the source is not indicated) suggests that the meaning 'disperse in flight, retreat precipitously' (Wright's gloss) is an American import. See Sleeth (1981:5), who also treats *long before* in EDD as wholly without merit. Given the meaning 'spill potatoes, coals, apples, and other substances falling from a moving cart,' one can imagine the facetious extension 'scatter like potatoes; put to flight,' but the change to the intransitive use 'flee' remains undocumented.

3. **The verb *skedaddle* is probably not a blend. It is rather an augmented, or extended form (*Streckform*, to use Schröder's term)**. In German, nearly all such forms are of regional origin. They have an expressive meaning and contain three syllables with stress on the middle one. The inserted syllables are *ab, eb, ap, af, am, aw, ag, ak, ad, at, ar, al, as,* and so so. Here are some German verbs with the meaning 'run fast, run about aimlessly' (the inserted syllables are given in parentheses): *b(aj)äckern, j(ad)ackern, sl(ad)acken, sch(aw)up-pen, kl(ad)astern,* and *kl(ab)astern* (H. Schröder [1906/7, 15, 95, 163, 172, and 189]). See also H. Schröder (1903), in which 53 forms are listed, and Behaghel (1923:183). The presence of extended forms in many languages can hardly be called into question. See HOBBLEDEHOY and RAGAMUFFIN, and in addition to Schröder and Behaghel, Gonda (1943: numerous examples from Indonesian; pp. 393 and 394-96 on German, Dutch, and French) and Gonda (1956; Classical Greek and Dutch).

The existence of a *Streckform* can be established only if the initial form has been recorded, and indeed *bäckern, jackern, slacken,* and the rest happen to be attested verbs in the same or neighboring dialects of German. E reg *scaddle* means 'scare, frighten; run off in a fright, dare one to do something' (EDD); it is a common verb, according to Haigh (1928). *Skedaddle* is its extended form, an expressive but not a 'fanciful' formation. In Green's opinion (1906:28), Lanc *skiddle* 'spill' is another form of *skedaddle,* "and perhaps has given rise to it by a sort of internal reduplication." That is almost exactly what Schröder would presumably have said. W.D. (1868:498) suggested a similar derivation before Green, though he traced *skaddle* to improbable sources. Scots *skedaddle* is, most likely, an extended form of *skiddle*, and its American doublet is an extended form of *scaddle* or **skeddle* (see below). If so, *skaddle* is not a jocular abbreviation of *skedaddle*, as Cohen et al (1979:21, with reference to Herman Rappaport) and Sleeth (1981:9) thought.

The persuasiveness of the idea that *skedaddle* is an extended form depends on supporting evidence. In Modern English, such forms are few; nearly all of them are regional frequentative verbs with stress on the second syllable, like *skedaddle.* The examples below are from EDD. *Fineney* 'mince, simper' is a doublet of *finey. Fandangle* 'ornaments, trinkets; capers' has stress on the first syllable; yet it looks like an extended form of *fangle* in *newfangled*. EDD glossed *fangle* as 'a conceit, whim; to trim showily, entangle; hang about, trifle, waste time.' *Fundawdle* 'caress' may be from *fondle*, and *gamawdled* 'slightly intoxicated' from *gaddle* 'drink greedily and hastily.' DARE and HDAS add nothing of importance to that short list. Extended forms with *-de-* ~ *-te-* in the middle are discussed in connection with *hobbledehoy*, in the entry *ragamuffin* (see those entries).

Finagle may belong with the verbs mentioned above. It surfaced in the 1920's in the United States and is not of Jewish origin (Gold, forthcoming). W^2 compares it to *fainaigue* [fə'ni:g] 'revoke at cards, renege, play truant, cheat, *etc*' from EDD. NED and NTCD suggest that *finagle* is the respelling of the family name of Gregor von Feinagle (?1765–1819), a German mesmerist and whist expert, often ridiculed in Germany and France. AHD defines *finagle* (also spelled *fenagle*) as 'achieve by dubious or crafty methods; wrangle; trick or delude; deceive craftily.' Griffith (1939:292) "grew up" with the meaning 'fuss and feather over a small matter with fakery in it, a lackadaisical effort to sell a bargain, a small bargain,' and it was he who derived this word from *Feinaigle.* He wondered whether *feinagle* might go back to Byron's usage in *Don Juan* I/11, but "more likely," he says, "it is the off-spring of the lampooning, local hit slang-inventiveness of music-hall taste; in England, 1805-1820, the 'popular' pronunciation of the foreign lecturer's name would have been 'Fee-nágle.'"

Most dictionaries prefer the first etymology, and it is indeed hard to reconcile Feinagle's fame with the apparently regional provenance of *finagle* and its late attestation. In light of the constant interchange of *-ddle* and *-ggle* in British English, one can assume *figgle* to be an alternate pronunciation of *fiddle* (OED gives only one example of *figgle* 'fidget about,' 1652, but this verb exists in modern dialects [EDD]); then *finagle* will emerge as *fi(na)gle*.

In H. Schröder's list, the intrusive syllable always ends in a consonant (*ad, al, an,* and so on), while the English augment is represented by open syllables like *na, ne, la,* and *du*, if for the sake of argument we accept the derivations *fi(na)gle, fi(ne)ney*, and the rest. But Behaghel (1906:401-02), who despite his disagreement with most of H. Schröder's etymologies accepted the idea of infixation in ludic forms (and only in them), cited the German regional verbs *kladatschen, strapantzen,* and *tralatschen* from *klatschen* 'clap,' *strantzen* 'steal,' and *tratschen* 'chat,' that is, *kla(da)tschen, stra(pa)ntzen,* and *tra(la)tschen* (Behaghel[1923:183]), with open syllables in the middle, as in English.

The point of division in *klabastern* versus *klastern* Schröder writes *kl(ab)astern,* though *kla(ba)stern* will yield the same result, and it is more natural to postulate insertion at the syllable boundary. Perhaps *-ba-, -da-,* and so on should sometimes have been put in place of *-ab-, -ad-,* and others. This ambiguity holds for all words with vowel harmony, such as *glockotzen* 'burp' from *glotzen* (*glo-ko-tzen* = *gl-ock-otzen*) (H. Schröder 1903/37). Only in words like *krabutzen* 'small children' from *krutzen* 'little child' (ib./44), the division is undoubtedly *kr-ab-utzen*. Schröder must have reasoned that *klabastern* and *krabutzen* have identical structure.

Skedaddle is rather *ske(da)ddle* than *sked(ad)dle*, despite the fact that the attested primary verb is *scaddle*, not **skeddle*. The pronunciation [e] for [æ] is widespread all over England.

Many similar-sounding words have been compared with *skedaddle*: OE *scēadan* 'divide' (E *shed*), OE *sceot* 'quick' (anonymous 1868b:138, Skeat 1875:372), E *scud* and *scuttle* (W.D. [1868]), and Du *schudden* 'shake, jolt' (Stormonth) among them. *Scuttle* (the same as reg *scuddle*), defined as 'run with quick hurried steps' but also used transitively (*scuttle an effort, scuttle a meeting* = 'bring to a speedy end'), is a variant of *skiddle* and *scaddle* ~ **skeddle* by secondary (false) ablaut. The verbs listed above were often recorded late, and it is not necessary to trace them to a common source. **Their origin is of no consequence for the etymology of *skedaddle*.** Once *skedaddle* struck root in the language, it joined the words beginning with *sk-* and implying quick, brisk movement: *scour, skip, scuttle, scuddle, scud, scutter, scoot, (helter-)skelter,* and *scamper* (Marchand [1969:410/7.50]). On *scadoodle* (probably a humorous variant of *skedaddle* rather than a blend) see Cohen (1979:24-25; 1985:53-54) and Liberman (1994b: 173-75).

SLANG (1756)

Slang, *ultimately of Scandinavian origin, may have existed in northern dialects before the 18*th *century, but it spread to the rest of the country after its meaning 'jargon,' the only one remembered today, reached the underworld of London. Its semantic development can be reconstructed as follows: 'a piece of land' → 'those who travel about this territory' (first and foremost, hawkers) → 'the manner of hawkers' speech' → 'low class jargon, argot.' Neither N reg* slengjeord *nor E* language ~ *F* langue *is its etymon, though* slang *was probably understood as* s-lang, *and that circumstance may have contributed to its rise and survival in the Standard.*

The sections are devoted to 1) the attestation and the various meanings of slang, *2) the hypotheses on its origin, and 3) the proposed reconstruction.*

1. OED lists several nouns spelled *slang*: 1) A species of cannon; a serpentine or culverin (only 16th-century examples; the last is dated 1600) from MDu or MLG *slange* 'snake'; 2) a long narrow strip of land (regional; alternating with *sling, slanget, slanket, slinget,* and *slinket)* of obscure origin; 3) I.a. The special vocabulary used by any set of persons of a low or disreputable character; language of a low and vulgar type. (Now merged in c.) According to the comment following that definition, the first quotation ("Thomas Throw had been upon the town, knew the slang well") may refer to customs or habits rather than language. But in the 1774 example, *slang* refers only to language; b. The special vocabulary... of a particular profession; c. Language of a highly colloquial type..., d. Abuse, impertinence (one 1825 citation). II. Humbug, nonsense (one 1762 citation). III. A line of work (one 1789 citation): "How do you work now? O, upon the old slang, and sometimes a little bully-prigging [= stealing]." IV. A license, especially that of a hawker (no citations before 1812). V. A traveling show (from 1859 onward), a performance (one citation, 1861); hence *slang cove, slang cull* 'showman'; VI. A short weight or measure (one citation, 1851). 4) A watch chain, a chain of any kind, apparently, like (1), from Du *slang* 'snake'; pl 'fetters, leg irons'.

The noun *slang* used attributively, means 'having the character of slang (language)' (1758); 'given to the use of slang, of a fast or rakish character, impertinent' (1818); 'extravagant' (of dress) (1828; possibly obsolete); 'rakish' (of tone) (1834); 'short, defective' (of measures; costers' slang) (1812). The verb *slang* has been recorded in the senses 'to exhibit at a fair or market' (one 1789 example); 'defraud, cheat; give short measure' (1812); 'make use of slang; abuse' (1828 and 1844 respectively). *Slang* (*sb*[3]) is a word of obscure origin. "It is possible that some of the senses may represent independent words" (OED).

Not listed in OED is *slang* 'water course,' known in some parts of the United States and Canada (H.R. [1890], Qui Tam [1890]) but not entered in dictionaries of Americanisms. A connection between *slang* 3 and *slang* 1-2 is probably unthinkable, though John Bee (1825:5) tries to establish it: "Slangs are the greaves with which the legs of convicts are fettered, having acquired that name from the manner in which they were worn, as they required a sling of string to keep them off the ground.... The irons were the slangs; and the slang-wearer's language was of course slanguous, as partaking much of the slang." Zeus (1853) and E. Coleman (1900) reproduced that quotation. According to WFl, *slang* 'watch chain' (obsolete; underworld use) owes its existence to rhyming slang: *clock and slang = watch and chain.* More likely, *slang* 'watch chain' and *slang(s)* 'fetter(s)' are one and the same word. R. Chapman states that *slang* originally meant both 'a kind of projectile hurling weapon' and 'the language of thieves and vagabonds.' A projectile hurling weapon means what OED calls 'a species of cannon.' The two words are homonyms.

The questions to be addressed are the unity of *slang* 3, which OED finds debatable, and the origin of *slang* 'thieves' cant'. **Since a search for pre-1756 records of *slang* has been unsuccessful, one can assume that the word had no currency in towns before the middle of the 18th century, but as soon as it caught the fancy of Londoners, it spread fast.** For example, Jack Slang, the horse doctor, was one of the company at "The Three Pigeons" whom Tony Lumpkin is going to meet in Act I of *She Stoops to Conquer.* Goldsmith's comedy was produced on March 15th, 1773, and the name may have had an allusive meaning, as Robins (1900) remarks. His observation did not make its way into the annotated editions of Goldsmith's work. Since Jack Slang has no lines written for him, we cannot form an opinion about his manner of speaking. He was certainly not genteel and may have been a cheat. Woty says in *Fugitive and Original Poems* (1786:28): "Did ever Cicero's correct harangue / Rival this flowing eloquence of slang?" The note added to this place ("A cant word for vulgar language") makes it clear that the word *slang* had not yet become universally known (Courtney [1900]).

The first lexicographer to recognize the present day meaning of *slang* was Grose (1785). S. Johnson (1755) may have ignored it, or it may have been too recent for inclusion. A professional lawyer, a character in Hugh Kelly's 1773 comedy *The School for Wives,* admits that he has never heard about "a little rum language" called *slang. Rum* (adj) is itself a cant word; see the discussion in Langenauer (1957). Throughout the 19th century, lexicographers defined *slang* as vulgar, low, and inelegant (Reves [1926]). As late as 1901, Greenough and Kittredge (1901:55) wrote: "Slang is a peculiar kind of vagabond language, always hanging on the outskirts of legitimate speech, but continually straying or forcing its way into the most respectable company." Their statement has often been quoted in linguistic works.

Nowadays, slang is understood as highly informal, expressive vocabulary. However, *slang* rose to its present day status from the lowest depths, whence the disgust of "the most respectable company." Chaucer's, let alone earlier, colloquialisms are hard to appreciate today, but the literary production of Shakespeare's contemporaries and the Restoration comedy are so unabashedly gross that the war declared on slang by later generations can have only one explanation: *slang* was at that time synonymous with *cant* and *flash*. Once the social stigma was removed, the disgust evaporated (see Gotti [1999:114-22]). But it is also true that although slang (in the modern meaning of the word) is a universal overlay on colloquial language, be it Classical Greek, Latin, or Modern English, the vastness and all-pervasiveness of English slang, from Canada to Australia, is a unique phenomenon. That is why the word *slang* gained popularity in many languages. Slang is volatile. Yet some slang words may remain substandard for centuries, while others become colorless and neutral (Hayward, as reported in anonymous [1894]; Maurer and High [1980]). In our understanding, slang is racy and in some circumstances inappropriate rather than vulgar.

2. **Three main approaches to the etymology of *slang* have been tried:** 1) **The originator of the first is I. Taylor whose ideas on the Romany origin of slang go back to Hotten**. Skeat[1] (*slang*) reproduced most of the relevant passage. Here it is in full: "In a wild district of Derbyshire, between Macclesfield and Buxton, there is a village called Flash, surrounded by uninclosed land. The squatters on these commons, with their wild gypsy habits, travelled about the neighbourhood from fair to fair, using a slang dialect of their own. They were called the Flash men, and their dialect Flash talk; and it is not difficult to see the stages by which the word *flash* has reached its present signification. A slang is a narrow strip of waste land by the roadside, such as those which are chosen by gypsies for their encampments. To be 'out on the slang,' in the lingo used by thieves and gypsies, means to travel about the country as a hawker, encamping by night on the roadside *slangs*. A travelling show is also called a *slang*. It is easy to see how the term [*slang*] was transferred to the language spoken by hawkers and itinerant showmen" (1865:450). This is a slightly modified version of Taylor (1864:471); the same text, with different italics, appears in Taylor (1873:308), the edition that Skeat used.

DDEL adopted Hotten and Taylor's explanation and said that *slang* is perhaps "of Gypsy origin." W (1864) and (1890) mention it but express doubts. Taylor failed to produce a credible Romany etymon of *slang*, and his derivation of *flash* 'argot,' which he allegedly found in Smiles is fanciful (nothing is said about Flash in Smiles 1861:II, 307). Skeat remarks that it is not "easy to see" how the term *slang* was transferred to the language spoken by hawkers and itinerant showmen, for "surely, no one would dream of calling thieves' language *a travelling-show*, or a *camping-place*. On the other hand, it is likely that *a slang* (from the verb *sling*, to cast) may have meant 'a cast' or 'a pitch'; for both *cast* and *pitch* were used to mean a camping-place, or a place where a travelling-show is exhibited; and, indeed, Halliwell notes that 'a narrow slip of ground' is also called a *slinget*."

Despite such objections, Platt (1903) defended Taylor's etymology. He returned to Skeat's statement that no one would dream of calling thieves' language a traveling show or a camping place and noted that in Urdu, *Urdu-zabān* (ODEE has *zabān i urdū*) means 'camp language.' "This curtailment of the phrase rather increases than diminishes the analogy with the English, since Fielding and all other early users of the term have *slang patter* instead of *slang*, which thus appears to be an abbreviation of same nature as *Urdu*. We cannot... call a language a camp, but we can call it camp patter." Taylor and Platt's reconstruction is then as follows: *slang* 'a piece of land' → 'the territory used by tramps for their wanderings' → 'their camps' → 'the language used in these camps.' The meaning 'jargon' may indeed have been secondary, and it is unfortunate that the above reasoning was not taken seriously; nor did Platt know that Sampson (1898) had anticipated him; see the end of the entry.

2) Taylor's idea did not survive the criticism of Skeat, who supported Wedgwood's etymology. **According to Wedgwood, *slang* is a word of Scandinavian origin. He referred to N reg *slengja* 'fling, cast,'** *slengja kjeften* 'make insulting allusions' (literally 'sling the jaw,' as in the English verb *slang = jaw*), and *slengjeord* 'slang words,' also 'new words taking rise from a particular occasion without having wider foundation' (all the definitions are his). With regard to *slang* 'long narrow strip of land,' Wedgwood cited Sw *släng* 'stroke' and noted that E *stripe* also combines the meanings 'blow, streak *or* stroke' and 'long narrow portion of surface.'

Skeat repeated Wedgwood's Norwegian examples (from Aasen), stated incorrectly that *slang* is derived from the past tense of *sling* (he meant that *slang* has the same grade of ablaut as the obsolete preterit of *sling*: in his terminology, the second stem of *sling*; see OED and compare G *schlingen—schlang* and the noun *Schlange* 'snake'), and noted that Icel *slyngr* and *slunginn* 'versed in a thing, cunning' (also derived from *sling-*) resemble *slang* 'cheat'. He could have added Sw *slängd* 'versed in something' (though neither *slyngr*, *slunginn* nor *slängd* refers to underhand dealings). All the Scandinavian words listed above are related to *sling* and its Germanic cognates, but the distance from 'throw, fling, sling, cast' to 'cheat, humbug' is long, even though *slengjeord* ('a slung word') 'nonce word, word coined on the spur of the moment, word blurted out,' *slengjenamn* 'nickname,' and *slengje kjeften* 'use insulting language' are transparent formations.

Wedgwood's etymology of *slang* found its way into many dictionaries. Boag and Craig, who borrowed their definition of *slang* from W (1828: 'low, vulgar, unmeaning language') but left out 'vulgar,' say curtly: "old preter[it] of *sling*"; others cite the alleged Norwegian etymon. Stormonth, W[1], and W[2] repeat Wedgwood's etymology. Mueller and OED had serious reservations, however. OED: "The date and early associations of the word make it unlikely that there is any connexion with certain Norw. forms in *sleng-* which exhibit some approximation in sense." Those reservations had little effect on Skeat, who did not change his opinion until the end. Weekley, Wyld (UED), Partridge (1958), Klein (CEDEL), and WNWD[1] mention *sling* as a seemingly obvious cognate of *slang* but state that the tie between *slang-* and *slengje-* is insecure. J. de Vries (NEW, *slang* 2) sides with OED. ODEE, after admitting the notable parallelism between the northern regional sense of 'abusive language' and the colloquial use of the verb *slang* 'abuse' on one hand and the corresponding Norwegian regional words and expressions on the other, resorts to its usual formula "no immediate connexion can be made out." The etymology of *slang* was written for OED by Craigie. Contrary to him, Bradley ("Slang" in EB[11]) found Wedgwood's derivation acceptable (see Bradley [1928:146], a reprint of the article in EB), and the disagreement between the editors of OED may explain why the etymology in ODEE differs (even if just slightly) from the one in its parent work.

Among Scandinavian lexicographers, FT gave Wedgwood their unlimited support (*slænge,* end of the entry), whereas Hellquist (SEO, *slang* 2) repeated the statement in OED. Spitzer (1952) tried to connect *slang* and *sling*, bypassing Norwegian. He took his inspiration from Partridge's idea that slang is 'slung language' (1940:175). Partridge cited the expressions *sling the bat* 'speak the vernacular,' *sling words* (or *language*) 'talk,' *sling off at* 'jeer at or taunt,' and *slanging*, a music hall term of the 1880's for 'singing,' from the practice of interpolating gags between the verses of a song. Spitzer added *mud slinging* and several examples of how in French, after it borrowed the Germanic verb, F *élinguer* (< OF *eslinguer*) 'throw stones with a sling' developed the meaning 'speak (rudely).' He concluded that judging by the examples in OED, *slang* must originally have meant 'banter of hawkers' rather than 'thieves' cant.'

Although Partridge presents the inconsistency of word formation as an insignificant detail, it invalidates the idea of 'slung language.' *Slang* is a late word. Classical ablaut was not productive in the 18th century, and new pairs like *shoot* (v)—*shot* (sb) and *ride—road* stopped appearing at least a thousand years before that time. No model existed that would have allowed S. Johnson's contemporaries to overcome the barrier between *sling* (or *slung*) and *slang*, just as it would not occur to us today to coin *slum* 'poor neighborhood' from *slim* 'poor' or *slam* 'beat.' Partridge, who was not schooled in historical linguistics, was dimly aware of that difficulty when he wrote (1940:175, note 1): "The fact that *slang* is nowhere recorded as a past participle may appear insuperable to many: but *slang* was originally a cant word; perhaps, therefore, a deliberate perversion of *slung* (recorded long before our noun *slang*)."

Unlike Partridge, Spitzer, an experienced etymologist, knew that there was a problem but dismissed it. "As to the phonetic form of *slang*," he observed, "I suggest a secondary *Ablaut* from *sling*. *Slang* as a variant of *sling* is also attested since 1610 by the NED in the meaning 'a long narrow strip of land' (from *sling* 'bond, rope') and, conversely, *sling* since 1590 as a variant of *slang* in the meaning 'a serpentine or culverin' (Germ. *Schlange* 'serpent')" (1952:103). Secondary ablaut, that is, alternation of vowels in later periods responsible for the coexistence of *keb* ~ *cub* ~ *cob*, *tit* ~ *tat* ~ *tot* (see COB, CUB and TOAD), and other similar forms, is always limited to the same part of speech; it never produces nouns from verbs. The border can be crossed only between nouns and adjectives, for nouns are regularly used attributively. If *sling* ~ *slang* is a pair like *big* ~ *bag* or *bag* ~ *bug* (see BEACON), two possibilities present themselves. Either *sling* (v) was the source of *slang* (v), which would mean that *slang* (sb) is derived from *slang* (v). Or *slang* (sb) goes back to *sling* (sb), but then phrases like N *slengje kjeften*, *sling the bat*, and *mudslinging*, as well as the French analogues of *sling* (v), lose their relevance. Obviously, neither alternative is acceptable. And *sling* 'projectile' could hardly be the etymon of *slang* 'abusive language.'

The similarity between N *slengjeord* and E *slang words* is undeniable, but Wedgwood's etymology has a weak point. Numerous words of Scandinavian origin in English dialects become known to linguists late because regional words remain tied to their home unless popular authors revive them (see CUSHAT), and researchers may not know that they exist. However, the northern form *sleng- if it had been current since the Vikings' times, would have yielded *sling, as O. Ritter (1906b:41) pointed out, because ME *eng* went over to *ing*. If an early date is improbable, *slang* must be a reshaping of a recent (18th-century?) noun. But such a conclusion is also untenable, for no group of Norwegians could have brought the posited regional word to England in the mid-seventeen hundreds and made it common among peddlers, showmen, and thieves. **Thus the near identity between N *slengjeord* and E *slang* is due to coincidence**, though, as will be shown in sec 3, they have the same root, and their similarity is not a mere caprice of word history. Barnhart emphasized the coincidental nature of that similarity: "...the remoteness of the borrowing is hard to overcome," but the conclusion "so that perhaps both English and Scandinavian are of a different common source" is insupportable: no asterisked common source can be reconstructed for *slang* and *slengjeord*.

3) Although coming at the end of this survey, the last etymology of *slang* to be considered is the earliest in the scholarly literature. Its originator was probably **Thomson**, who **derived *slang* 'corrupt or obsolete language' from F *langue* or L *lingua* and compared it with E *lingo***. A.G. (1850) notes that "... in the word *slang*, the *s*, which is there prefixed to *language*, at once destroys the better word, and degrades its meaning." According to Skeat[1], Wedgwood's hypothesis "is far preferable to the wholly improbable and unauthorized connection of *slang* with E. *lingo* and F. *langue*, without an attempt to explain the initial *s*, which has been put forward by some, but only as a guess." Despite his harsh verdict, *s* is easy to explain, and "the wholly improbable and unauthorized connection" is little more than a display of eloquence.

Mahn (W [1864]) wrote: "Said to be of Gypsy origin" and added: "But cf. *lingo*." Reference to *lingo* disappeared only in W (1890), which favors Wedgwood's etymology. Chambers repeated Thomson, while Mueller[1] noted that Wedgwood's explanation was not better than the old ones—from *lingua* and of Romany. Among the authors of modern etymological dictionaries Holthausen (EW[1-3]) considered the derivation of *slang* from F *langue* not improbable. However, outside lexicographical circles, that derivation had at least three distinguished advocates. O. Ritter (1906b) suggested that *slang* is the result of so-called attraction (its other name is metanalysis), the misdivision responsible for the emergence of *n-uncle, t-awdry*, and so forth. He traced *slang* to phrases like *beggars' lang, thieves' lang*, and the like, and *lang* to a clipped form of *language*. According to his hypothesis, *lang* 'language' was common in the 17th century. Horn (1921b:142) and Klaeber (1926) supported him but J. de Vries (NEW, *slang* 2) disagreed.

Most of Ritter's article is devoted to *s-mobile* in English (mainly in dialects), though he did not include *slang* among such words as *slam* versus OI *lemja* 'thrash, beat,' *slock* 'lure, entice' versus OI *loccian* (the same meaning), and *sclash, sclimb* = *clash, climb*. The most vulnerable part of Ritter's etymology is its dependence on *lang 'language.' If such a form existed, it must have been indistinguishable from F *langue*. *Lang* (< *language*) turns up neither in writing nor in living speech. Phrases like **beggars' (thieves', sailors', tinkers') lang* have not been recorded. F *langue* as the etymon of *slang* is even less convincing, for *slang* was not borrowed from French. In Guiraud's opinion, the etymon of *slang* is F *linguer* ~ *languer* 'prate, babble' from OF *eslanguer* 'tear off the tongue,' whose reflexes are extant in dialects in the sense 'chatter, speak rudely; revile, malign someone.' It remains unclear whether Guiraud meant that *slang* was borrowed from *Old* French (otherwise, where did *s-* come from?) or that *slang* is F reg *languer* with *s-* added. His conjecture appears in KS as an alternative to Wedgwood's. Ritter asserted that *slang* could not be *lang* with *s* appended to it. But if the clipped form *lang* existed, *s-lang* would be its viable doublet. Weekley (1921) cited N reg *slengjeord* as a possible etymon of *slang* but observed that "[s]ome regard it as an argotic perversion of F. *langue*, language (see *s-*)." His entry *s-*, which complements Ritter's material, contains many noteworthy facts. Those who seek the origin of *slang* in *language* or *langue* need not reject the idea of a modern version of *s-mobile*. See an early survey of the etymology of *slang* in G. Schröder (1893:17-19).

Several more conjectures on the etymology of

slang exist. Mackay (1877) endorsed the idea that *slang* was, in principle, L *lingua*, "literally the language of the gypsies," but since his goal was to discover the Gaelic origin of all words, he translated *slang*, allegedly 'the language of the vulgar,' into German, got *Pöbelsprache*, and cited "Gaelic *sluagh* 'a multitude, a people, a host, an army, a mob' and *theanga* 'tongue, speech, dialect,' pronounced *teanga* or *theanga*." A combination of those two words, both "abbreviated and corrupted into *slua* and *eanga*," is said to have yielded *sluaenga* and *slang*. The Gaelic root to which Mackay referred occurs in E *slogan* (< Gael *sluagh-ghairm*; *sluagh* 'host,' *gairm* 'shout, cry'). All etymologies in Mackay's 1877 book are such, but few are so contrived.

W. Barnes (1862:286) derived *slang*, which he defined as 'slack form of speech,' and *sling* from sl*ng, one of his heavy-duty roots. A.A. (1865) wondered whether *slang* might be a word of Italian origin. Since, in Italian, *s-* is a negative prefix, *slang* would turn out to be **slingua*, some sort of 'unlanguage.' Shipley (1945) reproduced, without reference, John Bee's derivation: Du *slang* 'snake' → chain, fetters → criminals → talk. Unfortunately for his explanation, he remarked "the word was used to refer to language before it was used to mean chains!" He was unacquainted with more recent theories. WNWD[1] mentions N *slengjeord*, suggests its relatedness to *sling*, and tentatively traces *slang* to **sling* ***language***, which it calls a cant clipped form. A blend is probably meant. This hypothesis seems to have been lifted from FW(NCSD), though as early as 1963 FW(SCD) called *slang* a word of uncertain etymology. Cohen (1972c:1, 5) traced *slang* to the root *lk/lg with the general meaning 'striking, cutting'; apparently, he derived it from *sling*. Mozeson (1989), the author of multifarious fantasies, derives *slang* from Hebr lsn (Hebr לשין 'language' in Genesis X:22). As he explains, "a #1—#2 letter swap allows SLAN(G) to be heard. Slander, language, and lozenge are also said to have this root, whereby Finnish seems to be of some help" (see Gold's scathing criticism [1990a]; *slang* is mentioned on p. 111).

Another ingenious suggestion is Riley's (1857). He thought that the starting point of the sought for etymology is not the noun *slang* 'cant language' but the verb *slang* 'abuse, use insulting language.' He said: "I would suggest that, in the latter sense, it may have been first used by our military men in the time of Queen Anne, and that it not improbably was derived from the name of the Dutch General, Slangenberg, who was notorious for his vituperative language and abuse, of Marlborough in particular; the consequences of which was, that he was ultimately removed from the command of the Dutch forces." Thanks to a reference in I. Taylor (the two first editions [1864:471-72; 1865:450]; later removed), Riley's opinion became widely known. One of its supporters was Van Lennep (1860): "In corroboration of his [Riley's] conjecture I may add that the sailors of our Royal Navy still... design a soldier under the name *slang*– "het is eén slang," meaning "it is a redcoat," whilst the substantive itself may very well have been employed as a *nom de guerre* for the Dutch General..., and afterwards applied to all soldiers indiscriminately." The situation Riley and Van Lennep reconstructed is not unthinkable (consider the history of E *martinet*), but the many meanings of *slang* make the hypothesis that *slang* is going back to a proper name unlikely (for a similar clash of incompatible suggestions see TROT). WNT does not list *slang* 'soldier.'

As always in controversial cases, some dictionaries (FW, W[2], W[3], SOD, RHD, and WNWD[2], among them) say "origin uncertain" or "of unknown origin". Others say only "of cant origin."

3. The etymology of *slang* will become clearer if instead of asking the only question that interests us (namely, how this designation of 'rum language' came into being), we look at the picture in its entirety. The best point of departure is the Scandinavian verbs for 'walk aimlessly, stroll,' most of which also mean 'throw': N *slenge* 'hang loose, sway, dangle, wobble (*gå og slenge* 'loaf'); throw, sling, fling, cast; wave one's arms; blurt out words'; Dan *slænge* 'throw, sling, fling, cast; wave one's arms, swing, hang loose'; Sw *slänga* means only 'throw, cast, fling' (Olson [1907: 75-76/13-16]). The meaning 'hang loose' is not too remote from 'twine, coil, wind around something' and 'creep, crawl,' as in G *schlingen*, whence G *Schlange* 'snake' and its Dutch cognate *slang*. Their common denominator seems to be 'move freely in any direction.' Dictionaries list several related verbs of nearly the same meaning and sound shape but offer few comments on their semantic history. See *slænge* (FT, DEO), *slänga* (SEO), and *slyngja* (AEW). E *sling* is not native in any of its meanings.

EDD cites Sc *slanger* 'linger, go slowly.' Whether *slanger* is related to *linger* is immaterial, for its kinship with the Scandinavian verbs discussed above is not in doubt; *slanger* is most probably a loanword. **Verbs of movement designating wandering have the tendency to associate themselves with the name of the territory in which the movement occurs**. However difficult it may be to unravel the knot consisting of E *stripe* 'narrow piece,' E *strip* 'run' (as in *outstrip*), E *strip* 'narrow piece,' G *streifen* 'roam, wander,' and G *Streifen* 'stripe, strip' (sb), the concepts 'stripe' and 'roam' will end up in close proximity. A similar development seems to have occurred in the *slang* group. **We have *slang* 'long narrow piece of land' and *slanger* 'linger, go slowly,' presumably from **slenge* 'wander, loaf.' The slang must have been the land, the territory over which one wandered. The word *slanget* looks like **sleng-et*, **släng-et*, or **slæng-et*, a neuter noun of some Scandinavian language with a postposed definite article**, for *-et* cannot be a relic of a French suffix in it. Dan *slæng* and N *sleng* 'gang, band' (that is, 'a group of strollers') are neuter; their definite forms are *slæng-et* and *sleng-et* respectively. With regard to semantics, OI *slangi* 'tramp' and *slangr* 'going astray' (said about sheep), versus the verb *slangra* 'sling' and 'stray' (said about sheep in pastures straying into another flock) present a parallel.

A prepositional phrase containing a noun with the definite article seems to have been borrowed from some Scandinavian language, for instance, **på slænget* '(out) on the slang.' **Slænget* or **slanget* must have meant the gang's turf (cf *policeman's beat*). *Slanket*, *slinget*, and *slang* are, in all likelihood, later modifications of *slanget*, though *slinget* may have been a parallel formation. **Those who traveled about the country or a certain area were thus 'on the slang' and judging by Dan *slæng* ~ N *sleng* 'gang,' were themselves called 'slang'**. The definition of *slang* in OED ('a long narrow strip of land') is insufficient. EDD adds 'a narrow piece of land running up between other and larger divisions of ground' and notes that *slang* is very common as a field name. Dodgson (1968:124) reconstructs OE **slang* 'sinuous, snake-like, long and narrow and winding, snake-like, a snake' (he cites OE *slingan* 'twist oneself, creep' and G *schlingen*, the same meaning). He considers as less probable the idea that Middle English adopted "Scandinavian and German or Dutch loan words in districts not apparently immediately susceptible to either, when those words do not themselves appear in the Danelaw and South-Eastern districts most susceptible to such loans." Dodgson's arguments are persuasive. However, **a southern noun for 'border' from OE *slingan* 'twist' and a northern one for 'piece of land' from *slenge* 'wander' may have met**.

The evidence of the almost certainly Scandinavian form *slanget* cannot be shaken off, and it is the northern word that is important for understanding the rise of *slang* 'jargon.' We do not know how long *slang* 'territory over which one strolls; gang; strollers' language' existed in the north. That word may never have surfaced in the Standard. For example, *keld*, a northern regional word for 'well, spring, fountain,' was first recorded in writing in 1697; *billow*, another loan from Scandinavian, did not occur in texts before the middle of the 16th century. *Slang*, a local term of vagabonds' language, had almost no chance to become part of the standard, and it is a small miracle that it did. **The sense 'narrow strip of land' (< 'border') is that of its southern cognate. The northern sense of *slang* must have been closer to 'wasteland.'**

Traveling actors, too, were 'on the slang.' Slangs were competitive, with different groups of hawkers, strolling showmen, itinerant mendicants, and thieves fighting for spheres of influence; hence *slang* 'hawker's license,' a permit that guaranteed the person's right to sell within a given 'precinct' (or slang). 'Humbug' is a predictable development of peddlers' activities, for mountebanks cannot be trusted. Hawkers use a special vocabulary and a special intonation when advertising their wares, and many disparaging, derisive names characterize their speech. Such is *charlatan*, ultimately from Ital *ciarlatano: ciarlare* means 'babble, patter' (though this derivation has been called into question: see Menges [1948-49]). Such is also *quack*, the stub of *quacksalver* 'one who goes "quack-quack" praising his salves.' Compare Grose's definition of *cant* 'pedlars' French.'

The earliest meaning of *slang* 'a kind of language' must have been 'hawkers' patter,' rather than 'secret language of thieves,' possibly from attributive use (see Platt above), as in *slang patter* 'the patter of the slang,' where *slang* designated either the area under vendors' control or the profession of people on the slang. Those who knew about the existence of Shelta, the secret language of wandering tinkers (cairds), may have used *slang* as its derogatory synonym. *Slang* 'abusive language' and 'speak insultingly' are the result of a negative attitude toward the language of the lowest strata of the population or of badgers' (hucksters') bickering with one another.

The reconstruction presented here accounts for all the recorded meanings of *slang* except 'cannon,' and 'fetters.' Both are related to *slang* 'jargon' but are different words. Their home, as OED states, is not in Scandinavia. *Slang* has come a long way from 'hawkers' jargon' to 'informal, expressive vocabulary,' but it is still 'meaningless prattle' to the uninitiated.

None of the derivations of *slang* in dictionaries and special publications produced convincing results, but some of them contained useful ideas. I. Taylor's attempt to connect *slang* 'piece of land' with vagabonds and their language should not have been dismissed in the peremptory way typical of Skeat. Nor was Platt too far from the truth. Spitzer made an astute observation that *slang* had originally meant 'the language of hawkers.' Mueller's suggestion that *slang* 'cant' goes back to a word like Dan *slæng* 'band, gang,' if noticed, might have stimulated a better informed search. Wedgwood rightly pointed to the northern origin of *slang*. *Slang* is not akin to *language* or F *langue,* but the survival of *slang* 'jargon' in Standard English may be partly due to the accidental closeness between it and *langue,* that is, to folk etymology. Given the power of *s-mobile* in modern dialects and unbuttoned speech, everybody sensed that *slang (s-lang)* was some kind of language. Efforts to discover the origin of the word *slang* were not completely successful, but they have not been wasted. With the publication of the letter *S* in OED all the pieces of the puzzle lay in full view, and one needed only a careful look at the larger picture to find a slot for each of them in the overall scheme.

The difference is apparent between a lucky guess and a reconstruction based on the wealth of material presented in OED and supported by reputable etymologists. But in all fairness it should be noted that the most convincing etymology of *slang* was offered more than a century ago. A correct solution appears in BL (*slang*), though Barrère and Leland attempted to combine Skeat's and Taylor's solutions. However, they say: "It is clear that in the sense of argot it is gypsy, the *slang* language originally meaning the language of the *slangs,* or shows, just as 'language de l'argot' meant the language of the brotherhood termed 'argot,' being afterwards shortened into argot and generalised." This is approximately the same etymology as in Platt's note. But the author of the first consistent explanation of the origin of *slang* is Sampson (1898). He did not bother to refute the views of his predecessors and published his observations in a local periodical called *Chester Courant.* Later they were reprinted in *The Cheshire Sheaf.* No one paid attention to them. Dodgson (1968) referred to an exchange of opinions about the exact meaning of *slang* 'strip of land' in *The Cheshire Sheaf* (see Holly [1898], E.G. [1898], James Hall [1898], and Sampson [1898]), but he did not say that Sampson's article contained in a nutshell everything needed for understanding the history of *slang* 'informal language.' Here is the relevant passage.

"As a student of Romani, may I point out that whatever the word 'slang' may be, it is certainly not of Gypsy origin. It is not found in a single English or continental Gypsy vocabulary, nor have I ever heard it used by Gypsies, even as a loan word... Nor, again, is the word 'slang' Shelta... As a cant word 'slang' exists; but it is, in my belief, of too recent an origin to have given birth to the field-name, though, as I will attempt to shew, the converse process may have taken place. I have heard the word used by itinerant hawkers and other non-Gypsy van dwellers: (1) In the common phrase *slanging the prads...* lit[erally] 'fielding the horses' – that is, turning them loose for the night in some farmer's field; (2) as a substantive 'slang' or 'slangs' bears the meaning of 'a hawker's license'; and (3) 'slang' now used to describe any racy colloquialism, was formerly used as a synonym for 'cant,' *that is,* the secret jargon of some vagabond or criminal set of people.

"Now it is worthy of note that these very different meanings may be harmonised and explained on the simple supposition that hawkers and other vagrants, who are often the conservators of interesting archaisms, should have preserved in their ordinary speech a genuine old English word 'slang' which meant 'field' or some form of field, and which gradually acquired various secondary meanings... Anyone familiar with the life of the roads knows that tramps and vagrants of different degrees meet together on camping grounds and in lodging-houses, and pick up and pass on each other's words, often with little regard to the true or original sense of the word borrowed... This explanation, of course, leaves the original question of the etymology of 'slang' as a field-name still to seek. But it may prevent its being sought in Romani where it does not exist, or in cant, which, if my contention be correct, owes the word to the field-name, and not *vice versa.*" The main correction of Sampson's hypothesis concerns "a genuine old English word 'slang.'"

SLOWWORM (900)

E slowworm *(< OE* slāwyrm*), Sw and OD* (orm)slå, *N* (orm)slo, *N reg* sleva, *and G* (Blind)schleiche *designate the same reptile, the lizard* Anguis fragilis. *The Scandinavian compounds also occur without* orm-. *Slowworm has been explained as a sloe eater, a slow creature, a slow biter, or a slayer. All those explanations are products of folk etymology. The second element,* -worm, *meant 'snake' (not 'worm'). A connection between* slā-, *etc with the Germanic word for 'slime' is unlikely, because the slowworm is not slimy. Most* *probably, the etymon of* slā- *is* *slanhō-, *related to OHG* slango *'snake', with* h *and* g *alternating by Verner's Law. If so, then* slāwyrm *is a tautological compound, 'snake-snake,' like OHG* lintwurm *'dragon' and Dan* ormeslange *'slowworm.' Given this etymology, N* sleva *and G* -schleiche *are not related to* slā- ~ slå- ~ slo- *or each other. The reverse order of the elements in E* slowworm, *as opposed to* ormslå ~ ormslo, *can be accounted for by the fact that since each part of the compound had the same meaning, it mattered little which of them occupied the first place. OHG* slango *(ModG* Schlange*) stands in ablaut relation with the verb* schlingen *'twist, bend' and is not akin to* slay *(G* schlagen *'strike'), whatever the original meaning of Gmc* *slahan *may have been.*

The sections are devoted to 1) the attested forms of the English word, 2) the early conjectures about its origin, 3) the effort by Scandinavian scholars to explain the origin of slå- ~ slo- ~ slā-, sleva, *and* -schleiche, *4) Svanberg's attempt to connect some of those words with* *slahan *'strike', and 5)* slowworm *among tautological compounds in and outside Germanic.*

1. **E *slow(worm),* Sw and OD *(orm)slå,* N *(orm)slo,* N reg *sleva,* and G *(Blind)schleiche* designate the same reptile, the lizard *Anguis fragilis.*** The elements *slow-* (< *slā-*), *slo-* (the Scandinavian words also occur without *orm-*), *sleva,* and *-schleiche,* particularly the first three, sound alike, but it remains a matter of debate whether some or all of them are related and what their origins are. *Blind-* in the lizard's name is not limited to German: cf E *blindworm* and Sw and Dan *blindorm.* Although the slowworm can see, references to its alleged blindness have been known since antiquity. Gk τυφλόν and L *caecilia* may have influenced the modern European forms (SN, 231: "Eidechse"). E *orvet,* if it goes back to L *orbus (luminis)* (Svanberg [1929:255]), likewise alludes to the deprivation of sight. A few older researchers mention the slowworm's large eyelids and the closing of its eyes at death as the reason for calling it blind, but later authorities unanimously speak of its small eyes. Sw *kopparorm* and N *stålorm,* literally 'copper snake' and 'steel snake' (Svanberg 1929:256), show that the 'metallic' skin is the lizard's other conspicuous feature.

No citations of *blindworm* predate 1450 in OED. By contrast, *slowworm* is old. OE *slāwyrm* and *slāwerm* "rendered various Latin names of serpents and lizards" (OED). The Old English form *slawwyrm(e),* as it appears in Somner and Lye, turns up in several dictionaries (it made its way even into Karsten [1900:243, note 1], and E. Fraenkel [1953:68]), but it is a ghost word, for the spelling with *-ww-* appeared only in the 16th century.

2. **The conjectures about the origin of *slowworm* in English dictionaries are not numerous.** Minsheu: "sloeworm, because it useth to creepe and liue on sloe-trees." This etymology finds no support in the lizard's habits. Yet Skinner, the anonymous author of *Gazophylacium* (who, as usual, copied from Skinner), and Boag repeated it. N. Bailey (1721 and 1730) assumed that slowworms were slow. Many lexicographers repeated his explanation. One of them was Richardson, who wrote: "*a slowe* [sic] a sloth or sluggard." E. Adams (1860-61:9) compared *slowworm* with *slugworm* and *lugworm.* Those words were recorded only in 1602 and 1799 respectively (OED). The slug is indeed a sluggard, but the noun *slug,* with or without *s-,* is not related to *slow* 'tardy,' whereas the history of *lug* 'a large marine worm' has not been clarified.

Wedgwood compared *slow-* with *-schleiche* (independently of Wachter, who predated him in this respect). He also cited a few Norwegian regional words, including *sleva,* which attracted the attention of Scandinavian researchers much later. His tentative hypothesis was that the slowworm got its name "from its slime." Skeat (as reported in anonymous [1881:177], and see Skeat[1]) traced *slow-* to **slaha* 'smiter.' Since the slowworm was considered to be venomous, it could have been called a slayer. Folk etymology anticipated Bailey (*slowworm* is the same as *slow worm*) and Skeat (the spelling *slay-worm* has been attested); the affinity between *slow-* and *slow* ~ *slay* is apparent. Skeat's initial gloss of *ormslå* as 'worm striker' carries little conviction, despite the fact that the slowworm feeds on insects, worms, and so forth, because *-worm* and *-orm* in the compounds discussed here mean 'snake,' not 'worm' (there is no disagreement on this point). Skeat never gave up his treatment of *slowworm* but later offered a more reasonable gloss, namely 'slay-worm, the snake that strikes,' and decided that OE *slā-* was borrowed from Scandinavian (he says: Icelandic). Numerous dictionaries copied Skeat's etymology (the same in Qui Tam [1890a:225] and Whitman [1907:392]). No one tried to explain the difference in the order of elements: *slow* + *worm* versus *orm* + *slå* ~ *slo.*

3. **Thus we have the slowworm understood as a sloe eater, a slow creature (a sluggard), or a slayer. If we follow Wedgwood's lead and make *slow-* akin to *-schleiche,* the lizard will emerge as a creeper or a slimy animal.** In dealing with *slowworm,* students of English accord the Swedish and Norwegian forms no special treatment. Onions (ODEE) only says that the first element of *slowworm,* which is of doubtful origin, had been assimi-

lated to *slow* and that it appears with or without *orm* in *ormslå* ~ *ormslo*. The main progress in investigating those words was made by Scandinavian scholars. **Johansson** (1889:302, note 2) **hesitatingly reconstructed the protoform of *slå-* ~ *slo-* as **slaihwō*, from **slingwan* 'bend'** (cf L *oblīquus* 'bending, slanting; crooked'). He cited Lith *slíekas* 'snail,' OPr *slayx* 'rainworm,' and Gk σκώληξ 'worm, larva, caterpillar' (< *'bending') among its congeners. Wood (1903:47, 1905:124/548), von Friesen (1906:11, note 1, cont on p. 12), and E. Fraenkel (1953:68 and LEW) supported his derivation. But in the next volume of *PBB* (1891:213) **Johansson noted that *slå-* ~ *slo-* might perhaps go back to **slanhō*, of which OHG *slango* 'snake' would be an alternate form by Verner's Law.** A. Kock (1916:198, note) found both hypotheses equally plausible, whereas A. Noreen (1894:184 and 1904:sec 73.2) preferred the second one. Noreen's lists contain no discussion.

In the meantime, Falk (1890:117-18), without references to his predecessors, suggested that the most important word in reconstructing the origin of *slå* ~ *slo* is E *slow(worm)*, which he interpreted as 'slow worm'; a reptile "whose bite is blunt" *(den, hvis bid er slövt)*, in contrast to the adder. This is an unpromising etymology, for the Old English and the Old Scandinavian words in question meant both 'slowworm' and 'adder.' Its sole advocate seems to have been H. Pipping (1904:160-61, esp note 4 on p. 160; 1905:37-38; and 1917:82-89), though he glossed **slaiwu* as 'a snake that does not bite' *(den orm, som ej biter)*, probably because he could not understand Falk's odd phrase. In FT, no trace of the blunt bite remained. The German translation repeats the Norwegian version verbatim; the supplement contains only bibliographical references (read there *Beitr. 14, 302* for *Beitr. 24, 302*). **Falk and Torp's starting point is Johansson's **slaihwō*. They cite the same Baltic words but give PIE **slîk*[w] the meaning 'slimy,' with *sleva* being an ablaut variant of *slå-* ~ *slo-* in the zero grade (**g* < **k* by Verner's Law).** PIE **slig*, as allegedly in MLG *slîk* and MHG *slîch* 'slime, ooze,' is called a synonym of **slei* (cf N *slim* 'slime,' Russ *slimak* 'snail,' etc). Unlike Johansson, who glossed *ormslå* ~ *ormslo* as 'writher,' **Falk and Torp's lizard turned out to be a slimy creature.** (See the most detailed discussion of the root **slei* in their entry *slesk* 'toady; unctuous.' Slipperiness and smoothness are lumped together among its reflexes, whence E *slick* ~ *sleek;* cf Weekley: *slowworm*.) **They contended that G *-schleiche*, in *Blindschleiche*, although akin to *slå-* ~ *slo-*, was at an early time associated with the verb *schleichen* 'creep.'**

Falk and Torp's derivation has the advantage of explaining *sleva* as a doublet of *slå-* ~ *slo-* (OE *slāwyrm*, made so much of in Falk [1890], is not mentioned), but assigning them to a root meaning 'slime' inspires little confidence, because neither *slāwyrm* nor *slå-* ~ *slo-* ~ *sleva* designated a slimy reptile. With or without minor variations, FT's etymology is reproduced in many dictionaries, including WP, though German researchers, who missed Wachter and Wedgwood's comparison of *slow-* with *-schleiche*, paid no attention to Falk and Torp's rediscovery of it. Nor were the Scandinavian forms drawn into the picture.

Kluge (in KL), who followed FT in his treatment of *slowworm*, disregarded it in the entry *Blindschleiche*, which first appeared in EWDS[7]. According to him, *Blindschleiche* meant *blinder Schleicher*, but he referred to Nehring (see SN, above), in whose opinion *blind-* might have been a folk etymological alteration of late L *ablinda* (the name of some reptile), an obscure Alpine word. Only Seebold (EWDS[23-24]) broke with that tradition and took into account the scholarship on the other Germanic names of the blindworm. He does not insist on the original tie between *-schleiche* and *schleichen* and remains noncommittal as to the word's descent. Lith *slíekas* has intervocalic *k*, a stop. The OS for OHG *blint(o)slîh(h)o* was *blindslîco* — apparently, not a cognate of the Baltic word (one expects intervocalic *h* in Germanic). **Perhaps, Seebold says, Gmc **sleihw-* became *-schleiche* under the influence of the verb *schleichen*, or in PIE **sloiwōn/n̥* 'worm, snake', *w* went over to *k* before syllabic *n*.**

The more special works surveyed above appeared long ago. Johansson set the tone for a serious discussion of *slowworm* and its congeners, and FT made the first of his ideas well-known. The other 'thick' dictionaries usually copy from FT or WP. 'Slimy' is the most common etymological gloss (still so in HD[1]). The small changes lexicographers introduce into the entry *slowworm* from one edition to another are arbitrary. For example, W[1] cites OE *slēan* 'slay' with a question mark, W[2] and HD[1] follow WP (that is, FT), while W[3] and HD[3-4] give no etymology at all. Pokorny (IEW) expunged *slå-* ~ *slā-* from his revision of Walde.

4. **The latest important contribution to the history of *slowworm* is Svanberg** (1928-29). **His central thesis is that 'strike,' the meaning of *schlagen* and its cognates, developed from 'make a quick movement' or 'move in a certain direction.'** He gives examples in which the verb *slá*, etc mean 'turn, twist; rush, dash; fall, move back and

forth; drive, swing.' His material is abundant, but in every sentence he cites the verb is followed by an object or has a prefix. In all the recorded Germanic languages, *slahan, slēan* and *slá* have the same connotations as do modern *schlagen* and *slå*. The numerous senses Svanberg lists are, according to him, "hardly secondary" (p. 242).

The meaning 'strike' in the languages of the world is indeed often secondary (derivative), but the origin of Gmc **slahan* has not been ascertained. Svanberg offers a new derivation of it, to reinforce his semantic analysis. *Slahan* has more or less secure cognates only in Celtic. According to Svanberg, *slahan* is related to OE *slingan* ~ OI *slyngva* 'creep' and OHG *slingan* 'swing; plait, braid.' He could cite only one allegedly similar case: PIE **svenk* ~ **sveng* versus **svek* ~ **sveg*, as in OHG *swingan* 'swing,' G *schwank* 'undecided, faltering' (MHG *swank* 'pliant'), Nynorsk *svaga* 'sway, roll, lurch from side to side,' and possibly, MLG *swaken* 'shake, wobble, lurch.' In light of his etymology he examines a number of words, including G *schwach* 'weak' (with /x/ from */k/), which is related to both Nynorsk *svaga* and G *schwank*. In the pairs *slingan* (< **slengwan*) and *svaga* ~ *swank*, the first one shows the loss of the labial element in **gw*, and the second is an example of the infix *n*.

Manuals of Old Germanic give few details on the development of intervocalic **hw* (cf the summary exposition in SB, sec 205, note 3); only Wood (1926) partly makes up for this deficiency. By contrast, in Scandinavian phonetics the history of **hw* is a major topic (the main works are A. Kock [1895], H. Pipping [1912], Lindroth [1911-12], and Olson [1915a and 1915b]). Assuming that *slahan* has cognates outside Germanic, its *h* must go back to **k* (PIE **slak-*). OE *slic* 'hammer, mallet' and *slecg* 'hammer' (> *sledge;* the latter corresponding to OI *sleggja*) look like being related to *slēan* ~ *slá* but have incompatible final consonants. One wonders what role sound imitation and sound symbolism played in the formation of those nouns. Svanberg's parallel *(*slahan : *slengwan* as *svaga : swingan)* has its limitations, because *-g-* in *swingan* is not necessarily a reflex of **gw*. We have only Go *afswaggjan** (the recorded form is *afswaggidai*, past participle, plural), tentatively glossed as 'make one waver,' a possible causative to *swingan*. The reliability of the attested form is in doubt, and the function of *w* (not a regular suffix of causative verbs) is unclear. Despite those difficulties, Svanberg's reconstruction need not be rejected out of hand. The original meaning of *slahan* may have been 'make a quick movement,' though if *slingan* and *slahan* are related, their root emerges only after the postradical consonants have been given the status of enlargements. In any case, tracing *slingan* and *slahan* to the same root is more credible than setting up a common etymon for *slîhhan* and *slingan*, as Osthoff (1910:169) suggested (this is why he easily connected *-schleiche, slango,* and the Baltic words, which are allegedly akin to *ormslå:* pp. 168-69).

When Svanberg began his investigation, he was apparently unaware of the fact that long before him Wood had used the same arguments, listed the same derivatives of *slahan* ~ *slagan* ~ *slá*, and arrived at the same conclusions about both *slahan* and *slowworm*. A brief reference to Wood close to the end of the article (Svanberg [1928-29:260, note 4]) is added almost in an afterthought. Wood (1903:40, 42; 1905-06:22-23) set up the root **sele-q^{u}a^x* and took the rest for granted. As usual, he strung dozens of forms from various languages, many of them of uncertain origin. Svanberg's work made no impact on further studies. Seebold refers to it in KS, but his reference is a mere formality. Wood's etymology of *slahan* and *slowworm* found no reflection in etymological dictionaries either. Unlike Wood, Svanberg tried to reveal the process by which *slahan* can be shown to belong with *slingan*.

In the final section of his article, Svanberg surveys the various hypotheses on the origin of *slowworm* ~ *omslå* ~ *ormslo* and registers some good points in every conjecture but emphasizes the fact that the slowworm is smooth rather than slimy and that its skin reminds one of a metallic surface. **Svanberg** was the only one to have discovered Du *slaaworm* 'the larva of the cockchafer' (p. 259, note 4) in the index to Nemnich. He **believed that *(orm)slå* is related to **slahan* and that **slanhō* is the sought-for link between the verb and **slengwan*** (p. 260). ***Sleva,* he points out, may be a separate word** (p. 259), **while *-schleiche* refers to the lizard's 'sleek' appearance** (p. 256). Even if *slahan* at one time combined the meanings 'make a quick movement' (hence 'writhe like a snake') and 'strike', we still do not know whether the protoform of *slā-* ~ *slå-* ~ *slo-* was **slaihwō* or **shanhō,* and this is the main question.

A hypothesis illuminating several forms is preferable to a series of conjectures, each of which purports to reconstruct the past of one word. **Slaihwō* allowed Johansson to trace *slo-* ~ *slå-* and *sleva* to different grades of ablaut of the same etymon. Yet he offered a second etymology of *slå-* ~ *slo-*, from **slanhō,* passed by *sleva,* and connected the forms in question with *slango.* As already stated, A. Kock could not decide which etymon is more convincing. Hellquist (1891:8) felt the same way and refused to commit himself even many years later: in SEO, he cautiously sided with FT.

Svanberg's etymology of the lizard's name is unsatisfactory. G *-schleiche* can be understood as 'sleek' only if the word's etymon is **(s)lei-* 'slime,' but then reference to a quick movement is no longer needed. Surprisingly, Svanberg accepted this part of FT's etymology to account for *Blindschleiche* after he implicitly rejected the rest of it for his material. If *slá* is derived from *slahan,* it cannot also be derived from **slengwan,* even assuming that the two verbs are cognate. Nor can the animal name *slá-* from *slahan* mean 'writher' or 'creeper' only because **slengwan* means 'writhe, creep.' Tracing this noun to *slahan* presupposes that at the moment of derivation *slahan* predominantly meant 'turn, twist,' and so forth. **Slanhō,* a congener of **slengwan* in a different grade of ablaut, indeed meant 'writher.' Unlike FT, Svanberg (and here he follows Johansson's second etymology) left N *sleva* without an explanation, and perhaps he was right. *Sleva* may have formed folk etymological ties with *slå-* ~ *slo-* late, whereas the slowworm was, in the past, taken for a snake, so that the idea of **slánhā-* > *slō-* versus **slanhố-* > *slango* is appealing.

5. **If we disassociate *slow(worm)* from **slaihwō* and from the Baltic words and agree that *slā-*, and *slå-* ~ *slo-* mean 'a kind of snake,' with **slanhố* being the generic term and **slánhō* designating the species, the freedom in ordering the elements of the compounds will stop being a puzzle. *Slāwyrm* and *ormslå* ~ *ormslo* will become transparent from the point of view of word formation: they will join other tautological compounds.** In 1901, Koeppel published a short article on such words. His most cogent examples are Go *þiumagus* 'servant' and *marisaiws** 'sea,' OHG *gomman* 'man' and *lintwurm* 'dragon,' MHG *diupstâle* (> ModG *Diebstahl*) 'theft,' as well as G *Salweide* 'willow' (the willow tree was known as *salaha* and as *wîda*) and *Sauerampfer* 'sorrel' (both OHG *sûr* and *ampfaro* meant 'sour'). In English, we have *gangway* with a specialized meaning (from OE *gang* and *weg* 'path'), *pathway, sledgehammer,* and *haphazard.* Cf also OE *mægencræft* and *mægenstrengo* ~ *mægenstrengðo* 'strength' (a counterpart of MHG *magenkraft*), *holtwudu* 'forest, grove,' *race(n)tēag* 'chain,' and *wordcwide* 'speech, utterance.' E *henbane* (each of its parts once meant 'death': see HENBANE), *courtyard,* and perhaps *mealtime* (one of the meanings of OE *mǣl* was 'fixed time'), along with G *lobpreisen* 'praise, glorify' (and *lobhudeln* 'praise excessively'), can be added to this list. Cf also what is said about F *bran de son* (BRAIN).

In addition, Koeppel cited Middle English hybrids of the *love-amour, wonder-mervaile,* and *cite-toun* type. Such hybrids (half-native, half-Romance) enjoyed some popularity (Kriebitzsch [1900:14-37], though his examples are not always convincing; other examples can be found in von Künßberg [1940]). G *klammheimlich* seems to be from L *clam* 'secret, unknown to' (the root also occurring in E *clandestine*) and G *heimlich;* then the adjective (students' slang, some wit's coinage?) has the structure comparable to that of *love-amour.* Koziol (1937:49, sec 89) repeats Koeppel's examples, but there must be many more such, and their existence was noticed long ago (cf Warwick [1856]). If *ragamuffin* (see RAGAMUFFIN) started as 'devil-a-devil,' it belongs here too.

Ershova and Pavlova (1984:39) point out that this type of word formation is productive in English dialects: cf *lass-quean, lad-bairn,* and *sea-loch;* the last one is an analogue of Go *marisaiws**. Russ *put'-doroga* 'way' (from *put'* 'way' and *doroga* 'road'; cited by Ershova and Pavlova) and *gore-zloschast'e* 'misfortune-mishap,' as well as the Irish epic name *Culhwych,* literally 'pig-pig' (Hamp [1986a]) show that such words are not limited to Germanic. See Liberman (2007).

If we derive animal names *slo-* ~ *slå-* and OHG *slango* from the same etymon, *ormslå* ~ *ormslo* will emerge as 'snake-snake.' Lindroth (1911:126) shared this view. Johansson and A. Noreen must have thought so too. This etymology helps explain why it was possible to reverse the elements (*slāwyrm* versus *ormslå* ~ *ormslo*): both had the same meaning. Cf Sw *regndusk* and N *duskregn* 'drizzle': it matters little whether one says *drizzle-rain* or *rain-drizzle.*

An ideal etymology of *slowworm, (orm)/slå* ~ *slo, sleva,* and *Blindschleiche* would show all of them to be cognates. With the facts at our disposal, such an etymology cannot be offered, because the origin of G *Blindschleiche* (unless it has always meant 'blinder Schleicher,' so that the similarity between *-schleiche* and the rest is fortuitous) is beyond reconstruction. N *sleva* is incompatible with **slanhō,* whereas **slaihwō* is not akin to OHG *slango.* Consequently, each choice presupposes a sacrifice. *Sleva,* a regional word, whose history is unknown, may be a smaller one. The closest analogues of *slowworm* and *ormslå* ~ *ormslo* will be OHG *lintwurm* and *lintdrache* 'dragon' (another snake-snake) and Dan *ormeslange* 'slowworm' (Liberman [2005]).

STRUMPET (1327)

Several Germanic roots that are sometimes hard to keep apart may have interacted or coalesced in the production of strumpet. *The first, meaning 'rough,' is seen in LG* Struwwel- *'tousle-head'; the second, meaning 'stump,' underlies G* Gestrüpp *'shrubbery' and MHG* strumpf *'stump' (later 'trouser leg' and 'stocking'). With the root designating things rough and sticking out, the original meaning of* strumpet *emerges as *'unpolished woman.' Compare MHG* strunze *'stump' and ModG* Strunze *'slattern.' Closely related are words for 'walk (in an ungainly way),' such as G* strunzen *'loaf,' whence the idea of* strumpet **'gadabout.' A third root unites many German and Scandinavian words meaning 'unwieldy receptacle' and 'unpleasant (ugly) person' (usually 'woman'): Icel* strympa *'bucket; big woman.' Icel* strunta *'small wooden vessel; grouchy man' is a cognate of G* Strunze. *The last root may not be different from the previous ones. English lacks the variety of forms and meanings found in German and Icelandic, which suggests that* strumpet *is probably a borrowing, more likely from Low German than from Scandinavian. It has not always referred to women, as follows from E reg* strumpet *'fat, hearty child,' but 'prostitute' has been its main meaning from the start.* Strumpet *is not an alteration of L* stuprum *'dishonor' or OIr* striapach *'prostitute'; only the suffix* -et *is of French origin.*

The sections are devoted to 1) the earliest etymologies of strumpet, *2) S. Johnson's derivation of* strumpet *from L* stuprum, *3)* strumpet *and its putative cognates in German, and 4)* strumpet *in a Scandinavian context.*

1. OED lists the following forms of *strumpet*: *strumpat, strompat, strompett(e), strompyd, stroumpet, strumpett(e), strumpytte, strompott,* and *strumpit*. With the exception of *strompott,* which probably owes its existence to an association with *pot,* they seem to reflect the pronunciation [strumpit] or [strumpət], later [strʌmpit]. In recorded texts, *strumpet* has always meant 'prostitute.' **Older dictionaries offered several etymologies for this word. OED treated all of them as unprofitable speculation, and at present the origin of *strumpet* is believed to be unknown.**

These are the earliest conjectures about the derivation of *strumpet*: from F *tromper* 'cheat, deceive,' especially in the sense 'jilt' (Minsheu; often repeated later), from the Greek noun μαστροπός 'pander' (Casaubon in Junius), from Du *stront-pot* 'dung pot or common Jakes' (N. Bailey's gloss [1730]: *Jake* means 'latrine,' that is, 'john'), and from Ir *striopach* 'prostitute' (Lye in Junius; Webster, from 1828 to 1847; Wedgwood, and Mackay [1877]). Tooke supported the dungpot hypothesis but explained *strumpet* as a compound of two Dutch participles. Ker (1837:II, 3) thought that *strumpet* consisted of three Dutch words. His candidates were the nouns *stier* ~ *steur* ~ *stuyr* (he believed that those were Dutch words for 'tax'), *ruymen* (that is, *ruimen*) 'make room,' and *bed* 'bed.' In passing, he accused Tooke of stupidity and arrogance. Ker's derivation of *strumpet* constituted only a small part of an embarrassingly vituperative entry (but Tooke was not more courteous). Thomson derived *strumpet* from *strum* 'fornicate.' No dictionary records this meaning of *strum*. In some languages, words for 'woman' begin with *str-*, Skt *strī́* 'woman, wife' and OHG *strîa* 'witch' among them (Mayrhofer [1952a:35-37], KEWA [522-23], Normier [1980:44-46], with further references). Even if some of them are related, none has anything to do with *strumpet.*

2. Johnson introduced L *stuprum* 'disgrace, licentiousness, whoredom' into the discussion of *strumpet* (as he pointed out, his source was Trévoux). His etymology proved especially long-lived. Todd (in Johnson-Todd) referred to Wachter, who cited *strüne*, a Low Saxon word for 'prostitute' (Todd left out the umlaut sign). Wach-ter mentions *strüne* in the entry on *Strunze,* where we also find OE *mylte streona*. He probably meant OE *myltestre* 'prostitute.' Speakers seem to have understood that noun as *mylte-stre,* because OE *myltenhūs* 'brothel' also existed. OE *meltan* 'consume by fire, burn up' and *mieltan* 'digest; purge; exhaust' suggest that *mylten-hūs* resembles such 15th-century words for 'brothel' as *kitchen* and *stew*: both refer to heat and its effect. *Miltestre* is usually explained as an Anglicized reflex of L *meretrix* 'prostitute' (a word that allegedly came to England with Roman soldiers), but Wachter, although he followed folk etymology, may have been close to the truth in treating *-stre* as an independent element, even if it was confused with the productive suffix *-stre* (see more on *myltestre* in Gusmani [1972], with references to earlier works). G *Strunze* 'slattern' must be related to the verb *strunzen* 'gad about, loaf' (the gloss for MHG *strunze* is 'Stumpf, Bengel,' that is, 'stump; boy, lad' in WHirt and 'stumpf, lanzensplitter,' that is, 'stump; brave knight' in Lexer). In the rare cases *Strunze* appears in German etymological dictionaries, it is never connected with E *strumpet.* G *strunzen* is a cognate of E *strunt* (a nasalized form of *strut*).

Ogilvie (ID) repeats the supposed French derivation of the English noun but modifies it slightly: *strumpet* may be, he says, a nasalized form of OF *(e)stropier* 'lame, maim' (v), in allusion to the effects of venereal diseases. In the versions of ID that appeared under his own name, Annandale mentions only OF *st(r)upre* (< *stuprum*). Weekley (1924 and only in that version of his dictionary) cites the mid-15th-century word *streppet* 'strumpet.' Partridge (1958) favors a Dutch etymon; he glosses MDu *strompen* as 'stride, stalk' and explains *strumpet* as a stalker of men. The other dictionaries copy from one of the above authors (most prefer the derivation from *stuprum*) or say that the origin of *strumpet* is unknown.

Skeat[4] suggested the Old French etymon **estrompette,* as though from MDu *strompe* 'stocking,' or a nasalized form of OF *strupe,* late L *strupum* 'dishonor, violation' (< L *stuprum*), with *m* "strengthening" the form **strup-et.* He admitted that the English word might be derived directly from OF **strupée* < late L **strupata,* a metathesized form of *stuprata,* the past participle of *stuprāre* (from *struprum,* sb). Skeat traced Ir and Gael *striopach* to the same Latin word. Alongside MDu *strompe,* he mentioned LG *strump* 'stocking,' N reg *strumpen* 'stumbling,' LG *strumpen, strumpeln* 'stumble,' *strumpeling* 'staggering, tottering in gait,' and MDu *strompelen* 'stagger, trip, reel.' "We might perhaps then explain *strumpet* as 'one who trips, or makes a false step,'" he says. He compared all those words with G *strampeln* 'kick' and found it remarkable that in Huntingdonshire *strumpet* means 'fat, hearty child,' that is, 'little kicker' (EDD). A Germanic section appeared in his entry on *strumpet* only in the fourth edition. Earlier he considered the Romance etymons as certain and gave the probable root as **stup* 'push, strike against' (as in Gk στῠφελίζω 'push, repulse'). G. Williams (1994) finds the derivation of *strumpet* from *stuprum* convincing, but his supporting example (*mastrupation* for *masturbation,* another form with metathesis) is nothing more than a learned folk etymology.

3. **Two closely related approaches to the etymology of *strumpet* are worthy of discussion. Germanic had the roots **struppan- ~ *strubbōn-* 'rough' and **strumpa- ~ *strunka- ~ *strunta-* 'stump'** (Lühr [1988:163-6, 278-9]). In some situations, they may have overlapped, for reference was to things both rough and sticking out. Many Germanic words beginning with *str-* have *s-mobile,* with *t* inserted between *s* and *r* (Wanner [1963], with reference to A. Noreen and Kluge). Among them are SwiG *rūb ~ strūb* and *Rŭbel ~ Strŭbel.* They designate things sticking out, truncated, or uneven. G *struppig* 'tousled,' *Gestrüpp* 'shrubbery,' *Strobel,* a regional word for *Struwwelpeter* (or *Strubbelpeter*) 'touslehead,' and *sträuben* 'ruffle,' belong here, as well as many words with nasalization, for example, *Strumpf* 'stump' and *Rumpf* 'rump.' The Swiss noun *Rŭbel* means 1. 'touslehead,' 2. 'rude man; bad-mannered young woman,' 3. 'stormy weather,' especially 'blizzard,' 4. 'great noise, quarrel.' A synonym of *Rŭbel* is *Strŭbel* (Wanner [1963:138]). Given the etymon designating 'rough (object),' all the meanings of *Rŭbel* are easy to explain, but they would be hard to predict or reconstruct.

Strump(et) looks like a cognate of *Strŭbel* 'rude, unpolished person of either sex.' In the beginning, such words often refer to both men and women and have relatively inoffensive meanings (see more at GIRL). *Harlot* started as 'vagabond, rascal, low fellow' (13th century). *Strumpet* may initially have been a term of abuse, something like *'cantankerous, querulous, ill-mannered person'; later this meaning may have been narrowed down to *'bad-mannered woman' and still later to 'prostitute,' though such intermediate meanings have not been attested.

Consequently, **we should search for the etymon of *strumpet* among words meaning 'rough, unpolished, bad-tempered person.'** Shrubs, stubs, and stumps would turn up in this search at every step because stumps are 'stiff' (H. Schröder [1908:521-24]) or because it is hard to walk gracefully over rough, 'stumpy' ground (Vercoullie, *struik;* Lindqvist [1918:111-12]). Consider also G *Strumpf* 'trouser leg, stocking.' Its original meaning was 'stub, stump' (KM, KS). The clue from *Strunze* should be considered too. Although here we may be dealing with a different etymon, the semantic spectrum is remarkable: ModG *Strunze* means 'slattern,' MHG *strunze* means 'stump,' whereas ModG *strunzen* means 'loaf' (v). Du *stront* is 'excrement, dung,' that is, 'droppings.' If *strunzen* is unrelated to *strunze ~ Strunze,* we have another word like *Strŭbel,* but it would be strange if *strunze ~ Strunze* and *strunzen* were not cognate.

Assuming that the German words listed above are akin to *strumpet,* a strumpet was either a rough (dirty, slatternly, unpolished) woman or a strunter ('strutter'). MHG *trunze* (*drunze, drumze*) 'piece of a broken spear, splinter' and *trunzen* 'curtail' are usually traced to OF *trons* 'fragment', *tronce* 'cut off' (compare E *truncate, truncheon,* and possibly *trounce*), but OI *trunsa ~ trumsa* 'snub, spurn,' and N *trunta* 'sulk' (reg) versus Dan *trunte* 'tree trunk, stump,' which are probably borrowings from Low German, suggest that *trunze* is a doublet of *strunze* and thus a word of Germanic origin. Among the authors of Scandinavian etymological dictionaries, Holthausen (VEW) seems to be the closest to the truth in dealing with those words. MHG *(s)trunze* 'stump,' ModG *Strunze* 'slattern,' and ModG *strunzen* 'gad about, loaf' testify to the fact that the words denoting 'uneven (object)' and 'walk in an untidy or clumsy manner' could be (near) homonyms and affect one another. See a detailed analysis of the root *strut* in Herbermann (1974:6-31).

4. **A somewhat different approach to *strumpet* is based mainly on the facts of Modern Icelandic.** ÁBM lists *strympa* (first recorded in the 17th century) 'dipper, tall or pointed hat, bucket, building with a cone-shaped roof; virago, big woman' (its more modern variant is *strumpa*). *Strympa* occurs in CV, where it is compared with OI *strompr* 'chimney stack.' ÁBM offers the same comparison. *Stromp(u)r* has more or less certain cognates in the other Scandinavian languages (the meanings are 'narrow wooden bucket,' 'whetstone,' 'barrel,' 'measuring vessel,' and 'upper part of a trouser leg'). **If 'dipper, tall hat, chimney stack,' 'stub,' and the rest go back to the same protomeaning *'stump-like,' we come back to the root discussed above, but the path from *strump-* 'stump' to 'prostitute' would go via 'unwieldy; like a vat,' rather than via 'rough, sticking out.'**

As long as a bond between the roots with and without *n* remained in the linguistic intuition, the idea of strutting could merge with the idea of 'arrogance' (consider ModI *struns* 'arrogance' borrowed from Low German in the 18th century) and 'loafing' (ModI *struns* also means 'loafing'). The 17th-century Icelandic verb *strunsa* 'mock, deceive' seems to be related to *strunsa* 'gad about, strut' and to *strunta* (18th century) 'small wooden vessel, *etc*; grouchy man.' G *Strunze* 'slattern' corresponds to 'small wooden vessel'. **It follows that the meaning 'virago, *etc*' may be a descendant of the ancient meaning of *strump-* 'stump' ('rough object,' with the influence from its homonym 'gad about') or a metaphor, from 'receptacle' ('unwieldy object') to '(unpleasant, unattractive) person.'**

The syncretism 'vessel' (especially often 'basket') / 'old, unattractive woman' is widespread in Germanic. Consider OI *skrukka* 'nickname of a troll woman' (in Modern Icelandic, 'old wrinked woman') and 'basket made of birch bark,' Bav *Krade* 'basket carried on one's back' and 'ugly woman,' G *Schachtel* 'box' and 'hag' (*alte Schachtel* 'old woman'), Sc *reiskie* 'beehive' and 'ungainly woman' (A.M. [1903]; W [1903]). Magnússon ([1957:239] and see ÁBM) mentions OI *bryðja* 'pot; giantess,' ModI *drylla* ~ *drulla* (first recorded in the 17th century) 'bucket, vat, narrow vessel; arrogant woman,' and *strylla* (a 15th-century word, perhaps from Low German) 'small pail, vat; single rock, pyramid, *etc*; troll woman.' One can add Icel *biða* 'vessel with a narrow neck, chimney stack' and 'fat woman' (also 'tiny tot'); OI *kolla* 'wooden vessel without a handle, mug' and 'woman' (now obsolete); Nynorsk *lodda* 'short woman' and 'half-stocking made of coarse fabric' (see LAD). Words for 'cavity, opening, hole' often become the etymons for 'woman' (Rooth [1963] discusses an especially imaginative example), but not all the vessels mentioned here got their names from 'opening' ('vagina').

E reg *strumpet* 'fat, hearty child' must originally have meant 'ugly or intractable child,' not 'little kicker,' for all words of this group have negative connotations. 'Fat, hearty child' and 'grouchy man' show that *strunt-* ~ *strump-* did not necessarily appy to women. Partridge (1949b) sees no problem in E *molly* 'fruit basket' ("if ever you have seen women in an orchard you will know what I mean"), but *molly* 'basket' ~ *moll(y)* 'prostitute' may be another example of the syncretism mentioned above. The root of E *strumpet*, G *Strunze*, and Icel *strympa* is Germanic; the meaning of the English and the Modern Icelandic words may have been influenced by Low German (the differences between the groups *-nt* ~ *-nz* and *-mp-* may perhaps be due to assimilation).

Although details remain hidden, the fact that English lacks the sound string *strump-* and *strunt-* in the names of receptacles (vessels) seems to indicate that E *strumpet* is a borrowing (more probably from Low German than from Scandinavian), with a French suffix added to turn a native *strunze* into a classy harlot. In similar fashion, *trull* coexists with *trollop*; both are related to *troll*. See more about the root *strot-* at TROT (sb). Ir *striopach* is so unlike *strump(et)* that borrowing, regardless of the direction, need not be considered. LE confirms the antiquity of the Irish word and shares the common opinion that *striopach* goes back to L *stuprum*, with metathesis. As we have seen, Skeat, too, had to introduce metathesis into his reconstruction of the Romance form. The derivation in LE (unless it can be shown that *striopach* is a bookish, churchy word) is as unappealing as the derivation of E *strumpet* from *stup-rum* (Liberman [1992a:87-91, 93-94]).

STUBBORN (1386)

The only cognate of stubborn, *with* s-mobile, *is Icel* þybbin *'obstinate,' which can be explained as either 'swollen' or 'firm.' The English word is thus not a derivative of* stub, *and* stubborn *does not mean 'immovable as a stub.' The al-*

ternation of the suffixes (-orn ~ -inn) *remains unexplained.*

The earliest forms of *stubborn* are *stibourne, stoburne*, and the like. Most explanations, including the one we find in modern dictionaries, have been of a folk etymological nature. Minsheu derived *stubborn* from *strout-born*, perhaps with reference to *strout*, a variant of *strut* (sb) 'strife, contention,' unless it is a misprint for *stout-born*, as N. Bailey (1721) must have thought. However, Skinner and N. Bailey (1730) repeat *strout-born*. **Beginning with Lye (in Junius), *stubborn* has been connected with *stub*, as though *stubborn* meant 'immovable as a stub.'** Both etymologies (from *stout-born* and from *stub*) sometimes appear as equally probable even much later (Graham [1843:61]). Old English had *stubb* and *stybb*, which (if *stubborn* is akin to them) would explain the Middle English doublets *stoburn*, pronounced with [u], and *stibourne*. Skeat[1] derived *stubborn* from *stybb* and ignored *stubb* (Ekwall [1903:64, note 5] pointed to the weakness of Skeat's derivation). He found only one example with *u* < *y* (*furze* < OE *fyrs*). However, words with ME *u* < *y* are common: *blush, clutch* (with [u] before [ʃ] and [tʃ]), *church, burden* (with [u] before *r*), *shut, shuttle, thrust*, and so forth (Luick 1964:secs 375 and 397). English dialectal dictionaries cite neither *stib* nor *stibborn*. OED does not object to *stub* as the etymon of *stubborn*, and Weekley (1921) gives a parallel from German: *Storren* 'stump' ~ *störrisch* 'obstinate, stubborn.'

The only unquestionable cognate of *stubborn* is ModI *þybbin* 'obstinate, dogged, sturdy,' though etymological dictionaries of English and Icelandic never mention the connection between them. *Þybbin* was first recorded in the 18th century; however, *þybbast* 'endure, resist' occurs in the works of Guðmundur Ólafsson, 1552-95 (Árni Böðvarsson, personal communication; ÁBM dates the verb to the 17th century). Both *stubborn* and *þybbin* seem to be old, even though both were recorded late. *Þybbin* may be related to words with the reconstructed root *tēu-, *təu-, *tū- ~ *tŭ-, as in OI *þúfa* 'mound,' and L *tūber* 'swelling, hump.' So IsEW (431), but AEW doubts that *tūber* belongs here and does not cite *þybbinn* in the discussion of *þúfa* (the same in ÁBM). Wood (1919:251/16 and 271/90) reconstructs the base *tu̯əbh- 'make firm, strong, secure' and compares OI *þopta* 'rower's bench' and L *tabula* 'board.' The first vowel of *þybbinn* is umlauted *u*, and the geminate is probably of expressive origin. The root of *stubborn* can be seen in OI *stúfr* and *stubbr* ~ *stubbi* (both mean 'stump').

Unlike E *stubborn*, Icel *þybbinn* has a well-attested suffix: compare Icel *feginn* 'glad,' *heiðinn* 'heathen,' *heppin* 'happy,' which shows that *-orn* in *stubborn* is a Middle English development. Skeat reconstructed *stubbor* with excrescent *-n*, as in *bittern*, and cited *slattern*, a word that periodically appeared in and disappeared from his entry, and *marten* < *martern* < *marter* (Skeat [1887 = 1892:372]). Nothing is known about the history of *-n* in *bittern*, whereas *slattern* is hardly from *slatter* + *n*; neither word is an adjective. Skeat believed that *stubborn* had emerged through a redistribution of morphemes in the noun: *stubborn-ess* < *stubbor-ness*, but OED points out that *-or* did not exist as a living suffix in Old English. Words with it were inherited and formed on verb, not noun, stems. Mätzner I:431 and Mueller mention OE *clibbor* 'adhesive' (a cognate of G *klebrig*), which was monomorphemic in Old English.

OI *þybbinn* presupposes ME *stybbin* or *stybben*, so that the substitution of an obscure suffix for a transparent one remains unexplained. However, the variation *-en* ~ *-ern* occurs not only in *stubborn*. English has *golden, wooden*, and *woolen*, whereas the German adjectives are *hölzern* 'made of wood,' *gläsern* 'made of glass,' and *zinnern* 'made of tin.' The variants with *-ern* in German are late, and details of their origin are in some cases unclear. Even less clear is the history of *-ern* in German verbs like *folgern* 'draw the conclusion, follow' and *steigern* 'raise' (Paul [1920:sec 66], Henzen [1965:secs 128 and 148]). The suffix in E *southern, northern, eastern*, and *western* is of a different origin than in *hölzern* and *gläsern*; see also the comment on the form *earthern* in OED. In Middle English, the sound string *-orn* existed as a borrowing from French in *aborne* ~ *alborne* 'auburn,' but *-orn* was at no time a productive suffix. **If *stubborn*, with *s-mobile*, is related to *þybbin*, it cannot be derived from *stub*.**

According to Spitzer (1954), *stubborn* is a word of Romance origin. He discusses F reg *estibourner* 'fortify the ground by stakes or palisades,' perhaps from OD *stibord* 'a board that stifles, stems, stays,' corresponding to OD *stigbord* 'sluice' (see EWFS, *étibois*). *Stubborn*, in his opinion, meant 'strong, resistant as a palisade.' But the English word cannot be separated from ModI *þybbin*, whereas *estibourner* may have been derived from ME *stibourne* rather than from Old Danish, unless the similarity between the Middle English and the French word is a coincidence. Thomson compared *stubborn* and *stiff* but found no supporters, though the earliest dictionaries (see N. Bailey and Junius) derived *stubborn* from Gk στιβαρός 'firm, strong' (N. Bailey

[1721], but badly misspelled in N. Bailey [1730]). Bailey's derivation recurs as late as 1847 (Talbot) and 1858 (Richardson). However, the Greek adjective represents the zero grade of the root **steibh-*, the same as in OE *stīf* 'stiff' (Frisk, 782; Chantraine, 1047; WP II:647; IEW, 1015). Curtius (1873:226) gives a different explanation of the Greek word, but he, too, dispenses with *stubborn*. *Stubborn* is unrelated to *stiff* and στιβαρός (Liberman [1986:111-14]).

TOAD (1000)

Toad is the continuation of OE tādige. *Beside* tādige, *Old English* tadde *and* tosca *(with the metathesized doublet* tocsa*), both meaning 'toad,' have been recorded. Middle English had* tāde *and* tadde. *The same root can be found in ModE* tadpole. *The etymology of* toad *hinges on two questions: 1) How are OE* tādige *and* tadde *related to OE* tosca? *2) What is the relationship between OE* tosca *and the Scandinavian forms: Dan* tudse, *Sw* tossa, *and N reg* tossa, *all of them meaning 'toad'? Dictionaries, with the exception of SEO, deny any links between* tādige *and the Scandinavian words, because OE* ā, *allegedly from* *ai, *is incompatible with* ă. *However,* tādige *appears to be the lengthened variant of* tadde *despite the common opinion that* tadde *has* a < ā *before an expressive geminate. The root of* tad-de *is probably the same as in Dan* tudse *and OE* tosca *(<* *tod-sca*). North Sea Germanic has numerous words with* t/d *+ vowel +* t/d *in the root designating small objects and small movements, such as E* tid(bit), tit(bit), tad, toddle, totter, dodder, *and the like. The toad must have been thought of as a small round creature. Perhaps its warts or manner of moving in short steps ('toddling') gave it its name. If so, the old idea that Dan* tudse *is related to OHG* zuscen *'burn' should be abandoned.*

The sections are devoted to 1) the proposed etymologies and the putative Scandinavian cognates of toad, *2) the origin of* ā *in OE* tādige, *3)* toad *among other words having the structure* t-d, *and 4) the etymology of* toadstool.

1. "The etymological jungle stretching around the designations of the toad is almost impassable, in a wide variety of languages. One encounters two independent sources of complications: (a) the luxuriant growth of rival words, not always geographically delimited; and (b) the opacity of the overwhelming majority of the lexical items at issue" (Malkiel [1985:242]; see the comparative material in Wilhelm Lehmann [1907:185, note 4]). English is no exception.

Old English had *tādige* and *tădde*. *Tadpole*, that is, 'toadhead,' has been recorded since the 15th century. Both *tadde* and *tāde* turned up in Middle English. **Secure cognates of *toad* are absent, but a few look-alikes exist**, OE *tosca* 'toad' being one of them; *tosca* yielded *tocsa* by metathesis (A. Campbell [1959:sec 359]). Similar forms are Dan *tudse* (OD *tudse* and *todze*), Sw reg *tossa* (earlier *tådsa* and *tussa*), N reg *tossa*, all meaning 'toad' (Rietz, *tossa;* SEO, *tossa;* DEO, *tudse*), along with Low German *Tutz(e)* ~ *Tuutz* and a few others like it (Claus [1956]). Other similar words begin with *p-*: ME *pad* (continued as E reg *pad* ~ *paddock*), OI *padda* 'frog, toad,' with correspondences elsewhere in West Germanic, and LG *Pogge* 'toad.'

OED and ODEE call *tādige* a word of unknown etymology and unusual formation. However, it resembles OE *bodig* 'body,' and the resemblance may not be fortuitous. No direct path leads from *tadde* to *pad*, but Dan *tudse* looks like a good match for *tadde*, the widespread opinion to the contrary notwithstanding. Kaluza (1906-07:I, sec 60a) lists *tādige* among the words with *ā* < **ai*, but he follows a mechanical pattern, according to which OE *ā* can have only one source. **Taidige* and **taid-* are fiction.

Toads play an outstanding role in folklore: they are held to be loathsome and poisonous, they are associated with witchcraft, and all kinds of diseases, from warts to angina pectoris, are ascribed to them. Taboo is prominent in the names of the toad, and this circumstance may be partly responsible for the opacity of words like L *būfō*, F *crapaud*, Ital *rospo*, G *Kröte*, and Russ *zhaba*. To complicate matters, the same name often applies to the frog, the toad, and occasionally the snake (compare G *Unke* 'orange-speckled toad' versus L *anguis* 'snake').

Inquiry into the etymology of *toad* has revealed few viable possibilities. Ihre (932) compared OSw *tossa* and OI *tað* 'dung' on account of the toad's ugliness but preferred to derive *tossa* from Gk τοξικός 'poisonous' (the same as late as Charnock [1889]). The first idea (*tossa* ~ *tað*) has some potential (see below), but the second is devoid of value. Thomson listed both (O)I *tad* (that is, *tað*) and Sw *tossa* at *toad*. *Tosse* (in this form) occurs in Minsheu, who also lists G *Tod* 'death' (spelled *todt*). *Tudse* appears in Skinner and Junius. Ettmüller (1851:530) tentatively derived ME *tāde* from OE **tihan* (that is, *tēon*), which he connected with *tācen* 'token': '(an animal) pointing to rain?' ('quasi pluviam indicans?'). Webster's dictionary between 1864 and 1880 gives *tad*, *tudse*, and *tossa* at *toad*. Since words for 'frog' and 'toad' have often been traced to verbs meaning 'swell,' Richardson thought of *toad* as a derivative of OE *tēon* 'extend, expand,' whereas Wedgwood looked on OI *tútna* 'swell' as the etymon of the English word (the same also Lynn [1881:249]). Neither Richardson nor Wedgwood paid attention to phonetic details, and Mueller was justified in rejecting Wedgwood's etymology.

The search for the origin of *toad* resolves itself into two questions: 1) How are OE *tādige* and *tadde* related to OE *tosca*? 2) Are *tādige* and *tadde* related to the Scandinavian words? Skeat and OED found it impossible to bridge OE *tādige* and Dan *tudse* because if *tādige* goes back to **taidige, ai* has to be separated from *u:* the zero grade of *ai* is *i,* not *u.* It is easy to write "*toad:* cf. Dan. *tudse,*" as do Whitman (1907:386) and DEO, but the invitation to "compare" these forms is vacuous.

2. Practically everyone who has written about the etymology of OE *tadde* has agreed that the geminate in it is of expressive origin (see Zachrisson [1934:401] and Coates [1982:213] among others and a list of words like *tadde,* generated from von Friesen [1897], in Kauffmann [1900]), whereas *a* is alleged to be the result of shortening before *dd.* OED refers to Björkman as the originator or a supporter of that view. FT (*tudse*), Torp (1909:168), and Torp (1919, *tossa;* both times with a question mark), WP I:768 (with reference to Torp [1909]), and IEW, 180, proposed a connection of *tosca* and *tudse* with OHG *zuscen* 'burn'. FT point out that *tudse* is not related to *tādige* or *tadde;* the other dictionaries do not mention the English word. Holthausen wondered what fire has to do with toads (is fire the poison they secrete?) but cited WP's etymology in AeW.

The comparison *tudse* ~ *tossa* ~ *zuscen* predates FT, for it appears in BT. The reviewer of BT wrote (anonymous [1898:96]): "Under *taxe* (frog or toad) it would have been worthwhile to suggest a comparison with the synonymous *tosca,* and *vice versâ;* the two words cannot well be etymologically connected as they stand, but they bear a suspiciously close resemblance to each other in form. The conjecture that *tosca* is related to the OHG *zuscen* to burn, seems decidedly unhappy." As we now know, *taxe* is a ghost word (Napier [1898:359]), but "the unhappy conjecture" is still alive.

It would be a rare coincidence if Germanic possessed two nearly identical but unrelated forms for 'toad' (*tādige* ~ *tadde* and *tudse*). They may be connected if we assume that *a* in *tadde* is not the result of *ā* shortened but that *ā* in *tādige* is the result of *ă* lengthened. No Old Germanic language had words with the root **taid-* ~ **taiþ-, *teid-* ~ **teiþ-,* and in Old English only *tādige* begins with *tād-*. Sequences of long vowels followed by long consonants in the root were rare in Old English, so that when words like *ǣdre* 'vein' and *ātor* 'poison' (all of them had *d* or *t* before *r*) developed geminates, the vowel was usually shortened (SB, 204, sec 299, and see A. Campbell [1959:sec 281]). If *tadde* with an original geminate underwent lengthening because of taboo or for emphasis, it would become **tāde,* rather than **tādde,* and the suffix *-ig,* as in *bodig* 'body,' would be added to *tād-,* not *tadd-*. LG *Pogge,* OE *bodig,* and OE *tādige* ~ *tadde* belong to the same semantic field; see sec 4.

Some of the words with traces of spontaneous lengthening may have changed their pronunciation because of their meaning and usage. Such is OE *wēl* 'well' (adv); *fraam* 'bold, strong' is another possible example of expressive lengthening. *Haam* 'shirt' and *goor* 'dung' are hard to explain (SB, 124, sec 137/6), but all those forms were recorded in the most ancient glosses, so that lengthening in them has nothing to do with early Middle English quantitative changes. If, however, as stated above, we assume that *tăd(d)-* was the original form, the origin of *toad* will stop being a mystery. Such a type of reverse reasoning (*tadd* > *tād,* not *tād* > *tadd*) always meets with resistance. Consider the puzzlement of de Saussure's contemporaries at the idea that in Proto-Indo-European one vowel with three unknown consonants alternated, rather than three vowels with one unknown consonant.

3. **English has a considerable number of monosyllables beginning with *t* and ending in *d*, all of them meaning 'small quantity.'** Here are some of them culled from OED and EDD. *Tad* 'child' (but also 'a quantity, a burden' and in northern British dialects 'dung, manure,' probably from 'pieces of manure'); *tid,* best known as the first component of *tidbit* (in dialects also 'teat, udder,' as well as a synonym of *ted* 'small cock of hay' and 'any great (!) weight, heap; bundle of hay'); *tod* 'fox' (a northern word) and 'load; bushy mass' (in this meaning an earlier southern word), *tod* ~ *toddie* ~ *todie* 'small round cake of any kind of bread, given to children to keep them in good humor' (cf *toddle* 'small cake' and *toddle* 'walk with short unsteady steps'); *tud* 'very small person.'

Most of those words have variants or synonyms with *d* in place of *t.* Both *tottle* and *doddle* exist, and *totter* is a synonym of *toddle. Tidbit* is a variant of *titbit.* One of the glosses of *tid,* as already mentioned, is 'teat.' Its vulgar synonym (variant) is *tit,* and dialects have *tet.* In *tit for tat,* both words are symbolic names for 'some quantity.' *Tit* is also 'small horse' and 'girl,' and the titmouse is a very small bird (the idea of smallness comes from *tit* because the German for *titmouse* is simply *Meise*).

Tatter is a borrowing from Scandinavian; obviously, tatters are small rags. J. de Vries (AEW) notes at *tág* 'twig, root' that Old Icelandic had surprisingly many words beginning with *t-* and meaning 'fiber' and 'fray.' His list is heterogeneous. However, he mentions *toddi* 'weight of wool, bit' and *tǫturr* 'rag'; see *toddi* also in Kauffmann (1900:256) and *tud* in FT. E *tatting* 'kind of knotted lace work' was first recorded in 1842, and its origin is obscure, but even if it is a humorous adaptation of a foreign word, the sound string *tat* fits the idea of knotted embroidery. *Tittle, tattle,* and *tittle-tattle* suggest 'smallness,' whether it be a small dot or small talk. *Tot* is 'anything very small; tiny child'; *tut* has numerous meanings, including 'small seat made of straw.' The interjection *tut-tut!* looks like one of the words listed above. The situation with *t–d* ~ *t–t* ~ *d–t* words is the same in all the Germanic languages; see von Friesen (1897:95-97) and Björkman (1912:269 and 273, footnote) (neither of them mentions OE *tadde* or Dan *tudse*).

When dealing with near synonyms and near homonyms like *tottle-toddle-totter-dodder, tid-tit-teat,* and *tad-tot,* an etymology that would more or less fit the entire group would be the best one, even though each word has its own history and deserves attention. Some of the English words listed here are borrowings from Scandinavian and Low German or Dutch, others may be borrowings, and still others are native. Yet a general conclusion is possible. We are facing a large set of Germanic nouns and verbs with the structure *t/d* + vowel + *t/d* referring to small, often round objects. Most of them are of northern origin.

Once a complex of this type has been discovered, little else can be done. Apparently, *tad, tod, ted, tid,* and *tud* are not onomatopoeic, and it is impossible to explain how this combination of sounds acquired the meaning preserved by North Sea Germanic. We are unable to trace such complexes to other conventional signs, and reconstructing a more ancient form with enlargements will not solve any problems. So when ODEE, following OED, says that the origin of *toddle,* to give a random example, is unknown, its verdict should not be taken as final. *Toddle* is a frequentative verb from the base *tod-* 'small quantity.' Further research is unlikely to disclose a deeper or subtler truth. Nor is setting up Gmc **tuððon* of unknown origin (so Orel [2003:411]) of much use.

Dan *tudse* and Sw *tossa* (< **todsa*) probably belong with the words discussed above. Perhaps the toad was thought of as a small round creature. Perhaps its warts gave it its name. Not inconceivably, the toad's manner of moving in short steps ('toddling, tottling') provided the sought-for connection. Hellquist (1903-04:63) and SEO (*tossa*) was the first to offer this approach to *tadde* and *tossa.* He believed that the meaning of the 'root' *tad* ~ *tod* ~ *tud* is 'swollen' (and this is probable: cf ModI *túði* 'young calf'), though 'small (and round)' seems to be preferable. The line between 'swollen' and 'small and round' is blurred, but in English the toad hardly got its name because it can make itself swell up. Since Hellquist did not touch on the length of *ā* in OE *tādige* and did not destroy the connection between *tudse* and *zuscen,* his etymology could not influence English etymologists interested in the history of *toad* (assuming that they were aware of his views).

4. At one time, a discussion arose on the origin of *toadstool* (Godfrey [1939]; Strachan [1939]). *Toadstool* is nothing more than *toad* + *stool.* Parallels in Dutch, Frisian, German, and Scandinavian support this etymology (in addition to Strachan [1939], see Bayne [1881]; E. Marshall [1881], who quotes Minsheu: "Toade-stoole, because the toades doe greatly love it. Belg. Padden-stoel, pad-stoel, bufonum sedes"; Terry [1881]; A.B.C. [1934], and Stapelkamp [1957b:13]). Strachan had a good reason not to look on *tod* 'weight of wool' as the etymon of *toad* in *toadstool,* but he shared the common opinion that *ā* in *tādige* is the original vowel (Liberman [2003:381-86]).

TRAIPSE (1593, v), (1676, sb)

G traben ~ draben *'wander,' Russ* drapat' *'run for one's life,' and the like, most probably of onomatopoeic origin, testify to the existence of a common European migratory verb meaning 'move about.' It seems to have spread to other languages from Low German.* Traipse *(sb, a doublet of* drab*) is 'a woman given to traipsing; slut.'*

The verb *traipse* means 'walk in a trailing or untidy way, tramp, tread' (OED). AHD glosses it 'walk about idly or intrusively,' but the word may be devoid of negative connotations (as in Jersey; Lee [1894:334]). According to W^2 and W^3, *traipse* is regional or colloquial. *Trape* (v), a doublet of *traipse,* also occurs in dialects (OED). *Traipse* or *trapes* (sb) is "an opprobrious name for a woman or a girl slovenly in person or habits, dangling slattern" (OED). The origin of the verb and the noun is obscure, but the two are probably related.

Similar-sounding verbs meaning 'be on the run' turn up in a number of European languages. Such are, for example, G *traben* 'trot' (< MHG *draben* ~ *draven*; OS *thraбon*, MDu *draven*), with the variation *t-* ~ *d-* common in German and *trapsen* 'tramp.' See Krogmann (1938b:188), who cites many verbs of this type, and Århammar (1986:22-23) on the unlikely ties between *traben* and the Old French etymon of E *travail* ~ *travel*.

According to KM, G *Trabant* 'satellite' is a borrowing from Czech (its original meaning was 'infantry man'), but KS admits some connection between *traben* and *Trabant*. KM mention almost identical nouns from Polish, Serbo-Croatian, Slovenian, Rumanian, and Hungarian. See also *Trabant* in Törnqvist (1960) and Knobloch (1971:313-14; he related *Trabant* to G *Treppe* 'stair'). Russ *drapat'* 'flee ignominiously, run for one's life' may belong to the same group. In most Slavic languages, the cognates of *drapat'* mean 'scratch, pinch,' and a link between 'scratch' and 'flee' is possible: compare Russ *udirat'* 'flee' (the same root as in *dergat'* 'pluck, pinch'). The Russian verb is believed to be related to Gk δρέπω 'I cut, pluck,' OI *trefr* pl 'fringes,' and so on (IEW, 211; Vasmer I:535; ESSI V:101-2; Chernykh I:267). The meaning 'flee' in *drapat'* has the support of Gk δραπέτης 'fugitive' (sb and adj), possibly Skt *drāpayati* 'causes to run' (rejected by Frisk, ἀπο-διδρᾱ́σκω), and at least one Iranian form (Abaev [1966:14]). The Old Frisian cognate of *traben* was *tro(u)wia*. Dan *trave*, N *trave* ~ *tråve*, and Sw *trava* are borrowings from West Germanic (according to KM, from Frisian; according to DEO, from Low German). E *trape* (reg) and *trapes* ~ *traipse* seem to have formed part of the *traben* / *drapat'* group. See also Ihrig (1916: 66, sec 25. 04). In all probability, *traben* and its cognates are of onomatopoeic origin.

In Smythe Palmer's opinion (1883), *trapes* ~ *traipse* go back to F *tre(s)passer*. He dissociated *trapes* 'wander or saunter about' from *trape* 'trail along in an untidy manner' and connected the noun *trapes* 'idle slatternly woman' with the verb *trapes*. The connection is probable, but the French as the source of the English verb is unlikely, for *trespass* has always meant what it means at present.

Skinner compared *traipse* and *traben*, and two and a half centuries later Weekley (1924) mentioned *traben* in his discussion of *drab*[2]. Both were probably right. *Traipse* is not a cognate of *traben* (since the etymon of *traben* ~ *draben* begins with *þ-*). Nor is Russ *drapat'* related to either of them, but in soldiers' language and in popular speech *drab-* ~ *trap-* became a migratory word understood from Hungary to England. The verb spread in several waves, came into contact with native homonyms, enriched their meaning, or ousted them. Consider the dates of the earliest attestations: *trape* 'tramp' (1400), G *Trabant* (1424), *drab* (sb; 1515), *traipse* (v; 1593), *traipse* (sb; 1676). Nasalized forms (like *tramp*) and forms in another grade of ablaut (like *trip*) were probably not felt to be related and did not influence the development of *trab-* ~ *drab-* in the languages of Europe.

Most likely, *trapes* (v) is a borrowing from German (before the change [a:] > [ei]), an Anglicized colloquialism, and *trapes* (sb) is 'woman given to trapsing,' hence 'slut.' Johnson and Kenrick defined *trape* as 'run idly and sluttishly about' and added: "It is used only of women"; according to OED, *trape* is "usually said of a woman or child." The alliterative phrase *traipsing and trolloping about* (L. Payne [1909:384], Alabama) confirms the connection of *traipse* with women, but the 18th-century meaning need not have been primary: it may have developed under the influence of the noun. *Drab* (sb) is a doublet of *trapse*. The spelling *traipse* disguised its etymology. At present, *traipse* is monosyllabic, "but many modern dialects have it as two syllables" (OED). The same is true of some American dialects (Lee [1894:334]). The second syllable can be an affectation or a trace of baby language (Liberman 1992a:91-92).

TROT (sb) (1352)

The closest cognate of trot *'old woman' is 18th-century G* trot *(the same meaning), which seems to be related to MHG* trut(e) *'female monster' and G* Drude *'sorceress; incubus.' If* Drude *is also related to Go* trudan *'tread' (and thereby to E* tread *and G* treten*),* trot *may originally have meant 'gadabout,' like* drab *and* traipse. *Not improbably,* trot *is a borrowing from German.*

Trot 'old woman' (usually disparaging), old beldame, hag' appears in texts almost simultaneously with the verb *trot* (1362). The earliest forms of *trot* are *trat, trate,* and *tratte*. Such spellings in Middle English neither presuppose nor exclude disyllabic pronunciation. ME *baudstrot* 'bawd' provides no clue to the etymology of *trot*, for the second component of *baudstrot* is *strot* rather than *-trot*, probably a variant of *strut*, of which G *strunz-* is a nasalized form; see further at STRUMPET. According to Weekley, *trot* is Dame Trot of Salerno, 11th-century doctor and witch (given with a question mark in 1921, without it in 1924, and not repeated in Weekley [1933]). Shipley (1984: index) says that *trot* is a reflex of PIE **dra*, which does not turn up in his book. This is a worthless idea.

In 1854 *trot* 'toddler' and in 1895 *trot* 'young animal' were first recorded in English books. OED (*trot sb*[4]) lists them among the other meanings of *trot* 'gait of a quadruped,' but neither toddlers nor young animals trot. On the other hand, children are often likened to feeble women and animals (see GIRL). Thackeray and Skelton, who were the first authors to use *trot* in those meanings, must have known a regional or slang word most people understood at their time. (Is this the reason why Dickens invented the name Trotwood and why Miss Betsey shortened David's "adopted name of Trotwood into Trot"? Her house became a "wood" in which the "trot" grew up. Dickens began publishing *David Copperfield* in 1849. *Trot* appears in Chapter 15. Hawes [1974:86] does not mention any works on the origin of *Trotwood*.) If *trot* 'hag' and *trot* 'toddler, young animal' belong together, Dame Trot fades out of the picture.

Trot is hardly an *s*-less variant of *strot*, for *trot* never meant 'prostitute' in English. Yet when *trot* 'old woman' became sufficiently well-known, it may have degraded into a term of abuse under the influence of other disparaging names beginning with *tr-* like *traipse* and *trollop*; see more at DRAB. If an early disyllabic word **trotte*, with the variant *tratte*, existed, we may be dealing with an expressive formation (the *o* ~ *a* alternation, especially next to *r*, is typical of many regional words; see them at HEIFER and RABBIT).

OED states that Gower used *trote* in one of his Anglo-French works but that it has not been found in Continental French. **Trot is, most likely, of Germanic origin. It may be related to G *Drude* ~ *Frau Trude* 'sorceress, incubus' and Late MHG *trut(e)* 'female monster'** (Lecouteux [1987:15-17]). *Drude* has Scandinavian cognates. Magnusen (FML, 971) compared it with the valkyrie name (OI) *þrúðr* ('strength'; see OE *þrȳð* in AEW), and J. Grimm first shared this idea, which was vastly superior to the old etymology *Drude* = Celt **druid* (see the comment in Andresen [1889:229]). WHirt and Hirt (1921:298) also give the equation *Drude* = *þrúðr*. A simpler etymology derives G *Trude* 'foolish woman' from the modern name *Gertrude* (Beysel [1925:116]), but the connection between the proper and the common name is probably secondary. Neither Reinius (1903:120) nor Sundén (1904:134) to whom Beysel refers (and gives wrong pages in both cases) supports his etymology.

The Grimms (DW) derived *Drude* from **drūd* 'lovable, lovely'. In their opinion, *Drude* may at one time have designated a beautiful woman; they saw no objections to treating the stem vowel in MHG *trute* as long. Kluge (EWDS[1-10]) accepted the Grimms' etymology. He thought that calling an incubus beautiful had been the result of taboo and mentioned the case of Gk Εὐμενίδες 'the gracious ones' (= the Erinyes).

EWDS[16] compared *Drude* with Go *trudan* 'tread' (*Drude* allegedly meant 'heavy walker'), which presupposes *ŭ* in MHG *trute*. This etymology survived Mitzka's editorship (KM), but Seebold (KS), although he does not reject it, considers it uncertain. However, it may be correct. See Knobloch (1989:284) and what is said about E *trull* at the end of the entry DRAB. WFl *truttelen* 'loiter, trifle' and Du reg *trut* 'female genitals' (Baskett [1920:117/127 E4]) may contain the same root, and again we get a familiar connection between walking and women. DW[2] mentions ModI *drútur* 'infertile egg' and *trutta* 'urge a horse to move faster' and refers them to onomatopoeia. On the face of it, the two words have nothing to do with *Drude*; neither, as it seems, does onomatopoeia.

More problematic is OIr *drúth* 'fool,' which split into the meanings 'feeble-minded' and 'prostitute.' G. Lane (1933:261) believed that they were homonyms, but Campanile (1970:36) is probably right in deriving both 'prostitute' and 'clown' from the base 'dishonest, filthy, contemptible.' OIr *drúth* cannot be separated from OE *trūð* 'actor' and OI *trúðr* 'clown,' but it is unclear whether the Germanic words are native or borrowed. Breeze (1995) argues for the Celtic origin of the Old English word. See *trúðr* in AEW and *trūð* in AeEW, which give further references and discuss a possible connection of *trūð* ~ *trúðr* with the root of Go *trudan* (OI *troða*).

No modern etymologist seems to have compared MHG *trute* and ME *trate(e)* ~ ModE *trot*, even though the development from 'incubus' to 'old hag' is perhaps more natural than from 'incubus' to 'sorceress.' In addition to *trotte, drutte,* and *drude*, Wachter cites G *trot* 'woman; old woman, fortune teller.' **If 18th-century G *trot* really meant 'old woman,' a link between E *trot* and G *Drude* can be viewed as almost established** (English borrowing from German?) and a search for an expressive formation of the *tratte* type becomes unnecessary. Only the origin of E *trot* 'toddler, young animal' remains partly unexplained.

Trot (v) may have influenced the meaning of *trot* (sb) ('bad women' were traditionally represented as loafers: see above and STRUMPET). The etymology of *trot* (v) is debatable. If the verb is of Germanic origin, it is related to *trot* (sb), but that is exactly the point of dispute. Junius's idea that *trot* is "such a one as hath trotted long up and down," is ingenious but not supported by any facts. Some of the cognates of E *trot* (sb) that one finds in dictionaries, namely OI *drós* 'girl' (CV; in modern usage, 'whore'), *þrot* 'destitution' (Junius), and *þreyta* 'exhaust' (Lye in Junius), are unrelated to it. Ital *drudo* 'lover' that CV give as the etymon of *drós* is from Gmc **drūd*, which J. Grimm believed to have been the etymon of G *Drude* (Liberman [1992a:91-92]).

UNDERSTAND (888)

In the Indo-European languages, many verbs of understanding consist of a prefix and a verbal root for 'stand,' but in the Germanic family only West Germanic has related forms and analogues of understand. *All of them developed from spatial metaphors whose idea was that standing in a certain position allows the observer to get to know the properties of the object. The root* -standan *might but did not necessarily have a transitive meaning. OE* (West Saxon) understandan *coexisted with a synonym* forstandan; *its cognate won out in Frisian* (ferstean), *Dutch* (verstaan), *and German* (verstehen). *Its other synonym was* undergi(e)tan. *The prefix* under- *had the syncretic meaning 'beneath' and 'among,' hence 'between.'*

If understandan *emerged relatively late, the ancient meaning of the prefix should interest us only insofar as it at one time determined the coining of other verbs like* undergietan, *but if all of those verbs arose after the etymological meaning of* under- *and* for- *had been forgotten, the situation in Proto-Indo-European is of limited value in the reconstruction of their semantic history. Given the existence of OE* forstandan *and* undergi(e)tan *(both meant 'understand'),* understandan *may have arisen as a blend of the two.* Understandan *and* forstandan *need not have been based on the same metaphor, for example, one of separation; 'in front of' seems to be a likelier sense of* for-. *It is unclear whether* understandan, forstandan, *and so forth were used in a neutral or an elevated style. The contrast between the metaphorical* forstandan ~ understandan *and the fully transparent Go* fraþjan *and OI* skilja *is striking.*

The sections are devoted to 1) the semantic structure of understand *and its analogues in Old West Germanic, 2) the semantic history of these verbs, especially G* verstehen, *and 3) attempts to find the distant origin of* understand *and its analogues. Section 4 contains a tentative etymology of* understand.

1. **The inner structure of the verb *understand* has not changed since the time it was first recorded (OE *understandan ~ understondan*). It is the meaning of the whole that is unexpected. Reflexes of two adverbs merged in Germanic, namely **n̥dher* 'under' (as in L *infrā*) and **n̥ter* 'between' (as in L *inter* 'between, among'), with *d* from **t* by Verner's Law.** This fact was not known before 1893 (Gneuss [1999:108], with reference to Delbrück), but the original meaning of *under-* in *understand* ('beneath,' 'among'?) was discussed as early as the 18th century.

***Under* 'among' rarely occurs in Old English. The only incontestable example is *under him* 'among them' (Alfred's *Orosius*). All the other sentences yield an equally good meaning (sometimes a better one) if *under* in them is interpreted as meaning 'under.'** Even the modern phrase *under the circumstances* is not unambiguous from this point of view. In contrast, German *unter* 'among' is still common, whether it is a native word or the result of French influence (compare G *unter uns* and F *entre nous* 'between ourselves').

Many Old English verbs beginning with *under-* occur only in glosses. Sweet may have been right in calling some of them unnatural words (see Gneuss [1999:114]), but such translation loans as OE *undercuman* 'assist' and *underhlystan* 'supply an omitted word' for L *subvenīre* and *subaudīre,* however "contrary to the genius of the language" (Sweet [1897:VIII], quoted by Gneuss), show that *under-* was a productive prefix and that the likes of *undercuman* were at least not stupid. The same is probably true of OHG *untarambahte* for L *subministrat* 'serves,' and so forth. Today the dullest glossator would not suggest even as a mnemonic device such monstrosities as *undercome* and *underlisten* despite the productivity of *under-* 'insufficiently' (compare the verbs *underestimate* and *underappreciate),* mainly in words of Romance origin.

The meaning of the resulting sum of *under* + verb, to the extent that we can trace it to the old period, is unpredictable. G *untergehen* means only 'go under' ('sink, go down, decline'), while OE *undergān* meant 'undermine, ruin,' and ModE *undergo* has acquired the sense 'endure, experience.' Compare also E *understand* and ModG *unterstehen* 'come under (the jurisdiction of), be subordinate to; dare (with *sich*).' Similar difficulties arise with the cognates of *-stand* outside Germanic, as seen in the much-discussed L *superstitio* 'superstition; excessive fear of the gods; religious rituals' and L *praestāre* 'stand before' and 'guarantee.'

Neither 'stand between, stand among' nor 'stand under' leads unambiguously to the meaning of ModE *understand,* but both can be interpreted in a satisfactory way: one 'stands under' and gets to the bottom of things, and while standing between or among things, one acquires the power of discrimination. *Understand* must originally have referred to the process of observation and learning rather than its result. We have in it a semantic analogue of such a preterit-present verb as Go *wait* 'I know' (from seeing to knowing) and of OIr *tucu* 'I understand' (originally the same as in the perfect forms of *do-biur* 'I bring': Buck

1205/17.16.3, with reference to Holger Pedersen), but today *verstehen* and *understand* designate rest, not motion (Weisweiler [1935:55]).

OE *understandan* and its Old English synonym *forstandan* have several analogues in West Germanic: MLG *understân,* MDu *onderstaen,* OFr *understān;* OHG *firstantan,* OS *farstandan,* MDu *verstaen,* OFr *forstān;* OFr *ūrstān,* and OHG *intstantan.* The Gothic for 'understand' was *fraþjan* (akin to Go *frōþs* 'clever, wise'); its Icelandic synonym is *skilja* (literally 'separate'). OE *underniman, underþencan,* and especially *undergi(e)tan* meant nearly the same as *understandan. Underþencan* is usually glossed 'consider,' but when used with a reflexive pronoun, it meant 'change one's mind, repent.' *Underniman* was the least specialized of those verbs: 'understand,' 'blame' and 'undertake' (so in Ælfric) and in medical texts also 'steal' (here the connotation of secrecy present in the prefix *under-* comes to the fore: *underniman* = 'take clandestinely'; see Newman [2001:192]).

2. The semantic history of those verbs has been the object of protracted debate. See a general survey of the material in Kroesch (1911; *understand,* pp. 470-71). No agreement exists even on the development of G *verstehen,* a deceptively transparent word. According to Schwenck's vague formulation, *verstehen* denotes the direction of thought toward a place or object that will become known. Kluge (EWDS[1-6], *Verstand*) admits that the sense development of *verstehen* is obscure and compares G *verstehen* and Gk ἐπίσταμαι 'be able, be experienced; know, consider, think.' Bréal (1898:59-60) repeated or made independently the same comparison. In his opinion, G *sich auf etwas verstehen* and the Greek verb describe the situation when one gets on top of something and comprehends its essence. He cited *understand* but did not elaborate. The Greek counterparts of *verstehen* and *understand* occurred to Junius and Schwenck. According to Harm (2003:117-24), ἐπίσταμαι is not an exact analogue of *verstehen* ~ *understand,* because it means 'put oneself on top *or* at the head of something.'

Kluge (EWDS,[7-9] *verstehen*) juxtaposed OHG *fir-* with Gk περί '(a)round,' as it allegedly occurs in Go *frisahts* 'image,' and mentioned OHG *antfristôn* 'interpret' with two prefixes (*ant-fri-stôn*). His gloss of *verstehen* 'place oneself around something' (*sich um etwas herumstellen*) looks odd (the same in DW and in Hirt 1921:248), and the origin of *frisahts* is unclear (*fri-sahts?, fris-ahts?*). OHG *antfristôn* only seems to refer to standing: it is *antfrist-ôn,* not *ant-fri-stôn* (*antfrist* has been explained as a calque of L *interpres* 'interpreter'). However, Kluge's mention of OE *wealhstod* 'interpreter, mediator' (EWD[10]) possibly deserves attention.

An unexpected parallel to *wealhstod* (a word of unknown etymology: see AeEW, *stōd*) is E *spokesman,* originally also 'interpreter' (OED), an early 16th-century noun with enigmatic ablaut. The ablaut relations in the pair OE *(-)standan* 'understand' ~ *(-)stōd* 'interpreter' are the inverse of Go *frōþs* 'wise' ~ *fraþjan* 'understand.' In case a *wealhstod* merely 'stood by' in communicating with foreigners (OE *wealh* 'foreigner, stranger'), the origin and meaning of that word shed no light on the history of *forstandan* and *understand,* but perhaps *-stōd* in *wealhstod* is the stem of some verb with the causative meaning 'make things understood.'

Götze (EWDS[11-15]) rewrote the entry, removed Kluge's speculation, and explained *verstehen* and *understand* as 'stand in front or beneath something, in order to get exact information.' Then Roland Martin wrote his groundbreaking article (1938) in which he traced *verstehen* to legal practice: from 'stand in front,' meaning 'vouch for, guarantee,' to 'comprehend.' E *understand,* he contended (p. 627, footnote), "is apparently nothing more than the generalization of the same basic legal meaning: I take it upon myself to speak in this case because I have grasped all the connections." Martin's formulation sounds more convincing in German than in English because the German for 'take it upon oneself' is *sich unterstehen* ("ich unterstehe mich, eine Sache zu vertreten, weil ich den Zusammenhang erfaßt habe"). The pun produces the impression that *sich unterstehen* is equivalent to *understand.*

EWDS[16-21] accepted Martin's etymology and KS has not dismissed it (likewise, Rix [1995:240]). But Schröpfer (1985:430), who sees in it an overzealous application of the principles of the Wörter und Sachen school ("when a word has an abstract meaning, try to find a situation in which the meaning was concrete"), seems to be closer to the truth. Harm (2003:112-13) cites an additional argument against Martin: *firstân* ~ *firstantan* never had the meaning 'present a case in court.' **It is not necessary to look for some everyday use of 'stand in front,' in order to reconstruct the meaning 'understand.'** L *praestāre* 'guarantee, vouch for' (literally 'stand in front') also acquired a legal sense at the end, rather than at the beginning of its semantic history (Beikircher [1992]). Despite Martin's explanation that the parallelism between *verstehen* and *understand* is far from obvious, both verbs are indeed based on spatial concepts. Germanic and comparative scholars have recognized this fact (see Buck 1205-06/17.16, Belardi [1976:86], and Poli

[1992:125]). Only the meaning of the prefixes continues to baffle etymologists.

ModE *understand* and OE *understandan* are dissimilar in that *understand* has no synonyms in the neutral style, whereas *understandan* competed with *undergi(e)tan* and partly with *underniman, underþencan* (the same prefix but different roots), and *forstandan* (the same root but a different prefix). Those five verbs were not always interchangeable, their frequency was different, and each gravitated toward a certain locality or school. Ono (1981a and b; 1984; 1986) has investigated the pair *understandan* (a West Saxon verb) ~ *undergietan*; it appears that neither monopolized the field the way ModE *understand* did. OE *under-* was, consequently, less 'marked' than its modern reflex. In some examples, *understandan* seems to have referred to the first step of comprehension and *undergietan* to the next (Ogura [1993:43]).

3. The proposal that *under-* in *understand* should be taken to mean 'between, among' is old. It occurs in Skinner, and Mueller observes that *understand* and its counterparts bring to the fore the idea of standing in the midst of things, withstanding, impeding, and boldly striving. Skeat explained *understand* as "stand under or among, hence to comprehend" and compared it with L **inter-ligere* 'choose between.' *Intelligere* is a common gloss for the Old English verbs of understanding, and Skinner, who wrote his dictionary in Latin, also glossed Flemish ("Belgian") *verstaen* with L *intelligere.*

The most innovative approach to *understand* and *verstehen* is Wood's (1899b:129-30). The subsequent exchange (Hempl [1899], Wood [1900]) adds only a few details to his main idea. It would be more profitable to quote him at lenght than to retell his text, which would amount to reproducing it almost verbatim. Wood says the following: "A term denoting insight, perception, understanding may primarily mean one of several things, the most common of which are: 'sharpness, keenness, acuteness'; 'grasping, comprehension'; 'separating, distinguishing.' The last mentioned class is very numerous. Thus: Lat. *cernō* 'separate, sift : distinguish, discern,' *discernō* 'separate : discern,' Gk. κρίνω 'separate : judge'; Lat. *distinguō* 'separate : distinguish,' *intelligō* ('choose between') : 'perceive, comprehend,' etc. So also in Germanic. Here the usual prefixes used in expressing separation are Goth. *fair-* 'for-,' OHG. *fir-*, etc; OE *tō-*, OS *ti-*, OHG *zir-*; OS *undar-*, OE *under-*, OHG. *untar-* 'unter.' In the sense 'between, apart,' OHG. *undar-*, etc, are to be compared with Lat. *inter,* which is used in the same way, and further with Gk. ἔντερον, Skt. *antara-m* 'entrails.'... In words expressing separation the meaning 'understand' may develop in two ways: 1. 'separate' : 'distinguish'; 2. 'separate, take away, take in' : 'perceive.' To the first class belong Lat. *cernō, distinguō;* to the second *intelligo, percipio....* To class 2. belong: OE *under-gietan* ('get apart, take to oneself,' as *forgietan* 'forget'–'love') : 'understand, perceive'... To these we can add OHG. *fir-stantan,* MHG. *ver-stān, -stēn* 'hinder from, intercept' : ('take to oneself') 'understand,' MHG *unter-stān* 'undertake, take upon oneself, seize, attain' : OE *under-standan* 'take for granted, perceive, understand.' That these words came to mean 'perceive, understand' through 'intercept, take to oneself' admits of but little doubt. This entirely explains their origin and use. Thus OE. *understandan* 'take for granted, assume' points plainly to this origin. A Gk. ἐπίσταμαι in explaining *verstehen, understand* is futile, since, in any case, the Gk. word developed its meaning differently. That, if from the root *stā-* 'stand,' would give 'stand over, oversee, care for, give attention to,' hence 'perceive, know, understand.'"

Here are Hempl's amendments to Wood's reconstruction (1899:234): "German *verstehen* and English *understand* are cases of class 1, not of class 2, and so is Greek ἐπίσταμαι. OE. *understandan* was originally simply 'to stand between,' and so 'to keep apart,' 'to separate,' and it, like Latin *distinguo,* German *unterscheiden,* etc., got the figurative meaning 'distinguish,' 'make out,' 'understand,' 'know how (to)' (and in German, *unterstehen* passed on to 'undertake (to),' 'presume (to)'). But the same is true of German *verstehen,* OE. *forstandan.* These originally meant 'to stand in front of,' 'to keep off (from some one [sic] else),' 'to separate,' and hence 'to distinguish,' 'to make out,' 'to understand.' Just so, Greek ἐπίστημι, ἐπίσταμαι originally means, as still shown in ἐπίστημι, ἐφίστημι 'to stand in front of,' 'to oppose,' 'to check,' 'to keep off.' Hence the meaning 'to separate' and metaphorically 'to distinguish,' 'to understand,' 'to know how,' as shown in ἐπίσταμαι."

In his rejoinder, Wood (1900:15-16) offers an interpretation of the Greek verbs different from Hempl's. With regard to Germanic, he cites the meanings "of MHG *understân* : 'keep, assume, reach, undertake; snatch something away from someone' of OE *understandan* : 'take for granted, assume, perceive, understand.' Germ. *unterstehen* carries out the idea contained in MHG. *understān, -stēn,* and did not pass through the meaning 'understand'.... OHG. *firstantan,* MHG. *verstān, -stēn* 'intercept' : 'notice,' 'perceive,' 'understand' show the same development of meaning as OE. *understandan*... Now it is possible that OE. *forstandan*, OHG *firstantan, firstān* 'verstehen' may have meant primarily 'stand before,' and hence 'watch, observe, perceive, understand.' So Schade, *Wb.*, explains them. This interpretation I considered when writing my first article on these words. But it seemed on the whole more probable that Germ. *verstehen, vernehmen*, OE *understandan, underniman, undergietan* all belonged to one class and were explained by OHG. *firneman* 'wegnehmen, im besitz nehmen, vernehmen, wahrnemen' ['take away, take in one's possession, learn, perceive']; and that *verstehen, understand* are both based on the transitive use of the root *stā-, stē-*, which is found by the side of the intransitive use from IE. time down to the present."

Gneuss (1999:119), an advocate of the idea that *under-* in *understandan* means 'among,' refers to Wood with approval and quotes L. Bloomfield (1933:425-26), who believed that "*I understand these things* may have meant, at first, 'I stand among these things'" (see also Bloomfield [1933:433] on the meaning of *understand*). However, as follows from the excerpts given above, Wood, unlike Hempl, thought of "standing among things" only in the sense of separating and appropriating them; compare his gloss of OE *undergietan* 'get apart, take to oneself.' Obviously, such a meaning could develop only with time, for the idea of separation is not present in OE *under-*. In *underþencan*, it would be even harder to come up with a gloss like 'get apart.' Wood's analysis presupposes, as he says at the end of his second article, the transitive use of *standan*.

OE *forstandan* is also troublesome. *For-* may be a cognate of Go *fra-*, so that *forstandan* (with transitive *-standan*) would have meant primarily 'snatch away,' but it may be a cognate of Go *faur-* (with intransitive *-standan*), and then the meaning would come out as 'stand in front.' The West Germanic cognates of Go *fra-*, *faur-* and *fair-* (was there also *fri-*, as in *frisahts*?) merged or were confused in many words. **Such divergent meanings of OE *forstandan* as 'defend, withstand, resist,' 'benefit, avail,' and 'understand; signify, be equal' did not necessarily spring up from a single source**. Wood admitted that two interpretations of *forstandan* and *firstantan* are possible, but the first was "on the whole" more probable. It is more probable only within the framework of his system. If we assume that verbs of understanding are based on the concept of separation, Wood's idea will be unobjectionable. However, even a viable general principle, if it is a product of induction, should be applied with care. OFr *ūrstān* and OHG *intstantan* bear out Wood's conclusion because *ūr-* and *int-* (ModG *ent-*) meant what Wood expected them to in such cases. It is *verstehen* and *understand* that remain problematic.

The sense of a prefixed word is frequently determined by the attraction of the semantic field rather than by the etymological meaning of the prefix. For example, we have OE *ofergitan* 'forget' and *undergi(e)tan* 'understand.' The contrast is between *ofer-* (to lose knowledge) and *under-* (to gain knowledge). However, one of the synonyms of *ofergitan* (with a cognate in the Frisian dialect of Sylt: Stiles [1997:341]) was *forgitan*, so that in the pair *forstandan* ~ *understandan*, the prefix *for-* and *under-* are interchangeable, while the verbs *forgitan* and *undergi(e)tan* are antonyms. If we did not know the meanings of E *oversee* and *overlook*, we would be unable to guess which means what. The German for both is *übersehen*. Ogura (1993:20) makes the same point for Old English, and see what is said in sec 1, above, about *undergo, untergehen*, and so forth.

In his analysis of Germanic verbs of forgetting, McLintock (1972) touches on OE *ongi(e)tan* and *undergitan*. He identifies *on-* in *ongietan* with Gmc *and-*; with respect to *under-*, its "likeliest interpretation," he says, "is that it is a semantic continuant of Gmc *uƀ*" (= Go *uf-*). "If *under-* were a replacement for *uƀ-* we might regard the triad *ongitan : undergitan : ofergitan* as parallel to Go. *andhausjan* ['listen'] : *ufhausjan* ['obey'] : **ufarhausijan* [*'forget, neglect'], the first two members in each being synonyms" (pp. 87-88). Like Wood, McLintock was motivated by the requirements of the system and the wish to find a single principle governing the use of the verbs he was examining. Yet he mentions other possibilities and explores them.

One such possibility is that *under-* in verbs of mental perception, such as *understand*, meant 'among.' But *under-* might be a doublet of Gmc **und-*. From a historical point of view, *under* is the comparative form of **und*. Gothic and Old Icelandic retained the simplexes. Gothic had *und* 'for, until,' which coexisted with the prefix *unþa-* (recorded only in *unþaþliuhan** 'escape,' a counterpart of G *entfliehen*) and *under* 'under' (also *undaro*), not used as a prefix. In Old Icelandic, *und* 'under' was a poetic doublet of *undir*; there also were OI *unz* (< *und es*) 'till' and *undan* (< **und-ana*) 'away from.' *Under-* in *undergietan* as a by-form of **und-* seemed acceptable to Seebold (1992:418: "[t]he verbal *un-*

der- is in this case... not taken from the free form OE *under-* but is a secondary extension of *und- by way of confusion with *under* 'below, beneath'"). He may not have been aware of McLintock's arguments, for he says: "It is difficult, if not impossible, to determine how many verbs with *under-* have shared this development... there is... no help to be found in analyzing *understandan*"). Gneuss (1999:115, note 20) rejected Seebold's reconstruction.

McLintock's (1972:88) comment is as follows: "Although in Gothic there is no semantic overlap between *and* and *und* as prepositions, the two are doubtless related by Ablaut. Furthermore, there is some evidence in Gothic that as verbal prefixes they were interchangeable... Outside Gothic we find evidence in OS *antthat* beside *untthat* for the interchangeability of the prepositions. Now the Gothic prefix *und-*, which occurs in *undgreipan* ['seize'], *undredan* ['provide, grant'], *undrinnan* ['fall to one's share'], has a by-form *unþa-* in *unþaþliuhan* ['escape'], whose cognates in OE are *ūþ-* in nominal and *oþ-* in verbal forms... Since Go. *unþaþliuhan* corresponds semantically to OHG *intfliohan*, we might regard Gmc. **und-, *unþa...* as one of the sources of OHG *ant-, int-*. We should then be able to link OHG *intstantan* 'to understand' with OE *understand* and see the Old High German pair *firstantan, intstantan* as parallel to OE *forstandan, understandan*."

Newman (2001) offers a brief survey of early scholarship (the main articles by Wood and Hempl; Jäkel [1995:224], and a few modern dictionaries) and reduces the hypotheses on the origin of *understand* to three types: 1) 'stand between' > 'separate' = 'keep x apart from y' > 'understand'; 2) 'stand between' > 'separate' = 'take something away from the rest, thereby bringing it to oneself' > 'perceive' > 'understand'; 3a) 'stand among' > 'be physically close to' > 'understand,' and 3b) 'stand under' > 'be physically close to' > 'understand.' "It is a problem for all three hypotheses," he says, "that there simply is no 'stand' meaning (e.g. 'stand between, stand among, stand next to, stand near, stand at, stand under') documented for OE *understandan* (with inseparable prefix)" (p. 189). Turning to *undergietan*, he adds that it "came into use as a more specifically abstract variant of *ongietan*. The emergence of *undergietan* is instructive because, like *understand*, when it makes its appearance, it is only used in the abstract sense of 'understand, perceive.' *Undergietan* is not used in any sense of 'take among, take between, take under' etc. There is no evidence that *undergietan* emerges gradually out of any immediately prior concrete sense" (p. 193). These observations are valid; compare the proposal in sec 4, below.

In Newman's opinion, *undergietan* was introduced "to carry the more abstract senses of another *-gietan* verb" and "*understandan* was introduced to carry the more abstract sense 'understand' of another *standan* verb, namely *forstandan* 'defend; obstruct, stop (way); understand; hinder from; help, avail, profit' " (p. 194). He believes that the starting point was *standan* *'stand upright,' for what is correct is straight. According to this reconstruction, the original meaning of *understand* must have been *'take a stance.' This result does not sound like a revelation, for 'stand' is 'stand.' With regard to *under-* we are only told that its semantic complexity is a factor to be reckoned with. The conclusion is so guarded as to be almost devoid of interest: "The points I have made concerning the semantics of OE *under-* and the semantic components of 'stand' have been made in order to establish motivations for the OE compound *understand*, distinct from the motivations for this compound proposed in previous scholarship. The motivations which I point to in Sections 3 and 4 need not to be thought of as replacing the earlier hypotheses. Rather, one might consider the motivations proposed here as constituting additional reasons for the emergence and consolidation of *understandan* in OE" (p. 198). The most valuable part of Newman's article is the one devoted to the interaction of synonyms for *understand* in Old English.

By contrast, Hough's suggestion (2004) seems unpromising. She quotes sentences in Old English in which *standan* is connected with light (*lēoht stōd, lēoma stōd*, etc) and sets up OE *standan* *'shine, gleam,' but does not discuss the role of *under-* in the history of *understand*. The meaning 'comprehend' could of course have developed from 'see (the) light'; yet the path from 'shine' to 'understand' is unimaginable, the more so because *standan* did not really mean 'shine': light "stood," as rivers "lay" in Old English; it is only our view that they shone and flowed.

According to Harm (2003:113-14, 123-24), OE *undestandan* and its Old High German counterparts developed from **and(a)standan* 'stand in front' but he, too, assumes that prefixes alternated in the *verba sentiendi*. This assumption seems to be the most reasonable starting point for the etymology of *understand*.

4. **The picture that emerges from the foregoing discussion can be summarized as follows**: 1) OE *understandan* is one of many verbs in the Indo-

European languages with a verbal root for 'stand' and a prefix, the whole meaning 'get to know, comprehend.' In West Germanic, *int-*, *fir-* (OHG), *for-* (OE), and *ūr-* (OFr) competed with *under-* and its cognates in the formation of such verbs. 2) Other verbal roots could be combined with *under-* and yield (almost) the same meaning, as in OE *understandan* and *undergi(e)tan*. OE *understandan* was first recorded in 888, but its actual age cannot be determined. 3) OE *under-* meant 'under' and 'between, among,' which poses the question of whether the reference was to standing under an object and exploring it from the bottom up or standing among several objects and being able to choose the right one. 4) If, however, *under-* is an extension of **und-*, the initial idea might have been one of separation, approximately 'stand against an object, in order to appropriate it.' The same interpretation of *understandan* is possible even if *under-* meant 'among.' 5) The origin of OE *forstandan* ~ OHG *firstantan* is not clear in all details. With so many similar verbs meaning 'understand,' it is not necessary to reconstruct a concrete situation (a legal process, for example) that gave rise to that verb. Since the origin of OE *for-* ~ OHG *fir-* is ambiguous (several ancient prefixes may have had *for-* ~ *fir-* as their reflexes), the initial meaning of the prefixed verbs is often opaque. If *for-* ~ *fir-* in *forstandan* ~ *firstantan* designated hindering, impeding, OE *forstandan* might be synonymous with *understandan* 'stand against, separate.' 6) Given a variety of prefixed verbs of understanding and forgetting, new verbs employing the same model arose easily. It would be enough to have *forstandan* and *undirgi(e)tan,* both meaning 'understand,' for *understandan* to come into being. In such a process, reminiscent of blending, the Indo-European etymology of *under-* would be of no consequence. This summary leaves open the questions about the origin of the earliest metaphor in OE *undergi(e)tan* and *forstandan* (assuming that both are older than *understandan*) and about the equivalence of *under-* and *for-* in them. (*Understand* is not the only word whose prefix *under-* has piqued the curiosity of linguists, philosophers, and specialists in logic: cf L *substantia* and Gk ὑπόστασις, both of which combine "under" and "stand.")

The data at our disposal are insufficient for drawing definitive conclusions about the origin of the West Germanic verbs of understanding. Research into the etymology of *understand* makes sense only as part of a broader investigation of the entire group. Although WGmc *under* had two meanings ('under' and 'among'), the line demarcating them is one of our own making. We have here an old preposition or adverb with a vague spatial meaning. Its referents depended on the situation. This is a common occurrence. The difference between E *in the library* ~ *at the library, in the street* ~ *on the street, above the river* ~ *over the river* is irrelevant for speakers of many other languages. The same, and much more frequently, happens to conjunctions. The German phrase *wenn du kommst* must be translated into English as 'when you come' or 'if you come,' but only exposure to foreign languages makes speakers of German (unless they are linguists) aware of the ambiguity of *wenn.* The alternative made much of by modern etymologists—is *understand* equal to 'stand under' or to 'stand between (among)'?—is an anachronism. The pair *undergi(e)tan* 'understand' ~ *ofergietan* 'forget' refers to *under-* 'under' as opposed to *ofer-* 'over,' while the pair of synonyms *forstandan* ~ *understandan* seems to refer to events on the surface.

The extent to which the idea of separation was prominent in the minds of those who first endowed verbal units like 'stand beneath ~ among,' 'stand in front,' 'stand against' with the meaning 'perceive, get to know, comprehend' is beyond reconstruction. Nor can we establish whether those words go back to popular usage or to the language of scholars (poets, priests). Go *fraþjan* ('be mindful of something, use one's mind' = 'understand') and OI *skilja* ('separate' = 'understand') are simpler and more transparent than their West Germanic counterparts.

WITCH (890)

Old English distinguished between wicca *(m) and* wicce *(f). The leveling of endings and apocope wiped out the difference between them, and ME* wicce *(m) was later replaced by* wizard. *The etymology of* wicca ~ wicce *seems to be almost within reach, yet it remains disputable, and dictionaries either reproduce uncritically one of the existing hypotheses or say "origin uncertain."* Wicca *and* wicce *have been compared with Gmc* *wīhs *'holy,' OE* wīglian *'foretell the future,' OE* wīcian *'yield' ~ OI* víkja *'turn aside,' L* vegēre *'excite, stir,' and with the verbs whose Modern German reflexes are* weigern *'refuse,'* wiegen *'sway,'* (be)wegen *'move,' and even* wiehern *'neigh.' Since the original functions of and the powers ascribed to the persons called* wicca ~ wicce *are unknown (one can rely solely on haphazard Latin glosses), the proposed interpretations differ widely and include 'divinator,' 'averter,' 'wise man (woman),' and 'necromancer.' It is suggested here that OE* wicca *goes back to the protoform* *wit-ja- *'one who knows,' in which* -tj- *merged with* -kj- *(>* ch*), as happened in several Old English words and presumably in the history of the verb* fetch < ? fetian. *If this etymology is correct,* wicca ~

wicce *will align themselves on the semantic plane with L* sāga, *Russ* ved'ma, *and E* wizard. *There can be little doubt that OE* wiccian *'use witchcraft' was derived from the noun, rather than being its source.*

The sections are devoted to 1) the naming of witches in various cultures, 2) the early attempts to connect wiccian *with the ancient custom of predicting the future by the neighing of horses (MDu* wijchelen*) and Grimm's derivation of OE* wiccian *and* wīglian *from* *wīhs, *3) the relationship between MDu* wichelen *and OE* wīglian *and between both of them and OE* wiccian *(*wiccian *appears to be unrelated to either, and the origin of* wicheln *is obscure), 4) the arguments against the derivation of* wicca *from* wītega, *5) other etymologies of* witch, *6) an attempt to understand* wicca *as 'necromancer,' and 7) the proposed etymology of* witch *from* *witja-. *Section 8 is an addendum on the origin of the words most often mentioned in connection with* witch, *namely* wicked, wile, wizard, wiseacre, *and* wight.

1. The earliest recorded form of *witch* is OE *wicca* (m) 'man practicing witchcraft' (*Laws of Ælfred*, 890). Its feminine counterpart *wicce* surfaced in 1000 (Ælfric; see both in OED). ModE *witch* usually refers to a woman and continues *wicce*, but the reflexes of *wicca* and *wicce* merged in Middle English because of the reduction of endings and apocope. Two main hypotheses compete in the attempts to etymologize *wicca* ~ *wicce*, though as usual, several less known conjectures also exist. The majority of recent dictionaries cite the Old and Middle English forms of *witch* and leave the question of origins open.

In reconstructing the history of words for '*witch*,' the most important question concerns the exact powers attributed to witches in a given society. The range goes all the way from divinators, that is, sorceresses and (presumably) wise soothsayers to charlatans and evil creatures. Among the examples are L *venēficus* ~ *venēfica* 'preparer of poison' (its Old English calque is *unlybwyrhta*) and MHG *goukelære* 'street entertainer, conjurer, magician,' (on which see GAWK). TOE I:16.01.04 lists sorceresses, divinators, and so forth. Most Old English words are compounds with the roots *drȳ-*, *lyb-*, *sige-*, *galdor-*, *scin-*, and *-rūn*. Other words glossed 'witch' include OI *vǫlva*, to be discussed below (sec 6), and OI *túnriða* ~ late MHG *zûnrite* 'fence rider.' See Buck (1497/22.43), Lauffer (1938:114-19), Poortinga (1968), and Pálsson (1991:158) for a survey of the properties ascribed to witches in medieval literature and of words designating *witch* in Indo-European languages.

In Germanic, especially difficult is G *Hexe* < OHG *hagzussa* (akin to OE *hægtesse*), a compound made up of two obscure elements; see it and E *hag* in etymological dictionaries. The most ingenious etymology of *hagzussa* is Bergkvist's (1937; 1938:14 and 17). He combined *hag-* 'wolf' (originally 'shaggy creature') and *-zussa* 'a kind of cloth' (named after its fabric: cf OE *tysse* 'coarse cloth') and obtained 'person in wolf's clothing,' like OI *úlfheðinn* 'wolf cloak' or *berserkr* 'berserk,' if the latter is understood as 'bearskin' rather than 'bareskin.' Güntert (1919:119) partly anticipated his explanation of *-zussa*. OE *wicca* ~ *wicce* are not compounds, but their etymon almost certainly contained a suffix and was longer than the earliest attested forms.

2. Kilianus cited Du *wichelen* and *wijchelen*, which he glossed 'hinnire' ('neigh') and 'hariolari' ('foretell the future, divine'). In present day Standard Dutch, *wijchelen* 'neigh' no longer exists. Even Hexham did not use it for glossing *neigh* and *whinny*. According to Duflou (1927:120), who refers to Kluyver (1884), Kilianus looked on *wichelen* and *wijchelen* as different meanings of the same word (the verb for neighing is probably onomatopoeic; it has an English regional cognate *wicker*) and quoted Tacitus's statement that "the *Germans*...did principally...divine and foretell things to come by whinnying and neighing of their horses." Minsheu, Blount (whose English version of Tacitus is given above), Skinner, the author of *Gazophylacium* (*witch*), Wachter (*wicker* 'divinator'), and VV (*wichelen*) repeated that quotation. Ten Kate (505) gives an excerpt from Tacitus. Franck (EWNT) is the only modern researcher who treated Kilianus's etymology of Du *wichelen* with some interest. Van Wijk expunged the reference to Tacitus from Franck's entry. We can disregard the alleged connection of OE *wicca* with MDu *wichelen* 'neigh,' but its relatedness to MDu *wijchelen* 'foretell the future' merits further discussion.

J. Grimm (1835: 581-82, see *witch* on p. 581; the same in the later editions) **cited OE *wiccian* 'use witchcraft' and *wīglian* 'take auspices, divine,' along with *wīglere* 'soothsayer, wizard,' *wīglung* and *gewīglung* 'soothsaying, augury, witchcraft, sorcery,' and their numerous Germanic cognates, and referred them to the root of Go *weihs* 'holy.'** (In the present entry, OE *wīglian* is given with a long vowel despite the lack of consensus on this subject.) Pictet (1859-63, II:643), Mueller, Leo (1877:494), and E. Zupitza (1896:142-43) supported J. Grimm's etymology, and after Osthoff (1896:44-45; 1899:184-85) connected the entire group with L *victima* 'sacrifice,' the existence of a verbal root 'separate' lost its hypothetical character. "In Lat[in] and esp[ecially] G[er]m[ani]c, this base was adapted for the notion 'sacred; forbidden to (separated from) humans'" (Feist-Lehmann, 398). See Berneker (1908:2), Torp (1909:408-09), WP I:392, 1. *u̯eiq-*, IEW 1128, 1. *u̯eik-*, IsEW 112, *u̯eiq-*, and AHD[1] 1548, *weik-*[2]: "In words connected with magic and religious notions (in Germanic and Latin)." Many authors believe that Go *weihs* and L *victima* belong together, but the situation with OE *wīglian* and *wiccian* and the origin of MDu *wijchelen* is less clear. (For a different etymology of *victima* see Odé [1927:98-99], who posits the root *g^{u}*ī*- 'live' in it and dissociates *victima* from Go *weihs*.)

The etymology proposed by Grimm appeared in Webster's dictionary in 1864 and stayed there until 1880. In 1882 Skeat[1] came out, and W 1890 changed its explanation of *witch*. But W[3] reinstated Grimm's idea. Partridge and Barnhart copied from W[3]. WNWD[1] follows W[3], except that the first edition gives the root **weiq-* 'violent strength' and cites L *vinco* 'conquer' as a cognate. Apparently, a wrong paragraph from IEW (1128: *u̯eik* 2) was reproduced; the mistake was caught later and not repeated, but it recurs in Limburg (1986:171).

3. In Go *weihs* 'holy,' *h* is not the product of devoicing before *s*, as follows from *gaweihan* 'consecrate,' and it corresponds regularly to *h* in the related forms elsewhere in Germanic (Feist). Sometimes *g* turns up in them. One of the variants of OE *wēofod* 'altar' (also *wēofud, wīobud,* and *wiohbed*) is Northumbr *wīgbed*, whose first component (*wīg-*) should be understood as a variant of *wīh-* by Verner's Law, especially because OE *wīg* 'idol, image' has been recorded. Although standard works on the history of English do not discuss the origin of *-g* in *wīg*, Barber (1932:98), in a book on Verner's Law, notes the alternation in question. Likewise, A. Noreen (1970:231, a) treated *-veig* in OI *Rannveig* and other women's names as related to *vé* < **wīha-* 'altar.' However, the etymology of OI *-veig* is debatable (see it in AEW). In OI *vígja* 'consecrate,' a weak *-ja-* verb, voicing is to be expected, but the proper name *Vígnir* shows that the root *víg-* had an independent existence in Icelandic word formation. Consequently, /g/in OE *wīglian* is not incompatible with /h/ in Go *weihs* and /k/ in L *victima*.

OE *wiccian* and *wīglian* also seem to be related, but the difference between /k:/ and /g/ poses problems even if the geminate is of expressive origin. Martinet (1937:179) pointed out that OE *fricca* 'herald' is a *nomen agentis* of the verb *frignan* 'ask, inquire.' The pair *frignan* ~ *fricca* would be a counterpart of *wīglian* ~ *wicca* if the etymology of *fricca* were more convincing. Why should a herald, a crier be called 'inquirer' or 'questioner'? Holthausen (AeEW), whose etymology Martinet must have used, compares *fricca* and Skt *praśnín-* 'one who asks' but offers no discussion. *Fricca*, more probably, is traceable to OE *fricgan* 'investigate' and *friclan* 'seek, desire,' but a herald is not a spy, and one has little choice but to agree with Förster (1908:337, note 2) that *fricca* has nothing to do with *fric, frec,* and so forth. ***Wīglian* ~ *wicca* and *frignan* ~ *fricca* look like forming a perfect group, but each pair is probably a mismatch.**

The etymology of MDu *wi(j)chelen* is debatable. Van Wijk (EWNT[2]) states that *k* in MDu *wîkelen*, a doublet of *wi(j)chelen*, and by implication, in OE *wiccian* cannot be old, because Gmc **k* in them would leave *g* in OE *wīglian* unexplained (he does not consider the possibility of Verner's Law in the forms with *g*), and traces it to the influence of some synonym. In his opinion, the source of /k:/ in words like OE *wiccian* was PIE **k̑n, *kn, *g̑hn,* or **ghn*. Thus he goes a step further than Kluge (1884:165), who listed a series of weak nouns with /k:/ but did not commit himself to their origin. However, he believed that OE *wicce* was related to OE *wīglian*.

Wood (1913-14:337/71 and 1923:336) connected OE *wicca* with the circle of G *wiegen* 'rock, sway' and MHG ~ MDu *wigelen* 'sway, shake.' He mentioned E *wiggle* but not OHG *wegan* 'weigh' (ModG *wägen*) or MHG ~ ModG *bewegen* 'move; induce,' though all of them may be related to one another and to MDu *wijchelen*. In focusing on the verbs of weighing, Wood possibly followed Wedgwood, who compared OE *wicca* and Du *wikken* 'weigh' (later 'consider, conjecture, predict'), even though, according to Wood, the meaning underlying the entire group of verbs is 'rock, swing, shake,' because conjurers used to roll violently. L *vātēs* 'prophet, seer' and Gk μάντις 'diviner, prophet,' he adds, received their names from frenzy: compare Gk μανία 'fury' and Go *wōds* 'furious, possessed' (ModG *Wut* < OHG *wuot* 'rage, fury').

If Motz (1980) had been aware of Wood's etymology, she would perhaps have explained OI *vǫlva* as 'one who wallows, rolls (in ecstasy).' She mentions *wallow* and its congeners but comes to different results (see the end of sec 6, below). As J. de Vries observes (NEW, *wichelen*), our insufficient knowledge of the practice of divination at a time when *wichelen* was coined makes such reconstructions unverifiable. In addition, he examines the hypotheses that bring the roots of such words as E *willow* and G *weigern* 'refuse' (v) into the picture. To complicate matters, owing to the workings of Verner's Law, at a certain point, the paths of Gmc **wīhan-* 'consecrate' and **wīgan* 'fight' crossed. Ettmüller (1851:134-37), for instance, listed them together (see OE *wicce* on p. 137).

A few tentative conclusions follow from the material presented so far. **Old English had the synonyms *wiccian* and *wīglian* 'foretell the future.' They may have been derived from the same root, but if they were, the relation between their postradical consonants remains unclear: neither the length of /k/ in *wiccian* nor the presence of a voiced stop in *wīglian* has been explained in a fully satisfactory way.**

The origin of MDu *wi(j)chelen* is equally problematic. Even if *wichelen* and *wiccian* are phonetic variants of the same earlier form, their kinship with Gmc **wīhs* 'holy' need not be taken for granted. Nothing points to the fact that Du *wichelaar* and OE *wiglere* (soothsayer) have ever been priests, though the line between an augur and a priest is admittedly blurred. 'Weigh' and 'move violently (in a state of ecstasy or religious frenzy)' are two other semantic bases that have been suggested for *wiccian*. A connection of *witch* with a Proto-Indo-European root for 'consecrate' (MA, 493) rests on a flimsy foundation. **OE *wicca* cannot be separated from *wiccian*, but *wicca* and *wīglian* should be assigned to the same etymon with reservations, if at all.**

4. For a long time etymologists tried to connect *witch* with *wise* and *wit*, a derivation partly inspired by *wizard*, always (and correctly) understood as 'wise man.' From a historical point of view, *witch* and *wizard* are not a perfect fit, because *witch* goes back to Old English, whereas *wizard* was first recorded and probably coined in the first half of the 15th century; its root is *wise*, not *wit*. Blount explained only *witch* according to Kilianus and Minsheu and traced *wizard* to OE *wītega* 'soothsayer, prophet.' Phillips, as usual, copied from Blount. But Lemon referred to his predecessors, including Casaubon, who treated *wise, wit, witch,* and *wizard* as related and akin to some forms of Gk Ϝεΐδω 'see,' Ϝοῖδα (perfect) 'be aware, know' (in his opinion, *witch* was derived from L *vātes*). Serenius allegedly supplied Sw *vita* (now *veta*) with the Latin gloss *fascinare* ('charm, enchant'), and Todd cited his gloss, but nothing similar appears in Serenius (1737) at Sw *weta*. Johnson did not propose any etymology of *witch*.

J. Grimm (1835:582) states that although the senses of OHG *wîzago* ~ OE *wīt(e)ga* and MDu *wichelen* refer to nearly the same reality, the sounds (he says: letters) do not match (*buchstäblich unverwandt*). For that reason, he **found it impossible to derive OE *wicce* from *wītega*.** With respect to meaning, *witch* 'wise, knowing woman' would correspond to L *sāga* 'seeress,' but since Grimm could not explain away the phonetic difference between *wicce* and *wît(e)ga*, he opted for **wīhs* as the root of *wichelen* and *wiccian*. Yet some books present *wizard, witch,* and *wit* as cognates (Talbot [1847:197], Cockayne [1861:356-57], Baly [1897:110], Swinton [1864:101], and Mitchell [1908:354]).

Skeat[1] supported the etymology that Grimm rejected. He called OE *wicca* "a corruption" of OE *wītga* and cited OI *vitki* 'conjurer, magician' derived from *vita* as proof. Skeat also noted that *wicca* "does not appear to be in very early use" and has no cognates except EFr *wikke* and LG *wikken*. In his opinion, both OE *wiccian* (but not *wicca*) and *wīglian* are related to OE *wīg* (= *wīh;* he follows Grein and glosses it 'temple'). "I do not see how we can possibly attribute *wicca* to the same root, as some propose to do," he says. ID, ED, and W (1890) quote Skeat and repeat his etymology.

Scott (CD) offered the most eloquent defense of Skeat's etymology (the text is identical in both editions). It is reproduced below in full. Witch "< ME. *witche, wicche, wichche, wiche*, a witch (man or woman), < AS. *wicca*, m., *wicce*, f. (pl. *wiccan* in both genders), a sorcerer or sorceress, a wizard or witch, = Fries. *wikke* = LG. *wikke*, a witch; cf. Icel. *vitki*, m., a witch, wizard, prob. after AS.; prob. a reduction, with shortened vowel and assimilation of consonants (*tg* > *tk* > *kk*, in AS. written *cc*), of AS. *wītga*, a syncopated form of *wītiga, wītega*, a seer, prophet, soothsayer, magician (cf. *deóful-wītga*, 'devil prophet,' wizard) (= OHG. *wīzago, wīzzago*, a prophet, soothsayer), < **wītig*, seeing, a form parallel to *witig* (with short vowel), knowing, *witan*, know, **wītan*, see: see *wit*[1], and cf. *witty*. The notion that *witch* is a fem. form is usually accompanied by the notion that the corresponding masc. is *wizard* (the two words forming one of the pairs of masc. and fem. correlatives given in the grammars); but *witch* is historically masc. as well as fem. (being indeed orig., in the AS. form *witga*, only masc.), and *wizard* has no immediate relation to *witch*. Cf. *wiseacre*, ult. < OHG *wīzago*, and so a doublet of *witch*. Hence ult. (< AS. *wicca*) ME. *wikke, wicke*, evil, wicked, and *wikked, wicked*, wicked: see *wick*[7] and *wicked*[1]. The change of form (AS. *wicca* < *wītiga*) is paralleled by a similar change in *orchard* (AS. *orceard* < *orcgeard* < *ortgeard*), and the development of sense ('wicked,' 'witched') is in keeping with the history of other words which have become ultimately associated with popular superstitions—superstition, whether religious or etymological, tending to pervert or distort the forms and meanings of words."

The main difficulty of J. Grimm's etymology consists in that a bridge has to be drawn from /χ/ in **wīchs* to /g/ in *wīglian* and from /χ/ or /g/ to /k:/ in *wiccian* and *wicce*. Some possibilities to overcome it exist, but as stated above, none is fully satisfactory. Skeat's etymology faces similar problems. Scott mentions the change *tg* > *tk* > *kk*, but later he says that the development of *cc* in *wicce*, with its palatalization of a later period (after which *ċċ* became an affricate), is paralleled by a similar change in *ortgeard* < *orcgeard* < *orceard*. His use of letters instead of phonetic symbols complicates his exposition. Medially, OE *g* designated [j] between front vowels and a resonant. Before a back vowel, [j] was possible only if it followed a product of *i*-umlaut, as in *bīegan* 'bend' (the causative of *būgan* 'bend, bow') and *fēgan* 'join' (Old Saxon had *fôgian*). Elsewhere in the middle of a word, it designated [ɣ], a voiced velar spirant (A. Campbell [1959:sec 429]).

At first sight, *wītiga* and *wītega*, with *g* between a front and a back vowel were pronounced *['wi:tiɣa] and *['wi:teɣa]. Syncope would not have changed the status of [ɣ] in *witga* (assuming vowel shortening), which would have retained the value of a velar spirant. Proximity to [t] would at most have devoiced it, so that the result would have been [witχa]. The group [tχ] was impossible in Old English. It might have produced [k:], but usually, when a stop and a spirant found themselves in contact in Old Germanic, the stop suffered spirantization; [þχ] would have been a more likely result. The change [tk] > [t:] is not unthinkable (though only in Old Icelandic; cf OI *etki* 'not' > *ekki*), but the change of [t:] to [k̇:] would still remain unexplained and improbable.

The case of *ortgeard* (that is, *ort-geard*) is different, for in initial position, OE *g* had the value of [j] before front vowels. *Geard* was [jeard], and [j] has been preserved to this day in *yard*, the modern reflex of OE *geard*. In *ortgeard* and *orcgeard*, the stop, whether [k] or [t], always stood before [j] and only the variation [kj] ~ [tj] (> [k̇k̇] > [tʃ]) has to be accounted for, whereas in *wīt(e)ga* we must go the long way from [tɣ] to the rather implausible geminate [t:] and then to [k:] and [tʃ].

In all probability, Scott had a more realistic string of changes in mind. OE *wītiga*, like its cognate OHG *wîzzago*, is a substantivized adjective (the alternation *-ig-* ~ *-ag-* is the same as in OE *īfig* ~ OHG *ebah*: see IVY). The suffix *-ig* was pronounced [ij]. This follows from the modern pronunciation of adjectives like *witty* and *heavy* (OE *wittig, hefig*) and nouns like *ivy* and *body* (OE *īfig, bodig*). OE *wītiga* continued into the 13th century, and its Middle English spelling *witie* (OED) shows that *witiga* was never pronounced with [ɣ]. Scott may have reconstructed the palatalization process so: from [wi:tija] to [witja] (with [*t*] palatalized) and then to [wiṫ:a] and [wik̇:a]. Given this order of events, *orchard* and *witch* can be understood as similar cases, except that Skeat and Scott took the shortening of *ī* in *wītga* too lightly. In Old English disyllabic words, vowel shortening has been attested before geminates and *ht*. No examples resembling *wītga* > *wĭtga* occur in SB, sec 138. Grimm's etymology also passed over some problems of vowel length (see EWNT[2], *wichelen*), but an erratic development of consonants overshadowed them.

The reconstruction from *wītga*, whatever its pronunciation, to *wicca* is burdened with one more inconsistency that neither Skeat nor CD noted. OE *wīt(i)ga* (897) and *wicca* (890) were recorded at almost the same time, and Skeat's statement that *wicca* does not appear to be in very early use is wrong. To accept his etymology, we need to assume that already at the earliest period, *witga*, the syncopated variant of *wītiga*, split off from its maternal form and turned into *wicca*. The proposed change [ṫ:] > [k̇:] must have been completed and forgotten by 890 for scribes to adopt the spelling *wicca* of the word that had once been *wītga* or *witga*. But *wītga* occurred in Old English beside *wicca*, and the coexistence of the synonyms *wītga* < *wītega* and *wicca* < *wītega* is unlikely. **The derivation of *wicca* from *wītega* has no more appeal than its derivation from *wīh* ~ *wīg* and *wīglian*. In both etymologies, a few important phonetic problems have not been solved.**

5. As already pointed out, in addition to two most influential etymologies of *witch*—from OE *wīglian* (an alleged cognate of *wiccian*, supposedly related to Go *weihs* and L *victima*) and from OE *wītiga*—there have been others. Junius's entry is short. He refers only to Lindenbrogius, that is, probably to his *Codex Legum Antiquarum*, 1613 (Mayou [1999:125]). There *witch* is said to be akin to L *vegius*, a word that occurs in British Latin, and nowhere else. Du Cange's explanation of it needs no corrections: *vegius* 'hariolus' is a Latinized form of OE *wīglere* 'soothsayer.' In later lexicography, only Mueller[1] mentions Lindenbrogius's derivation (without references to him or Junius). Quite possi-

bly, medieval scholars and priests noticed the similarity between OE *wīglian* and L *vegēre* 'excite, arouse, stir' and decided that a soothsayer was 'a vigilant one.' They must also have noticed the closeness of *wīglian* and *wiccian* and pondered the nature of that closeness, but no extant gloss connects *wicca* and *vegius*.

Tooke (1798-1805:II, 313) explained *wicked* as *(be)witched*, a past participle of OE *wiccian* 'practice sorcery' (his gloss is 'incantare'). He treated nearly all English nouns as past participles; in this case, his explanation happened to be partly acceptable. Webster (1828), too, used *wicked* as his starting point in reconstructing the ancient meaning of *witch*. However, he compared *wicked* with OE *wīcan* 'recede, slide, fall away' (his glosses) and *wicelian* 'vacillate, stumble.' "It seems to be connected in origin with *wag*," he says. "The primary sense is, to wind and turn, or to depart, to fall away." Did he think of a witch as a stumbler, an anomaly, or an apostate? OE *wiclian*, which Webster found in Somner, is, most likely, a ghost word (W. S. Morris [1967:46]). ID[1] copied Webster's etymology.

Mahn (W 1864) followed J. Grimm, while W (1890) substituted Skeat's etymology for Mahn's. W[1] cites LG *wikken* 'predict' and Icel *vitki* 'wizard' ~ *vitka* 'bewitch,' "perhaps akin to E. *wicked*." W[2] removed the Icelandic word but added hesitatingly L *victima* as a cognate. W[3] lists OE *wiccian* 'practice witchcraft,' MHG *wicken* 'bewitch, divine' and OE *wīgle* 'divination,' along with OE *wīg* 'idol, image' and OI *vé* 'temple.' Grimm's and Osthoff's etymology has returned, with none of its obscure points illuminated.

Levitskii (2000-03:II, 249, *wīh*[1]) admits that OE *wicca* may go back to the root of Go *weihs*. "The concept of witchcraft," he remarks, "is more often connected with the idea of cutting, but OI *seið-* 'witchcraft' has been traced to IE *sēi-* 'bind' (see *seið*[2]). Therefore, Gmc *wīh* ~ *wikk* can be a derivative of the root *u̯ei̯k-* ~ *u̯ei̯g-* 'bend, turn'; in all probability, this root had the syncretic meaning 'bind together ~ separate' (see *wið-*)." At *wið*, II:248-49, he says nothing new about *witch*.

The equation 'bewitched' = 'spellbound' is common. Holbrooke (1910:267) cites *witch* in a list so long and heterogenous that it cannot be put to any use; L *vincere* 'bind' turns up in it among many other words. Enchantment is connected with the power of speech or singing, whence *incantare* and *enchant*. Lessiak (1912:146-47), who traced the names of several diseases to magic, searched for a bond between *witch* and L *vox* 'voice' and related forms (he gave the Proto-Indo-European root as **veqᵘ-*) but dissociated it from OE *wīgol*.

OE *wicce* has thus been assigned to various Proto-Indo-European roots, namely **weik-* (Gmc **wīh-*) 'holy, sacred' (J. Grimm, Osthoff, and their numerous followers), ****wīg-*, which is on one hand a variant of **wīh-* by Verner's Law but on the other an independent root meaning 'fight'** (see Ettmüller's multiple glosses of *vîhan* ~ *vîgan*: 'facere, conficere; premere, pugnare; sacrare, colere; ariolari, incantare'), ****weik-* 'turn, move'** (this is the root of Webster's *wīcan*), **and *wekᵘ-* 'speak'** (Lessiak's **veqᵘ-*). Levitskii considers **wīh-* to be possibly related to **weik-*.

Skeat never gave up his idea of the origin of *witch* but relegated it to a kind of footnote: "... also explained as a corruption of OE *wītga*" (Skeat[4], *witch*; in CED, 1910, even that brief mention is absent). In his latest version of the etymology of *witch*, he makes no concessions to Grimm. He lists OE *wiccian* (but not *wīglian*) and other related forms with *-kk-* (*-ck-*, *-cc-*) and refers to OI *víkja* 'move, turn, push aside' and N *vikja* 'turn aside, conjure away' (it is an error: the *Bokmål* form is *vike* 'retreat, etc'). OI *víkja* is a cognate of OE *wīcan* that attracted Webster's attention. **Skeat concluded that *wicca* was perhaps at one time understood as an averter** (he did not specify of what). *Witch* the averter does not solve the problem, but a partial revival of Webster's etymology is curious. AeEW gives *wīcan* as a cognate or the etymon of *wicca*, but in the entry *wīgle*, *wicca* appears again. Webster's idea that OE *wīglian* may be a congener of ModE *wag* also reemerged, though in a revised form, in later research. In his discussion of *witch*, Wood mentioned E *wiggle*. *Wiggle* is related by ablaut to *waggle*, a frequentative (iterative) verb derived from *wag*.

These then are the verbs that have been proposed as more or less remote cognates of *witch*: *wiegen*, *wegen*, *wägen*, *weichen*, *wiehen*, and *weigern* (Modern German); *wijchelen* (Middle and Modern Dutch); *víkja* (Old and Modern Icelandic); *wīcan*, *wiccian*, and *wīglian* (Old English); *wag* and *wiggle* (Modern English). Their history can be traced to the older periods of Germanic with the help of numerous etymological dictionaries. The quickest search will reveal the fact that **the only reliable connection is between OE *wicca* and OE *wiccian* (and the almost identical verb in Low German); the other leads are of little value.** It appears that today we do not know much more about the origin of *witch* than did our predecessors four, three, and two centuries ago. Even J.

Grimm failed to break the spell laid by language on this word.

The authors of popular books on the history of Germanic and English words and on matters not directly connected with etymology take their information from some easily available sources. Wesche (1940:99) repeats J. Grimm. Bleckert and Westerberg (1986:372) do the same. Makovskii (1999a) mentions the Proto-Indo-European root *u̯eg- 'bind (with charms)' but considers the possibility that *wicca* is a cognate of OE *swegel* 'sky' and *swegle* 'brilliant, shining,' because witches are seers; then the original root of *wicce* is PIE *u̯ig- 'twinkle, glitter' (the postulated development is from 'glitter' to 'see'). He adds that it is important to take into consideration OE *swincian* 'deceive.' This verb cannot be taken into consideration, because it did not exist, whereas OE *swincan* meant 'work, struggle, languish.' Perhaps G *schwindeln* was meant. A. Hall (1906) gives another exotic list of the cognates of *witch*.

6. **Huld** (1979) **made the only serious recent attempt to look at *witch* in a new way**. He points out that in an 11th-century gloss, OE *wiccecræft* 'witchcraft' glosses L *necromantia* and makes that fact a cornerstone of his reconstruction. He quotes Wulfstan's *Sermo ad Anglos* in which the phrase *wiccan and wælcyrian* 'witches and valkyries' occurs and says: "This would be well justified if witches were necromancers and also dealt like valkyries with the dead. This interpretation is supported not only by many early Germanic references to necromantic practices but also by the following etymology of *wicca. Wicca* reflects P[roto-] G[ermanic] */wikyoon/, which cannot, as Skeat saw, be related to P[roto-]I[ndo-]E[uropean] */u̯eḱ/ 'be holy.' It is instead related to PIE */u̯eǵ/ 'stir, make live,' the same root [as] in OE *wacian* 'wake,' *weccan* 'awaken' and Lat[in] *vegēre* 'be lively, stir up'. *Wicca* is then 'waker (of the dead)' reflecting PIE */u̯eǵ-ioon/" (pp. 37-38).

J. Puhvel suggested to Huld that */u̯eǵ-ioon/ can be interpreted as 'the wakeful one,' but he preferred not to change the gloss 'waker' (note 8 on pp. 38-39). In his opinion, the witch of the Anglo-Saxons was not unlike the Icelandic *draugr* 'revenant.' He drew a parallel between English and Scandinavian beliefs concerning female necromancers: "By far the most famous necromantic operation is Óðinn's consultation with the spirit of a *vǫlva* in the *Vǫluspá*" (p. 38).

Huld's treatment of word formation is realistic. OED states that *wicce* and *wicca* are "app[arently] derivative of *wiccian*." This derivation looks like a tribute to J. Grimm, who based his etymology of *wicca* on the meanings of the verbs *wīglian* and *wiccian*. But *wicca* cannot owe its origin to *wiccian*. As Huld notes (p. 36), the geminate in *wiccian*, a second class weak verb, is impossible to explain from **wikōjan*. If *wiccian* were a reflex of **wikōjan*, one would also expect a geminate in OE *locian* 'look,' *macian* 'make,' and so forth, but the weak verbs of the second class are subject to neither umlaut nor West Germanic gemination. **Therefore, *wiccian* must have been derived from *wicce*, and not the other way around.**

The chronology available to us also runs counter to the idea that *wicca* ~ *wicce* were back formation from *wiccian* (even if such an idea had merit). OE *wiccian* surfaced in texts in the year 1000 (see *witch, v* in OED), 110 years later than *wicca*. The implication need not be that *wiccian* was coined late, but the opposite conclusion (an early date of the verb) would be equally unwarranted. However, even Weekley and Wyld (UED) did not dare contradict OED and repeated the etymology of *witch* offered in its pages. (ODEE says diplomatically that *wicce* is related to *wiccian*; the same in the later editions of SOD.) Huld's Proto-Indo-European protoform **weǵiōn-* has another advantage in that it accounts for *-cc-* in *wicce* without an ad hoc reference to expressive gemination. Yet his reconstruction is not without problems.

The putative Proto-Indo-European base of *wake* is represented in Germanic almost exclusively by the *a*-grade: compare Go *wakan** 'awake, be awake,' OI *vaka* 'be awake,' OE *-wacan*, their weak counterparts (like OE *wacian*), and their causatives having the umlaut of *a* in the root. Gothic had *ō* in the noun *wokains** 'watch.' The congeners of Go *wokrs** 'interest on money' (originally 'fruit, progeny') do not seem to belong with *wakan** (Feist-Lehmann). **Given Huld's etymology, OE *wicca* and its nearest cognates in Frisian and Middle Low German will be the only Germanic reflexes of **weǵ-* in the *e*-grade**. If *wicca* had been recorded with the meaning 'awakener,' it would have been recognized as related to *-wacan*, but since the existence of this meaning is what has to be proved, the entire reconstruction becomes unsafe. Note that the Latin words beginning with *veg-* ~ *vig-* refer to vegetation, vigor and vigil, rather than being awake. Nor has Huld dealt with all the semantic difficulties.

In the Middle Ages, various kinds of witchcraft were associated with acquiring mantic knowledge, that is, they presupposed contacts with the dead. Kögel (1894:207-08) cited OE *heagorūn* 'witchcraft,' glossed as 'nicromancia' [sic]; see also Güntert

(1919:121). OE *hellerūne* is 'sorceress' and 'demon' (the latter in Ælfric), but OE *hellirūne* was likewise glossed as 'necromantia' (one can assume without much risk the existence of OE **heagorūne*), and Jordanes glossed sorceresses 'haliurunnas' (Motz [1980:204-05). Apparently, **necromancy was not a function associated with, let alone unique to the** ***wicce***. Perhaps *necromantia* became a synonym for black magic and sorcery, not tied to the magician's ability to conjure up the spirits of the dead. Therefore, caution is required in etymologizing *wicce* as 'necromancer.'

The *vǫlva* of ancient Scandinavians must have been endowed with the powers similar to those of the *hellerūne* ~ **heagorūne*. The etymology of the word *vǫlva* is debatable. Motz (1980) undermined the idea that *vǫlva* is connected with *vǫlr* 'round stick,' but her explanation of *vǫlva* as 'a hidden one' (this is exactly how Güntert understood G *Hexe*) is not convincing, because 'roll' and 'wallow' do not mean 'draw the borders, circumscribe' and by implication, 'conceal.' Be that as it may, the Icelandic *vǫlva* never raised anyone from the dead: it was she whom Óðinn woke up to learn the secrets of the subterranean kingdom. She was neither 'a waker' nor 'a wakeful one.' The same holds for the revenants of Icelandic folklore. They did not need anyone to wake them up; on the contrary, they could not be put to rest.

Finally, as regards necromancy, the phrase *wiccan and wælcyrian* is not a strong argument for a particular closeness between witches and valkyries in England at the epoch of the Viking raids. Whatever the etymology of *wicca*, it had become obscure by Wulfstan's time, whereas *wælcyrie* 'corpse chooser' was a transparent word. Wulfstan's use of alliteration is a prominent feature of his rhetoric. Both witches and valkyries designated (demonic?) individuals capable of laying spells and perhaps murdering people rather than animating the dead. Their vicious power made them good companions of the plunderers, robbers, and despoilers mentioned in the passage Huld quotes. All were abominable creatures, and *wiccan* and *wælcyrian*, the names of two pagan figures, formed an alliterative binomial. Wulfstan did not pass up such an opportunity.

Huld's etymology found its way into AHD[3-4]. *Witch*, or rather *wicce*, was reassigned from **weik-* to the root **weg-* 'be strong, be lively' and defined 'necromancer.'

7. **The etymology proposed below retains some elements of Skeat's and Scott's, as well as Huld's etymologies. It is based on the supposition that the protoform of OE** ***wicca*** **was** ****wit-ja-*****.** Old English seems to have distinguished between *wita* 'wise man,' *wīt-ig-a* (or *wīt-eg-a*) 'wise man, prophet, soothsayer,' and **wit-ja*, originally 'divinator' or perhaps 'healer' ('witch doctor'), like Russ *znakhar'* 'physician, specialist in folk medicine' (from *znat'* 'know'). The negative connotations inherent in ModE *witch* probably appeared late. Nothing testifies to the *wicca* ~ *wicce* as an ancient seer. The English counterpart of OI *vǫlva* was *hellerūne*. The value of L *(h)ariolus, parcae,* and *pytho*, used to gloss OE *wicca* ~ *wicce*, should not be overestimated in the reconstruction of the English protoform, because most medieval glosses are approximate. Scribes knew the meanings of the words of their native language but often strung Latin synonyms indiscriminately. To them *wicca* and *hellerūne* were not interchangeable, and they strove to attain ever subtler distinctions (otherwise they would not have borrowed *drȳ* 'magician' from Irish), but the Latin nouns were in their memory mere labels belonging to the sphere of the supernatural, from foretelling the future to determining one's destiny.

Wita and *wītiga* yielded *wite* and *witie* respectively and had a short life in Middle English, whereas **witja-* presumably became **witta* (with palatalized /t:/) and then *wicca* and continued into the modern period. Whether *wicce* goes back to **wit-jō-* or was formed as the feminine counterpart of *wicca* cannot be decided and is of marginal importance for its etymology. A derivational analogue of *wicca* from **witja-* would be *wræcca* 'outcast, exile' (ModE *wretch*) from **wrakja-*, with the immediately noticeable difference between *-tj-* in the first word and *-kj-* in the second.

Scott (CD), who traced *wicca* to *wīt(i)ga*, cited the history of the affricate in *orchard* as evidence that *t'* might become *ḱ*. A stronger case is E *fetch* (v) from OE *fecc(e)an*, believed to be an alteration of *fetian*. Scott preferred to ally OE *fecc(e)an* with OE *facian* 'try to obtain, reach,' because "[a] change such as that of *fetian* to *feccan, fecchen* (*ti ty*), > *ci (ki, ky)*, > *ch, tch (ch)* is... otherwise unexampled in AS., though a common fact in later LL, Rom, ME, etc (*fetch*)." When writing the etymology of *witch*, he did not treat that change as unexampled. Bülbring (1900b:77-80) explained how, in his opinion, *fetian* became *fecc(e)an*, but the problem remains partly unsolved.

Despite the uncertainty about the origin of *fetch* and the exact time when *kj* and *tj* merged in Old English, the fact of their occasional merger before the date of the first occurrence of *wicca* in texts cannot be disputed. The examples given in grammars are not numerous. *Fetch* and *orchard* are the main among them, but also of interest is the spelling *cræfca* 'craftsman' beside *cræftca* and *cræftga*, all of them from *cræft-ig-a*, a substantivized adjective like *wīt-ig-a*. See SB, secs 196.2, 206.8, and 227, note 3, Kaluza (1906-07:I, sec 84b), Luick (1964:secs 668, note 2, and 686), and A. Campbell (1959:sec 486, note 1). Those forms could have been used to support Skeat's etymology of *witch* < *wītega* but for the problem of shortened *ī* and the competition between ME *wicce* and *witie*, allegedly from the same etymon.

The crowding of near synonyms, which also happened to be near homonyms (*wita, wītiga,* and **witja-*), must have accelerated the change **witja-* > *wicca*. The verb *witan* 'know' often referred to people's familiarity with arcane things. This follows from Rittershaus's survey of Go *witan* and its cognates with and without prefixes (1899:73-77). OE *witt* (that is, *wit-t*) meant not only 'knowledge' but also 'understanding, consciousness, conscience,' whereas OI *vitt* meant only 'witchcraft, charms.' L *saga* and OE *wītiga* ~ OHG *wîzzago* show that a 'sagacious' and 'witty' person was intelligent and privy to things hidden from others, especially events to come. A close parallel to *witch* derived from **wit-ja-* is Russ *ved'ma* (morphologically *ved'-m-a*). ORuss *vĕd'* meant both 'knowledge' and 'witchcraft.' Otkupshchikov (1977:271 = 2001:235) suggested in passing that *witch* is related to *wit* but offered only typological arguments; his topic was the origin of two Baltic words.

The idea that *wicce* goes back to **witja* retains the semantic base of Skeat's etymology, Scott's phonetic reasoning, and Huld's derivational model. Since **witja-* is an asterisked form, its existence is bound to remain hypothetical. However, this hypothesis seems to be less vulnerable (it is less daring and less speculative) than the others discussed in secs 1-6.

8. Several English words are sometimes mentioned in connection with the etymology of *witch*. A brief discussion of them below will be confined only to the facts relevant for understanding the origin of OE *wicca* ~ *wicce*.

1) *Wicked*. ME *wicke* (1200) 'wicked' has an obscure history. It is identical with either the noun *wicce* (< *wicca*) or OE *wicci* 'wicked,' an adjective recorded only once (1154). *Wicked* (1275) looks like a past participle but is probably an adjective of the type represented by *wretched* (1200). Weekley followed Skeat and said that *wicked* is related to *weak*. However, he connected *witch* with Go *weihs* and L *victima*. His etymologies are incompatible, for *wicked* is akin to OE *wicca*, whereas *weihs* and *weak* are not allied. Skeat thought that *wicked* had originally been a past participle meaning 'rendered evil.' This is unlikely because no evidence exists that the *wicca* of the Anglo-Saxons was wicked. In Skeat's opinion, OE *wiccian* was derived from the adjective *wikke* (in its Old English form).

2) *Wile* (1154). A connection between *wile* and *guile* is a matter of debate. OE *wīl* may be akin to the verb *wīglian* 'practice sorcery'; compare the Old Kentish gloss *wīlung* 'divinatio' and OE *wīgle* 'divination.' However, if the word *wīl* was borrowed from Scandinavian, its etymon was akin to OI *vél* 'device, machine; trick' from **vihl-*, a form related to OE *wīgle* by Verner's Law (ODEE; OED is more cautious). The etymon will turn out to be the same in both cases. Since *wicca* has probably nothing to do with *wīglian*, the etymology of *wile* is irrelevant in the present context.

3) *Wizard* (1400; the meaning 'man skilled in occult arts' was recorded only in 1550). This word deserves mention here because at present *wizard* is understood to be a male counterpart of *witch*. It is a coinage made up of the root of *wisdom* and a suffix, as in *coward, drunkard*, and the like.

4) *Wiseacre* (1595). *Wiseacre* is believed to be an alteration of MDu *wijssegher* 'soothsayer,' literally 'wise sayer.' The ironic connotations that have always been present in *wiseacre* make the idea of a borrowing from Dutch credible. Weekley quotes Blount: "One that knows or tells truth, but we commonly use it in *malam partem* for a fool." G *Wahrsager* is a folk etymological reshaping of OHG *wîz(z)ago*, a cognate of OE *wītega*, discussed at length above.

5) *Wight*. OE *wiht* has numerous cognates: Go *waihts*, (M)Du *wicht*, OS and OHG *wiht*, and OI *vættr*, with meanings ranging from 'thing' to 'creature' and 'demon; dwarf; elf' (compare also E *whit*). In his discussion of OE *wicca*, J. Grimm suggested that all these words are related to Go *weihs*. The development would then be from 'spirit' to 'living creature, child, (girl),' and further to 'thing.' The span is broad, but any attempt to explain *waihts* has to come to grips with an unusual diversity of meanings. Although Grimm's etymology may be the best there is, even Feist does not mention it in his survey of the literature. The difference between the full grade in *weihs* and the zero grade in *waihts* is probably not fatal for connecting them. According to the etymology proposed here, **wīh-* and *wicca* are unrelated. Consequently, further discussion of Grimm's hypothesis, however per-

suasive, is not warranted in this entry. Yet it is interesting to observe how many of the words mentioned above turn up in the recorded approaches to explain the origin of *waihts*, L *vox*, L *vegēre*, and OE *wegan* being among them. There is also Russ *veshch'* 'thing,' an important cognate of E *wight*, with congeners elsewhere in Slavic.

YET (888)

The Old English for yet *was* gīet(a), gīt(a), gȳt(a), *and* gēt(a). *In the Anglian dialects, those forms competed with* gēn(a) *and* gīn(a), *neither of which continued into Middle English. It has always been understood that* yet *was originally a compound, and early researchers often cited Gk* ἔτι *'still' as its cognate. Of the numerous attempts to find an adverbial phrase that later became* yet, *the most convincing one is Berneker's. He traced MHG* je zuo (> G jetzt) *'now' and E* yet *to the combination* *iu-ta, *with* iu *'already' and the enclitic* -ta (< *-dō), *the latter having secure cognates outside Germanic. The development must have been from* *íuta *to* *iúta, *which means that the earliest form of E* yet *was* gȳta, *not* gēta (gīeta *and* gīta *are side forms of* gȳta). *Unlike* gȳta, OE gēta cannot go back to *iūta. *Its possible etymon is* *ē²-ta, *whose* *ē² *can be associated with the locative of the adverb* *ei. *The initial consonant of* gēta *seems to have arisen under the influence of* gȳta *and its variants. The existence of* *j *in the Proto-Indo-European protoform is less likely.*

The phrases *iu-ta *and* *ē²-ta *must have been synonymous in Early Germanic. In Old English, the meanings of* gȳta *and* gēta *are indistinguishable. It is argued here that OFr* ēta *and* ieta *preserved the reflexes of the oldest alternation. No etymology of OE* gēta ~ gȳta *is valid unless it also explains the Frisian forms. MHG* je zuo *is akin to* yet, *though* zuo *in it may be an adverb. The Middle Low German cognates of* yet (jetto, jutto, *etc) are genuine counterparts of OE* gēt *and* gȳta. *Like* yet *and the later Frisian forms,* jetto *and* jutto *underwent the shortening of the radical vowel. Despite some uncertainty about the history of* oo- *in Du* ooit *'ever,'* ooit *is another cognate of* yet.

Beside the reflexes of the synonyms *iu-ta *and* *ei-ta (?*jei-ta), gēna *and* gīena *were current in Old English, with a doublet* geona, *apparently having a short vowel. The enclitic* -na *occurs elsewhere in Germanic: in OE* þēana (= þēah) *'though,' OI* hérna *'here,' and adverbs like Go* aftana *'from behind.' The coexistence of* gȳta *and* gȳt, gēna *and* gēn *has many parallels; one of them is OHG* ûzana *and* ûzan *'outside.' In Early Germanic, the enclitics* *-tō ~ *-ta *and* *-nō ~ *-na, *each with its distinct etymology, must have had the same meaning pairwise. ModE* yit, *still in use in the 17ᵗʰ century, might continue OE* gȳt(a), gīet(a), *or* gīta, *whereas* yet *is apparently the continuation of* gēt(a).

The sections are devoted to 1) the use of gīet *and its variants in Old English and the possible causes of vowel shortening in those forms, 2) attempts by lexicographers from Casaubon to our contemporaries to etymologize* yet, *3) conjectures in the non-lexicographical literature on the word group of which OE* gīeta *and* gīena *are later contractions, 4) Berneker's reconstruction and the etymology of* -na *in* gī(e)na, *5) the development of OE* gēta *from* *ēta, *different from* *iu-ta, *and the origin of* g- *in it, and 6) the etymology of Du* ooit. *Section 7 is the conclusion.*

1. OE *gīet* (*gīt, gȳt, gēt*), *gīeta, gēta,* and their Middle English reflexes meant 'besides, moreover, more' (preserved in *yet again, yet once more*), 'even, still,' to strengthen a comparative (as in ModE *yet more closely*), 'still' (in the archaic *you look ill yet*), 'till now' (familiar from *not yet*), and as a conjunction. The later use (as in ModE *the splendid yet useless imagery*) developed from 'besides, moreover,' but the earliest examples of it do not antedate the beginning of the 13ᵗʰ century. In present day English, *yet* alternates with *still* and *already*. Cf *Has he come yet? ~ Yes, he has already arrived. / No, not yet* and *He is still here ~ He is not here yet* (see OED). OE *gīet* is glossed as 'still; besides; hitherto; hereafter; even, even now'; *þā gīet*, as 'yet, still; further, also'; *nū gīet*, as 'until now, hitherto, formerly; any longer' (Clark Hall; see a similar list in BT). The glosses of *gēn (gīen, gēna, gīena)* are nearly the same.

Only one addition may be in order here. The adverb *still* 'without moving,' as in *stand still*, acquired the meaning 'always, ever, continually,' known from Shakespeare (for example, *Thou still hast been the father of good news—Hamlet* II ii, 42). Apparently, in some dialects, *yet* has the same meaning, though neither OED nor EDD mentions it. According to Hales (1884b), the lines from Wordsworth's sonnet: "So didst thou travel on life's common way / In cheerful godliness; and yet thy heart / The lowliest duties on herself did lay" ("Milton! thou shouldst be living at this hour...") are misunderstood by "the general reader" (*yet* in them means 'always,' not 'however'). He quotes a native of Cumberland, who wanted to say that in a certain part of the county a spectator could keep the harriers long in sight and expressed his thought so: "You can see them *yet* all along the fellside." *Yet* here corresponds to Hales's Latin gloss *adhūc* 'still, until now.' A similar medley of meanings can be observed in G *noch*: *noch nicht* 'not yet,' *noch drei Stunden* 'three more hours,' *noch besser* 'still (even) better,' *noch hier* 'still here,' *immernoch* 'constantly.'

The first vowel in *gēta* and *gēna* is long. J. Grimm (1822-37:120 = 1890:113) erred in positing *gĕta* with old *ĕ*. Sweet (1885:526) also gives *gĕt* (in his dictionary [1897], the form appears as *gīet*), and Kügler (1916:57) is based on Grimm's reconstruction. Sievers (1885:500) emphasized that *ē* was long in *gēna*, but his reference to velar umlaut in *geona* (ASG[2], sec 157.2) presupposes **ĕ*, because velar umlaut does not affect long vowels (see the discussion in E. Brown [1892:250]). The form *geona* in ASG[1] (the same section) has a length sign. In ASG[3] (sec 74, note 1), Sievers supplies the vowels with macrons but calls their history "unclear." Jordan (1906:49-50) does not object to positing *ĕo* in *geona* and *ĕ* in *gieta* and admits that *gīeta* may not reflect the original form. Whatever the ultimate etymon of *gīet(a)* ~ *gēt(a)* and its synonyms *gīena* ~ *gēna,* the root vowels in both probably had the same origin, and the diphthong in *gīeta* is believed to reflect **ē*[2] after /j/ (SB [sec 45.6 and 91d], A. Campbell [1959:sec 185], G. Schmidt [1963:122]). Since the origin of *gēta* and *gēna* remains to a certain extent obscure, it is better to follow Luick's example (1964:secs 172.2 and 173, note 2) and in the early stages of the investigation stay away from reconstructed protoforms.

Gēna was an Anglian form (Hart [1892], Jordan [1906:50]). Hempl's attempt to prove that it had wider distribution was unsuccessful. In poetry, West Saxon and Anglian forms alternated (see Jordan [1906:62] and the examples from *Beowulf,* below), but in prose West Saxon scribes either did not understand *gēn(a)* or considered it as an oddity and wrote *gīeta* instead (J. Campbell [1952:383-84]).

In Early Modern English, the vowel in both *gīt* and *gȳt* underwent shortening, which Luick (1964:sec 354.1) **ascribed with some hesitation to the lack of stress**. However, judging by their use in poetry, *gīt* and *gȳt* did not always occupy a weak position. In *Beowulf* and "The Fight at Finnsburg," *gīt* and *gȳt* occur eighteen times (in addition to the glossary in Klaeber [1950], see Jordan [1906:62-63]). In the adverbial group *þā gȳt* 'further, besides' (eight occurrences), *gȳt* does not carry stress, but in *nū gȳt* it does. Hempl (1892a:124) called attention to the fact that in the early literature *gīet* or *gīen* alone seldom express the temporal meaning 'still': in the past, *þā gīet* is used, and in the present, *nū gīet,* less often *gīet oð þisne dæg*. He adds: "The two latter expressions are clearly emphatic, but it would be very difficult to find in the *þa* and *nu* any force other than that of the tense, which is also expressed by the verb. At times one might translate *þagiet* 'then still' or *nugiet* 'now till' or 'even now,' but I know of no cases where 'still' or 'yet' is not fully as satisfying, and in the great majority of cases this is the only admissible translation. Indeed, *nugiet* may, like simple *giet*, be strengthened by *todæge*."

Gȳt and *gīt* may begin or conclude the line (compare ModE *and `yet this is `true* versus *it's not `over yet*), and sometimes, when they are not line final, they alliterate with other *g*-words. The syntax of *yet* has not changed too much since the days of *Beowulf* (except that *yet* no longer needs props like *nū* and *þā*): cf *gyf hēo gȳt lyfað* 'if he yet [= still] lives' (944b) and *gȳt ic wylle* 'yet I wish' (2512b; the lines as in Klaeber [1950]). *Gēn* occurs ten times and *gēna* twice in *Beowulf.* The contexts are largely the same as for *gȳt* ~ *gīt*. In the phrases *þā gēna* and *þā gēn,* the second adverb is unstressed. It is also unstressed in the two verses in which it is not preceded by *þā* or *nū*. In the phrase *þā gēn,* which turns up three times, *gēn* carries stress only in line 2677, and it is stressed in both occurrences of *nū gēn.*

The words for 'yet' had short vowels already in Old English (note especially OE *gett* [SB, 65, sec 91d]), which may have been caused by the variation *'nū gȳt* ~ *þa 'gȳt* (that is, *'nū *gȳ̆t* ~ *þa 'gȳ̆t*). The other forms probably lost their length later when massive shortening occurred before dentals, as in *bread, breath, threat,* and the like. *Yit* is also an old form, predating early Modern English by many centuries. It was regular in the seventeen-hundreds, but *i* in it is believed to be a reflex of *e* before dentals rather than the continuation of *ī* or *ȳ*. **More likely, *yit* continues OE *gȳt(a)* ~ *gī(e)ta,* whereas *yet* is a reflex of *gēta*** (Luick [1964:secs 379, 540-41]; HL, 133; Jordan [1968, secs 34.1 and 78, note]).

2. **The origin of *yet* has been an object of endless speculation**: 1) Casaubon (1650:264) proposed the connection between *yet* and Gk ἔπι 'beyond, besides.' N. Bailey (1721) alone endorsed his proposal. It is absent even from N. Bailey (1730). 2) Minsheu glossed *yet* in Hebrew, Greek, and Latin. Townsend (1824:123) and Bosworth (1838) looked on Hebr עוד (*'od*) 'beyond, further, *etc*' as a cognate of *yet*. 3) Junius made a more realistic conjecture. He compared *yet* with Gk ἔτι 'until now, still, besides' and εἶτα 'back; again; after; in (one's) turn' and mentioned Welsh *etwa* ~ *etto* 'already; now; also; even; still; again.' Nugent (1801:392), like Junius, derived *yet* from εἶτα. 4) Whiter accepted Junius's etymology, added L *etiam* 'also, even, still' (*etiam* is one of Junius's glosses of *etto*) and G *jetzt* 'now' and suggested that the root of *yet* is the same as in E *it* and L *id* 'this or that thing' (Whiter's gloss). In his opinion, *yet* may have been the compound *y-et*.

5) True to his plan to derive English words from imperatives, Tooke (1798-1805:I, 178) ex-

plained *yet* as *get!* (= OE *giet!*) and *still* as *stell!* (OE *stellan* 'put'). Todd (in Johnson-Todd) mentions only Tooke's etymology of *yet*. Richardson had access to Junius but sided with Tooke: "*Yet*, meaning *get*, must be interpreted as equivalent to being or having been *got* or *gotten*." Tooke's idea found its way into W (1828), Kaltschmidt (*jetzt*), and Diefenbach (1851:II, 411). Mueller[1] cites *get* as a possible etymon of *yet*, but in the second edition, he calls that combination unlikely. Tooke's etymology has analogues in contemporary research. For example, Seebold (KS, *auch*) did not discard attempts to connect Go *auk* 'for; and; but' with the imperative of *aukan** 'increase.'

6) Jamieson (1814:137) found Tooke's explanation unacceptable, doubted that *yet* was of native origin, and derived it from Gk ἔτος 'year' (dative: ἔτει). He added Hebr עוד 'yet,' among others, for "[t]hose who are attached to oriental etymons." As an anonymous reviewer put it: "If the word is originally Egyptian, it must have had a long journey northwards" (anonymous [1815-16: 109]). Bosworth (1838) copied Jamieson's etymology (without referring to it) and added a new idea. Since he thought that the basic meaning of *yet* was 'movement beyond a certain point,' he numbered OE -*giht* 'going (in *gebedgiht* 'evening,' literally 'bed going'), which he glossed as 'time,' among the possible etymons of *yet*. Such fantasies have never been repeated, but ἔτι as a putative cognate of *yet* did not lose its appeal for a few more decades (so Cockayne [1861:sec 351]).

7) Graff compared *je zuo* (since it is a late phrase, it appears in parentheses) and Go *hita*, the neuter accusative of a pronoun that occurs only in the phrase *und hita (nu)* 'until now, hitherto.' J. Grimm (1822-37:III, 120 = 1890:III, 113) rejected Graff's comparison. He was unwilling to ascribe a pronominal origin to an adverb of time, saw no possibility to connect Go *h*- with OE *g*-, and dissociated OE *gēta* from the numerous recorded forms of G *jetzt*. Despite his objections, Schwenck adopted Graff's etymology; both Hempl and H. Schröder offer variations of the same idea (see sec 3, below).

The pair E *yet* ~ G *jetzt*, which Graff noted, constitutes a special problem. Diefenbach (1851:I, 123) treated *yet* as a cognate of *jetzt*, and before him Webster (1828) did the same, but Mueller[2] followed J. Grimm and called the similarity between *yet* and *jetzt* deceptive. Nor does *yet* appear in the entry *jetzt* in any edition of EWDS. See more about *jetzt* in sec 4, below.

Cosijn (1888:56) probably followed Graff but gave no references. He only said that *git* is not a good example of the change /g/ > /j/ because it goes back to *ja* + *te*, as does *gieta*, allegedly from *ja* + *tō*. It is unclear what *ja* is supposed to mean, but *te* must be a form of the preposition.

8) The broad range of cognates—from Welsh *etto* to Gr ἔτι—pleased Wedgwood, who did not go further than Junius. 9) Skeat[1] analyzed OE *gēta* into **ge-tō* 'and too, moreover.' That compound looks like MHG *je zuo* 'jetzt,' even though OE *ge* 'and' has a short vowel and the first component of *ietzt* is believed to mean 'ever, always' rather than 'and.' 10) Scott (CD) accepted Skeat's derivation but added an important remark and a disclaimer. He said that MHG *je* in *je zuo* is either 'ever' or a form cognate with OE *ge* and that *zuo* in *je zuo* "may merely simulate *zuo*." 11) Weekley repeated Skeat's explanation without comments. 12) Among the modern dictionaries, only RHD invites us "to compare" *jeze* and *yet*. 13) OED and ODEE relegated *yet* to words of obscure or unknown origin. 14) W[1], W[2], W[3], EW, and UED do not venture any hypotheses on *yet*.

3. *Yet* has also been an object of several special investigations outside dictionaries. 15) Kluge (1895:333) derived -*a* in OE *sōna* 'soon' and *gēna* ~ *gēta* from *-*ā*, which he traced to an adverb meaning 'always, ever' (OE *āwa*, Go *aiw*). Pogatscher (1898:100, 1902:15-16) and Luick (1964:sec 313) supported Kluge's idea. 16) Brunner (SB, sec 317) asserted that -*a* in *gēta*, and so on goes back to *-*ā* < *-*ō*, this **ō* being the Proto-Indo-European ablative ending *-*ōd* ~ *-*ēd*. 17) Kaluza (1906-07:I, 320, sec 193) posited the adjectival endings *-*om* and **ōd* as the etymons of -*a* in adverbs and extended his reconstruction to such adverbs as have no correlates among adjectives, for example, *gēta, gēna, gēara* 'once,' *giestra* 'yesterday,' *sōna* 'soon,' *ofta* 'often,' and others.

In KL, Kluge repeated his derivation of *sōna* (*soon*) but gave no etymology of *gēta* (*yet*). Whatever the origin of *sōna*, at first sight, there may be some justification in dividing it into *sōn-a*. *Gēara, ofta*, and so forth are *gēar-a* and *oft-a*, but *gēna, gēta* are not necessarily *gēn-a, gēt-a* or *gē-na, gē-ta*. Besides that, even a convincing etymology of -*a* leaves the origin of *gēn*- and *gēt*- unexplained. Kluge may not have known that he was not the first to compare -*a* in the *gīeta* group with OE *ā* 'always, ever.' Hempl (1892a:124) pointed out that in Thomas Miller's edition of Bede (1890-91) *gȳta* occurs each of three times with an accent over -*a*. No other unstressed -*a* in adverbs has a similar distinction. Since lengthening in an unstressed syllable is out of the question (one could rather expect shortening), Hempl asked whether *gȳta* might not be a conglomeration of *gīet* and *ā* 'ever.' It will be shown later that Kluge's and Hempl's suggestions are wrong. Both fell into the same trap as Old English scribes, who, guided by one of the meanings of *gȳta*, interpreted the adverb as *gȳt* + *ā*. This is folk etymology.

18) Hempl (1891) had offered another etymology of *gēna* ~ *gēta* before he noticed accents over *-a*. He supposed "the words to be composed of *iú*, *géo* [sic] (Goth. *ju*) 'once, already, now, still,' and the adverbial accusative: masc. (with 'day' understood), and neut., of the demonstrative *hi-*, which was preserved in Gothic only in forms used as temporal adverbs (d. *himma daga* and a. *hina dag* 'today, heretofore'; *und hita* 'thus far')." Hempl's scheme is as follows. Gmc **iu hinō-* yielded Go **ju hina* and OE **gēohin*. Depending on whether umlaut and breaking before *h* affected the form **geohin*, the reflexes were **gīehin* and *gīen* (West Saxon) or **gēhin* > *gēn* and **gēohin* > *gēon* (Anglian); later, *gīena, gēona*. Likewise, Gmc **iu hitō* allegedly produced Go **iu hita* and OE **gēohta*. From **gēohta* we have **giehit, gīet* (West Saxon) and **gēhit* > *gēt, *gēohit* > *gēot* (Anglian). "The forms in *-a*," Hempl concludes, "may be wholly due to the analogy of other temporal adverbs in *-a*... or the way may have been led by forms in *-e* like *hine*, Germ[anic] *hinōn-*." Further discussion (Mayhew [1891b], E. Brown [1892], and Hart [1892]) concerns details rather than the principle according to which *gēta* and *gēna* were formed.

Kaluza (1906-07:I, sec 147.4; *-gȳt* < **jau hit*) and Mayhew (1891b) accepted Hempl's etymology, but later research passed it by, except perhaps Partridge (1958), who suggests, in his familiar confusing way, that *yet* may be akin to Go *ju* 'now, already,' "hence to L *iam* (ML *jam*)." L *jam* 'now, already' is related to Go *ja* 'yes,' not Go *ju*. Jordan (1906:49) dismissed Hempl's reconstruction without offering any arguments, probably because he shared Kluge's idea that *yet* and *jetzt* are unrelated. Hempl's etymon **iuhinō* ~ **iuhitō* and Graff's *and hita* share common ground in that they contain an oblique case of the same demonstrative pronoun (the first elements they proposed are different).

19) H. Schröder (1910:61-62) suggested an etymology reminiscent of Hempl's. He was obviously unaware of a predecessor, but he did not refer to Graff either. Of all the attempts to connect *jetzt* (and by implication *yet*) with the pronominal root **hi-* Schröder's is the most resourceful. He begins by stating what had always been sensed, namely, that the meaning 'jetzt' ('now') cannot be obtained from 'ever' with a preposition or an adverb after it. The Middle Low German cognates of *jetzt* are *jetto, gitto,* and *jutto* 'until now; already; further' and *juttonigen* 'now, already,' whereas in Austrian dialects their analogues are *hiazunder, hietz, hietza, hietzen, hietzunder, hiez* and *hiaz*. Schröder, like Lexer and Schmeller before him (see his references), believed that *h-* in the Austrian forms is old and reconstructed the following string of changes: **hiu-to* > **(h)iúo* > *jutto; *hío-to* > **híeto* > **(h)iéto* > *jetto*, and HG **hío-zuo* > **híezuo* > **(h)iézuo* > *jetzo, jetzt*. The history of G *heute* < OHG **hiu-tagu* constitutes, in Schröder's opinion, a parallel to *jetzt* < **hio-zuo*.

His is an ingenious reconstruction. The shift of stress in the diphthong *iu* occurred many times. For example, the reflex of OHG *iu* merged with MHG *ǖ*. The merger could have happened only if *iu* was pronounced *iú*. The German adverb *je* 'ever' developed from a form like *eo*. See also Luick (1964:secs 265-66) on similar processes in the history of English. The meaning 'jetzt' ('now') matches exactly that of **hio zuo*. WP I:453 and IEW (609) repeat Schröder's etymology of *jetzt*. Although well thought out and elegant, it is not flawless, because it presupposes the loss of *h-* in MLG *jetto* and so forth and in HG *jetzt*. Contrary to *jetzt, heute* has preserved *h-*. The idea of an early addition of *h-* to Bavarian forms under the influence of words like *heute* and *hīer* should not be disregarded. Such is also the opinion of G. Schmidt (1963:125).

20) AHD[1,3,4] refers *yet* to the Proto-Indo-European root **i-*, a pronominal stem (see it in IEW, 281, 3. *e-*). Once again a pronoun emerges as the etymon of *yet*, but this time it has been detected in the first element of the English adverb. Under the root **i-*, AHD lists E *ilk, yon, yond, yea (yes), yet,* and *if*. However, OE *gēt(a)* does not appear in WP or IEW. Probably for this reason, AHD says the following about *yet*: "preform uncertain." Shipley (1984) asserts that *yet* is from **i*, as in L *id*. He mentions *yet* under this root in the index, but it does not appear in the main part of the book.

21) Bammesberger (1990:258-59) proposes a different version of the etymology that we find in AHD. His starting point is the protoform **jē²-t-a-*, with *-a* being of the same origin as in OE *sōna* (see Kluge's reconstruction above). He admits that the radical vowel, most likely **ē²*, has an obscure history but suggests that perhaps it is a lengthened (vrddhi) grade of PIE **yod*, the neuter of the pronominal stem **yō-*, so that **j-e-at-a* resulted in **jē²ta-*. With *yet* traced to **i* ~ **yō-*, we are

back to where Junius and Whiter sought the origin of *yet* but at cross-purposes with J. Grimm, who was reluctant to reconstruct a pronominal stem in a temporal adverb. In his review, J. Klein (1992:140) called Bammesberger's etymology bizarre. It is not bizarre, but too speculative.

4. **Despite the obscurity enveloping the history of *gēta* and *gēna*, the efforts to etymologize them have not been wasted. A consensus exists that both adverbs were at one time compounds. Direct comparison with Hebrew, Greek, Welsh, and so forth was a mistake, because all such forms have postvocalic *t* instead of the expected *d*. However, if the words to be compared are from the historical point of view ἔ-τι, *e-t(t)o*, and *gē-ta*, their first syllables can be cognate. The same holds for MHG *ie-ze, ie-zuo*.**

Some compounds meaning 'still, yet, already' are transparent (for example, L *adhūc*), but most of them are short and opaque. Such are the words from Greek, Latin, and Welsh cited above, as well as Russ *eshche* 'yet' and *uzh(e)* 'already,' with cognates in other Slavic languages (in Russian, they are stressed on the last syllable). Both L *aut* 'or' and Go *auk* 'too' (unless the latter is an imperative, which seems unlikely) also consist of two elements. Graff's and especially Hempl's reconstruction incorporates *yet* into the group of which ἔτι and the rest are legitimate members. Their approach is more promising than Kluge's, because Kluge accounts for the origin of *-a* but says nothing about *gēt-* and *gēn-*.

If the morphemic cut in OE *gēta* ~ *gēna* was at one time after *gē*, *-ta* and *-na* may go back to some enclitic. Germanic enclitics are numerous but are distributed unevenly in the extant vocabulary, and their frequency is an unsafe clue to their role at earlier periods. For example, *-(u)h* is common in the text of the Gothic Bible, but in Old High German it can be detected only in *doh* 'yet' and *noh* 'yet, still' (see G *doch, noch,* Go *nauh,* OI *þó*, and OE *þēah* ~ ModE *though* in etymological dictionaries). The Old Icelandic negative enclitics *-a* and *-at* have no counterparts anywhere in Germanic, whereas Go *-hun* and OI *-gi* ~ *-ki* are akin to OE *-gen* ~ OHG *-gin*. In some monosyllabic adverbs and pronouns, final *-t* goes back to a demonstrative pronoun: see the history of E *what*, Russ *tut* 'here,' and Russ *net* 'no.'

The problem consists in finding cognates of OE *-t(a)* and *-n(a)* that have a similar function and match them phonetically. Hempl's etymology meets those demands, though it involves many intermediate steps—a circumstance that weakens its explanatory power. His initial idea was that *-a* in *gīeta* ~ *gīena* arose under the influence of other adverbs ending in *-a*. Such adverbs were not numerous: *gegnunga* 'immediately, certainly, *etc*,' *geostra* 'yesterday,' *tela* 'well' (and *untela* 'badly'), *singala* 'always,' *gēara* 'formerly,' *sōna* 'soon,' *fela* 'much,' and those with the second component *-hwega* 'about, somewhat' (Nicolai [1907:sec 26]). Even though Hempl's idea is realistic, certain considerations make it unlikely. Such forms as Go *ufta*, OFr *ofte*, OS *ofto*, and OHG *ofto* 'often,' coexisting with OE *oft*, OI *opt*, OS *oft* (the latter alternated with *ofto*, mentioned above) show that we are dealing with ancient doublets. The words for 'yet' must have belonged with *oft* ~ *ofta*.

22) Berneker (1899:157) compared the cognates of Russ *uzh(e)*, Lith *jaũ*, and others, related to them, not only with Go *ju* but also with *ie-*, as in MHG *je zuo* 'now' and *iesâ* 'at once.' As already mentioned, G *jetzt*, despite its seemingly transparent inner form, baffles etymologists, because the sum *io* 'ever' and *zuo* 'to' does not yield the meaning 'at present.' Kluge said so in the first edition of EWDS, and Seebold is no closer to the solution in KS. H. Schröder had every reason to give up the traditional etymology of *jetzt*, but he did not know that Berneker had partly anticipated his conclusions.

Jezuo appeared in German texts in the second half of the 12th century (Bahder [1929; see the details on p. 432]) and developed several variants. The one current in Modern German had excrescent *-t* (as in *Artzt* 'doctor' and *Obst* 'fruit,' for example), but the meaning of *jetzt* has not changed since roughly 1150. From the semantic point of view, it is unlike E *yet*. Kluge (EWDS[9]) cited G *immerzu* as a structural analogue of MHG *je zuo*, but *immerzu* means 'constantly,' that is, exactly what is expected of *immer* + *zu*; apparently, *zu* could be added to another adverb for reinforcement.

Berneker, whose opening statement is almost verbatim the same as H. Schröder's, written eleven years later, guessed correctly: ***je* in *je zuo* is related not to OHG *io* 'always, ever' but to Go *ju* 'already, now.'** The occurrence of Go *juþan* 'already' shows how easily **iu* entered into adverbial phrases. The following adverbs should not be confused: Go *aiw* 'ever' (OHG, OS *êo, io*; MHG *ie*; OE *ā, ō*; OI *æ, ei, ey*; they are discussed at EVER) and Go *ju* 'already, now' (OHG, OS *iu*; no corresponding form in Old English except presumably in *gīt, gīeta*). Kluge proposed OHG *io* as a cognate of *ie* in *je zuo*, but the correct choice is OHG *iu*. Tracing the first component of *yet* and *jetzt* to **iu* overcomes the main flaw of H. Schröder's etymology, namely, the presumed loss of initial *h-*.

Berneker compared *zuo* in *je zuo* with Slavic *-da*, as in OSl *što-da* 'what,' *dže-da* 'where,' Russ *pokida* 'as long as' (the form in the modern Standard is *pokuda;* stress on the second syllable), and Pol *nedaktory* 'no one' with *-t* in E *yet*. He pointed to the parallelism between Go *ju ni* 'no more' and E *not yet*. The problem of OE *gȳta* (Berneker referred only to ModE *yet*) was solved: *-ta* in *gȳta* is the same element as *-ta* in Go *þata* 'that' (n). However, with regard to G *je-zuo* Berneker probably erred in that he looked on *-zuo* as an incontestable cognate of Sl *-da*. Scott (CD) remarked that ***zuo* in *je zuo* may merely simulate *zuo*** (see the end of sec 2, above). Since the earliest extant German form is not old, *zuo* need not be a reflex of an ancient enclitic. Perhaps it is a homonym of the enclitic preserved in OE *gȳta*, but the existence of *immerzu* makes the simplest reconstruction more likely. We may assume that *zuo* in *je zuo* is an adverb.

The hypotheses by Berneker, Hempl, and H. Schröder are based on the assumption that *iu-* in **iuta* went from a falling to a rising diphthong (*íu* > *iú*). An acceptance of this development means that **the most ancient form of *yet* was not *gēta* but *gȳta*, whereas *gī(e)ta* arose under the influence of *ǵ* (palatal)**. According to G. Schmidt (1963:123), *-t(a)* in *gīet(a)* continues Gmc **tō* ~ **ta* 'to.' **Tō* may be the same word as the adverb and preposition *tō*. Cases of an adverb used in other adverbs as an enclitic are known. Compare, in addition to G *immerzu*, OI *hingat* and *þangat* from **hinn-veg-at* 'here' and **þan(n)-veg-at* 'there' (AEW, ÁBM). Perhaps G *dort* 'there' (< OHG *tharot* ~ *dorot*) and its cognates (see them in KM and KS at *dort*) also belong here. The element *-ta* in Go *þata* goes back to a Proto-Indo-European pronoun, and it is unclear whether it has the same etymon as the preposition *tō*. On Slav *da* see ESSI IV, 180-81: *da* and VI, 7: *e da*, and Vasmer I, 400: *gde* 'where,' 480: *da*; II, 399: *kuda*. Slavic adverbs ending in *-gda*, such as Russ *kogda* 'when,' *togda* 'then,' and *vsegda* 'always,' constitute a special group.

23) J. Zupitza (1880:25 and 1883) advanced two arguments against the kinship between E *yet* and G *jetzt*. The first concerns the Middle High German diphthong *ie*, which, in his opinion, was incompatible with /j/ in OE *gēta*. Kluge reconstructed the shift of stress in *ie* (*íe* > **ié* > *je*) and disposed of that problem. Secondly, Zupitza believed that WGmc **t* would have become *ss*, rather than *z*, in *jeze* if it were related to *yet* (cf E *water* and G *Wasser* < OHG *wazzar*). This is a particularly weak objection. The group *je zuo* consisted of two independent words, and the initial consonant in *zuo* is a regular reflex of WGmc **t* (cf E *ten* and G *zehn*).

After Berneker's remarks, the following became clear: 1) MHG *je* in *je zuo* goes back to **iu* 'already, now,' so that *je zuo* is a reinforced variant of *ie*, whatever the distant origin of *zuo* here, and the mystery of its meaning exists no longer; 2) OE *gȳta* should be divided *gȳ-ta*, with *gȳ-* corresponding to MHG *ie* and *-ta* corresponding to Slav *-da* (the protoform of both must have been **dō*).

If *gȳta* is *gȳ-ta*, *gēna* is, in all likelihood, *gē-na*. **The element *-na* is easier to etymologize than *-ta* because it is not isolated in Germanic word formation**. It turns up in OE *þēana* 'nevertheless, yet,' a sum of *þēah* 'although; however; still, yet' and *-na* (*þēana* < **þau-h-na*). Old Icelandic has *hérna* 'here,' *þarna* 'there,' and *svána* 'so.' In Gothic, *-na* was a productive suffix of local adverbs, for example, in *aftana* 'from behind,' *hindana* 'from beyond,' *ūtana* 'from outside,' and *innana* '(from) within' (with cognates elsewhere in the Germanic languages); *-na* has been traced to PIE **-nē*. See these words in Feist (*-na*), AEW, ÁBM, and G. Schmidt (1963:259-61).

Here, too, shortened variants occur: Go *aftana, hindana, innana*, and *ūtana* coexisted with OE *æftan*, OS *(at)aftan*, MHG *aften*, OI *aptan*; OE, OS *hindan* (OHG *hintana*); OE, OS, OI *innan* (OHG *innana*), and OE, OS, OI *ūtan* (OHG *ûzan* and *ûzana*). If *-n(a)* is akin to the pronominal stem in E *yo-n*, G *je-n-er* 'that (one),' Go *jai-n-s* (the same meaning), and others, the parallelism between, for example, Go *þa-ta* ~ OE *gē-na* and OE *þat* ~ OE *gēt* is complete, since *-t(a)* is also of pronominal origin. OE *gīena* and *gēna* left no traces in Modern English.

5. Of all the Old English forms for *yet*, to the extent that they end in *-t(a)*, the hardest one to explain is *gēt(a)*, which occurs only in the Anglian dialects. If, as has been proposed above, *īe* in *gīeta* is not the product of **ē²* diphthongized after /j/ but a side form of *ȳ* from **iu* and if *g-* goes back to **i* (non-syllabic) rather than *ǵ* (palatal), then *gēta* and *gīeta* cannot be directly related. Nevertheless, OE *gēta* is a legitimate form, not a chance hybrid (*Mischform*) or *gīeta* with *īe* monophthongized for an unknown reason. This follows from the pair *ēta* and *ieta* in Old Frisian.

G. Schmidt (1963:123), who, like all his predecessors, considered OE *gēta* to be the primary form and the etymon of *gīeta* and *gȳta*, traced *ē* in *gēta* to an adverb in the locative, namely, PIE **ĕi*, which, despite the absence of length in the diphthong, became Gmc *ē². **More probably, *ē-ta (< *ei-ta) at one time alternated with *iu-ta, as OE *nū gȳt* alternated with *þā gȳt*.** If that supposition is correct, Old Frisian retained the reflexes of the ancient alternation: *ēta* < *ē²-tā (< *ei-to) alongside *ieta* (< *ȳtā < *iútō). EDD cites *jit* ~ *jət* (phonetic spellings), *īt* ~ *it*. The regular spellings are *yit, yut*, and three forms without a palatal onset: *eet, et*, and *it(t)*. Doublets with and without /j/ occur elsewhere in Germanic. Compare ModE *if*, from OE *gif* ~ *gyb*, and OFr *jef* ~ *ef* and *jof* ~ *of*, coexisting with OHG *ibu*, and so forth. OHG *jâmerlîh* 'miserble' had a side form *âmerlîh* in Notker.

In all probability, *g-* in OE *gēta* is not 'organic' and must have been added under the influence of *gīeta*, unless the badly understood protoform (here given as *ei) contained *j* (compare Bammesberger's *yod). Holthausen (AaEW) calls OE *geona* a word of unknown origin and adds in parentheses: "The onset [*Anlaut*] is doubtful." At *gīeta*, he leaves out the statement about the origin (no etymology is offered) and reproduces only the parentheses. **If *gīet(a)* and *gīt* from *gȳt(a)* and *gēt(a)* are reflexes of ancient synonyms, rather than four continuations of the same protoform, then *g-* in *gȳta* ~ *gīeta* ~ *gīt* goes back to *i̯*, whereas *g* in *gēta* is due to analogy.** The case of OE *gēta* is not unique, as OS *êo* and *io* alongside *gio* 'always, ever' and OHG *jenêr* 'that' alongside *enêr* show (see Go *jains* in Feist).

6. The only incontestable cognates of OE *gȳt* have been found in Old Frisian. As we have seen, the affinity between E *yet* and G *jetz(t)* needs special proof. The Middle Low German forms belong to the same problematic group. Thus we have OE *gȳt, gīt, gīeta, gēta*; OFr *ēta, iēta, (ita)*; MLG *jetto, gitto, jutto*, and MHG *je zuo* and *jeze*, spelled as two words or together. The Middle Low German adverbs underwent the same vowel shortening that occurred in the history of *yet*. Fifteenth-century West Frisian also had *jetta* (Holthausen [1929b:425, a comment on sec 82.5]). Du *ooit* 'ever' and *nooit* 'never' seem to be related to *gȳt* and the rest.

ModDu *(n)ooit* is pronounced in two syllables, that is, [(n)o:-it]. Franck (1898) showed that in Middle Dutch the pronunciation of *ooit* was the same as now and supposed that its etymon was *au-aiw-wiht 'at that time,' with *au being a pronoun 'that one.' His etymology is stillborn. The most authoritative works on the history of *(n)ooit* are Psilander (1900 and 1902). According to him, *-it* in *ooit* is identical with E *yet* < *gīet*, whereas *oo-* goes back to OFr *ā* < *aiw 'ever,' because Franconian *â* could have yielded *ê*. In addition to *ooit* and *nooit*, the forms *ooint, nooint* and MDu *iewent* (< *iewet*) have been recorded. Psilander (1900:147) compared them with OE *gēn* ~ *gīen* and derived *ē* from *ē². If *ooit* is a reflex of *ā-iet, we obtain a mirror image of what Hempl, Kluge, and Old English scribes, all of them inspired by folk etymology, detected in OE *gīeta*, allegedly from *gīet-a, only *ā*, instead of being an enclitic appears in pre-position. Psilander (1900:146) cites OE *ǣfre gīet* and *nǣfre gīet*, literally 'ever yet' and 'never yet,' as other examples of intensified adverbial phrases.

Heeroma (1941:99) pointed out that OFr *ā-ieta did not exist and that since *ooit* and *nooit* had wide currency in Middle Dutch, they do not look like Frisian imports. Those are valid objections, but the solution he offers is hardly credible. In his opinion, *nooit* arose under the influence of pairs like Du *ie* 'ever' ~ *nie* 'never' and *ergens*.

Between 1900 and 1902, Psilander changed his views on *-n-* in *ooint*. In the later article (p. 123), he calls *-n-* a mere insertion. Psilander (1902) was a response to Kern (1901), who believed that *ooit* developed from *jo-tît (*tît* 'time') and referred to *aait* from *altit* in the dialect of Twente. The experience of Franck, Hempl, Kluge, and Schröder shows that combinations of this type are easy to invent. The group *jo-tît might have yielded *ooit*, though the loss of *-t-* poses a problem, but it is preferable to agree on an etymology that takes care of both *ooit* and *yet*. Inasmuch as OE *tīd* has no relation to *yet*, Kern's reconstruction should be rejected. EWNT² and NEW accept Psilander's ideas, but both expresses doubts about *oo*. If Dutch had cognates of OE *gēna*, then *ooint* and *iewent* are hybrid forms. A direct comparison between OE *gēt* and Du *ooit* (so Björkman [1916:248]) is to be avoided. In any case, **-it in Du *ooit* is akin to E *yet*** (Heeroma thinks so too) **and all the words listed at the beginning of this section.**

7. The verdict of English etymological lexicography that *yet* is a word of unknown origin lacks foundation. *Yet* has cognates in Frisian, Dutch, Low and High German, and German linguists need not repeat Grimm's statement that *jetzt* is not related to *yet*. OE *gīet(a)* consists of two demotivated elements, *gīe-* and *-t(a)*, not *gīet-* and *-a*. Consequently, *-a* should be separated from *ā* 'ever.' OE *gīen(a)* had a similar structure: *gie-n(a)*. These facts are no longer controversial.

The second components of *gīet(a)* and *gīen(a)* go back to pronominal stems occurring outside Germanic; *-na* is a common Germanic element. Not only did *gīe* attract different enclitics; the same enclitic was sometimes added to different roots. It may seem natural to posit OE *gēt(a)* with *ē[2] and trace *gīet(a), gīt,* and *gȳt(a)* to it. Likewise, MHG *je zuo* looks like a continuation of **ja zuo*, with **ja* < *ē[2]. However, such a reconstruction does not hold for OFr *īeta* and *ēta* because neither OFr *īe* can be derived from *ē*, coexisting with it, nor *ē* from *īe*. Therefore, it has been suggested here that OE *gēta* and *gēna* have an etymon different from that of *gīet(a)* and *gīen(a)*.

The *gīe-* part of *gīet(a)* goes back to **iu* 'already,' with stress on *u*. The form **iút(a)* became *gȳt; gīet(a)* and *gīt(a)* are its variants. *Gīen(a)* must have developed from *gēna*. If the first syllable of OFr *ēta* and OE *gēta* is traceable to **ei, g* in *gēt(a)* arose under the influence of *gīeta* and *gȳt*, and it is not necessary to reconstruct *j* in the protoform. The absence of **gȳna* makes the history of *g-* in *gēna* less clear.

The existence of competing adverbial phrases like **iu-ta* and **ei-ta* is not unusual: compare OE *nū gȳt* and *þā gȳt*. In East Slavic, two Proto-Indo-European words merged: Proto-Slavic **ju(že)* and **u* (Vasmer IV:151-52, *uzhe* 'already'). Slav *ešče* 'yet, still' has been derived from **etsque, *adsque*, and **jest-je*. None of the proposed etymons is fully convincing, but none is improbable (Vasmer II:30-31, *eshche*).

The oldest meaning of *iu-ta* seems to have been 'already' and 'at this moment,' preserved by MHG *je zuo* (> *jetzt*). Phrases like *nū gȳt* and *þā gȳt* acquired the meanings 'until now, formerly' and 'yet, still, further, in addition.' At first, *gȳt* in them only reinforced *nū* and *þā* ('right now' and 'just then'); later it began to convey the same meaning alone. We no longer say **now yet* and **then yet*, but phrases like *now then* show how unpredictable and illogical such combinations sometimes are. The distance from 'right now' to 'still' and from 'just then' to 'yet' was relatively easy to cover. The abstract meaning 'however' must have been the last to appear. Although the paths of E *yet* and *ever* crossed more than once (cf *ǣfre gīet*), the origins of those adverbs are different.

The shortening of the vowel in *yet* and in its Frisian and Low German cognates should probably be accounted for by sentence stress. But the formula 'loss of length in an unstressed position' would be misleading, because in everyday speech *gȳt* was sometimes stressed and sometimes unstressed. Germanic generalized the shortened form. By contrast, Slav **ače* 'if, though, *etc*,' a word group reminiscent of L *atque* 'and, and also,' has lengthened *a*, ascribed, for want of a better explanation, to emphasis (ESSI I:36-37).

Not every detail in the etymology of *yet* and its cognates is clear, but in such matters absolute clarity is unachievable. It is more surprising how thoroughly historical linguists have investigated the origin of *yet* and how little of the obtained knowledge is reflected in our best dictionaries.

BIBLIOGRAPHY

In using the bibliography, the following has to be remembered: 1) Umlauted letters, namely *ä*/*æ*, *ö*/*ø*, and *ü*, are treated as *ae*, *oe*, and *ue* respectively. Consequently, *Hoeufft* follows rather than precedes *Höfler* (as would have happened if *ö* were equal to *o*). Likewise, *Brøndal* stands between *Brocket* and *Brogyanyi*, and *Mueller, Eduard* follows *Mūlenbachs* and precedes *Müller, Ernst*. However, *å* is treated like *a*, not like *aa*, and no distinction is made between *c* and *č*. 2) If a book has been published in more than one volume, this fact is mentioned only if each volume has its own pagination. 3) Cross-references are given not only to joint authors but also to the editors of all books. This system makes the general picture more transparent, especially because the same people often appear as editors and as contributors. 4) The names of publishers are given exactly as they appear on the title page: C. Winter, Carl Winter, Carl Winter's Universitätsverlag, Carl Winter Universitätsverlag, and so forth. Nor have prepositions been deleted: At the Clarendon Press, Gedruckt bey Joseph Kaestner, Apud Joh. Frid. Gleditschi B. Filium, and the like. The places of publication appear in their natural guise, for example, Firenze, München, and Sankt-Peterburg, not Florence, Munich, or St. Petersburg. 5) In references to *Notes and Queries*, the roman number designates the series. 6) The titles of the works in Russian, Ukrainian, and Czech have been translated by the editor.

Abbreviations of Journal Titles and Book Series

(See abbreviated book titles like KLNM and RGA in the bibliography.)

A&A — Anglistica and Americana. Hildesheim, New York: G. Olms.

Aarbøger — Aarbøger for nordisk oldkyndighet og historie, udgivne af Det Kongelige Nordiske Oldskrift Selskab. II. Række. Kjøbenhavn: I Commission i den Gyldendalske Boghandel.

AB — *Anglia Beiblatt* (= *Beiblatt zur Anglia*)

ABÄG — *Amsterdamer Beiträge zur älteren Germanistik*

ABibl — Altdeutsche Bibliothek. Tübingen: Max Niemeyer.

AC — *Archaeologica Cambrensis*

AF — Anglistische Forschungen. Heidelberg: Carl Winter.

AG — *Americana Germanica*

AGDSZ — Abhandlungen herausgegeben von der Gesellschaft für deutsche Sprache in Zürich. Zürich: E. Speidel, Akadem. Verlagsbuchhandlung/Druck und Verlag von Züricher & Furrer.

AGI — *Archivio glottologico italiano*

AGSM — Abhandlungen der Geistes- und sozialwissenschaftlichen Klasse. Verlag der Akademie der Wissenschaften und der Literatur in Mainz. Wiesbaden: Verlag der Akademie der Wissenschaften und der Literatur in Mainz, in Kommission bei F. Steiner.

AIAVS — Arbeiten aus dem Institut für Allgemeine und Vergleichende Sprachwissenschaft. Wien: Gerold & Co.

AIL — *Anales del Instituto de Lingüística de la Universidad Nacional de Cuyo.*

AION-FG — *AION–Filologia germanica*

AION-SL — *AION–Sezione linguistica*

AJ — Acta Jutlandica/Aarsskrift for Aarhus Universitet. København: Levin & Munksgaard.

AJGLL — *American Journal of Germanic Languages and Literatures*

AJP — *The American Journal of Philology*

AK — *Archiv für Kulturgeschichte*

Bibliography

AL — *Archivum Linguisticum*

ALLG — *Archiv für lateinische Lexikographie und Grammatik*

AM — *The Atlantic Monthly*

ANF — *Arkiv för nordisk filologi*

ANQ — *American Notes and Queries*

ANVA — Avhandlinger utgitt av Det Norske Videnskaps-Akademi i Oslo. II. Hist-filos. Klasse. Oslo: Universitetsforlaget.

APS — *Acta Philologica Scandinavica*

ArA — Archaeologica Austrica. Wien: Franz Deuticke, Horn: Ferdinand Berger und Söhne OHG.

Archaeologia — *Archaeologia: Or Miscellaneous Tracts Related to Antiquity*

Archiv — *Archiv für das Studium der neueren Sprachen und Literaturen*

AS — *American Speech*

ASNSP — *Annali della Scuola Normale Superiore di Pisa*

ASP — Archiv für slavische Philologie

ASTHLS: ACL — Amsterdam Studies in the Theory and History of Linguistic Sciences: Amsterdam Classics in Linguistics. Amsterdam, Philadelphia: John Benjamins B.W.

ASTHLS: CILT — Amsterdam Studies in the Theory and History of Linguistic Sciences: Current Issues in Linguistic Theory. Amsterdam, Philadelphia: John Benjamins Publishing Company.

ASTHLS/IV — Amsterdam Studies in the Theory and History of Linguistic Science. Series IV: Current Issues in Linguistic Theory. Amsterdam, Philadelphia: John Benjamins Publishing Company.

ATS — *Antiqvarisk tidskrift för Sverige*

AUU — Acta Universatits Umensis/Umeå Studies in the Humanities. Umeå Universitet

Avh. NVAO — Avhandlinger utgitt av Det Norske Videnskaps-Akademi i Oslo. II. Hist-filos. Klasse. Ny Serie. Oslo: Universitetsforlaget.

AWL — Akademie der Wissenschaften und der Literatur. Abhandlungen der Geistes- und sozialwissenschaftlichen Klasse. Verlag der Akademie der Wissenschaften und der Literatur in Mainz. Wiesbaden: Kommission bei Franz Steiner Verlag GMBH.

AYR — *All the Year Round*

BAVSS — *Beiträge zur Assyrologie und vergleichenden semitischen Sprachwissenschaft*

BB — [Bezzenberger's] *Beiträge zur Kunde der indogermanischen Sprachen*

BBA — Bibliothèque Bretonne Armoricaine publiée par la Faculté des Lettres de Rennes. Rennes: J. Plihon and L. Hervé.

BCILL — Bibliothèque des Cahiers de l'Institut de Linguistique. Louvain-la Neuve: Peeters.

BFH — Biblioteca Filología Hispánica. Madrid: Consejo Superior de Investigaciones Científicas.

BG — Bibliotheca Germanica. Bern: A. Francke AG. Verlag, München: Leo Lehnen Verlag GMBH.

BH — Biblioteca di Helikon. Rivista di tradizione e cultura classica dell'Università di Messina. Roma: Herder Editrice e Libreria.

BM — Bibliothèque du *Muséon*. Louvain: Publications Universitaires. Institut Orientaliste.

BMDC — Bijdragen en Mededelingen der Dialect-Commissie van de Koninklijke Nederlandse Akademie van Wetenschappen te Amsterdam. Amsterdam: N.V. Noord-Hollandsche Uitgevers Maatschappij.

BN — *Beiträge zur Namenforschung*

BNL — Beiträge zur neueren Literaturgeschichte. Heidelberg: Carl Winter.

BRH — Biblioteca Románica Hispánica. Madrid: Editorial Gredos.

BRLF — Biblioteca di Ricerche Linguistiche e Filologiche. Università di Roma: Istituto di Glottologia.

BSGLN — Bouwstoffen en studien voor de geschiedenis en de lexicografie van het Nederlands. Het Belgisch Interuniversitair Centrum voor Neerlandistiek.

BSLP *Bulletin de Société de Linguistique de Paris*
BT/RB *Belgisch Tijdschrift voor Philologie en Geschiedenis/Revue Belge de Philologie et d'Histoire*
BTLV *Bijdragen tot de taal-, land- en volkenkunde van Nederlandsch-Indië*
CE *College English*
CF Collectanea Friburgensia / Veröffentlichungen der Universität Freiburg (Schweiz) N.F. Freiburg, Schweiz: St. Paulusdruckerei. Freiburg (Schweiz): Kommissions-Verlag Universitätsbuchhandlung Gebr. Hess & Co.
CFR English Linguistics 1500-1800. A Collection of Facsimile Reprints Selected and Edited by R. C. Alston. Menston, England: The Scolar Press.
CG *Colloquia Germanica*
ChEJ *Chambers' English Journal*
ChJ *Chambers' Journal of Popular Literature, Science, and Arts*
CJL *Canadian Journal of Linguistics*
CLSLP Collection Linguistique publiée par La Société de Linguistique de Paris. Paris: Librairie Ancienne Honoré Champion.
CM *Collegium Medievale*
CMHS Collections of the Maine Historical Society. Portland: Bailey and Noyes.
CoE *Comments on Etymology*
CP *Classical Philology*
CQ *Classical Quarterly*
CR *The Classical Review*
CRew *Chiba Review*
CS *The Cheshire Sheaf*
CSP Camden Society [Publications]. Oxford: Printed for the Camden Society.
DAWW Denkschriften der Akademie der Wissenschaften in Wien. Philosophisch-historische Classe. Wien: [no indication of publisher].
DB *Driemaandelijke bladen*
DCNQ *Devonshire and Cornwall Notes and Queries*
DFm 6 Danmarks folkeminder 6. Fra dansk folkemindesamling 3: Meddelelser og optegnelser. København: Det Schønbergske forlag, 1910.
DLZ *Deutsche Literaturzeitung*
DMT Durham Medieval Texts [no indication of publisher].
DN *Dialect Notes.* Norwood, MA, *etc*: J. S. Cushing & Co, *etc.*
DS *Danske studier*
DTg *De Nieuwe Taalgids*
EAO Episteme dell'Antichità e oltre. Roma: Il Calamo.
EB Erlanger Beiträge zur Sprach- und Kunstwissenschaft. Nürnberg: H. Carl.
EDSP English Dialect Society Publications. Publ for the English Dialect Society by N. Trübner & Co; [later] London: Henry Frowde.
EETS Early English Text Society. London: Trübner & Co. and Oxford University Press.
EG *Études Germaniques*
EGS *English and Germanic Studies*
ELN *English Language Notes*
ER *Essex Review*
ES *English Studies*
ESELL Essays and Studies on English Language and Literature. Uppsala: A.-B. Lundequistska Bokhandeln, Copenhagen: Einar Munksgaard, Cambridge, MA: Harvard University Press.
ESt *Englische Studien*
ET *English Today*
FA Forum Anglicum. Frankfurt am Main, *etc*: Peter Lang.
FC Filologia e critica. Roma: Edizioni dell'Ateneo & Bizzarri.

FJ *Frysk Jierboek*. Assen: Van Gorcum & Camp. N. V.
FL *Forum Linguisticum*
FLH *Folia Linguistica Historica*
FM *Fraser's Magazine*
FS *Frühmittelalterliche Studien*
FSt Französische Studien. Heilbronn: Verlag von Gebr. Henninger.
FVC Forhandlinger i Videnskabs-Selskabet i Christiania. In Commission bei Jacob Dybwad (A. W. Brøggers Buchdruckerei).
GA Germanistische Abhandlungen. Breslau: M. & H. Marcus.
GAG Göppinger Arbeiten zur Germanistik. Göppingen: Kümmerle Verlag.
GASK Germanistische Arbeiten zu Sprache und Kulturgeschichte. Frankfurt am Main, *etc:* Verlag Peter Lang.
GB/I Germanische Bibliothek. I. Sammlung germanischer Elementar- und Handbücher. 1. Reihe: Grammatiken; 4. Reihe: Wörterbücher. Heidelberg: Carl Winter.
GB/II Germanische Bibliothek. II. Untersuchungen und Texte. I. Beiträge zur germanischen Sprach- und Kulturgeschichte. Heidelberg: Carl Winter.
GBDP Gießener Beiträge zur deutschen Philologie. Gießen: Von Münchowsche Universitäts-Druckerei Otto Kindt GmbH.
GBESKEN *Giessener Beiträge zur Erforschung der Sprache und Kultur Englands und Nordamerikas*
GGA *Göttingsche Gelehrte Anzeigen*
GH Germanische Handbibliothek. Halle (Saale): Buchhandlung des Waisenhauses.
GHÅ Göteborgs Högskolas Årsskrift. Göteborg: Wettergren & Kreber.
GKVVSH Göteborgs Kungl. Vetenskaps- och Vitterhets- Samhälles Handlingar. Göteborg: Wald. Zachrissons Boktryckeri.
GL *General Linguistics*
GLL *German Life and Letters*
GLM Grazer Linguistische Monographien. Graz: Institut für Sprachwissenschaft der Universität Graz.
GM *The Gentleman's Magazine*
GRM *Germanisch-Romanische Monatsschrift*
GUÅ Göteborgs Universitets Årsskrift/Acta Universitatis Gothoburgensis. Stockholm: Almqvist & Wiksell.
HBV *Hessische Blätter für Volkskunde*
HFM Historisk-filosofiske Meddelelser af Det Kongelige Danske Videnskabernes Selskab. København: Munksgaard.
HKZM *Handelingen der Koninklijke Zuidnederlandse Maatschappij voor Taal- en Letterkunde en Geschiedenis*
HLQ *The Huntington Library Quarterly*
HM *Historical Magazine*
HS *Historische Sprachforschung/Historical Linguistics*
HSCL Harvard Studies in Comparative Literature. Cambridge: Harvard University Press.
HSCP *Harvard Studies in Classical Philology*
HT *Historisk tidskrift*
HUA Universität Hamburg. Abhandlungen aus dem Gebiet der Auslandskunde. Reihe B. Völkerkunde, Kulturgeschichte und Sprachen. Hamburg: Cram, de Gruyter & Co.
IaRD *Iazyk i rechevaia deiatel'nost'*
IARL *International Anthropological and Linguistic Review*
IB Indogermanische Bibliothek. Heidelberg: Carl Winter. Universitäts-buchhandlung.
IBK Innsbrucker Beiträge zur Kulturwissenschaft, herausgegeben von der Innsbrucker Gesellschaft zur Pflege der Geisteswissenschaften. Innsbruck: AMŒ
IBS Innsbrucker Beiträge zur Sprachwissenschaften. Innsbruck: Institut für Sprachwissenschaft der Universität Innsbruck.

ICQ	*Irish Church Quarterly*
IF	*Indogermanische Forschungen*
IF(A)	*Indogermanische Forschungen (Anzeiger)*
IFil	*Inozemna filolohija*
IJGLSA	*Interdisciplinary Journal for Germanic Linguistics and Semiotic Analysis*
IJP	*The International Journal of Psychoanalysis*
IJVS	*Innsbrucker Jahrbuch für Volkskunde und Sprachwissenschaft*
IORIS	*Izvestiia Otdeleniia russkogo iazyka i slovesnosti Rossiiskoi Akademii nauk*
JAF	*Journal of American Folklore*
JAOS	*Journal of the American Oriental Society*
JCS	*The Journal of Celtic Studies*
JDSG	*Jahrbuch der Deutschen Shakespeare-Gesellschaft*
JEGP	*The Journal of English and Germanic Philology*
JEP	*Journal of English Philology*
JGP	*The Journal of Germanic Philology*
JIES	*Journal of Indo-European Studies*
JIES-MS	Journal of Indo-European Studies. Monograph Series. Washington, D.C.: Institute for the Study of Man.
JL	Janua Linguarum. The Hague, Paris: Mouton.
JLR	*Jewish Language Review*
JLS	*Jewish Language Studies*
JPh	*Jahrbuch für Philologie*
JREL	*Jahrbuch für romanische und englische Literatur*
KCMS	*King's College Medieval Studies. King's College London: Centre for Late Antique and Medieval Studies.*
KVNS	*Korrespondenzblatt des Vereins für niederdeutsche Sprachforschung*
KZ	[Kuhn's] *Zeitschrift für vergleichende Sprachforschung auf dem Gebiete der indogermanischen Sprachen*
LACUS	*LACUS* [Linguistic Association of Canada and the United States] *Forum*
LangM	Language Monographs. Philadelphia: Linguistic Society of America.
LB	*Leuvense Bijdragen*
LCD	*Literarisches Centralblatt für Deutschland*
LD	Linguistic Dissertations. Philadelphia: LSA, University of Pennsylvania.
Lg	*Language*
LiB	*Linguistica Baltica*
Lit.bl.	*Literaturblatt für germanische und romanische Philologie*
LL	*Lore and Language*
LM	*Lippincott's Magazine*
LNS	Lundastudier i nordisk språkvetenskap. Lund: G. W. K. Gleerup.
LP	*Lingua Posnaniensis*
LSA	Linguistic Society of America
LSE	Lund Studies in English. Lund: C. W. K. Gleerup, Copenhagen: Ejnar Munksgaard
LSFU	Lexica Societatis Fenno-Ugricae. Helsinki: Suomalais-ugrilainen seura.
LSG	Linguistic Studies in Germanic. Chicago: The University of Chicago Press.
LUÅ	Lunds Universitets Årsskrift. Lund: G. W. K. Gleerup, Leipzig: Otto Harrassowitz.
MA	Meijerbergs arkiv för svensk ordforskning. Göteborg: Styrelsen för Meijerbergs Institut vid Göteborgs Universitet.
MacMag	*MacMillan's Magazine*
MÆ	*Medium Ævum*
MarM	*Mariner's Mirror*
MART	Medieval Academic Reprints for Teaching. Toronto, Buffalo: University of Toronto Press in association with the Medieval Academy of America.

MBG Marburger Beiträge zur Germanistik. Marburg: N.G. Elwert Verlag.
MCNQ *Manchester City Notes and Queries*
ME Manuales y anejos de "Emerita." Madrid: Instituto "Antonio de Nebrija".
MF Münstersche Forschungen. Münster, Köln: Böhlau.
MGS *Michigan Germanic Studies*
MKAW Mededeelingen der Koninklijke Akademie van Wetenschappen. Afdeeling Letterkunde. Amsterdam: Uitgave der Koninklijke Akademie van Wetenschappen te Amsterdam.
MLN *Modern Language Notes*
MLQ *Modern Language Quarterly*
MLR *Modern Language Review*
MM *Maal og Minne*
MMS Münstersche Mittelalter-Schriften. München: Wilhelm Fink Verlag.
MNQ *Manchester Notes and Queries*
MO *Le Monde Oriental*
MPh *Modern Philology*
MR *The Monthly Review*
MS *Moderna Språk*
MSGV *Mitteilungen der Schlesischen Gesellschaft für Volkskunde*
MSN Mémoires de la Société Néo-philologique. Helsingfors: Neuphilologischer Verein.
MSp Monographien zur Sprachwissenschaft. Heidelberg: Carl Winter.
MSt Mitteldeutsche Studien. Halle (Saale): VEB Max Niemeyer Verlag
NAWG Nachrichten der Akademie der Wissenschaften in Göttingen. Philologisch-historische Klasse. Göttingen: Vandenhoeck & Ruprecht.
NB *Namn och Bygd*
NBRW *Nieuwe bijdragen voor regtsgeleerdheid en wetgeving*
NC *The Nineteenth Century and After*
NDL Neudrucke deutscher Litteraturgeschichte des XVI. und XVII. Jahrhunderts. Halle an der Saale: Max Niemeyer.
NdM *Niederdeutsche Mitteilungen*
NG Nomina Germanica. Uppsala: Almqvist & Wiksells boktryckeri, A.-B.
NGN *Nomina Geographica Neerlandica*
NJ *Niederdeutsches Jahrbuch. Jahrbuch des Vereins für niederdeutsche Sprachforschung*
NJES *Nordic Journal of English Studies*
NJKAGDL(P) *Neue Jahrbücher für das Klassische Altertum, Geschichte und deutsche Literatur (und Pädagogik)*
NJP *Neue Jahrbücher für Pädagogik*
NKGWG Nachrichten von der Königlichen Gesellschaft der Wissenschaften zu Göttingen. Philologisch-historische Klasse. Göttingen: Dietrichsche Buchhandlung.
NM *Neuphilologische Mitteilungen*
NoB *Namn och Bygd*
NOWELE *North-Western European Language Evolution*
Nph *Neophilologus*
NQ *Notes and Queries*
NR NORNA-Rapporter. Uppsala: NORNA-Förlaget.
NS Niederdeutsche Studien. Köln, Graz: Böhlau Verlag.
NSST *The New Shakspere Society's Transactions*
NSt *Nysvenska studier*
NTF *Nordisk Tidsskrift for Filologi*
NTg *Nieuwe Taalgids*
NTU Nordiska texter och undersökningar. Stockholm: Hugo Gebers Förlag, København: Levin & Munksgaard, *etc.*

NVES — A New Variorum Edition of Shakespeare. Philadelphia & London: J. B. Lippincott Company.
NW — *Niederdeutsches Wort*
NYTM — *The New York Times Magazine*
NZV — *Niederdeutsche Zeitschrift für Volkskunde*
O&S — *Ord og sag*
OO — *Onomasiology Online.* http://www.onomasiology.de
OT — *Onze Taaltuin*
PADS — Publications of the American Dialect Society. Publ for the American Dialect Society by the University of Alabama Press.
PAFS — Publications of the American Folklore Society. American Folklore Society.
PAPA — Proceedings of the American Philological Association. Hartford.
PBB — [Paul und Braune's] *Beiträge zur Geschichte der deutschen Sprache und Literatur*
PDS — *Prager Deutsche Studien*
PFLUS — Publications de la Faculté des Lettres de l'Université de Strassbourg. Macon: Protat Frères.
PG — Philologica Germanica. Wien: Wilhelm Braumüller, Universitätsbuchhandlung GmbH.
PLi — *Papiere zur Linguistik*
PLL — *Papers on Language and Literature*
PLPLS — Proceedings of the Leeds Philosophical and Literary Society. Leeds: The Society.
PMLA — *Publications of the Modern Language Association of America*
PPS — *Proceedings of the Philological Society*
PPSoc — Publications of the Philological Society. Oxford: Oxford University Press; London: Humphrey Milford.
PQ — *Philological Quarterly*
PSAS — Proceedings of the Society of Antiquaries of Scotland. Edinburgh: Printed for the Society by Neill and Company Ltd.
PVFGH — Populärt vetenskapliga föreläsningar vid Göteborgs Högskola. Stockholm: Albert Bonniers Förlag.
QALT — *Quaderni dell'Atlante Lessicale Toscano. Regione Toscana.*
QF — Quellen und Forschungen zur Sprach- und Culturgeschichte der germanischen Völker. Strassburg: K. J. Trübner.
QLF — *Quaderni linguistici e filologici*
QPL — Quaderni Patavini di linguistica. Publicazione del Dipartimento di Linguistica dell'Università di Padova e del Centro per gli Studi di Fonetica del C. N. R. Padova: Unipress.
QR — *The Quarterly Review*
RBDSL — Regensburger Beiträge zur deutschen Sprach- und Literaturwissenschaft. Frankfurt a. M.: Peter Lang.
RBMÆS — Rerum Britannicarum Medii Ævi Scriptores, or Chronicles and Memorials of Great Britain and Ireland. London: Longman, etc.
RES — *Review of English Studies*
RF — *Romanische Forschungen*
RGW — Rijksuniversiteit te Gent. Werken uitgegeven door de Faculteit van de Wijsbegeerte en Letteren. Antwerpen: De Sikkel, s'-Gravenhage: Martin Nijhoff.
RH — Romanica Helvetica. Genève: Librairie E. Droz.
RHR — *Revue de l'Histoire des Religions*
RIL — *Rendiconti del'Istituto Lombardo. Accademia di Scienze e Lettere. Classe di Lettere e Scienze Morali e Storiche*
RLR — *Revue de linguistique romane*
RMP — *Rheinisches Museum für Philologie*
RP — *Romance Philology*

Runrön Runologiska bidrag utgivna av Institutionen för nordiska språk vid Uppsala universitet. Uppsala.

S&S *Språk och Stil*

Sächs. Ges. Wiss. Berichte über die Verhandlungen der Königlichen Sächsischen Gesellschaft der Akademie der Wissenschaften zu Leipzig. Philologisch-historische Klasse. Leipzig: Bei B. C. Teubner.

Saga-Book *Saga-Book of the Viking Society for Northern Research*

SAJL/SATT *South African Journal of Linguistics / Suid-Afrikaanse Tydskrif vir Taalkunde* SAMLA-ADS South-Atlantic Modern Language Association, American Dialect Society.

SBAW Sitzungsberichte der Bayerischen Akademie der Wissenschaften. Philosophisch-historische Abteilung. München: Verlag der Bayerischen Akademie der Wissenschaften.

SBS Slaviska och baltiska studier. Lund: Slaviska Institutionen vid Lunds Universitet.

SCCS Smith College Classical Studies. Northampton, MA.

ScNQ *Scottish Notes and Queries*

SDNQ *Somerset & Dorset Notes & Queries*

SDSÖ Schriften zur deutschen Sprache in Österreich. Wien: Wilhelm Braunmüller.

SEC *Studia Etymologica Cracoviensia*

SEP Studien zur englischen Philologie. Halle (Saale): Max Niemeyer.

SFR Scholars' Facsimiles & Reprints. Delmar, New York.

SG *Studi Germanici*

SGEH Sammlung germanischer Elementar- und Handbücher. Heidelberg: Carl Winter's Universitätsbuchhandlung.

SGLH Sammlung germanischer Lehr- und Handbücher. Heidelberg: Carl Winter's Universitätsbuchhandlung.

SGP Schriften zur germanischen Philologie. Berlin: Weidmannsche Buchhandlung.

SHAW Sitzungsberichte der Heidelberger Akademie der Wissenschaften. Philosophisch-historische Klasse. Heidelberg: Carl Winter's Universitätsbuchhandlung.

SI *Scripta Islandica*

SID Scripta Instituti Donneriani Aboensis. Publ by The Donner Institute for Research in Religious and Cultural History, Åbo, Finland. Stockholm: Almquist & Wiksell.

SIDS Schriften des Instituts für Deutsche Sprache. Düsseldorf: Pädagogischer Verlag Schwann.

SILH Sammlung indogermanischer Lehr- und Handbücher. Heidelberg: Carl Winter's Universitätsbuchhandlung.

SINS Skrifter utgivna av Institutionen för nordiska språk vid Uppsala Universitet.

SK *Sprog og kultur*

SKAW Sitzungsberichte der Philosophisch-historischen Classe der Kaiserlichen Akademie der Wissenschaften. Wien: [variously commissioned].

SKGGD Sammlung kurzer Grammatiken germanischer Dialekte. Tübingen, Halle (Saale): Max Niemeyer.

SKPAW Sitzungsberichte der Königlich Preussischen Akademie der Wissenschaften zu Berlin: Verlag der Akademie der Wissenschaften.

Skr. Krist. Skrifter utgit av Videnskapsselskapet i Kristiania. Historisk-filosofisk Klasse. Kristiania: In Kommission bei Jacob Dybwad, A. W. Brøggers boktrykkeri A/S.

Skr. Lund Skrifter utgivna av Vetenskaps-Societeten i Lund. Lund: C. W. K. Gleerup.

Skr. Up(p)s. Skrifter utg. av Kungl. Humanistiska Vetenskaps-Samfundet i Up(p)sala. Uppsala: A-B. Akademiska bokhandeln i kommission, *etc.*; Leipzig: Otto Harrassowitz.

SKS Sprog og Kulturs Skriftrække, udgivet af Institut for Jysk Sprog- og Kulturforskning. Aarhus: Universitetsforlaget.

SLG Studia Linguistica Germanica. Berlin, New York: Walter de Gruyter.

SM *Sønderjydsk maanedsskrift*

SMS	Studia Medievalia Septentrionalia. Wien: Fassbaender.
SN	*Studia Neophilologica*
SNF	Studier i nordisk filologi. Helsingfors: Svenska Litteratursällskapet i Finland.
SÖAW	Sitzungsberichte der Österreichischen Akademie der Wissenschaften. Philosophisch-historische Klasse. Wien: Gerold, [later] Verlag der Österreichischen Akademie der Wissenschaften.
SoS	*Språk och stil*
SOSÅ	Sydsvenska ortnamnsällskapets Årsskrift. Lund: Sydsvenska ortnamnsällskapets förlag.
SP	*Studies in Philology*
SPE	Society for Pure English. [Oxford]: At the Clarendon Press.
SR	*The Saturday Review*
SS	*Scandinavian Studies*
Ssb	Skandinavskii sbornik. Tallinn: Eesti raamat.
SSL	Skrifter utgivna av Svenska Litteratursällskapet i Finland. Upsala: Akademiska boktryckeriet.
SSLL	Stanford Studies in Language and Literature. Stanford, CA: Stanford University Press.
SSp	Saecula Spiritualia. Baden-Baden: Verlag Valentin Koerner.
SSUF	Språkvetenskapets Sällskaps i Uppsala Förhandlingar. Uppsala: University Press (Edv. Berling); Almqvist & Wiksell.
ST	Studia Transylvanica. Köln, Wien: Böhlau.
STT	Suomalaisen Tiedeakatemian Toimitukjia/Annales Academiæ Scientiarum Fennicæ, Saria./Ser. B. Helsinki: Suomalainen Tiedeakatemia.
SvLm	(Nyare bidrag till kännedom om de) Svenska landsmål och svenskt folklif/folkliv. Stockholm: Samson & Wallin, *et al.*
SySe	*Syn og Segn*
TAPA	*Transactions of the American Philological Association*
TAPS	*Transactions of the American Philological Society*
TB	*Taalkundige Bijdragen*
TBL	Tübinger Beiträge zur Linguistik. Tübingen: Gunter Narr Verlag.
TCPS	Transactions of the Cambridge Philological Society
THL	Theory and History of Folklore. Minneapolis: University of Minnesota Press.
TLb	*De Taal- en Letterbode*
TLS	*The Times Literary Supplement*
TLSM	Trends in Linguistics. Studies and Monographs. Berlin, New York: Mouton de Gruyter.
TM	*Taalkundig Magazin*
TNTL	*Tijdschrift voor Nederlandsche Taal- en Letterkunde*
TODL	Trudy otdela drevnerusskoi literatury. Leningrad: Akademiia nauk SSSR.
TPS	*Transactions of the Philological Society*
TT	*Taal en Tongval*
TVUB	*Tijdschrift van de Vrije Universiteit Brussel*
TYDS	*Transactions of the Yorkshire Dialect Society*
UCPL	*University of California Publications in Linguistics*
UGDS	Untersuchungen zur Geschichte der deutschen Sprache. Halle (Saale): Max Niemeyer Verlag.
UMIS	University of Manitoba Icelandic Studies. Manitoba: University of Manitoba Press.
UNC: SGLL	University of North Carolina. Studies in the Germanic Languages and Literatures. Chapel Hill: The University of North Carolina Press.
UUÅ	Uppsala Universitets Årsskrift. Filosofi, språkvetenskap och historiska vetenskaper. Uppsala: University Press (Edv. Berling); Almqvist & Wiksell.

UVGGS	Untersuchungen zur vergleichenden Grammatik der germanischen Sprachen. Heidelberg: Carl Winter. Universitätsverlag.
UW	*Us Wurk*
VIa	*Voprosy iazykoznaniia*
VMKANTL	Verslagen en Mededelingen van de Koninklijke Academie voor Nederlandse Academie voor Nederlandse Taal- en Letterkunde.
VMKVATL	Verslagen en Mededelingen der/van de Koninklijke Vlaamse/Vlaamsche Academie voor Taal- en Letterkunde
WA	*The Western Antiquary*
(W)AMB	*(Walford's) Antiquarian Magazine and Bibliographer*
WF	*Western Folklore*
WuS	*Wörter und Sachen*
WW	*Wirkendes Wort*
YAJ	*Yorkshire Archaeological Journal*
ZCP	*Zeitschrift für celtische Philologie*
ZD	*Zeitschrift für Deutschkunde*
ZDA	*Zeitschrift für deutsches Altert(h)um und deutsche Lit(t)eratur*
ZDA(A)	*Anzeiger für Deutsches Altert(h)um und deutsche Lit(t)eratur (Anzeiger)*
ZDD	*Zeitchrift für deutsche Dialekte*
ZDL	*Zeitschrift für Dialektologie und Linguistik*
ZDM	*Zeitschrift für deutsche Mundarten*
ZDMG	*Zeitschrift der deutschen Morgenländischen Gesellschaft*
ZDP	*Zeitschrift für deutsche Philologie*
ZDR	*Zeitschrift für deutsches Recht und deutsche Rechtswissenschaft*
ZDS	*Zeitschrift für deutsche Sprache*
ZDW	*Zeitschrift für deutsche Wortforschung*
ZFf	*Zbornik Filozofske fakultete*
ZFSL	*Zeitschrift für französische Sprache und Literatur*
ZII	*Zeitschrift für Indologie und Iranistik*
ZMu	*Zeitschrift für Mundartforschung*
ZNF	*Zeitschrift für Namenforschung*
ZONF	*Zeitschrift für Ortsnamenforschung*
ZPh	*Zeitschrift für Phonetik (und allgemeine Sprachwissenschaft)*
ZRP	*Zeitschrift für romanische Philologie*
ZSP	*Zeitschrift für slavische Philologie*
ZSSR(GA)	*Zeitschrift der Savigny-Stiftung für Rechtsgeschichte* (Germanistische Abteilung)
ZV	*Zeitschrift für Volkskunde*

A.A. 1865. Slang : Slog. *NQ* III/8, 187–88.

Abaev, V. I. 1966. Etimologicheskie zametki [Etymological Notes]. In *Studia Linguistica Slavica Baltica. Canuto-Olavo Falk Sexagenario a collegis, amicis, discipulis oblata*. SBS 8, 1–25.

________. 1997. Corrections and Additions to the Ossetic Etymological Dictionary. *Historical, Indo-European, and Lexicographical Studies: A Festschrift for Ladislav Zgusta on the Occasion of his 70th Birthday*, ed. Hans Heinrich Hock. TLSM 90, pp. 197–219.
See also IESOI.

A.B.C. 1934. Derivation of 'Toadstool.' *NQ* 166, 315.

ÁBM = Ásgeir Blöndal Magnússon, *Íslensk orðsifjabók*. Orðabók Háskólans, 1989.

Abrahams, Roger D., and Lois Rankin, eds. 1980. *Counting-Out Rhymes: A Dictionary*. PAFS. Bibliographical and Special Series 31. Austin and London: University of Texas Press.

ACD = *The American College Dictionary*. New York: Random House, 1947.

Adams, Douglas Q. 1985. Latin *mas* and *masturbari*. *Glotta* 63, 241–47.
See also MA.

Adams, Ernest. 1858. On the Names of Ants, Earwigs and Beetles. *TPS*, 93–107.

________. 1859. On the Names of Spiders. *TPS*, 216–27.

________. 1860. On the Names of the Wood-Louse. *TPS* 7, 8–19.

Adams, F. 1896. Round Robin. *NQ* VIII/10, 391–92.

________. 1897. Round Robin. *NQ* VIII/11, 177.

Adams, James D. 1963. *The Magic and Mystery of Words*. New York, Chicago, San Francisco: Holt, Reinhart and Winston.

Adams, Ramon F. 1968. *Western Words: A Dictionary of the American West*. Norman: University of Oklahoma Press.

Addis, John, Jun. 1868. Rabbit. *NQ* IV/1, 207.

Ader, Dorothea. 1958. *Studien zur Sippe von d.* schlagen. Diss. Münster (Westf.). Mülheim: Mülheimer Druckereigesellschaft m.b.H.

AeEW = Ferdinand Holthausen, *Altenglisches etymologisches Wörterbuch*. Heidelberg: Carl Winter, 1934. 2nd ed: 1963, 3rd ed: 1974.

AEW = Jan de Vries, *Altnordisches etymologisches Wörterbuch*. Leiden: E. J. Brill, 1957–61. 2nd ed: 1962, 3rd ed: 1977.

AfW = Ferdinand Holthausen, *Altfriesisches Wörterbuch*. GBI/5, 1925; 2nd ed, by Dietrich Hofmann. Heidelberg: Carl Winter, 1985.

A.G. 1850. Origin of the Word "snob." *NQ* I/2, 250.

AHD = *The American Heritage Dictionary of the English Language*. William Morris, ed. Boston, *etc*: American Heritage Publishing Co., Inc. and Houghton Mifflin Company, 1969. 2nd ed: 1973, 3rd ed: 1992, 4th ed: 2000.

Ahlbäck, Tore. *See* Elmevik, Lennart. 1990.

Ahlqvist, August. 1875. *Die Kulturwörter der westfinnischen Sprachen. Ein Beitrag zu der älteren Kulturgeschichte der Finnen.* Helsingfors: Verlag der Wasenius'schen Buchhandlung.

AHW = *Althochdeutsches Wörterbuch...* founded by Elisabeth Karg-Gasterstädt, et al, ed by Rudolf Grosse. Berlin: Akademie-Verlag, 1952–.

Alessio, Giovanni. 1969. Etimologie latine. In *Studia classica et orientalia Antonino Pagliaro oblata*, vol. 1, 75–94. Roma: no indication of publisher.
See also Battisti, Carlo.

Alexander, Henry. 1944. Words and the War. *AS* 19, 276–80.

Allen, F. Sturges. *See* Webster, Noah. 1909.

Allen, Hope E. 1936. The Influence of Superstition on Vocabulary: Robin Goodfellow and his Louse. *PMLA* 51, 904–20.

Allen, R. E. *See* COD8.

Althaus, Hans P. 1963. Zur Etymologie von *schummeln, beschummeln*. *ZMu* 30, 66–69.

A.M. 1903. The Words *reiskie* and *treviss*. ScNQ II/5, 75.

Ambrosini, Riccardo. 1956. *ΖΕΦΥΡΟΣ*: un problema etimologico antico e moderno. ASNSP. Lettere, Storia e Filosofia II/25, 142–47.

AMG = *The Annotated Mother Goose: Nursery Rhymes Old and New.* Arranged and Explained by William S. Baring-Gould and Ceil Baring-Gould. The World Publishing Co., 1967.

Amosova, N. N. 1956. *Etimologicheskie osnovy slovarnogo sostava sovremennogo angliiskogo iazyka [The Etymological Foundations of Modern English Vocabulary].* Moskva: Izdatel'stvo literatury na inostrannykh iazykakh.

AND = *The Australian National Dictionary: A Dictionary of Australianisms on Historical Principles.* William Stanley Ramson, ed. Melbourne and New York: Oxford University Press, 1988.

Andersen, Harry. 1930. Karving. *DS*, 178–79.

Andersen, Torben A. 1982. Stodder, enke, fok—jyske betegnelser for sidste neg og sidste læs. *A&S* 2, 12–22.

Andersson, Fritz. 1936. Låset, regeln och nyckeln. II. NTU 9, 81–88.

Andersson, Linda. *See* Liberman, Anatoly. 2002a.

Andreev (a.k.a. Andreyew), N. D. 1986. *Ranneindoevropeiskii iazyk [Early Indo-European].* Leningrad: Nauka.

________. 1994. Early Indo-European Typology. *IF* 99, 1–20.

Andrén, Anders. *See* Arvidsson, Stefan.

Andresen, Karl. 1889. *Über Deutsche Volksetymologie.* 5th ed. Heilbronn a/N: Verlag von Gebr. Henninger.

Andrésson, Guðmundur = Gudmundus Andreæ, *Lexicon Islandicum sive Gothicæ Runæ vel Lingvæ Septentrionalis Dictionarium....* Petrus J. Resenius, ed. Havniæ: Sumptibus C. Gerhardi. Repr Reykjavík: Orðabók Háskolans, 1999.

Annandale, Charles, ed. 1892. *The Imperial Dictionary....* Chicago: Belford Publishing Co.
See also ID2.

Anonymous. 1815. [Rev of] Jamieson, John. 1814. *QR* 14, 96–113.

________. 1822a. [Rev of] Nares, Robert. 1822. *The Academy* 28: 328–29.

________. 1822b. [Rev of] Nares, Robert. 1822. *GM* 92/II, 523–24, 614–18.

________. 1826. [Rev of] Thomson, John. 1826. *MR*, Series 3, 3/II, 110–2.

________. 1829. [Rev of] Brocket, John T. 1829 [see Brocket, John T. 1846]. *GM* 99/II, 141–43.

________. 1845. Archæology of the Word 'Cockney.' *ChEJ* 3, 225–27.

________. 1857. Cob. *ChJ* 183, 14–16.

________. 1859. [Rev of] Richard S. Charnock, *Local Etymology: A Derivational Dictionary of Geographical Names*. London: Houlston and Wright, 1859. *The Athenæum*/I, 578–79.

________. 1861. Wandering Words. *AYR* 5, 140–44.

________. 1864a. [Rev of] Hotten, John C. 1864. *The Athenæum*/II, 557–59.

________. 1864b. [Rev of] Hotten, John C[3]. *SR* 18, 544–45.

________. 1865. [Rev of] Dwight, Benjamin W. 1859. *SR* 19, 180–81.

________. 1868a. [Rev of] Atkinson, John C. 1868. *The Athenæum*/II, 835–36.

________. 1868b. Wordborough Mint. *AYR* 19, 135–39.

________. 1870. [Rev of] Höfer, Albert. 1870a. *LCD*, 497–98.

________. 1872. [Report of the meeting of the Philological Society on March 1, 1872.] *The Athenæum*/I, 310.

________. 1877a. [An entry in The Contributors' Club]. *AM* 40/II, 233–35, 748.

________. 1877b. [Report of a meeting of the Philological Society]. *The Academy* 12, 498.

________. 1878. [Rev of] Bartlett, John R. 1877. *The Nation* 26, 171–72.

________. 1881. [Report of Walter W. Skeat's paper on etymology]. *TCPS* 2, 177–79.

________. 1885a. Philological [Report of Walter W. Skeat's paper on etymology]. *(W)AMB* 8, 284.

________. 1885b. Philological Society [Report of Walter W. Skeat's paper on etymology]. *Academy* 28, 328–9.

________. 1887. [Untitled]. *(W)AMB* 12, 188.

________. 1889a. Whence the Name "Welsh Rabbit." *ANQ* 3, 49–50.

________. 1889b. The Word Cockney. *ANQ* 4, 1–6.

________. 1890. [A survey of journals, *etc.*] *The Nation* 50, 80. Repr in *ANQ* 5, 30.

________. 1894. [Report of] Arthur C. Hayward, Elizabethan Slang. *The Academy* 45, 232–33.

________. 1897. [Rev of] Sweet, Henry. 1897. *The Athenæum*/I, 610–11.

________. 1898. [Rev of] BT. *The Anthenæum*/II, 95–96.

________. 1901a. Philological. *The Athenæum*/I, 600.

________. 1901b. [Rev of] OED. *—L—Lap*. *The Athenæum*/I, 588.

________. 1904. Philological. *The Athenæum*/I, 791.

________. 1912. Capabarre. *MarM* 2, 64.

________. 1935. Dorset Local Words. *SDNQ* 21, 177–79.

________. 1939. Een vijftiende-eeuwse straatroep. *NTg* 33, 40.

________. 1963. Leute machen Sprachgeschichte. *Der Sprachdienst* 7, 164–66.

Apperson, George L. 1892. Etymological Diversions. *GM*/I, 132–39.

Arbeitman, Yoël L. 1980. Look Ma, What's Become of the Sacred Tongues. *Maledicta* 4, 71–88.
See also Lockwood, William B. 1981a and Puhvel, Jaan. 1988.

Arcamone, Maria G. 1982. Italiano antico *mucciare* e voci toscane connesse. *QALT*. 167–92.

________. 1983. Nuove prove linguistiche della presenza langobarda nel Ducato di Spoleto. In *Atti del 9 Congresso Internationale di studi sull'alto Medioevo, Spoleto, 27 settembre–2 ottobre 1982*, vol. 2, 759–79. Spoleto: Centro Italiano di studi sull'alto Medioevo.

Arditti, Adolfo. 1987. Some "Dirty Words" in Modern Salonica, Istanbul, and Jerusalem Judezmo. *JLR* 7A, 209–18.

Argent, Joseph E. 1996. The Etymology of a Dystopia: Laputa Reconsidered. *ELN* 34, 36–40.

Århammar, Nils R. 1986. Etymologisches um den 'Streß' mit einem Exkurs zum älteren Einfluß des Niederländischen auf das Nordfriesische. In *Wortes anst / verbi gratia. Donum natalicium Gilbert A.R. de Smet*, eds. H. L. Cox, V. F. Vanacker, and E. Verhofstadt. pp. 19–28. Leuven/Amersfoort: Uitgeverij Acco.

________. 2001. Das Nordfriesische im Sprachkontakt (unter Einschluß der Nordfriesischen Lexikologie). In HF, 313–53. *See also* Hofmann, Dietrich. 1984 and Roelandts, Karel. 1984.

Arndt, Walter W. *See* Robinson, Fred C. 1967.

Arnoldson, Torild W. 1915. *Parts of the Body in Older Germanic and Scandinavian*. Diss. The University of Chicago. LSG 2.

Arntz, Helmut. *See* Jensen, Hans. 1936.

Arvidsson, Stefan. 2005. Slita dvärg. Om frånvaron av arbete i Nibelungentraditionen. In *Hededomen i historiens spegel*, eds. Catharina Raudvere, Anders Andrén, and Kristina Jennbert, 97–132. Lund: Nordic Academic Press.

ASG = Sievers, Eduard. *Angelsächsische Grammatik*. SKGGD I/3, 1882. 2nd ed: 1886, 3rd ed: 1898. For the later editions see SB.

Ash, John. 1775. *The New and Complete Dictionary of the English Language*. London: Printed for E. & C. Dilby, *etc*.

ASh = *King Lear*. The Aldus Shakespeare... 67. New York: Bigelow Smith & Co., 1909.

Atkinson, John C. 1868. *A Glossary of the Cleveland Dialect; Explanatory, Derivative, and Critical*. London: John Russell Smith.

Audrey, Samuel. 1883–84. Fefnicute, Eem, and Keigh-Neyve. *MNQ* 5, 309–10.

Aufrecht, Th. 1885. Miscellanea. *KZ* 27, 219–21.

Augst, Gerhard. 1970. *"Haupt" und "Kopf." Eine Wortgeschichte bis 1550*. Diss. Mainz. Giessen: no indication of publisher.

Austin, William M. 1958. Germanic Reflexes of Indo-European *-Hy-* and *-Hw-*. *Lg* 34, 203–11.

Avis, Walter S. *See* DC.

Baader, Theodor. 1953. Zur westfälischen Wortkunde. Erläuterungen zu dem Aufsatz Ferdinand Holthausens Nd. Jb. 71/73 (1948/50) 311ff. *NJ* 75, 38–43.

Babcock, C. Merton. 1950. The Vocabulary of Social Life on the American Frontier. *WF* 9, 136–43.

Bachofer, Wolfgang. *See* Rooth, Erik. 1963.

Bächtold-Stäubli, Hanns. *See* HDA 2.

Bäck, Hilding. 1934. *The Synonyms for "Child," "Boy," "Girl" in Old English: An Etymological-Semasiological Investigation*. LSE 2.

Bagg, L. G. 1935. Dorset Local Words. *SDNQ* 21, 208–09.

Bahder, K. von. 1903. Zur hochdeutschen Lautlehre (hd. *f* = wgerm. *b*). *IF* 14, 258–65.

________. 1929. Jetzt, jetzund, jetzo. *PBB* 53, 431–54.

Bailey, H. W. 1959. Iranian *arya-* and *daha-*. *TPS*, 71–115.

Bailey, Nathan. 1721. *An Universal Etymological English Dictionary*. London: Printed for E. Bell, *etc*. Repr as A&A 52, 1969.

________. 1730. *Dictionarium Britannicum*. London: Printed for T. Cox, *etc*. Repr as A&A 50, 1969.

Bailey, Richard W. *See* Read, Allen W. 2002.

Bain, David. 1991. Six Greek Verbs of Sexual Congress (*βινῶ, κινῶ, πυγίζω, ληκῶ, οἴφω, λαικάζω*). *CQ* 41, 51–77.

Baist, G. 1880. [Untitled]. *ZRP* 4, 474–75.

Baker, Sheridan. 1956. Swift, "Lilliputian," and Catullus. *NQ* 201, 477–79.

Ball, C. J. E. 1970. [Rev of] CEDEL. *Lingua* 25, 64–70.

Ball, J. *See* RHHDAS.

Balliolensis. 1853. Coniger, &c. *NQ* I/7, 368.

Baly, J. 1897. *Eur-Aryan Roots*.... London: Kegan Paul.

Bammesberger, Alfred. 1990. *Die Morphologie des urgermanischen Nomens*. UVGGS 2.

________. 1996. [Rev of] Beekes, Robert S. P. *HS* 109, 310–14.

________. 1999. *Mannum/Manno* bei Tacitus und der Name der *m*-Rune. *BN* 34 (NF), 1–8.

________ [and] Joachim Grzega. 2001. Modern English *girl* and Other Terms for 'Young Female Person' in English Language History. *OO* 2, 1–8 [in *OO* each article has its own pagination].

Barber, Charles C. 1932. *Die vorgeschichtliche Betonung der germanischen Substantiva und Adjektiva*. IB 12.

Barbier, Paul. 1932–35. Miscellanea Lexicographica 10: Etymological and Lexicographical Notes on the French Language and on the Romance Dialects of France. *PLPLS* 3, 73–136, 257–316.

________. 1938–43. Miscellanea Lexicographica 23: Etymological and Lexicographical Notes on the French Language and on the Romance Dialects of France. *PLPLS* 5, 294–332.

Barclay, James. 1835. *A Complete and Universal English Dictionary:* no indication of place or publisher.

Bardsley, Charles W. 1884. *English Surnames: Their Sources and Signification*. 3rd ed. London: Chatto and Windus. Repr Rutland, VT: C.E.

Tuttle, Co., [1968] and Newton Abbot: David & Charles Reprints, 1969.
Baring-Gould, Ceil. *See* AMG.
Baring-Gould, William S. *See* AMG.
Barlow, Frederick. 1772–73. *The Complete English Dictionary....* London: Printed for the author.
Barnes, Michael P. 1994. *The Runic Inscriptions of Maeshowe, Orkney.* Runrön 8.
Barnes, William. 1862. *TIW; or a View of the Roots and Stems of the English as a Teutonic Tongue.* London: John Russell Smith.
Barnhart, Clarence L. *See* WBD.
Barnhart, Robert K., ed., Sol Steinmetz, managing ed. 1988. *The Barnhart Dictionary of Etymology.* [Bronx, N.Y.]: The H. W. Wilson Company.
Barrère, Albert. *See* BL.
Barry, Michael V. 1967. Yorkshire Sheep-Scoring Numerals. *TYDS* XII/67, 21–31.
________. 1969. Traditional Enumeration in the North Country. *Folk Life* 7, 75–91.
Bartholomae, Christian. 1901. Arica. XIV. *IF* 12, 92–150.
Bartlett, John R. 1860. *Dictionary of Americanisms....* 3rd ed. Boston: Little, Brown, and Company.
Bartsch, Karl. *See Nib.*
Baskakov, N.A., and A.N. Kononov. 1985. *Tiurkskaia leksika v "Slove o polku Igoreve."* [*Turkic Words in* The Lay of Igor's Host]. Moskva: Nauka.
Baskett, William D. 1920. *Parts of the Body in the Later Germanic Languages.* Diss. The University of Chicago. LSG 5.
Battisti, Carlo, and Giovanni Alessio. 1950–57. *Dizionario etimologico italiano.* Firenze: G. Barbèra, Edittore.
Bause, Joh. 1907. Katthagen (kathāgɔn). *KVNS* 28, 81–82.
Bayne, Tomas. 1881. Toadstool. *NQ* VI/4, 452.
BE = Wilhelm Braune, *Althochdeutsche Grammatik.* SKGGD 5. 14th ed, by Hans Eggers. Tübingen: Max Niemeyer, 1987.
Beale Paul. *See* Patridge, Erik. 1961.
Bechtel, Fritz. 1877. Germanisch *zd. ZDA* 21, 214–29.
Beck, Heinrich. *See* Meid, Wolfgang. 1992.
Beckh, Hermann. 1954. *Neue Wege zur Ursprache. Sprachwissenschaftliche Studien.* Stuttgart: Urachhaus. (First published in 1921.)
Beddoe, John, and Joseph H. Rowe. 1907. The Ethnology of West Yorkshire. *YAJ* 19, 31–60.
Bee [= Badcock], John. 1825. *Sportsman's Slang: A New Dictionary and Varieties of Life.* London: Printed for the author.
Beekes, Robert S. P. 1994. "Right," "Left" and "Naked" in Proto-Indo-European. *Orbis* 37, 87–96.
________. 1995. *Comparative Indo-European Linguistics: An Introduction.* Amsterdam, Philadelphia: John Benjamins.
________. 1996. Ancient European Loanwords. *HS* 109, 215–36.
See also Schwartz, Martin.
Beeler, Madison S. 1970. Etymological Layers of the English Lexicon. [Rev of] ODEE. *RP* 23, 312–23.
Behaghel, Otto. 1906. [Rev of] Schröder, Heinrich. 1906. *Lit.bl.* 27, 401–02.
________. 1923. Humor und Spieltrieb in der deutschen Sprache. *Neophilologus* 8, 180–93.
See also Heliand und Genesis.
Behr, Ursula. 1935. *Wortkontaminationen in der neuenglischen Schriftsprache.* Diss. Berlin. Würzburg: Richard Mayr.
Beikircher, Hugo. 1992. Zur Etymologie und Bedeutungsentwicklung von *praestare. Glotta* 70, 88–95.
Belardi, Walter. 1976. *Superstitio.* BRLF 5.
Bell, Robert. *See* BPW; TC-B.
Benediktsson, Hreinn. 1959. The Vowel System of Icelandic: A Survey of Its History. *Word* 15, 282–312.
Benfey, Theodor. 1875. [Rev of] Anonymous [preface signed F. L. C. Frh. v. M.], *Der Hopfen. Seine Herkunft und Benennung. Zur vergleichenden Sprachforschung.* Homburg vor der Höhe: Buchdruckerei von J. G. Steinhäußer. *GGA,* 208–20.
Benois-Thomas = Eugène Benois and Émile Thomas, *Poésie de Catulle....* Vol 2. Paris: Hachette et Cie, 1882–90.
Bense, J. F. 1939. *A Dictionary of the Low-Dutch Element in the English Vocabulary.* The Hague: Martinus Nijhoff.
Benveniste, Émile. 1931. Avestique *mrzu-. BSLP* 31, 80.
________. 1937. Expression indo-européenne de l'eternité. *BSLP* 38, 103–12.
Berg, Arne et al. 1966. Lås. In: KLNM 11, 48–73.
Berg, B. van den. *See* Van den Berg, B.
Berg, Jan van den. *See* Van den Berg, Jan.

Bergdal, Ed. 1929. Hamlet's Name. *SS* 10, 159–75 (printed immediately after p. 154).

_______. 1931. The Hamlet *yrya. SS* 11, 79–89.

Bergerson, Jeremy. 2002. The Etymology of Afrikaans botje and English buddy, Boots. LB 91, 63–71.

_______. 2004. Emphatic *-s* in Modern Germanic. *IJGLSA* 9, 83–100.

Bergin, Osborn. *See* Vendryes, Joseph. 1912.

Bergkvist, Erik. 1937. Die Etymologie von westfries. heks < nhd. hexe < ahd. hagazussa. FJ 1937, 9–19.

_______. 1938. Westfries. *kôl* 'Blesse', nl. *kol* 'Hexe' und schwed. *Blå-kulla* 'die Blaue Jungfrau'; 'Hölle'. Ein Beitrag zur vergleichenden Sprachforschung und Mythologie. FJ 1938, 9–22.

Bergsten, Nils. 1911. A Study on Compound Substantives in English. Diss. Uppsala. Uppsala: Almquist & Wiksell.

[Bernard, Edward]. *Vocabulorum Anglicorum & Brittanicorum origines Russicæ, Slavonicæ, Persicæ & Armenicæ.* Publ anonymously as *Etymologicon Britannicum* in George Hickes, *Institutiones Grammaticæ et Moeso-gothicæ.* Oxoniæ: E Theatro Sheldoniano. Repr as CFR 277, 1971. (The name of the author is given in the editor's preface.)

Berndt, Rolf. 1960. *Einführung in das Studium des Mittelenglischen....* Halle (Saale): VEB Max Niemeyer.

Berneker, Erich. 1898. Etymologisches. *IF* 9, 360–64.

_______. 1899. Von der Vertretung des idg. *ĕu* im baltisch-slavischen Sprachzweig. *IF* 10, 145–67.

_______. 1908. Weihen. *PDS 8. Untersuchungen und Quellen zur germanischen und romanischen Philologie (Johann von Kelle dargebracht)*, part 1, 1–8.

_______. 1908–13. *Slavisches etymologisches Wörterbuch.* Vol. 1. IB I/2/2.

Bertoldi, Vittorio, 1928. Sprachliches und Kulturhistorisches über die Eibe und den Faulbaum. *WuS* 11, 145–61.

Bertoni, Giulio. 1914. *L'elemento germanico nella lingua italiana.* Genova: A.F. Formiggini.

Bessason, Haraldur. *See* Hale, Christopher S.

Bett, Henry. 1936. *Wanderings among Words.* London: George Allen & Unwin Ltd.

Beysel, Karl. 1925. Die Namen der Blutverwandtschaft im Englischen. *GBESKEN* 3, 89–152.

Bezzenberger, Adalbert. 1878. Zu den beiden gutturalreihen. *BB* 2, 151–58.
See also Stokes, Whitley. 1894.

_______. 1880. [Footnote to Fick, August. 1880, p 168.]

_______. 1890. [Rev of] Feist, Sigmund. 1890. *DL* 11, 14.

Bezzenberger, Adalbert, and August Fick. 1881. Nachträge zum indogermanischen Wörterbuch. *BB* 6, 235–40.

Bickel, Ernst. 1953. Salaputium: mentula salax. *RMP* 96, 94–95.

Bickerton, Derek. 1982. An Afro-Creole Origin for *eena meena mina mo. AS* 57, 225–28.

Bierbaumer, Peter. 1974. Ae. *fornetes folm*—eine Orchideenart. *Anglia* 92, 172–76.
See also BWA.

Bierwirth, H. C. 1891. Zur geschichte des wortes *schmetterling. PBB* 15, 387–89.

Bilderdijk, Willem. 1822. *Geslachtlijst der Nededuitsche Naamwoorden, op stellige taalgronden gevestigt.* 2 vols. Amsterdam: J. C. Sepp en Zoon.

Bindseil, Heinrich E. *See* Pott, August F. 1859–76.

Bingham, G. W. 1862. Rabbit. *NQ* III/2, 18.

Binnig, Wolfgang. 1984. Got. *hraiwadūbo* (Luk 2, 24). In *Philologische Untersuchungen gewidmet Elfriede Stutz zum 65. Geburtstag*, ed. Alfred Ebenbauer. PG 7, 41–50.

Binz, Gustav. 1906. Engl. *oats;* deutsch *erbse;* engl. *ant, emmet,* deutsch *ameise. ZDP* 38, 369–72.

_______. 1927. [Rev of] Weekley, Ernest 1921 and 1924. *AB* 38, 176–83.

Birlinger, A. 1870. [Rev of] Anonymous, *Das Brot im Spiegel schweizerdeutschen Volkssprache und Sitte. Lese schweizerischer Gebäcknamen. Aus den Papieren des Schweizerischen Idiotikons.* Leipzig: S. Hirzel, 1868. *KZ* 19, 144–52.

_______. 1872. Zur deutschen wortforschung: *mûch-, mauch-. KZ* 20, 316–20.

Birnbaum, Salomo A. 1935. Hebräische Etymologien im Deutschen. *ZDP* 59, 238–41.

_______. Der Mogel. 1955. *ZDP* 74, 225–50.

Bishop, Joseph W. Jr. 1946. American Army Speech in the European Theater. *AS* 21, 241–52.

BjL = Harald Bjorvand and Frederik O. Lindeman, *Våre arveord. Etymologisk ordbok.* Oslo: Novus Forlag, 2000.

Björkman, Erik. 1899. Altvile im Sachsenspiegel. *ZDA* 43, 146–50.

________. 1900. *Scandinavian Loan-Words in Middle English.* Halle a. S.: Max Niemeyer. Repr New York: Greenwood Press /Haskell House Publishers, 1969.

________. 1901. Die Pflanzennamen der althochdeutschen Glossen. *ZDW* 2, 202–33.

________. 1903–05. Etymological Notes. *JEGP* 5, 501–04.

________. 1908. Zur Etymologie von *cub.* Archiv CXVIII, S. 389f. *Archiv* 119, 189.

________. 1911 [Rev of] Mutschmann, Heinrich. *Archiv* 126, 448–52.

________. 1912. Neuschwed. *gosse* 'Knabe, Junge', eine semasiologische Studie. *IF* 30, 252–78.

________. 1916 [Rev of] Kügler, Hermann. *AB* 27, 246–49.

Bjorvand, Harald. 1994. *Holt og holtar. Udviklingen av det indoeuropeiske kollektivum i norrønt.* Oslo: Solum Forlag.
See also BjL.

BL = Albert Barrère and Charles G. Leland. *A Dictionary of Slang, Jargon & Cant.* London: George Bell & Sons, 1897. Repr Book Tower, Detroit: Gale Research Company, 1967.

Blackley, William Lewery. 1869. *Word Gossip: A Series of Familiar Essays on Words and their Peculiarities.* London: Longmans, Green, and Co.

Bleckert, Lars, and Anna Westerberg. 1986. Germanic Synthesis of Question ALE-QI: 503, "Witch." In *Aspects of Language: Studies in Honour of Mario Alinei. Papers Presented to Mario Alinei by his Friends and Colleagues of the* Atlas Linguarum Europae *on the Occasion of his 60th Birthday*, 364–79. Amsterdam: Rodopi.

Bliss, A. J. 1951–52. Three Etymological Notes. *EGS* 4, 20–30.

Bloch, Oscar. *See* BW.

Blok, Henk, and Herman ter Stege. 1995. *De Nederlandse vogelnamen en hun betekenis.* Leidschendam: H. Blok, Waalre: H.J. ter Stege.

Bloomfield, Leonard. 1909–10. A Semasiologic Differentiation in Germanic Secondary Ablaut. *MPh* 7, 245–88, 345–82. Also publ in book form as Chicago diss. Chicago: Chicago University Press, 1909.

________. 1912. Etymologisches. *PBB* 37, 245–61.

________. 1925. Einiges vom germanischen Wortschatz. In *Germanica. Eduard Sievers zum 75. Geburtstage 25. November*, 90–106. Halle: Niemeyer.

________. 1930. Salic *litus.* In *Studies in Honor of Hermann Collitz, Professor of Germanic Philology, Emeritus, in the Johns Hopkins University, Baltimore, Maryland, Presented by a Group of his Pupils and Friends on the Occasion of his Seventy-Fifth Birthday, February 4, 1930,* 83–94. Baltimore, Maryland: The Johns Hopkins Press.

________. 1933. *Language.* New York: Henry Holt and Company.

Bloomfield, Maurice. 1895. On Assimilation and Adaptation in Congeneric Classes of Words. *AJP* 16, 409–34.

Blount, Thomas. 1656. *Glossographia: or, A Dictionary, Interpreting All Such Hard Words....* London: Printed by Tho. Newcomb. Repr as CFR 153, 1969.

Blunt, Christopher. *See* Feilitsen, Olof von, and Christopher Blunt.

Bo, L.L. *See* De Bo, L.L.

Boag, John. [1850] *The Imperial Lexicon of the English Language....* Edinburgh, London, and Glasgow: A. Fullarton & Co, New York: Fullarton, Macnab & Co.

Boase, C. W. 1881. [Rev of] Grant Allen, *Anglo-Saxon Britain.* London: Society for Promoting Christian Knowledge. *The Academy* 20, 377–78.

Bodelsen, C. A. *See* Pedersen, Holger. 1930.

Böðvarsson, Árni. 1951. "áttur um malfræ istörf Eggerts Ólafssonar. *Skírnir* 125, 156–72.

Bøgholm, N. *See* Pedersen, Holger. 1930.

Bohn, Henry G. *See* Butler, Samuel. 1859.

Boisacq, Émile. 1950. *Dictionnaire étymologique de la langue grecque étudiée dans ses rapports avec les autres langues indo-européennes.* Heidelberg: Carl Winter Universitätsverlag.

Bolton, Henry C. 1888. *The Counting-Out Rhymes of Children: Their Antiquity, Origin, and Wide Distribution. A Study in Folk-Lore.* New York: D. Appleton & Co. Repr Detroit: Singing Tree Press, Book Tower, 1969.

Bomhard, Allan R., and John C. Kerns. 1994. *The Nostratic Macrofamily: A Study in Distant Linguistic Relationship.* TLSM 74.
See also Lockwood, William B. 1981a.

Bonfante, Giuliano. 1974. Latini e germani in Italia. In his *Scritti scelti.* Renato Gendre, ed. Alessandria: Edizioni dell'Orso, 1–73. (Repr of the 4th ed of this work, 1977.)

Bont, A. P. de. *See* De Bont, A.P.

Boor, Helmut de. *See* De Boor, Helmut.

Booth, David. 1836. *An Analytical Dictionary of the English Language....* A corrected edition. London: Simpkin, Marshall, and Co.

Borck, Karl Heinz. *See* Foerste, William. 1964b.

Borgato, Gianluigi. *See* Rocchi, Luciano.

Bosworth, Joseph. 1838. *A Compendious Anglo-Saxon and English Dictionary.* London: Reeves and Turner.
See also BT.

Both, Martin. 1909. *Die konsonantischen Suffixe altenglischer Konkreta und Kollektiva.* Diss. Kiel. Kiel: Druck von Schmidt & Klaunig.

Botha, Theunis J.R., editor-in-chief. 1989. *Inleiding tot die Afrikaanse taalkunde.* 2nd ed. Pretoria: Academica.

Boutkan, Dirk F. H. 1999. Pre-Germanic Fish in Old Saxon Glosses. On Alleged Ablaut Patterns and Other Formal Deviations in Gmc. Substratum Words. *ABÄG* 52, 11–26.

________ and Maarten Kossman. 1998. Etymologische Betrachtungen zur Dialekt-geographie von *Raupe, rups. ABÄG* 50, 5–11.

Boys, Thomas. 1857. West-country "Cob." *NQ* II/4, 65–66.

BPW = Robert Bell, ed, *Poetical Works of Geoffrey Chaucer...* Vol. 1. London: George Bell and Sons, 1888.

Brachet, Auguste. [n. d.]. *Dictionnaire étymologique de la langue française....* New ed. Paris: J. Hetzel.

Bradley, Henry. 1877. The Ancient British Numerals. *The Athenæum*/II, 402–03.

________. 1894. The Etymology of "lad" and "lass." *The Athenæum*/I, 744.

________. 1910. Slang. EB[11]. Repr in: *The Collected Papers of Henry Bradley,* 145–56. Oxford: At the Clarendon Press, 1928.

________. 1916. Some Emendations in Old English Texts. *MLR* 11, 212–15.

________. 1920. 'Cursed Hebenon' (or 'Hebona'). *MLR* 15, 85–87.

________. 1928. *See* Bradley, Henry. 1910.
See also Stratman, Francis H.

Bradtke, P. von. 1886. Beiträge zur altindischen Religions- und Sprachgeschichte. *ZDMG* 40, 347–64.

Brand, John. 1849. *Observations on the Popular Antiquities of Great Britain: Chiefly Illustrating the Origin of Our Vulgar and Provincial Customs, Ceremonies, and Superstitions.* London: George Bell. (First published in three volumes in 1841 by Charles Knight and Co. of London and reprinted in the original format–Detroit: Singing Tree Press, Book Tower, 1969, and New York: AMS Press, Inc., 2003.)

Brandenstein, Wilhelm. *See* SIG.

Brandl, A. *See* BZ.

Brandreth, E. L. 1885. Untitled. *TPS* 21 (1885–87), vi–viii.

Brasch, Carl. 1910. *Die Namen der Werkzeuge im Altenglischen.* Diss. Kiel. Leipzig: August Hoffmann.

Braune, Wilhelm T., ed. 1879. Johann Lauremberg, *Niederdeutsche Scherzgedichte.* NDL 16–17.

________. 1897. Neue Beiträge zur Kenntnis einiger romanischer Wörter deutscher Herkunft. *ZRP* 21, 213–24.

________. 1912. *Deutsche Etymologieen.* Wissenschaftliche Beilage zum Jahresbericht des Königl. Luisengymnasiums zu Berlin. Ostern 1912. Berlin: Druck von W. Pormetter.
See also BE.

Braune, Theodor. *See* Braune, Wilhelm T.

Bréal, Michel. 1898. Étymologies. *MSLP* 10, 59–70.

Brechenmacher, Josef K. 1957. *Etymologisches Wörterbuch der deutschen Familiennamen.* 2nd ed. Limburg a. d. Lahn: C. A. Starke.

Breeze, Andrew. 1995. Ælfric's *truð* 'buffoon': Old Irish *druth* 'buffoon.' *NQ* 42 (n.s.), 155–57.

Bremmer, Rolf H. Jr. 1992. [Rev of] De Vries, J., and F. de Tollenaere, in collaboration with A.J. Persijn. 1991. *Etymologisch Woordenboek.* 15th ed. Utrecht, Antwerpen: Het Spectrum. *Forum der Letteren* 33, 63–67.

________. 1993. Dutch and/or Frisian: North Sea Germanic Aspects in Dutch Etymological Dictionaries in Past and Future. In *Current Trends in West Germanic Etymological Lexicography: Proceedings of the Symposium Held in Amsterdam 12–13 June 1989*, eds. Rolf H. Bremmer Jr and Jan van den Berg, 17–36. Leiden, New York, Köln: E. J. Brill.
See also Stanley, E. G. 1990.

Brendal, John M. [?1908]. *Some Substantive Synonyms in Anglo-Saxon.* ?Hallock, MN: unpublished.

Brewer, Ebenezer C. 1873. Curmudgeon : Scrupulous. *NQ* IV/11, 408.

________. 1882. *Etymological and Pronouncing*

Dictionary of Different Words. London: Ward, Lock & Co.
Brewster, K. G. *See* NCD.
Brink, Bernhard ten. *See* Ten Brink, Bernhard.
Brocket, John T. 1846. *A Glossary of North Country Words*. 3rd ed. Newcastle upon Tyne: Emerson Charnley; London: Simpkin, Marshall. First publ in 1829.
Brøndal, Viggo. 1917. *Substrater og Laan i Romansk og Germansk. Studier i Lyd- og Ordhistorie*. Kjøbenhavn: G. E. C. Gad. Transl *Substrat et emprunt en roman et en germanique. Étude sur l'histoire des sons et des mots*. København: Ejnar Munksgaard.
________. 1928–29. Mots "scythes" en nordique primitif. *APS* 3, 1–31.
Brøndum-Nielsen, Johannes. 1924. Om ordet *kisselinke* letfærdigt pigebarn. In *Festskrift tillägnad Hugo Pipping på hans sextioårsdag den 5 november 1924*, 51–55. Helsingfors: Mercators tryckeri aktiebolag.
________. 1931–32. Problemet *lykil : nykil*. *APS* 6, 171–90.
________. 1933–34. Om *nykil : lykil*. *APS* 8, 90–93.
________. 1971–73. Problemet *lykill ~ nykill*. *APS* 29, 164–67.
Brogyanyi, Bela. *See* Malkiel, Yakov. 1979.
Brok, H. J. T. M. *See* Heukels, H. 1987.
Brouwer, J. H. 1964. *Boai, poai* en *poalle* yn it nijfrysk. *TT* 16, 65–67.
Brown, Alan. 1972. Heifer. *Neophilologus* 56, 79–85.
________. 1973. Some Further Etymologies of Heifer. *Neophilologus* 57, 94.
Brown, Edward M. 1892. Anglo-Saxon *gīen, gī ena*. *MLN* 7, 250–51.
Brown, S. Dickson. *See* Prevost, E. W.
Bruckner, Wilh. 1899. *Charakteristik der germanischen Elemente im Italienischen*. Wissenschaftliche Beilage zum Bericht über das Gymnasium in Basel. Schuljahr 1898–99. Basel: Fr. Reinhardt, Universitäts-Buchdruckerei.
Brüch, Josef. 1917. Zu Meyer-Lübkes etymologischem Wörterbuch. *ZRP* 38, 676–702.
________. 1919. Zu Meyer-Lübkes etymologischem Wörterbuch. *ZRP* 39, 200–11.
Brückmann, Patricia C. 1974. Lilliputian. *ANQ* 13, 4.
Brüll, Hugo. 1913. *Untergegangene und veraltete Worte des Französischen im heutigen Englisch: Beiträge zur französischen und englischen Wortforschung*. Halle a. S.: Max Niemeyer.
Brugmann, Karl. 1897–1916. *Grundriss der vergleichenden Grammatik der indogermanischen Sprachen*. 2nd ed. Strassburg: Karl J. Trübner.
________. 1905–06. Alte Wortdeutungen in neuer Beleuchtung. *IF* 18, 423–39.
________. 1906. Verdunkelte Nominalkomposita des Lateinischen und des Griechischen. Sächs. Ges. Wiss. 58, 158–78.
________. 1907. *Νυός, nurus, snuṣā́* und die griechischen und italischeń femininen substantiva auf *-os*. *IF* 21, 315–22.
________. 1913. Griechisch *ἅπτω* und seine außergriechischen Verwandten. *IF* 32, 319–26.
Brugmann, Karl, and Berthold Delbrück. 1906. *Grundriß der vergleichenden Grammatik der indogermanischen Sprachen...*, vol. 2, part 1. Strassburg: Karl J. Trübner.
Brumbaugh, Thomas B. 1965. In Regard to "Skedaddling." *AS* 40, 306–07.
Brunner, Karl. *See* SB.
Brunner, Linus. 1969. *Die gemeinsamen Wurzeln des semitischen und indogermanischen Wortschatzes. Versuch einer Etymologie*. Bern, München: Francke Verlag.
Brunovicus. 1868. [Untitled]. *HM* 3, 180.
Brusendorff, Aage. *See* Pedersen, Holger. 1930.
BT = *An Anglo-Saxon Dictionary. Based on the Manuscript Collection of the Late Joseph Bosworth*, edited and enlarged by T. Northcote Toller. Oxford: At the Clarendon Press, 1898. Repr 1929, 1954, 1972, 1973. *Supplement* by T. Northcote Toller. Oxford University Press, 1921. Repr 1955 and 1960.
Buck, Carl D. 1949. *A Dictionary of Selected Synonyms in the Principal Indo-European Languages....* Chicago: The University of Chicago Press. Repr 1988.
Budes, Antonio L. *See* Gold, David L. forthcoming.
Bülbring, Karl D. 1900a. Zur altenglischen Diphthongierung durch Palatale. *AB* 11, 80–119.
________. 1900b. Zur alt- und mittelenglischen Grammatik. *ESt* 27, 73–89.
Bugge, Sophus. 1874. Étymologies françaises et romanes. *Romania* 3, 145–63.
________. 1888a. Svensk ordforskning. [Rev of] Erik Brate "Schwedische Wortforschung" (in *Beiträge zur Kunde der indogermanischen*

Sprachen 13, 21–53) og *Äldre Vestmannalagens ljudlära*. Upsala 1887. *ANF* 4, 115–40.

________. 1888b. Etymologische studien über germanische Lautverschiebung. *PBB* 13, 167–87, 311–39.

________. 1899. Beiträge zur vorgermanischen Lautgeschichte. *PBB* 24, 425–63.

________. 1904. *Fricco, Frigg* und *Priapos*. FVC 3.

Burchfield, R. W. 1972. Four-Letter Words. *TLS,* October 13, 1233. Repr in *Lexicography and Dialect Geography: Festgabe for Hans Kurath*, eds. Harald Scholler and John Reidy. *ZDL*, Beihefte, N. F. 9 der ZDM, pp. 84–89. Wiesbaden: Franz Steiner Verlag GMBH, 1973.

________. 1973. Some Aspects of the Historical Treatment of Twentieth-Century Vocabulary. In *Tavola rotonda sui grandi lessici storici*, pp. 31–35. Firenze: Accademia della Crusca. *See* also ODEE *and* Murray, K. M. Elisabeth. 1977.

Burton, Jill. *See* Burton T. L. 1988.

Burton, T. L. 1988. Drudgery, Bludgery, and Fudgery: Lexicography for Editors of Middle English Texts. In *Lexicographical and Linguistic Studies: Essays in Honour of G. W. Turner*, eds. T. L. Burton and Jill Burton, pp. 19–30. Cambridge [England], Wolfebro, NH: D.S. Brewer.

Bury, John B. 1883. Untitled. *BB* 7, 78–84.

Busse, W. *See* Ostheeren, Klaus.

Butler, Samuel. 1859. *Hudibras....* with variorum notes selected principally from Grey and Nash. Vol 2. London: Henry G. Bohn.

B.W. 1946. Jeep. *ANQ* 6, 96.

BW = Oscar Bloch and Walther von Wartburg. *Dictionnaire étymologique de la langue française*. 7th ed. Paris: Presses Universitaires de France, 1986.

BWA = Bierbaumer, Peter. *Der botanische Wortschatz des Altenglischen*. 3 vols. Bern: Herbert Lang, Frankfurt am Main: Peter Lang, 1975–79.

BWb = Eberhard Tiling, *Versuch eines bremisch-niedersächsichen wörterbuchs....* Bremen: Georg L. Förster, 1767–71. Repr Osnabrück: H. Th. Wenner, 1975.

Byskov, J. 1909. Dissimilation og Ordet *Nögle*. *ANF* 25, 179–90.

BZ = Alois Brandl and Otto Zippel. *Mittelenglische Sprach- und Literaturproben*. Berlin: Weidmannsche Buchhandlung, 1917. 2nd ed: 1927.

Cahen, Maurice. 1923. [Rev of] Jungner, Hugo. 1922. *RHR* 87, 145–47.

Cameron, A. Guyot. 1892. Beekenes. *MLN* 7, 220–21.

Campanile, Enrico. 1969. Sulle isoglosse lessicali celtogermaniche. *AION-SL* 9, 1–27, 220–21.

________. 1970. Sulle isoglosse lessicali celtogermaniche. *AION-SL* 9, 13–39.

Campbell, Alistair. 1959. *Old English Grammar*. Oxford: At the Clarendon Press.

________. 1969. [Rev of] Herbert D. Meritt, *Some of the Hardest Glosses in Old English*. *MÆ* 38, 306–08.

Campbell, J. J. 1952. The OE Bede: Book III, Chapters 16 to 20. *MLN* 67, 381–86.

Cardona, George. *See* Dyen, Isidore. 1970.

Carey, John. 1822. Untitled. *GM* 92, 326–27.

Carhart, Paul W. *See* Webster, Noah. 1934.

Carl, Helmut. 1957–58. Tiernamen bilden Verben. *WW* 8, 353–57.

Carnoy, Albert. 1955. *Dictionnaire étymologique du proto-indo-européen*. BM 39.

Carominas, Joan = Corominas, Juan.

Carpentier, L. J. *See* NC.

Carr, Gerald F. *See* Ivanov, Vyacheslav V. 1999a *and* Liberman, Anatoly. 1998.

Carr, Joseph W. 1907. A Word-List from Hampstead, E. E. New Hampshire. *DN* 3, 177–204.

Carstens, Heinrich. 1879a. Beeken. *KVNS* 4, 16.

________. 1879b. Beeken. *KVNS* 4, 93–94.

________. 1908. Katthagen. *KVNS* 29, 25.

Casaubon, Meric. 1650. *De Lingua Hebraica et De Lingua Saxonica*. Londini: Typis J. Flesher.

Cassidy, Frederick G. 1958. Report of a Recent Project of Collecting. *PADS* 29, 19–41. *See also* DARE.

Catullus 1554 = *Catvllvs, et in evum commentarivs M. Antonii Mvreti ab eodem correcti, & scholiis illvstrati, Tibvllvs, et Propertivs*. Venetiis: Aldvs, 1554.

Catullus 1686 = *Catvllvs, Tibvllvs, Propertivs, cum C. Galli fragmentis*. Serio Castigati. Amsteledami: Apud Isbrandum Haring, 1686.

Catullus 1702 = *Catulli, Tibulli, et Propertii Opera. Ad optimorum Exemplarium fidem recensita. Accesserunt Variæ Lectiones, Quæ in Libris MSS. & Eruditorum Commentariis notatu digniores occurrunt*. Cantabrigiæ: Typis Academicis,

Impensis Jacobi Tonson Bibliopolæ Londin, 1702.
Catullus 1715 = *Catulli, Tibulli, et Propertii Opera.* Londini: Ex Officinâ Jacobi Tonson, & Johannis Watts, 1715.
CD = *The Century Dictionary: An Encyclopedic Lexicon of the English Language.* William D. Whitney, ed. New York: The Century Co., 1889–1911. Rev by Benjamin E. Smith, 1911.
CDIL = *Contributions to a Dictionary of the Irish Language.* Dublin: Published by the Royal Irish Academy, 1964–.
CED = Walter W. Skeat, *A Concise Etymological Dictionary of the English Language.* Oxford: At the Clarendon Press, 1882. The last ed: 1910.
CEDEL = Ernest Klein, *A Comprehensive Etymological Dictionary of the English Language.* Amsterdam, London and New York: Elsevier Publishing Company, 1966; repr 1967, 1969, and 1971.
CEDHL = Ernest Klein, *A Comprehensive Etymological Dictionary of the Hebrew Language for Readers of English.* New York: Macmillan, London: Collier Macmillan, 1987.
Ceelen, F. 1958. Klimop (Hedera helix). *TT* 10, 16–31.
Celander, Hilding. 1925. Orden *fock, focka* och deras släktingar. GHÅ 31, 112–17.
Chakhoian, L. P. *See* Voronin, S. V.
Chamberlain, A. F. 1889. Welsh Rabbit. *ANQ* 3, 103–04.
Chambers, William. 1867. *Etymological Dictionary of the English Language.* James Donald, ed. London and Edinburgh: W. & R. Chambers. Rev by Andrew Findlater, 1882. (Numerous reprints.)
Chance, Frank. 1862. Rabbit. *NQ* III/1, 490–91.
________. 1887. Hobbledehoy. *NQ* VII/4, 523–25.
________. 1889. Lilliput. *NQ* VII/7, 506.
________. 1890a. Cockney. *The Academy* 37, 13–14.
________. 1890b. Cockney. *The Academy* 38, 367.
________. 1897. Round Robin. *NQ* VIII/11, 130–31.
Chantraine = Pierre Chantraine. *Dictionnaire étymologique de la langue grecque. Histoire des mots.* Paris: Éditions Klincksieck, 1968–80.
Chapman, Bruce. 1947. *Why Do We Say Such Things? The Stories behind the Words We Use.* New York: Miles-Emmett.
Chapman, Robert L, ed. 1995. *Dictionary of American Slang*, 3rd ed. New York: Harper Collins.
Chapple, William. 1785. *A Review of Part of Risdon's Survey of Devon....* Exeter: Printed... by R. Thorn.
Charnock, Richard S. 1868. *Ludus Patronymicus; or, The Etymology of Curious Surnames.* London: Trübner & Co. Repr Book Tower, Detroit: Gale Research Company, 1968.
________. 1889. *Nuces Etymologicæ.* London: Trübner & Co.
Charpentier, Jarl. 1912. Zur altindischen Etymologie. *MO* 6, 118–60.
________. 1918. Zur italischen Wortkunde. *Glotta* 9, 33–69.
Chemodanov, N. S. 1962. Mesto germanskikh iazykov sredi drugikh indoevropeiskikh iazykov [The Place of Germanic among the Other Indo-European Languages]. In SGGI I, 19–113.
Chernykh, P. Ia. 1993. *Istoriko-etimologicheskii slovar' sovremennogo russkogo iazyka* [*A Historical and Etymological Dictionary of Modern Russian*]. Moskva: Russkii iazyk.
Child, Francis J., ed. 1860. *English and Scottish Ballads.* Vol. 8. Boston: Little, Brown and Co.
Christensen, Arthur. 1916. Reste von Manu-Legenden in der iranischen Sagenwelt. In *Festschrift Friedrich Carl Andreas zur Vollendung des siebzigsten Lebensjahres am 14. April 1916, dargebracht von Freunden und Schülern.* Leipzig: Otto Harrassowitz, 63–69.
Christmas, Henry. *See* Pegge, Samuel, 3rd ed.
Ciardi, John. 1980. *A Browser's Dictionary and Native's Guide to the Unknown American Language.* New York: Harper & Row.
Claiborne, Robert. 1989. *The Roots of English: A Reader's Handbook of Word Origins.* Times Book.
Clapin, Sylva. 1902. *A New Dictionary of Americanisms.* New York: Louis Weiss & Co. Repr Book Tower, Detroit: Gale Research Company, 1968.
Clark, Paul O. 1953. A "Gulliver" Dictionary. *SP* 50, 592–624.
Classen, Karl. 1931. Die kulturgeschichtliche Bedeutung des Hafers, der Ziege und des Haushuhns. *IF* 49, 253–66.
Claus, Helmut. 1956. Schleswigsch *tūts* 'Kröte.' *KVNS* 63, 44–45.
Cleasby, Richard. *See* CV.
Cleland, John. 1766. *The Way to Things by*

Words.... London: L. Davis and C. Reymers. Repr as CFR 122, 1968.
Clemoes, Peter. *See* Feilitzen, Olof von.
Coates, Richard. 1982. Phonology and the Lexicon: A Case Study of Early English Forms in *-gg-*. *IF* 87, 195–222.
Cockayne, Thomas Oswald. 1861. *Spoon and Sparrow, ΣΠΕΝΔΕΙΝ* and *ΨΑΡ, Fvndere and Passer; or, English Roots in the Greek, Latin, and Hebrew*.... London: Parker, Son, and Bourn.
________. 1864–66. *Leechdoms, Wortcunning, and Starcraft*.... *RBMÆS* 35:1–2.
COD = *The Concise Oxford Dictionary*. 5th ed, by E. McIntosh. Etymologies revised by G. W. S. Friedrichsen. Oxford: At the Clarendon Press, 1964; 6th and 7th eds, by J. B. Sykes, 1976 and 1982; 8th ed, by R. E. Allen, 1990; 9th ed, by Della Thompson, 1995; 10th ed, by Judy Pearsall, 1999. (All publ by The Clarendon Press.)
Coetzee, Anna E. 1995. *Kaboems, kabolder, kerjakker, karbonkel, karfoefel:* Vanwaar de hele kaboedel. *SATT*, Supplement 28, 27–44.
Cohen, Gerald L. 1972a. English: Lad. *CoE* I/9, 2–3
________. 1972b. GL Root in Indo-European. *CoE* I/14, 1–8.
________. 1972c. LK/LG Root. *CoE* I/12, 1–5.
________. 1975. Proto-Germanic **Par-* (= Bull, Calf) As a Borrowing from Semitic *Par* (= Bull, Young Bull). *CoE* V/3, 1–5.
________. 1976. Skedaddle. *CoE* V/12–13, 1–8.
________. 1979. *Skedaddle* Revisited. *CoE* VIII/10–11, 1–42.
________. 1982. More on the Possibility of Semitic Borrowings into Proto-Germanic. *CoE* XI/9–10, 1982, 13–17.
________. 1985a. Etymology of *Skedaddle* and Related Forms. In Cohen 1985b, 29–63.
________. 1985b. *Studies in Slang, Part 1*. FA 14/1.
________. 1987. Drat. *CoE* XVII/3–4, 3–4.
________. 1989. *Studies in Slang*, Part 2. FA 16.
________. 1997. *Studies in Slang*, Part 5. FA 22.
________ et al. 1979. Concerning *skedaddle*. *CoE* VIII/15, 20–24.
See also Gore, Willard C.
Colby, Elbridge. 1942. *Army Talk: A Familiar Dictionary of Soldier Speech*. Princeton: Princeton University Press.
Coleman, Everard H. 1900. Slang. *NQ* IX/5, 212.
Coleman, Julia. 1992. Sexual Euphemism in Old English. *NM* 93, 93–98.
Coles, Elisha. 1676. *An English Dictionary*. London: Printed for Samuel Crouch. Repr as CFR 268, 1971.
Collinder, Björn. 1932. Wortgeschichtliches aus dem Bereich der germanisch-finnischen und germanisch-lappischen Lehnbeziehungen. *APS* 7, 193–225.
Collyns, Wm. 1857. West-country "Cob." *NQ* II/4, 258.
Colman, Fran. 1986. *cæġ* to Old English Syllable Structure. In *Linguistics across Historical and Geographical Boundaries: In Honour of Jacek Fisiak on the Occasion of his Fiftieth Birthday. Vol 1: Linguistic Theory and Historical Linguistics*, eds. Dieter Kastovsky and Aleksander Szwedek, 225–30. TLSM 32.
Colodny, J. *See* Hixson, Jerome C.
Cook, Albert S. 1890. Etymological Notes: "Cockney," "Clock," "Coble." *The Academy* 37, 390.
Cooke, W. G. 1988. *The Tournament of Tottenham:* Provenance, Text, and Lexicography. *ES* 69, 113–16.
Čop, Bojan. 1955a. Etyma. *ZFf* 2, 393–410.
________. 1955b. Etyma. *Linguistica* 1, 28–32.
________. 1957. Beiträge zur indogermanischen Wortforschung. 2. *Die Sprache* 3, 135–49.
________. 1964. Zur hetitischen Schreibung und Lautung. *Linguistica* 5, 21–46.
Cope, William H. 1883. *A Glossary of Hampshire Words and Phrases*. EDSP 40.
Corèdon, Christopher. *See* DMTP.
Cornu, Jules. 1880. Étymologies espagnoles et portugaises. *Romania* 9, 129–37.
________. 1881. Étymologies espagnoles. *Romania* 10, 404–05.
Corominas, Joan. 1942. [Note 1 to Spitzer (1942:18)].
________. 1961. *Breve diccionario etimológico de la lengua castellana*. Madrid: Editorial Gredos. *See also* DCECH.
Cortelyou, John van Zandt. 1906. *Die altenglischen Namen der Insekten, Spinnen- und Krustentiere*. AF 19.
Cosijn, P. J. 1879. De oudste Westsaksische chroniek. *TB* 2, 259–77.
________. 1888. *Altwestsächsische Grammatik*. Haag: Martinus Nijhoff.
Cotgrave, Randle. 1611. *A Dictionarie of the French and English Tongues*. London: Printed

by Adam Islip. Repr Columbia: University of South Carolina Press, 1950; as CFR 82, 1968; *and* Amsterdam: New York: Theatrum Orbis Terrarum Ltd / Da Capo Press, 1971.
Cottle, Basil. 1978. *The Penguin Dictionary of Surnames*. 2nd ed, by Allen Lane.
Coulson, Jessie. *See* SOD.
Courtney, W. P. 1900. *Slang*, When First Used. *NQ* IX/5, 28.
Cowan, H. K. J. 1974. Proto-Indo-europese relicten in de Nederlanden. II. *LB* 63, 215–60.
Cox, H. L. *See* Århammar, Nils R.
Craig, John. 1848–49. *A New Universal Technological Etymological Dictionary of the English Language....* London: Henry George Collins.
Craig, W. J., ed. [1907] *The Works of Shakespeare. The Tragedy of King Lear.* Indianapolis: The Bowen-Merrill Co.
Craigie, William A. *See* CV, DAE, and DOST.
Craik, T. W. *See* LC.
Crespo, Roberto. *See* Markey, Thomas L. 1987.
Crook, Eugene J. *See* Jordan, Richard. 1974.
Crook, Keith. 1998. *A Preface to Swift.* London and New York: Longman.
Curtis, J. Lewelyn. 1852. Camden's Definition of Cockney. *NQ* I/6, 149.
Curtius, Georg. 1873. *Grundzüge der griechischen Etymologie.* 4th ed. Leipzig: B. G. Teubner.
Curzan, Anne. *See* Liberman, Anatoly. 2004b.
CV = *An Icelandic-English Dictionary initiated by Richard Cleasby, subsequently revised, enlarged and completed by Gudbrand Vigfusson....* Oxford: At the Clarendon Press, 1874. 2nd ed with a supplement, by William A. Craigie, 1957.
Daa, Lewis K. 1856. On the Affinities between the Languages of the Northern Tribes of the Old and New Continents. *TPS*, 251–94.
DAE = *A Dictionary of American English on Historical Principles.* William A. Craigie and James R. Hulbert, eds. Chicago: The University of Chicago Press, 1938–44.
Dahlberg, Torsten. 1955. *Mittelhochdeutsches* wurpôz *'radix,'* bôze *'Flachsbündel,'* bŏz *'stoss.' Geographie und Etymologie.* GUÅ 61/1.
Dal, Erik. *See* Nielsen, Niels Å.
Dal', Vladimir. 1955. *Tolkovyi slovar' zhivogo velikorusskogo iazyka* [*A Comprehensive Dictionary of the Living Russian Language*]. Moskva: Gosudarstvennoe izdatel'stvo inostrannykh i natsional'nykh slovarei.
DARE = *Dictionary of American Regional English.* Frederic G. Cassidy, chief ed., Joan H. Hall, associate ed. Cambridge, Massachusetts, and London, England: The Bellknap Press of Harvard University Press, 1985– .
Davies, John. 1855. On the Races of Lancashire, as Indicated by the Local Names and the Dialect of the County. *TPS*, 210–84.
________. 1880a. The Celtic Element of the English People. *AC* IV/11, 10–24, 97–105.
________. 1880b. The Celtic Languages in Relation to Other Aryan Tongues. *Y Cymmrodoar* III/1, 1–51.
________. 1885. The Celtic Element in the Dialectic Words of the Counties of Northampton and Leister. *AC* 5th series, V/2, 1–32, 81–96, 161–82.
Davis, M.D. 1895. The Word "Graffe" in Chaucer. *NQ* VIII/7, 226–27.
DC = *A Dictionary of Canadianisms on Historical Principles.* Walter S. Avis et al., eds. The Lexicographical Center for Canadian English, University of Victoria, British Columbia. Toronto: Gage, 1967.
DCECH = Joan Corominas, with the assistance of José A. Pascual, *Diccionario crítico etimológico castellano e hispánico.* BRH V. Diccionarios 7, 1980–91.
DDEL = Anonymous, *A Dictionary of the Derivations of the English Language*. Glasgow, Edinburgh: Collins, New York: Putnam's Sons, 1872.
De Bo, Leonard L. 1892. *Westvlaamsch Idioticon.* Joseph Samyn, ed. Gent: Alfons Siffer.
De Bont, A. P. 1948. Over beduit(je) en wat dies meer zij. *TNTL* 66, 23–42.
________. 1973. Fiets. *NTg* 66, 49–54.
De Boor, Helmut. 1924. Der Zwerg in Skandinavien. In *Festschrift Eugen Mogk zum 70. Geburtstag 19. Juli 1924,* 536–70. Halle an der Saale: Max Niemeyer.
See also Nib.
De Hoog, W. 1909. *Studiën over de Nederlandsche en Engelsche Taal- en Letterkunde en haar Wederzijdschen invloed.* Dordrecht: J. P. Revers.
De Jager, A. *See* WF.
De Lagarde, Paul. *See* Lagarde, Paul de.
De Montigny, Allen H. K. 1953. Legends or Facts? Yes, There Were Giants and Dwarves! *IALR* I/1, 68–70.
De Morgan, A. 1869. Hanne-bane; Hyocyamus. *The Athenæum*/II, 253.

De Sainte Palaye, La Curne. *See* Sainte-Palaye, La Curne de.

De Schutter, G. 1996. De woordenschat van het Nederlands en van het Engels, een vergelijkende studie. *VMKANTL*, 41–59.

De Tollenaere, Francien. 1969. Problemen van het Nederlands etymologisch woordenboek. *TNTL* 85, 212–47.
See also NEW.

De Vaan, Michiel. 2000. Reconsidering Dutch rups, G Raupe 'caterpillar.' *ABÄG* 54, 151–74.

________. 2003. [Rev of] *Proceedings of the Twelfth Annual UCLA Indo-European Conference. Los Angeles, May 26–28, 2000*. JISM 40. *ABÄG* 58, 283–88.

De Vries, Jan. 1935–37. *Altgermanische Religionsgeschichte. Grundriss der germanischen Philologie* 12/1–2. Berlin and Leipzig: Walter de Gruyter.

________. 1956a. *Altgermanische Religionsgeschichte* 1. *Grundriss der germanischen Philologie* 12/1. Berlin: Walter de Gruyter.

________. 1956b. Die altnordischen Wörter mit *gn-*, *hn-*, *kn-*Anlaut. *IF* 62, 136–50.

________. 1959. Das -r- emphaticum im Germanischen. In *Mélanges de Linguistique et de Philologie Fernand Mossé in memoriam*, 467–85. Paris: Didier.
See also AEW *and* NEW.

De Vries, W. 1914. Etymologische aanteekeningen. *TNTL* 33, 143–49.

________. 1915. Etymologische aanteekeningen. *TNTL* 34, 1–22.

________. 1919. Etymologische aanteekeningen. *TNTL* 38, 257–301.

________. 1923 Gotisch *fitan*. *TNTL* 42, 25–27.

________. 1924. Etymologische aanteekeningen. *TNTL* 43, 129–44.

Debrunner, Albert. 1918. Die Besiedlung des alten Griechenland im Licht der Sprachwissenschaft. *NJKAGDL(P)* 21, 433–48.

Del Rosal, Francisco. 1992. *Diccionario etimológico....* BFH 10.

Delatte, F. 1935. The Etymology of "Mug" = "Face." *NQ* 168, 196.

Delbrück, Berthold. 1870. Die declination der substantiva im germanischen insonderheit im gotischen. *ZDP* 2, 381–407.
See also Brugmann, Karl, and Berthold Delbrück. 1906.

Della Volpe, Angela. *See* Liberman, Anatoly. 1998.

Dent, Alan. 1971. *World of Shakespeare: Plants*. Reading, Berkshire: Osprey.

DEO = Niels Å. Nielsen, *Dansk etymologisk Ordbog. Ordenes Historie*. 3rd ed. Gyldendal, 1989, 4th ed: 1997.

Derocquigny, Jules. 1904. *A Contribution to the Study of the French Element in English*. Lille: Le Bigot Bros.

Derolez, René. 1945. Germ. "*du̯erga-." *BT/RB* 24, 164–69.

Detter, Ferdinand. 1892. Die Hamletsage. *ZDA* 36, 1–25.

________. 1897. *Deutsches Wörterbuch*. Leipzig: G. J. Göschen'sche Verlagshandlung.

________. 1898. Etymologien. *ZDA* 42, 53–58.

Devoto, Giacomo. 1968. *Avviamento alla etimologia italiana. Dizionario etimologico*. 2nd ed. Firenze: Felice le Monnier.

Diefenbach, Lorenz. 1851. *Vergleichendes Wörterbuch der gothischen Sprache*. Frankfurt am Main: Joseph Baer. Repr Wiesbaden: Dr. Martin Sändig, 1967.

________. 1857. *Glossarium latino-germanicum mediae et infimae aetatis....* Francofurti ad Moenum: Sumptibus Josephi Baer Bibliopolae.

Diensberg, Bernhard. 1978. Zur Etymologie von ne. *boy*. *Sprachwissenschaft* 3, 345–56.

________. 1981. The Etymology of Modern English *Boy:* A New Hypothesis. *MÆ* 50, 79–85.

________. 1984. The Etymology of Modern English *Girl*. An Old Problem Reconsidered. *NM* 85, 473–75.

________. 1985a. The Lexical Fields *boy/girl—servant—child* in Middle English. *NM* 86, 328–36.

________. 1985b. *Untersuchungen zur phonologischen Rezeption romanischen Lehnguts im Mittel- und Frühneuenglischen. Die Lehnwörter mit mittelenglisch* oi/ui *und ihre phonologische Rezeption*. TBL 268.

________. 1994. Towards a Revision of the Oxford Dictionary of English Etymology. In *Symposium on Lexicography VI: Proceedings of the Sixth International Symposium on Lexicography May 7–9, 1992 at the University of Copenhagen*, 207–33. Karl Hyldgaard-Jensen and Viggo H. Pedersen, eds. Tübingen: Max Niemeyer Verlag.

________. 1999. Linguistic Change in English. The Case of the Great Vowel Shift from the Perspective of Phonological Alternations Due to the Wholesale Borrowing of Anglo-French Loanwords. *FLH* 19, 103–18.

Dietz, Klaus. 1967. Zur neuenglischen Etymologie. *Archiv* 204, 354–65.

________. 1981a. Mittelenglisches *oi* in heimischen Ortsnamen und Personennamen. *BN.* N. F. 16, 269–340, 361–405.

________. 1981b. Me *oi* heimischer Provenienz. In *Weltsprache Englisch in Forschung und Lehre. Festschrift für Kurt Wächtler*, eds. Peter Kunsmann and Ortwin Kuhn, 81–109. Berlin: Erich Schmidt Verlag.

________. 2000. [Rev of] *Interdigitations: Essays for Irmengard Rauch*, eds. Gerald F. Carr, Wayne Harbert, and Lihua Zhang, pp. 1–24. New York: Peter Lang, 1999. *BN* 35 (N.F.), 77–81.

See also Jordan, Richard. 1925, 3rd ed.

Diez, Friedrich. 1887. *Etymologisches Wörterbuch der romanischen Sprachen.* 5th ed. Bonn: Bei Adolph Marcus.

Dinneen, Patrick S. 1927. *Foclóir Gae˙dilge agus béarla. An Irish-English Dictionary.* Dublin: Publ for the Irish Texts Society, 1927. Repr with additions, 1934; repr 1953.

Disterheft, Dorothy. *See* Greppin, John A. C.

Dittmann, Wolfgang. *See* Rooth, Erik. 1963.

DLLA = *Dizionario letterario del lessico amoroso.* Torino: Utet, 2000.

DMTP = Christopher Corèdon, with Ann Williams, *A Dictionary of Medieval Terms and Phrases.* Cambridge: D. S. Brewer, 2004.

DNZE = *The Dictionary of New Zealand English: A Dictionary of New Zealandisms on Historical Principles.* H. W. Orsman, ed. Auckland, New York: Oxford University Press, 1997.

Dobozy, Maria, translator. 1999. *The Saxon Mirror: A* Sachsenspiegel *of the Fourteenth Century.* Philadelphia: University of Pennsylvania Press.

Dobson, Eric, J. 1940. The Etymology and Meaning of *Boy. MÆ* 9, 121–54.

________. 1943. Middle English and Middle Dutch *Boye. MÆ* 12, 71–76.

________. 1957. *English Pronunciation 1500–1700.* Vol. 2: *Phonology.* Oxford: At the Clarendon Press. 2nd ed: 1968.

Dodgson, John M. 1968. Cheshire Field-Name Elements. *NQ* 213, 123–24.

DOE = Antonette di Paolo Healey. *Dictionary of Old English* (microfiche), 1986. Venezky, Richard L., *A Microfiche Concordance to Old English: The High-Frequencey Words*, 1985. Toronto, Ont.: Publ for the Dictionary of Old English Project Centre for Mediaeval Studies of Toronto, by the Pontifical Institute.

Dörner, Hans H. 1993. Der Totschlag an Ymir. *ABÄG* 37, 1–17.

Dolle, Rudolf. 1912. *Graphische und lautliche Untersuchung von Dan Michels 'Ayenbite of Inwyt'.* Diss. Bonn. Bonn: Carl Georgi.

Donald, James. *See* Chambers, William.

Donaldson, David. *See* Jamieson, John. 1879–82.

Doornkaat Koolman, Jan ten. *See* Ten Doornkaat Koolman, Jan.

DOPE = Thomas Wright, *Dictionary of Obsolete and Provincial English....* London: Henry G. Bohn, 1857. Repr Book Tower, Detroit: Gale Research Co., 1967.

DOST = William A. Craigie et al., eds., *A Dictionary of the Older Scottish Tongue from the Twelfth Century to the End of the Seventeenth.* Chicago: The University of Chicago Press, London: Humphrey Milford/Oxford University Press, Aberdeen University Press, [1937] –.

Douce, Francis. 1807. *Illustrations of Shakespeare, and of Ancient Manners: With Dissertations on the Clowns and Fools of Shakespeare....* 2 vols. London: Longman, *etc.*

Draat, P. Fijn van. *See* Van Draat, P. Fijn.

Drake, Allison E. 1907. *Discoveries in Hebrew, Gaelic, Gothic, Anglo-Saxon, Latin, Basque and Other Caucasic Languages Showing Fundamental Kinship of the Aryan Tongues and of Basque with the Semitic Tongues.* Denver: The Herrick Book & Stationery Company; London: Kegan Paul, Trench, Trübner & Company, Ltd.

Drees, Ludwig. 1974. *Der Kult des Mannus in den Ardennen. Die heidnische Kultstätte von Malmedy und ihre Christianisierung.* Schriftreihe des Geschichtsvereins "Zwischen Venn und Schnefel" St. Vith 7 (= Sonderdruck aus den Annalen des Historischen Vereins für den Niederrhein, insbesondere das alte Erzbistum Köln 175, 1973, 7–62). Düsseldorf: L. Schwann.

Drexel, Albert. 1926. Die Krisis in der vergleichenden Sprachwissenschaft. *IJVS* 1, 109–16.

Drosdowski, Günther. 1950. *Studien zur*

Bedeutungsgeschichte angelsächsischer_ Zeitbegriffswörter. Diss. Freie Universität zu Berlin. Unpublished.

Du Cange, Carolus du Fresne (Charles). 1954. *Glossarium mediae et infimae latinitatis....* Graz: Akademische Druck- und Verlagsanstalt. Repr of the 1883–1887 ed. First publ in 1678.

Duckett, Eleanor S. 1925. *Catullus in English Poetry*. SCCS 6.

Duden 7 = *Duden 7. Das Herkunftswörterbuch. Eine Etymologie der deutschen Sprache....* Mannheim, Wien, Zürich, Dudenverlag, 1963.

Duden 8 = *Duden 8. Die Sinn- und Sachverwandten Wörter....* Mannheim, Wien, Zürich, Dudenverlag, 1986.

Duflou, G. 1927. Wichelaar en wikkelaar. In *Album opgedragen aan Prof. Dr. J. Vercoullie door ambtgenooten, ould-leerlingen en vereerders, ter gelegenheid van zijn zeventigsten verjaardag en van zijn emeritaat*, 119–23. Brussel: Paginæ.

DW = *Deutsches Wörterbuch von Jacob Grimm und Wilhelm Grimm*. Leipzig: Verlag von S. Hirzel, 1854–1971. Repr 1965–89.

DW[2] = *Deutsches Wörterbuch von Jacob und Wilhelm Grimm. Neubearbeitung*. Leipzig: S. Hirzel Verlag, 1965–.

Dwight, Benjamin W. 1859. *Modern Philology: Its Discoveries, History and Influence....* New York: A. S. Barnes & Burr.

Dyen, Isidore. 1970. Background 'Noise' or 'Evidence' in Comparative Linguistics: The Case of the Austronesian-Indo-European Hypothesis. In *Indo-European and Indo-Europeans: Papers Presented at the Third Indo-European Conference at the University of Pennsylvania*, eds. George Cardona, Henry M. Hoenigswald, and Alfred Senn. Philadelphia: University of Pennsylvania Press, 431–40.

Earle, John. 1888. *A Hand-Book to the Land-Charters, and Other Saxonic Documents*. Oxford: At the Clarendon Press.

________. 1890. [Untitled]. *The Academy* 37, 339.

EB = *Encyclopaedia Britannica*. 11th, 12th, and 13th eds.

E.B. 1877. Americanisms in England. *LM* 19, 513–14.

Ebbinghaus, Ernst A. 1989a. [Rev of] EWA 1. *GL* 29, 135–38.

________. 1989b. The Cognomenta of Two Germanic Matronae. In *Hanjamana*, ed. Subhadra K. Sen, pp. 4–5. Calcutta: Calcutta University Press.

Ebenbauer, Alfred. *See* Binnig, Wolfgang.

Ebener, Frederick. *See* EG.

ED = Robert Hunter, ed, *The Encyclopædic Dictionary....* London, *etc*: Cassell & Company, Limited, 1892–98.

EDD = *The English Dialect Dictionary*. Joseph Wright, ed. London, *etc*: H. Frowde, 1898–1905. Repr London: Oxford University Press, 1970.

Edda = Gustav Nechel, ed. *Edda. Die Lieder des Codex Regius nebst verwandten Denkmälern*, vol 1. 4th ed, by Hans Kuhn. Heidelberg: Carl Winter. Universitätsverlag, 1962.

Edlinger, August V. 1886. *Erklärung der Tier-Namen aus allen Sprachgebieten*. Landshut: Krüll.

Edwards, Eliezer. 1881. *Words, Facts, and Phrases. A Dictionary of Curious, Quaint, & Out-of-the-Way Matters*. Philadelphia: J. B. Lippincott and Co. Repr Book Tower, Detroit: Gale Research Company, 1968.

Edwards, Philip, ed. 1985. [Cambridge Shakespeare.] *Hamlet, Prince of Denmark*. Cambridge, *etc*.: Cambridge University Press.

Edye, L. 1886–87. "Faggot" As a Term of Reproach. *WA* 6, 196.

E.G. 1898 (publ 1899). 'Slang' As a Field Name. *CS* III/2, 34.

EG = Frederick Ebener and Edward Greenway, Jr. 1871. *Words: Their History and Derivation*. Baltimore: Sold by Turnbull Brothers, London: Trübner & Co.

Egger, Hans-Jürgen. 1981. *Zur Schichtung der germanischen Körperteilnamen*. Diss. Gießen. Unpublished.

Eggers, Hans. *See* BE.

Egilsson, Sveinbjörn. *See LP*.

Ehrlich, Hugo. 1907. Zur Mythologie. *KZ* 41, 283–304.

Eichner, Heiner. 1994. Zur Frage der Gültigkeit Boppscher sprachgeschichtlicher Deutungen aus der Sicht der modernen Indogermanistik. In *Bopp-Symposium 1992 der Humboldt-Universität zu Berlin. Akten der Konferenz vom 24.3–26.3.1992 aus Anlaß von Franz Bopps zweihundertjährigem Geburtstag am 14.9.1991*, ed. Reinhard Sternemann, 72–90. Heidelberg: Universitätsverlag C. Winter.

Eisiminger, Sterling. 1979. Acronyms and Folk Etymology. *JAF* 91, 582–84.

________. 1984. Etymology Unknown: The Crème de la Crème de la Crème. *AS* 59, 90–96.

Ejder, Bertil. 1961–62. Var på din vakt! Om några ord med betydelsen 'vaktställe,' 'vårdkase' o.dyl. SOSÅ 1961–62, 59–99.

Ekwall, Eilert. 1903. *Shakspere's Vocabulary: Its Etymological Elements.* Diss. Uppsala. Uppsala: At the University Press. Also publ as: UUÅ 21/2.

________. 1908. Engl. *heather* 'Heidekraut.' *Archiv* 121, 135–39.

________. 1928. *English River-Names.* Oxford: At the Clarendon Press.

________. 1938. [Rev of] Rolf Kaiser, *Zur Geographie des mittelenglischen Wortschatzes.* Palaestra 205. Leipzig: Mayer & Müller, 1937. *ES* 20, 257–59.

________. 1960. *Concise Oxford Dictionary of English Place-Names.* 4th ed. Oxford: At the Clarendon Press.

Eliasson, Stig. *See* Polomé, Edgar C. 1997.

Ellekilde, Hans. 1937–38. "Folk," "Hundneg" og "Basse" imellen Aabenraa og Flensborg Fjord. *SM* 14.

Ellert, Ernest E. 1946. *The Etymology and Semantic Development of Words of Family Relationship in the Germanic Languages.* North Carolina University (Chapel Hill) Ph. D. dissertation. Unpublished.

Ellis, Alexander J. 1867. On Paleotype. Supplement 1. *TPS.* [Printed at the end of the volume with its own pagination. 66 pp.]

________. 1870. On Glosik, a Neu Sistem ov Engglish Speling.... *TPS,* 89–118.

________. 1871. *On Early English Pronunciation....* Vol. 3. London: Publ for the Philological Society by Asher & Co., and for the Early English Text Society, and the Chaucer Society by Trubner & Co. Repr New York, N.Y.: Haskell House Publishers Ltd, 1969.

________. 1877. The Ancient British Numerals. *The Athenæum*/II, 371.

Ellmers, Detter. *See* Meid, Wolfgang. 1992.

Ellwood, T. 1877. The Ancient British Numerals. *The Athenæum*/II, 433.

Elmevik, Lennart. 1971. Till härledningen av ordet kvi(a) 'kreatursfålla' m. m. *NSt* 51, 58–82.

________. 1974. Kǫgurr och Kägra. In: *Nordiska namn. Festskrift till Lennart Moberg 13 december 1974,* 187–98. Uppsala: Lundequistska bokhandeln.

________. 1984. Två ordstudier. Bernt Fossestøl et al, eds. *Festskrift til Einar Lundeby 3. oktober 1984,* 130–40. Oslo: Novus forlag.

________. 1986. On Some Scandinavian Words for "Weasel." In *Aspects of Language: Studies in Honour of Mario Alinei: Papers Presented to Mario Alinei by his Friends, Colleagues and Former Students on the Occasion of his 60th Birthday.* Vol. 1: *Geolinguistics,* eds. Nils Århammar, et al, 79–89. Amsterdam: Rodopi.

________. 1990. Aschw. *Lytis* in Ortsnamen. Ein kultisches Element oder ein profanes? In *Old Norse and Finnish Religions and Cultic Place-Names. Based on Papers Read at the Symposium on Encounters between Religions in Old Nordic Times and on Cultic Place-Names, Held at Åbo, Finland on the 19th–21st of August 1987,* ed. Tore Ahlbäck, pp. 490–507. SID 13.

EM = Alfred Ernout, and Antoine Meillet, *Dictionnaire étymologique de la langue latine.* 5th ed. Paris: Librairie C. Klincksieck, 1985.

Emery, H. G. *See* NCD.

Emmons, Kimberly. *See* Liberman, Anatoly. 2004b.

Engelstoft, L. *See* Outzen, Nicolaus.

Engler, A. *See* Hehn, Victor.

EONSS = Jakob Jakobsen, *Etymologisk ordbog over de norrøne sprog på Shetland.* København: Vilhelm Priors Kgl. Hofboghandel, 1921.

Erdmann, Oskar. *See* Otfrid.

Ernout, Alfred. *See* EM.

Ernst, C. W. 1894 Cockney. *NQ* VIII/6, 64.

Eroms, Hans-Werner. *See* Hiersche, Rolf. 1984.

Ershova, I.A. and O. A. Pavlova. 1984. "O nekotorykh osobennostiakh leksiki angliiskikh territorial'nykh dialektov." *Vestnik Moskovskogo universiteta,* Seris 9, Filologiia, No. 4, 31–44.

ErW = Hans Heestermans, ed., *Erotisch woordenboek.* Vijverhof Baarn: Erven Thomas Rap, 1977. Repr Utrecht: Spectrum, 1980.

ES = Robert M. Estrich and Hans Sperber, *Three Keys to Language.* New York: Rinehart & Company, Inc., 1952.

E.S.C. 1872. Cater-Cousins. *NQ* IV/9, 517.

Espy, Willard R. 1978. *O Thou Improper, Thou Uncommon Noun.* New York: Clarkson N. Potter, Inc.

ESRI = *Etimologicheskii slovar' russkogo iazyka* [*Russian Etymological Dictionary*]. N. M. Shanskii, ed. Moskva: Izdatel'stvo Moskovskogo universiteta, 1963–82 (A-K).

ESSI = *Etimologicheskii slovar' slavianskikh*

iazykov. Praslavianskii leksicheskii fond [*An Etymological Dictionary of the Slavic Languages. Proto-Slavic Vocabulary*]. O. N. Trubachev, ed. Moskva: Nauka, 1974–.

Estrich, Robert M. *See* ES.

Etter, Annemarie. *See* Polomé, Edgar C. 1986.

Ettmüller, Ludovicus (= Ettmüller, Ernst Moritz Ludwig). 1851. *Vorda Wealhstôd Engla and Seaxna. Lexicon Anglosaxonicum....* Quedlinburg and Leipzig: Gottfr. Basse.

Euling, Karl. *See* Paul, Hermann. 1897, 4th ed.

Evans, Arthur B. 1844. Untitled. *GM*/I, 383–84.

EW = Ferdinand Holthausen, *Etymologisches Wörterbuch der englischen Sprache*. Leipzig: Bernhard Tauchnitz, 1917. 2nd ed: 1927; 3rd ed: 1949.

EWA = Albert L. Lloyd, Rosemarie Lühr, and Otto Springer, *Etymologisches Wörterbuch des Althochdeutschen*. Göttingen, Zürich: Vandenhoeck & Ruprecht, 1988–.

EWD = Wolfgang Pfeifer, ed, *Etymologisches Wörterbuch des Deutschen*. Berlin: Akademie-Verlag, 1989.

EWDS = Friedrich Kluge, *Etymologisches Wörterbuch der deutschen Sprache*. Straßburg: Karl J. Trübner. 1st and 2nd eds: 1883, 3rd ed: 1884 (unchanged), 4th ed: 1889, 5th ed: 1894, 6th ed: 1899 (repr without changes in 1905), 7th ed: 1910, 8th ed: 1915, 9th ed: 1921, 10th ed: 1924, 11th ed, by Alfred Götze in collaboration with Wolfgang Krause: 1934, 12th–13th (1943) and 14th (1948) eds (unchanged), 15th ed, by Alfred Götze with the assistance of Hans Krahe, completed by Alfred Schirmer: 1951, 16th ed (unchanged): 1953, 17th ed, by Alfred Schirmer, rev by Walther Mitzka: 1957, 18th through 21st eds, by Walther Mitzka [KM]: 1960, 1963, 1967, 21st ed (unchanged): 1975, 22nd, 23rd and 24th eds, by Elmar Seebold [KS]: 1989, 1995, 2003. (The post-1915 eds were publ by Walter de Gruyter [Berlin, New York].)

Ewen, C. L'Estrange. 1931. *A History of Surnames of the British Isles: A Concise Account of their Origin, Evolution, Etymology and Legal Status*. London: Kegan Paul, Trench, Trubner & Co. Ltd. Repr Book Tower, Detroit: Gale Research Company, 1968.

________. 1938. *A Guide to the Origin of British Surnames*. London: John Gifford Limited, Repr Book Tower, Detroit: Gale Research Company, 1969.

EWFS = Ernst Gamillscheg, *Etymologisches Wörterbuch der französischen Sprache*. Heidelberg: Carl Winter's Universitätsbuchhandlung, 1928.

EWNT = Johannes Franck, *Etymologisch woordenboek der Nederlandsche taal*. 's-Gravenhage: Martinus Nijhoff, 1892. 2nd ed, by N. van Wijk: 1912, Supplement by C. B. van Haeringen. 's-Gravenhage: Martinus Nijhoff, 1936. Repr in one volume, 1949.

Faiss, Klaus. 1978. *Verdunkelte Compounds im Englischen. Ein Beitrag zu Theorie und Praxis der Wortbildung*. Tübingen: TBL-Verlag Gunter Narr.

Falileyev, Alexander and Graham Isaac. 1998. Welsh *cabl* "calumny, blame, blasphemy." *IF* 103, 202–06.

Falk, Hjalmar. 1890. Vexlen *ā : ō* i nordisk. *ANF* 6, 113–20.

________. 1896. Om indskud af *j* med forsterkende og navnlig nedsættende betydning i nordiske ord. *Sproglig-historiske studier tilegnede Professor C.R. Unger*. Kristiania: H. Aschehoug & Co.

________. 1918–19. Schloß und Schlüssel. In *RGA* 4, 134.

________. 1919. *Altwestnordische Kleiderkunde mit besonderer Berücksichtigung der Terminologie*. Skr. Krist. 1918/3.

________. 1925a. Die altnordischen Namen der Beizvögel. In *Germanica. Eduard Sievers zum 75. Geburtstage 25. November 1925*, 236–46. Halle an der Saale: Max Niemeyer.

________. 1925b. Svensk ordforskning. *ANF* 41, 113–39.

See also FT(G), FT(N), *and* Torp, Alf.

Fanego, Teresa. *See* Vennemann, Theo. 2002.

Farmer, John S. 1900. *The Public School Word-book*. London: Privately issued for Subscribers Only by Hirshfeld Brothers. Repr Book Tower, Detroit: Gale Research Company, 1968.

Faulmann, Karl. 1893. *Etymologisches Wörterbuch der deutschen Sprache nach eigenen neuen Forschungen*. Halle a. S.: Ehrhardt Karras' Verlag.

Fay, Edwin W. 1895. Agglutination and Adaptation. *AJP* 16, 1–27.

________. 1905. A Semantic Study of Indo-Iranian Nasal Verbs 2. *AJP* 26, 172–203.

________. 1906. Latin Word-Studies. *TAPA* 37, 5–24.

________. 1913. The Root STHA in Composition. *AJP* 34, 15–42.

F.C.H. 1868. Rabbit. *NQ* IV/1, 207.

Fehr, Bernhard. 1910. Zur Agglutination in der englischen Sprache. In *Festschrift zum 14. Neuphilologentage in Zürich 1910*, 303–34. Zürich: Züricher & Furrer.

Feilberg, H. F. 1886–1914. *Bidrag til en ordbog over jyske almuesmål.* Kjøbenhavn: H. H. Thieles bogtrykkeri.

Feilitzen, Olof von, and Christopher Blunt. 1971. Personal Names on the Coinage of Edgar. In *England before the Conquest: Studies in Primary Sources Presented to Dorothy Whitelock*, eds. Peter Clemoes and Kathleen Hughes, pp. 183–214. Cambridge: At the University Press.

Feist, Sigmund. 1888. *Grundriß der gotischen Etymologie.* Sammlung indogermanischer Wörterbücher 2. Straßburg: Karl J. Trübner.

________. 1909. *Vergleichendes Wörterbuch der gotischen Sprache.* Halle a. S.: Verlag von Max Niemeyer. 2nd ed: 1924, 3rd ed: 1939; 4th ed, by Winfred P. Lehmann, 1986. The last two eds, Leiden: E. J. Brill.

Feitsma, Tony. 1962. Sproglige berøringer mellem Frisland og Skandinavien. *SK* 23, 97–121.

Fernández, L. Gil. 1959. *Nombres de insectos en griego antiguo.* ME 18.

FEW = Walther von Wartburg, *Französisches etymologisches Wörterbuch....* Leipzig, Berlin: Verlag B. G. Teubner, *etc.,* Basel: Zbinden Druck und Verlag AG, 1934–[98].

FH = French, Walter H., and Charles B. Hale, eds., *Middle English Metrical Romances.* New York: Prentice-Hall, Inc., 1930. Repr New York: Russell & Russell, Inc., 1964, 2 vols.

Fick, August. 1874–76. *Vergleichendes Wörterbuch der indogermanischen Sprachen.* 3rd ed, Göttingen: Vandenhoeck. 4th ed: 1890–1909. Repr 1979.

________. 1880. Zum schwâ im griechischen. *BB* 5, 166–68.

________. 1891. Etymologien. *BB* 17, 319–24.

________. 1892. [Rev of] Walter Prellwitz. *GGA* 227–48.

See also Bezzenberger, Adalbert, and August Fick.

Findlater, Andrews. *See* Chambers, Williams.

Fischer, Frank. 1909. *Die Lehnwörter des Altwestnordischen.* Palaestra 85. Berlin: Mayer & Müller.

Fishwick, H. 1883. Caterways. *NQ* VI/7, 354.

Fisiak, Jacek. *See* Terasawa, Yoshio. 1993.

F.J.J. 1876. Skid. *NQ,* V/5, 337–38.

Flasdieck, Hermann M. 1937. Harlekin. Germanischer Mythos in romanischer Wandlung. *Anglia* 61, 225–340.

________. 1958. Die Entstehung des engl. Phonems [ʃ], zugleich ein Beitrag zur Geschichte der Quantität. *Anglia* 76, 339–410.

Fleece, Jeffrey. 1943. A Word-Creator. *AS* 18, 1943, 68–69.

Fleissner, Robert F. 1983. Dickens' *Oliver Twist. The Explicator* 41/3, 30–32.

Flexner, Stuart B. 1976. *I Hear America Talking: An Illustrated Treasury of American Words and Phrases.* New York, *etc*: Van Nostrand Reinhold Company.

See also WFl and RHD[2].

Flom, George T. 1900. *Scandinavian Influence on Southern Lowland Scotch: A Contribution to the Study of the Linguistic Relations of English and Scandinavian.* Diss. Columbia. New York: Press of The New Era Printing Company.

________. 1913. Semological Notes on Old Scand. *flík* and Derived Forms in the Modern Scandinavian Dialects. *JEGP* 12, 78–92.

Florio, John. 1611. *Queen Anna's New World of Words.* London: Printed by Melch. Bradwood. Repr as CFR 105, 1968.

FML = Finn Magnusen, *Priscæ Veterum Borealium Mythologiae Lexicon....* Havniæ: Typis Jani H. Schultz, 1828.

Foerste, William. 1954. Die niederländischen und westniederdeutschen Bezeichnungen des Klees. In *Festschrift für Jost Trier zu seinem 60. Geburtstag am 15. Dezember 1954*, eds. Benno von Wiese and Karl H. Borck, pp. 395–416. Meisenheim/Glan: Westkulturverlag Anton Hain.

________. 1955. Westfaalse en Nederlandse expansie. Lezingen, gehouden voor de Dialecten-Commissie der Koninklijke Nederlandse Akademie van Wetenschappen op 27 October 1954 door Prof. Dr. W. Foerste en Prof. D. K. Heeroma, 1–38. BMDC 15.

________. 1964a. Schummeln. *NW* 4, 79.

________. 1964b. Bild. Ein etymologischer Versuch. In *Festschrift für Jost Trier zum 70. Geburstag*, eds. William Foerste and Karl H. Borck, pp. 112–45. Köln, Graz: Böhlau Verlag.

Förstemann, Ernst. 1900. *Altdeutsches Namenbuch*. Vol 1. 2nd ed. Bonn: P. Hanstein's Verlag.

Förster, Max. 1902. Frühmittelenglische und anglofranzösische Glossen aus Digby 172. *Archiv* 109, 314–37.

________. 1908. Beiträge zur altenglischen wortkunde aus ungedruckten volkskundlichen texten. *ESt* 39, 321–55.

________. 1917. Die altenglische glossenhandschrift Plantinus 32 (Antwerpen) und Additional 32246 (London). *Anglia* 41, 94–161.

________. 1941. *Der Flußname Themse und seine Sippe. Studien zur Anglisierung keltischer Eigennamen und zur Lautchronologie des Altbritischen.* SBAW 1941/1.

Fokkema, K. 1959. Over *veiling* en de etymologie van fri. *feil(j)e*. *TNTL* 77, 63–64.

Forby, Robert. 1830. *The Vocabulary of East Anglia....* London: Printed by and for J. B. Nichols and Son. Repr New York: A. M. Kelly, Newton Abbot: David and Charles, 1970. *See also* Rye, Walter.

Fordyce, C. J., ed. 1961. *Catullus*. Oxford University Press. Repr with corrections, 1978.

Fort, Marron C. 1971. De slangwoorden van Nederlandse afkomst in het Amerikaans. *HKZM* 25, 135–39.

Fossestøl, Bernt. *See* Elmevik, Lennart. 1984.

Fowler, H. W. 1965. *A Dictionary of Modern English Usage*. 2nd ed, by Ernest Gowers. Oxford: At the Clarendon Press. *See also* SOD.

Fraenkel, Ernst. 1953. Glück Heil. *Lexis* 3, 64–68. *See also* LEW.

Fraenkel, Meir. 1960. *Schmuh*. *Muttersprache* 70, 18–19.

________. 1966. Bemerkungen zu Lutz Mackensen: Deutsche Etymologie. *Sprachwart* 16, 87–89.

Franck, Johannes. 1883. [Rev of] *EWDS* (1883). *ZDA(A)* 11, 1–31.

________. 1893. *Notgedrungene Beiträge zur Etymologie. Eine Abrechnung mit Prof. Jan te Winkel.* Bonn: Verlag von Friedrich Cohen.

________. 1898. Eine Bemerkung über *nooit*. *TNTL* 17, 81–83.

________. 1910. *Mittelniederländische Grammatik mit Lesestücken und Glossar*, 2nd ed. Leipzig: Chr. Herm. Tauchnitz. *See also* EWNT.

Frank, Roberta. 1972. Some Uses of Paronomasia in Old English Scriptural Verse. *Speculum* 47, 207–26.

Frankis, P. G. 1960. A Middle English Crux *nere*, with a Note on Initial Consonant Mutation in English. *NM* 61, 373–87.

Fraser, W. 1853. A Cob-wall. *NQ* I/8, 279.

French, Walter H. *See* FH.

Friederici, Georg. 1947. *Amerikanistisches Wörterbuch*. HUA 53 (B:29).

Friedrich, Gustav, ed. 1908. *Catulli Veronensis Liber*. Leipzig and Berlin: Druck und Verlag von B. G. Teubner.

Friedrich, Johannes. *See* HW.

Friedrichsen, G. W. S. *See* ODEE, SOD, and COD5.

Friesen, Otto von. 1897. *Om de germanska mediageminatorna med särskild hänsyn till de nordiska språken*. UUÅ 2, 1897. Also published as Diss. Upsala. Upsala: Akademiska boktryckeriet Edv. Berling.

________. 1906. *Till den nordiska språkhistorien. Bidrag II.* Skr. Up(p)s. IX/6.

Friesinger, Herwig. *See* Steinhauser, Walter.

Frings, Theodor. 1943. Französisch und Fränkisch 4. Franz. *hache* = deutsch *Häpe, Hippe*. *ZRP* 63, 174–78. *See also* AHW.

Frings, Theodor, and Gertraud Müller. 1951. Das Wort *keusch*. In *Erbe der Vergangenheit. Germanistische Beiträge. Festgabe für Karl Helm zum 80. Geburtstage 19. Mai 1951*, 109–35. Tübingen: Max Niemeyer Verlag.

Frisk, Hjalmar. 1931. Griechische Wortdeutungen. *IF* 49, 97–104. *See also* GrEW.

Fritzner, Johan. 1883. Þing eðr þjóðarmál. *ANF* 1, 22–32. *See also* ODGNS.

Froehde, Friederich. 1886. Etymologien. *BB* 10, 294–301.

FT(G)* = Hjalmar Falk and Alf Torp, *Norwegisch-dänisches etymologisches Wörterbuch*. Heidelberg: Carl Winter's Universitätsbuchhandlung, 1910–11. Repr as 2nd ed by the same publisher in cooperation with Universitetsforlaget (Oslo, Bergen).

FT(N)* = Hjalmar Falk and Alf Torp, *Etymologisk ordbog over det norske og det danske*

* FT in the text means that the information in FT(G) and FT(N) coincides.

sprog. Kristiania: H. Aschehoug (W. Nygaard), 1903–06.

Funk, Charles E. *See* FW(NCSD)

Furness, Horace H., ed. 1877. *Hamlet*. Vol 1. NVES 3.

________., ed. 1880. *King Lear*. NVES 5.

________., ed. 1895. *The Merchant of Venice*. NVES 7.

________., ed. 1901. *Twelfth Night, Or, What You Will*. NVES 13.

Futrell, Allan W. *See* Maurer, David W.

FW = *A Standard Dictionary of the English Language*. New York, London and Toronto: Funk and Wagnalls Company, 1890. Repr regularly, later as Funk & Wagnalls *New "Standard" Dictionary of the English Language*.

FW(NCSD) = *Funk and Wagnalls New College Standard Dictionary*. Charles E. Funk, ed. New York: Funk & Wagnalls Company, 1947.

FW(SCD) = *Funk and Wagnalls Standard College Dictionary*. New York: Harcourt, Brace & World, Inc, 1963.

FWSD = Maria Leach, ed., *Funk and Wagnalls Standard Dictionary of Folklore, Mythology and Legend*. 2 vols. New York: Funk and Wagnalls Company, 1949–50.

Gabriel, Eugen. 1986. Allgäuische Einflüsse in der Sprachgeographie von Vorarlberg. *Jahrbuch des Vorarlberger Landesmuseumvereins Freunde der Landeskunde* (Bregenz), 151–82.

Gajek, Bernhard. *See* Hiersche, Rolf. 1984.

Gallée, Johan H. 1885. Uitzonderingen op de wet der klankverschuiving. In *Études archéologiques, linguistiques et historiques dédiées à Mr. le Dr. G. Leemans, à l'occasion du cinquantième anniversaire de sa nomination aux fonctions de Directeur du Musée archéologique de Pays-Bas*, 379–82. Leiden: E. J. Brill.

________. 1901. *Henne, hunne* en *hune* en hunne samenstellingen. *TNTL* 20, 46–58.

________. 1902. Nog eens *henne-hunne*. *TNTL* 21, 34–35.

Gamillscheg, Ernst. 1921. Französische Etymologien 4. *ZRP* 41, 631–47.

________. 1926. Germanisches im Französischen. In *Festschrift der Nationalbibliothek herausgegeben zur Feier des 200 jährigen Bestehens des Gebäudes*, 235–50. Wien: Druck und Verlag der Österreichischen Staatsdruckerei. Repr in: *Ausgewählte Aufsätze von Ernst Gamillscheg. Festschrift zu seinem 50. Geburtstage am 28. Oktober 1937*, 210–27. *ZFSL*. Supplementheft 15. Jena and Leipzig: Verlag von Wilhelm Gronau (W. Agricola), 1937.

________. 1927. Zur Methodik der etymologischen Forschung. *ZFSL 50*, 216–99. *See also* EWFS.

Gamkrelidze, Thomas V. *See* GI.

Garcia de Diego, Vicente. [1968]. *Diccionario de voces naturales*. Madrid: Aguilar.

________. 1985. *Diccionario etimológico español e hispánico*. Madrid: Espasa-Calpe, S.A.

Gardner, John D. 1871. Skedaddle. *NQ* IV/7, 351.

Garmonsway, G. N. *See* PED.

Garrison, Webb B. [1955]. *Why You Say It*. New York, Nashville: Abingdon Press.

Garrod, H. W. 1914. Salapantivm disertvm. *CQ* 8, 48–49.

Gazophylacium Anglicanum. 1689. London: Printed by E. H. and W. H. Repr as CFR 166, 1969.

Gebhardt, August. 1911. [Rev of] FT(G). *DLZ* 32, 1890–97.

Gendre, Renato. *See* Bonfante, Giuliano.

George. 1887. More Vulgar Words and Phrases. *(W)AMB* 12, 91–95.

Georgiev, Vladimir. 1953. Tri slova, oboznachaiushchie "topor," i nedostatki sravnitel'no-istoricheskogo metoda [Three Words for 'Ax' and Some Drawbacks of the Comparative Method]. With a summary in French. *LP* 4, 109–10.

Gepp, Edward. [1920]. *A Contribution to an Essex Dialect Dictionary*. London: George Routledge & Sons, Ltd.

________. 1922. A German Professor on our Dialect. *ER* 31, 105–08.

________. 1923. *An Essex Dialect Dictionary*. London: George Routledge & Sons, Ltd., New York: E. P. Dutton & Co.

Gering, Hugo. 1920. [Rev of] Feilberg, H. F. 1886–1914. *ZDP* 48, 291–315.

________. 1927. *Kommentar zu den Liedern der Edda*, posthumous ed by B. Sijmons. GH VII/3, Part 1.

Gerland, Georg. 1861. Hüne, Haune. *KZ* 10, 275–88.

________. 1869a. Bauernwenzel, ziegenpeter, mums. *ZDP 1*, 309–12.

________. 1869b. *Intensiva und Iterativa und ihr Verhältnis zu einander. Eine sprachwiszenschaftliche* [sic] *Abhandlung*. Leipzig: Verlag von Friedrich Fleischer.

Gerson, Stanley. 1983. *Cockney* As a Term of Abuse. *MS* 77, 1–12.

Gervasi, Teresa. *See* Scardigli, Piergiuseppe, and Teresa Gervasi.

GEW = Ferdinand Holthausen, *Gotisches etymologisches Wörterbuch. Mit Einschluß der Eigennamen und der Lehnwörter im Romanischen.* GB I/8, 1934.

GI = Gamkrelidze, T. V., and Viach. Vs. Ivanov. 1984. *Indoevropeiskii iazyk i indoevropeitsy. Rekonstruktsiia i istoriko-tipologicheskii analiz praiazyka i protokul'tury.* 2 vols. Tbilisi: Izdatel'stvo Tbilisskogo universiteta. English translation by Johanna Nichols, Thomas V. Gamkrelidze, and Vjačeslav V. Ivanov, *Indo-European and the Indo-Europeans: A Reconstruction and Historical Analysis of a Proto-Language and a Proto-Culture.* 2 vols. TLSM 8, 1995.

Gibbens, V. E. 1955. Shifts in Gender and Meaning of Nouns Designating the Sexes. *AS* 30, 296–98.

Ginneken, Jacob van. *See* Van Ginneken, Jacob.

Glatthaar, Michael. *See* Mordek, Hubert, and Michael Glatthaar.

Glendinning, Robert J. *See* Hale, Christopher S.

Glendinning, Victoria. 1998. *Jonathan Swift.* London: Hutchinson.

Glenvarloch. 1892. Good Old (or New?) Etymologies. *ANQ* 8, 230.

G.L.G. 1883. Caterways. *NQ* VI/7, 354.

Gneuss, Helmut. 1999. Zur Etymologie von englisch *under.* In *Grippe, Kamm und Eulenspiegel. Festschrift für Elmar Seebold zum 65. Geburtstag,* 105–24. Berlin, New York: Walter de Gruyter.

Goblirsch, Kurt G. *See* Vennemann, Theo. 1997.

Godefroy, Frédéric. 1880–1902. *Dictionnaire de l'ancienne langue française et de tous ses dialectes du IXe au XVe siècle....* Paris: F. Vieweg.

Godfrey, Rafaela. 1939. 'Toadstool': Derivation. *NQ* 176, 226.

Goedel, Gustav. 1902. *Etymologisches Wörterbuch der deutschen Seemannssprache.* Kiel, Leipzig: Verlag von Lipsius & Tischer.

Görlach, Manfred. 1996. Relic Words As Tools for Linguistic Geography. In *Speech Past and Present: Studies in English Dialectology in Memory of Ossi Iholainen,* 72–79. Juhani Klemola, Merja Kytö, and Matti Rissanen, eds. Frankfurt am Main, *etc.*: Peter Lang.

Goetz, Dieter. 1971. *Studien zu den verdunkelten Komposita im Englischen.* EB 40.

Götze, Alfred. 1921. Review of EWDS[9]. *ZDP* 49, 282–89.

See also EWDS[11].

Gold, David L. 1984 [Rev of] F. Mish et al, eds, *Webster's Ninth New Collegiate Dictionary.* Springfield, MA: Merriam-Webster, Inc., 1983. *Dictionaries* 6, 200–35.

________. 1985. [Rev of] Poetto, 1984. *JLR* 5, 315–18.

________. 1989. On the Supposed Yiddish Origin of the English noun *gozump.* (With an Appendix on Other Words of Yiddish or Supposed Yiddish Origin). *JLS* 1, 26–34.

________. 1990a. Fiction or Medieval Philology. [Rev of Mozeson, Isaac E. 1989.] *JLS* 2, 105–33.

________. 1990b. Some Yiddish, Judezmo, and Hebrew Children's Counting-Out Rimes in their European Context and Evidence Against the Suggestion that the First Line of the English Children's Counting-Out Rime *eena meena mina mo* May Be of São Tomense Origin. *JLS* 2, 84–104.

________. 1990c. Untitled [=316/5–21]. *JLS* 2, 524–25.

________. 1992. On the Fourth Edition of *A Dictionary of South African English. Lexicos* 2 (Afrilex-Reeks/Series 2), 85–136.

________. 1995a. A Contribution to Semantics, Etymology, and Anthropology: The Lexical Pairing of Sexuality and Food, with Examples from Afrikaans, Chinese, Dutch, English, French, High German, Hungarian, Japanese, Latin, Polish, Spanish, Yiddish, and Possibly Italian. *SAJL/SATT* 13, 128–30.

________. 1995b. When Religion Intrudes into Etymology (On *The Word: The Dictionary That Reveals the Hebrew Source of English*). In *Cultures, Ideologies, and the Dictionary: Studies in Honor of Ladislav Zgusta,* eds. Braj B. Kachru and Henry Kahane, pp. 369–80. Tübingen: Max Niemeyer.

________. (forthcoming). A Hitherto Unrecognized Non-Jewish Family of Words Going Back in One Way or Another to Hebrew *chaver:* Australian English *cobber,* European Dutch *gabber,* New Zealand English *cobber,* Rotwelsch *Cabber* ~ *Kabber,* San *gaba,* South African *chabba* ~ *gabba* ~ *gubba,* and Spanish *háber.* In his *Studies in Etymology and Etiology (With Emphasis on Germanic, Jewish,*

Romance, and Slavic Languages). Selected and edited, with a foreword, by Félix R. González and Antonio L. Buades.

Goldberger, Walter. 1930. Kraftausdrücke im Vulgärlatein. *Glotta* 18, 8–65.

________. 1932. Kraftausdrücke im Vulgärlatein. *Glotta* 20, 101–50.

Goldschmidt, Moritz. 1887. *Zur Kritik der altgermanischen Elemente im Spanischen.* Diss. Bonn. Lingen: Druck von J. L. v. d. Velde Veldemann.

Gollancz, Israel. 1898. *Hamlet in Iceland....* London: David Nutt.

Gonda, Jan. 1943. Indonesische lasvormen. *BTLV* 102, 371–440.

________. 1956. 'Streckformen' in Greek. *Mnemosyne* IV/9, 134–35.

Gonzalez, Félix R. *See* Gold, David L., forthcoming.

Goodrich, Chauncey A. *See* Webster, Noah. 1847 and 1864.

Gore, Willard C. 1993. Student Slang. *CoE* XXII/7, 1–47. Repr in Cohen, Gerald L., 1997, 1–50.

Gotti, Maurizio. 1999. *The Language of Thieves and Vagabonds: 17th and 18th Century Canting Lexicography in England.* Lexicographica. Series Maior 94. Tübingen: Niemeyer.

Gottlieb, Eugene. 1931. *A Systematic Tabulation of Indo-European Animal Names.* LD 8.

Gottlund, Carl A. 1853. *Försök att förklara de finska stamordens uppkomst.* Diss. Kejserl. Alexanders Universitet. Helsingfors: Frenckell & Son.

Gottschald, Max. 1954. *Deutsche Namenkunde. Unsere Familiennamen nach ihrer Entstehung und Bedeutung.* 3rd ed. Berlin: Walter de Gruyter; 4th ed, by Rudolf Schützeichel, 1971.

Gould, Chester N. 1929. Dwarf-Names: A Study in Old Icelandic Religion. *PMLA* 44, 939–67.

Gove, Philip B. *See* Webster, Noah. 1961.

Gowers, Ernest. *See* Fowler, H. W. 1965.

G.P. 1885–86. Faggot As a Term of Reproach. *WA* 5, 106.

GPC = *Geiriadur Prifysgol Cymru. A Dictionary of the Welsh Language.* Caerdydd: Gwasg Prifysgol Cymru, [1950]–.

Gradl, Heinrich. 1870. Zur kunde deutscher mundarten. *KZ* 19, 125–30.

Graff, Eberhard G. 1834–46. *Althochdeutscher Sprachschatz....* Beim Verfasser und in commission der Nikolaischen Buchhandlung. Berlin, Darmstadt: Wissenschaftliche Buchgesellschaft. Repr Hildesheim: Georg Olms Verlagsbuchhandlung, 1963.

Graham, William. 1843. *Exercises on Etymology.* Edinburgh: Publ by William and Robert Chambers.

Grant, William. *See* SND.

Graßmann, Hermann. 1863a. Über die aspiraten und ihr gleichzeitiges vorhandensein im an- und auslaute der wurzel. *KZ* 12, 81–110.

________. 1863b. Über das ursprüngliche vorhandensein von wurzeln, deren anlaut und auslaut eine aspirate enthielt. *KZ* 12, 110–38.

Grau, Gustav. 1908. *Quellen und Verwandtschaften der älteren germanischen Darstellungen des Jüngsten Gerichts.* SEP 31.

Gray, Louis H. 1930. Indo-European Comparative Linguistics As an Aid to Romance Etymology. In *Todd Memorial Volumes: Philological Studies* 1, 185–99. New York: Columbia University Press.

Green, J. Hanson. 1906. A Handful of Derivations. *TYDS* I/7, 25–42.

Greene, David. 1992. [Indo-European Numerals:] Celtic. In *Indo-European Numerals*, ed. Jadranka Gvozdanović, TLSM 57, 497–554.

Greenough, James B., and George L. Kittredge. 1901. *Words and their Ways in English Speech.* New York: The Macmillan Co. Repr Boston: Beacon Press, [1962].

Greenway, Edward. *See* EG.

Grein, C. W. M. 1912. *Sprachschatz der angelsächsischen Dichter.* New ed by J. J. Köhler, in collaboration with F. Holthausen. GB I/4/4.

Greppin, John A.C. 1983. "An Etymological Dictionary of the Indo-European Components of Armenian." *Bazunavep* 141, 234–323.

________. 1997. A Note on the Etymology of English Horehound. In *Studies in Honor of Jaan Puhvel. Part One: Ancient Languages and Philology*, eds. Dorothy Disterheft, Martin Huld, and John Greppin. JIES-MS 20, 71–74 .

GrEW = Hjalmar Frisk, *Griechisches etymologisches Wörterbuch.* IB II, 1960–66.

Grienberger, Theodor von. 1900. *Untersuchungen zur gotischen Wortkunde.* SÖAW 142/8.

________. 1913. [Rev of] Schönfeld, Moritz. 1911. *IF(A) 32*, 42–54.

Griffith, R. H. 1939. Phenagling. *MLN* 54, 291–92.

Grimm, Jacob. 1822–37. *Deutsche Grammatik*, 2nd ed. Göttingen: Dietrichsche Buchhandlung 3rd ed: 1890.

________. 1835. *Deutsche Mythologie*. Göttingen: Dietrichsche Buchhandlung. Repr Frankfurt am Main: Keip Verlag, 1985; 2nd ed: 1844; 4th ed, by Elard H. Meyer. Gütersloh: G. Bertelsmann (and other publishers), 1875–78. (Engl, transl *Teutonic Mythology* by James S. Stallybrass. London: W. Swan Sonnenschein & Allen, 1880; repr London: Routledge-Thoemmes Press, 1999).

________. 1848. *Geschichte der deutschen Sprache*. Leipzig: Verlag von S. Hirzel. 3rd ed: 1868.

________. 1865. Über Marcellus Burdigalensis. In *KSchr* II: 114–51. First publ in 1847.

________. 1875 – 78. *See* Grimm, Jacob. 1835.

________. 1890. *See* Grimm, Jacob, 1822–37, 3rd ed.

________. 1966. Über diphthonge nach weggefallnen consonanten. In *KSchr*, 103–70. First presented in 1845.

________. 1983. *Deutsche Rechtsaltertümer*. Darmstadt: Wissenschaftliche Buchgesellschaft. A reprint of the 1955 ed (Wiesbaden: Dieterich'sche Verlagsbuchhandlung), which reproduces the 4th ed by Andreas Heusler and Rudolf Hübner. First publ 1828.
See also DW *and* KSchr.

Grimm, Wilhelm. 1848. Wiesbader Glossen. *ZDA* 6, 321–40.
See also DW.

Grinda, Klaus. *See* Terasawa, Yoshio.

Grindon, Leo H. 1883. *The Shakspere Flora: A Guide to All the Principal Passages in Which Mention Is Made of Trees, Plants, Flowers, and Vegetable Production; with Comments and Botanical Particulars.* Manchester: Palmer & Howe, London: Simpkin, Marshall, & Co.

Gröber, G. 1886. Vulgärlateinische Substrate romanischer Wörter. *ALL* 3, 507–34.

Gröger, Otto. 1911. *Die althochdeutschen und altsächsischen Kompositionsfuge mit Verzeichnis der althochdeutschen und altsächsischen Composita.* AGDSZ 11.

Grootaers, L. 1954. *Veil* 'klimop' in Zuid-Nederland. *TT* 6, 89–93.

Grose, Francis. 1785. *A Classical Dictionary of the Vulgar Tongue*. London: Printed for S. Hooper. Repr as CFR 80, 1968. 4th ed: *Lexicon Balatronicum. A Dictionary of Buckish Slang, University Wit, and Pickpocket Eloquence.* London: Printed for C. Chappel, 1811.

Grosse, Rudolf. *See* AHW.

Grot, Ia. K. 1899. O nazvaniiakh aista v Rossii. In *Trudy Ia. K. Grota. Filologicheskie razyskaniia* 2 (1852–1892). Sankt-Peterburg: Tipografiia Ministerstva putei soobshcheniia.

Groth, Christian E. P. 1922. Curmudgeon. *NQ* XII/11, 191.

Grube, F. W. 1934. Cereal Foods of the Anglo-Saxons. *PQ* 13, 140–58.

Grundy, Lynn. *See* TOE.

Grzega, Joachim. *See* Bammesberger, Alfred, and Joachim Grzega. 2001.

Gülzow, Erich. 1938. Katschüse. *KVNS* 51, 7.

________. 1943–49. Katschüse. *KVNS* 56, 56.

________. 1950. Katschüse. *KVNS* 57, 29.

Güntert, Hermann. 1915. *Eine etymologische Deutung von griech. ἄνθρωπος*. SHAW 1915/10. Heidelberg: Carl Winter.

________. 1919. *Kalypso. Bedeutungsgeschichtliche Untersuchungen auf dem Gebiet der indogermanischen Sprachen.* Halle a. S.: Verlag von Max Niemeyer.

________. 1928. Weiteres zum Begriff "Winkel" im ursprünglichen Denken. *WuS* 11, 124–42.

________. 1930. Zur Frage nach der Urheimat der Indogermanen. In *Deutschkundliches. Friedrich Panzer zum 60. Geburtstage, überreicht von Heidelberger Fachgenossen.* Hans Teske, ed. BNL. NF 16, 1–33.

________. 1932. *Labyrinth. Eine sprachwissenschaftliche Untersuchung*. SHAW 23/1.

Guiraud, Pierre. 1982. *Dictionnaire des étymologies obscures.* Paris: Payot.

Gunnell, Terry. 2001. *Hof*, Halls, *Goðar* and Dwarves: An Examination of the Ritual Space in the Pagan Icelandic Hall. *Cosmos* 17, 3–36.

________. 2003. *Höf, höll, goð* (*a*-) and *dvergar*: Ritual Space in the Pagan Icelandic *Skáli*. In *Scandinavia and Christian Europe in the Middle Ages: Papers of the 12th International Saga Conference*, eds. Rudolf Simmek and Judith Meurer, Bonn/Germany, 28th July–2nd August 2003, 187–97. Bonn: Hausdruckerei der Universität Bonn.

Guralnik, David B. *See* WNWD[2, 3].

Gusmani, Roberto. 1972. Anglo-sassone *myltestre* "meretrix." *SG* 10, 157–67.

Gutenbrunner, Siegfried. 1955. Eddastudien 1. Über die Zwerge in der Völospa Str. 9–13. *ANF* 70, 61–75.

Gvozdanović, Jadranka. *See* Greene, David.

G.W. 1850. Haviour, Haver, Hyfr. *NQ* I/1, 342.

Gysseling, Maurits. 1987. Substratwörter in den germanischen Sprachen. *NOWELE* 10, 47–62.

Haeringen, C. B. van. *See* Van Haeringen, C.B., *and* EWNT.

Haeserijn, R. 1954. Bijnamen in de oudste rekening van Aardenburg a[0] 1309–1310. *VMKVATL* 109–74.

Hagen A. *See* Weijnen, Antonius A. 1965.

Haigh, Walter E. 1928. *A New Glossary of the Dialect of the Huddersfield District.* Oxford: Oxford University Press; London: Humphrey Milford.

Haldeman, Samuel S. 1872. *Pennsylvania Dutch: A Dialect of South German with an Infusion of English.* Philadelphia: Reformed Church Publication Board.

Hale, Charles, B. *See* FH.

Hale, Christopher S. 1983. The River Names in *Grímnismál* 27–29. In *Edda: A Collection of Essays*, eds. Robert J. Glendinning and Haraldur Bessason, UMIS 4, 165–86.

Hales, John W. 1875. [Rev of] Alexander Schmidt, *Shakespeare-Lexicon: A Complete Dictionary of All the English Words, Phrases and Constructions in Works of the Poet.* Vol 1: A–L. Berlin: Georg Reimer, London: Williams & Norgate, 1874. *The Academy* 7, 286–87. Repr in: Hales, John W. 1884a, 174–78.

________. 1884a. *Notes and Essays on Shakespeare.* London: G. Bell and Sons.

________. 1884b. "Yet" in Wordsworth. *The Athenæum*/I, 98.

________. 1891. Cock's Eggs. *The Academy* 39, 91.

Hall, A. 1890. Rabbit : Riot. *NQ* VII/10, 230–31.

________. 1894. Celtic Numerals. *Antiquary* 29, 87–88.

________. 1904. The Word "lad." *The Academy* 67, 346.

________. 1906. German Etymology. *The Academy* 70, 604–05.

Hall, James. 1898 (publ 1899). The Field-Name Slang. *CS* III/2, 36.

Hall, Joan H. *See* DARE.

Hall, J. R. Clark. 1984. *A Concise Anglo-Saxon Dictionary.* 4th ed, with a supplement, by Herbert D. Meritt. MART 14.

Halliwell, James O. 1855. *A Dictionary of Archaic and Provincial Words....* London: Thomas and William Boone. Repr New York: AMS Press, 1973.

See also Nares, Robert. 1822.

Hamp, Eric P. 1971–73. Lykill ~ nykill. *APS* 29, 163.

________. 1974. 'Ivy' in Italic and Celtic. *JIES* 2, 87–93.

________. 1981. Two Young Animals. *PLi* 24, 39–43.

________. 1984. On Criteria for Northwest Germanic. *LP* 27, 7–11.

________. 1985. Old English *Bēacon* 'beacon,' *Beckon*, etc. *CoE* XV/5–6, 9–10.

________. 1986a. *Culwch*, the Swine. *Zeitschrift für Celtische Philologie* 41, 257–58.

________. 1986b. German *Baum*, English *Beam.* In *Linguistics across Historical and Geographical Boundaries: In Honour of Jacek Fisiak on the Occasion of his Fiftieth Birthday.* Vol 1: *Linguistic Theory and Historical Linguistics*, eds. Dieter Kastovsky and Aleksander Szwedek, pp. 345–46. Berlin, New York, Amsterdam: Mouton de Gruyter.

________. 1988a. Footnote to "On Criteria for Northwest Germanic." *LP* 31, 45.

________. 1988b. The Indo-European Terms for "Marriage." In *Languages and Cultures: Studies in Honor of Edgar C. Polomé*, eds. Mohammad A. Jazayery and Werner Winter, pp. 179–82. Berlin, New York, Amsterdam: Mouton de Gruyter.

________. 1989. On Some Celtic Bird Names. *ZCP* 43, 196–98.

________. 1994. English *Elk. NOWELE* 24, 47–48.

Hanley, Louise. *See* Thornton, Richard H. 1912–1939.

Harbert, Wayne. *See* Ivanov, Vyacheslav V. 1999a. *and* Liberman, Anatoly. 1999.

Hargrave, Basil. 1925. *Origins and Meanings of Popular Phrases and Names....* London: T. Werner Laurie Ltd. Repr Book Tower, Detroit: Gales Research Company, 1968. First publ 1911.

Harm, Volker. 2003. Zur semantischen Vorgeschichte von dt. *Verstehen*, e. *understand* und agr. *ἐπίσταμαι. HS* 116, 108–27.

Harris, W. T. *See* Webster, Noah. 1909.

Harrison, Henry. 1912. *Surnames of the United Kingdom: A Concise Etymological Dictionary.* London: The Eaton Press.

Harrison, W. A. 1880–82. Hamlet's Juice of Cursed Hebona. *NSST,* 295–321.

Hart, J. M. 1892. The Anglo-Saxon *gīen, gīena. MLN* 7, 61–62.

Hauch, Karl. *See* Kuhn, Hans. 1952.

Haupt, Karl J. T. 1870. *Alvil des Sachsenspiegels und seine Verwandten. Ein Beitrag zur vergleichenden Mythologie.* Separat-Abdruck aus dem 47. Bande des *Neuen Lausitsischen Magazins.* Liegnitz: Max Cohn (formerly H. Krumbhaar).

Haupt, Moritz. 1848. Altvil. *ZDA* 6, 400.

Haupt, Paul. 1889–90. Ergebnisse einer erneuten Collation der Izdubar-Legenden. *BAVSS* 1, 94–150.

________. 1906. Some Germanic Etymologies. *AJP* 27, 154–65.

Hauschild, Oskar. 1899–1900. Die Bedeutung der Assonanz und des Ablautes für die Wortbildung im Niederdeutschen. *KVNS* 21, 3–9.

Hawes, Donald. 1974. David Copperfield's Names. *The Dickensian* 74, 81–87.

Hayward, Arthur C. *See* Anonymous, 1894.

H.B.F. 1872. Hobbledehoy. *NQ* IV/9, 147–48.

H.C.C. 1853. Derivation of "lad" and "lass." *NQ* I/7, 256–57.

H.C.K. 1858. Difficulties of Chaucer. *NQ* II/5, 511–12.

HDA = Hanns Bächtold-Stäubli, ed, with the special assistance of E. Hoffmann-Krayer, *Handwörterbuch des deutschen Aberglaubens.* Vol 2. Berlin and Leipzig: Walter de Gruyter & Co., 1927–42.

HDGFU = Keith Spalding, *An Historical Dictionary of German Figurative Usage.* Oxford: Basil Blackwell, 1952– .

Healey, Antonette di Paolo. *See* DOE.

HED = Jaan Puhvel, *Hittite Etymological Dictionary.* Berlin, New York, Amsterdam: Mouton Publishers, 1984– .

Heeroma, K. 1937. Aantekeningen bij dialektkaartjes. *TNTL* 56, 241–65.

________. 1941–42. Etymologische aantekeningen. *TNTL* 61, 45–77, 81–117.

________. 1949. De taalgeschiedenis van het oosten. *DB* 1 (N. S.), 21–32.

Heestermans, Hans. *See* ErW.

Hehn, Victor. 1894. *Kulturpflanzen und Haustiere in ihrem Übergang aus Asien nach Griechenland und Italien sowie in das übrige Europa. Historisch-linguistische Skizzen.* 6th ed, by Oskar Schrader and notes on botany by A. Engler. Berlin: Gebrüder Borntraeger, Ed. Eggers. (Engl transl of the 1885 ed: *The Wanderings of Plants and Animals from their First Home,* ed. by James S. Sonnenschein, repr in 1891 as a cheap edition under the title *Cultivated Plants and Domesticated Animals in their Migration from Asia to Europe: Historico-linguistic Studies.* London: Stallybrass, 1885. Repr as ASTHLS: ACL I/7, 1976 and 2003, with a bio-bibliographical account of Hehn and a survey of the research in Indo-European prehistory by James P. Mallory.)

Heidermanns, Frank. 1993. *Etymologisches Wörterbuch der germanischen Primäradjektive.* SLG 33.

Heinertz, N. Otto. 1927. *Etymologische Studien zum Althochdeutschen.* Skr. Lund 7.

Heizmann, Wilhelm. *See* Liberman, Anatoly. 2002c.

Heliand und Genesis, ed. by Otto Behaghel. 7th ed, by Walter Mitzka. ABibl 4.

Heller, Karin. *See* Schmidt, Klaus T., and Klaus Strunk.

Hellquist, Elof. 1891. Bidrag till läran om den nordiska nominalbildningen. *ANF* 7, 7–62, 142–74.

________. 1903–04. Några bidrag till nordisk språkhistoria. *NTF* III/12, 49–70.

________. 1912. Fornsvensk tillnamn. In *Xenia Lideniana. Festskrift tillägnad Professor Evald Lidén på hans femtiårsdag den 3 october 1912,* 84–114. Stockholm: P. A. Norstedt & Söners förlag.

________. 1915. Ett par fågelnamn. *SoS* 15, 144–51.

________. 1929–30. *Det svenska ordförrådets ålder och ursprung.* Lund: C. W. K. Gleerups förlag. *See also* SEO.

Helm, G. L. van den. *See* Van den Helm, G. L.

Helm, Karl. 1903. [Rev of] *Germanistische Abhandlungen. Hermann Paul zum 17. März 1902 dargebracht. HBV* 2, 82–85.

________. 1905. Germanisch **hūniz* 'schwarz.' *PBB* 30, 328–33.

Helten, W. L. van. *See* Van Helten, W. L.

Helvigius, Andreæ. 1620. *Origines dictionvm germanicarvm, ex tribvs illis nobililus atiquitatis erudiæ Linguis, Latina, Græca, Hebræa, derivatarvm.* Hanoviæ: Impensis Conradi Eifridi.

Hempl, George. 1889. The Etymology of O. E. *ǽbre, ǽfre*, E. *ever*. *MLN* 4, 209.
_______. 1891. The Etymology of "yet," O. E. "gíet." *The Academy* 40, 564.
_______. 1892a. The Anglo-Saxon *gīen(a), gī et(a)*. *MLN* 7, 1892, 123–25.
_______. 1892b. "Ever" and "yet." *The Academy* 41, 472.
_______. 1899. The Semasiology of *ἐπίσταμαι, verstehen, understand, unterstehen, gestehen, unternehmen, undertake*, etc. *MLN* 14, 233–34.
_______. 1901. Etymologies. *AJP* 22, 426–31.
Henke, James T. 1979. *Courtesans and Cuckolds: A Glossary of Renaissance Dramatic Bawdy (Exclusive of Shakespeare)*. New York and London: Garland Publishing, Inc.
Henne, Helmut. *See* Paul, Hermann. 1897, 6th ed.
Henrion, Pierre. 1962. *Jonathan Swift Confesses: 1. Gulliver's Secret / Jonathan Swift Avoue: 1. Le secret de Gulliver*. Versailles: Published by the author.
Henry, Victor. 1900. *Lexique étymologique des termes les plus usuels du Breton Moderne*. BBA 3.
Henzen, Walter. 1965. *Deutsche Wortbildung*. SKGGD B/5. Tübingen: Max Niemeyer.
Herbermann, Clemens-Peter. 1974. *Etymologie und Wortgeschichte. Die indogermanische Sippe des Verbums* strotzen. MBG 45.
Herescu, N. J. 1959–60. Sur le sens "érotique" de sedere. *Glotta* 38, 125–34.
Hermann, Eduard. 1918. Sachliches und Sprachliches zur indogermanischen Großfamilie. NAWG, 204–32.
Hermodsson, Lars. 1990. Pflanzennamen und verschollenes Wortgut. Zur Deutung von *Himbeere, Hirschbeere, Hindläufte, Hindlaub*. *SN* 62, 79–84.
_______. 1991. Deutsche etymologische Lexikographie aus West und Ost. *SN* 63, 223–33.
Herrtage, Sidney J. H., ed. 1872. *Catholicon Anglicum, An English-Latin Wordbook Dated 1483*. CSP, N. S. 30.
See also Tusser, Thomas.
Hester, D. H. 1964–65. Pelasgian—A New Indo-European Language? *Lingua* 13, 335–89.
Hettema, M. de Haan. 1856. Hints on the Thesis "The Old-Friesic above All Others the *Fons et Origo* of the Old-English." *TPS* 1856, 196–215.
Hettrich, Heinrich. *See* Rix, Helmut. 1995.
Heukels, H. 1987. *Woordenboek der Nederlandsche volksnamen von planten*, ed, with an introduction, by H. J. T. M. Brok, and Heukel's biography by P. Smit. Utrecht: Koninklijke Nederlandse Natuurhistorische Vereniging.
Heusler, Andreas. *See* Grimm, Jacob. 1983.
H.E.W. 1883. Caterways : Catering. *NQ* VI/7, 476.
Hewett, W.T. 1884. [Rev of] EWDS². *AJP* 5, 243–5.
Hexham, Hendrik. 1678. *Dictionarium, ofte, Woorden-Boeck, Begrijpende den Schat der Nederlandsche Tale, met de Engelsche Uytlegginge....* Ed. by Daniel Manly. Tot Rotterdam: By de Weduwe van Arnout Leers.
Heyne, Moritz. 1899. *Fünf Bücher deutscher Hausaltertümer von den ältesten geschichtlichen Zeiten bis zum 16. Jahrhundert. 1. Wohnung—Das deutsche Wohnungswesen*. Leipzig: Verlag von S. Hirzel.
_______. 1908. *Das altdeutsche Handwerk*. Straßburg: Karl J. Trübner.
HF = Horst H. Munske, ed., *Handbuch des Friesischen / Handbook of Frisian Studies*. Tübingen: Max Niemeyer Verlag, 2001.
Hibbard, G.R. 1977. Ben Jonson's Use of "Pimp." *NQ* 222, 522.
Hibyskwe. 1885–86. *Faggot* As a Term of Reproach. *WA* 5, 85.
Hickes, George. 1703–05. *Linguarum Vett*. 2 vols. Oxoniæ: E Theatro Sheldoniano. Repr as CFR 248, 1970.
Hiersche, Rolf. 1984. Indoarisch-germanische Isoglossen und die Ausgliederung des Germanischen. In *Studia Linguistica et Philologica. Festschrift für Klaus Matzel zum sechzigsten Geburtstag, überreicht von Schülern, Freunden und Kollegen*, eds. Hans-Werner Eroms, Bernhard Gajek, and Herbert Kolb. Heidelberg: Carl Winter.
_______. 1986–. *Deutsches etymologisches Wörterbuch*. Heidelberg: Carl Winter. Universitätsverlag.
High, Ellesa C. *See* Maurer, David W.
Hildebrand, Rudolf. *See* Weiske, Julius, ed, 5th ed.
Hill, David, and Sheila Sharp. 1997. An Anglo-Saxon Beacon System. In *Names, Places and People: An Onomastic Miscellany in Memory of John McNeal Dodgson*, eds. Alexander R. Rumble and A. D. Mills, pp. 157–65. Stamford: Paul Watkins.

Hills, A. C. 1945. Jeep. *NQ* 188, 87.

Hilmer, Hermann. 1914. *Schallnachahmung, Wortschöpfung und Bedeutungswandel. Auf Grundlage der Wahrnehmungen von Schlag, Fall, Bruch und derartigen Vorgängen dargestellt an einigen Lautwurzeln der deutschen und der englischen Sprache.* Halle a. S.: Verlag von Max Niemeyer.

________. 1918. The Origin and Growth of Language. *JEGP* 17, 21–60.

Hines, Carole P. *See* Stanley, Julia.

Hintner, Val. 1874. Worterklärungen. *ZDP* 5, 66–69.

Hirt, Herman. 1921. *Etymologie der neuhochdeutschen Sprache.* Handbuch des deutschen Unterrichts IV/2. München: C. H. Beck'sche Verlagsbuchhandlung. Repr 1968.

________. 1927. *Indogermanische Grammatik* 1. SILH I/1.

See also WHirt *and* Weigand, Friedrich L. K.

Hixson, Jerome C., and J. Colodny. 1939. *Word Ways: A Study of Our Living Language.* New York, *etc*: American Book Company. Repr 1946.

HL = Wilhelm Horn, *Laut und Leben*, ed. by Martin Lehnert. Berlin: Deutscher Verlag der Wissenschaften, 1954.

Hoad, T. F. 1986. *The Concise Oxford Dictionary of English Etymology.* Oxford: At the Clarendon Press.

Hock, Hans Heinrich. *See* Abaev, V. I.

Höfer, Albert. 1870a. *Altvile im Sachsenspiegel.* Halle: Verlag der Buchhandlung des Waisenhauses.

________. 1870b. Zur Laut-, Wort- und Namenforschung. *Germania* 15, 411–19.

________. 1873. Nochmals Altvile im Sachsenspiegel. *Germania* 18, 29–34.

Höfer, Matthias. 1815. *Etymologisches Wörterbuch der in Oberdeutschland, vorzüglich aber der in Oesterreich üblichen Mundart.* Linz: Gedruckt bey Joseph Kastner.

Höfler, Otto. 1934. *Kultische Geheimbünde der Germanen.* Vol. 1. Frankfurt am Main: Moritz Diesterweg. (No more published.)

Hoekstra, Erik. 2001. Frisian Relics in the Dutch Dialects. HF, 138–42.

Hoenigswald, Henry M. *See* Dyen, Isidore. 1970.

Hoeufft, J. H. 1835. Taalkundige Aanteekeningen 3. *TM* 1, 291–303.

Hofmann, Dietrich. 1961. *Die k-Diminutiva im Nordfriesischen und in Verwandten Sprachen.* NS 7.

________. 1984. Das altfriesiche Wortpaar *flêta* und *fleia/fleina* 'wegschaffen, beiseite schaffen.' In *Miscellanea Frisica: In nije bondel Fryske stúdzjes, een nieuwe bundel Friese studies, a new collection of Frisian studies.* [Bundel aangeboden aan Prof. dr. H. T. J. Miedema ter gelegenheid van zijn pensionering als bijzonder hooglerar Friese taal- en letterkunde aan de Rijksuniversiteit te Utrecht], eds. N. R. Århammar et al, pp. 79–87. Assen: Van Gorcum.

See also AfW, *and* Kuhn, Hans. 1969–78.

Hofmann, Erich. *See* LEW.

Hofmann, Johann. B. 1950. *Etymologisches Wörterbuch des Griechischen.* München: Verlag von R. Oldenbourg.

See also WH.

Hoffmann-Krayer, E. *See* HDA 2.

Hogenhout-Mulder, Maaike. *See* NEW.

Hogg, Richard M. 1979. Old English Palatalization. *TPS*, 89–113.

Holbrooke, George O. 1910. *Âryan Word-Building.* New York: The Knickerbocker Press.

Holder, Alfred. 1896. *Alt-celtischer Sprachschatz.* Vol 1. Leipzig: B. G. Teubner. Repr Graz: Akademische Druck- und Verlaganstalt, 1961.

Holloway, William. 1838. *A General Dictionary of Provincialisms...* Lewes: Sussex Press; Baxter and Son.

Holly. 1898 (publ 1899). The Meaning of the Word 'Slang' in Field Names. *CS* III/2, 21–22.

Holm, Gösta. 1993. Etymologiska metoder. In *Studier i svensk språkhistoria 3. Förhandlingar vid Tredje Sammankomsten för svenska språkets historia, Uppsala 15–17 oktober 1992*, ed. Lars Wollin, pp. 109–20. SINS 34. Uppsala: Institutionen för nordiska språk vid Uppsala universitet.

Holmboe, Chr. Andr. 1852. *Det norske Sprogs væsentligste Ordforraad sammenlignet med Sanskrit og andre Sprog af samme Æt. Bidrag til en norsk etymologisk Ordbog.* Wien: Trykt i det keiserlig-kongelige Hof- og Stats-Trykkerie.

Holthausen, Ferdinand. 1886. Miscellen. *PBB* 11, 548–56.

________. 1894. [Rev of] George Hempl, *Old-English Phonology.* Boston: D. C. Heath & Co. *AB* 4, 131.

________. 1896. [Rev of] Oliver F. Emerson, *The*

History of the English Language. New York: Macmillan & Co., 1894. *Lit.bl.* 17, 264–66.
_______. 1900. Kegel und Verwandtes. *Archiv* 105, 365–66.
_______. 1901. Etymologien. *Archiv* 107, 379–82.
_______. 1903a. [Rev. of] Max Kaluza, *Historische Grammatik der englischen Sprache*. Berlin: E. Felber, 1900–01. *Litt.bl.* 24, 329–34.
_______. 1903b. [Rev of] Walter Skeat, *A Concise Etymological Dictionary of the English Language*. Oxford: At the Clarendon Press, 1901. *AB* 14, 33–40.
_______. 1904–05. Etymologien. *IF* 17, 293–96.
_______. 1909. Etymogien 2. *IF* 25, 147–54.
_______. 1912. Etymologien 3. *IF* 30, 47–49.
_______. 1913. Wortdeutungen. *IF* 32, 333–39.
_______. 1918a. Beiträge zur englischen wortkunde 2. *AB* 29, 250–56.
_______. 1918b. Etymologisches. *KZ* 48, 237–39.
_______. 1921. *Altsächsisches Elementarbuch*, 2nd ed. GB I/I/5.
_______. 1923. Zur englischen Wortkunde. *AB* 34, 342–52.
_______. 1924. [Rev of] SEO[1]. *ZDA(A)* 43, 113–18.
_______. 1929a. Gotische Wörter im Romanischen. In *Behrens-Festschrift. Dietrich Behrens zum siebzigsten Geburtstag dargebracht von Schülern und Freunden*, 106–09. *ZFSL*. Supplementheft 13. Jena and Leipzig: Verlag von Wilhelm Gronau (W. Agricola).
_______. 1929b. [Rev of] Godard Gosses, *De friesche oorkonden uit het archief van het St. Anthony-Gasthuis te Leeuwarden 1. Een bydrag tot de kennis der historische grammatika van het Westfriesch*. Bolsward: A. J. Osinga, 1928. *Lit. bl.* 50, 424–25.
_______. 1932. Worterklärungun 1. *GRM* 20, 65–68.
_______. 1934. [Rev of] EWDS[11]. *AB* 45, 34–36.
_______. 1935. [Rev of] EWDS[11]. *AB* 46, 165–70.
_______. 1935–36. Zur neuenglischen Etymologie. *ESt* 70, 324–30.
_______. 1941. [Rev of] SEO[2]. *ZDA* 78, 78–82.
_______. 1942a. Etymologisches und Grammatisches. *PBB* 66, 265–75.
_______. 1942b. Zum altenglischen Wortschatz 2. *AB* 53, 35–37.
_______. 1951–52. Beiträge zur englischen Etymologie. *Anglia* 70, 1–21.
_______. 1952. Etymologien. *IF* 60, 277–81.
_______. 1955. Wortkundliches 2. *KZ* 72, 198–208.
_______. 1955–1956. Wortkundliches 3. *KZ* 73, 95–103.
See also AeEW, AfW, EW, GEW; Grein, C. W. M. 1912; *and* VEW.
Homeyer, Carl G., ed. 1830. *Des Sachsenspiegels zweiter Theil, nebst den verwandten Rechtsbüchern. 1. Das sächsische Lehnrecht und der Richtsteig Lehnrechts*. Berlin: Bei Ferdinand Dümmler.
Hoog, W. de. *See* De Hoog, W.
Hooper, James. 1897. Round Robin. *NQ* VIII/11, 177.
Hoops, Johannes. 1889. *Über die altenglischen Pflanzennamen*. Diss. Freiburg i. B. Freiburg i. B. Universitäts-Buchdruckerei von Chr. Lehmann.
_______. 1902. Hunnen und Hünen. In *Germanistische Abhandlungen. Hermann Paul zum 17. März 1902 dargebracht*, 167–80. Strassburg: Karl J. Trübner.
_______. 1903. Alte *k*-Stämme unter den germanischen Baumnamen. *IF* 14, 478–85.
_______. 1905. *Waldbäume und Kulturpflanzen im germanischen Altertum*. Straßburg: Verlag von Karl J. Trübner.
_______. 1913–15. Hafer. RGA II, 352–59.
_______. 1920. [Rev of] Richard Loewe, *Germanische Pflanzennamen. Etymologische Untersuchungen über* Hirschbeere, Hindbeere, Rehbockbeere *und ihre Verwandten*. GB II/6, 1913. *IF(A)* 38–39, 34–43.
See also RGA.
Hopkinson, S. D. 1890. Rabbit and Riot. *NQ* VII/10, 122–23.
Hoptman, Ari. 2000. *Finger* and Some Other *f-* and *fl-*Words. *NOWELE* 36, 77–91.
Horn, Wilhelm. 1901. *Beiträge zur Geschichte der englischen Gutturallaute*. Berlin: W. Gronau.
_______. 1921a. *Sprachkörper und Sprachfunktion*. Palaestra 135. Berlin: Mayer & Müller.
_______. 1921b. [Rev of] EW. *Archiv* 142, 140–43.
_______. 1935. Zur englischen Bühnensprache. *Archiv* 166, 40–49.
_______. 1950. *Beiträge zur englischen Wortgeschichte*. *AWL* 23.
See also HL.
Hornscheidt, Antje. *See* Liberman, Anatoly. 2006.

Hortling, Ivar. 1944. *Svenska fågelnamn. Försök till tydning av deras innebörd.* Stockholm: Bokförlaget Natur och Kultur.

Hotten, John C. 1859. *The Slang Dictionary.* London: John C. Hotten. 3rd ed: 1864, 5th ed: 1903. London: Chatto and Windus.

Hough, Carole. 2004. New Light on the verb "understand." In *New Perspectives on English. Historical Linguistics: Selected Papers from 12 ICEHL, Glasgow, 21–26 August 2002. Volume 2: Lexis and Transmission*, eds. Christian Kay, Carole Hough, [and] Irené Wortherspoon, pp. 139–149. ASTHLSV/IV 252.

H.R. 1890. Slang. *ANQ* V/3, 28.

Hubschmid, Johannes. 1943. Bezeichnungen für 'Kaninchen'—'Höhle'—'Steinplatte.' In *Sache. Ort und Wort. Jakob Jud zum sechzichsten Geburtstag 12. Januar 1942*, 246–80. RH 20.

________. 1953. Fr. *laîche*, dt. *lische*: eine gallische und germanische Wortfamilie. *ZCP* 24, 81–90.

Hudson, Wilson M. 1950–51. Whitaker's Attack on Johnson's Etymologies. *HLQ* 14, 285–97.

Hübner, Rudolf . *See* Grimm, Jacob. 1983.

Hughes, Geoffrey. 1988. *A History of English Words.* Oxford: Blackwell.

________. 1991. *Swearing: A Social History of Foul Language, Oaths and Profanity in English.* Oxford: Blackwell.

Hughes, John P. 1954. On "h" for "r" in English Proper Names. *JEGP* 53: 601–12.

Hughes, Kathleen. *See* Feilitzen, Olof von.

Huisman, J. A. 1953. Ekliptik und Nord/ Südbezeichnung im Indogermanischen. *KZ* 71, 97–108.

Hulbert, James R. *See* DAE.

Huld, Martin E. 1979. English *witch. MGS* 5, 36–39.

See also Greppin, John A. C., *and* Liberman, Anatoly. 2001b.

Hunter, Robert. *See* ED.

Huss, Richard. 1935. Die sogenannten Labiovelaren. In, *Atti del III Congresso Internazionale dei Linguisti / Actes du III Congrès International de Linguistes.* Roma, 19–26 settembre 1933, eds. Bruno Migliorini and Vittore Pisani, pp. 202–14. Firenze: Felice le Monnier. Repr Kraus Repr Nendeln/ Liechtenstein, 1972.

H.W. 1944. Jeep. *ANQ* 4, 26–27.

HW = Johannes Friedrich, *Hethitisches Wörterbuch. Kurzgefasste kritische Sammlung der Deutungen hethitischer Wörter.* Heidelberg: Carl Winter Universitätsverlag, 1952.

Hyldgaard-Jensen, Karl. *See* Diensberg, Bernhard. 1994.

Iago, W. 1903. Anglo-Saxon Names and Titles. *NQ* IX/12, 268.

ID = *The Imperial Dictionary of the English Language.* John Ogilvie, ed. London: Blackie & Son, 1850. 2nd ed, by Charles Annandale, 1882. *See also* Annandale, Charles.

IESOI = V. I. Abaev, *Istoriko-etimologicheskii slovar' osetinskogo iazyka* [A Historical and Etymological Dictionary of the Ossetic Language]. 4 vols. Moskva-Leningrad: Izdatel'stvo Akademii Nauk SSSR; Leningrad: Nauka, 1958–89.

IEW = Julius Pokorny, *Indogermanisches etymologisches Wörterbuch.* Bern and München: Francke, 1959.

Ihre, Johan. 1769. *Glossarium Suiogothicum....* Upsaliæ: Typis Edmannianis.

Ihrig, Roscoe M. 1916. *The Semantic Development of Words for "Walk, Run" in the Germanic Languages.* Diss. The University of Chicago. LSG 4.

Illich-Svitych, V. M. 1976. *Opyt sravneniia nostraticheskikh iazykov [An Attempt at a Comparison of the Nostratic Languages.*], vol. 2. Moscow: Nauka.

Ipsen, Gunther. 1924. Der alte Orient und die Indogermanen. In *Stand und Aufgaben der Sprachwissenschaft. Festschrift für Wilhelm Streitberg*, 200–37. Heidelberg: Carl Winter's Universitätsbuchhandlung.

Isaac, Graham. *See* Falileyev, Alexander, and Graham Isaac.

IsEW = Alexander Jóhannesson, *Isländisches etymologisches Wörterbuch.* Bern: Francke, 1956.

Ising, Gerhard. 1960. Zu den Tiernamen in den ältesten niederdeutschen Bibeldrucken. *NJ* 83, 41–58.

Itkonen, Erkki. *See* SKES *and* SSA.

Ivanov, Vyacheslav V. 1999a. Traces of Indo-European Medical Magic in an Old English Charm. In *Interdigitations: Essays for Irmengard Rauch*, eds. Gerald F. Carr, Wayne Harbert, and Lihua Zhang, pp. 1–24. New York: Peter Lang.

________. 1999b. Comparative Notes on Hurro-Urartian, Northern Caucasian and Indo-European. In UCLA Indo-European Studies 1,

eds. Vyacheslav V. Ivanov and Brent Vine, pp. 147–264.
See also GI.

Jaeger, P. L. *See* Schröer, M. M. Arnold.

Jäkel, Olaf. 1995. The Metaphorical Conception of Mind: 'Mental activity is manipulation'. In *Language and the Cognitive Construal of the World*, eds. John R. Taylor and Robert E. MacLaury, pp. 197–229. TLSM 82.

Jager, A. de. *See* De Jager, A.

Jahr, Ernst H. *See* Polomé, Edgar C. 1997.

Jakobsen, Jakob. *See* EONSS.

James, Charles. 1802. *A New and Enlarged Military Dictionary....* London: Printed for T. Egerton at the Military Library.

Jamieson, John. 1808. *An Etymological Dictionary of the Scottish Language*. Edinburgh: Printed for Archibald Constable, *etc.* Repr 1818. *Supplement*, 1825.

________. 1814. *Hermes Scythicus: Or, The Radical Affinities of the Greek and Latin Languages to the Gothic: Illustrated from the Moeso-Gothic, Anglo-Saxon, Francic, Alemannic, Scio-Gothic, Islandic, &c. To Which is Prefixed, a Dissertation on the Historical Proofs of the Scythian Origin of the Greeks.* Edinburgh: Printed at the University Press; for Longman, etc.

________. 1867. *Dictionary of the Scottish Language*. Edinburgh: William P. Nimmo. .

________. 1879–82. *An Etymological Dictionary of the Scottish Language.* Ed. by John Longmuir. Paisley: Alexander Gardner. *Supplement...* by David Donaldson, 1887.

Janko, Josef. 1926. O slovích *spiknutí, piksa, pikel-fig(e)l* [On the Words *spiknutí, piksa, pikel-fig(e)l*]. In *Μνῆμα. Sborník vydaný na pamět' čtyřicítiletého učitelského pusobení Prof. Josefa Zubatého na Universitě Karlově 1885–1925.* [Praha]: Jednota českých filologů v Praze, 1–16.

Janni, Pietro. 1978. *Etnografia e mito. La storia dei Pigmei.* FC 30.

________. 1985. I Pigmei in Scandinavia: vicende di una leggenda etnografica. In *Cultura classica e cultura germanica settentrionale. Atti del Convegno internazionale di studi, Università di Macerata, Macerata—S. Severino Marche, 2–4 maggio 1985*, eds. Pietro Janni, Diego Poli, [and] Carlo Santini. QLF 3, 113–23.

Janz, Brigitte. 1989. *Rechtssprichwörter im Sachsenspiegel. Eine Untersuchung zur Text-Bild-Relation in den Codices picturati.* GASK 13.

Jazayery, Mohammad A. *See* Hamp, Eric P. 1988b.

J.C.M. 1864. Curmudgeon. *NQ* III/5, 319.

________. 1868. Rabbit it. *NQ* IV/1, 280.

J.C.R. 1880. Skedaddle. *MCNQ* 3, 20 (No. 1529).

Jellinghaus, Hermann F. 1898a. Angelsächsisch-neuenglische Wörter, die nicht niederdeutsch sind. *Anglia* 20, 463–66.

________. 1898b. [Rev of] Arnold Wall, A Contribution towards the Study of the Scandinavian Element in the English Dialects. *Anglia* 20, 189, 45–135. *KVNS* 20, 28–32.

Jenkins, Harold. 1982. *Hamlet.* The Arden Edition of the Works of William Shakespeare. London and New York: Methuen.

Jennbert, Kristina. *See* Arvidsson, Stefan.

Jensen, Hans. 1908. *Die Verbalflexion im 'Ayenbite of Inwyt.'* Diss. Kiel. Kiel: no indication of publisher.

________. 1936. Indogermanisch und Koreanisch. In *Germanen und Indogermanen. Volkstum, Sprache, Heimat, Kultur. Festschrift für Herman Hirt*. Vol. 2: *Ergebnisse der Sprachwissenschaft*, ed. Helmut Arntz. IB III/15 (2), 159–70.

________. 1951. "Was bedeutet 'Mensch'?" *ZPh* 5, 244–47.

Jespersen, Otto. 1909. *A Modern English Grammar on Historical Principles* 1. SGEH I/9.

________. 1962. *Growth and Structure of the English Language.* 9th ed. Oxford: Basil Blackwell.

Jessen, E. 1893. *Dansk Etymologisk Ordbog.* Kjøbenhavn: Gyldendal.

Jirlow, Ragnar. 1936. Låset, regeln och nycheln. 1. Ordgeografi och språkhistoria. NTU 9, 74–80.

J.N. *See* Pegge, Samuel, 2nd ed.

Jóhannesson, Alexander. 1927. *Die Suffixe im Isländischen.* Fylgir Árbók Háslola Íslands 1927. Reykjavík: Prentsmiðjan Gutenberg.

________. 1932. *Die Mediageminata im Isländischen.* Fylgir Árbók Háskóla Íslands 1929–30. Reykjavík: Ríkisprentsmiðjan Gutenberg.

________. 1940. Torskilin orð í íslenzku. In *Afmælisrit helgað Einari Arnórssyni Hæstaréttardómara Dr. Juris sextugum 24. febrúar 1940*, 1–8. Reykjavík: Ísafoldarprentsmiðja, H. F.

_______. 1942. Isländische Beiträge zum indogermanischen Wörterbuch. *KZ* 67, 220–23.
See also IsEW.

Johansson, Karl F. 1889. Über die idg. verbindungen von *s(z)* + guttural + *l, m, n* in den germanischen sprachen. *PBB* 14, 289–368.

_______. 1890. Etymologische Beiträge. *KZ* 30, 346–51, 428–52.

_______. 1891. Nachtrag zu *Betr.* 14, 289 f. *PBB* 15, 212–13.

_______. 1900. Anlautendes indogerm. *b. KZ* 36, 342–90.

Johnson, Samuel. 1755. *A Dictionary of the English Language.* London: Printed by W. Strahan for J. and P. Knapton, *etc.* Repr New York: AMS Press Inc, 1967. 2nd ed, by H. J. Todd. London: Longman, *etc.*, 1827.

Joki, Aulis J. *See* SKES.

Jones-Bley, Karlene. *See* Liberman, Anatoly. 2002.

Jónsson, Finnur. 1907. Tilnavne i den islandske oldlitteratur. Aarbøger 22, 161–381.

_______. 1916. Navne på fjorde, vige m. m. på Island. *NB* 4, 73–86.
See also LP.

Jordan, Richard. 1903. *Die altenglischen Säugetiernamen.* AF 12.

_______. 1906. *Eigentümlichkeiten des anglischen Wortschatzes. Eine wortgeographische Untersuchung mit etymologischen Anmerkungen.* AF 17.

_______. 1925. *Handbuch der mittelenglischen Grammatik.* Heidelberg: Carl Winter. 2nd ed, by H. Ch. Matthes: 1934, 3rd ed, with a bibliographical supplement, by Klaus Dietz: 1968.

_______. 1974. *Handbook of Middle English Grammar: Phonology.* 4th ed. Trans and rev by Eugene J. Crook. JL. Series Practica 218. The Hague, Paris: Mouton.

Jungner, Hugo. 1922. *Gudinnan Frigg och Als härad. En studie i Västergötlands religions-, språk- og bebyggelsehistoria.* Diss. Uppsala. Uppsala: Wretmans boktryckeri.

Junius = Francisci Junii Francisci filii *Etymologicum Anglicanum*: Ex Autographo descripsit & accessionibus permultus auctum edidit Edwardus Lye. Oxonii: E Theatro Sheldoniano, 1743. Repr Los Angeles: Sherwin & Freutel, 1970.

Juret, A. 1942. *Dictionnaire étymologique grec et latin.* PFLUS 98.

Kachru, Braj B. *See* Gold, David L. 1995b.

Kähler, Hans. 1952. Bemerkungen zu Hans Jensen: *Was bedeutet 'Mensch'? ZPh* 6, 252–53.

Kaestner, Walter. 1970. Boofke und Piefke. *KVNS* 77, 10–11.

Kahane, Henry. *See* Gold, David L. 1995b.

Kahle, Bernard. 1903. Altwestnordische Namenstudien. *IF* 14, 133–224.

_______. 1910. Die altwestnordischen Beinamen bis etwa zum Jahre 1400. *ANF* 26, 142–202, 227–60.

Kalb, Hans. 1937. *Die Namen der Säugetiere im Mittelenglischen.* Diss. Berlin. Bottrop i. W.: Wilh. Postberg.

Kalkar, Otto. *See* OÆDS.

Kaltschmidt, Jakob H. 1839. *Sprachvergleichendes Wörterbuch der deutschen Sprache.* Leipzig: Verlag der J. C. Hinrichschen Buchhandlung.

Kaluza, Max. 1906–07. *Historische Grammatik der englischen Sprache.* 2 vols., 2nd ed. Berlin: Felber.

Karaliūnas, Simas. 1993. Some Remarks on the Names for Pigeon in Lithuanian. *LiB* 2, 109–13.

Karg-Gasterstädt, E. 1941. Aus der Werkstatt des althochdeutschen Wörterbuches. *PBB* 65, 185–213.
See also AHW.

Karsten, Torsten E. 1895–1900. *Studier öfver de nordiska språkens primära nominalbildning.* 2 vols. Helsingfors: Finska litteratur-sällskapets tryckeri.

_______. 1900. *Studier öfver de nordiska språkens primära nominalbildning II.* Helsingfors: Finska litteratur-sällsk. tryckeri.

_______. 1902. Beiträge zur germanischen Wortkunde. *MSN* 3, 399–442.

Karulis, Konstantīns, 1992. *Latviešu etimologijas vārdnīca.* Rīga: Avots.

Kaspers, Willy. 1938. Der Name Kettwig, Katwijk; Kat(t)-, Katz- in Ortsnamen; der Tiername 'Katze.' *ZNF* 13, 213–25.

_______. 1945. Zur Etymologie von ahd. *chūski* 'keusch.' *PBB* 67, 151–54.

Kastovsky, Dieter. *See* Colman, Fran; Hamp, Eric P. 1986, *and* Ono, Shigeru. 1986.

Kate, Lambert ten. *See* Ten Kate, Lambert.

Katz, Joshua T. 1998. Testimonia ritus italici: Male Genitalia, Solemn Declarations, and a New Latin Sound Law. *HSCP* 98, 183–217.

Kauffmann, Friedrich. 1887. Zur geschichte des germanischen consonantismus. *PBB* 12, 504–47.

________. 1894. Mythologische Zeugnisse aus Romischen [sic] Inschriften. *PBB* 18, 134–94.

________. 1900. [Rev of] Friesen, Otto von. 1897. *ZDP* 32, 255–56.

Kay, Christian. *See* Hough, Carole *and* TOE.

KD = *The Kenkyusha Dictionary of English Etymology*. Kenkyusha Limited, 1997.

Keightley, Thomas. 1862a. Rabbit. *NQ* III/1, 403.

________. 1862b. Rabbit. *NQ* III/1, 491.

Keintzel-Schön, Fritz. 1976. *Die siebenbürgisch-sächsischen Familiennamen.* ST 3.

Keller, A. von. 1871. Kleine Bemerkungen. *Germania* 16, 78–79.

Keller, Hennig. 1967. [Rev of] ODEE. *Archiv* 204, 294–99.

Keller, Margrit. [?]1938. *Die Frau und das Mädchen in den englischen Dialekten.* Diss. Zürich: no indication of place or publisher.

Kelling, H. D. 1951. Some Significant Names in *Gulliver's Travels. SP* 48, 761–78.

Kelly, Walter K. 1854. *Erotica: The Poems of Catullus and Tibullus and the* Vigil of Venus: *A Literal Prose Translation with Notes....* London: G. Bells and Sons.

Kempe Valk, C. van. *See* Van Kempe Valk, C.

Kenrick, William. 1773. *A New Dictionary of the English Language....* London: Printed for John and Francis Rivington, *etc.*

Ker, John B. 1837. *An Essay on the Archæology of our Popular Phrases and Nursery Rhymes.* 2 vols. A new ed. London: Longman, *etc.*

Kerchler, Helga. *See* Steinhauser, Walter.

Kern, J. Hendrick. 1901. Ooit. *TNTL* 19, 201–03.

Kerns, John C. *See* Bomhard, Allan R., and John C. Kerns.

KEWA = Manfred Mayrhofer, *Kurzgefaßtes etymologisches Wörterbuch des Altindischen. A Concise Etymological Sanskrit Dictionary.* Heidelberg: Carl Winter, 1956–80.

KEWAS = Christianus C. Uhlenbeck, *Kurzgefaßtes etymologisches Wörterbuch der altindischen Sprache.* Amsterdam: Johannes Müller, 1898–99.

KEWGS = Christianus C. Uhlenbeck, *Kurzgefaßtes etymologisches Wörterbuch der gotischen Sprache.* Amsterdam: Verlag von Joh. Müller, 1896. 2nd ed: 1900.

Keyworth, Thomas. 1880. Skedaddle. *MCNQ* 3 (No. 1529), 20.

Kilianus, Cornelius [a.k.a. Kiel, Corneille]. 1599. *Etymologicum teutonicæ linguæ....* Antverpiæ: Ex Officina Plantiniana, apud Joannem Moretum. Repr Traiecti Batavorum: Apud Roelandum de Meyere, 1777. Repr Amsterdam: Adolf M. Hakkert, 1972.

King, Arthur G. 1962. 'Jeep' and 'Peep,' 'Pipable' and 'Jeepable.' *AS* 37, 77–78.

Kitson, P. R. 1997. Old English Bird-Names 1. *ES* 78, 481–505.

Kittredge, George L. *See* Geenough, James B.

KL = F. Kluge and F. Lutz, *English Etymology....* Boston, New York, Chicago: D. C. Heath & Co; London: Blackie & Son, 1899.

Klaeber, Friedrich. 1905. [Rev of] Wood 1902. *Archiv* 114, 201–03.

________. 1912. Die christlichen Elemente im Beowulf. *Anglia* 35, 111–36.

________. 1926. Concerning the Etymology of "Slang". *AS* 1, 368.

________., ed. 1950. *Beowulf and the Fight at Finnsburg.* 3rd ed with First and Second Supplements. Lexington, MA: D. C. Heath and Company.

Klein, Erich. 1911. *Die verdunkelten Wortzusammensetzungen im Neuenglischen.* Diss Königsberg i. Pr. Königsberg i. Pr.: Druck von Karg und Manneck.

Klein, Ernest. *See* CEDEL *and* CEDHL.

Klein, Jared S. 1992. [Rev of] Bammesberger, Alfred. 1900. *Kratylos* 37, 136–42.

Klein, Thomas. 1977. 'Ramschoup' und 'iwin loup.' Bemerkungen zu Parz. 459, 11; 486, 7f. *ZDA* 106, 358–67.

Kleinpaul, Rudolf. 1885. *Menschen- und Völkernamen. Etymologische Streifzüge auf dem Gebiete der Eigennamen.* Leipzig: Verlag von Carl Reissner.

Klemola, Juhani. *See* Görlach, Manfred.

KLNM = *Kulturhistoriskt Lexikon för nordisk medeltid från vikingatid till reformationstid.* Malmö: Allhems förlag, 1956–78.

Kluge, Friedrich. 1884. Die germanische Konsonantendehnung. *PBB* 9, 149–86.

________. 1889. *Kater* und verwantes. *PBB* 14, 585–87.

________. 1895. Englische Etymologien. *EST* 20, 333–35.

________. 1897. [Rev of] KEWAS[1] (1896). *Lit.bl.* 18, 1.

_______. 1901a. Anglo-Saxon Etymologies. In *An English Miscellany Presented to Dr. Furnivall in Honour of His Seventy-Fifth Birthday,* 199–200. Oxford: At the Clarendon Press.

_______. 1901b. *Geschichte der englischen Sprache.* In Paul's *Grundriss der germanischen Philologie.* 2nd ed, 926–1151. Straßburg: Karl J. Trübner.

_______. 1901c. *Rotwelsch....* Straßburg: Karl J. Trübner.

_______. 1901–02. Tuisco deus et filius Mannus Germ 2. *ZDW* 2, 43–45.

_______. 1906. [Rev of] Schröder, Heinrich. 1906. *Lit.bl.* 27, 393–401.

_______. 1913. *Urgermanisch. Vorgeschichte der altgermanischen Dialekte.* Strassburg: Karl J. Trübner.

_______. 1916a. Etymologien. *PBB* 41, 180–82.

_______. 1916b. Germanisches Reckentum. *Frankfurter Zeitung,* Erstes Morgenblatt, Juni 21, 2.

_______. 1921. Zur Wortgeschichte. *ZRP* 41, 678–85.

_______. 1922. Germanisches Reckentum: frz. garçon. *MLN* 37, 385–90.

_______. 1926. *Nominale Stammbildungslehre der altgermanischen Dialekte.* SKGGD, Ergänzungsreihe, 1. Halle (Saale): Max Niemeyer Verlag.
See also EWDS *and* KL.

Kluyver, A. 1884. *Proeve eener critiek op het woordenboek van Kiliaan.* Diss. Leiden. 's-Gravenhage: Martinus Nijhoff.

KM = Kluge-Mitzka. *See* EWDS[17–21].

Knobloch, Johann. 1959. [Rev of] *IEW*, fasc. 1–11. *Kratylos* 4, 29–41.

_______. 1969. Catull c 53, 5 und Cicero. *RMP* 112, 23–29.

_______. 1971. Deutsche historische Wortforschung. (Aus Anlass der 20. Auflage des 'Kluge-Mitzka.') *Lingua* 26, 294–314.

_______. 1972. Jakob. In *Festschrift Matthias Zender. Studien zu Volkskultur, Sprache und Landesgeschichte,* eds. Edith Ennen and Günter Wiegelmann, in collaboration with Branimir Bratanić, et al. Bonn: Ludwig Röhrscheid.

_______. 1980. Germanische und indogermanische Verwandte von burgenländisch *Hotter* und siebenbürgisch-sächsisch (m.) 'Grenze, Gemarkung, Feld.' In *Sprache und Name in Österreich. Festschrift für Walter Steinhauser zum 95. Geburtstag,* ed. Peter Wiesinger. SDSÖ 6, 197–201.

_______. 1987. Die Kleidung der Indogermanen und ihrer Erben: Schuwerk. In *Studien zum indogermanischen Wortschatz,* ed. Wolfgang Meid. IBS 52, 65–66.

_______. 1989. Alb und Vamp. Die Internationalität des Aberglaubens. *Sprachwissenschaft* 14, 282–84.

_______. 1995. Etymologische Beobachtungen zum deutschen Wortschatz. *Muttersprache* 105, 141–48.

Knott, Thomas A. *See* Webster, Noah. 1934.

Koch, C. Friedrich. 1867. [Rev of] Mueller, Eduard. 1865–67. *JREL* 8, 318–24.

_______. 1873. Englische Etymologien. *ZDP* 4, 135–43.

_______. 1882. *Historische Grammatik der englischen Sprache* 1. Kassel: Georg H. Wigand. (A repr of the 1863 ed.)

Kock, Axel. 1895. Zur Frage über den *w*-Umlaut, sowie über den Verlust des *w* in den altnordischen Sprachen. *IF* 5, 153–67.

_______. 1895–98. *Belysning af några svenska ord ock uttryck. ATS* 16:3.

_______. 1916. Undersökningar i fornnordisk grammatik. *ANF* 32, 176–200.

Kock, Ernst A. 1940. *Notationes norroenæ. Anteckningar till* Edda *och skaldediktning* 27. LUÅ. NF. Avd. 1, 37/2.

Kögel, Rudolf. 1892. [Rev of] Ferdinand Wrede, *Über die Sprache der Ostgoten in Italien.* QF 68. *ZDA(A)* 18, 43–60.

_______. 1893. Beowulf. *ZDA* 37, 268–76.

_______. 1894–97. *Geschichte der deutschen Literatur bis zum Ausgang des Mittelalters.* Vol I: 1–2. Straßburg: Karl Trübner.

Köhler, J. J. *See* Grein, C. W. M.

Koeppel, Emil. 1901. Tautological Compounds of the English Language. In *An English Miscellany Presented to Dr. Furnivall in Honour of his Seventy-Fifth Birthday,* pp. 201–04. Oxford: Clarendon Press.

_______. 1904. Zur englischen Wortbildungslehre. *Archiv* 25–66.

Körting, Gustav. 1923. *Lateinisch-romanisches Wörterbuch. Etymologisches Wörterbuch der romanischen Hauptsprachen.* 3rd ed. New York: G. E. Stechert & Co.

Kohl, J. G. 1869. *A History of the State of Maine.* CMHS II/1.

Kolb, Herbert. *See* Hiersche, Rolf. 1984.

Koolman, J. ten Doornkaat. *See* Ten Doornkaat Koolman, J.
Kononov, A. N. *See* Baskakov, N.A.
Koppmann, K. 1876. Altvil. *KVNS* 1, 6.
________. 1899–1900. Zur Assonanz im Niederdeutschen. *KVNS* 21, 35–47.
Korhammer, Michael. *See* Sauer, Hans. 1992, *and* Seebold, Elmar. 1992.
Korsch, Th. 1886. [Rev of] Miklosich, Franz R. von. 1884. *ASP* 9, 487–520.
Kosegarten, Johann G. L. 1859–60. *Wörterbuch der Niederdeutschen Sprache.* Greifswald: C. A. Kunike.
Kossmann, Maarten. *See* Boutkan, Dirk F. K., and Maarten Kossmann.
Koziol, Herbert. 1937. *Handbuch der englischen Wortbildung*. GB/I/21. Repr 1972.
See also Luick, Karl. 1964.
Krahe, Hans. 1929. Illyrisch und Germanisch. *IF* 47, 321–28.
See also EWDS[15] *and* KrM.
Kralik, Dietrich von. 1914. [Rev of] Suolahti, Hugo. 1909. *GGA* 179/3, 129–68.
Krause, K. E. H. 1888. Kalmäuser Klamüser. *KVNS* 13, 55–56.
Krause, Wolfgang. 1958. [Rev of] *AEW* 1–3. *GGA* 212, 49–57.
See also EWDS[11].
Kretschmer, Paul. 1933. Literaturbericht für das Jahr 1930: Griechisch. *Glotta* 21, 153–83.
Kriebitzsch, Paul. 1900. *Beiträge zur deutschen Etymologie*. Wissenschaftliche Beilage zum Jahresbericht des Königlichen Gymnasiums zu Spandau.
KrM = Hans Krahe, *Germanische Sprachwissenschaft*. Vol 3. 7th ed, by Wolfgang Meid. Berlin and New York: Walter de Gruyter, 1969.
Kroes, H. W. J. 1955. Gotica. *GRM* 36, 265.
Kroesch, Samuel. 1911. The Semasiological Development of Words for 'Perceive, Understand, Think, Know,' in the Old Germanic Dialects. *MPh* 8, 461–510. Offprint from the journal, publ with a word index as University of Chicago Dissertation.
Krogmann, Willy. 1933. Ae. *dyde*. *Anglia* 57, 377–95.
________. 1934–35. Germ. **du̯erga-* "Zwerg." *KZ* 62, 143.
________. 1936. Zwei ae. Wortdeutungen. *Anglia* 60, 33–38.
________. 1938a. Adebar. *Korr.bl.* 51, 71–73.
________. 1938b. Tropf. *ZDP* 63, 184–88.
________. 1938c. Adel und Udel. *ZDP* 63, 189–91.
________. 1952. Scorlemorle. *KVNS* 59, 28–29.
Kronasser, Heinz. 1962. *Etymologie der hethitischen Sprache I. Zur Schreibung und Lautung des Hethitischen* 1. Wiesbaden: Otto Harrassowitz.
Kruijsen, J. *See* Weijnen, Antonius A. 1975.
Kruppa-Kusch, Veronika, and Felix Wortmann. 1964. Norddeutsche Bezeichnungen des weiblichen Schaflamms. *NW* 4, 1–52.
KS = Kluge-Seebold. *See* EWDS[22–24].
KSchr = Jacob Grimm, *Kleinere Schriften*. Vols. 1–8. Gütersloh: Ferd. Dümmlers Verlagsbuchhandlung/ Druck und Verlag von G. Bertelsmann, 1866–90; repr Hildesheim: Georg Olms Verlagsbuchhandlung, 1965–66.
Kubriakova, E. S. 1963. Morfologicheskaia struktura slova v drevnikh germanskikh iazykakh [The Morphological Structure of the Word in Old Germanic]. SGGI III, 7–131.
Kück, Eduard. 1905. *Niederdeutsche Beiträge zum Deutschen Wörterbuch*. Beilage zum Jahresbericht des Gymnasiums zu Friedenau. Ostern 1905. Friedenau: Druck von Leo Schultz.
Kügler, Hermann. 1916. ie *und seine Parallelformen im Angelsächsischen*. Berlin: In Kommission bei Mayer & Müller.
Künßberg, Ebenhard F. von. 1940. Aus der Werkstatt des Rechtswörterbuches. In *Festschrift Ernst Heymann… überreicht von Freunden, Schülern und Fachgenossen*, 102–09. Weimar: Verlag Hermann Böhlaus Nachfolger.
Küpper, Heinz. *See* WDU-1963 and WDU-1970.
Kuethe, J. Louis. 1941. Notes on the DAE, Volume II, Corn Pit–Honk. *AS* 16, 54–56.
Kuhn, Adalbert. 1852. *Τελχίν, θέλγω*. *KZ* 1, 193–205.
________. 1853. Über die durch nasale erweiterten verbalstämme. *KZ* 2, 455–71.
________. 1861. Scharn-, wodeskerne, schierling. *KZ* 10, 317.
Kuhn, Hans. 1938. Das Zeugnis der Sprache über Alter und Ursprung der Runenschrift. In *Beiträge zur Runenkunde und nordischen Sprachwissenschaft. Gustav Neckel zum 60. Geburtstag*, 54–74. Leipzig: Otto Harrassowitz. Repr in Kuhn, Hans. 1969–78, III, 469–85.

________. 1941. Hadbarden und Hadraumer. *NB* 29, 84–116. Repr in Kuhn 1969–78, III, 6–30.

________. 1952. Heldensage vor und ausserhalb der Dichtung. In *Edda, Skalden, Saga. Festschrift zum 70. Geburtstag von Felix Genzmer*, ed. Hermann Schneider, 262–78. Heidelberg: C. Winter. Repr in *Zur germanisch-deutschen Heldensage…*, ed. Karl Hauch. Wege der Forschug 14, 173–94. Darmstadt: Wissenschaftliche Buchgesellschaft, 1965, and in Kuhn, Hans. 1969–78, II, 102–18.

________. 1954. Ablaut, *a* und Altertumskunde. *KZ* 71, 129–61. Repr in Kuhn, Hans. 1969–78, II, 219–45.

________. 1962. Angelsächsisch *cōp* "Kappe" und Seinesgleichen. In *Festgabe für L. L. Hammerich. Aus Anlass seines siebzigsten Geburtstags*, 113–24. Kopenhagen: Naturmetodens Sproginstitut. Repr in Kuhn, Hans, 1969–78, I, 390–99.

________. 1972. Das römische Kriegswesen im germanischen Wortschatz. *ZDA* 101, 13–53. Repr in Kuhn, Hans. 1969–78, IV, 23–60.

________. 1969–78. *Kleine Schriften*. 4 vols. Dietrich Hofmann, ed., in collaboration with Wolfgang Lange and Klaus von See. Berlin: Walter de Gruyter & Co. (vol. II: 1971, vol. III: 1972).

See also Edda.

Kumada, Kazunori. 1994. The Semantic Development of the Indo-European Root **pelə-, plā-*. *Asterisk* 3, 15–16.

Kunsmann, Peter. *See* Diez, Klaus. 1981b.

Kurath, Hans. *See* MED.

Kure, Henning. 2003. In the Beginning was the Scream: Conceptual Thought in the Old Norse Myth of Creation. In *Scandinavia and Christian Europe in the Middle Ages: Papers of the 12th International Saga Conference*, Bonn/ Germany, 28th July–2nd August 2003, eds. Rudolf Simmek and Judith Meurer, 311–19. Bonn: Hausdruckerei der Universität Bonn.

Kurt, Ortwin. *See* Diez, Klaus. 1981b.

Kytö, Merja. *See* Görlach, Manfred.

L. 1853. "Namby Pamby," and Other Words of the Same Form. *NQ* I/8, 390–92.

Läffler, L. Fr. 1911. Det evigt gränskande trädet vid Uppsala. *MM* (= *Festskrift til H. F. Feilberg*), 617–96.

Lagarde, Paul de. 1877. *Armenische Studien*. Osnabrück: Otto Zeller Verlag. Repr 1970.

Laistner, Ludwig. 1888. Über den Butzennamen. *ZDA* 32, 145–95.

Lane, Allen. *See* Cottle, Basil.

Lane, G. S. 1933. The Germano-Celtic Vocabulary. *Language* 9, 244–64.

Lange, Wolfgang. *See* Kuhn, Hans. 1969–78.

Langenauer, Ilse. 1957. [Untitled] *Anglia* 70, 102–04.

Langenhove, G. van. *See* Van Langenhove, G.

Lanman, Charles R. 1906. *A Sanskrit Reader: With Vocabulary and Notes.* Boston: Ginn and Company.

Larin, B. A. *See* Vasmer, Max.

Larson, Pär. 1990. Tra "garzoni" e "guarcini": note etimologiche. *AGI* 75, 74–90.

Lass, Roger. 1995. Four Letters in Search of an Etymology. *Diachronica* 12, 99–111.

Last, Werner. 1925. *Das Bahuvrîhi-Compositum im Altenglischen, Mittelenglischen und Neuenglischen.* Greifswald: Buchdruckerei Hans Adler.

Latendorf, Friedrich. 1877. Altvil. *KVNS* 2, 25.

________. 1880. Altvil noch am Leben. *KVNS* 5, 17–18.

Latham, Robert G. 1866–70. *A Dictionary of the English Language*. London: Green & Co., *etc*.

Latham, Ronald E. 1965. *Revised Medieval Latin Word List from British and Irish Sources.* Under the direction of a committee appointed by the British Academy. London: Oxford University Press (for the British Academy).

Lauffer, Otto. 1938. Die Hexe als Zaunreiterin. In *Volkskundliche Ernte, Hugo Hepding dargebracht am 7. September 1938 von seinen Freunden.* GBDP 60, 114–30.

LC = J. M. Lothian and T. W. Craik, eds., *Twelfth Night.* The Arden Edition of the Works of William Shakespeare. London: Methuen & Co Ltd, 1975.

LE = Joseph Vendryes, *Lexique étymologique de l'irlandais ancien.* Dublin: Institute for Advanced Studies, Paris: Centre National de la Recherche Scientifique, 1959–.

Leach, Maria. *See* FWSD.

Lebrun, Yvan. 1969–70. Het lot van de "obscene" woorden in de angelsaksische landen. *TVUB* 12, 55–59.

Lecouteux, Claude. 1981. Zwerge und Verwandte. *Euphorion* 75, 366–78.

________. 1987. Mara—Ephialtes—incubus. Le Cauchemar chez les peuples germaniques. *EG* 42, 1–24.

Lee, Francis B. 1894. Jerseyisms. *DN* 1, 327–34.
Leendertz, P. Jr. 1918. Kenne, kene, boye, kier. *TNTL* 37, 269–70.
LeFanu, William. 1988. *A Catalogue of Books Belonging to Dr Jonathan Swift*.... Cambridge: Bibliographical Society.
Lehman, B. H. 1922. Additional Words from the Northwest. *DN* 5, 181.
Lehmann, Paul. *See* MlW.
Lehmann, Wilhelm. 1906. Zum ae. wortschatz. *AB* 17, 296–300.
________. 1907. Anmerkungen zum ae. Sprachschatz. *Archiv* 119, 184–89.
________. 1908. Irische Etymologien. *ZCP* 6, 433–38.
Lehmann, Winfred P. 1966–67. [Rev of] CEDEL and ODEE. *CE* 28, 625–28.
See also Feist, Sigmund , 4th ed.
Lehnert, Martin. *See* HL.
Leland, Charles G. *See* BL.
Lemon, George W. 1783. *English Etymology*. London: G. Robinson.
Lenz, Philipp. 1898. *Vergleichendes Wörterbuch der neuhochdeutschen Sprache und der handschuhsheimer Dialekts*. Baden-Baden: Ernst Kölblin, Hof-Buchdruckerei.
Leo, Heinrich 1842. Zur Lex Salica. *ZDA* 2, 500–33.
________. 1877. *Angelsächsisches Glossar*.... Halle: Verlag der Buchhandlung des Waisenhauses.
Lerchner, Gotthard. 1965. *Studien zum nordwestgermanischen Wortschatz. Ein Beitrag zu den Fragen um Aufbau und Gliederung des Germanischen*. MSt 28.
Le Roy Andrews, A. 1914. Old Norse Notes. *MLN* 29, 133–36.
Lessen, Jacoba, H. van. *See* Van Lessen, Jacoba H.
Lessiak, Primus. 1912. Gicht. Ein Beitrag zur Kunde deutscher Krankheitsnamen. *ZDA* 53, 101–82.
Leumann, Manu. 1954. Vokaldehnung, Dehnstufe und Vrddhi. *IF* 61, 1–16.
Leverkus. *See* Lübben, August. 1871.
Levin, Jules F. 1992. Pigeons, Cows and April in Lithuania. *LiB* 2, 85–91.
Levin, Saul. 1976. The English and the American Robin. *LACUS* 3, 128–36.
________. 1995. *Semitic and Indo-European. The Principal Etymologies, with Observations on Afro-Asiatic*. ASTHLS: CILT 129.
Levitskii, V.V. 2000–03. *Etimologicheskii slovar' germanskikh iazykov* [*Germanic Etymological Dictionary*]. 4 vols. Chernovtsy: Ruta.
LEW = Ernst Fraenkel, *Litauisches etymologisches Wörterbuch*. 2 vols. Vol. 2, with the assistance of Annemarie Slupski, continued by Erich Hofmann and Eberhard Tangl. Heidelberg: Carl Winter, Universitätsverlag; Göttingen: Vandenhoeck & Ruprecht, 1962–65.
Lewis, Henry. 1923. [Untitled.] *The Bulletin of the Board of Celtic Studies* 1, 9–15.
Lexer, Matthias. 1869–78. *Mittelhochdeutsches Handwörterbuch*. Leipzig: Verlag von S. Hirzel.
Liberman, Anatoly. 1986. Two Icelandic Etymologies. *GL* 26, 106–14.
________. 1988a. The Etymology of Modern English *Heifer*. *GL* 28, 163–75.
________. 1988b. Two Dialectal Words for 'Pig.' *GL* 28, 104–18. Partly repr in: Liberman 1994c, 254–63.
________. 1988c. The Origin of the Eddic Animal Names *Heiðrún* and *Eykþyrnir*. *GL* 28, 32–48. Repr in Liberman 1994c, 237–52.
________. 1990. Etymological Studies 3: Some Germanic Words Beginning with *fl-*. Language at Play. *GL* 30, 1–27. Repr in Liberman 1994c, 264–91.
________. 1991. [Rev of] ÁBM. *SS* 63, 221–29. Repr in Liberman 1994c, 292–302.
________. 1992a. Etymological Studies 5: Some English Words Related to Sex and Prostitution. GL 32, 71–94.
________. 1992b. Snorri and Saxo on Útgarðaloki, with Notes on Loki Laufeyjarson's Character, Career, and Name. In *Saxo Grammaticus. Tra storiografia e letteratura*, ed. Carlo Santini, pp. 91–158. Roma: Il Calamo. Repr in: Liberman 1994c, 176–234.
________. 1994a. An Analytic Dictionary of English Etymology. *Dictionaries* 15, 1–29.
________. 1994b. Etymological Studies 6: Some Obscure English Words. (From the Files of *An Analytic Dictionary of English Etymology*.) *GL* 33, 164–78.
________. 1994c. *Word Heath. Wortheide. Orðheiði: Essays on Germanic Literature and Usage (1972–1992)*. EAO 1.
________. 1995. [Rev of] Barnes, Michael P. 1994. *Scandinavica* 34, 263–66.
________. 1996a. Etymologies [in *The Century Dictionary*]. *Dictionaries* 17, 29–54.

________. 1996b. Ten Scandinavian and North English Etymologies. *ALVÍSSmál* 6, 69–98.

________. 1997. Etymological Studies 7: A Small Animal Farm. *GL* 35, 97–130.

________. 1998. English *Girl* under the Asterisked Sky of the Indo-Europeans. In *Proceedings of the Seventh UCLA Indo-European Conference, Los Angeles, 1995,* ed. Angela della Volpe, in collaboration with Edgar C. Polomé. JIES-MS 27, 150–72.

________. 1999a. The English *F*-Word and its Kin. In *Interdigitations: Essays for Irmengard Rauch,* eds. Gerald F. Carr, Wayne Harbert, and Lihua Zhang, pp. 107–20. New York: Peter Lang.

________. 1999b. Fonosemantika i etimologiia [Phonosemantics and Etymology]. *IaRD* 2, 94–102.

________. 2001a. The Etymology of English *beacon, boy,* and *buoy. AJGLL* 12, 201–34.

________. 2001b. The Etymology of Some Germanic, Especially English, Plant Names (*Henbane, Hemlock, Horehound*). In *Proceedings of the Twelfth Annual UCLA Indo-European Conference, Los Angeles, May 26–28, 2000,* eds. Martin Huld et al. JIES-MS 40, 132–46.

________. 2002a. A Cobweb of Dwarves and Dweebs (An Exercise in Very Close Reading and Germanic Etymology). In *"A Certain Text": Close Readings and Textual Studies on Shakespeare and Others in Honor of Thomas Clayton,* eds. Linda Andersson and Janis Lull, 173–92. Newark: University of Delaware Press, London: Associated University Presses.

________. 2002b. English *ivy* and German *Epheu* in their Germanic and Indo-European Context. In *Proceedings of the Thirteenth Annual UCLA Indo-European Conference, Los Angeles, November 9–10, 2001,* eds. Karlene Jones-Bley, et al. JIES-MS 44, 129–44.

________. 2002c. What Happened to Female Dwarfs? In *Mythological Women: Studies in Memory of Lotte Motz,* eds. Rudolf Simek and Wilhelm Heizmann. SMS 7, 257–63.

________. 2003. *Bird* and *Toad.* In *Runica—Germanica—Medieaevalia,* eds. Wilhelm Heizmann and Astrid van Nahl. Ergänzungsbände zum *Reallexikon der Germanischen Altertumskunde* 37, 375–88. Berlin, New York: Walter de Gruyter.

________. 2004a. An Etymologist Looks at Gray Matter. (On the Origin and History of English *brain,* German *Hirn,* and Some of their Synonyms). In *Worlds of Words: A Tribute to Arne Zettersten,* ed. Cay Dollerup. *NJES* 3 (special issue), 45–59.

________. 2004b. Extended forms (*Streckformen*) in English. In *Studies in the History of the English Language II: Unfolding Conversations,* eds. Anne Curzan [and] Kimberly Emmons, 85–110. Topics in Linguistics 45 . Berlin, New York: Mouton de Gruyter.

________. 2005. The Relation of English *slowworm,* Swedish and Older Danish *ormslå,* Norwegian Dialectal *sleva,* and German *Blindschleiche* to **slahan* 'strike,' with a Note on Tautological Compounds. In *Papers on Scandinavian and Germanic Language and Culture, Published in Honour of Michael Barnes*... *NOWELE* 46–47, 119–32.

________. 2006. Etymological Devilry: Swedish *raggere/raggen,* English *ragamuffin,* Lithuanian *rãgana/rãgius,* and Italian *ragazzo.* In *Grenzgänger. Festschrift zum 65. Geburtstag von Jurij Kusmenko,* eds. Antje Hornscheidt, et al, 191–200. Berliner Beiträge zur Skandinavistik 9. Berlin: Nordeuropa-Institut der Humboldt-Universität.

________. 2007. An Additional Note on Tautological Compounds. *NOWELE* 52, 67–73. *See also* Propp, Vladimir.

Lidén, Evald. 1937. Wortgeschichtliches. In: *Mélanges Linguistiques offerts à M. Holger Pedersen à l'occasion de son soixante-dixième anniversaire 7 avril 1937,* 88–94. AJ IX/1.

Liebert, Gösta. 1949. *Das Nominalsuffix* -ti- *im Altindischen. Ein Beitrag zur altindischen und vergleichenden Wortbildungslehre.* Diss. Göteborg. Lund: Håkon Ohlssons boktryckeri.

Lighter, J. E. *See* RHHDAS.

Limburg, Peter R. 1986. *Stories behind Words: The Origins and Histories of 285 English Words.* H. W. Wilson Company.

Lind, E. H. 1905–15. *Norsk-isländska dopnamn ock fingerade namn från medeltiden.* Uppsala: A.-B. Lundequistska bokhandeln, Leipzig: Otto Harassowitz.

________. 1920–21. *Norskisländska personbinamn från medeltiden....* Uppsala: A. B. Lundequistska Bokhandeln.

Lindeman, Frederik O. *See* BjL.

Lindquist, Ivar. 1956. *Die Urgestalt der* Hávamál.

Ein Versuch zur Bestimmung auf synthetischem Wege. LNS 11.
Lindqvist, Axel. 1918. Vom Anlautwechsel *STR : R* im Germanischen. *PBB* 43, 100–13.
Lindroth, Hjalmar. 1911. Studier i svensk etymologi och ordhistoria. In *Festskrift till K. F. Söderwall på hans sjuttioårsdag den 1 januari 1912*, 121–76. Lund: C. W. K. Gleerup.
________. 1911–12. Beiträge zur altnordischen Lautlehre. *IF* 29, 129–200.
Linnig, Franz. 1895. *Bilder zur Geschichte der deutschen Sprache.* Paderborn: Druck und Verlag von Ferdinand Schöningh.
Little, William. *See* SOD.
Littmann, Enno. 1924. *Morgenländische Wörter im Deutschen.* 2nd ed. Tübingen: Verlag von J. C. B. Mohr (Paul Siebeck).
Littré, Émile. 1875–89. *Dictionnaire de la langue française....* 2nd ed. Paris: Librarie Hachette et Cie. Repr Paris: Gallimard-Hachette, 1959–61. (Édition intégrale.)
Llewellyn, E. C. 1936. *The Influence of Low Dutch on the English Vocabulary.* PPSoc 12.
Lloyd, Albert L. *See* EWA.
Lochner-Hüttenbach, Fritz. 1967. Zum Namen der Habergeiß. In *Beiträge zur Indogermanistik und Keltologie. Julius Pokorny zum 80. Geburtstag gewidmet,* ed. Wolfgang Meid. IBK 13, 51–55.
Lockwood, William B. 1981a. Etymological Observations on Brambling, Bunting, Fieldfare, Godwit, Wren. In *Bono Homini Donum: Essays in Historical Linguistics in Memory of J. Alexander Kerns*, eds. Yoël L. Arbeitman and Allan R. Bomhard. ASTHLS IV/16, 187–201.
________. 1981b. Wortkundliche Parerga. *ZCP* 38, 179–86.
________. 1984. *The Oxford Book of British Bird Names.* Oxford, New York: Oxford University Press.
________. 1995a. Etymological Notes on Some British Bird Names. *LL* 13, 67–72.
________. 1995b. Philology and Folklore: The Case of *Adebar* and *Storch*. *GLL* 48, 371–75.
Löfstedt, Ernst. 1948. Nordfriesische Beiträge 3. *NdM* 4, 74–81.
________. 1963–65. Beiträge zur nordseegermanischen und nordseegermanischnordischen [sic] Lexikographie. *NdM* 19–21, 281–345.
________. 1969. Beiträge zur nordseegermanischen und nordseegermanisch-nordischen [sic] Lexikographie. *NdM* 25, 25–45.
Loewe, Richard. 1910. *Deutsches Wörterbuch.* Leipzig: G. J. Göschen'sche Verlagshandlung.
________. 1935. Etymologische und wortgeschichtliche Bemerkungen zu deutschen Pflanzennamen. *PBB* 59, 244–60.
________. 1938. Etymologische und wortgeschichtliche Bemerkungen zu deutschen Pflanzennamen 5. *PBB* 62, 43–54.
Loewenthal, John. 1915. Drei Götternamen. *ANF* 31, 153–54.
________. 1916. Zur germanischen Wortkunde. *ANF* 32, 270–301.
________. 1917. Zur germanischen Wortkunde. *ANF* 33, 97–131.
________. 1927. Fricco. *PBB* 50, 287–96.
________. 1928. Etymologica. *PBB* 52, 457–59.
Logeman, H. 1906. On Some Cases of Scandinavian Influence in English. *Archiv* 117, 29–46, 268–86.
Logeman, Willem S. 1891. Bird. *NQ* VII/11, 116.
Lommatzsch, Erhard. *See* TL.
Long, Harry A. 1883. *Personal and Family Names.* London: Hamilton, Adams & Co., *etc.* Repr Book Tower, Detroit: Gale Research Company, 1968.
Longman 1984 = *Longman Dictionary of the English Language.* Longman Group Limited, 1984.
Longman Dictionary of the English Language. New [2nd] ed, 1991. Longman.
Longman's English Larousse. Paris: Moreau & Cie, Librairie Larousse, 1968. Repr as *Longman Modern English Dictionary. Longman.* Owen Watson, ed., 1976.
Longmuir, John. *See* Jamieson, John. 1879–82.
Lothian, J. M. *See* LC.
Lower, Mark A. 1875. *English Surnames: An Essay on Family Nomenclature, Historical, Etymological, and Humorous.* 2 vols. London: John Russell Smith. Repr Book Tower, Detroit: Gale Research Company, 1968.
LP = Sveinbjörn Egilsson, *Lexicon poeticum antiquæ linguæ septentrionalis. Ordbog over det norsk-islandske skjaldesprog.* 2nd ed, by Finnur Jónsson. København: Atlas bogtryk, 1966.
Lubotsky, Alexander. 1988. *The System of Nominal Accentuation in Sanskrit and Proto-Indo-European.* Leiden; New York: E.J. Brill.

See also Schrijver, Peter. 1997, *and* Schwartz, Martin
Luce, Morton, ed. 1937. *The Works of Shakespeare. Twelfth Night, or What You Will.* London: Methuen and Co. Ltd.
Lübben, August. 1871. Altvil. *ZDP* 3, 317–31 (pp. 317–23 were written by Leverkus; p. 331 contains a few remarks by J. Zacher).
________. 1876. [Altvil] Antwort. *KVNS* 1, 6.
See also MW.
Lühr, Rosemarie. 1982. *Studien zur Sprache des Hildebrandliedes.* Part 1: *Herkunft und Sprache.* Europäische Hochschulschriften I/568. RBDSL 22.
________. 1988. *Expressivität und Lautgesetz im Germanischen.* MSp 15.
See also EWA.
Luick, Karl. 1897. [Rev of] Skeat, Walter W. 1896. *AB* 8, 129–32.
________. 1897–98. Die herkunft des ne. *girl. AB* 8, 235–36.
________. 1964. *Historische Grammatik der englischen Sprache*, posthumous ed, by Friedrich Wild and Herbert Koziol. Cambridge, MA: Harvard University Press. First publ 1914–40.
Luiselli, Bruno. 1992. *Storia culturale dei rapporti tra mondo romano e mondo germanico.* BH 1.
Lull, Janis. *See* Liberman, Anatoly. 2002a.
Lund, Johannes J. 1935. *The History of Words Pertaining to Certain Crafts in the Principal Indo-European Languages.* Private Edition, distributed by the University of Chicago Libraries. Chicago, Illinois.
Lutjens, August. 1911. *Der Zwerg in der deutschen Heldendichtung des Mittelalters.* GA 38.
Lutz, F. *See* KL.
Lydekker, R. 1907. The "Coney" of the Bible. *Knowledge... A Monthly Record of Sience* 30, 248–50.
Lye, Edward [Edvardvs]. 1772. *Dictionarium Saxonico et Gothico-Latinum*, ed by Owen Manning. Londini: B. White, *etc.*
See also Junius.
Lynn, W. T. 1881. Toadstool. *NQ* VI/4, 249.
________. 1884. Ashkey. *NQ* VI/9, 27.
________. 1889. Chiddingstone : To Chide. *NQ* VII/7, 445–46.
MA = J.P. Mallory and D.Q. Adams, eds., *Encyclopedia of Indo-European Culture.* London and Chicago: Fitzner Dearborn Publishers, 1997.
Maak, Hans-Georg. 1974. Germ. **dall-/*dill-/*dull-. NM* 75, 377–85.
MacBain, Alexander. 1982. *An Etymological Dictionary of the Gaelic Language.* Glasgow: Gairm Publications, vol. 57. Repr of the 2nd ed. First publ Inverness: The Northern Counties Printing and Publishing Company, Ltd, 1896; 2nd rev ed, Stirling: E. Mackay, 1911.
MacGillivray, Hugh S. 1902. *The Influence of Christianity on the Vocabulary of Old English.* SEP 8.
Machan, Tim W., ed. 1988. *Vafþrúðnismál.* DMT 6.
Mackay, Charles. 1877. *The Gaelic Etymology of the Languages of Western Europe and More Especially of the English and Lowland Scotch, and of their Slang, Cant, and Colloquial Dialects.* London: Publ for the author by N. Trübner and Co.
________. 1887. *A Glossary of Obscure Words and Phrases in the Writings of Shakespeare and his Contemporaries Traced Etymologically to Ancient Language of the British People As Spoken before the Irruption of the Danes and Saxons.* London: Sampson Low, *etc.*
________. 1888. *A Dictionary of Lowland Scotch.* Edinburgh: Privately Printed at the Ballantyne Press.
MacKay, L. A. 1933. Catullus 53.5. *CR* 47, 220.
Mackel, Emil. 1887. *Die germanischen Elemente in der französischen und provenzalischen Sprache.* FSt VI/1.
________. 1905. Romanisches und Französisches im Niederdeutschen. *Festschrift Adolf Tobler zum siebzigsten Geburtstage...*, 263–73. Braunschweig: George Westermann.
Mackensen, Lutz. 1985. *Ursprung der Wörter. Etymologisches Wörterbuch der deutschen Sprache.* München: Südwest Verlag.
MacLaury, Robert E. *See* Jäkel, Olaf.
MacRitchie, David. 1911. The Speech of the Roads. *NC* 70, 545–54.
________. 1915. The Celtic Numerals of Strathclyde. PSAS 1914–1915, 276–85.
Mätzner, Eduard. 1860. *Englische Grammatik.* Vol 1. *Die Lehre vom Worte.* Berlin: Weidmannsche Buchhandlung.
________. 1878–85. *Altenglische Sprachproben nebst einem Wörterbuche.* Berlin: Weidmann.
Magnusen, Finn. 1828. *See* FML.

Magnússon, Ásgeir Blöndal. 1953. Endurtekningarsagnir með *t*-viðskeyti í íslenzku. In *Afmæliskveðja til Próf. Dr. Phil. Alexanders Jóhannessonar Háskólarektors 15. júli 1953 frá samstarfsmönnum og nemendum*, 9–41. [Reykjavík]: Helgafell.

________. 1957. [Rev of] AEW [1st ed, fasc 1]. *Skírnir* 131, 236–41.

________. 1989. *Íslensk orðsifjabók*. [Reykjavík]: Orðabók Háskólans.

See also ÁBM.

Majut, Rudolf. 1963. Himmelsziege und Verwandtes. *ZDS* 19, 1–38.

Makaev, È. A. 1962. Sistema soglasnykh fonem v germanskikh iazykakh [The System of Consonant Phonemes in Germanic]. SGGI II, 11–71.

________. 1970. *Struktura slova v indoevropeiskikh i germanskikh iazykakh* [*The Structure of the Word in the Indo-European and Germanic Languages*]. Moskva: Nauka.

Makovskii, M. M. [a.k.a. Makovskij, M. M.] 1964. Interaction of Areal Slang Variants and their Correlation with Standard Language. *Linguistics* 7, 42–54.

________. 1968. "Geografiia slov" i leksicheskie sviazi germanskikh iazykov i dialektov ["The Geography of Words" and Lexical Connections in Germanic Languages and Dialects]. *VIa* 3, 126–35.

________. 1971. *Teoriia leksicheskoi attraktsii. (Opyt funktsional'noi tipologiii leksiko-semanticheskikh sistem.)* [*Theory of Lexical Attraction.* (*An Attempt at a Functional Typology of Lexico-Semantic Systems*)]. Moskva: Nauka.

________. 1977. Sootnoshenie neobkhodimosti i svobody v leksiko-semanticheskikh preobrazovaniiakh [The Relationship between Necessity and Freedom in Lexico-Semantic Transformations]. *VIa* 3, 55–72.

________. 1980. *Sistemnost' i asistemnost' v iazyke. Opyt issledovaniia antinomii v leksike i semantike* [*System and Lack of System in Language: An Attempt at an Investigation of the Antinomy in Lexis and Semantics*]. Moskva: Nauka.

________. 1985. *Problemy lingvisticheskoi kombinatoriki* [*Problems of Combinatorial Linguistics*]. *VIa* 3, 43–57.

________. 1986. *Angliiskaia etimologiia* [*English Etymology*]. Moscow: Vysshaia shkola.

________. 1988a. *Lingvisticheskaia kombinatorika. Opyt topologicheskoi stratifikatsii iazykovykh struktur* [*Combinatorial Linguistics: An Attempt at a Topological Stratification of Language Structures*]. Moskva: Nauka (Glavnaia redaktsiia vostochnoi literatury).

________. 1988b. [Rev of] Feist[4]. *VIa* 5, 140–46.

________. 1988c. [Rev of] Stuart E. Mann, 1984–87. *VIa* 3, 135–41.

________. 1989a. [Rev of] Starck, Taylor, and J. C. Wells, *Althochdeutsches Glossenwörterbuch....* Heidelberg: Carl Winter. *VIa* 1, 134–41.

________. 1989b. *Udivitel'nyi mir slov i znachenii. Illiuzii i paradoksy v leksike i semantike* [*A Wonderful World of Words and Meanings: Illusions and Paradoxes in Vocabulary and Semantics*]. Moskva: Vysshaia shkola.

________. 1991. [Rev of] *EWD*. *VIa* 3, 138–44.

________. 1992a. "Kartina mira" i miry obrazov (lingvokul'turologicheskie etiudy) ["A Picture of the World" and the Worlds of Images (Etudes on Language and Culture)]. *VIa* 6, 36–53.

________. 1992b. *Lingvisticheskaia genetika. Problemy ontogeneza slova v indoevropeiskikh iazykakh* [*Linguistic Genetics: The Ontogenesis of the Word in the Indo-European Languages*]. Moskva: Nauka.

________. 1993. [Rev of] HED. *VIa* 4, 128–39.

________. 1995. Kompendium slavianskoi i indoevropeiskoi etimologii. (K dvadtsatiletiiu vykhoda v svet pervogo vypuska "Etimologicheskogo slovaria slavianskikh iazykov") [A Compendium of Slavic and Indo-European Etymology. (On the 20th Anniversary of Volume 1 of *ESSI*)]. *VIa* 5, 127–41.

________. 1996. [Rev of] T. V. Toporova, *Kul'tura v zerkale iazyka: drevnegermanskie dvuchlennye imena sobstvennye [Culture in the Mirror of Language: Two-Element Proper Names in Germanic*]. Moskva: Shkola "Iazyki russkoi kul'tury." *VIa* 4, 120–28.

________. 1998. Metamorfozy slova. (Tabuiruiushchie markery v indoevropeiskikh iazykakh) [The Metamorphoses of the Word. (Taboo Markers in the Indo-European Languages)]. *VIa* 4, 151–79.

________. 1999a. *Istoriko-etimologicheskii slovar' sovremennogo angliiskogo iazyka. Slovo v zerkale chelovecheskoi kul'tury* [*A Historico-Etymological Dictionary of Modern English: The Word in the Mirror of Human Culture*]. Moskva: Izdalel'skii dom "Dialog." [The date on the title page is 2000.]

________. 1999b. Mifopoetika pis'ma v indoevropeiskikh iazykakh. [The Mythopoetics of Writing in the Indo-European Languages]. *VIa* 4, 73–86.

________. 2000a. [Rev of] *Iazyk i rechevaia deiatel'nost'* 1–2. Sankt-Peterburg: Sankt-Peterburgskii Universitet, 1998. *VIa* 3, 132–48.

________. 2000b. *Fenomen tabu v traditsiakh i v iazyke indoevropeitsev. Sushchnost'—formy—razvitie. [Taboo in the Traditions and Language of the Indo-Europeans: Its Essence, Forms, and Development].* Moscow: Azbukovnik.

________. 2002. Semiotika iazycheskikh kul'tov. (Mifopoeticheskie etiudy) [The Semiotics of Pagan Cults. (Mythopoetical Etudes.) *Vla* 6, 55–81.

Malkiel, Yakov. 1979. Semantic Universals, Lexical Polarization, Taboo: The Romance Domain of 'Left' and 'Right' Revisited. In *Studies in Diachronic, Synchronic, and Typological Linguistics: Festschrift for Oswald Szemerényi on the Occasion of his 65th Birthday*, ed. Bela Brogyanyi. ASTHLS IV/11, 507–27.

________. 1985. The Differentiation of Two Hispanic Zoönyms Based on Latin *curtus* 'short'. In *Studi linguistici e filologici per Carlo Alberto Mastrelli*, 233–46. Pisa: Pacini editore.

Mallory, James P. *See* Hehn, Victor. 1894.

Malone, Edmond. *See* MSh.

Malone, Kemp. 1923. *The Literary History of* Hamlet *1. The Early Tradition.* AF 59. Repr New York: Haskell House, 1964.

________. 1927. Etymologies for Hamlet. *RES* 3, 257–71.

________. 1928. More Etymologies for Hamlet. *RES* 4, 257–69.

________. 1929. Hamlet and Oskeladd. *SS* 10, 138–41 (printed at the end of the volume; duplicate the same page numbers from a different article in the middle).

________. 1952. [Rev of] IsEW, Fasc. 1. *Lg* 28, 527–33.

________. 1955. On the Etymology of *filch. MLN* 70, 165–68.

________. 1956. [Rev of] IsEW, Fasc. 6–7. Bern: A. Francke, 1955. *Lg* 32, 340–51.

Mańczak, Witold. 1987. *Frequenzbedingter unregelmässiger Lautwandel in den germanischen Sprachen.* Wrocław, *etc.*: Wydawnictwo Polskiej Akademii nauk.

________. 1998. Étymologie de l'allemand *Mann. SEC* 3, 25–26.

Mandel, Jerome. 1975. "Boy" As Devil in Chaucer. *PLL* 11, 407–11.

Manly, Daniel. *See* Hexham, Hendrik.

Mannhardt, Wilhelm. 1884. *Mythologische Forschungen aus dem Nachlasse von Wilhelm Mannhardt.* Karl Müllenhoff and Wilhelm Scherer, eds. QF 51.

Manning, Owen. *See* Lye, Edward.

Mansion, J. 1928. Twee Zeeuwsche *-kerke-*namen. *NGN* 6, 88–93.

Marchand, Hans. 1969. *The Categories and Types of Present-Day English Word-Formation: A Synchronic-Diachronic Approach.* 2nd ed. München: C. H. Beck.

Markey, Thomas L. 1976. *A North Sea Germanic Reader.* München: Wilhelm Fink Verlag.

________. 1979. Nfr *kūch*, Engl. 'key,' and the Unshifted Consonant Question. *ZDL* 46, 41–55.

________. 1980. [Rev of] Piergiuseppe Scardigli and Teresa Gervasi, 1978. *CG* 13, 177–79.

________. 1983. Gmc. **Baina-* 'Bone' and Other Monstrosities. *NOWELE* 2, 93–107.

________. 1986. The Lexical Semantics of Western Indo-European 'Girl.' In *Aspects of Language: Studies in Honour of Mario Alinei: Papers Presented to Mario Alinei by his Friends, Colleagues and Former Students on the Occasion of his 60th Birthday.* Vol. 2: *Theoretical and Applied Semantics*, eds. Nils Århammar, et al, 275–89. Amsterdam: Rodopi.

Marsh, George P. 1865. Notes on Mr. Hensleigh Wedgwood's Dictionary of English Etymology, and on Some Words Not Discussed by Him. *TPS*, 187–200. *See also* Wedgwood, Hensleigh. 1859–65.

Marshall, Ed. 1881. Toadstool. *NQ* VI/4, 452.

________. 1897. Round Robin. *NQ* VIII/11, 131.

Marshall, Julian. 1890. *Cockney. NQ* VII/9, 74.

Marstrander, Carl. *See* Vendryes, Joseph. 1912.

Martin, Ariadna Y. *See* Propp, Vladimir.

Martin, Bernhard. 1923. Wortgeographische Studien in Hessen-Nassau. *ZDD* 18/3–4 (= *Festschrift Ferdinand Wrede zu seinem sechzigsten Geburtstage, gewidmet von seinen Freunden und Schülern*), 254–57.

Martin, Ernst. 1907. *Der Versbau des* Heliand *und der altsächsischen* Genesis. QF 100.

Martin, Ralph G. 1944. The Biography of a Jeep. *NYTM*, July 2, 22, 38, 39.

Martin, Richard P. *See* Propp, Vladimir.
Martin, Roland. 1938. Können wir das Wort 'verstehen' verstehen? Ein Versuch. *ZD* 52, 626–29.
Martinet, André. 1937. *La gémination consonantique d'origine expressive dans les langues germaniques.* Copenhagen: Levin & Munksgaard, Paris: Klincksieck.
Martinius = Matthiæ Martini, *Lexicon Philologicum....* Amstelodami: Apud Johannem Ludovicum de Lorme, 1701.
Marzell, Heinrich. 1943–79. *Wörterbuch der deutschen Pflanzennamen.* Leipzig and Stuttgart: S. Hirzel; Wiesbaden: Franz Steiner.
Matthes, H. Ch. *See* Jordan, Richard, 2nd ed.
Matthews, Constance M. 1966. *English Surnames.* London: Weidenfeld and Nicolson.
Maurer, David W., assisted by Ellesa C. High. 1980. New Words—Where Do They Come from and Where Do They Go? *AS* 55, 184–94.
________. 1981. *Language of the Underworld.* Collected and Edited by Allan W. Futrell & Charles B. Wordell. Lexington, KY: The University Press of Kentucky.
See also Mencken, H. L.
Mawer, Allen. 1937. English Place-Names and English Philology. *TPS,* 120–33.
Maxwell, Herbert. 1891a. Bird. *NQ* VII/11, 63.
________. 1891b. Bird. *NQ* VII/11, 177.
May, Martin, 1893. *Beiträge zur Stammkunde der deutschen Sprache nebst einer Einleitung über die keltgermanischen Sprachen und ihr Verhältnis zu allen anderen Sprachen....* Leipzig: F. W. v. Biedermann.
Mayhew, Anthony L. 1890. The Etymology of "Cockney." *The Academy* 37, 338.
________. 1891a. Bird. *NQ* VII/11, 116.
________. 1891b. The Etymology of "yet," O. E. "gíet." *The Academy* 40, 564.
________. 1891c. *Synopsis of Old English Phonology.* Oxford: At the Clarendon Press.
________. 1891d. [Rev of] *CD. ESt* 15, 447–57.
________. 1894. Larrikin. *NQ* VIII/5, 447–48.
________. 1900. Hun-Barrow. *NQ* IX/5, 87.
________. 1912. On Some Etymologies of English Words. *MLR* 7, 318–25, 499–507.
Mayhew, Anthony L., and Walter W. Skeat. 1888. *A Concise Dictionary of Middle English from A.D. 1150 to 1580.* Oxford: At the Clarendon Press.
Mayou, Martha B. 1999. The Sources of the *Etymologicum Anglicanum* (1743) by Francis Junius. *Dictionaries* 20, 90–150.
See also Vennemann, Theo. 1997.
Mayrhofer, Manfred. 1952a. Gibt es ein indogermanisches **sor* "Frau"? *SIG,* 32–39.
________. 1952b. Indogermanische Wortforschung seit Kriegsende. *SIG,* 39–55.
See also KEWA.
McArthur, Roshan. 1996. Taboo Words in Print. *ET* 12:3, 50–58.
McCloskey, Richard G. 1943. Jeep. *ANQ* 3, 136–37.
McDavid, Raven I., Jr. 1967. [Rev of] DC. *CJL* 13, 55–57.
See also Mencken, H. L.
McFarlane, W. C. 1943. Jeep. *ANQ* 3, 155.
McIntoch, E. *See* COD5.
McKinley, Richard. 1990. *A History of British Surnames.* London and New York: Longman.
McLintock, D. R. 1972. 'To forget' in Germanic. *TPS,* 79–93.
McMullen, Edwin W. Jr. 1953. *English Topographic Terms in Florida 1563–1874.* Gainesville: University of Florida Press.
McPeek, James A. S. 1939. *Catullus in Strange and Distant Britain.* HSCL 15.
ME = Manuales y anejos de "Emerita." Madrid: Instituto "Antonio de Nebrija".
MED = *Middle English Dictionary.* Hans Kurath et al, eds. Ann Arbor: University of Michigan Press, 1956–2001.
Meech, Sanford B. 1940–41. Proverbs in Rawlinson MS D328. *MP* 38, 111–32.
Meer, Geart van der. *See* Van der Meer, Geart.
Meid, Wolfgang. 1992. Die germanische Religion im Zeugnis der Sprache. In *Germanische Religionsgeschichte. Quellen und Quellenprobleme,* eds. Heinrich Beck, Detlev Ellmers, and Kurt Schier, 486–507. Berlin, New York: Walter de Gruyter.
See also KrM *and* Lochner-Hüttenbach, Fritz.
Meidinger, Heinrich. 1836. *Vergleichendes etymologisches Wörterbuch der gothisch-teutonischen Mundarten.* 2nd ed. Frankfurt am Main: Bei Johann V. Meidinger.
Meier, Harri. 1976. Garçon, valet, vassal. In *Scritti in onore di Giuliano Bonfante,* 473–87. Brescia: Paideia Editrice.
Meillet, Antoine. *See* EM.
Meißner, Rudolf. 1927. Der Name Hamlet. *IF* 45, 370–94.
Melefors, Evert. 1984. *Ling* och *graun*—

växtbeteckningar i ortnamn på Gotland. In *Florilegium Nordicum: En bukett nordiska språk- och namnstudier tillägnade Sigurd Fries den 22 april 1984.* AUU 61, 176–90.

Melioranskii, P. 1902. Turetskie elementy v iazyke "Slova o polku Igoreve" [Turkic Elements in the Language of *The Lay of Igor's Host.*] IORIS VII/2, 273–302.

Ménage [a.k.a. Menagius], Gilles. 1694. *Dictionnaire étymologique ou les origines de la langue françoise....* Paris: J. Anisson. 2nd ed, Paris: Briasson, 1750. Repr Gèneve: Slatkin Reprints, 1973.

Mencken, Henry L. 1936. *The American Language.* New York: Alfred A. Knopf. Supplement I, 1945. 4th ed and the Two Supplements, abridged, with annotations and new material by Raven I. McDavid, Jr. with the assistance of David W. Maurer, 1967.

Méndez-Naya, Belen. *See* Vennemannn, Theo. 2002.

Menges, Karl H. 1948–49. It. *ciarlatano,* Fr. *charlatan* – Altaic Loan Words. *RP* 2, 229–31.

________. 1951. *The Oriental Elements in the Vocabulary of the Oldest Russian Epos,* The Igor' Tale. *Word.* Supplement 7.

Mentz, F. 1905. Altvil. Ein neuer Erklärungsversuch. *NJ* 31, 1–19.

________. 1908. Zu altvil. *KVNS* 29, 18–19.

Menzel, Wolfgang. 1861. Die Heimchen. *Germania* 6, 129–43.

Meringer, Rudolf. 1892. *Beiträge zur Geschichte der indogermanischen Declination.* SKAW 125/2.

________. 1904–05. Wörter und Sachen 2. *IF* 17, 100–66.

________. 1907. Wörter und Sachen 5. *IF* 21, 277–314.

________. 1908. Wörter und Sachen 3. *IF* 18, 204–96.

Meritt, Herbert D. 1959. *The Old English Prudentius Glosses at Boulogne-sur-Mer.* SSLL 16.
See also Hall, J. R. Clark.

Merkulova, V. A. 1967. *Ocherki po russkoi narodnoi nomenklature rastenii. Travy, griby, iagody* [Studies in Popular Russian Plant Names. Herbs, Mushrooms, Berries]. Moskva: Nauka.

Meulen , van der R. *See* Van der Meulen, R.

Meurer, Judith. *See* Gunnell, Terry, *and* Kure, Henning.

Meyer, Elard H. *See* Grimm, Jacob. 1875.

Meyer, Johannes. 1880. *Die drei Zelgen. Ein Beitrag zur Geschichte des alten Landbaus.* Ostprogramm der Thurangischen Kantonsschule. Frauenfeld: J. Huber.

Meyer, Leo. 1901–02. *Handbuch der griechischen Etymologie.* Leipzig: Verlag von S. Hirzel.

________. 1902. [Report of his book] *Handbuch der griechischen Etymologie.* Vol 4. Leipzig: Verlag von S. Hirzel, 1901–02. *GGA* 164, 409–13.

Meyer, W. 1888. [Etymologisches]. *ZRP* 11, 250–57.

Meyer-Lübke, Wilhelm. 1905. *Romanische Namenstudien. 1. Die altportugiesischen Personennamen germanischen Ursprungs.* SKAW 149/2.
See also ML.

Mezger, Fritz. 1946. Some Indo-European Formatives. *Word* 2, 229–40.

Michiels, Hubert. 1912. *Über englische Bestandteile altdeutscher Glossenhandschriften.* Bonn: Peter Hanstein.

Migliorini, Bruno. *See* Huss, Richard.

Miklosich, Franz R. von. 1884. *Die türkischen Elemente in den südost- und osteuropäischen Sprachen....* DAWW 34–35. Separately printed in the same year. Wien: In Commission bei K. Gerold.

Miller, Thomas, ed. 1890–91. *The Old English Version of Bede's* [Ecclesiastical History of the English People]. EETS 95–96. Repr Millwood, NY: Kraus Reprint Co, 1978.

Miller, Wsewolod. 1907. Beiträge zur ossetischen Etymologie. *IF* 21, 323–34.

Mills, A. D. *See* Sties, Patrick V.

Minsheu [a.k.a. Minshæus], John. 1617. *Ductor in linguas. The Guide into the Tongues....* London: Publ by the author. Repr with *Vocabularium Hispanicolatinum. A Most Copious Spanish Dictionary,* with an introduction by Jürgen Schäfer, as SFR 321, 1978. 2nd ed. London: John Haviland, 1627.

Mish, Frederick C. *See* WCD[10].

Mitchell, James. 1908. *Significant Etymology or Roots, Stems, and Branches of the English Language.* Edinburgh and London: William Blackwood & Sons.

Mitscha-Märheim, Herbert. *See* Steinhauser, Walter.

Mitzka, Walter. *See* EWDS[17–21] *and Heliand und Genesis.*

ML = Wilhelm Meyer-Lübke, *Romanisches etymologisches Wörterbuch,* 3rd ed. Heidelberg: Carl Winter. Universitätsverlag, 1935. Repr as 5th ed, 1972.

MlW = Otto Prinz, Johannes Schneider, eds., *Mittellateinisches Wörterbuch... bis zum ausgehenden 13. Jahrhundert.* München: Beck, 1959– .

Moberg, Lennart. 1971. Växtnamnet grön. SNF 58, 174–84.

Modéer, Ivar. 1937. *Namn- och ordgeografiska studier.* UUÅ 1937/12.

________. 1943. Fvn. *bákn,* sv. *båken* och besläktade ord. *NoB* 31, 131–49.

Möller, Hermann. 1879. Epenthese vor k-lauten im germanischen als wirkung des velaren oder palatalen charakters des wurzelauslauts. *KZ* 24, 427–522.

________. 1880. Zu declination. Germanisch in den endungen des *o* (a_2). *PBB* 7, 482–547.

________. 1911. *Vergleichendes indogermanisch-semitisches Wörterbuch.* Göttingen: Vandenhoeck & Ruprecht.

Møller, Kristen. 1943–45. Diminutiver i moderne Dansk. *APS* 17, 1–124.

Moerdijk, Alfons. 1994. (Mis)use of Semantic Parallelism: Robinson's Etymology of English Girl. *NOWELE* 24, 49–65.

Mogk, Eugen. 1880. Untersuchungen über die Gylfaginning 2. *PBB* 7, 203–318.

________. 1918–19. Zwerg. *RGA* 4, 591–98.

Mohr, Wolfgang. 1939. Wortschatz und Motive der jüngeren Eddalieder mit südgermanischem Stoff. *ZDA* 76, 149–217.

Molbech, C. *See* Outzen, Nicolaus.

Montgomerie-Fleming, J.B. 1899. *Desultory Notes on Jamieson's Scottish Dictionary.* Glasgow and Edinburgh: William Hodge & Company.

Montgomery, Marshall. 1920. 'Cursed Hebenon' (or 'Hebona'). *MLR* 15, 304–06.

Montigny, Allen H. K. de. *See* De Montigny, Allen H. K.

Mordek, Hubert, and Michael Glatthaar. 1993. Von Wahrsagerinnen und Zauberern. Ein Beitrag zur Religionspolitik Karls des Großen. *AK* 75, 33–64.

Morgan A., de. *See* De Morgan, A.

Morley, Henry, ed. 1890. *Gulliver's Travels: Exactly Reprinted from the First Edition and Other Works by Jonathan Swift....* London: George Routledge and Sons.

Morris, Richard. 1903. *Historical Outlines of English Accidence.* 2nd ed. London: Macmillan.

Morris, William. *See* AHD.

Morris, William S. 1967. *Possible Solutions to Some Old English Words of Uncertain Etymology.* Ph.D. Diss. Stanford University. Unpubl.

Morsbach, Lorenz. 1888. *Über den Ursprung der neuenglischen Sprache.* Heilbronn: Verlag von Gebr. Henninger.

________. 1896. *Mittelenglische Grammatik.* SKGGD 7.

Mossé, Ferdinand. 1933. [Rev of] AeEW, 1–3. *ES* 15, 60–65.

Motz, Lotte. 1973. New Thoughts on Dwarf-Names in Old Icelandic. *FS* 7, 100–17.

________. 1973–74. On Elves and Dwarfs. *Arv* 29–30, 93–127.

________. 1980. Old Icelandic *völva.* A New Derivation. *IF* 85, 196–206.

________. 1983. *The Wise One of the Mountain. Form, Function and Significance of the Subterranean Smith: A Study in Folklore.* GAG 379.

________. 1993. The Host of Dvalinn: Thoughts on Some Dwarf-Names in Old Icelandic. *CM,* 81–96.

Mozeson, Isaac E. 1989. *The Word: The Dictionary that Reveals the Hebrew Source of English.* New York: Shapolsky Publishers.

MSh = *The Plays and Poems of William Shakespeare with the Corrections and Illustrations of Various Commentators: Comprehending a Life of the Poet and an Enlarged History of the Stage,* by the Late Edmond Malone. With a New Glossarial Index. London: Printed for F. C. and J. Rivington, *etc,* 1821.

Much, Rudolf O. 1893. Die Südmark der Germanen. *PBB* 17, 1–136.

________. 1895. Germanische Völkernamen. *ZDA* 39, 20–52.

________. 1901–02. Worterklärungen. *ZDW* 2, 283–87.

________. 1909. Holz und Mensch. *WuS* 1, 39–48.

________. 1924. Balder. *ZDA* 61, 93–126.

________. 1932. Oheim. *ZDA* 69, 46–48.

Mühlenbachs, K. 1955. *Latviešu valodas vārdnīca. Lettisch-deutsches Wörterbuch.* Ed. by J. Endzelīn. Chicago: Publ by der Gruppe der lettischen Baltologen in Chikago [sic]. First publ in 1923.

Müllenhoff, Karl. 1900. *Deutsche Altertumskunde*, vol. 4: *Die Germania des Tacitus erläutert.* Berlin: Weidemann.
See also Mannhardt, Wilhelm.

Mueller, Eduard. 1865–67. *Etymologisches Woerterbuch der englischen Sprache*. Coethen: Druck und Verlag von Paul Schettler. 2nd ed: 1878 (the names of the author and the town are given as *Müller* and *Cöthen*).

Müller, Ernst E. 1968. Synchronie–Diachronie an einem Beispiel aus der Wortgeschichte: Knabe, Bube, Junge. In *Sprache, Gegenwart und Geschichte. Probleme der Synchronie und Diachronie. Sprache der Gegenwart*. SIDS 1969. Jahrbuch 1968, 129–46.

Müller, Friedrich Max. 1890. Cockney. *The Academy* 38, 73.

________. 1897. *Beiträge zur etymologischen Erklärung der griechischen sprache*. SÖAW 136/4.

Müller, Gertraud. *See* Frings, Theodor. 1951.

Müller, Josef. 1911. [Rev of] *Wörterbuch der Elberfelder Mundart nebst Abriß der Formenlehre und Sprachproben. ZDM* 6, 181–83.
See also RhW.

Müller, Max. *See* Müller, Friedrich Max.

Müller-Graupa, Edwin. 1957. Verbale Tiermetaphern. *PBB* (H) 79, 456–91.

Muir, Kenneth, ed. 1952. *King Lear.* The Arden Edition of the Works of William Shakespeare. Rev ed: 1972. London: Methuen & Co Ltd.

Muller, J. W. 1891. Glimp—glimpen. *TNTL* 10, 14–31.

________. 1916. Vaak. *TNTL* 35, 142–49.

________. 1938–39. Booi. *TNTL* 58, 177–84.

Munske, Horst H. *See* HF.

Murray, James A. H. 1890a. Cockney. *The Academy* 37, 320–21. (The end of the article repr in *ANQ* 8, 1890, 92.)

________. 1890b. The English Diphthong "-ay." *The Academy* 37, 357.

________. 1890c. Cockney. *The Academy* 37, 426–27.

________. 1890d. Cockney. *The Academy* 37, 445.

________. 1891. Bird. *NQ* VII/11, 115–16.
See also OED.

Murray, K. M. Elisabeth. 1977. *Caught in the Web of Words: James A. H. Murray and the Oxford English Dictionary.* With a Preface by R. W. Burchfield. New Haven and London: Yale University Press.

Muss-Arnolt, William. 1890. Semitic and Other Glosses to Kluge's *Etymologisches Wörterbuch der deutschen Sprache* 1. *MLN* 45, 245–52.

Must, Gustav. 1957. The Etymology of German *Hengst* 'Stallion', Swedish *Häst* 'Horse'. *JEGP* 56, 60–64.

Mutschmann, Heinrich. 1909. *A Phonology of the North-Eastern Scotch Dialect on an Historical Basis.* Bonner Studien zur englischen Philologie 1. Bonn: Hanstein.

MW = Karl Schiller and August Lübben, *Mittelniederdeutsches Wörterbuch.* Bremen: J. Kühtmann, 1875–81. Repr Wiesbaden: Dr. Martin Sändig OHG in collaboration with Aschendorffsche Verlagsbuchhandlung, Münster, 1969.

Naarding, J. 1954. Hondemiegersholt. *DB* 6, 94–96.

________. 1960. Ar-. *DB* 12, 1–5.

Nahl, Astrid von. *See* Liberman, Anatoly 2003.

Napier, Arthur S. 1898. On Some Old English Ghost-Words. *JGP* 2, 359–62.
See also NS.

Nares, Robert. 1822. *A Glossary; or, Collection of Words, Phrases, Names, and Allusions to Customs, Proverbs, etc., Which have been Thought to Require Illustration, in the Works of English Authors, Particularly Shakespeare and his Contemporaries.* A new ed by James O. Halliwell and Thomas Wright. London: John Russell Smith, 1872.

NC = Fr. Noël & L. J. Carpentier. *Dictionnaire étymologique.... Pour servir à l'histoire de la Langue Française.* Paris: Librairie le Normant, 1857.

NCD = *The New Century Dictionary of the English Language....* H. C. Emery and K. G. Brewster, eds. New York, London: D. Appleton-Century, 1927.

Neckel, Gustav. *See Edda.*

Nehring, A. *See* SN.

Neilson, William A. *See* Webster, Noah. 1934.

Nemnich, Philipp A. 1793–98. *Allgemeines Polyglotten-Lexicon der Naturgeschichte mit erklärenden Anmerkungen.* Hamburg: L. Nemnich; Halle: J. J. Gebauer.

NEO = Alf Torp, *Nynorsk etymologisk ordbok.* Kristiania: Aschehoug & Co. W. Nygaard, 1919. Repr 1963.

Nerman, Birger. 1954. Rígsþula 16:8 *dvergar á ǫxlom,* arkeologiskt belyst. *ANF* 69, 210–13.

Neufeldt, Victoria. *See* WNWD³.

Neumann, Friedrich. 1881. Tell—Dellingr—Heimdall. *Germania* 26, 343–48.

Neumann, Günter. 1971. *Substrate im Germanischen?* NAWG 1971/4 (= pp. 74–99 of the entire volume). *See also* Tischler, Johann.

Neumann, J. H. 1943. Jonathan Swift and the Vocabulary of English. *MLQ* 4, 191–204.

Neuss, Elmar. 1973. *Studien zu althochdeutschen Tierbezeichnungen der Handschriften Paris lat. 9344, Berlin Lat. 8⁰ 73, Trier R. III. 13 und Wolfenbüttel 10.3. Aug. 4⁰* MMS 16.

NEW = Jan de Vries, *Nederlands etymologisch woordenboek*. Leiden, *etc.*: E. J. Brill, 1971; 2nd ed, 1987; 3rd ed, by Francien de Tollenaere, in collaboration with Maaike Hogenhout-Mulder, 1992; 4th ed, 1997.

Newell, William W. 1883 *Games and Songs of American Children*. New York: Harper & Brothers.

Newman, John. 2001. How to understand *understand*. *NM* 102, 185–99.

Newton, Alfred. 1893–96. *A Dictionary of Birds*. London: Adam and Charles Black.

Nib = Karl Bartsch and Helmut de Boor, eds, *Das Nibelungenlied*, 21st ed., 1979. Wiesbaden: F. A. Brockhaus.

Nichols, Johanna. *See* GI.

Nicholson, B. 1880–82. Hamlet's Cursed Hebenon. *NSST*, 21–31.

Nicklin, T. 1904. Girl. *NQ* X/1, 245–46.

Nicolai, Otto. 1907. *Die Bildung des Adverbs im Altenglischen*. Diss Kiel. Kiel: Druck von H. Fiencke.

Niedermann, Max. 1911. [Rev of] Alois Walde, *Lateinisches etymologisches Wörterbuch*, 2nd ed. Heidelberg: Carl Winter, 1910. *IF(A)* 29, 29–37.

Nielsen, Niels Å. 1964. Etymologiske noter. In *Danica. Studier i dansk sprog. til Aage Hansen 3. 9. 1964*, eds. Erik Dal et al. SKS 1, 195–201. *See also* DEO.

Niermeyer, Jan F. 1976. *Mediae Latinitatis Lexicon Minus*. Leiden: E. J. Brill.

Nigra, C. 1903. Lat. *bŏa, bŏva*; fr. *bouée*. *ZRP* 27, 341–43.

Nilsson, Jan. 1984. Om det isländska växtnamnet *smári* n. 'smäre, klöver.' In *Florilegium Nordicum. Et bukett nordiska språk- och namnstudier tillägnade Sigurd Fries den 22 april 1984*. AUU 61, 201–10.

Noël, Fr. *See* NC.

Nörrenberg, Erich. *See* Woeste, Friedrich. 1930.

Noguchi, Rei R. 1996. On the Historical Longevity of One Four-Letter Word: The Interplay of Phonology and Semantics. *Maledicta* 12, 29–43.

Norberg, Rune. 1967. Nøkler. *KLNM* 12, 470–77.

Nordfelt, A. 1927. Om det äldre Hamletproblemet. Namnet och typen. UUÅ 6. SSUF Jan. 1925–Dec. 1927, 55–94.

Noreen, Adolf. 1894. *Abriss der urgermanischen Lautlehre mit besonderer Rücksicht auf die nordischen Sprachen*. Strassburg: Verlag von Karl J. Trübner.

________. 1897. *Svenska etymologier*. Skr Up(p) s. V/3.

________. 1904. *Altschwedische Grammatik mit Einschluss des Altgutnischen*. SKGGD VIII/2.

________. 1909. *Ordlista öfver Dalmålet. Tillägg och rättelser*. SvLm IV/2, 226–40.

________. 1918. Urkon Auðhumla och några hennes språkliga släktingar. *NB* 6, 169–72.

________. 1970. *Altnordische Grammatik*. SKGGD A/4. 5th ed.

Normier, Rudolf. 1980. Nochmals zu **sor*. *IF* 85, 43–80.

NS = Arthur S. Napier and W. H. Stevenson. *Anecdota Oxoniensia: The Crawford Collection of Early Charters and Documents Now in the Bodleian Library*. Oxford: At the Clarendon Press, 1895.

NTCD = *Webster's New Twentieth Century Dictionary of the English Language*. 2nd ed. William Collins Publishers, Inc, 1955.

Nugent, T. 1801. *The Primitives of the Greek Tongue*.... Translated from the French of Messieurs De Port Royal. A new ed... by N. Salmon. London: Printed for F. Wingrave and J. Mawman.

Nutt, Alfred. 1900. The Origin of "dude." *The Athenæum* 2, 481.

OÆDS = Otto Kalkar, *Ordbog til det ældre danske sprog (1300–1700)*. København: Thieles bogtrykkeri, 1881–1918. Repr with corrections Odense: Akademisk forlag, 1976.

Objartel, Georg. *See* Paul, Hermann. 1897 , 6th ed.

Ochs, Ernst. 1921. *Rôrea gafaclita*. *NM* 22, 124–28.

________. 1954. Eine Hocke mittelhochdeutscher Nüsse. STT 84, 149–54.

O'Connor, J. *See* RHHDAS.

OD = *Odhams Dictionary of the English Language*. A. H. Smith and J. L. N. O'Loughlin, eds. London: Odhams Press Limited, 1946.

Odé, A. W. M. 1927. Reflexe von "Tabu" und "Noa" in den indogermanischen Sprachen. MKAW, A/63, 73–100.

ODEE = C. T. Onions, ed., with the assistance of G. W. S. Friedrichsen and R. W. Burchfield, *The Oxford Dictionary of English Etymology.* Oxford: At the Clarendon Press, 1966.

ODGNS = Johan Fritzner, *Ordbog over Det gamle norske Sprog....* 4th ed. Oslo, Bergen, Tromsø: Universitetsforlaget, 1972–73.

ODS = *Ordbog over det Danske Sprog....* København: Gyldendalske Boghandel, Nordisk Forlag, 1919–1956.

OED = *The Oxford English Dictionary.* James A. H. Murray, et al, eds. Oxford: At the Clarendon Press, 1884–1928; 2nd ed, by J. A. Simpson and E. S. C. Weiner. Oxford: Oxford University Press, 1992.

Oehl, Wilhelm. 1921–22. Elementare Wortschöpfung. *Anthropos* 16–17, 765–800.

________. 1933a. *Das Lallwort in der Sprachschöpfung.* Rede gehalten am 15. November 1932 zur feierlichen Eröffnung des Studienjahres. Freiburg, Schweiz: St. Paulusdruckerei.

________. 1933b. *Fangen—Finger—fünf. Studien über elementarparallele Sprachschöpfung.* CF 22 (31 of the entire series).

Ölberg, Hermann M. *See* Schröpfer, Johannes.

OFED = Dirk Boutkan and Sjoerd Michiel Siebenga. *Old Frisian Etymological Dictionary.* Leiden: E.J. Brill, 2005.

Ogilvie, John. *See* ID.

Ogonov'ska, O. V. 1989. Deiakĭ slov'ians'kĭ zapozichennia v davn'oanglĭis'kĭi movĭ [Some Slavic Borrowings in Old English.]. *IFil* 93, 33–36.

Ogura, Michico. 1993. Verbs Prefixed with *ofer-* and *under-* in OE and ME. *CRev* 15, 19–49.

Oizumi, Akio. *See* Terasawa, Yoshio. 1993.

Okasha, Elisabeth. 1976. "Beacen" in Old English Poetry. *NQ* 221, 200–07.

Olck, Franz. 1905. Epheu. PW V/2, 2826–47.

O'Loughlin, J. L. N. *See* OD.

Olrik, Axel. 1910. Irminsul og gudestøtter. *Maal og Minne,* 1–9.

Olsen, Bernard. 1910. Det sidste neg. *DFm* 6, 1–18.

Olsen, Birgit. 1988. *The Proto-Indo-European Instrument Suffix* *-tlom *and its Variants.* HFM 55.

Olsen, Magnus. 1940. Kǫgurbarn og kǫgursveinn. *MM,* 9–16.

________. 1964. *Edda- og skaldekvad. Forarbeider til kommentar.* Avh. NVAO 5.

Olson, Emil. 1907. Några ord med bet. "slå dank." *SoS* 7, 66–80.

________. 1915a. Om behandlingen av urgerm. *hw* i de nordiska språken. *ANF* 31, 1–25.

________. 1915b. Kritiska anmärkningar till frågan om samnordisk förlust av *w. ANF* 31, 115–53.

Olybrius. 1943. Jeep. *NQ* 184, 349.

O'Muirithe, Diarmaid. 1997. *A Word in Your Ear.* Dublin: Four Courts Press.

Onions, C. T. *See* ODEE, SG, *and* SOD.

Ono, Shigeru. 1981a. The Old English Equivalents of Latin *cognoscere* and *intelligere*: The Dialect and Temporal Distribution of Vocabulary. In *Eigi no rekishi to kozo Miyabe Kikuo kyoju kanreki kinen ronbun shu* [*History and Structure of the English Language: Festschrift in Honor of Kikuo Miyabe*], eds. Yoshio Terasawa, et al, 117–45. Tokyo: Kenkyusha.

________. 1981b. Supplementary Notes on *ongietan, undergietan* and *understandan. Poetica* (Tokyo) 12, 94–97.

________. 1984. *Understandan* As a Loan Translation, a Separable Verb and an Inseparable Verb. In *Studies in English Philology and Linguistics in Honour of Dr. Tamotsu Matsunami,* 3–13. Tokyo: Shubun International.

________. 1986. *Undergytan* As 'Winchester' Word. In *Linguistics across Historical and Geographical Boundaries: In Honour of Jacek Fisiak on the Occasion of his Fiftieth Birthday. Vol. 1: Linguistic Theory and Historical Linguistics,* eds. Dieter Kastovsky and Aleksander Szwedek, 569–77. Berlin, New York: Mouton de Gruyter.

OO = Iona Opie and Peter Opie, eds., *The Oxford Dictionary of Nursery Rhymes.* Oxford: At the Clarendon Press, 1951.

________, eds. 1983. *The Oxford Book of Narrative Verse.* Oxford, New York: Oxford University Press.

Opie, Iona. *See* OO.

Opie, Peter. *See* OO.

O'Reilly, Edward. 1821. *An Irish-English Dictionary....* Dublin: Printed, for the author, by A. O'Neil.

Orel, Vladimir. 2003. *A Handbook of Germanic Etymology.* Leiden, Boston: Brill.

Orsman, H. W. *See* DNZE.

Orton, Harold. *See* SED.

Ostheeren, Klaus. 1992. Altenglisch *dream* 'Freude'—interkulturell. In *Anglistentag 1991 Düsseldorf.* Proceedings of the Conference of the German Association of University Professors of English / Tagungsberichte des Anglistentags Verbands Deutscher Anglisten 13, ed. Wilhelm Busse, 40–50. Tübingen: Max Niemeyer.

Osthoff, Hermann. 1890. Die lautgruppe *mr* im lateinischen, germanischen und altindischen. In Hermann Osthoff and Karl Brugmann, *Morphologische Untersuchungen auf dem Gebiete der indogermanischen Sprachen* 5. Leipzig: S. Hirzel.

________. 1896. Griechische und lateinische Wortdeutungen. *IF* 6, 1–47.

________. 1899. Allerhand zauber etymologisch beleuchtet. *BB* 24–25, 109–73, 177–213.

________. 1901. *Etymologische Parerga 1.* Leipzig: Verlag von S. Hirzel.

________. 1910. Zur Entlabilisierung der Labiovelare im Keltischen. *IF* 27, 161–93.

Oswald, John. 1866. *A Dictionary of Etymology of the English Language: And of English Synonymes and Paronymes.* 12th ed. Edinburgh: Adam & Charles Black.

Otfrid = Oskar Erdmann, ed., *Otfrids Evangelienbuch.* GH 5. Halle a. S.: Verlag der Buchhandlungen des Waisenhauses, 1881.

Otkupshchikov, Iu.V. 1961. K etimologii irlandskogo *brán* [Concerning the Etymology of Irish *brán*]. *Uchenye zapiski Leningradskogo gosudarstvennogo universiteta* 299. Seriia filologicheskikh nauk 59, 143–47. Repr Otkupshchikov, Iu.V. 2001. *Ocherki po etimologii* [*Essays on Etymology*]. [St. Petersburg]: Izdatel'stvo S.-Peterburgskogo universiteta, 2001, 332–36.

________. 1977. O proiskhozhdenii lit., ltsh. *ragana* 'ved'ma' [On the Origin of Lith., Latv. *ragana* 'witch']. *Baltistica* 13, 271–75. Repr in Otkupshchchikov, Iu. V. 2001, 234–39.

________. 2001. *Ocherki po etimologii* [*Essays on Etymology*]. Sankt-Peterburg: Izdatel'stvo Sankt-Peterburgskogo universiteta.

Ott, J. H. 1892. Beacon, Beekenes. *MLN* 7, 254.

Outzen, Nicolaus. 1837. *Glossarium der friesischen Sprache, besonders in nordfriesischer Mundart.* Posthumous ed, by L. Engelstoft and C. Molbech. Kopenhagen: Gyldendal. Repr Wiesbaden: Dr. Martin Sändig OHG, 1969.

Page, R. J. 1975. [Rev of] Alistair Campbell, *An Anglo-Saxon Dictionary Based on the Manuscript Collection of Joseph Bosworth: Enlarged Addenda and Corrigenda to the Supplement by T. Northcote Toller.* Oxford: At the Clarendon Press, 1972. *MÆ* 44, 65–68.

Palander, Hugo [a.k.a. Hugo Suolahti]. 1905. Volksetymologische Umbildungen im Englischen. *NM* 7, 125–27.

Paley, F. A. 1882. On the Antiquity of Some of our Familiar Agricultural Terms. *FM* 26, 458–68.

Palmer, Abram Smythe. *See* Smythe Palmer, A.

Palmer, Robert E. A. 1972. Ivy and Jupiter Priest. In *Homenaje a Antonio Tovar ofrecido por sus discípulos, colegas y amigos*, 341–47. Madrid: Editorial Gredos.

Pálsson, Gísli. 1991. The Name of the Witch: Sagas, Sorcery and Social Context. In *Social Approaches to Viking Studies*, ed. Ross Samson, 157–68. Glasgow: Cruithne Press.

Parkhurst, John. 1792. *An Hebrew and English Lexicon, Without Points: In Which the Hebrew and Chaldee Words of the Old Testament are explained in their leading and derived Senses....* London: Printed for G. G. J. and J. Robinson.

Paroissien, David. 1984. "What's in a Name?" Some Speculations about Fagin. *The Dickensian* 80, 41–45.

________. 1986. *Oliver Twist: An Annotated Bibliography.* New York and London: Garland Publishing, Inc.

Paros, Lawrence. 1984. *The Erotic Tongue: A Sexual Lexicon.* Seattle: Madrona Publishers.

Parr, D. Kermode. [1900]. *Whitcombe's School Etymological Dictionary....* Ernest Weekley, ed. Auckland, *etc.*: Whitcombe & Tombs Ltd.

Parry, David. *See* SOD: DG.

Partridge, Eric. 1933. *Slang Today and Yesterday. With a Short Historical Sketch and Vocabularies of English, American, and Australian Slang.* London: G. Routledge & Sons, Ltd. [Several later editions.]

________. 1940. *Slang.* SPE, Tract 55. (The volume includes Tracts 51–60, with consecutive pagination. Tract 55: pp. 173–96.)

________. 1947a. *Shakespeare's Bawdy: A Literary and Psychological Essay and a Comprehensive*

Glossary. London: Routledge and Kegan Paul. 2nd ed: 1955; 3rd ed: 1968.

_______. 1947b. Thanks to the War.... *QR* 285, 139–51.

_______. 1949a (= 1950). *A Dictionary of the Underworld.* London: Routledge & Kegan Paul Ltd.

_______. 1949b. *Name into Word: Proper Names That Have Become Common Property: A Discursive Dictionary.* London: Secker and Warburg.

_______. 1958. *Origins: A Short Etymological Dictionary of Modern English.* Oxford: At the Clarendon Press. 2nd ed: 1966.

_______. 1961. *A Dictionary of Slang and Unconventional English.* New York: The Macmillan Company. 8th ed, by Paul Beale. New York: Routledge, 2002.

Paschall, Clarence. 1943. The Semasiology of Words Derived from Indo-European **nem-.* *UCPL* 1, 1–9.

Pascual, José A. *See* DCECH.

Paul, Hermann. 1897. *Deutsches Wörterbuch....* Halle a. S.: Verlag von Max Niemeyer. 2nd ed: 1908, 3rd ed: 1921; 4th ed, by Karl Euling, 1935; 5th ed, by Alfred Schirmer, 1957–66; 6th ed, by Helmut Henne and Georg Objartel, 1992.

_______. 1920. *Deutsche Grammatik.* 5 vols. Halle a. S.: Verlag von Max Niemeyer.

Pauli, Ivan. 1919. *'Enfant' 'garçon' 'fille' dans les langues romanes. Essai de lexicologie comparée.* Lund: A.-B. Ph. Lundstedts Univ.-bokhandel.

Pauly, August. *See* PW.

Pavlova, O.A. *See* Ershova, I.A.

Payne, L. W., Jr. 1909. Word-List from East Alabama. *DN* 3, 343–91.

Payne, W. *See* Tusser, Thomas. 1878.

Peacock, Edward. 1889. *A Glossary of Words Used in the Wapentakes of Manley and Corringham, Lincolnshire.* 2nd ed. EDSP 58–59.

Pearsall, Judy. *See* COD10.

PED = G. N. Garmonsway with Jacqueline Simpson, *The Penguin English Dictionary.* [London]: Allen Lane, 1965.

Pedersen, Holger. 1893. *r-n*-stämme. *KZ* 32, 240–73.

_______. 1895. Das indogermanische *s* im Slavischen. *IF* 5, 33–86.

_______. 1907–08. Die idg.-semitische Hypothese und die idg. Lautlehre. *IF* 22, 341–65.

_______. 1909. *Vergleichende Grammatik der keltischen Sprachen* 1. *Einleitung und Lautlehre.* Göttingen: Vandenhoeck & Ruprecht. Repr 1976.

_______. 1930. Oldengelsk *fæmme.* In *A Grammatical Miscellany Offered to Otto Jespersen on his Seventieth Birthday*, eds. N. Bøgholm, Aage Brusendorff, [and] C. A. Bodelsen, 55–68. Copenhagen: Levin & Munksgaard, London: Allen & Unwin Ltd.

_______. 1941–42. Angl. *wife* et *woman. SN* 14, 252–54.

_______. 1949–50. Old Irish *ainder,* 'a young woman.' *JCS* 1, 4–6.

Pedersen, Viggo H. *See* Diensberg, Bernhard. 1994.

Pegge, Samuel. 1803. *Anecdotes of the English Language; Chiefly Regarding the Local Dialect of London and its Environs.* London: J. B. Nichols and Son. 2nd ed, by J. N., 1814; 3rd ed, by Henry Christmas, 1844.

Penagi, Oswald. *See* Schmidt, Klaus T., and Klaus Strunk.

Persson, Per. 1904. Små bidrag till germansk etymologi. In *Nordiska studier tillegnade Adolf Noreen på hans 50-årsdag den 13 mars 1904 af studiekamrater och lärjungar,* 54–62. Uppsala: K. W. Appelbergs boktryckeri.

_______. 1912. *Beiträge zur indogermanischen Wortforschung.* Skr. Upps. 12:1, 2.

Peterson, Lena. *See* Strandberg, Svante.

Petersson, Herbert. 1906–07. Etymologische Beiträge. *IF* 20, 367–68.

_______. 1908–09. Got. *ibuks. IF* 23, 160–61.

_______. 1914. Einige Tier- und Pflanzennamen aus idg. Sprachen. *KZ* 46:128–50.

_______. 1915. *Vermischte Beiträge zur Wortforschung.* Från Filologiska Föreningen i Lund. Språkliga uppsatser 4. Lund: Berling.

_______. 1916. Beiträge zur armenischen Wortkunde. *KZ* 47, 240–91.

_______. 1918. *Baltische und slavische Wortstudien.* LUÅ, N.F., Avd. 1, XIV/31.

_______. 1921. Beiträge zur lateinischen und griechischen Etymologie. In *Commentationes in honorem Fridolfi Gustafsson in Universitate Helsingforsiensi professoris romanarum litterarum emeriti.* Helsinki: Suomal. Kirjall. Seuran kirjapaino osakeyhtiö. [Each article in this volume has its own pagination. Petersson's contribution, pp. 1–22, is the last one.]

Pethtel, Lillian. 1965. Name Lore Around Kamiah. *WF* 24, 281–84.

Pfannenschmid, Heino. 1865. Der mythische Gehalt der Tellsage. Ein Beitrag zur deutschen Mythologie. *Germania* 10, 1–40.

Pfeifer, Wolfgang. *See* DEW.

Pheifer, J. D. 1974. *Old English Glosses in the Épinal-Erfurt Glossary.* Oxford: At the Clarendon Press.

Phillips, Edward. 1658. *The New World of Words: Or, a Universal English Dictionary.* London: Printed by E. Tyler, for Nath. Brooke. Repr as CFR 162, 1969. 5th ed, London: Printed for R. Bently, 1696.

Pianigiani, Ottorino. [1937] *Vocabolario etimologico della lingua italiana.* Milano: Casa editrice Sonzogno. Repr: Edizioni Polaris, 1991 and 1993.

Pictet, Adolphe. 1859–63. *Les origines indo-européennes.* 2 vols. Paris: Joël Cherbuliez (vol 1: 1859, vol 2: 1863).

PII = *Problemy indoevropeiskogo iazykoznaniia. Etiudy po sravnitel'no-istoricheskoi grammatike indoevropeiskikh iazykov [Problems of Indo-European Linguistics: Essays on the Comparative-Historical Grammar of the Indo-European Languages].* V.N. Toporov, ed. Moskva: Nauka, 1964.

Pinkerton, Edward C. 1982. *Word for Word.* A Verbatim Book. Distributed… by Gale Research Company, Detroit, MI.

Pipping, Hugo. 1904. Germanische Miszellen. *NM* 6, 145–67.

_______. 1905. *Grammatiska studier.* GHÅ XI/3.

_______. 1912. Zur Lehre vom *w*-Verlust in den altnordischen Sprachen. In *Xenia Lideniana. Festskrift tillägnad Professor Evald Lidén på hans femtioårsdag den 3 oktober 1912.* Stockholm: P.A. Norstedt & Söner, 138–75.

_______. 1917. *Urgermanskt* aiw *i nordiska språken.* SNF VIII/1.

_______. 1928. *Eddastudier 3.* SNF 18/4.

Pipping, Rolf. 1933–34. Lås och nycklar. *APS* 8, 78–90.

Pisani, Vittore. 1953. Zur lateinischen Wortgeschichte. *RMP* N.F. 96, 181–83.

_______. 1959. Altlateinisches *iopetoi* und die Duenos-Inschrift. *RMP* N. F. 102, 303–07.

_______. 1968. *Lezioni sul lessico inglese.* Brescia: Paideia.

_______. 1979. Ludi etymologici. *RIL* 314–20. *See also* Huss, Richard.

Plate, Rudolf. 1934. *Englische Wortkunde auf sprach- und kulturgeschichtlicher Grundlage.* München: Max Hueber.

Platt, James Jun. 1892. The Etymology of "ever." *The Academy* 41, 41.

_______. 1903. Slang. *NQ* IX/11, 166–67.

Poetto, Massimo. 1984. Inglese d'America *futz. Paideia* 39, 198–200.

Pogatscher, Alois. 1898. Altenglisch *br* aus *mr.* In *Festschrift zum VIII. Allgemeinen Deutschen Neuphilologentage in Wien, Pfingsten 1898,* ed. J. Schipper, 97–106. Wien and Leipzig: Wilhelm Braunmüller.

_______. 1900. Englische Etymologien. *ESt* 27, 217–27.

_______. 1901. [Rev of] F. Roeder, *Die Familie bei den Angelsachsen. Eine kultur- und litteraturhistorische Studie auf Grund gleichzeitiger Quellen. Erster Hauptteil: Mann und Frau.* Halle: Max Niemeyer, 1899. *AB* 12, 193–99.

_______. 1902. Etymologisches. *AB* 13, 233–36.

_______. 1903. Etymologisches. *AB* 14, 181–85.

Pokorny, Julius. 1949–50. Some Celtic Etymologies. *JCS* 1, 129–35. *See also* IEW *and* WP.

Poli, Diego. 1992. Dissezioni di membra e tassonomie di valori. In *Storia, problemi e metodi del comparativismo linguistico. Atti del Convegno della Società Italiana di Glottologia.* Bologna 29 novembre–1 dicembre 1990, 115–40. Pisa: Giardini. *See also* Janni, Pietro. 1985.

Polomé, Edgar C. 1951. [Rev of] Buck, Carl D., 1949. *BT/RB* 29, 1183–98.

_______. 1952. Zum heutigen Stand der Laryngaltheorie. *BT/RB* 30, 444–71.

_______. 1953. L'étymologie du terme germanique **ansuz* "dieu souverain." *EG* 8, 36–44.

_______. 1957. Germanisch und Venetisch. In *ΜΝΗΜΣ ΧΑΡΙΝ. Gedenkschrift Paul Kretschmer. 2. Mai 1866–9. März 1956.* Vol 2, 86–98. Wien: Im Verlag der Wiener Sprachgesellschaft; Wiesbaden: Otto Harrassowitz; Wien: Brüder Hollinek.

_______. 1980. Remarques sur quelques isoglosses germano-indo-aryennes. *FLH* 1, 109–16.

_______. 1983. The Problem of Etymological Dictionaries: The Case of German. *JIES* 11, 45–58.

________. 1985. Problems in Germanic Etymology. *CoE* XV/3–4, 6–13.

________. 1986a. The Non-Indo-European Component of the Germanic Lexicon. In *o-o-pe-ro-si. Festschrift für Ernst Risch zum 75. Geburtstag*, ed. Annemarie Etter, 661–72. Berlin, New York: Walter de Gruyter.

________. 1986b. Some Comments on Germano-Hellenic Lexical Correspondences. In *Aspects of Language: Studies in Honour of Mario Alinei: Papers Presented to Mario Alinei by his Friends, Colleagues and Former Students on the Occasion of his 60th Birthday*. Vol. 2: *Theoretical and Applied Semantics*, eds. Nils Århammar, et al, 171–98. Amsterdam: Rodopi.

________. 1987. Who are the Germanic People? In *Proto-Indo-European. The Archaeology of a Linguistic Problem: Studies in Honor of Marija Gimbutas*, eds. Susan Nacev Skomal and Edgar C. Polomé, 216–44. Washington, D. C.: Institute for the Study of Man.

________. 1997. Notes on the Dwarfs in Germanic Tradition. In *Language and its Ecology: Essays in Memory of Einar Haugen*, eds. Stig Eliasson and Ernst H. Jahr, 441–50. Berlin, New York: Mouton de Gruyter.
See also Liberman, Anatoly, 1998.

Pons, E. 1936. Rabelais et Swift. À propos du Lilliputien. In *Mélanges offerts à M. Abel Lefranc, professeur au Collège de France, membre de l'Académie des Inscriptions et Belles-lettres, par ses élèves et ses amis*, 219–28. Paris: Librairie E. Droz.

Poortinga, Y. 1968. Tsjoensters—Hexenwesen in Friesland. In *Philologia Frisica Anno 1966. Lêzingen en neipetearen fan it 4de Fryske Filologenkongres, august–septimber 1966*, 88–104 [includes discussion]. Grins: Wolters-Noordhoff N. V.

Porter, Noah. *See* Webster, Noah. 1864 and 1890.

Porzig, Walter. 1927. Kleinasiatisch-Indische Beziehungen. *ZII* 5, 265–80.

Pott, August F. 1833. *Etymologische Forschungen auf dem Gebiete der Indo-Germanischen Sprachen....* Lemgo: Im Verlage der Meyerschen Hofbuchhandlung.

________. 1859–76. *Etymologische Forschungen auf dem Gebiete der Indo-Germanischen Sprachen....* 2nd ed. Lemgo and Detmold: Meyer'sche Hofbuchhandlung (Gebrüder Klingenberg). Vol. I, 1859; vol. II/1, 1861; vol. II/2, 1867: beginning with this volume, now also called *Wurzel-Wörterbuch der Indogermanischen Sprachen*, the numbering starts anew. Vol. II/2 (this number is not given on the title page) = vol. I; vol. II, 1869; vol. II/2, 1870; vol. III, 1871; vol. IV, 1873; vol. V, 1873; additional vol., index to vols. I–V: *Wurzel-, Wort-, Namen-, und Sachregister* by Heinrich E. Bindseil, 1876.

Potter, Charles. 1949–50a. Eeny, meeny, miny, mo. *FWSD*, 339–40.

________. 1949–50b. Shepherd's score. *FWSD*, 1006–07.

Powell, Thomas. 1877. The Ancient British Numerals. *The Athenæum*/II, 629–30.

P.P. 1872. Cater-Cousins. *NQ* IV/9, 517.

Prellwitz, Walther. 1889. *Ἐκεῖνος—κῆνος*, äol. *κῆ* und verwandtes. *BB* 15, 154–58.

________. 1892. *Etymologisches Wörterbuch der griechischen Sprache mit besonderer Berücksichtigung des Neuhochdeutschen und einem deutschen Wörterverzeichnis.* Göttingen: Vandenhoeck & Ruprecht.

Prescott, R. G. W. 1995. Muffy, Moffradite, Hermaphrodite. *MarM* 81, 222–23.

Princi Braccini, Giovanna. 1984. Recupero di un lemma germanico e connesse questioni etimologiche (*wala-paus* in Rotari, *wala* nel *Beowulf*, francese *galon*, italiano *gola*, e tedesco *posse*). *AION-FG* 27, 135–205.

Prior, R. C. A. 1870. *On the Popular Names of British Plants....* Edinburgh: Williams and Norgate.

Propp, Vladimir. 1984. *Theory and History of Folklore.* Translated by Ariadna Y. Martin and Richard P. Martin. Edited with an Introduction and Notes, by Anatoly Liberman. THL 5.

Prevost, E. W. 1905. *A Supplement to the Glossary of the Dialect of Cumberland.* With a Grammar of the Dialect by S. Dickson Brown. London: Henry Frowde, and Carlisle: C. Thurnam & Sons.

Psilander, Hjalmar. 1900. De etymologie van Nederlandsch *ooit*. *NJ* 26, 146–47.

________. 1902. Ooit. *TNTL* 21, 123–30.

Puhvel, Jaan. 1988. 'Shoulder' and 'Corner' in Hittite. In *A Linguistic Happening in Memory of Ben Schwartz: Studies in Anatolian, Italic, and Other Indo-European Languages*, ed. Yoël L. Arbeitman, BCILL 42, 255–58.
See also HED.

PW = *Pauly's Realencyclopädie der classischen*

Altertumswissenschaft, new ed. by Georg Wissowa, vol V/2 (half-volume 10). Stuttgart: Alfred Druckenmüller Verlag, 1905. Repr 1958.

Pyles, Thomas. 1971. The Porn is Green. [Rev of] *A Supplement to the Oxford English Dictionary 1....* *AS* 46, 237–46.

Quigley, John. 1917. The History of the Irish Bible. *ICQ* 10, 49–69.

Qui Tam. 1890a. Good Old Etymologies. *ANQ* 5, 225.

________. 1890b. Slang. *ANQ* V/4, 47.

Q.W. 1944. Jeep, *ANQ* 4, 26–27.

Radcliffe, Jno. N. 1853. Huggins and Muggins. *NQ* I/8, 503.

Ramat, Paolo. 1963a. I problemi della radice indoeuropea **bhāg-*. *AION-SL* 33–57.

________. 1963b. Il gotico *manna* e i suoi composti. *Die Sprache* 9, 23–34.

Ramson, W. S. *See* AND.

Rankin, Lois. *See* Abrahams, Roger D.

Rapkin, Maurice. 1945. *Jeep*. *NQ* 188, 215–16.

Rapp, Karl M. [a.k.a. Rapp, Moriz]. 1855. *Grundriss der grammatik des indisch-europäischen sprachstammes* 2. *Wurzelbüchlein: die weitest verbreiteten sprachwurzeln des indisch-europäischen stammes.* Tübingen: J. G. Cotta.

Rauch, Irmengard. 1975. What Can Generative Grammar Do for Etymology? An Old Saxon Hapax. *Semasia* 2, 249–60.

Raucq, Elisabeth. 1939. *Contribution à la linguistique des noms d'animaux en indo-européen.* RGW 88.

Raudvere, Catharina. *See* Arvidsson, Stefan.

Rawson, Hugh. 1989. *Wicked Words: A Treasury of Curses, Insults, Put-Downs, and Other Formerly Unprintable Terms from Anglo-Saxon Times to the Present.* New York: Crown Publishers.

Ray, John. 1874. *A Collection of English Words, Not Generally Used...*, ed. by Walter W. Skeat. EDSP 2. First publ in 1674.

R.D.S. 1880a. Skedaddle. *MCNQ* 3, 6.

________. 1880b. Skedaddle. *MCNQ* 3, 20.

Read, Allen W. 1934. An Obscenity Symbol. *AS* 9, 264–78. Repr in Read, Allen W. 2002, 251–69.

________. 1976. An Obscenity Symbol after Four Decades. Paper given before the Conference "Perspective on Language" at the University of Louisville, Louisville, Kentucky, May 7, 1976. Unpublished. (From the archive of Jesse Sheidlower.)

________. 2002. *Milestones in the History of English in America.* Ed. by Richard W. Bailey. PADS 86. Publ by Duke University Press for the American Dialect Society. Annual Supplement to *American Speech.*

Reaney, Percy H. 1976. *A Dictionary of British Surnames.* 2nd rev ed. London and Boston: Routledge and Kegan Paul; 3rd ed, by R. M. Wilson. London and New York: Routledge, 1991.
See also RW.

Rédei, Károly. 1986. *Zu den indogermanisch-uralischen Sprachkontakten.* SÖAW 468.

Redslob, Walter. 1913–14. Die Worte: *Plürr, Kattrepel, Slammátje, böten* und *Kuddel-muddel.* *KVNS* 34, 31–33.

Rees, Nigel. 1987. *Why Do We Say ...? Words and Sayings and Where They Come From.* London, New York, Sydney: Blandford Press.

Regel, Karl. 1862. Zur dialectforschung. *KZ* 11, 104–23.

Reichborn-Kjennerud, I. 1931. Dvergnavnet Móðsognir. *MM,* 116–17.

________. 1934. Den gamle dvergtro. In *Studia Germanica tillägnade Ernst Albin Kock den 6 december 1934,* 278–88. Lund: Carl Blom.

Reichl, Karl. *See* Sauer, Hans. 1992.

Reid, Alexander. 1846. *A Dictionary of the English Language.* Edinburgh: Oliver & Boyd.

Reidy, John. *See* Burchfield R. W. 1972.

Reinisch, Leo. 1873. *Der einheitliche Ursprung der Sprachen der alten Welt....* Wien: W. Braumüller. Repr Vaduz, Liechtenstein: Sändig Reprints Verlag, 1986.

Reinius, Josef. 1903. *On Transferred Appellations of Human Beings, Chiefly in English and German. Studies in Historical Sematology.* Göteborg: Wald. Zachrissons boktryckeri A.-B. Also in: GKVVSH, 4th series, V–VI.

Resenius, Peder J. *See* Andrésson, Guðmundur.

Restle, David. *See* Schrijver, Peter.

Revard, Carter. 1977. Deciphering the Four-Letter Word in a Medieval Manuscript's Satire on Friars. *Verbatim* IV/1, 1, 3.

Reves, Haviland F. 1926. What is Slang? A Survey of Opinion. *AS* 1, 216–20.

RGA = *Reallexikon der germanischen Altertumskunde.* Johannes Hoops, ed. Straßburg: Verlag von Karl J. Trübner, 1911–19.

RHD = *The Random House Dictionary of the English Language*. Jess M. Stein, ed. New York: Random House, 1966; 2nd ed, by Stuart B. Flexner: 1987.

RHHDAS = J. E. Lighter, ed., J. Ball, J. O'Connor, assistant eds, *Random House Historical Dictionary of American Slang*. New York: Random House, 1994–.

RhW = *Rheinisches Wörterbuch...*, ed by Josef Müller. Bonn: Fritz Klopp, 1928–71.

Riccius, Christian G. 1750. *Spicilegium Juris Germanici ad illustris domini Jo. Rudolphi Engau Elementa juris Germanici civilis....* Gottingae: Apud Jo. Guiluil. Schmid.

Richards, Thomas. 1815. *Antiquæ Linguæ Britannicæ Thesaurus: Being a British, or Welsh-English Dictionary*. Dolgelley: Gomerian Press.

Richardson, Charles. 1858. *A New Dictionary of the English Language, Combining Explanation with Etymology.* London: Bell and Daldy.

Richthofen, Karl F. 1840. *Altfriesisches Wörterbuch.* Göttingen: Dieterichsche Buchhandlung.

Riecke, Jörg. 1997. Ahd *dwesban, fehtan* und die starken Verben der III. Ablautreihe. *Sprachwissenschaft* 22, 207–19.

Riese, Alexander, ed. 1884. *Die Gedichte des Catullus.* Leipzig: Druck und Verlag von B. G. Teubner.

Rietz, Johan E. 1867. *Svenskt dialektlexikon. Ordbok öfver svenska allmogespråket.* Lund: N. P. Lundberg.

Riley, Henry T. 1857. To Slang: Origin of the Term. *NQ* II/3, 445.

Rissanen, Matti. *See* Görlach, Manfred.

Ritter, George W. 1943–44. Jeep. *ANQ* 3, 155–56.

Ritter, Otto. 1904. Zur herkunft von ne. *elk. AB* 15, 301–03.

________. 1906a. Englische Etymologien. *Archiv* 117, 148–50.

________. 1906b. Zur Herkunft von ne. *slang.* Mit einem Anhang über das 'bewegliche *s*' im Englischen. *Archiv* 116, 41–49.

________. 1908. Englische Etymologien. *Archiv* 120, 429–33.

________. 1910. Etymologieen. *Anglia* 33, 471–79.

________. 1922. *Vermischte Beiträge zur englischen Sprachgeschichte, Etymologie, Ortsnamenkunde, Lautlehre.* Halle (Saale): Max Niemeyer.

________. 1936. [Rev of] R. E. Zachrisson, English Place-Name Puzzles.... *Studia Neophilologia* 5, 1–69. *ZONF* 12, 1936, 82–97.

Rittershaus, Adeline. 1899. *Die Ausdrücke für Gesichtsempfindungen in den altgermanischen Dialekten. Ein Beitrag zur Bedeutungslehre.* Part 1. AGDSZ 3.

Rix, Helmut. 1995. Griechisch ἐπίσταμαι. Morphologie und Etymologie. In *Verba et structurae. Festschrift für Klaus Strunk zum 65. Geburtstag*, eds. Heinrich Hettrich et al. IBS 83, 237–47.

Roberts, Jane. *See* TOE.

Robins, Alfred F. 1900. Slang. *NQ* IX/5, 212.

Robinson, Fred C. 1967. European Clothing Names and the Etymology of *Girl.* In *Studies in Historical Linguistics in Honor of George Sherman Lane*, eds. Walter W. Arndt et al, 233–40. UNC: SGLL 58.

________. 1993. European Clothing Names and the Etymology of *Girl.* In his *The Tomb of Beowulf and Other Essays on Old English,* 175–81. Oxford, UK & Cambridge, USA: Blackwell.

Rocchi, Luciano. 1989. A. nord. *pika,* baltofinn. **piika* "ragazza; serva". In *Dialettologia e varia linguistica per Manlio Cortelazzo*, eds. Gianluigi Borgato and Alberto Zamboni. QPL, Monografie 6, 301–06.

Rochholz, Ernst L. 1871. Mundartliche namen des cretinismus. *ZDP* 3, 331–42.

Roeder, F. 1909. Zur Deutung der angelsächsischen Glossierungen von 'paranymphus' und 'paranympha' ('pronuba'). Ein Beitrag zur Kenntnis des ags. Hochzeitsrituels. NKGWG, 14–41.

Roelandts, Karel. 1966. Familiarismen met anorganische konsonant (types Jakke, Witte, Pelle enz.). VMKVATL, 213–98.

________. 1984. De etymologie von Fries *boai,* Engels *boy* en Middelnederlands *boye.* In *Miscellanea Frisica. In nije bondel Fryske stúdzjes. Een nieuwe bundel Friese studies. A New Collection of Frisian Studies*, eds. N. R. Århammar et al, 123–36. Fryske Akademy 634. Assen: Van Gorcum.

Rogström, Lena. 1998. *Jacob Serenius lexikografiska insats.* Diss. Göteborg. MA 22.

Root, Robert K. *See* TC-R.

Rooth, Erik. 1962. Mittelniederdeutsche Wortstudien. *NdM* 18, 5–82.

________. 1963. Küfig und Kebse. Ein etymologischer Versuch. In *Festgabe für Ulrich Pretzel zum 65. Geburtstag, dargebracht von Freunden und Schülern*, eds. Werner Simon,

Wolfgang Bachofer, and Wolfgang Dittmann, 301–07. [Berlin]: Erich Schmidt Verlag.

Roquefort, Jean B. B. de. 1829. *Dictionnaire étymologique de la langue françoise...,* 2 vols. Paris: Goeury.

Roscoe, E. Haigh. 1944. *Jeep. TLS,* May 6, 223.

Rosenfeld, Hans-Friedrich. 1947. Zu dem pommerschen Haustierbezeichnungen. Aus der Werkstatt des Pommerschen Wörterbuches. *NdM* 3, 54–81.

________. 1955. Vom studentischen *Fuchs* und von *Rauchfliess. PBB* (H) 77, 246–305.

________. 1958. Germ. *fīs (t)* in seiner Entfaltung in übertragenem Sinn. *PBB* (H) 80, 357–420.

Ross, Alan S. C. 1932–35. Names of a Hare. *PLPLS* 3, 347–77.

________. 1937. *Studies in the Accidence of the Lindisfarne Gospels.* Printed by Titus Wilson of Kendal for members of the School of English Language in the University of Leeds.

Ross, Hans. 1895. *Norsk Ordbog.* Christiania: Alb. Cammermeyers Forlag (Lars Swanstrøm).

Rotermund, G. 1895. *Der Sachsenspiegel (Landrecht).* Hermannsburg: Druck und Verlag der Missionshandlung.

Rowe, Joseph H. *See* Beddoe, John.

Ruhlen, Merritt. 1994. *On the Origin of Languages: Studies in Linguistic Taxonomy.* Stanford University Press.

Rule, Frederick. 1873. Word-Lore. *NQ* IV/11, 361.

Rumble, Alexander R. *See* Stiles, Patrick V.

Russell, T. Baron. 1893. The American Language. *GM*/II, 529–33.

Rye, Walter. 1895. *A Glossary of Words Used in East Anglia Founded on That of Forby. With Numerous Corrections and Additions.* EDSP 26/2. London: Henry Frowde.

Sabaliauskas, A. 1964. Iz istorii terminologii zhivotnovodstva v baltiiskikh iazykakh [From the History of Cattle Breeding Terminology in the Baltic Languages]. In PII, 59–65.

Sabler, Georg von. 1892. Etymologien nebst laut- und formgeschichtlichen bemerkungen. *KZ* 31, 274–85.

Sachsse. 1853. Bemerkungen zum Sachsenspiegel. *ZDR* 14, 1–45.

Sahlgren, Jöran. 1928. Nordiska ordstudier. *ANF* 44, 253–85.

Sainéan, Lazare. 1907. *La création métaphorique en français et en roman. Images tirées du monde des animaux domestiques: le chien et le porc, avec des appendices sur le loup, le renard et les batraciens.* Beihefte zur *ZRP* 10. Halle a. S.: Verlag von Max Niemeyer.

________. 1925–30. *Les sources indigènes de l'étymologie française.* 3 vols. Paris: E. de Boccard, éditeur.

Sainte-Palaye, La Curne de. 1875–82. *Dictionnaire historique de l'ancien langage françois....* Niort: L. Favre, Paris: H. Champion.

Samelson, A. 1880. Skedaddle. *MCNQ* 3, 20.

Sampson, John. 1898 [publ 1899]. The Word *Slang* As a Field Name. *CS* III/2, 85–86.

Samson, Ross. *See* Pálsson, Gísli.

Samyn, Joseph. *See* De Bo, L. L. 1892.

Sandahl, Bertil. 1958. *Middle English Sea Terms 2: Masts, Spars, and Sails.* ESELL 20.

Sands, Donald B. ed. 1966. *Middle English Verse Romances.* New York, *etc.*: Holt, Rinehart and Winston, Inc. Repr as 2nd ed: University of Exeter, 1986.

Santangelo, Paolo E. 1953. *Fondamenti di una scienza della origine del linguaggio e sua storia remota* [1]. Milano: Santangelo.

Santini, Carlo. *See* Janni, Pietro. 1985, *and* Liberman, Anatoly. 1992b.

Sapir, Edward. 1937. Hebrew "Helmet," a Loanword, and its Bearing on Indo-European Phonology. *JAOS* 57, 73–77.

Sarrazin, Gregor. 1911. Englisch 'henbane,' 'Bilsenkraut.' *Festschrift zur Jahrhundertfeier der Universität zu Breslau.* MSGV 13–14, 552–53.

Sauer, Hans. 1992. Towards a Linguistic Description and Classification of the Old English Plant Names. In *Words, Texts and Manuscripts: Studies in Anglo-Saxon Culture Presented to Helmut Gneuss on the Occasion of his Sixty-Fifth Birthday*, ed. Michael Korhammer, in collaboration with Karl Reichl and Hans Sauer, 381–408. Cambridge: D. S. Brewer.

Sauvageot, Aurélien. 1930. *Recherches sur le vocabulaire des langues ouralo-altaïques.* CLSLP 30.

Savage, Frederick G. 1923. *The Flora and Folk Lore of Shakespeare.* Cheltenham and London: Ed. J. Burrow & Co. Ltd.

Sayce, O.L. *See* Wright, Joseph. 1954.

SB = Karl Brunner, *Altenglische Grammatik, nach*

der angelsächsischen Grammatik von Eduard Sievers. SKGGD A/3. 3rd ed., 1965.

Scardigli, Piergiuseppe, and Teresa Gervasi. 1978. *Avviamento all'etimologia inglese e tedesca. Dizionario comparativo dell'elemento germanico comune ad entrambe le lingue*. Firenze: Le Monnier.

Scarpat, Giuseppe. 1969. Il fico e le sue foglie nella tradizione classica e cristiana. In *Studi linguistici in onore di Vittore Pisani*, 871–89. Brescia: Editrice Paideia.

Schachmatov, Alexis. 1912. Slavische Wörter für Epheu. In *Festschrift Vilhelm Thomsen zur Vollendung des siebzigsten Lebensjahres am 25. Januar 1912, dargebracht von Freunden und Schülern*, 192–97. Leipzig: Otto Harrassowitz.

Schade, Oskar. 1882. *Altdeutsches Wörterbuch*. 2nd ed. Halle a. d. Saale: Verlag der Buchhandlung des Waisenhauses.

Schäfer, Jürgen. *See* Minsheu, John.

Schele de Vere, M. 1872. *Americanisms; The English of the New World*. New York: Charles Scribner & Company.

Scheler, Auguste. 1862. *Dictionnaire d'étymologie française d'après les résultats de la science moderne*. Bruxelle: C. Muquart. 2nd ed: 1873, 3rd ed: 1888.

Scherer, Wilhelm. *See* Mannhardt, Wilhelm.

Schier, Kurt. *See* Meid, Wolfgang. 1992.

Schiller, Karl. *See* MW.

Schipper, J. *See* Pogatscher, Alois. 1898.

Schirmer, Alfred. *See* EWDS17 *and* Paul, Hermann. 1897, 5th ed.

Schleicher, August. 1871. *Compendium der vergleichenden Grammatik indogermanischen Sprachen*. 2nd ed. Weimar: Hermann Böhlau.

Schlutter, Otto B. 1907. [Rev of] Cortelyou, John van Zandt. 1906. *ESt* 38, 297–305.

________. 1908a. Anglo-Saxonica. *Anglia* 31, 55–71.

________. 1908b. Gildas, *Libellus querulus de excidio britannorum* As a Source of Glosses in the *Cottoniensis (Cleopatra A III = WW. 338–473)* and the *Corpus Glossary*. *AJP* 29, 432–48.

________. 1913a. Glossographische Beiträge zur deutschen Wortgeschichte im Anschluß an Kluges Etym. Wörterbuch 1. *ZDW* 14, 137–60.

________. 1913b. Weitere Beiträge zur altenglischen Wortforschung. *Anglia* 37, 42–43.

________. 1923. Is There Any Evidence for OE *weargingel* 'butcher-bird'? *Neophilologus* 8, 206–08.

Schmid, M. Johann Christoph. 1831. *Schwäbisches Wörterbuch mit etymologischen und historischen Anmerkungen*. Stuttgart: E. Schweizerbart's Verlagshandlung.

Schmidt, Gernot. 1963. *Studien zum germanischen Adverb*. Diss. Freie Universität Berlin. Berlin: Ernst-Reuter-Gesellschaft der Förder und Freunde der Freien Universität Berlin, e. V.

Schmidt, Johannes. 1893. [Footnote to Pedersen, Holger. 1893, p. 253.]

________. 1895. *Kritik der Sonantentheorie. Eine sprachwissenschaftliche Untersuchung*. Weimar: Hermann Böhlaus Nachfolger.

Schmidt, Klaus T., and Klaus Strunk. 1989. Toch. B *kuīpe* "Scham; Schande," A *kip* 'Scham' und germ. **wība* 'Weib'. In *Indogermanica Europaea. Festschrift für Wolfgang Meid zum 60. Geburtstag am 12. 11. 1989*, eds. Karin Heller, Oswald Penagi, and Johann Tischler. GLM 4, 251–84.

Schmidt, Lothar. 1961. *Wringen—Dweran—Torquere. Etymologische Untersuchungen*. Diss. Münster (Westf.). Münster: Max Kramer.

Schmitt, Rüdiger. *See* Szemerényi, Oswald. 1962.

Schmitt-Brandt, Robert. *See* Vermeer, Hans J.

Schneider, Hermann. *See* Kuhn, Hans. 1952.

Schönfeld, Moritz. 1911. *Wörterbuch der altgermanischen Personen- und Völkernamen nach der Überlieferung des klassischen Altertums bearbeitet*. GB I/2. Heidelberg: Carl Winter's Universitätsbuchhandlung. Repr: 1965.

Sholler, Harald. *See* Burchfield, R. W. 1972.

Schrader, Oskar. 1901. *Reallexikon der indogermanischen Altertumskunde. Grundzüge einer Kultur- und Völkergeschichte Alteuropas*. Strassburg: Verlag von Karl J. Trübner. *See also* Hehn, Victor, *and* SN.

Schrijnen, Joseph. 1904. Guttural-sigmatische wisselformen. *TNTL* 23, 81–98, 299–315.

Schrijver, Peter. 1997. Animal, Vegetable and Mineral: Some Western European Substratum Words. In *Sound Law and Analogy: Papers in Honor of Robert S.P. Beekes on the Occasion of his 60th Birthday*, ed. Alexander Lubotsky, 293–316. Amsterdam, Atlanta: Rodopi.

________. 2002. Irish *ainder*, Welsh *anner*, Breton *annoar*, Basque *andere*. In *Sounds and Systems. Studies in Structure and Change: A Festschrift for Theo Vennemann*, eds. David Restle and Dietmar Zaefferer. TLSM 141, 205–19.

Schröder, Edward. 1909. *Balz. ZDA(A)* 33, 120–21.
Schröder, Franz R. 1941. *Untersuchungen zur germanischen und vergleichenden Religionsgeschichte 1: Ingunar-Freyr.* Tübingen: Verlag von J. C. B. Mohr (Paul Siebeck).
Schröder, Georg. 1893. *Über den Einfluss der Volksetymologie auf den Londoner slang-Dialekt.* Diss. Rostock. Rostock: Carl Boldt'sche Hof-Buchdruckerei.
Schröder, Heinrich. 1903. Streckformen. *PBB* 29, 346–54.
________. 1906. *Streckformen. Ein Beitrag zur Lehre von der Wortentstehung und der germanischen Wortbetonung.* GB II/1.
________. 1908. Die germ. Wurzeln *stel-* und *ster-* und ihre durch *p, k, t* erweiterten Formen. *IF* 18, 509–28.
________. 1909. [Rev of] FT(N). *GRM* 1, 587–88.
________. 1910. *Ablautstudien.* GB II/1:2.
Schröer, M. M. Arnold. 1937–70. *Englisches Handwörterbuch in genetischer Darstellung auf Grund der Etymologien und Bedeutungsentwicklungen...* P. L. Jaeger, ed. Heidelberg: Carl Winter.
Schröpfer, Johannes. 1985. Etymologien im Jagdbereich, gewonnen durch Bezeichnungsver-gleich. In *Sprachwissenschaftliche Forschungen. Festschrift für Johann Knobloch zum 65. Geburtstag am 5. Januar 1984, dargebracht von Freunden und Kollegen*, eds. Hermann M. Ölberg et al, in collaboration with Heinz Bothien. IBK 23, 429–36.
Schuchardt, Hugo. 1901. Franz. bouée—mhd. bouchen. *ZRP* 25, 345–47.
________. 1903. Zur Methodik der Wortgeschichte. *ZRP* 27, 609–15.
________. 1905. *Hugo Schuchardt an Adolf Mussafia.* Graz: no indication of publisher.
Schütte, Otto. 1902. Dôkmâget. *KVNS* 23, 70–71.
________. 1912. Helferling = Zwitter. *KVNS* 33, 41.
Schützeichel, Rudolf. *See* Gottschald Max, 1954, 4th ed.
Schüwer, Helmut. 1977. Knochen, Knoten, Knopf, Knubbe und verwandte Bildungen. Eine bedeutungsgeschichtliche Studie zur indogermanischen Wurzel **gen-*. *NW* 17, 115–23.
Schultz, Franz. *See* Wuttke, Dieter.
Schumann, C. 1904. Göre. *KVNS* 25, 52.
Schur, Norman. 1994. *2000 Most Challenging and Obscure Words.* New York: Galahad Books.
Schuster-Šewc. *See* WONS.
Schutter, G. de. *See* De Schutter, G.
Schwabe, H. O. 1916–17. Germanic Coin-Names 2. *MPh* 14, 105–20.
________. 1917. Etymological Notes. *MLN* 32, 222–25.
Schwartz, Martin. 1992. Relative Chronology in and across Formal and Semantic Hierarchies: The History of **dhwer(E)* 'go apart' in Indo-European. In *Rekonstruktion und relative Chronologie. Akten der VIII. Fachtagung der Indogermanischen Gesellschaft. Leiden, 31. August–4. September 1987*, eds. Robert Beekes, Alexander Lubotsky, and Jos Weitenberg. IBS 65, 391–410.
Schwarz, Ernst. 1951. *Goten, Nordgermanen, Angelsachsen. Studien zur Ausgliederung der germanischen Sprachen.* BG 2.
Schwenck, Konrad. 1834. *Wörterbuch der deutschen Sprache in Beziehung auf Abstammung und Begriffsbildung.* Frankfurt am Main: Druck und Verlag von Johann D. Sauerländer. 2nd ed: 1837; 3rd ed: 1838; 4th ed: 1855.
Schwentner, Ernst. 1951. Etymologische Miszellen. *KZ* 69, 244–47.
Scott, Charles P. G. 1890. The Etymology of Cockney. *The Nation* 50, 468–69. Repr in *ANQ* 8, 1890, 92.
________. 1892. English Words Which hav Gaind or Lost an Initial Consonant by Attraction. *TAPS* 23, 179–305.
________. 1893. English Words Which hav Gaind or Lost an Initial Consonant by Attraction. *TAPS* 24, 89–155.
________. 1894. English Words Which hav Gaind or Lost an Initial Consonant by Attraction. *TAPS* 25, 82–139.
Searle = William G. Searle, *Onomasticon Anglo-Saxonicum: A List of Anglo-Saxon Proper Names from the Time of Beda to That of King John.* Cambridge: University Press, 1877. Repr Hildesheim: Georg Olms Verlagsbuchhandlung, 1969.
SED = Harold Orton and Martyn F. Wakelin, eds., *Survey of English Dialects: The Basic Material.* 4 vols. Publ for the University of Leeds by E. J. Arnold & Son Limited, Leeds. 1962–1968.
SED: DG = Clive Upton, David Parry, and J. D. A. Widdowson, *Survey of English Dialects: The*

Dictionary and Grammar. London and New York: Routledge, 1994.
See, Klaus von, et al. 1997. *Kommentar zu den Liedern der Edda.* Vol. 2. Heidelberg: Universitätsverlag C. Winter.
See also Kuhn, Hans. 1969–78.
Seebold, Elmar. 1967. Die Vertretung von idg $g^{u}h$ im Germanischen. *KZ* 81, 104–33.
________. 1970. *Vergleichendes und etymologisches Wörterbuch der germanischen starken Verben.* JL. Series practica 85.
________. 1992. Kentish—and Old English Texts from Kent. In *Words, Texts and Manuscripts: Studies in Anglo-Saxon Culture Presented to Helmut Gneuss on the Occasion of his Sixty-Fifth Birthday,* ed. Michael Korhammer, 409–34. Cambridge: D. S. Brewer.
________. 1997. *Zapfen, Zipfel, Zopf, zupfen* und die 'mots populaires' in den germanischen Sprachen. *HS* 110, 146–60.
See also EWDS[22–24].
Seelmann, Erich. 1932–33. Kuckuck. In HDA 5, 690–751.
Sehrt, Edward H. 1925. *Vollständiges Wörterbuch zum* Heliand *und zur altsächsischen* Genesis. Hesperia 14. Göttingen: Vandenhoeck & Ruprecht, Baltimore: The Johns Hopkins Press.
Seiler, Hansjakob. 1953. *Ἄνθρωπος. Glotta* 32, 225–36.
Sen, Subhadra K. *See* Ebbinghaus, Ernst A. 1989b.
Senn, Alfred. 1933. Nachträge zu Kluge's Wörterbuch. *JEGP* 32, 504–29.
See also Dyen, Isidore. 1970.
SEO = Elof Hellquist, *Svensk etymologisk ordbok.* 3rd ed. Lund: C. W. K. Gleerup, 1948. 1st ed: 1920–22; 2nd ed: 1939.
Serenius, Jacob. 1737. *Dictionarium anglo-svethico-latinum...* Hamburgi: Apud Rudolphum Beneken.
________. 1757. *An English and Swedish Dictionary.* Printed at Harg and Stenbro near Nykoping [sic] in Sweden, by Pet Momma.
SG = C. T. Onions, *A Shakespeare Glossary.* 2nd ed. Oxford: At the Clarendon Press, 1946.
SGGI = *Sravnitel'naia grammatika germanskikh iazykov* [*A Comparative Germanic Grammar*]. Moskva: Izdatel'stvo Akademii nauk SSSR, 1962–66 (vol. I, 1962; vol. II, 1962; vol. III, 1965).
Shanskii, N. M. *See* ESRI.
Sharp, Sheila. *See* Hill, David, and Sheila Sharp.
Sharypkin, D. M. 1973. 'Rek Boian i Khodyna...' (K voprosu o poèzii skal'dov i 'Slove o polku Igoreve') ['Rek Boian i Khodyna...' (On Skaldic Poetry and *The Lay of Igor's Host*)]. Ssb 18, 195–202.
________. 1976. Boian v 'Slove o polku Igoreve' i poeziia skal'dov [Boian in *The Lay of Igor's Host* and Skaldic Poetry]. TODL 31, 14–22.
Shchur, G. S. 1982. [Rev of] Makovskii, M. M. 1980. *VIa* 2, 153–56.
Sheidlower, Jesse, ed. 1995. *The F Word.* New York: Random House. 2nd ed: 1999.
Shipley, Joseph T. 1945. *Dictionary of Word Origins.* New York: The Philosophical Library, 3. 2nd ed, New York: Greenwood Press, 1969.
________. 1977. The Origin of our Strongest Taboo-Word. *Maledicta* 1, 23–29.
________. 1984. *The Origins of English Words: A Discursive Dictionary of Indo-European Roots.* Baltimore and London: The Johns Hopkins University Press.
Shores, David L. *See* Stanley, Julia.
Shulman, David. 1948. N. P. Willis and the American Language. *AS* 23, 39–47.
SI = *Wörterbuch der schweizerdeutschen Sprache (Schweizerisches Idiotikon).* Frauenfeld: Verlag von J. Huber, 1881–[2003].
Siebs, Theodor. 1889. *Zur Geschichte der englisch-friesischen Sprache.* Halle a. S.: Max Niemeyer. Repr Wiesbaden: Dr. Martin Sändig OHG, 1966.
________. 1892. Beiträge zur deutschen Mythologie. *ZDP* 24, 145–57.
________. 1904. Anlautstudien. *KZ* 37, 277–324.
________. 1930. Von Henne, Tod und Teufel. *ZV* 40, 49–61.
Siefert, Georg. 1902. Zwerge und Riesen. *NJKAGDLP* 10 (= *NJP* 5), 362–94, 433–49, 473–95.
Sievers, Eduard. 1878. Kleine Beiträge zur deutschen grammatik 4. Das nominalsuffix *tra* im germanischen. *PBB* 5, 519–38.
________. 1884. *Miscellen zur angelsächsischen Grammatik. PBB* 9, 197–300.
________. 1885. Zur Rhythmik des germanischen Alliterationsverses 2. *PBB* 10, 451–545.
________. 1894. Germanisch *ll* aus *ðl. IF* 4, 335–40.
See also ASG and SB.
SIG = *Studien zur indogermanischen*

Grundsprache. Wilhelm Brandenstein ed. AIAVS 4, 1952.
Sigfússon, Björn. 1934–35. Names of Sea-Kings (*heiti sækonunga*). *MPh* 32, 125–42.
Sigismund R. 1885. Über die Wirkung des Hebenon im Hamlet und eine damit verglichene Stelle bei Plutarch. *JDSG* 20, 320–24.
Sigma. 1890. Dorset Words. *SDNQ* 1, 125–26.
Sijmons, B. *See* Gering, Hugo. 1927.
Simmek, Rudolf. *See* Gunnell, Terry; Kure, Henning; *and* Liberman, Anatoly. 2003.
Simon, Werner. *See* Rooth, Erik. 1963.
Simpson, J. A. *See* OED[2].
Simpson, Jacqueline. *See* PED.
Simpson, R. R. 1947. How Did Hamlet's Father Die? *The Listener* 37, 581–82.
Singer, S. 1924. Verlorene Wörter. *ZDM* 19, 1–2 [*Festschrift Albert Bachmann*], 225–37.
Skalmowski, Wojciech. 1998. A Note on Greek *ἄνθρωπος*. *SEC* 3, 103–06.
SKCW = Walter W. Skeat, ed, *The Complete Works of Geoffrey Chaucer....* Vol. 2, 1894; Vol. 5, 1924. Oxford: At the Clarendon Press.
Skeat, Walter W., ed. 1867. *Parallel Extracts from Twenty-Nine Manuscripts of Piers Plowman...* EETS 28. Repr 1898.
________. 1868. Rabbit. *NQ* IV/1, 279–80.
________. 1875. Skid. *NQ*, V/4, 371–72.
________. 1882. *An Etymological Dictionary of the English Language.* Oxford: At the Clarendon Press. 2nd ed: 1884, 3rd ed: 1897, 4th ed: 1910.
________. 1883. Caterways. *NQ* VI/8, 74.
________, ed. 1885. *The Vision of William Concerning Piers Plowman....* IV/2. EETS 81.
________. 1885–87. Notes on English Etymology. *TPS* 21, 1–12, 283–333, 690–722.
________. 1886a. Cushat. *The Academy* 29, 311.
________, ed. 1886b. *The Vision of William Concerning Piers the Plowman in Three Parallel Texts...* 2 vols. Oxford: At the Clarendon Press.
________. 1887. *Principles of English Etymology.* Oxford: At the Clarendon Press. 2nd ed: 1892.
________. 1894. Cockney. *NQ* VIII/6, 135.
________. 1895. Haggaday. *Antiquary* 31, 288.
________. 1896. *A Student's Pastime.* Oxford: At the Clarendon Press.
________. 1897. *See* Skeat, Walter W., 1882, 3rd ed.
________. 1899–1902. Notes on English Etymology. *TPS (May 12)*, 261–90, 440–68, 651–73.
________. 1901. *Notes on English Etymology.* Oxford: At the Clarendon Press.
________. 1903–06. Notes on English Etymology. *TPS* 247–60.
________. 1907–10. Notes on English Etymology. *TPS*, 332–58.
________. 1909. Untitled. *AJP* 30, 351–52.
________. 1911–16. The Friesic Element in English; and Some Etymologies. *TPS*, 27–51.
Skeat[1, 2, 3, 4]. *See* Skeat, Walter W. 1882. *See also* CED; Mayhew, Anthony L., 1888; Ray, John; SKCW; *and* TC-B.
SKES = Erkki Itkonen and Aulis J. Joki, *Suomen kielen etymologinen sanakirja.* LSFU XII:1–7, 1975–81.
Skinner, Stephen. 1671. *Etymologicon Linguæ Anglicanæ....* Londini: Typis T. Roycroft. Repr Los Angeles: Sherwin & Freutel, 1970.
Skomal, Susan N. *See* Polomé, Edgar C. 1987.
Sleeth, Charles. 1981. Skedaddle. *CoE* XI/5–6, 4–9.
Slupski, Annemarie. *See* LEW.
Smiles, Samuel. 1861. *Lives of the Engineers.* London: John Murray.
Smit, P. *See* Heukels, H. 1987.
Smith, A. H. 1956. *English Place-Name Elements.* 2 vols. Cambridge University Press. *See also* OD.
Smith, Benjamin E. *See* CD.
Smith, C. J. 1865. *Common Words with Curious Derivations.* London: Bell and Daldy.
Smith, Elsdon C. 1956. *Dictionary of American Family Names.* New York: Harper & Brothers Publishers.
________. 1969. *American Surnames.* Philadelphia, New York, London: Chilton Book Company.
Smith, Lloyd E. 1926. Morsels for Puzzle Fans. *AS* 1, 210–15.
Smith, Roland M. 1954. Swift's Little Language and Nonsense Names. *JEGP* 43, 178–96.
Smithers, G.V. 1954. Some English Ideophones. *AL* 6, 73–111.
Smits, A. A. 1870. [Rev of] Höfer, Albert. 1870a. *NBRW* 20, 148–57.
Smythe Palmer, A. 1876. *Leaves from a Word-Hunter's Note-Book: Being Some Contributions to English Etymology.* London: Trübner & Co.
________. 1883. *Folk-Etymology: a Dictionary of Verbal Corruptions or Words Perverted in Form or Meaning, by False Derivation or Mistaken Analogy.* London: Henry Holt & Co. Repr

New York: Greenwood Press Publishers, 1969.

_______. 1910. Folk-Lore in Word-Lore. *NC* 68, 545–57.

SN = Otto Schrader. *Reallexikon der indogermanischen Altertumskunde.* 2nd ed, by A. Nehring. Berlin: Walter de Gruyter, 1929.

SND = *The Scottish National Dictionary.* William Grant, ed. Edinburgh: The Scottish National Dictionary Association Ltd, [1931]–76.

SOD = *The Shorter Oxford English Dictionary on Historical Principles,* prepared by William Little, H. W. Fowler, Jessie Coulson, rev. and ed. by C. T. Onions. Oxford: At the Clarendon Press, 1933. 2nd ed: 1936, 3rd ed: 1944; 3rd ed completely reset with etymologies rev by G. W. S. Friedrichsen and with rev addenda, 1973 (= SOD[3a]).

Söderlind, Johannes. 1968. The Word *Lilliput.* *SN* 40, 75–79.

Söhns, Franz. 1888. *Die Parias unserer Sprache. Eine Sammlung von Volksausdrücken.* Heilbronn a./R.: Verlag von Gebr. Henninger.

Solmsen, Felix. 1904. Beiträge zur geschichte der lateinischen sprache. *KZ* 37, 1–26.

_______. 1908. Über einige slavische Wörter mit dem Wurzelelement *mar-*. In *Zbornik u slavu Vatroslava Jagića*, 576–82. Berlin: Weidmannsche Buchhandlung.

Sommer, Ferdinand. 1924. Zur venetischen Schrift und Sprache. *IF* 42, 90–132.

Somner, William. 1650. [Gvilelmi Somneri]. *De Lingua Hebraica et, De lingua Saxonica.* Londini: Typis J. Flesher.

_______. 1659. *Dictionarium Saxonico Latino-Anglicum...* Oxonii: Excudebat Gvliel. Hall, pro Authore. Repr CFR 247, 1970.

Sonnenschein, James S. *See* Hehn, Victor.

Spalding, Keith. *See* HDGFU.

Specht, Franz. 1944. *Der Ursprung der indogermanischen Deklination.* Göttingen: Vandenhoeck & Ruprecht.

Sperber, Hans. 1912. Über den Einfluß sexueller Momente auf Entstehung der Sprache. *Imago* 1, 405–53.
See also ES.

Spillner, Paul W. 1963. Jeep. *Der Sprachdienst* 7, 176.

Spitzer, Leo. 1915. [Rev of] Sperber 1912. *WuS* 6, 206–15.

_______. 1917. [Rev of] Kluge 1916. *LBl* 38, 302–03.

_______. 1921. Französische Etymologien. *ZRP* 41, 161–75.

_______. 1925. Aus der Werkstatt des Etymologen. *JPh* 1, 129–59.

_______. 1942a. Curmudgeon 'miser.' *JEGP* 41, 150–51.

_______. 1942b. Estudios etimológicos 2. *AIL* 2, 1–43.

_______. 1947. Ragamuffin, Ragman, Rigmarole, Rogue. *MLN* 62, 85–93.

_______. 1951. Two Anglo-French Etymologies. *Word* 7, 211–21.

_______. 1952. Slang. *MLN* 67, 99–103.

_______. 1954. Stubborn. *MLN* 69, 550–51.

Sprenger, R. 1887. Etepetete. *KVNS* 12, 43.

_______. 1905. Gör = unmündiges Alter? *KVNS* 26, 19.

Springer, Otto. *See* EWA.

SSA = Erkki Itkonen, *Suomen sanojen alkuperä. Etymologinen sanakirja.* Helsinki: Suomalaisen Kirjallisuuden Seura, Kotimaisten kielten tutkimuskesus, 1992–95.

Stallybrass, James S. *See* Grimm, Jacob. 1835, *and* Hehn, Victor. 1894.

Stalmaszczyk, Piotr, and Krzysztof T. Witczak. 1991–92. The Celtic Word for 'oats, avena sativa' and its Indo-European Equivalents. *LP* 34, 83–87.

Stanley, E. G. 1968. [Rev of] CEDEL, vol. 2. *NQ* 213, 108–10.

_______. 1990. J. Bosworth's Interest in 'Friesic' for his Dictionary of the Anglo-Saxon Language (183): 'The Friesic is far the most important language for my purpose.' *ABÄG* 31–32 (= *Estrikken* 69: Rolf H. Bremmer Jr, Geart van der Meer, and Oebele Vries, eds, *Aspects of Old Frisian Philology*), 428–52.

Stanley, Julia P. 1977. Paradigmatic Woman: The Prostitute. In *Papers in Language Variation*, eds. David L. Shores and Carole P. Hines, 303–21. SAMLA-ADS Collection. The University of Alabama Press.

Stapelkamp, Chr. 1946. Einige merkwürdige mittelniederdeutsche Wörter. *NdM* 2, 56–62.

_______. 1950a. Breegns–bragen. *DB* 2, 53–54.

_______. 1950b. Frisiaca. *It Beaken* 12, 100–5, 148–55.

_______. 1957a. Lexicografische aantekeningen. *NTg* 50, 227–30.

_______. 1957b. Podde-hoed. *UW* 6, 12–13.

Starck, Taylor, and J.C. Wells. 1971–87. *Althochdeutsches Glossenwörterbuch. (Mit*

Stellennachweis zu sämtlichen gedruckten althochdeutschen und verwandten Glossen.) GB/ II. Heidelberg: Carl Winter.

Stave, Joachim. 1965. Raffke–Piefke–Boofke. Ein Sprachbeitrag zum Bilde des häßlichen Deutschen. *WW* 15, 127–37.

Štech, Svatopulk. 1959. Zur Etymologie des tschechischen Wortes *pampeliska* und *Verwandtes*. *ZSP* 28, 153–59.

Stege, Herman ter. *See* Blok, Henk, and Herman ter Stege.

Stein, Jess M. *See* RHD.

Steinhauser, Walter. 1976. Das Hunaland und die Kimmerier. In *Festschrift für Richard Pittioni zum siebzigsten Geburtstag. Vol. 1: Urgeschichte*, eds. Herbert Mitscha-Märheim, Herwig Friesinger, and Helga Kerchler. ArA 13, 504–37.

Steinmetz, Sol. *See* Barnhart, Robert K.

Steller, Walther. 1928. *Abriss der altfriesischen Grammatik....* SKGGD C 5.

Sternemann, Reinhard. *See* Eichner, Heiner.

Stevens, James. 1925. Logger Talk. *AS* 1, 135–40.

Stevenson, W. H. *See* NS.

Stewart, Doug. 1992. Hail to the Jeep! Could we have won without it? *Smithsonian* 23/8, 60–73.

Stibbe, Hildegard. 1935. *„Herr" und „Frau" und verwandte Begriffe in ihren altenglischen Äquivalenten.* AF 80. Heidelberg: Carl Winter.

Stiles, Patrick V. 1997. Old English *halh* 'slightly raised ground isolated by marsh.' In *Names, Places and People: An Onomastic Miscellany in Memory of John McNeal Dodgson*, eds. Alexander R. Rumble and A. D. Mills, 330–44. Stamford: Paul Watkins.

Stock, Elliott. *See* Swainson, Charles.

Stoddart, John. 1845. Grammar. In *The Encyclopaedia Metropolitana* 1, 1–192. London: B. Fellowes, *etc.*

Stoett, F. A. 1917. *Fokken, foppen. TNTL* 36, 61–66. *See also* VV.

Stokes, Whitley. 1894. *Urkeltischer Sprachschatz.* Translated, rev., and publ. by Adalbert Bezzenberger. In Fick[4], Part 2.

________. 1897. Celtic Etymologies. *BB* 23, 41–65.

Stoltz, G. 1935. Kunavn fra Radøen. *MM*, 50–55.

Stone, Leo. 1954. On the Principal Obscene Word of the English Language. *IJP* 35, 30–56.

Stopa, R. 1972. Influssi africani sulla struttura dell'indoeuropeo. In *Le lingue dell'Europa. Atti del V Convegno internazionale di linguisti tenuto a Milano nei giorni 1–5 settembre 1969.* Istituto Lombardo Accademia di Scienze e Lettere Sodalizio Glottologico Milanese. Istituto di Glottologia, Università di Milano. Special supplement to volume 22 of *Atti del S. G. M.*, 194–96. Brescia: Paideia editrice. [The text is in English.]

Storm, Johan. 1876. Mélanges étymologiques. *Romania* 5, 165–88.

________. 1881. *Englische Philologie. Anleitung zum wissenschaftlichen Studium der englischen Sprache. Die lebende Sprache.* Heilbronn: Verlag von Gebr. Henninger.

Stormonth, James. 1885. *A Dictionary of the English Language....* New York: Harper & Brothers.

Strachan, L. R. M. 1939. 'Toadstool': Derivation. *NQ* 176, 266–67.

Strandberg, Svante. 1993. *Budde.* Hypokorism eller deappellativiskt binamn? In *Personnamn i nordiska och andra germanska fornspråk.* Handlingar från NORNA:s artonde symposium i Uppsala 16–19 augusti 1991 , ed. Lena Peterson. NR 51, 141–52.

Stratmann, Francis H. 1867. *A Dictionary of the Old English Language....* Krefeld: Printed for the author by Kramer and Brown. 2nd ed: 1873, 3rd ed: 1878; a new ed, by Henry Bradley, Oxford: At the Clarendon Press, 1891; repr 1911, 1951, 1954.

________. 1883. *ESt* 6, 441–42.

Streitberg, Wilhelm. 1896. *Urgermanische Grammatik. Einführung in das vergleichende Studium der altgermanischen Dialekte.* GB I/I.

________. 1897. [Rev of] KEWAS[1] (1896) [and four more books]. *IF(A)* 7, 248–55.

Stroebe, Lilian L. 1904. *Die altenglischen Kleidernamen. Eine kulturgeschichtlich-etymologische Untersuchung.* Borna-Leipzig: Robert Noske.

Strömbäck, Dag. 1928. Lytir—en fornsvensk gud? In *Festskrift til Finnur Jónsson 29. Maj 1928*, 283–93. København: Levin & Munksgaards Forlag.

Strons, Johannes. *See* MlW.

Strunk, Klaus. *See* Schmidt, Klaus T.

Stuart, Heather. 1976. The Anglo-Saxon Elf. *SN* 48, 313–20.

________. 1977. 'Spider' in Old English. *Parergon* 18, 17–42.

Stürmer, F. 1929. Etymologische Fragen und Vermutungen. (Die idg. Wortsippe **(s)mē*.)

In *Donum Natalicium Schrijnen. Verzameling van opstellen door oud-leeringen en bevriende vakgenooten opgedragen aan Mgr. Prof. Dr. Jos. Schrijnen. Bij Gelegenheid van zijn zestigsten verjaardag 3 Mei 1929,* 333–41. Nijmegen-Utrecht: N.V. Dekker & Van de Vegt.

Sturtevant, Albert M. 1928–29. Certain Old Norse Suffixes. *MPh* 26, 467–76.

Sturtevant, Edgar H. 1928. Initial *sp* and *st* in Hittite. *Lg* 4, 1–6.

________. 1942. *The Indo-Hittite Laryngeals.* Baltimore: Linguistic Society of America. At the Waverly Press, Inc.

Sundén, Karl F. 1904. *Contributions to the Study of Elliptical Words in Modern English.* Diss. Upsala. Upsala: Almquist & Wiksell.

Suolahti, Hugo [a.k.a. Hugo Palander]. 1909. *Die deutschen Vogelnamen. Eine wortgeschichtliche Untersuchung.* Straßburg: Verlag von Karl J. Trübner.

Svanberg, Nils. 1928–29. Das Verbum *schlagen,* westnord. *sløgr* und schwed. *ormslå.* Eine etymologische Studie. *APS* 3, 234–63.

Sverdrup, Jakob. 1916. Maalvitskap og Kultursoga. *SySe* 22, 34–42, 264–78.

Swainson, Charles. 1886. *The Folk Lore and Provincial Names of British Birds.* London: Publ for the Folk Lore Society by Elliott Stock. (First publ as EDS 47, 1885.)

Swann, H. Kirke. 1913. *A Dictionary of English and Folk-Names of British Birds.* London: Witherby & Co.

Sweet, Henry. 1885. *The Oldest English Texts....* London: N. Trübner & Co. for the Early English Text Society; repr. Folcroft, PA: Folcroft Library Editions, 1978.

________. 1888. *A History of English Sounds from the Earliest Period, with Full Word-Lists.* Oxford: At the Clarendon Press. Repr Vaduz: Kraus Reprint, 1965.

________. 1897. *The Student's Dictionary of Anglo-Saxon.* London: Henry Frowde; New York: Oxford University Press. Repr: 1911.

Swinton, William. 1864. *Rambles among Words: Their Poetry, History and Wisdom.* New York: Dion Thomas.

Sydow, Rudolf von. 1828. *Darstellung des Erbrechts nach den Grundsätzen des Sachsenspiegels, mit Rücksicht auf die verwandten Quellen.* Berlin: Bei Ferdinand Dümmler.

Sykes, J. B. *See* COD$^{6-7}$.

Szemerényi, Oswald. 1962. Principles of Etymological Research in the Indo-European Languages. In *II. Fachtagung für Indogermanische und Allgemeine Sprachwissenschaft. Innsbruck 10–15. Oktober 1961.* IBK 15, 175–212. Repr in *Etymologie,* ed. Rüdiger Schmitt, Wege der Forschung 373, 286–346. Darmstadt: Wissenschaftliche Buchgesellschaft.

________. 1989. Germanica II (6–10). In *Indogermanica Europaea. Festschrift für Wolfgang Meid zum 60. Geburtstag am 12. 11. 1989,* 367–84. GLM 4.

Szwedek, Aleksander. *See* Colman, Fran; Hamp, Eric P. 1986, *and* Ono, Shigeru. 1986.

Talbot, H. Fox. 1847. *English Etymologies....* London: J. Murray.

Tamm, Fredrik. 1890–1905. *Etymologisk svensk ordbok* 1. Uppsala: Akademiska boktryckeriet. Edv. Berling. (No more published.)

Tangl, Eberhard. *See* LEW.

Tavernier-Vereecken, C. 1968. *Gentse naamkunde van ca. 1000 tot 1253. Een bijdrage tot de kennis van het oudste Middelnederlands.* BSGLN 11.

Taylor, Isaac. 1864. *Words and Places: or, Etymological Illustrations of History, Ethnology, and Geography.* London: Macmillan and Co.; 2nd ed: 1865; 3rd ed: 1873; 4th ed: 1877.

________. 1877. The Ancient British Numerals. *The Athenæum*/II, 338, 371, 433.

Taylor, John R. *See* Jäkel, Olaf.

Taylor, Joseph. 1818. *Antiquitates Curiosæ: The Etymology of Many Remarkable Old Sayings, Proverbs, and Singular Customs....* London: Printed for T. and J. Allman.

Taylor, Marvin. *See* Vennemann, Theo. 1997.

TC-B = *Poetical Works of Geoffrey Chaucer....* Robert Bell, ed. With a Preliminary Essay by W.W. Skeat. London: George Bell and Sons, 1880.

TC-R = *The Book of* Troilus and Criseyde *by Geoffrey Chaucer.* Robert K. Root, ed. London: Humphrey Milford Oxford University Press; Princeton: Princeton University Press, 1926.

TC-W = *A Seventeenth-Century Modernisation of the First Three Books of Chaucer's "Troilus and Criseyde."* Herbert G. Wright, ed. Bern: Francke Verlag, 1960.

TDW = *Trübners Deutsches Wörterbuch.* Berlin (and Leipzig): Walter de Gruyter & Co., 1936–1957.

Ten Brink, Bernhard. 1884. *Chaucers Sprache und Verskunst.* Leipzig: [T. O. Weigel].

Ten Doornkaat Koolman, Jan. 1879–84. *Wörterbuch der ostfriesischen Sprache etymologisch bearbeitet.* Norden: Verlag von Herm. Braams. Repr Wiesbaden: Dr. Martin Sändig, 1965.

Tengvik, Gösta. 1938. *Old English Bynames.* Diss. Uppsala. NG 4.

Ten Kate = Lambert ten Kate. *Aenleiding tot de kennisse van het verhevene deel der Nederdeuitsche Sprake....* Part 2. Amsterdam: Rudolph en Gerard Wetstein, 1723.

Terasawa, Yoshio. 1993. Some Etymological and Semasiological Notes on *Girl.* In *Anglo-Saxonica. Beiträge zur Vor- und Frühgeschichte der englischen Sprache und zur altenglischen Literatur. Festschrift für Hans Schabram zum 65. Geburtstag*, eds. Klaus R. Grinda and Claus-Dieter Wetzel, 335–45. München: Wilhelm Fink Verlag. Repr in *English Historical Linguistics and Philology in Japan*, eds. Jacek Fisiak and Akio Oizumi, TLSM 109, 1998, 401–16.
See also Ono, Shigeru, 1981.

Terry, F.C. Birkbeck. 1881. "Quest" or "Quist" = Wood-Pigeon. *NQ* VI/3, 349.

________. 1881. Toadstool. *NQ* VI/4, 451–52.

________. 1883. Caterways. *NQ* VI/7, 354.

Ter Stege, Herman. *See* Blok, Henk, and Herman ter Stege.

Terwen, J. L. 1844. *Etymologisch Handwoordenboek der nederduitsche taal, of proeve van een geregeld overzigt van de afstamming der nederduitsche woorden.* Gouda: G. B. van Goor.

Tew, Edmund. 1868. Rabbit. *NQ* IV/1, 207.

Te Winkel, Jan, ed. 1875. *Jacob van Maerlants* Roman van Torec. Leiden: E. J. Brill.

________. 1893. [Rev of] Franck, Johannes. 1893. *LCD* 7, 51–54.

Thaning, Kirstine. 1904. *Besejrede oldengelske Ord. Betragtninger over Sprog som Udtryk for Tanke.* Kjøbenhavn: Gyldendalske Boghandel, Nordisk Forlag.

Thielmann, Ph. 1887. Salaputtium. *ALLG* 4, 601–02.

Thieme, Paul. 1953. *Die Heimat der indogermanischen Gemeinsprache.* Akademie der Wissenschaften und der Literatur. AGSM 11.

Thiselton-Dyer, William T. 1916. Natural History: Plants. In *Shakespeare's England: An Account of the Life and Manners of his Age.* Vol. 1, 500–14. Oxford: At the Clarendon Press.

Thomas, Émile. *See* Benois-Thomas.

Thomas, S. Pantzerhielm. 1909–10. Ne. fidge(t), oe. ficol og deres gruppe. *NTF* III/8, 47–48.

Thompson, Della. *See* COD[9].

Thompson, G.H. 1887. Dr. Johnson and Oats. *NQ* VII/3, 26.

Thomsen, Vilhelm. 1869. *Den gotiske sprogklasses indflydelse på den finske. En sproghistorisk undersøgelse.* Repr in his *Samlede afhandlinger* 2, 49–238 (with a postscript: 239–64). København and Kristiania: Gyldendalske boghandel, Nordisk forlag, 1920.

Thomson, John. 1826. *Etymons of English Words.* Edinburgh: Oliver & Boyd, London: Longman, *etc.*

Thornton, Richard H. 1912–1939. *An American Glossary...* Philadelphia: J. B. Lippincott Company; London: Francis & Co. 2 vols. Vol. 3, ed. by Louise Hanley. Madison, WI: The American Dialect Society, 1939.

________. 1962. *An American Glossary* 2. New York: Frederick Ungar Publishing Co.

Tiling, Eberhard. *See* BWb.

Timmermann, Ulf. 2001. Nordfriesische Personennamen. In HF, 381–95.

Tischler, Johann. 1977–[1990]. *Hethitisches etymologisches Glossar.* Mit Beiträgen von Günter Neumann. IBS 20.
See also Schmidt, Klaus T., and Klaus Strunk.

TL = Adolf Tobler and Erhard Lommatzsch, *Altfranzösisches Wörterbuch.* Berlin: Weidmannsche Buchhandlung, Wiesbaden: Franz Steiner Verlag, 1925–.

TNJC-1 = *Tiomna Nuadh ar Dtighearna Agus ar Slanaightheora Josa Criosd. Ar na Tarrujng gu fjrjnneach as Gréigis gu gádjohejlg, Re Hujlljam o Domhnujll.* Ata so ar na a Golo a mbajlé ... sé Seon Francke, 1602.

TNJC-2 = *Tiomna Nuadh ar Dtighearna Agus ar Slanaigheora Iosa Criosd. Ar na t˙arrving go fírińeac as Greigis go Goid˙eilg. Re Huilliam o Domhnuill.* A Lunnduin, Ar na c'ur a goló re Robert Ebheringt˙am [= Everingham], agus ata sé sé ré na dhiól ag Beniamin Túc ag com˙arta na luinge a Relic t˙eampuil Phóil, 1681.

TNJC-3 = *Tiomna Nuadh ar Dtighearna Agus ar Slanaigheora Iosa Criosd. Ar na tharruing go firinneach as an ghreigs ughdarach.* Ris an tathair is onoruighthe a ndia Uilliam o Domhnuill, Ardeaspug Thuaim. London: For the British and Foreign Bible Society, 1817.

Tobler, Adolf. 1896. Etymologisches. SKPAW, 851–72.
See also TL.

Tobler, Friedrich. 1912. *Die Gattung Hedera. Studien über Gestalt und Leben des Efeus, seine Arten und Geschichte.* Jena: Verlag von Gustav Fischer.

Tobler, Ludwig. 1868. *Über die Wortzusammensetzung nebst einem Anhang über die verstärkenden Zusammensetzungen. Ein Beitrag zur philosophischen und vergleichenden Sprachwissenschaft.* Berlin: Ferd. Dümmlers Verlagsbuchhandlung; Harrwitz und Gossmann.

Todd, H. J. *See* Johnson, Samuel.

TOE = Jane Roberts and Christian Kay with Lynne Grundy, *A Thesaurus of Old English.* KCMS 11, 1995.

Törnqvist, Nils. 1959. Westfälisch *blage* 'Kind.' *KVNS* 66, 13–15.

________. 1960. Nhd *Trabant. PBB* (H) 82, 146–51.

________. 1969. Zwei seemännische Wörter dunkler Herkunft. *KVNS* 76, 9–10.

________. 1970. Nd. *brise*–Ndl. *bries. KVNS* 77, 22–23.

Toll, Johannes-Michael. 1926. *Niederländisches Lehngut im Mittelenglischen.... Ein Beitrag zur englischen Wortgeschichte mit Benutzung einer von Dr. O. Zippel handschriftlich hinterlassenen Materialsammlung.* SEP 69.

Tollenaere, F. de. *See* De Tollenaere, F.

Toller, Northcote T. *See* BT.

Tommaseo = Tommaseo, Nicoló, et al., *Dizionario della lingua italiana...* Torino: Unione tipografico-Editrice, [1861–79].

Tooke, Horne J. 1798–1805. *EPEA PTEROENTA. Or, the Diversions of Purley.* 2 vols. London: Printed for the author at J. Johnson's. Repr as SFR 127, 1968.

Toone, William. 1832. *A Glossary and Etymological Dictionary of Obsolete and Uncommon Words....* London: William Pickering.

Toporov, V.N. *See* PII.

Torp, Alf, in collaboration with Hjalmar Falk. 1909. *Wortschatz der Germanischen Spracheinheit.* In Fick[4], Part 3.
See also FT *and* NEO.

Torpusman, Rachel. 1998. [An annotated translation of Catullus's selected poems into Russian]. *Solnechnoe spletenie* (Jerusalem) 2, 27–31.

Townsend, Joseph. 1824. *Etymological Researches....* Bath: Printed by Gye and Son.

T.R. 1945. Neither Fish nor Flesh, nor Good Red Herring. *ANQ* 5, 125.

Trévoux = *Dictionnaire universel françois et latin, vulgairement appelé dictionnaire de Trévoux....* Nouvelle ed. Paris: Associés, Chez Estienne Ganneau libraire de Paris, 1704; 2nd ed: 1721, 3rd ed: 1732; the last ed before the publication of Samuel Johnson's dictionary: 1750.

Trier, Jost. 1947. Vater. *ZSSR(GA)* 65, 232–60.

________. 1952. *Holz. Etymologien aus dem Niederwald.* MF 6.

________. 1963. *Venus. Etymologien um das Futterlaub.* MF 15.

Trubachev, O. N. 1960. Slavianskie etimologii 24–27 [Slavic Etymologies 24–27]. In *Ezikovedsko-etnografski izsledvaniia v pamet na akademik Stoian Romanski,* 137–43. Sofiia: Bulgarska akademiia na naukite. Otdelenie za ezikoznanie, literaturoznanie i etnografiia.

________. 1980. Rekonstruktsiia slov i ikh znachenii [Reconstruction of Words and their Meanings]. *VIa* 3, 3–14.
See also EESI *and* Vasmer, Max.

Trumbull, J. Hammond. 1871. A Mode of Counting, Said to Have Been Used by the Wawenoc Indians of Maine. Summary in Third Annual Session, held at New Haven, July 1871, 13–15 (appended to the 1871 vol of TAPA). Hartford, 1872.

________. 1871. On Algonkin Names for Man. *TAPA* [2], 138–59.

________. 1877. The Ancient British Numerals. *The Athenæum*/II, 662.

Trutmann, Albertine. 1972. *Studien zum Adjektiv im Gotischen.* QF (NF) 47 (171). Berlin, New York: Walter de Gruyter.

T.T.W. 1872. Cater-Cousins. *NQ* IV/9, 456.

Tucker, T. G. [no date]. *Notes on Indo-European Etymologies: Preliminary to a Full Discussion of I.-E. Roots and their Formation.* Halle (Saale): Karras, Kröber & Nietschmann.

Tullberg, Hampus K. 1868. *Bidrag till etymologiskt lexikon över främmande ord i svenska språket.* Lund: Af Håkon Ohlssons tryckeri.

Tusser, Thomas. 1878. *Fiue Hundred Pointes of*

Good Husbandrie, ed by W. Payne and Sydney J. Herrtage. EDSP 8. First publ in 1557.

Tylor, E.B. 1874. The Philology of Slang. *MacMag* 29, 502–13.

Tyrwhitt, T. 1775 = *The Canterbury Tales of Chaucer...*, vol 5. London: Printed for T. Payne and Son. Repr New York: AMS Press, 1972.

Üçok, Necip. 1938. *Über die Wortgruppen weltanschaulichen und religiösen Inhalts in der Bibelübersetzung Ulfilas*. Diss. Heidelberg. Heidelberg: Druckerei Winter.

UED = *The Universal Dictionary of the English Language*. Henry C. Wyld, ed. London: Routledge & Kegan Paul Limited, 1932 (numerous reprints).

Uhlenbeck, Christianus C. 1894. Etymologisches. *PBB* 19, 326–33.

________. 1896. Etymologisches. *PBB* 21, 98–106.

________. 1901. Zur deutschen etymologie. *PBB* 26, 290–312.

________. 1905. Bemerkungen zum gotischen wortschatz. *PBB* 30, 252–327.

________. 1909. Zur deutschen etymologie. *PBB* 35, 161–80.

See also KEWAS *and* KEWGS.

Ulenbrook, Jan. 1967. Einige Übereinstimmungen zwischen dem Chinesischen und dem Indogermanischen. (Vorläufiger Bericht.) *Anthropos* 62, 535–51.

Ulrix, Eugeen. 1907. *De germaansche Elementen in de Romaansche Talen. Proeve van een Germaansch-Romaansch Woordenboek*. Gent: A. Siffer.

Ulving, Tor. 1968–69. Indo-European Elements in Chinese. *Anthropos* 63–64, 944–51.

Upton, Clive. *See* SOD: DG.

Uspenskij, Fjodor. 2000. Towards Further Interpretation of the Primordial Cow Auðhumla. *SI* 51, 119–32.

Vaan de, Michiel. *See* De Vaan, Michiel.

Vanacker, V. F. *See* Århammar, Nils R. 1986.

Van den Berg, B. 1938. Een amsterdamsche scheldroep uit de 15d eeuw. *NTg* 32, 366–67.

________. 1954. De namen van de klaver. *NGN* 14, 183–93.

Van den Berg, Jan. *See* Bremmer, Rolf H. Jr.

Van den Helm, G. L. 1861. Etymologische onderzoekingen. *TNLT* 3, 203–10.

Van der Meer, Geart. *See* Stanley, E. G. 1900.

Van der Meulen, R. 1917. Robbedoes. *TNTL* 36, 1–9.

Van Draat, P. Fijn. 1940. Reduplicatory Emphasis. *ESt* 74, 156–67.

Van Ginneken, Jacob. 1941. De tweede aflevering van onzen Nederlandschen taalatlas. *OT* 9, 353–84.

Van Haeringen, C. B. 1921. Sporen van Fries buiten Friesland. *TNTL* 40, 269–300.

See also EWNT.

Van Helten, Willem L. 1873. Epea pteroenta XIV–XXI. *TLb* 4, 213–51.

________. 1905. Grammatisches. *PBB* 30, 213–51.

________. 1908–09. Zu einigen germanischen Benennungen für *cunnus* und *veretrum*. *ZDW* 10, 195–97.

Vaniček, Alois. 1881. *Etymologisches Wörterbuch der lateinischen Sprache*, 2nd ed. Leipzig: B. G. Teubner.

Van Kempe Valk, C. 1880. Eenige voorbeelden van opmerkelijke etymologie in de Engelsche taal. *Taalstudie* 2, 162–73.

Van Langenhove, G. 1928. [Rev of] WP II/1. *RB* 7, 157–62.

Van Lennep, J. H. 1860. To Slang. *NQ* II/9, 471.

Van Lessen, Jacoba H. 1928. *Samengestelde naamwoorden in het Nederlandsch*. Groningen, Den Haag: Bij J. B. Wolters' U. M.

________. 1934. *Gorlegooi*. *TNTL* 53, 92–95.

Van Veen, P. A. F. 1989. *Etymologisch woordenboek. De herkomst van onze woorden.* Utrecht, Antwerpen: Van Dale Lexicografie.

Van Wijk, Nicolaas. 1909. Germanische Etymologien. *IF* 24, 30–37.

See also EWNT.

Van Windekens, A. J. 1957. Die Herkunft von ai. *aravinda* 'Lotosblume' und *taru-* 'Baum.' *ZDMG* 107, 554–56.

Vasmer, Max. 1950–58. *Russisches etymologisches Wörterbuch*. Heidelberg: Carl Winter. Russian ed: M. Fasmer, *Etimologicheskii slovar' russkogo iazyka*. Translated and enlarged by O. N. Trubachev, edited and with an introduction by B. A. Larin. Moskva: Progress, 1964–73.

Veen, P. A. F. von. *See* Van Veen, P. A. F.

Venables, Edmund. 1875. To Miche. *The Athenæum*/II, 650.

Vendryes, Joseph. 1912. À propos des groupes initiaux *dentale + v*. In *Miscellany Presented to Kuno Meyer by Some of his Friends and Pupils on the Occasion of his Appointment to the Chair of Celtic Philology in the University of Berlin*, eds.

Osborn Bergin and Carl Marstrander, 286–90. Halle a.S.: Max Niemeyer.
See also LE.

Venezky, Richard L. *See* DOE.

Venmans, L. A. W. C. 1930. *Σέρφος*. *Mnemosyne* 58, 58–73.

Vennemann, Theo. 1995. Etymologische Beziehungen im Alten Europa. *Der Ginkgo-Baum* 13, 39–115.

_______. 1997. Zur Etymologie der Sippe von engl. *knife*, franz. *canif*, bask. *kaniber*. In *Germanic Studies in Honor of Anatoly Liberman*, eds. Kurt G. Goblirsch, Martha B. Mayou, and Marvin Taylor, *NOWELE* 31/32, 443–62.

_______. 2000. Zur Entstehung des Germanischen. *Sprachwissenschaft* 25, 233–69.

_______. 2002. *Key* Issues in English Etymology. In *Sounds, Words, Texts, and Change*: *Selected Papers from 11 ICEHL, Santiago de Compostela, 7–11 September 2000*, eds. Teresa Fanego and Belén Méndez-Naya, 227–52. Amsterdam: John Benjamins Publishing Company.

Vercoullie, Jozef. 1890. *Beknopt etymologisch Woordenboek der Nederlandsche Taal*. Gent: J. Vuylsteke, 's-Gravenhage: Martinus Nijhoff. 2nd ed: 1898; 3rd ed, 's-Gravenhage: Martinus Nijhoff, Gent: Van Rysselberghe & Rombaut, 1925.

_______. 1920. Etymologisch Kleingoed. VMKVATL, 789–95, 936.

Verdam, Jacob. 1897. Dietsche verscheidenheden. *TNTL* 16, 1–20, 163–75.
See also VV.

Verhofstadt, E. *See* Århammar, Nils R. 1986.

Vermeer, Hans J. 1971. "Indisch" *boy*. In *Donum indogermanicum. Festgabe für Anton Scherer zum 70. Geburtstag*, ed. Robert Schmitt-Brandt, 70–81. Heidelberg: Carl Winter.

Verwijs, E. *See* VV.

VEW = Ferdinand Holthausen, *Vergleichendes und etymologisches Wörterbuch des Altwestnordischen (Altnorwegisch-isländischen)*.... Göttingen: Vandenhoeck & Ruprecht, 1948.

Vidos, B. E. 1957. Étymologie organique. *RLR* 21, 93–105.

Vigfusson, Gudbrand (a. k. a. Vigfússon, Guðbrandur). *See* CV.

Vine, Brent. *See* Ivanov, Vyacheslav V. 1999.

Visio Willi de Petro Plowman, item visiones ejusdem de Dowel, Dobet, et Dobest. Or The Vision of William concerning Piers Ploughman, and the Visions of the same concerning the Origin, Progress, and Perfection of the Christian Life. Ascribed to William Langland... Printed... together with an introductory discourse, a perpetual commentary, annotations, and a glossary. By Thomas D. Whitaker... London: Printed for John Murray, 1813.

Voronin, S. V. 1997. Fonosemantika i etimologiia [Phonosemantics and Etymology]. In *Diakhronicheskaia germanistika*. Mezhvuzovskii sbornik, ed. L. P. Chakhoian, 131–77. Sankt-Peterburg: Sankt-Peterburgskii universitet.

Voyles, Joseph. 1968. Gothic and Germanic. *Lg* 44, 720–46.

Vries, Jan de. *See* De Vries, Jan.

Vries, Oebele. *See* Stanley, E. G. 1990.

Vries, W. de. *See* De Vries, W.

VV = E. Verwijs and J. Verdam, completed by F. A. Stoett. *Middelnederlandsch Woordenboek*. 's-Gravenhage: Martinus Nijhoff, 1885–1941.

W = Webster.

W[1, 2, 3]. *See* Webster, Noah, 1909, 1934, 1961.

W. 1868. Curmudgeon. *NQ* IV/2, 355.

_______. 1903. The Words Reiskie and Treviss. *ScNQ* II/5, 95.

Wachter, Johann G. 1737. *Glossarium Germanicum*.... Lipsiæ: Apud Joh. Frid. Gleditschii B. Filium. Repr Hildesheim, NY: G. Olm, 1975.

Wackernagel, Wilhelm. 1860. Die deutschen Appellativnamen. *Germania* 4, 129–59; 5, 290–356. Repr in Wackernagel, Wilhelm. 1874b, 59–177.

_______. 1861. *Die Umdeutschung fremder Wörter*. In Programm der Promotionsfeier des Pädagogiums in Basel 1861. Repr in a revised form in Wackernagel, Wilhelm. 1874b, 252–333.

_______. 1874a. ΕΠΕΑ ΠΤΕΡΟΕΝΤΑ. *Ein Beitrag zur vergleichenden Mythologie*. In Wackernagel, Wilhelm. 1874b, 178–251.

_______. 1874b. *Kleinere Schriften*, vol. 3. Leipzig: Verlag von S. Hirzel. Repr: Göttingen: Vandenhoeck and Ruprecht, [1955].

Wadstein, Elis. 1918–22. *Friesische Lehnwörter im Nordischen*. Skr. Ups. 21:3.

_______. 1925. *Norden och Västeuropa i gammal tid*. PVFGH, NF 22.

_______. 1932. Våra förfäder och de gamla

friserna. Från vår historias gryningstid. *HT* 52, 81–88.

________. 1936. On the Relations between Scandinavians and Frisians in Early Times. *Saga-Book* 11, 5–25.

Wagner, Norbert. 1994. Lateinisch-germanisch *Mannus. HS* 107, 143–46.

Wakelin, Martyn F. 1971. OE. *bræȝȝen, braȝȝen. Nph* 58, 108.

________. 1972. Dialectal "Skippet": Consonant Mutations in Cornwall. *DCNQ* 32, 152–53.

________. 1979. OE. *bræȝȝen, braȝȝen:* A Further Note. *Orbis* 28, 369–71.
See also SED.

Walde, Alois. 1906. Aspiratendissimilation im Latein. *IF* 19, 98–111.
See also WH.

Wall, Arnold. 1898. A Contribution towards the Study of the Scandinavian Element in the English Dialects. *Anglia* 20, 45–135.

Wallenberg, J. K. 1923. *The Vocabulary of Dan Michel's 'Ayenbite of Inwyt.'* Diss. Uppsala. Uppsala: Appelbergs boktryckeri Aktienbolag.

Walsh, Chad. 1939. Catercornered. *AS* 14, 205.

Walshe, M. O'C. 1951. *A Concise German Etymological Dictionary*. London: Routledge & Kegan Paul Ltd.

Waltemath, Wilhelm. 1885. *Die fränkischen Elemente in der französischen Sprache.* Paderborn and Münster: Druck und Verlag von Ferdinand Schöningh.

Walther, C. 1893. Zu den Königsberger Pflanzenglossen im Ndd. Jahrbuch XVII, 81 ff. *NJ* 18, 130–40.

Wanner, Hans. 1963. Wortpaare vom Typus *recken : strecken* im Schweizerdeutschen. In *Sprachleben der Schweiz. Sprachwissenschaft, Namenforschung, Volkskunde*, ed. Paul Zinsli, 133–39. Bern: Francke.

Wartburg, Walther von. *See* BW *and* FEW.

Warwick, Eden. 1856. Meaning of Leckerstone. *NQ* II/2, 290–91.

Wasserzieher, Ernst. 1923. *Spaziergänge durch unsere Muttersprache. Neue sprachliche Plaudereien.* Berlin: Verlag des Deutschen Sprachvereins.

Wasson, George S. 1928–29. Our Heritage of Old Sea Terms. *AS* 4, 377–84.

Watson, Owen. *See Longman English Larousse.*

WBD = Clarence L. Barnhart, editor-in-chief, *The World Book Dictionary.* Chicago, *etc.*: Publ for Field Enterprises Educational Corporation. [A Thorndike-Barnhart Dictionary, copyright by Doubleday & Company, Inc.], 1963.

WCD[10] = Frederick C. Mish, editor-in-chief, *Merriam-Webster's Collegiate Dictionary*, 10th ed. Springfield, MA: Merriam-Webster, Inc., 1993.

W.D. 1868. Skedaddle. *NQ*, IV/6, 498.

WDU-1963 = Heinz Küpper, *Wörterbuch der deutschen Umgangssprache.* Hamburg: Claassen Verlag, 1963.

WDU-1970 = Heinz Küpper, *Wörterbuch der deutschen Umgangssprache.* Vol 6: *Jugenddeutsch von A bis Z.* Hamburg: Claassen Verlag, 1970.

Webb, J. Barry. 1989. *Shakespeare's Erotic Word Usage.* Hastings, E. Sussex: Cornwallis Press.

Weber, Gerd W. 1993. Of Trees and Men: Some Stray Thoughts on Kennings and Metaphors– and on Ludvig Holberg's Arboresque Anthropology. *NOWELE* 21–22, 419–46.

Webinger, Alfred. 1937a. Vom Butz und Bitzel. *ZV* 7, 157–60.

________. 1937b. Zu 'Balz' und 'balzen.' *ZV* 7, 160–61.

Webster, H. T. 1943. The Canting Language: Some Notes on Old Underworld Slang. *CE* 4, 230–35.

Webster, Noah. 1828. *An American Dictionary of the English Language.* New York: S. Converse. Repr New York and London: Johnson Reprint Corporation, 1970.

________. 1847. *An American Dictionary of the English Language.* Chauncey A. Goodrich, ed. Springfield, MA: G. & C. Merriam Company.

________. 1864. *An American Dictionary of the English Language.* Chauncey A. Goodrich and Noah Porter, eds. Springfield, MA: G. & C. Merriam Company.

________. 1880. *An American Dictionary of the English Language.* Chauncey A. Goodrich and Noah Porter, eds. Springfield, MA: G. & C. Merriam Company.

________. 1890. *Webster's International Dictionary of the English Language.* Noah Porter, ed. Springfield, MA: G. & C. Merriam Company.

________. 1909. *Webster's New International Dictionary of the English Language.* W. T. Harris and F. Sturges Allen, eds. Springfield, MA: G. & C. Merriam Company (= W[1]).

________. 1934. *Webster's New International Dictionary of the English Language.* 2nd ed.

William A. Neilson, Thomas A. Knott, and Paul W. Carhart eds. Springfield, MA: G. & C. Merriam Company (= W^2).

________. 1961. *Webster's New International Dictionary of the English Language.* 3rd ed. Philip B. Gove, ed. Springfield, MA: G. & C. Merriam Company (= W^3).

Wedgwood, Hensleigh. 1852–53. On Words Admitting of Being Grouped around the Root *flap* or *flak*. *PPS* 6, 143–52.

________. 1855. English Etymologies. *TPS*, 104–18.

________. 1856. On the Connexion of the Finn and Lapp with Other European Languages. *TPS*, 1–18.

________. 1859–65. *A Dictionary of English Etymology....* London: Trübner & Co.; 2nd ed: 1872, 3rd ed: 1878, 4th ed: 1888. 1st American ed, by George P. Marsh; only vol. 1: A-D. New York: Sheldon and Co., Boston: Gould and Lincoln, 1862.

________. 1882. *Contested Etymologies in the Dictionary of the Rev. W. W. Skeat.* London: Trübner & Co.

________. 1890a. Cockney. *The Academy* 38, 52.

________. 1890b. Cockney. *The Academy* 38, 452.

Weekley, Ernest. 1907–10. Anglo-Norman Etymologies. *TPS*, 205–52.

________. 1909. [Report of a paper on] Anglo-Romance Etymologies. *The Athenæum*/I, 107–08.

________. 1910. Etymologies, Chiefly Anglo-French. *TPS* 27, 288–331.

________. 1915. Curmudgeon. *NQ* XI/11, 429.

________. 1921. *An Etymological Dictionary of Modern English.* London: John Murray. Repr New York: Dover Publications, 1967.

________. 1924. *A Concise Etymological Dictionary of Modern English.* London: John Murray. Repr New York: Dutton, 1952.

________. 1933. *Words and Names.* New York: Dutton.

________. 1937. *Surnames.* 3rd ed. New York: E. P. Dutton and Company, Inc.
See also Parr, D. Kermode.

Weigand, Friedrich L. K. 1857–1871. *Deutsches Wörterbuch.* 3rd ed. Gießen: Alfred Töpelmann; Gießen: J. Ricker'sche Buchhandlung (vol. I, 1857; vol. II, 1860–71).
See also WHirt.

Weijnen, Antonius A. 1939–40. Raggen. *OT* 8, 326–30.

________. 1965. Oude Engels-Nederlandse parallellen. VMKVATL, 385–401. Repr in *Algemene en vergelijkende dialectologie / General and Comparative Dialectology. Een verzameling studies van A. Weijnen.* Ed. by A. Hagen and J. Kruijsen, with an introduction, bibliography, and summaries in English, on the occasion of his 65th birthday, 173–87. Amsterdam: Holland University Pers, 1976.

________. 1981. Hiltiken. *TT* 33, 131–37.

________. 1998. Etymologische invallen. *TT* 50, 150–63.

Weiner, E. S. C. *See* OED^2.

Weinstock, Horst. 1968. *Mittelenglisches Elementarbuch....* Berlin: Walter de Gruyter & Co.

Weise, Benno von. *See* Foerste, William. 1954.

Weise, O. 1902. Worterklärungen. *ZDW* 3, 241–49.

Weiser, Lily. 1926 Germanische Hausgeister und Kobolde. *NZV* 4, 1–19.

Weiske, Julius, ed. 1840. *Der Sachsenspiegel.* Leipzig: Verlag von Jon. Fr. Hartknoch. 5th ed, by Rudolf Hildebrand. Leipzig: O. R. Reisland, 1876.

Weißbrodt, Ernst. 1935. Mogeln. *ZDP* 60, 211–13.

Weisweiler, Josef. 1924. Geschichte des ahd. Wortes *euua*. In *Stand und Aufgaben der Sprachwissenschaft. Festschrift für Wilhelm Streitberg,* 419–62. Heidelberg: Carl Winter's Universitätsbuchhandlung.

________. 1935. [Rev of] Klara H. Collitz, *Verbs of Motion in their Semantic Divergence.* LangM 8. *IF* 53, 54–56.

Weitenberg, Jos. *See* Schwartz, Martin.

Wells, A.Wade. 1946. *Hail to the Jeep. A Factual and Pictorial History of the Jeep.* New York and London: Harper & Brothers.

Wells, J.C. *See* Starck, Taylor, and J.C. Wells.

Wentworth, Harold. *See* WFl.

Wesche, Heinrich. 1940. *Der althochdeutsche Wortschatz im Gebiete des Zaubers und der Weissagung.* UGDS 1.

Wescott, Roger W. 1977a. Ideophones in Bini and English. *FL* 2, 1–13.

________. 1977b. Ooglification in American English Slang. *Verbatim* 3/4, 5.

Westerberg, Anna. *See* Bleckert, Lars.

Westwood, J. O. 1877. The Ancient British Numerals. *The Athenæum*/II, 371.

Wetzel, Claus-Dieter. *See* Terasawa, Yoshio.

WF = A. de Jager, *Woordenboek der*

frequentatieven in het Nederlandsch. Gouda: G. B. van Goor Zonen, 1875–78.
WFl = Wentworth, Harold, and Stuart B. Flexner, *Dictionary of American Slang.* 2nd Supplemented Edition. New York: Thomas Y. Crowell, 1975.
WFT = *Wurdboek fan de Fryske taal / Woordenboek der Friese Taal.* Lióuwerd—Leeuwarden: Fryske Akademy/De Tille, 1984– .
WH = Alois Walde, *Lateinisches etymologisches Wörterbuch.* 3rd ed, by Johann B. Hofmann. Heidelberg: Carl Winter, 1938–54.
Whallon, William. 1987. Greek Cognates of the Vilest Words in English. *NM* 88, 35–37.
Whatmough, Joshua. 1953. On the Name of the Genius Cucullatus. *Ogam* 5, 65–66.
WHirt = L. K. Weigand, *Deutsches Wörterbuch.* 5th ed, by Herman Hirt. Gießen: Verlag von Friedrich Alfred Töpelmann, 1909–10.
Whitaker, John. 1771–75. *The History of Manchester in Four Books.* [London]: n. p. (See "A Specimen of an English-British Dictionary," vol. 2 [1775], 240–326.)
Whitaker, Thomas D. *See Visio Willi de Petro Ploughman....*
White, Holt A. 1858. Cob at Lyme Regis. *NQ* II/5, 258.
Whitehall, Harold. 1939. On the Etymology of 'lad.' *PQ* 18, 19–24.
Whiter, Walter. 1822–25. *Etymologicon Universale; or, Universal Etymological Dictionary.* 3 vols. Cambridge: At the University Press for Richard Priestley.
Whiting, Bartlett J. 1968. With the collaboration of Helen Wescott Whiting. *Proverbs, Sentences and Proverbial Phrases from English Writings Mainly before 1500.* Cambridge, MA: The Belknap Press of Harvard University Press.
Whiting, Helen Wescott. *See* Whiting, Bartlett J. 1968.
Whitman, Charles H. 1898. The Birds of Old English Literature. *JEP* 2, 149–98.
________. 1907. The Old English Animal Names: Mollusks; Toads, Frogs; Worms; Reptiles. *Anglia* 30, 380–93.
Whitney, William D. *See* CD.
Wiarda, Tileman D. 1786. *Altfriesisches Wörterbuch.* Aurich: Bey August F. Winter.
Widdowson, John D. A. 1971. The Bogeyman: Some Preliminary Observations on Frightening Figures. *Folklore* 82, 99–115. *See also* SED: DG.
Wiedemann, Oskar. 1893. Nachtrag [zu s. 479–484 des vorigen bandes]. *KZ* 32, 149–52.
________. 1904. Etymologien. *BB* 28, 1–83.
Wiese, Benno von. *See* Foerste, William. 1954.
Wiesinger, Peter. *See* Knobloch, Johann. 1980.
Wijk, Nicolaas van. *See* Van Wijk, Nicolaas van.
Wilbraham, Roger. 1821. An Attempt at a Glossary of Some Words Used in Cheshire. *Archaeologia* 19, 19–42.
Wild, Friedrich. *See* Luick, Karl. 1964.
Wilken, E. 1872. [Rev of] MW, Fsc. 1. *GGA* 441–57.
Wilkes, G. A. 1996. *A Dictionary of Australian Colloquialisms,* 4th ed. South Melbourne, Australia: Oxford University Press.
Williams = Robert Williams, *Lexicon Cornu-Brittannicum: A Dictionary of the Ancient Celtic Language of Cornwall....* Llandonvert: Roderic; London: Trubner & Co., 1865.
Williams, Ann. *See* DMTP.
Williams, Gordon. 1994. *A Dictionary of Sexual Language and Imagery in Shakespearean and Stuart Literature.* London and Atlantic Highlands, N. J.: The Athlone Press.
________. 1997. *A Glossary of Shakespeare's Sexual Language.* London & Atlantic Highlands, N. J.: Athlone.
Williams, Harold. 1932. *Dean Swift's Library....* Cambridge: At the University Press.
Wilson, Edward. 1993. A 'Damned F__in Abbot' in 1528: The Earliest English Example of a Four-Letter Word. *NQ* 238, 29–34.
Wilson, J. Dover. 1934. *The Manuscript of Shakespeare's* Hamlet *and the Problems of its Transmission: An Essay in Critical Bibliography.* Vol. 2: *Editorial Problems and Solutions.* Cambridge: At the University Press.
Wilson, R. M. *See* Reanly, Percy H., 3rd ed.
Winkel, Jan te. *See* Te Winkel, Jan.
Winter, Werner. *See* Hamp, Erik P. 1988b.
Wissowa, Georg. *See* PW.
Witczak, Krzysztof. *See* Stalmaszczyk, Piotr.
Wittmann, Henry. 1964. Some Hittite Etymologies. *Die Sprache* 10, 144–48.
Witty, J. R. 1927. Sheep and Sheep-scoring. *TYDS* IV/28, 41–49.
WNT = *Woordenboek der Nederlandsche taal.* 's-Gravenhage: Nijhoff, Leiden: Sijthoff, 1882–.
WNWD = *Webster's New World Dictionary of the American Language.* Cleveland and New York: The World Publishing Company, 1951. 2nd ed, by David B. Guralnik, 1970; 3rd ed, by Victoria

Neufeldt and David Guralnik, 1986. New York: Webster's New World.
Woeste, Friedrich. 1857. Schnitzel aus dem niederd. Wörterbuche. *KZ* 6, 429–35.
________. 1871. Beiträge aus dem niederdeutschen. *ZDP* 3, 356–58.
________. 1875. Beiträge aus dem niederdeutschen. *ZDP* 6, 207–16.
________. 1876. Kuvern, kuwern. *KVNS* 1, 55.
________. 1930. *Wörterbuch der westfälischen Mundart.* Erich Nörrenberg, ed. Norden: Dietrich Soltau. Repr Wiesbaden: Martin Sändig, 1966. First publ in 1882 as: Verein für niederdeutsche Sprachforschung. Wörterbücher 1.
Wolf, Siegmund A. 1956. *Wörterbuch des Rotwelschen. Deutsche Gaunersprache.* Mannheim: Bibliographisches Institut.
________. 1962. Verkannte jiddische Etymologien. *Muttersprache* 72, 184–85.
Wolff, Ludwig. 1976. Zu Walthers Liede 42, 31 *Wil ab iemen wesen frô* und 'Heide' als Namen der 'erica.' *ZDA* 105, 255–57.
Woll, Dieter. 1986. Frz. *flatter, flétrir* und verwandtes—Etymologie und Wortgeschichte. *RF* 98, 1–16.
Wollin, Lars. *See* Holm, Gösta.
WONS = H. Schuster-Šewc, *Historisch-etymologisches Wörterbuch der ober- und niedersorbischen Sprache.* Bautzen: VEB Domowina-Verlag, 1978–89.
Wood, Francis A. 1899a. The Semasiology of Words for 'smell' and 'see.' *PMLA* 14, 299–346.
________. 1899b. *Understand, guess, think, mean,* Semasiologically Explained. *MLN* 14, 129–31.
________. 1899–1900. Germanic Etymologies. *AG* 3, 309–25.
________. 1900. The Semasiology of *understand, verstehen, ἐπίσταμαι. MLN* 15, 14–16.
________. 1902. Color-Names and their Congeners: A Semasiological Investigation. Halle a. S.: Max Niemeyer.
________. 1903. The IE. Root *selo-*. *AJP* 24, 40–61.
________. 1904. Some Derived Meanings. *MLN* 19, 1–5.
________. 1905. *Indo-European* $a^x : a^xi : a^xu$: *A Study in Ablaut and in Wordformation.* Strassburg: Verlag von Karl J. Trübner.
________. 1905–06. How Are Words Related? *IF* 18, 1–49.
________. 1907–08. Studies in Germanic Strong Verbs 2. *MPh* 5, 265–90.
________. 1910–11. Iteratives, Blends, and "Streckformen." *MPh* 9, 157–94.
________. 1913. *Some Parallel Formations in English.* Hesperia, Ergänzungsreihe, Vol. 1. Göttingen: Vandenhoeck & Ruprecht; Baltimore: The Johns Hopkins Press.
________. 1913–14. Germanic Etymologies. *MPh* 11, 315–38.
________. 1914a. Etymological Notes. *MLN* 29, 69–72.
________. 1914b. Germanic Etymologies. *JEGP* 13, 499–507.
________. 1919. Greek and Latin Etymologies. *CP* 14, 245–72.
________. 1919–20. The IE. Root **qēu-:* 'nuere, nutare, cevere; quatere, cudere; cubare, incumbere.' *MPh* 17, 331–50, 567–80.
________. 1920. Names of Stinging, Gnawing, and Rending Animals. *AJP* 41, 223–39, 336–54.
________. 1923. Augurs and Omens, Gods and Ghosts. In *The Manly Anniversary Studies in Languages and Literature,* 328–39. Chicago, IL: The University of Chicago Press.
________. 1926. *Post-Consonantal* W *in Indo-European.* LangM 3.
________. 1931. Prothetic Vowels in Sanskrit, Greek, Latin, and Germanic. *AJP* 52, 105–44.
Worcester, Joseph E. 1860. *A Dictionary of the English Language....* Philadelphia: J. B. Lippincott.
Wordell, Charles B. *See* Maurer, David W.
Wotherspoon, Irené. *See* Hough, Carole.
Wortmann, Felix. 1964. Kibbe (Bezeichnung für kleine Tiere) und verwandte Bildungen. Eine bedeutungsgeschichtliche Studie. *NW* 4, 53–76.
See also Kruppa-Kusch, Veronika, and Felix Wortmann.
Woty, William. 1786. *Fugitive and Original Poems.* Derby: Printed for the author by J. Drewry.
WP = Alois Walde, *Vergleichendes Wörterbuch der indogermanischen Sprachen.* Julius Pokorny, ed. Berlin: Walter de Gruyter, 1927–32. Repr 1973.
WPP = Thomas Wright, ed., *The Vision and Creed of Piers Ploughman.* 2nd ed. London: Reeves and Turner, 1883.
WPW = Thomas Wright, ed., *The Poetical Works of Geoffrey Chaucer. A New Text, with Illustrative Notes.* Philadelphia: J. B. Lippincott & Co, 1880.
Wright, Elizabeth M. *See* Wright, Joseph, and Elizabeth M. Wright.

Wright, Herbert G. *See* TC-W.

Wright, Joseph. 1954. *Grammar of the Gothic Language....* 2nd ed. with a Supplement to the Grammar by O.L. Sayce. Oxford: At the Clarendon Press.

________. 1968. *The English Dialect Grammar.* Oxford University Press. First publ as part of vol. 5 of EDD.
See also EDD.

Wright, Joseph, and Elizabeth M. Wright. 1914. *Old English Grammar.* 2nd ed. London, etc.: Humphrey Milford Oxford University Press.

Wright, Thomas. *See* DOPE; Nares, Robert; WPP; *and* WPW.

Wright, William A., ed. 1877. *King Lear.* Clarendon Press Series. Shakespeare, *Select Plays.* Oxford: At the Clarendon Press.

Wüst, Walther. 1956. *Idg.* *pélek̑u *'Axt, Beil.' Eine paläo-linguistische Studie.* STT B/93 (1). Helsinki.

Wuttke, Dieter, ed. 1994. Sebastian Brant, *Das Narrenschiff.* Facsimile of the first ed, Basel 1494, with a postscript by Franz Schultz (Straßburg 1912). SSp 6.

W.W.E.T. 1852. Sir Hobbard de Hoy. *NQ* I/5, 468.

Wyld, Henry C. 1899–1902. Apparent Irregularities in English Guttural Sounds. *NQ* IX/3, 20–22.

________. 1899. Contributions to the History of the Guttural Sounds in English. *TPS* 1898–1902, 129–260. Publ in book form as *Contributions to the History of the English Gutturals.* Hertford: Printed by Stephen Austin & Sons for the Philological Society, 1899.

________. 1920. *A History of Modern Colloquial English.* New York: E. P. Dutton and Company. 3rd ed. Oxford: Basil Blackwell.
See also UED.

Zabel, Hartie E. 1922. *The Semantic Development of Words for Mental Aberration in Germanic.* Diss. The University of Chicago.

Zaccaria, D. Enrico. 1901. *L'elemento germanico nella lingua italiana. Lessico con appendice e prospetto cronologico.* Bologna: Libreria editrice Treves di Luigi Beltrami. Repr 1986.

Zacher, Julius. *See* Lübben, August. 1871.

Zachrisson, R. E. 1934. Germanic Etymologies. In *Studia Germanica tillägnade Ernst Albin Kock den 6 december 1934,* 400–13. Lund: Carl Bloms boktryckeri.

Zaeffer, Dietmar. *See* Schrijver, Peter.

Zamboni, Alberto. *See* Rocchi, Luciano. 1989.

Zehetmayr, Seb. 1879. *Analogisch-vergleichendes Wörterbuch über das Gesammtgebiet der indogermanischen Sprachen....* Leipzig: F. A. Brockhaus.

Zettersten, Arne. 1965. *Studies in the Dialect and Vocabulary of the* Ancrene Riwle. LSE 34.

Zeus. 1853. Etymology of Slang. *NQ* 7, 511.

Zhang, Lihua. *See* Ivanov, Vycheslav V. 1999a *and* Liberman, Anatoly. 1999a.

Zimmer, Heinrich. 1879. Keltische studien. *KZ* 24, 201–26.

Zimmermann, Fritz. 1961. *Chadalrich* und *Chadalhoch* in Burgenland. In *Atti del VII Congresso internazionale di Scienze Onomastiche,* 517–47. Firenze: Tipografia Giuntina.

Zinsli, Paul. *See* Wanner, Hans.

Zippel, O. *See* BZ *and* Toll, Johannes-Michael.

Zollinger, Gustav. 1952. *TAU oder TAU-t-an und das Rätsel der sprachlichen und menschlichen Einheit.* Bern: A. Francke AG Verlag.

Zubatý, Josef. 1898. Etymologický příspěvek [An Etymological Note]. In *Rozpravy filologické věnované Janu Gebauerovi,* 166–74. Praha: Tiskem F. Šimáčka

Zupitza, Ernst. 1896. *Die germanischen Gutturale.* SGP 8.

________. 1899. Etymologien. *BB* 25, 89–105.

________. 1900. Über doppelkonsonanz im irischen. *KZ* 36, 202–45.

________. 1904. Miscellen. *KZ* 37, 387–406.

Zupitza, Julius. 1880. [Rev of] Karl Böddeker, ed, *Altenglische Dichtungen des MS. Harl. 2253 mit Grammatik und Glossar.* Berlin: Weidmannsche Buchhandlung, 1878. *ZDA(A)* 6, 1–38.

________. 1883. [Rev of] Immanuel Schmidt, *Grammatik der englischen Sprache für obere Klassen höherer Lehranstalten.* 3rd ed. Berlin: Haude und Spener, 1883. *DLZ* 4, 1163.

________. 1884. Etymologie von neuengl. *loose. Anglia Anzeiger* 7, 152–55.

INDEX OF SUBJECTS

INDEX OF WORDS

The index contains over 6000 words in over eighty languages and periods from nearly the whole world. Below, they are classified by family, group, language, and period. The languages represented by fewer than three words have not been included. It has also been considered unnecessary to include such multiple forms as *stroumpat, strompette, strompott*, and three more ('strumpet'), all of which occur on the same page in the text and would have followed one another in the index. The summaries of the entries also have not been indexed. Although every word has been checked in the best dictionaries available, a few suspect forms remain. Rather frequently a reliable author would cite a word from Old Irish or Frisian (to give the most characteristic examples) that does not appear in any dictionary consulted. Some such words remain in the text but do not show up in the index. Obviously, I had minimal control over regional (dialectal) words, even in English; my main source for English was EDD. The orthography of some languages has changed (occasionally more than once) since the time they became the object of etymological research, and Sanskrit is now transliterated differently from how it was done in the 19th century. Except in quotations from dictionaries, all words are given in the form familiar today. Only *ß* in German words is spelled according to the pre-reform norm. References to the order of letters in the ALPHABET of some languages, to the extent that this order is specific, appear at the beginning of the lists.

Contents

MODERN ENGLISH

(Includes early modern and obsolete words; regional words given in italics. Head words of the entries are given in small caps)

MIDDLE ENGLISH

OLD ENGLISH

(æ is equal to ae; *þ and ð are not differentiated, and follow* t*)*

MODERN DUTCH

(Includes early modern and obsolete words; regional words given in italics)

MIDDLE DUTCH

FLEMISH

FRISIAN

(Old, modern, and dialectal foms undifferentiated)

MODERN GERMAN

(Includes early modern and obsolete words; regional words are given in italics and have not been capitalized. The words are spelled according to the pre-reform orthography)

MIDDLE HIGH GERMAN

MIDDLE LOW GERMAN

OLD HIGH GERMAN

OLD SAXON

MODERN DANISH

(Includes early modern and obsolete words. Æ, ø, and å follow z.)

OLD DANISH

FAROESE

ICELANDIC

(Includes early modern and obsolete words. Old and Modern words are undifferentiated. D *is equal to* ð; þ, æ, *and* ö *follow* z.)

NORWEGIAN (BOKMÅL)

(Regional words are given in italics. Æ, ø, and å follow z.)

NORWEGIAN (NYNORSK)

MODERN SWEDISH

(Regional words are given in italics. Å, ä, and ö follow z.)

OLD SWEDISH

GOTHIC

HITTITE

ARMENIAN

LATVIAN

LITHUANIAN

BRETON

CORNISH

IRISH

OLD IRISH

SCOTTISH GAELIC

WELSH

GREEK

(Digamma does not influence the alphabetization.)

AVESTAN

OSSETIC

PERSIAN

(Modern, Old, and Middle)

SANSKRIT

(Includes Vedic Sanskrit. The words have been transliterated but follow the order accepted in Sanskrit dictionaries.)

MODERN FRENCH

(Includes early and obsolete words; regional words are given in italics.)

OLD FRENCH

(Includes Middle French. Anglo-French and Provençal words are given in italics.)

ITALIAN

(Regional words are given in italics.)

LATIN

(Medieval Latin words are given in italics.)

PORTUGUESE
(Modern and Old)

SPANISH
(Old Spanish words are italicized)

OLD SLAVIC

POLISH

RUSSIAN

BASQUE

FINNISH

ARABIC

HEBREW

(The words transliterated in the text)

INDEX OF PERSONAL AND PLACE NAMES